June 22–27, 2014
Snowbird, UT, USA

Association for
Computing Machinery

Advancing Computing as a Science & Profession

PODS'14

Proceedings of the 33rd ACM SIGMOD-SIGACT-SIGART Symposium on Principles of Database Systems

Sponsored by:

ACM SIGACT, ACM SIGART, ACM SIGMOD

Supported:

Goldman Sachs, Microsoft, Oracle, AT&T, Baidu, Facebook, Google, IBM Research, Pivotal, SAP, Tableau, WalmartLabs, Intel, NEC, Yahoo! Labs, Morgan & Claypool Publishers, Elsevier, & Springer

Association for
Computing Machinery

Advancing Computing as a Science & Profession

The Association for Computing Machinery
2 Penn Plaza, Suite 701
New York, New York 10121-0701

Notice to Past Authors of ACM-Published Articles
ACM intends to create a complete electronic archive of all articles and/or other material previously published by ACM. If you have written a work that has been previously published by ACM in any journal or conference proceedings prior to 1978, or any SIG Newsletter at any time, and you do NOT want this work to appear in the ACM Digital Library, please inform permissions@acm.org, stating the title of the work, the author(s), and where and when published.

ISBN: 978-1-4503-2375-8 (Digital)

ISBN: 978-1-4503-3109-8 (Print)

Additional copies may be ordered prepaid from:

ACM Order Department
PO Box 30777
New York, NY 10087-0777, USA

Phone: 1-800-342-6626 (USA and Canada)
+1-212-626-0500 (Global)
Fax: +1-212-944-1318
E-mail: acmhelp@acm.org
Hours of Operation: 8:30 am – 4:30 pm ET

Printed in the USA

PODS 2014 General Chair Welcome Message

It is our great pleasure to welcome you to the 33rd ACM Symposium on Principles of Database Systems – PODS 2014, held in Snowbird, Utah, on June 22-25, 2014, in conjunction with the 2014 ACM SIGMOD International Conference on Management of Data. This year's symposium continues its tradition of being the premier international conference on the theoretical and foundational aspects of data management. Since the first edition of the symposium in 1982, the PODS papers are distinguished by a rigorous approach to widely diverse problems in data management, often bringing to bear techniques from a variety of different areas, including computational logic, finite model theory, computational complexity, algorithm design and analysis, programming languages, and artificial intelligence. The interested reader is referred to the PODS web pages at http://www.sigmod.org/the-pods-pages for information on the history of this conference series.

The PODS Symposia study data management challenges in a variety of application contexts, including more recently probabilistic data, streaming data, graph data, information retrieval, ontology and semantic web, and data-driven processes and systems. This year the program includes a workshop on Big Uncertain Data, co-chaired by Kristian Kersting and Benny Kimelfeld, which continues recent activity in the PODS community to explore principles underlying "Big Data", in this instance by bringing together researchers from the database and AI communities.

We had an excellent team that has worked very hard to create PODS 2014. We are particularly grateful to the Program Chair, Martin Grohe, who did an outstanding job in selecting and coordinating the program committee members, and to the whole program committee, who worked very hard in reviewing papers and providing feedback for authors. We are also grateful to the SIGMOD 2014 General Chairs, Curtis Dyreson and Feifei Li, for their excellent coordination of the overall SIGMOD/PODS 2014 conference, and their collaboration and support in all the issues requiring coordination between SIGMOD and PODS. Finally, we thank André Hernich, the PODS 2014 Proceedings Chair; Wim Martens, for maintaining the PODS web; and all our sponsors, in particular the ACM Special Interest Groups on Theoretical Computer Science, on Management of Data, and on Artificial Intelligence, for their invaluable support.

We wish you an inspiring and enjoyable stay in Park City, and we hope that you will find the PODS 2014 program informative, intriguing, and thought provoking, in the best tradition of the PODS Symposia.

Richard Hull
PODS 2014 General Chair
ACM, USA

PODS'14 Program Chair's Welcome Message

This volume contains the proceedings of the thirty-third ACM SIGMOD-SIGACT-SIGART Symposium on Principles of Database Systems (PODS 2014), held in Snowbird, Utah, USA, on June 22-25, 2014, in conjunction with the 2014 ACM SIGMOD International Conference on Management of Data. Associated with PODS'14 was a workshop on Big Uncertain Data.

The proceedings include papers based on the keynote address by Leonid Libkin (University of Edinburgh), two invited tutorials by Peter J. Haas (IBM Almaden) and Benny Kimelfeld (LogicBlox), and 22 contributions that were selected by the program committee for presentation at the symposium.

The contributed papers were selected from 67 submissions. Most of the 22 accepted papers are extended abstracts. While all submissions have been reviewed by at least three program committee members, they have not been formally refereed. It is expected that much of the research described in these papers will be published in detail in scientific journals.

An important and pleasant task for the program committee was the selection of the PODS 2014 Best Paper Award. The committee selected the paper

- "Weaker Forms of Monotonicity for Declarative Networking: a more fine-grained answer to the CALM-conjecture" by Tom J Ameloot, Bas Ketsman, Frank Neven and Daniel Zinn.

On behalf of the committee, I would like to extend my sincere congratulations to the authors. Since 2008, PODS gives the ACM PODS Alberto O. Mendelzon Test-of-Time Award to a paper or a small number of papers published in the PODS proceedings ten years prior that had the most impact over the intervening decade. This year's committee, consisting of Wenfei Fan (chair), Floris Geerts, and Dan Suciu, selected the following two papers:

- "Composing Schema Mappings: Second-Order Dependencies to the Rescue" by Ronald Fagin, Phokion G. Kolaitis, Lucian Popa, and Wang Chiew Tan,
- "Foundations of Semantic Web Databases" by Claudio Gutiérrez, Carlos A. Hurtado, and Alberto O. Mendelzon.

Congratulations to the authors!

I thank all authors who submitted papers to the symposium. I would also like to thank all members of the Program Committee and all external referees for the enormous amount of work they have done. The program committee did not meet in person, but carried out extensive discussions during the electronic PC meeting using the EasyChair System. I thank the PODS General Chair Richard Hull and the PODS executive committee for their support at all phases of the PC work. I am particularly grateful to Wenfei Fan and Michael Benedikt, the two previous PODS PC chairs, for their help and advice. Special thanks go to André Hernich, the Proceedings and Publicity Chair of PODS 2014.

Martin Grohe
PODS 2014 Program Chair

Table of Contents

PODS 2014 Symposium Organization

General Chair: Richard Hull *(IBM T.J. Watson Research Center, USA)*

Program Chair: Martin Grohe *(RWTH Aachen University, Germany)*

Proceedings & Publicity Chair: André Hernich *(University of Liverpool, UK)*

Program Committee:
Serge Abiteboul *(INRIA Saclay, France)*
Pablo Barceló *(Universidad de Chile, Chile)*
Jan van den Bussche *(Hasselt University, Belgium)*
Andrea Calì *(Birkbeck College, UK)*
Sara Cohen *(Hebrew University of Jerusalem, Israel)*
Dario Colazzo *(Université Paris Sud, France)*
Claire David *(Université Paris Est MLV, France)*
Daniel Deutch *(Ben Gurion University, Israel)*
Thomas Eiter *(TU Wien, Austria)*
Alexandre Evfimievski *(IBM Almaden Research Center, USA)*
Roberto Grossi *(Università di Pisa, Italy)*
Sudipto Guha *(University of Pennsylvania, USA)*
André Hernich *(University of Liverpool, UK)*
David Karger *(MIT, USA)*
Kristian Kersting *(University of Bonn, Germany)*
Jure Leskovec *(Stanford University, USA)*
Sebastian Maneth *(University of Edinburgh, UK)*
Gabriele Puppis *(LaBRI, France)*
Dan Suciu *(University of Washington, USA)*
Tony Tan *(Hasselt University, Belgium)*
Wang-Chiew Tan *(University of California, Santa Cruz, USA)*
Yufei Tao *(Chinese University of Hong Kong, China)*
Ke Yi *(Hong Kong University of Science and Technology, China)*

Additional reviewers:
Foto Afrati
Peyman Afshani
Alexandr Andoni
Marcelo Arenas
Leopoldo Bertossi
Pierre Bourhis
James Cheney
Alin Deutsch
Travis Gagie
Olivier Gauwin
Amélie Gheerbrant
Georg Gottlob
Michael Hay
Xiaocheng Hu
Zengfeng Huang
George Kollios
Chao Li
Leonid Libkin
Ashwin Machanavajjhala
Julian McAuley
Andrew McGregor
Yakov Nekrich
Jorge Perez
Jeff Phillips
Lucian Popa
Vibhor Rastogi

Additional reviewers (continued):

Cristian Riveros
Isabelle Stanton
Slawek Staworko
Balder ten Cate
Konstantinos Tsakalidis
Victor Vianu
Søren Vind
Domagoj Vrgoc
Zhewei Wei
Oren Weimann
Xiaokui Xiao
Qin Zhang

Alberto O. Mendelzon Test-of-Time Award Committee:

Wenfei Fan (Chair) *(University of Edinburgh, UK)*
Floris Geerts *(University of Antwerp, Belgium)*
Dan Suciu *(University of Washington, USA)*

PODS 2014 Sponsors & Supporters

Sponsors:

Platinum Supporters:

Gold Supporters:

Silver Supporters:

Platinum Publisher:

Silver Publishers:

Incomplete Data: What Went Wrong, and How to Fix It

Leonid Libkin
School of Informatics
University of Edinburgh
libkin@inf.ed.ac.uk

ABSTRACT

Incomplete data is ubiquitous: the more data we accumulate and the more widespread tools for integrating and exchanging data become, the more instances of incompleteness we have. And yet the subject is poorly handled by both practice and theory. Many queries for which students get full marks in their undergraduate courses will not work correctly in the presence of incomplete data, but these ways of evaluating queries are cast in stone – SQL standard. We have many theoretical results on handling incomplete data but they are, by and large, about showing high complexity bounds, and thus are often dismissed by practitioners. Even worse, we have a basic theoretical notion of what it means to answer queries over incomplete data, and yet this is not at all what practical systems do.

Is there a way out of this predicament? Can we have a theory of incompleteness that will appeal to theoreticians and practitioners alike, by explaining incompleteness and being at the same time implementable and useful for applications? After giving a critique of both the practice and the theory of handling incompleteness in databases, the paper outlines a possible way out of this crisis. The key idea is to combine three hitherto used approaches to incompleteness: one based on certain answers and representation systems, one based on viewing incomplete databases as logical theories, and one based on orderings expressing relative value of information.

Categories and Subject Descriptors

H.2.1 [**Database Management**]: Logical Design—*Data Models*; H.2.1 [**Database Management**]: Languages—*Query Languages*; H.2.4 [**Database Management**]: Systems—*Query Processing*

PODS'14, June 22–27, 2014, Snowbird, UT, USA.

ACM 978-1-4503-2375-8/14/06 ...$15.00. http://dx.doi.org/10.1145/2594538.2594551

Keywords

Incomplete information, query evaluation

1. INTRODUCTION

The need to handle incomplete data was recognized early in the development of relational database systems: already in the 1970s, Codd developed the basis of what would become null-related features of commercial DBMSs [21, 22]. His proposal for a single one-size-fits-all null value, its propagation through arithmetic and Boolean operations, and the use of the three-valued logic for computing with nulls was largely reflected in the SQL standard. It has, however, quickly become apparent that the adopted design of null-related features has a number of deficiencies, and it has become one of the most criticized aspects of SQL design [24, 26].

To illustrate one of the best known points of such criticism, consider a database of orders and payments, with relations `Order(o_id,product)` and `Pay(p_id,order,amount)`: the first gives order ids and products they are for, the other indicates that a payment with a given id was made for an order. We want to check if there are unpaid orders. A student who has taken a basic database course will immediately produce

```
SELECT o_id FROM Order
WHERE o_id NOT IN (SELECT order FROM Pay)
```

expecting to get full marks. But now take `Order` $= \{(\text{oid1}, \text{pr1}), (\text{oid2}, \text{pr2})\}$, and `Pay` $= \{(\text{pid1}, \bot, 100)\}$, where $\bot$ indicates null value. We know that at least one order has not been paid for, and yet the above query happily returns the empty set, indicating that no customers need to be chased for their payments! The problem easily confounds SQL programmers: consider a simple query $R - S$, where R and S are single-attribute relations, written as `SELECT R.A FROM R WHERE R.A NOT IN (SELECT S.A FROM S)`. It will produce the empty set if S contains just a null value, no matter what R contains. This goes against our intuition, of course: we know that if $|R| > |S|$, then $R - S$ cannot possibly be empty, but SQL tells us that it is. As [26] nicely put it, *"those SQL features are ... fundamentally at odds with the way the world behaves"*; a more damning assertion *"you can never trust the answers you get from a database with nulls"* is found in [24].

How did we get there? The approach to evaluating queries with nulls dates back to Codd's paper [21] from 1975, in which the 3-valued logic approach is advocated. Problems with it were caught early [37]: a simple query

```
SELECT p_id
FROM Pay
WHERE order = "oid1"  OR  order <> "oid1"
```

when evaluated on the database shown above, produces the empty table, and yet intuitively we expected the answer to be 'pid1'. Indeed, no matter what non-null value we replace the null with, this is what the query will produce.

The idea of answering queries consistently with every possible interpretation of nulls, first proposed in [37] as a way of fixing some problems with Codd's 3-valued approach, led to the notion of *certain answers*, now the standard way of answering queries over incomplete databases. It was first properly defined by [54]. The definition relies on the notion of a *semantics* of an incomplete database D, denoted by $[\![D]\!]$, which is the set of all complete databases D' that D can represent. For instance, such databases can be obtained by replacing nulls by values (but this is not the only possibility). Then, given a relational query Q and an incomplete database D, certain answers were defined as

$$\mathsf{certain}(Q, D) = \bigcap \{Q(D') \mid D' \in [\![D]\!]\}, \qquad (1)$$

i.e., they consist of tuples that belong to the answer no matter how the missing information is interpreted.

In the theory community, certain answers have become *the* way for answering queries over incomplete databases, used across a variety of applications such as query answering using views [1, 39], data integration [43], data exchange [7], inconsistency management [15], and data cleaning [30].

However, this more disciplined approach, compared to SQL's 3-valued logic, does not come for free. Let Q be a Boolean (i.e., true/false) query. Then $\mathsf{certain}(Q, D)$ is true iff Q is true in every $D' \in [\![D]\!]$. Thus computing certain answers becomes a form of *validity* (i.e., checking if a sentence is true in all structures). In fact, when Q comes from relational calculus, then under the open-world-semantics (to be defined later), finding certain answers is exactly the validity problem. However, this is an undecidable problem, as was shown by Church and Turing back in the 1930s. Actually, the problem we look at is slightly different – we are only concerned about finite structures – but that does not make it easier. A detailed study of the complexity of finding certain answers was initiated by [3] which showed hardness results, coNP-hard and up. In fact, high complexity bounds are widespread in applications of incompleteness as well, with classes such as coNP, Π_2^p, PSPACE, coNEXP, and so on being regularly mentioned, even for *data* complexity.

So, where does this bring us? We can summarize the state of affairs roughly as follows:

Practice:
- sacrifice correctness for efficiency;
- the same query evaluation engine for complete and incomplete data;

Theory:
- correctness at the expense of efficiency;
- new semantics for query answering in the presence of incompleteness.

The picture looks quite bleak: it is almost 40 years since nulls were introduced, and yet the practice has taught generations to live with incorrect answers, while the theory is not really addressing the right problems. What can we do?

First, we have to recognize that we live in the real world, and no database vendors will change their products if we offer them radical solutions, like completely new query evaluation algorithms. Indeed, it took them many years to make DBMSs as efficient as they are today, and significant changes in basic query processing algorithms will result in years worth of work to adjust other elements of their products. We can, perhaps, suggest small and easily implementable changes. And we definitely can suggest new algorithms for specialized products.

Second, we must develop a theory applicable to a variety of models: relational, XML, graph data, with different types of incomplete information. But we also need a good testbed for such a general theory. Nulls seen in earlier examples correspond to SQL's view of missing information in standalone databases. But we can have incompleteness due to a multitude of other reasons, in particular, data interoperability. Incompleteness inevitably arises when we move data between different applications, such as in data integration and exchange scenarios [5, 7, 29, 43]. For example, suppose that from the `Order` relation, we want to build a database of customers and their preferences. Such a transformation is usually specified by rules known as schema mappings [7], for instance,

$$\texttt{Order}(i, p) \rightarrow \texttt{Cust}(x), \texttt{Pref}(x, p)$$

saying that if an order was placed for a product p, then a customer x must exist who placed that order, and that customer x prefers product p. From the tuple `Order`(oid1,pr1), this rule will generate tuples `Cust`($\bot$) and `Pref`($\bot$,pr1), and from the tuple `Order`(oid2,pr2) it will generate `Cust`($\bot'$) and `Pref`($\bot'$,pr2). Note that it is important for us to remember that, while the values $\bot$ and $\bot'$ are not yet known, when $\bot$ is replaced by some value c in `Cust`($\bot$), it must be replaced by the *same* value c in `Pref`($\bot$,pr1), and likewise for $\bot'$. On the other hand, $\bot$ and $\bot'$ may be replaced by the same, or by different constants – there are no restrictions.

What this example tells us is that we must have a mechanism for saying that some nulls should always be replaced by the same constant. Such nulls are known as *naïve*, or *marked* nulls [2, 40]. They are the most common model of nulls used in integration/exchange tasks [7, 29, 43] and in fact have been implemented as part of schema mapping and data exchange tools [38, 55].

Thus, while the approach to incompleteness we are about to present does not assume any particular data model, we shall be using, as the main illustration, the model of naïve nulls in relations (of course SQL's nulls are just a special case of it). In this model the standard interpretation of nulls is that a value is missing. This is not the only possibility: other nulls, such as 'non-applicable' or 'no-information' exist as well [44, 67]. However, all the results that we show here apply regardless of the nature of nulls: all that we need is a definition of the semantics of incomplete databases for results to work.

Plan of the paper Our goal is to make an attempt at building applicable theory of incompleteness. We start by recalling the basics of existing relational theory of incomplete information in Section 2. In Section 3 we discuss a number of serious shortcomings of this theory.

In Section 4 we explain the basics of a different approach to incompleteness, based on a duality between objects and queries. Combining the two, we present a simple model of incomplete objects (not just relational databases) that lets us define the notion of certainty in a principled way. We do it in Section 5, and show that there are actually two different notions of certainty: one represents it as an object, and the other as the knowledge we possess about that object.

We then use the new notions of certainty to apply them to query answers and extract what should rightly be called certain answers to queries. This is done in Section 6, which shows that sometimes it is actually very easy to compute certain answers using existing query evaluation technology. The key is the right notion of the semantics, of both input databases and query answers, and the right representational mechanism for query answers. Section 7 outlines directions for further work.

2. RELATIONAL INCOMPLETENESS

We now present formal definitions for some of the basic notions related to incomplete information in relational databases, see [2, 34, 40, 66]. But first, we briefly recall the main languages we deal with here, cf. [2]. The basic language will be *relational algebra*, on the procedural side, and *first-order logic* (FO), or relational calculus, on the declarative side. The selection-projection-join-union fragment of relational algebra is also referred to as the *positive* relational algebra (the difference operator is removed). Logically, it corresponds to the $\exists, \wedge, \vee$-fragment of FO, also known as existential positive formulae. In terms of its expressiveness, it is exactly the same as *unions of conjunctive queries*, denoted by UCQ. Recall that conjunctive queries are select-project-join, or $\exists, \wedge$-queries; queries in UCQ are their unions.

Incomplete databases and their semantics

We assume that databases are populated by two types of elements: constants (such as numbers, strings, etc.) and nulls. The set of constants is denoted by Const and the set of nulls by Null. These are countably infinite sets. Nulls will be denoted by $\bot$, sometimes with sub- or superscripts.

A relational schema is a set of relation names with associated arities. An incomplete relational instance D assigns to each k-ary relation symbol S from the schema a k-ary relation over $\mathsf{Const} \cup \mathsf{Null}$, i.e., a finite subset of $(\mathsf{Const} \cup \mathsf{Null})^k$. Such incomplete relational instances are referred to as *naïve* databases [2, 40]; note that a null $\bot \in \mathsf{Null}$ can appear multiple times. If each null $\bot \in \mathsf{Null}$ appears at most once, we speak of *Codd* databases; these model SQL's nulls. If we talk about single relations, it is common to refer to them as naïve tables and Codd tables.

We write $\mathsf{Const}(D)$ and $\mathsf{Null}(D)$ for the sets of constants and nulls that occur in a database D. The *active domain* of D is $\mathrm{adom}(D) = \mathsf{Const}(D) \cup \mathsf{Null}(D)$. A *complete* database D has no nulls, i.e., $\mathrm{adom}(D) \subseteq \mathsf{Const}$.

Below, R is a naïve table and S is a Codd table:

R:

$\bot$	1	$\bot'$
2	$\bot'$	$\bot$

S:

$\bot_1$	1	$\bot_2$
2	$\bot_3$	$\bot_4$

with $\mathsf{Const}(R) = \mathsf{Const}(S) = \{1, 2\}$ and $\mathsf{Null}(R) = \{\bot, \bot'\}$ and $\mathsf{Null}(S) = \{\bot_1, \bot_2, \bot_3, \bot_4\}$.

Each incomplete database can represent many possible complete databases. The exact set of complete databases it represents is the *semantics* of an incomplete database. The semantics is by no means unique, but in this paper we concentrate on the two most common ones, based on *open-world* and *close-world* assumptions [40, 58], usually abbreviated as OWA and CWA. The key notion for both is a *valuation* of nulls, which is a mapping $v : \mathsf{Null}(D) \to \mathsf{Const}$. This mapping associates a constant value with each null. It naturally extends to databases: $v(D)$ is simply the result of replacing each null $\bot \in \mathrm{adom}(D)$ by $v(\bot)$.

With that, we define CWA and OWA semantics as follows:

$$\begin{aligned} [\![D]\!]_{\mathrm{CWA}} &= \{D' \mid D' = v(D),\ v \text{ is a valuation}\} \\ [\![D]\!]_{\mathrm{OWA}} &= \{D' \mid D' \supseteq v(D),\ v \text{ is a valuation}\} \end{aligned}$$

Under CWA, we believe that an incomplete database represents information fully, except some missing values. Thus, databases represented by it are obtained by substituting values for nulls. Under OWA, the database is open to adding new facts: thus, after substituting values for nulls, one can add new tuples.

For instance, relation R_1 below belongs to both $[\![R]\!]_{\text{CWA}}$ and $[\![R]\!]_{\text{OWA}}$, for R depicted above (as it is obtained by valuation $\bot \mapsto 3$, $\bot' \mapsto 4$), and relation R_2 is in $[\![R]\!]_{\text{OWA}}$, as it also adds the tuple $(5, 6, 7)$:

R_1:

3	1	4
2	4	3

R_2:

3	1	4
2	4	3
5	6	7

A more expressive representation mechanism for incomplete information is that of *conditional tables*. Such a table is of the form

$$D = \left(\begin{array}{|c|c|} \hline & \text{condition} \\ \hline t_1 & c_1 \\ \hline \dots & \dots \\ \hline t_n & c_n \\ \hline \end{array} , \; c \right)$$

where $t_1, \dots, t_n$ are tuples and $c, c_1, \dots, c_n$ are *conditions*: Boolean combinations of statements $x = y$, where $x, y \in \mathsf{Const} \cup \mathsf{Null}$. Note that conditions may use nulls not present in the tuples. Conditional tables are usually viewed under the closed-world semantics $[\![D]\!]_{\text{CWA}}$ which consists of databases $\{v(t_i) \mid v(c_i) = \text{true}, \; i \leq n\}$, where v is a valuation so that $v(c)$ is true. For example, consider a conditional table

$$D = \left(\begin{array}{|c|c|} \hline & \text{condition} \\ \hline 1 & \bot = 1 \\ \hline 0 & \bot = 0 \\ \hline \end{array} , \; (\bot = 0) \vee (\bot = 1) \right)$$

The only valuations satisfying $(\bot = 0) \vee (\bot = 1)$ are $\bot \mapsto 0$ and $\bot \mapsto 1$. Hence $[\![C]\!]_{\text{CWA}} = \{\{0\}, \{1\}\}$; conditional tables thus can encode disjunctions: C says that either 0 or 1 is in the database.

Query answering

Fix a semantics $[\![\,]\!]$ of incompleteness, and assume we are given a query Q and an incomplete database D. Of course we know how to evaluate Q on complete databases. So the key object for us to work with is

$$Q([\![D]\!]) = \{Q(D') \mid D' \in [\![D]\!]\}$$

of query answers on all databases that are possibly represented by D. If we have an incomplete database that represents this set, then we have our query answer. That is, if there is a table A (for *answer*) such that

$$[\![A]\!] = Q([\![D]\!]), \tag{2}$$

then we declare A to be the answer to Q on D. Indeed, we get a single table that captures exactly the space of all possible query answers. If this happens for all incomplete database from some class $\mathcal{K}$ (Codd/naïve/conditional tables, or others) and for all queries Q from a language $\mathcal{L}$, then we say that $\mathcal{K}$ forms a *strong representation system* for $\mathcal{L}$ under $[\![\,]\!]$.

Strong representation systems, as the name suggest, are quite strong, and thus are hard to come by. The best known example is that of conditional tables for full relational algebra (equivalently, first-order logic) under the closed-world semantics $[\![\,]\!]_{\text{CWA}}$, see [40]. To give an example, let us revisit the query $R - S$. If our database D has $R = \{1, 2\}$ and $S = \{\bot\}$, then $Q([\![D]\!]_{\text{CWA}}) = \{\{1, 2\}, \{1\}, \{2\}\}$, depending on whether the null $\bot$ is instantiated into 1, or 2, or another constant. This can be represented by a conditional table

	condition
1	$\bot' = 1 \vee \bot' = 2$
2	$\bot' \neq 1$

Indeed, going over possible values of $\bot'$, one can see that it generates exactly $Q([\![D]\!]_{\text{CWA}})$. One problem with such an answer is that it is hardly meaningful to humans, and one probably would not be happy getting this answer from a DBMS.

Since (2) is too strong a condition, one tries to replace it by

$$[\![A]\!] \sim Q([\![D]\!]) \tag{3}$$

where $\sim$ is some equivalence relation. This idea led to the notion of a *weak representation system* based on the following equivalence. For two sets of instances, $\mathcal{I}_1$ and $\mathcal{I}_2$, and a query language $\mathcal{L}$, we let $\mathcal{I}_1 \sim_{\mathcal{L}} \mathcal{I}_2$ if

$$\bigcap\{q(D') \mid D' \in \mathcal{I}_1\} = \bigcap\{q(D') \mid D' \in \mathcal{I}_2\}$$

for each query q in $\mathcal{L}$. If (3) holds for $\sim_{\mathcal{L}}$ over a class $\mathcal{K}$ of instances for each query $Q \in \mathcal{L}$, we say that $\mathcal{K}$ forms a weak representation system for $\mathcal{L}$ under semantics $[\![\,]\!]$. The best known examples are, under both $[\![\,]\!]_{\text{OWA}}$ and $[\![\,]\!]_{\text{CWA}}$:

- Codd tables for selection/projection queries; and
- Naïve tables for UCQs (positive relational algebra).

The key reason weak representation systems are of interest is that they let us compute certain answers. Given an instance D, let D^{cmpl} be the complete part of it, i.e., all the tuples in D without nulls. Then, if we have a weak representation system, it follows that $A^{\text{cmpl}} = \mathsf{certain}(Q, D)$. Thus, certain answers are obtained by keeping the complete portion of the answer given by (3).

What makes the connection particularly attractive is that sometimes A is just $Q(D)$, i.e., one *naïvely* evaluates Q on D as if nulls were the usual values. In such a case, when A in (3) equals $Q(D)$, we say that *naive evaluation works for* Q. It then follows that

$$Q(D)^{\text{cmpl}} = \mathsf{certain}(Q, D). \tag{4}$$

It is known that naïve evaluation works for UCQs under both open and closed world semantics [40]. Moreover, under OWA, the result is optimal for FO: if we have a Boolean (yes/no) FO query and naïve evaluation works for it, then it is equivalent to a UCQ, i.e., a positive relational algebra query [51]. To see how naïve evaluation fails for non-positive queries, consider the query $\pi_A(R - S)$ where $R = \{(1, \bot)\}$ and $S = \{(1, \bot')\}$ are relations over attributes A, B. Then naïve evaluation computes $\{1\}$, while the certain answer is $\emptyset$.

If naïve evaluation works, i.e., (4) holds, computing certain answers can be done by a straightforward query evaluation following by an extra selection operation, throwing out tuples with nulls (or simply adding `IS NOT NULL` conditions in the `WHERE` clause of the original query). Thus, we do not need to invent new evaluation techniques.

As for the complexity of computing certain answers, for full relational algebra (first-order logic) it is undecidable under $[\![\,]\!]_{\text{OWA}}$ and coNP-complete under $[\![\,]\!]_{\text{CWA}}$, for data complexity (that is, for a fixed query, when only database is the input), see [3, 33]. This makes it prohibitively expensive under CWA, and plain impossible under OWA, but the good news is that due to (4), the complexity is very low ($\text{AC}^0 \subsetneq$ DLogSpace) for positive relational algebra queries.

It is a general phenomenon that by going away from positive queries, one loses tractability of finding certain answers, demonstrated for many problems related to handling incompleteness in databases [7, 13, 15, 17, 18, 29, 43, 53, 62, 66]. There are some classes extending UCQs for which certain answers can be computed tractably – for instance, Boolean combinations of conjunctive queries [33] – but the algorithms, despite having polynomial time bounds, are too complicated to be efficiently implemented on top of existing DBMSs.

3. CRITIQUE OF THEORY

There has been plenty of criticism of practical approaches to incomplete information, in particular SQL's treatment of nulls, see, e.g., [24, 25, 26], but the theoretical approaches have so far been spared. We put an end to it now. In fact much of theoretical research on incomplete information took the notions of *strong and weak representation systems* and *certain answers* as sacrosanct but we shall argue that their untouchable status needs to be re-examined.

Semantics of query answers. Let us look at the seemingly uncontroversial (2) saying that if we are lucky enough to get A satisfying $[\![A]\!] = Q([\![D]\!])$, then A should be viewed as the answer to Q on D. At the first glance it looks like a reasonable condition, but nonetheless there is one assumption built into it that is not unassailable. Note that (2) requires that both the input database D, and the answer A, be interpreted under the *same* semantics $[\![\,]\!]$. However, a priori, there is no reason for it. Why, for instance, should the answer to a query be interpreted under CWA if this is the semantics of the input?

Why intersection? The equivalence $\sim_{\mathcal{L}}$ used in the definition of weak representation systems looks quite ad hoc. Actually it is: it was defined that way to ensure compositionality, but its essence is really going from the very strong requirement (2) to a weaker one that only certain answers need to be produced. And certain answers are defined as the intersection of all possible answers. Again, at first this looks very reasonable: we want tuples that will be in the answer no matter how nulls are interpreted. But a closer examination reveals some problems. To start with, there are models other than relational. What can one do, for instance, for XML queries returning documents? (A side remark: much of the work on incompleteness in XML has been restricted to XML-to-relational queries, for this very reason [4, 9, 13, 33].) But even more importantly, how do we know that we do not lose important information by taking intersection and removing information from the answer?

Are certain answers certain? Actually, the standard intersection-based certain answers need not be. Intersection takes some tuples away from potential answers. At first the intuition appears to be fine: removing tuples from what is certain, we seem to retain only information we are certain about. However, removing tuples amounts to removing *data*, not information. In fact, the process can actually *add* information: for instance, under CWA, by removing a tuple we gain information that it is not in the answer. Hence, certain answers defined by (1) cannot be called certain in all scenarios.

Semantics and informativeness. Above, we alluded to the possibility of comparing incomplete databases in terms of their informativeness. This is a line of work that was pursued in the 1990s, rather independently of the rest of the work on incompleteness [16, 49, 57, 64]. The idea was to define orderings stating that one database has more information than another, albeit for primitive models, such as Codd tables. Having an ordering describing informativeness could be important for deciding what the proper semantics of query answers is, bringing us back to our first point of discussion. Indeed, it is expected that one should get more informative answers from more informative databases. However, there was no real attempt to tie the ordering-based approach with the basics such as representation systems and certain answers, and this needs to be done.

Are objects sufficiently expressive to be query answers? We are used to queries returning database objects – tables, XML documents, graphs. But are these sufficiently expressive to describe answers on incomplete databases? Specifically, are these sufficiently expressive to represent sets $Q([\![D]\!])$? Such sets may well be infinite, and describing them may require a more complex representation mechanism than simple database objects: an example of that was already seen when we looked at conditional tables. But is it always possible – and necessary – to have representations that look like database relations, while they are not?

Can high complexity bounds be avoided? Too much work has been done on showing high complexity bounds. A typical picture looks like this: a class of queries, often a fragment of positive relational algebra, can be evaluated efficiently; beyond that, intractability or even undecidability of data complexity is shown. Such results, while occasionally requiring nontrivial machinery, are becoming completely standard – but is this really the direction the field should be going in? And how much of this owes to the rigid setting (basic semantics, certain answers) that one is unwilling to tweak and experiment with? In fact, very often high complexity is shown in the setting where the semantics of input databases is the same as the semantics of query answers. So perhaps there is another reason to reconsider that assumption.

Thus, despite an extensive literature and cast-in-stone notions of representation systems and certain answers, theoreticians do not actually know that much about handling incomplete information in databases. There are very basic questions that are still lacking adequate answers; among them:

- What is the semantics of query answers? When can/should it be the same as the semantics of input databases?
- Is taking intersection the only way to define certain answers?
- What does it mean to have a more informative data set?
- How do informativeness and semantics relate?
- How can we represent answers to queries over incomplete databases?
- When can we rely on existing query evaluation algorithms to produce meaningful answers?

It may seem that neither theory nor practice has good answers to a persistent and ubiquitous problem of handling incomplete information. But perhaps we can view this positively rather than negatively: this simply means that we are back at square one, and an effort must be made to develop a proper theory and to apply it. Both sides must show some flexibility – in tweaking both definitions and products – but first questions posed above (and many others) need to be answered. This paper does not claim to provide all such answers, far from it. But we shall at least attempt to outline an approach: one has to start somewhere, after all. Our idea is to bind together three directions of work on incomplete information:

1. the standard database approach based on representation systems and certain answers;
2. the approach from the knowledge representation community, based on viewing databases as logical theories, pioneered by Reiter [58, 60] in the 1980s; and
3. the approach based on the ideas from programming semantics that used orderings to describe information content, proposed in the 1990s [16, 49].

4. DUALITY: INCOMPLETE DATA AS QUERIES

We now describe an alternative way of looking at incomplete databases that dates back to [58, 60]. It proved to be more popular with the knowledge representation community than with the mainstream database community. More importantly for us, it developed the idea of duality between queries and databases (first noticed in [19]) for incompletely specified databases.

We start with an example. Consider an incomplete relation $R = \{(1, \bot), (\bot, 2)\}$. It can be viewed as a tableau of a Boolean conjunctive query $Q_R = \exists x\ R(1, x) \wedge R(x, 2)$. Complete databases satisfying this query are precisely the databases in the semantics of R under OWA. If we let $\mathsf{Mod}_\mathsf{C}(\varphi)$ stand for all the models of a formula φ among complete databases, then our observation can be formulated as

$$\mathsf{Mod}_\mathsf{C}(Q_R) \;=\; [\![R]\!]_{\text{OWA}}\,. \tag{5}$$

This tells us that the semantics of an incomplete database can be defined by a logical formula. This can be extended for other semantics: for instance, the formula

$$Q_R^{\text{CWA}} = \exists x \begin{pmatrix} R(1,x) \wedge R(x,2) \\ \wedge\ \forall y,z\ (R(y,z) \rightarrow \begin{pmatrix} & y = 1 \wedge z = x \\ \vee & y = x \wedge z = 2 \end{pmatrix} \end{pmatrix}$$

has the property that $\mathsf{Mod}_\mathsf{C}(Q_R^{\text{CWA}}) = [\![R]\!]_{\text{CWA}}$. In general, the approach of [58, 60] was to view a database as a logical theory, i.e., a collection Φ of formulae. A finite $\Phi = \{\varphi_1, \ldots, \varphi_n\}$ can of course be viewed as a single formula $\varphi_1 \wedge \ldots \wedge \varphi_n$.

What is the advantage of viewing incomplete databases as logical theories? An immediate benefit is that we can cast the query answering problem as logical implication, or, closer to the database language, as query containment.

Indeed, suppose we have an database D given as a theory Φ so that $\mathsf{Mod}_\mathsf{C}(\Phi) = [\![D]\!]$. Take a Boolean query Q. For it to be true in every database in $[\![D]\!]$ it has to be true in every model of Φ; thus, Q is true with certainty iff it is *logically implied* by Φ, i.e., $\Phi \models Q$. If Φ happens to be a single query Q', as in our examples above, this amounts to checking implication $Q' \models Q$, or, as database literature prefers to call it, *containment* of Q' in Q. Thus, finding certain answers is a special case of logical implication or query containment.

The connection gives us further insights. Suppose we have an incomplete database D, a Boolean conjunctive query Q, and we would like to know whether the certain answer to Q is true on D. As in (5), we have a Boolean conjunctive query Q_D so that $\mathsf{Mod}_\mathsf{C}(Q_D) = [\![D]\!]_{\text{OWA}}$. Thus, under OWA, $\mathsf{certain}(Q, D)$ is true iff Q_D is contained in Q. By a well known fact about conjunctive queries, this happens if and only if the tableau of Q_D satisfies Q – but the tableau of Q_D is D itself. Hence, the certain answer is true iff $D \models Q$. Thus, viewing incomplete databases as formulae, we can use known results on containment to find cases when naïve evaluation works.

One may notice that we used conjunctive queries together with the OWA semantics, which is described as the models of conjunctive queries. Is this a coincidence? Is it possible, for instance, to use naïve evaluation for a larger class of queries under CWA, since the formula describing $[\![\,]\!]_{\text{CWA}}$ uses features beyond those of conjunctive queries? We shall see later that the answer is positive.

5. INCOMPLETENESS AND CERTAINTY: A NEW LOOK

With this dual look at incomplete information – as formulae and as structures – we now start addressing questions posed at the end of Section 3. We want to deal with them in a setting that is independent of a particular data model – and yet applicable to all of them. In other words, we do not want to provide definitions that will apply specifically to relational databases, or to XML documents, or to graph databases. What we want instead is a *minimalistic* approach that will use only the key concepts of incompleteness. In fact, it is easier to work in a general setting so that details of a concrete data model would not obscure the picture. We now present such a minimalist model of incompleteness, following [51, 52].

5.1 Representation systems

To talk about incomplete information, one needs three key notions: of *objects*, of *complete objects*, which form a subset of the set of objects, and of *semantics* of incompleteness, which associates with every object a set of complete objects represented by it.

To formalize this, we consider triples $\langle \mathcal{D}, \mathcal{C}, [\![\,]\!] \rangle$, where

- $\mathcal{D}$ is a set of database objects (e.g., relational databases over the same schema),
- $\mathcal{C} \subseteq \mathcal{D}$ is the set of complete objects (e.g., databases without nulls);
- $[\![\,]\!]$ is a function from $\mathcal{D}$ to subsets of $\mathcal{C}$; the set $[\![x]\!] \subseteq \mathcal{C}$ is the semantics of object x.

We have not imposed any conditions at all, but some of them are needed to make this definition reflect the reality of incomplete data models. For instance, we expect a complete object c in the semantics of an incomplete object x to have more information than x. To express this, we fulfill our promise and bring the third line of work on incompleteness – based on orderings – into the picture. We define the *information ordering* as

$$x \preceq y \;\Leftrightarrow\; [\![y]\!] \subseteq [\![x]\!].$$

The intuition is that the more objects an incomplete object can potentially denote, the less information it contains (in the extreme case, if we have no information at all, every object is a possibility). We then impose two conditions on triples $\langle \mathcal{D}, \mathcal{C}, [\![\,]\!] \rangle$:

1. a complete object c denotes at least itself: $c \in [\![c]\!]$;
2. a complete object c is more informative than any incomplete object x it may represent: if $c \in [\![x]\!]$, then $x \preceq c$.

These conditions hold for $[\![\,]\!]_{\text{OWA}}$, $[\![\,]\!]_{\text{CWA}}$, and many other semantics of incompleteness.

We want to incorporate all approaches to incompleteness even at this general level, so we now bring in logical formulae. Let us assume that we have a set $\mathbb{F}$ of formulae and the satisfaction relation $\models$ between objects and formulae: $x \models \varphi$ means that φ is true in x. We write $\mathsf{Th}(x)$ for the *theory* of x:

$$\mathsf{Th}(x) \;=\; \{\varphi \mid x \models \varphi\}$$

is the set of formulae true in x. We write $\mathsf{Mod}(\varphi)$ for *models* of φ:

$$\mathsf{Mod}(\varphi) \;=\; \{x \mid x \models \varphi\}$$

is the set of all objects satisfying φ. These are extended to sets in the usual way:

$$\mathsf{Th}(X) = \bigcap_{x \in X} \mathsf{Th}(x) \quad \text{and} \quad \mathsf{Mod}(\Phi) = \bigcap_{\varphi \in \Phi} \mathsf{Mod}(\varphi).$$

Also, as before, we write $\mathsf{Mod}_{\mathcal{C}}(\varphi)$ for $\mathsf{Mod}(\varphi) \cap \mathcal{C}$.

Now we turn tuples $\langle \mathcal{D}, \mathcal{C}, [\![\,]\!], \mathbb{F} \rangle$ into *representation systems* that let us talk at once about objects, their semantics, logical representation, and information orderings. For that, we add the following conditions.

For formulae. Logical formulae must have enough power to define the semantics, as in (5), and must respect the informativeness of the objects.

Formally, for each object x there must be a formula δ_x so that $\mathsf{Mod}_{\mathcal{C}}(\delta_x) = [\![x]\!]$. Furthermore, $x \preceq y$ and $x \models \varphi$ imply $y \models \varphi$ for every formula φ. We also require that formulae be closed under conjunction.

For objects. Sets of objects cannot be too thin: thinking of relational databases, nulls should be replaceable by sufficiently many constants. That is, there must be sufficiently many valuations v of nulls so that $v(D) \in [\![D]\!]$; this is definitely true in standard semantics of incompleteness.

To state what 'sufficiently many' means, note that for every finite set $C \subset \mathsf{Const}$, we have an equivalence relation $\approx_C$ between databases: $D \approx_C D'$ says that there is an isomorphism f between D and D' that preserves constants in C (technically, both f and f^{-1} are the identity on C). Then, for every D, there is a valuation v so that $v(D) \approx_C D$. Indeed, we can just replace nulls with distinct constants outside of the finite set C. Thus, we have infinitely many equivalence relations $\approx_C$ such that for every database D, and every such relation, there is $D' \in [\![D]\!]$ so that $D' \approx_C D$.

Equivalence relations $\approx_C$ satisfy some basic properties. For instance, a formula that only mentions constants in C cannot distinguish two equivalent databases with respect to $\approx_C$. Also, if $D \approx_{C \cup C'} D$, then $D \approx_C D'$ and $D \approx_{C'} D'$.

These conditions can easily be formalized in our basic model. We assume that there is a family $\text{Iso} = \{\approx_j\}_{j \in J}$ of equivalence relations on $\mathcal{D}$ so that:

- The set $\{c \in [\![x]\!] \mid x \approx_j c\}$ is nonempty for each $x \in \mathcal{D}$ and $j \in J$;
- for all $j, j' \in J$, there is $k \in J$ so that $x \approx_k y$ implies both $x \approx_j y$ and $x \approx_{j'} y$; and
- for each formula $\varphi \in \mathbb{F}$, there must be $j \in J$ so that $x \approx_j y$ implies $x \models \varphi \Leftrightarrow y \models \varphi$.

Of course these three conditions hold for the family $\{\approx_C \mid C \text{ is a finite subset of } \mathsf{Const}\}$. From now on, we assume all the above conditions. We then call:

- $\mathbb{D} = \langle \mathcal{D}, \mathcal{C}, [\![\,]\!], \text{Iso} \rangle$ a *domain*, and
- $\mathbb{RS} = \langle \mathbb{D}, \mathbb{F} \rangle$ a *representation system.*

We now give examples of those and show how they help us define the notion of certainty.

5.2 OWA and CWA representation systems

We now provide examples of representation systems corresponding to relational OWA and CWA semantics. Let $\mathcal{D}(\sigma)$ and $\mathcal{C}(\sigma)$ be the sets of all relational databases, and of all complete databases (not having nulls) of schema σ. The domains will be of the form $\mathbb{D}_*(\sigma) = \langle \mathcal{D}(\sigma), \mathcal{C}(\sigma), [\![\,]\!]_*, \text{Iso} \rangle$, where $*$ is OWA or CWA. The relations in Iso are, as seen earlier, of the form $\approx_C$ when C ranges over finite subsets of Const.

Under OWA, the set of formulae $\mathbb{F}$ can be taken to be UCQ, unions of conjunctive queries. Thus, $\mathbb{RS}_{\text{OWA}}(\sigma) = \langle \mathbb{D}_{\text{OWA}}(\sigma), \mathsf{UCQ} \rangle$ is a representation system under OWA. The formula δ_D is simply $\exists \bar{x}\ \text{PosDiag}(D)$, where $\text{PosDiag}(D)$, the positive diagram of D, is the conjunction of all atoms in D, where each null $\bot_i$ is associated with a variable x_i. For instance, if D contains a relation $R = \{(1,2), (2, \bot_1), (\bot_1, \bot_2)\}$, then $\text{PosDiag}(D) = R(1,2) \wedge R(2, x_1) \wedge R(x_1, x_2)$.

Under CWA, we used different features in the formula describing $[\![R]\!]_{\text{CWA}}$ in Section 4. Such formulae use universal quantification and implication, although in a limited way: the antecedent in implication was a relational atom. Such a class of formulae was already studied a long time ago [23]. Recall that *positive* FO formulae are those that do not use negation: they are formed from atomic formulae using $\wedge, \vee, \exists$, and $\forall$. We now extend this class to *positive formulae with universal guards*, denoted by $\mathsf{Pos}^{\forall \mathsf{G}}$. Such formulae are closed under $\wedge, \vee, \exists, \forall$ and the following rule: if $\varphi(\bar{x}, \bar{y})$ is a $\mathsf{Pos}^{\forall \mathsf{G}}$ formula in which all variables in $\bar{x}$ are distinct, and R is a relation symbol of the arity $|\bar{x}|$, then $\forall \bar{x}\ (R(\bar{x}) \rightarrow \varphi(\bar{x}, \bar{y}))$ is a $\mathsf{Pos}^{\forall \mathsf{G}}$ formula. In Section 6 we also describe this fragment in terms of relational algebra operators.

Then the CWA representation system is defined as $\mathbb{RS}_{\text{CWA}}(\sigma) = \langle \mathbb{D}_{\text{CWA}}(\sigma), \mathsf{Pos}^{\forall \mathsf{G}} \rangle$. For each D with $\mathsf{Null}(D) = \{\bot_1, \ldots, \bot_n\}$, the formula δ_D is

$$\exists x_1, \ldots, x_n \Big(\text{PosDiag}(D) \wedge \bigwedge_{R \in \sigma} \forall \bar{y}\ \big(R(\bar{y}) \rightarrow \bigvee_{\bar{t} \in R^D} \bar{y} = \bar{t} \big) \Big),$$

where the length of $\bar{y}$ and $\bar{t}$ is the arity of R, and $\bar{y} = \bar{t}$ means $\bigwedge_{i \leq \text{arity}(R)} (y_i = t_i)$.

We can also describe orderings $\preceq_{\text{OWA}}$ and $\preceq_{\text{CWA}}$ corresponding to $[\![\,]\!]_{\text{OWA}}$ and $[\![\,]\!]_{\text{CWA}}$. Recall that a *homomorphism* $h : D \to D'$, where D and D' are two databases of the same schema, is a mapping h from $\text{adom}(D)$ to $\text{adom}(D')$ so that $h(a) = a$ whenever $a \in \mathsf{Const}$, and for each tuple $\bar{t}$ in relation R of D, the tuple $h(\bar{t})$ is in the relation R of D', cf. [2, 7]. That is, h replaces nulls with either other nulls or constants, and leaves constants intact. A homomorphism is called *strong onto* if every tuple in D' is the image of a tuple in D, i.e., if $D' = h(D)$. Then [32, 51]:

- $D \preceq_{\text{OWA}} D' \quad \Leftrightarrow \quad \exists$ homomorphism $h : D \to D'$;
- $D \preceq_{\text{CWA}} D' \quad \Leftrightarrow \quad \exists$ strong onto homomorphism $h : D \to D'$.

The OWA and CWA semantics are not the only possible ones of course. For instance, one can use a weaker version of CWA, in which tuples can be added, as long as they do not add new elements to the active domain [59]. Then a representation system for this semantics will use the class of positive FO formulae, and the ordering is given by the existence of onto homomorphisms, which map $\text{adom}(D)$ onto $\text{adom}(D')$ [32, 52].

We can also connect representation systems and orderings. It can be shown that $\mathsf{Mod}(\delta_x) = \uparrow x = \{y \mid x \preceq y\}$, i.e., the set of all models of δ_x is the set of more informative objects.

5.3 Certainty in representation systems

Recall that to define certain answers to queries, we had to determine certain information contained in the set $Q([\![D]\!])$. Thus, the central problem for us is to understand how to define certainty contained in a set $X \subseteq \mathcal{D}$ of objects. With the dual view of objects as elements of an ordered set and as formulae, we have two approaches to defining certainty: as *knowledge* about the collection X, and as an *object* representing what is known about it. In general, the former is more flexible: we have already seen this in the example of conditional tables, which are just encodings of formulae. Trying to represent certainty as another object of the same kind can tie our hands too much, although in many important cases it can be done.

Certain information represented as knowledge The first attempt to describe with certainty information contained in a set X of objects is to find a formula φ so that $\mathsf{Mod}(\varphi) = X$. This is the approach of strong representation systems which look for an object A so that $[\![A]\!] = Q([\![D]\!])$; indeed, by the duality between formulae and objects, this is the same as requiring $\mathsf{Mod}_{\mathsf{C}}(\delta_A) = Q([\![D]\!])$. The problem is that not all sets X are of the form $\mathsf{Mod}(\varphi)$, for formula coming from logics of interest to us (of course we could use a highly expressive formalism but such a formalism would hardly be useful).

So following the approach of weak representation systems, we go for the next best thing, and replace equality by an equivalence relation. But equivalence between what? We now appeal to the duality again, and view X as a *theory*, i.e., $\mathsf{Th}(X)$, which says what we know about X with certainty in a given logical language. Indeed, $\mathsf{Th}(X)$ contains formulae φ which are true in *all* objects of X.

We now must find a formula φ representing this certain knowledge $\mathsf{Th}(X)$. Since two sets of formulae are equivalent if they have the same models, we need a formula φ such that $\mathsf{Mod}(\varphi) = \mathsf{Mod}(\mathsf{Th}(X))$. This is our certain knowledge of X, denoted by $\mathsf{certain}_{\mathcal{K}}X$. To summarize,

$$\mathsf{Mod}(\mathsf{certain}_{\mathcal{K}}X) = \mathsf{Mod}(\mathsf{Th}(X)). \quad (6)$$

It is easy to show that if $\mathsf{Mod}(\varphi) = X$, or if $\mathsf{Mod}_{\mathsf{C}}(\varphi) = X$, then $\varphi = \mathsf{certain}_{\mathcal{K}}X$. Thus, (6) is a relaxation of the very strong notion of strong representation systems.

Certain information represented as object We appeal to the ordering-based approach to incompleteness. To represent what we know about X with certainty by an object y, this object must be less informative than any object $x \in X$ (as it reflects knowledge contained in all other objects in X as well). If we have two such objects y and y', and $y' \preceq y$, then of course we prefer y as it is giving us more information.

Thus, the object that we seek must be less informative than all objects in X, and at the same time the most informative among such objects. This is precisely the *greatest lower bound* of X, with respect to $\preceq$ (or $\bigwedge X$, using the standard order-theoretic notation). We denote it by $\mathsf{certain}_{\mathcal{O}}X$. To summarize,

$$\mathsf{certain}_{\mathcal{O}}X = \bigwedge X. \quad (7)$$

A few remarks are in order. Neither $\mathsf{certain}_{\mathcal{K}}X$ nor $\mathsf{certain}_{\mathcal{O}}X$ need exist in general. When they exist, they may not be unique, but they are equivalent. That is, we may have different formulae φ and ψ satisfying (6) but they are equivalent: $\mathsf{Mod}(\varphi) = \mathsf{Mod}(\psi)$. Likewise, the greatest lower bound is not unique, but for every two objects x, x' satisfying the condition of being $\bigwedge X$ we have $x \preceq x'$ and $x' \preceq x$, which means $[\![x]\!] = [\![x']\!]$, i.e., x and x' are equivalent. The idea of using formula/object duality to define certain answers first appeared in [28], albeit in a very limited context, when $\mathbb{F} = \mathcal{D}$ and $x \models y$ was a shorthand for $y \preceq x$. The definitions we are using here, as well as the results below, are from [52].

These notions of certainty have some of the expected properties. For instance, the certain knowledge about $[\![x]\!]$ is δ_x, and its object representation is x itself: $\mathsf{certain}_{\mathcal{K}}[\![x]\!] = \delta_x$ and $\mathsf{certain}_{\mathcal{O}}[\![x]\!] = x$. In particular, $\mathsf{certain}_{\mathcal{O}}[\![x]\!] \models \mathsf{certain}_{\mathcal{K}}[\![x]\!]$, although in general $\mathsf{certain}_{\mathcal{O}}X \models \mathsf{certain}_{\mathcal{K}}X$ need not hold. Also the theory of all objects represented by x is the same as the theory of x, i.e., $\mathsf{Th}([\![x]\!]) = \mathsf{Th}(x)$.

Moreover, $\mathsf{certain}_{\mathcal{K}}X$ can be viewed as a greatest lower bound in a well-known ordering on formulae: implication $\psi \vdash \varphi$, which holds if every model of ψ is a model of φ. Thus, for a set of formulae Φ, we can look at its greatest lower bound in this preorder, denoted by $\bigwedge \Phi$. This is the most specific formula ψ that implies every $\varphi \in \Phi$ (i.e., every other formula that implies Φ must imply ψ as well). Note that since $\vdash$ is a preorder, technically $\bigwedge \Phi$ is a set of formulae, all of which, however, are equivalent.

Now the following is an alternative description of certain knowledge:

$$\mathsf{certain}_{\mathcal{K}}X = \bigwedge \mathsf{Th}(X). \quad (8)$$

With this understanding of how to extract certain information, we are now going to apply it to sets $Q([\![D]\!])$, to see how certain answers must be defined.

6. MAKING CERTAIN ANSWERS EASY

We now want to use concepts from Section 5 to define certain answers to queries and to see when they can be computed efficiently, essentially using the existing technology. But first let us revisit the standard intersection-based notion of certain answers (1) to see what may go wrong if we use it. Take a very simple example: we have a database containing relation $R = \{(1,2),(2,\bot)\}$, and a query Q that just returns R. Following (1), $\mathsf{certain}(Q,R) = \{(1,2)\}$ under both OWA and CWA. This is, however, problematic for a number of reasons. First of all, such an answer misses information that there is a tuple whose first component is 2. Even more importantly, using intersection blindly for defining certain answers leads to counterintuitive results. Appealing to orderings describing the degree of incompleteness, we would expect $\mathsf{certain}(Q,R)$ not to exceed the level of informativeness of $Q(R')$ for each $R' \in [\![R]\!]$, as it presents information *common* to all such $Q(R')$. Under OWA, this is easily true, as $\{(1,2)\} \preceq_{\text{OWA}} R'$ for each $R' \in [\![R]\!]_{\text{OWA}}$. However, under CWA, exactly the opposite is true: $\{(1,2)\} \not\preceq_{\text{CWA}} R'$ for each $R' \in [\![R]\!]_{\text{CWA}}$. So in what sense $\{(1,2)\}$ is a certain answer under CWA is quite mysterious.

What causes this problem is the fact that intersection, in general, does *not* correspond to the ordering and the semantics of query answers. It may do so, but only under very limited conditions [52]. And if we want to define certainty as the greatest lower bound for the right ordering, as in (7) and (8), we need to understand what the orderings are. Note that we are defining orderings on query answers, so we are back to one of our basic questions: what is the semantics of query answers?

To answer this, we use a very basic principle:

> *if we know more about the input of a query, then we should know more about its output.*

However simple and natural this principle is, it is ignored by most approaches to incompleteness, starting with the definitions of strong and weak representation systems that somehow assume the same semantics for inputs and outputs.

6.1 Queries and naıve evaluation

To state results in a way independent of a particular data model, we view queries as mappings $Q : \mathbb{D} \to \mathbb{D}'$ between two domains $\mathbb{D} = \langle \mathcal{D}, \mathcal{C}, [\![\,]\!], \text{Iso}\rangle$ and $\mathbb{D}' = \langle \mathcal{D}', \mathcal{C}', [\![\,]\!]', \text{Iso}'\rangle$. The basic principle stated above, that more informative inputs produce more informative outputs, is then the *monotonicity* of queries: if $x \preceq y$ then $Q(x) \preceq' Q(y)$, where $\preceq'$ is the ordering associated with the semantics $[\![\,]\!]'$. In particular, using blindly the same semantics for both databases and query results (as is often actually done) does not necessarily make sense.

Certain answer to Q on an object x represents certain information in $Q([\![x]\!])$. We have shown how to define it as knowledge, and as object, and the former requires a representation system $\mathbb{RS} = \langle \mathbb{D}', \mathbb{F}\rangle$ on query answers. In its presence, we can define certain answers as

$$\begin{array}{lrcl} \text{objects:} & \mathsf{certain}_{\mathcal{O}}(Q,x) & = & \mathsf{certain}_{\mathcal{O}}Q([\![x]\!]), \\ \text{knowledge:} & \mathsf{certain}_{\mathcal{K}}(Q,x) & = & \mathsf{certain}_{\mathcal{K}}Q([\![x]\!]). \end{array}$$

Then the following holds [52]: if Q is both monotone and generic, then

$$\mathsf{certain}_{\mathcal{O}}(Q,x) = Q(x) \quad (9)$$

$$\mathsf{certain}_{\mathcal{K}}(Q,x) = \delta_{Q(x)} \quad (10)$$

That is, naïve evaluation works: simply applying Q, without doing anything else, is what we need. By *genericity* we mean the standard notion of independence of query results under permutation: in the above setting, it is stated as follows: for every j, there is k so that $x \approx_k y$ implies $Q(x) \approx'_j Q(y)$. Relational queries under the standard interpretation of $\approx$ satisfy it.

This is great news: we can get properly defined certain answers without, seemingly, doing anything special. But a question remains: why do we need representation systems and (10) when we already have (9) at the level of objects? The answer is: because in the absence of a representation system, (9) need not be true; in fact, one first needs to establish (10) and then derive (9) as a corollary, as shown in [52].

Thus, if we want to rely on existing query evaluation techniques to produce correct answers in the presence of incompleteness, we need two things:

1. A proper semantics for query answers that ensures that more informative inputs produce more informative outputs; and
2. a representation system for that semantics.

We now show how to achieve these for relational databases under OWA and CWA.

6.2 Naıve evaluation under OWA and CWA

We now look at what naïve evaluation gives us when, as had been done before, we use the same semantics for query inputs and query answers; the semantics will be $[\![\,]\!]_{\text{OWA}}$ and $[\![\,]\!]_{\text{CWA}}$. Relational queries expressed in FO, or relational algebra, are guaranteed to be generic. Thus, we need to understand when they are monotone.

For now, look at a Boolean query Q, and the description of orderings $\preceq_{\text{OWA}}$ and $\preceq_{\text{CWA}}$. Then monotonicity simply means that if $D \models Q$ and $h : D \to D'$ is a homomorphism, for OWA (or strong onto homomorphism, for CWA), then $D' \models Q$. In other words, Q is *preserved under homomorphisms* (or strong onto homomorphisms).

Homomorphism preservation is a well known concept in logic; in particular, homomorphism preservation theorems give syntactic descriptions of classes of formulae satisfying these semantic conditions. Most of them are proved for infinite structures, but some work in the finite case too [20]. For instance, an FO sentence is preserved under homomorphisms iff it is equivalent to a union of conjunctive queries [63]. Preservation results for onto homomorphisms, however, only work in the infinite case, and are known to fail in the finite [6, 65]. Nonetheless, one can take advantage of sufficient conditions for preservation: for instance, it is known that the class of $\mathsf{Pos}^{\forall \mathsf{G}}$ formulae is preserved under strong onto homomorphisms [32].

We can now show when naïve evaluation works under OWA and CWA, if we use the same semantics for databases and query answers. Let Q be a query that is defined on databases of schema σ and produces databases of schema σ'. We say that $*$-*naïve evaluation works for* Q, where $*$ is OWA or CWA, if $\mathsf{certain}_{\mathcal{O}}(Q,D) =$

$Q(D)$, where we view Q as a mapping from $\mathbb{D}_*(\sigma)$ to $\mathbb{D}_*(\sigma')$ (remember that we need a semantics of answers specified in order to define the lower bound which gives us the notion of $\mathsf{certain}_{\mathcal{O}}$).

Then, combining (9) with the preservation result of [63] and the fact that UCQs form a representation system under OWA, we obtain:

- OWA-naïve evaluation works for UCQs, i.e., for positive relational algebra queries.

By combining (9) with the preservation result for $\mathsf{Pos}^{\forall\mathsf{G}}$ [32] and the fact that $\mathsf{Pos}^{\forall\mathsf{G}}$ forms a representation system under CWA, we obtain

- CWA-naïve evaluation works for $\mathsf{Pos}^{\forall\mathsf{G}}$ queries.

Can we get a better intuition of the power of $\mathsf{Pos}^{\forall\mathsf{G}}$ queries? Clearly they add something to the positive relational algebra, and clearly it cannot be the difference operator. Recall that many real-life queries with *for-all* conditions can be written using the *division* operator of relational algebra. If we have a relation R with attributes $A_1, \ldots, A_m, B_1, \ldots, B_k$ and a relation S with attributes $B_1, \ldots, B_k$, then $R \div S$ contains tuples of A-attributes of R that appear in R in every possible combination with a tuple from S, i.e., $R \div S = \{\bar{t} \in \pi_{\bar{A}}(R) \mid \forall \bar{s} \in S : (\bar{t}, \bar{s}) \in R\}$. Division is a derived operation of relational algebra, it can be expressed with $\sigma, \pi, \times, \cup, -$.

The easy way to think of the class $\mathsf{Pos}^{\forall\mathsf{G}}$ is that it adds to the positive relational algebra the operation of diving by a base relation (i.e., S in $R \div S$ must be a relation in the database). In fact, the class is slightly more expressive, and defined as follows.

Let Δ be the query returning $\{(a, a) \mid a \in \mathrm{adom}(D)\}$; it is easily definable in positive relational algebra. Let $\mathsf{RA}(\Delta, \pi, \times, \cup)$ be the class of relational algebra queries obtained from base relations and Δ by closing them under π, $\times$, and $\cup$. Now we define $\mathsf{RA}_{\mathrm{CWA}}$ as follows:

- Each relation name is an $\mathsf{RA}_{\mathrm{CWA}}$ query;
- $\mathsf{RA}_{\mathrm{CWA}}$ is closed under $\sigma, \pi, \times$, and $\cup$ (i.e., all operations except difference);
- if Q is an $\mathsf{RA}_{\mathrm{CWA}}$ query, and Q' is an $\mathsf{RA}(\Delta, \pi, \times, \cup)$ query, then $Q \div Q'$ is in $\mathsf{RA}_{\mathrm{CWA}}$.

One can then show the following.

- $\mathsf{RA}_{\mathrm{CWA}} = \mathsf{Pos}^{\forall\mathsf{G}}$, and consequently:
- CWA-naïve evaluation works for $\mathsf{RA}_{\mathrm{CWA}}$.

Thus, we have two large classes of queries for which simply evaluating queries using existing technology does produce correct answers.

7. WHERE DO WE GO FROM HERE?

Summary

We started with a rather bleak assessment of the practical use of nulls: *"If you have any nulls in your database, you're getting wrong answers to some of your queries. What's more, you have no way of knowing, in general, just which queries you're getting wrong answers to; all results become suspect. You can never trust the answers you get from a database with nulls"* [24]. We then analyzed the state of theoretical research on incompleteness in databases, and concluded that it was in disarray as well.

But by answering some of the questions posed at the end of Section 3, we can alleviate some of the fears expressed in [24]. Not *all* results become suspect. You can *sometimes* trust the result you get from a database with nulls. One precondition for it is to have naïve, or marked nulls, but this, as mentioned already, is doable, and implemented in existing DBMS [38]. Then one can fully trust answers to positive relational algebra queries, even extended with a rather liberal use of the division operator under the closed-world semantics. In general, if the semantics of the answers is right, one *can* trust the answers provided by the standard query evaluation.

As for the key questions about the state of the theory of incompleteness, we provided a few answers. We argued that the semantics of query answers need not be the same as the semantics of input databases, and that it should be chosen in a way that more informative inputs provide more informative outputs. Intersection is not the only way to define certain answers – in fact sometimes it is a plain wrong way to define certain answers. We should be open to viewing query answers as both objects and a representation of knowledge about all possible answers. And we should be free to go back and forth between several paradigms for dealing with incompleteness: the standard object-based view, the logical-theory view, and the ordering view.

Future directions

More expressive queries We have seen how to handle positive relational algebra queries and their extension with the division operator. Can we push this further? Of course yes: (9) and (10) tell us that there is no limit as long as the semantics is chosen correctly. So the next obvious step is to analyze semantic requirements for different types of queries, and see when they can be used together with the standard query evaluation techniques.

Evaluation techniques Naïve evaluation simply applies existing query evaluation as is, and it produces the right answers under the right semantics. But we are assuming we actually know how to apply a given query to a database with nulls, and this need not always be the case. There are a variety of possible evaluation techniques that need to be investigated. Returning to our example from the introduction, it is quite bad that the query says no payments are missing, but at least we are not chasing good guys – there are no false positives. Can this always be guaranteed? Sound evaluation has been addressed before [61], but we do not fully understand efficient query evaluation techniques with nulls and their interaction with the right notions of certainty. The logical approach to incomplete databases also fits in well with the three-value semantics of SQL: theories representing databases need not be complete and may lead to unknown answers [42, 60]. One can also consider applying existing reasoning procedures with unknown outcomes (e.g., [48]) to databases with nulls.

Handling constraints This subject has been addressed, in particular for functional dependencies, with several different attempts to define when an incomplete database satisfies a constraint, see, e.g., [12, 46]. Some of these results were also applied to database design, both relational and beyond [8, 47]. However, unlike in the case of querying, little attention has been paid to the role of the semantics. But constraints are queries, after all, and we should be able to apply techniques developed here to their study. Most constraints, however, involve universal quantification, and thus special care needs to be taken in evaluating them.

Beyond relations: XML and graphs We have looked only at relational databases but of course there are other models of data. Already a long time ago, analogs of the basic concepts from [40] were worked out for nested relations [45]. More recently, there was some activity in studying incompleteness in XML [4, 13, 27, 28]. One of the key differences is that not only data but also some structural features can be missing, although it was shown that structural incompleteness leads to intractability very quickly. Most of these papers used XML-to-relations queries to define certain answers by means of intersection; an exception is [28] in which a rudimentary version of (6) was given. To extend our techniques to XML, we would need to find classes of queries satisfying homomorphism preservation conditions, which is not a trivial task at all for tree-like structures [11] and it becomes even harder with data present. A few initial results in this direction were very recently reported in [31]. And in the case of graph databases we know even less; see [14, 56] for attempts at defining incompleteness over graph data and RDF.

Applications Some of the most important applications of incomplete data occur in tasks such as data integration, data exchange, and consistent query answering: in fact, in all three of them, the standard semantics of query answering is based on certain answers. The need to apply techniques from incomplete databases in these areas is well recognized, see, e.g., [1, 35, 41] for data integration and [10, 36, 50] for data exchange. However, in all the cases, the standard intersection-based definition is used, and with few exceptions, OWA is the dominating semantics. In fact quite often naïve evaluation is used for query answering in cases where it is known not to work (as explained in [7, 50]). It thus seems to be a natural next step to apply the notions of certainty we presented here in these applications. This may well involve rethinking several of the semantic assumptions made in the past.

Acknowledgments I am very grateful to Marcelo Arenas, Pablo Barceló, Diego Figueira, Amélie Gheerbrant, Filip Murlak, Juan Reutter, and Cristina Sirangelo for reading earlier drafts and providing many helpful comments. Thanks also to Serge Abiteboul, Claire David, Giuseppe de Giacomo, Maurizio Lenzerini, Wim Martens, Antonella Poggi, Lucian Popa, and Domagoj Vrgoč for comments, discussions, and questions reflected in this paper. This work is partly supported by EPSRC grant J015377.

8. REFERENCES

[1] S. Abiteboul, O. Duschka. Complexity of answering queries using materialized views. In *PODS'98*, pages 254–263.

[2] S. Abiteboul, R. Hull, and V. Vianu. *Foundations of Databases.* Addison-Wesley, 1995.

[3] S. Abiteboul, P. Kanellakis, and G. Grahne. On the representation and querying of sets of possible worlds. *Theoretical Computer Science*, 78(1):158–187, 1991.

[4] S. Abiteboul, L. Segoufin, and V. Vianu. Representing and querying XML with incomplete information. *ACM TODS*, 31(1):208–254, 2006.

[5] S. Abiteboul et al. *Web Data Management.* Cambridge University Press, 2011.

[6] M. Ajtai and Y. Gurevich. Monotone versus positive. *J. ACM*, 34(4):1004–1015, 1987.

[7] M. Arenas, P. Barceló, L. Libkin, and F. Murlak. *Foundations of Data Exchange.* Cambridge University Press, 2014.

[8] M. Arenas and L. Libkin. A normal form for XML documents. *ACM TODS*, 29(1):195–232, 2004.

[9] M. Arenas and L. Libkin. XML data exchange: Consistency and query answering. *J. ACM*, 55(2), 2008.

[10] M. Arenas, J. Pérez, and J. L. Reutter. Data exchange beyond complete data. *J. ACM*, 60(4), 2013.

[11] A. Atserias, A. Dawar, and P. Kolaitis. On preservation under homomorphisms and unions of conjunctive queries. *J. ACM*, 53(2):208–237, 2006.

[12] P. Atzeni and N. M. Morfuni. Functional dependencies in relations with null values. *IPL*, 18(4):233–238, 1984.

[13] P. Barceló, L. Libkin, A. Poggi, and C. Sirangelo. XML with incomplete information. *J. ACM*, 58(1), 2010.

[14] P. Barceló, L. Libkin, and J. Reutter. Querying regular graph patterns. *J. ACM*, 61(1), 2014.

[15] L. Bertossi. *Database Repairing and Consistent Query Answering.* Morgan&Claypool Publishers, 2011.

[16] P. Buneman, A. Jung, A. Ohori. Using powerdomains to generalize relational databases. *TCS*, 91(1):23–55, 1991.

[17] A. Calì, D. Lembo, and R. Rosati. On the decidability and complexity of query answering over inconsistent and incomplete databases. In *PODS*, pages 260–271, 2003.

[18] D. Calvanese, G. D. Giacomo, and M. Lenzerini. Semi-structured data with constraints and incomplete information. In *Description Logics*, 1998.

[19] A. K. Chandra, P. M. Merlin. Optimal implementation of conjunctive queries in relational data bases. In *STOC'77*, pages 77–90.

[20] C. Chang, H. Keisler. *Model Theory.* North Holland, 1990.

[21] E. F. Codd. Understanding relations (installment #7). *FDT - Bulletin of ACM SIGMOD*, 7(3):23–28, 1975.

[22] E. F. Codd. Extending the database relational model to capture more meaning. *ACM TODS*, 4(4):397–434, 1979.

[23] K. Compton. Some useful preservation theorems. *Journal of Symbolic Logic*, 48(2):427–440, 1983.

[24] C. J. Date. *Database in Depth - Relational Theory for Practitioners*. O'Reilly, 2005.

[25] C. J. Date. A critique of Claude Rubinson's paper 'Nulls, three-valued logic, and ambiguity in SQL: critiquing Date's critique'. *SIGMOD Record*, 37(3):20–22, 2008.

[26] C. J. Date and H. Darwin. *A Guide to the SQL Standard*. Addison-Wesley, 1996.

[27] C. David, A. Gheerbrant, L. Libkin, and W. Martens. Containment of pattern-based queries over data trees. In *ICDT*, pages 201–212, 2013.

[28] C. David, L. Libkin, and F. Murlak. Certain answers for XML queries. In *PODS*, pages 191–202, 2010.

[29] R. Fagin, P. G. Kolaitis, R. J. Miller, and L. Popa. Data exchange: Semantics and query answering. *Theoretical Computer Science*, 336:89–124, 2005.

[30] W. Fan and F. Geerts. *Foundations of Data Quality Management*. Morgan&Claypool Publishers, 2012.

[31] D. Figueira and L. Libkin. Pattern logics and auxiliary relations. In *LICS*, 2014.

[32] A. Gheerbrant, L. Libkin, and C. Sirangelo. When is naïve evaluation possible? In *PODS*, pages 75–86, 2013.

[33] A. Gheerbrant, L. Libkin, and T. Tan. On the complexity of query answering over incomplete XML documents. In *ICDT*, pages 169–181, 2012.

[34] G. Grahne. *The Problem of Incomplete Information in Relational Databases*. Springer, 1991.

[35] G. Grahne. Information integration and incomplete information. *IEEE Data Eng. Bull.*, 25(3):46–52, 2002.

[36] G. Grahne and A. Onet. Representation systems for data exchange. In *ICDT*, pages 208–221, 2012.

[37] J. Grant. Null values in a relational data base. *Inf. Process. Lett.*, 6(5):156–157, 1977.

[38] L. M. Haas, M. A. Hernández, H. Ho, L. Popa, and M. Roth. Clio grows up: from research prototype to industrial tool. In *SIGMOD*, pages 805–810, 2005.

[39] A. Halevy. Theory of answering queries using views. *SIGMOD Record*, 29(1):40–47, 2000.

[40] T. Imielinski and W. Lipski. Incomplete information in relational databases. *J. ACM*, 31(4):761–791, 1984.

[41] D. Lembo, M. Lenzerini, and R. Rosati. Source inconsistency and incompleteness in data integration. In *Description Logics*, 2002.

[42] M. Lenzerini. Type data bases with incomplete information. *Inf. Sci.*, 53(1-2):61–87, 1991.

[43] M. Lenzerini. Data integration: a theoretical perspective. In *PODS*, pages 233–246, 2002.

[44] N. Lerat and W. L. Jr. Nonapplicable nulls. *Theor. Comput. Sci.*, 46(3):67–82, 1986.

[45] M. Levene and G. Loizou. Semantics for null extended nested relations. *ACM TODS*, 18(3):414–459, 1993.

[46] M. Levene and G. Loizou. Axiomatisation of functional dependencies in incomplete relations. *Theor. Comput. Sci.*, 206(1-2):283–300, 1998.

[47] M. Levene and G. Loizou. Database design for incomplete relations. *ACM TODS*, 24(1):80–125, 1999.

[48] H. J. Levesque. A completeness result for reasoning with incomplete first-order knowledge bases. In *KR*, pages 14–23, 1998.

[49] L. Libkin. A semantics-based approach to design of query languages for partial information. In *Semantics in Databases*, LNCS vol. 1358, pages 170–208. Springer, 1995.

[50] L. Libkin. Data exchange and incomplete information. In *PODS*, pages 60–69, 2006.

[51] L. Libkin. Incomplete information and certain answers in general data models. In *PODS*, pages 59–70, 2011.

[52] L. Libkin. Certain answers as objects and knowledge. In *Principles of Knowledge Representation and Reasoning (KR)*, 2014.

[53] L. Libkin and C. Sirangelo. Data exchange and schema mappings in open and closed worlds. *J. Comput. Syst. Sci.*, 77(3):542–571, 2011.

[54] W. Lipski. On semantic issues connected with incomplete information databases. *ACM TODS*, 4(3):262–296, 1979.

[55] B. Marnette, G. Mecca, P. Papotti, S. Raunich, and D. Santoro. ++Spicy: an opensource tool for second-generation schema mapping and data exchange. *PVLDB*, 4(12):1438–1441, 2011.

[56] C. Nikolaou and M. Koubarakis. Incomplete information in RDF. In *RR*, pages 138–152, 2013.

[57] A. Ohori. Semantics of types for database objects. *Theoretical Computer Science*, 76:53–91, 1990.

[58] R. Reiter. On closed world data bases. In *Logic and Data Bases*, pages 55–76, 1977.

[59] R. Reiter. Equality and domain closure in first-order databases. *J. ACM*, 27(2):235–249, 1980.

[60] R. Reiter. Towards a logical reconstruction of relational database theory. In *On Conceptual Modelling*, pages 191–233, 1982.

[61] R. Reiter. A sound and sometimes complete query evaluation algorithm for relational databases with null values. *J. ACM*, 33(2):349–347, 1986.

[62] R. Rosati. On the decidability and finite controllability of query processing in databases with incomplete information. In *PODS*, pages 356–365, 2006.

[63] B. Rossman. Homomorphism preservation theorems. *J. ACM*, 55(3), 2008.

[64] B. Rounds. Situation-theoretic aspects of databases. In *Situation Theory and Applications*, volume 26 of *CSLI*, pages 229–256. 1991.

[65] A. Stolboushkin. Finitely monotone properties. In *LICS*, pages 324–330, 1995.

[66] R. van der Meyden. Logical approaches to incomplete information: A survey. In *Logics for Databases and Information Systems*, pages 307–356, 1998.

[67] C. Zaniolo. Database relations with null values. *J. Comput. Syst. Sci.*, 28(1):142–166, 1984.

Expressive Languages for Querying the Semantic Web

Marcelo Arenas
Dept. of Computer Science
PUC Chile
Av. Vicuña Mackenna 4860
Santiago, Chile
marenas@ing.puc.cl

Georg Gottlob
Dept. of Computer Science
University of Oxford
Parks Road OX1 3JP
Oxford, United Kingdom
georg.gottlob@cs.ox.ac.uk

Andreas Pieris
Dept. of Computer Science
University of Oxford
Parks Road OX1 3JP
Oxford, United Kingdom
andreas.pieris@cs.ox.ac.uk

ABSTRACT

The problem of querying RDF data is a central issue for the development of the Semantic Web. The query language SPARQL has become the standard language for querying RDF, since its standardization in 2008. However, the 2008 version of this language missed some important functionalities: reasoning capabilities to deal with RDFS and OWL vocabularies, navigational capabilities to exploit the graph structure of RDF data, and a general form of recursion much needed to express some natural queries. To overcome these limitations, a new version of SPARQL, called SPARQL 1.1, was recently released, which includes entailment regimes for RDFS and OWL vocabularies, and a mechanism to express navigation patterns through regular expressions. Unfortunately, there are still some useful navigation patterns that cannot be expressed in SPARQL 1.1, and the language lacks of a general mechanism to express recursive queries.

To the best of our knowledge, there is no RDF query language that combines the above functionalities, and which can also be evaluated efficiently. It is the aim of this work to fill this gap. Towards this direction, we focus on the OWL 2 QL profile of OWL 2, and we show that every SPARQL query enriched with the above features can be naturally translated into a query expressed in a language which is based on an extension of Datalog which allows for value invention and stratified negation. However, the query evaluation problem for this language is highly intractable, which is not surprising since it is expressive enough to encode some inherently hard queries. We identify a natural fragment of it, and we show it to be tractable and powerful enough to define SPARQL queries enhanced with the desired functionalities.

Categories and Subject Descriptors

H.2.3 [**Database Management**]: Languages–*Data manipulation languages, query languages*

Keywords

Semantic Web; RDF; SPARQL; Query Answering; Datalog-based Languages

PODS'14, June 22–27, 2014, Snowbird, UT, USA.

ACM 978-1-4503-2375-8/14/06 ...$15.00.
http://dx.doi.org/10.1145/2594538.2594555.

1. INTRODUCTION

The Resource Description Framework (RDF) is the W3C recommendation data model to represent information about World Wide Web resources. An atomic piece of data in RDF is a *Uniform Resource Identifier (URI)*. In the RDF data model, URIs are organised as RDF graphs, that is, labeled directed graphs where node labels and edge labels are URIs. As with any data structure designed to model information, the natural problem of querying RDF data has been widely studied. Since its release in 1998, several designs and implementations of RDF query languages have been proposed [16]. In 2004, a first public working draft of a language, called SPARQL, was released by the W3C, which is in fact a graph-matching query language. Since then, SPARQL has been adopted as the standard language for querying the Semantic Web, and in 2008 it became a W3C recommendation [29].

One of the distinctive features of Semantic Web data is the existence of vocabularies with predefined semantics: the *RDF Schema (RDFS)* [7] and the *Ontology Web Language (OWL)* [24], which can be used to derive logical conclusions from RDF graphs. Thus, it would be desirable to have an RDF query language equipped with reasoning capabilities to deal with these vocabularies. Besides, it has also been recognised that navigational capabilities are of fundamental importance for data models with an explicit graph structure such as RDF [2, 4, 5, 15, 27], and, more generally, it is also well-accepted that a general form of recursion is a central feature for a graph query language [5, 23, 30]. Thus, it would also be desirable to have an RDF query language with such functionalities.

Unfortunately, the 2008 version of SPARQL missed the above crucial functionalities. To overcome these limitations, a new version of SPARQL, called SPARQL 1.1 [21], was recently released, which includes entailment regimes for RDFS and OWL vocabularies, and a mechanism to express navigation patterns through regular expressions. However, it has already been proved that there exist some very natural and useful queries that require of a more general form of recursion and cannot be expressed in SPARQL 1.1 [23, 30].

To the best of our knowledge, there is no RDF query language that combines all the functionalities mentioned above. Thus, it is the precise aim of the current work to bridge the gap between the existing RDF query languages and the three desired functionalities. Our ultimate goal is to propose an expressive query language that supports these features, and which can also be evaluated efficiently. Towards this direction, we first need to answer the following key question: what is the right syntax for such a language? Interestingly, Datalog with stratified negation [1, 13] has been shown to be expressive enough to represent every SPARQL query [2, 3, 4, 28, 31], so it has been used as a natural platform for the extensions of SPARQL with richer navigation capabilities and recursion mechanisms [23, 30]. Besides, some extensions of Datalog with existential quantification in the heads of rules have shown to be appropriate to encode some inferencing mechanisms in OWL [8].

Therefore, Datalog and some of its extensions – in particular, the members of the recently introduced Datalog$^{\pm}$ family of knowledge representation and query languages [10] – appear as a natural option for our purposes. However, for the language obtained by extending Datalog with existential quantification, the query evaluation problem is undecidable (this is implicit in [6]). In fact, undecidability holds even in the case of *data complexity* [32], that is, when the input query is fixed, and only the extensional database (or the RDF graph) is considered as part of the input [8]. It is thus a very important and challenging task to single out an expressive RDF query language that: (1) is based on Datalog, and thus enables a modular rule-based style of writing queries; (2) is expressive enough for being useful in real Semantic Web applications, and in particular to support reasoning and navigational capabilities, as well as a general form of recursion; (3) ensures the decidability of the query evaluation problem; and (4) has good complexity properties in the case the input query is fixed. This latter issue is of fundamental importance, as a low data complexity is considered to be a key condition for a query language to be useful in practice.

Our contributions can be summarised as follows:

1. We introduce in Section 4 a *modular* query language where reasoning capabilities, navigation capabilities and recursion mechanisms can be placed in different modules. This language is called *triple query language* (TriQ), and it is based on stratified Datalog$^{\exists,\neg,\bot}$, that is, Datalog extended with existential quantifiers in the heads of rules, stratified negation, and negative constraints expressed by using the symbol $\bot$ (*false*) in the heads of rules. In Section 4, we show this language to be expressive enough for encoding some useful but costly queries. In fact, we show that the data complexity of the query evaluation problem for this language is EXPTIME-complete.

2. We show that the modular structure of TriQ queries is very convenient to deal with SPARQL queries over the OWL vocabulary. More precisely, we focus in Section 5 on the profile of OWL, called OWL 2 QL, that is designed to be used in applications where query answering is the most important reasoning task. Then we prove that every SPARQL query under the entailment regime for OWL 2 QL [17, 22] can be naturally translated into a TriQ query. Moreover, we also show in Section 5 that the use of TriQ allows us to formulate SPARQL queries in a simpler way, as a more natural entailment regime described in that section can be easily defined by using this query language.

3. Given the high data complexity of the query evaluation problem for TriQ, we investigate in Section 6 whether the results proved in Section 5 can also be obtained for a tractable fragment of this query language. More precisely, we identify in Section 6 a natural restriction on TriQ queries that gives rise to a language, called TriQ-Lite, with the desired properties. In particular, we prove that the data complexity of the query evaluation problem for this language is PTIME-complete.

4. A key advantage of the modular nature of TriQ-Lite is the fact that, whenever the user wants to pose a new query over an RDF graph, (s)he does not need to modify the module which encodes the OWL 2 QL ontology. In Section 7, we show that this favorable behaviour cannot be achieved if we consider modular Datalog$^{\neg s,\bot}$. In particular, we introduce a novel notion of expressiveness which allows us to collect the queries that can be answered via a fixed program, and we show that TriQ-Lite is more expressive than modular Datalog$^{\neg s,\bot}$ under this notion. Notice that the crucial feature to establish such a result is the existential quantification.

The organisation of the paper is described in the summary of our contributions. Let us just say that in Section 2 we give an example which motivates our query languages, the notation used in the paper is introduced in Section 3, and that some concluding remarks are given in Section 8.

Due to lack of space, we do not give full proofs of the formal results of this paper, however, we provide proof sketches and/or sufficient evidence for the validity of the main results.

2. MOTIVATING EXAMPLE

The goal of this section is to show some of the difficulties encountered when querying RDF data with SPARQL, which motivated us to design an RDF query language based on Datalog and some of its extensions. Assume that G_1 is an RDF graph containing the following triples:

(dbUllman, is_author_of, "The Complete Book")
(dbUllman, name, "Jeffrey Ullman").

The first triple indicates that the object with URI dbUllman is one of the authors of the book "The Complete Book", while the second triple indicates that the name of dbUllman is "Jeffrey Ullman".

To retrieve the list of authors mentioned in G_1 we can use the following SPARQL query:

$$\text{SELECT } ?X \quad (?Y, \text{is\_author\_of}, ?Z) \text{ AND } (?Y, \text{name}, ?X). \quad (1)$$

We use here the algebraic syntax for SPARQL introduced in [26], which is formally defined in Section 3. In the query above, variables starts with the symbol ?. Thus, the triple $(?Y, \text{is\_author\_of}, ?Z)$ is used to retrieve the pairs (a, b) of elements from G_1, which are stored in the variables $?Y$ and $?Z$, such that a is an author of b. In the same way, the triple $(?Y, \text{name}, ?X)$ is used to retrieve the pairs (a, c) of elements from G_1, which are stored in the variables $?Y$ and $?X$, such that c is the name of a. Moreover, the operator AND in used to join the results of the triples, while SELECT $?X$ indicates that we are only interested in the values stored in the variable $?X$.

As mentioned in Section 1, one of the distinctive features of Semantic Web data is the use of the RDFS and OWL vocabularies. As an example of this, assume that G_2 is an RDF graph consisting of the following triples:

(dbUllman, is_author_of, "The Complete Book")
(dbUllman, name, "Jeffrey Ullman")
(dbAho, is_coauthor_of, dbUllman)
(dbAho, name, "Alfred Aho")
(r_1, rdf:type, owl:Restriction)
(r_1, owl:onProperty, is_coauthor_of) (2)
(r_1, owl:someValuesFrom, owl:Thing)
(r_2, rdf:type, owl:Restriction)
(r_2, owl:onProperty, is_author_of)
(r_2, owl:someValuesFrom, owl:Thing)
(r_1, rdfs:subClassOf, r_2).

In G_2, the URIs with prefix rdfs: are part of the RDFS vocabulary, while the URIs with prefix owl: are part of the OWL vocabulary. More precisely, the third triple above indicates that the object with URI dbAho is a coauthor of the object with URI dbUllman. The fifth, sixth and seventh triples of G_2 define r_1 as the class of URIs a for which there exists a URI b such that $(a, \text{is\_coauthor\_of}, b)$ holds, while the following three triples of this graph define r_2 as the class of URIs a for which there exists a URI b such that the triple $(a, \text{is\_author\_of}, b)$ holds. Finally, the last triple of G_2 indicates that r_1 is a subclass of r_2.

The last seven triples of G_2 indicate that for every pair a, b of elements such that $(a, \text{is\_coauthor\_of}, b)$ holds, it must be the case that a is an author of some publication. Thus, if we want to retrieve the list of authors mentioned in G_2, then we expect to find dbAho in this list. However, the answer to the SPARQL query (1) over G_2 does not include this URI, and we are forced to encode the semantics of the RDFS and OWL vocabularies in the query. In fact, even if we try to obtain the right answer by using SPARQL 1.1 under the entailment regimes for these vocabularies, we are forced by the restrictions of the language [17] to replace the triple $(?Y, \text{is\_author\_of}, ?Z)$ in (1) by:

$$\begin{aligned}&(?Y, \text{rdf:type}, ?Z) \text{ AND}\\ &\quad (?Z, \text{rdf:type}, \text{owl:Restriction}) \text{ AND}\\ &\quad (?Z, \text{owl:onProperty}, \text{is\_author\_of}) \text{ AND}\\ &\quad (?Z, \text{owl:someValuesFrom}, \text{owl:Thing}),\end{aligned}$$

which indicates that we are looking for the objects that are authors of some publication (that is, the objects of type r_2).

As the reader may have noticed, the resulting query is very complicated. In the query language proposed in this paper, the user can use separate modules to encode reasoning capabilities and actual queries. In particular, the user first needs to utilise a module for the RDFS and OWL vocabularies (or for some fragment of them), that could consist of Datalog$^{\exists,\neg,\bot}$ rules such as the following:

$$\begin{aligned}&\text{triple}(?X, \text{rdf:type}, ?Y),\\ &\text{triple}(?Y, \text{rdf:type}, \text{owl:Restriction}),\\ &\text{triple}(?Y, \text{owl:onProperty}, ?Z),\\ &\text{triple}(?Y, \text{owl:someValuesFrom}, ?U) \rightarrow\\ &\qquad\qquad \exists ?W\, \text{triple}(?X, ?Z, ?W).\end{aligned}$$

In this module, the predicate triple is used to store the triples of the RDF graphs. Notice that the rules of the module are used to encode the semantics of the respective vocabulary. Besides, these rules are fixed, they do not depend on the query that the user is trying to answer. Thus, to pose the desired query, the user just need to write on top of this module a simple query similar to (1):

$$\begin{aligned}&\text{triple}(?Y, \text{is\_author\_of}, ?Z),\\ &\qquad \text{triple}(?Y, \text{name}, ?X) \rightarrow \text{query}(?X). \quad (3)\end{aligned}$$

In particular, (s)he does not need any prior knowledge about the semantics and inference rules for the respective vocabulary. In fact, the module for encoding this vocabulary can be publicly available, thus greatly simplifying the process of writing queries.

It is a very common practice in the Web to have several URIs for the same object. For example, the following are URIs of Jeffrey Ullman in DBpedia (the RDF version of Wikipedia) and the semantic knowledge base YAGO:

http://dbpedia.org/resource/Jeffrey_Ullman,

http://yago-knowledge.org/resource/Jeffrey_Ullman,

respectively. To alleviate the issue of having pieces of information about the same object that use distinct URIs for this object, the OWL vocabulary includes the keyword owl:sameAs to indicate that two URIs represent the same element. For example, this keyword is used in the following RDF graph G_3 to indicate that dbUllman and yagoUllman are URIs for the same object:

(dbUllman, is_author_of, "The Complete Book")

(dbUllman, owl:sameAs, yagoUllman)

(yagoUllman, name, "Jeffrey Ullman").

Assume now that we want to retrieve the list of authors mentioned in G_3. If we try to use again the SPARQL query (1), then we obtain the empty answer as the semantics of owl:sameAs is not taken into consideration. To solve this problem, one has to use the following query:

$$\begin{aligned}&\text{SELECT } ?X\\ &\Big(((?Y, \text{is\_author\_of}, ?Z) \text{ AND } (?Y, \text{name}, ?X)) \qquad (4)\\ &\quad \text{UNION}\\ &\quad ((?Y, \text{is\_author\_of}, ?Z) \text{ AND } (?Y, \text{owl:sameAs}, ?W)\\ &\qquad\qquad \text{AND } (?W, \text{name}, ?X))\Big),\end{aligned}$$

where the operator UNION is used to obtain the union of the results of two queries, and the query after this operator is used to encode the semantics of the owl:sameAs keyword. Thus, as in the previous example, the user is forced to encode the semantics of the OWL vocabulary in the SPARQL query. And, as the reader may have noticed already, the situation gets even worse if we consider the graph G_2 in (2) but with the first two triples replaced by the triples in G_3. Fortunately, all these problems can be easily solved in our framework by just incorporating a fixed module encoding the semantics of the keyword owl:sameAs, which could consist of Datalog$^{\exists,\neg,\bot}$ rules of the form:

$$\begin{aligned}&\text{triple}(?X_1, \text{owl:sameAs}, ?X_2),\\ &\text{triple}(?Y_1, \text{owl:sameAs}, ?Y_2),\\ &\text{triple}(?X_1, ?U, ?Y_1) \rightarrow\\ &\qquad\qquad \text{triple}(?X_2, ?U, ?Y_2),\end{aligned}$$

and then using the same query (3) on top of the necessary modules.

3. DEFINITIONS AND BACKGROUND

Let $\mathbf{U}$, $\mathbf{B}$, $\mathbf{V}$ be pairwise disjoint infinite countable sets. The elements of $\mathbf{U}$ are called URIs, the elements of $\mathbf{B}$ are called blank nodes, and the elements of $\mathbf{V}$ are called variables and are assumed to start with the symbol ?. The sets $\mathbf{U}$ and $\mathbf{B}$ are used when defining both relational databases and RDF graphs, and we also refer to them as constants and (labeled) nulls, respectively.

RDF and the query language SPARQL. A triple $(s, p, o) \in \mathbf{U} \times \mathbf{U} \times \mathbf{U}$ is called an RDF triple. An RDF graph is a finite set of RDF triples. We use here an algebraic formalisation of SPARQL proposed in [26]. We start by defining the notion of SPARQL *built-in condition*, which is used in filter expressions. Formally, (1) if $?X, ?Y \in \mathbf{V}$ and $c \in \mathbf{U}$, then $?X = c$, $?X = ?Y$ and bound$(?X)$ are (atomic) built in-conditions; and (2) if R_1 and R_2 are built-in conditions, then $(\neg R_1)$, $(R_1 \vee R_2)$ and $(R_1 \wedge R_2)$ are built-in conditions. Then the set of (SPARQL) *graph patterns* is defined recursively as follows: (1) a set $\{\mathbf{t_1}, \ldots, \mathbf{t_n}\}$, where every $\mathbf{t_i} \in (\mathbf{U} \cup \mathbf{B} \cup \mathbf{V}) \times (\mathbf{U} \cup \mathbf{B} \cup \mathbf{V}) \times (\mathbf{U} \cup \mathbf{B} \cup \mathbf{V})$ $(1 \leq i \leq n)$, is a graph pattern (called a basic graph pattern); (2) if P_1 and P_2 are graph patterns, then $(P_1 \text{ UNION } P_2)$, $(P_1 \text{ AND } P_2)$, $(P_1 \text{ OPT } P_2)$ are graph patterns; (3) if P is a graph pattern and R is a SPARQL built-in condition, then $(P \text{ FILTER } R)$ is a graph pattern; and

(4) if P is a graph pattern and W is a finite set of variables, then (SELECT W P) is a graph pattern. From now on, given a graph pattern P, we define var(P) as the set of variables occurring in P, and likewise for var(R) for a built-in condition R. Moreover, we assume that for every graph pattern (P FILTER R), it holds that $\text{var}(R) \subseteq \text{var}(P)$. Finally, we usually omit curly brackets in singleton basic graph patterns, that is, we replace $\{\mathbf{t}\}$ by $\mathbf{t}$, where $\mathbf{t} \in (\mathbf{U} \cup \mathbf{B} \cup \mathbf{V}) \times (\mathbf{U} \cup \mathbf{B} \cup \mathbf{V}) \times (\mathbf{U} \cup \mathbf{B} \cup \mathbf{V})$.

To define the semantics of SPARQL, we need to introduce some extra terminology. A *mapping* μ is a partial function $\mu : \mathbf{V} \to \mathbf{U}$. Abusing notation, for a basic graph pattern $P = \{\mathbf{t}_1, \ldots, \mathbf{t}_n\}$, we denote by $\mu(P)$ the basic graph pattern obtained by replacing the variables occurring in P according to μ. The *domain* of μ, denoted by dom(μ), is the subset of $\mathbf{V}$ where μ is defined. Two mappings μ_1 and μ_2 are *compatible*, denoted by $\mu_1 \sim \mu_2$, when for all $?X \in \text{dom}(\mu_1) \cap \text{dom}(\mu_2)$, it is the case that $\mu_1(?X) = \mu_2(?X)$, i.e. when $\mu_1 \cup \mu_2$ is also a mapping. Moreover, given a mapping μ and a set of variables W, the *restriction of μ to W*, denoted by $\mu_{|W}$, is a mapping such that $\text{dom}(\mu_{|W}) = (\text{dom}(\mu) \cap W)$ and $\mu_{|W}(?X) = \mu(?X)$ for every $?X \in (\text{dom}(\mu) \cap W)$. Finally, given a function $h : \mathbf{B} \to \mathbf{U}$, we denote by $h(P)$ the basic graph pattern obtained from P by replacing the blanks nodes occurring in P according to h.

To define the semantics of graph patterns, we first need to introduce the notion of satisfaction of a built-in condition by a mapping, and then we need to introduce some operators for mappings. More precisely, given a mapping μ and a built-in condition R, we say that μ *satisfies* R, denoted by $\mu \models R$, if (omitting the usual rules for Boolean connectives): (1) R is bound($?X$) and $?X \in \text{dom}(\mu)$; (2) R is $?X = c$, $?X \in \text{dom}(\mu)$ and $\mu(?X) = c$; and (3) R is $?X = ?Y$, $?X, ?Y \in \text{dom}(\mu)$ and $\mu(?X) = \mu(?Y)$. Moreover, given sets Ω_1 and Ω_2 of mappings, the *join* of, the *union* of, the *difference* between and the *left outer-join* between Ω_1 and Ω_2 are defined as follows:

$$\Omega_1 \bowtie \Omega_2 = \{\mu_1 \cup \mu_2 \mid \mu_1 \in \Omega_1, \mu_2 \in \Omega_2 \text{ and } \mu_1 \sim \mu_2\},$$
$$\Omega_1 \cup \Omega_2 = \{\mu \mid \mu \in \Omega_1 \text{ or } \mu \in \Omega_2\},$$
$$\Omega_1 \smallsetminus \Omega_2 = \{\mu \in \Omega_1 \mid \forall \mu' \in \Omega_2 : \mu \not\sim \mu'\},$$
$$\Omega_1 ⟕ \Omega_2 = (\Omega_1 \bowtie \Omega_2) \cup (\Omega_1 \smallsetminus \Omega_2).$$

Then given an RDF graph G and a graph pattern P, the evaluation of P over G, denoted by $[\![P]\!]_G$, is recursively defined as follows: (1) if P is a basic graph pattern, then $[\![P]\!]_G = \{\mu \mid \text{dom}(\mu) = \text{var}(P)$ and there exists $h : \mathbf{B} \to \mathbf{U}$ such that $\mu(h(P)) \subseteq G\}$; (2) if P is (P_1 AND P_2), then $[\![P]\!]_G = [\![P_1]\!]_G \bowtie [\![P_2]\!]_G$; (3) if P is (P_1 OPT P_2), then $[\![P]\!]_G = [\![P_1]\!]_G ⟕ [\![P_2]\!]_G$; (4) if P is (P_1 UNION P_2), then $[\![P]\!]_G = [\![P_1]\!]_G \cup [\![P_2]\!]_G$; (5) if P is (P_1 FILTER R), then $[\![P]\!]_G = \{\mu \mid \mu \in [\![P_1]\!]_G \text{ and } \mu \models R\}$; and (6) if P if (SELECT W P_1), then $[\![P]\!]_G = \{\mu_{|W} \mid \mu \in [\![P_1]\!]_G\}$.

Notice that according to the semantics of SPARQL [21, 29], the scope of an occurrence of a blank node in a graph pattern is the basic graph pattern containing it. This is reflected in the item (1) of the previous definition, where the existence of function $h : \mathbf{B} \to \mathbf{U}$ is checked at the level of basic graph patterns. In fact, if P is a graph pattern, P_1 is a basic graph pattern occurring in P, B is a blank node occurring in P_1, and P' is the graph pattern obtained from P by replacing every occurrence of B in P_1 by a fresh blank node B', then P and P' are equivalent graph patterns according to the previous definition.

Relational databases and Datalog$^{\exists,\neg s,\bot}$ queries. A *term* t is a constant ($t \in \mathbf{U}$), labeled null ($t \in \mathbf{B}$), or variable ($t \in \mathbf{V}$). An *atom* has the form $p(t_1, \ldots, t_n)$, where p is an n-ary predicate, and $t_1, \ldots, t_n$ are terms. For an atom $\underline{a}$, we denote by dom($\underline{a}$) and var($\underline{a}$) the set of its terms and the set of its variables, respectively; these notations extend to sets of atoms. We refer to the predicate of an atom $\underline{a}$ by pred($\underline{a}$). An *instance* I is a (possibly infinite) set of atoms $p(\mathbf{t})$, where $\mathbf{t}$ is a tuple of constants and labeled nulls. A *database* D is a finite instance where only constants occur; we refer to the constants in D as dom(D).

A Datalog$^{\exists,\neg}$ rule ρ is an expression of the form[1]

$$\underline{a}_1, \ldots, \underline{a}_n, \neg \underline{b}_1, \ldots, \neg \underline{b}_m \to \exists ?Y_1 \ldots \exists ?Y_k\, \underline{c},$$

where: (1) $n \geqslant 1$ and $m, k \geqslant 0$; (2) every $\underline{a}_i$ ($1 \leq i \leq n$) is an atom with terms from ($\mathbf{U} \cup \mathbf{V}$); (3) every $\underline{b}_i$ ($1 \leq i \leq m$) is an atom with terms from ($\mathbf{U} \cup \mathbf{V}$); (4) $\text{var}(\{\underline{b}_1, \ldots, \underline{b}_m\}) \subseteq \text{var}(\{\underline{a}_1, \ldots, \underline{a}_n\})$; (5) $\text{var}(\{\underline{a}_1, \ldots, \underline{a}_n, \underline{b}_1, \ldots, \underline{b}_m\}) \cap \{?Y_1, \ldots, ?Y_k\} = \varnothing$; and (6) $\underline{c}$ is an atom with terms from ($\mathbf{U} \cup \{?Y_1, \ldots, ?Y_k\} \cup \text{var}(\{\underline{a}_1, \ldots, \underline{a}_n\})$). The set $\{\underline{a}_1, \ldots, \underline{a}_n\}$ is denoted by body$^+(\rho)$, while $\{\underline{b}_1, \ldots, \underline{b}_m\}$ is denoted by body$^-(\rho)$. The *body* of ρ, denoted body(ρ), is defined as (body$^+(\rho) \cup$ body$^-(\rho)$). The atom $\underline{c}$ is the *head* of ρ, denoted by head(ρ). A *Datalog$^{\exists,\neg}$ program* Π is a finite set of Datalog$^{\exists,\neg}$ rules. Let sch(X), where X is either a program or a set of atoms, be the set of predicates occurring in X. A *stratification* of Π is a function $\sigma : \text{sch}(\Pi) \to [0, \ell]$, where $\ell \geqslant 0$, such that, for each $\rho \in \Pi$ with $p = \text{pred}(\text{head}(\rho))$: (1) $\sigma(p) \geqslant \sigma(p')$, for each $p' \in \text{sch}(\text{body}^+(\rho))$; and (2) $\sigma(p) > \sigma(p')$, for each $p' \in \text{sch}(\text{body}^-(\rho))$. For each $i \in [0, \ell]$, let $\Pi_i = \{\rho \mid \rho \in \Pi \text{ and } \sigma(p) = i\}$. We say that Π is *stratified* if there exists a stratification of Π.

A *constraint* ν is an assertion of the form $\underline{a}_1, \ldots, \underline{a}_n \to \bot$, where $n \geqslant 1$ and every $\underline{a}_i$ ($1 \leq i \leq n$) is an atom with terms from $\mathbf{U} \cup \mathbf{V}$. The *body* of ν, denoted body(ν), is the set $\{\underline{a}_1, \ldots, \underline{a}_n\}$. A *Datalog$^{\exists,\neg,\bot}$ program* Π is a finite set of Datalog$^{\exists,\neg}$ rules and constraints. Moreover, we denote by ex(Π) the set of Datalog$^{\exists,\neg}$ rules in Π, and we say that Π is *stratified* if ex(Π) is stratified. An *answer rule* w.r.t. a program Π is a Datalog$^{\exists,\neg}$ rule ρ without existentially quantified variables and negated atoms (i.e., a plain Datalog rule) such that $\text{sch}(\text{body}(\rho)) \subseteq \text{sch}(\Pi)$ and $\text{pred}(\text{head}(\rho)) \notin \text{sch}(\Pi)$. A *stratified Datalog$^{\exists,\neg,\bot}$ query* Q is a pair (Π, Λ), where Π is a stratified Datalog$^{\exists,\neg,\bot}$ program, and Λ is a set of answer rules w.r.t. Π. Henceforth, for brevity, we write Datalog$^{\exists,\neg s,\bot}$ for stratified Datalog$^{\exists,\neg,\bot}$ programs and queries. Moreover, a supra-index can be removed from Datalog$^{\exists,\neg s,\bot}$ to indicate that the corresponding feature is disallowed. For example, in a Datalog$^{\neg s}$ program neither existential variables in the heads of rules nor constraints are allowed.

Due to the lack of space, we do not formally define the semantics of a Datalog$^{\exists,\neg s,\bot}$ query. Instead, we explain how the chase of a database with a Datalog$^{\exists,\neg s}$ program is computed, and then how the semantics of a Datalog$^{\exists,\neg s,\bot}$ query can be defined in terms of this chase. More precisely, a *homomorphism* from a set of atoms X to a set of atoms X' is a partial function $h : \mathbf{U} \cup \mathbf{B} \cup \mathbf{V} \to \mathbf{U} \cup \mathbf{B} \cup \mathbf{V}$ such that: (1) $t \in \mathbf{U}$ implies $h(t) = t$, and (2) $p(t_1, \ldots, t_n) \in X$ implies $p(h(t_1), \ldots, h(t_n)) \in X'$. Then a Datalog$^{\exists,\neg s}$ rule ρ is said to be *applicable* to an instance I if there exists a homomorphism h such that $h(\text{body}^+(\rho)) \subseteq I$ and $h(\text{body}^-(\rho)) \cap I = \varnothing$. Moreover, the result of applying ρ to I in this case is an instance $I' = I \cup h'(\text{head}(\rho))$, where h' is a homomorphism such that $h'(?X) = h(?X)$ if $?X \in \text{var}(\text{body}(\rho)) \cap \text{var}(\text{head}(\rho))$ and $h'(?Y)$ is a fresh null if $?Y \in \text{var}(\text{head}(\rho)) \setminus \text{var}(\text{body}(\rho))$. Finally, the chase of a database D with a Datalog$^{\exists,\neg s}$ program Π is

[1]For the sake of brevity, in the rest of the paper we may write rules with more than one atom in the head. This is not a problem as such rules can be transformed into an equivalent set of rules with just one head-atom; see, e.g., [11].

an instance chase(D,Π) constructed as follows. Let $\sigma : \text{sch}(\Pi) \to [0,\ell]$ be a stratification of Π, and let $\Pi_0, \ldots, \Pi_\ell$ be the partition of Π induced by σ. To construct chase(D,Π), we first construct $I_0 = \text{chase}(D,\Pi_0)$ by exhaustively applying the rules of Π_0 starting from D. Then we construct $I_1 = \text{chase}(I_0,\Pi_1)$, but this time by exhaustively applying the rules of Π_1 starting from I_0. In general, we define $I_{i+1} = \text{chase}(I_i,\Pi_{i+1})$ for $i \in \{0,\ldots,\ell-1\}$, and we define chase$(D,\Pi)$ as I_ℓ.

Let $Q = (\Pi,\Lambda)$ be a Datalog$^{\exists,\neg s,\bot}$ query and D a database. The evaluation of Q over D, denoted by ans(Q,D), is defined as follows. If there is a constraint ν in Π for which there exists a homomorphism h such that $h(\text{body}(\nu)) \subseteq \text{chase}(\text{ex}(\Pi),D)$, then D is *inconsistent* w.r.t. Q; otherwise, D is *consistent* w.r.t. Q. If D is inconsistent w.r.t. Q, then we define ans(Q,D) as $\top$, where $\top$ is a special symbol used to indicate such inconsistency. If D is consistent w.r.t. Q, which is the case we are really interested on, then ans(Q,D) is defined as:

$$\left\{ p(h(t_1),\ldots,h(t_n)) \;\middle|\; \begin{array}{l} \exists \rho \in \Lambda\ \exists \text{ homomorphism } h\text{:} \\ h(\text{body}(\rho)) \subseteq \text{chase}(\text{ex}(\Pi),D), \\ \text{head}(\rho) = p(t_1,\ldots,t_n), \text{ and} \\ h(t_i) \in \mathbf{U} \text{ for every } i \in [1,n] \end{array} \right\}$$

The decision problem associated to query evaluation is as follows: given an atom $p(\mathbf{t})$, a Datalog$^{\exists,\neg s,\bot}$ query Q, and a database D, decide whether $p(\mathbf{t}) \in \text{ans}(Q,D)$. In this work we are interested on the *data complexity* of this problem, i.e., the complexity calculated by considering Q as fixed.

Guardedness. The problem of evaluating Datalog$^{\exists,\neg s,\bot}$ queries is undecidable; this is implicit in [6, 8]. Several decidability restrictions have been proposed in the literature. The restriction which is relevant for the present work is based on the notion of guardedness. Before we proceed further, let us recall the notion of the affected position [8]. A *position* $p[i]$ identifies the i-th attribute of a predicate p. We refer to the *arity* of p by arity(p). Given a set of predicates X, the set of positions of X, denoted pos(X), is the set $\{p[i] \mid p \in \text{sch}(X) \text{ and } i \in [1,\text{arity}(p)]\}$. Given a Datalog$^{\exists,\neg s}$ program Π, the set of *affected positions* of sch(Π), denoted by affected(Π), is defined as follows: (1) if there exists $\rho \in \Pi$ such that at position π an existentially quantified variable occurs, then $\pi \in \text{affected}(\Pi)$; and (2) if there exists $\rho \in \Pi$ and a variable $?V$ that occurs in body$^+(\rho)$ only at positions of affected(Π), and $?V$ appears in head(ρ) at position π, then $\pi \in \text{affected}(\Pi)$. Let nonaffected$(\Pi)$ be the set $(\text{pos}(\Pi) \setminus \text{affected}(\Pi))$.

Example 1. Consider the Datalog$^{\exists,\neg s}$ program Π:

$$\begin{array}{rcl} p(?X,?Y), s(?Y,?Z) & \to & \exists ?W\, t(?Y,?X,?W) \\ t(?X,?Y,?Z) & \to & \exists ?W\, p(?W,?Z) \\ p(?X,?Y), \neg r(?X) & \to & \exists ?Z\, q(?X,?Z). \end{array}$$

Due to the existentially quantified variables, we get that $t[3]$, $p[1]$ and $q[2]$ belong to affected(Π). Since the variable $?Z$ occurs in the body-atom of the second rule at position $t[3]$ which is affected, and also at position $p[2]$ in the head of the same rule, $p[2] \in \text{affected}(\Pi)$. Similarly, $t[2]$ and $q[1]$ are affected positions of sch(Π). Notice that, although $?Y$ occurs in the body of the first rule at the affected position $p[2]$, and also at position $t[1]$ in the head of the same rule, $t[1]$ is not affected since $?Y$ occurs also at position $s[1] \notin \text{affected}(\Pi)$. Finally, observe that $q[1]$ is affected, even if $?X$ occurs in the body of the third rule at the non-affected position $r[1]$, since we consider only positive atoms. □

A Datalog$^{\exists,\neg s}$ program Π is *weakly-guarded* if for each $\rho \in \Pi$, there exists $\underline{a} \in \text{body}^+(\rho)$, called *weak-guard*, which contains all the variables of var(body(ρ)) that appear in body$^+(\rho)$ only at positions of affected(Π) [8]. Observe that the program Π in Example 1 is weakly-guarded. A *weakly-guarded Datalog*$^{\exists,\neg s,\bot}$ *query* is a Datalog$^{\exists,\neg s,\bot}$ query (Π,Λ) where ex(Π) is weakly-guarded.

4. MODULAR QUERIES

The main goal of this paper is to construct a query language with reasoning capabilities to deal with the OWL vocabulary, navigational capabilities to exploit the graph structure of RDF data, and a general form of recursion much needed to express some natural and useful queries. To this end, we introduce in this section a query language where these functionalities can be placed in different modules. In this paper, we exploit this modular structure and show it to be very convenient to deal with SPARQL queries over the OWL vocabulary (Section 5) and to find a tractable query language with the desired features (Section 6). Besides, this modularity allows us, for example, to easily replace a translation of a SPARQL query by a more efficient encoding if needed.

We now introduce our main language called *triple query language* (TriQ). A modular Datalog$^{\exists,\neg s,\bot}$ query M is a pair $[Q_1,Q_2]$, where both Q_1 and Q_2 are Datalog$^{\exists,\neg s,\bot}$ queries. A TriQ query is a modular Datalog$^{\exists,\neg s,\bot}$ query $[Q_1,Q_2]$, where both Q_1 and Q_2 are weakly-guarded. In order to define the semantics of modular Datalog$^{\exists,\neg s,\bot}$, we first need to define when a database D is consistent w.r.t. a modular Datalog$^{\exists,\neg s,\bot}$ query $M = [Q_1,Q_2]$. Formally, if D is inconsistent w.r.t. Q_1 or ans(Q_1,D) is inconsistent w.r.t Q_2 in the sense defined in Section 3, then we say that ans$(M,D) = \top$. Otherwise, the evaluation of M over D is performed in a modular way, that is, ans(M,D) is defined as ans$(Q_2,\text{ans}(Q_1,D))$.

In this paper, we consider modular queries with *two* modules, as these are enough for our purpose. It should be noted that, however, these queries can be easily extended to handle an arbitrary number of modules. In particular, the semantics of a modular query of the form $M = [Q_1,Q_2,\ldots,Q_k]$ is defined by considering a sequence $D_1,\ldots,D_k$ of databases such that $D_1 = \text{ans}(Q_1,D)$ and $D_{i+1} = \text{ans}(Q_{i+1},D_i)$ $(1 \le i < k)$, and then letting ans(M,D) be D_k.

A natural question at this point is how expressive TriQ is. Interestingly, we show in the next example that this language is expressive enough for encoding some very useful but costly queries; e.g., whether a graph contains a clique of size k.

Example 2. Let $G = (V,E)$ be an undirected graph with $n > 0$ vertices, and let $k > 0$. We will construct a database D and a TriQ query $M = [(\Pi_{aux},\Lambda_{copy}),(\Pi_{clique},\Lambda_{clique})]$ such that G contains a k-clique iff yes() $\in$ ans(M,D). The database D encodes the graph G and the value k. More precisely, for each node $c \in V$, D contains atom node$_0(c)$, and for each edge $(v,w) \in E$, D contains edge$_0(v,w)$. Moreover, number k is encoded in D by using atoms succ$_0(0,1),\ldots,$ succ$_0(k-1,k)$. The set of rules Π_{aux} is used to compute some auxiliary relations that are needed when checking whether G contains a k-clique. More precisely, Π_{aux} contains two rules to define the usual linear order on $[0,k]$:

$$\begin{array}{rcl} \text{succ}_0(?X,?Y) & \to & \text{less}_0(?X,?Y) \\ \text{succ}_0(?X,?Y), \text{less}_0(?Y,?Z) & \to & \text{less}_0(?X,?Z), \end{array}$$

and contains the following rules to define the minimum and maximum elements of this linear order:

$$\begin{array}{rcl} \text{less}_0(?X,?Y) & \to & \text{not\_max}(?X) \\ \text{less}_0(?X,?Y) & \to & \text{not\_min}(?Y) \\ \text{less}_0(?X,?Y), \neg\text{not\_min}(?X) & \to & \text{zero}_0(?X) \\ \text{less}_0(?Y,?X), \neg\text{not\_max}(?X) & \to & \text{max}_0(?X). \end{array}$$

The set of answer rules Λ_{copy} is just used to copy the atoms of D and the results of Π_{aux} into a new schema that can be queried by $(\Pi_{clique}, \Lambda_{clique})$. In fact, for each predicate p_0 occurring in D or Π_{aux}, we have a rule $p_0(\mathbf{X}) \rightarrow p(\mathbf{X})$.

Let us now give the key idea underlying Π_{clique}. Intuitively, Π_{clique} constructs a tree of mappings (rooted at some dummy mapping), where a mapping at level $i \in [1, k]$ actually maps the set of integers $[1, i]$ to the vertices of G. Each mapping μ at level $i < k$ has n child-mappings, one for each node of G. The child-mapping μ' of μ (for a node v) simply extends μ by mapping $(i + 1)$ to v. The k-th level of the tree contains all the possible n^k mappings $\mu : [1, k] \rightarrow V$. It is then easy to check whether there exists a mapping that maps $[1, k]$ to a clique of G.

Now we define Π_{clique}. In this program, apart from the predicates occurring in the head of the rules of Λ_{copy}, we also have the following predicates: (1) ism; the atom $\text{ism}(\mu, i)$ says that μ is a mapping at level i of the tree; (2) map; the atom $\text{map}(\mu, i, v)$ says that $\mu(i) = v$; (3) next; the atom $\text{next}(\mu, v, \mu')$ encodes the fact that μ' is obtained from μ by mapping $(i + 1)$ to v (assuming that μ is a mapping at level i); (4) noclique; the atom $\text{noclique}(\mu)$ says that μ does not map to a clique; and (5) clique_k; which is a propositional predicate used to indicate that some k-clique has been found. Moreover, the program Π_{clique} consists of the following rules:

$$\text{zero}(?X) \rightarrow \exists ?Y\, \text{ism}(?Y, ?X)$$

$$\text{ism}(?X, ?Y), \text{succ}(?Y, ?Z), \text{node}(?W) \rightarrow$$
$$\exists ?U\, \text{next}(?X, ?W, ?U), \text{ism}(?U, ?Z), \text{map}(?U, ?Z, ?W)$$

$$\text{next}(?X, ?Y, ?Z), \text{map}(?X, ?U, ?V) \rightarrow \text{map}(?Z, ?U, ?V)$$

$$\text{less}(?X, ?Y), \text{map}(?Z, ?X, ?W),$$
$$\text{map}(?Z, ?Y, ?U), \neg\text{edge}(?W, ?U) \rightarrow \text{noclique}(?Z)$$

$$\text{less}(?X, ?Y), \text{map}(?Z, ?X, ?W),$$
$$\text{map}(?Z, ?Y, ?W) \rightarrow \text{noclique}(?Z)$$

$$\text{ism}(?X, ?Y), \text{max}(?Y), \neg\text{noclique}(?X) \rightarrow \text{clique}_k()$$

Notice that the purpose of the fifth rule is to avoid that the same node is used more than once in a clique (which can happen if G contains self-loops). Finally, Λ_{clique} contains the single answer rule $\text{clique}_k() \rightarrow \text{yes}()$, which returns "yes" if a k-clique has been found. □

The previous example gives evidence that the data complexity of the query evaluation problem for TriQ is intractable. In what follows, we show that this problem is indeed EXPTIME-complete. The lower bound follows immediately from the fact that the same problem for weakly-guarded Datalog$^{\exists}$ queries is already EXPTIME-hard in data complexity [8]. The problem of deciding whether a database D is inconsistent w.r.t. a weakly-guarded Datalog$^{\exists,\neg s,\bot}$ query can be reduced to the problem of query evaluation for weakly-guarded Datalog$^{\exists,\neg s}$ queries. Thus, to establish the desired upper bound, it suffices to show that the evaluation problem for weakly-guarded Datalog$^{\exists,\neg s}$ queries is feasible in EXPTIME. This can be established by a careful extension of the existing alternating algorithm for weakly-guarded Datalog$^{\exists}$ queries.

THEOREM 1. *The query evaluation problem for* TriQ *is* EXPTIME-*complete in data complexity.*

It is important to mention that recently, independently from our work, it has been shown that weakly-guarded Datalog$^{\exists,\neg s}$ can express all the queries that can be evaluated in exponential time in data complexity [19]. Combining this result with the upper bound in Theorem 1, we obtain that weakly-guarded Datalog$^{\exists,\neg s}$ captures EXPTIME. This result implies that TriQ and weakly-guarded Datalog$^{\exists,\neg s}$ are equally expressive query languages. However, the modular nature of TriQ allows us to write more intuitive and succinct queries than weakly-guarded Datalog$^{\exists,\neg s}$.

5. FROM SPARQL OVER OWL 2 QL TO TRIQ

The first version of the Web ontology language OWL was released in 2004 [24]. The second version of this language, which is called OWL 2, was released in 2012 [20]. This new version includes three profiles that can be implemented more efficiently [25]. One of these profiles, called OWL 2 QL, is based on the description logic DL-Lite$_{\mathcal{R}}$ [12] and is designed to be used in applications where query answering is the most important reasoning task. As the main goal of our paper is to design a query language that naturally embeds the fundamental features for querying RDF, we focus on OWL 2 QL in this section, and show that every SPARQL query under the OWL 2 direct semantics entailment regime [17, 22] can be naturally translated into a TriQ query. But not only that, a second goal of this section is to show that the use of TriQ allows us to formulate SPARQL queries in a simpler way, as a more natural notion of entailment can be easily encoded by using this query language.

For the sake of presentation, we first disregard the direct semantics entailment regime and show in Section 5.1 that each SPARQL query can be translated into a modular Datalog$^{\neg s}$ query. Then we extend this translation in Section 5.2 to prove that every SPARQL query under the direct semantics entailment regime can be transformed into a TriQ query. Moreover, we show in Section 5.3 that a more natural notion of entailment, which is obtained by removing a restriction from the regime proposed in [17], can also be encoded in TriQ. It should be noticed that it is known that SPARQL can be translated into Datalog$^{\neg s}$ [2, 3, 4, 28, 31], if one focuses on RDF graphs with RDFS vocabulary extended with a special symbol to represent the null value (and with a built-in predicate to check for this symbol). Thus, the goal of Section 5.1 is not to prove that SPARQL can be embedded into modular Datalog$^{\neg s}$, but instead to propose a translation that does not need to use a special symbol for the null value, and which can be easily extended to deal not only with the RDFS vocabulary but also with the vocabulary used in OWL 2 QL ontologies (as shown in Section 5.2).

5.1 Translating SPARQL into modular Datalog$^{\neg s}$

In this section, we show that every SPARQL query can be easily translated into a modular Datalog$^{\neg s}$ query. The main ingredients of this translation are shown in the following example. From now on, given an RDF graph G, assume that $\tau_{\text{db}}(G)$ is the instance of the relational schema $\{\text{triple}(\cdot, \cdot, \cdot)\}$ naturally associated with G, that is, a tuple (a, b, c) is in the relation triple in $\tau_{\text{db}}(G)$ if and only if $(a, b, c) \in G$.

Example 3. Let P_1 be the graph pattern $(?X, \text{name}, ?Y)$, where name is a constant, which is asking for the list of pairs (a, b) of elements from an RDF graph G such that b is the name of a in G. This graph pattern can be easily represented as a Datalog program over $\tau_{\text{db}}(G)$:

$$\text{triple}(?X, \text{name}, ?Y) \quad \rightarrow \quad \text{query}_{P_1}(?X, ?Y).$$

The predicate query_{P_1} is used in this program to store the answer to the graph pattern P_1. Now assume that P_2 is the graph pattern

$(?X, \text{name}, B)$, where B is a blank node. This time we are asking for the list of elements in an RDF graph G that have a name (the blank node B is used in P_2 to indicate that $?X$ has a name, but that we are not interested in retrieving it). As in the previous case, this graph pattern can be easily represented as a Datalog program over $\tau_{\text{db}}(G)$:

$$\text{triple}(?X, \text{name}, ?Y) \rightarrow \text{query}_{P_2}(?X). \tag{5}$$

Given that blank nodes are used as existential variables in basic graph patterns, variable $?Y$ is used in the previous rule to represent blank node B. However, this time we do not include variable $?Y$ in the head of the rule as we are not interested in retrieving names. As a third example, consider the following graph pattern P_3:

$$(?X, \text{name}, ?Y) \quad \text{OPT} \quad (?X, \text{phone}, ?Z),$$

where phone is a constant. For every constant a in an RDF graph G, this graph pattern is asking for the name and phone number of a, if the information about the phone number of a is available in G, and otherwise it is only asking for the name of a. To represent this graph pattern in Datalog$^{\neg s}$, we first assume that Q_1, Q_2 are basic graph patterns $(?X, \text{name}, ?Y)$ and $(?X, \text{phone}, ?Z)$, respectively, and we construct, as before, the following rules to represent them:

$$\text{triple}(?X, \text{name}, ?Y) \rightarrow \text{query}_{Q_1}(?X, ?Y) \tag{6}$$
$$\text{triple}(?X, \text{phone}, ?Z) \rightarrow \text{query}_{Q_2}(?X, ?Z). \tag{7}$$

Predicates query_{Q_1} and query_{Q_2} are used in the representation of graph pattern P_3 in Datalog$^{\neg s}$. More precisely, we first construct a set of rules for the cases where the information about phone numbers is available:

$$\text{query}_{Q_1}(?X, ?Y), \text{query}_{Q_2}(?X, ?Z) \rightarrow \text{query}_{P_3}(?X, ?Y, ?Z) \tag{8}$$
$$\text{query}_{Q_1}(?X, ?Y), \text{query}_{Q_2}(?X, ?Z) \rightarrow \text{compatible}_{P_3}(?X). \tag{9}$$

As for the previous graph patterns, we use a predicate query_{P_3} to store the answers to the query. But in this case, we also include a predicate compatible_{P_3}, which is used to store the list of individuals with phone numbers. This predicate is used in the definition of the third rule utilised to represent graph pattern P_3, which takes care of the individuals without phone numbers:

$$\text{query}_{Q_1}(?X, ?Y), \neg\text{compatible}_{P_3}(?X) \rightarrow \text{query}^{\{3\}}_{P_3}(?X, ?Y). \tag{10}$$

Notice that in this case a binary predicate $\text{query}^{\{3\}}_{P_3}$ is used to store the answer, which has a supra-index $\{3\}$ to indicate that the third argument in the answer to P_3 is missing (which is the phone number). □

The approach shown in Example 3 can be generalised to represent any graph pattern. To formally prove this claim, we need to introduce some terminology. Assume first that $P = \{\mathbf{t}_1, \ldots, \mathbf{t}_n\}$ is a basic graph pattern such that $\mathbf{t}_i = (u_i, v_i, w_i)$ for every $i \in \{1, \ldots, n\}$, and $\text{var}(P) = \{?X_1, \ldots, ?X_k\}$. Then define as follows a Datalog program $\tau_{\text{bgp}}(P)$ encoding P. Assume that ς is a substitution such that for every symbol u occurring in P, it holds that $\varsigma(u) = u$ if $u \in (\mathbf{U} \cup \mathbf{V})$, and $\varsigma(u)$ is a fresh variable if u is a blank node. Then $\tau_{\text{bgp}}(P)$ is defined as:

$$\text{triple}(\varsigma(u_1), \varsigma(v_1), \varsigma(w_1)), \ldots, \text{triple}(\varsigma(u_n), \varsigma(v_n), \varsigma(w_n)) \rightarrow \text{query}_P(?X_1, \ldots, ?X_k)$$

For example, if P_2 is the basic graph pattern $(?X, \text{name}, B)$ mentioned in Example 3, then $\tau_{\text{bgp}}(P_2)$ consists of the rule (5). Now assume that P is a graph pattern. Then define $\tau_{\text{bgp}}(P)$ as the Datalog program consisting of the rules $\tau_{\text{bgp}}(Q)$ for every basic graph pattern Q occurring in P. For example, if P_3 is the pattern

$$(?X, \text{name}, ?Y) \ \text{OPT} \ (?X, \text{phone}, ?Z)$$

mentioned in Example 3, then $\tau_{\text{bgp}}(P_3)$ consists of the rules (6) and (7). Moreover, define $\tau_{\text{opr}}(P)$ as a Datalog$^{\neg s}$ program representing the non-basic graph patterns occurring in P. Due to the lack of space, we do not provide these rules here, we just point out that these rules are used to encode the semantics of the SPARQL operators occurring in P as shown in Example 3. In fact, if P_3 is again the graph pattern $(?X, \text{name}, ?Y)$ OPT $(?X, \text{phone}, ?Z)$ mentioned in this example, then $\tau_{\text{opr}}(P_3)$ consists of the rules (8), (9) and (10).

Let P be a graph pattern. The union of $\tau_{\text{bgp}}(P)$ and $\tau_{\text{opr}}(P)$ forms the translation of P. Notice that $\tau_{\text{bgp}}(P)$ and $\tau_{\text{opr}}(P)$ are kept separately, as $\tau_{\text{bgp}}(P)$ is used as a bridge from the data stored in an RDF graph and the Datalog$^{\neg s}$ program $\tau_{\text{opr}}(P)$ used to compute the answers to P. Thus, the modular Datalog$^{\neg s}$ query representing P is defined as:

$$\tau_{\text{dat}}(P) = [(\varnothing, \tau_{\text{bgp}}(P)), (\tau_{\text{opr}}(P), \tau_{\text{out}}(P))],$$

where $\tau_{\text{out}}(P)$ is a set of answer rules for the Datalog$^{\neg s}$ program $\tau_{\text{opr}}(P)$, which is defined as follows. Recall that some atoms of the form $\text{query}^J_P(?X_1, \ldots, ?X_k)$ occur in $\tau_{\text{opr}}(P)$, where J is a set of indexes. For example, if P_3 is defined as in the previous paragraph, then $\text{query}_{P_3}(?X, ?Y, ?Z)$ and $\text{query}^{\{3\}}_{P_3}(?X, ?Y)$ occur in $\tau_{\text{opr}}(P_3)$ (if $J = \varnothing$, then we use $\text{query}_P(?X_1, \ldots, ?X_k)$ instead of $\text{query}^{\varnothing}_P(?X_1, \ldots, ?X_k)$). Then for every atom $\text{query}^J_P(?X_1, \ldots, ?X_k)$ occurring in P, the following copying rule is included in $\tau_{\text{out}}(P)$:

$$\text{query}^J_P(?X_1, \ldots, ?X_k) \rightarrow \text{answer}^J_P(?X_1, \ldots, ?X_k).$$

In order to prove the correctness of our translation, we need to define one last term. Let P be a graph pattern, G an RDF graph and $\underline{a} = \text{answer}^J_P(t_1, \ldots, t_k)$ an atom in $\text{ans}(\tau_{\text{dat}}(P), \tau_{\text{db}}(G))$. By construction, in the set of answer rules $\tau_{\text{out}}(P)$ there is a single atom $\text{answer}^J_P(?X_1, \ldots, ?X_k)$ having answer^J_P as its predicate (which may occur in several rules). Then define as follows a mapping $\mu_{\underline{a},P}$ corresponding to $\underline{a}$ given P: $\text{dom}(\mu_{\underline{a},P}) = \{?X_1, \ldots, ?X_k\}$ and $\mu_{\underline{a},P}(?X_i) = t_i$ for every $i \in \{1, \ldots, k\}$. Moreover, define as follows a set of mappings corresponding to the answers of $\tau_{\text{dat}}(P)$ given $\tau_{\text{db}}(G)$:

$$[\![(\tau_{\text{dat}}(P), \tau_{\text{db}}(G))]\!] = \{\mu_{\underline{a},P} \mid \underline{a} \in \text{ans}(\tau_{\text{dat}}(P), \tau_{\text{db}}(G))\}.$$

With this notation, we are ready to prove that our translation is correct.

THEOREM 2. *For every graph pattern P and RDF graph G, it holds that $[\![P]\!]_G = [\![(\tau_{dat}(P), \tau_{db}(G))]\!]$.*

5.2 SPARQL entailment regime and TriQ

As pointed out before, several functionalities were included in SPARQL 1.1 [21] to overcome some of the limitations of the first version of this language. In particular, SPARQL 1.1 includes an entailment regime to deal with RDFS and OWL vocabularies [17, 22]. In this section, we show that this functionality can be encoded by using TriQ.

We start by indicating how OWL 2 QL ontologies are stored as RDF graphs in our setting. In the specification of OWL 2 [20], it is defined a standard syntax to represent OWL 2 ontologies as RDF triples. For the sake of readability, we use here a simplified version of this syntax, having in mind that the results of this section can be readily adapted to the standard syntax. More precisely, define the vocabulary Σ of an OWL 2 QL ontology as a finite set of unary and binary predicates, which are called classes and properties, respectively. Moreover, define a basic property over Σ as either p or p^-, where p is a property in Σ, and define a basic class over Σ as either a or $\exists r$, where a is a class in Σ and r is a basic property over Σ. Then to represent an OWL 2 QL ontology over a vocabulary Σ, we first include the following triples to indicate what the classes and properties in Σ are. For every class a in Σ, we include the triple $(a, \text{rdf:type}, \text{owl:Class})$. Notice that this triple uses the reserved URIs rdf:type and owl:Class, and indicates that a is of type (rdf:type) class (owl:Class). Moreover, for every property p in Σ, we include the following triples:

$$
\begin{array}{ll}
(p, \text{rdf:type}, \text{owl:Prop}) & (p, \text{owl:inv}, p^-) \\
(p^-, \text{rdf:type}, \text{owl:Prop}) & (p^-, \text{owl:inv}, p) \\
(\exists p, \text{owl:rest}, p) & (\exists p, \text{rdf:type}, \text{owl:Class}) \\
(\exists p^-, \text{owl:rest}, p^-) & (\exists p^-, \text{rdf:type}, \text{owl:Class})
\end{array}
$$

The triples $(p, \text{rdf:type}, \text{owl:Prop})$, $(p^-, \text{rdf:type}, \text{owl:Prop})$ indicate that p and p^- are properties (owl:Prop). It is important to notice that p and p^- are assumed to be (distinct) URIs. The triple $(p^-, \text{owl:inv}, p)$ indicates that p^- is the inverse property of p, while triples $(\exists p, \text{owl:rest}, p)$, $(\exists p^-, \text{owl:rest}, p^-)$ indicate that $\exists p$ and $\exists p^-$ are restrictions of p and p^-, respectively, where $\exists p$ and $\exists p^-$ are also assumed to be URIs. Finally, $(\exists p, \text{rdf:type}, \text{owl:Class})$ and $(\exists p^-, \text{rdf:type}, \text{owl:Class})$ indicate that $\exists p$ and $\exists p^-$ are classes. It is important to notice that the notation used above is a simplification of the notation used in OWL 2, as owl:Prop, owl:inv and owl:rest correspond to the OWL 2 keywords owl:ObjectProperty, owl:inverseOf and owl:Restriction, respectively. Besides, a triple such as $(\exists p, \text{owl:rest}, p)$ is represented by means of several triples in OWL 2, as shown in Section 2.

In order to represent the axioms in an OWL 2 QL ontology, we include the following triples. To indicate that a basic class b_1 is a sub-class of a basic class b_2, we include the triple $(b_1, \text{rdfs:sc}, b_2)$. Similarly, to indicate that a basic property r_1 is a sub-property of a basic property r_2, we include the triple $(r_1, \text{rdfs:sp}, r_2)$. Finally, to indicate that basic classes b_1 and b_2 are disjoint, we include the triple $(b_1, \text{owl:disj}, b_2)$. It should be noticed that, as before, rdfs:sc, rdfs:sp and owl:disj are shorthands for the keywords rdfs:subClassOf, rdfs:subPropertyOf and owl:disjointWith, respectively, which can be used in OWL 2.

Finally, in order to represent the membership assertions in an OWL 2 QL ontology, we include the following triples. To indicate that a constant a belong to a basic class b, we include the triple $(a, \text{rdf:type}, b)$. Similarly, to indicate that a constant a_1 is related to a constant a_2 through a property p, we include the triple (a_1, p, a_2).

From now on, we say that an RDF graph G represents an OWL 2 QL ontology if there exists an OWL 2 QL ontology $\mathcal{O}$ such that, the translation into RDF of $\mathcal{O}$ according to the previous rules generates G.

As a second step in our construction, we show how a graph pattern is evaluated under the OWL 2 direct semantics entailment regime defined in [17]. To compute the answer to a graph pattern, this regime is first applied at the level of basic graph patterns, and then the results of this step are combined using the standard semantics for the SPARQL operators [22]. Thus, we only need to define the OWL 2 direct semantics entailment regime for basic graph patterns.

Assume that P is a basic graph pattern. Under the OWL 2 direct semantics entailment regime, the evaluation of P over an RDF graph G adopts an active domain semantics, that is, it uses the notion of entailment in OWL 2 QL (which corresponds to the notion of entailment in DL-Lite$_{\mathcal{R}}$) but allowing the variables and blank nodes in P to take only values from G. For example, assume that we are given an RDF graph G consisting of the following triples:

$$(\text{dog}, \text{rdf:type}, \text{animal}) \;\; (\text{animal}, \text{rdfs:sc}, \exists\text{eats}), \qquad (11)$$

which indicate that dog is an animal, and every animal eats something. Moreover, assume that we want to retrieve the list of elements of G that eat something. The natural way to formulate this query is by using a graph pattern of the form $(?X, \text{eats}, B)$, where B is a blank node. However, the answer to this query is empty under the OWL 2 direct semantics entailment regime, as there are no elements a, b in G that can be assigned to $?X$ and B in such a way that the triple (a, eats, b) is implied by the axioms in G. In other words, the answer to $(?X, \text{eats}, B)$ is empty under the active domain semantics adopted in SPARQL 1.1. To obtain a correct answer in this case, we can consider the graph pattern $(?X, \text{rdf:type}, \exists\text{eats})$, as the triples in G can be used to infer the triple $(\text{dog}, \text{rdf:type}, \exists\text{eats})$, from which the correct answer dog is obtained.

Let G be an RDF graph representing an OWL 2 QL ontology. Given a triple $\mathbf{t} \in \mathbf{U} \times \mathbf{U} \times \mathbf{U}$, we use notation $G \models \mathbf{t}$ to indicate that $\mathbf{t}$ is implied by G as defined in [25, 17], which in turn is based on the notion of entailment for DL-Lite$_{\mathcal{R}}$ [12]. Moreover, given a basic graph pattern P, the evaluation of P over G under the OWL 2 direct semantics entailment regime, denoted by $[\![P]\!]_G^{\mathbf{U}}$, is defined as:

$$\{\mu \mid \text{dom}(\mu) = \text{var}(P) \text{ and there exists } h : \mathbf{B} \to \mathbf{U} \text{ such that for every } \mathbf{t} \in \mu(h(P))\text{: } G \models \mathbf{t}\}. \qquad (12)$$

Notice that the supra-index $\mathbf{U}$ in $[\![P]\!]_G^{\mathbf{U}}$ is used to indicate that every variable and blank node in P has to be assigned a constant, as $\mathbf{U}$ is the range of functions h and μ in the previous definition. Moreover, the evaluation of a graph pattern P over an RDF graph G under the OWL 2 direct semantics entailment regime, denoted by $[\![P]\!]_G^{\mathbf{U}}$, is recursively defined as the usual semantics for graph patterns (which is given in Section 3) but replacing the rule for evaluating basic graph patterns by rule (12). In what follows, we define a fixed Datalog$^{\exists,\neg s,\bot}$ program τ_{owl2ql} that is used to encode the semantics $[\![\cdot]\!]_G^{\mathbf{U}}$. In this program, we first include a Datalog rule to store in a unary predicate C all the URIs from the graph (recall that we assume that an RDF graph does not contain any blank nodes):

$$\text{triple}(?X, ?Y, ?Z) \;\to\; \text{C}(?X), \text{C}(?Y), \text{C}(?Z). \qquad (13)$$

Then we define some Datalog rules that store the different elements in the ontology:

$$
\begin{array}{rcl}
\text{triple}(?X, \text{rdf:type}, ?Y) & \to & \text{type}(?X, ?Y) \\
\text{triple}(?X, \text{rdfs:sp}, ?Y) & \to & \text{sp}(?X, ?Y) \\
\text{triple}(?X, \text{owl:inv}, ?Y) & \to & \text{inv}(?X, ?Y) \\
\text{triple}(?X, \text{owl:rest}, ?Y) & \to & \text{rest}(?X, ?Y) \\
\text{triple}(?X, \text{rdfs:sc}, ?Y) & \to & \text{sc}(?X, ?Y) \\
\text{triple}(?X, \text{owl:disj}, ?Y) & \to & \text{disj}(?X, ?Y) \\
\text{triple}(?X, ?Y, ?Z) & \to & \text{triple}_1(?X, ?Y, ?Z)
\end{array}
$$

If we have triples $(a, \text{rdf:type}, b)$, $(b, \text{rdfs:sc}, \exists r)$ in an OWL 2 QL ontology, then the Datalog$^{\exists,\neg s,\bot}$ program τ_{owl2ql} will create a triple of the form (a, r, z), where z is a null value. If (a, r, z) is stored in the relation triple, then by using rule (13) we will conclude that $\text{C}(z)$ holds, violating the intended interpretation of predicate C. To solve this problem, we include the last Datalog rule above to produce a copy of the predicate triple in the predicate triple_1. In this way, the new values are added to triple_1, that is, we do not modify the predicate triple but instead we have that both $\text{triple}_1(a, \text{rdf:type}, b)$ and $\text{triple}_1(b, \text{rdfs:sc}, \exists r)$ hold, from which we conclude that $\text{triple}_1(a, r, z)$ also holds. Moreover, we include the following rules to reason about properties:

$$\begin{aligned} &\text{sp}(?X_1, ?X_2), \text{inv}(?Y_1, ?X_1), \\ &\qquad \text{inv}(?Y_2, ?X_2) \rightarrow \text{sp}(?Y_1, ?Y_2) \\ &\text{type}(?X, \text{owl:Prop}) \rightarrow \text{sp}(?X, ?X) \\ &\text{sp}(?X, ?Y), \text{sp}(?Y, ?Z) \rightarrow \text{sp}(?X, ?Z) \end{aligned}$$

we include the following rules to reason about classes:

$$\begin{aligned} &\text{sp}(?X_1, ?X_2), \text{rest}(?Y_1, ?X_1), \\ &\qquad \text{rest}(?Y_2, ?X_2) \rightarrow \text{sc}(?Y_1, ?Y_2) \\ &\text{type}(?X, \text{owl:Class}) \rightarrow \text{sc}(?X, ?X) \\ &\text{sc}(?X, ?Y), \text{sc}(?Y, ?Z) \rightarrow \text{sc}(?X, ?Z) \end{aligned}$$

and we include the following rule to reason about disjointness constraints:

$$\begin{aligned} &\text{disj}(?X_1, ?X_2), \text{sc}(?Y_1, ?X_1), \\ &\qquad \text{sc}(?Y_2, ?X_2) \rightarrow \text{disj}(?Y_1, ?Y_2) \end{aligned}$$

Finally, we include the following rules to reason about membership assertions:

$$\begin{aligned} &\text{triple}_1(?X, ?U, ?Y), \text{sp}(?U, ?V) \rightarrow \text{triple}_1(?X, ?V, ?Y) \\ &\text{triple}_1(?X, ?U, ?Y), \text{inv}(?U, ?V) \rightarrow \text{triple}_1(?Y, ?V, ?X) \\ &\text{type}(?X, ?Y), \text{rest}(?Y, ?U) \rightarrow \exists ?Z\, \text{triple}_1(?X, ?U, ?Z) \\ &\text{type}(?X, ?Y), \text{sc}(?Y, ?Z) \rightarrow \text{type}(?X, ?Z) \\ &\text{triple}_1(?X, ?U, ?Y), \text{rest}(?Z, ?U) \rightarrow \text{type}(?X, ?Z) \\ &\text{type}(?X, ?Y), \text{type}(?X, ?Z), \text{disj}(?Y, ?Z) \rightarrow \bot \end{aligned}$$

Given a graph pattern P and an RDF graph G, to compute $[\![P]\!]_G^{\mathbf{U}}$ we need to include τ_{owl2ql} in the modular Datalog$^{\neg s}$ query $\tau_{\text{dat}}(P)$ defined in Section 5.1. More precisely, assuming that $\tau_{\text{dat}}(P) = [(\varnothing, \tau_{\text{bgp}}(P)), (\tau_{\text{opr}}(P), \tau_{\text{out}}(P))]$, we need to replace $\varnothing$ by τ_{owl2ql} in the first component of $\tau_{\text{dat}}(P)$, but taking into consideration the active domain semantics in the entailment regime just defined. For example, assume that P is the basic graph pattern $(?X, \text{eats}, B)$ and G is the RDF graph in (11) storing information about animals. Then we have that $\tau_{\text{bgp}}(P)$ is the following answer rule:

$$\text{triple}(?X, \text{eats}, ?Y) \quad \rightarrow \quad \text{query}_P(?X). \tag{14}$$

In order to combine this rule with τ_{owl2ql}, we first need to consider the fact that all the triples inferred by using the axioms in G are stored in the predicate triple_1. Thus, we need to replace triple by triple_1 in the rule (14):

$$\text{triple}_1(?X, \text{eats}, ?Y) \quad \rightarrow \quad \text{query}_P(?X).$$

Moreover, we need to enforce the constraint that every variable and blank node in P can only take a value from G (the active domain semantics restriction), which is done by including the predicate C:

$$\text{triple}_1(?X, \text{eats}, ?Y), \text{C}(?X), \text{C}(?Y) \quad \rightarrow \quad \text{query}_P(?X). \tag{15}$$

Thus, given a graph pattern P, let $\tau_{\text{bgp}}^{\mathbf{U}}(P)$ be the set of answer rules obtained from $\tau_{\text{bgp}}(P)$ by first replacing triple by triple_1 in every rule of $\tau_{\text{bgp}}(P)$, and then adding $\text{C}(?X)$ in the body of every resulting rule ρ if $?X$ occurs in ρ. Moreover, let $\tau_{\text{dat}}^{\mathbf{U}}(P) = [(\tau_{\text{owl2ql}}, \tau_{\text{bgp}}^{\mathbf{U}}(P)), (\tau_{\text{opr}}(P), \tau_{\text{out}}(P))]$. Then it is possible to prove that:

THEOREM 3. *For every graph pattern P and RDF graph G, it holds that* $[\![P]\!]_G^{\mathbf{U}} = [\![(\tau_{dat}^{\mathbf{U}}(P), \tau_{db}(G))]\!]$.

Moreover, we have that:

PROPOSITION 4. *For every graph pattern P, $\tau_{dat}^{\mathbf{U}}(P)$ is a* TriQ *query.*

5.3 Removing the active domain restriction

Consider the basic graph pattern:

$$Q_0 \quad = \quad \{(?X, \text{eats}, B), (B, \text{rdf:type}, \text{plant\_material})\},$$

which is asking for the lists of animals that eat some plant material, and assume that G is an RDF graph. Under the active domain semantics, a is an answer to Q_0 over G if we can replace blank node B by a specific plant material b such that G implies $(?X, \text{eats}, b)$. But what happens if such a concrete witness cannot be found in G, and we can only infer that a is an answer to Q_0 by using the axioms in the ontology. For example, this could happens if G stores information only about herbivores, so it includes the axiom $(\exists\text{eats}^-, \text{rdfs:sc}, \text{plant\_material})$. In this case, Q_0 has to be replaced by a basic graph pattern of the form:

$$\{(?X, \text{rdf:type}, \exists\text{eats}), (\exists\text{eats}^-, \text{rdfs:sc}, \text{plant\_material})\}$$

in order to obtain the correct answers. And even worse, what happens if the query has to be distributed over several RDF graphs, which is a very common scenario in the Web. Then the user is forced to use a graph pattern of the form:

$$\begin{aligned} &\{(?X, \text{eats}, B), (B, \text{rdf:type}, \text{plant\_material})\} \text{ UNION} \\ &\{(?X, \text{rdf:type}, \exists\text{eats}), (\exists\text{eats}^-, \text{rdfs:sc}, \text{plant\_material})\}, \end{aligned}$$

in which some inferences have to be encoded. All these issues can be solved if we do not force B to take values only in G, as this allows us to use the initial basic graph pattern Q_0. This gives rise to the semantics $[\![P]\!]_G^{\text{ALL}}$ that is defined exactly as $[\![P]\!]_G^{\mathbf{U}}$, but considering every basic graph pattern as a conjunctive query, and treating blank nodes as existential variables that are not forced to take only values in G (they can take values in the interpretations of G).

At this point, one may be tempted to think that the semantics $[\![\cdot]\!]^{\text{ALL}}$ can be directly defined by transforming every basic graph pattern into a conjunctive query, which has to be evaluated over a DL ontology. In fact, this approach works well with our initial query Q_0, which can be transformed into the conjunctive query $\exists Y\, \text{eats}(X, Y) \wedge \text{plant\_material}(Y)$. However, there are simple queries for which this approach does not work. For instance, consider the basic graph pattern $(?X, \text{rdfs:sc}, \exists\text{eats})$. Given that $?X$ is used to store class names, this pattern cannot be transformed into a conjunctive query in order to define its semantics; instead we need to replace $?X$ by every class name C, and then verify whether the inclusion $C \sqsubseteq \exists\text{eats}$ is implied by the DL ontology in order to define its semantics. Thus, the goal of this section is to show that the more natural semantics $[\![\cdot]\!]^{\text{ALL}}$ can be easily defined by using modular Datalog$^{\exists, \neg s, \bot}$, without needing to differentiate between variables that are used to store individuals, classes or properties.

Given a basic graph pattern Q, let $\tau_{\text{bgp}}^{\text{ALL}}(Q)$ be the answer rule obtained from $\tau_{\text{bgp}}^{\mathbf{U}}(Q)$ by removing every atom of the form $\text{C}(?X)$ such that $?X \notin \text{var}(Q)$ (that is, every atom $\text{C}(?X)$ such that $?X$ is a variable associated to a blank node occurring in Q). For example, assume that P is the basic graph pattern $(?X, \text{eats}, B)$. Then we have that $\tau_{\text{bgp}}^{\mathbf{U}}(P)$ is the rule (15), from which we conclude that $\tau_{\text{bgp}}^{\text{ALL}}(P)$ is the following rule:

$$\text{triple}_1(?X, \text{eats}, ?Y), \text{C}(?X) \quad \rightarrow \quad \text{query}_Q(?X).$$

Moreover, given a graph pattern P, define $\tau_{\text{bgp}}^{\text{ALL}}(P)$ as the Datalog program consisting of the rules $\tau_{\text{bgp}}^{\text{ALL}}(Q)$ for every basic graph pattern Q occurring in P. Finally, define $\tau_{\text{dat}}^{\text{ALL}}(P)$ as $[(\tau_{\text{owl2ql}}, \tau_{\text{bgp}}^{\text{ALL}}(P)), (\tau_{\text{opr}}(P), \tau_{\text{out}}(P))]$. With this very simple modification of $\tau_{\text{dat}}^{\text{U}}(P)$, we can formally define the semantics $[\![\cdot]\!]^{\text{ALL}}$:

Definition 1. Given a graph pattern P and an RDF graph G, define $[\![P]\!]_G^{\text{ALL}}$ as $[\![(\tau_{\text{dat}}^{\text{ALL}}(P), \tau_{\text{db}}(G))]\!]$.

We conclude by pointing out that $\tau_{\text{dat}}^{\text{ALL}}(P)$ is a TriQ query, for every graph pattern P. Thus, this query language is expressive enough to represent the OWL 2 direct semantics entailment regime for the case of OWL 2 QL ontologies, even if the active domain restriction is not imposed.

6. A TRACTABLE QUERY LANGUAGE

TriQ forms a natural language which embeds the fundamental features for querying RDF, as shown in Section 5. Unfortunately, Theorem 1 shows that this language is highly intractable in data complexity. Then the question that comes up is whether a fragment of this language exists which is powerful enough for expressing every SPARQL query under the entailment regime for OWL 2 QL, and at the same time ensures the tractability of query evaluation. Towards the identification of such a sublanguage, we single out a fragment of TriQ for which the query evaluation problem can be reduced in polynomial time to the query evaluation problem for linear Datalog$^{\exists}$. Recall that a rule ρ is called linear if body(ρ) contains only one atom. Interestingly, the query evaluation problem for linear Datalog$^{\exists}$ can be reduced to first-order query evaluation [9]. Thus, our reduction allows us not only to find the desired tractable fragment, but also to exploit the mature and efficient relational database technology to answer queries in this fragment.

6.1 The query language TriQ-Lite

After a careful analysis of ex(τ_{owl2ql}), that is, the program obtained after eliminating the constraint occurring in τ_{owl2ql}, we observed that it enjoys the following interesting property. Let D be a database and $\rho \in$ ex(τ_{owl2ql}). If ρ is triggered with a homomorphism h during the construction of chase(ex(τ_{owl2ql}), D), then for each body-variable $?V$ of ρ that participates in a join operation (i.e., appears more than once in body(ρ)) we have that $h(?V) \in$ dom(D). Inspired by this observation, we introduce a syntactic condition that is sufficient to ensure the above semantic property.

Let Π be a Datalog$^{\exists,\neg s,\perp}$ program. Π is called *constant-join* if for every $\rho \in$ ex(Π) and every variable $?V \in$ var(body(ρ)) that occurs more than once in body(ρ), it holds that $?V$ appears in body$^{+}(\rho)$ at a position of nonaffected(ex(Π)).

Example 4. Consider the Datalog$^{\exists,\neg s}$ program Π:

$$\begin{aligned} p(?X,?Y), s(?Y,?Z) &\rightarrow \exists ?W\, t(?Y,?X,?W) \\ t(?X,?Y,?Z) &\rightarrow \exists ?W\, p(?W,?Z) \\ s(?X,?Y), \neg r(?X), \neg r(?Y) &\rightarrow \exists ?Z\, q(?X,?Z). \end{aligned}$$

Clearly, affected(Π) $= \{t[3], p[1], q[2], p[2], t[2]\}$. The first rule is constant-join since at least one occurrence of the variable $?Y$ appears at the non-affected position $s[1]$. The second rule is trivially constant-join since each variable occurs in its body only once. Finally, the third rule is constant-join since both $?X$ and $?Y$ occur in a positive atom at a non-affected position. Therefore, Π is a constant-join program. □

A Datalog$^{\exists,\neg s,\perp}$ query (Π, Λ) is constant-join if the program Π is constant-join. A modular Datalog$^{\exists,\neg s,\perp}$ query $[Q_1, Q_2]$ is called constant-join if both Q_1 and Q_2 are constant-join. Finally, a TriQ-Lite query is defined as a constant-join TriQ query. Then we have that:

PROPOSITION 5. *For every graph pattern P, both $\tau_{dat}^{\text{U}}(P)$ and $\tau_{dat}^{\text{ALL}}(P)$ are* TriQ-Lite *queries.*

By combining Theorem 3 and Proposition 5, we immediately get that:

COROLLARY 6. *Every SPARQL query under the entailment regime for OWL 2 QL can be expressed as a* TriQ-Lite *query.*

After posing the constant-join condition on TriQ, we obtain a language for which the query evaluation problem is tractable in data complexity:

THEOREM 7. *Query evaluation for* TriQ-Lite *is* PTIME-*complete in data complexity.*

Since every Datalog program is a weakly-guarded constant-join Datalog$^{\exists,\neg s,\perp}$ program, every Datalog query can be rewritten as an equivalent TriQ-Lite query. This allows us to deduce the lower bound in Theorem 7, as the query evaluation problem for Datalog is PTIME-hard in data complexity (see, e.g., [14]). Thus, the rest of this section is devoted to establish the membership of our problem in PTIME.

The problem of checking whether a database D is inconsistent w.r.t. a TriQ-Lite query $M = [Q_1, Q_2]$ can be reduced to the query evaluation problem for weakly-guarded constant-join Datalog$^{\exists,\neg s}$. To check whether D is inconsistent w.r.t. $Q_1 = (\Pi_1, \Lambda_1)$, we first construct the weakly-guarded constant-join Datalog$^{\exists,\neg s}$ query $Q_1' = (\text{ex}(\Pi), \Lambda \cup \Gamma)$, where Γ contains an answer rule body$(\nu) \rightarrow p_\nu()$ for each constraint ν in Π (notice that these constraints are the only source of inconsistency). Then we check whether an atom $p_\nu()$ belongs to ans(Q_1', D), which implies that ν is violated and, thus, D is inconsistent w.r.t. Q_1. In the same way, we check whether the instance ans(Q_1, D) is inconsistent w.r.t. Q_2.

Whenever the input database is inconsistent with the given query M, we return the symbol $\top$. Otherwise, we continue by focusing on the query obtained from M by eliminating the constraints. By definition of the semantics of modular queries, to show that the query evaluation problem for TriQ-Lite is in PTIME in data complexity, it suffices to show that the same problem is in PTIME for weakly-guarded constant-join Datalog$^{\exists,\neg s}$. Thus, Theorem 7 follows from the following result.

PROPOSITION 8. *The query evaluation problem for weakly-guarded constant-join Datalog$^{\exists,\neg s}$ is in* PTIME *in data complexity.*

The key idea underlying the proof of this proposition is to construct a polynomial-time reduction, from the query evaluation problem for weakly-guarded constant-join Datalog$^{\exists,\neg s}$ to the query evaluation problem for linear Datalog$^{\exists}$. This reduction is computed in two steps. In the first step, we eliminate the negation from the given query (Π, Λ) to produce (Π^{+}, Λ). More specifically, assume that $\rho \in \Pi$ and $?V$ is a variable occurring in an atom of body$^{-}(\rho)$. Then $?V$ must occur in an atom of body$^{+}(\rho)$ and, therefore, $?V$ must appear at a non-affected position due to the constant-join condition. Hence, in the computation of the chase of a database D with Π, every predicate in body$^{-}(\rho)$ can store only constants occurring in D. Thus, given that Π is stratified, Π^{+} can be computed from Π in a standard way, by replacing each negated atom $\neg p(\mathbf{t})$ with a

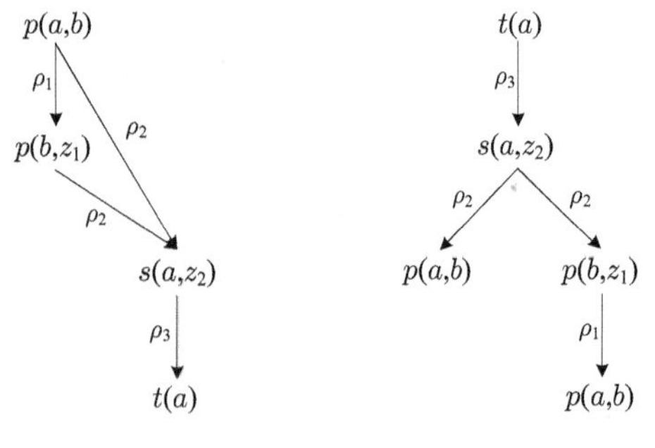

(a) (b)

Figure 1: (a) The part of chase(D, Π) which entails $\underline{a} = t(a)$; (b) The proof-tree for $\underline{a} = t(a)$ w.r.t. D and Π.

positive atom $\bar{p}(\mathbf{t})$, where the relation $\bar{p}$ stores the complement of p with respect to the ground chase (that is, the atoms of the chase with only constants).

The second step is to convert each non-linear rule in Π^+ into a linear one. Assume that $\rho \in \Pi$ and $\underline{a}$ is the weak-guard of ρ. Since Π^+ is both weakly-guarded and constant-join, if ρ is triggered during the construction of the chase, then every atom in body$(\rho) \setminus \{\underline{a}\}$ is mapped only to the ground chase. Thus, to convert ρ into a linear rule, we just need to keep the rule $h(\underline{a}) \rightarrow h(\text{head}(\rho))$, for every homomorphism h that maps the atoms in body$(\rho) \setminus \{\underline{a}\}$ to the ground chase. Let us now give some more details regarding the two steps just described.

6.1.1 From Weakly-guarded constant-join Datalog$^{\exists,\neg_s}$ to linear Datalog$^{\exists}$

It is clear that the ground part of the chase plays a central role in our reduction. In what follows, we first explain how this part of the chase is computed. Then we explain more formally how negation can be eliminated, and how non-linear rules can be transformed into linear ones.

Computing the ground chase. The *ground chase* of a database D with a Datalog$^{\exists}$ program Π, denoted by $chase_{\downarrow}(D, \Pi)$, is defined as $\{\underline{a} \in \text{chase}(D, \Pi) \mid \text{dom}(\underline{a}) \subset \mathbf{U}\}$. This instance is constructible in polynomial time w.r.t. D when Π is constant-join (recall that Π is assumed to be fixed). To prove this, it suffices to show that the problem of deciding whether a ground atom $\underline{a}$ belongs to chase(D, Π) is feasible in polynomial time w.r.t. D. We propose a recursive alternating algorithm, called Proof, which solves the above problem by constructing a proof-tree of $\underline{a}$ w.r.t. D and Π (if it exists). Such a proof-tree is a tree-like representation of the part of the chase on which $\underline{a}$ depends on. For example, if Π is

$$\begin{array}{lcl} \rho_1 & : & p(?X, ?Y) \rightarrow \exists ?Z\, p(?Y, ?Z) \\ \rho_2 & : & p(?X, ?Y), p(?Y, ?Z) \rightarrow \exists ?W\, s(?X, ?W) \\ \rho_3 & : & s(?X, ?Y) \rightarrow t(?X), \end{array}$$

$D = \{p(a, b)\}$ and $\underline{a} = t(a)$, then the part of the chase on which $\underline{a}$ depends on is depicted in Figure 1(a), while a proof-tree for $\underline{a}$ w.r.t. D and Π is shown in Figure 1(b).

Proof$(\underline{a}, D, \Pi)$ constructs a proof-tree (if it exists) by starting from $\underline{a}$ and applying resolution steps until the database D is reached. Whenever a rule ρ is used in a resolution step, the variables of body(ρ) which are not in a join and do not appear in head(ρ) are replaced by the special symbol $\star$, which plays the role of a witness for them. It is clear that for such non-join variables, what is important is not their actual value but the existence of a witness. Then each atom of body(ρ) is considered as a new ground atom which is proved recursively in a universal branch (recall that Proof is an alternating algorithm). At each step of the computation of Proof at most polynomially many constants of dom(D) must be remembered. This can be achieved using logarithmically many bits on $|\text{dom}(D)|$, and thus Proof needs logarithmic space w.r.t. D at each step of its computation. Since ALOGSPACE = PTIME, we immediately get that our algorithm describes a polynomial time procedure w.r.t. D, and the next crucial technical result follows:

LEMMA 9. *Consider a database D and a constant-join Datalog$^{\exists}$ program Π. Then, $chase_{\downarrow}(D, \Pi)$ is constructible in polynomial time w.r.t. D.*

Consider a weakly-guarded constant-join Datalog$^{\exists,\neg_s}$ query $Q = (\Pi, \Lambda)$ and a database D. Having Lemma 9 in place, we are now ready to show how negation can be eliminated, and how non-linear rules can be transformed into linear ones, in order to obtain a linear Datalog$^{\exists}$ query $Q_L = (\Pi_L, \Lambda)$ and a database $D_L \supseteq D$ such that ans$(Q, D) =$ ans(Q_L, D_L).

Eliminating negation. Since Π is stratified, there is a stratification σ : sch$(\Pi) \rightarrow \{0, \ldots, k\}$. Let $\Pi_0, \ldots, \Pi_k$ be the partition of Π induced by σ. Then we denote by Π_i^+ $(i \in [1, k])$ the program obtained from Π_i by replacing each negative atom $\neg p(\mathbf{t})$ with the positive atom $\bar{p}(\mathbf{t})$. Let $sch^-(\Pi_i)$ be the set of predicates occurring in Π_i in at least one negative atom. We inductively define $D_k^\star$ and $\Pi_k^\star$ as: (1) $D_0^\star = D$ and $\Pi_0^\star = \Pi_0$; and (2) for each $i \in [1, k]$, $D_i^\star = (D_{i-1}^\star \cup C_{i-1})$, where C_i is the set:

$$\left\{ \bar{p}(\mathbf{u}) \;\middle|\; \begin{array}{l} p \in sch^-(\Pi_i), \mathbf{u} \in (\text{dom}(D))^{\text{arity}(p)} \\ \text{and } p(\mathbf{u}) \notin chase_{\downarrow}(D_{i-1}^\star, \Pi_{i-1}^\star) \end{array} \right\},$$

and $\Pi_i^\star = \Pi_{i-1}^\star \cup \Pi_i^+$. For each $i \in [1, k]$, $\Pi_{i-1}^\star$ is constant-join. Thus, we have by Lemma 9 that C_{i-1} can be constructed in polynomial time. Hence, $D_k^\star$ and $\Pi_k^\star$ are both constructible in polynomial time w.r.t. D. Let $D_L = D_k^\star$. It is easy to verify that ans$(Q, D) =$ ans$((\Pi_k^\star, \Lambda), D_L)$.

Constructing linear Datalog$^{\exists}$ program Π_L. Observe that $\Pi_k^\star$ can be partitioned into $\{\Pi_1, \Pi_2\}$, where Π_1 consists of the linear rules of $\Pi_k^\star$ and $\Pi_2 = \Pi_k^\star \setminus \Pi_1$. Clearly, Π_2 is a weakly-guarded constant-join Datalog$^{\exists}$ program. For a rule $\rho \in \Pi_2$, let guard(ρ) be the weak-guard of ρ, and side(ρ) be the set of atoms (body$(\rho) \setminus \{\text{guard}(\rho)\}$). For each $\rho \in \Pi_2$, let H_ρ be the set of substitutions $\{h \mid h : \text{var}(\text{side}(\rho)) \rightarrow \text{dom}(D)\}$. Moreover, let Π_2' be the program $\{h(\text{guard}(\rho)) \rightarrow h(\text{head}(\rho)) \mid \rho \in \Pi_2, h \in H_\rho$ and $h(\text{side}(\rho)) \subseteq chase_{\downarrow}(D_k^\star, \Pi_k^\star)\}$. We have that $\Pi_L = \Pi_1 \cup \Pi_2'$ is a linear Datalog$^{\exists}$ program such that ans$((\Pi_k^\star, \Lambda), D_L)$ and ans$((\Pi_L, \Lambda), D_L)$ coincide. Clearly, for each $\rho \in \Pi_2$, $|H_\rho| = n^k$, where $n = |\text{dom}(D)|$ and $k = |\text{var}(\text{side}(\rho))|$, which implies that H_ρ can be constructed in polynomial time w.r.t. D. Hence, Π_L is of polynomial size w.r.t. D, and it can be constructed in polynomial time w.r.t. D by Lemma 9.

Having the above reduction in place, it is easy to see that query evaluation for weakly-guarded constant-join Datalog$^{\exists,\neg_s}$ is feasible in polynomial time in data complexity. At this point, it is important to clarify that the linear Datalog$^{\exists}$ program Π_L is not fixed since it depends on the database D. However, the problem of computing ans$((\Pi_L, \Lambda), D_L)$ is feasible in polynomial time as Λ is fixed (this is implicit in [18]), from which the desired upper bound follows.

7. PROGRAM EXPRESSIVE POWER

We have shown that TriQ-Lite is expressive enough to represent the OWL 2 entailment regime for the case of OWL 2 QL. In fact, as shown in Section 5, given a graph pattern P and an RDF graph G, the natural semantics $[\![P]\!]_G^{\text{ALL}}$ can be computed via the TriQ-Lite query $\tau_{\text{dat}}^{\text{ALL}}(P) = [(\tau_{\text{owl2ql}}, \tau_{\text{bgp}}^{\text{ALL}}(P)), (\tau_{\text{opr}}(P), \tau_{\text{out}}(P))]$. Importantly, the program τ_{owl2ql} does not depend on P. In other words, given a new graph pattern P', we just need to construct the programs $\tau_{\text{bgp}}^{\text{ALL}}(P')$, $\tau_{\text{opr}}(P')$ and $\tau_{\text{out}}(P')$ without altering τ_{owl2ql} to compute $[\![P']\!]_G^{\text{ALL}}$. This is quite beneficial in practice since, whenever the user wants to pose a new query over an RDF graph, (s)he does not need to change the part of the modular query which encodes the OWL 2 QL ontology. A natural question at this point is whether this favorable behavior can be achieved if τ_{owl2ql} is replaced by a Datalog$^{\neg s,\perp}$ program, i.e., without allowing existentially quantified variables in the heads of rules in this program. In this section, we give a negative answer to this question. Given a Datalog$^{\neg s,\perp}$ program Π, define $\tau_{\text{dat},\Pi}^{\text{ALL}}(P)$ as the query $[(\Pi, \tau_{\text{bgp}}^{\text{ALL}}(P)), (\tau_{\text{opr}}(P), \tau_{\text{out}}(P))]$, i.e., the query obtained by replacing τ_{owl2ql} in $\tau_{\text{dat}}^{\text{ALL}}(P)$ with Π. Then we can show that:

THEOREM 10. *There exist an RDF graph G and a graph pattern P such that, for every Datalog$^{\neg s,\perp}$ program Π, $[\![P]\!]_G^{\text{ALL}} \neq [\![(\tau_{dat,\Pi}^{\text{ALL}}(P), \tau_{db}(G))]\!]$.*

Let us construct an RDF graph G and a graph pattern P satisfying the statement of Theorem 10. Consider the basic classes b_1 and b_2, and the basic property p. Let $\mathcal{O}$ be the OWL 2 QL ontology which encodes the following:

1. b_1 is a sub-class of b_2;
2. b_2 is a sub-class of $\exists p$;
3. $\exists p^-$ is a sub-class of b_2; and
4. the constant a belongs to b_1.

Assume that G is the RDF graph which encodes the ontology $\mathcal{O}$ according to the rules given in Section 5.2. Moreover, consider the graph pattern P:

$$\{(?X, p, B_1), (B_1, p, B_2)\} \text{ UNION } \{(?X, p, B_3), (B_3, p, ?Y)\}$$

where each B_i $(1 \leq i \leq 3)$ is a blank node. Recall that $\tau_{\text{dat}}^{\text{ALL}}(P)$ is the TriQ-Lite query $[(\tau_{\text{owl2ql}}, \tau_{\text{bgp}}^{\text{ALL}}(P)), (\tau_{\text{opr}}(P), \tau_{\text{out}}(P))]$, while $\tau_{\text{db}}(G)$ is the instance associated to G. It is not difficult to verify that the atom $\underline{a} = \text{answer}_P^{\{2\}}(a)$ belongs to $\text{ans}(\tau_{\text{dat}}^{\text{ALL}}(P), \tau_{\text{db}}(G))$, which in turn implies that $\mu_{\underline{a},P} \in [\![(\tau_{\text{dat}}^{\text{ALL}}(P), \tau_{\text{db}}(G))]\!]$. However, for every $\underline{a}_b = \text{answer}_P(a, b)$, where $b \in \mathbf{U}$, it holds that $\underline{a}_b \notin \text{ans}(\tau_{\text{dat}}^{\text{ALL}}(P), \tau_{\text{db}}(G))$, and thus $\mu_{\underline{a}_b,P} \notin [\![(\tau_{\text{dat}}^{\text{ALL}}(P), \tau_{\text{db}}(G))]\!]$. But, we can show that for every Datalog$^{\neg s,\perp}$ program Π, $\underline{a}$ belongs to $\text{ans}(\tau_{\text{dat},\Pi}^{\text{ALL}}(P), \tau_{\text{db}}(G))$ if and only if there exists $b \in \mathbf{U}$ such that $\underline{a}_b \in \text{ans}(\tau_{\text{dat},\Pi}^{\text{ALL}}(P), \tau_{\text{db}}(G))$. From the previous discussion, we conclude that for every Datalog$^{\neg s,\perp}$ program Π, it must be the case that $[\![(\tau_{\text{dat}}^{\text{ALL}}(P), \tau_{\text{db}}(G))]\!] \neq [\![(\tau_{\text{dat},\Pi}^{\text{ALL}}(P), \tau_{\text{db}}(G))]\!]$. Theorem 10 follows since $[\![P]\!]_G^{\text{ALL}} = [\![(\tau_{\text{dat}}^{\text{ALL}}(P), \tau_{\text{db}}(G))]\!]$.

This result is a strong sign that the existential quantification in rule-heads allows us to obtain a modular query language which is more powerful than Datalog$^{\neg s,\perp}$. In what follows, we give a formal proof of this fact. However, before showing this for modular query languages, we would like to concentrate first on non-modular query languages, and show that weakly-guarded constant-join Datalog$^{\exists,\neg s,\perp}$ is more expressive than Datalog$^{\neg s,\perp}$ – towards this direction, we introduce the notion of *program expressive power*. This is an interesting result on its own, stressing out the importance of the existentially quantified variables in rule-heads even for non-modular query languages. Henceforth, given a (modular) query language $\mathcal{L}$, a program that can appear in a (modular) query which falls in $\mathcal{L}$ is called $\mathcal{L}$-program.

Consider a query language $\mathcal{L}$, and a program Π. The program expressive power of Π relative to $\mathcal{L}$, denoted by $\mathsf{Pep}_{\mathcal{L}}[\Pi]$, is defined as the set of triples $(D, \Lambda, \underline{a})$ such that (Π, Λ) is a query in $\mathcal{L}$, and $\underline{a} \in \text{ans}((\Pi, \Lambda), D)$. Notice that if Π is not an $\mathcal{L}$-program, then $\mathsf{Pep}_{\mathcal{L}}[\Pi] = \varnothing$. In fact, $\mathsf{Pep}_{\mathcal{L}}[\Pi]$ encodes the set of atoms that can be inferred from a database D via a query Q in $\mathcal{L}$, where Π is the program of Q. It is now natural to define the program expressive power of $\mathcal{L}$ as $\mathsf{Pep}[\mathcal{L}] = \{\mathsf{Pep}_{\mathcal{L}}[\Pi] \mid \Pi \text{ is an } \mathcal{L}\text{-program}\}$. In other words, $\mathsf{Pep}[\mathcal{L}]$ is a family of sets of triples, where each of its members encodes the program expressive power of an $\mathcal{L}$-program relative to $\mathcal{L}$. Given two languages $\mathcal{L}$ and $\mathcal{L}'$, we write $\mathcal{L}' \preceq_{\mathsf{Pep}} \mathcal{L}$ if $\mathsf{Pep}[\mathcal{L}'] \subseteq \mathsf{Pep}[\mathcal{L}]$. Finally, we say that $\mathcal{L}$ is more expressive than $\mathcal{L}'$ w.r.t. the program expressive power, written as $\mathcal{L}' \prec_{\mathsf{Pep}} \mathcal{L}$, if $\mathcal{L}' \preceq_{\mathsf{Pep}} \mathcal{L}$ and $\mathcal{L} \not\preceq_{\mathsf{Pep}} \mathcal{L}'$. By exploiting the construction given in the proof of Theorem 10, we can show the following result:

THEOREM 11. *It holds that,*

$$\textit{Datalog}^{\neg s,\perp} \prec_{\mathsf{Pep}} \textit{Weakly-guarded constant-join Datalog}^{\exists,\neg s,\perp}.$$

Notice that the same result can be shown for other Datalog-based languages such as guarded Datalog$^{\exists,\neg s,\perp}$ [9]. Let us now focus on modular query languages. Before we formally state the desired result, we first need to adapt the notion of program expressive power for modular query languages; this will give rise to the notion of *modular program expressive power*.

Consider a modular query language $\mathcal{L}$, a query language $\mathcal{L}'$ and a program Π. The modular program expressive power of Π relative to $\mathcal{L}$ and $\mathcal{L}'$, denoted by $\mathsf{MPep}_{\mathcal{L},\mathcal{L}'}[\Pi]$, is defined as the set of 4-tuples $(D, \Lambda, Q, \underline{a})$ such that $M = [(\Pi, \Lambda), Q]$ is a modular query in $\mathcal{L}$, Q is in $\mathcal{L}'$, and $\underline{a} \in \text{ans}(M, D)$. Notice that if Π is not an $\mathcal{L}$-program, then $\mathsf{MPep}_{\mathcal{L},\mathcal{L}'}[\Pi] = \varnothing$. Intuitively, $\mathsf{MPep}_{\mathcal{L},\mathcal{L}'}[\Pi]$ encodes the set of atoms that can be inferred from a database D via a modular query $[Q_1, Q_2]$ in $\mathcal{L}$, where Π is the program of Q_1 and Q_2 is a query in $\mathcal{L}'$. We now define the modular program expressive power of $\mathcal{L}$ relative to $\mathcal{L}'$ as $\mathsf{MPep}_{\mathcal{L}'}[\mathcal{L}] = \{\mathsf{MPep}_{\mathcal{L},\mathcal{L}'}[\Pi] \mid \Pi \text{ is an } \mathcal{L}\text{-program}\}$. In other words, $\mathsf{MPep}_{\mathcal{L}'}[\mathcal{L}]$ is a family of sets of 4-tuples, where each of its members encodes the modular program expressive power of an $\mathcal{L}$-program relative to $\mathcal{L}$ and $\mathcal{L}'$. Given two modular query languages $\mathcal{L}$ and $\mathcal{L}'$, we write $\mathcal{L}' \preceq_{\mathsf{MPep}} \mathcal{L}$ if $\mathsf{MPep}_{\mathcal{L}\cap\mathcal{L}'}[\mathcal{L}'] \subseteq \mathsf{MPep}_{\mathcal{L}\cap\mathcal{L}'}[\mathcal{L}]$[2]. Finally, we say that $\mathcal{L}$ is more expressive than $\mathcal{L}'$ w.r.t. the modular program expressive power, written as $\mathcal{L}' \prec_{\mathsf{MPep}} \mathcal{L}$, if $\mathcal{L}' \preceq_{\mathsf{MPep}} \mathcal{L}$ and $\mathcal{L} \not\preceq_{\mathsf{MPep}} \mathcal{L}'$. As for Theorem 11, by exploiting the construction given in the proof of Theorem 10, we obtain that:

THEOREM 12. *Modular Datalog$^{\neg s,\perp}$ $\prec_{\mathsf{MPep}}$ TriQ-Lite.*

Notice that modular Datalog$^{\neg s,\perp}$ and Datalog$^{\neg s,\perp}$ are equally expressive in the classical sense. However, we need to use modular Datalog$^{\neg s,\perp}$ in the statement of Theorem 12 as we are comparing modular program expressive powers in this theorem.

Several query languages that enhance SPARQL with navigation capabilities and/or recursion mechanisms have been proposed, most notably nSPARQL [27], PSPARQL [2], recursive triple algebra [23], and NEMODEQ [30]. Each one of these languages $\mathcal{L}$ is contained in Datalog$^{\neg s,\perp}$, in the sense that every $\mathcal{L}$-query can be expressed as a Datalog$^{\neg s,\perp}$ query. Therefore, we can consider the Datalog version $\mathcal{L}^{\text{dat}}$ of $\mathcal{L}$, and then we can use $\mathcal{L}^{\text{dat}}$ (resp., modular $\mathcal{L}^{\text{dat}}$) in order to compare the program expressive power (resp., modular program expressive power) of $\mathcal{L}$ and weakly-guarded constant-join Datalog$^{\exists,\neg s,\perp}$ (resp., TriQ-Lite); notice that modular $\mathcal{L}^{\text{dat}}$ is as expressive as $\mathcal{L}^{\text{dat}}$ in the usual sense. Then, from Theorems 11 and 12 we obtain the following result:

[2]Notice that we also use $\mathcal{L}\cap\mathcal{L}'$ as a (non-modular) query language.

COROLLARY 13. *Assume that $\mathcal{L}$ is one of the query languages nSPARQL, PSPARQL, recursive triple algebra and NEMODEQ. Then, the following hold:*

1. $\mathcal{L}^{\text{dat}} \prec_{\text{Pep}}$ *Weakly-guarded constant-join Datalog*$^{\exists,\neg s,\bot}$;
2. *Modular* $\mathcal{L}^{\text{dat}} \prec_{\text{MPep}}$ TriQ-Lite.

8. CONCLUSIONS

We considered the problem of bridging the gap between the existing RDF query languages and key features for querying RDF data such as reasoning capabilities, navigational capabilities, and a general form of recursion. A modular query language has been proposed which is expressive enough to encode every SPARQL query under the entailment regime for OWL 2 QL. Moreover, this language allows us to formulate SPARQL queries in a simpler way, as it can easily encode a more natural notion of entailment. Interestingly, the proposed language incorporates the main RDF query languages that can be found in the literature.

9. ACKNOWLEDGMENTS

Part of the work of M. Arenas was performed while visiting Oxford, UK, while part of the work of A. Pieris was performed while visiting Santiago, Chile. M. Arenas was supported by the Millennium Nucleus Center for Semantic Web Research under Grant NC120004 and Fondecyt grant 1131049, G. Gottlob was supported by ERC grant 246858 (DIADEM), and A. Pieris was supported by EPSRC grant EP/J008346/1 (PrOQAW). We thank the anonymous referees for many helpful comments.

10. REFERENCES

[1] S. Abiteboul, R. Hull, and V. Vianu. *Foundations of Databases*. Addison-Wesley, 1995.

[2] F. Alkhateeb, J.-F. Baget, and J. Euzenat. Extending SPARQL with regular expression patterns (for querying RDF). *J. Web Sem.*, 7(2):57–73, 2009.

[3] R. Angles and C. Gutierrez. The expressive power of SPARQL. In *ISWC*, pages 114–129, 2008.

[4] M. Arenas, C. Gutierrez, and J. Pérez. Foundations of RDF databases. In *RW*, pages 158–204, 2009.

[5] P. Barceló. Querying graph databases. In *PODS*, pages 175–188, 2013.

[6] C. Beeri and M. Y. Vardi. The implication problem for data dependencies. In *ICALP*, pages 73–85, 1981.

[7] D. Brickley and R. Guha. RDF vocabulary description language 1.0: RDF schema. W3C Recommendation 10 February 2004, `http://www.w3.org/TR/rdf-schema`.

[8] A. Calì, G. Gottlob, and M. Kifer. Taming the infinite chase: Query answering under expressive relational constraints. *J. Artif. Intell. Res.*, 48:115–174, 2013.

[9] A. Calì, G. Gottlob, and T. Lukasiewicz. A general Datalog-based framework for tractable query answering over ontologies. *J. Web Sem.*, 14:57–83, 2012.

[10] A. Calì, G. Gottlob, T. Lukasiewicz, B. Marnette, and A. Pieris. Datalog+/-: A family of logical knowledge representation and query languages for new applications. In *LICS*, pages 228–242, 2010.

[11] A. Calì, G. Gottlob, and A. Pieris. Towards more expressive ontology languages: The query answering problem. *Artif. Intell.*, 193:87–128, 2012.

[12] D. Calvanese, G. De Giacomo, D. Lembo, M. Lenzerini, and R. Rosati. Tractable reasoning and efficient query answering in description logics: The DL-Lite family. *J. Autom. Reasoning*, 39(3):385–429, 2007.

[13] S. Ceri, G. Gottlob, and L. Tanca. *Logic Programming and Databases*. Springer, 1990.

[14] E. Dantsin, T. Eiter, G. Georg, and A. Voronkov. Complexity and expressive power of logic programming. *ACM Comput. Surv.*, 33(3):374–425, 2001.

[15] V. Fionda, C. Gutierrez, and G. Pirrò. Semantic navigation on the web of data: specification of routes, web fragments and actions. In *WWW*, pages 281–290, 2012.

[16] T. Furche, B. Linse, F. Bry, D. Plexousakis, and G. Gottlob. RDF querying: Language constructs and evaluation methods compared. In *Reasoning Web*, pages 1–52, 2006.

[17] B. Glimm and C. Ogbuji. SPARQL 1.1 entailment regimes. W3C Recommendation 21 March 2013, `http://www.w3.org/TR/sparql11-entailment/`.

[18] G. Gottlob, G. Orsi, and A. Pieris. Ontological queries: Rewriting and optimization. In *ICDE*, pages 1–13, 2011.

[19] G. Gottlob, S. Rudolph, and M. Simkus. Expressiveness of guarded existential rule languages. In *PODS*, 2014. To appear.

[20] W. O. W. Group. OWL 2 web ontology language document overview (second edition). W3C Recommendation 11 December 2012, `http://www.w3.org/TR/owl2-overview/`.

[21] S. Harris and A. Seaborne. SPARQL 1.1 query language. W3C Recommendation 21 March 2013, `http://www.w3.org/TR/sparql11-query/`.

[22] I. Kollia, B. Glimm, and I. Horrocks. SPARQL query answering over owl ontologies. In *ESWC (1)*, pages 382–396, 2011.

[23] L. Libkin, J. L. Reutter, and D. Vrgoc. Trial for RDF: adapting graph query languages for RDF data. In *PODS*, pages 201–212, 2013.

[24] D. L. McGuinness and F. van Harmelen. OWL web ontology language overview. W3C Recommendation 10 February 2004, `http://www.w3.org/TR/owl-features/`.

[25] B. Motik, B. C. Grau, I. Horrocks, Z. Wu, A. Fokoue, and C. Lutz. OWL 2 web ontology language profiles (second edition). W3C Recommendation 11 December 2012, `http://www.w3.org/TR/owl2-profiles/`.

[26] J. Pérez, M. Arenas, and C. Gutierrez. Semantics and complexity of sparql. *ACM Trans. Database Syst.*, 34(3), 2009.

[27] J. Pérez, M. Arenas, and C. Gutierrez. nSPARQL: a navigational language for RDF. *J. Web Sem.*, 8(4):255–270, 2010.

[28] A. Polleres. From sparql to rules (and back). In *WWW*, pages 787–796, 2007.

[29] E. Prud'hommeaux and A. Seaborne. SPARQL query language for RDF. W3C Recommendation 15 January 2008, `http://www.w3.org/TR/rdf-sparql-query`.

[30] S. Rudolph and M. Krötzsch. Flag & check: data access with monadically defined queries. In *PODS*, pages 151–162, 2013.

[31] S. Schenk. A SPARQL semantics based on Datalog. In *KI*, pages 160–174, 2007.

[32] M. Y. Vardi. The complexity of relational query languages. In *STOC*, pages 137–146, 1982.

Expressiveness of Guarded Existential Rule Languages

Georg Gottlob
Department of Computer Science and Oxford Man Institute
University of Oxford, UK
georg.gottlob@cs.ox.ac.uk

Sebastian Rudolph
Institute of Artificial Intelligence
Technische Universität Dresden, Germany
sebastian.rudolph@tu-dresden.de

Mantas Šimkus
Institute of Information Systems
Vienna University of Technology, Austria
simkus@dbai.tuwien.ac.at

ABSTRACT

The so-called *existential rules* have recently gained attention, mainly due to their adequate expressiveness for ontological query answering. Several decidable fragments of such rules have been introduced, employing restrictions such as various forms of *guardedness* to ensure decidability. Some of the more well-known languages in this arena are *(weakly) guarded* and *(weakly) frontier-guarded* fragments of existential rules. In this paper, we explore their relative and absolute expressiveness. In particular, we provide a new proof that queries expressed via frontier-guarded and guarded rules can be translated into plain Datalog queries. Since the converse translations are impossible, we develop generalizations of frontier-guarded and guarded rules to *nearly frontier-guarded* and *nearly guarded* rules, respectively, which have exactly the expressive power of Datalog. We further show that weakly frontier-guarded rules can be translated into weakly guarded rules, and thus, weakly frontier-guarded and weakly guarded rules have exactly the same expressive power. Such rules cannot be expressed in Datalog since their query answering problem is ExpTime-complete in data complexity. We strengthen this completeness result by proving that on ordered databases with input negation available, weakly guarded rules capture all queries computable in exponential time. We then show that weakly guarded rules extended with *stratified negation* are expressive enough to capture all database queries decidable in exponential time, without any assumptions on the input databases. Finally, we note that the translations of this paper are, in general, exponential in size, but lead to worst-case optimal algorithms for query answering with the considered languages.

Categories and Subject Descriptors

H.2 [**Database Management**]: General

Keywords

Existential rules; Expressiveness; Descriptive Complexity

PODS'14, June 22–27, 2014, Snowbird, UT, USA.

http://dx.doi.org/10.1145/2594538.2594556.

1. INTRODUCTION

Rule-based logical formalisms play a pivotal role in databases and knowledge representation. They are used in databases as expressive constraint and query languages, and in knowledge representation for declarative problem solving via various forms of logic programming, and, more recently, to represent and reason about ontological information.

Consequently, rule languages can be employed in at least two different ways: as ontology languages and as query languages. In the ontological setting, a set of facts and rules may be used to specify domain knowledge, in this way forming a *knowledge base*. In this setting, we are interested in answering user queries over a knowledge base, where queries may be expressed in a standard query language such as *conjunctive queries*. Alternatively, the rule part can be understood as part of the specification of a query that is executed over a plain database (such queries are sometimes called *ontology-mediated queries*[12]).

Given the plethora of different rule (and thus querying) languages, it is of utmost importance to understand and determine their expressivity. Facing with the problem of picking an adequate query language for some scenario, one has to have a clear picture of which information needs the languages at hand can express, which other query languages they subsume and also if they allow to express all possible queries whose answers can be computed at a certain cost.

To support this crucial considerations, database theory has come up with appropriate notions to compare and characterize query languages: *relative* and *absolute expressiveness*. Relative expressiveness considers if, given two query languages, every query formulated in the first language can be expressed by means of the second (and vice versa). Note that two languages might be equally expressive and still differ significantly in terms of the size of expressions needed to express the same query. Such *succinctness* differences impact the combined complexity of the corresponding entailment problem, whereas the data complexity (where only the database is assumed to vary while the query is fixed) of two equally expressive query languages must be the same. On the other hand, two query languages with coinciding data complexity do not necessarily have the same expressivity. Hence it makes sense to identify the query languages with a certain data complexity that have the maximal expressiveness. This leads us to *absolute expressiveness*, where expressive power is measured in terms of complexity classes using *descriptive complexity theory* [21]. A query language is said to *capture* a complexity class $\mathcal{C}$ if it can express any query that can be answered by a computation in $\mathcal{C}$. Such a language is guaranteed to semantically subsume all other query languages with the same data complexity, and can therefore be considered as the best value-for-money (i.e. expressiveness for computation cost) choice in class $\mathcal{C}$.

This paper provides an expressivity analysis for important query languages based on the so-called *existential* rules, which support *value invention.* They allow to reason about objects whose identity is unknown yet whose existence is implied by the specified knowledge. This basic form of inference with incomplete information also lies at the core of reasoning in ontology languages such as *description logics* [5].

Existential rules are first-order logic sentences of the form $\forall\vec{x}\forall\vec{y}\alpha(\vec{x},\vec{y}) \rightarrow \exists\vec{z}\beta(\vec{y},\vec{z})$, where α, β are conjunctions of atoms over constants and variables. Such rules occur in many scenarios and are widely known under different names such as *tuple-generating dependencies* or *Datalog with value invention* in databases [2, 19], *Datalog±* in ontological knowledge representation (see [14] and references there in), and *conceptual graph rules* in diagrammatic reasoning [26].

The typical reasoning problem considered in the context of existential rules is whether a ground atom is logically *entailed* by a collection of ground atoms and existential rules.

EXAMPLE 1. *As a running example we use the set* Σ_p *of rules, which describe (a part of) a publication database:*

$$\sigma_1 = \mathsf{Publication}(x) \rightarrow \exists k_1, k_2.\mathsf{Keywords}(x, k_1, k_2),$$

$$\sigma_2 = \mathsf{Keywords}(x, k_1, k_2) \rightarrow \mathsf{hasTopic}(x, k_1),$$

$$\sigma_3 = \mathsf{hasTopic}(x, z),\ \mathsf{hasAuthor}(x, u),\ \mathsf{hasAuthor}(y, u),\ \mathsf{hasTopic}(y, z'),\ \mathsf{Scientific}(z'), \mathsf{citedIn}(y, x) \rightarrow \mathsf{Scientific}(z).$$

In particular, the above rules state that every publication must have at least two keywords, where the first keyword describes the (main) topic of the publication at hand. The last rule provides a recipe to infer scientific topics: a topic is scientific if it is a topic of a paper that cites a scientific paper and shares with it a coauthor.

Suppose we are interested in persons who have authored scientific publications. This can be expressed using the following rule, which we add to Σ_p*:*

$$\sigma_4 = \mathsf{hasAuthor}(x, y), \mathsf{hasTopic}(x, z), \mathsf{Scientific}(z) \rightarrow \mathsf{Q}(y)$$

We consider the following atom set $D = \{\mathsf{Publication}(\mathrm{p}_1), \mathsf{Publication}(\mathrm{p}_2), \mathsf{citedIn}(\mathrm{p}_1, \mathrm{p}_2), \mathsf{hasAuthor}(\mathrm{p}_1, \mathrm{a}_1), \mathsf{hasAuthor}(\mathrm{p}_2, \mathrm{a}_1), \mathsf{hasAuthor}(\mathrm{p}_2, \mathrm{a}_2), \mathsf{hasTopic}(\mathrm{p}_1, \mathrm{t}_1), \mathsf{Scientific}(\mathrm{t}_1)\}$. *Intuitively,* Σ_p *and* D *together entail* $\mathsf{Q}(\mathrm{a}_1)$ *and* $\mathsf{Q}(\mathrm{a}_2)$*, thus* a_1 *and* a_2 *are answers to our query.*

Entailment checking over existential rules is nontrivial, because in the general case there is no bound on the number of unnamed objects that need to be considered for inferring the relevant information. In fact, theories of existential rules are undecidable already in very restricted cases [6]. To circumvent this, several syntactic and semantic conditions defining decidable fragments of existential rules have been introduced, inspired by positive decidability results in modal and description logics.

For many widely known existential rule languages, decidability is guaranteed by means of various versions of *guardedness.* Among the most expressive such fragments are *guarded and weakly guarded* rules [14] as well as *frontier-guarded* and *weakly frontier-guarded* rules [6]. In a nutshell, a rule is guarded (resp., frontier-guarded) if it has a body atom

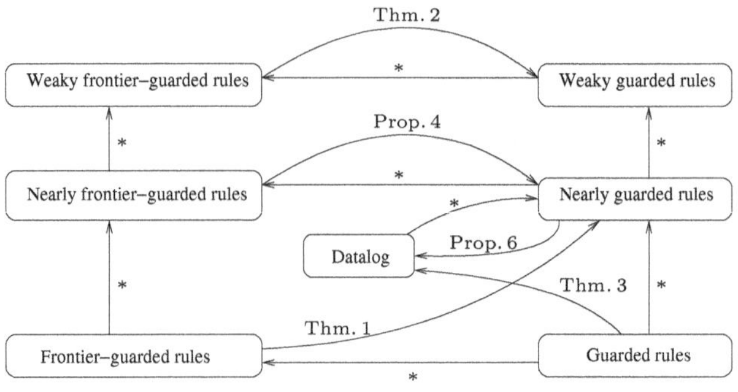

Figure 1: Semantic relations between the considered languages. An arrow from a fragment $\mathcal{L}$ to a fragment $\mathcal{L}'$ indicates that $\mathcal{L}'$ can be expressed in $\mathcal{L}$. Here '*' indicates syntactic membership.

that contains (i.e.,"guards") all the universally quantified variables of the rule (resp., of the rule head). The *weakly* guarded and the *weakly* frontier-guarded fragments are obtained by restricting guarding to only "dangerous" variables, i.e. the ones that may be forced to be instantiated with unnamed objects. Our paper focuses on the above formalisms, plain Datalog, as well as the *nearly guarded* and *nearly frontier-guarded* rules that we introduce in this paper.

While there are several results on the combined and the data complexity of these fragments, little is known about their relative and absolute expressiveness. A notable exception is the sketch in [7] and the thorough proof in [8] that frontier-guarded rules are expressible in Datalog. Importantly, such rules can be translated into a small fragment of Datalog, where e.g. FO-rewritability is decidable [8, 10].

In this paper we close significant gaps concerning relative and absolute expressiveness and more practicable translations between the mentioned fragments. Our main contributions are as follows (Figure 1 summarizes the relationships between the considered formalisms):

- We show that all considered query languages with PTIME data complexity have the same expressive power as Datalog. This is a crucial insight as it shows that query answering in those languages can be realized via appropriate translations and subsequent execution on one of the existing optimized Datalog engines.

- In particular, noting that weakly (frontier-)guarded rules have EXPTIME data complexity and thus unfortunately cannot be expressed in Datalog, we introduce *nearly guarded* and *nearly frontier-guarded* rules, which retain as much expressivity of weakly (frontier-)guarded rules (such as syntactically containing plain Datalog) as possible while still being in PTIME and thus expressible in Datalog.

- To show our claims, we propose several translations between rule fragments. These do not depend on an input database and preserve entailment of ground atoms as well as answers to conjunctive queries. Moreover, compared to previously presented translations [7, 8], ours are modular, demonstrably worst-case optimal, much more goal-directed, and hence well-suited for an effective implementation.

(i) We provide a translation from frontier-guarded into nearly guarded rules (Theorem 1). The translation capitalizes on a suitable characterization of the relevant models of a frontier-guarded theory in terms of tree-shaped structures.

(ii) The above translation can be lifted to translate nearly frontier-guarded rules into nearly guarded rules (Proposition 4) and weakly frontier-guarded rules into weakly guarded rules (Theorem 2).

(iii) We show that nearly guarded rules can be translated into plain Datalog. This result is established by first providing a resolution based translation from fully guarded rules to plain Datalog (Theorem 3). We then show certain modularity properties that allow to extend the translation to cover nearly guarded rules as well (Proposition 6).

- Our results also show that answering conjunctive queries in knowledge bases where a database is enriched with nearly frontier-guarded rules, can be reduced to answering a Datalog query over the same database.

- Although the presented translations are not polynomial in general, they yield worst-case optimal algorithms for the considered problems. These findings allow to conclude that in most cases, the exponential blow-ups are unavoidable.

- We take a closer look at weakly guarded and weakly frontier-guarded rules, which are known to have EXPTIME-complete data complexity. We strengthen this result by showing that on ordered databases with input negation available, weakly guarded rules in fact *capture* all queries computable in exponential time. This result is reminiscent of the fact that semipositive Datalog on ordered databases captures exactly queries computable in polynomial time [31, 28] (see [1] for an overview of this fundamental result).

- We show that weakly guarded rules extended with *stratified negation* are expressive enough to capture EXPTIME, without any assumptions on the input databases. Consequently, despite being a rather plain query language, weakly guarded rules endowed with a mild form of negation subsume all languages with EXPTIME data complexity. This supplements Cabibbo's proof that existential rules equipped with stratified negation capture all computable queries [13], and also exposes the expressive power of TriQ, a recent RDF query language based on stratified weakly guarded rules [3].

In summary, we show that (a) all considered notions of guardedness for which the data complexity is in PTIME can be expressed in plain Datalog and that (b) the variants with EXPTIME data complexity, endowed with a very moderate form of negation, actually capture this complexity class, that is, they are able to express all other EXPTIME query languages including formalisms as powerful as second-order logic extended with a least fixed point operator.

The paper is organized as follows. After introducing the considered fragments of existential rules and recalling the standard notion of database *chase*, we show in Section 4 that the chase of a frontier-guarded rule set can be seen as a specially constructed tree. In Section 5, we exploit this property to provide translations from frontier-guarded and nearly frontier-guarded rules to nearly guarded rules, and a translation from weakly frontier-guarded rules to weakly guarded rules. In Section 6 we specially tailored inference rules to translate guarded rules into Datalog rules. We then lift this translation to nearly guarded rules. By composing the introduced transformations, we obtain the desired translations. In Section 7 we discuss how our results apply to the problem of answering conjunctive queries over databases enriched with existential rules. In Section 8 we present the capturing result, and then discuss some related work and conclude in Sections 9 and 10.

2. PRELIMINARIES

Existential Rules Let Δ_c, Δ_n and Δ_v be infinite mutually disjoint sets of *constants*, *labeled nulls*, and *variables*, respectively. Elements in $\Delta_c \cup \Delta_n \cup \Delta_v$ are *terms*. An *atom* α is an expression of the form $R(t_1, \dots, t_n)$, where R is a *relation name* with *arity* n, and $t_1, \dots, t_n$ are terms. We let $\mathsf{terms}(\alpha) = \{t_1, \dots, t_n\}$ and $\mathsf{vars}(\alpha) = \mathsf{terms}(\alpha) \cap \Delta_v$. If $\mathsf{terms}(\alpha) \subseteq \Delta_c$, then α is *ground*. For a set Γ of atoms, we let $\mathsf{terms}(\Gamma) = \bigcup_{\alpha \in \Gamma} \mathsf{terms}(\alpha)$ and $\mathsf{vars}(\Gamma) = \mathsf{terms}(\Gamma) \cap \Delta_v$. An *(existential) rule* σ is an expression of the form

$$B_1 \wedge \dots \wedge B_n \to \exists y_1, \dots, y_k . H_1 \wedge \dots \wedge H_m, \qquad (1)$$

where $B_1, \dots, B_n$, with $n \geq 0$, and $H_1, \dots, H_m$, with $m \geq 1$, are atoms with terms from $\Delta_c \cup \Delta_v$ only. We let $\mathsf{body}(\sigma) := \{B_1, \dots, B_n\}$ and $\mathsf{head}(\sigma) := \{H_1, \dots, H_m\}$. Let $\mathsf{terms}(\sigma) = \mathsf{terms}(\mathsf{body}(\sigma)) \cup \mathsf{terms}(\mathsf{head}(\sigma))$ and $\mathsf{vars}(\sigma) = \mathsf{terms}(\sigma) \cap \Delta_v$. Moreover, we let $\mathsf{uvars}(\sigma) = \mathsf{vars}(\mathsf{body}(\sigma))$, and let $\mathsf{evars}(\sigma) = \{y_1, \dots, y_k\}$. The sets $\mathsf{uvars}(\sigma)$ and $\mathsf{evars}(\sigma)$ contain the *universal* and *existential* variables of σ, respectively. The set $\mathsf{fvars}(\sigma) = \mathsf{vars}(\mathsf{head}(\sigma)) \setminus \mathsf{evars}(\sigma)$ is called the *frontier* of σ. We assume that all rules are *safe*, i.e. $\mathsf{fvars}(\sigma) \subseteq \mathsf{vars}(\mathsf{body}(\sigma))$. If $\mathsf{evars}(\sigma) = \emptyset$, then σ is a *Datalog* rule.

A set Σ of rules is called a *theory*. A *Datalog program* is a theory consisting of Datalog rules only.

Databases A *database* D is any set of atoms with terms from $\Delta_c \cup \Delta_n$.[1] Given a set of atoms Γ and a database D, a *homomorphism* from Γ into D is a mapping $h : \Delta_c \cup \Delta_n \cup \Delta_v \to \Delta_c \cup \Delta_n$ such that

(i) $h(c) = c$ for each $c \in \Delta_c$;

(ii) if $R(t_1, \dots, t_n) \in \Gamma$, then $R(h(t_1), \dots, h(t_n)) \in D$.

A database D *satisfies* a rule σ if for any homomorphism h from $\mathsf{body}(\sigma)$ into D, there exists a homomorphism h' from $\mathsf{head}(\sigma)$ into D such that $h'(x) = h(x)$ for all $x \in \mathsf{uvars}(\sigma)$. A database D *satisfies* a theory Σ if D satisfies each $\sigma \in \Sigma$. Given a database D and a theory Σ, a *solution* to (Σ, D) is a database D' such that $D \subseteq D'$ and D' satisfies Σ. Given a ground atom α, we write $\Sigma, D \models \alpha$ if $\alpha \in D'$ for every solution D' to (Σ, D).

Queries A *query* is a pair (Σ, Q), where Σ is a theory and Q is a relation symbol. Given a query (Σ, Q) and a database D, we let $\mathsf{ans}((\Sigma, Q), D) = \{\vec{c} \in (\Delta_c)^n \mid \Sigma, D \models Q(\vec{c})\}$, where n is the arity of Q. We call Q the *output relation* of (Σ, Q) and $\mathsf{ans}((\Sigma, Q), D)$ the *answer* to (Σ, Q) over D.

Chase We recall the notion of *(oblivious) chase* [24, 11]. Assume a database D, a rule σ and a homomorphism h from $\mathsf{body}(\sigma)$ into D. A set of atoms Γ is called a *consequence* of σ w.r.t. D and h if Γ can be obtained from $\mathsf{head}(\sigma)$ by replacing each universal variable x by $h(x)$ and each existential variable by a fresh null $c \in \Delta_n$ not occurring in D. A *chase* of a database D w.r.t. a theory Σ is a potentially infinite sequence $D_0, D_1, \dots$ of databases such that:

(a) $D_0 = D$;

[1]Whenever a database D is part of an input in a computational problem, D is assumed to be finite.

(b) for each $i > 0$, D_i is a consequence of some $\sigma \in \Sigma$ w.r.t. $D_0 \cup \ldots \cup D_{i-1}$ and some h;

(c) if there is some $\sigma \in \Sigma$, $i \geq 0$, and a homomorphism h from $\mathsf{body}(\sigma)$ into $D_0 \cup \ldots \cup D_i$, then there is $j \geq 0$ s.t. D_j has a consequence of σ w.r.t. $D_0 \cup \ldots \cup D_i$ and h.

Let $\mathsf{chase}(\Sigma, D) = \bigcup_{i \geq 0} D_i$. We remind the reader that $\mathsf{chase}(\Sigma, D)$ is unique up to homomorphic equivalence. It is also well known that $\mathsf{chase}(\Sigma, D)$ is a *universal solution* to (Σ, D), i.e. $\mathsf{chase}(\Sigma, D)$ is a solution to (Σ, D), and there is a homomorphism from $\mathsf{chase}(\Sigma, D)$ into any solution D' to (Σ, D) (see [14]). Observe that due to the universality of the chase, $\Sigma, D \models \alpha$ iff $\alpha \in \mathsf{chase}(\Sigma, D)$, for any ground atom α. This also implies that, given an n-ary relation symbol Q, $\mathsf{ans}((\Sigma, Q), D)$ equals the set constant tuples $\vec{c}$ with $Q(\vec{c}) \in \mathsf{chase}(\Sigma, D)$. With a slight abuse of notation, we will later write $\mathsf{chase}(\Sigma, D) \subseteq \mathsf{chase}(\Sigma', D')$ if there is a homomorphism from $\mathsf{chase}(\Sigma, D)$ to $\mathsf{chase}(\Sigma', D')$. If $\mathsf{chase}(\Sigma, D)$ and $\mathsf{chase}(\Sigma', D')$ are homomorphically equivalent, then we simply write $\mathsf{chase}(\Sigma, D) = \mathsf{chase}(\Sigma', D')$.

Relation name annotations It will sometimes be useful to encode some information as part of relation names. To this end, we will consider *annotated* relation names that have the form $R[\vec{t}]$, where $\vec{t}$ is a tuple of terms. A theory Σ is *safely annotated* if the following is true for every rule $\sigma \in \Sigma$:

(i) If $R[\vec{t}](\vec{v})$ is an atom in σ, then none of the variables of $\vec{t}$ occurs as an argument in an atom of σ.

(ii) If $x \in \Delta_v$ occurs in the annotation of an atom in $\mathsf{head}(\sigma)$, then x also occurs in the annotation of some atom in $\mathsf{body}(\sigma)$.

Further Notions We assume a unary *active constant domain* relation ACDom whose extension is fixed: for any database D, $\mathsf{ACDom}(c) \in D$ iff c occurs in some atom $R(\vec{v}) \in D$ with $R \neq \mathsf{ACDom}$. This assumption will help presentation, but won't affect generality. We also prohibit ACDom from rule heads.

For a possibly partial function f, let $\mathsf{dom}(f)$ and $\mathsf{ran}(f)$ denote the domain and the range of f, respectively. For a set of variables X, $\vec{X}$ is the tuple obtained by enumerating X. The enumeration of variable sets is globally fixed, i.e. for two sets X, Y of variables, $X = Y$ implies $\vec{X} = \vec{Y}$.

3. VARIATIONS OF GUARDED RULES

We remind that syntactic restriction on existential rules are required to ensure decidability of the basic reasoning tasks such as query answering. In this section we recall the so-called guarded, frontier-guarded, weakly guarded and weakly frontier-guarded rules. We also define nearly guarded and nearly frontier-guarded rules.

DEFINITION 1. *((Frontier-)Guarded rules) We say a rule σ is* guarded *(resp.,* frontier-guarded*) if there exists an atom $\alpha \in \mathsf{body}(\sigma)$ such that $\mathsf{uvars}(\sigma) \subseteq \mathsf{vars}(\alpha)$ (resp., such that $\mathsf{fvars}(\sigma) \subseteq \mathsf{vars}(\alpha)$). A theory is* guarded *(resp.,* frontier-guarded*) if all its rules are guarded (resp., frontier-guarded). For a frontier-guarded rule σ, let $\mathsf{fg}(\sigma)$ be an arbitrary but fixed frontier-guard α in σ, i.e. an atom containing all the variables of $\mathsf{fvars}(\sigma)$.*

EXAMPLE 2. *It is easy to see that Σ_p as defined in Example 1 is frontier-guarded. In Figure 2 we present the corresponding chase(Σ_p, D), witnessing $\Sigma_p, D \models \mathsf{Q}(\mathrm{a}_1)$ and $\Sigma_p, D \models \mathsf{Q}(\mathrm{a}_2)$.*

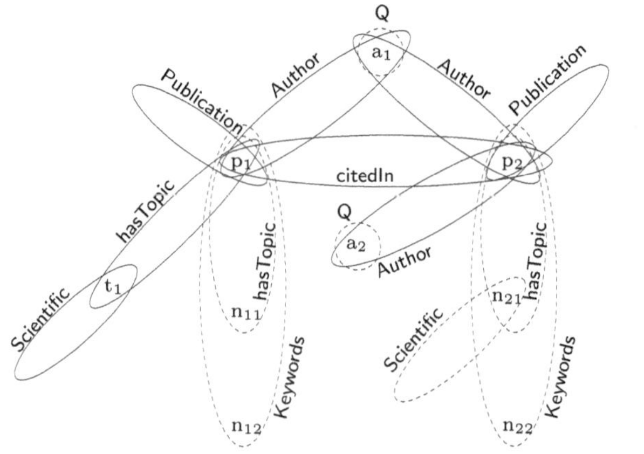

Figure 2: Illustration of *chase*(Σ_p, D) for Σ_p and D from Ex. 1. The solid ellipses indicate the atoms of D and dashed ones indicate the inferred atoms.

Guarded and frontier-guarded theories cannot express all Datalog queries. To see this, assume a query (Σ, Q), where Σ is a frontier-guarded theory with no constants. It can be easily seen that for any tuple $\vec{c} \in \mathsf{ans}((\Sigma, Q), D)$, where D is a database, all constants from $\vec{c}$ must occur together in some database fact $R(\vec{t}) \in D$. In other words, Σ cannot relate constants that are not explicitly related in the input database (allowing for constants in Σ does not solve the issue in general). This property rules out using frontier-guarded rules to query e.g. the transitive closure of a binary relation, which is a classic task for Datalog.

The above expressiveness limitations can be resolved by employing weakly (frontier-)guarded theories, obtained by relaxing (frontier-)guardedness.

DEFINITION 2. *(Weakly (frontier-)guarded rules) Given a variable x and a set of atoms Γ, let $\mathsf{pos}(\Gamma, x)$ be the set of pairs (R, i) such that Γ has an atom $R(t_1, \ldots, t_n)$ with $t_i = x$, i.e. Γ has an atom where x occurs in position i. We collect the* affected positions *in relations of a theory Σ. Let $\mathsf{ap}(\Sigma)$ be the smallest set such that:*

i) $\mathsf{pos}(\mathsf{head}(\sigma), x) \subseteq \mathsf{ap}(\Sigma)$ for all $\sigma \in \Sigma$ and $x \in \mathsf{evars}(\sigma)$, i.e. all positions where existential variables occur are affected; and

ii) if $\sigma \in \Sigma$ and $x \in \mathsf{uvars}(\sigma)$ is such that $\mathsf{pos}(\mathsf{body}(\sigma), x) \subseteq \mathsf{ap}(\Sigma)$, then $\mathsf{pos}(\mathsf{head}(\sigma), x) \subseteq \mathsf{ap}(\Sigma)$, i.e. if all positions where x occurs in the body are affected, then all positions where x occurs in the head are affected as well.

Assume a theory Σ. We say a variable x of a rule σ is unsafe *w.r.t. Σ if $\mathsf{pos}(\mathsf{body}(\sigma), x) \subseteq \mathsf{ap}(\Sigma)$. We use $\mathsf{unsafe}(\sigma, \Sigma)$ to denote the variables of σ that are unsafe w.r.t. Σ. We say a rule σ is* weakly guarded *(resp.,* weakly frontier-guarded*) in Σ if it has a body atom B that contains all the variables of $\mathsf{uvars}(\sigma) \cap \mathsf{unsafe}(\sigma, \Sigma)$ (resp., of $\mathsf{fvars}(\sigma) \cap \mathsf{unsafe}(\sigma, \Sigma)$). Then Σ is* weakly guarded *(resp.,*weakly frontier-guarded*) if each rule of Σ is weakly-guarded (resp., weakly frontier-guarded) w.r.t. Σ.*

Weakly guarded and weakly frontier-guarded theories are significantly more expressive than plain Datalog. This is due to the fact that query answering in these languages is

EXPTIME-hard in data complexity [14]. Since query answering in plain Datalog is PTIME-complete in data complexity (see e.g. [16]), one generally cannot convert a query (Σ, Q), where Σ is weakly guarded or weakly frontier-guarded, into a Datalog query while preserving the query answers.

We introduce next *nearly guarded* and *nearly frontier-guarded* rules, which strictly extend guarded and frontier-guarded rules, yet less expressive than weakly guarded and weakly-frontier guarded theories, respectively. We will see later that they have exactly the expressive power of Datalog.

DEFINITION 3. *(Nearly (frontier-)guarded rules) We say a rule σ is* nearly guarded *(resp.,* nearly frontier-guarded*) in a theory Σ if*

(i) σ is guarded (resp., frontier-guarded), or

(ii) $\mathsf{unsafe}(\sigma, \Sigma) = \mathsf{evars}(\sigma) = \emptyset$.

Then Σ is nearly guarded *(resp.,* nearly frontier-guarded*) if each rule of Σ is nearly guarded (resp., nearly frontier-guarded) w.r.t. Σ.*

Intuitively, every non-guarded rule of a nearly guarded theory only "operates" on constants from the input database. This is similar in spirit to the definition of description logics extended with *DL-safe* rules [25].

Normalization To make presentation easier, we will manipulate structurally simplified theories, defined as follows:

DEFINITION 4. *(Normalized theories) A theory Σ is in* normal form *(or, is* normal*) if the following are satisfied:*

(i) For every $\sigma \in \Sigma$, we have $|\mathsf{head}(\sigma)| = 1$.

(ii) Every $\sigma \in \Sigma$ with $\mathsf{evars}(\sigma) \neq \emptyset$ is guarded. In other words, if σ is not guarded, then it is a Datalog rule.

(iii) If $\sigma \in \Sigma$ has an occurrence of a constant, then σ is of the form $\rightarrow R(c)$.

PROPOSITION 1. *Every query (Σ, Q) can be transformed in logarithmic space into a query (Σ', Q') such that*

(a) Σ' is normal;

(b) $\mathsf{ans}((\Sigma, Q), D) = \mathsf{ans}((\Sigma', Q'), D)$ *for any database D;*

(c) if Σ is weakly frontier-guarded (resp., weakly guarded, nearly frontier-guarded, nearly guarded), then Σ' is weakly frontier-guarded (resp., weakly guarded, nearly frontier-guarded, nearly guarded);

4. CHASE TREE

The translations of this paper build on the fact the chase of a database w.r.t. a frontier-guarded theory has the shape of a tree. It is a known fact that $\mathsf{chase}(\Sigma, D)$, where Σ is weakly-guarded, has treewidth that is polynomial in the size of Σ and D [14]. We will (indirectly) make use of this property. We show that the chase of a frontier-guarded theory can be seen as the construction of a tree (the *chase tree*), whose root stores the atoms over the original constants of the input database, while the non-root nodes store atoms with labeled nulls. This representation turns out to be more informative than the existing representations in terms of tree decompositions. In particular, we exploit the fact that the structure of non-leaf nodes is only dependent on the theory and is independent from the database.

DEFINITION 5. *(Minimal nodes) Assume a tree T whose nodes are sets of atoms. Given a set C of terms, a node d in T is called C-*minimal *if $C \subseteq \mathsf{terms}(d)$ and d has no parent d' with $C \subseteq \mathsf{terms}(d')$.*

We are ready to the define the notion of *chase tree.*

DEFINITION 6. *(Chase tree) Assume a database D, a normal frontier-guarded theory Σ, and suppose*

$$D, \{R_1(\vec{t_1})\}, \{R_2(\vec{t_2})\} \ldots$$

is a chase of D w.r.t. Σ. Suppose each $\{R_i(\vec{t_i})\}$ is a consequence of $\sigma_i \in \Sigma$ w.r.t. $D \cup \{R_1(\vec{t_1})\} \cup \ldots \cup \{R_{i-1}(\vec{t}_{i-1})\}$ and a homomorphism h_i. Then a chase tree *T of D w.r.t. Σ is a tree built as follows. Initially, T consists of the single node*

$$d_0 = D \cup \{R(c) \mid \rightarrow R(c) \in \Sigma\}.$$

Subsequently each $R_i(\vec{t_i})$ from $R_1(\vec{t_1}), R_2(\vec{t_2}), \ldots$ is added to T in the given order as follows:

(C1) if T has a node d with $\vec{t_i} \subseteq \mathsf{terms}(d)$, then add $R_i(\vec{t_i})$ to a $\vec{t_i}$-minimal node in T;

(C2) otherwise, create a new node $\{R_i(\vec{t_i})\}$ and set it as a child of some $\{h(x_0), \ldots, h(x_n)\}$-minimal node of T, where $\{x_0, \ldots, x_n\} = \mathsf{fvars}(\sigma_i)$.

PROPOSITION 2. *Assume a database D, a normal frontier-guarded theory Σ, and let T be a chase tree of D w.r.t. Σ. Let m be the highest relation arity over all relations in Σ, and let k be the number of constants occurring in rules of Σ (recall that due to normalization such rules have the form $\rightarrow R(c)$). Then the following hold:*

(P1) $|\mathsf{terms}(d_0)| \leq |\mathsf{terms}(D)| + k$ for the root d_0 of T,

(P2) $|\mathsf{terms}(d)| \leq m$ for all non-root nodes d of T.

(P3) For any set C of terms, there is at most one C-minimal node in T.

The above proposition also shows the small tree-width of $\mathsf{chase}(\Sigma, D)$ for frontier-guarded rules. Take the chase tree T of D w.r.t. Σ and take the function L that maps each node d in T to $\mathsf{terms}(d)$. As easily seen, (T, L) is a tree decomposition of (the hypergraph of) $\mathsf{chase}(\Sigma, D)$ of width $max(|D|+k, m)$ with m the highest relation arity in Σ and k the number of constants in Σ. We only note that the satisfaction of the *connectedness condition* for (T, L) is guaranteed by the uniqueness of C-minimal nodes in T (the property (P3)). Indeed, if T had a term t that would induce several disconnected trees in T, then there would exist several $\{t\}$-minimal nodes in T.

5. FROM FRONTIER-GUARDEDNESS TO GUARDEDNESS

We start by providing a translation from frontier-guarded rules to nearly guarded rules. We then extend it to also cover nearly frontier-guarded and weakly frontier-guarded rules.

5.1 From Frontier-guarded to Nearly Guarded Rules

We show how a normal frontier-guarded theory Σ can be rewritten into a nearly guarded theory $\mathsf{rew}(\Sigma)$ such that $\Sigma, D \models \alpha$ iff $\mathsf{rew}(\Sigma), D \models \alpha$ for any database D and a ground atom $\alpha = R(\vec{t})$, where R is a relation from Σ. Note that this implies $\mathsf{ans}((\Sigma, Q), D) = \mathsf{ans}((\mathsf{rew}(\Sigma), Q), D)$ for any query (Σ, Q) and database D, where Σ is frontier-guarded. The translation exploits the fact that frontier-guarded theories enjoy universal solutions that can be represented as trees (see Proposition 2).

Clearly, the difficult part is that $\mathsf{body}(\sigma)$ of a frontier-guarded rule σ can be seen as a complex (possibly cyclic) structure whose variables may have to be mapped rather arbitrarily into labeled nulls during the construction of the chase. This is in contrast to weakly and nearly guarded theories, where the possibly "cyclic part" of a body of a each rule only maps to original constants. Nevertheless, due to Proposition 2, the chase of a frontier-guarded theory is tree-like, and hence the relevant homomorphisms from $\mathsf{body}(\sigma)$ are only the ones that map into tree-like structures, given by partially constructed chase trees. In our translation we capture the set such homomorphisms for σ by a (potentially exponential) set of nearly guarded rules.

We first define the notion of *selection* in a rule. Intuitively, we select a set variables and obtain a group of at most k variables, where k is the maximal arity over all relations appearing in Σ.

DEFINITION 7. *(Selection) Let Σ be a normal frontier-guarded theory and assume $\sigma \in \Sigma$. A selection for σ is a partial function μ from $\mathsf{uvars}(\sigma)$ to $\mathsf{uvars}(\sigma)$ such that $|\mathsf{ran}(\mu)| \leq k$ with k the maximal arity over all relations appearing in Σ. Given a set Γ of atoms, we use $\mu(\Gamma)$ to denote the result of replacing in Γ each variable $x \in \mathsf{dom}(\mu)$ by $\mu(x)$.*

We collect the rule atoms that are *covered* by a selection:

DEFINITION 8. *(Covered atoms) Assume a normal frontier-guarded theory Σ, $\sigma \in \Sigma$, and a selection μ for σ. We define the following:*

$$\mathsf{cov}(\sigma, \mu) = \{B \in \mathsf{body}(\sigma) \mid \mathsf{vars}(B) \subseteq \mathsf{dom}(\mu)\}.$$

We will use two kinds of transformations. Intuitively, given a rule σ and a selection μ, the first transformation will pull out from σ all the atoms that are covered by μ. The second one will instead pull out of σ all the atoms that are *not* covered by μ. The removed atoms will be moved to a fresh rule. To preserve soundness, we must keep track of variables that occur both in the range of the selection and in a body atom not covered by the selection. The same holds for variables that occur in the head of σ.

DEFINITION 9 (VARIABLES TO KEEP). *Assume a normal frontier-guarded theory Σ, $\sigma \in \Sigma$, and a selection μ for σ. We let $\mathsf{keep}(\sigma, \mu)$ be the set of all $\mu(x)$ such that $x \in \mathsf{dom}(\mu)$ and x occurs in $\mathsf{body}(\sigma) \setminus \mathsf{cov}(\sigma, \mu)$ or $\mathsf{head}(\sigma)$.*

We are now ready to define the two rewriting steps that we use. In both cases, a frontier-guarded rule σ is split into a pair σ', σ'' of rules, where one of them becomes guarded, while the other one is frontier-guarded but structurally less complex than σ. In the rewriting we employ annotated relation names, but they will only become relevant in next section for dealing with weakly frontier-guarded rules.

DEFINITION 10. *(Remove-covered (rc)) Assume a non-guarded Datalog rule σ in a normal frontier-guarded theory Σ, and a selection μ for σ. An* rc-rewriting *of σ w.r.t. μ is any pair of σ', σ'' of rules obtained as follows:*

(i) $\sigma' = R(\vec{x}) \wedge \mu(\mathsf{cov}(\sigma, \mu)) \rightarrow H(\vec{y})$, where

- *(a) (guarding) R is an arbitrary relation from Σ, and $\vec{x}$ contains each variable of σ',*
- *(b) (variable projection) $\mu(\mathsf{cov}(\sigma, \mu))$ has a variable z such that $z \notin \vec{y}$, and*
- *(c) (fresh atom) H is a fresh relation name and $\vec{y} = \mathsf{keep}(\sigma, \mu)$. H has the annotation of $\mathsf{head}(\sigma)$.*

(ii) $\sigma'' = H(\vec{y}) \wedge \mu(\mathsf{body}(\sigma) \setminus \mathsf{cov}(\sigma, \mu)) \rightarrow \mu(\mathsf{head}(\sigma))$.

EXAMPLE 3. *Consider the rule $\sigma = R(x_0, x_1)$, $R(x_1, x_2)$, $R(x_2, x_3)$, $R(x_3, x_4)$, $R(x_4, x_1) \rightarrow P(x_1)$. Clearly, σ is not guarded, but is frontier-guarded. Take the partial function $\mu = \{x_4 \rightarrow x_2, x_2 \rightarrow x_2, x_3 \rightarrow x_3\}$. Then $\mathsf{cov}(\sigma, \mu) = \{R(x_2, x_3), R(x_3, x_4)\}$ and $\mathsf{keep}(\sigma, \mu) = \{x_2\}$. An rc-rewriting σ', σ'' of σ w.r.t. μ can be obtained as follows. Let*

$$\sigma'' = R(x_0, x_1), R(x_1, x_2), R(x_2, x_1), A(x_2) \rightarrow P(x_1),$$

where A is a fresh relation name. In case, Q is a relation in Σ of arity 3, we can let

$$\sigma' = R(x_2, x_3), R(x_3, x_2), Q(x_2, x_3, y) \rightarrow A(x_2).$$

Observe that σ' is guarded, while σ'' is not guarded but frontier-guarded with the variables x_4, x_3 vanished.

EXAMPLE 4. *Recall the rule σ_4 from Example 1. Take the function $\mu = \{x \rightarrow x, z \rightarrow z\}$. Then $\mathsf{cov}(\sigma_4, \mu) = \{\mathsf{hasTopic}(x, z), \mathsf{Scientific}(z)\}$ and $\mathsf{keep}(\sigma_4, \mu) = \{x\}$. Then the following pair is an rc-rewriting of σ_4 w.r.t. μ:*

$$\mathsf{hasAuthor}(x, y), \mathsf{Aux}(x) \rightarrow \mathsf{Q}(y),$$
$$\mathsf{Keywords}(x, z, u), \mathsf{hasTopic}(x, z), \mathsf{Scientific}(z) \rightarrow \mathsf{Aux}(x),$$

where $\mathsf{Aux}(y)$ is a fresh relation name. In this example, we use $\mathsf{Keywords}(y, z, u)$ as a guard in the second rule. Observe that the two resulting rules are guarded.

DEFINITION 11. *(Remove-non-covered (rnc)) Assume a non-guarded Datalog rule σ in a normal frontier-guarded theory Σ, and a selection μ for σ. An* rnc-rewriting *of σ w.r.t. μ is any pair of σ', σ'' of rules obtained as follows:*

(i) $\sigma' = R(\vec{x}) \wedge \mu(\mathsf{body}(\sigma) \setminus \mathsf{cov}(\sigma, \mu)) \rightarrow H(\vec{y})$, where

- *(a) (frontier-guarding) R is a relation from Σ and $\vec{x}$ contains each variable in $\vec{y}$;*
- *(b) (variable projection) $\vec{x}$ has a variable z such $z \notin \vec{y}$ and z occurs in $\mu(\mathsf{body}(\sigma) \setminus \mathsf{cov}(\sigma, \mu))$;*
- *(c) (fresh atom) H is a fresh relation name and $\vec{y} = \mathsf{keep}(\sigma, \mu)$; H has the annotation of $\mathsf{head}(\sigma)$;*

(ii) $\sigma'' = P(\vec{z}) \wedge H(\vec{y}) \wedge \mu(\mathsf{cov}(\sigma, \mu)) \rightarrow \mu(\mathsf{head}(\sigma))$, where

- *(guarding) P is a relation from Σ and $\vec{z}$ contains each variable of σ''.*

EXAMPLE 5. *Assume the rule $\sigma = R(x_1, x_2)$, $R(x_2, x_3)$, $R(x_3, x_4)$, $R(x_4, x_1)$, $R(x_4, x_5) \rightarrow P(x_1, x_2)$. Again, σ is not guarded, but is frontier-guarded. Take the partial function $\mu = \{x_1 \rightarrow x_1, x_2 \rightarrow x_2, x_3 \rightarrow x_3\}$. Then $\mathsf{cov}(\sigma, \mu) = \{R(x_1, x_2), R(x_2, x_3)\}$ and $\mathsf{keep}(\sigma, \mu) = \{x_1, x_3\}$. An rnc-rewriting σ', σ'' of σ w.r.t. μ can be obtained as follows. Let σ' be the next rule:*

$$W(x_1, x_3, x_4), R(x_3, x_4), R(x_4, x_1), R(x_4, x_5) \rightarrow A(x_1, x_3),$$

where A is a fresh relation name and W is a ternary relation in Σ. In case Q is a relation in Σ of arity 3, we can let σ'' be as follows:

$$Q(x_1,x_3,x_2), A(x_1,x_3), R(x_1,x_2), R(x_2,x_3) \to P(x_1,x_2).$$

We have that σ'' is guarded, while σ' is frontier-guarded.

EXAMPLE 6. *Recall the rule σ_3 from Example 1. As in the previous example, take the function $\mu = \{x \to x, z \to z\}$. Then $\mathsf{cov}(\sigma_3,\mu) = \{\mathsf{hasTopic}(x,z), \mathsf{Scientific}(z)\}$ and $\mathsf{keep}(\sigma_3,\mu) = \{x\}$. Then the following pair of rules is an rnc-rewriting of σ_3 w.r.t. μ:*

$$\begin{array}{rcl} \mathsf{hasAuthor}(x,u), \mathsf{hasAuthor}(y,u), & & \\ \mathsf{hasTopic}(y,z'), \mathsf{Scientific}(z'), \mathsf{citedIn}(y,x) & \to & \mathsf{Aux}(x) \\ \mathsf{Keywords}(x,z,u), \mathsf{hasTopic}(x,z), \mathsf{Aux}'(x) & \to & \mathsf{Scientific}(z), \end{array}$$

where $\mathsf{Aux}'(y)$ is a fresh relation. The atom $\mathsf{Keywords}(y,z,u)$ is used as a guard in the second rule. Observe that the first rule is frontier-guarded and second rule is fully guarded.

An *expansion* of a frontier-guarded theory is obtained by closing it under rc-rewritings and rnc-rewritings.

DEFINITION 12. *(Expansion) An* expansion $\mathsf{ex}(\Sigma)$ *of a normal frontier-guarded theory Σ is obtained by exhaustively adding rules to Σ as follows: for each Datalog rule $\sigma \in \Sigma$ and each selection μ for σ, add to Σ all the rc-rewritings and rnc-rewritings of σ w.r.t. μ.*

Note that applying an rc-rewriting or an rnc-rewriting on a non-guarded rule leads to a guarded rule and a frontier-guarded rule that has, due to variable projection, strictly less variables that do not occur in a frontier guard. Thus the expansion can be computed in exponential time in the size of the input theory.

We can now finalize our transformation from frontier-guarded rules to nearly guarded rules. To this end, we simply add atoms of the form $\mathsf{ACDom}(x)$ to bodies of rules in $\mathsf{ex}(\Sigma)$ to ensure near guardedness of the resulting theory.

DEFINITION 13. *(Rewriting) The* rewriting $\mathsf{rew}(\Sigma)$ *of a normal frontier-guarded theory Σ is obtained from $\mathsf{ex}(\Sigma)$ by adding to each non-guarded rule $\sigma \in \mathsf{ex}(\Sigma)$ the atom $\mathsf{ACDom}(x)$ for each universal variable x of σ.*

The translation above leads to a nearly guarded theory.

PROPOSITION 3. *Let Σ be a normal frontier-guarded theory. Then $\mathsf{rew}(\Sigma)$ is nearly guarded.*

We are ready to state the main result of this section.

THEOREM 1. *Let Σ be a normal frontier-guarded theory. Then $\Sigma, D \models \alpha$ iff $\mathsf{rew}(\Sigma), D \models \alpha$ for any database D and ground atom α over Σ.*

PROOF SKETCH. To prove the claim, it suffices to show that $\alpha \in \mathsf{chase}(\Sigma, D)$ iff $\alpha \in \mathsf{chase}(\mathsf{rew}(\Sigma), D)$. For the "if" direction, one can show that, considering only atoms over the signature of Σ, each inference of an atom made in the construction of $\mathsf{chase}(\mathsf{rew}(\Sigma), D)$ can also be made by employing rules of Σ. For the "only if" direction, we can employ Proposition 2. Assume a non-guarded rule $\sigma \in \Sigma$ and suppose $\mathsf{body}(\sigma)$ has a homomorphism h into the (partially constructed) $\mathsf{chase}(\Sigma, D)$ that maps m variables to labeled nulls. By Proposition 2, $\mathsf{chase}(\Sigma, D)$ can be decomposed into a tree of atom sets such that each non-leaf node is over at most k constants, where k is the maximal arity of relations in Σ. Take a node d such that d has an atom from $h(\mathsf{body}(\sigma))$ and no descendant of d has an atom from $h(\mathsf{body}(\sigma))$. In case $h(\mathsf{fg}(\sigma)) \notin d$ (resp., $h(\mathsf{fg}(\sigma)) \in d$), one can pick a selection μ and define an rc-rewriting (resp., rnc-rewriting) of σ', σ'' of σ together with respective homomorphisms that give the same consequence as σ. Importantly, if the rewriting produces a non-guarded rule, then its body homomorphism employs strictly less than d labeled nulls. In this way one shows that every ground $\alpha \in \mathsf{chase}(\Sigma, D)$ can be derived by rules in $\mathsf{ex}(\Sigma)$ that are either guarded or don't employ labeled nulls in body homomorphisms. $\square$

For the class of frontier-guarded theories with singleton heads, our translation into nearly guarded rules does not increase the maximal arity of relations. Entailment of ground atoms in frontier-guarded theories with singleton heads is 2-EXPTIME-hard even in case relation arities are bounded by a constant [7]. On the other hard, the same problem under bounded arities is EXPTIME-complete for weakly-guarded rules [14]. Thus the existence of polynomial arity-preserving translation would imply 2-EXPTIME = EXPTIME.

It is not difficult to extend the previous translation to cover nearly frontier-guarded rules. Assume a nearly frontier-guarded theory Σ. If a rule $\sigma \in \Sigma$ is not frontier guarded, then by definition of near frontier-guardedness, σ has no unsafe variable and thus during chasing its body is never mapped to labeled nulls. Such rules simply need no rewriting, which we see more formally as follows.

DEFINITION 14. *Assume a nearly frontier-guarded theory Σ. Let Σ_f denote the frontier-guarded rules in Σ and let $\Sigma_d = \Sigma \setminus \Sigma_f$ (note that $\mathsf{unsafe}(\sigma,\Sigma) = \mathsf{evars}(\sigma) = \emptyset$ for all $\sigma \in \Sigma_d$). We define $\mathsf{rew}(\Sigma) = \mathsf{rew}(\Sigma_f) \cup \Sigma_d$.*

PROPOSITION 4. *Assume a query (Σ, Q) with Σ a normal nearly frontier-guarded theory. We have that $\mathsf{rew}(\Sigma)$ is nearly guarded and $\mathsf{ans}((\Sigma,Q),D) = \mathsf{ans}((\mathsf{rew}(\Sigma),Q),D)$ for any database D.*

Axiomatizing the Relation ACDom Due to Definition 13, the theory $\mathsf{rew}(\Sigma)$ resulting from a theory Σ may contain atoms of the form $\mathsf{ACDom}(x)$. Such atoms can be eliminated from $\mathsf{rew}(\Sigma)$ while preserving ground atomic consequences, modulus renaming of relation names.

DEFINITION 15. *Assume a nearly guarded theory Σ. For every relation R of Σ, let R^* be a fresh relation of the same arity as R. Note that this includes the fresh relation ACDom^* in case ACDom occurs in Σ. Let Σ^* be the theory obtained from Σ by replacing every atom $R(\vec{t})$ by $R^*(\vec{t})$ and adding the following rules:*

(a) $R(x_1,\ldots,x_n) \to R^*(x_1,\ldots,x_n)$ for every n-ary R of Σ,

(b) $R(x_1,\ldots,x_n) \to \mathsf{ACDom}^*(x_i)$ for every n-ary relation R of Σ and $i \in \{1,\ldots,n\}$, and

(c) $\to \mathsf{ACDom}^*(c)$ for every constant c of Σ.

The following is not difficult to check:

PROPOSITION 5. *Assume a query (Σ, Q) with Σ nearly guarded. Then (Σ^*, Q^*) is a query such that*

i) Σ^* is a nearly guarded theory with no occurrences of the built-in relation ACDom, and

ii) $\mathsf{ans}((\Sigma,Q),D) = \mathsf{ans}((\Sigma^*,Q^*),D)$, for any database D.

5.2 Translating Weakly Frontier-guarded Rules

We have seen above a translation from frontier-guarded and nearly frontier-guarded rules to nearly guarded rules. We show next that it can be extended to also cover weakly frontier-guarded rules. Such rules are treated in three steps:

(a) converting them into frontier-guarded rules by removing the terms occurring in non-affected positions from atoms and storing them in relation annotations,

(b) converting the resulting frontier-guarded theory into a nearly guarded theory using the translation of the previous section, and

(c) reconstructing original atoms from relation annotations, thus obtaining a weakly guarded theory.

We make this more precise next.

To simplify presentation, we will use a convent ordering of positions in relations of a weakly frontier-guarded theory.

DEFINITION 16. *(Proper theories) We say a weakly frontier-guarded theory* Σ *is* proper *if the following holds:* $(R,i) \notin \mathsf{ap}(\Sigma)$ *with* $i \geq 1$ *implies* $(R, i+1) \notin \mathsf{ap}(\Sigma)$.

In other words, if Σ is proper, then each atom $R(\vec{t})$ in Σ has an initial sequence of terms in affected positions, followed by terms that appear in non-affected positions only. For the rest of the section, we w.l.o.g. assume only proper theories. Any theory can be transformed in logarithmic space into a proper theory by reordering arguments in atoms.

We next define how atoms with terms in non-affected positions are converted into atoms where such terms are moved into a relation's annotation.

DEFINITION 17. *Assume a weakly frontier-guarded theory* Σ. *We let* $a_\Sigma(R(t_1, \dots, t_n)) = R[t_{i+1}, \dots, t_n](t_1, \dots, t_i)$, *where* i *is the last affected position in* R. *Given a database* D, *we let* $a_\Sigma(D) = \{a_\Sigma(A) \mid A \in D\}$. *Finally, we let* $a(\Sigma)$ *denote the theory obtained from* Σ *by replacing each atom* A *of* Σ *with* $a_\Sigma(A)$.

As easily seen, if Σ is weakly frontier-guarded, then $a(\Sigma)$ is frontier-guarded. We are ready to finalize the translation from weakly frontier-guarded theories:

DEFINITION 18. *For a frontier-guarded theory* Σ *with a safe annotation, we use* $a^-(\Sigma)$ *to denote the theory obtained from* Σ *by replacing each atom* $R[\vec{v}](\vec{t})$ *by* $R(\vec{t}, \vec{v})$.

For a normal weakly frontier-guarded theory Σ, *we let* $\mathsf{rew}(\Sigma) = a^-(\mathsf{rew}(a(\Sigma)))$.

We are ready to state the main result of this section.

THEOREM 2. *Take a query* (Σ, Q) *with* Σ *a normal weakly frontier-guarded theory. Then* $\mathsf{rew}(\Sigma)$ *is weakly guarded and* $\mathsf{ans}((\Sigma, Q), D) = \mathsf{ans}((\mathsf{rew}(\Sigma), Q), D)$ *for any database* D.

PROOF SKETCH. For the second part of the claim, assume (Σ, Q) as above and let D be a database. For a theory Σ', let $\mathsf{pg}(\Sigma, D)$ denote the theory that can be obtained from Σ' by all possible substitutions of safe variables by constants in D. Let $\Sigma_{pg} = \mathsf{pg}(\Sigma, D)$. It can be verified that $\mathsf{ans}((\Sigma, Q), D) = \mathsf{ans}((\Sigma_{pg}, Q), D)$ and

$$\mathsf{ans}((\mathsf{rew}(\Sigma), Q), D) = \mathsf{ans}((\mathsf{pg}(\mathsf{rew}(\Sigma), D), Q), D).$$

Thus due to Theorem 1, to prove the claim it suffices to show that $\mathsf{rew}(a(\Sigma_{pg}))$ and $a(\mathsf{pg}(\mathsf{rew}(\Sigma), D))$ have the same ground consequences from $a_\Sigma(D)$. This true because the two theories are equal modulo renaming of variables and auxiliary relation symbols introduced during the rewritings. □

$$\frac{\alpha \to \beta \wedge A}{\alpha \to A} \quad A \text{ has no existential variables}$$

$$\frac{\alpha \to \beta \quad \gamma_1 \wedge \gamma_2 \to \delta}{\alpha \wedge h(\gamma_1) \to \beta \wedge h(\delta)} \quad \begin{array}{l}\gamma_1 \wedge \gamma_2 \to \delta \text{ is a Datalog rule,} \\ h \text{ is a homomorphism from} \\ \gamma_2 \text{ to } \beta \text{ with } \mathsf{vars}(h(\gamma_1)) \subseteq \\ \mathsf{vars}(\alpha).\end{array}$$

$$\frac{\alpha \to \beta}{g(\alpha) \to g(\beta)} \quad g : \mathsf{vars}(\alpha) \to \mathsf{vars}(\alpha)$$

Figure 3: Inference Rules

6. FROM NEARLY GUARDED RULES TO DATALOG

In this section, we give a translation from nearly guarded rules to Datalog. In line with the previous sections, the translation preserves answers to ground atomic queries. We first translate fully guarded theories in Datalog. The translation is based on specially tailored inference rules, which we use to saturate the input set of guarded rules. The desired Datalog program is obtained by dropping all existential rules. We then show that this methods easily extends to translate nearly guarded rules into Datalog.

DEFINITION 19. *For a guarded theory* Σ, *let* $\Xi(\Sigma)$ *be the closure of* Σ *under the inference rules in Figure 3. Let* $\mathsf{dat}(\Sigma)$ *be the set of Datalog rules obtained from* $\Xi(\Sigma)$ *by dropping all rules containing existential variables in the head.*

We note that applying any of the inference rules to guarded rules, only guarded rules will be produced. Consequently $\Xi(\Sigma)$ (and thus $\mathsf{dat}(\Sigma)$) is guarded whenever Σ is.

THEOREM 3. *Let* Σ *be a guarded theory. Then* $\Sigma, D \models \alpha$ *iff* $\mathsf{dat}(\Sigma), D \models \alpha$, *for any ground atom* α *and database* D.

EXAMPLE 7. *We provide an illustrative example. Let our rule set* Σ *contain the rules*

- $\sigma_1 = \mathsf{A}(x) \to \exists y.\mathsf{R}(x, y)$,
- $\sigma_2 = \mathsf{R}(x, y) \to \mathsf{S}(y, y)$,
- $\sigma_3 = \mathsf{S}(x, y) \to \exists z.\mathsf{T}(x, y, z)$,
- $\sigma_4 = \mathsf{T}(x, x, y) \to \mathsf{B}(x)$,
- $\sigma_5 = \mathsf{C}(x), \mathsf{R}(x, y), \mathsf{B}(y) \to \mathsf{D}(x)$.

Let our database D *consist of* $\mathsf{A}(c)$ *and* $\mathsf{C}(c)$, *and let our query* α *be* $\mathsf{D}(c)$. *The following chase confirms the query:*

$\{\mathsf{A}(c), \mathsf{C}(c)\}$
$\Longrightarrow \{\mathsf{R}(c, n_1)\}$ — *apply* σ_1 *with* $x \mapsto c$
$\Longrightarrow \{\mathsf{S}(n_1, n_1)\}$ — *apply* σ_2 *with* $y \mapsto n_1$
$\Longrightarrow \{\mathsf{T}(n_1, n_1, n_2)\}$ — *apply* σ_3 *with* $x \mapsto n_1, y \mapsto n_1$
$\Longrightarrow \{\mathsf{B}(n_1)\}$ — *apply* σ_4 *with* $x \mapsto n_1, y \mapsto n_2$
$\Longrightarrow \{\mathsf{D}(c)\}$ — *apply* σ_5 *with* $x \mapsto c, y \mapsto n_1$.

We now show how this query can be answered using only the datalog program $\mathsf{dat}(\Sigma)$. *To this end, we first provide derivations of new rules from* Σ

- $\sigma_6 = \mathsf{S}(y,y) \rightarrow \exists z.\mathsf{T}(y,y,z)$
(from σ_3 via third rule with $g = \{x \mapsto y, y \mapsto y, z \mapsto z\}$),
- $\sigma_7 = \mathsf{S}(y,y) \rightarrow \exists z.\mathsf{T}(y,y,z) \wedge B(y)$
(from σ_6 and σ_4 via second rule, $\gamma_1 = \emptyset$, $h = \{x \mapsto y, y \mapsto z\}$),
- $\sigma_8 = \mathsf{S}(y,y) \rightarrow \mathsf{B}(y)$ *(from σ_7 via first rule),*
- $\sigma_9 = \mathsf{A}(x) \rightarrow \exists y.\mathsf{R}(x,y) \wedge \mathsf{S}(y,y)$
(from σ_1 and σ_2 via second rule, $\gamma_1 = \emptyset$, $h = id$),
- $\sigma_{10} = \mathsf{A}(x) \rightarrow \exists y.\mathsf{R}(x,y) \wedge \mathsf{S}(y,y) \wedge \mathsf{B}(y)$
(from σ_9 and σ_8 via second rule, $\gamma_1 = \emptyset$, $h = id$),
- $\sigma_{11} = \mathsf{A}(x) \wedge \mathsf{C}(x) \rightarrow \exists y.\mathsf{R}(x,y) \wedge \mathsf{S}(y,y) \wedge \mathsf{B}(y) \wedge \mathsf{D}(x)$
(from σ_{10} and σ_5 via second rule, $\gamma_1 = \mathsf{C}(x)$, $h = id$),
- $\sigma_{12} = \mathsf{A}(x) \wedge \mathsf{C}(x) \rightarrow \mathsf{D}(x)$, *(from σ_{11} via first rule).*

Clearly, σ_{12} is contained in $\mathsf{dat}(\Sigma)$ as it is a plain Datalog rule. Now it is straightforward to see that $\mathsf{D}(c)$ can be derived from $\{\mathsf{A}(c), \mathsf{C}(c)\}$ by one application of σ_{12}.

We saw how a (fully) guarded theory can be converted into a Datalog program while preserving atomic consequences. We show here that the method can also be applied to nearly guarded theories.

PROPOSITION 6. *Let Σ be a nearly guarded theory, α a ground atom, and D a database. Let Σ_g denote the guarded rules in Σ and let $\Sigma_d = \Sigma \setminus \Sigma_g$. Then $\Sigma, D \models \alpha$ iff $\mathsf{dat}(\Sigma_g) \cup \Sigma_d, D \models \alpha$.*

In other words, a nearly guarded theory Σ is translated into the Datalog program $\mathsf{dat}(\Sigma_g) \cup \Sigma_d$ while preserving ground atomic consequences of Σ.

The above translation leads to a Datalog program that is of size double exponential in the size of the input guarded or nearly-guarded theory. To see this, assume a nearly guarded theory Σ. Let Σ_g denote the guarded rules in Σ and let $\Sigma_d = \Sigma \setminus \Sigma_g$. Let v be the maximal number of variables per rule in Σ, and let p be the maximal arity of relations in Σ, and let c be the number of constants in Σ. Observe that the rewriting of Σ_g into the datalog program $\mathsf{dat}(\Sigma_g)$ does not introduce new variables, new constants or new relation symbols into the constructed rules, but may introduce new atoms in rule bodies and heads (see the second rule in Figure 3). Assuming the number of relation symbols in Σ is m, the number of possible rules is bounded by $2^{(v+c)^p m}$. In case the arity of the relations in Σ is bounded by a constant, the number of rules resulting from the translation in 19 is single exponential in the size of Σ.

The above translation does not increase the number of variables per rule. If we place this as a requirement, which is reasonable for practical purposes, then the double exponential blow-up in the size of the input theory Σ is unavoidable. This follows from the 2-EXPTIME-hardness of query answering in guarded theories [14]. Indeed, a (singly) exponentially sized Datalog program could be evaluated in single exponential time because the grounding of the program would remain of single exponential size. The double exponential blowup, under the common assumptions in complexity theory, is unavoidable even if we relax the requirement a bit: instead of preserving the number of variables per rule, we require the maximal predicate arity to be preserved. In this case, querying the resulting program would be feasible in NEXPTIME to due the fact that query answering in Datalog under bounded predicate arities is in NP [17].

7. CONJUNCTIVE QUERY ANSWERING

We look next at conjunctive queries over databases enriched with existential rules (see e.g. [9, 14] for similar results and motivation), which are fully supported in our setting. A *knowledge base query* is of the form $(\Sigma \cup \{\alpha \rightarrow Q(\vec{x})\}, Q)$, where Σ is a weakly frontier-guarded theory and Q does not occur in Σ. Note that $\alpha \rightarrow Q(\vec{x})$ need not be weakly frontier-guarded in $\Sigma \cup \{\alpha \rightarrow Q(\vec{x})\}$. However, by employing the built-in relation ACDom, the rule $\alpha \rightarrow Q(\vec{x})$ can be converted into a weakly frontier-guarded rule. Indeed, $(\Sigma \cup \{\alpha \rightarrow Q(\vec{x})\}, Q)$ and the weakly frontier-guarded query $(\Sigma \cup \{\alpha \wedge \mathsf{ACDom}(x_1) \wedge \ldots \wedge \mathsf{ACDom}(x_n) \rightarrow Q(x_1, \ldots, x_n)\}, Q)$ output the same for any database D, where $\langle x_1, \ldots, x_n \rangle = \vec{x}$.

We recall that checking $\Sigma, D \models \alpha$, where Σ is weakly frontier-guarded, is 2-EXPTIME-complete in combined complexity [30]. It is not difficult to see that the translations of this paper provide an alternative proof for the double exponential time upper bound. The high-level procedure to check $\Sigma, D \models \alpha$ is as follows:

1. Compute the weakly guarded theory $\mathsf{rew}(\Sigma)$.
2. Compute the *partial grounding* Σ_1 of $\mathsf{rew}(\Sigma)$ w.r.t. D. That is, Σ_1 is the set of rules that can be obtained from $\mathsf{rew}(\Sigma)$ by instantiating variables in non-affected positions with constants from D. The resulting Σ_1 is guarded, is of exponential size in the size of Σ and D, but has linearly many variables per rule.
3. Translate Σ_1 into Datalog with the translation of the previous section, obtaining $\Sigma_2 = \mathsf{dat}(\Sigma_1)$. The resulting Σ_2 is of double exponential size in the size of Σ and D, but has linearly many variables per rule.
4. Ground Σ_2 with the constants of D, obtaining a ground theory Σ_3 with doubly exponentially many rules.
5. If $\Sigma_3, D \models \alpha$, then $\Sigma, D \models \alpha$. Otherwise, $\Sigma, D \not\models \alpha$.

8. CAPTURING QUERIES COMPUTABLE IN EXPONENTIAL TIME

We have seen that many of the query languages investigated here can be expressed by plain Datalog queries. However, queries based on weakly frontier-guarded or weakly guarded rules cannot be expressed in Datalog due to the increase in data complexity from completeness for PTIME to EXPTIME [14]. We next explore settings in which these formalisms capture *all* queries computable in exponential time.

We first show that all exponential time computable queries posed over *string databases* can be expressed by weakly guarded theories. We later show that weakly guarded theories extended with *stratified negation* are in fact expressive enough to capture *all queries* computable in exponential time, without any assumptions about input databases.

DEFINITION 20. *(String databases and queries) Assume an integer k and a set Ω of k-ary relation symbols. Assume also k-ary relations $\mathsf{First}^k, \mathsf{Last}^k$, and a $2k$-ary relation Next^{2k}. A database D is called a* string database *(of degree k) if it has the following properties:*

- *Let Dom be the set of constants in D. Then for all k-tuples $\vec{v} \in Dom^k$, there is exactly one $\sigma \in \Omega$ such that $\sigma(\vec{v}) \in D$.*
- *The relation $\{(\vec{v}_1, \vec{v}_2) \mid \mathsf{Next}^{2k}(\vec{v}_1, \vec{v}_2) \in D, \vec{v}_1, \vec{v}_2 \in Dom^k\}$ is a successor relation from some total $<$ order on Dom^k. Moreover, $\mathsf{First}^k(\vec{v}_1)$ and $\mathsf{Last}^k(\vec{v}_2)$ are true exactly for the minimal and the maximal element in $<$, respectively.*

We let $w(D) \in \Omega^*$ denote the word such that, for each $1 \leq i \leq |Dom^k|$, the ith symbol of $w(D)$ is exactly the symbol $\sigma \in \Omega$ such that $\sigma(\vec{v}) \in D$, where $\vec{v}$ is the ith smallest element in $<$. In other words, $w(D)$ extracts the string encoded in D.

A string query *is a triple (k, Ω, T), where k and Ω are as above, and T is a set of string databases of degree k such that T is closed under isomorphic databases. We say (k, Ω, T) is* decidable in exponential time *if there is deterministic Turing machine M with alphabet Ω that accepts exactly the language $\{w(D) \in \Omega^* \mid D \in T\}$, and M operates in time that is bounded by an exponential in the size D.*

THEOREM 4. *Any string query (k, Ω, T) decidable in exponential time can be expressed as a query (Σ, Q) where Σ is weakly guarded.*

PROOF SKETCH. One shows that from a Turing machine M to decide (k, Ω, T) one can build a query (Σ_M, Q), where Σ_M is weakly guarded and Q is 0-ary (i.e. a propositional variable), such that $D \in T$ iff $\Sigma_M, D \models Q$. In particular, one can write a theory Σ_M to implement an alternating polynomial space algorithm for checking whether M accepts $w(D)$. □

Weakly guarded rules do not capture all database queries decidable in exponential (or, even polynomial) time. E.g. due to monotonicity of query answers with plain existential rules, it is impossible to express a query that checks whether the number of constants occurring in a database is even. This already hints that we need to add some non-monotonicity to the formalism in order to also cover non-monotonic queries. But first, we define our goal more formally.

DEFINITION 21. *A* (generic) Boolean database query *is a tuple (A, BQ), where is A is a set of relation names (a signature), and BQ is a set of databases over A such that BQ is closed under isomorphic databases. We assume a coding C that encodes databases over A into words, such that a database D with d constants is encoded as a string of length d^k over a fixed alphabet Ω, where k is a sufficiently large yet fixed constant k.*[2] *We say BQ is* decidable in exponential time *if there is an exponential time bounded deterministic Turing machine M that decides, for any database D over A, whether $C(D) \in \{C(D') \mid D' \in BQ\}$ holds.*

Assume (A, BQ) as above. Observe that there is only one problem that needs to be resolved before we can employ the previous result for string databases to show that (A, BQ) can also be captured. We need a set of rules to implement an encoding C. In particular, it suffices to define a theory Σ_{code} to transform an input database D into a string database D_s of level k, for some fixed k, with $C(D)$ being the string written in D_s, i.e. with $w(D_s) = C(D)$.

Implementing Σ_{code} is straightforward, assuming each input database provides via relations Succ, Min and Max a total order over its constants, and we have means to infer the absence of tuples in the input database. We sketch such an encoding for the case A has only one n-ary relation R. We employ a standard semipositive Datalog program, which we in fact also introduce formally later. Let Ω consist of n-ary relations Zero and One. The first step is to define relations First^n, Next^{2n} and Last^n to store a lexicographically ordered sequence of n-tuples of constants from D, which can be done using plain Datalog rules [16]. We then can simply use the rules $R(\vec{x}) \to \mathsf{One}(\vec{x})$ and $\neg R(\vec{x}) \wedge \mathsf{ACDom}(x_1) \wedge \ldots \wedge \mathsf{ACDom}(x_n) \to \mathsf{Zero}(\vec{x})$ to represent the characteristic function of R in D, where $\langle x_1, \ldots, x_n \rangle = \vec{x}$. Thus we can infer that weakly guarded rules extended with negation on input relations capture all exponential time computable queries over ordered databases.

We next show that the desired total order (represented by Succ, Min and Max) can be generated by weakly guarded rules with *stratified negation*, which generalizes negation on input relations. Thus weakly guarded rules with stratified negation capture all exponential time computable queries, without any assumptions on the input databases.

DEFINITION 22. *(Stratified theories – syntax) An existential rule with negation is an expression of the form*

$$B_1 \wedge \ldots \wedge B_n \to H_1 \wedge \ldots \wedge H_m, \quad (2)$$

where $B_1, \ldots, B_n$ can be atoms $R(\vec{t})$ or negated atoms $\neg R(\vec{t})$. Negated atoms are called negative*; the remaining atoms are called* positive. *We consider* safe *theories where every variable of a negative body atom also occurs in some positive body atom. A theory Σ is called* stratified *if it can be partitioned into mutually disjoint $\Sigma_1, \ldots, \Sigma_n$ such that:*

- *if Σ_i has a body atom $A(\vec{t})$, then there is no rule in $\Sigma_{i+1} \cup \ldots \cup \Sigma_n$ with A in the head;*
- *if Σ_i has a body atom $\neg A(\vec{t})$, then there is no rule in $\Sigma_i \cup \ldots \cup \Sigma_n$ with A in the head.*

If $n = 1$, then Σ is semipositive.

The semantics of such theories is given by an iterative chasing following the stratification, which we recall here [15].

DEFINITION 23. *(Stratified theories – semantics) Let Σ be a stratified theory and D a database. For every $\neg A(\vec{t})$ in Σ we introduce a predicate name $\bar{A}$ of the same arity as A. We also define $p(\Sigma)$ to be the theory obtained by uniformly replacing each atom $\neg A(\vec{t})$ in Σ by the atom $\bar{A}(\vec{t})$.*

The semantics is defined inductively. Assume a database D and Σ with stratification $\Sigma_1, \ldots, \Sigma_n$. We define the following databases:

- *$S_0 = D$, and*
- *For each $1 \leq i \leq n$, the database S_i is obtained by restricting $chase(p(\Sigma_i), S'_{i-1})$ to the original symbols of Σ, where $S'_{i-1} = S_{i-1} \cup \{\bar{A}(\vec{t}) \mid A(\vec{t}) \notin S_{i-1}\}$.*

We let $chase(\Sigma, D) = S_n$.

Introducing negation requires to revisit the notion of weak guardedness. Assume a stratified theory Σ and let Σ' be the theory obtained from Σ by dropping all negative atoms. We say Σ is *weakly guarded* if every rule $\sigma \in \Sigma$ has a body atom that contains all the variables of $\mathsf{unsafe}(\sigma, \Sigma') \cap \mathsf{uvars}(\sigma)$.

[2]Note that this is possible due to the fixed signature. We assume that D has at least two constants.

It has been shown in [3] that query answering in stratified weakly guarded theories is ExpTime-complete in data complexity, i.e. stratified negation does not increase the complexity of reasoning with weakly guarded rules.

Theorem 5. *Any Boolean database query (A, BQ) decidable in exponential time can be expressed as a query (Σ, Q) where Σ is a stratified, weakly guarded theory.*

Proof Sketch. We only define using a stratified theory (a variant of) the relations Succ, Min and Max to store a total order over the constants of the input database. To this end, we write a program Σ_{succ} that creates an infinite forest such that each possible total ordering of constants of an input database is represented by a prefix of a branch. At the end, each different total ordering will be represented by a distinct null value, and all relevant facts regarding a specific ordering will be indexed by the null value corresponding to that ordering.

In particular, we use the following relations:

- $\mathsf{Min}(a, u)$ means that a constant a is the smallest element of the ordering identified by u.
- $\mathsf{Max}(a, u)$ means that a constant a is the greatest element of the ordering identified by u.
- $\mathsf{Lt}(a, b, u)$ means that a precedes b in the ordering identified by u.
- $\mathsf{Succ}(a, b, u)$ means that b is the immediate successor of a in the ordering identified by u.
- $\mathsf{Good}(u)$ means that u effectively represents a linear ordering over the set of constants in the input database.
- $\mathsf{Repetition}(u)$ means that u *does not* represent a linear ordering due to a cycle in the Succ relation.
- $\mathsf{Omission}(u)$ means that u *does not* represent a linear ordering due to a missing element.
- $\mathsf{New}(a, u)$ means that a is the new element introduced for a candidate ordering u.
- $\mathsf{Old}(a, u)$ means that a is an element already treated in the construction of the current ordering.

We will employ the active constant domain relation ACDom, which can be axiomatized as discussed previously. The theory Σ_{succ} has the following rules:

(1) $\mathsf{ACDom}(x) \to \exists u.\mathsf{Min}(x, u) \wedge \mathsf{New}(x, u)$.

(2) $\mathsf{New}(x, u), \mathsf{ACDom}(y) \to \exists v.\mathsf{Succ}(x, y, u, v) \wedge \mathsf{New}(y, v)$.

(3) $\mathsf{New}(x, u) \to \mathsf{Old}(x, u)$.

(4) $\mathsf{Succ}(x, y, u, v), \mathsf{Old}(x', u) \to \mathsf{Old}(x', v)$.

(5) $\mathsf{Succ}(x, y, u, v), \mathsf{Min}(x', u) \to \mathsf{Min}(x', v)$.

(6) $\mathsf{Succ}(x, y, u, v), \mathsf{Succ}(x', y', u) \to \mathsf{Succ}(x', y', v)$.

(7) $\mathsf{Succ}(x, y, u) \to \mathsf{Lt}(x, y, u)$

(8) $\mathsf{Lt}(x, y, u), \mathsf{Lt}(y, z, u) \to \mathsf{Lt}(x, z, u)$.

(9) $\mathsf{Lt}(x, x, u) \to \mathsf{Repetition}(u)$.

(10) $\mathsf{Old}(y, u), \mathsf{ACDom}(x), \neg\mathsf{Old}(x, u) \to \mathsf{Omission}(u)$.

(11) $\mathsf{Old}(x, u), \neg\mathsf{Repetition}(u), \neg\mathsf{Omission}(u) \to \mathsf{Good}(u)$.

(12) $\mathsf{New}(x, u), \mathsf{Good}(u) \to \mathsf{Max}(x, u)$.

For each u for which $\mathsf{Good}(u)$ holds, the relations $\mathsf{Min}(\cdot, u)$, $\mathsf{Max}(\cdot, u)$, and $\mathsf{Succ}(\cdot, \cdot, u)$ jointly constitute a (u-"labeled") linear order on the constants of an input database. Viceversa, for each such linear order, some u exists such that $\mathsf{Good}(u)$ holds and the order is represented by the relations $\mathsf{Min}(\cdot, u)$, $\mathsf{Max}(\cdot, u)$, and $\mathsf{Succ}(\cdot, \cdot, u)$. □

We remark that the above capturing result cannot be obtained for semipositive weakly guarded theories. This is because queries (Σ, Q), where Σ is semipositive, are monotonic on full databases (where all relations have all possible tuples). For this reason, it is impossible to express e.g. the query to check whether the input database is full and its domain has an odd number of constants.

9. RELATED WORK

There exists prior work on translations from frontier-guarded rules to Datalog [7, 8]. Exploiting a boundedness property, these earlier approaches essentially enumerate all (i.e., best-case exponentially many) possible queries with a certain number of variables. Contrarily, our approach was designed to be much more selective. In fact, methods which are close in spirit (i.e., inspired by knowledge compilation and consequence-driven reasoning) have been successfully implemented and evaluated for related but easier logics (cf. [4, 20, 18, 22]) As another difference, we give an intermediate translation into nearly guarded rules, which takes only single exponential time and generalizes nicely to a translation from weakly frontier-guarded to weakly-guarded rules. These results, which are based on new ideas and a new class of rules, and are proven from first principles, are of their own interest; they provide interesting insights and do not follow from previous work.

Recently, Bienvenu et al. have investigated the expressiveness of queries formulated by coupling a standard query language (e.g. conjunctive queries) and various description logics, and also richer logics such as extensions of the guarded fragment [12]. The authors show that such queries can be expressed in various fragments of disjunctive Datalog and also provide descriptive complexity results by establishing a tight connection with constraint satisfaction problems. We note that the query rewriting technique of [12] does not easily apply in our non-disjunctive setting, as it intrinsically relies on disjunctive rules to, intuitively speaking, compute the possible consistent completions of the database with ground atoms. Several further data-independent reformulations of query answering in description logics in terms of Datalog have been developed previously, e.g. for instance queries [20, 29, 27] and conjunctive queries [18]. All query languages above are not harder than NP in data complexity, and thus are subsumed by stratified weakly guarded existential rules.

Translations between existential rule fragments have been used to provide expressiveness and complexity results: in particular, there is a polynomial translation from weakly (frontier-)guarded into (frontier-)guarded rules [7] to show that they have the same combined complexity, however, this translation is not data-independent. Translations into Datalog exist for other existential rule fragments, e.g., for those based on notions of acyclicity [23].

The calculus from Definition 19 is inspired by results in description logics, where similar procedures have been developed for $\mathcal{EL}$ [4] and Horn-$\mathcal{SHIQ}$ [22].

10. CONCLUSION

In this paper, we have explored the relative and absolute expressiveness of diverse database query languages based on existential rules with various forms of guardedness.

We have seen that the considered languages with polynomial time data complexity (all up to nearly frontier-guarded theories) can in fact be expressed in plain Datalog. To this end, we have provided translations which are worst-case optimal in terms of the incurred blow-up of the query size.

For the discussed languages with exponential time data complexity (i.e. weakly guarded and weakly frontier-guarded rules), we showed that, extended with negation on input facts, they capture all exponential time computable queries over ordered databases. For arbitrary databases, an extension with stratified negation is required in order to fully capture ExpTime. This result has far-reaching implications—it shows that queries with stratified weakly guarded rules can express an overwhelming range of query formalisms: first-order and second-order logic (even extended via least fixed point operators), any of the known concrete decidable fragments of existential rules or formalisms based on descriptions logics (to the best of our knowledge, no such formalisms with data complexity beyond ExpTime have been proposed).

Exploring existential rules under more fine grained notions of expressiveness such as *modular expressive power* [3] is a natural next step for future work.

11. ACKNOWLEDGMENTS

We thank the anonymous reviewers for their helpful comments. This work was partially supported by the Austrian Science Fund's (FWF) projects P25518-N23 and P25207-N23. Georg Gottlob's work was supported by the European Research Council under grant FP7/2007-2013/ERC 246858 "DIADEM"; Georg Gottlob is a James Martin Senior Fellow.

12. REFERENCES

[1] S. Abiteboul, R. Hull, and V. Vianu. *Foundations of Databases*. Addison-Wesley, 1995.

[2] S. Abiteboul and V. Vianu. Datalog extensions for database queries and updates. *Journal of Computer and System Sciences*, 43(1):62 – 124, 1991.

[3] M. Arenas, G. Gottlob, and A. Pieris. Expressive languages for querying the semantic web. In *Proc. of PODS'14*. ACM Press, 2014.

[4] F. Baader, S. Brand, and C. Lutz. Pushing the el envelope. In *In Proc. of IJCAI 2005*, pages 364–369. Morgan-Kaufmann Publishers, 2005.

[5] F. Baader, D. Calvanese, D. McGuinness, D. Nardi, and P. Patel-Schneider, editors. *The Description Logic Handbook: Theory, Implementation, and Applications*. Cambridge University Press, second edition, 2007.

[6] J.-F. Baget, M. Leclère, M.-L. Mugnier, and E. Salvat. On rules with existential variables: Walking the decidability line. *Artif. Intell.*, 175(9-10):1620–1654, 2011.

[7] J.-F. Baget, M.-L. Mugnier, S. Rudolph, and M. Thomazo. Walking the complexity lines for generalized guarded existential rules. In *Proc. of IJCAI' 11*, pages 712–717. IJCAI/AAAI, 2011.

[8] V. Bárány, M. Benedikt, and B. ten Cate. Rewriting guarded negation queries. In *Proc. of MFCS' 13*, pages 98–110. ACM, 2013.

[9] V. Barany, G. Gottlob, and M. Otto. Querying the guarded fragment. *Logic in Computer Science, Symposium on*, 0:1–10, 2010.

[10] V. Bárány, B. ten Cate, and M. Otto. Queries with guarded negation. *PVLDB*, 5(11):1328–1339, 2012.

[11] C. Beeri and M. Y. Vardi. A proof procedure for data dependencies. *J. ACM*, 31(4):718–741, Sept. 1984.

[12] M. Bienvenu, B. ten Cate, C. Lutz, and F. Wolter. Ontology-based data access: A study through disjunctive datalog, CSP, and MMSNP. In *Proc. of PODS' 13*. ACM Press, 2013.

[13] L. Cabibbo. The expressive power of stratified logic programs with value invention. *Information and Computation*, 147(1):22 – 56, 1998.

[14] A. Calì, G. Gottlob, and M. Kifer. Taming the infinite chase: Query answering under expressive relational constraints. *J. Artif. Intell. Res.*, 48:115–174, 2013.

[15] A. Calì, G. Gottlob, and T. Lukasiewicz. A general datalog-based framework for tractable query answering over ontologies. *J. Web Sem.*, 14:57–83, 2012.

[16] E. Dantsin, T. Eiter, G. Gottlob, and A. Voronkov. Complexity and expressive power of logic programming. *ACM Computing Surveys*, 33(3):374–425, 2001.

[17] T. Eiter, W. Faber, M. Fink, and S. Woltran. Complexity results for answer set programming with bounded predicate arities and implications. *Ann. Math. Artif. Intell.*, 51(2-4):123–165, 2007.

[18] T. Eiter, M. Ortiz, M. Simkus, T.-K. Tran, and G. Xiao. Query rewriting for horn-shiq plus rules. In *Proc. of AAAI' 2012*. AAAI Press, 2012.

[19] R. Hull and M. Yoshikawa. Ilog: Declarative creation and manipulation of object identifiers. In *Proc. VLDB 1990*, pages 455–468. Morgan Kaufmann, 1990.

[20] U. Hustadt, B. Motik, and U. Sattler. Reasoning in description logics by a reduction to disjunctive datalog. *J. Autom. Reasoning*, 39(3):351–384, 2007.

[21] N. Immerman. *Descriptive complexity*. Graduate texts in computer science. Springer, 1999.

[22] Y. Kazakov. Consequence-driven reasoning for horn shiq ontologies. In *Proc. of IJCAI'09*, pages 2040–2045, 2009.

[23] M. Krötzsch and S. Rudolph. Extending decidable existential rules by joining acyclicity and guardedness. In *Proc. of IJCAI' 11*, pages 963–968, 2011.

[24] D. Maier, A. O. Mendelzon, and Y. Sagiv. Testing implications of data dependencies. *ACM Trans. Database Syst.*, 4(4):455–469, Dec. 1979.

[25] B. Motik, U. Sattler, and R. Studer. Query answering for OWL-DL with rules. *Web Semantics*, 3(1), 2005.

[26] M.-L. Mugnier. Conceptual graph rules and equivalent rules: A synthesis. In *Proc. of ICCS 2009*, 2009.

[27] M. Ortiz, S. Rudolph, and M. Simkus. Worst-case optimal reasoning for the horn-dl fragments of owl 1 and 2. In *Proc. of KR'10*. AAAI Press, 2010.

[28] C. H. Papadimitriou. A note the expressive power of prolog. *Bulletin of the EATCS*, 26:21–22, 1985.

[29] S. Rudolph, M. Krötzsch, and P. Hitzler. Type-elimination-based reasoning for the description logic SHIQbs using decision diagrams and disjunctive datalog. *Logical Methods in Comp. Science*, 8(1), 2012.

[30] M. Thomazo, J.-F. Baget, M.-L. Mugnier, and S. Rudolph. A generic querying algorithm for greedy sets of existential rules. In *Proc. of KR 2012*, 2012.

[31] M. Y. Vardi. The complexity of relational query languages. In *Proc. of STOC' 82*. ACM, 1982.

Containment and Equivalence of Well-Designed SPARQL

Reinhard Pichler
Vienna University of Technology
pichler@dbai.tuwien.ac.at

Sebastian Skritek
Vienna University of Technology
skritek@dbai.tuwien.ac.at

ABSTRACT

Query containment and query equivalence constitute important computational problems in the context of static query analysis and optimization. While these problems have been intensively studied for fragments of relational calculus, almost no works exist for the semantic web query language SPARQL. In this paper, we carry out a comprehensive complexity analysis of containment and equivalence for several fragments of SPARQL: we start with the fundamental fragment of well-designed SPARQL restricted to the AND and OPTIONAL operator. We then study basic extensions in the form of the UNION operator and/or projection. The results obtained range from NP-completeness to undecidability.

Categories and Subject Descriptors

H.2.3 [**Database Management**]: Query languages

Keywords

SPARQL; RDF; Semantic Web; query containment

1. INTRODUCTION

Query containment and query equivalence constitute important computational problems in the context of static query analysis and optimization. Indeed, optimization ultimately comes down to replacing a given query by an *equivalent* one with better computational properties. Equivalence thus naturally plays an important role in this area. Containment is closely related to equivalence since the equivalence of two queries holds if and only if both directions of containment hold. Moreover, containment is also interesting in its own right: for instance, for query approximation, where we seek to replace a query by a simpler one which may not yield all answers of the original query but guarantees to yield only correct answers. In other words, we search for a simpler query that is *contained* in the original one.

PODS'14, June 22–27, 2014, Snowbird, UT, USA.

http://dx.doi.org/10.1145/2594538.2594542.

Consequently, the containment and equivalence problem have always played a prominent role whenever computational properties of a query language have been analysed. For instance, in the relational calculus, many classical results of database theory deal with containment and equivalence of various fragments. Of course, by Trakhtenbrot's Theorem, we know that containment and equivalence are undecidable for the full relational calculus. Hence, the attention of database theory research has been directed to interesting fragments of relational calculus: starting with one of the most fundamental fragments – conjunctive queries (CQs) – and continuing with basic extensions thereof, such as unions of CQs, CQs with inequalities, etc. [4, 18, 11].

The rise of the web has brought about an enormous increase of non-relational data. Hence, query languages designed for these data formats are gaining more and more importance. In case of the *semantic web*, the dedicated data format is RDF [7] and the tailor-made query language is SPARQL [17]. The **goal of this work** is to initiate a systematic study of the containment and equivalence problem for this query language. Since SPARQL has equal expressive power as the relational calculus [16, 1], containment and equivalence are undecidable for full SPARQL. Hence, we shall follow the line of research on relational query languages and direct our attention to interesting fragments. We shall thus start with one of the most fundamental fragments of SPARQL – well-designed SPARQL [15] – and continue with basic extensions thereof, such as union and/or projection.

The vision of the semantic web is to make information on the web readable not only by humans but also by machines. The data model proposed for this purpose is the *Resource Description Framework* (RDF) [7], which allows one to specify data in the form of directed, arc-labelled graphs. SPARQL (a recursive acronym which stands for "SPARQL Protocol and RDF Query Language") has been released as a W3C Recommendation in 2008 [17] and extended to SPARQL 1.1 in 2013 [8] as the dedicated query language for RDF data. A brief introduction to RDF and SPARQL is given in Section 2. The following example illustrates some basic features.

Example 1.1 (adapted from [15]) *Consider an RDF graph G storing information about professors in a university with the following triples, and the pattern P:*

$(R_1$, *name*, *paul*$)$, $(R_1$, *phone*, *777-3426*$)$,
$(R_2$, *name*, *john*$)$, $(R_2$, *email*, *john@acd.edu*$)$,
$(R_3$, *name*, *george*$)$, $(R_3$, *webPage*, *www.george.edu*$)$,
$(R_4$, *name*, *ringo*$)$, $(R_4$, *email*, *ringo@acd.edu*$)$,
$(R_4$, *webPage*, *www.starr.edu*$)$, $(R_4$, *phone*, *888-4537*$)$

$$P = (((?A, name, ?N) \text{ AND } (?A, email, ?E)) \\ \text{OPT } (?A, webPage, ?W))$$

If we evaluate P over G, then intuitively we retrieve the name and email of the resources in G, and, optionally, we retrieve the web page if it exists. In this example, the evaluation of P over G yields the set of mappings $[\![P]\!]_G = \{\mu_1, \mu_2\}$ *with*

$$\mu_1 = \{?A \to R_2, ?N \to john, ?E \to john@acd.edu\}, \\ \mu_2 = \{?A \to R_4, ?N \to ringo, ?E \to ringo@acd.edu, \\ ?W \to www.starr.edu\}.$$

An RDF graph is composed of RDF triples of the form (s, p, o), whose components are referred to as "subject, predicate, and object". The basic construct in SPARQL is the *triple pattern*, which is essentially an RDF triple that can have variables. Identifiers starting with "?" are used to denote these variables. We follow here the algebraic-style notation of RDF and SPARQL used in [15] rather than the blank-separated triple notation from the W3C Recommendations.

SPARQL provides several operators such as AND, OPTIONAL, UNION, and FILTER to combine triple patterns. If we restrict SPARQL to the AND operator, we simply get conjunctive queries without existentially quantified variables. A characteristic feature of semantic web queries is the *optional matching* realized via the OPTIONAL operator (abbreviated to OPT in the remainder of the paper). Its idea is to allow information to be added if it is available, and to leave some variables unbound if no matching for them exists. The OPT operator thus corresponds to the left outer join. *Projection* is realized in SPARQL by wrapping a SPARQL graph pattern into a SELECT-statement where we may explicitly specify the variables of interest. For instance, in Example 1.1, we could wrap the pattern P into a statement of the form SELECT ?A, ?N, ?W WHERE $\{P\}$ to project out the email.

As far as the expressive power of SPARQL is concerned, it was shown in [16, 1] that SPARQL is relational complete. Consequently, the SPARQL query evaluation problem (i.e., given an RDF graph G, a SPARQL query Q, and a set μ of variable bindings, check if μ is a solution) was shown PSPACE-complete (combined complexity) [15, 19]. The OPT operator was identified as one of the main sources of complexity. Indeed, it was shown in [19] that the PSPACE-completeness of SPARQL query evaluation holds even if we restrict SPARQL to the AND and OPT operator. The reason for this high complexity is the unrestricted use of variables inside and outside an OPT-expression. Therefore, in [15], the class of *well-designed* SPARQL graph patterns was introduced. The restriction imposed there is that if a variable occurs on the right-hand side of an OPT-expression and anywhere else in the SPARQL graph pattern, then it must also occur on the left-hand side of the OPT-expression. It was shown that the complexity of the evaluation problem for the well-designed fragment drops to coNP-completeness [15].

Apart from few exceptions ([20, 6, 12, 13]), containment and equivalence of fragments of SPARQL have hardly been studied so far. However, neither in [20] nor [6] the OPT operator is considered, which is at the heart of well-designed SPARQL studied here. The equivalence of well-designed SPARQL restricted to the AND and OPT operator was shown NP-complete in [12]. If also projection is allowed, equivalence was shown to be Π_2^P-hard in [13] but no matching upper bound was provided. Actually, we shall show here that the problem is even undecidable.

In [15], *subsumption* was defined as a variant of containment. We say that query Q_1 is subsumed by Q_2 (written as $Q_1 \sqsubseteq Q_2$) if, for every RDF graph G, every solution of Q_1 *can be extended* to a solution of Q_2. In [12], subsumption was studied for well-designed SPARQL restricted to AND and OPT. It was shown that, analogously to containment, two queries are equivalent if and only if both directions of subsumption hold. Moreover, subsumption was proved Π_2^P-complete in [12]. In [13], this Π_2^P-completeness result was extended to well-designed SPARQL with projection. However, it was also shown in [13] that in the presence of projection, both directions of subsumption no longer suffice to enforce equivalence, i.e., it may happen that $Q_1 \sqsubseteq Q_2$ and $Q_2 \sqsubseteq Q_1$ hold and, nevertheless, Q_1 and Q_2 are *not equivalent*. In this paper, we show that also for the extension of well-designed SPARQL with UNION (but without projection), the two directions of subsumption do not suffice to enforce equivalence.

The **main results of this paper** are summarized in Tables 1 and 2. We use the abbreviations "NP-c.", "Π_2^P-c.", and "Π_2^P-h." for "NP-completeness", "Π_2^P-completeness", and "Π_2^P-hardness", respectively. Moreover, we write CONTAINMENT$[S_1,S_2]$ to denote the containment problem of $Q_1 \subseteq Q_2$ where, for each $i \in \{1, 2\}$, Q_i is a query from well-designed SPARQL (using the AND and OPT operator) plus the extensions listed in S_i. We write $\cup$ to denote UNION and π to denote projection. For instance, the entry in the last line, first column states that the containment problem of $Q_1 \subseteq Q_2$ is NP-complete if Q_1 is allowed to use AND and OPT together with UNION and projection, while Q_2 is restricted to AND and OPT.

Analogously, we write EQUIVALENCE$[S_1,S_2]$ to denote the equivalence problem for well-designed SPARQL – possibly extended by UNION and/or projection. Clearly, the EQUIVALENCE$[S_1,S_2]$ problem is symmetric in S_1 and S_2. Hence, only the lower triangle of the table has been filled in. In contrast, the CONTAINMENT$[S_1,S_2]$ problem displays a surprising asymmetry. For instance, testing $Q_1 \subseteq Q_2$ is NP-complete if Q_1 uses projection and Q_2 is restricted to AND and OPT. However, the problem becomes undecidable if we change the roles of Q_1 and Q_2.

In addition, we show that the subsumption problem remains in Π_2^P for well-designed SPARQL with UNION and projection, thus extending the result of [13].

In summary, our main results are a complete complexity classification of the containment and subsumption problem of well-designed SPARQL – possibly extended by UNION and/or projection – as well as an almost complete complexity classification of the EQUIVALENCE$[S_1,S_2]$ problem. The only case left open is $S_1 = \{\pi\}$ and $S_1 = \{\cup\}$. We comment in Section 5 on the difficulties encountered for this case.

The paper is organized as follows. After recalling some basic notions and results in Section 2, we classify in Section 3 the complexity of containment for all decidable cases (i.e., the first two columns in Table 1) and of subsumption. Section 4 deals with the undecidable cases of containment (i.e., the last two columns in Table 1). In Section 5, we establish all results of Table 2 for equivalence. A conclusion and discussion of future directions for research are given in Section 7.

$\downarrow S_1$ / $S_2 \rightarrow$	$\emptyset$	$\{\cup\}$	$\{\pi\}$	$\{\cup,\pi\}$
$\emptyset$	NP-c.	Π_2^P-c.	undec.	undec.
$\{\cup\}$	NP-c.	Π_2^P-c.	undec.	undec.
$\{\pi\}$	NP-c.	Π_2^P-c.	undec.	undec.
$\{\cup,\pi\}$	NP-c.	Π_2^P-c.	undec.	undec.

Table 1: CONTAINMENT[S_1,S_2]

$\downarrow S_1$ / $S_2 \rightarrow$	$\emptyset$	$\{\cup\}$	$\{\pi\}$	$\{\cup,\pi\}$
$\emptyset$	NP-c. [12]	–	–	–
$\{\cup\}$	Π_2^P-c.	Π_2^P-c.	–	–
$\{\pi\}$	Π_2^P-c.	Π_2^P-h.	undec.	–
$\{\cup,\pi\}$	Π_2^P-c.	undec.	undec.	undec.

Table 2: EQUIVALENCE[S_1,S_2]

2. RDF, SPARQL, AND PATTERN TREES

RDF. In this article we focus on ground RDF graphs and assume them to be composed of URIs only. Formally, let $\mathbf{U}$ be an infinite set of URIs. An *RDF triple* is a tuple in $\mathbf{U} \times \mathbf{U} \times \mathbf{U}$, and an *RDF graph* is a finite set of RDF triples. The active domain $\text{dom}(G) \subseteq \mathbf{U}$ of an RDF graph G is the set of URIs actually appearing in G.

SPARQL Syntax. SPARQL [17] is the standard query language for RDF. Following the presentation in [15], we next recall the formalization of its graph pattern matching facility, which forms the core of the language. Let $\mathbf{V}$ be an infinite set of variables with $\mathbf{U} \cap \mathbf{V} = \emptyset$. We write variables in $\mathbf{V}$ with a leading question mark, as in $?X$. A *SPARQL triple pattern* is a tuple in $(\mathbf{U}\cup\mathbf{V})\times(\mathbf{U}\cup\mathbf{V})\times(\mathbf{U}\cup\mathbf{V})$. More complex patterns studied in this article are constructed using the operators AND, OPT, and UNION. We omit further operators specified by [17] and [8], including the FILTER operator. Formally, *SPARQL graph patterns* (or simply *graph patterns*, for short) are recursively defined as follows. (1) a triple pattern is a graph pattern, and (2) if P_1 and P_2 are graph patterns, then $(P_1 \circ P_2)$ is a graph pattern for $\circ \in \{\text{AND}, \text{OPT}, \text{UNION}\}$. Let P be a graph pattern or a set of graph patterns, we write $\text{vars}(P)$ to denote the set of variables occurring in P.

SPARQL Semantics. For defining the semantics of SPARQL graph patterns, we again follow closely the definitions proposed in [15]. A *mapping* is a function $\mu\colon A \rightarrow \mathbf{U}$ for some $A \subset \mathbf{V}$. For a triple pattern t with $\text{vars}(t) \subseteq \text{dom}(\mu)$, we write $\mu(t)$ to denote the triple obtained by replacing the variables in t according to μ. Two mappings μ_1 and μ_2 are called compatible (written $\mu_1 \sim \mu_2$) if $\mu_1(?X) = \mu_2(?X)$ for all $?X \in \text{dom}(\mu_1) \cap \text{dom}(\mu_2)$. A mapping μ_1 is subsumed by μ_2 (written $\mu_1 \sqsubseteq \mu_2$) if $\mu_1 \sim \mu_2$ and $\text{dom}(\mu_1) \subseteq \text{dom}(\mu_2)$. In this case, we also say that μ_2 is an extension of μ_1. Subsumption is naturally extended to sets of mappings, e.g., $\mu \sqsubseteq M$ for a set M of mappings, if $\mu \sqsubseteq \mu'$ for some $\mu' \in M$.

We formalize the evaluation of graph patterns over an RDF graph G as a function $[\![\cdot]\!]_G$ that, given a graph pattern, returns a set of mappings. For a graph pattern P, it is defined recursively as follows [15]:

1. $[\![t]\!]_G = \{\mu \mid \text{dom}(\mu) = \text{vars}(t) \text{ and } \mu(t) \in G\}$ for a triple pattern t.
2. $[\![P_1 \text{ AND } P_2]\!]_G = \{\mu_1 \cup \mu_2 \mid \mu_1 \in [\![P_1]\!]_G, \mu_2 \in [\![P_2]\!]_G, \text{ and } \mu_1 \sim \mu_2\}$.
3. $[\![P_1 \text{ OPT } P_2]\!]_G = [\![P_1 \text{ AND } P_2]\!]_G \cup \{\mu_1 \in [\![P_1]\!]_G \mid \forall \mu_2 \in [\![P_2]\!]_G \colon \mu_1 \not\sim \mu_2\}$.
4. $[\![P_1 \text{ UNION } P_2]\!]_G = [\![P_1]\!]_G \cup [\![P_2]\!]_G$.

We extend the definition of $[\![\cdot]\!]_G$ to a set $\mathcal{P} = \{t_1, \ldots, t_n\}$ of triple patterns as $[\![\mathcal{P}]\!]_G := [\![(t_1 \text{ AND } \ldots \text{ AND } t_n)]\!]_G$. Note that, as in [15], we assume set semantics, while the W3C Recommendation specifies bag-semantics [17].

Well-designed SPARQL. In [15], the authors identify several classes of graph patterns. One of these classes, which is at the heart of our study, is formed by the so-called *well-designed* SPARQL graph patterns. A graph pattern P built only from AND and OPT is well-designed if there does not exist a subpattern $P' = (P_1 \text{ OPT } P_2)$ of P and a variable $?X \in \text{vars}(P_2)$ that occurs in P outside P', but not in P_1. A graph pattern $P = P_1 \text{ UNION } \ldots \text{ UNION } P_n$ is well-designed if each subpattern P_i is UNION free and well-designed. Thus, as in [15], when including the UNION operator, we only allow it to appear outside the scope of other operators. We note that the definition of well-designed graph patterns in [15] includes also the FILTER operator. However, as mentioned earlier, in this work we do not consider FILTER expressions

Pattern trees. Another class of graph patterns defined in [15] are graph patterns in OPT *normal form*. A pattern containing only the operators AND and OPT is in OPT normal form if the OPT operator never occurs in the scope of an AND operator. It was shown that every well-designed graph pattern can be transformed into OPT normal form in polynomial time. Moreover, such graph patterns allow for a natural tree representation, formalized by so-called *pattern trees* in [12]. A *pattern tree (PT)* $\mathcal{T}$ is a pair $(T, \mathcal{P})$ where $T = (V, E, r)$ is a rooted, unordered, tree and $\mathcal{P} = (P_n)_{n \in V}$ is a labelling of the nodes in V, s.t. P_n is a non-empty set of triple patterns for every $n \in V$. The following example, which slightly extends Example 1.1, illustrates this idea.

Example 2.1 *Consider the graph pattern*

$P =$
$(((?A, \mathit{name}, ?N) \text{ AND } (?A, \mathit{email}, ?E))$
$\text{OPT } (?A, \mathit{web}, ?W))$
$\text{OPT } ((?A, \mathit{phone}, ?P)$
$\text{OPT } (?A, \mathit{fax}, ?F))$

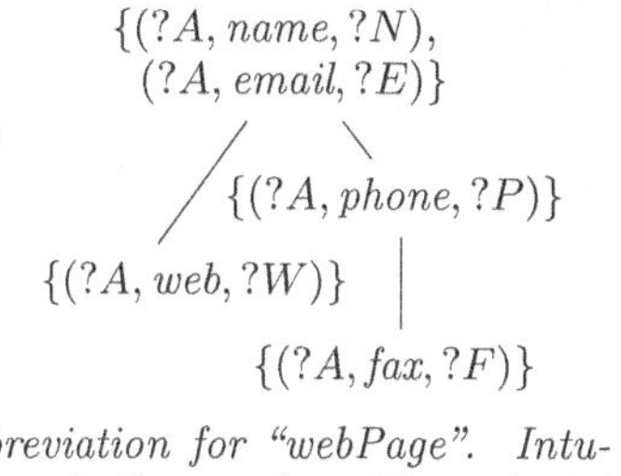

where we use "web" as abbreviation for "webPage". Intuitively, the graph pattern extends the one from Example 1.1 as follows. If name and email of a person are known, then, independent of the available information on a web page, the query also tries to retrieve the phone number of that person. If also this information is known, it asks for a fax number. The corresponding pattern tree is shown on the right.

Like the pattern P in the example, graph patterns in OPT normal form consist of conjunctive parts (represented by the nodes of the pattern tree) that are located in a structure of nested OPT operators (modelled by the tree-structure). Note that the order of child nodes in such a tree does not matter. This is due to the fact that, for a well-designed graph pattern P, any subpattern of the form $((P_1 \text{ OPT } P_2) \text{ OPT } P_3)$ may be replaced by $((P_1 \text{ OPT } P_3) \text{ OPT } P_2)$ yielding an equivalent pattern P' [14]. We thus get a natural translation (formalized in [12]) from graph patterns in OPT normal form to pattern trees, and vice versa.

Components of a pattern tree. Let $\mathcal{T} = ((V, E, r), \mathcal{P})$ be a pattern tree. We call a PT $\mathcal{T}' = ((V', E', r'), (P_n)_{n \in V'})$ a *subtree of* $\mathcal{T}$ if (V', E', r') is a subtree of T. $\mathcal{T}'$ is a *subtree of* $\mathcal{T}$ *containing the root* if $r' = r$. Throughout this article, we only consider subtrees containing the root, and will thus refer to them simply as "subtrees", omitting the phrase "containing the root". An *extension* or *supertree* $\hat{\mathcal{T}}'$ of a subtree $\mathcal{T}'$ of $\mathcal{T}$ is a subtree $\hat{\mathcal{T}}'$ of $\mathcal{T}$, s.t. $\mathcal{T}'$ is in turn a subtree of $\hat{\mathcal{T}}'$. That is, we do not consider arbitrary supertrees, but only extensions within $\mathcal{T}$. A subtree or extension is *proper* if some node of the bigger tree is missing in the smaller tree.

Given $\mathcal{T}$, we write $V(\mathcal{T})$ to denote the set V of vertices. For a PT $\mathcal{T} = (T, (P_n)_{n \in V(\mathcal{T})})$, we denote with $pat(\mathcal{T}')$ the set $\bigcup_{n \in V(\mathcal{T}')} P_n$ of triple patterns occurring in $\mathcal{T}'$. We write $\text{vars}(\mathcal{T})$ (resp. $\text{vars}(n)$) as an abbreviation for $\text{vars}(pat(\mathcal{T}))$ (resp. $\text{vars}(pat(n))$. These notions extend naturally to sets of nodes. Given a node $n \in V(\mathcal{T})$, we define $\text{branch}(n) = n^1, \ldots, n^k$ with $n^1 = r$ and $n^k = n$ as the unique sequence of nodes from the root r to n. For nodes $n, \hat{n} \in V(\mathcal{T})$, s.t. $\hat{n}$ is the parent of n, let $\text{newvars}(n) = \text{vars}(n) \setminus \text{vars}(\text{branch}(\hat{n}))$. A node n is a child of a PT $\mathcal{T}$ if $n \notin V(\mathcal{T})$ and n is the child of some node $n' \in V(\mathcal{T})$. Moreover, we call n a *nearest descendant* of $\mathcal{T}$ satisfying some property p if n satisfies p, node n is a descendant of some node $n' \in V(\mathcal{T})$, and no node on the path from n' to n satisfies p.

Well-designed pattern trees. A *well-designed pattern tree (wdPT)* is a pattern tree $\mathcal{T} = (T, \mathcal{P})$ where for every variable $?X \in V(\mathcal{T})$, the nodes $\{n \in V(\mathcal{T}) \mid ?X \in \text{vars}(n)\}$ induce a connected subgraph of T. This restriction ensures that the result of the natural translation from a wdPT into a graph pattern is well-designed. Conversely, also every PT derived from a well-designed graph pattern in OPT normal form yields a wdPT. This provides a polynomial time transformation from wdPTs into equivalent well-designed graph patterns, and vice versa (the semantics of wdPTs will be discussed in the next paragraph). Another property of wdPTs $\mathcal{T}$ is that for every variable $?X \in \text{vars}(\mathcal{T})$, there is a unique node $n \in V(\mathcal{T})$, s.t. $?X \in \text{newvars}(n)$ and all other nodes $n' \in V(\mathcal{T})$ with $?X \in \text{vars}(n')$ are descendants of n. Given $?X \in \text{vars}(\mathcal{T})$, we denote this node n with $\text{new-node}_{\mathcal{T}}(?X)$ (omitting $\mathcal{T}$ if clear from the context). A wdPT $\mathcal{T}$ is said to be in NR normal form, if $\text{newvars}(n) \neq \emptyset$ for every $n \in V(\mathcal{T})$ [12]. It was shown in [12], that every wdPT can be transformed efficiently into an equivalent wdPT in NR normal form. We therefore assume w.l.o.g. that all wdPTs dealt with in this paper are in NR normal form.

Semantics of pattern trees. Analogously to graph patterns, the result of evaluating a wdPT $\mathcal{T}$ over some RDF graph is denoted by $[\![\mathcal{T}]\!]_G$. In [12], the set $[\![\mathcal{T}]\!]_G$ of solutions was defined via a translation to graph patterns. However, for wdPTs in NR normal form, the set of solutions $[\![\mathcal{T}]\!]_G$ has a nice direct characterization in terms of maximal subtrees of $\mathcal{T}$. In this article, we will use this characterization.

Lemma 2.2 ([12]) *Let $\mathcal{T}$ be a wdPT in NR normal form and G an RDF graph. Then $\mu \in [\![\mathcal{T}]\!]_G$ iff there exists a subtree $\mathcal{T}'$ of $\mathcal{T}$, s.t. (1) $\text{dom}(\mu) = \text{vars}(\mathcal{T}')$, and (2) $\mathcal{T}'$ is the maximal subtree of $\mathcal{T}$, s.t. $\mu \sqsubseteq [\![pat(\mathcal{T}')]\!]_G$.*

It can be easily checked that $\mathcal{T}'$ is uniquely defined by $\text{dom}(\mu)$. We refer to this tree as $\mathcal{T}_\mu$.

Projection. For studying projection in this article, we follow the approach of SPARQL 1.0. That is, projection is not considered as part of a graph pattern, but as the SELECT result modifier on top of a graph pattern (or, equivalently, of a pattern tree). For a mapping μ and a set $\mathcal{X}$ of variables, let $\mu_{|\mathcal{X}}$ denote the projection of μ to the variables in $\mathcal{X}$, that is, the mapping μ' defined as $\text{dom}(\mu') := \mathcal{X} \cap \text{dom}(\mu)$ and $\mu'(?X) := \mu(?X)$ for all $?X \in \text{dom}(\mu')$.

The result of projecting a graph pattern P to $\mathcal{X}$ is defined as $[\![(P, \mathcal{X})]\!]_G = \{\mu_{|\mathcal{X}} \mid \mu \in [\![P]\!]_G\}$. Analogously, we define $[\![(\mathcal{T}, \mathcal{X})]\!]_G = \{\mu_{|\mathcal{X}} \mid \mu \in [\![\mathcal{T}]\!]_G\}$ for a wdPT $\mathcal{T}$. We refer to the pair $(\mathcal{T}, \mathcal{X})$ as *projected wdPT (pwdPT)*, and refer to $\text{vars}(\mathcal{T}) \cap \mathcal{X}$ as the free variables ($\text{fvars}(\mathcal{T})$) and to $\text{vars}(\mathcal{T}) \setminus \text{fvars}(\mathcal{T})$ as the existential variables in $\mathcal{T}$ ($\text{evars}(\mathcal{T})$). Analogously, we write $\text{fvars}(n)$ and $\text{evars}(n)$, respectively, for nodes $n \in V(\mathcal{T})$. Moreover, for $n \in V(\mathcal{T})$, let $\text{newfvars}(n) = \text{newvars}(n) \cap \text{fvars}(n)$. W.l.o.g., we assume that existential variables in pwdPTs are always renamed apart, i.e., $\text{evars}(\mathcal{T}_1) \cap \text{evars}(\mathcal{T}_2) = \emptyset$ for any two distinct pwdPTs $\mathcal{T}_1$ and $\mathcal{T}_2$.

A pwdPT $(\mathcal{T}, \mathcal{X})$ is in NR normal form if $\mathcal{T}$ is. For pwdPTs, a similar characterization of solutions as Lemma 2.2 for wdPTs exists.

Lemma 2.3 ([13]) *Let $(\mathcal{T}, \mathcal{X})$ be a pwdPT in NR normal form, G an RDF graph and μ a mapping with $\text{dom}(\mu) \subseteq \mathcal{X}$. Then $\mu \in [\![(\mathcal{T}, \mathcal{X})]\!]_G$ iff there exists a subtree $\mathcal{T}'$ of $\mathcal{T}$, s.t. (1) $\text{dom}(\mu) = \text{fvars}(\mathcal{T}')$, and (2) there exists a mapping $\lambda\colon \text{evars}(\mathcal{T}') \to \text{dom}(G)$, s.t. $\mu \cup \lambda \in [\![\mathcal{T}]\!]_G$.*

SPARQL allows the use of blank nodes in graph patterns (see [8] for details), which we do not consider here. This is however no restriction, since every well-designed graph pattern with blank nodes is equivalent to a well-designed graph pattern with projection but without blank nodes.

Union. The UNION operator was not studied in [13]. We thus need to extend the concept of PTs to capture the UNION operator. Recall that, in well-designed SPARQL graph patterns as introduced in [15], UNION occurs only on top-level. Hence, we can transform every well-designed SPARQL graph pattern $P = P_1 \text{ UNION } \ldots \text{ UNION } P_k$ in UNION normal form into a set $\{\mathcal{T}_1, \ldots, \mathcal{T}_k\}$ of wdPTs. Such sets will be referred to as *well-designed pattern forests (wdPF)* $\mathcal{F}$. Analogously, a *projected well-designed pattern forest (pwdPF)* $(\mathcal{F}, \mathcal{X})$ is a set of pwdPTs $\{(\mathcal{T}_1, \mathcal{X}), \ldots, (\mathcal{T}_k, \mathcal{X})\}$. We define the set of solutions of a wdPF $\mathcal{F}$ and of a pwdPF $(\mathcal{F}', \mathcal{X})$ over an RDF graph G as $[\![\mathcal{F}]\!]_G := \bigcup_{\mathcal{T} \in \mathcal{F}} [\![\mathcal{T}]\!]_G$ and $[\![(\mathcal{F}', \mathcal{X})]\!]_G := \bigcup_{(\mathcal{T}, \mathcal{X}) \in \mathcal{F}'} [\![(\mathcal{T}, \mathcal{X})]\!]_G$, respectively.

All notions introduced for (p)wdPTs extend naturally to (p)wdPF; e.g., a subtree $\mathcal{T}'$ of a (p)wdPF $\mathcal{F}$ is a subtree for some (p)wdPT $\mathcal{T} \in \mathcal{F}$. (Recall that throughout this paper, we write "subtree" to refer to a *subtree containing the root*.) A subforest of $\mathcal{F}$ is a set of subtrees of $\mathcal{F}$. Moreover, we define $pat(\mathcal{F}) = \bigcup_{\mathcal{T} \in \mathcal{F}} pat(\mathcal{T})$, and analogously $\text{vars}(\mathcal{F})$.

Problems studied in this article. The different classes of well-designed SPARQL graph patterns studied in this article will be referred to as wd-SPARQL[S] where $S \subseteq \{\cup, \pi\}$. We thus study well-designed graph patterns which use the AND and OPT operator and which may be extended by UNION (if $\{\cup\} \subseteq S$) and/or projection (if $\{\pi\} \subseteq S$).

Given two graph patterns P_1 and P_2, they are *equivalent* (denoted as $P_1 \equiv P_2$) if $[\![P_1]\!]_G = [\![P_2]\!]_G$ for every RDF graph G. Similarly, P_1 *is contained in* P_2 ($P_1 \subseteq P_2$) if $[\![P_1]\!]_G \subseteq [\![P_2]\!]_G$ for every RDF graph G. Finally, P_1 *is subsumed by* P_2 ($P_1 \sqsubseteq P_2$), if for every $\mu \in [\![P_1]\!]_G$ there exists a $\mu' \in [\![P_2]\!]_G$, s.t. $\mu \sqsubseteq \mu'$. For every $S_1, S_2 \subseteq \{\cup, \pi\}$, we thus study the following problems in this article:

CONTAINMENT[S_1,S_2]		
Input:	graph patterns	P_1 from wd-SPARQL[S_1], P_2 from wd-SPARQL[S_2].
Question:	does $P_1 \subseteq P_2$ hold?	

EQUIVALENCE[S_1,S_2]		
Input:	graph patterns	P_1 from wd-SPARQL[S_1], P_2 from wd-SPARQL[S_2].
Question:	does $P_1 \equiv P_2$ hold?	

SUBSUMPTION[S_1,S_2]		
Input:	graph patterns	P_1 from wd-SPARQL[S_1], P_2 from wd-SPARQL[S_2].
Question:	does $P_1 \sqsubseteq P_2$ hold?	

3. DECIDABLE CONTAINMENT

We start our complexity analysis of the CONTAINMENT[S_1,S_2] problem with the decidable cases, i.e., S_1 is an arbitrary subset of $\{\cup, \pi\}$ and S_2 must not contain π. We thus fill in the first two columns of Table 1. Clearly, membership results always propagate from the more general case to the more specific one. Likewise, hardness results propagate in the other direction. Below, we thus prove the following complexity results:

- NP-membership of CONTAINMENT[$\{\cup, \pi\}$,$\emptyset$]
- Π_2^P-membership of CONTAINMENT[$\{\cup, \pi\}$,$\{\cup\}$]
- Π_2^P-hardness of CONTAINMENT[$\emptyset$,$\{\cup\}$]

The NP-hardness of CONTAINMENT[$\emptyset$,$\emptyset$] follows immediately from the NP-hardness of EQUIVALENCE[$\emptyset$,$\emptyset$] shown in [12]. Recall from Section 2 the close connection between well-designed SPARQL graph patterns and pattern trees/forests. Hence, to prove our results for SPARQL we shall use pattern trees/forests.

For the NP-membership of CONTAINMENT[$\{\cup, \pi\}$,$\emptyset$], we concentrate on CONTAINMENT[$\{\pi\}$,$\emptyset$]. The extension to CONTAINMENT[$\{\cup, \pi\}$,$\emptyset$] is straightforward. Below we give a necessary and sufficient criterion for $(\mathcal{T}_1, \mathcal{X}) \subseteq \mathcal{T}_2$.

Theorem 3.1 *Let $(\mathcal{T}_1, \mathcal{X})$ be a pwdPT and let $\mathcal{T}_2$ be a wdPT. Then $(\mathcal{T}_1, \mathcal{X}) \subseteq \mathcal{T}_2$ iff for every subtree $\mathcal{T}_1'$ of $\mathcal{T}_1$,*

(1) either there exists a child node n of $\mathcal{T}_1'$ and a homomorphism $h\colon pat(n) \to pat(\mathcal{T}_1')$ with $h(?X) = ?X$ for all $?X \in \mathrm{vars}(n) \cap \mathrm{vars}(\mathcal{T}_1')$

(2) or there exists a subtree $\mathcal{T}_2'$ of $\mathcal{T}_2$, s.t.

(a) $\mathrm{fvars}(\mathcal{T}_1') = \mathrm{vars}(\mathcal{T}_2')$,

(b) $pat(\mathcal{T}_2') \subseteq pat(\mathcal{T}_1')$, and

(c) for all extensions $\hat{\mathcal{T}}_2'$ of $\mathcal{T}_2'$ there exists an extension $\hat{\mathcal{T}}_1'$ of $\mathcal{T}_1'$ and a homomorphism $h\colon pat(\hat{\mathcal{T}}_1') \to pat(\mathcal{T}_1') \cup pat(\hat{\mathcal{T}}_2')$ with $h(?X) = ?X$ for all $?X \in \mathrm{vars}(\mathcal{T}_1')$.

PROOF IDEA. Let G be an arbitrary RDF graph. We have to test for every subtree $\mathcal{T}_1'$ of $\mathcal{T}_1$ and every mapping σ with $\mathrm{dom}(\sigma) = \mathrm{vars}(\mathcal{T}_1')$, if $\sigma \in [\![\mathcal{T}_1]\!]_G$, then also $\sigma_{|\mathcal{X}} \in [\![\mathcal{T}_2]\!]_G$.

Case (1) in the theorem captures the situation that every mapping σ with $\mathrm{dom}(\sigma) = \mathrm{vars}(\mathcal{T}_1')$, such that σ sends $\mathcal{T}_1'$ into G can be extended to one of the child nodes of $\mathcal{T}_1'$. In other words, such mappings σ cannot be in $[\![\mathcal{T}_1]\!]_G$.

Case (2) captures the situation that $\mathcal{T}_1$ admits solutions σ with $\mathrm{dom}(\sigma) = \mathrm{vars}(\mathcal{T}_1')$. To check if every such σ also gives rise to a solution $\mu = \sigma_{|\mathcal{X}}$ in $[\![\mathcal{T}_2]\!]_G$, we consider as RDF graph G the frozen database of $\mathcal{T}_1'$. Conditions (2a) and (2b) guarantee that μ also maps $\mathcal{T}_2'$ into G, and is thus a candidate for a solution on $\mathcal{T}_2$ as well. The only reason why it may possibly not be a solution of $\mathcal{T}_2$ is if there exists some extension μ' of μ with $\mu' \in [\![\mathcal{T}_2]\!]_G$. In this case, $\mathcal{T}_{2,\mu'}$ is an extension of $\mathcal{T}_2'$. Now property (2c) guarantees that if such a μ' exists, regardless of the mappings on the existential variables in $\mathcal{T}_1$, σ can also be extended to a mapping σ' that binds at least one additional variable in $\mathcal{T}_1$. But then σ is not in $[\![\mathcal{T}_1]\!]_G$ either. □

We demonstrate the main ideas of this algorithm in the following example.

Example 3.2 *Consider the pwdPT $(\mathcal{T}_1, \mathcal{X})$ with $\mathcal{X} = \{?X_1, ?X_2, ?X_3\}$ and wdPT $\mathcal{T}_2$ as depicted below.*

$r_1\colon \{(?X_1, b, ?X_1), (?Y_1, c, ?Y_1), (?Y_1, d, ?Y_1)\}$

$n_1\colon \{(?X_1, e, ?X_1), (?X_2, f, ?X_2)\}$ $\quad$ $n_1'\colon \{(?X_3, c, ?X_3), (?X_3, d, ?X_3)\}$

$r_2\colon \{(?X_1, b, ?X_1), (?X_3, c, ?X_3), (?X_3, d, ?X_3)\}$

$n_2\colon \{(?X_2, f, ?X_2)\}$

To check $(\mathcal{T}_1, \mathcal{X}) \subseteq \mathcal{T}_2$, we have to test for each of the four subtrees of $\mathcal{T}_1$ induced by the vertex sets $\{r_1\}$, $\{r_1, n_1\}$, $\{r_1, n_1'\}$, and $\{r_1, n_1, n_1'\}$ if either property (1) or (2) from Theorem 3.1 is satisfied.

As it turns out, the test fails for the subtree of $\mathcal{T}_1$ that contains r_1 and n_1'. Properties (2a) and (2b) are clearly satisfied by the subtree of $\mathcal{T}_2$ that contains exactly the node r_2. Observe that this means that for every RDF graph G and solution $\mu \in [\![(\mathcal{T}_1, \mathcal{X})]\!]_G$, the first property from Lemma 2.2 is satisfied for μ and $\mathcal{T}_2$. However, for $\mu \in [\![\mathcal{T}_2]\!]_G$, also the second property stated in the lemma must be satisfied. This is checked by (c). However, (c) is not satisfied when extending r_2 by n_2: It can be easily seen that there does not exist the required homomorphism from $pat(n_1)$ into $pat(r_1) \cup pat(n_1') \cup pat(r_2) \cup pat(n_2)$.

In order to see that this indeed contradicts $(\mathcal{T}_1, \mathcal{X}) \subseteq \mathcal{T}_2$, consider the RDF graph $G = \{(x_1, b, x_1), (y_1, c, y_1), (y_1, d, y_1), (x_2, f, x_2)\}$. Then clearly $\mu \cup \lambda \in [\![\mathcal{T}_1]\!]_G$ for $\mu(?X_1) := x_1$, $\mu(?X_3) = y_1$, and

$\lambda(?Y_1) := y_1$, *and thus* $\mu \in [\![(\mathcal{T}_1, \mathcal{X})]\!]_G$. *However,* $\mu \notin [\![\mathcal{T}_2]\!]_G$ *because of the extension* μ' *of* μ *with* $\mu'(?X_2) := x_2$ *and* $\mu'(pat(n_2)) \subseteq G$.

If we redefine $pat(n_2)$ *as* $pat(n_2) := \{(?X_2, f, ?X_2), (?X_1, e, ?X_1)\}$, *then the required homomorphism* h *exists (e.g., take* h *to be the identity), and thus (2) is now satisfied. In fact, then* $(\mathcal{T}_1, \mathcal{X}) \sqsubseteq \mathcal{T}_2$.

To see that this is correctly identified by the characterization, assume in the following $pat(n_2)$ *to contain also the triple pattern* $(?X_1, e, ?X_1)$.

Now consider the subtree of $\mathcal{T}_1$ *that contains exactly* r_1. *Then (2) is again not satisfied, since there does not exist a subtree of* $\mathcal{T}_2$ *that satisfies (a). Observe however, that this time there does not exist any RDF* G *and solution* $\mu \in [\![(\mathcal{T}_1, \mathcal{X})]\!]_G$ *with* $?X_3 \notin \text{dom}(\mu)$*: For every RDF graph* G, *every mapping* μ' *with* $\mu'(pat(r_1)) \subseteq G$ *can be extended to a mapping* μ'' *with* $\mu''(pat(n_1')) \subseteq G$ *by defining* $\mu''(?X_3) = \mu'(?Y_1)$. *Since there does not exist any solution to* $(\mathcal{T}_1, \mathcal{X})$ *with domain* $?X_1$, *it is not required that such solutions are also retrieved on* $\mathcal{T}_2$. *Thus (2) need not be satisfied. Instead, the homomorphism* $h\colon pat(n_1') \to pat(r_1)$ *with* $h(?X_3) = ?Y_1$ *satisfies (1). The same argument applies to the subtree of* $\mathcal{T}_1$ *containing* r_1 *and* n_1.

Thus it only remains to check if the complete tree $\mathcal{T}_1$ *satisfies (2), which is clearly the case (with* $\mathcal{T}_2$ *being the corresponding "subtree" of* $\mathcal{T}_1$*).*

An immediate consequence of the theorem is that $\text{vars}(\mathcal{T}_2) = \text{fvars}(\mathcal{T}_1)$ is a necessary condition for $(\mathcal{T}_1, \mathcal{X}) \sqsubseteq \mathcal{T}_2$. Since this condition is easy to test, we may assume w.l.o.g. that $\text{vars}(\mathcal{T}_2) = \text{fvars}(\mathcal{T}_1)$ holds whenever this is helpful.

In principle, the above theorem can be directly translated into an algorithm for deciding $(\mathcal{T}_1, \mathcal{X}) \sqsubseteq \mathcal{T}_2$. However, this would mean that we end up with a Π_2^P-algorithm, because we would essentially test for *all subtrees* $\mathcal{T}_1'$ of $\mathcal{T}_1$, that a subtree $\mathcal{T}_2'$ of $\mathcal{T}_2$ with the desired properties exists. To push the complexity down to NP, we have to eliminate one source of non-determinism. Indeed, we show below that it suffices to test a *polynomial number of subtrees* of $\mathcal{T}_1$. The correctness of the resulting algorithm will then be shown by proving that the conditions of Theorem 3.1 are indeed fulfilled by *all subtrees* of $\mathcal{T}_1$. The polynomially many subtrees of interest are defined via the *closure of a variable.*

Definition 3.3 (Closure $(C_1(?X), C_2(?X))$ of a variable) *Let* $(\mathcal{T}_1, \mathcal{X})$ *be a pwdPT and let* $\mathcal{T}_2$ *be a wdPT with* $\text{vars}(\mathcal{T}_2) = \text{fvars}(\mathcal{T}_1)$. *Consider* $?X \in \text{fvars}(\mathcal{T}_1)$. The closure of $?X$ in $(\mathcal{T}_1, \mathcal{X})$ and $\mathcal{T}_2$ *is the pair* $(C_1(?X), C_2(?X))$, *where* $C_i(?X)$ *(for* $i \in [2]$*) is a subtree of* $\mathcal{T}_i$ *such that the following conditions are met:*

(1) $\text{branch}(\text{new-node}_{\mathcal{T}_1}(?X)) \subseteq V(C_1(?X))$,

(2) $r_2 \in V(C_2(?X))$,

(3) $\text{fvars}(C_1(?X)) = \text{vars}(C_2(?X))$, *and*

(4) $C_1(?X)$ *and* $C_2(?X)$ *are minimal w.r.t. properties 1–3.*

Minimality in (4) means that for all subtrees $\mathcal{D}_1$ *of* $\mathcal{T}_1$ *and* $\mathcal{D}_2$ *of* $\mathcal{T}_2$, *if* D_1 *and* D_2 *satisfy conditions 1–3 (substituting* D_i *for* C_i*), then* $V(C_1) \subseteq V(D_1)$ *and* $V(C_2) \subseteq V(D_2)$.

Recall that we may assume w.l.o.g., that $\text{fvars}(\mathcal{T}_1) = \text{vars}(\mathcal{T}_2)$ holds. Hence, the closure always exists.

Proposition 3.4 *Let* $(\mathcal{T}_1, \mathcal{X})$ *be a pwdPT and let* $\mathcal{T}_2$ *be a wdPT with* $\text{fvars}(\mathcal{T}_1) = \text{vars}(\mathcal{T}_2)$. *Then the closure* $(C_1(?X), C_2(?X))$ *exists and can be efficiently computed.*

Proof idea. The computation of the closure starts with $C_1(?X) = \text{branch}(\text{new-node}_{\mathcal{T}_1}(?X))$ and setting $V(C_2(?X)) = \{r\}$ for the root r of $\mathcal{T}_2$. We alternately add nodes to either $C_2(?X)$ or $C_1(?X)$ so as to add (free) variables contained in one of the $C_i(?X)$'s but not in the other. More precisely, if $\text{vars}(C_2(?X)) \subset \text{fvars}(C_1(?X))$, we add $\text{branch}(\text{new-node}_{\mathcal{T}_2}(?Y))$ to $C_2(?X)$ for all variables $?Y \in \text{fvars}(C_1(?X)) \setminus \text{vars}(C_2(?X))$. Likewise, if $\text{vars}(C_2(?X)) \supset \text{fvars}(C_1(?X))$, we add $\text{branch}(\text{new-node}_{\mathcal{T}_1}(?Y))$ to $C_1(?X)$ for all variables $?Y \in \text{vars}(C_2(?X)) \setminus \text{fvars}(C_1(?X))$. By the condition $\text{fvars}(\mathcal{T}_1) = \text{vars}(\mathcal{T}_2)$, this procedure of alternately extending $C_1(?X)$ and $C_2(?X)$ will eventually reach a fixpoint. It is easy to check that this is indeed the least fixpoint. □

The intuition of the alternating extension of $C_1(?X)$ and $C_2(?X)$ in the computation of the closure is as follows: suppose that a solution μ of $(\mathcal{T}_1, \mathcal{X})$ is defined on some free variable $?Y$. Then, in order to obtain this solution also in $\mathcal{T}_2$, μ must also bind all variables that occur in $\mathcal{T}_2$ on the branch from the root to the node n where $?Y$ is introduced. Analogously, if some variable $?Y$ is bound by a solution μ of $\mathcal{T}_2$, then μ must also bind all free variables in $(\mathcal{T}_1, \mathcal{X})$ along the branch from the root to the first occurrence of $?Y$.

We now use the closure $(C_1(?X), C_2(?X))$ to formulate the following characterization of $(\mathcal{T}_1, \mathcal{X}) \sqsubseteq \mathcal{T}_2$. It tells us that, instead of testing the conditions of Theorem 3.1 for all (exponentially many) subtrees of $(\mathcal{T}_1, \mathcal{X})$ it suffices to inspect all (polynomially many) closures $(C_1(?X), C_2(?X))$.

Theorem 3.5 *Let* $(\mathcal{T}_1, \mathcal{X})$ *be a pwdPT and let* $\mathcal{T}_2$ *be a wdPT. Then* $(\mathcal{T}_1, \mathcal{X}) \sqsubseteq \mathcal{T}_2$ *iff* $\text{fvars}(\mathcal{T}_1) = \text{vars}(\mathcal{T}_2)$ *and for every* $?X \in \text{fvars}(\mathcal{T}_1)$

(1) $pat(C_2(?X)) \subseteq pat(C_1(?X))$,

(2) for every $n \in V(C_1(?X)) \setminus \text{branch}(\text{new-node}_{\mathcal{T}_1}(?X))$, *there exists a homomorphism* $h_1\colon pat(n) \to pat(\text{branch}(\hat{n})) \cup pat(\text{branch}(\text{new-node}_{\mathcal{T}_1}(?X)))$ *(where* $\hat{n}$ *is the parent node of* n *in* $\mathcal{T}_1$*) with* $h_1(?X) = ?X$ *for all* $?X \in \text{vars}(n) \cap \big(\text{vars}(\text{branch}(\hat{n})) \cup \text{vars}(\text{branch}(\text{new-node}_{\mathcal{T}_1}(?X)))\big)$, *and*

(3) for every child node m *of* $C_2(?X)$, *and for every variable* $?Y \in \text{newvars}(m)$, *the following property holds: let* $n \in \text{branch}(\text{new-node}_{\mathcal{T}_1}(?Y))$. *Then there exists a homomorphism* $h_2\colon pat(n) \to pat(C_1(?X)) \cup pat(m) \cup pat(\text{branch}(\hat{n}))$ *(where* $\hat{n}$ *is the parent node of* n*) with* $h_2(?X) = ?X$ *for all* $?X \in \text{vars}(n) \cap \big(\text{vars}(C_1(?X)) \cup \text{vars}(\text{branch}(\hat{n}))\big)$.

Proof idea. Let G be an arbitrary RDF graph. Condition (1) makes sure that, whenever a mapping σ sends $C_1(?X)$ into G then also $\mu = \sigma_{|\mathcal{X}}$ sends $C_2(?X)$ into G. Condition (2) guarantees that, every solution σ of $\mathcal{T}_1$ with $?X \in \text{dom}(\sigma)$ indeed sends all of $C_1(?X)$ into G. Finally, condition (3) is the analog of condition (2c) in Theorem 3.1: it considers the case that $\mu = \sigma_{|\mathcal{X}}$ with $\text{dom}(\mu) = \text{vars}(C_2(?X))$ sends $C_2(?X)$ into G but is not a solution of $\mathcal{T}_2$ because it can be extended to some child of $C_2(?X)$. In this case, it must be possible to extend also σ to some child of $C_1(?X)$.

It is easy to check that these conditions are necessary for $(\mathcal{T}_1, \mathcal{X}) \subseteq \mathcal{T}_2$. To show that they are also sufficient, we have to verify the conditions of Theorem 3.1. We thus consider an arbitrary subtree $\mathcal{T}_1'$ of $\mathcal{T}_1$. If $\mathcal{T}_1'$ does not correspond exactly to the union of several closures then it can be shown that $\mathcal{T}_1'$ satisfies condition (1) in Theorem 3.1. If $\mathcal{T}_1'$ can be defined as the union of several closures, then $\mathcal{T}_1'$ is a tree of the second kind described in Theorem 3.1, and the properties (2a) – (2c) are ensured by the conditions (1) – (3) of the current theorem. □

Theorem 3.6 CONTAINMENT[$\{\cup, \pi\}$,$\emptyset$] *is in* NP.

PROOF. First of all, the characterization in Theorem 3.5 can be decided in NP: it suffices to guess a polynomial number of homomorphisms, whose size is of course polynomially bounded. For each guess, the conditions of Theorem 3.5 can be tested in polynomial time.

Moreover, observe that for a pwdPF $(\mathcal{F}, \mathcal{X})$ and a wdPT $\mathcal{T}$ we have $(\mathcal{F}, \mathcal{X}) \subseteq \mathcal{T}$ iff $(\mathcal{T}_i, \mathcal{X}) \subseteq \mathcal{T}$ for every $(\mathcal{T}_i, \mathcal{X}) \in (\mathcal{F}, \mathcal{X})$. □

Next, we show that the CONTAINMENT[$\{\cup, \pi\}$,$\{\cup\}$] problem is in Π_2^P. For the formulation of a necessary and sufficient condition of containment, it is convenient to introduce the notion of a *renamed proper extension of a wdPF*. Let $\mathcal{F} = \{\mathcal{T}_i \mid \text{ with } 1 \leq i \leq k\}$ be a wdPF and $\mathcal{F}'$ a subforest of $\mathcal{F}$. For every $\mathcal{T}_i \in \mathcal{F}$, consider an injective renaming function ρ_i with $\text{dom}(\rho_i) = \text{vars}(\mathcal{T}_i)$ s.t. (i) $\rho_i(?X) = ?X$ for all $?X \in \text{vars}(\mathcal{F}')$, and (ii) $\rho_i(?X) \neq \rho_j(?Y)$ for every $?X \in \text{vars}(\mathcal{T}_i) \setminus \text{vars}(\mathcal{F}')$, $i \neq j \in \{1, \dots, k\}$ and $?Y \in \text{dom}(\rho_j)$. Finally, let $\hat{\mathcal{F}}$ be the wdPF $\{\rho_i(\mathcal{T}_i) \mid 1 \leq i \leq k\}$. Then a renamed proper extension of $\mathcal{F}'$ is a subforest of $\hat{\mathcal{F}}$ that has $\mathcal{F}'$ as a proper subforest. We are now ready to present a characterization for CONTAINMENT[$\{\cup, \pi\}$,$\{\cup\}$].

Theorem 3.7 *Let $(\mathcal{T}_1, \mathcal{X})$ be a pwdPT and let $\mathcal{F}_2$ be a wdPF. Then $(\mathcal{T}_1, \mathcal{X}) \subseteq \mathcal{F}_2$ iff for every subtree $\mathcal{T}_1'$ of $(\mathcal{T}_1, \mathcal{X})$*

(1) either there exists a child node n of $\mathcal{T}_1'$ s.t. there is a homomorphism h: $pat(n) \to pat(\mathcal{T}_1')$ with $h(?X) = ?X$ for all $?X \in \text{vars}(n) \cap \text{vars}(\mathcal{T}_1')$

(2) or there exists a subtree $\mathcal{T}_2'$ of $\mathcal{F}_2$ with $\text{vars}(\mathcal{T}_2') = \text{fvars}(\mathcal{T}_1')$ and $pat(\mathcal{T}_2') \subseteq pat(\mathcal{T}_1')$ s.t. every renamed proper extension $\mathcal{F}_2'$ of $\{\mathcal{T}_2'\}$ in $\mathcal{F}_2$ satisfies one of the following properties:

(a) there exists a proper renamed extension $\hat{\mathcal{F}}_2'$ of $\mathcal{F}_2'$ and a homomorphism h_a: $pat(\hat{\mathcal{F}}_2') \to pat(\mathcal{F}_2')$ with $h(?X) = ?X$ for all $?X \in \text{vars}(\hat{\mathcal{F}}_2') \cap (\text{vars}(\mathcal{F}_2') \cup \text{vars}(\mathcal{T}_1'))$, or

(b) there exists an extension $\hat{\mathcal{T}}_1'$ of $\mathcal{T}_1'$ and a homomorphism h_b: $pat(\hat{\mathcal{T}}_1') \to pat(\mathcal{F}_2') \cup pat(\mathcal{T}_1')$ with $h(?X) = ?X$ for all $?X \in \text{vars}(\mathcal{T}_1')$, or

(c) case (a) does not apply and there exists a tree $\mathcal{T} \in \mathcal{F}_2'$ with $\text{vars}(\mathcal{T}) = \text{fvars}(\mathcal{T}_1')$.

PROOF IDEA. The conditions given in this theorem extend the containment criterion from Theorem 3.1 to the situation where $\cup$ is allowed in S_2. Let G be an arbitrary RDF graph. As in Theorem 3.1, we have to inspect every subtree $\mathcal{T}_1'$ of $(\mathcal{T}_1, \mathcal{X})$ and check for every mapping σ sending $\mathcal{T}_1'$ into G that either σ can be extended to some child node of $\mathcal{T}_1'$ or $\sigma_{|\mathcal{X}} \in [\![\mathcal{F}_2]\!]_G$. Condition (1) here is analogous to condition (1) in Theorem 3.1. Condition (2) here extends condition (2) from Theorem 3.1 in the following way: as in condition (2a) and (2b) of Theorem 3.1, there must exist some subtree $\mathcal{T}_2'$ of $\mathcal{F}_2$ with $\text{vars}(\mathcal{T}_2') = \text{fvars}(\mathcal{T}_1')$ and $pat(\mathcal{T}_2') \subseteq pat(\mathcal{T}_1')$. The difficult part is to extend condition (2c) of Theorem 3.1. Now, it does not suffice to extend $\mathcal{T}_2'$ by a child node n such that $\mu = \sigma_{|\mathcal{X}}$ also sends n into G. Since we have a pattern forest, μ might still be a solution of another tree in $\mathcal{F}_2$. We now have to extend *all subtrees* in $\mathcal{F}_2$ with $\text{vars}(\mathcal{T}_2') = \text{fvars}(\mathcal{T}_1')$ and $pat(\mathcal{T}_2') \subseteq pat(\mathcal{T}_1')$ to cover the case that μ is not a solution of $\mathcal{F}_2$ but extensions of μ are solutions. This is why we have to consider *renamed proper extensions*. By conditions (2a) and (2c), we only need to check condition (2b) for *renamed proper extensions* that satisfy a certain maximality condition (this is done by (2a)) and that indeed extend every relevant subtree $\mathcal{T}_2'$ of $\mathcal{F}_2$ (this is done by (2c)). The renaming is needed so that, in condition (2b), we only check for the existence of a homomorphism h_b that maps $\hat{\mathcal{T}}'$ into a single subtree of $\mathcal{F}_2$, and not into the union of several subtrees. □

Theorem 3.8 CONTAINMENT[$\{\cup, \pi\}$,$\{\cup\}$] *is in* Π_2^P.

PROOF. The characterization in Theorem 3.7 can be directly translated into a Σ_2^P-algorithm for testing $(\mathcal{T}_1, \mathcal{X}) \not\subseteq \mathcal{F}_2$: first guess $\mathcal{T}'$ and the proper renamed extension $\hat{\mathcal{F}}_2'$, and then test by a coNP-oracle that there does not exist a child node n and homomorphism h as described by property (2b).

The Π_2^P-membership of CONTAINMENT[$\{\cup, \pi\}$,$\{\cup\}$] follows immediately. Indeed, to test $(\mathcal{F}_1, \mathcal{X}) \subseteq \mathcal{F}_2$ we just need to test if $(\mathcal{T}_i, \mathcal{X}) \subseteq \mathcal{F}_2$ holds for every $(\mathcal{T}_i, \mathcal{X}) \in (\mathcal{F}_1, \mathcal{X})$. □

As for the *hardness* results, we already noted that the NP-hardness of CONTAINMENT[$\emptyset$,$\emptyset$] follows from the NP-completeness of EQUIVALENCE[$\emptyset$,$\emptyset$] [12]. It thus only remains to show the Π_2^P-hardness of CONTAINMENT[$\emptyset$,$\{\cup\}$].

Theorem 3.9 CONTAINMENT[$\emptyset$,$\{\cup\}$] *is* Π_2^P*-hard.*

PROOF IDEA. All Π_2^P-hardness proofs in this paper are by reduction from the Π_2^P-complete problem 3-QSAT$_{\forall,2}$. An instance of this problem is given by a formula $\Phi = \forall\vec{x}\exists\vec{y}\Psi$, where Ψ is a Boolean formula in CNF over the variables $\vec{x} \cup \vec{y}$. The question is if every assignment I on the variables in $\vec{x}$ can be extended to an assignment J on $\vec{y}$, s.t. $J \models \Psi$.

From an arbitrary instance of 3-QSAT$_{\forall,2}$, we construct an instance of CONTAINMENT[$\emptyset$,$\{\cup\}$] as follows: The wdPT $\mathcal{T}_1$ consists of the root and two child nodes n_i, n_i' for every variable $x_i \in \vec{x}$ plus one additional child node n_0 containing the variables in $\vec{y}$ and an encoding of the formula Ψ. Every subtree $\mathcal{T}_1'$ of $\mathcal{T}_1$ which, for every i, contains exactly one of the nodes n_i, n_i', encodes an assignment on the variables in $\vec{x}$. The difficulty in the construction of the wdPF $\mathcal{F}_2$ consists in dealing with "unintended" subtrees of $\mathcal{T}_1'$ of $\mathcal{T}_1$ which, for some i, contain zero or two of the nodes n_i, n_i'. For all these cases, certain wdPTs are added to $\mathcal{F}_2$. Finally, we also add one wdPT to $\mathcal{F}_2$ which contains the triples encoding the formula Ψ in its root plus the child nodes n_i, n_i'. This latter wdPT produces the solutions of all "intended" subtrees of $\mathcal{T}_1'$ if and only if every assignment I on the variables in $\vec{x}$ can be extended to an assignment J on $\vec{y}$, s.t. $J \models \Psi$. □

We conclude this section by settling the complexity of the SUBSUMPTION[S_1,S_2] problem for every $S_1, S_2 \subseteq \{\cup, \pi\}$. It was shown in [12], that the simplest case where $S_1 = S_2 = \emptyset$ holds, is Π_2^P-complete. In [13], the Π_2^P-membership (and, hence, the Π_2^P-completeness) was extended to the case where $S_1 = S_2 = \{\pi\}$ holds. To further extend the Π_2^P-completeness to arbitrary $S_1, S_2 \subseteq \{\cup, \pi\}$, it suffices to show the Π_2^P-membership for the most general case.

Theorem 3.10 SUBSUMPTION[$\{\cup,\pi\}$,$\{\cup,\pi\}$] *is in* Π_2^P.

PROOF SKETCH. Let $(\mathcal{F}_1, \mathcal{X})$ and $(\mathcal{F}_2, \mathcal{X})$ be two pwdPFs. It can be shown that $(\mathcal{F}_1, \mathcal{X}) \sqsubseteq (\mathcal{F}_2, \mathcal{X})$ iff for every subtree $\mathcal{T}_1'$ of $\mathcal{F}_1$, there exists a subtree $\mathcal{T}_2'$ of $\mathcal{F}_2$, s.t.

(1) $\text{fvars}(\mathcal{T}_1') \subseteq \text{fvars}(\mathcal{T}_2')$ and

(2) there exists a homomorphism $h\colon pat(\mathcal{T}_2') \to pat(\mathcal{T}_1')$ with $h(?X) = ?X$ for all $?X \in \text{fvars}(\mathcal{T}_1')$.

This criterion can be immediately turned into a Π_2^P-algorithm, i.e.: for all subtrees $\mathcal{T}_1'$ of $\mathcal{F}_1$ check that there exists a subtree $\mathcal{T}_2'$ of $\mathcal{F}_2$ together with a homomorphism of the desired property. □

As pointed out in [15], subsumption is an interesting concept in its own right. Moreover, it was shown in [12] that for graph patterns in wd-SPARQL[$\emptyset$], subsumption can be used to characterize equivalence. That is, for graph patterns P_1, P_2 in wd-SPARQL[$\emptyset$], we have $P_1 \equiv P_2$ iff $P_1 \sqsubseteq P_2$ and $P_2 \sqsubseteq P_1$ hold. However, in [13], it was shown that this characterization of equivalence no longer works for graph patterns in wd-SPARQL[$\{\pi\}$]. This negative result can be even strengthened to equivalence between one pattern from wd-SPARQL[$\{\pi\}$] and one pattern from wd-SPARQL[$\emptyset$]. The same is also true for patterns P_1 in wd-SPARQL[$\emptyset$] and P_2 in wd-SPARQL[$\{\cup\}$].

Proposition 3.11 *There exist pairs P_1, P_2 of graph patterns P_1 from wd-SPARQL[$\emptyset$] and P_2 from either wd-SPARQL[$\{\pi\}$] or wd-SPARQL[$\{\cup\}$], s.t. $P_1 \sqsubseteq P_2$ and $P_2 \sqsubseteq P_1$ hold but $P_1 \not\equiv P_2$.*

PROOF SKETCH. We first provide an example for P_1 from wd-SPARQL[$\emptyset$] and P_2 from wd-SPARQL[$\{\cup\}$]. Consider the graph patterns $P_1 = t_1$ OPT t_2 and $P_2 = (t_1)$ UNION $(t_1$ AND $t_2)$, for distinct triple patterns t_1, t_2. Then $P_1 \sqsubseteq P_2$ and $P_2 \sqsubseteq P_1$ can be easily seen, while $P_1 \not\equiv P_2$ does not hold since, the disjunct t_1 in P_2 may produce solutions which are not solutions of P_1 (even though they can of course be extended to solutions of P_1).

Now consider the following pair P_1, P_2 for P_1 from wd-SPARQL[$\emptyset$] and P_2 from wd-SPARQL[$\{\pi\}$], with $P_1 = (?X_1, a, ?X_2)$ OPT $((?X_3, a, ?X_2)$ AND $(?X_3, a, ?X_3))$ and $P_2 = ((?X_1, a, ?X_2)$ AND $(?Y_1, a, ?Y_2))$ OPT $((?X_3, a, ?X_2)$ AND $(?X_3, a, ?X_3)$ AND $(?Y_3, a, ?Y_2)$ AND $(?Y_3, a, ?Y_3))$ and $\mathcal{X} = \{?X_1, ?X_2, ?X_3\}$. It can now be checked that $P_1 \sqsubseteq (P_2, \mathcal{X})$ and $(P_2, \mathcal{X}) \sqsubseteq P_1$, but $P_1 \not\equiv (P_2, \mathcal{X})$. To see this, note that P_1 and P_2 coincide on the triple patterns which contain only free variables. In addition, P_2 contains some triple patterns with existential variables, such that there is a homomorphism from the latter into the former. Hence, one can easily verify that $P_1 \sqsubseteq (P_2, \mathcal{X})$ holds (actually, even $P_1 \subseteq (P_2, \mathcal{X})$). However, in the other direction, we have $(P_2, \mathcal{X}) \sqsubseteq P_1$ but, in general, $(P_2, \mathcal{X}) \not\subseteq P_1$ since, by appropriate choice of graph G and appropriate instantiation of the existential variables $?Y_1, ?Y_2$ in the root of P_2, one can block the extension of a mapping to the child node. □

4. UNDECIDABLE CONTAINMENT

In this section, we prove that the CONTAINMENT[S_1,S_2] problem becomes undecidable as soon as $\pi \in S_2$. Hence, in order to fill in the entire last two columns of Table 1, it suffices to establish the undecidability of the simplest case, i.e., $S_1 = \emptyset$ and $S_2 = \{\pi\}$. Our undecidability proof will be by reduction from a classical database problem, which has received renewed interest in the context of information integration, namely the problem of conjunctive query answering under integrity constraints in the form of tuple generating dependencies (tgds) [9, 3]. Several adaptations of the original result are needed to make it suitable for a reduction to the problems studied here: first, it is important to note that the undecidability results in [9, 3] refer to *arbitrary* (i.e., possibly infinite) databases. This is problematical in our case, where we deal with RDF graphs, which are *finite*. Moreover, RDF graphs contain only triples, while in [9, 3], predicates of arbitrary arity are allowed. Finally, for our problem reduction, it turns out to be convenient to restrict the set of tgds in the original problem to a single tgd.

We start by introducing some additional terminology that we need to formally define the problem of conjunctive query answering under tgds and to adapt the existing undecidability results to our needs.

A *tuple generating dependency (tgd)* is a first-order formula of the form $\forall \vec{x}(\phi(\vec{x}) \to \exists \vec{y}\psi(\vec{x}, \vec{y}))$ where $\phi(\vec{x})$ and $\psi(\vec{x}, \vec{y})$ are conjunctive queries and all variables in $\vec{x}$ indeed occur in $\phi(\vec{x})$. To simplify the notation, the $\forall$-quantifiers are usually omitted. Satisfaction of a tgd τ by a database instance I (denoted by $I \models \tau$) is defined like the usual satisfaction relation for first-order formulas. By the specific form of tgds, satisfaction can also be defined in terms of homomorphisms: $I \models \tau$ holds, if for every homomorphism $h\colon \phi(\vec{x}) \to I$ (mapping constants onto themselves), there exists an extension of h to a homomorphism $h'\colon \psi(\vec{x}, \vec{y}) \to I$. For a set Σ of tgds, $I \models \Sigma$ holds if $I \models \tau$ for every $\tau \in \Sigma$.

A *Boolean Conjunctive Query (BCQ)* is a set of atoms. A BCQ Q evaluates to *true* over a database instance I (denoted as $Q(I) =$ *true* or $I \models Q$) if there exists a homomorphism $h\colon Q \to I$ that maps constants onto themselves. For a set Σ of tgds, a database instance I and a BCQ Q, we say that $I, \Sigma \models Q$ holds, if for every (possibly infinite) database instance (or *model*) M, s.t. $M \models \Sigma$ and $I \subseteq M$ (also denoted by $M \models I$), we also have $M \models Q$. Note that by slight abuse of notation we do not distinguish between models and database instances. We write $I, \Sigma \models_f Q$ if only *finite* models M are allowed.

To distinguish between variables occurring in tgds and BCQs and variables in graph patterns, we denote variables in the relational context with lower case letters, like x, y, z.

We study the following two problems on query answering under tgds, where either arbitrary or only finite models are considered:

BCQ-UNDER-TGDs

Input:	set Σ of tgds, database instance I, BCQ Q.
Question:	does $\Sigma, I \models Q$ hold?

FINITE-BCQ-UNDER-TGDs	
Input:	set Σ of tgds, database instance I, BCQ Q.
Question:	does $\Sigma, I \models_f Q$ hold?

To prove the undecidability of CONTAINMENT[S_1,S_2] whenever $\pi \in S_2$ holds, we proceed as follows: first we establish the undecidability of FINITE-BCQ-UNDER-TGDs by adapting the undecidability proof from [3] for BCQ-UNDER-TGDs. We then strengthen this result by showing that FINITE-BCQ-UNDER-TGDs remains undecidable even if all predicates are restricted to arity 2 and only a single tgd is allowed. This restricted version of FINITE-BCQ-UNDER-TGDs will then be reduced to CONTAINMENT[$\emptyset$,$\{\pi\}$] to settle all undecidable cases of CONTAINMENT[S_1,S_2].

The undecidability proof of BCQ-UNDER-TGDs in [3] goes by reduction from the HALTING problem. The crucial idea is to encode the initial configuration of the Turing machine (TM) in the instance I and to define tgds that describe the transitions of the TM. The query Q is used to encode the halting condition. It is then shown that the Turing Machine halts iff $\Sigma, I \models Q$ holds. In particular, if the Turing Machine does not halt, then one can construct a counter-model M for $\Sigma, I \models Q$ (i.e., a model M of Σ, I that does not satisfy Q) by taking M as the straightforward encoding of the infinite run of the TM. Clearly, this M is infinite.

It is easy to see that this reduction does not work for the FINITE-BCQ-UNDER-TGDs problem. Indeed, observe that asking if $I, \Sigma \models Q$ holds is semi-decidable, since the problem is obviously equivalent to the unsatisfiability of the set of FO formulas $I, \Sigma, \neg Q$. The latter problem is clearly semi-decidable. Hence, the co-problem of BCQ-UNDER-TGDs *is not semi-decidable*. On the other hand, the co-problem of FINITE-BCQ-UNDER-TGDs (i.e., testing if $I, \Sigma \not\models_f Q$ holds) obviously *is semi-decidable*, since we can enumerate all finite models M (up to isomorphism) and decide for every M if $M \models I$, $M \models \Sigma$ and $M \not\models Q$ hold. But then the reduction from the HALTING problem given in [3] cannot work for finite models, since this would give a reduction from co-HALTING to the semi-decidable co-FINITE-BCQ-UNDER-TGDs problem. Nevertheless we can show the following result:

Theorem 4.1 *FINITE-BCQ-UNDER-TGDs is undecidable.*

PROOF IDEA. Analogously to the reduction from HALTING to BCQ-UNDER-TGDs given in [3], we use atoms of the form *state*(x,q), *cursor*(x,p), and *contains*(x,y,s) to represent the configurations of the Turing machine (TM). We can thus express that, at some time instant x, the TM is in state q, the cursor is at position p and the tape content of tape cell y is s. In addition, a successor relation *next*(x,x') is defined that can be applied to time instants and tape positions.

As in [3], the initial configuration of the TM is encoded in the instance I and the transitions of the TM are encoded by the tgds. We adapt the reduction given in [3] in such a way that we reduce the *co-problem* of HALTING to FINITE-BCQ-UNDER-TGDs. This adaptation implements two main ideas: First, we introduce a relation *smaller*$(\cdot,\cdot)$ and add tgds which ensure that this relation contains the transitive closure of *next*$(\cdot,\cdot)$. Second, the query Q now asks for *smaller*(x,x); i.e. if there exists some "loop" in the time instants.

It can then be shown that $I, \Sigma \models_f Q$ holds iff the TM does not halt: Indeed, if the TM halts, a simple counter-model M of $I, \Sigma \models_f Q$ is obtained by the natural encoding of the (*halting*) run of the TM, using the numbers $1,\dots,n$ to encode the time instants and tape positions. Now suppose that TM does not halt. Then every model M of I, Σ contains an encoding of the infinite number of steps in the (*non-halting*) run of the TM. Since each step is identified by some time instant and M is finite, at least one symbol a must be used to encode more than one time instant. Thus *smaller*$(a,a) \in M$. □

Next, we strengthen the undecidability result from Theorem 4.1 to make it better suited for our undecidability proofs in the context of SPARQL. We have already recalled above that RDF graphs contain only triples. Alternatively, we can represent these triples as atoms $p(s,o)$ provided that the triples (s,p,o) do not contain variables in the middle-position (i.e, the "predicate"). We thus show that FINITE-BCQ-UNDER-TGDs remains undecidable if we only allow binary relation symbols. Moreover, it will be convenient to also restrict the set of tgds in FINITE-BCQ-UNDER-TGDs to a singleton.

Theorem 4.2 *FINITE-BCQ-UNDER-TGDs is undecidable, even if the arity of every relation symbol is at most two and even if Σ consists of a single tgd.*

PROOF IDEA. We construct a single tgd τ from Σ by combining all antecedents of the tgds in Σ to the antecedent in τ (after renaming variables apart), and analogously for the consequent of τ. Now the idea is to implement "switches" for each tgd $\tau_i \in \Sigma$ such that, for every i, if the i-th switch is turned on, then for all $j \neq i$, the j-th switch may be turned off. Turning the j-th switch off means that all parts in τ stemming from τ_j are trivially satisfied. Hence, if all switches except for the i-th one are turned off then τ is satisfied iff τ_i is. In other words, we can thus simulate the "firing" of a single tgd. The switches are realized by introducing a new variable v_i for every $\tau_i \in \Sigma$. Moreover, every atom in τ that stems from τ_i is extended with this variable. Then the instance is extended in such a way that mapping a variable v_i to a certain value indeed "switches off" the tgd τ_i.

For the reduction to binary atoms, we replace every atom of arity $k > 2$ by k binary atoms in such a way that the following chain of equivalences holds: for any such binary atom in the tgd or query, there exists a homomorphism into an instance I iff the homomorphism can be extended to map all k atoms into I iff this homomorphism is also a homomorphism in the original non-binary case. □

We are now ready to prove the main result of this section:

Theorem 4.3 CONTAINMENT[$\emptyset$,$\{\pi\}$] *is undecidable.*

PROOF IDEA. The proof is by reduction from FINITE-BCQ-UNDER-TGDs containing a single tgd. We construct a wdPT $\mathcal{T}_1$ and a pwdPT $(\mathcal{T}_1, \mathcal{X})$, each consisting of a root with one child node. Both roots contain the antecedent of the single tgd τ and the instance I, as well as additional auxiliary triple patterns. The root r_2 of $\mathcal{T}_2$ contains in addition another copy of the antecedent of τ, such that this copy is realized by existential variables in evars(r_2).

The child nodes in both trees contain the consequent of the tgd as well as some further auxiliary triple patterns. In addition, the child node n_1 in $\mathcal{T}_1$ contains the query. The child node n_2 in $\mathcal{T}_2$ contains in addition another copy of the consequent of τ realized by existential variables in evars(n_2). The auxiliary graph patterns are needed to compensate for the lack of projection in $\mathcal{T}_1$: they deal with the query variables that must occur in $\mathcal{T}_2$ as well.

The construction ensures that $\mathcal{T}_1 \sqsubseteq (\mathcal{T}_2, \mathcal{X})$ holds. Hence, the only reason for $\mathcal{T}_1 \not\subseteq (\mathcal{T}_2, \mathcal{X})$ is that for some RDF graph G, we have the following situation: some solution $\mu \in [\![\mathcal{T}_1]\!]_G$ sends the root into G but cannot be extended to n_1, while in $(\mathcal{T}_2, \mathcal{X})$ every extension of μ to the existential variables in the root can be further extended so as to send also the child node n_2 into G. From this we can deduce three facts:

(1) Q is not satisfied by G: indeed, n_2 consists of triples from n_1 plus the triples encoding the BCQ Q. Since, n_2 can be mapped into G by an extension of μ, this is also true for all triple patterns in n_1 except for those encoding Q.

(2) G satisfies τ: indeed, recall that $\mathcal{T}_2$ uses existential variables to encode a copy of the antecedent of τ in the root and a copy of the consequent of τ in n_2, respectively. We are assuming that every mapping on vars(r_2) that maps the root into G can be extended to the existential variables in n_2 s.t. n_2 is mapped into G. Hence, G satisfies τ by the homomorphism criterion recalled previously in this section.

(3) I must be contained in G, since we are assuming that μ sends the root of both, $\mathcal{T}_1$ and $\mathcal{T}_2$, into G.

Thus, G provides a counter-model for $I, \tau \models_f Q$. $\square$

5. EQUIVALENCE

For the CONTAINMENT[S_1,S_2] problem, the borders between NP-completeness and Π_2^P-completeness on the one hand, and between decidability and undecidability on the other hand, were clearly determined by the language features allowed in S_2. In this section, we study the complexity of the EQUIVALENCE[S_1,S_2] problem, see Table 2. It turns out that the border between decidability and undecidability is not so clear-cut any more. In particular, equivalence may be decidable for two SPARQL queries even if one of the two directions of containment would be undecidable.

In our complexity analysis of EQUIVALENCE[S_1,S_2] we again make use of the fact that membership (resp. hardness) results propagate to the more special (resp. more general) case. Moreover, we now also have the symmetry between S_1 and S_2. We prove the following results:

- Π_2^P-membership of EQUIVALENCE[$\{\cup, \pi\}$,$\emptyset$]
- Π_2^P-hardness of EQUIVALENCE[$\{\cup\}$,$\emptyset$]
- Π_2^P-hardness of EQUIVALENCE[$\{\pi\}$,$\emptyset$]
- undecidability of EQUIVALENCE[$\{\cup, \pi\}$,$\{\cup\}$]
- undecidability of EQUIVALENCE[$\{\pi\}$,$\{\pi\}$]

The NP-completeness of EQUIVALENCE[$\emptyset$,$\emptyset$] was shown in [12]. The Π_2^P-membership of EQUIVALENCE[$\{\cup\}$,$\{\cup\}$] follows immediately from the Π_2^P-membership of the CONTAINMENT[$\{\cup\}$,$\{\cup\}$] problem and the Π_2^P-hardness of EQUIVALENCE[$\{\cup\}$,$\emptyset$] to be shown below. Hence, the above listed 6 cases indeed cover the entire Table 2. Note that for EQUIVALENCE[$\{\pi\}$,$\cup$] we only manage to establish the Π_2^P-hardness (which carries over both from EQUIVALENCE[$\{\pi\}$,$\emptyset$] and from EQUIVALENCE[$\{\emptyset\}$,$\cup$]). Proving a matching upper bound (or a higher lower bound) is left as an open problem for future work.

We present the complexity results of the EQUIVALENCE[S_1,S_2] problem per column in Table 2, so to speak. That is, we first consider the case $S_2 = \emptyset$ and establish Π_2^P-completeness if $S_1 \neq \emptyset$. To this end, we prove the Π_2^P-membership of the most general case (i.e., $S_1 = \{\cup, \pi\}$) and then prove the Π_2^P-hardness of the two incomparable cases $S_1 = \{\cup\}$ and $S_1 = \{\pi\}$, respectively.

Theorem 5.1 *Let $\mathcal{T}$ be a wdPT and $(\mathcal{F}, \mathcal{X})$ be a pwdPF. Then $\mathcal{T} \equiv (\mathcal{F}, \mathcal{X})$ iff*

(1) $\mathcal{T} \sqsubseteq (\mathcal{F}, \mathcal{X})$ and

(2) $(\mathcal{F}, \mathcal{X}) \subseteq \mathcal{T}$.

PROOF SKETCH. Properties (1) and (2) are clearly necessary for equivalence. To prove that they are also sufficient, it suffices to show that under the assumption that (2) is satisfied, the following equivalence holds: $\mathcal{T} \sqsubseteq (\mathcal{F}, \mathcal{X})$ iff $\mathcal{T} \subseteq (\mathcal{F}, \mathcal{X})$.

The "only if" direction of this equivalence is trivial. For the "if" direction, suppose to the contrary that $\mathcal{T} \sqsubseteq (\mathcal{F}, \mathcal{X})$ holds but $\mathcal{T} \subseteq (\mathcal{F}, \mathcal{X})$ does not. That is, for some graph G, there exists a solution μ of $\mathcal{T}$ that is not a solution of $(\mathcal{F}, \mathcal{X})$ but some extension μ' of μ is a solution of $(\mathcal{F}, \mathcal{X})$. Then μ' is a proper extension of μ. But then, by condition (2), μ' is also a solution of the wdPT $\mathcal{T}$. This is a contradiction, since it cannot happen that a mapping μ and a proper extension μ' of μ are both a solution of a wdPT. $\square$

By Theorems 3.10 and 3.6, properties (1) and (2) from the above theorem can be decided in Π_2^P and NP, respectively. From this we immediately get the following upper-bound.

Theorem 5.2 EQUIVALENCE[$\emptyset$,$\{\cup, \pi\}$] *is in* Π_2^P.

Towards the Π_2^P-completeness of EQUIVALENCE[S_1,S_2] if $S_1 \neq \emptyset$ and $S_2 = \emptyset$ hold, we prove the following two Π_2^P-hardness results.

Theorem 5.3 EQUIVALENCE[$\emptyset$,$\{\cup\}$] *is* Π_2^P*-hard.*

PROOF IDEA. In the proof of Theorem 3.9, we started with an arbitrary instance Φ of 3-QSAT$_{\forall,2}$ and constructed a wdPT $\mathcal{T}_1$ and a wdPF $\mathcal{F}_2$, such that Φ is valid iff $\mathcal{T}_1 \subseteq \mathcal{F}_2$ holds. An inspection of $\mathcal{T}_1$ and $\mathcal{F}_2$ reveals, that they always satisfy the condition $\mathcal{T}_1 \supseteq \mathcal{F}_2$. Hence, in this particular case, $\mathcal{T}_1 \subseteq \mathcal{F}_2$ holds iff $\mathcal{T}_1 \equiv \mathcal{F}_2$ holds. The problem reduction of Theorem 3.9 therefore also proves the current theorem. $\square$

Theorem 5.4 EQUIVALENCE[$\emptyset$,$\{\pi\}$] *is* Π_2^P*-hard.*

PROOF IDEA. Again, the proof is by reduction from 3-QSAT$_{\forall,2}$. Consider an arbitrary instance $\Phi = \forall\vec{x}\exists\vec{y}\Psi$ of 3-QSAT$_{\forall,2}$. We construct a wdPT $\mathcal{T}_1$ and a pwdPT $(\mathcal{T}_2, \mathcal{X})$ as follows: both trees consist of the root plus $k+1$ child nodes with $|\vec{x}| = k$. The variables in $\vec{x}$ are encoded by existential variables which are introduced in the root of $\mathcal{T}_2$ and which also occur in the child nodes. The $(k+1)$-st child contains an encoding of the clauses in Ψ, where the variables in $\vec{y}$ are encoded by further existential variables. $\mathcal{T}_1$ and $(\mathcal{T}_2, \mathcal{X})$ are constructed in such a way that $\mathcal{T}_1 \supseteq (\mathcal{T}_2, \mathcal{X})$ holds. Now consider an arbitrary subtree $\mathcal{T}_1'$ of $\mathcal{T}_1$. Truth assignments I of $\vec{x}$ are encoded by the subset S of the first k leaf nodes of $\mathcal{T}_1$ which are contained in $\mathcal{T}_1'$. More precisely, setting x_i to true in I is encoded by putting the i-the child node into S. It can be shown that a solution μ of $\mathcal{T}_1$ sending the root together with the nodes in S and the $(k+1)$-st leaf node of $\mathcal{T}_1$ into the RDF graph is also a solution of $\mathcal{T}_2$ iff the assignment I can be extended to an assignment J with $J \models \Psi$. □

We now proceed to the second column of Table 2. That is, we consider the EQUIVALENCE$[S_1,S_2]$ problem for the cases where $S_2 = \{\cup\}$ holds. It only remains to consider the cases $S_1 = \{\pi\}$ and $S_1 = \{\cup, \pi\}$. We will comment on the former case at the end of this section. The latter case is shown undecidable below.

Theorem 5.5 EQUIVALENCE$[\{\cup,\pi\},\{\cup\}]$ *is undecidable.*

PROOF IDEA. The undecidability is shown by adapting the reduction from FINITE-BCQ-UNDER-TGDs to CONTAINMENT$[\emptyset,\{\pi\}]$ in Theorem 4.3. Let an arbitrary instance of FINITE-BCQ-UNDER-TGDs be given by a tgd τ, an instance I, and a BCQ Q. From this we construct an instance of EQUIVALENCE$[\{\cup,\pi\},\{\cup\}]$ defined by a pwdPF $\{(\mathcal{T}_1,\mathcal{X}),(\mathcal{T}_2,\mathcal{X})\}$ and a wdPF $\{\mathcal{S}_1,\mathcal{S}_2,\mathcal{S}_3\}$. $\mathcal{S}_1$ is almost like the wdPT in the proof of Theorem 4.3: it has the root plus a child node encoding the BCQ Q; but now S_1 has an additional child node of the root which is isomorphic to the other child node (introducing fresh variables). Likewise, $\mathcal{T}_1$ is like the pwdPT in the proof of Theorem 4.3 (encoding the tgd), augmented by the same second child of the root as $\mathcal{S}_1$. Hence, we have exactly the same equivalence as in the proof of Theorem 4.3, namely $\mathcal{S}_1 \subseteq (\mathcal{T}_1,\mathcal{X})$ iff $I,\{\tau\} \models Q$. The remaining pattern trees are needed to guarantee the containment $\{(\mathcal{T}_1,\mathcal{X}),(\mathcal{T}_2,\mathcal{X})\} \subseteq \{\mathcal{S}_1,\mathcal{S}_2,\mathcal{S}_3\}$.

The key idea is to define $\mathcal{S}_2$ and $\mathcal{T}_2$ like $\mathcal{S}_1$ but deleting the first child of the root (i.e., they encode the query Q via the fresh variables introduced for the second child of the root in $\mathcal{S}_1$ and $\mathcal{T}_1$). Hence, these pattern trees have a strictly smaller set of (free) variables. Their purpose is as follows: whenever a mapping μ on the root of $\mathcal{T}_1$ and $\mathcal{S}_1$ can be extended to the first child of the root of $\mathcal{S}_1$ but not to the first child of $\mathcal{T}_1$ (due to a "bad" choice of the binding of the existential variables), then μ can also be extended to the second child of the root of $\mathcal{S}_1$ and of $\mathcal{T}_1$. But then $\mathcal{T}_1$ gives rise to a solution which is actually contained in the wdPF, namely in $\mathcal{S}_2$. Finally, $\mathcal{S}_3$ is essentially like $\mathcal{T}_1$ but omitting all triples that contain an existential variables. It guarantees that also the remaining solutions of $\mathcal{T}_1$ are contained in the wdPF. □

Finally, we consider the EQUIVALENCE$[S_1,S_2]$ problem with $S_1 = S_2 = \{\pi\}$. The undecidability in this case is shown by another adaptation of the reduction from FINITE-BCQ-UNDER-TGDs to CONTAINMENT$[\emptyset,\{\pi\}]$ in Theorem 4.3.

Theorem 5.6 EQUIVALENCE$[\{\pi\},\{\pi\}]$ *is undecidable.*

We conclude this section by a brief discussion of the only case that has been left open in our complexity analysis, namely the problem EQUIVALENCE$[\{\pi\},\{\cup\}]$. As mentioned above, Π_2^P-hardness carries over from two special cases – replacing either $\{\pi\}$ or $\{\cup\}$ by $\emptyset$. A matching upper bound is open. Actually, at this point, we cannot even exclude undecidability. To illustrate the difficulties of this case, we inspect the two "neighbouring" cases so to speak and point out why the proof ideas applied there do not work for EQUIVALENCE$[\{\pi\},\{\cup\}]$.

For a possible Π_2^P-membership proof, look at the proof of Theorem 5.1, where $S_1 = \{\pi,\cup\}$ and $S_2 = \emptyset$. The crucial idea is that the "difficult" direction of containment (i.e., the one where π is allowed on the right-hand side) can be replaced by a subsumption test. However, if $S_2 = \{\cup\}$, the final argument in the proof of Theorem 5.1 does not work any more. Indeed, it may happen that both some mapping μ and a proper extension μ' of μ are solutions of a pattern *forest*, namely of two different trees within this forest.

For a possible undecidability proof, look at the proof of Theorem 5.5, where $S_1 = \{\pi,\cup\}$ and $S_2 = \{\cup\}$. The crucial idea of this problem reduction is to define the pattern forest without projection in such a way that its trees have different sets of variables. However, in the setting where S_1 is restricted to $S_1 = \{\pi\}$ it can be easily shown that $\text{fvars}(\mathcal{T}) = \text{vars}(\mathcal{T}_i)$ for every $\mathcal{T}_i \in \mathcal{F}$ is a necessary condition for the equivalence $\mathcal{F} \equiv (\mathcal{T},\mathcal{X})$.

6. RELATED WORK

As mention earlier, containment and equivalence of fragments of SPARQL have hardly been studied so far.

In [20], containment and equivalence of two fragments of the RDF query language RQL (introduced in [10]) were investigated. The authors provide algorithms for deciding query containment and performing query minimization, but do not perform a detailed complexity analysis of these problems. Moreover, note that the fragments studied in [20] do not contain the OPT operator, which is at the heart of well-designed SPARQL studied here.

In [5], a 2-EXPTIME upper bound was proved for containment under RDFS entailment of SPARQL queries that contain only the AND and UNION operator as well as property paths. For a similar query fragment, but instead of RDFS taking ontologies in the Description Logic $\mathcal{SHI}$ into account, the same upper bound was proved in [6]. In both papers, the 2-EXPTIME upper bound was shown by translating the problem into the μ-calculus. However, lower bounds as well as the OPT operator have not been considered in either of the two articles.

Equivalence of graph patterns was also studied in [14] and [15]. However, there the goal was not to actually decide whether two given graph patterns are equivalent. Instead, the authors provide several equivalence preserving transformation rules for graph patterns. These rewriting rules are then used for identifying several normal forms of graph patterns. A similar approach was taken in [19], where further equivalence preserving rewriting rules were introduced.

The works most closely related to our paper are [12] and [13]. In [12], EQUIVALENCE$[\emptyset,\emptyset]$ was already shown NP-complete (where the NP-membership is the difficult part). Moreover, EQUIVALENCE$[\{\pi\},\{\pi\}]$ was shown to be Π_2^P-hard in [13] but no matching upper bound was provided. Thus, concerning the equivalence problem, the current paper extends these works significantly by including UNION and projection. Also, by heavily using the containment problem for deciding equivalence, we take a different approach than in [12]. Finally, the containment problem for well-designed SPARQL has not been studied before.

7. CONCLUSION

Containment and equivalence are two fundamental computational problems for query languages. We have drawn a fairly complete picture of the complexity of these problems for well-designed SPARQL queries restricted to the AND and OPT operator and possible extensions by UNION and/or projection. Our complexity results reach from NP-completeness to undecidability. On the road to the undecidability proofs we had to extend the undecidability of a classical database problem, namely the problem of conjunctive query answering under integrity constraints in the form of tuple generating dependencies.

Our first goal for future work is, of course, to determine the precise complexity of the EQUIVALENCE[$\{\pi\}$,$\{\cup\}$] problem. Another obvious line for future work is the inclusion of more SPARQL operators to the study of containment and equivalence such as the FILTER operator or property paths (introduced in SPARQL 1.1). Moreover, observe that in the definition of well-designed queries, we followed the approach of [15] where the UNION operator is allowed to occur only "outside" AND and OPT expressions. Lifting this restriction is another future work. A possible way of extending well-designedness to "nested" UNION has been suggested, but not further studied, in [16]. Of course, relaxing the well-designedness condition is also an interesting extension. Another extension of our work will incorporate ontologies of various Description Logics into our study of containment and equivalence analogously to [6].

Containment and equivalence are problems which naturally arise in the context of query optimization. Thus the intractability results provided in this paper represent rather "bad news". An investigation of tractable fragments for these problems is therefore be of highest interest. Observe that one big source of intractability is to check the existence of suitable homomorphisms. Thus studying the influence of e.g. restricting the set of triple patterns in each node to acyclic sets may be a first starting point.

Towards a strong theory of query optimization in SPARQL, the study of the containment and equivalence problems has to be complemented by the search for powerful transformations (in particular, simplifications) of SPARQL queries. In [15] and [12], simple transformations are given to obtain the OPT-normal form and NR-normal form, respectively, mentioned in this paper. A list of transformation rules on relational algebra expressions, which are also applicable to SPARQL graph patterns, is given in [19]. The search for transformation rules should be continued.

Finally, recall that we have pointed out that for graph patterns P_1 and P_2 containing UNION and projection, $P_1 \sqsubseteq P_2$ and $P_2 \sqsubseteq P_1$ need not imply $P_1 \equiv P_2$. However, in the presence of the OPT operator, subsumption sometimes seems to be the more natural concept than containment (cf. [2]). It is thus of interest to investigate if there are cases that would benefit from an alternative notion of equivalence, defined via mutual subsumption.

Acknowledgements

This work was supported by the Vienna Science and Technology Fund (WWTF), project ICT12-15 and by the Austrian Science Fund (FWF): P25207-N23.

8. REFERENCES

[1] R. Angles and C. Gutierrez. The expressive power of SPARQL. In *ISWC*, volume 5318 of *LNCS*, pages 114–129. Springer, 2008.

[2] M. Arenas and J. Pérez. Querying semantic web data with SPARQL. In *PODS*, pages 305–316. ACM, 2011.

[3] A. Calì, G. Gottlob, and M. Kifer. Taming the infinite chase: Query answering under expressive relational constraints. In *KR*, pages 70–80. AAAI Press, 2008.

[4] A. K. Chandra and P. M. Merlin. Optimal implementation of conjunctive queries in relational data bases. In *STOC*, pages 77–90. ACM, 1977.

[5] M. W. Chekol, J. Euzenat, P. Genevès, and N. Layaïda. SPARQL query containment under RDFS entailment regime. In *IJCAR*, volume 7364 of *LNCS*, pages 134–148. Springer, 2012.

[6] M. W. Chekol, J. Euzenat, P. Genevès, and N. Layaïda. SPARQL query containment under SHI axioms. In *AAAI*. AAAI Press, 2012.

[7] R. Cyganiak, D. Wood, and M. Lanthaler. RDF 1.1 concepts and abstract syntax. W3C Recommendation, Feb. 2014. `http://www.w3.org/TR/rdf11-concepts`.

[8] S. Harris and A. Seaborne. SPARQL 1.1 Query Language. W3C Recommendation, Mar. 2013. `http://www.w3.org/TR/sparql11-query`.

[9] D. S. Johnson and A. C. Klug. Testing containment of conjunctive queries under functional and inclusion dependencies. *JCSS*, 28(1):167–189, 1984.

[10] G. Karvounarakis, A. Magkanaraki, S. Alexaki, V. Christophides, D. Plexousakis, M. Scholl, and K. Tolle. Querying the semantic web with RQL. *Computer Networks*, 42(5):617–640, 2003.

[11] A. C. Klug. On conjunctive queries containing inequalities. *J. ACM*, 35(1):146–160, 1988.

[12] A. Letelier, J. Pérez, R. Pichler, and S. Skritek. Static analysis and optimization of semantic web queries. In *PODS*, pages 89–100. ACM, 2012.

[13] A. Letelier, J. Pérez, R. Pichler, and S. Skritek. Static analysis and optimization of semantic web queries. *ACM Trans. Database Syst.*, 38(4):25, 2013.

[14] J. Pérez, M. Arenas, and C. Gutierrez. Semantics and complexity of SPARQL. In *ISWC*, volume 4273 of *LNCS*, pages 30–43. Springer, 2006.

[15] J. Pérez, M. Arenas, and C. Gutierrez. Semantics and complexity of SPARQL. *ACM TODS*, 34(3), 2009.

[16] A. Polleres. From SPARQL to rules (and back). In *WWW*, pages 787–796. ACM, 2007.

[17] E. Prud'hommeaux and A. Seaborne. SPARQL Query Language for RDF. W3C Recommendation, Jan. 2008. `http://www.w3.org/TR/rdf-sparql-query`.

[18] Y. Sagiv and M. Yannakakis. Equivalences among relational expressions with the union and difference operators. *J. ACM*, 27(4):633–655, 1980.

[19] M. Schmidt, M. Meier, and G. Lausen. Foundations of SPARQL query optimization. In *ICDT*, pages 4–33. ACM, 2010.

[20] G. Serfiotis, I. Koffina, V. Christophides, and V. Tannen. Containment and minimization of RDF/S query patterns. In *ISWC*, volume 3729 of *LNCS*, pages 607–623. Springer, 2005.

On Scale Independence for Querying Big Data

Wenfei Fan
University of Edinburgh
& RCDB and SKLSDE Lab,
Beihang University
Edinburgh & Beijing
wenfei@inf.ed.ac.uk

Floris Geerts
Dept. of Mathematics and
Computer Science
University of Antwerp
Antwerpen, Belgium
floris.geerts@uantwerpen.be

Leonid Libkin
School of Informatics
University of Edinburgh
Edinburgh, UK
libkin@inf.ed.ac.uk

ABSTRACT

To make query answering feasible in big datasets, practitioners have been looking into the notion of scale independence of queries. Intuitively, such queries require only a relatively small subset of the data, whose size is determined by the query and access methods rather than the size of the dataset itself. This paper aims to formalize this notion and study its properties. We start by defining what it means to be scale-independent, and provide matching upper and lower bounds for checking scale independence, for queries in various languages, and for combined and data complexity. Since the complexity turns out to be rather high, and since scale-independent queries cannot be captured syntactically, we develop sufficient conditions for scale independence. We formulate them based on access schemas, which combine indexing and constraints together with bounds on the sizes of retrieved data sets. We then study two variations of scale-independent query answering, inspired by existing practical systems. One concerns incremental query answering: we check when query answers can be maintained in response to updates scale-independently. The other explores scale-independent query rewriting using views.

Categories and Subject Descriptors: H.2.1 [**Database Management**]: Logical Design – *Data Models*; H.2.1 [**Database Management**]: Systems – *Query Processing*
General Terms: Theory, Languages, Algorithms
Keywords: Scale independence; big data; query answering

1. INTRODUCTION

Big data introduces challenges to the scalability of query answering. Given a query Q and a dataset D, it is often prohibitively costly to compute the answers $Q(D)$ to Q in D when D is big, *e.g.*, of PetaByte (10^{15} bytes) or ExaByte (10^{18}) size. To this end, one may want to use heuristics, "quick and dirty" algorithms which return approximate answers. However, in many applications it is a must to find exact query answers.

PODS'14, June 22–27, 2014, Snowbird, UT, USA.

ACM 978-1-4503-2375-8/14/06 ...$15.00
http://dx.doi.org/10.1145/2594538.2594551.

To cope with these, practitioners have been studying scale independence (*e.g.*, [4–6]). A query Q is said to be *scale-independent* in a dataset D *w.r.t.* M if $Q(D)$ can be computed by accessing a set D_Q of at most M tuples in D, *independent of* the size of the underlying dataset D. Here M is a non-negative integer, indicating the capacity of our available resources, such as time and space.

The need for scale independence is evident in practice. It allows us to answer Q in big D within our available resources. Moreover, if Q is scale-independent in all datasets, we can answer Q without performance degradation when D grows, *i.e.*, make Q scalable.

Scale independence per se is not easy to achieve, nor is it easy to test for, as we shall show. Nonetheless, there are many practical scenarios where scale independence is achievable, roughly classified into three groups below.

(1) Additional information about accessing information in a dataset, which is typically provided in the form of indices and/or cardinality constraints, can make rather expressive classes of queries scale-independent. Such access information is in fact commonly available in many large datasets being used in the real world.

(2) Even if a query Q is not scale-independent, we may still make it feasible to query big data *incrementally*, *i.e.*, to evaluate Q incrementally in response to changes ΔD to D, by accessing an M-fraction of the dataset D. That is, we compute $Q(D)$, once and offline, as precomputation, and then incrementally answer Q on demand.

(3) Additionally, we can sometimes achieve *scale independence using views*, *i.e.*, when a set $\mathcal{V}$ of views is defined, we rewrite Q into Q' using $\mathcal{V}$, such that for any dataset D, we can compute $Q(D)$ by using Q', which accesses materialized views $\mathcal{V}(D)$ and only a bounded amount of data from D (this is subject to the storage and maintenance costs of $\mathcal{V}(D)$).

We now illustrate these three scenarios by examples.

Example 1.1: Some real-life queries are actually scale-independent. For example, below are (slightly modified) queries taken from Graph Search of Facebook [11].

(a) Query Q_1 is to find all friends of a person p who live in NYC, from a dataset D_1. Here D_1 consists of two relations specified by $\mathsf{person}(\mathsf{id}, \mathsf{name}, \mathsf{city})$ and $\mathsf{friend}(\mathsf{id}_1, \mathsf{id}_2)$, recording the basic information of people (with a key id) and their friends, respectively. Query Q_1 can be written as follows:

$$Q_1(\mathsf{p}, \mathsf{name}) = \exists \mathsf{id}\big(\mathsf{friend}(\mathsf{p}, \mathsf{id}) \wedge \mathsf{person}(\mathsf{id}, \mathsf{name}, \mathrm{NYC})\big).$$

In personalized social searches we do not want to compute the entire answer to Q_1, but rather do it for a specified person p_0; that is, given p_0, we want to find all values of name so that (p_0, name) is in the answer to Q_1.

The dataset D_1 is often big in real life: Facebook has more than 1 billion users with 140 billion friend links [10]. A naive computation of the answer to Q_1, even if p_0 is known, may fetch the entire D_1, and is cost prohibitive.

Nonetheless, we can compute $Q_1(p_0, D_1)$ by accessing only a small subset D_{Q_1} of D_1. Indeed, Facebook has a limit of 5000 friends per user (cf. [5]), and id is a key of person. Thus by using indices on id attributes, we can identify D_{Q_1}, which consists of a subset D_f of friend including all friends of p_0, and a set D_p of person tuples t such that $t[\text{id}] = t'[\text{id2}]$ for some tuple t' in D_f. Then $Q_1(p_0, D_{Q_1}) = Q_1(p_0, D_1)$. Moreover, D_{Q_1} contains at most 10000 tuples of D_1, and is much smaller than D_1. Thus Q_1 is scale-independent in D_1 *w.r.t.* $M \geq 10000$.

This illustrates the key ingredients of the recipe for scale independence. First, we may have to fix values of some parameters of the query (p_0 for p above). Second, we may need access information telling us that based on some key values, tuples can be fetched efficiently, and there is an upper limit on the number of tuples fetched.

(b) Query Q_2 is to find from D_2 all restaurants rated A in NYC, where p's friends in NYC have been. Dataset D_2 consists of four relations: person and friend as above, and relations specified by restr(rid, name, city, rating) (with rid as a key) and visit(id, rid). Here Q_2 is

$$Q_2(\text{p}, \text{rn}) = \exists \text{id}, \text{rid}, \text{pn}\big(\text{friend}(\text{p}, \text{id}) \wedge \text{visit}(\text{id}, \text{rid}) \wedge \text{person}(\text{id}, \text{pn}, \text{NYC}) \wedge \text{restr}(\text{rid}, \text{rn}, \text{NYC}, A)\big).$$

Again, we want to find the answers for a given person p_0. However, unlike D_1, dataset D_2 imposes no restriction on the number of restaurants in NYC or on the number of restaurants which a person visits.

Nonetheless, in this case we can *incrementally* evaluate Q_2 scale-independently, leveraging the old output $Q_2(p_0, D_2)$. Given a set ΔD_2 of insertions to visit, one can compute $Q_2(D_2 \cup \Delta D_2)$ by fetching at most $3|\Delta D_2|$ tuples from D_2, where $|S|$ denotes the number of tuples in S. Indeed, for each tuple (id, rid) in ΔD_2, we fetch the restaurant identified by the key rid, the friend of p_0 identified by id, and person tuple (identified by id) to verify that the friend lives in NYC, via indexing. Let S be the set of the names of the restaurants that are fetched and visited by NYC friends. Then $S \cup Q_2(D_2) = Q_2(D_2 \cup \Delta D_2)$. Note that ΔD_2 is often small in practice. If $3|\Delta D_2| \leq M$, then the *incremental evaluation* of Q_2 is scale-independent *w.r.t.* M.

(c) Assume that two views are defined: V_1 contains all restaurants in NYC, and V_2 is a subset of visit(id, rid) such that id lives in NYC (restaurants visited by NYC locals). Using V_1 and V_2, query Q_2 can be rewritten as:

$$Q_2'(\text{p}, \text{rn}) = \exists \text{id}, \text{rid}\big(\text{friend}(\text{p}, \text{id}) \wedge V_2(\text{id}, \text{rid}) \wedge V_1(\text{rid}, \text{rn}, A)\big).$$

Then for all datasets D_2, by using materialized views $V_1(D_2)$ and $V_2(D_2)$, Q_2' needs to fetch at most 5000 friend tuples from D_2 for $\text{p} = p_0$, *i.e.*, for a fixed p, Q_2 is scale-independent in all D_2 by using V_1 and V_2. Here we assume that the views are cached in memory and can be efficiently retrieved. That is, for scale independence using views to be effective, the materialized views should be of small size. □

All three examples thus show that it is feasible to answer a query Q in a big dataset D by accessing a bounded amount of data. To make practical use of scale independence, however, several questions have to be answered. Given Q and D, can we decide whether Q is scale-independent in D? If such an identification is expensive, can we find sufficient conditions for scale independence, perhaps using indices and other access information? If Q is determined to be scale-independent in D, can we effectively identify a small $D_Q \subseteq D$ such that $Q(D) = Q(D_Q)$ and $|D_Q| \leq M$, by using available indices? And can we achieve reasonable time bounds for finding this set and for evaluating the query over it? Similar questions also arise for incremental scale independence and scale independence using views.

Contributions. Our goal is to give a formal definition of scale independence (this has not been previously done) and study the above questions along the following three lines.

Complexity of scale independence. We look at the problem of deciding, given a query Q, a dataset D, and a bound M, whether Q is scale-independent in D *w.r.t.* M, *i.e.*, $Q(D)$ can be computed by accessing at most M tuples in D. We call it QDSI (with QD emphasizing that both Q and D are inputs). We establish both combined and data complexity bounds for QDSI, when Q is a conjunctive query (CQ), a union of conjunctive queries (UCQ), or in first-order logic (FO). We also study a special case when M is a constant, *i.e.*, when the capacity of our resources is fixed. Moreover, we study another problem, QSI, to check whether Q is scale-independent in *all instances* D of a relational schema.

Most of the results are negative: for FO queries, QSI is undecidable, and few sensible CQ queries are scale-independent in all instances, while the complexity of QDSI also tends to be rather high. This naturally brings us to the next theme of our investigation.

Sufficient conditions for scale independence. Not only is the complexity of QDSI and QSI rather high, it is also impossible to capture scale-independent queries syntactically. Thus, we need to find sufficient conditions for scale independence, with additional access information.

Such additional information comes in the form of *access schemas* $\mathcal{A}$ that specify what parts of data can be efficiently retrieved from D by using indices, as practiced in real life, and in addition give cardinality restrictions on such retrieved sets of tuples. We then provide a sufficient syntactic condition for an FO query to be scale-independent under $\mathcal{A}$. The class of queries we define is compositional: it is given by a set of rules forming new queries from existing ones, and we show that each rule is optimal, *i.e.*, it cannot get any tighter. We then show that the syntactic class of queries guarantees scale independence under $\mathcal{A}$. For instance, the query Q_1 we have seen above is an example of such a query: our conditions say that when the person is fixed, and if the Facebook restriction on the number of friends applies, then the query can be executed scale-independently.

Furthermore, we introduce *embedded* access schemas to incorporate constraints commonly found in practice, such as functional dependencies. We show that some queries that are not scale-independent may become so under embedded $\mathcal{A}$ with simple constraints.

Two variants of scale independence. Finally, we extend our study to incremental scale independence and scale independence using views, which have been used in practice [6]. We investigate the following problems.

(a) ΔQSI is to decide whether *for all small updates* ΔD to D, the answer to Q on the updated database can be incrementally computed from $Q(D)$ by using at most M additional tuples from base relations in D.

(b) VQSI is to decide whether a query Q can be rewritten to another query Q' using a set $\mathcal{V}$ of views, such that *for all datasets* D, $Q(D)$ can be computed by using Q', which accesses materialized views $\mathcal{V}(D)$ and at most M tuples in the data source D.

We provide complexity bounds for these problems, and sufficient conditions for queries to be incrementally scale-independent and scale-independent using views.

To the best of our knowledge, this work is the first effort to give a formal treatment of scale independence, a notion recently proposed and implemented [4–6]. Our results provide a comprehensive picture of complexity bounds for the problem, help us identify a bounded amount of data from a large dataset for query evaluation, and suggest what indices to build on our datasets. The lower bounds also justify the adoption of approximate query answering.

Related work. The notion of scale independence was proposed in [5], to guarantee that a bounded amount of work (key/value store operations) is required to execute all queries in an application, regardless of the size of the underlying data. An extension to SQL was developed in [4] to enforce scale independence, which allows users to specify bounds on the amount of data accessed and the size of intermediate results; when the data required exceeds the bounds, only top-k items are retrieved to meet the bounds. View selection and maintenance were studied in [6], such that a bounded amount of work is needed to answer queries by query rewriting using views and materialized (precomputed) views.

The goal of this work is to give a precise notion of scale independence and study its properties. We identify problems fundamental to scale independence, provide matching complexity bounds, propose access schemas to formulate data access via indexing and constraints, and give sufficient conditions for scale independence (incrementally, or using views). The results tell us what is doable and what is not. To the best of our knowledge, no prior work has studied these.

Related to our notion of access schemas is the notion of access patterns. Access patterns require that a relation can only be accessed by providing certain combinations of attribute values. Query processing under limited access patterns has been extensively studied, *e.g.,* [7, 9, 22, 24]. In contrast to the prior work, we use access schemas to combine indexing and the amount of data retrieved, and embed cardinality constraints in an access schema. Our goal is to provide a sufficient condition for identifying what queries are scale-independent with indices and constraints, rather than to study the complexity or executable plans for answering queries under access patterns [7,9,22,24].

There has been a host of work on incremental query answering (surveyed in [15]) and query rewriting using views (surveyed in [16,19]). The prior work has mostly focused on improving performance by making maximum use of precomputed query answers or views. In contrast, incremental scale independence and scale independence using views aim to *access a minimum amount of data* in data sources, to cope with the sheer volume of big data. There has also been prior work on bounded incremental computation [28], self-maintainable views [27], queries independent of updates [21] and view complements [25], which also access limited source data or no source data at all. We will clarify the difference between those previous works and ours in Sections 5 and 6.

Related to problem QDSI is the relatively complete database problem (RCDP) studied in [12]. Given a query Q, a database D, master data D_m, a set Σ of containment constraints on D and D_m, RCDP is to decide whether D has complete information to answer Q relative to D_m and Σ, *i.e.,* for all extensions D' of D, if D' and D_m satisfy Σ, then $Q(D) = Q(D')$. In contrast, QDSI is to decide whether there exists a $D_Q \subseteq D$ such that $Q(D) = Q(D_Q)$ and $|D_Q|$ is below a bound M. The two problems are quite different, from complexity bounds to proofs. For instance, when Q is in CQ and constraints in Σ are expressed in CQ, RCDP is NEXPTIME-complete, while QDSI is Σ_3^p-complete.

There has also been recent work on querying big data, *e.g.,* on the communication complexity of parallel query evaluation [17, 18], the complexity of query processing in terms of MapReduce rounds [2,30], and the study of query classes that are tractable on big data [13]. In contrast, this work studies whether it is feasible to compute query answers in big data by accessing a small subset of the data, and if so, how to efficiently identify this subset.

Organization. Section 2 presents notations. Section 3 establishes the complexity bounds for QDSI and QSI, and Section 4 deals with conditions for scale independence under access schemas. Sections 5 and 6 investigate ΔQSI and VQSI, respectively. Conclusions are in Section 7.

2. PRELIMINARIES

A relational schema $\mathcal{R}$ consists of a collection of relation names $(R_1, \ldots, R_n)$, with each R_i having a fixed set of attributes. We assume a countably infinite set U from which elements populating databases are drawn. That is, an instance D of $\mathcal{R}$ associates with each $R \in \mathcal{R}$ having m attributes an m-ary relation R^D over U, *i.e.,* a subset of U^m. When there is no confusion, we omit the superscript D. The set of all elements of U present in relations in D is called the *active domain* of D and is denoted by $adom(D)$.

We shall use logical languages for expressing queries declaratively. The languages $\mathcal{L}$ used here are standard relational languages (see [1] for details). We list them now, together with their relational algebra equivalents.

- Conjunctive queries (CQ) are built up from relation atoms $R_i(\bar{x})$ (for $R_i \in \mathcal{R}$), and equality atoms $x = y$ or $x = c$ (for constant c), by closing them under conjunction $\wedge$ and existential quantifier $\exists$ (*i.e.,* the class SPJ of select-project-join queries);
- Unions of conjunctive queries (UCQ) are queries of the form $Q_1 \cup \cdots \cup Q_k$, where each Q_i is in CQ for $i \in [1, k]$ (equivalently, SPJU queries);
- First-order logic queries (FO) are built from atomic formulas by using $\wedge$, $\vee$, negation $\neg$, and quantifiers $\exists$ and $\forall$ (equivalently, the full relational algebra).

If $\bar{x}$ is the tuple of free variables of Q, we shall also write $Q(\bar{x})$. Given a query $Q(\bar{x})$ with $|\bar{x}| = m$ and a database D, the answer to Q in D, denoted by $Q(D)$, is the set of tuples $\{\bar{a} \in adom(D)^m \mid D \models Q(\bar{a})\}$.

Often we need to fix values for some free variables. For a query $Q(\bar{x}, \bar{y})$ with $|\bar{y}| = m$ and a tuple $\bar{a}$ of values for $\bar{x}$, $Q(\bar{a}, D)$ denotes $\{\bar{b} \in adom(D)^m \mid D \models Q(\bar{a}, \bar{b})\}$.

If Q is a sentence (*i.e.,* it has no free variables), we refer to it as a *Boolean query*; such a query returns true or false. To distinguish queries that have free variables, we shall call them *data selecting* queries; for such a query Q, the answer $Q(D)$ is a set of (nonempty) tuples.

Remark. All our complexity results for CQ also hold for UCQ. Hence, in what follows, we will only mention CQ and FO when reporting complexity bounds.

3. SCALE-INDEPENDENT QUERIES

The key idea behind scale independence is that we can find a small subset of a database D so that a query Q can be answered over that subset, rather than over the entire D. In this section we define the notion of scale independence formally, study its basic properties, and establish the complexity of problems associated with it.

Let $\mathcal{R}$ be a relational schema, D a database of this schema, Q a query in language $\mathcal{L}$, and M a non-negative integer. Let $|D|$ denote the size of D, measured as the total number of tuples in relations of D.

We say that Q is *scale-independent in D* w.r.t. M if there exists a subset $D_Q \subseteq D$ such that

- $|D_Q| \leq M$ and
- $Q(D_Q) = Q(D)$.

That is, to answer Q in D, we need only to fetch at most M tuples from D, *regardless of how big D is.*

We refer to D_Q as a *witness* for scale independence of Q in D *w.r.t.* M. We write $\mathsf{SQ}_{\mathcal{L}}(D, M)$ for the set of all $\mathcal{L}$ queries that are scale-independent in D *w.r.t.* M.

We say that Q over schema $\mathcal{R}$ is *scale-independent* w.r.t. M if Q is scale-independent in D *w.r.t.* M for *all databases* D of $\mathcal{R}$, and write $\mathsf{SQ}_{\mathcal{L},\mathcal{R}}(M)$ for the set of all $\mathcal{L}$ queries Q that are scale-independent *w.r.t.* M.

For instance, for $Q_1(\mathsf{p}, \mathsf{name})$ and D_1 given in Example 1.1, the query $Q_1(p_0, \mathsf{name})$ with a given person p_0 is in both $\mathsf{SQ}_{\mathcal{L}}(D_1, 10000)$ and $\mathsf{SQ}_{\mathcal{L},\mathcal{R}}(10000)$, under the constraints that limit 5000 friends per person and id is a key of person.

These two notions lead to two problems of determining scale independence, *i.e.,* whether there exists a witness at all, denoted by QDSI and QSI. They are stated as follows.

- Problem QDSI($\mathcal{L}$):
  - INPUT: A relational schema $\mathcal{R}$, an instance D of $\mathcal{R}$, a query $Q \in \mathcal{L}$ over $\mathcal{R}$, and $M \geq 0$.
  - QUESTION: Is Q in $\mathsf{SQ}_{\mathcal{L}}(D, M)$?
- Problem QSI($\mathcal{L}$):
  - INPUT: A schema $\mathcal{R}$, a query $Q \in \mathcal{L}$ over $\mathcal{R}$, and $M \geq 0$.
  - QUESTION: Is Q in $\mathsf{SQ}_{\mathcal{L},\mathcal{R}}(M)$?

Problem QDSI tests *query-database* scale independence. It is highly relevant in practice since one often wants to know whether a query is scale-independent for the database at hand. The need for this is particularly evident for *e.g.,* Facebook: it maintains a single dataset D for its social data (when D is updated, we only need to consider incremental scale independence). Problem QSI is "stronger": it tests *query* scale independence for *all instances* of a schema.

For problem QDSI($\mathcal{L}$) we also have two versions to study: *data complexity*, when schema and query are fixed, but database and M may vary; and *combined complexity*, when everything $(\mathcal{R}, Q, D, M)$ is a parameter.

We now study the complexity of these problems. *All the lower bounds of this paper also hold when schema $\mathcal{R}$ is fixed.* We also study the case when M is fixed too.

Query-database scale independence. We first deal with the problem QDSI in which both the query and the database are part of the input. We start with combined complexity. The first result is for data-selecting queries, and we show that the problem is necessarily in the polynomial hierarchy even for simple classes of queries, and it is in PSPACE for FO.

Theorem 3.1: For data selecting queries, the combined complexity of QDSI($\mathcal{L}$) is

- Σ_3^p-complete when $\mathcal{L}$ is CQ; and
- PSPACE-complete when $\mathcal{L}$ is FO. □

Proof sketch. (1) Upper bounds. We first consider a simpler *witness problem.* That problem asks, given Q, D, M and $D' \subseteq D$ with $|D'| \leq M$, whether $Q(D) = Q(D')$, *i.e.,* it checks whether a given D' witnesses scale independence. It can be verified that the witness problem is Π_2^p-complete for CQ and PSPACE-complete for FO. Observe that solving QDSI just adds an existential guess of D' on top of the witness problem, thus taking us to the third level of the polynomial hierarchy for CQ, and staying in PSPACE for FO.

(2) Lower bounds. QDSI(CQ) is verified by reduction from the $\exists^*\forall^*\exists^*$3CNF problem, which is known to be Σ_3^p-complete [29]. The latter problem is to decide, given a sentence $\varphi = \exists X \forall Y \exists Z\, \psi(X, Y, Z)$, whether φ is true, where $\psi(X, Y, Z)$ is an instance of 3SAT, *i.e.,* ψ is $C_1 \wedge \cdots \wedge C_r$, and each C_i is a disjunction of three literals (variables or negations of variables in X, Y or Z).

To show that QDSI(FO) is PSPACE-hard, we use reduction from Q3SAT, which is PSPACE-complete (cf. [26]). Given a sentence $\varphi = P_1 x_1 \ldots P_m x_m\, \psi(x_1, \ldots, x_m)$, Q3SAT is to decide whether φ is true, where P_i is either $\exists$ or $\forall$, and ψ is an instance of 3SAT. The reduction uses a Boolean FO query and a constant M. □

Boolean queries. For Boolean queries, QDSI becomes much simpler for CQ. Indeed, if $Q(D)$ is true, then $Q(D_Q)$ is true for some D_Q such that $|D_Q| \leq \|Q\|$. For a CQ Q, we measure $\|Q\|$ as the size of the tableau of Q. This follows from the standard homomorphism semantics of CQ (see [1]). For a UCQ $Q = Q_1 \cup \cdots \cup Q_k$, we define $\|Q\|$ to be $\max\{\|Q_i\| \mid i \in [1, k]\}$. In practice, typically $\|Q\| \ll M \ll |D|$.

Since the PSPACE lower bound of Theorem 3.1 was verified by using a Boolean FO query, in the case of FO there is no lowering of the complexity. Thus, we have:

Corollary 3.2: For Boolean queries Q, QDSI($\mathcal{L}$) is

- in constant time (if $\|Q\| \leq M$) when $\mathcal{L}$ is CQ; and
- PSPACE-complete when $\mathcal{L}$ is FO.

for the combined complexity. □

A similar analysis gives a bound for M when Q is a data-selecting CQ query. Since for each tuple $\bar{a}$ in $Q(D)$

Query languages	Data selecting		Boolean	
	combined (Th 3.1)	data (Th 3.3)	combined (Cor 3.2)	data (Th 3.3)
CQ, UCQ	Σ_3^p-complete	NP-complete	O(1)-time	O(1)-time
FO	PSPACE-complete	NP-complete	PSPACE-complete	NP-complete
	Special case: when M is a constant			
	combined (Prop 3.4)	data (Prop 3.4)	combined (Th 3.4)	data (Th 3.4)
CQ, UCQ	Π_2^p-complete	PTIME	O(1)-time	O(1)-time
FO	PSPACE-complete	NP-complete	PSPACE-complete	PTIME

Table 1: Complexity bounds for QDSI (O(1) cases hold when $\|Q\| \leq M$)

we need at most $\|Q\|$ tuples in D to witness it, for each $M \geq \min\{|D|, |Q(D)| \cdot \|Q\|\}$, we have $Q \in \mathsf{SQ}_{\mathcal{L}}(D, M)$.

Data complexity. Fixing query Q makes our lives easier. For data selecting queries, QDSI($\mathcal{L}$) is down to NP-complete for all the languages. This is because the data complexity of all the languages is in PTIME. For Boolean queries, the problem is easy for CQ, but remains NP-complete for full FO.

Theorem 3.3: The data complexity of QDSI($\mathcal{L}$) for data selecting queries is NP-complete for $\mathcal{L}$ ranging from CQ to FO. For Boolean queries, it is in O(1)-time for CQ (if $\|Q\| \leq M$) but NP-complete for FO. □

Proof sketch. (1) Upper bounds. It suffices to give an NP algorithm for checking whether $Q \in \mathsf{SQ}_{\mathcal{L}}(D, M)$ when Q is a fixed FO data-selecting query. Observe that the witness problem (see proof of Theorem 3.1) is in PTIME for FO when data complexity is concerned. Hence, the additional existential guess needed to solve QDSI brings us to NP. Boolean CQ queries inherit the O(1) bound from Corollary 3.2.

(2) Lower bounds. For both fixed data-selecting query Q in CQ and fixed Boolean Q in FO, we show that QDSI is NP-hard by reductions from the set covering problem (SCP), which is known to be NP-complete (cf. [26]). Given a finite set X, a family $F = \{C_1, \ldots, C_n\}$ of subsets of X, and a positive integer k, SCP is to decide whether there exist k subsets in F whose union is X. □

When M is fixed. When we have a fixed set of resources, the bound M is a constant. Fixing M simplifies the analysis of QDSI. The combined complexity drops one level in the polynomial hierarchy for CQ, but it remains intact for FO. Data complexity becomes tractable, even for data-selecting FO queries, since only fixed-size subsets need to be checked.

Proposition 3.4: When M is fixed, the combined complexity of QDSI($\mathcal{L}$) is

- Π_2^p-complete for data-selecting queries, and is in O(1)-time for Boolean queries if $\|Q\| \leq M$, for CQ;
- PSPACE-complete for both data-selecting queries and Boolean queries in FO.

The data complexity of QDSI($\mathcal{L}$) is the same as in Theorem 3.3 except that it becomes PTIME for FO. □

Proof sketch. (1) Upper bounds. When M is fixed, we give a Π_2^p algorithm to check whether Q is in $\mathsf{SQ}_{\mathcal{L}}(D, M)$ when Q is a data-selecting query in CQ, and a PTIME algorithm when Q is a fixed data-selecting FO query. More precisely, we have a Σ_2^p algorithm for the complement problem in which the guess of D' and the guess of a witness of $Q(D') \neq Q(D)$ are combined. The O(1) and PSPACE bounds are inherited from Corollary 3.2 and Theorem 3.1, respectively.

(2) Lower bounds. For data-selecting CQ, we show it is Π_2^p-hard by reduction from $\forall^*\exists^*$3CNF [29]. It is to decide, given a sentence $\varphi = \forall X \exists Y\, \psi(X, Y)$, whether φ is true, where $\psi(X, Y)$ is an instance of 3SAT (see the proof of Theorem 3.1 for 3SAT). For Boolean FO queries, the proof of Theorem 3.1 already verified the PSPACE-hardness by using $M = 3$. □

Table 1 summarizes the complexity results for QDSI.

Query scale independence, We now look at the problem QSI($\mathcal{L}$) that checks scale independence for *all* databases. For queries Q in CQ or UCQ, the answer is 'no' in the absence of constraints on databases, unless Q is trivial (*e.g.*, it returns a constant tuple over all databases). This is due to the monotonicity of queries: we can always add tuples to the database that generate new tuples in the answer if Q is non-trivial. For full FO, as expected, the problem is undecidable. Indeed, for $M = 0$, the problem asks whether Q or its negation is finitely valid (*i.e.*, true in every finite structure), which is undecidable (cf. [23]).

Proposition 3.5: The problem QSI is undecidable even for Boolean FO queries and every fixed M. In fact for a schema $\mathcal{R}$ and $M \geq 0$, the set $\mathsf{SQ}_{\mathsf{FO},\mathcal{R}}(M)$ is not even recursively enumerable. □

Note that $Q \in \mathsf{SQ}_{\mathcal{L}}(D, |D|)$ for every language $\mathcal{L}$ and every query Q: all this says is that Q can be answered on D itself. The question is whether the $|D|$ bound can be lowered, ideally to a constant. For general data-selecting queries this may not be doable over all databases, *e.g.*, when the queries need to look at the entire input such as those that simply return the input database. But what about Boolean queries?

We say that a Boolean query Q *does not use its input fully* if there is a function $f_Q : \mathbb{N} \to \mathbb{N}$ such that $f_Q(n) < n$ for all sufficiently large n and $Q \in \mathsf{SQ}_{\mathcal{L}}(D, f_Q(|D|))$ for every D. Otherwise a query fully uses its input.

Clearly every Boolean CQ does not use its input fully: it only needs a portion of it of the size $\|Q\|$. But when it comes to FO, this is not the case. Indeed, one can easily find Boolean FO queries that fully use their input.

Proposition 3.6: There are FO Boolean queries that fully use their input. □

The results above might look negative: testing scale independence is computationally hard in the presence of data (which may be of very large size), or undecidable when we want to check whether it works on all databases (or, worse yet, the answer is simply negative). Nonetheless, this is not an atypical situation in databases, and it simply tells us that we should look for meaningful restrictions on queries to achieve scale independence. This is what we do next.

4. QUERY ANSWERING WITH ACCESS SCHEMAS

The results of the previous section indicate that without additional knowledge about the class of databases on which queries are posed, it is hard to achieve scale independence and hard to test it. We now introduce additional restrictions that will allow us to define an expressive fragment of FO admitting scale independence.

The motivation for the type of restrictions we want to use comes from access methods used in practice, and it is already implicit in Example 1.1. There are three reasons why Q_1 can be answered fast. First, Facebook imposes a limit on the number of friends. Second, for each person id, we can retrieve his/her friends (as well as other information) quickly, due to the presence of an index. And third, the query used constant person id p_0.

Thus, to be able to state that some queries are scale-independent, we need information about *access to data*: both on the speed of access, and on the amount of data that can be retrieved. We formalize this in terms of a notion of access schemas. Then we show when the combination of the syntactic shape of queries, constants used in them, and access constraints guarantees scale independence.

Access schemas and scale independence. For a relational schema $\mathcal{R} = (R_1, \ldots, R_n)$, an *access schema* $\mathcal{A}$ over $\mathcal{R}$ is a set of tuples (R, X, N, T) where

- R is a relation name in $\mathcal{R}$,
- X is a set of attributes of R, and
- $N, T \in \mathbb{N}$.

A database D *conforms to the access schema* $\mathcal{A}$ if two conditions hold for each $(R, X, N, T) \in \mathcal{A}$:

- for each tuple of values $\bar{a}$ of attributes of X, the set $\sigma_{X=\bar{a}}(R)$ has at most N tuples; and
- $\sigma_{X=\bar{a}}(R)$ can be retrieved in time at most T.

That is, one has an index on X that allows efficient retrieval of tuples from the database, and in addition there is a bound N on the number of such tuples (in the simplest case, when X is a key, the bound is 1). Moreover, the N tuples can be retrieved in T time units by using the index.

In our Facebook example, we would have a tuple $(\mathsf{friend}, \mathsf{id}_1, 5000, T)$ for some value T in the access schema, indicating that if id_1 is provided, at most 5000 tuples with such an id exist in friend, and it takes time T to retrieve those. In addition, we would have a tuple $(\mathsf{person}, \mathsf{id}, 1, T')$, saying that id is a key for person with a known time T' for retrieving the tuple for a given id.

Given a relation schema $\mathcal{R}$, an access schema $\mathcal{A}$, and a query $Q(\bar{x}, \bar{y})$, we say that Q is *$\bar{x}$-scale-independent under $\mathcal{A}$* if for each database D that conforms to $\mathcal{A}$ and each tuple $\bar{a}$ of values for $\bar{x}$, the answer $Q(\bar{a}, D)$ can be found in time that depends only on $\mathcal{A}$ and Q, but not on D. In analogy to data complexity, when the query Q is fixed but the access schema $\mathcal{A}$ may vary, we say that Q is *efficiently* $\bar{x}$-scale-independent under $\mathcal{A}$ if the time to answer $Q(\bar{a}, D)$ is polynomial in $\mathcal{A}$.

Consider again the Facebook example:

$Q_1(\mathsf{p}, \mathsf{name}) = \exists \mathsf{id}\big(\mathsf{friend}(\mathsf{p}, \mathsf{id}) \wedge \mathsf{person}(\mathsf{id}, \mathsf{name}, \mathrm{NYC})\big)$.

Then, under the access schema given above, Q_1 is p-scale-independent: for each given person p_0, the answers to Q_1 can be found in time determined by the access schema alone.

Controllability and scale independence. It is undecidable whether a query is $\bar{x}$-scale-independent under access schema $\mathcal{A}$, even if $\mathcal{A}$ is empty. Even more, the set of scale-independent queries is not recursively enumerable, as we have seen in Proposition 3.5, which rules out the existence of an effective syntax for it.

However, the lack of effective syntactic characterizations of classes of queries is common in databases. It is typically overcome by finding good and practically relevant sufficient conditions that guarantee desired properties of queries.

This is exactly what we do now: we define a syntactic class of $\bar{x}$-controlled queries for a given access schema, where $\bar{x}$ is a subset of free variables of a query, and show that each $\bar{x}$-controlled query under $\mathcal{A}$ is efficiently $\bar{x}$-scale-independent under $\mathcal{A}$. That is, an $\bar{x}$-controlled query becomes scale-independent under $\mathcal{A}$ once we fix values $\bar{a}$ for $\bar{x}$.

We now inductively define the class of *$\bar{x}$-controlled* FO queries under an access schema $\mathcal{A}$. We also say that $Q(\bar{x})$ is *controlled* if it is $\bar{x}$-controlled, *i.e.*, controlled by providing values for all its free variables. The rules for $\bar{x}$-controlled formulae are as follows:

atoms: if (R, X, N, T) is in $\mathcal{A}$, then $R(\bar{y})$ is $\bar{x}$-controlled under $\mathcal{A}$, where $\bar{x}$ is the subtuple of $\bar{y}$ corresponding to attributes in X;

conditions: if $Q(\bar{x})$ is a Boolean combination of equalities among variables in $\bar{x}$, then Q is $\bar{x}$-controlled;

disjunction: if $Q_i(\bar{y})$ is $\bar{x}_i$-controlled under $\mathcal{A}$ for $i = 1, 2$, then $Q_1(\bar{y}) \vee Q_2(\bar{y})$ is $(\bar{x}_1 \cup \bar{x}_2)$-controlled;

conjunction: if $Q_i(\bar{x}_i, \bar{y}_i)$ is $\bar{x}_i$-controlled under $\mathcal{A}$ for $i = 1, 2$, then $Q_1 \wedge Q_2$ is controlled under $\mathcal{A}$ by both $\bar{x}_1 \cup (\bar{x}_2 - \bar{y}_1)$ and $\bar{x}_2 \cup (\bar{x}_1 - \bar{y}_2)$;

safe negation: If $Q(\bar{y})$ is $\bar{x}$-controlled under $\mathcal{A}$, and $Q'(\bar{z})$ with $\bar{z} \subseteq \bar{y}$ is controlled under $\mathcal{A}$, then $Q \wedge \neg Q'$ is $\bar{x}$-controlled under $\mathcal{A}$;

existential quantification: if $Q(\bar{y})$ is $\bar{x}$-controlled under $\mathcal{A}$ and $\bar{z}$ is a subtuple of $\bar{y} - \bar{x}$, then $\exists \bar{z}\, Q$ is $\bar{x}$-controlled under $\mathcal{A}$;

universal quantification: if $Q(\bar{x}, \bar{y})$ is $\bar{x}$-controlled under $\mathcal{A}$, and $Q'(\bar{z})$ with $\bar{z} \subseteq \bar{x} \cup \bar{y}$ is controlled under $\mathcal{A}$, then $\forall \bar{y}\, \big(Q(\bar{x}, \bar{y}) \rightarrow Q'(\bar{z})\big)$ is $\bar{x}$-controlled under $\mathcal{A}$;

expansion: if $Q(\bar{y})$ is $\bar{x}$-controlled under $\mathcal{A}$ and $\bar{x} \subseteq \bar{x}' \subseteq \bar{y}$, then Q is $\bar{x}'$-controlled under $\mathcal{A}$.

Remark. We use set-theoretic operations for tuples of free variables to avoid cumbersome notations, as the meaning of those is clear from the context: for instance, $\bar{x} \cup \bar{y}$ is the tuple of all the variables used in $\bar{x}$ and $\bar{y}$, while $\bar{x} - \bar{y}$ is the subtuple of $\bar{x}$ from which variables occurring on $\bar{y}$ are eliminated.

Example 4.1: For example, under the access schema shown earlier, the query $Q_1(\mathsf{p}, \mathsf{name})$ is p-controlled. Indeed, the access schema tells us that $\mathsf{friend}(\mathsf{p}, \mathsf{id})$ is p-controlled and $\mathsf{person}(\mathsf{id}, \mathsf{name}, \mathrm{NYC})$ is id-controlled, and hence their conjunction is p-controlled. After adding an existential quantifier over id, the whole Q_1 is still p-controlled.

As another example, consider query Q_3, which revises Q_2 of Example 1.1 to find all restaurants in NYC that are rated A and were visited in a given year by p_0's friends who lived in NYC. Relation $\mathsf{visit}(\mathsf{id}, \mathsf{rid})$ is extended by including attributes yy, mm, dd, indicating that person id visited restaurant rid on a given date. Then:

$$Q_3(\mathsf{rn},\mathsf{p},\mathsf{yy}) = \exists \mathsf{id},\mathsf{rid},\mathsf{pn},\mathsf{mm},\mathsf{dd}\big(\mathsf{friend}(\mathsf{p},\mathsf{id}) \wedge \mathsf{visit}(\mathsf{id},\mathsf{rid},\mathsf{yy},\mathsf{mm},\mathsf{dd}) \wedge \mathsf{person}(\mathsf{id},\mathsf{pn},\mathrm{NYC}) \wedge \mathsf{restr}(\mathsf{rid},\mathsf{rn},\mathrm{NYC},A)\big).$$

Under the same access schema $\mathcal{A}$ as before, one can derive that all base relations are only controlled by all their free variables, except for friend that is deduced by the atom rule also p-controlled, and person that is id-controlled. We have just seen that $\mathsf{friend}(\mathsf{p},\mathsf{id}) \wedge \mathsf{person}(\mathsf{id},\mathsf{pn},\mathrm{NYC})$ is p-controlled. Processing the remaining conjunctions in this way, one can see that this the subquery of Q_3 is $\{\mathsf{p},\mathsf{rid},\mathsf{yy},\mathsf{mm},\mathsf{dd},\mathsf{rn}\}$-controlled. After adding the existential quantification $\exists\mathsf{id},\mathsf{rid},\mathsf{pn},\mathsf{mm},\mathsf{dd}$, the corresponding rule tells us that Q_3 is not scale-independent. Indeed, the existential quantification "forgets" that one needs to specify values for rid, mm, dd as specified by the controlling attributes. We will see below how to enrich the access schema $\mathcal{A}$ with embedded constraints to make Q_3 scale-independent. □

We now state the main result that the syntactic condition of controllability indeed guarantees the semantic condition of scale independence.

Theorem 4.2: If an FO query Q is $\bar{x}$-controlled under an access schema $\mathcal{A}$, then it is efficiently $\bar{x}$-scale-independent under $\mathcal{A}$. □

Proof sketch. We show by induction on $Q(\bar{x},\bar{y})$ how to retrieve a set $D_Q(\bar{a}) \subseteq D$ on which $Q(\bar{a},\cdot)$ can be evaluated, *i.e.*, $Q(\bar{a},D) = Q(\bar{a},D_Q(\bar{a}))$, for a given set of values $\bar{a}$ for $\bar{x}$, and provide polynomial bounds for its size and query evaluation time. The base case is provided by the access schema. We now sketch the conjunction case; others are similar. Assume we have $Q_i(\bar{x}_i,\bar{y}_i)$ which are $\bar{x}_i$-controlled for $i=1,2$; also let $\bar{x}_2'$ stand for the subtuple of $\bar{x}_2$ consisting of variables that occur in $\bar{y}_1$, and $\bar{x}_2''$ for the remaining variables of $\bar{x}_2$, *i.e.*, $\bar{x}_2'' = \bar{x}_2 - \bar{y}_1$. Given values $\bar{a}_1$ and $\bar{a}_2''$ for $\bar{x}_1$ and $\bar{x}_2''$, proceed as follows. Find $D_{Q_1}(\bar{a}_1)$ by using, *e.g.*, indices. Since $Q(\bar{a}_1,D) = Q(\bar{a}_1,D_{Q_1}(\bar{a}_1))$, the number of tuples $\bar{b}$ in $Q(\bar{a}_1,D)$ is bounded too. For each such tuple $\bar{b}$, let $\bar{b}_2$ stand for the part of it corresponding to the variables in $\bar{x}_2$. Then for each tuple $(\bar{b}_2,\bar{a}_2'')$ we can find $Q_2(\bar{b}_2,\bar{a}_2'',D)$ effectively by constructing a subset $D_{Q_2}(\bar{b}_2,\bar{a}_2'')$ and evaluating the query on it; this shows that the whole conjunction (join) is scale-independent once $\bar{a}_1$ and $\bar{a}_2''$ are known. □

Intuitively, Theorem 4.2 suggests the following. First, guided by an access schema $\mathcal{A}$, we can build up indices on certain attributes of relations in an instance of schema $\mathcal{R}$. Second, capitalizing on the indices, for all instances D of $\mathcal{R}$, we can answer FO queries Q that are $\bar{x}$-controlled under $\mathcal{A}$ by retrieving a small subset $D_Q \subseteq D$, such that $Q(D) = Q(D_Q)$ and $|D_Q| \leq M$, where M can be derived from the N-values in $\mathcal{A}$. Furthermore, there exists an effective plan for identifying D_Q, which can be derived from $\mathcal{A}$ and an inductive analysis of the structure of Q. In particular, this confirms our intuition that for a fixed p_0, the query Q_1 in our example can be evaluated in a scale-independent way.

Even though the rules might look rather easy and perhaps limited in some cases (e.g., the universal quantification rule only guarantees controllability with all free variables), it is the *combination* of rules that lets us derive nontrivial controllability statements. For instance, the universal quantification rule can be used in conjunction with another query, and then it provides genuinely new information.

To give an example, assume that we have a schema with relations $R(A,B)$, $S(A,B,C)$, and $T(A,B,C)$, and suppose that (R,A,N,T) is in the access schema for some N and T. Now we are given a query

```
SELECT A, B FROM R
WHERE A=1 AND
  NOT EXISTS (SELECT * FROM S
       WHERE R.A=S.A AND R.B=S.B AND
         NOT EXISTS (SELECT * FROM T
           WHERE T.A=S.A AND T.B=S.B AND T.C=S.C))
```

What are the conditions on S and T that will make this query scale-independent? Using our rules we can quickly answer this. The query is equivalent to $R(x,y) \wedge (x=1) \wedge \forall z\,\big(S(x,y,z) \rightarrow T(x,y,z)\big)$. Applying the conjunction and universal quantification rules, we see that it suffices for S to be (A,B)-controlled, and T to be controlled by any set of attributes (in particular, (A,B,C)-controlled) for the whole query to be scale-independent. This suggests building an index on A,B for S and an arbitrary index for T.

Optimality of the rules. One may wonder whether the rules for controllability for FO queries are optimal, *i.e.*, can they be relaxed so that they provide us with a "tighter" notion of controllability in terms of the number of values needed to guarantee scale independence? The answer is negative. Indeed, the rules – for queries of that syntactic shape – are optimal. In general, each rule is a template that applies to many queries of the same shape. Each of those templates has many instances of the form: under an access schema $\mathcal{A}$, if $Q(\bar{x})$ is $\bar{x}_1$-controlled and $Q'(\bar{y})$ is $\bar{y}_1$-controlled, then some query $Q''(\bar{z})$, built from Q and Q', is controlled by tuples $\bar{z}_1,\ldots,\bar{z}_k$ (for some of them, Q' is not needed).

We say that such a rule is *optimal* if there exists an instance of it in which the query Q'' is not controlled by any subtuple $\bar{z}$ of a minimal tuple among the $\bar{z}_i$'s. That is, in full generality, we cannot achieve smaller controlling tuples. Then the following can be easily verified.

Proposition 4.3: Each of the rules for defining the classes of controlled queries is optimal. □

Complexity of controllability. As controllability, unlike scale independence, is a purely syntactic condition, one can expect it to be decidable. In fact we pinpoint the exact complexity of it. The conjunction rule above involves two possibilities, indicating that some guessing is needed while looking for tuples controlling a query. This intuition is confirmed by NP-completeness of two problems shown below. For the second one, we say that Q is *minimally* controlled by $\bar{x}$ if it is $\bar{x}$-controlled but not $\bar{x}'$-controlled for any subtuple $\bar{x}'$ of $\bar{x}$.

- Problem QCntl:
  - INPUT: An access schema $\mathcal{A}$, a number $K > 0$, an FO query $Q(\bar{y})$.
  - QUESTION: Is there $\bar{x}$ with $|\bar{x}| \leq K$ so that Q is $\bar{x}$-controlled?

- Problem $\mathsf{QCntl}_{\mathsf{min}}$:
  - INPUT: An access schema $\mathcal{A}$, an FO query $Q(\bar{y})$, a variable x.
  - QUESTION: Is Q minimally controlled by some $\bar{x}$ containing x?

Theorem 4.4: The problems QCntl and $\mathsf{QCntl}_{\mathsf{min}}$ are NP-complete. They remain NP-hard for CQ. □

Proof sketch. We use reductions from problems related to candidate keys and prime attributes, cf. [1]. □

Embedded controllability and query answering under constraints. So far we have looked at access schemas, which tell us that, given values of certain attributes, there is a bound on the set of tuples having those attribute values. But we often have cases when such constraints are *embedded*, *i.e.,* they do not apply to the whole set of attributes. For instance, consider a relation visit(id, restaurant, yy, dd, mm) indicating that a person id visited a restaurant on a given date. Then we can add to the access schema information stating that for every year yy, there is a limit on the number of retrieved months (mm) and days (dd) (namely 366), and those values can be efficiently found.

Another reason to consider such embedded statements is that they make it possible to incorporate constraints such as functional dependencies (FDs) into access schemas: an FD $X \to Y$ says that once X is fixed, we have just one possibility for the values of Y.

Formally, embedded constraints in an access schema are tuples $(R, X[Y], N, T)$ with $X \subseteq Y$ being sets of attributes of R, indicating that for a given tuple $\bar{a}$ of values of X, the result of $\pi_Y(\sigma_{X=\bar{a}}(R))$ has at most N tuples and can be found in time T. Note that previous statements (R, X, N, T) are just a special case when $Y = attr(R)$, the set of all attributes in R. An FD $X \to Y$ with a time guarantee T to retrieve values of Y for given values of X is just $(R, X[X \cup Y], 1, T)$ in the access schema.

We can then extend the rules of controllability to define what it means for a query $Q(\bar{z})$ to be $\bar{x}[\bar{y}]$-controlled (under $\mathcal{A}$) when $\bar{x} \subseteq \bar{y} \subseteq \bar{z}$. Most of the rules just mimic those for controllability except two that are similar to inference rules for FDs. Below we give two sample controllability rules (rules 1,2) and the two inference rules (rules 3,4).

1. if $(R, X[Y], N, T)$ is in $\mathcal{A}$, then $R(\bar{z})$ is $\bar{x}[\bar{y}]$-controlled, where $\bar{x}$ and $\bar{y}$ are subtuples of $\bar{z}$ corresponding to attributes in X and Y;
2. if $Q_i(\bar{x}_i, \bar{z}_i)$ is $\bar{x}_i[\bar{y}_i]$-controlled $i = 1, 2$, then $Q_1 \wedge Q_2$ is $(\bar{x}_1 \cup (\bar{x}_2 - \bar{y}_1))[\bar{x}_1\bar{x}_2\bar{y}_1\bar{y}_2]$-controlled (and likewise for the symmetric case);
3. if $Q(\bar{z})$ is $\bar{x}[\bar{y}]$-controlled and $\bar{x}' \subseteq \bar{z}$, then Q is $(\bar{x} \cup \bar{x}')[\bar{y} \cup \bar{x}']$-controlled;
4. $Q(\bar{z})$ is $\bar{x}[\bar{y}]$-controlled and $\bar{x}'[\bar{y}']$-controlled for $\bar{x}' \subseteq \bar{y}$, then Q is $\bar{x}[\bar{y} \cup \bar{y}']$-controlled.

Then one adapts the proof of Theorem 4.2 to show:

Proposition 4.5: If $Q(\bar{x}, \bar{y}, \bar{z})$ is $\bar{x}[\bar{x} \cup \bar{y}]$-controlled under $\mathcal{A}$, then $\exists \bar{z}\ Q(\bar{a}, \bar{y}, \bar{z})$ is efficiently scale-independent under $\mathcal{A}$ for each $\bar{a}$. □

By Proposition 4.5, we can process some queries scale-independently under constraints, as shown below.

Example 4.6: As we have seen in Example 4.1, query Q_3 is not scale-independent, even if p and yy are fixed. In contrast, below we show that Q_3 becomes scale-independent after adding two embedded statements to the access schema. One is (visit, yy[yy, dd, mm], 366, T), which simply says that a year has at most 366 days; and the other is an FD id, yy, dd, mm $\to$ rid, saying that on a given day, each person id dines out at most once, even in NYC (we assume the FD to be effective).

Given these two embedded statements, one can apply the rules to derive that subquery visit is (id, yy)-controlled. Together with the assumption that id forms an index for person and that restr is city-controlled, this shows that query Q_3 is (p, yy)-controlled. Thus, if we want to find, for instance, all A-rated NYC restaurants that were visited by a NYC friends of p_0 in 2013, we can pose the query $Q_3(\mathsf{rn}, p_0, 2013)$, which is now scale-independent. □

5. INCREMENTAL SCALE INDEPENDENCE

While some queries Q may not be in $\mathsf{SQ}_{\mathcal{L}}(D, M)$ for a database D, they may be incrementally scale-independent in D [6]. That is, we can compute $Q(D)$ *once* as precomputation, and then incrementally evaluate Q *on demand* in response to changes to D, by accessing at most M tuples from D. Incremental scale independence allows us to answer online queries efficiently, by making maximum use of previous computation.

In this section, we first formally specify incremental scale independence, and then establish its complexity. Finally, we identify sufficient conditions for a query to be scale-independent for incremental evaluation.

Incremental scale independence. We consider updates $\mathbf{\Delta} D = (\Delta D, \nabla D)$ to D that consist of a list of tuples ΔD to be inserted into D and a list ∇D of tuples to be deleted. It is required that ∇D be contained in D and ΔD be disjoint from D; in particular, $\Delta D \cap \nabla D = \emptyset$. We write $D \oplus \mathbf{\Delta} D$ to denote the database obtained by applying $\mathbf{\Delta} D$ to D, *i.e.,* $(D - \nabla D) \cup \Delta D$ (where updates are applied relation-wise).

The setting of *incremental query answering* is as follows. We are given a query Q and its answer $Q(D)$ on a database D. Now, for an update $\mathbf{\Delta} D$, we want to compute $Q(D \oplus \mathbf{\Delta} D)$, *i.e.,* we want a pair of queries $\mathbf{\Delta} Q = (\nabla Q, \Delta Q)$ that take $\mathbf{\Delta} D$ and D as inputs so that

$$Q(D \oplus \mathbf{\Delta} D) = Q(D) \oplus \mathbf{\Delta} Q(\mathbf{\Delta} D, D).$$

We use the notation $Q(D) \oplus \mathbf{\Delta} Q(\mathbf{\Delta} D, D)$ to denote $(Q(D) - \nabla Q(\mathbf{\Delta} D, D)) \cup \Delta Q(\mathbf{\Delta} D, D)$.

As shown in [14], for FO queries Q, we can effectively find ∇Q and ΔQ in FO so that $\nabla Q(\mathbf{\Delta} D, D) \subseteq Q(D)$ and $\Delta Q(\mathbf{\Delta} D, D)$ is disjoint from $Q(D)$. Typically such queries are found by propagating changes through relational algebra expressions [15]. Such queries can often be evaluated much faster than computing $Q(D \oplus \mathbf{\Delta} D)$ from scratch, if $\mathbf{\Delta} D$ is small compared to D, as found in practice [15].

To give an example, recall Q_2 and ΔD_2 from Example 1.1, where ΔD_2 inserts tuples into visit, denoted by Δvisit(id$_2$, rid). From Q_2 we derive ΔQ_2(rn, p) as:

$$\Delta Q_2(\mathsf{rn}, \mathsf{p}) = \exists \mathsf{id}_2, \mathsf{rid}\big(\mathsf{friend}(p_0, \mathsf{id}_2) \wedge \Delta\mathsf{visit}(\mathsf{id}_2, \mathsf{rid}) \wedge \mathsf{restr}(\mathsf{rid}, \mathsf{rn}, \mathrm{NYC}, A)\big).$$

Here ΔQ_2 finds tuples to be inserted into $Q_2(D_2)$, such that $Q_2(D_2 \oplus \Delta D_2) = Q_2(D_2) \cup \Delta Q_2(\Delta D_2, D_2)$.

We say that Q is *incrementally scale-independent in* D w.r.t. (M, k) *if for all updates* $\mathbf{\Delta} D$ to D with $|\mathbf{\Delta} D| \leq k$, there exists a subset $D_Q \subseteq D$ with $|D_Q| \leq M$ such that $Q(D \oplus \mathbf{\Delta}D) = Q(D) \oplus \mathbf{\Delta}Q(\mathbf{\Delta}D, D_Q)$. That is, to incrementally answer Q in D in response to $\mathbf{\Delta}D$, we need to access no more than M tuples from D, *independent of the size of the underlying* D. We consider updates $\mathbf{\Delta}D$ with a bounded number of tuples since in real life updates are typically frequent but *small*, very often consisting of single tuple insertions or deletions.

We write $\Delta\mathsf{SQ}_{\mathcal{L}}(D, M, k)$ for the set of all $\mathcal{L}$ queries that are incrementally scale-independent in D *w.r.t.* (M, k). For instance, Q_2 above is in $\Delta\mathsf{SQ}_{\mathcal{L}}(D_2, M, k)$ if $M \geq 3k$, when some constraints state that only updates allowed to D_2 are insertions $\Delta\mathsf{visit}(\mathsf{id}_2, \mathsf{rid})$.

We study the *incremental scale-independence problem*, denoted by $\Delta\mathsf{QSI}(\mathcal{L})$, which is stated as follows.

- PROBLEM: $\Delta\mathsf{QSI}(\mathcal{L})$.
  - INPUT: A schema $\mathcal{R}$, a query $Q \in \mathcal{L}$ over $\mathcal{R}$, an instance D of $\mathcal{R}$, and $M, k \geq 0$.
  - QUESTION: Is Q in $\Delta\mathsf{SQ}_{\mathcal{L}}(D, M, k)$?

Complexity. We next give the complexity of ΔQSI. For full FO, ΔQSI matches the bound of QDSI for scale-independent query answering, even in simple settings, for combined complexity, and moves one level up in the polynomial hierarchy for data complexity.

Theorem 5.1: When $\mathcal{L}$ is FO, $\Delta\mathsf{QSI}(\mathcal{L})$ is

- PSPACE-complete for combined complexity, even for Boolean queries, and even if M is fixed; and
- Π_2^p-complete for data complexity (when both queries Q and $\mathbf{\Delta}Q$ are fixed), and coNP-complete if in addition, M is fixed. □

Proof sketch. Since guessing is free in PSPACE, and since the combined complexity of FO is in PSPACE as well, the definition of incremental scale independence naturally translates into a PSPACE algorithm. For the PSPACE hardness, we use reduction from Q3SAT for Boolean FO by using a fixed M.

For the lower bounds for data complexity, we use reductions from the $\forall^*\exists^*$3CNF problem and the complement of 3SAT, when M is not fixed and fixed, respectively. □

We next look at the case of CQ. It turns out that we have rather high bounds.

Theorem 5.2: The complexity of $\Delta\mathsf{QSI}(\mathsf{CQ})$ is

- Π_4^p-complete, or Π_2^p-complete if M also is fixed, for combined complexity, assuming that the maintenance queries $\mathbf{\Delta}Q$ are CQ as well; and
- Π_2^p-complete, or coNP-complete when M is in addition fixed, for data complexity. □

Proof sketch. The upper bounds follow essentially from parsing the definitions of being incrementally scale-independent and using the tableau representation of a CQ, except the case for fixed M, which is more involved. For data complexity, the maintenance query is allowed to be in FO, which also has PTIME data complexity.

The lower bounds are verified by reductions from satisfiability problems: $\forall^*\exists^*\forall^*\exists^*$3CNF for Π_4^p, $\forall^*\exists^*$3CNF for Π_2^p, and the complement of 3SAT for coNP. The coding for the data complexity with variable M is more involved, to cope with various ΔD and ∇D. □

The condition that maintenance queries are in CQ is true for insertion-only updates; in fact in this case the maintenance query can be computed in polynomial time [14]. An example of arbitrary updates admitting CQ maintenance query is when Q is key-preserving [8], if the projection attributes of Q include a key of each occurrence of base relations that are involved in Q.

Under access schemas. We now look at incremental scale independence under access schemas. Given a relational schema $\mathcal{R}$, an access schema $\mathcal{A}$, and a query $Q(\bar{x}, \bar{y})$, we say that Q is *$\bar{x}$-incrementally scale-independent under $\mathcal{A}$* if for each tuple $\bar{a}$ of values for $\bar{x}$, and each update $\mathbf{\Delta}D$, the answer to maintenance queries $\mathbf{\Delta}Q(\bar{a}, \mathbf{\Delta}D, D)$ can be found in time that depends on Q, $\mathcal{A}$ and $\mathbf{\Delta}D$ only, but not on D. Note that $\mathbf{\Delta}Q$ has the same free variables $\bar{x}, \bar{y}$ as Q, but takes as its input both D and $\mathbf{\Delta}D$. Efficient incremental scale independence under $\mathcal{A}$ is defined along the same lines as its counterpart given in Section 4.

From results of Section 4, we immediately obtain:

Corollary 5.3: If queries $\mathbf{\Delta}Q(\bar{x}, \bar{y})$ are $\bar{x}$-controlled under an access schema $\mathcal{A}$ for a query Q in FO, then Q is efficiently incremental $\bar{x}$-scale-independent under $\mathcal{A}$. □

In the literature on view maintenance and incremental recomputation, queries $\mathbf{\Delta}Q$ are commonly derived for relational algebra queries. They are not queries that are written by the user, but rather automatically generated by the DBMS; hence it is better to produce them in their procedural version, to avoid an extra compilation stage [15]. We now show how to achieve incremental scale independence for relational algebra queries. As an intermediate step, we also show how to achieve scale independence for relational algebra.

The idea is as follows. The analog of a tuple $\bar{x}$ of variables in $\bar{x}$-controlled queries is now a set of attributes X of an expression E of relational algebra. We then produce results on scale independence when the X attributes are fixed, *i.e.*, on scale independence of queries $\sigma_{X=\bar{a}}(E)$. For each expression E we next introduce expressions E^{∇} and E^{Δ}, and, for an access schema $\mathcal{A}$, inductively generate the set $\mathsf{RA}_{\mathcal{A}}$ of pairs (E, X), where E is an expression, or an expression annotated with Δ or ∇, and X is a set of its attributes. These will tell us whether the expression is (incrementally) scale-independent for fixed values of attributes in X.

Formally, let $attr(E)$ be the set of attributes of the output of a relational algebra expression E. We assume that all selection conditions θ in σ_θ are conjunctions of equalities and inequalities. Then, for an access schema $\mathcal{A}$, the set $\mathsf{RA}_{\mathcal{A}}$ is defined inductively as follows:

Relational algebra rules:

- if $(R, X, N, T) \in \mathcal{A}$, then $(R, X) \in \mathsf{RA}_{\mathcal{A}}$;
- if $(E, X) \in \mathsf{RA}_{\mathcal{A}}$ and $X \subseteq Y$, then $(\pi_Y(E), X) \in \mathsf{RA}_{\mathcal{A}}$;
- if $(E, X) \in \mathsf{RA}_{\mathcal{A}}$ and θ is a condition, then $(\sigma_\theta(E), X - X') \in \mathsf{RA}_{\mathcal{A}}$, where X' is the set of attributes A for which θ implies that $A = a$;
- if $(E_1, X_1), (E_2, X_2) \in \mathsf{RA}_{\mathcal{A}}$ and $attr(E_1) = attr(E_2)$, then $(E_1 \cup E_2, X_1 \cup X_2) \in \mathsf{RA}_{\mathcal{A}}$;
- if $(E_1, X_1), (E_2, attr(E_2)) \in \mathsf{RA}_{\mathcal{A}}$ and $attr(E_1) = attr(E_2)$, then $(E_1 - E_2, X_1) \in \mathsf{RA}_{\mathcal{A}}$;

- if (E_1, X_1) and (E_2, X_2) are in $\mathsf{RA}_\mathcal{A}$, then $(E_1 \bowtie E_2, X_1 \cup (X_2 - attr(E_1)) \in \mathsf{RA}_\mathcal{A}$;
- if $(E, X) \in \mathsf{RA}_\mathcal{A}$ and $X \subseteq Y \subseteq attr(X)$, then $(E, Y) \in \mathsf{RA}_\mathcal{A}$.

We now show rules for expressions E^∇ and E^Δ. For this, we use queries for propagating changes through relational expressions, and apply relational algebra rules to them. We use maintenance queries from [14] since, unlike others proposed in the literature, those guarantee that $E^\nabla \subseteq E$ and $E^\Delta \cap E = \emptyset$. To give an example, consider the propagation expression $(E_1 - E_2)^\nabla = (E_1^\nabla - E_2) \cup (E_2^\Delta \cap E_1)$. If we know that E_1^∇ is controlled by a set X of attributes, and E_2 is controlled by any set of attributes (and thus by $attr(E_2)$), then $E_1^\nabla - E_2$ is controlled by X. Likewise, if E_2^Δ is controlled by Z and E_1 is controlled by anything (and thus by $attr(E_1)$), then $E_2^\nabla \cap E_1$ is controlled by Z, and $(E_1 - E_2)^\nabla$ by $X \cup Z$. Now we list the rules for E^∇ and E^Δ.

Decrement rules:

- if $R \in \mathcal{R}$, then $(R^\nabla, \emptyset) \in \mathsf{RA}_\mathcal{A}$;
- if (E^∇, X), (E, X) and (E^Δ, X) are in $\mathsf{RA}_\mathcal{A}$, and $X \subseteq Y$, then $((\pi_Y(E))^\nabla, X) \in \mathsf{RA}_\mathcal{A}$;
- if $(E^\nabla, X) \in \mathsf{RA}_\mathcal{A}$, then $((\sigma_\theta(E))^\nabla, X) \in \mathsf{RA}_\mathcal{A}$;
- if (E_i^∇, X_i), $(E_i, attr(E_i))$, and $(E_i^\Delta, attr(E_i))$ are all in $\mathsf{RA}_\mathcal{A}$ for $i = 1, 2$, then $((E_1 \cup E_2)^\nabla, X_1 \cup X_2) \in \mathsf{RA}_\mathcal{A}$;
- if (E_1^∇, X), (E_2^Δ, Z), and $(E_i, attr(E_i))$ are all in $\mathsf{RA}_\mathcal{A}$ for $i = 1, 2$, then $((E_1 - E_2)^\nabla, X \cup Z) \in \mathsf{RA}_\mathcal{A}$;
- if (E_i^∇, X_i) and (E_i, Y_i) are all in $\mathsf{RA}_\mathcal{A}$ for $i = 1, 2$, then $((E_1 \bowtie E_2)^\nabla, X_1 \cup X_2 \cup (Y_1 - attr(E_2)) \cup (Y_2 - attr(E_1)))$ is in $\mathsf{RA}_\mathcal{A}$.

Increment rules:

- if $R \in \mathcal{R}$, then $(R^\Delta, \emptyset) \in \mathsf{RA}_\mathcal{A}$;
- if (E^Δ, X) and (E, X) are in $\mathsf{RA}_\mathcal{A}$, and $X \subseteq Y$, then $((\pi_Y(E))^\Delta, X) \in \mathsf{RA}_\mathcal{A}$;
- if $(E^\Delta, X) \in \mathsf{RA}_\mathcal{A}$, then $((\sigma_\theta(E))^\Delta, X) \in \mathsf{RA}_\mathcal{A}$;
- if (E_i^∇, X_i) and $(E_i, attr(E_i))$ are all in $\mathsf{RA}_\mathcal{A}$ for $i = 1, 2$, then $((E_1 \cup E_2)^\Delta, X_1 \cup X_2) \in \mathsf{RA}_\mathcal{A}$;
- if (E_1^Δ, X_i), (E_i^∇, Z_i), and $(E_i, attr(E_i))$ are all in $\mathsf{RA}_\mathcal{A}$ for $i = 1, 2$, then $((E_1 - E_2)^\Delta, X_1 \cup Z_2) \in \mathsf{RA}_\mathcal{A}$;
- if (E_1^Δ, X_i), $(E_i^\nabla, attr(E_i))$, and (E_i, Y_i) are all in $\mathsf{RA}_\mathcal{A}$ for $i = 1, 2$, then $((E_1 \bowtie E_2)^\Delta, X_1 \cup X_2 \cup (Y_1 - attr(E_2)) \cup (Y_2 - attr(E_1))) \in \mathsf{RA}_\mathcal{A}$.

These rules tell us when relational algebra expressions are scale-independent, both in the usual way and with respect to incremental computation. We can also construct the set D_Q for maintenance queries, by applying the standard pushing selection optimizations through the expressions.

Theorem 5.4: Assume that E is a relational algebra expression, and let $\mathcal{A}$ be an access schema. Then

- if $(E, X) \in \mathsf{RA}_\mathcal{A}$, then $\sigma_{X=\bar{a}}(E)$ is scale-independent under $\mathcal{A}$; and
- if (E^Δ, X) and (E^∇, X) are in $\mathsf{RA}_\mathcal{A}$, then $\sigma_{X=\bar{a}}(E)$ is incrementally scale-independent under $\mathcal{A}$. □

Proof sketch. The first item is by induction on relational algebra expressions, similar to the proof of Theorem 4.2. For the second item, we use change propagation expressions for relational algebra queries given in [14], and analyze them to find controlling sets of attributes. □

Leveraging the special shape of maintenance queries, we have the following result for CQ. Let $\mathcal{A}(R)$ be an access schema obtained from $\mathcal{A}$ by adding $(R, \emptyset, 1, 1)$ stating that one can obtain the entire relation R in constant time. Note that it is *easier* to answer queries scale independently under $\mathcal{A}(R)$ than under $\mathcal{A}$ alone.

Proposition 5.5: Let $Q(\bar{x}, \bar{y})$ be a CQ, and $\mathcal{A}$ an access schema. (1) If Q is $\bar{x}$-scale-independent under $\mathcal{A}(R)$, then Q is incrementally $\bar{x}$-scale-independent under $\mathcal{A}$ when updates are insertions into relation R. (2) If it is also derivable by $\mathsf{RA}_\mathcal{A}$ rules that Q is controlled by all of its attributes, then Q is incrementally $\bar{x}$-scale-independent under $\mathcal{A}$ for arbitrary updates on R. □

Example 5.6: Recall query Q_2 from Example 1.1 (also used earlier in this section). Query Q_2 was not p-controllable, but when $(\mathsf{visit}, \emptyset, 1, 1)$ is added to the access schema, ΔQ_2 becomes p-controllable, and therefore, $\Delta Q_2(\mathsf{rn}, p_0)$ can be found scale independently for a fixed p_0. □

Connections with view maintenance. We conclude with a few remarks relating our notions here with several problems from incremental view maintenance.

One is the problem of self-maintainability. A query Q is *self-maintainable* if there exists a set $\mathcal{V}$ of views such that given updates $\mathbf{\Delta} D$ to D, both $Q(D \oplus \mathbf{\Delta} D)$ and $\mathcal{V}(D \oplus \mathbf{\Delta} D)$ can be computed from $Q(D)$, $\mathcal{V}(D)$ and $\mathbf{\Delta} D$, without accessing the underlying database D [27]. This notion is stronger than incremental scale independence, but only in the presence of views that need to be maintained themselves.

Even stronger than self-maintenance is the notion of *queries independent of updates* [21]: *i.e.*, whether for all databases D and $\mathbf{\Delta} D$, we have $Q(D) = Q(D \oplus \mathbf{\Delta} D)$. In fact, [21] looks at more complex updates generated by other queries. This implies incremental scale independence even with $M = 0$, but is much more restrictive.

Finally, to analyze incremental algorithms, [28] proposes to use $|\mathsf{CHANGED}| = |\mathbf{\Delta} D| + |\mathbf{\Delta} S|$, the size of the changes in the input and output. An incremental algorithm is said to be *bounded* if its cost can be expressed as a function of only $|\mathsf{CHANGED}|$, not of $|D|$. In contrast to $\Delta\mathsf{QSI}$, bounded incremental query answering concerns the size of $\mathbf{\Delta} Q(\mathbf{\Delta} D, D)$ rather than the number of tuples in D accessed. Nonetheless, if Q is in $\Delta\mathsf{SQ}_\mathcal{L}(D, M, k)$, the cost of computing $\mathbf{\Delta} Q(\mathbf{\Delta} D, D)$ is a function of $|\mathbf{\Delta} D|$ and M for all $\mathbf{\Delta} D$ with $|\mathbf{\Delta} D| \le k$.

6. SCALE INDEPENDENCE USING VIEWS

We may also approach a query Q that is not scale-independent by using views [6]. The idea is to maintain a set $\mathcal{V}(D)$ of views of a database D, and compute $Q(D)$ from $\mathcal{V}(D)$ and at most M additional tuples from D.

This section studies scale independence using views. We state the problem, provide its complexity, and give sufficient conditions for scale independence by using views.

Scale independence using views. Assume a set $\mathcal{V}$ of views defined over a schema $\mathcal{R}$, in a query language $\mathcal{L}$. Consider an $\mathcal{L}$ query Q. Let Q' be a query over $\mathcal{R}$ expanded with relations that hold the views from $\mathcal{V}$. Then Following [20], we say Q' is *a rewriting of* Q *using* $\mathcal{V}$ if $Q(D) = Q'(D, \mathcal{V}(\mathcal{D}))$ for every database D of $\mathcal{R}$, *i.e.*, $Q(D)$ can be computed by Q' and leveraging the materialized view extents $\mathcal{V}(D)$. We consider Q' that is in the same language $\mathcal{L}$, and is *polynomially bounded, i.e.*, its size is bounded by a polynomial in the size $|Q|$ of query and the size $|\mathcal{V}|$ of view definitions, since queries of exponential size are not much of practical use.

For instance, Example 1.1 gives a rewriting Q_2' of Q_2 using views V_1 and V_2.

A query Q is said to be *scale-independent* w.r.t. M *using* $\mathcal{V}$ if there exists a rewriting Q' of Q using $\mathcal{V}$ such that for all instances D of $\mathcal{R}$, there is a subset $D_Q \subseteq D$ with $|D_Q| \leq M$ satisfying $Q(D) = Q'(D_Q, \mathcal{V}(D))$. That is, for *all databases* D, we can compute $Q(D)$ by using materialized views $\mathcal{V}(D)$ and by accessing at most M additional tuples from in D.

We denote by $\mathsf{VSQ}_{\mathcal{L}}(\mathcal{V}, M)$ the set of $\mathcal{L}$ queries that are scale-independent *w.r.t.* M using $\mathcal{V}$.

We investigate the *scale-independence problem using views*, denoted by $\mathsf{VQSI}(\mathcal{L})$. It is stated as follows.

- PROBLEM: $\mathsf{VQSI}(\mathcal{L})$.
  - INPUT: A schema $\mathcal{R}$, a query $Q \in \mathcal{L}$, a set of $\mathcal{V}$ of $\mathcal{L}$-definable views over $\mathcal{R}$, and $M \geq 0$.
  - QUESTION: Is Q in $\mathsf{VSQ}_{\mathcal{L}}(\mathcal{V}, M)$?

In contrast to QDSI and ΔQSI that focus on a given database D, VQSI is to decide whether a query Q is scale-independent in *all instances* D of $\mathcal{R}$ by using $\mathcal{V}$, as in the study of query rewriting using views [16, 19] (hence we do not distinguish the combined and data complexity of VQSI). As opposed to QSI, VQSI explores rewriting Q' of Q to achieve scale independence by using views, when Q is not scale-independent itself. Note that QSI is a special case of VQSI when $\mathcal{V}$ is empty.

Complexity bounds. As opposed to QDSI and ΔQSI, the problem VQSI is undecidable for FO. Moreover, the complexity bounds for VQSI are rather robust: they remain intact for both data selecting and Boolean queries; and fixing M does not simplify the analysis of VQSI.

Theorem 6.1: The problem $\mathsf{VQSI}(\mathcal{L})$ is

- NP-complete when $\mathcal{L}$ is CQ; and
- undecidable when $\mathcal{L}$ is FO,

for both data selecting and Boolean queries. The complexity remains the same when M is a constant. □

Proof sketch. We show that VQSI is NP-hard for CQ by reduction from the 3-colorability problem, which is NP-complete (cf. [26]). We verify the undecidability of VQSI for FO by reduction from the satisfiability of FO, whose undecidability can be proved by using FO queries over a single binary relation schema (cf. [23]). In light of this, we prove the lower bounds using fixed $\mathcal{R}$. Moreover, the reductions use Boolean queries and a constant M.

To show that VQSI is in NP for CQ, we need to characterize what CQ rewritings are scale-independent using views. We start with the following notations. A CQ rewriting $Q'(\bar{x})$ of a CQ $Q(\bar{x})$ using $\mathcal{V}$ is of the form:

$$Q'(\bar{x}) = \exists \bar{w} \ (\bigwedge_{i=1}^{p} R_i(\bar{x}_i) \wedge \bigwedge_{j=1}^{q} V_j(\bar{y}_j) \wedge \phi),$$

where R_j is a relation atom in $\mathcal{R}$, V_j is a view literal in $\mathcal{V}$, and ϕ is a conjunction of equality atoms. We write $Q' = \exists \bar{w} \ (Q_b' \wedge Q_v')$, where $Q_b' = \bigwedge_{i=1}^{p} R_i(\bar{x}_i)$ and $Q_v' = \bigwedge_{j=1}^{q} V_j(\bar{y}_j)$, referred to as the *base* and *view* part of Q', respectively. We eliminate ϕ by replacing a variable x with a constant c if $x = c$ can be derived from ϕ via the transitivity of its equality atoms, and enforce $x = y$ in ϕ by using the same variable.

Variables in $\bar{x}$ are called *distinguished.* We say that a variable x in $\bar{x}$ is *constrained* in Q' if either x has been instantiated to a constant c; or it is not "connected" to a base relation in Q_b' via a chain of joins, *i.e.*, there exists no set of atoms $\{S_i(\bar{v}_i) \mid 1 \leq i \leq l\}$ in Q' so that $S_1, \ldots, S_{l-1} \in \mathcal{V}$, $S_l \in \mathcal{R}$, $x \in \bar{v}_1$, and $\bar{v}_i \cap \bar{v}_{i+1} \neq \emptyset$ for all $i < l-1$. It is called *unconstrained* otherwise.

For instance, in the rewriting $Q_2'(\mathsf{p}, \mathsf{rn})$ from Example 1.1, the variable rn is unconstrained in Q_2' since it connects to base relation friend via joins.

We then show that a data selecting CQ $Q(\bar{x})$ is scale-independent *w.r.t.* M using CQ views $\mathcal{V}$ if and only if there exists a rewriting $Q'(\bar{x}) = \exists \bar{w} \ (Q_b' \wedge Q_v')$ of $Q(\bar{x})$ using $\mathcal{V}$ such that (a) all the distinguished variables in $\bar{x}$ are constrained in Q', and (b) $\|Q_b'\| \leq M$. For Boolean CQ, condition (b) alone suffices. The same characterization remains intact when Q, $\mathcal{V}$ and Q' are in UCQ.

Based on this, we develop an NP algorithm to check whether Q is in $\mathsf{VSQ}_{\mathcal{L}}(\mathcal{V}, M)$, for UCQ Q and $\mathcal{V}$. □

Conditions for scale independence using views. Following Section 4, we say that a query Q is *$\bar{x}$-scale-independent under an access schema $\mathcal{A}$ using* $\mathcal{V}$ if there exists a rewriting Q' of Q using $\mathcal{V}$, such that for each database D that conforms to $\mathcal{A}$ and each tuple $\bar{a}$ of values for $\bar{x}$, the answer $Q'(\bar{a}, D)$ can be found in time that depends only on $\mathcal{A}$, Q and $\mathcal{V}(D)$ only, but not on $|D|$.

Consider a rewriting Q' of a CQ $Q(\bar{x})$ using $\mathcal{V}$, where $Q'(\bar{x}) = \exists \bar{w} \ (Q_b' \wedge Q_v')$ (see the proof of Theorem 6.1). We say that $Q'(\bar{x})$ is *$\bar{y}$-controlled under $\mathcal{A}$ using* $\mathcal{V}$ if its base part Q_b' is $\bar{y}$-controlled under $\mathcal{A}$, following the rules for the controllability of CQ given in Section 4. Then the characterization given in the proof of Theorem 6.1 tells us that under $\mathcal{A}$, Q is $\bar{y}$-scale-independent using $\mathcal{V}$ if $Q'(\bar{x})$ is $\bar{y}$-controlled under $\mathcal{A}$ using $\mathcal{V}$ and $\bar{y}$ includes all the unconstrained distinguished variables in $\bar{x}$.

We also give a sufficient condition for an FO query Q to be scale independence using FO views. Given an FO rewriting Q' of Q, we define the *expansion* Q_e' of Q' to be the query that unfolds Q' by substituting the definition of view V for each occurrence of $V \in \mathcal{V}$ in Q'.

From Theorem 4.2 and the proof of Theorem 6.1, one can readily get the following corollary.

Corollary 6.2: (1) For a query Q and a set $\mathcal{V}$ of views in FO, if Q has a rewriting Q' whose expansion Q_e' is $\bar{x}$-controlled under an access schema $\mathcal{A}$, then Q is $\bar{x}$-scale-independent under $\mathcal{A}$ using $\mathcal{V}$. (2) For Q and $\mathcal{V}$ in CQ, if Q has a $\bar{y}$-controlled rewriting $Q'(\bar{x})$ under $\mathcal{A}$ using $\mathcal{V}$ and if $\bar{y}$ contains all unconstrained variables of Q' in $\bar{x}$, then Q is $\bar{y}$-scale-independent of under $\mathcal{A}$ using $\mathcal{V}$. □

Example 6.3: For instance, consider again the rewriting $Q_2'(\mathsf{p}, \mathsf{rn})$ using views $\mathcal{V} = \{V_1, V_2\}$ given in Example 1.1,

Under an access schema $\mathcal{A}$ that limits 5000 friends per person, its base part friend(p, id) is p-controlled using $\mathcal{V}$, and hence, so is Q'_2. As a result, Q_2 is p-scale-independent under $\mathcal{A}$ using $\mathcal{V}$. In contrast, under the same $\mathcal{A}$, Q_2 is not p-scale-independent *in the absence of* $\mathcal{V}$. □

Connections. Finally, we relate scale independence using views with prior work on the study of views.

A *complete rewriting* of Q using $\mathcal{V}$ is a rewriting of Q built up with only literals in $\mathcal{V}$ and equality predicates [20]. Obviously, if Q has a complete rewriting using $\mathcal{V}$, then Q is scale-independent using $\mathcal{V}$ with $M = 0$. That is, the former is a special case of the latter.

Given a set $\mathcal{V}$ of views over a schema $\mathcal{R}$, the study of view complements (*e.g.,* [25]) is to find a (minimal) set $\mathcal{V}_c$ of views such that for all instances D of $\mathcal{R}$, D can be reconstructed from $\mathcal{V}(D)$ and $\mathcal{V}_c(D)$. When both $\mathcal{V}$ and $\mathcal{V}_c$ are available, all queries Q is scale-independent using $\mathcal{V}$ and $\mathcal{V}_c$, with $M = 0$, without accessing D. However, it is not very practical to approach scale independence by using views and their complements: $\mathcal{V}(D)$ and $\mathcal{V}_c(D)$ are no smaller than D, and it is nontrivial to compute a minimal set $\mathcal{V}_c$ of view complements.

7. CONCLUSION

We have given a formal treatment of scale independence, incremental scale independence and scale independence using views. We have established complexity bounds of QDSI, QSI, ΔQSI and VQSI for CQ, UCQ and FO, for Boolean and data selecting queries, and for combined and data complexity. We have also provided sufficient conditions for FO queries to be scale-independent under (embedded) access schemas, specifying indices and constraints. The conditions also suggest how we can efficiently identify a small subset D_Q of a database D for a query Q such that $Q(D) = Q(D_Q)$.

In the future we want to study, when Q is not scale-independent in D *w.r.t.* M, what the best performance ratio is if we approximately compute $Q(D)$ by accessing at most M tuples from D. We want to strike a balance between the accuracy of the inexact query answers and the bound on the amount of data retrieved. Another question concerns the design of access schemas. In particular, we would like to see how to optimally design access schemas for a given query workload. Furthermore, an interesting extension is to consider query languages that support grouping and aggregation. We believe that sufficient conditions for scale independence can also be developed to that setting. Finally, we want to investigate how the techniques from [3] can be used for incremental scale-independent queries.

Acknowledgments. Fan and Libkin are supported in part by EPSRC EP/J015377/1, UK. Fan is also supported by 973 Programs 2012CB316200 and 2014CB340302, NSFC 61133002, Shenzhen Peacock Program 1105100030834361 and Guangdong Innovative Research Team Program 2011D005, China.

8. REFERENCES

[1] S. Abiteboul, R. Hull, and V. Vianu. *Foundations of Databases.* Addison-Wesley, 1995.

[2] F. N. Afrati and J. D. Ullman. Optimizing joins in a map-reduce environment. In *EDBT*, 2010.

[3] Y. Ahmad, O. Kennedy, C. Koch, and M. Nikolic. Dbtoaster: Higher-order delta processing for dynamic, frequently fresh views. *PVLDB*, 5(10):968–979, 2012.

[4] M. Armbrust, K. Curtis, T. Kraska, A. Fox, M. J. Franklin, and D. A. Patterson. PIQL: Success-tolerant query processing in the cloud. In *VLDB*, 2011.

[5] M. Armbrust, A. Fox, D. A. Patterson, N. Lanham, B. Trushkowsky, J. Trutna, and H. Oh. Scads: Scale-independent storage for social computing applications. In *CIDR*, 2009.

[6] M. Armbrust, E. Liang, T. Kraska, A. Fox, M. J. Franklin, and D. Patterson. Generalized scale independence through incremental precomputation. In *SIGMOD*, 2013.

[7] V. Bárány, M. Benedikt, and P. Bourhis. Access patterns and integrity constraints revisited. In *ICDT*, 2013.

[8] G. Cong, W. Fan, F. Geerts, J. Li, and J. Luo. On the complexity of view update analysis and its application to annotation propagation. *TKDE*, 24(3), 2012.

[9] A. Deutsch, B. Ludäscher, and A. Nash. Rewriting queries using views with access patterns under integrity constraints. *TCS*, 371(3), 2007.

[10] Facebook. *http://newsroom.fb.com.*

[11] Facebook. Introducing graph search. *https://en-gb.facebook.com/about/graphsearch*, 2013.

[12] W. Fan and F. Geerts. Relative information completeness. *TODS*, 35(4), 2010.

[13] W. Fan, F. Geerts, and F. Neven. Making queries tractable on big data with preprocessing. In *VLDB*, 2013.

[14] T. Griffin, L. Libkin, and H. Trickey. An improved algorithm for the incremental recomputation of active relational expressions. *TKDE*, 9(3):508–511, 1997.

[15] A. Gupta and I. Mumick. *Materialized Views.* MIT Press, 2000.

[16] A. Y. Halevy. Answering queries using views: A survey. *VLDB J.*, 10(4):270–294, 2001.

[17] J. M. Hellerstein. The declarative imperative: experiences and conjectures in distributed logic. *SIGMOD Record*, 39(1):5–19, 2010.

[18] P. Koutris and D. Suciu. Parallel evaluation of conjunctive queries. In *PODS*, 2011.

[19] M. Lenzerini. Data integration: A theoretical perspective. In *PODS*, 2002.

[20] A. Y. Levy, A. O. Mendelzon, Y. Sagiv, and D. Srivastava. Answering queries using views. In *PODS*, 1995.

[21] A. Y. Levy and Y. Sagiv. Queries independent of updates. In *VLDB*, 1993.

[22] C. Li. Computing complete answers to queries in the presence of limited access patterns. *VLDB J.*, 12(3), 2003.

[23] L. Libkin. *Elements of Finite Model Theory.* Springer, 2004.

[24] A. Nash and B. Ludäscher. Processing first-order queries under limited access patterns. In *PODS*, 2004.

[25] A. Nash, L. Segoufin, and V. Vianu. Views and queries: Determinacy and rewriting. *TODS*, 35(3), 2010.

[26] C. H. Papadimitriou. *Computational Complexity.* Addison-Wesley, 1994.

[27] D. Quass, A. Gupta, I. S. Mumick, and J. Widom. Making views self-maintainable for data warehousing. In *PDIS*, 1996.

[28] G. Ramalingam and T. Reps. On the computational complexity of dynamic graph problems. *TCS*, 158(1-2), 1996.

[29] L. J. Stockmeyer. The polynomial-time hierarchy. *TCS*, 3(1):1–22, 1976.

[30] Y. Tao, W. Lin, and X. Xiao. Minimal MapReduce algorithms. *SIGMOD*, 2013.

The ACM PODS Alberto O. Mendelzon Test-of-Time Award 2014

In 2007, the PODS Executive Committee decided to establish a Test-of-Time Award, named after the late Alberto O. Mendelzon, in recognition of his scientific legacy, and his service and dedication to the database community.

Mendelzon was an international leader in database theory, whose pioneering and fundamental work has inspired and influenced both database theoreticians and practitioners, and continues to be applied in a variety of advanced settings. He served the database community in many ways; in particular, he served as the General Chair of the PODS conference, and was instrumental in bringing together the PODS and SIGMOD conferences. He also was an outstanding educator, who guided the research of numerous doctoral students and postdoctoral fellows. The Award is to be awarded each year to a paper or a small number of papers published in the PODS proceedings ten years prior, that had the most impact (in terms of research, methodology, or transfer of practice) over the intervening decade. The decision was approved by SIGMOD and ACM. The funds for the Award were contributed by IBM Toronto.

The PODS Executive Chair has appointed us to serve as the Award Committee for 2014. After careful consideration and soliciting external assessments, we have decided to select the following two papers as the award winners for 2014:

Composing Schema Mappings: Second-Order Dependencies to the Rescue

Ronald Fagin, Phokion G. Kolaitis, Lucian Popa, Wang Chiew Tan

Foundations of Semantic Web Databases

Claudio Gutierrez, Carlos A. Hurtado, Alberto O. Mendelzon

The first paper proposed a general semantics for composing schema mappings. Schema mappings study how the data from one application is to be mapped to another with a different data format, typically specified by source-to-target tuple-generating dependencies (st-tgds). The paper proved that the composition of st-tgd mappings is not necessarily an st-tgd mapping. In light of this impossibility result, it introduced the language of second-order st-tgds (SO-tgds), and showed that the class of mappings defined by SO-tgds is closed under composition. Moreover, it showed that this class preserves good properties of st-tgds for data exchange. It also proved that every SO-tgd defines the composition of a finite number of st-tgd mappings. This definition of the composition operator for schema mappings has been adopted as a standard in the area of data exchange.

The second paper was the first paper in PODS about semantic Web databases, and was among the first efforts to study fundamental problems associated with RDF graphs pre-dating SPARQL. It provided clean, elegant and simple formalizations of the main concepts related to the use of blank nodes and RDFS vocabulary in RDF, formalized the inference and query answering problems for RDF in this general context, and established the computational complexity of these problems. This paper was instrumental in bringing traditional database techniques into semantic Web, showing how fundamental theoretical results in database theory can be carried over to an important domain. Both papers have received hundreds of citations, and have had an impact on subsequent research on data exchange and semantic Web databases, respectively. In particular, the Test-of-Time Award for the second paper is a posthumous recognition of the great work of the late Alberto O. Mendelzon.

Wenfei Fan
University of Edinburgh, UK

Floris Geerts
University of Antwerp, Belgium

Dan Suciu
University of Washington, USA

The Alberto O. Mendelzon Test-of-Time Award Committee for 2014

Weaker Forms of Monotonicity for Declarative Networking: a More Fine-grained Answer to the CALM-conjecture

Tom J. Ameloot*
Hasselt University & transnational University of Limburg
tom.ameloot@uhasselt.be

Bas Ketsman
Hasselt University & transnational University of Limburg
bas.ketsman@uhasselt.be

Frank Neven
Hasselt University & transnational University of Limburg
frank.neven@uhasselt.be

Daniel Zinn
LogicBlox, Inc
daniel.zinn@logicblox.com

ABSTRACT

The CALM-conjecture, first stated by Hellerstein [23] and proved in its revised form by Ameloot et al. [13] within the framework of relational transducer networks, asserts that a query has a coordination-free execution strategy if and only if the query is monotone. Zinn et al. [32] extended the framework of relational transducer networks to allow for specific data distribution strategies and showed that the non-monotone win-move query is coordination-free for domain-guided data distributions. In this paper, we complete the story by equating increasingly larger classes of coordination-free computations with increasingly weaker forms of monotonicity and make Datalog variants explicit that capture each of these classes. One such fragment is based on stratified Datalog where rules are required to be connected with the exception of the last stratum. In addition, we characterize coordination-freeness as those computations that do not require knowledge about *all* other nodes in the network, and therefore, can not globally coordinate. The results in this paper can be interpreted as a more fine-grained answer to the CALM-conjecture.

Categories and Subject Descriptors

H.2 [**Database Management**]: Languages; H.2 [**Database Management**]: Systems—*Distributed databases*; F.1 [**Computation by Abstract Devices**]: Models of Computation

*PhD Fellow of the Fund for Scientific Research, Flanders (FWO).

PODS'14, June 22–27, 2014, Snowbird, UT, USA.
Copyright 2014 ACM 978-1-4503-2375-8/14/06 ...$15.00.
http://dx.doi.org/10.1145/2594538.2594541.

Keywords

Distributed database, relational transducer, consistency, coordination, expressive power, cloud programming

1. INTRODUCTION

Declarative networking is an approach where distributed computations are modeled and programmed using declarative formalisms based on extensions of Datalog. On a logical level, programs (queries) are specified over a global schema and are computed by multiple computing nodes over which the input database is distributed. These nodes can perform local computations and communicate asynchronously with each other via messages. The model operates under the assumption that messages can never be lost but can be arbitrarily delayed. An inherent source of inefficiency in such systems are the global barriers raised by the need for synchronization in computing the result of queries.

This source of inefficiency inspired Hellerstein [11] to formulate the *CALM-principle* which suggests a link between logical monotonicity on the one hand and distributed consistency without the need for coordination on the other hand.[1] A crucial property of monotone programs is that derived facts must never be retracted when new data arrives. The latter implies a simple coordination-free execution strategy: every node sends all relevant data to every other node in the network and outputs new facts from the moment they can be derived. No coordination is needed and the output of all computing nodes is consistent. This observation motivated Hellerstein [23] to formulate the CALM-conjecture which, in its revised form[2], states

> *"A query has a coordination-free execution strategy iff the query is monotone."*

Ameloot, Neven, and Van den Bussche [13] formalized the conjecture in terms of relational transducer networks and provided a proof. Zinn, Green, and Ludäscher [32] subsequently showed that there is more to this story. In particular, they obtained that when computing nodes are increas-

[1]CALM stands for Consistency And Logical Monotonicity.
[2]The original conjecture replaced monotone by Datalog [13].

ingly more knowledgeable on how facts are distributed, increasingly more queries can be computed in a coordination-free manner. Zinn et al. [32] considered two extensions of the original transducer model introduced in [13]. In the first extension, here referred to as the *policy-aware* model, every computing node is aware of the facts that should be assigned to it and can consequently evaluate negation over schema relations. In the second extension, referred to as the *domain-guided* model, data distribution is restricted as follows: each possible domain value d is assigned to at least one node; and, when an input fact contains value d, this fact is given to all nodes that d is assigned to. It was shown in [32] that the coordination-free computations within the original, policy-aware, and domain-guided models form a strict hierarchy and that the non-monotone win-move query can be computed by a coordination-free domain-guided transducer network. *The central objective of this paper is to characterize these increasingly larger classes of coordination-free computations in terms of increasingly weaker forms of monotonicity thereby obtaining a more fine-grained answer to the CALM-conjecture.*

Towards this goal, we introduce the set of *domain-distinct-monotone* and the set of *domain-disjoint-monotone* queries, which we denote by $\mathcal{M}_{distinct}$ and $\mathcal{M}_{disjoint}$, respectively. Recall that a query is monotone if the output does not decrease (w.r.t. set inclusion) when new facts are added. The classes of domain-distinct-monotone and domain-disjoint-monotone queries then correspond to queries with non-decreasing output (again w.r.t. set inclusion) when only facts are added that contain *at least one* and *only* new domain elements, respectively. While $\mathcal{M}_{distinct}$ is a reformulation of the class of queries preserved under extensions (c.f., Section 3.2), $\mathcal{M}_{disjoint}$ appears to be a new class. We semantically characterize the coordination-free computations within the policy-aware and domain-guided model in terms of $\mathcal{M}_{distinct}$ and $\mathcal{M}_{disjoint}$, respectively, to obtain the following answer to the CALM-conjecture: for a query Q,

(*i*) Q can be computed by a coordination-free (original) transducer network iff Q is monotone; [13]

(*ii*) Q can be computed by a coordination-free policy-aware transducer network iff $Q \in \mathcal{M}_{distinct}$; and,

(*iii*) Q can be computed by a coordination-free domain-guided transducer network iff $Q \in \mathcal{M}_{disjoint}$.

It is tricky to formally define coordination-freeness because ideally it should forbid communication for coordination purposes but it should allow communication to exchange data values, for instance, to compute joins. We employ the formalization of coordination-freeness as introduced in [13]. While we do not claim this notion of coordination-freeness to be the only possible one, the results in this paper imply that it is a sensible one. In particular, we show that coordination-free computations can not globally coordinate across *all* computing nodes. This is made precise by proving that every coordination-free transducer is equivalent to one that has no knowledge of all other nodes in the network. We refer to Section 4.1.5 and Section 4.3 for a more thorough discussion.

In its original formulation [23], the CALM-conjecture did not refer to the general class of monotone queries, but rather to the monotone queries definable in Datalog. Therefore, it is interesting to investigate subclasses of Datalog with negation that remain within $\mathcal{M}_{distinct}$ and $\mathcal{M}_{disjoint}$, respectively. As mentioned before, $\mathcal{M}_{distinct}$ corresponds to the well-known class of queries which are preserved under extensions, denoted by $\mathcal{E}$. Afrati et al. [6] obtained that semi-positive datalog, denoted SP-Datalog, is included in $\mathcal{E}$, while Cabibbo [18] showed that SP-Datalog extended with value invention captures $\mathcal{E}$ and therefore $\mathcal{M}_{distinct}$. We show that *semi-connected stratified Datalog*, denoted semicon-Datalog$^{\neg}$, a fragment of stratified Datalog where only 'connected' rules are allowed (except for the last stratum) and which contains SP-Datalog, is included in $\mathcal{M}_{disjoint}$ and that this fragment extended with value invention captures precisely $\mathcal{M}_{disjoint}$. Furthermore, all queries definable in SP-Datalog and semicon-Datalog$^{\neg}$ are coordination-free within the policy-aware and domain-guided transducer network model, respectively.

The results of this paper are summarized in Figure 2.

Outline. In Section 2, we introduce the necessary definitions. In Section 3, we investigate the classes $\mathcal{M}_{distinct}$ and $\mathcal{M}_{disjoint}$. In Section 4, we semantically characterize coordination-free transducer networks in the policy-aware and domain-guided models. In Section 5, we consider Datalog fragments for $\mathcal{M}_{distinct}$ and $\mathcal{M}_{disjoint}$. We discuss related work in Section 6 and conclude in Section 7.

2. DEFINITIONS

Queries and instances. We assume an infinite set **dom** of data values. A *database schema* σ is a collection of relation names R where every R has arity $ar(R)$. We call $R(\bar{d})$ a *fact* when R is a relation name and $\bar{d}$ is a tuple in **dom**. We say that a fact $R(d_1, \ldots, d_k)$ is *over* a database schema σ if $R \in \sigma$ and $ar(R) = k$. A *(database) instance* I over σ is simply a finite set of facts over σ. We denote by $adom(I)$ the set of all values that occur in facts of I. When $I = \{\mathbf{f}\}$, we simply write $adom(\mathbf{f})$ rather than $adom(\{\mathbf{f}\})$. By $|I|$ we denote the number of facts in I. A *query* over a schema σ to a schema σ' is a generic mapping Q from instances over σ to instances over σ'. Genericity means that for every permutation π of **dom** and every instance I, $Q(\pi(I)) = \pi(Q(I))$. For a set of facts I and a schema σ, we write $I|_{\sigma}$ to denote the maximal subset of I that is over σ.

For convenience, we restrict our attention to schemas for which all relations have arity greater than zero. In particular, this means that queries, and therefore also Datalog programs, can not define nullary relations. We address how the addition of nullary facts changes our results in Section 7.

Datalog with negation. Let **var** be the universe of variables, disjoint from **dom**. An *atom* is of the form $R(u_1, \ldots, u_k)$ where R is a relation name and each $u_i \in$ **var**. We call R the *predicate*. A *literal* is an atom or a negated atom and is called *positive* in the former case and *negative* in the latter case.

We recall Datalog with negation [4], abbreviated Datalog$^{\neg}$. Formally, a Datalog$^{\neg}$ *rule* φ is a quadruple $(head_{\varphi}, pos_{\varphi}, neg_{\varphi}, ineq_{\varphi})$ where $head_{\varphi}$ is an atom; pos_{φ} and neg_{φ} are sets of atoms; $ineq_{\varphi}$ is a set of inequalities $(u \neq v)$ with $u, v \in$ **var**; and, the variables of φ all occur in pos_{φ}. The components $head_{\varphi}$, pos_{φ} and neg_{φ} are called respectively the *head*, the *positive body atoms* and the *negative body atoms*. We refer to $pos_{\varphi} \cup neg_{\varphi}$ as the *body atoms*. Note, neg_{φ}

contains just atoms, not negative literals. Every Datalog¬ rule φ must have a head, pos_φ must be non-empty and neg_φ may be empty. If $neg_\varphi = \emptyset$ then φ is called *positive*. Of course, a rule φ may be written in the conventional syntax. For instance, if $head_\varphi = T(u,v)$, $pos_\varphi = \{R(u,v)\}$, $neg_\varphi = \{S(v)\}$, and $ineq_\varphi = \{u \neq v\}$, with $u,v \in \mathbf{var}$, then we can write φ as $T(u,v) \leftarrow R(u,v), \neg S(v), u \neq v$. The set of variables of φ is denoted $vars(\varphi)$. A rule φ is said to be *over schema* σ if for each atom $R(u_1,\ldots,u_k) \in \{head_\varphi\} \cup pos_\varphi \cup neg_\varphi$, the arity of R in σ is k. A Datalog¬ *program* P *over* σ is a set of Datalog¬ rules over σ. We write $sch(P)$ to denote the (minimal) database schema that P is over. We define $idb(P) \subseteq sch(P)$ to be the database schema consisting of all relations in rule-heads of P. We abbreviate $edb(P) = sch(P) \setminus idb(P)$. As usual, the abbreviation "idb" stands for "intensional database schema" and "edb" stands for "extensional database schema" [4]. A *valuation for* a rule φ in P w.r.t. an instance I over $edb(P)$, is a total function $V : vars(\varphi) \to \mathbf{dom}$. The *application* of V to an atom $R(u_1,\ldots,u_k)$ of φ, denoted $V(R(u_1,\ldots,u_k))$, results in the fact $R(a_1,\ldots,a_k)$ where $a_i = V(u_i)$ for each $i \in \{1,\ldots,k\}$. This is naturally extended to a set of atoms, which results in a set of facts. The valuation V is said to be *satisfying for* φ on I if $V(pos_\varphi) \subseteq I$, $V(neg_\varphi) \cap I = \emptyset$, and $V(u) \neq V(v)$ for each $(u \neq v) \in ineq_\varphi$. If so, φ is said to *derive* the fact $V(head_\varphi)$.

Positive and semi-positive Datalog. A Datalog¬ program P is *positive* if all rules of P are positive. We say that P is *semi-positive* if for each rule $\varphi \in P$, the atoms of neg_φ are over $edb(P)$. We now give the semantics of a semi-positive Datalog¬ program P [4]. First, let T_P be the *immediate consequence operator* that maps each instance J over $sch(P)$ to the instance $J' = J \cup A$ where A is the set of facts derived by all possible satisfying valuations for the rules of P on J. Let I be an instance over $edb(P)$. Consider the infinite sequence I_0, I_1, I_2, etc, inductively defined as follows: $I_0 = I$ and $I_i = T_P(I_{i-1})$ for each $i \geq 1$. The *output of P on input I*, denoted $P(I)$, is defined as $\bigcup_j I_j$; this is the *minimal fixpoint* of the T_P operator.

We denote by Datalog, Datalog($\neq$), and SP-Datalog the the class of positive Datalog¬ programs without inequalities, the positive Datalog¬ programs, and the class of semi-positive Datalog¬ programs, respectively. Note that the last two classes may use inequalities.

Stratified semantics. We say that P is *syntactically stratifiable* if there is a function $\rho : sch(P) \to \{1,\ldots,|idb(P)|\}$ such that for each rule $\varphi \in P$, having some head predicate T, the following conditions are satisfied: (1) $\rho(R) \leq \rho(T)$ for each $R(\bar{u}) \in pos_\varphi \cap idb(P)$; and, (2) $\rho(R) < \rho(T)$ for each $R(\bar{u}) \in neg_\varphi \cap idb(P)$. For $R \in idb(P)$, we call $\rho(R)$ the *stratum number* of R. Intuitively, ρ partitions P into a sequence of semi-positive Datalog¬ programs $P_1,\ldots,P_k$ with $k \leq |idb(P)|$ such that for each $i = 1,\ldots,k$, the program P_i contains the rules of P whose head predicate has stratum number i. This sequence is called a *syntactic stratification* of P. We can now apply the *stratified semantics* to P: for an input I over $sch(P)$, we first compute the fixpoint $P_1(I)$, then the fixpoint $P_2(P_1(I))$, etc. The *output of P on input I*, denoted $P(I)$, is defined as $P_k(P_{k-1}(\ldots P_1(I)\ldots))$. It is well known that the output of P does not depend on the chosen syntactic stratification (if more than one exists). Not all Datalog¬ programs are syntactically stratifiable. By

$$
\begin{array}{ccccccc}
\mathcal{M} & & & & & & \\
\cup| & & & & & & \\
\mathcal{M}_{distinct} & \subsetneq & \mathcal{M}^{i+1}_{distinct} & \subsetneq & \mathcal{M}^{i}_{distinct} & \subsetneq & \mathcal{M}^{1}_{distinct} \\
\cup| & & \cup| & & \not\cup| & & \cup| \\
\mathcal{M}_{disjoint} & \subsetneq & \mathcal{M}^{i+1}_{disjoint} & \subsetneq & \mathcal{M}^{i}_{disjoint} & \subsetneq & \mathcal{M}^{1}_{disjoint} \\
 & & & & & & \cup| \\
 & & & & & & \mathcal{C}
\end{array}
$$

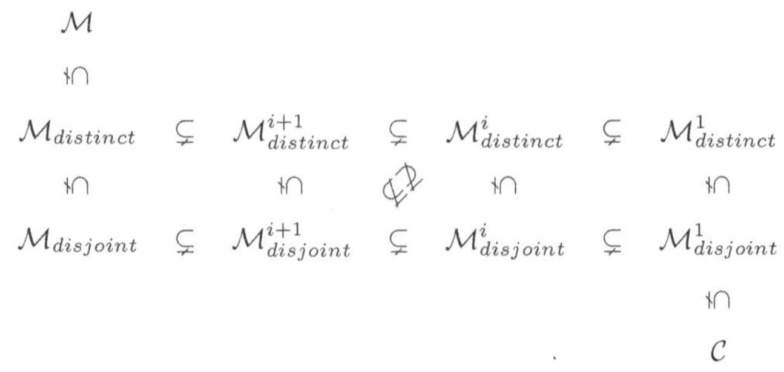

Figure 1: Monotonicity hierarchy

stratified Datalog we refer to all Datalog¬ programs which are syntactically stratifiable.

Since we only consider syntactically stratifiable programs in this paper, we denote from now on the class of stratified Datalog¬ programs simply by Datalog¬.

Computing Queries. For a query Q with input schema σ and output schema σ', and a stratifiable Datalog¬ program P, we say that P *computes* Q if $Q(I) = P(I)|_{\sigma'}$ for all instances I over σ.

We assume that for each Datalog¬ program some *idb*-relations are marked as the intended output. In our example Datalog¬ programs, we use the convention that relation 'O' denotes that output. The input relations are recognizable as the *edb*-relations.

In the sequel, we overload notation and denote both the fragment of Datalog¬ programs as well as the queries expressed by programs in that class with the same notation. For instance, we use SP-Datalog to denote both the class of semi-positive Datalog¬ programs as well as the queries which are expressible by a semi-positive Datalog¬ program.

In examples, we use a unary *idb*-relation $Adom$ that contains the active domain of the input. This predicate is computed as the union of the projections of all positions of all *edb*-relations. We omit the rules to compute $Adom$.

3. WEAKER FORMS OF MONOTONICITY

We introduce in Section 3.1 two weaker forms of monotonicity that will be used in Section 4 to characterize classes of coordination-free transducers. In Section 3.2, we relate these notions with the well-known classes of queries preserved under homomorphisms and extensions.

3.1 Domain distinct & disjoint monotonicity

We say that a fact $\mathbf{f}$ is *domain distinct* from instance I when $adom(\mathbf{f}) \setminus adom(I) \neq \emptyset$ (i.e., $\mathbf{f}$ should contain a new domain element not occurring in I); $\mathbf{f}$ is *domain disjoint* when $adom(\mathbf{f}) \cap adom(I) = \emptyset$. Furthermore, an instance J is domain distinct (resp., domain disjoint) from I, when every fact $\mathbf{f} \in J$ is domain distinct (resp., domain disjoint) from I.

We introduce two weaker forms of monotonicity by restricting the set of instances for which the monotonicity condition should hold:

Definition 1. Let Q be a query. Then,

- Q is *monotone* if $Q(I) \subseteq Q(I \cup J)$ for all database instances I and J;

- Q is *domain-distinct-monotone* if $Q(I) \subseteq Q(I \cup J)$ for all instances I and J for which J is domain distinct from I; and,
- Q is *domain-disjoint-monotone* if $Q(I) \subseteq Q(I \cup J)$ for all instances I and J for which J is domain disjoint from I.

We denote the class of monotone, domain-distinct-monotone, and domain-disjoint–monotone queries by $\mathcal{M}$, $\mathcal{M}_{distinct}$, and $\mathcal{M}_{disjoint}$, respectively. Next, we restrict the monotonicity definitions to sets J of bounded size. More precisely, for $i \geq 1$, we say that Q is i-monotone, i-domain-distinct-monotone, and i-domain-disjoint-monotone when in the corresponding definition J is restricted to a size of at most i. We denote the respective classes by $\mathcal{M}^i$, $\mathcal{M}^i_{distinct}$, and $\mathcal{M}^i_{disjoint}$. By definition, $\mathcal{M} \subseteq \mathcal{M}_{distinct} \subseteq \mathcal{M}_{disjoint}$ and $\mathcal{M}^i \subseteq \mathcal{M}^i_{distinct} \subseteq \mathcal{M}^i_{disjoint}$.

The following theorem provides some insight in how the above classes are related. Separating examples can all be expressed in fragments of Datalog$^\neg$. A more visual representation is provided in Figure 1. We denote the class of all computable queries by $\mathcal{C}$.

THEOREM 3.1. *For every $i, j \geq 1$ with $i < j$,*

1. $\mathcal{M} \subsetneq \mathcal{M}_{distinct} \subsetneq \mathcal{M}_{disjoint} \subsetneq \mathcal{C}$;
2. $\mathcal{M} = \mathcal{M}^i$;
3. $\mathcal{M}_{distinct} \subsetneq \mathcal{M}^{i+1}_{distinct} \subsetneq \mathcal{M}^i_{distinct}$;
4. $\mathcal{M}_{disjoint} \subsetneq \mathcal{M}^{i+1}_{disjoint} \subsetneq \mathcal{M}^i_{disjoint}$;
5. $\mathcal{M}^i_{distinct} \subsetneq \mathcal{M}^i_{disjoint}$;
6. $\mathcal{M}^j_{disjoint} \not\subseteq \mathcal{M}^i_{distinct}$; *and,*
7. $\mathcal{M}^i_{distinct} \not\subseteq \mathcal{M}^j_{disjoint}$.

PROOF. We focus on the inequalities and sketch the separating examples. All queries are over directed graphs that are defined over the binary edge relation E.

For (1), first, $\mathcal{M} \subsetneq \mathcal{M}_{distinct}$ follows from SP-Datalog $\subseteq \mathcal{M}_{distinct}$. Second, we show $Q_{\overline{TC}} \in \mathcal{M}_{disjoint} \setminus \mathcal{M}_{distinct}$, where $Q_{\overline{TC}}$ is the query that computes the complement of the transitive closure of the edge relation. To see $Q_{\overline{TC}} \in \mathcal{M}_{disjoint}$, for all instances I with a path missing from vertex a to vertex b, i.e., $(a, b) \in Q_{\overline{TC}}$, the addition of domain-disjoint subgraphs will not create this path. To see $Q_{\overline{TC}} \notin \mathcal{M}_{distinct}$, the addition of domain-distinct subgraphs can create a path $E(a, c), E(c, b)$, where c is a new vertex. Third, for $\mathcal{M}_{disjoint} \subsetneq \mathcal{C}$, take the query that outputs all triangles on condition that no two disjoint triangles exist.

For (2), by definition, $\mathcal{M}^{i+1} \subseteq \mathcal{M}^i$. We show that $\mathcal{M}^i \subseteq \mathcal{M}^{i+1}$. Let $Q \in \mathcal{M}^i$ and let I and J be arbitrary instances such that $|J| \leq i + 1$. Pick an arbitrary fact $\mathbf{f} \in J$ and set $J' = J \setminus \{\mathbf{f}\}$. By assumption, $Q(I) \subseteq Q(I \cup J')$ and $Q(I \cup J') \subseteq Q((I \cup J') \cup \{\mathbf{f}\})$. Hence, $Q(I) \subseteq Q(I \cup J)$.

For (3), it suffices to show that $\mathcal{M}^i_{distinct} \setminus \mathcal{M}^{i+1}_{distinct} \neq \emptyset$. Ignoring the direction of edges, let Q^k_{clique} be the query that outputs the edge relation when no clique of k vertices exists and the empty relation otherwise. We show $Q^{i+2}_{\text{clique}} \in \mathcal{M}^i_{distinct} \setminus \mathcal{M}^{i+1}_{distinct}$. Let I be an input not containing $(i+2)$-size cliques, upon which the output is thus nonempty. To expose the non-monotone behavior of Q^{i+2}_{clique}, we can try to extend any $(i+1)$-size cliques in I to $(i+2)$-size cliques by adding a domain-distinct instance J. For this to work, J needs to contain a star: one new value is the center and it points at old clique vertices of I, requiring $|J| \geq i+1$. Such instances J are not considered in the definition of $\mathcal{M}^i_{distinct}$, but they are considered in the definition of $\mathcal{M}^{i+1}_{distinct}$.

For (4), again, we only show that $\mathcal{M}^i_{disjoint} \setminus \mathcal{M}^{i+1}_{disjoint} \neq \emptyset$. Let Q^k_{star} be the query that outputs the edge relation when there is no star with k spokes in the input and the empty relation otherwise. Clearly, $Q^{i+1}_{\text{star}} \notin \mathcal{M}^{i+1}_{disjoint}$ as $i+1$ domain-disjoint edges suffice to create an entirely new star with $i+1$ spokes. On the other hand, if there is not already a star with $i+1$ spokes in the input, we can never create one by adding i domain-disjoint edges.

For (5), using similar arguments as for (3) above, we can see that $Q^{i+1}_{\text{clique}} \notin \mathcal{M}^i_{distinct}$ and $Q^{i+1}_{\text{clique}} \in \mathcal{M}^i_{disjoint}$.

For (6), we show $Q^{j+1}_{\text{star}} \in \mathcal{M}^j_{disjoint} \setminus \mathcal{M}^i_{distinct}$, where Q^{j+1}_{star} is the query that outputs the edge relation when there is no star with $j+1$ spokes in the input and the empty relation otherwise. To see $Q^{j+1}_{\text{star}} \in \mathcal{M}^j_{disjoint}$, if we may only add j domain-disjoint edges, we can not extend a star with less than $j+1$ spokes to a star with $j+1$ spokes, and we can also not create a completely new star with $j+1$ spokes. To see $Q^{j+1}_{\text{star}} \notin \mathcal{M}^i_{distinct}$, when the input already contains a star with j spokes, we can increase the number of spokes to $j+1$ by adding one additional edge containing the old central vertex and one new value.

Finally, for (7), we can only prove the stated result for a schema that grows with j. Therefore, let $R_1, \ldots, R_j$ be binary predicates and define $Q^j_{\text{duplicate}}$ as the query that gives as output the relation R_1 when the (global) intersection of all relations is empty, and the emptyset otherwise. We first argue $Q^j_{\text{duplicate}} \in \mathcal{M}^i_{distinct}$. Let I be an arbitrary instance where the intersection of all relations is empty. Instances J that are domain-distinct with respect to I can not replicate any existing tuples of I over all relations. Moreover, if $|J| \leq i$ with $i < j$ then J can not even replicate a completely new tuple over all relations. To see $Q^j_{\text{duplicate}} \notin \mathcal{M}^j_{disjoint}$, a domain-disjoint instance J with $|J| = j$ can replicate a new tuple over all relations. □

3.2 Correspondence with other classes

We relate the above classes to those defined in terms of preservation of properties. Let I and J be two instances over σ. A *homomorphism* from I to J is mapping h from $adom(I)$ to $adom(J)$ such that $R(\bar{d}) \in I$ implies $R(h(\bar{d})) \in J$ for every $R \in \sigma$ and $\bar{d} \in adom(I)^{ar(R)}$. We say that h is *injective* if $h(d) \neq h(d')$ whenever $d \neq d'$. An instance J is called an *induced subinstance* of I if $J = \{\mathbf{f} \in I \mid adom(\mathbf{f}) \subseteq adom(J)\}$.

Definition 2. Let Q be a query. Then,

- Q is *preserved under (injective) homomorphisms* if for all instances I and J, and for every (injective) homomorphism $h : adom(I) \to adom(J)$, $R(\bar{d}) \in Q(I)$ implies $R(h(\bar{d})) \in Q(J)$ for all facts $R(\bar{d})$.
- Q is *preserved under extensions* if for all instances I and J for which J is an induced subinstance of I, $R(\bar{d}) \in Q(J)$ implies $R(\bar{d}) \in Q(I)$ for all facts $R(\bar{d})$.

We denote by $\mathcal{H}$, $\mathcal{H}_{\text{inj}}$, and $\mathcal{E}$ the class of queries preserved under homomorphisms, injective homomorphisms, and extensions, respectively. Sometimes $\mathcal{H}$ is also referred to as the class of *strongly monotonic queries* (e.g., [6, 26]).

LEMMA 3.2. $\mathcal{H} \subsetneq \mathcal{H}_{inj} = \mathcal{M} \subsetneq \mathcal{E} = \mathcal{M}_{distinct}$.

PROOF. We only argue that $\mathcal{E} = \mathcal{M}_{distinct}$ as the rest is folklore (see, e.g., [6, 26, 29]). The equality follows immediately as J is an induced subinstance of I iff $I \setminus J$ is domain distinct from J. □

4. COORDINATION-FREENESS

A *relational transducer* is essentially a collection of queries that transforms a sequence of input facts to a sequence of output facts while maintaining a relational state [5, 20, 21]. In the distributed context, the functionality at each node of a network can be described via a relational transducer, giving rise to so-called relational transducer networks [13]. Subsequently, relational transducer networks have been extended in two ways to give nodes restricted access to *distribution policies* [32]. Such policies model deterministic input data distributions based on hashing. In this section, we review these two extensions, here referred to as *policy-aware* and *domain-guided* transducer networks, and characterize the corresponding classes of coordination-free queries. In particular, we show the following: the queries that are *coordination-free* in policy-aware transducer networks and domain-guided transducer networks correspond to the query classes $\mathcal{M}_{distinct}$ and $\mathcal{M}_{disjoint}$, respectively. It was shown in [13] that coordination-free queries in the original transducer networks correspond precisely to the set $\mathcal{M}$ of all monotone queries. The results in this section therefore provide a refinement of the CALM-conjecture in terms of weaker forms of monotonicity.

We formalize the transducer networks in Section 4.1 and then present the results in Section 4.2. We provide some additional discussion in Section 4.3.

4.1 Transducer models

We review the two extensions of Zinn et al. [32] to the original transducer network model [13]. Here, we refer to these extensions as *policy-aware* and *domain-guided* transducer networks, respectively.

4.1.1 Networks, data distribution, and policies

A *network* $\mathcal{N}$ is a nonempty finite set of values from **dom**, which we call *nodes*. Let σ be a database schema. A *distributed database instance* H over σ and $\mathcal{N}$ is a function that maps each $x \in \mathcal{N}$ to an instance over σ. A distributed database instance H over σ models a distribution with potential replication of data over the schema σ.

For a set X, let $\mathcal{P}^+(X) = \mathcal{P}(X) \setminus \{\emptyset\}$ denote the set of all non-empty subsets of X. We write *facts*(σ) to denote the set of all possible facts over σ, i.e., using all possible values from **dom**. A *distribution policy* $\boldsymbol{P}$ *for* σ *and* $\mathcal{N}$ is a total function from *facts*(σ) to $\mathcal{P}^+(\mathcal{N})$. Intuitively, $\boldsymbol{P}$ says how to distribute any instance I over σ to the nodes of $\mathcal{N}$, possibly with replication. Concretely, we define $dist_{\boldsymbol{P}}(I)$ to be the distributed database instance H over σ and $\mathcal{N}$ that satisfies $H(x) = \{\mathbf{f} \in I \mid x \in \boldsymbol{P}(\mathbf{f})\}$ for each $x \in \mathcal{N}$.

A *domain assignment* $\boldsymbol{\alpha}$ *for* $\mathcal{N}$ is a total function from **dom** to $\mathcal{P}^+(\mathcal{N})$. A distribution policy $\boldsymbol{P}$ for σ and $\mathcal{N}$ is called *domain-guided* if there exists a domain assignment $\boldsymbol{\alpha}$ for $\mathcal{N}$ such that for each $R(a_1, \ldots, a_k) \in$ *facts*(σ) we have $\boldsymbol{P}(R(a_1, \ldots, a_k)) = \bigcup_{i=1}^{k} \boldsymbol{\alpha}(a_i)$.[3] Intuitively, for each value $a \in$ **dom**, function $\boldsymbol{\alpha}$ says which nodes get input facts containing a.

EXAMPLE 4.1. *Suppose* **dom** *is the set* $\mathbb{N}$ *of natural numbers. Let* $\mathcal{N} = \{1, 2\}$ *be a two-node network and let the schema* σ *contain the single relation symbol* E *of arity* 2. *Consider the following distribution policy* $\boldsymbol{P}_1$ *for* σ *and* $\mathcal{N}$:

$$\boldsymbol{P}_1(\,\mathtt{E}(a,b)\,) = \begin{cases} \{1\} & \text{if } a \text{ is odd} \\ \{2\} & \text{otherwise} \end{cases}$$

for each $a, b \in \mathbb{N}$. *Note that* $\boldsymbol{P}_1$ *partitions any input* I *over* σ *based on its first attribute. If* $I = \{\mathtt{E}(1,3), \mathtt{E}(3,4), \mathtt{E}(4,6)\}$, *the distributed database instance* $dist_{\boldsymbol{P}_1}(I)$ *is*

$$\{1 \mapsto \{\mathtt{E}(1,3), \mathtt{E}(3,4)\}, 2 \mapsto \{\mathtt{E}(4,6)\}\}.$$

This input I *demonstrates that* $\boldsymbol{P}_1$ *is not a domain-guided policy: neither node is assigned all facts containing domain value* 4.

A domain-guided policy assigns domain values (rather than facts) to nodes in the network. Consider the domain assignment $\boldsymbol{\alpha}$ *for* $\mathcal{N}$ *that maps odd numbers to* $\{1\}$ *and even numbers to* $\{2\}$. *The corresponding domain-guided distribution policy* $\boldsymbol{P}_2$ *for* σ *and* $\mathcal{N}$ *allocates a fact* $\mathbf{f}$ *to node* 1 *if* any *of its two values is odd; to node* 2 *if* any *of its two values is even. For the specific input* I *from above, the instance* $dist_{\boldsymbol{P}_2}(I)$ *is*

$$\{1 \mapsto \{\mathtt{E}(1,3), \mathtt{E}(3,4)\}, 2 \mapsto \{\mathtt{E}(3,4), \mathtt{E}(4,6)\}\}.$$

Note that node identifiers can occur as data in relations. □

4.1.2 Policy-aware relational transducers

In the following, we write $R^{(k)}$ to denote a relation symbol R of arity k. A *(policy-aware) transducer schema* Υ is a tuple $(\Upsilon_{\text{in}}, \Upsilon_{\text{out}}, \Upsilon_{\text{msg}}, \Upsilon_{\text{mem}}, \Upsilon_{\text{sys}})$ of database schemas with disjoint relation names, with the additional restriction that

$$\Upsilon_{\text{sys}} = \{\mathtt{Id}^{(1)}, \mathtt{All}^{(1)}, \mathtt{MyAdom}^{(1)}\} \cup \{\mathtt{policy}_R^{(k)} \mid R^{(k)} \in \Upsilon_{\text{in}}\}.$$

These schemas are called respectively "input", "output", "message", "memory", and "system".

A *(policy-aware relational) transducer* Π over Υ is a quadruple $(Q_{\text{out}}, Q_{\text{ins}}, Q_{\text{del}}, Q_{\text{snd}})$ of queries having the input schema $\Upsilon_{\text{in}} \cup \Upsilon_{\text{out}} \cup \Upsilon_{\text{msg}} \cup \Upsilon_{\text{mem}} \cup \Upsilon_{\text{sys}}$ and such that

- query Q_{out} has target schema Υ_{out};
- queries Q_{ins} and Q_{del} both have target schema Υ_{mem};
- query Q_{snd} has target schema Υ_{msg}.

These queries form the mechanism by which a node on a network produces output, updates its memory (through insertions and deletions), and sends messages.

We note that the transducers in [13] do not have the relations MyAdom and $\mathtt{policy}_R$ (with R in Υ_{in}).

4.1.3 Policy-aware transducer networks

A *(policy-aware) transducer network* $\boldsymbol{\Pi}$ is a quadruple $(\mathcal{N}, \Upsilon, \Pi, \boldsymbol{P})$ where $\mathcal{N}$ is a network, Υ is a transducer schema, Π is a transducer over Υ, and $\boldsymbol{P}$ is a distribution policy for Υ_{in} and $\mathcal{N}$. We say that $\boldsymbol{\Pi}$ is *domain-guided* if the distribution policy $\boldsymbol{P}$ is domain-guided. Note that domain-guided transducer networks are a special kind of policy-aware transducer networks.

[3]Recall that we have assumed $k \geq 1$ throughout the paper.

Intuition. We will next give the semantics of $\mathbf{\Pi}$ on an input I over Υ_{in}. We start with the underlying intuition. Intuitively, we put a copy of transducer Π on each node of $\mathcal{N}$, and the policy $\boldsymbol{P}$ tells us how to initialize each node with a fragment of I. Then we choose an arbitrary node $x \in \mathcal{N}$ and make it "active": we execute the queries of Π on the union of the local input facts at x, the output and memory facts stored at x, any message facts (over Υ_{msg}) received by x, and also some facts over Υ_{sys}. The facts over Υ_{sys} consist of the following: relation `Id` provides the identifier of x (i.e., just 'x'); relation `All` provides the identifiers of all nodes in the network; relation `MyAdom` provides for convenience the active domain that x knows about (either from its local facts or from received messages); and, the relations $\texttt{policy}_R$ provide the set of facts over this active domain that x is responsible for (i.e., that are assigned to x) in policy $\boldsymbol{P}$.[4] Intuitively, by considering only $\texttt{policy}_R$-facts over the active domain at x, we provide "safe" access to the distribution policy, i.e., we prevent x from using values outside $adom(I) \cup \mathcal{N}$.[5] Next, the queries of Π update the output and memory at x, and generate new messages that are sent to the other nodes. Such an active moment of a node is called a *transition* of $\mathbf{\Pi}$. The semantics of $\mathbf{\Pi}$ is described by so-called *runs* which are infinite sequences of transitions.

EXAMPLE 4.2. *Recall* **dom**, $\mathcal{N}$, σ, *and* $\boldsymbol{P}_1$ *from Example 4.1. Consider a policy-aware transducer network* $\mathbf{\Pi} = (\mathcal{N}, \Upsilon, \Pi, \boldsymbol{P}_1)$ *with* $\Upsilon_{\text{in}} = \sigma$. *We leave* Υ_{out}, Υ_{msg}, *and* Υ_{mem} *unspecified. Let us focus on the node* 1. *On input* $I = \{\texttt{E}(1,3), \texttt{E}(3,4), \texttt{E}(4,6)\}$, *at least the following facts will be exposed to node* 1 *during each transition: the local input facts* $\texttt{E}(1,3)$ *and* $\texttt{E}(3,4)$; *the system facts* $\texttt{Id}(1)$, $\texttt{All}(1)$, $\texttt{All}(2)$, $\texttt{MyAdom}(a)$ *for each* $a \in \{1,2,3,4\}$, *and* $\texttt{policy}_{\texttt{E}}(a,b)$ *with* $a \in \{1,3\}$ *and* $b \in \{1,2,3,4\}$. *If node* 1 *would later receive (and store) the value* 6, *then also* $\texttt{MyAdom}(6)$ *will be exposed, and the* $\texttt{policy}_{\texttt{E}}(a,b)$*-facts with* $a \in \{1,3\}$ *and* $b = 6$. *Also, note that node* 1 *can in principle deduce that* $\texttt{E}(3,2)$ *is not part of* I *since* $\texttt{policy}_{\texttt{E}}(3,2)$ *is present at node* 1 *but not* $\texttt{E}(3,2)$. □

Formal semantics. Let $\mathbf{\Pi} = (\mathcal{N}, \Upsilon, \Pi, \boldsymbol{P})$ be a policy-aware transducer network. A *configuration* of $\mathbf{\Pi}$ is a pair $\rho = (s, b)$ of functions s and b such that:

- s maps each $x \in \mathcal{N}$ to a set of facts over $\Upsilon_{\text{out}} \cup \Upsilon_{\text{mem}}$;
- b maps each $x \in \mathcal{N}$ to a multiset of facts over Υ_{msg}.

We call s and b respectively the *state* and *(message) buffer*. Intuitively, s specifies for each node what output and memory facts it has locally available, and b specifies for each node what messages have been sent to it and that are not yet delivered. The reason for having multisets for the buffers, is that the same message can be sent multiple times to the same recipient and thus multiple copies can be floating around in the network simultaneously. The *start configuration* of $\mathbf{\Pi}$ is the unique configuration $\rho = (s, b)$ that satisfies $s(x) = \emptyset$ and $b(x) = \emptyset$ for each $x \in \mathcal{N}$.

[4]The relations $\texttt{policy}_R$ were previously called '$\texttt{local}_R$' [32]. Here, we have chosen a new predicate name to avoid confusion with local input facts at a node.

[5]This safety restriction also makes our model more realistic: in general, a node still needs to communicate with other nodes before it can draw global conclusions about the input or network.

A *transition of* $\mathbf{\Pi}$ *on an input* I *over* Υ_{in} is a quadruple (ρ_1, x, m, ρ_2) where $\rho_1 = (s_1, b_1)$ and $\rho_2 = (s_2, b_2)$ are configurations of $\mathbf{\Pi}$, $x \in \mathcal{N}$, m is a submultiset of $b_1(x)$, and, letting

$$
\begin{aligned}
H &= dist_{\boldsymbol{P}}(I),\\
M &= m \text{ collapsed to a set},\\
J &= H(x) \cup s_1(x) \cup M,\\
A &= \mathcal{N} \cup \bigcup_{\mathbf{f} \in J} adom(\mathbf{f}),\\
S &= \{\texttt{Id}(x)\} \cup \{\texttt{All}(y) \mid y \in \mathcal{N}\} \cup \{\texttt{MyAdom}(a) \mid a \in A\} \cup\\
&\quad \{\texttt{policy}_R(a_1, \ldots, a_k) \mid R^{(k)} \in \Upsilon_{\text{in}}, \{a_1, \ldots, a_k\} \subseteq A,\\
&\quad x \in \boldsymbol{P}(R(a_1, \ldots, a_k))\},\\
D &= J \cup S,
\end{aligned}
$$

for the state s_2 we have

$$
\begin{aligned}
s_2(x)|_{\Upsilon_{\text{out}}} &= s_1(x)|_{\Upsilon_{\text{out}}} \cup Q_{\text{out}}(D),\\
s_2(x)|_{\Upsilon_{\text{mem}}} &= \left[s_1(x)|_{\Upsilon_{\text{mem}}} \cup (Q_{\text{ins}}(D) \setminus Q_{\text{del}}(D))\right]\\
&\quad \setminus (Q_{\text{del}}(D) \setminus Q_{\text{ins}}(D)),\\
s_2(y) &= s_1(y) \text{ for each } y \in \mathcal{N} \setminus \{x\},
\end{aligned}
$$

and for the buffer b_2 we have (using multiset difference and union)

$$
\begin{aligned}
b_2(x) &= b_1(x) \setminus m,\\
b_2(y) &= b_1(y) \cup Q_{\text{snd}}(D) \text{ for each } y \in \mathcal{N} \setminus \{x\}.
\end{aligned}
$$

We call ρ_1 and ρ_2 respectively the *source* and *target* configuration of the transition and we refer to x as the active node. If $m = \emptyset$, then we call the transition a *heartbeat*.

For an input I over Υ_{in}, a *run* $\mathcal{R}$ *of* $\mathbf{\Pi}$ *on* I is an infinite sequence of transitions of $\mathbf{\Pi}$ on I, such that the start configuration of $\mathbf{\Pi}$ is used as the source configuration of the first transition, and the target configuration of each transition is the source configuration of the next transition. Note that runs represent nondeterminism: each transition can choose what node becomes active and what messages to deliver from the buffer of that node. We consider only *fair* runs. These are the runs that satisfy the following additional conditions: *(i)* each node is the active node in an infinite number of transitions; and, *(ii)* if a fact occurs infinitely often in the message buffer of a node then this fact is infinitely often delivered to that node. Intuitively, the last condition demands that no sent messages are infinitely delayed.

4.1.4 Computing queries

We are interested in transducers that produce the same facts over Υ_{out} regardless of the network, the distribution policy, and the order of transitions. These transducers are said to compute a query.

Formally, let Q be a query with input schema σ_1 and output schema σ_2. Further, let $\mathbf{\Pi} = (\mathcal{N}, \Upsilon, \Pi, \boldsymbol{P})$ be a policy-aware transducer network. We define the output of a run $\mathcal{R}$ of $\mathbf{\Pi}$, denoted $out(\mathcal{R})$, to be the union of all output facts jointly produced by the nodes of $\mathcal{N}$ during $\mathcal{R}$, i.e., all facts over Υ_{out}. Note that once a fact is added to Υ_{out}, it can never be retracted. We say that $\mathbf{\Pi}$ *computes* Q if *(i)* $\Upsilon_{\text{in}} = \sigma_1$ and $\Upsilon_{\text{out}} = \sigma_2$; and, *(ii)* for each input I over σ_1, every (fair) run $\mathcal{R}$ of $\mathbf{\Pi}$ on I satisfies $out(\mathcal{R}) = Q(I)$.

Now, we say that a policy-aware transducer Π over transducer schema Υ *(distributedly) computes* Q *(for all policies)* if for all networks $\mathcal{N}$ and all distribution policies $\boldsymbol{P}$ for Υ_{in} and $\mathcal{N}$, the policy-aware transducer network $(\mathcal{N}, \Upsilon, \Pi, \boldsymbol{P})$ computes Q. We say that Π *(distributedly) computes Q under domain-guidance* if for all networks $\mathcal{N}$ and all domain-guided policies $\boldsymbol{P}$ for Υ_{in} and $\mathcal{N}$, the transducer network $(\mathcal{N}, \Upsilon, \Pi, \boldsymbol{P})$ computes Q.

4.1.5 Coordination-freeness

We define coordination-freeness for policy-aware transducers similarly as for the original transducer model [13].

Definition 3. Let Π be a policy-aware transducer over a schema Υ. We say that Π is *coordination-free* if (1) Π distributedly computes a query Q, and (2) for all networks $\mathcal{N}$, for all inputs I for Q, there is a distribution policy $\boldsymbol{P}$ for Υ_{in} and $\mathcal{N}$ such that the policy-aware transducer network $(\mathcal{N}, \Upsilon, \Pi, \boldsymbol{P})$ has a run on input I in which $Q(I)$ is already computed in a prefix consisting of only heartbeat transitions.[6]

Similarly, we say that Π is *coordination-free under domain-guidance* if (1) Π distributedly computes a query Q under domain-guidance, and (2) if for all networks $\mathcal{N}$, for all inputs I for Q, there is a domain-guided policy $\boldsymbol{P}$ for $\mathcal{N}$, such that the transducer network $(\mathcal{N}, \Upsilon, \Pi, \boldsymbol{P})$ has a run on input I in which $Q(I)$ is already computed in a prefix consisting of only heartbeat transitions.

We write $\mathcal{F}_1$ to denote the set of queries distributedly computed by coordination-free policy-aware transducers. We write $\mathcal{F}_2$ to denote the set of queries distributedly computed by policy-aware transducers that are coordination-free under domain-guidance.

It is useful to reflect on what it means to be coordination-free. Of course, one could prohibit any form of communication but that would be too drastic and unworkable when data is distributed and communication is already needed for the simple purpose of exchanging data (for instance, to compute joins). Therefore, the present formalization tries to separate the 'data'-communication (that can never be eliminated in a distributed setting) from the 'coordination'-communication by requiring that there is some 'ideal' distribution on which the query can be computed without any communication.[7] The intuition is as follows: because on the ideal distribution there is no coordination (as communication is prohibited), and the transducer network has to correctly compute the query on *all* distributions, communication is only used to transfer data on non-ideal distributions and is not used to coordinate. While we do not claim our notion of coordination-freeness to be the only possible one, the results in Section 4.3 confirm that the just described intuition is not too far off. Indeed, it follows that coordination-freeness corresponds precisely to those computations that do not require the knowledge about *all* other nodes in the network, and hence, can not globally coordinate. Specifically, we show that when a node has no complete overview of *all* the nodes in the network, which can be achieved by removing the relation `All`, then every transducer is coordination-free.

[6]Technically, heartbeat transitions allow to send messages but not to read them. So, 'only heartbeat' transitions effectively means 'no communication'.

[7]We remark that in this ideal distribution it is not always sufficient to give the full input to all nodes (see, e.g., [13]). Furthermore, the network is not necessarily aware that the data is ideally distributed as it can not communicate.

More importantly, the converse holds true as well. That is, we show that every coordination-free transducer is equivalent to one that does not use the relation `All`.

4.2 Characterization

We characterize the classes $\mathcal{M}_{distinct}$ and $\mathcal{M}_{disjoint}$ by coordination-free transducers.

THEOREM 4.3. *$\mathcal{F}_1 = \mathcal{M}_{distinct}$.*

PROOF. We sketch the proof.

$\boxed{\mathcal{F}_1 \subseteq \mathcal{M}_{distinct}}$ Let Q be a query from σ to σ' distributedly computed by a coordination-free policy-aware transducer Π. Let I and J be two input instances for Q, such that J is domain-distinct from I. Let $\mathbf{f} \in Q(I)$. We show $\mathbf{f} \in Q(I \cup J)$. Because Π distributedly computes Q, transducer Π also computes Q on a network $\mathcal{N}$ with at least two nodes. By coordination-freeness, there is a distribution policy $\boldsymbol{P}_1$ for σ and $\mathcal{N}$ such that the transducer network $\mathbf{\Pi}_1 = (\mathcal{N}, \Upsilon, \Pi, \boldsymbol{P}_1)$ when given input I, has a run $\mathcal{R}_1$ in which $Q(I)$ is already computed in a prefix consisting of only heartbeat transitions. Let $x \in \mathcal{N}$ be a node that outputs $\mathbf{f}$ in this prefix. We can make x output $\mathbf{f}$ on input $I \cup J$, so that $\mathbf{f} \in Q(I \cup J)$.

To do this, fix an arbitrary node $y \in \mathcal{N} \setminus \{x\}$. Consider the following distribution policy $\boldsymbol{P}_2$ for σ and $\mathcal{N}$: $\boldsymbol{P}_2(\mathbf{g}) = \{y\}$ for all $\mathbf{g} \in J$, and $\boldsymbol{P}_2(\mathbf{g}) = \boldsymbol{P}_1(\mathbf{g})$ for all $\mathbf{g} \in \mathit{facts}(\sigma) \setminus J$. Denote $\mathbf{\Pi}_2 = (\mathcal{N}, \Upsilon, \Pi, \boldsymbol{P}_2)$. It can be verified that $\mathbf{\Pi}_2$ on input $I \cup J$ gives to x the same local input facts as $\mathbf{\Pi}_1$ on input I. So, when running $\mathbf{\Pi}_2$ on input $I \cup J$, if we initially do only heartbeats with active node x, the node x goes through the same state changes as in the heartbeat-prefix of $\mathcal{R}_1$. So after a while, say after k heartbeats, node x outputs $\mathbf{f}$. This finite prefix can be extended to a full fair run $\mathcal{R}_2$ of $\mathbf{\Pi}_2$ on input $I \cup J$, for which $\mathit{out}(\mathcal{R}_2) = Q(I \cup J)$ holds by assumption on Π. Hence, $\mathbf{f} \in Q(I \cup J)$.

$\boxed{\mathcal{M}_{distinct} \subseteq \mathcal{F}_1}$ Let $Q \in \mathcal{M}_{distinct}$. Let I be an input for Q that is distributed over a network $\mathcal{N}$. We say that a subset $C \subseteq \mathit{adom}(I) \cup \mathcal{N}$ is *complete* at a node $x \in \mathcal{N}$, when x knows for every fact $\mathbf{f} \in \mathit{facts}(\sigma)$ with $\mathit{adom}(\mathbf{f}) \subseteq C$ whether $\mathbf{f} \in I$ or $\mathbf{f} \notin I$. If C is indeed complete at x, node x will output $Q(I')$ where $I' = \{\mathbf{f} \in I \mid \mathit{adom}(\mathbf{f}) \subseteq C\}$. Note that $Q(I') \subseteq Q(I)$ by domain-distinct-monotonicity of Q. We will construct a policy-aware transducer that postpones executing Q at a node x until the system relation `MyAdom` is complete at x.

To implement this idea, the nodes broadcast their locally given input facts. Each node x stores every received input fact. This way, the system relation `MyAdom` grows at x. During each transition, x checks for each input relation $R^{(k)}$ and each k-tuple $(a_1, \ldots, a_k)$ over $\texttt{MyAdom}^k$ whether the fact $\texttt{policy}_R(a_1, \ldots, a_k)$ is shown to x. If so, then x is reponsible for the fact $R(a_1, \ldots, a_k)$ under the distribution policy. In that case, if $R(a_1, \ldots, a_k)$ is absent in the local input at x, node x can conclude that $R(a_1, \ldots, a_k)$ is actually globally absent from the entire input. Then x broadcasts the absence of this fact. These absences are also accumulated at all nodes. Now, consider a transition of node x, and let $I' \subseteq I$ denote the set of collected input facts at x so far. For each potential input fact $\mathbf{f}$ over `MyAdom`, node x checks whether $\mathbf{f} \in I'$ or that node x knows $\mathbf{f} \notin I$ (by means of the explicit absences). If this is so then `MyAdom` is complete at x, and x subsequently computes Q on I'.

We have already ensured that no wrong outputs are produced. To show that at least $Q(I)$ is produced, we note that at some point, each node x has received all available input facts and all absences of facts over $adom(I) \cup \mathcal{N}$. At that moment, x computes Q on I, causing at least $Q(I)$ to be output in each run.

Transducer Π is indeed coordination-free according to the formal definition: for all networks $\mathcal{N}$, and for all inputs I, the full output will be computed at some node x with only heartbeats when x is made responsible (under the distribution policy) for all facts over Υ_{in} made with the values $adom(I) \cup \mathcal{N}$; then x will immediately detect that relation MyAdom is complete. □

THEOREM 4.4. *$\mathcal{F}_2 = \mathcal{M}_{disjoint}$.*

PROOF. We sketch the proof. The proof of $\mathcal{F}_2 \subseteq \mathcal{M}_{disjoint}$ is similar to the proof of $\mathcal{F}_1 \subseteq \mathcal{M}_{distinct}$.

$\boxed{\mathcal{M}_{disjoint} \subseteq \mathcal{F}_2}$ Let $Q \in \mathcal{M}_{disjoint}$. Let I be an input for Q that is distributed over a network $\mathcal{N}$, by means of a domain-guided distribution policy. We call a subset $C \subseteq adom(I) \cup \mathcal{N}$ *complete* at a node x when x knows it has collected all facts $\mathbf{f} \in I$ for which $adom(\mathbf{f}) \cap C \neq \emptyset$. If C is indeed complete at x, node x will compute $Q(I')$ where $I' = \{\mathbf{f} \in I \mid adom(\mathbf{f}) \cap C \neq \emptyset\}$. Note that $Q(I') \subseteq Q(I)$ by domain-disjoint-monotonicity of Q. We will construct a policy-aware transducer that postpones executing Q at a node x until the system relation MyAdom is complete at x.

To implement this idea, the nodes broadcast the active domain of their local input fragment. These values are accumulated at each node. Note that when a node x has some value a in relation MyAdom, node x is responsible for a under the domain assignment if and only if $\texttt{policy}_R(a, \ldots, a)$ is shown to x for at least one input relation R. If x is indeed responsible for a then x is already locally given all facts of I containing a (because the distribution policy is domain-guided). Now, when x is not responsible for a, node x will send out the request (x, a). Any node y responsible for a under the domain assignment will then send all input facts containing a to x. When x has acknowledged all these facts to y, node y will send "OK(x, a)". Now, consider a transition of x, and let $I' \subseteq I$ denote the set of collected input facts at x so far. Node x checks for each value a in MyAdom whether x is responsible for a or that x has "OK" for a. If this is so, the protocol above implies that x has obtained all input facts containing values from MyAdom, i.e., that MyAdom is complete at x. Subsequently, x computes Q on I'.

We have already argued that no wrong outputs are produced. To see that at least $Q(I)$ is computed, we note that each node x eventually knows of the entire active domain (because the broadcasted domain will eventually arrive), and will thus at some point compute Q on the entire set of collected input facts.

The transducer is coordination-free according to the formal definition: for all networks $\mathcal{N}$, and all inputs I, the output will be computed with only heartbeats at some node x when x is made responsible (under the domain assignment) for all values $adom(I) \cup \mathcal{N}$; then x will immediately detect that relation MyAdom is complete. □

4.3 Discussion

We contrast the evaluation algorithms in the above proofs for $\mathcal{M}_{distinct}$ and $\mathcal{M}_{disjoint}$ with that for $\mathcal{M}$. It is important to realize that the formulated algorithms are naive in the sense that the whole database is sent to all nodes and every node computes the result of the query. It is the type of monotonicity that determines when a node can start producing output:

- $\mathcal{M}$: every node broadcasts all local input facts; output is generated for every newly received fact;
- $\mathcal{M}_{distinct}$: every node broadcasts all local input facts as well as non-facts (missing input facts that the node is responsible for); output is generated for every complete (cf. proof of Theorem 4.3) subset of facts; and,
- $\mathcal{M}_{disjoint}$: every node broadcasts the active domain of the local input facts; whenever a new domain element is received that the node is not responsible for, a coordination protocol is initiated with nodes responsible for this value; output is generated for every complete (cf. proof of Theorem 4.4) subset of facts.

While it might seem contradictory that the coordination-free evaluation of queries in $\mathcal{M}_{disjoint}$ requires the use of a coordination protocol, it is important to realize that this coordination is only determined by the way data is distributed and does not require *global* coordination between *all* nodes. Indeed, we show below that transducers that do not access the system relation All, containing the names of all the nodes in the network, are automatically coordination-free. Moreover, the classes of queries that are distributedly computed by policy-aware transducers without relation All still capture $\mathcal{M}_{distinct}$ and $\mathcal{M}_{disjoint}$. That is, in absence of relation All, we do not need the notion of coordination-freeness to characterize $\mathcal{M}_{distinct}$ and $\mathcal{M}_{disjoint}$.

Formally, to prevent usage of relation All, at a node x we modify the semantics of transitions from Section 4.1.3 as follows: we define the set A now as $A = \{x\} \cup \bigcup_{\mathbf{f} \in J} adom(\mathbf{f})$; and, the set S is defined as before, but now without the All-facts. For this resulting model, let $\mathcal{A}_1$ denote the set of queries distributedly computed by policy-aware transducers, and let $\mathcal{A}_2$ denote the set of queries distributedly computed by policy-aware transducers under domain-guidance.

THEOREM 4.5. *$\mathcal{A}_1 = \mathcal{M}_{distinct}$ and $\mathcal{A}_2 = \mathcal{M}_{disjoint}$*

PROOF. First, the transducers constructed for the proofs of directions $\mathcal{M}_{distinct} \subseteq \mathcal{F}_1$ and $\mathcal{M}_{disjoint} \subseteq \mathcal{F}_2$ can be used unmodified to respectively show that $\mathcal{M}_{distinct} \subseteq \mathcal{A}_1$ and $\mathcal{M}_{disjoint} \subseteq \mathcal{A}_2$, because they do not use All.

We sketch the proof of $\mathcal{A}_1 \subseteq \mathcal{M}_{distinct}$. Let Q be a query that is distributedly computed by a policy-aware transducer Π without All. By assumption, transducer Π also computes Q on a single-node network $\{x\}$. So, on input I, the single-node transducer network will produce $Q(I)$ with just heartbeats (no messages can be sent). Let J be an input instance for Q that is domain-distinct from I. To show $Q(I) \subseteq Q(I \cup J)$, we consider a two-node network $\{x, y\}$ on which we run Π, and consider the distribution policy that assigns J to just y and the other facts to x. Then x is still given precisely I when the two-node transducer network is given $I \cup J$ as input. Now, if we do only heartbeats at x, then x will behave the same as on the single-node network because it can not detect the difference with the two-node network in absence of relation All. So, x will produce $Q(I)$ after a finite number of heartbeats. This prefix can be extended to a full fair run of the two-node transducer network on input $I \cup J$.

The inclusion $\mathcal{A}_2 \subseteq \mathcal{M}_{disjoint}$ can be shown similarly, except that now we assign all values of $adom(J)$ to y and all other domain values to x. □

It is interesting to note what happens when transducers are not aware of the distribution policies, i.e., when we do not provide the $\texttt{policy}_R$-relations. In the resulting model, the set $\mathcal{F}_0$ of queries distributedly computed by coordination-free transducers is precisely the set $\mathcal{M}$ of monotone queries; and, relating to the above, the set $\mathcal{A}_0$ of queries distributedly computed by transducers without relation `All` is also $\mathcal{M}$ [13].

For completeness, we also mention the existence of so-called *oblivious* transducers in the original transducer model of Ameloot et al. [13]: these transducers may use neither relation `Id` nor relation `All`. The set of queries distributedly computed by oblivious transducers is again the set $\mathcal{M}$.

COROLLARY 4.6. $\mathcal{F}_0 = \mathcal{A}_0 = \mathcal{M}$.

5. DATALOG FRAGMENTS

5.1 Semi-connected Datalog$^\neg$

As mentioned in the introduction, the original formulation of the CALM-conjecture links coordination-free computation to Datalog. It is therefore interesting to investigate subclasses of Datalog with negation that remain within $\mathcal{M}_{distinct}$ and $\mathcal{M}_{disjoint}$. While SP-Datalog $\subseteq \mathcal{M}_{distinct}(= \mathcal{E})$ [6], it is not known whether SP-Datalog can be further extended while remaining within $\mathcal{E}$.

We next identify a fragment of Datalog$^\neg$ which is domain-disjoint-monotone. Let φ be a Datalog$^\neg$ rule. We define $graph^+(\varphi)$ as the graph where nodes are the variables in positive body atoms of φ, and there is an edge between two variables if they occur together in a positive body atom of φ. We say φ is *connected* if $graph^+(\varphi)$ is connected. We say that an SP-Datalog program is *connected* when all rules are connected.

Definition 4. Let P be a program in Datalog$^\neg$. Then P is a *connected stratified datalog program*, when there is a stratification for P such that all strata are connected SP-Datalog programs. We say that P is *semi-connected* when there is a stratification such that all strata except possibly the last one are connected SP-Datalog programs.

In the following, we denote the class of connected and semi-connected stratified Datalog$^\neg$ programs by con-Datalog$^\neg$ and semicon-Datalog$^\neg$, respectively. Then *(i)* SP-Datalog $\subsetneq$ semicon-Datalog$^\neg$, *(ii)* SP-Datalog $\not\subseteq$ con-Datalog$^\neg$, and *(iii)* con-Datalog$^\neg \subsetneq$ semicon-Datalog$^\neg$.

EXAMPLE 5.1. *Consider the following Datalog$^\neg$ program P_1*

$$\begin{aligned} T(x) &\leftarrow E(x,y), E(y,z), E(z,x), y \neq x, y \neq z, x \neq z \\ O(x) &\leftarrow \neg T(x), Adom(x) \end{aligned}$$

Then, P_1 is in con-Datalog$^\neg$, but $P_1 \notin \mathcal{M}_{distinct}$. Indeed, $P_1(\{E(a,b)\}) \neq \emptyset$, while $P_1(\{E(a,b)\} \cup \{E(b,c), E(c,a)\}) = \emptyset$. Therefore, $P_1 \notin$ SP-Datalog.

Consider the program P_2 which is not a semicon-Datalog$^\neg$ program:

$$\begin{aligned} T(x,y,z) &\leftarrow E(x,y), E(y,z), E(z,x), y \neq x, y \neq z, x \neq z \\ D(x_1) &\leftarrow T(x_1,x_2,x_3), T(y_1,y_2,y_3), \textstyle\bigwedge_{1\leq i,j\leq 3} x_i \neq y_j \\ O(x) &\leftarrow \neg D(x), Adom(x) \end{aligned}$$

Note that the expressed query is not in $\mathcal{M}_{disjoint}$. As we will see shortly, this implies that the query itself can not be defined by any semicon-Datalog$^\neg$ program. □

We next relate connected programs to distributed evaluation over components. An instance J is a *component* of an instance I when $J \subseteq I$, $J \neq \emptyset$, $adom(J) \cap adom(I \setminus J) = \emptyset$ and J is minimal with this property. That is, there is no strict nonempty subset J' of J for which $adom(J') \cap adom(I \setminus J') = \emptyset$. Intuitively, a component is complete w.r.t. its active domain as it either contains all the facts in I in which a certain domain element occurs, or it contains none of these facts. Denote by $co(I)$ the components of I.

Definition 5. A query Q *distributes over components* if for all instances I: (1) $Q(I) = \bigcup_{C \in co(I)} Q(C)$; and, (2) $adom(Q(C)) \cap adom(Q(C')) = \emptyset$ for all $C, C \in co(I)$ with $C \neq C'$.

The lemma below highlights an important property of con-Datalog$^\neg$ and forms a crucial part of the proof of Theorem 5.3. We omit the proof because of space limitations.

LEMMA 5.2. *Every query in con-Datalog$^\neg$ distributes over components.*

We are now armed to prove the following theorem:

THEOREM 5.3. *semicon-Datalog$^\neg \subseteq \mathcal{M}_{disjoint}$*

PROOF. Let P be a semicon-Datalog$^\neg$ program with stratification $P_1, \ldots, P_s$ where P_i is a connected SP-Datalog program for $i < s$. Define $P_{\leq i}$ as the composition $P_i \circ \cdots \circ P_1$ of the first i strata. Clearly, $P = P_{\leq s} = P_s \circ P_{\leq s-1}$. Let I and J be two domain disjoint instances. Then by Lemma 5.2, $P_{\leq s-1}(I)$ is domain disjoint from $P_{\leq s-1}(J)$. By domain-disjoint-monotonicity of SP-Datalog programs, it follows that

$$P_s(P_{\leq s-1}(I)) \subseteq P_s(P_{\leq s-1}(I) \cup P_{\leq s-1}(J)). \qquad (\dagger)$$

We next show that

$$P_{\leq s-1}(I) \cup P_{\leq s-1}(J) = P_{\leq s-1}(I \cup J), \qquad (\ddagger)$$

which together with (†) implies that $P(I) \subseteq P(I \cup J)$ and therefore $P \in \mathcal{M}_{disjoint}$.

It remains to prove (‡). Lemma 5.2 implies that $P_{\leq s-1}(I) = \bigcup_{C \in co(I)} P_{\leq s-1}(C)$, $P_{\leq s-1}(J) = \bigcup_{D \in co(J)} P_{\leq s-1}(D)$ and $P_{\leq s-1}(I \cup J) = \bigcup_{K \in co(I \cup J)} P_{\leq s-1}(K)$. Since I and J are domain disjoint, $co(I) \cup co(J) = co(I \cup J)$. Therefore,

$$\begin{aligned} & P_{\leq s-1}(I) \cup P_{\leq s-1}(J) \\ &= \textstyle\bigcup_{C \in co(I)} P_{\leq s-1}(C) \cup \bigcup_{D \in co(J)} P_{\leq s-1}(D) \\ &= \textstyle\bigcup_{K \in co(I \cup J)} P_{\leq s-1}(K) \\ &= P_{\leq s-1}(I \cup J). \end{aligned}$$

This completes the proof. □

5.2 Datalog$^\neg$ with value invention

The classes $\mathcal{M}$ and $\mathcal{E}$ (and therefore $\mathcal{M}_{distinct}$) are captured by fragments of ILOG$^\neg$, a declarative formalism in the style of stratified Datalog$^\neg$ originally introduced in the context of object databases by Hull and Yoshikawa [24].

We follow Cabibbo [18] for the definition of ILOG$^\neg$ and assume the existence of *invention relations*. These are relations with a distinguished first position, called the *invention position* or the *invention attribute*. An *invention atom* is an atom of the form $R(*, u_1, \ldots, u_k)$, where R is an invention relation and each $u_i \in \mathbf{var}$. The symbol $*$ is called the *invention symbol*. An ILOG$^\neg$ program P over σ is a Datalog program with negation over σ where we allow head atoms to be either (ordinary) relation atoms or invention atoms.

Before defining the semantics of ILOG$^\neg$, we associate to each invention relation R a distinct *Skolem functor* f_R of arity $ar(R) - 1$. The *Skolemization* of P, denoted by $Skol(P)$, is the set of rules in P where every occurrence of the invention symbol is replaced by appropriate Skolem functor terms. For example, the Skolemization of the rule

$$R(*, x_1, x_2) \leftarrow E(x_1, x_2)$$

is

$$R(f_R(x_1, x_2), x_1, x_2) \leftarrow E(x_1, x_2).$$

The semantics of ILOG$^\neg$ is defined similar to the semantics of Datalog with negation, but valuations are applied on the Skolemized rules instead of the rules itself and are w.r.t. the Herbrand universe $\mathcal{H}_P$ for P which is the set of all ground terms built using elements from **dom** and Skolem functors for invention relations in P. When the repeated application of the immediate consequence operator eventually gives rise to relations of infinite size, the output of the program is undefined, otherwise the output consists of the facts in the output relations.

An ILOG$^\neg$ program P is *safe* when the output contains no invented values. Although safety is an undecidable property, there are syntactical restrictions that ensure safe programs. One of these is called weakly safe which we define next. We consider the set of *unsafe positions* in atoms of P. This is the smallest set S containing pairs of the form (R, i), where R is a relation name and $i \leq ar(R)$, such that

- $(R, 1) \in S$ for every invention relation R; and,
- if $(R, i) \in S$ and there is a rule φ in P such that $R(x_1, \ldots, x_k) \in pos_\varphi$, $T(y_1, \ldots, y_\ell) = head_\varphi$, and x_i and y_j refer to the same variable, then $(T, j) \in S$.

An ILOG$^\neg$ program P is *weakly safe* when the output relations of P do not contain unsafe positions. Note that a weakly safe program is always safe. We denote weakly safe ILOG$^\neg$ by wILOG$^\neg$. Furthermore, wILOG$^\neg$ where negation is restricted to predicates in $edb(P)$ is denoted by SP-wILOG for semi-positive wILOG$^\neg$. Stratification can be defined for wILOG$^\neg$ in the same way as for Datalog$^\neg$. As before, we only consider stratified negation in this paper.

Cabibbo investigated the expressiveness of ILOG$^\neg$ over relational databases [18] and obtained the following results: stratified wILOG$^\neg$ programs with two strata capture the class of all computable queries; wILOG$^\neg$ programs where negation is restricted to inequalities and extensional database predicates captures $\mathcal{M}$ and $\mathcal{E}$, respectively.

We introduce the class of *semi-connected wILOG$^\neg$* programs and show that it captures precisely the domain-disjoint-monotone queries. Analogous to the definitions for Datalog$^\neg$, we say that a SP-wILOG program is *connected* when all rules are connected. A wILOG$^\neg$ program P is *semi-connected* when there is a stratification for P such that all strata, except possibly the last one, are connected SP-wILOG programs. Due to space restrictions, the proof of the next result is omitted.

THEOREM 5.4. *Semi-connected wILOG$^\neg$ computes precisely all queries in $\mathcal{M}_{disjoint}$.*

6. RELATED WORK

Declarative networking. Hellerstein [23] argues that the theory of declarative database query languages can provide a foundation for the next generation of parallel and distributed programming languages and formulates a number of related conjectures for the PODS community. Datalog has previously been considered for distributed systems, see e.g. [25, 1, 28].

Ameloot et al. [13] have introduced the framework of relational transducer networks to formalize and prove the CALM-conjecture. The formalism was then parameterized by Zinn et al. [32] to allow for specific data distribution strategies. These authors showed that the classes of coordination-free queries in the original transducer network model ($\mathcal{F}_0$), in the policy-aware transducer network model ($\mathcal{F}_1$), and in the domain-guided transducer network model ($\mathcal{F}_2$) form a strict hierarchy. In particular, they showed that the non-monotone win-move query is in $\mathcal{F}_2$. Some further work on relational transducer networks was done by Ameloot and Van den Bussche who studied decidability of confluence [14] and consistency [12]. The CRON-conjecture, which relates the causal delivery of messages to the nature of the computations that those messages participate in (like monotone versus non-monotone) is treated by Ameloot and Van den Bussche [15].

Zinn introduced in [31] the idea of domain-distinct- and domain-disjoint-monotone queries (albeit under a different name). He defined these as $\mathcal{M}^1_{distinct}$ and $\mathcal{M}^1_{disjoint}$, respectively, and used them to show the corresponding version of Theorem 4.3 and Theorem 4.4. Although the proof and statement of the results are incorrect, the proposed approach did already contain the ideas on which the proofs presented in this paper are based. In fact, it was the enthusiasm of the first three authors over the approach in [31] that in a collaborative effort with the fourth author led to the present paper. In this way, Section 4.2 of the present paper can be seen as an extension and correction of [31]. The results in Section 3, Section 4.3, and Section 5 are not discussed in [31].

The networked relational transducer model is just one paradigm for studying distributed query evaluation. Another notable model (or language) is WebdamLog [3], which is a Datalog-variant for declarative networking. This language supports *delegation*, where a node can send rules to another node instead of just facts; transmitted rules can then be locally evaluated at the addressee. In general, the distributed computations expressed by WebdamLog do not assume a fixed set of nodes, but they allow previously unseen nodes to participate.

Another model, called the massively parallel (MP) model, is introduced by Koutris and Suciu [27]. Here, computation proceeds in a sequence of parallel steps, each followed by global synchronization of all servers. In this model, evaluation of conjunctive queries [27, 17] as well as skyline queries [8] have been considered.

Related to the MP model, is the MapReduce framework where the evaluation of queries has been considered by a number of researchers. Afrati and Ullman [9] study the evaluation of join queries and take the amount of commu-

Datalog($\neq$)	$\subsetneq$	wILOG($\neq$)	$\overset{[18]}{=}$	$\mathcal{M}$	$\overset{[13]}{=}$	$\mathcal{F}_0$	$\overset{[13]}{=}$	$\mathcal{A}_0$
$\subsetneq$		$\subsetneq$		$\boldsymbol{\subsetneq}$		$\subsetneq^{[32]}$		$\boldsymbol{\subsetneq}$
SP-Datalog	$\subsetneq$	SP-wILOG	$\overset{[18]}{=}$	$\boldsymbol{\mathcal{M}_{distinct}}$	**=**	$\mathcal{F}_1$	**=**	$\boldsymbol{\mathcal{A}_1}$
$\boldsymbol{\subsetneq}$		$\boldsymbol{\subsetneq}$		$\boldsymbol{\subsetneq}$		$\subsetneq^{[32]}$		$\boldsymbol{\subsetneq}$
semicon-Datalog$^{\neg}$	$\boldsymbol{\subsetneq}$	**semicon-wILOG$^{\neg}$**	**=**	$\boldsymbol{\mathcal{M}_{disjoint}}$	**=**	$\mathcal{F}_2$	**=**	$\boldsymbol{\mathcal{A}_2}$

Figure 2: Main results of this work: query classes introduced and relationships obtained in this paper are shown in bold-face. Non-bold-face relationships without annotation are part of database folklore.

nication, calculated as the sum of the sizes of the input to reducers, as a complexity measure. Evaluation of transitive closure and datalog queries in MapReduce has been investigated in [7, 10].

Lastly, in Active XML [2], a distributed system is represented as a collection of XML documents in which some vertices contain calls to remote webservices. Any data returned by the calls is incorporated into the calling document.

Finite model theory. The expressiveness of (extensions of) Datalog and its relation to monotonicity have been previously investigated. We discuss some of the results relevant to the present paper. It is known that Datalog and Datalog($\neq$) are strictly included in $\mathcal{H}$ and $\mathcal{M}$, respectively (c.f., e.g., [6, 26]). As mentioned before, Afrati et al. [6] obtained that SP-Datalog $\subseteq \mathcal{E}$. Feder and Vardi [22] showed that all queries in SP-Datalog that are preserved under homomorphisms can already be expressed in Datalog. That is, SP-Datalog$\cap\mathcal{H}$ = Datalog. Dawar and Kreutzer [19] showed that the latter result can not be extended to least fixed-point logic (LFP): LFP $\cap\, \mathcal{H} \not\subseteq$ Datalog. The status of SP-Datalog w.r.t. $\mathcal{E}$ is less clear. It is, for instance, not known whether SP-Datalog $= \mathcal{E} \cap$ Datalog$^{\neg}$. A related result here is the one by Rosen [29], who showed that FO[$\exists^*\forall\exists$]$\cap\mathcal{E} \subseteq$ SP-Datalog, where FO[$\exists^*\forall\exists$] denotes first-order logic formulas of the form $\exists\bar{x}\forall y\exists z\,\psi$ where ψ is quantifier-free. We note that Tait's counterexample [30] separating $FO[\exists]$ from $\mathcal{E} \cap FO$ is definable in SP-Datalog [29]. Atserias et al. [16] study $\mathcal{E}$ in relation to FO over restricted classes of structures.

7. CONCLUSION

Figure 2 summarizes the main findings of this paper. At the same time the figure formulates a more fine-grained answer to the CALM-conjecture which stipulates that a program has a coordination-free execution strategy if and only if the program is monotone. In particular, our results equate increasingly larger classes of coordination-free computations with increasingly weaker forms of monotonicity and make Datalog variants explicit for each of these classes. Furthermore, the last two columns, as already explained in Section 4.1.5 and Section 4.3, confirm that the notion of coordination-freeness as proposed in [13] is a sensible one. Indeed, the notion corresponds to the intended semantics in that coordination-freeness avoids global synchronization barriers through the absence of knowledge about *all* the nodes in the network. That said, we do not claim that our notion is the only possible one. Indeed, one could argue that, especially within $\mathcal{F}_1$ and $\mathcal{F}_2$, even though there is no global synchronization barrier, computing nodes are still prone to wait until complete subsets of the input data have been accumulated (cf. Section 4.2). Of course, the semantical characterizations in terms of weaker forms of monotonicity make precise that this waiting is determined by the way data is distributed. The query evaluation algorithms in the proofs in Section 4.2 are inefficient in that they require all data to be sent to all nodes, it remains to investigate how the insights obtained in this paper can lead to more practical algorithms.

Another contribution of this paper is the identification of (semi-)connected Datalog variants which to the best of our knowledge have not been considered before. We can prove that the connected variant of Datalog under the well-founded semantics, making use of the well-known "doubled program" approach, remains within $\mathcal{M}_{disjoint}$ which implies a simpler proof of the fact that win-move is in $\mathcal{M}_{disjoint}$ (one of the main results in [32]). It is open whether semi-connected Datalog under the well-founded semantics is in $\mathcal{M}_{disjoint}$. A direction for future work is to study the properties of connected Datalog.

As is to be expected, deciding whether a query class belongs to one of the monotonicity classes quickly turns undecidable. Still, it would be interesting to find decidable subclasses or identify sufficient conditions as this would provide insight on the way queries can be distributedly computed. In Section 3, we introduced the bounded classes $\mathcal{M}^i_{distinct}$ and $\mathcal{M}^i_{disjoint}$ mainly because of the mismatch with [31] as explained in Section 6. It remains to investigate their relationship with distributed evaluation of queries.

We avoided the use of nullary relations. This is not a fundamental restriction but a practical one. With general policies, all results in this paper carry over to programs with schemas that can derive nullary relations unaltered. For domain-guided policies, definitions need to be slightly adapted: a nullary fact is never domain disjoint from any relation. Furthermore, in a domain-guided distribution policy, all nullary facts always have to be assigned to all computing nodes, and the definition of a component has to be extended to include all nullary facts. We will provide all details in the journal version of this paper.

Acknowledgments.

We thank Georg Gottlob, Thomas Eiter, and Phokion Kolaitis for answering our questions on Datalog. We also thank Phokion Kolaitis for bringing [29] to our attention.

8. REFERENCES

[1] S. Abiteboul, Z. Abrams, S. Haar, and T. Milo. Diagnosis of asynchronous discrete event systems:

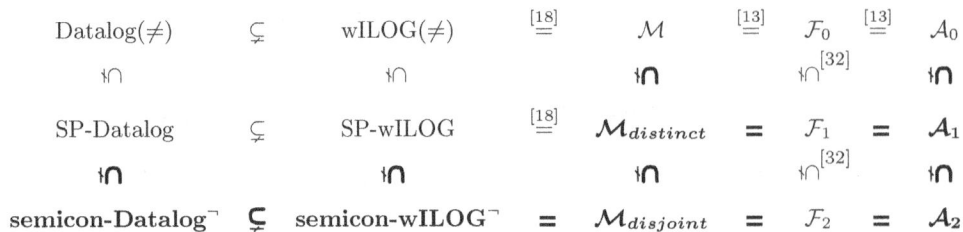

Datalog to the rescue! In *PODS*, pages 358–367. ACM, 2005.

[2] S. Abiteboul, O. Benjelloun, and T. Milo. The active xml project: An overview. *The VLDB Journal*, 17(5):1019–1040, 2008.

[3] S. Abiteboul, M. Bienvenu, A. Galland, and E. Antoine. A rule-based language for Web data management. In *PODS*, pages 293–304. ACM Press, 2011.

[4] S. Abiteboul, R. Hull, and V. Vianu. *Foundations of Databases*. Addison-Wesley, 1995.

[5] S. Abiteboul, V. Vianu, B. Fordham, and Y. Yesha. Relational transducers for electronic commerce. *J. Comput. Syst. Sci.*, 61(2):236–269, 2000.

[6] F. Afrati, S. S. Cosmadakis, and M. Yannakakis. On Datalog vs polynomial time. *Journal of computer and system sciences*, 51:177–196, 1995.

[7] F. N. Afrati, V. R. Borkar, M. J. Carey, N. Polyzotis, and J. D. Ullman. Map-reduce extensions and recursive queries. In *ICDE*, pages 1–8, 2011.

[8] F. N. Afrati, P. Koutris, D. Suciu, and J. D. Ullman. Parallel skyline queries. In *ICDT*, pages 274–284, 2012.

[9] F. N. Afrati and J. D. Ullman. Optimizing joins in a map-reduce environment. In *EDBT*, pages 99–110, 2010.

[10] F. N. Afrati and J. D. Ullman. Transitive closure and recursive Datalog implemented on clusters. In *EDBT*, pages 132–143, 2012.

[11] P. Alvaro, N. Conway, J. Hellerstein, and W. R. Marczak. Consistency analysis in bloom: a calm and collected approach. In *CIDR*, pages 249–260, 2011.

[12] T. J. Ameloot. Deciding correctness with fairness for simple transducer networks. In *ICDT*, 2014.

[13] T. J. Ameloot, F. Neven, and J. Van den Bussche. Relational transducers for declarative networking. *J. ACM*, 60(2):15, 2013.

[14] T. J. Ameloot and J. Van den Bussche. Deciding eventual consistency for a simple class of relational transducer networks. In *ICDT*, pages 86–98, 2012.

[15] T. J. Ameloot and J. Van den Bussche. On the CRON conjecture. In *Datalog*, pages 44–55, 2012.

[16] A. Atserias, A. Dawar, and M. Grohe. Preservation under extensions on well-behaved finite structures. *SIAM J. Comput.*, 38(4):1364–1381, 2008.

[17] P. Beame, P. Koutris, and D. Suciu. Communication steps for parallel query processing. In *PODS*, pages 273–284, 2013.

[18] L. Cabibbo. The expressive power of stratified logic programs with value invention. *Information and Computation*, 147(1):22–56, 1998.

[19] A. Dawar and S. Kreutzer. On Datalog vs. LFP. In *ICALP*, pages 160–171, 2008.

[20] A. Deutsch, L. Sui, and V. Vianu. Specification and verification of data-driven Web applications. *J. Comput. Syst. Sci.*, 73(3):442–474, 2007.

[21] A. Deutsch, L. Sui, V. Vianu, and D. Zhou. Verification of communicating data-driven Web services. In *PODS*, pages 90–99. ACM Press, 2006.

[22] T. Feder and M. Y. Vardi. Homomorphism closed vs. existential positive. In *LICS*, pages 311–320, 2003.

[23] J. M. Hellerstein. The declarative imperative: experiences and conjectures in distributed logic. *SIGMOD Record*, 39(1):5–19, 2010.

[24] R. Hull and M. Yoshikawa. ILOG: Declarative creation and manipulation of object identifiers. In *VLDB*, pages 455–468, 1990.

[25] T. Jim and D. Suciu. Dynamically distributed query evaluation. In *PODS*, pages 28–39. ACM, 2001.

[26] P. G. Kolaitis and M. Y. Vardi. On the expressive power of Datalog: Tools and a case study. In *PODS*, pages 61–71, 1990.

[27] P. Koutris and D. Suciu. Parallel evaluation of conjunctive queries. In *PODS*, pages 223–234, 2011.

[28] B. Loo, T. Condie, et al. Declarative networking: Language, execution and optimization. In *Proceedings of the 2006 ACM SIGMOD International Conference on Management of Data*, pages 97–108. ACM, 2006.

[29] E. Rosen. *Finite Model Theory and finite Variable Logics*. PhD thesis, University of Pennsylvania, 1995.

[30] W. W. Tait. A counterexample to a conjecture of Scott and Suppes. *The journal of Symbolic Logic*, 24(1):15–16, 1959.

[31] D. Zinn. Weak forms of monotonicity and coordination-freeness. *CoRR*, abs/1202.0242, 2012.

[32] D. Zinn, T. J. Green, and B. Ludäscher. Win-move is coordination-free (sometimes). In *ICDT*, pages 99–113, 2012.

Model-Data Ecosystems: Challenges, Tools, and Trends

Peter J. Haas
IBM Almaden Research Center
650 Harry Road
San Jose, CA 95120-6099 U.S.A.
phaas@us.ibm.com

ABSTRACT

In the past few years, research around (big) data management has begun to intertwine with research around predictive modeling and simulation in novel and interesting ways. Driving this trend is an increasing recognition that information contained in real-world data must be combined with information from domain experts, as embodied in simulation models, in order to enable robust decision making under uncertainty. Simulation models of large, complex systems (traffic, biology, population well-being) consume and produce massive amounts of data and compound the challenges of traditional information management. We survey some challenges, mathematical tools, and future directions in the emerging research area of model-data ecosystems. Topics include (i) methods for enabling data-intensive simulation, (ii) simulation and information integration, and (iii) simulation metamodeling for guiding the generation of simulated data and the collection of real-world data.

Categories and Subject Descriptors

H.4.2 [**Information Systems Applications**]: Types of Systems—*decision support*; I.6 [**Simulation and Modeling**]: Simulation Support Systems

General Terms

Algorithms, Design

Keywords

Simulation, data assimilation, information integration, decision support

1. INTRODUCTION: DATA IS STILL DEAD

In their *VLDB 2011* paper, "Data is dead...without what-if analytics", Haas et al. [27] point out that, outside of scientific or historical investigations and monitoring-type applications, the essential motivation underlying data processing and analytics is the need to support enterprise decision making under uncertainty. Thus the ultimate goal is to support deep predictive analytics that incorporate domain expertise in order to robustly predict the future consequences of decisions made today. From this perspective, data by itself is indeed "dead", reflecting the past state of the world. Descriptive analytics—such as simple querying, OLAP, data mining, machine learning, and time-series analysis—find important patterns and relationships in existing data, leading to insights about the real world as it currently stands. A "shallow" predictive approach that simply extrapolates current patterns into the future, however, can lead to very brittle predictions and subsequent bad decisions because it does not account for the fact that the mechanisms that generated the existing data can change. Figure 1 illustrates this point. A simple time series model was fit to median U.S. housing prices from 1970 to 2006 and then extrapolated to 2011. As can be seen, the resulting prediction failed spectacularly because it ignored expert information from economists, financial analysts, behavioral scientists, and others that might have helped in modeling the housing-price collapse that began in 2006. Thus data must be supplemented by models that embody expert knowledge about the constituent parts of systems and the way they behave and interact. For systems characterized by uncertainty, these models often take the form of stochastic simulations.

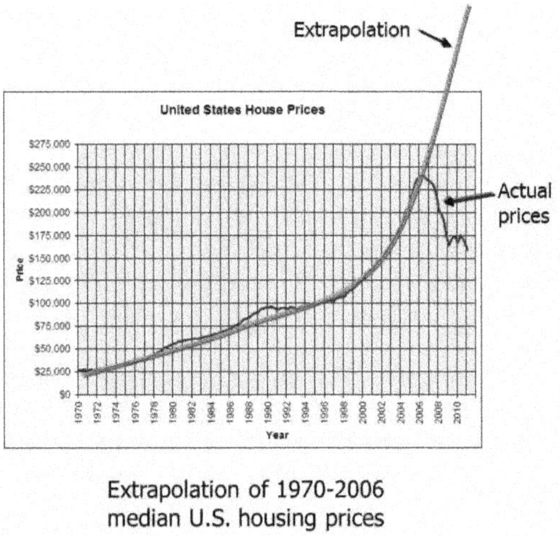

Figure 1: The dangers of extrapolation

Eric Bonabeau, the author of *Swarm Intelligence*, makes a similar point in one of his blogs [9]:

> There is no doubt that the more *information* is used in building a model, the more accurate the model is likely to be. However, the notion that quantitative, nu-

PODS'14, June 22–27, 2014, Snowbird, UT, USA.

ACM 978-1-4503-2375-8/14/06 ...$15.00.
http://dx.doi.org/10.1145/2594538.2594562.

merical data are the *only* type of information needed to build an accurate model is flawed. In fact, I believe that the typical business obsession with numeric data can do more damage than good.

He then asserts the need for fundamental system information possessed by domain experts and gives as an example the problem of reducing traffic jams. A data-centric approach would collect large amounts of data about current traffic speeds, volumes, and delays, and attempt to discover correlations between time of day and average speed, between number of cars and delay lengths, and so on. This approach ignores crucial information possessed by traffic experts, such as that we slow down at certain rates when someone appears in front of us, that we accelerate to a driver-dependent "comfortable" speed when the road is clear, that we may switch lanes if they are open, and so on. "This kind of information is critical because it is at the heart of what creates traffic. And yet, typical data-driven approaches would have no way whatsoever of including this domain knowledge along with the numerical data." Bonabeau then shows how simple agent-based simulations that incorporate such behavior can accurately imitate traffic jams observed in the real world. In this context, data is key to parametrizing and calibrating such models.

Perhaps because of their increasing awareness of the need for interplay between models and data within a coherent ecosystem, researchers in the fields of information management and system simulation have interacted more and more over the past several years, and this trend will most likely continue. In a striking example of this confluence of interests, the *2014 Winter Simulation Conference (WSC)*—the premier venue of the stochastic simulation community—has chosen for its theme "exploring big data through simulation". Research on model-data ecosystems, however, is clearly in its infancy. Indeed, even the Conference Chair of WSC 2014 has expressed uncertainty about the precise meaning of the theme.

We therefore provide a survey of research pertaining to the emerging model-data ecosystem. Each topic will be treated via specific examples, presented in a tutorial style. The selection of topics is admittedly idiosyncratic, reflecting the author's interests and experience as a member of both the database and simulation communities. The goal is both to spark interest in some of these topics and to indicate some system prototypes and mathematical tools—some of which are perhaps more familiar to the modeling community than to the database community—that are being used to attack some of the new research questions. Overall, we distinguish three main topics:

1. *Data-intensive simulation* Modern simulation models can consume and produce massive amounts of data, which creates opportunities to improve simulation performance by deploying data-management technologies within simulation environments. These include (i) incorporating stochastic simulation functionality into database systems, (ii) developing methods for massive scale time series transformations between models using MapReduce and related technologies, (iii) extending techniques for query optimization to the setting of simulation-run optimization, and (iv) querying simulated data as part of the simulation process.

2. *Simulation and information integration* An interesting line of thought views simulation, especially agent-based simulation (ABS), as a tool for combining disparate real-world data. A related topic is "data assimilation", which is concerned with fusing simulated and real-world sensor data to get a clearer picture of an evolving real-world phenomenon such as a forest fire.

3. *Simulation metamodeling* Metamodeling techniques provide a powerful set of tools both for controlling the amount of simulated data that is generated and for guiding the collection of real-world data.

In the following sections we will cover each of these topics in turn.

2. DATA-INTENSIVE SIMULATION

Traditionally, a simulation analysis would start with a small to medium set of input data and produce a medium to "large" set of output data. Both the input data and output data would themselves be the result of a data reduction process. Typical input data, for example, might comprise a so-called "reproduction number" for use in an epidemic simulation or some mean and variance parameters of a lognormal distribution for use in a financial simulation; such inputs would typically be the result of a statistical estimation procedure. This situation has changed dramatically with the introduction of agent-based simulation—see, e.g., [2, 7, 39]. ABS is an approach to modeling systems comprising individual, autonomous, interacting "agents". With roots going back at least to the 1970's [48], ABS has surged in popularity in recent years as computational power has grown. An ABS often involves massive numbers of agents, e.g., in simulations of regional or national populations at the individual level. Thus the input data requirements can be huge. The output of the simulation, which can comprise a time series of snapshots of the state of the agent population, can also be massive. Even when ABS is not used *per se*, the scale, complexity, and granularity of simulations is growing rapidly, commensurate with increases in both computing power and the amount of available data. Running a modern simulation therefore requires managing large amounts of data, and there have been a number of attempts to leverage the expertise of the information-management community when designing simulation platforms.

2.1 Simulation in the database

One line of research has attempted to incorporate stochastic simulation functionality into database systems, with a goal of avoiding the need to reduce, extract, and load the data into a separate simulation engine and then later integrate the simulation results back into the database. Examples of this type of system are given by the *Monte Carlo Database System (MCDB)* and *SimSQL*. The MCDB system [33] allows an analyst to attach arbitrary stochastic models to a relational database. In more detail, the analyst can specify, in addition to the ordinary tables in the database, "stochastic" tables that contain "uncertain" data. Such data are not represented by specific data values, but rather by stochastic models that describe the probability distribution over possible values. The models are implemented as user- and system-defined libraries of external C++ programs called *Variable Generation functions*, or VG functions for short. A call to a VG function generates a realization of uncertain data values in the form of a pseudorandom sample from the underlying probability distribution. The sample can correspond to the value of a single data element or to a set of correlated elements residing in various row and column positions. The possible actions of a VG function range from simple generation of a sample from a normal distribution, to executing a backward random walk starting at a given current price in order to estimate missing prior prices, to simulating a sequence of stock prices in order to return a sample of the value of a stock option one week from now. As another example, a customer's random demand for an item, given its price, might be computed by fitting a parametric global demand model based on data from all customers, and then computing a customized demand distribution for each customer using the customer's individual purchase history together with Bayes' Theorem. Then one can ask queries such as "how would the revenue from East Coast customers under thirty years old have been affected by a 5% price increase?".

In MCDB, the VG functions are parametrized on the current state of the non-random tables (e.g., tables of historical sales data or delivery times). As a very simple example, consider the following specification of a random table of blood pressure data:

```
CREATE TABLE SBP_DATA(PID, GENDER, SBP) AS
 FOR EACH p in PATIENTS
  WITH SBP AS Normal (
   SELECT s.MEAN, s.STD
   FROM SPB_PARAM s)
  SELECT p.PID, p.GENDER, b.VALUE
  FROM SBP b
```

A realization of SBP_DATA is generated by looping over the set of patients and using the Normal VG function to generate a row for each patient. These rows are effectively UNIONed to create the realization of SBP_DATA. The FOR EACH clause specifies this outer loop. The Normal VG function simple generates a sample from the normal distribution. This function is parametrized with a mean and standard deviation, which are obtained via a SELECT query over the (single row, two column) SBP_PARAM table; in general a VG function can be parametrized using a general SQL query over the set of all non-random relations in the database.

Generating a sample of each uncertain data value creates a *database instance*, i.e., a realization of an ordinary database. Running an SQL query over the database instance generates a sample from the query-result distribution. Iteration of this process yields a collection of samples from this distribution that can then be used to estimate distribution features of interest such as moments and quantiles. To ensure acceptable performance, MCDB employs query processing techniques that execute a query plan only once, processing "tuple bundles" rather than ordinary tuples. A tuple bundle encapsulates the instantiations of a tuple over a set of Monte Carlo iterations. MCDB runs on a parallel relational database platform, and so can exploit parallel database technology for scalability. Subsequent work [5, 42] demonstrates how MCDB can be extended to deal with risk analysis (by efficiently estimating extreme quantiles) and with threshold queries of the form "Which regions will see more than a 2% decline in sales with at least 50% probability?".

SimSQL [11] is a re-implementation and extension of MCDB. SimSQL allows data in stochastic database tables to be used to parametrize the VG functions that generate the data in other stochastic database tables. Moreover, SimSQL allows both versioning and recursive definitions of stochastic database tables. For example, data in stochastic table A can be used to parametrize the stochastic generation of table B, which in turn can be used to parametrize the stochastic generation of a second version of table A, and so on. Whereas MCDB merely allowed generation of sample realizations of a stochastic database D—in other words, a static database-valued random variable—the foregoing extensions enable SimSQL to generate realizations of a database-valued Markov chain $D[0], D[1], D[2], \ldots$. That is, the stochastic mechanism that generates a realization of the ith database state $D[i]$ may explicitly depend on the prior state $D[i-1]$. As with MCDB, queries are expressed in SQL; unlike MCDB, SimSQL executes queries using the Hadoop [4] MapReduce implementation in order to scale to massive data.

Besides being well suited to scalable Bayesian machine learning (see [11]), SimSQL can also be used to implement massive stochastic ABS models inside the database. The idea is to build on work by Wang et al. [55], who observed that a step in an agent-based simulation can be viewed as a self-join. That is, the data in each row of a table represent the internal state of an agent, so the self-join step allows agents to interact with other agents. A key observation is that agents typically interact only with a relatively small group of "nearby" agents. Thus (with a little care) the join can be parallelized among groups of agents, and well known parallel database technology can be applied to achieve good performance. The work in [55] applies primarily to deterministic simulations; SimSQL can potentially be used to extend those ideas to stochastic simulations.

2.2 Data Harmonization at Scale

The need for transforming large datasets is certainly not new. The scientific community, especially, has long been concerned with transforming spatio-temporal data as part of a scientific workflow, both to combine disparate datasets and to conform datasets to the formats expected by analysis programs. Over the past few years, however, demand for efficient data transformations at scale has increased even further, driven by the rise of composite simulation modeling.

Decision-makers increasingly need to bring together multiple models across a broad range of disciplines to guide investment and policy decisions around highly complex issues such as population well-being; see, e.g., [23, 32] in the setting of food, climate, and health. Consequently, there have been a number of efforts to develop composite modeling tools that can leverage both new and existing models developed by domain experts. Examples include CIShell [10], Open Services Gateway initiatives (OSGi) framework, the High Level Architecture for U.S. Department of Defense simulations [35], the DEVS discrete-event simulation framework [54], and targeted simulation frameworks such as the STEM epidemiological model [18] and the Community Climate System Model [13], in which component models are written in a specified language (Java and Fortran 90) and compiled together to create the simulation program. All of these frameworks require major re-coding of existing models and/or strict enforcement of a common platform, API, or communication protocol—a nearly impossible task when dealing with experts in vastly different domains.

In response to these issues, systems such as the IBM Splash prototype (Smarter Planet Platform for the Analysis and Simulation of Health) [26, 28, 53] have attempted to synthesize simulation and data-integration techniques, permitting loose coupling of models via data exchange; that is, models communicate by reading and writing datasets. When model and data contributors initially register their models and datasets with Splash, they provide metadata that enables drag-and-drop composite-model creation, automatic detection of data mismatches between upstream "source" and downstream "target" models, and graphical tools for specifying needed data transformations, which are then compiled into runtime code. For a stochastic composite model, data transformations must be performed at every Monte Carlo repetition, so that efficiency a is major concern.

The database community has lent its expertise to improving data-transformation technology in several ways. For example, Howe and Maier [31] provide an algebra of "gridfields" to allow for efficient optimization and query processing of gridded data in a relational database, especially when the grids are irregular. A *grid*, in their terminology, is a collection of heterogeneous abstract *cells* of various dimensions. A grid also has an incidence relation $\preceq$ between cells, where $x \preceq y$ means that either $x = y$ or $\dim(x) < \dim(y)$ and x "touches" (i.e., is adjacent to) y. For example, cell x might correspond to a line segment and cell y might correspond to a square, so that $x \preceq y$ if x coincides with a side of the square. A variety of set-like operations can be defined on grids. A *gridfield* results from binding data to a grid by specifying, for each dimension k, a function f_k that operates on cells of dimension k and returns a data value of some type τ_k. A variety of operations can be defined on gridfields, with the most important operation in the current context being "regrid". The regrid operator maps a source gridfield's cells onto a target gridfield's cells via a many-to-one assignment function and then aggregates the data values bound to the mapped cells via an aggregation function. The authors show, for example that certain "restriction" operations—which are analogous to standard relational selection operations—can commute with the regrid operator, creating opportunities for optimization. This technology was originally applied to the CORIE system, which supports simulations of the Columbia River Estuary and other coastal regions.

As another example, the Splash system, discussed earlier, uses Hadoop for data transformations between models. Hadoop is used both to execute *schema alignment* and *time alignment* transformations on massive time series with many time ticks and large amounts of data per tick. The former type of transformation typically handles "format" discrepancies between source-model outputs and target-model inputs at any given point of simulated time, whereas time alignment deals with the orthogonal problem of time-scale discrepancies between models. To specify schema transformations, Splash uses Clio++, an extension of the Clio schema mapping tool [24] to allow users to graphically define a schema mapping. For time-alignment transformations, the time aligner tool determines the class of time alignment needed—e.g., aggregation if the target model has coarser time granularity than the source model or interpolation if the target has finer granularity—and provides a GUI that lets the user specify an appropriate alignment method from a menu. Graphical specifications of data transformations are then automatically compiled into Hadoop runtime code.

Some time alignment operations are non-trivial to implement efficiently in a MapReduce setting. Consider interpolation, for example, where the input is a time series $S = \langle(s_0,d_0),\ldots,(s_m,d_m)\rangle$ for some $m \geq 0$; here s_i is the time of the ith observation and d_i is the associated data observed at time s_i. Each d_i can be viewed as a k-tuple for some $k \geq 1$. The output is a target dataset $T = \langle(t_0,\tilde{d}_0),\ldots,(t_n,\tilde{d}_n)\rangle$. To exploit parallelization, Splash computes *windows* of the form $W = \langle(s_j,d_j),(s_{j+1},d_{j+1})\rangle$. Each window is used to compute data at target points $\{t_i : s_j \leq t_i < s_{j+1}\}$. The windows can be processed in parallel and then the target time series can be assembled via a parallel sort. A novel challenge arises when computing a natural cubic spline interpolation, one of the most common interpolations used in practice. The interpolation formula is

$$\tilde{d}_i = \frac{\sigma_j}{6h_j}(s_{j+1}-t_i)^3 + \frac{\sigma_{j+1}}{6h_j}(t_i - s_j)^3 + \left(\frac{d_{j+1}}{h_j} - \frac{\sigma_{j+1}h_j}{6}\right)(t_i - s_j) + \left(\frac{d_j}{h_j} - \frac{\sigma_j h_j}{6}\right)(s_{j+1} - t_i),$$

where $h_j = s_{j+1} - s_j$ and $\sigma_0,\sigma_1,\ldots,\sigma_m$ are *spline constants* that depend on the entire input dataset and are computed as the solution to linear equation system of the form $Ax = b$, where A is an $(m-1)\times(m-1)$ tridiagonal matrix. For massive time series with fine granularity, m can be huge, and the matrix A can contain millions of rows and millions of columns. Virtually all known methods for solving such massive systems do not translate well to a MapReduce environment, because massive amounts of data shuffling are required.

The technique used in [28] is to transform the problem of solving the tridiagonal linear system into the problem of choosing x to minimize $L(x) = \|Ax - b\|^2$—where $\|z\|$ denotes the euclidean norm—and then to apply a *distributed stochastic gradient descent* (DSGD) approach [21]. Ordinary stochastic gradient descent (SGD), minimizes L by taking downhill steps, using "quick and dirty" approximations of the true gradient. In more detail, we first write $L(x) = \sum_{i=1}^{m-1} L_i(x)$, where $L_i(x) = (A_{i\cdot}x - b_i)^2$ and $A_{i\cdot}$ denotes the ith row of A. The SGD algorithm starts with an initial guess $x^{(0)}$ for x, then picks a row I at random from $\{1,2,\ldots,m-1\}$, computes the gradient component $\nabla L_I(x^{(0)})$, then approximates the overall gradient $\nabla L(x^{(0)})) = \sum_{i=0}^{m} \nabla L_i(x^{(0)})$ by $Y_0 = m\nabla L_I(x^{(0)})$, and finally updates the solution by setting $x^{(1)} = x^{(0)} - \varepsilon_0 Y_0$. Such downhill steps are iterated using a carefully chosen sequence $\{\varepsilon_n\}_{n\geq 0}$ of step sizes; for step sizes of the form $\varepsilon_n = n^{-\alpha}$, SGD is provably convergent under mild conditions, provided that $1 \leq \alpha < 2$.

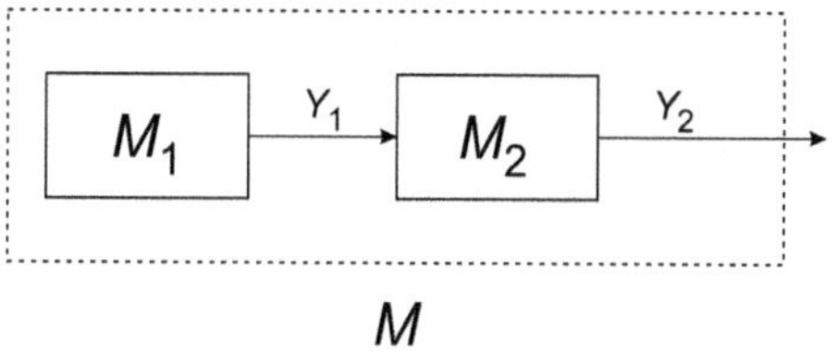

Figure 2: A simple composite simulation model

The SGD approach has long been known to work well in sequential settings [43] but it has not been obvious how to distribute the algorithm across a cluster. This problem was addressed in [21], originally in the context of matrix completion problems arising in recommendation systems. The idea is to partition the data into *strata*; the strata are carefully defined so that execution of SGD within a stratum can be parallelized. The DGSD algorithm runs within a chosen stratum for a period of time, then switches to another stratum, and so on. For the cubic spline problem, the first stratum S_1 comprises the data in rows $1,4,7,\ldots$ of the linear system. If row $i = 1$ is selected at random in SGD, the tridiagonal structure of A guarantees that the resulting update to x will only involve entries x_1 and x_2. Similarly, an update to row $i = 4$ will only involve entries x_3, x_4, and x_5. Thus rows 1 and 4 can be sampled in either order, or in parallel, and indeed the data in S_1 can be partitioned among the processing nodes and processed in parallel by the SGD algorithm. Similarly, SGD can be run in parallel over data in stratum $S_2 = \{2,5,8,\ldots\}$ and in $S_3 = \{3,6,9,\ldots\}$. Observe that when running in a given stratum S_i, SGD is minimizing the "wrong" function because the data in the other strata are being ignored. It is shown in [21], however, that if the process switches randomly from one stratum to another according to a "regenerative" process, and if equal time is spent in each stratum in the long run, then the algorithm will converge to the overall solution with probability 1. Moreover, the amount of data that needs to be shuffled is negligible, which results in superior performance on MapReduce platforms. Recent experiments indicate that the DSGD idea also leads to best-of-breed matrix completion algorithms on a variety of architectures [40].

2.3 Optimizing Simulation Runs

Optimizing the efficiency of simulation execution is another challenge where the simulation community can benefit from the experience of the database community. In particular, composite-modeling platforms such as Splash need to execute queries in order to harmonize data between models during a simulation run, so that the problem of simulation-experiment optimization subsumes the problem of query optimization. The challenges go further, however, to include issues such as how best to move data to models, or vice versa, in a distributed execution environment, how to schedule execution of components to minimize the overall run time, and so on.

We briefly discuss an example, taken from [25], of an optimization problem specific to stochastic composite simulation but with links to classical query optimization technology. To motivate the problem, consider a composite model M comprising two component models M_1 and M_2 in series, as shown in Figure 2. An execution of M proceeds by first executing M_1, which produces a random output Y_1 that is written to disk. Then M_2 is executed, taking Y_1 as input (after appropriate transformation) and generating a final output Y_2, where Y_2 is distributed according to a conditional cumulative distribution function $F_2(\cdot|Y_1)$. For example, M_1 might be a demand model that generates a sequence Y_1 of customer arrival times. The data in Y_1 might then fed into a queuing model M_2, which in turn produces an output Y_2, which might correspond to the average waiting time of the first 100 customers. To generate independent and identically distributed (i.i.d.) samples $Y_{2;1}, Y_{2;2}, \ldots, Y_{2;n}$ from the distribution of Y_2, one could execute the composite model n times, thereby executing M_1 and M_2 a total of n times each. Suppose, however, that M_1 is in fact deterministic, so that the same output Y_1 is produced every time the model is executed. Rather than repeatedly executing M_1. It is clearly more efficient to cache the output Y_1 of M_1 during the first execution of the composite model M and then, for each of the remaining $n-1$ executions, to read Y_1 from disk instead of re-executing M_1. If the cost of executing M_1 is large relative to the cost of executing M_2, then the cost savings can be significant. The general question, then, is how to optimally reuse results for a general composite model in which each component model might be stochastic.

The result-caching (RC) technique for the case of two stochastic models in series in considered in [25]. Here the goal of the simulation is to estimate $\theta = E[Y_2]$, the expected value of the (real valued) output from M_2. For n simulation replications of M_2, only $m_n = \lceil \alpha n \rceil$ replications of M_1 are executed, where $\alpha \in (0,1]$ is called the *replication fraction*.[1] We write the output of M_1 to disk after each of the first m_n simulation replications and then repeatedly cycle through these outputs in a fixed order to obtain inputs to M_2. Thus each M_1 output is used in approximately n/m_n executions of M_2. The deterministic cycling scheme produces a stratified sample of the outputs of M_1 and helps minimize estimator variance. Finally, θ is estimated as $\theta_n = (1/n)\sum_{l=0}^{n-1} Y_{2;l}$.

To precisely formulate the notion of "increasing the efficiency" of a simulation run, suppose that we are given a large but finite computing budget c. Denote by C_n the cost of generating n outputs from M_2 under the RC strategy; this cost comprises the cost of creating, transforming, and storing m_n outputs from M_1 plus the cost of creating n outputs from M_2. Under a budget c, the number of M_2 outputs that can be generated is $N(c) = \sup\{n \geq 0 : C_n \leq c\}$, resulting in the estimate $U(c) = \theta_{N(c)}$. Denote by c_1 and c_2 the expected computation costs for the first run of M_1 and M_2, respectively (so that the costs of transforming and storing the output from M_1 are included). Also denote by V_1 the variance of an output from M_2 and by V_2 the covariance of two outputs from M_2 when they share a common input from M_1; assume that $V_2 \geq 0$, as is usually the case in practice. Finally, set $r_\alpha = \lfloor 1/\alpha \rfloor$. It can be shown that $U(c) \to \theta$ with probability 1 and $c^{1/2}[U(c) - \theta] \Rightarrow \sqrt{g(\alpha)}N(0,1)$ as $c \to \infty$, where "$\Rightarrow$" denotes convergence in distribution, $N(0,1)$ denotes a standard (mean 0, variance 1) normal random variable, and

$$g(\alpha) = (\alpha c_1 + c_2)\Big(V_1 + [2r_\alpha - \alpha r_\alpha(r_\alpha + 1)]V_2\Big).$$

[1] Throughout, $\lfloor x \rfloor$ and $\lceil x \rceil$ denote the largest integer less than or equal to x and the smallest integer greater than or equal to x.

Thus $U(c)$ is a strongly consistent estimator of θ and, for a large budget c, is approximately normally distributed with mean θ and variance $g(\alpha)$. Following [19, 22], one can then define (asymptotic) efficiency as $1/g(\alpha)$, so that maximizing efficiency is equivalent to minimizing the variance of a budget-constrained simulation-based estimator. It can be seen that $g(\alpha)$ is the amortized total cost to produce an output from M_2 times the variance of such an output. This product-form balancing of simulation cost and variance in order to obtain an overall measure of efficiency was originally proposed by Hammersley and Handscomb in 1964 [29]; consideration of the asymptotic behavior of budget-constrained simulations, as above, provide a rigorous justification for this type of efficiency measure.

To gain insight into the nature of the optimal solution for the two-model problem, approximate r_α by $1/\alpha$ and write $g(\alpha) \approx \tilde{g}(\alpha) \stackrel{\text{def}}{=} (\alpha c_1 + c_2)\big(V_1 + (\alpha^{-1} - 1)V_2\big)$. It is then easy to verify that $\tilde{g}(\alpha)$ is maximized by setting $\alpha = \alpha^*$, where

$$\alpha^* = \left(\frac{c_2/c_1}{(V_1/V_2) - 1}\right)^{1/2}.$$

(Truncate α^* at $1/n$ or 1 as needed to ensure a feasible solution. Note that $V_1/V_2 \geq 1$ by the Cauchy-Schwarz inequality.) If c_1 is large relative to c_2, so that M_1 is relatively expensive to execute, then α^* is small, and it is optimal to execute M_1 a relatively small number of times. If M_2 is relatively insensitive to the input from M_1, so that most of the variability arises from randomness within M_2, then $V_2 \ll V_1$, and again we simulate M_1 only a small number of times. In the extreme case where $V_2 = 0$, we simulate M_1 only once, thereby recapturing the scenario in which M_1 is deterministic. If, on the other hand, M_2 is a deterministic function of its inputs and M_1 is stochastic, then $V_1 = V_2$ and it is optimal to run n replications of M_1. In this case, M_2 is merely a transformer of the output of M_1. Overall, it is clear that, depending on the values of c_1/c_2 and V_1/V_2, arbitrarily large efficiency improvements are possible in principle.

A key issue is how to estimate the statistics $\mathscr{S} = (c_1, c_2, V_1, V_2)$. Note that there is some tolerance for error: inaccuracies in the estimates of $\mathscr{S}$ might result in slightly suboptimal simulation performance but correctness is not an issue. Indeed, the foregoing results show that the simulation estimates are asymptotically valid for any value of α. Also note that a composite modeling system such as Splash is oriented toward re-use of models, and important performance characteristics of a model can be stored as part of the model's metadata. Thus the cost of executing pilot runs to estimate the statistics in $\mathscr{S}$ can be amortized over multiple model executions. Moreover, as the component models are used in production runs, their behavior can be observed and used to continually refine the statistics in $\mathscr{S}$, and hence to continually improve performance. The issues here are analogous to the issues encountered in estimating catalog statistics for a relational database system, and thus techniques from traditional query optimization can potentially be leveraged in the simulation setting and combined with metamodeling ideas as in Section 4 below and perhaps ideas from machine learning; see [25] for further discussion.

2.4 Querying Data During a Simulation

As we have seen with systems such as MCDB and SimSQL, one way to leverage information-management technology in data-intensive simulation is to incorporate simulation functionality into a database system. Another approach—as embodied in the Indemics simulation model for large scale epidemics [6]—is to divide the simulation work between a high-performance cluster (HPC) that performs compute-intensive tasks and a relational database engine that performs data-intensive tasks.

In more detail, Indemics uses a network model of disease transmission, where nodes represent individuals and edges represent social contacts between individuals. The nodes have attributes representing the health and behavioral state of an individual, along with static demographic information, and the edges have attributes that specify, e.g., contact duration and type. The model also comprises transition functions that modify nodes and/or edges, and hence specify changes in disease progression and behavioral status (e.g., fear level), as well as changes in social interactions (formation of new edges due to new contacts, deletion of edges due to quarantine, and so on). The HPC updates the state of the network in between observation times. At an observation time, the experimenter can issue SQL queries to assess the state of the network model. Such queries select subsets of individuals and run aggregation queries on each subset to summarize the state of the subpopulations (e.g., percent infected). Queries can also be used compute values of performance measures that are to be optimized (e.g., number of infected cases or economic damage). Finally, SQL queries can be used to specify complex interventions by specifying subsets of individuals together with the actions to be performed on each subset. An action on a subset S corresponds to modifying the states of the nodes corresponding to the individuals in S and/or the edges incident on the individuals in S. Algorithm 1, adapted from [6], indicates how an intervention strategy can be specified using SQL. When executed by the experimenter after pausing the simulation, this type of intervention represents an interactive extension to traditional "partially observed Markov decision processes".

Algorithm 1 Vaccinate preschoolers if more than 1% are sick

```
CREATE TABLE Preschool(pid) AS
  (SELECT pid FROM Person WHERE 0 ≤ age ≤ 4);
/* Based on demographic data */
DEFINE nPreschool AS (SELECT COUNT(pid) FROM Preschool);
for day = 1 to 300 do
   /* Based on demographic and disease dynamic data */
   WITH InfectedPreschool (pid) AS
    (SELECT pid FROM Preschool, InfectedPerson
     WHERE Preschool.pid = InfectedPerson.pid);
   DEFINE nInfectedPreschool AS
    (SELECT COUNT(pid) FROM InfectedPreschool);
   if nInfectedPreschool > 1% × nPreschool then
       Apply vaccines to SELECT( pid FROM Preschool);
       /* Intervention subpopulation and action */
   end if
end for
```

This division of labor between an HPC and an RDBMS yields a highly extensible and flexible system for specifying disease transmission models together with complicated intervention policies. This approach can potentially be applied to other large scale agent-based simulations.

We briefly mention another type of querying inside simulations, specifically, inside parallel discrete-event simulations of agent-based systems. Such simulations are studied in [52], for a simulation platform called PDES-MAS. In such simulations, parallel "agent logical processes" (ALPs) simulate the simultaneous behavior of massive numbers of agents. Each agent operates in a repeating cycle of "sense-think-response". A key part of the "sense" stage is discovering nearby agents via an instantaneous *range* query, e.g., "find all agents who are, right now, within one mile and who are over 25 years old". In the PDES-MAS distributed architecture, a set of "communication logical processes" (CLPs) maintains, in a distributed manner, a collection of "shared-state variables" (SSVs) that describe the state of the environment as well as the externally viewable characteristics of the agents such as physical location. CLPs in fact maintain a history of SSV values over time. In the PDES-MAS system, LPs communicate through ports; the CLPs are arranged in a treelike structure with leaves corresponding to ALPs, in such a manner as to balance accesses to the SSVs. The tree of CLPs is dynamic, with possible reconfiguration of the tree structure and migration of SSVs and/or ALPs in a continual attempt to move SSVs closer to the ALPs that are accessing them. Because the ALPs may progress through simulated time at different rates, answering range queries correctly becomes extremely challenging. The authors in [52] provide some initial range-query algorithms and test them empirically; there is still a need for theoretical analysis of such algorithms.

3. INFORMATION INTEGRATION

The discussion so far has concerned the combination of information-management and simulation methods to create simulation tools that can handle massive data. Another set of interesting ideas concerns information integration, both the integration of heterogeneous real-world datasets and the integration of real-world and simulated data. We discuss these two aspects below.

3.1 Simulation as an integration tool

In his keynote speech at WSC 2013 [8], Eric Bonabeau postulated that agent-based simulations can be viewed as a powerful tool for data integration and an essential means for making sense of big data. As one concrete example, he described issues that arise in marketing. Typically the available datasets are quite disparate in nature and measured at a variety of granularities. These include data about

1. Individual consumer behaviors (purchasing, use of product, communicating about product)
2. Aggregate customer profiles (drivers, awareness, perceptions)
3. Network data (connections, relationships, influence)
4. Touch points (channel affinities, media impact, reach and frequency)
5. Decisionmaking (rationality, emotion, social norms)

The claim is that big data investments alone will not solve the forecasting problem, because such investments merely provide non-overlapping perspectives on individuals from disparate data sources characterized by varying levels of aggregation. To address this problem, an ABS approach can be used to simulate synthetic personas created from these heterogeneous data sources. The key is then to *calibrate* the model using statistical and machine learning techniques in order to approximately match existing datasets. This integrated model can then be used to understand and predict the effect of different types of touch points, perception changes, social network influence, stages of the purchase "journey", and thus to forecast volatility, risk, and reward associated with marketing strategies. In more detail, a brand tracker or survey data can provide customer properties, media and sales data describe marketing effectiveness, industry or product reports cover the product or offer, and social tracking data describe word-of-mouth events and behaviors. The ABS model brings together these four disparate datasets in an integrated way and yields rich insights into consumer behavior that go far beyond mere sales.

Research on calibrating agent-based models is still at an early stage. Many of the existing quantitative techniques developed so far have come from the econometrics community, which has enthusiastically embraced the use of agent-based models. The traditional approach to estimating parameters is the method of *maximum likelihood* [37]. As a simple example, consider data $X = (X_1, X_2, \ldots, X_n)$ representing a sample of i.i.d. draws from the exponential density function $f(x;\theta) = \theta e^{-\theta x}$ for $x \geq 0$. The likelihood of seeing the given data points is $L(\theta;X) = \prod_{i-1}^{n} f(X_i;\theta) = \theta^n e^{-\sum_i X_i}$. The maximum likelihood estimate (MLE) $\hat{\theta}_n$ of θ is obtained by choosing θ to maximize $L(\theta;X)$ (or, equivalently, the logarithm of the likelihood L). A simple calculation yields $\hat{\theta}_n = 1/\bar{X}_n$, where $\bar{X}_n$ is the average of the X_i's. Although MLEs have many desirable properties, the output of an ABS is usually highly nonlinear and complex, so that the likelihood can only be obtained in rare cases; see [1] for an example.

Because of these difficulties, attempts at quantitative calibration have primarily relied on adaptations of the *method of moments* (MM). For the simple exponential example, it is known that the mean of an exponential random variable is given by $E[X] = 1/\theta$. The method of moments proceeds by replacing $E[X]$ by its empirical counterpart $\bar{X}_n$ and solving for θ, which in this case yields the MLE estimator (although in general the MM and MLE estimators do not coincide). For, e.g., a normal distribution, two equations in two unknowns would be used, equating the first two moments to the sample mean and sample variance. More generally, the procedure centers on a vector of observed statistics $Y = (Y^{(1)}, Y^{(2)}, \ldots, Y^{(m)})$ and, for $\theta = (\theta_1, \theta_2, \ldots, \theta_m)$, solves the system $\bar{Y}_n - m(\theta) = 0$, where $Y_1, Y_2, \ldots, Y_n$ are i.i.d. samples of Y and $m(\theta) = E[Y|\theta]$.

The extension of this method to ABS calibration is usually called the *method of simulated moments* (MSM), and is usually attributed to McFadden [41]. In this more general setting, the observations $Y_1, Y_2, \ldots, Y_n$ may represent a stationary ergodic sequence; i.i.d. observations are a special case. Moreover, $m(\theta)$, which is usually too complex to be calculated analytically, is approximated by a simulation-based estimate $\hat{m}(\theta)$, typically obtained by averaging i.i.d. samples of Y from simulation runs having parameter values equal to θ. Finally, the problem of solving $G_n = \bar{Y}_n - \hat{m}(\theta) = 0$ is usually relaxed to the problem of minimizing the generalized distance $J(\theta) = G_n^\top W G_n$, where W is chosen to boost statistical efficiency; see [30] for some relevant theory. Typically—see, e.g., [20]—W is chosen to be an estimate of the inverse of the variance-covariance matrix of the random vector G_n.

The main difficulty encountered in calibration of this sort is that $\hat{m}(\theta)$ is usually expensive to compute for even a single value of theta, so that the stochastic optimization problem of minimizing $J(\theta)$ is highly cost intensive. Recently, researchers have begun to apply some techniques from the field of simulation-based optimization to develop workable algorithms. For example, Fabretti [17] uses heuristic optimization methods, such as Nelder-Mead and genetic algorithms, to try and quickly locate the optimal parameter value. While this approach is a vast improvement over random sampling of θ values, the computational requirements can still be high. An alternative approach in [45] carefully uses *design of experiment* (DOE) techniques—in particular, a nearly-orthogonal Latin hypercube design (see Section 4.2 below)—to select representative values of θ to simulate. The method then uses a flexible surface-fitting technique called "kriging" to approximate the function $\hat{m}(\theta)$, and hence $J(\theta)$. This approximated function (also called a *simulation metamodel*) is then minimized to find the desired calibrated values of θ; see Section 4 below for a discussion of metamodeling. Both of these techniques implicitly assume that the simulation is deterministic in nature; other methods that explicitly consider stochastic model response are potentially applicable here. For example, the kriging method used in [45] could potentially be replaced by stochastic kriging and extensions—see, e.g., [44]—which incorporate simulation variability into the fitting algorithm.

Overall, there are ample research opportunities around the use of simulation as a data integration tool, especially with respect to model calibration. As indicated above, algorithm development is still at an early, largely ad hoc stage. Another interesting question is how to extend existing approaches, which calibrate against a small number of population summary statistics, to calibrate at a finer granularity. Such fine-grained calibration might have the potential for avoiding situations where multiple calibrations are all deemed acceptable but lead to very different predictions [51]. Principled methods for avoiding overfitting during the calibration process are also of great interest, since simulation-model calibration is known to be vulnerable to such issues [36, p. 266]. One advantage of the MSM method is that regularization terms can potentially be incorporated into the objective function J to avoid overfitting.

3.2 Combining real and simulated data

Besides integrating disparate real-world datasets, there is an increasing interest in combining simulated and real world data in order to more deeply integrate domain expertise into data analysis. One method receiving attention is *data assimilation* via *particle filtering*. As an example, the work in [56, 57] concerns the problem of monitoring a wildfire. Domain experts have developed simulation models that capture the probabilistic mechanism by which a fire spreads over terrain. During an actual fire, real-world temperature data from the affected region is available as a stream of time-varying readings from a set of sensors. Particle filtering can be used to combine sensor readings with simulated data to yield more accurate estimates of the fire status than could be obtained from either data source alone.

We give a brief introduction to particle filtering, following [16], and then indicate how particle filtering can be used for data assimilation. Particle filtering (also called "bootstrap" filtering) algorithms are a subclass of *sequential Monte Carlo* methods, which in turn are a subclass of *importance sampling* (IS) methods. We discuss each class of methods in turn. Suppose that, for some $n \geq 1$, our goal is to obtain a Monte Carlo approximation of a probability density $\pi_n(x_{1:n}) = \gamma_n(x_{1:n})/Z_n$ on $\mathscr{X}^n$, where $\mathscr{X}$ denotes the common state space of the x_i's and $z_{i:j}$ denotes the vector $(z_i, z_{i+1}, \ldots, z_j)$. Here γ_n is an unnormalized probability density and $Z_n = \int \gamma_n(x_{1:n})\,dx_{1:n}$ is a normalizing constant. A standard Monte Carlo approach draws N independent samples $\{X_{1:n}^i\}_{1 \leq i \leq N}$ from π_n and then approximates π_n by

$$\hat{\pi}_n(x_{1:n}) = (1/N) \sum_{i=1}^{N} \delta_{X_{1:n}^i}(x_{1:n}),$$

where $\delta_{x_0}(x)$ denotes the Dirac density function with unit probability mass at x_0. An expected value $\int g(x_{1:n})\pi_n(x_{1:n})\,dx_{1:n}$ can then be approximated by $\int g(x_{1:n})\hat{\pi}_n(x_{1:n})\,dx_{1:n} = (1/N)\sum_{i=1}^{N} g(X_{1:n}^i)$. This standard approach may fail however, if the dimension n is large and π_n is highly complex, so that sampling is either impossible or too expensive, e.g., with costs proportional to n. Computation of the normalizing constant is often the culprit with respect to high cost.

Importance sampling methods try to address the foregoing problems using a simple but powerful idea: to sample from a complicated distribution, first sample from a tractable distribution and then "correct" the sampled value via a multiplicative *weight*. In particular, suppose that for some $n \geq 1$ we want to approximate a distribution π_n from which it is hard to sample and there exists a *proposal density* q_n (also called an *importance density*) such that (i) it is relatively easy to sample from q_n and (ii) $q_n(x_{1:n}) > 0$ whenever

$\pi_n(x_{1:n}) > 0$. Then, trivially,

$$\pi_n(x_{1:n}) = w_n(x_{1:n})q_n(x_{1:n})/Z_n \qquad (1)$$

and

$$Z_n = \int w_n(x_{1:n})q_n(x_{1:n})\,dx_{1:n}, \qquad (2)$$

where w_n is the *unnormalized weight function*

$$w(x_{1:n}) = \gamma_n(x_{1:n})/q_n(x_{1:n}).$$

Thus we can (easily) draw N independent samples $\{X^i_{1:n}\}_{1\le i\le N}$ from q_n and insert the resulting Monte Carlo approximation of q_n into (1) and (2) to obtain

$$\hat{\pi}_n(x_{1:n}) = \sum_{i=1}^{N} W^i_n \delta_{X^i_{1:n}}(x_{1:n})$$

and

$$\hat{Z}_n = \frac{1}{N}\sum_{i=1}^{N} w_n(X^i_{1:n}),$$

where the *normalized weights* are given by

$$W^i_n = \frac{w_n(X^i_{1:n})}{\sum_{j=1}^{N} w_n(X^j_{1:n})}.$$

The samples are often called *particles*. Note that this method requires a priori knowledge only of γ_n and not π_n, so there is no need to know the value of the (hard-to-compute) constant Z_n in advance.

A sequential version of the above procedure, called *sequential importance sampling* (SIS) can be applied when the goal is to approximate a sequence $\{\pi_n\}_{n\ge 1}$ of probability measures of increasing dimension. SIS is recursive, so that only an $O(1)$ cost is incurred at each time point. The idea is to use an importance density having a Markov structure, i.e.,

$$q_n(x_{1:n}) = q_1(x_1)\prod_{k=2}^{n} q_k(x_{1:k} \mid x_{1:k-1}) \quad \text{for } n > 1,$$

which can be evaluated recursively. Using the Markov structure, some algebra shows that the unnormalized weights can also be computed recursively: $w_n(x_{1:n}) = w_{n-1}(x_{1:n-1})\alpha(x_{1:n})$, where

$$\alpha_n(x_{1:n}) = \frac{\gamma_n(x_{1:n})}{\gamma_{n-1}(x_{1:n-1})q_n(x_n \mid x_{1:n-1})}.$$

The method as described so far has a severe drawback. As n increases the IS estimate involves the product of more and more random weights, which can cause the variance of the estimate to grow exponentially or can cause $\hat{\pi}_n$ to "collapse", in that one weight will tend to 1 while the rest tend to 0. A solution to this problem is to obtain a new sample of size N at the end of each iteration by resampling the foregoing set of N particles according to their normalized weights $W^1_n,\ldots,W^N_n$. Each element in the new set of particles is independently sampled and is assigned a weight of $1/N$, thus preventing collapse or exponential growth. Note that the new set of particles is a sample from $\hat{\pi}_n$, and hence approximately a sample from π_n. The resulting method is called sequential importance sampling with resampling (SIR).

We now return to the particle filtering method, which starts with a *hidden Markov model* (also called a *state space model*), comprising (i) a discrete-time Markov chain $\{X_n\}_{n\ge 1}$ specified by an initial distribution $p_1(x_1)$ and transition probabilities $p_n(x_n|x_{n-1})$ for $n \ge 2$, and (ii) an *observation process* $\{Y_n\}_{n\ge 1}$ with associated probabilities $p_n(y_n|x_n)$ for $n \ge 1$. The goal is to infer at each time n the conditional probability density $p_n(x_n \mid y_{1:n})$ of the true state, given the observations. The particle filtering algorithm is obtained by specializing the SIR algorithm. Specifically, take $\gamma_n(x_{1:n}) = p_n(x_{1:n}, y_{1:n})$, so that $\pi_n(x_{1:n}) = p_n(x_{1:n} \mid y_{1:n})$. Based on the foregoing discussion, we obtain Algorithm 2. It can be shown that the proposal density $q^*_n(x_n \mid x_{n-1}, y_n) \propto p_n(x_n \mid x_{n-1})p_n(y_n \mid x_n)$ is "optimal" for this algorithm in that it minimizes the variance of the random weights.

Algorithm 2 Particle Filtering

```
1: Sample {X_1^i}_{1≤i≤N} from q_1(x_1 | y_1)
2: Compute weights w_1(X_1^i) = p_1(X_1^i) p_n(y_1 | X_1^i) / q_n(X_1^i | y_1) for 1 ≤ i ≤ N
3: Compute normalized weights {W_1^i}_{1≤i≤N}
4: Resample {(W_1^i, X_1^i)}_{1≤i≤N} to obtain {(1/N, X̄_1^i)}_{1≤i≤N}
5: for n ≥ 2 do
6:     Sample {X_n^i}_{1≤i≤N} from q_n(x_n | y_n, X̄_{n-1}^i)
7:     for i = 1,2,...,N do
8:         Compute weight α_n^i =
               p_n(y_n | X_n^i) p_n(X_n^i | X̄_{n-1}^i) / q_n(X_n^i | y_n, X̄_{n-1}^i)
9:     end for
10:    Compute normalized weights W_n^i = α_n^i / Σ_{j=1}^N α_n^j for 1 ≤ i ≤ N
11:    Resample {(W_n^i, X_n^i)}_{1≤i≤N} to obtain {(1/N, X̄_n^i)}_{1≤i≤N}
12: end for
```

In [56], Xue et al. exploit the particle filtering algorithm to combine simulated data and sensor measurements. Their modified version of the DEVS-FIRE model simulates the stochastic progression of a wildfire over a gridded representation of terrain, where the current fire state records for each cell whether the cell is unburned, burning, or burned and, if burning, the intensity of the fire. The state of the fire after the nth simulation step and the corresponding sensor data correspond to x_n and y_n as above. The goal is therefore to compute the conditional density $p_n(x_n \mid y_n)$, i.e., to use the sensor data to "correct" the simulation or, looked at another way, to use the simulation to infer the state of the fire from the sensor data. The simulation steps correspond to increments of Δt simulated time units, where Δt is determined by the sensor measurement frequencies and the model's time-scale granularity. Based on scientific studies, the authors obtain a Gaussian model of sensor behavior, which leads to a closed-form expression for the observation function $p_n(y_n \mid x_n)$ as required in Steps 2 and 8. The original formulation in [56] uses the state transition probability $p_n(x_n \mid x_{n-1})$ as the proposal density q_n for $n > 1$ and uses $p_1(x_1)$ for q_1. With these choices, the formulas for the weights reduce to an evaluation of the observation function in Steps 2 and 8. Moreover, the task of sampling from $q_n(x_n \mid y_n, \bar{X}^i_{n-1})$ in Step 6 reduces to sampling from $p_n(x_n \mid \bar{X}^i_{n-1})$; this sampling is accomplished simply by setting the state of the simulation to $\bar{X}^i_{n-1}$ and then simulating for Δt time units. (The initial sampling in Step 1 is handled similarly.)

Note that, unlike the optimal proposal density q^*_n, the foregoing version of q_n ignores the sensor data y_n. Experiments with the model showed, perhaps not surprisingly, that accuracy degrades when the transition density $p_n(x_n \mid x_{n-1})$ is far from the optimal proposal density q^*_n mentioned above. The authors address this issue in [57], where they provide a proposal density that is sensitive to the sensor measurements. In brief, the process starts by first generating a fire state x from $p_n(x_n \mid x_{n-1})$ as described earlier. Then, based on sensor readings, another fire state x' is generated from x by (i) randomly igniting unburned cells in x that are deemed to have sufficiently high sensor temperatures and (ii) "turning off" the fire for x cells where sensor temperatures are deemed sufficiently cool. Then either x or x' is selected at random, according to a probability that is based on the relative "confidence" in the sensors and in the simulation model, and the selected state is returned as the sample from q_n. To obtain analytical expressions for both $p_n(X_n^i \mid \bar{X}_{n-1}^i)$ and for $q_n(X_n^i \mid y_n, \bar{X}_{n-1}^i)$, as are needed to compute the weights in Step 8, $M > 1$ additional samples are drawn from these distributions using the methods discussed above and then the density functions are estimated using a standard *kernel density estimator* (KDE). For example, given samples $x_1, x_2, \ldots, x_M$ from the density $f_n(x) = p_n(x \mid \bar{X}_{n-1}^i)$, the density function is estimated as $\hat{f}_n(x) = (Mh)^{-1} \sum_{i=1}^{M} K\big((x - x_i)/h\big)$, where $h > 0$ is the KDE "bandwidth" and K is the KDE "kernel". The kernel is a nonnegative symmetric function such that $K(0) > 0$ and $K(x)$ is non-increasing in $|x|$, e.g., $K(x) = e^{-|x|}$; see [49] for a classical treatment and [15] for a discussion of more advanced kernel density methods. Finally, the method sets $p_n(X_n^i \mid \bar{X}_{n-1}^i) = \hat{f}_n(X_n^i)$ in Step 8, and the q_n term is handled analogously. Preliminary experiments indicate that the new proposal distribution can potentially lead to improvements in accuracy. As with model calibration, there are many opportunities for research in this area.

4. SIMULATION METAMODELING

We now focus our attention on the data generated from simulation models. Large, high-resolution models can easily generate terabytes of data during a run. Moreover, simulation models often have many input parameters, so there can be a combinatorially huge parameter space to explore, with large amounts of data being generated for each parameter-value combination simulated. For stochastic models, the amount of data generated is multiplied by the number of Monte Carlo replications. These challenges are exacerbated in composite modeling systems such as Splash. To fully exploit the potential of simulation models as tools for understanding complex systems, it is crucial that the generation of simulated data be carefully controlled and efficient.

Often, the first task in understanding a model is to identify the input parameters to which the model is most sensitive. Such sensitivity analysis can drastically reduce the size of the input parameter space by decreasing its dimensionality. Knowing which parameters are the most important can also guide the input-data collection process by focusing resources on data that yields sharper estimates of the important parameters. Often the parameters correspond to decision variables, and the goal is to identify optimal parameter settings that maximize or minimize some performance measure of interest. As discussed previously, the problem of model calibration falls into this category, where the performance measure to be minimized is the discrepancy between simulated and observed data. More generally, engineers and scientists have a set of questions that they want to answer using the model. One approach to controlling the amount of simulated data that is generated is to try and simulate just enough to capture the features pertinent to the questions of interest. Specifically, the use of statistical experimental-design methodology can reduce data-generation requirements by orders of magnitude. As discussed in what follows, the key concept underlying experimental design is simulation metamodeling.

4.1 Simple and Complex Metamodels

A simulation metamodel is a simplified functional representation of a simulation model, i.e., a response surface, that approximates the model response as a function of the input parameters. For a stochastic model, the response is often an expected value of some quantity of interest, such as profit. An appealing property of a metamodel is that is supports "simulation on demand": once a metamodel has been fit to the simulation data, then an approximation of the model output corresponding to given input values can be obtained almost instantly, allowing for exploration of a model in real time. For simplicity, we focus on real-valued responses throughout.

Metamodels vary in their complexity. The classic *polynomial model* relates the model response $Y(\mathbf{x})$ to the input parameters $\mathbf{x} = (x_1, x_2, \ldots, x_n)$ via

$$\begin{aligned} Y(\mathbf{x}) = &\beta_0 + \beta_1 x_1 + \beta_2 x_2 + \cdots + \beta_n x_n + \beta_{1,2} x_1 x_2 + \cdots \\ &+ \beta_{1,2,3} x_1 x_2 x_3 + \cdots + \beta_{1,2,\ldots,n} x_1 x_2 \cdots x_n + \varepsilon, \end{aligned} \tag{3}$$

where the β coefficients are real-valued constants and ε is a zero-mean random variable that encapsulates the stochastic variability. (Dropping ε in the above equation thus yields a model of the expected model response.) When only $\beta_0, \beta_1, \ldots, \beta_n$ are positive, we obtain a *linear model*, perhaps the simplest possible metamodel. (Sometimes, confusingly, the full polynomial model is referred to as a "linear model" because it is linear in the β coefficients.) The terms of the form $\beta_i x_i$ represent "main effects", whereas the remaining terms model second-order interaction effects, third-order effects, and so on.

At the other end of the complexity spectrum are *Gaussian process* metamodels. For deterministic models, perhaps the simplest form of such a model is

$$Y(\mathbf{x}) = \beta_0 + M(\mathbf{x}), \tag{4}$$

where the constant β_0 represents the mean response and $M(\mathbf{x})$ is a *stationary Gaussian process* (also called a *stationary Gaussian random field*), that is, a real-valued random process such that for any finite collection of points $\mathbf{x}_1, \mathbf{x}_2, \ldots, \mathbf{x}_r$ the random vector

$$V = \big(M(\mathbf{x}_1), M(\mathbf{x}_2), \ldots, M(\mathbf{x}_r)\big)$$

has a multivariate normal distribution with, $E[V] = (0, 0, \ldots, 0)$. In applications, the covariance matrix is often defined as

$$\Sigma_M(\mathbf{x}_i, \mathbf{x}_j) = Cov[M(\mathbf{x}_i), M(\mathbf{x}_j)] = \tau^2 \prod_{k=1}^{n} \exp\big(-\theta_j (x_{i,k} - x_{j,k})^2\big) \tag{5}$$

for each i and j. When the simulation is run at a set of *design points* $\mathbf{x}_1, \mathbf{x}_2, \ldots, \mathbf{x}_r$, the stochasticity of M models the uncertainty associated with the output of the simulation when run at a point $\mathbf{x}_0$ that is not one of the design points. Given the observed model outputs at the design points, it can be shown [3] that the optimal estimator (in terms of minimizing mean square error) is

$$\hat{Y}(\mathbf{x}_0) = \beta_0 + \Sigma_M(\mathbf{x}_0, \cdot)^\top \Sigma_M^{-1} (\bar{Y} - \beta_0 \mathbf{1}_r), \tag{6}$$

where $\Sigma_M(\mathbf{x}_0, \cdot) = \big(\Sigma_M(\mathbf{x}_0, \mathbf{x}_1), \ldots, \Sigma_M(\mathbf{x}_0, \mathbf{x}_r)\big)$, the vector $\bar{Y}$ is given by $\big(Y(\mathbf{x}_1), \ldots, Y(\mathbf{x}_r)\big)$, the $r \times r$ matrix Σ_M is the covariance matrix of the design points, and $\mathbf{1}_r = (1, 1, \ldots, 1)$ is a vector of length r. The main observations are that $\hat{Y}(\mathbf{x}_i)$ coincides with the observed value $Y(\mathbf{x}_i)$ at each design point $\mathbf{x}_i$ and, for an arbitrary point $\mathbf{x}_0$, the centered estimator $\hat{Y}(\mathbf{x}_0) - \beta_0$ is a linear combination of $Y(\mathbf{x}_1) - \beta_0, Y(\mathbf{x}_2) - \beta_0, \ldots, Y(\mathbf{x}_r) - \beta_0$. In practice the various parameters that appear in (6)—such as β_0, Σ_M, and so on—are estimated from the data.

For stochastic simulations, the jth observation at design point $\mathbf{x}_i$ is modeled as in (4), except with an additional additive term $\varepsilon_j(\mathbf{x})$ that represents the random variability between simulation runs at a given design point. Here, for each i, the random variables $\varepsilon_1(\mathbf{x}_i), \varepsilon_2(\mathbf{x}_i), \ldots$ are i.i.d. normal with mean 0 and variance $V(\mathbf{x}_i)$, independent of M and of $\varepsilon_j(\mathbf{x}_h)$ for all j and $h \neq i$. The estimator $\hat{Y}(\mathbf{x}_0)$ is defined almost as in (6) above, but the ith element of $\bar{Y}$ is now the average result over all simulation runs at design point $\mathbf{x}_i$ and the term Σ_M^{-1} is replaced by $[\Sigma_M + \Sigma_\varepsilon]^{-1}$, where Σ_ε is the

	Parameters						
Run	x_1	x_2	x_3	x_4	x_5	x_6	x_7
1	-1	-1	-1	1	1	1	-1
2	1	-1	-1	-1	-1	1	1
3	-1	1	-1	-1	1	-1	1
4	1	1	-1	1	-1	-1	-1
5	-1	-1	1	1	-1	-1	1
6	1	-1	1	-1	1	-1	-1
7	-1	1	1	-1	-1	1	-1
8	1	1	1	1	1	1	1

Figure 3: Resolution III design for seven parameters

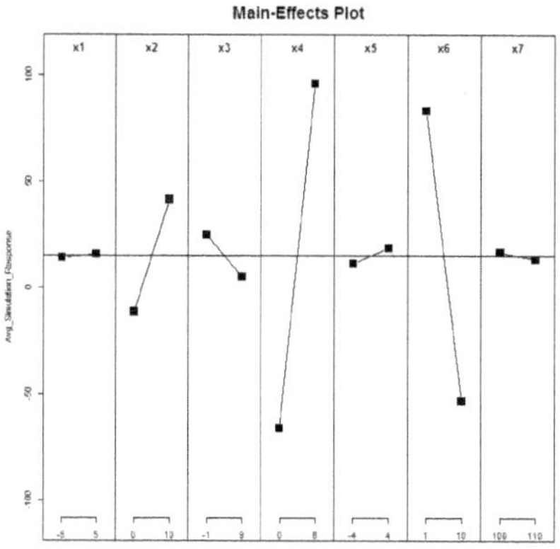

Figure 4: Main-effects plot for seven parameters

Run	x_1	x_2
1	-4	-3
2	-3	4
3	-2	-1
4	-1	2
5	0	0
6	1	-2
7	2	1
8	3	-4
9	4	3

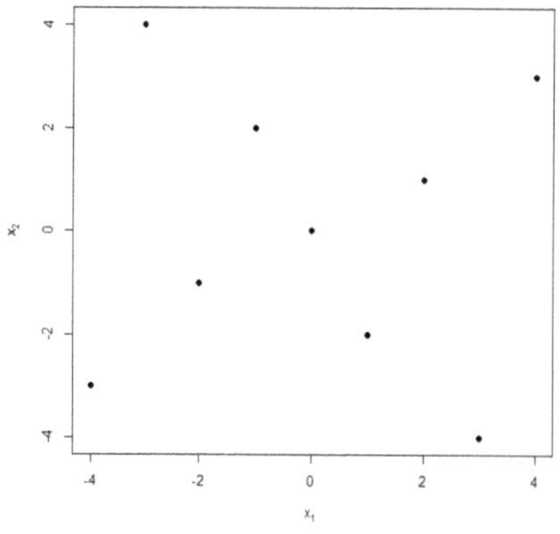

Figure 5: Latin hypercube design for two factors and nine runs

covariance matrix given by

$$\Sigma_\varepsilon(h,i) = Cov\Big[(1/n_h)\sum_{j=1}^{n_h} \varepsilon_j(\mathbf{x}_h), (1/n_i)\sum_{j=1}^{n_i} \varepsilon_j(\mathbf{x}_i)\Big]$$

and n_j denotes the number of Monte Carlo replications at $\mathbf{x}_j$.

Some good discussions of Gaussian process metamodels for deterministic and stochastic simulations can be found in [47] and [3], respectively. The basic ideas extend to more general settings where, for deterministic simulations, the metamodel has the form (4) but the random field M need not necessarily be Gaussian and the constant β_0 may be replaced by a more general regression model, e.g., as in (3). In this more general context, the metamodeling technique is often called *kriging*, after mining engineer D. G. Krige. The authors in [3] denote by *stochastic kriging* their extension of kriging obtained by adding a term ε_j, as discussed previously, to encompass stochastic models. See [44] for a recent example of stochastic kriging using a random field more complex than a basic Gaussian field.

4.2 Metamodeling and Experimental Design

The parameters of a metamodel encapsulate salient characteristics of simulation-model behavior. Selection of a particular metamodel leads to specific procedures for fitting the metamodel parameters. The power of experimental design lies in the observation that, if a relatively simple metamodel suffices to represent the simulated response, then the parameters of the metamodel—i.e., the key features of the simulation response—can often be estimated by exploring a very small but carefully selected subset of the parameter space, thereby reducing the amount of data that needs to be generated.

To illustrate, consider the polynomial model in (3) and suppose that $n = 7$. Of particular interest in this setting are the coefficients β_1 through β_7, which are called "main effects" or "sensitivities" and describe the change in simulation response corresponding to a given change in the parameter value while holding all other parameters constant. In classical experimental design, low and high values that represent ranges of feasibility or of problem-specific interest would be determined for each parameter, based on the experimenter's domain expertise. (Parameter values are usually called "factor levels" in experimental design terminology.) A naive "full factorial design" would then run simulations at all of the $2^7 = 128$ possible combinations of parameter values. Suppose, however, that prior knowledge leads one to believe that the higher-order terms in (3) can be ignored, so that a simple linear model adequately captures the shape of the response surface. One can then use a "resolution III fractional factorial design" as shown in Figure 3 to estimate the main effects using only eight simulation runs; in the figure, the symbols "-1" and "1" correspond to low and high values. For fractional factorial designs, the columns are orthogonal, which facilitates the ensuing statistical analysis. Note that, under the linearity assumption, the main effects capture virtually all model behavior of interest. Main effects are often displayed as in Figure 4. In this "main effects plot", each factor is characterized by two points, where the left (resp., right) point is the average simulation response over all runs where the parameter is set to its low (resp., high) value; these values are shown beneath the points. Main effects plots are typically accompanied with diagnostics that assess the statistical significance of the effect sizes, such as "half-normal plots", also called "Daniel plots" [14].

In a similar manner, if only third-order and higher effects can be ignored, one can estimate main effect using a resolution IV design that requires 16 runs. If the goal is to estimate both main and second-order effects, and if one can ignore third-order and higher effects, then a resolution V design requires only 32 runs. Thus experimental design methodology can be used to minimize the amount of data generated based on the both complexity of the response and the response characteristics of interest.

Rather than using only extreme values of the parameters as in fractional factorial designs, it is often desirable to use design points spread out evenly across the parameter space, especially when fitting complex nonlinear metamodels. A number of authors [3, 45] propose variants of *Latin hypercube* (LH) designs as providing a good compromise between covering the parameter space and minimizing the number of experiments. The basic procedure for a "randomized" LH with n parameters and $r \geq n$ design points—where r is typically of the form 2^k or $2^k + 1$ for some $k \geq 1$—is as follows. Determine r equally-spaced levels for each parameter and generate an $n \times r$ design matrix where each column is a random permutation of $\{1, 2, \ldots, r\}$. Then the ith row gives the levels to use for the ith simulation run. Figure 5 shows a randomized LH design for $n = 2$ parameters and $r = 9$ levels (and design points), where the levels are designated as $-4, -3, -2, -1, 0, 1, 2, 3, 4$, along with a plot of the design points. The chief characteristic of an LH design is that each possible x_1 value appears once, as does each possible x_2 value. In general, randomized LH designs may not work well unless $r \gg n$. LH designs, however, are usually well behaved when the columns of the design matrix are orthogonal. (The LH design in Figure 5 is in fact orthogonal.) Because orthogonal designs can be rather hard to create, schemes for *nearly orthogonal LH* (NOLH) designs have been developed that provide good space-filling and orthogonality properties while being computationally efficient [12].

Because of its practical importance and theoretical elegance, the literature on experimental design is enormous. Treatments that are oriented toward stochastic simulation include the book of Kleijnen [34] and the tutorial paper of Sanchez and Wan [46]; the latter reference contains a nice table summarizing a wide variety of modern experimental designs. In [26], the authors describe the experiment management capabilities of the Splash composite-modeling platform, where metadata is used to provide an experimenter with a unified view of composite model parameters. Splash also provides a facility for specifying experimental designs as well as runtime support for setting parameter values by automatically synthesizing, via a templating mechanism, the input files that each component model expects.

4.3 Metamodeling and Factor Screening

Factor screening refers to the process of identifying the subset of parameters to which the simulation response is most sensitive. As mentioned previously, focusing on the key factors can greatly reduce the amount of generated data and experimentation effort. This problem is intimately related to metamodeling because, as we have seen, metamodel coefficients can quantify the sensitivity of the simulation output to changes in parameter values. Thus these metamodel coefficients can be used to classify model parameters as "important" or "unimportant".

For example, if a linear metamodel suffices, the observation noise can be modeled as Gaussian, and the main-effect coefficients are positive, then efficient *sequential bifurcation* methods can be used to identify important factors from among a potentially large set [50]. This type of procedure starts by dividing the set of parameters into two groups, and testing each group to decide if it contains at least one important parameter; such group testing is much faster than testing each individual parameter. If a group contains no important parameters, then it is discarded; otherwise, the group is again divided in two, and the testing procedure continues recursively.

For complex metamodels, the screening problem is much more difficult, and is a topic of ongoing research. Consider, for example, the Gaussian process metamodel in Section 4.1. It follows from (5) that a plausible measure for the importance of the jth factor is the coefficient θ_j: a very low value for θ_j implies a correlation function that approximately equals 1, so that there is no variability in model response as the value of the jth parameter changes. A number of studies have looked at the factor screening problem in this context; see, for example, [38].

5. CONCLUSION

To effectively support decisions in the enterprise, the information contained in big data must be combined with the information known to domain experts. Consequently, the fields of information management and of system simulation are intermingling more and more over time. Many of the questions concerning the interplay between models and data have not been formulated very precisely, and many of the techniques developed so far have been ad hoc. The PODS community is well poised to address the many issues around the increasingly important topic of model-data ecosystems.

Acknowledgments

The author wishes to thank Eric Bonabeau and Haidong Xue for providing materials and support and Ron Fagin for providing helpful feedback.

6. REFERENCES

[1] S. Alfarano, F. Wagner, and T. Lux. Estimation of agent-based models: the case of an asymmetric herding. *Comput. Econ.*, 26:19–49, 2005.

[2] T. T. Allen. *Introduction to Discrete Event Simulation and Agent-Based Modeling*. Springer, 2011.

[3] B. E. Ankenman, B. L. Nelson, and J. Staum. Stochastic kriging for simulation metamodeling. *Oper. Res.*, 58(2):371–382, 2010.

[4] Apache Hadoop. https://hadoop.apache.org.

[5] S. Arumugam, R. Jampani, L. Perez, F. Xu, C. Jermaine, and P. J. Haas. MCDB-R: Risk analysis in the database. In *VLDB*, pages 782–793, 2010.

[6] K. R. Bisset, J. Chen, S. Deodhar, X. Feng, Y. Ma, and M. V. Marathe. Indemics: An interactive high-performance computing framework for data-intensive epidemic modeling. *ACM Trans. Model. Comput. Simul.*, 24(1):4, 2014.

[7] E. Bonabeau. Agent-based modeling: Methods and techniques for simulating human systems. *Proc. Nat. Acad. Sci.*, 99(3):7280–7287, 2002.

[8] E. Bonabeau. Big data and the bright future of simulation: The case of agent-based modeling. Keynote address, *Winter Simulation Conference*, December 2013.

[9] E. Bonabeau. Building accurate predictive models "without data". *Icosystem Blog*, accessed March 31. `http://www.icosystem.com/building-accurate-predictive-models-without-data`, 2014.

[10] K. Börner. Plug-and-play macroscopes. *Commun. ACM*, 54(3):60–69, 2011.

[11] Z. Cai, Z. Vagena, L. L. Perez, S. Arumugam, P. J. Haas, and C. M. Jermaine. Simulation of database-valued Markov chains using SimSQL. In *SIGMOD*, pages 63–7–648, 2013.

[12] T. M. Cioppa and T. W. Lucas. Efficient nearly orthogonal and space-filling Latin hypercubes. *Technometrics*, 49(1):45–55, 2007.

[13] W. D. Collins, C. M. Bitz, M. L. Blackmon, G. B. Bonan, C. S. Bretherton, J. A. Carton, P. Chang, S. C. Doney, J. J. Hack, T. B. Henderson, J. T. Kiehl, W. G. Large, D. S. Mckenna, B. D. Santer, and R. D. Smith. The community climate system model version 3 (CCSM3). *J. Climate*, 19:2122–2143, 2006.

[14] C. Daniel. Use of half-normal plots in interpreting factorial two-level experiments. *Technometrics*, 1(4):311–341, 1959.

[15] L. Devroye and G. Lugosi. *Combinatorial Methods in Density Estimation*. Springer, 2001.

[16] A. Doucet and A. M. Johansen. A tutorial on particle filtering and smoothing: fifteen years later. In D. Crisan and B. Rozovskii, editors, *The Oxford Handbook of Nonlinear Filtering*. Oxford University Press, 2011.

[17] A. Fabretti. On the problem of calibrating an agent based model for financial markets. *J. Econ. Interact. Coord.*, 8:277–293, 2013.

[18] D. A. Ford, J. H. Kaufman, and I. Eiron. An extensible spatial and temporal epidemiological modelling system. *Int. J. Health Geographics*, 5(4), 2006.

[19] B. L. Fox and P. W. Glynn. Discrete-time conversion for simulating finite-horizon Markov processes. *SIAM J. Appl. Math*, 50(5):1457–1473, 1990.

[20] R. Franke and F. Westerhoff. Structural stochastic volatility in asset pricing dynamics: Estimation and model contest. *J. Econ. Dynam. Control*, 36:1193–1211, 2012.

[21] R. Gemulla, E. Nijkamp, P. J. Haas, and Y. Sismanis. Large-scale matrix factorization with distributed stochastic gradient descent. In *KDD*, pages 69–77, 2011.

[22] P. W. Glynn and W. Whitt. The asymptotic efficiency of simulation estimators. *Oper. Res.*, 40(3):505–520, 1992.

[23] H. Godfray, J. Pretty, S. Thomas, E. Warham, and J. Beddington. Linking policy on climate and food. *Science*, 331(6020):1013–1014, 2011.

[24] L. M. Haas, M. A. Hernández, H. Ho, L. Popa, and M. Roth. Clio grows up: From research prototype to industrial tool. In *SIGMOD Conference*, pages 805–810, 2005.

[25] P. J. Haas. Improving the efficiency of stochastic composite simulation models via result caching. 2014. Submitted for publication.

[26] P. J. Haas, N. C. Barberis, P. Phoungphol, I. Terrizzano, W.-C. Tan, P. G. Selinger, and P. P.Maglio. Splash: Simulation optimization in complex systems of systems. In *50th Allerton Conf.*, 2012.

[27] P. J. Haas, P. P. Maglio, P. G. Selinger, and W. C. Tan. Data is dead... without what-if models. *PVLDB*, 4(12):1486–1489, 2011.

[28] P. J. Haas and Y. Sismanis. On aligning massive time-series data in splash. In *VLDB Big Data Workshop*, 2012. Available at `researcher.watson.ibm.com/researcher/files/us-phaas/mta.pdf`.

[29] J. M. Hammersley and D. C. Handscomb. *Monte Carlo Methods*. Chapman and Hall, 1964.

[30] L. P. Hansen. Large sample properties of generalized method of moments estimators. *Econometrica*, 50(4):1029–1054, 1982.

[31] B. Howe and D. Maier. Algebraic manipulation of scientific datasets. *VLDB J.*, 14(4):397–416, 2005.

[32] T. T. Huang, A. Drewnowski, S. K. Kumanyika, and T. A. Glass. A systems-oriented multilevel framework for addressing obesity in the 21st century. *Preventing Chronic Disease*, 6(3), 2009.

[33] R. Jampani, F. Xu, M. Wu, L. L. Perez, C. Jermaine, and P. J. Haas. The Monte Carlo Database System: Stochastic analysis close to the data. *TODS*, 36(3):1–41, 2011.

[34] J. P. C. Kleijnen. *Design and Analysis of Simulation Experiments*. Springer, 2008.

[35] F. Kuhl, R. Weatherly, and J. Dahmann. *Creating Computer Simulation Systems: An Introduction to the High Level Architecture*. Prentice Hall, New Jersey, 1999.

[36] A. M. Law. *Simulation Modeling and Analysis*. McGraw-Hill, sixth edition, 2014.

[37] E. L. Lehmann and G. Casella. *Theory of Point Estimation*. Springer, second edition, 1998.

[38] C. Linkletter, D. Bingham, N. Hengartner, and K. Q. Ye. Variable selection for Gaussian process models in computer experiments. *Technometrics*, 48(4):478–490, 2006.

[39] C. M. Macal and M. J. North. Introductory tutorial: Agent-based modeling and simulation. In *Proc. Winter Simul. Conf.*, pages 362–376, 2013.

[40] F. Makari, C. Teflioudi, R. Gemulla, P. J. Haas, and Y. Sismanis. Shared-memory and shared-nothing stochastic gradient descent algorithms for matrix completion. *Knowl. Info. Sys.*, 2014. In press.

[41] D. McFadden. A method of simulated moments for estimation of discrete response models without numerical integration. *Econometrica*, 57(5):995–1026, 1989.

[42] L. L. Perez, S. Arumugam, and C. M. Jermaine. Evaluation of probabilistic threshold queries in MCDB. In *SIGMOD*, pages 687–698, 2010.

[43] H. Robbins and S. Monro. A stochastic approximation method. *Ann. Math. Statist.*, 22:400–407, 1951.

[44] P. Salemi, J. Staum, and B. L. Nelson. Generalized integrated brownian fields for simulation metamodeling. In *Proc. Winter Simul. Conf.*, pages 543–554, 2013.

[45] I. Salle and M. Yildizoglu. Efficient sampling and metamodeling for computational economic models. *Comput. Econ.*, 2013. DOI 10.1007/s10614-013-9406-7.

[46] S. M. Sanchez and H. Wan. Work smarter, not harder: a tutorial on designing and conducting simulation experiments. In *Proc. Winter Simul. Conf.*, page 170, 2012.

[47] T. J. Santner, B. J. Williams, and W. I. Notz. *The Design and Analysis of Computer Experiments*. Springer, 2003.

[48] T. C. Schelling. Dynamic models of segregation. *J. Math. Sociol.*, 1:143–186, 1971.

[49] D. W. Scott. *Multivariate Density Estimation: Theory Practice, and Visualization*. Wiley, 1992.

[50] H. Shen and H. Wan. A hybrid method for simulation factor screening. In *Proc. Winter Simul. Conf.*, pages 382–389, 2006.

[51] D. Shi and R. J. Brooks. The range of predictions for calibrated agent-based simulation models. In *Proc. Winter Simul. Conf.*, pages 1198–1206, 2007.

[52] V. Suryanarayanan and G. K. Theodoropoulos. Synchronised range queries in distributed simulations of multiagent systems. *ACM Trans. Model. Comput. Simul.*, 23(4):25, 2013.

[53] W. C. Tan, P. J. Haas, R. L. Mak, C. A. Kieliszewski, P. G. Selinger, P. P. Maglio, S. Glissmann, M. Cefkin, and Y. Li. Splash: a platform for analysis and simulation of health. In *ACM Intl. Health Informatics Symp. (IHI)*, pages 543–552, 2012.

[54] G. A. Wainer. *Discrete-Event Modeling and Simulation: A Practitioner's Approach*. CRC Press, 2009.

[55] G. Wang, M. Vaz Salles, B. Sowell, X. Wang, T. Cao, A. Demers, J. Gehrke, and W. White. Behavioral simulations in MapReduce. *Proc. VLDB*, 3(1):952–963, 2010.

[56] H. Xue, F. Gu, and X. Hu. Data assimilation using sequential Monte Carlo methods in wildfire spread simulation. *ACM Trans. Model. Comput. Simul.*, 22(4):23, 2012.

[57] H. Xue and X. Hu. An effective proposal distribution for sequential Monte Carlo methods-based wildfire data assimilation. In *Proc. Winter Simul. Conf.*, pages 1938–1949, 2013.

All-Distances Sketches, Revisited: HIP Estimators for Massive Graphs Analysis

Edith Cohen
Microsoft Research SVC
editco@microsoft.com

ABSTRACT

Graph datasets with billions of edges, such as social and Web graphs, are prevalent. To be feasible, computation on such large graphs should scale linearly with graph size. All-distances sketches (ADSs) are emerging as a powerful tool for scalable computation of some basic properties of individual nodes or the whole graph.

ADSs were first proposed two decades ago (Cohen 1994) and more recent algorithms include ANF (Palmer, Gibbons, and Faloutsos 2002) and hyperANF (Boldi, Rosa, and Vigna 2011). A sketch of logarithmic size is computed for each node in the graph and the computation in total requires only a near linear number of edge relaxations. From the ADS of a node, we can estimate neighborhood cardinalities (the number of nodes within some query distance) and closeness centrality. More generally we can estimate the distance distribution, effective diameter, similarities, and other parameters of the full graph. We make several contributions which facilitate a more effective use of ADSs for scalable analysis of massive graphs.

We provide, for the first time, a unified exposition of ADS algorithms and applications. We present the Historic Inverse Probability (HIP) estimators which are applied to the ADS of a node to estimate a large natural class of queries including neighborhood cardinalities and closeness centralities. We show that our HIP estimators have at most half the variance of previous neighborhood cardinality estimators and that this is essentially optimal. Moreover, HIP obtains a polynomial improvement over state of the art for more general domain queries and the estimators are simple, flexible, unbiased, and elegant.

The ADS generalizes Min-Hash sketches, used for approximating cardinality (distinct count) on data streams. We obtain lower bounds on Min-Hash cardinality estimation using classic estimation theory. We illustrate the power of HIP, both in terms of ease of application and estimation quality, by comparing it to the HyperLogLog algorithm (Flajolet et al. 2007), demonstrating a significant improvement over this state-of-the-art practical algorithm.

We also study the quality of ADS estimation of distance ranges, generalizing the near-linear time factor-2 approximation of the diameter.

1. INTRODUCTION

Massive graph datasets are prevalent and include social and Web graphs. Due to sheer size, computation over these graphs should scale nearly linearly with the number of edges. One task that received considerable attention is computing the distance distribution. The distance distribution of a node i contains, for each distance d, the number of nodes that are of distance d from i, that is, the cardinality of the d-neighborhood of i. The distance distribution of a graph is the number of pairs of nodes for each distance d. The distance distribution captures important properties of nodes and of the whole network, reflecting on performance and information propagation, and incorporates parameters such as node centrality, spid, and effective diameter [25, 41, 21, 8, 9, 4].

The distance distributions for all nodes can be computed through an all-pairs shortest paths, which is computationally expensive, even with state-of-the-art methods [37, 2], and not feasible for very large networks. Efficient algorithms which approximate the distance distributions were proposed in the last two decades [14, 41, 18, 21, 8]. Implementations [4] based on ANF [41] and hyperANF [8] , and more recently, [15], based on [14, 18], target social graphs with billions of edges.

At the core of all these algorithms [14, 41, 18, 21, 8] is a computation of a sketch for each node, which we call the *All Distances Sketch (ADS)*. The ADS of a node v contains a random sample of nodes, where the inclusion probability of a node u decreases with its distance from v (more precisely, inversely proportional to the number of nodes closer to v than u). For each included node, the ADS also contains its distance from v. The ADSs of different nodes are *coordinated*, which means that the inclusions of each particular node in the ADSs of other nodes are positively correlated. Coordination is an artifact of the way the ADSs are computed (we could not compute independent sketches as efficiently) but also enables further applications such as estimating similarity between neighborhoods of two nodes [14], their distance, and their closeness similarities [15].

An ADS is an extension of the simpler and better-known *Min-Hash* sketch [29, 14] (term min-wise/min-hash was coined later by Broder [13]): The ADS of a node v is essentially the union of coordinated Min-Hash sketches of all the sets of the i closest nodes to v (for all possible values of i.) Min-Hash sketches are extensively used for approximate distinct counting [29, 14, 24, 5] and similarity estimation [14, 13, 12] and come in three flavors, which correspond to sampling schemes: A k-min sketch [29, 14] is a k sample obtained with replacement, a bottom-k sketch [14] is a k sample without replacement, and a k-partition sketch [29] samples one from each of the k buckets in a random partition. All three flavors were studied because they provide different tradeoffs between update costs, information, and maintenance costs. In all three, the integer parameter $k \geq 1$ controls a tradeoff between the information content (and accuracy of attainable estimates) of the sketch and resource usage (for storing, updating, or querying the sketch). Coordination of the sketches corresponds to coordination of the underlying samples, a concept that can be traced back four decades [11]. Accordingly, ADSs come in the same three flavors: k-mins [14, 41], bottom-k [14, 18], and k-partition [8], and have

PODS'14, June 22–27, 2014, Snowbird, UT, USA.

ACM 978-1-4503-2375-8/14/06 ...$15.00.
http://dx.doi.org/10.1145/2594538.2594546.

expected size $\leq k \ln n$. Our detailed presentation of all flavors, provided in Section 2, facilitates a unified study of estimators.

Algorithms which compute the set of ADSs are based on classic shortest-paths algorithms: BFS, which performs pruned Breadth First Searches (or Dijkstra when edges are weighted) [14], and DP [41, 8], which uses dynamic programming and applies when edges are unweighted (ADS computation is implicit in [41, 21, 8], as entries are computed but not retained.) Both BFS and DP use $O(km \log n)$ edge relaxations (where m is the number of edges and n the number of nodes). They have similar main-memory single-processor performance, but different implementation advantages.

Our main technical contributions are in the *estimation* component, where we use the ADSs to estimate the distance distribution, closeness centralities, and more general queries that are useful for analysis of social and other massive graphs. Our estimators, while clean and elegant, are geared for practice: getting the most from the information present in the sketch (in an exact, rather than an asymptotic sense), in terms of minimizing variance. Specifically, we use the Coefficient of Variation (CV), which is the ratio of the standard deviation to the mean,

Prior to our work, ADS-based neighborhood cardinality estimators [14, 18, 41, 28, 8] were applied by obtaining from the ADS a corresponding Min-Hash sketch of the neighborhood and applying a cardinality estimator [14, 29, 24, 28] to that Min-Hash sketch. We refer to these estimators as *basic*.

Cardinality estimators through the lens of estimation theory: In Section 3 we review Min-Hash cardinality estimators. Our exposition provides new insights from estimation theory on the optimality of these seemingly ad-hoc estimators. Our analysis also facilitates the comparison of basic estimators with the new estimators we propose here. The first-order term (and an upper bound) on the CV of the basic estimators is $1/\sqrt{k-2}$. We show, using the Lehmann-Scheffé theorem, that these estimators are the (unique) optimal unbiased estimators, in terms of minimizing variance.

Historic Inverse Probability (HIP) estimators: In Section 4 we present the novel HIP estimators, which improve over the basic estimators. The improvement is possible by utilizing all information present in the ADS (or accumulated during its computation), rather than only looking at the Min-Hash sketch of the estimated neighborhood. We show that for neighborhood cardinalities, the HIP estimators obtain a factor-2 reduction in variance over basic estimators, with CV upper bounded by the first-order term $1/\sqrt{2(k-1)}$). We further show that our HIP estimators are essentially optimal for ADS-based neighborhood cardinality estimates, and nearly match an asymptotic (for large enough cardinality) lower bound of $1/\sqrt{2k}$ on the CV. Moreover, the HIP estimates can be integrated in existing implementations (ANF [41] and hyperANF [8]) and replace the basic estimators essentially without changing the computation. We perform simulations that demonstrate a factor $\sqrt{2}$ gain in both mean square error and mean relative error of HIP over basic estimators.

Moreover, our HIP estimates have a linear form which makes them useful for an expressive general class of queries. Each node j has a nonnegative estimate $a_{ij} \geq 0$, which we refer to as *adjusted weight* on its presence with respect to i. The adjusted weight is unbiased (has expectation 1 for any j reachable from i). It is strictly positive $a_{ij} > 0$ if and only if $j \in \text{ADS}(i)$, in which case it can be computed from $\text{ADS}(i)$.

The cardinality of the d-neighborhood of i can be estimated by the sum of the adjusted weights of nodes in $\text{ADS}(i)$ that are of distance at most d from i. More generally, we can obtain unbiased and nonnegative estimates for arbitrary queries of form

$$Q_g(i) = \sum_{j | d_{ij} < \infty} g(d_{ij}, j) , \tag{1}$$

where $g(j, d_{ij}) \geq 0$ is a function over both node IDs and distances. The respective estimate $\hat{Q}_g(i) = \sum_{j \in \text{ADS}(i)} a_{ij} g(j, d_{ij})$ is a sum over (the logarithmically many) nodes in $\text{ADS}(i)$. Choosing $g(d_{ij}) = d_{ij}$, $Q_g(i)$ is the sum of distances from i, which is (the inverse of) the classic Bavelas closeness centrality measure [6]. Decay of relevance with distances [20, 44] and meta-data based node filters are captured by queries of the form:

$$C_{\alpha,\beta}(i) = \sum_{j | d_{ij} < \infty} \alpha(d_{ij}) \beta(j) , \tag{2}$$

where $\alpha \geq 0$ is monotone non-increasing and $\beta \geq 0$ is a nonnegative function over node IDs. The function β facilitates measuring centrality with respect to a filter applied to the meta-data of each node. For example, β can be a predicate that depends on gender, locality, or age in a social network or the topic in a Web graph. When using $\beta \equiv 1$, neighborhood cardinality is expressed using $\alpha(x) = 1$ if $x \leq d$ and $\alpha(x) = 0$ otherwise. Choosing $\alpha(x) \equiv 1$ gives the number of reachable nodes from i, $\alpha(x) = 2^{-x}$ gives exponential attenuation with distance [22], and $\alpha(x) = 1/x$ gives the (inverse) harmonic mean of distances from i [40, 10]).

In [20, 17] we estimated (2) from the ADS of i for any (non-increasing) α. The handling of a general β, however, required an ADS computation specific to β. We obtained unbiased nonnegative estimators through a reduction to basic neighborhood cardinality estimators, with the same CV of $1/\sqrt{k-2}$. On the same problem, our ADS HIP estimators:

$$\hat{C}_{\alpha,\beta}(i) = \sum_{j \in \text{ADS}(i)} a_{ij} \alpha(d_{ij}) \beta(j) , \tag{3}$$

have CV upper bounded by $1/\sqrt{2(k-1)}$. Moreover, we are also able to obtain unbiased estimates for general queries when the filter β in (2) (or the function g in (1)) are specified after the sketches are computed. This flexibility of using the same set of sketches for many queries is important in many conceivable applications of social networks or Web graphs analysis. For such queries, our HIP estimators obtain up to an (n/k)-fold improvement in variance over state of the art, which we believe is a subset-weight estimator applied to the Min-Hash sketch of all reachable nodes (by taking the average of $g(d_{ij}, j)$ over the k samples, multiplied by a cardinality estimate of the number of reachable nodes n).

HIP estimators for approximate distinct counting: Almost all streaming distinct counters [29, 14, 24, 5, 32, 30] maintain a Min-Hash sketch of the distinct elements. To answer a query (number of distinct elements seen so far), a "basic" estimator is applied to the sketch. In Section 5 we instead apply our HIP estimators. To do that, we consider the sequence of elements which invoked an update of the Min-Hash sketch over time (this corresponds to entries in the ADS computed with respect to distance rather than time). Even though the entry is not retained, (the streaming algorithm only retains the Min-Hash sketch), we can compute the adjusted weight of the new distinct element that invoked the update. These adjusted weights are added up to obtain a running estimate. To apply HIP, we therefore need to maintain the Min-Hash sketch and an additional approximate (non-distinct) counter, which maintains an approximate count of distinct elements. The approximate counter is updated (by a positive amount which corresponds to the adjusted weight of the element) each time the sketch is updated.

We experimentally compare our HIP estimator to the HyperLogLog approximate distinct counter [28], which is considered to be the state of the art practical solution. To facilitate comparison, we apply HIP to the same Min-Hash sketch with the same parametrization that the HyperLogLog estimator was designed for. Nonetheless, we demonstrate significantly more accurate estimates using HIP. Moreover, our HIP estimators are unbiased, principled, and do not require ad-hoc corrections. They are flexible in that they apply to all Min-Hash sketch flavors and can be further parametrized according to application needs or to obtain even better accuracy for the same memory.

Permutation estimators: The basic and HIP estimators have CV that is essentially independent of cardinality (the neighborhood size). When we have an upper bound on the domain size (total number of nodes), we can improve our cardinality estimates for sets that comprise a good fraction of the domain. The *permutation estimator* (presented in Section 4.4) is a variation on our HIP estimators. We experimentally show that permutation improves over plain HIP when the cardinality is a good fraction (at least 20%) of the total number of nodes.

Estimation quality for distance ranges: The *cummulative* distance distribution, that is, the number of pairs within distance at most d, can be estimated with small relative error. For the number of pairs of distance *equal to* d, we do not have the same guarantees. The estimators are nonnegative and unbiased, and in practice have small relative error [21, 8], but since the problem generalizes estimating the graph diameter [1, 42] we can not expect theoretical guarantees using our near-linear time sketch computation.

In Section 6 we explore the estimation quality for exact distances. For directed and undirected graphs, we explain the good performance in practice by the expansion of "real" graphs. For undirected graphs, we provide a guarantee that holds regardless of expansion: We show that for any two nodes (i, j), our estimate on the number of pairs with an endpoint in $\{i, j\}$ with distance in $[d_{ij}/2, 3d_{ij}/2]$ has CV that is $O(1/\sqrt{k})$. This result extends the best-known near-linear time diameter approximation factor of 2.

2. ALL-DISTANCES SKETCHES

We start with a brief review of Min-Hash sketches. The Min-Hash sketch summarizes a subset N of items (from some domain U) and comes in three flavors, k-mins, k-partition, and bottom-k, where the parameter k determines the sketch size.

The sketch is randomized and defined with respect to (one or more, depending on flavor) random permutations of the domain U. It is convenient to specify a permutation by assigning random *rank* values, $r(j) \sim U[0, 1]$, to items. The permutation is the list of items sorted by increasing rank order. To specify multiple permutations, we use multiple rank assignments. A k-mins sketch [29, 14] includes the item of smallest rank in each of k independent permutations and corresponds to sampling k times with replacement. A k-partition sketch [29, 28, 36] first maps items uniformly at random to k buckets and then includes the item with smallest rank in each bucket. A bottom-k sketch [14, 12] (also known as KMV sketch [5], coordinated order samples [11, 43, 39], or CRC [35]) includes the k items with smallest rank in a single permutation and corresponds to sampling k times without replacement. For $k = 1$, all three flavors are the same.

Min-Hash sketches of different subsets N are *coordinated* if they are generated using the same random permutations (or mappings) of the domain U. The notion of coordination can be traced to [11] and in the CS literature to [14, 12].

Before continuing to graphs, we introduce some terminology. For a set N and a numeric function $r : N$, the function $\mathrm{k}^{\mathrm{th}}_r(N)$ returns the kth smallest value in the range of r on N. If $|N| < k$ then we define $\mathrm{k}^{\mathrm{th}}_r(N)$ to be the supremum of the range of r (we mostly use $r \in [0, 1]$ and the supremum is 1.) We consider directed or undirected, weighted or unweighted graphs. For nodes i, j, let d_{ij} be the distance from i to j. For an interval J and node i, $N_J(i) = \{j | d_{ij} \in J\}$ is the set of nodes with distance in J from i, and $n_J(i) = |N_J(i)|$ is the cardinality of $N_J(i)$. For a distance d, we use the shorthand $N_{[0,d]} \equiv N_d$ and $n_{[0,d]} \equiv n_d$. We use the notation $\Phi_{<j}(i)$ for the set of nodes that are closer to node i than node j and $\pi_{ij} = 1 + |\Phi_{<j}(i)|$ for the *Dijkstra rank* of j with respect to i (j's position in the nearest neighbors list of i).

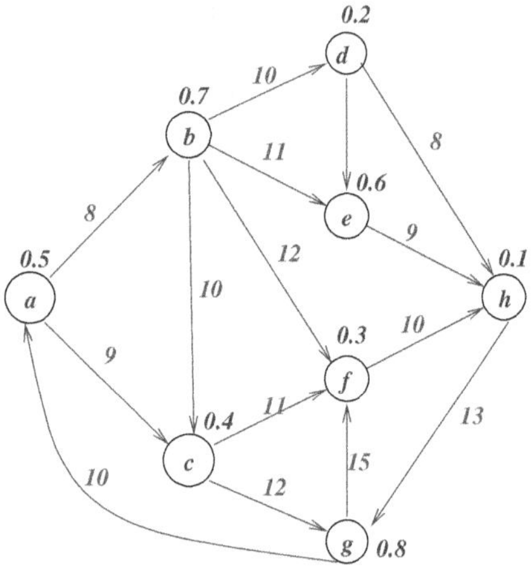

Figure 1: A directed graph with random rank values associated with its nodes.

The ADS of a node i, ADS(i), is a set of node ID and distance pairs. The included nodes are a sample of the nodes reachable from i and with each included node $j \in \text{ADS}(i)$ we store the distance d_{ij}. ADS(i) is the union of coordinated Min-Hash sketches of the neighborhoods $N_d(i)$ (for all possible values of d). The ADSs are defined with respect to random mappings/permutations of the set of all nodes and come in the same three flavors, according to the underlying Min-Hash sketches: Bottom-k, k-mins, and k-partition. For $k = 1$, all flavors are equivalent. For simplicity, our definitions of ADS(i) assume that distances d_{ij} are unique for different j (Which can be achieved using tie breaking).

A *bottom-k* ADS [18] is defined with respect to a single random permutation. ADS(i) includes a node j if and only if the rank of j is one of the k smallest ranks amongst nodes that are at least as close to i:

$$j \in \text{ADS}(i) \iff r(j) < \mathrm{k}^{\mathrm{th}}_r(\Phi_{<j}(i)) \,. \tag{4}$$

A *k-partition* ADS (implicit in [8]) is defined with respect to a random partition BUCKET : $V \to [k]$ of the nodes to k subsets $V_h = \{i | \text{BUCKET}(i) = h\}$ and a random permutation. The ADS of i contains j if and only if j has the smallest rank among nodes in its bucket that are at least as close to i.

$$j \in \text{ADS}(i) \iff$$
$$r(j) < \min\{r(h) \mid \text{BUCKET}(h) = \text{BUCKET}(j) \wedge h \in \Phi_{<j}(i)\} \,.$$

A k-mins ADS [14, 41] is simply k independent bottom-1 ADSs, defined with respect to k independent permutations.

As mentioned, the term All-Distances Sketch reflects the property that the sketch "contains" a Min-Hash sketch with respect to any distance d. We briefly explain how a Min-Hash sketch of a neighborhood $N_d(v)$ can be obtained from the ADS of a node v. This can be done for any $d \geq 0$ and in the context of Min-Hash sketches, $N_d(v)$ is treated as a subset of nodes.

For a k-mins ADS, we are interested in the k-mins Min-Hash sketch of $N_d(v)$ which is, for each of the k permutations r, $x \leftarrow \min_{u \in N_d(v)} r(u)$. The value for a given permutation is the minimum rank of a node of distance at most d in the respective bottom-1 ADS. The k minimum rank values $x^{(t)}$ $t \in [k]$ we obtain from the different permutations are the k-mins Min-Hash sketch of $N_d(v)$. Similarly, the bottom-k Min-Hash sketch of $N_d(v)$ includes the k nodes of minimum rank in $N_d(v)$, which are also the k nodes of minimum rank in ADS(v) with distance at most d. A k-partition Min-Hash sketch of $N_d(v)$ is similarly obtained from a k-partition ADS by taking, for each bucket $i \in [k]$, the smallest rank value in $N_d(v)$ of a node in bucket i. This is also the smallest value in ADS(v) over nodes in bucket i that have distance at most d from v.

Some of our analysis assumes that the rank $r(j)$ and (for k-partition ADSs) the bucket BUCKET(j) are readily available for each node j. This can be achieved using random hash functions.

For directed graphs, we consider both the *forward* and the *backward* ADS, which are specified with respect to forward or reverse paths from i. When needed for clarity, we augment the notation with $\overrightarrow{X}$ (forward) and $\overleftarrow{X}$ (backward) when X is the ADS, N, or n.

EXAMPLE 2.1. *Consider the graph of Figure 1. To determine the forward ADS of node a, we sort nodes in order of increasing distance from a. The order is a, b, c, d, e, f, g, h with respective distances $(0, 8, 9, 18, 19, 20, 21, 26)$. For $k = 1$, the (forward) ADS of a is: $\overrightarrow{ADS}(a) = \{(0, a), (9, c), (18, d), (26, h)\}$. The first value in each pair is the distance from a and the second is the node ID. To compute the reverse ADS of b, we look at nodes in sorted reverse distance from b: b, a, g, c, h, d, e, f with respective reverse distances $(0, 8, 18, 30, 31, 39, 40, 41)$. We obtain $\overleftarrow{ADS}(b) = \{(0, b), (8, a), (30, c), (31, h)\}$. The bottom-2 forward ADS of a contains all nodes that have one of the 2 smallest ranks in the prefix of the sorted order: so it also includes $\{(8, b), (20, f)\}$.*

The expected number of nodes in ADS(i) is $\leq k \ln(n)$, where n is the number of reachable nodes from i: This was established in [14] for k-mins ADS and in [19] for bottom-k ADS.

LEMMA 2.2. *[14, 19] The expected size of a bottom-k ADS is*

$$k + k(H_n - H_k) \approx k(1 + \ln n - \ln k) ,$$

where $H_i = \sum_{j=1}^{i} 1/j$ is the ith Harmonic number and n is the number of nodes reachable from v. The expected size of a k-partition ADS is accordingly $kH_{n/k} \approx k(\ln n - \ln k)$.

PROOF. For bottom-k ADS, we consider the nodes sorted by increasing distance from v, assuming unique distances. The ith node is included in the bottom-k ADS of v with probability $p_i = \min\{1, k/i\}$. Node inclusions are independent (when distances are unique, but otherwise are negatively correlated). The expected size of the ADS of v is the sum of node inclusions which is

$$\sum_{i=1}^{n} p_i = k + k(H_n - H_k) .$$

Similarly, for k-partition, (assuming a random partition and permutation), the expected number of included nodes from each bucket is $\ln(n/k)$ (since each bucket includes in expectation n/k nodes) and therefore the total expected size is $k \ln(n/k)$. □

Base-b ranks: The ADS definition as provided includes node IDs, that is, unique identifiers for nodes. Unique IDs are of size $\lceil \log_2 n \rceil$ and allow us to obtain unique ranks and also support queries involving meta-data based node selections. For many queries, including neighborhood cardinality estimation, we can use ranks that have a smaller representation: For some base $b > 1$, we use the rounded rank values $r'(j) = b^{-h_j}$, where $h_j = \lceil -\log_b r(j) \rceil$. The rounded rank can be represented by the integer h_j. The value of the base b trades-off the sketch size and the information it carries, where both increase when b is closer to 1.

With base-b ranks, the expected value of the largest h_j, which corresponds to the smallest $r(j)$, is $\log_b n$. Thus, the representation size of the rounded smallest rank is $\log_2 \log_b n$. The expected deviation from the expectation is $\leq \log_b 2$, which means that a set of k smallest ranks in a neighborhood or the k smallest ranks in different permutations can be compactly represented using an expected number of $\log_2 \log_2 n + k \log_b 2$ bits.

In the sequel, we consider full ranks and then point out the implication of using base-b ranks.

3. MIN-HASH CARDINALITY ESTIMATE

In this section we review estimators for the cardinality $|N| = n$ of a subset N that are applied to a Min-Hash sketch of N.

The cardinality of $N_d(v)$ can be estimated by obtaining its Min-Hash sketch from ADS(v) and applying a cardinality estimator to this Min-Hash sketch. This also applies to directed graphs, in which case we can estimate the size of the outbound d-neighborhood $\overrightarrow{n}_d(v)$ from $\overrightarrow{\text{ADS}}(v)$ and similarly estimate the size of the inbound d-neighborhood $\overleftarrow{n}_d(v)$ from $\overleftarrow{\text{ADS}}(v)$.

As mentioned in the introduction, we use the CV to measure the quality of the estimates. The CV of an estimator $\hat{n}$ of n is $\sqrt{\mathsf{E}[(n - \hat{n})^2]}/n$. For the same value of the parameter k, the bottom-k sketch contains the most information, but all flavors are similar when $n \gg k$. We first consider full precision ranks and then explain the implication of working with base-b ranks. For illustrative purposes, we start with the k-mins sketch. We then consider the more informative bottom-k sketch. The lower bound for the k-partition sketch is implied by the bound for the other flavors.

3.1 k-mins estimator

The k-mins sketch has the vector form x_i $i \in [k]$. The cardinality estimator $\frac{k-1}{\sum_{i=1}^{k} -\ln(1-x_i)}$ was presented and analysed in [14]. It is unbiased for $k > 1$. Its variance is bounded only for $k > 2$ and the CV is equal to $1/\sqrt{k-2}$. The Mean Relative Error (MRE) is

$$\frac{2(k-1)^{k-2}}{(k-2)! \exp(k-1)} \approx \sqrt{\frac{2}{\pi(k-2)}} .$$

This estimator can be better understood when we view the ranks as exponentially distributed with parameter 1 (rather than uniform from $U[0, 1]$). This is equivalent, as we can use a simple 1-1 monotone transformation $y = -\ln(1 - x)$ which also preserves the Min-Hash definition. In this light, the minimum rank is exponentially distributed with parameter n. Our estimation problem is to estimate the parameter of an exponential distribution from k independent samples and we use the estimator $\frac{k-1}{\sum_{i=1}^{k} y_i}$, where $y_i = -\ln(1 - x_i)$.

We now apply classic estimation theory to better understand how well this estimator uses the information available in the Min-Hash sketch.

LEMMA 3.1. *Any unbiased estimator applied to the k-mins Min-Hash sketch must have CV that is at least $1/\sqrt{k}$.*

PROOF. For cardinality n, each of the k entries (minimum ranks) is an exponentially distributed random variable and therefore has density function ne^{-nx}.

Since entries in the k-mins sketch are independent, the density function (likelihood function) of the sketch is the product of the k density functions $f(\boldsymbol{y}; n) = n^k e^{-n\sum_{i=1}^k y_i}$. Its logarithm, the log likelihood function, is $\ell(\boldsymbol{y}; n) = k \ln n - n \sum_{i=1}^k y_i$. The Fisher information, $I(n)$, is the negated expectation of the second partial derivative of $\ell(\boldsymbol{y}; n)$ (with respect to the estimated parameter n). We have

$$\frac{\partial^2 \ell(\boldsymbol{y}; n)}{\partial^2 n} = -\frac{k}{n^2} .$$

This is constant, and equal to its expectation. Therefore $I(n) = k/n^2$.

We now apply the Cramér-Rao lower bound which states that the variance of any unbiased estimator is at least the inverse of the Fisher information: $\frac{1}{I(n)} = \frac{n^2}{k}$. A corresponding lower bound of $\frac{1}{\sqrt{k}}$ on the CV is obtained by taking the square root and dividing by n. □

We next show that the sum $\sum_{i=1}^k y_i$ captures all necessary information to obtain a minimum variance estimator for n.

LEMMA 3.2. *The sum of the minimum ranks $\sum_{i=1}^k y_i$ is a sufficient statistics for estimating n from a k-mins sketch.*

PROOF. The likelihood function $f(\boldsymbol{y}; n) = n^k e^{-n\sum_{i=1}^k y_i}$ depends on the sketch only through the sum $\sum_{i=1}^k y_i$. □

Therefore, from the Rao-Blackwell Theorem [7, 33], a minimum variance estimator applied to the sketch may only depend on $\sum_{i=1}^k y_i$. We can further show that $\sum_{i=1}^k y_i$ is in fact a *complete* sufficient statistics. A sufficient statistics T is complete if any function g for which $E[g(T)] = 0$ for all n must be 0 almost everywhere (with probability 1). The Lehmann-Scheffé Theorem [34] states that any unbiased estimator which is a function of a complete sufficient statistics must be the unique Uniform Minimum Variance Unbiased Estimator (UMVUE). Since our estimator is unbiased, it follows that it is the unique UMVUE. That is, there is no other estimator which is unbiased and has a lower variance! (for any value of the parameter n).

This optimality results provides an interesting insight to the thread of research on approximate distinct counting (and to practice). One can easily come up with several ways of using the sketch information to obtain an estimator: taking the median, averaging quantiles, removing the two extreme values, and so on. The median specifically had been considered [14, 3, 5] because it is more amenable to obtaining concentration bounds. We now understand that while these estimators can have variance that is within a constant factor of optimal, estimation theory shows that (in terms of variance) the average, and the average alone, carries all the information we need and anything else is strictly inferior.

3.2 Bottom-k estimator

The bottom-k estimator includes the k smallest rank values in N, and we use the estimator $\frac{k-1}{\tau_k}$, where $\tau_k = \mathrm{k}_r^{\mathrm{th}}(N)$ is the kth smallest rank in N. This estimator is a conditional inverse-probability estimator [31]: For each element in N we consider its probability of being included in the Min-Hash sketch, conditioned on fixed ranks of all other elements. This estimator is therefore unbiased. The conditioning was applied with priority sampling [23] (bottom-k [19]) subset sum estimation.

The information content of the bottom-k sketch is strictly higher than the k-mins sketch [18]. We show that the CV of this estimator is upper bounded by the CV of the k-mins estimator:

LEMMA 3.3. *The bottom-k estimator has CV $\leq 1/\sqrt{k-2}$.*

PROOF. We interpret the bottom-k cardinality estimator as a sum of n negatively correlated inverse-probability [31] estimates for each element, which estimate the presence of the element in N. (That is, for each $v \in N$, estimating its contribution of "1" to the cardinality and for each $v \notin N$, estimating 0). The inclusion probability of an element is with respect to fixed ranks of all other elements. In this case, an element is one of the $k-1$ smallest ranks only if its rank value is strictly smaller than the $k-1$ smallest rank amongst the $n-1$. For elements currently in the sketch, this threshold value is τ_k. These estimates (adjusted weights) are equal and positive only for the $k-1$ elements of smallest rank. The variance of the adjusted weight conditioned on fixing the rank values of other elements is $1/p-1$, where p is the probability that the rank of our element is smaller than the threshold.

When ranks are exponentially distributed (which is convenient choice for analysis), the distribution of the $k-1$ smallest amongst $n-1$ is the sum of $k-1$ exponential random variables with parameters $n-1, n-1, \ldots, n-k+1$. We denote the density and CDF functions of this distribution by $b_{n-1,k-1}$ and $B_{n-1,k-1}$, respectively. We have $p = 1 - \exp(-x)$ and the adjusted weight of each element has variance of $1/p - 1 = \frac{\exp(-x)}{1-\exp(-x)}$ (conditioned on x). We now compute the expectation of the variance according to the distribution of x.

We denote by $s_{n,k}$ and $S_{n,k}$ the respective distribution function of the sum of k exponentially distributed random variables with parameter n.

$$\begin{aligned}
\mathsf{Var}[\hat{a}_v] &= \int_0^\infty b_{n-1,k-1}(x)\frac{e^{-x}}{1-e^{-x}}dx \leq \int_0^\infty s_{n-1,k-1}(x)\frac{1}{x}dx \\
&= \int_0^\infty \frac{(n-1)^{k-1}x^{k-2}}{(k-2)!}e^{-(n-1)x}\frac{1}{x}dx \\
&= \frac{(n-1)^{k-1}}{(k-2)!}\frac{(k-3)!}{(n-1)^{k-2}} = \frac{n-1}{k-2} .
\end{aligned}$$

The first inequality follows from $\frac{e^{-x}}{1-e^{-x}} \leq 1/x$ and $\forall x$, $B_{n,k}(x) \leq S_{n,k}(x)$, that is, $B_{n,k}$ is dominated by the sum of k exponential random variables with parameter n. We then substitute the probability density function [26] (also used for analyzing the k-mins estimator in [14])

$$s_{n,k} = \frac{n^k x^{k-1}}{(k-1)!}e^{-nx} .$$

The second to last equality uses $\int_0^\infty x^a e^{-bx}dx = a!/b^{a+1}$ for natural a, b,

Estimates for different elements are negatively correlated (an element being sampled makes is slightly less likely for another to be sampled) and thus, the variance on the cardinality estimate is at most the sum of variances of the n elements. The CV is therefore at most

$$\sqrt{\frac{1-\frac{kn-k+1}{n^2}}{k-2}} \leq \sqrt{\frac{1}{k-2}} .$$

□

The improvement of bottom-k over the k-mins estimator is more pronounced when the cardinality n is smaller and closer to k. The first order term, however, is the same and when $n \gg k$, the CV of the bottom-k estimator approaches $\sqrt{\frac{1}{k-2}}$.

We now consider this estimator from the estimation theoretic lens. When $n \leq k$, the variance is clearly 0. Therefore, any meaningful lower bound must depend on both n, k.

LEMMA 3.4. *Any unbiased estimator applied to the bottom-k Min-Hash sketch must satisfy*

$$\lim_{n \to \infty} CV(n, k) \geq 1/\sqrt{k} \,.$$

PROOF. Let $x_1, x_2, \ldots, x_k$ be the k smallest ranks in increasing order. From basic properties of the exponential distribution, the minimum rank $y_0 \equiv x_1$ is exponentially distributed with parameter n. For $i > 0$, the difference between the ith smallest and the $i-1$th smallest ranks, $y_i \equiv x_{i+1} - x_i$, is exponentially distributed with parameter $n - i$. Moreover, these differences y_i are independent. We can therefore equivalently represent the information in the bottom-k sketch by $(y_0, \ldots, y_{k-1})$, where y_i is independently drawn from an exponential distribution with parameter $n - i$. The joint density function is the product $f(\boldsymbol{y}; n) = \prod_{i=0}^{k-1}(n-i)e^{-(n-i)y_i}$. The Fisher information is $I(n) = \sum_{i=0}^{k} \frac{1}{(n-i)^2}$. We obtain a lower bound on the CV of at least $\frac{1}{\sqrt{\sum_{i=0}^{k-1} \frac{n^2}{(n-i)^2}}}$. When $n \gg k$, the expression approaches $\frac{1}{\sqrt{k}}$. □

LEMMA 3.5. *x_k (the kth smallest rank) is a sufficient statistics for estimating n from a bottom-k sketch.*

PROOF. We can express the joint density function $f(\boldsymbol{y}; n)$ as a product of an expression that does not depend on the estimated parameter n and $e^{-n\sum_{i=0}^{k-1} y_i} \prod_{i=0}^{k-1}(n-i)$. Therefore, $x_k = \sum_{i=0}^{k-1} y_i$ is a sufficient statistics. □

From Rao-Blackwell Theorem, the kth minimum rank captures all the useful information contained in the bottom-k sketch for obtaining a minimum variance estimator for n. Since it is a complete sufficient statistics, and our estimator is unbiased, it follows from the Lehmann-Scheffé theorem [34] that it is the unique UMVUE.

3.3 k-partition estimator

The estimator examines the $1 < k' \leq k$ nonempty buckets, and is conditioned on k'. The size of each bucket has distribution $1 + B(n - k', 1/k')$, where B is the Binomial distribution. We can approximate bucket sizes by n/k' and apply the k'-mins estimator (analysis holds for k' equal buckets). The estimate is $\frac{k'(k'-1)}{-\sum_{t=1}^{k} \ln(1-x^{(t)})}$, where $x^{(t)}$ is the minimum rank in partition t. When $n \gg k$, the k-partition estimator performs similarly to the bottom-k and k-mins estimators. When $n < k$, there are effectively only $k' < k$ nonempty buckets. Even when $n = O(k)$, the expected size of k' is significantly smaller than k, and the CV is more similar to that of a k'-mins estimate, and therefore, can be expected to be $\sqrt{k/k'}$ larger. Moreover, the k-partition estimator is biased down: In particular, when $k' = 1$, an event with positive probability, the estimate is 0. The probability of $k' = 1$ for cardinality n is $p = (1/k)^{n-1}$. Since we do not generally know n, we can not completely correct for this bias.

3.4 Min-Hash sketches with base-b ranks

We considered cardinality estimators for sketches with "full" ranks taken from the domain $[0, 1]$. If we work with truncated ranks but ensure that there are no rank collisions, the full-rank estimators can be applied by uniformly at random "filling in" missing bits to the desired precision or better yet, computing the expectation of the estimator over these random completions. A hash range of size n^c and representation $c \log n$ implies that with probability $1/n^{c-1}$ there are no rank collisions between any two nodes in a set of size n.

A uniform random completion of the truncated ranks is an equivalent replacement to the full rank when all elements with the same base-b rank that "contend" for a sketch entry are actually represented in the sketch. If this condition does not hold, the expected full-rank completions are more likely to be smaller than uniform completions and estimates obtained with uniform completion will be biased.

To satisfy this condition we need to ensure that there are no rank collisions along the "inclusion" threshold. With bottom-k this means that the base-b kth smallest rank is strictly smaller than the base-b $(k+1)$th smallest rank. With k-mins (k-partition) it means that the base-b minimum is unique in each permutation (bucket).

If we choose $b = 1 + 1/k^c$, probability of collision is at most $1/k^{c-1}$. In this case, the expected size of the (integer exponent of the) minimum rank is $\log_2 \log_b n \approx \log_2 \log_2 n + \log_2 k^c \approx \log_2 \log_2 n + c \log k$. Moreover, we recall that the expected size of the offset from this expectation is constant times $\log_b 2$. Substituting $b \approx 1/k^c$ we obtain an expected offset of the order of $c \log k$, so we can compactly represent the sketch using $\log_2 \log_2 n + ck \log k$ bits.

If we work with a larger base, collisions are more likely and introduce bias. The estimators then need to compensate for the bias. Specialized estimators for base-2 ranks with k-mins sketches were proposed in [29] and for k-partition sketches in [28]. The HIP estimators we present next naturally apply with base-b ranks.

4. THE HIP ESTIMATOR

The *Historic Inverse Probability (HIP)* estimators we present here gain from using the complete information present in $\text{ADS}(v)$ rather than extracting from it a Min-Hash sketch of the neighborhood whose size we want to estimate, and apply a cardinality estimator to that sketch. HIP estimators can be computed for all three ADS flavors and naturally extend to base-b ranks. We show that the HIP estimators obtain a factor 2 improvement in variance over the respective basic estimator and also show that they are asymptotically optimal. We also present a variant of HIP, the *permutation* cardinality estimator, which applies to bottom-k ADSs when ranks are a strict permutation of a domain $[n]$. This estimator improves over plain HIP when the cardinality is good fraction of n.

The HIP estimator is computed by scanning entries in $\text{ADS}(i)$ in order of increasing distance from i. For each node $j \in \text{ADS}(i)$ we compute an estimate $a_{ij} > 0$ on its presence in $\text{ADS}(i)$ which we call the *adjusted weight* of j. These adjusted weights are *conditioned* inverse probability estimates, a twist on a classic Horvitz-Thompson [31] estimator which applies it conditioned on the ranks of nodes that are closer to i than j. A similar conditioning technique, in a different context, was used in [23, 19]. The adjusted weight $a_{ij} \geq 0$ has expectation $\mathsf{E}[a_{ij}] = 1$ and is positive if and only if $j \in \text{ADS}(i)$.

As noted in the introduction, we can estimate $Q_g(i)$ (see (1)) from $\text{ADS}(i)$ using

$$\hat{Q}_g(i) = \sum_j a_{ij} g(d_{ij}, j) = \sum_{j \in \text{ADS}(i)} a_{ij} g(d_{ij}, j) \,. \quad (5)$$

Unbiasedness follows from linearity of expectation, since each adjusted weight is unbiased. The second equality holds since only nodes $j \in \text{ADS}(i)$ have positive $a_{ij} > 0$. We note that the estimate can be easily computed from $\text{ADS}(i)$, since for each included node j we have the distance d_{ij}.

When we are only interested in queries Q_g where $g(d_{ij})$ only depends on the distance and not on the node ID j, we can compress the ADS representation to a list of distance and adjusted weights pairs: For each unique distance d in $\text{ADS}(i)$ we associate an adjusted weight equal to the sum of the adjusted weights of included nodes in $\text{ADS}(i)$ with distance d.

To finish the presentation of the HIP estimators, we need to explain how the adjusted weights are computed for $j \in \text{ADS}(i)$. We focus in detail on bottom-k ADSs and start with full ranks $r(i) \sim U[0,1]$.

4.1 HIP estimate for bottom-k ADS

Consider a node v and list nodes by increasing Dijkstra rank with respect to v, that is node i has $\pi_{vi} = i$.

For node i, we define the threshold value

$$\tau_i = \mathrm{k}_r^{\text{th}}\{\Phi_{<i}(v) \cap \text{ADS}(v)\} . \tag{6}$$

The adjusted weights a_{vi} for node i are 0 if $i \notin \text{ADS}(v)$ and $1/\tau_i$ if $i \in \text{ADS}(v)$. Note that τ_i, and hence a_{vi}, can be computed from $\text{ADS}(v)$ for all $i \in \text{ADS}(v)$.

The adjusted weights are inverse-probability estimates with respect to the probability τ_i of including i in $\text{ADS}(v)$, conditioned on fixing the ranks of the nodes $1, \ldots, i-1$:

LEMMA 4.1. *Conditioned on fixed rank values of all nodes in $\Phi_{<i}(v)$, the probability of $i \in \text{ADS}(v)$ is τ_i.*

PROOF. Node i is included if and only if $r(i) < \mathrm{k}_r^{\text{th}}\{\Phi_{<i}(v)\}$, that is, i's rank is smaller than the kth smallest rank amongst nodes that are closer to v than i. Note that it is the same as the kth smallest rank among nodes that are in $\text{ADS}(v)$ and closer to v than i, since $\text{ADS}(v)$ must include all these nodes. When $r(i) \sim U[0,1]$, this happens with probability τ_i. □

Since these are inverse-probability weights, they are clearly unbiased when $\tau_i > 0$, which happens with probability 1. Note that for $i \leq k$ (when i is one of the k closest nodes to v), by definition $i \in \text{ADS}(v)$, $\tau_i \equiv 1$, and therefore $a_{vi} = 1$, since the first k nodes are included with probability 1. Also note that the adjusted weights of nodes in $\text{ADS}(v)$ are increasing with the distance d_{vi} (or Dijkstra rank π_{vi}). This is because the inclusion probability in the ADS decreases with distance. In particular this means that the variance of a_{vi} increases with d_{vi}.

We show that the variance of the HIP neighborhood cardinality estimator is at least a factor of 2 smaller than the variance of the basic bottom-k cardinality estimator, which in turn dominates the basic k-mins estimator.

THEOREM 4.1. *The CV of the ADS HIP estimator for a neighborhood of size n is*

$$\leq \frac{\sqrt{1 - \frac{n+k(k-1)}{n^2}}}{\sqrt{2(k-1)}} \leq \frac{1}{\sqrt{2(k-1)}} .$$

PROOF. When $n_d(v) \leq k$, the estimate is exact (variance is 0). Otherwise, (assuming nodes are listed by Dijkstra ranks $\pi_{vi} \equiv i$), the variance on i is $\mathsf{E}[1/p - 1]$ where p is the probability that the rank of v_i is smaller than the kth smallest rank among $v_1, \ldots, v_{i-1}$. We adapt the analysis of Lemma 3.3 for the variance of the bottom-k estimator. We use exponentially distributed ranks, and have, conditioned on kth smallest rank τ_i in $\Phi_{<i}(v)$ variance $\exp(-\tau_i)/(1-\exp(-\tau_i))$. We compute the expectation of the variance for τ_i distributed according to $b_{i-1,k}$. This is a similar computation to the proof of Lemma 3.3 and we obtain that the variance of the adjusted weight a_{vi} is bounded by $\frac{i-1}{k-1}$. Estimates for different i are again negatively correlated and thus the variance of the neighborhood estimate on n is upper bounded by $\sum_{i=k+1}^{n} \frac{i-1}{k-1} = \frac{n^2-n-k^2-k}{2(k-1)}$ and the upper bound on the CV follows. □

The bound of Theorem 4.1 extends to distance-decay closeness centralities.

COROLLARY 4.2. *For a monotone non-increasing $\alpha(x) \geq 0$ (we define $\alpha(\infty) = 0$), $\hat{C}_\alpha(i) = \sum_{j \in \text{ADS}(i)} a_{ij}\alpha(d_{ij})$ is an unbiased estimator of $C_\alpha(i) = \sum_j \alpha(d_{ij})$ with CV that is at most $1/\sqrt{2(k-1)}$.*

The Corollary holds for the more general form (2) when ADSs are computed with respect to the node weights $\beta(i)$. Otherwise, when estimating $Q_g(v)$ using (5), the variance is upper bounded as follows:

COROLLARY 4.3.

$$\mathsf{Var}[\hat{Q}_g(v)] \leq \sum_{i | v \leadsto i \wedge \pi_{vi} > k} g(i, d_{vi})^2 \frac{\pi_{vi} - 1}{k-1} .$$

In contrast, we can consider the variance of the naive estimator for $Q_g(v)$ that is mentioned in the introduction. That estimator uses a Min-Hash sketch, which is essentially a random sample of k reachable nodes. Since inclusion probabilities are about $\approx k/n$ The variance in this case is about $\frac{n-1}{k-1} \sum_i g(i, d_{vi})^2$. We can see that when $g(i, d_{vi})$ are concentrated (have higher values) on closer nodes, which the Min-Hash sketch is less likely to include, the variance of the naive estimate can be up to a factor of n/k higher, where n is the number of reachable nodes from v.

4.2 HIP estimate for k-mins and k-partition

We briefly present the HIP estimators for k-mins and k-partition ADS. Similarly, the adjusted weight is 0 if $i \notin \text{ADS}(v)$ and is $1/\tau_i$ otherwise, where the inclusion threshold τ_i is computed as follows. For k-mins, a node i is included in $\text{ADS}(v)$ only if it has rank value strictly smaller than the minimum rank in $\Phi_{<i}(v)$ in at least one of the k assignments r_h $h \in [k]$. Conditioned on fixed ranks of all the nodes $\Phi_{<i}(v)$, the inclusion threshold is

$$\tau_i = 1 - \prod_{h=1}^{k}(1 - \min_{j \leq i-1} r_h(j)) . \tag{7}$$

For k-partition ADS, we again fix both the rank values and the partition mapping (to one of the k buckets $V_1, \ldots, V_k$) of all nodes in $\Phi_{<i}(v)$. We then compute the inclusion threshold, which is the probability that $i \in \text{ADS}(v)$ given that conditioning. This is with respect to a uniform mapping of node i to one of the k buckets and random rank value. We obtain inclusion threshold

$$\tau_i = \frac{1}{k} \sum_{h=1}^{k} \min_{j \in V_h \cap \Phi_{<i}(v)} r(j) , \tag{8}$$

defining the minimum rank over an empty set $V_h \cap \Phi_{<i}(v)$ to be 1. Note that the threshold τ_i, and therefore the respective adjusted weight a_{vi}, can be computed from $\text{ADS}(v)$.

4.3 Lower bound on variance

We show that the variance of the HIP estimates is asymptotically optimal for $n \gg k$:

THEOREM 4.2. *The first order term, as $n \gg k$, of the CV of any (unbiased and nonnegative) linear (adjusted-weights based) estimator of $n_d(v)$ applied to $\text{ADS}(v)$ must be $\geq 1/\sqrt{2k}$.*

PROOF. The inclusion probability of the ith node from v $i \geq k$ in a bottom-k ADS(v) is $p_i = k/i$. If we had known p_i, the best we could do is use inverse probability weighting, that is, estimate 0 if not sampled and $1/p_i$ if the node is included. The variance of this ideal estimator is $1/p_i - 1$. There are very weak negative correlations between inclusions of two nodes, making them almost independent (for $i \gg k \gg 1$): The probability p_i given that $j < i$ is included is $\geq (k-1)/i$ and given that j is not included is $k/(i-1)$. The covariance is therefore $O(1/i)$. The sum of all covariances involving node i is therefore $O(1)$ and the sum of all covariances is $O(n)$. The variance of this ideal estimator on a neighborhood of size $n > k$ is at least the sum of variances minus an upper bound on the sum of covariances $\mathsf{Var}[\hat{n}] = \sum_{i=k+1}^{n} \frac{i-k}{k} = \frac{(n+k+1)(n-k)}{2k} - (n-k) - O(n)$. The CV, $\sqrt{\mathsf{Var}[\hat{n}]}/n$, has first order term for $n \gg k$, of $1/\sqrt{2k}$.

Similar arguments apply to k-mins and k-partition ADS. For k-mins ADS, the inclusion probability in ADS(v) of the ith node from v is $p_i = 1-(1-1/i)^k \approx k/i$, and we obtain the same sum for $i = 1, \ldots, n$ as with bottom-k ADS. For k-partition, the inclusion probability is $p_i = \mathsf{E}[1/(1+x)]$ where $x \sim B[i, 1/k]$. □

4.4 Permutation estimator

The permutation estimator we present here is applied to a bottom-k ADS that is computed with respect to ranks $\sigma_i \in [n]$ that constitute a random permutation of $[n]$. In terms of information content, permutation ranks dominate random ranks $r(i) \sim U[0,1]$, since random ranks can be associated based on the permutation ranks σ. The main advantage of the permutation estimator is that we obtain tighter estimates when the cardinality we estimate is a good fraction of n. The permutation estimator is only evaluated experimentally.

The permutation estimator, similarly to HIP, is viewed as computed over a stream of elements. In the graph setting, the stream corresponds to scanning of nodes so that first occurrences of nodes are according to increasing distance from v. The entries in ADS(v) correspond to nodes on which the sketch was updated. A positive weight is then associated with these updates. The weight is an estimate of the number of distinct elements scanned from the previous update (or the beginning if it is the first update) to the current one. We maintain a running estimate $\hat{s}$ on the cardinality s of the set S of distinct elements seen so far. When there is an update, $\hat{s}$ is increased by its weight w.

The first k updates corresponds to the first k distinct elements. Each of these updates has weight 1 and when the cardinality $s \leq k$, our estimate is exact $\hat{s} = s$.

Consider now an update that occur after the first k distinct elements. Let $\mu > k$ be the kth smallest rank in S (which is the kth smallest permutation rank in the bottom-k sketch).

We now argue that after an update, the expected number of distinct nodes until we encounter the next update is $w' = \frac{n-s+1}{\mu-k+1}$. To see this, note that the number of nodes in S with permutation rank μ or below is k. So there are $\mu - k$ remaining nodes with rank smaller than μ amongst those in $[n] \setminus S$. The expectation is that of sampling without replacement until we find a node with permutation rank below μ.

When the update occurs, we would like to compute w' and update our estimate $\hat{s}$. But we actually do not know s. So instead we plug-in the unbiased estimate $\hat{s}$ to obtain $w = \frac{n-\hat{s}+1}{\mu-k+1}$. We then update the bottom-k sketch (and μ if needed) and $\hat{s} \leftarrow \hat{s} + w$.

Note that when $\mu = k$, that is, the k smallest elements of the permutation, those with $\sigma_i \leq k$, are included in S, the probability of an update is 0 as the sketch is saturated. We then need to correct the estimate to account for the number of nodes that are farther than the nodes with permutation rank $[k]$. The correction is computed as follows.

If the cardinality is x, then conditioned on it including all the elements with permutation ranks $[k]$, the expected number of elements that are farther than all the elements with permutation ranks in $[k]$ is $\frac{x-k}{k+1}$. So the expected number of elements till the last update is $x' = x - \frac{n-k}{k+1}$. Note that our estimate $\hat{s}$ was unbiased for x'.

Solving $x - \frac{x-k}{k+1} = x'$ for x we obtain the relation $x = x'\frac{k+1}{k} - 1$. We plug-in $\hat{s}$ for x' and obtain the correction $\hat{x} = \hat{s}\frac{k+1}{k} - 1$. This correction is used when our sketch contains the k elements of permutation ranks $[k]$.

4.5 Simulations

We use simulations to study the Normalized Root Mean Square Error (NRMSE), which corresponds to the CV when estimator is unbiased, and the *Mean Relative Error* (MRE), defined as $\mathsf{E}[|n - \hat{n}|]/n$ of the basic, HIP, and permutation neighborhood-cardinality estimators. We evaluated the basic estimators for all three flavors and the bottom-k HIP estimators. We use sketches with full ranks, because the optimal basic estimators are well understood with full ranks. Actual representation size for "full" ranks is discussed in Section 3.4.

The cardinality $n_d(v)$ is estimated from nodes in ADS(v) of distance at most d. The structure of the ADS and the behavior of the estimator as a function of the cardinality $n_d(v)$ do not depend on the graph structure. When nodes are presented in increasing distance from v, the ADS only depends on the ranks assigned to these nodes. Our simulation is therefore equivalently performed on a stream of n distinct elements, and ADS content is built from the randomized ranks assigned to these elements. After processing i distinct element, we obtain an estimate of i from the current ADS. We do so for each cardinality. We use multiple runs of the simulation, which are obtained by different randomization of ranks. In case of the permutation estimator, the ranks we use are permutation ranks from a random permutation on all n nodes. For other estimators, the estimate for a certain cardinality does not depend on the total number of nodes.

Figure 2 shows the NRMSE and the MRE estimates by average of multiple simulation runs. We also provide, for reference, the exact values of the CV ($1/\sqrt{k-2}$) and MRE ($\approx \sqrt{2/(\pi(k-2))}$) of the k-mins basic estimator. These values are independent of cardinality and upper bounds the respective measures for the basic bottom-k estimator.

Looking at basic estimators, we can see that (as expected from analysis) for $n \gg k$, the error is similar for all three flavors and the NRMSE is around $1/\sqrt{k-2}$. For smaller values of n, the bottom-k estimator is more accurate than the k-mins which in turn is more accurate than the k-partition estimator: The bottom-k estimator is exact for $k \leq n$ and then the relative error slowly increases until it meets the k-mins error. We can observe that, as explained by analysis, the k-partition estimator is less accurate for $n \leq 2k$.

The figures also include the first-order term (upper bound) for HIP. The results for the bottom-k HIP estimator clearly demonstrate the improvement of the HIP estimators: We can see that the error of the bottom-k HIP estimator is a factor of $\sqrt{2}$ smaller than that of the basic bottom-k estimator. The figures also demonstrate the benefit of using our permutation estimator: The NRMSE and MRE of the permutation estimate were always at most that of HIP. The two are comparable when the estimated cardinality is at most $0.2n$. When it exceeds $0.2n$, we observe a significant advantage for the permutation estimator over plain HIP.

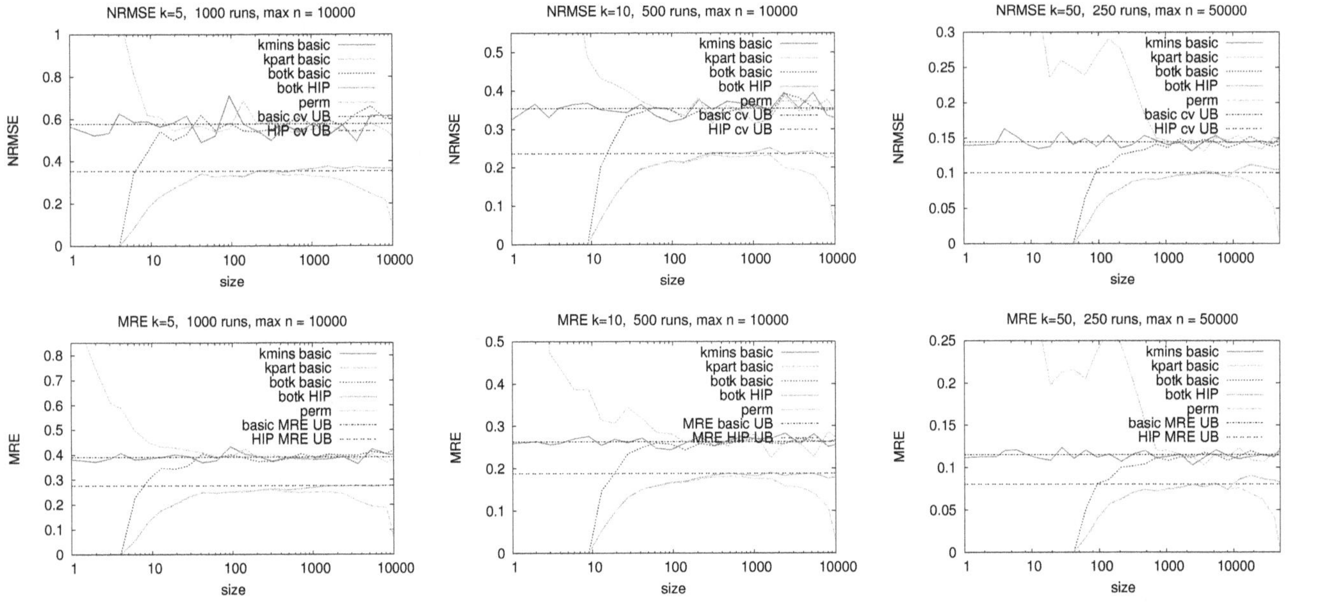

Figure 2: NRMSE (normalized root mean square error) and MRE (mean relative error) of neighborhood size estimators with $k = 5, 10, 50$, as a function of neighborhood size, averaged over multiple runs. We show k-mins, bottom-k, and k-partition basic estimators and our bottom-k HIP and permutation estimators. For reference, we also show the exact values $1/\sqrt{k-2}$ and $1/\sqrt{2(k-1)}$ of the CV of the basic and HIP k-mins estimators. These are upper bounds on the CV of respective bottom-k estimators. We also show $\sqrt{\frac{2}{\pi(k-2)}}$ for the MRE of the basic k-mins estimator and $\sqrt{\frac{1}{\pi(k-1)}}$ as a reference MRE for HIP.

4.6 HIP with base-b ranks

The application and analysis of HIP estimators carries over naturally, retaining unbiasedness even with collisions. Recall that the adjusted weight of i is obtained by first computing a threshold value, based on fixing ranks (and partition) of nodes closer to v than i. We then use an inverse probability estimate, based on the probability of being below the threshold. The necessary property for unbiasedness of inverse probability estimators, which is satisfied with base-b ranks, is that for any legal threshold τ, there is nonzero probability of having rank that is below τ.

When using base-b ranks, however, the threshold probability p_i we obtain will be "rounded down" from the corresponding full rank probability. Since the probability is strictly smaller than with the full ranks, the threshold inclusion probability τ is lower and therefore the contribution to the variance of the estimate, which is $1/\tau - 1$, is higher. We perform a back-of-the-envelope calculation which shows that τ can be expected to increase by a factor of $\frac{1+b}{2}$, which implies the same-factor increase in variance: Considering a range between discretized values, $a = 1/b^i$ and $ba = 1/b^{i-1}$, and assuming the full rank x lies uniformly in that interval. The full-rank inclusion probability is x whereas the rounded-down one is a. We consider the expectation of the ratio x/a. This expectation is

$$\frac{1}{a(b-1)} \int_a^{ba} \frac{x}{a} dx = \frac{b+1}{2} .$$

Simulations in the next section show that this calculation is fairly accurate. We can use this calculation to find a sweet spot for the base b, considering the tradeoff between representation size and variance. The CV as a function of k, b is $\sqrt{\frac{(1+b)}{4(k-1)}}$. The representation size depends on application. If sketch is only used for counting, maintaining few bits for counter, there is diminishing value with smaller bases. If the sketch is used as a sample (which supports selection queries) and stores meta-data (or node IDs), then k is the dominant term and it is beneficial to work with full ranks.

5. APPROXIMATE DISTINCT COUNTING

Our HIP estimators (with full or base-b ranks) can be used to approximate the number of distinct elements in a stream. A Min-Hash sketch is maintained for the distinct elements on the prefix of the stream that is processed.

To apply HIP, we augment the Min-Hash sketch with an additional register which maintains an approximate count of the number of distinct elements. Each time the sketch is updated, we compute the adjusted weight of the element and accordingly increase the count by that amount. Since the expected total number of updates is $\leq k \ln n$, where n is the number of distinct elements in the stream (see Lemma 2.2), the additional work performed for an update balances out as a diminishing fraction of the total stream computation.

An explicit representation of the additional counter as an approximate counter (see Appendix A) would require storing the exponent, which is of size $\lceil \log \log n \rceil + 1$ and $\lceil \log_2 \sqrt{(4k/3)} + 4 \rceil$ significant bits (precision with respect to the CV of HIP). The exponent can more efficiently be stored as an offset to the exponent values stored in the sketch, removing its dependence on n. Thus, using only $O(\log_2 k)$ for the approximate count. An even more compact representation of the approximate count also eliminates the dependence on k, and requires only few bits in total. To do that we represent the HIP estimate as a correction of a basic estimate obtained from the Min-Hash sketch. The correction can be expressed as a signed multiplier of $\hat{n}/\sqrt{k}$ using a fixed number of bits. When the sketch is updated, we recompute the basic estimate $\hat{n}$ and accordingly update the correction to be with respect to the new HIP estimate.

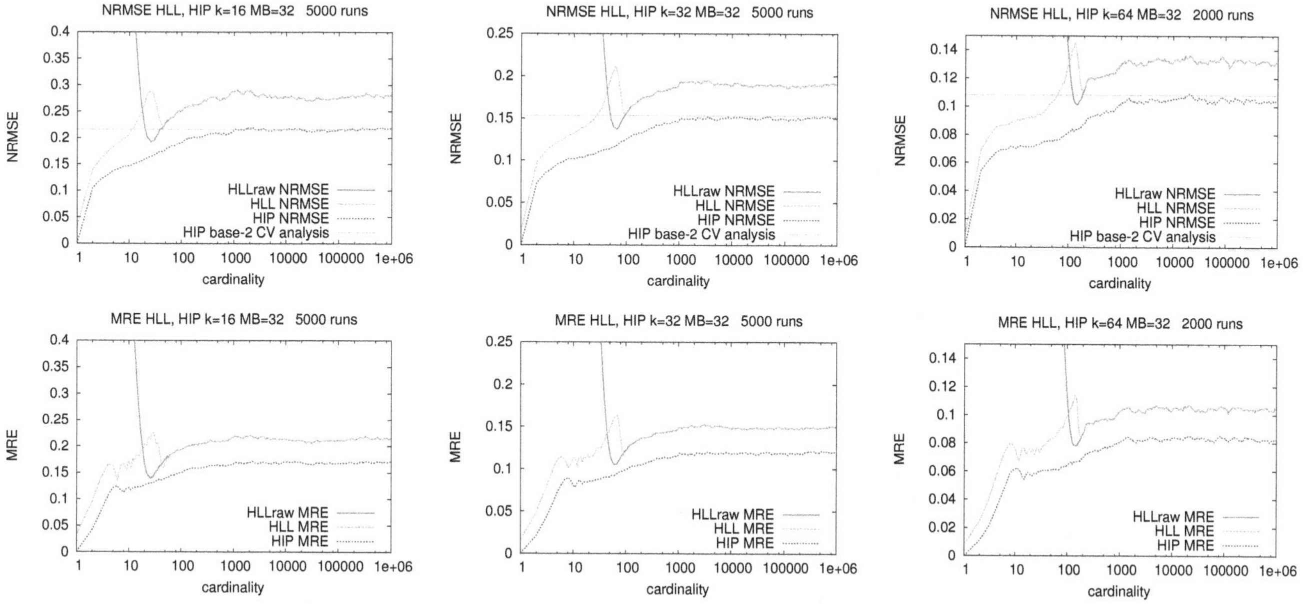

Figure 3: HIP and HLL raw and bias-corrected estimators. Applied with $k = 16, 32, 64$ and 5-bit counters. (k-partition base-2 Min-Hash sketches)

HIP is very flexible. It applies to all three sketch flavors, to full and to base-b ranks, and also works with truncated registers that can get saturated. In this case we simply take the update probability of a saturated register to be 0. The HIP estimate quality gracefully degrades with the number of saturated registers. Eventually, if all registers are saturated, the HIP estimate saturates and becomes biased. In order to compare the HIP estimate with HyperLogLog (HLL) [28, 30], which is the state of the art approximate distinct counter, we implemented it on the same Min-Hash sketch that is used by HLL. HLL uses k-partition Min-Hash sketches with base-2 ranks. The registers have 5 bits and are thus saturated at 31. Pseudo code for the HIP estimator when applied to the HLL sketch is provided in Figure 4.

Require: Random uniform hash functions: $\text{BUCKET}(v)$: $[k]$, $r(v)$: first 32 bits of $U[0, 1]$.

Initialization:
for $i = 1, \ldots, k$ **do** $M[i] \leftarrow 0$ ▷ $M[i]$ are 5-bit registers
$c \leftarrow 0$ ▷ c is an approximate counter

Processing stream element v**:**
$h(v) \leftarrow \min\{31, \lceil -\log_2 r(v) \rceil\}$
if $h(v) > M[\text{BUCKET}(v)]$ **then**
  $c \leftarrow c + \left(\sum_{i=1}^{k} I_{M[i]<31} 2^{-M[i]}\right)^{-1}$
  $M[\text{BUCKET}(v)] \leftarrow h(v)$

Figure 4: Pseudo code for HIP on the HyperLogLog Min-Hash sketches: k-partition, base-2, each register uses 5 bits. To apply HIP we maintain an additional register c.

Figure 3 shows results for the performance of the HIP and HLL estimators. Noting again that each simulation can be performed on any stream of distinct elements (multiple occurrences do not update the sketch or the estimate). We implemented HyperLogLog using the pseudocode provided in [28]. We show both the raw estimate and the improved bias corrected estimate as presented. The Figure also shows the back-of-the-envelope approximate bound we calculated for the CV of HIP, $\sqrt{\frac{b+1}{4(k-1)}}$, and we can see that it approximately matches simulation results.

A more recent and more complicated implementation of HLL [30] obtains improved performance. The improvement amounts to smoothing out the "bump" due to the somewhat ad-hoc bias reducing component, but the asymptotic behavior is the same as the original hyperLogLog. We can see that HIP obtains an asymptotic improvement over HLL and also has a smooth behavior. Moreover, HIP is unbiased (unless all counters are saturated) and elegant, and does not require corrections and patches as with [28, 30].

We quantify the improvement more precisely in terms of the number k of registers: The NRMSE of HLL is $\approx 1.08/\sqrt{k}$ versus $\approx \sqrt{3/(4k)} \approx 0.866/\sqrt{k}$ of HIP. This means that an HLL estimator requires $\approx 0.56k$ more registers for the same square error as a HIP estimator. As discussed above, HIP requires an additional register c, but its benefit, in terms of accuracy outweighs the overhead.

Some encoding optimizations that were proposed for HLL [30] and elsewhere [32] can also be integrated with HIP. In particular, the content of the k registers is highly correlated can be represented compactly by storing only one value and offsets for others (the expected size of each offset is constant). Recall that the "exponent" component of the approximate count c can also be represented as an offset (see discussion above).

We note that HIP permits us to work with a different base, and get further improvements with respect to HyperLogLog. Consider using base $b = 2^{1/i}$ for $i \geq 1$. With smaller base, we need larger counters but we also have a smaller variance. We need about $\log_2 \log_b n$ bits per register, for counting up to cardinality (number of distinct elements) $n/16$ (since we want to have the counters large enough so that at most a fraction of them get saturated). Since $\log_2 \log_b n = \log_2(\log_2 n / \log_2 b) = \log_2 \log_2 n - \log_2 \log_2 b \approx \log_2 \log_2 n + \log_2 i$, it means we need about $\log_2 i$ additional bits per register relative to base-2. The CV is $\approx \sqrt{\frac{b+1}{4(k-1)}}$. So with $i=1$ (base $b=2$) we had CV $\approx 0.866/\sqrt{k}$, with $i=2$ ($b=\sqrt{2}$), we need 1 additional bit per register but the CV is $\approx 0.777/\sqrt{k}$, meaning that we need 20% fewer registers for the same error as when using base-2. The advantage of base-$\sqrt{2}$ kicks in when n exceeds about 3×10^8. If the counting algorithm also retains a sample of distinct elements (such as with reservoir sampling) and thus IDs of sampled elements are retained, representation size is dominated by $k\log n$ in which case we might as well use full ranks for the approximate distinct count.

Our evaluation aims at practice and we mention some differences with the theory literature. First, our analysis applies to random hash functions. This is justified by simulation results with standard generators. We mention that a lower bound of Alon et al. [3] on the sketch size has logarithmic dependence on the cardinality (and there is a matching upper bound by Kane et al. [32]) whereas the HLL sketch has a much smaller, double logarithmic, size. The reason is that the lower bound "includes" the encoding of the hash function as part of the sketch, a requirement which is not justified when many counters use the same hash function.

Lastly, we comment on the mergeability of our extended Min-Hash sketches. Mergeability means that we can obtain a sketch of the union of (overlapping) data sets from the sketches of the sets. This property is important when parallelizing or distributing the computation. The Min-Hash component of the extended sketch are mergeable, but to correctly merge the counts, we need to estimate the overlap between the sets. This can be done using the similarity estimation hat of Min-Hash sketches. We leave further details for future work.

6. DISTANCE RANGES

We can obtain a small relative error (CV of $1/\sqrt{2(k-1)}$ with HIP) for estimating neighborhood cardinalities, that is, $n_d(v)$ for any v and d. In this section we explore the estimation quality For $n_J(v)$, where J is an arbitrary interval J, and in particular for estimating the number of nodes within distance exactly d from v. These problems generalize diameter estimation. The best known approximation of the diameter D that can be obtained in near linear time is $[0.5D, D]$: we pick an arbitrary node v and perform a single source shortest paths computation to find the farthest node from v. When the graph is undirected, the distance to the farthest node is at least $0.5D$. It is widely believed that a better approximation requires polynomially more time.

Consider estimating $n_{(a,b]}(v)$ from ADS(v) using the HIP estimator $\sum_{j\in N_{(a,b)}(v)} a_{vj}$. For a node j, the probability that $j\in$ ADS(v) is $\min\{1, k/\pi_{vj}\}$. The expected number of nodes from $N_{(a,b]}(v)$ in ADS(v) is $k(H_{n_b(v)}-H_{n_a(v)})\approx k\ln(n_b(v)/n_a(v))$. Since inclusions are negatively correlated, the variance of the HIP estimate is $\leq \sum_{i=n_a(v)+1}^{n_b(v)}\frac{i-1}{k-1} = \frac{1}{k-1}\frac{(n_b(v)+n_a(v)+1)(n_b(v)-n_a(v))}{2}$ and the CV, which is the ratio of the square-root of the variance to the mean $(n_b(v)+n_a(v))$, is $\leq \sqrt{\frac{1}{k-1}\frac{n_b(v)+n_a(v)}{2(n_b(v)-n_a(v))}}$. We can see that when $n_b(v) \gg (1+1/k)n_a(v)$, that is, when there is sufficient expansion, we obtain a vanishing CV with k.

For undirected graphs, we are able to provide bounds that do not depend on expansion: We show that when there is a pair with distance d in the graph, then with high probability there must be a sampled pair, that is a pair i,j such that $i\in$ ADS(j) or vice versa, so that $d_{ij}\in J=[d/2,3d/2]$. Moreover, for any i,j of distance d we can estimate with good relative error the number of pairs of nodes $n_J(i)+n_J(j)$ that are within distance that is in J from either i or j. These bounds match and extend what we can do for the diameter in near-linear time.

THEOREM 6.1. *For an undirected graph, for all i,j, and $J=[d_{ij}/2, 3d_{ij}/2]$, the HIP estimator $\hat{n}_J(i)+\hat{n}_J(j)$ has CV $\leq \sqrt{\frac{2}{k-1}}$.*

PROOF. Let $d\equiv d_{ij}$ and $J=[d/2,3d/2]$. Clearly, $N_{(0,d/2)}(i)$ and $N_{(0,d/2)}(j)$ are disjoint, $N_{(0,d/2)}(i)\subset N_J(j)$, and vice versa.

We first consider the covariances of the adjusted weight a_{jh} (for $h\in N_J(j)$) and $a_{i\ell}$ (for $\ell\in N_J(i)$). The covariance $\mathsf{Cov}[a_{hj}, a_{\ell i}]$ is not zero only when $\ell=h$. In this case, there is positive correlation and $\mathsf{Cov}[a_{jh}, a_{ih}] \leq \max\{\mathsf{Var}[a_{ih}], \mathsf{Var}[a_{jh}]\}$.

As a coarse upper bound,

$$\mathsf{Var}[\hat{n}_J(i)+\hat{n}_J(j)] \leq 2(\sum_{h|d_{ih}\in J}\mathsf{Var}[a_{ih}] + \sum_{\ell|d_{j\ell}\in J}\mathsf{Var}[a_{j\ell}]) . \quad (9)$$

We have

$$\begin{aligned}
\sum_{h|d_{ih}\in J}\mathsf{Var}[a_{hi}] &= \sum_{h=n_{(0,d/2)+1}(i)}^{n_{(0,3d/2]}(i)}\frac{h-1}{k-1} \\
&= \frac{1}{2(k-1)}(n_{(0,3d/2]}(i)+n_{(0,d/2]}(i)-2)n_J(i) \\
&\leq \frac{1}{2(k-1)}(n_J(i)+2n_{(0,d/2]}(i))n_J(i) \\
&\leq \frac{1}{2(k-1)}(n_J(i)+2n_J(j))n_J(i) = \frac{n_J(i)^2+2n_J(i)n_J(j)}{2(k-1)} .
\end{aligned}$$

The last inequality uses the fact that $N_{(0,d/2]}(i)\subset N_J(j)$ and therefore $n_{(0,d/2]}(i)\leq n_J(j)$. Substituting in (9) we obtain

$$\begin{aligned}
\frac{\mathsf{Var}[\hat{n}_J(i)+\hat{n}_J(j)]}{(n_J(i)+n_J(j))^2} &\leq \frac{1}{k-1}\frac{n_J(i)^2+4n_J(i)n_J(j)+n_J(j)^2}{(n_J(i)+n_J(j))^2} \\
&= \frac{1}{k-1}\frac{(n_J(i)+n_J(j))^2+2n_J(i)n_J(j)}{(n_J(i)+n_J(j))^2} \\
&\leq \frac{1.5}{k-1}
\end{aligned}$$

□

Conclusion

ADSs, introduced two decades ago, are emerging as a powerful tool for scalable analysis of massive graphs. We introduce HIP estimators, which apply to an extensive class of natural queries and significantly improve over state of the art. For neighborhood cardinalities and closeness centralities, HIP estimators have at most half the variance of previous estimators. Moreover, HIP estimators outperform state of the art practical estimators for approximate distinct counting on data streams. In follow-up work we apply HIP for ADS-based estimation of closeness similarity [15] and timed influence [16] queries.

7. REFERENCES

[1] D. Aingworth, C. Chekuri, P Indyk, and R. Motwani. Fast estimation of diameter and shortest paths (without matrix multiplication). *SIAM J. Comput.*, 28(4):1167–1181, 1999.

[2] T. Akiba, Y. Iwata, and Y. Yoshida. Fast exact shortest-path distance queries on large networks by pruned landmark labeling. In *SIGMOD*, pages 349–360, 2013.

[3] N. Alon, Y. Matias, and M. Szegedy. The space complexity of approximating the frequency moments. *J. Comput. System Sci.*, 58:137–147, 1999.

[4] L. Backstrom, P. Boldi, M. Rosa, J. Ugander, and S. Vigna. Four degrees of separation. In *WebSci*, pages 33–42, 2012.
[5] Z. Bar-Yossef, T. S. Jayram, R. Kumar, D. Sivakumar, and L. Trevisan. Counting distinct elements in a data stream. In *RANDOM*. ACM, 2002.
[6] A. Bavelas. A mathematical model for small group structures. *Human Organization*, 7:16–30, 1948.
[7] D. Blackwell. Conditional expectation and unbiased sequential estimation. *Annals of Mathematical Statistics*, 18(1), 1947.
[8] P. Boldi, M. Rosa, and S. Vigna. HyperANF: Approximating the neighbourhood function of very large graphs on a budget. In *WWW*, 2011.
[9] P. Boldi, M. Rosa, and S. Vigna. Robustness of social networks: Comparative results based on distance distributions. In *SocInfo*, pages 8–21, 2011.
[10] P. Boldi and S. Vigna. Axioms for centrality. *Internet Mathematics*, 2014.
[11] K. R. W. Brewer, L. J. Early, and S. F. Joyce. Selecting several samples from a single population. *Australian Journal of Statistics*, 14(3):231–239, 1972.
[12] A. Z. Broder. On the resemblance and containment of documents. In *Proceedings of the Compression and Complexity of Sequences*, pages 21–29. IEEE, 1997.
[13] A. Z. Broder. Identifying and filtering near-duplicate documents. In *Proc.of the 11th Annual Symposium on Combinatorial Pattern Matching*, volume 1848 of *LNCS*, pages 1–10. Springer, 2000.
[14] E. Cohen. Size-estimation framework with applications to transitive closure and reachability. *J. Comput. System Sci.*, 55:441–453, 1997.
[15] E. Cohen, D. Delling, F. Fuchs, A. Goldberg, M. Goldszmidt, and R. Werneck. Scalable similarity estimation in social networks: Closeness, node labels, and random edge lengths. In *COSN*, 2013.
[16] E. Cohen, D. Delling, T. Pajor, and R. Werneck. Influence computation scaled-up in sketch space, 2014. Manuscript.
[17] E. Cohen and H. Kaplan. Spatially-decaying aggregation over a network: model and algorithms. *J. Comput. System Sci.*, 73:265–288, 2007. Full version of a SIGMOD 2004 paper.
[18] E. Cohen and H. Kaplan. Summarizing data using bottom-k sketches. In *Proceedings of the ACM PODC'07 Conference*, 2007.
[19] E. Cohen and H. Kaplan. Tighter estimation using bottom-k sketches. In *Proceedings of the 34th VLDB Conference*, 2008.
[20] E. Cohen and M. Strauss. Maintaining time-decaying stream aggregates. *J. Algorithms*, 59:19–36, 2006.
[21] P. Crescenzi, R. Grossi, L. Lanzi, and A. Marino. A comparison of three algorithms for approximating the distance distribution in real-world graphs. In *TAPAS*, 2011.
[22] Ch. Dangalchev. Residual closeness in networks. *Phisica A*, 365, 2006.
[23] N. Duffield, M. Thorup, and C. Lund. Priority sampling for estimating arbitrary subset sums. *J. Assoc. Comput. Mach.*, 54(6), 2007.
[24] M. Durand and P. Flajolet. Loglog counting of large cardinalities (extended abstract). In *ESA*, 2003.
[25] D. Eppstein and J. Wang. Fast approximation of centrality. In *SODA*, pages 228–229, 2001.
[26] W. Feller. *An introduction to probability theory and its applications*, volume 2. John Wiley & Sons, New York, 1971.
[27] P. Flajolet. Approximate counting: A detailed analysis. *BIT*, 25, 1985.
[28] P. Flajolet, E. Fusy, O. Gandouet, and F. Meunier. Hyperloglog: The analysis of a near-optimal cardinality estimation algorithm. In *Analysis of Algorithms (AOFA)*, 2007.
[29] P. Flajolet and G. N. Martin. Probabilistic counting algorithms for data base applications. *J. Comput. System Sci.*, 31:182–209, 1985.
[30] S. Heule, M. Nunkesser, and A. Hall. HyperLogLog in practice: Algorithmic engineering of a state of the art cardinality estimation algorithm. In *EDBT*, 2013.
[31] D. G. Horvitz and D. J. Thompson. A generalization of sampling without replacement from a finite universe. *Journal of the American Statistical Association*, 47(260):663–685, 1952.
[32] D. M. Kane, J. Nelson, and D. P. Woodruff. An optimal algorithm for the distinct elements problem. In *PODS*, 2010.
[33] J. C. Kiefer. *Introduction to statistical inference*. Springer-Verlag, New York, 1987.
[34] E. L. Lehmann and H. Scheffé. Completeness, similar regions, and unbiased estimation. *Sankhya*, 10(4), 1950.
[35] P. Li, , K. W. Church, and T. Hastie. One sketch for all: Theory and application of conditional random sampling. In *NIPS*, 2008.
[36] P. Li, A. B. Owen, and C-H Zhang. One permutation hashing. In *NIPS*, 2012.
[37] M. H. Malewicz, G.and Austern, A.J.C Bik, J. C. Dehnert, I. Horn, N. Leiser, and G. Czajkowski. Pregel: a system for large-scale graph processing. In *SIGMOD*. ACM, 2010.
[38] R. Morris. Counting large numbers of events in small registers. *Comm. ACM*, 21, 1977.
[39] E. Ohlsson. Sequential poisson sampling. *J. Official Statistics*, 14(2):149–162, 1998.
[40] T. Opsahl, F. Agneessens, and J. Skvoretz. Node centrality in weighted networks: Generalizing degree and shortest paths. *Social Networks*, 32, 2010.
[41] C. R. Palmer, P. B. Gibbons, and C. Faloutsos. ANF: a fast and scalable tool for data mining in massive graphs. In *KDD*, 2002.
[42] L. Roditty and V. Vassilevska Williams. Fast approximation algorithms for the diameter and radius of sparse graphs. In *STOC*. ACM, 2013.
[43] B. Rosén. Asymptotic theory for order sampling. *J. Statistical Planning and Inference*, 62(2):135–158, 1997.
[44] M. Rosenblatt. Remarks on some nonparametric estimates of a density function. *The Annals of Mathematical Statistics*, 27(3):832, 1956.

APPENDIX

A. APPROXIMATE COUNTING

An approximate counter is a applied to a stream of positive integers $\{w_i\}$ and represents $n = \sum_i w_i$ approximately. Whereas an exact representation takes $\lceil \log_2 n \rceil$ bits, an approximate counter that uses only $O(\log \log n)$ bits was proposed by Morris [38] and analysed and extended by Flajolet [27]. This *Morris counter* is an integer $x \geq 0$ and the estimate is $\hat{n} = b^x - 1$, where the (fixed) base $b > 1$ controls a tradeoff between approximation quality and representation size. Since originally presented only for increments of 1, we provide procedures here for efficient weighted updates and for merges of two counters. An update of Y to a counter x is performed as follows: Let $i \leftarrow \lfloor \log_b(Y/b^x - 1) \rfloor$ be the maximum such that increasing the counter by i would increase the estimate by at most Y. We then compute the leftover $\Delta \leftarrow Y - b^x(b^i - 1)$ and update $x \leftarrow x + i$. Lastly, we increase x by 1 with probability $\Delta/(b^x(b-1))$ (this is an inverse probability estimate of Δ). Merge of two Morris counters x_1, x_2 is handled the same as incrementing x_1 with $b^{x_2} - 1$. The estimator $\hat{n}$ is clearly unbiased (by induction on updates). It is easy to show that the variance is dominated by the analysis in [38, 27] for increments, since it can only improve when two consecutive updates are combined to a single update with the sum of their values. Intuitively, only the "leftover" part of the updates contributes to the variance at all. This is relevant to us since we use an approximate counter in our HIP approximate distinct counter. The update magnitudes are increasing and typically are about $1/k$ of the total, therefore, with the choice of $b \leq 1 + 1/k$, the variance is significantly lower than in [38, 27]. The number of bits needed for counter representation is $\log_2 \log_b n \approx \log_2 \log_2 n + \log_2(1/(b-1))$ and the CV is about $(b-1)$. When using $b = 1 + 1/2^j$ we obtain that with j additional bits in the representation we can obtain relative error of $1/2^j$.

Composable Core-sets for Diversity and Coverage Maximization

[Extended Abstract]

Piotr Indyk
Massachusetts Institute of Technology
Cambridge, MA
indyk@mit.edu

Sepideh Mahabadi
Massachusetts Institute of Technology
Cambridge, MA
mahabadi@mit.edu

Mohammad Mahdian
Google, Inc.
Mountain View, CA
mahdian@alum.mit.edu

Vahab S. Mirrokni
Google, Inc.
New York, NY
mirrokni@gmail.com

ABSTRACT

In this paper we consider efficient construction of "composable core-sets" for basic diversity and coverage maximization problems. A core-set for a point-set in a metric space is a subset of the point-set with the property that an approximate solution to the whole point-set can be obtained given the core-set alone. A composable core-set has the property that for a collection of sets, the approximate solution to the union of the sets in the collection can be obtained given the union of the composable core-sets for the point sets in the collection. Using composable core-sets one can obtain efficient solutions to a wide variety of massive data processing applications, including nearest neighbor search, streaming algorithms and map-reduce computation.

Our main results are algorithms for constructing composable core-sets for several notions of "diversity objective functions", a topic that attracted a significant amount of research over the last few years. The composable core-sets we construct are small and accurate: their approximation factor almost matches that of the best "off-line" algorithms for the relevant optimization problems (up to a constant factor). Moreover, we also show applications of our results to diverse nearest neighbor search, streaming algorithms and map-reduce computation. Finally, we show that for an alternative notion of diversity maximization based on the maximum coverage problem small composable core-sets do not exist.

PODS'14, June 22–27, 2014, Snowbird, UT, USA.
ACM 978-1-4503-2375-8/14/06.
http://dx.doi.org/10.1145/2594538.2594560 .

Categories and Subject Descriptors

F.2.2 [**Nonnumerical Algorithms and Problems**]: Geometrical problems and computations; G.1.6 [**Optimization**]: Constrained optimization

Keywords

Core-set; Diversity; Streaming; Nearest Neighbor; Map-reduce;

1. INTRODUCTION

One of the most popular approaches to processing massive data is to first extract a compact representation (or synopsis) of the data and then perform further processing only on the representation itself. This approach significantly reduces the cost of processing, communicating and storing the data, as the representation size can be much smaller than the size of the original data set. Typically, the representation provides a smooth tradeoff between its size and the representation accuracy. Examples of this approach include techniques such as sampling, sketching, core-sets and mergeable summaries.

In this paper we focus on computing efficient representations for the purpose of *diversity-aware summarization and search,* a topic that has attracted significant attention over the last few years [20, 41, 7, 26, 40, 38, 18, 1, 32]. The goal of this line of research is to design efficient methods for searching and summarizing large data sets in a way that preserves the diversity of the data. In most formulations, the summary is a sub-set of the original data of some predefined size (say k) that maximizes a certain *diversity objective.* For example one could require that the minimum distance between any pair of points in the summary is as large as possible, i.e., the summary does not contain two "highly similar" items. Many other, more refined, diversity objectives have been studied, see Figure 1 for an overview.

In this paper we study specific diversity-aware representations called *composable core-sets.* An α-approximate *composable core-set* for a diversity objective is a mapping from a set S to a subset of S with the following property: for a collection of sets, the maximum diversity of the union of those sets is within an α factor of the maximum diversity of the union of the corresponding core-sets. That is, one can construct an approximately optimal solution for a given data set by partitioning it into several (possibly overlapping) blocks, computing a core-set for each block, and then solving the problem for the union of the core-sets. Composable core-sets naturally lead to divide-and-conquer solutions to a collection of massive data processing problems. In particular, they have been used for the following tasks:

- Streaming computation: In the data stream model, a sequence of n data elements needs to be processed "on-the-fly" while using only limited storage. Such an algorithm can be easily obtained using composable core-sets [22, 5][1]. Specifically, if a composable core-set for a given problem has size k, we start by dividing the stream of data into $\sqrt{n/k}$ blocks of size $s = \sqrt{nk}$. The algorithm then proceeds block by block. Each block is read and stored in the main memory, its core-set is computed and stored, and the block is deleted. At the end, the algorithm solves the problem for the union of the core-sets. The whole algorithm takes only $O(\sqrt{kn})$ space. The storage can be reduced further by utilizing more than one level of compression, at the cost of increasing the approximation factor.

- Distributed data processing: composable core-sets can be also used to process data in a distributed system, where each machine holds a block of the data. The algorithm is virtually identical to the one for streaming data: for each block, a composable core-set is computed and sent to the central server, where the computation is completed. As an example, this idea is directly applicable in the map-reduce framework [17] and gives an approximation algorithm in one round of map-reduce: Using $\sqrt{n/k}$ mappers, each mapper gets $\sqrt{kn}$ points as input and computes a composable core-set of size k for this set. These sets will be passed to a single reducer. The input of this reducer is the union of the core-sets, which is of size at most $k\sqrt{n/k} = \sqrt{kn}$. It computes and outputs a solution on this union, which by the definition of core-sets is a good approximation to the original problem. Recently, variants of this technique have been applied for optimization under map-reduce framework [28, 31, 8].

- Similarity search: recently, composable core-sets have been used to construct efficient near neighbor search algorithms that maximize the diversity of the answers, both in theory [2] and in practice [1]. This is done by observing that several similarity search algorithms (notably those based on the *Locality-Sensitive Hashing* technique) proceed by hashing each point into multiple buckets. Each query is then answered by retrieving the points stored in the buckets that the query is mapped into. Since the number of points stored in a bucket might be large (which is the case, e.g., when the data set contains one big cluster of close points), the query answering procedure might be slow. To improve the performance, the paper [1] proposed to replace the content of each bucket by its core-set. By collecting the core-sets stored in all relevant buckets and performing the computation over the their union, the algorithm reports a diverse summary of the points close to the query in time that depends on the number of buckets, not the size of the whole data set. This is discussed in more details in Appendix A.

The broad applicability of composable core-sets motivates the study of efficient methods for constructing them. This is the task we undertake in this paper.

Our results. In this paper we present a thorough study of composable core-sets for several well-studied diversity maximization problems. Suppose that the set S of interest lives in some metric space $(\Delta, dist)$, and let $div(S)$ be any function that maps a set into a non-negative real number. The goal of the diversity maximization problem is to find a subset S' of S of size k that maximizes the diversity objective.

The specific diversity functions div considered in this paper are described in Figure 1, following the taxonomy of dispersion measures introduced in [13]. For each dispersion function we provide the approximation factor of the composable core-set that we obtain for that function. We note that for all core-sets the approximation factor matches that of the best "off-line" algorithm for the corresponding diversity maximization problem [13] (up to a constant factor). All core-sets are of size k.

The interpretation of the diversity measures is as follows. First, remote-edge [1] and remote-clique [20] correspond to the well-studied diversity notions where the objective is to ensure that no two pairs of points are too "close" to each other, or that an average pair distance of points is not too "low", respectively. Remote-pseudoforest falls in between the two notions, as its goal is to ensure that the *average* distance of a point to its *nearest* neighbor is not too "low". Remote-pseudoforest can be viewed as a diversity analog of the well-studied Chamfer distance [27]. Remote-tree and remote t-tree measure the diversity by the cost of clustering the data using the Single Link algorithm [37]. Similarly, remote-star measures the diversity by the cost of connecting the points to the best center[2]. Finally, remote-matching, remote-cycle and remote-bipartition are more "exotic" combinatorial variations of the aforementioned measures. We include them to complete the table of [13].

All aforementioned notions of diversity are "pairwise", i.e., they are a function of the pair-wise distances between the selected items. We also consider a basic "higher order" notion of diversity which has been previously discussed in the context of diversity maximization[3, 10]. Intuitively, the idea is to model diversity by considering a set of topics that each item covers, and exploring the diversity or the union of topics *covered* by a set of items. More specifically, we consider the scenario where the items are binary vectors of topics, and the diversity of a set of items is equal to their *coverage* over another set of topics, i.e., the weight of the coordinate-wise OR of the item vectors. As before, the goal is to choose a set of size k which maximizes the total coverage. This is directly related to the maximum k-coverage problem that admits a tight $1 - 1/e$-approximation algorithm [19]. We show in Section 4 that this problem does not support composable core-sets of size *polynomial* in k. In particular, for

[1]The paper [22] introduced this approach for the special case of k-median clustering. More general formulation of this method with other applications appeared in [5].

[2]Note that the values of remote-clique and remote-star objectives are within a factor of $\Theta(k)$ from each other, and thus the core-sets for the two objectives are equivalent up to constant factors.

Problem	Diversity of the point set S	Approx. factor
Remote-edge	$\min_{p,q \in S} dist(p,q)$	$O(1)$
Remote-clique	$\sum_{p,q \in S} dist(p,q)$	$O(1)$
Remote-tree	$wt(MST(S))$, weight of the minimum spanning tree of S	$O(1)$
Remote-cycle	$\min_C wt(C)$ where C is a TSP tour on S	$O(1)$
Remote t-trees	$\min_{S=S_1\|...\|S_t} \sum_{i=1}^t wt(MST(S_i))$	$O(1)$
Remote t-cycles	$\min_{S=S_1\|...\|S_t} \sum_{i=1}^t wt(TSP(S_i))$	$O(1)$
Remote-star	$\min_{p \in S} \sum_{q \in S \setminus \{p\}} dist(p,q)$	$O(1)$
Remote-bipartition	$\min_B wt(B)$, where B is a bipartition (i.e., bisection) of S	$O(1)$
Remote-pseudoforest	$\sum_{p \in S} \min_{q \in S \setminus \{p\}} dist(p,q)$	$O(\log k)$
Remote-matching	$\min_M wt(M)$, where M is a perfect matching of S	$O(\log k)$
Max k-Coverage	$\sum_{i \le d} \max_{p \in S} p_i$, where p_i denotes the ith coordinate of p	no $\frac{\sqrt{k}}{\log k}$-approx. core-set of size k^β

Table 1: Notions of diversity considered in this paper. We use $S = S_1|...|S_t$ to denote that $S_1 \ldots S_t$ is a partition of S into t sets.

any $\alpha \le \frac{\sqrt{k}}{\log k}$ and any constant $\beta > 0$, there exists a set of instances for which no α-approximate core-set of size k^β exists. As an illustrative example of submodular maximization [33, 25], the maximum coverage problem has been recently studied from distributed computation perspective [16], e.g., in the map-reduce framework [15, 29]. Our negative result for existence of core-sets for this problem implies that one cannot use the simple core-set approach to solve this problem in distributed or streaming settings.

Our techniques. Our techniques for constructing composable core-sets rely on off-line algorithms that solve the corresponding diversity maximization problems. The three algorithms are given in Preliminaries. Our contribution is to show that the solutions produced by those algorithms satisfy the composable core-set properties. The basic idea is to show that, for each algorithm, one can construct a mapping from each element in the optimum solution (to the whole data set) and an element of the core-set. This correspondence is then used to bound the error incurred by the core-set. Note that for the remote-edge diversity measure, this analysis is analogous to the analysis in [2] (although that analysis was focused on the k-center clustering as opposed to the diversity maximization).

Related Work.

Composable core-sets: The notion of core-sets has been introduced in [5]. Informally, a core-set for an optimization problem is a subset of the data with the property that solving the underlying problem on the subset gives an approximate solution for the original data. The notion is somewhat generic, and many variations of core-sets exist. The notion of composable core-sets used in this paper has been implicit in earlier works that used core-sets for streaming applications. For example, the paper [5] (Section 5) specifies composability properties of ϵ-kernels (a variant of core-sets) that are very similar to ours. To avoid confusion, in this paper the term "core-set" always means "composable core-set" according to the definition in the introduction.

The notion of composable core-sets is related to the notion of merge-able summaries introduced in [4]. The main difference between the two notions is that aggregating merge-able summaries does *not* increase the approximation error, while in our case the error amplifies (similarly to [22]). In particular, every merge-able summary that is obtained by taking a sub-set of the data is also a composable core-set, but the opposite does not hold.

Diversity Maximization: The diversity maximization problem studied in this paper generalizes the maximum dispersion problem [24, 20, 9]. This problem has been explored in the context of diversity maximization for recommender systems [20], and commerce search [9]. A 2-approximation greedy algorithm has been developed for the unconstrained variant of this problem [24], and the variant with knapsack constraints [9]. More recently, local search algorithms have been developed to get a 2-approximation algorithm for the maximum dispersion problem under matroid constraints [3, 10].

Diversity in Recommender Systems and Web Search: Ranking and relevance maximization along with diversification have been extensively studied in recommender systems, web search, and database systems. In the context of web search, maximizing diversity has been explored as a post-processing step [11, 39]. Other papers explore ranking while taking into account diversity by a query reformulation for re-ranking the top searches [34] or by sampling the search results by reducing homogeneity [6]. Other methods are based on clustering results into groups of related topics [30], or expectation maximization for estimating the model parameters and reaching an equilibrium [35]. Moreover, in the context of recommender systems, diversification has been explored in various recent papers [41, 40]. For example, topical diversity maximization is discussed in [41], and explanation-based diversity maximization is explored in [40]. Finally, this topic has been also explored in database systems for example by presenting decision trees to users [14].

2. PRELIMINARIES

We start by formalizing the notion of diversity used in this paper.

Definition 1. For a given set $S \subset \Delta$, its **k-diversity** is defined as $div_k(S) = \max_{S' \subset S, |S'|=k} div(S')$. We also refer to the maximizing subset S' as the **optimal k-subset** of S. Note that k-diversity is not defined in the case where $|S| < k$.

Definition 2. Let div be a diversity function defined for subsets of Δ. A function $c(S)$ that maps a set $S \subset \Delta$ into one of its subsets is called an *α-composable core-set* ($\alpha \geq 1$) for *div*, if for any collection of sets $S_1 \ldots S_L \subset \Delta$ with $|S_i| \geq k$, we have

$$div_k(c(S_1) \cup \ldots \cup c(S_L)) \geq \frac{1}{\alpha} \cdot div_k(S_1 \cup \ldots \cup S_L)$$

The core-set is of size k' if for every S, $|c(S)| \leq k'$. Note that in general k' does not need to be the same as k. For example, in all applications mentioned in the previous section, a core-set of size k^2 would work as well when k is a constant. However, as it turns out, all our positive results give core-sets of size k.

Our algorithms for constructing core-sets are based on existing off-line approximation algorithms for the corresponding diversity maximization problems. In the rest of this section we review three such algorithms: GMM, Local Search and Prefix.

2.1 GMM Algorithm

In this paper we use the following slight variation of the "GMM" algorithm introduced in [21, 36]. The algorithm receives a set of points S, and the parameter k as the input. Initially, it chooses some arbitrary point $a \in S$. Then it repeatedly adds the next point to the output set until there are k points. More precisely, in each step, it greedily adds the point whose minimum distance to the currently chosen points is maximized. This algorithm was also utilized in [13] to find approximation algorithms for several dispersion problems.

Algorithm 1 GMM

Input S: a set of points, k: size of the subset
Output S': a subset of S of size k.

$S' \leftarrow$ An arbitrary point a
for $i = 2, \ldots, k$ **do**
  find $p \in S \setminus S'$ which maximizes $\min_{x \in S'} dist(p, x)$
  $S' \leftarrow S' \cup \{p\}$
end for
return S'

It is easy to see that the running time of the algorithm is $O(nk)$. Also, observe that if we define the radius value $r = \min_{p,q \in S'} dist(p, q)$ as the minimum pairwise distance in the set S', it is easy to see that the following two properties hold:

- $\forall p \in S' : dist(p, S' \setminus \{p\}) \geq r$
- $\forall p \in S : dist(p, S') \leq r$

Such sets S' are said to have the *anticover* property.

2.2 Local Search Algorithm

Algorithm 2 shows the local search algorithm. This was used in [3] to find a subset with approximate maximum diversity under matroid constraints for the case of Remote Clique. The algorithm iteratively improves the current solution by a factor of $(1 + \epsilon/n)$ and finds a more diverse set of k points. Since the initial set contains the two farthest points, the total number of iterations needed is at most $\log_{1+\epsilon/n}(k^2) = O(\frac{n}{\epsilon} \log k)$.

Algorithm 2 Local Search Algorithm

Input S: a set of points, k: size of the subset
Output S': a subset of S of size k.

$S' \leftarrow$ An arbitrary set of k points which contains the two farthest points
while there exists $p \in S \setminus S'$ and $p' \in S'$ such that $div(S' \setminus \{p'\} \cup \{p\}) \geq div(S')(1 + \frac{\epsilon}{n})$ **do**
  $S' \leftarrow S' \setminus \{p'\} \cup \{p\}$
end while
return S'

2.3 Prefix Algorithm

The Prefix algorithm was introduced in [13] which is used to solve the approximate maximum dispersion problem in the case of Remote Pseudo-forest and Remote Matching. Note that the algorithm works only in the case when $k \leq n/2$.

Algorithm 3 PREFIX Algorithm

Input S: a set of points, k: size of the subset
Output S': a subset of S of size k.

Run GMM obtaining a set $Y = \{y_1, \cdots, y_k\}$ with corresponding radii $r_1, \cdots, r_k$.
$q \leftarrow$ the value from the set $\{1, \cdots, k-1\}$ which maximizes $q \cdot r_q$.
$Y_{q+1} \leftarrow$ the prefix subsequence of Y of length $q + 1$
$Q_i \leftarrow$ vertices of distance at most $r_q/2$ from y_i for $i = 1, \cdots, q+1$.
$z \leftarrow \lfloor (q+1)/2 \rfloor$.
$\{Q_{i_1}, \cdots, Q_{i_z}\} \leftarrow$ the z sparsest spheres.
$S' \leftarrow$ the centers of $\{Q_{i_1}, \cdots, Q_{i_z}\}$
Add any set of $k - z$ vertices from $S \setminus \bigcup_{j=1}^{z} Q_{i_j}$ to S'
return S'

3. COMPOSABLE CORE-SETS FOR DIVERSITY MAXIMIZATION

This section provides algorithms for finding composable core-sets for different notions of diversity defined in Table 1. That is, we run one of the algorithms defined in Preliminaries to get k points in each of the instances of the problem and prove their union is an approximate core-set for the union of the instances.

In all of the following cases, we let $S_1, \cdots, S_L \subset \Delta$ be the subsets of Δ that correspond to the instances of the problem and let $S = \bigcup_{i=1}^{L} S_i$ denote their union. For each such instance S_i, we find a core-set T_i and we let $T = \bigcup_{i=1}^{L} T_i$ denote the union of the core-sets. Also we let $O = \{o_1, \cdots, o_k\}$ be the optimal k-subset of S, that is the subset of k points which maximizes the diversity. Moreover, we define $O_i = \{o \in O \cap S_i | \forall j < i : o \notin S_j\}$ to be the set of points from the optimal set in each of the instances (we impose extra condition in order to make O_i's a partition of O).

Next, for each notion of diversity, we describe how to choose T_i and compare k-diversity of T with that of S, which is equal to the diversity of O.

3.1 Remote Edge

LEMMA 1. *The GMM algorithm computes a 3-approximate composable core-set for the Remote Edge problem.*

PROOF. We run the GMM algorithm on each of the sets S_i and let $T_i = GMM(S_i)$ be the point set returned by the GMM and we let r_i denote the radius of T_i. Let $T = \bigcup_{i=1}^{L} T_i$ denote the union of the core-sets, and set $r = \max_i r_i$ to be the maximum radius over the instances. The goal is to prove that $div_k(T) \geq div_k(S)/3$.

Define a mapping $f : O_i \to T_i$ which maps each point $o \in O_i$ to one of its closest points in the set T_i, i.e., $dist(o, f(o)) = dist(o, T_i)$. By the anticover property of GMM we have $dist(o, f(o)) \leq r_i \leq r$. Note that since O_i's form a partition of O, for any $o \in O$, we can define $f(o) = f_i(o)$ if $o \in O_i$.

It is easy to see that for any i, since T is a superset of T_i, then $div_k(T) \geq div(T_i) = r_i$ and thus $div_k(T) \geq r$. Next, note that if for two points $o_1, o_2 \in O$, we have $f(o_1) = f(o_2)$, then

$$div(O) \leq dist(o_1, o_2) \leq dist(o_1, f(o_1)) + dist(o_2, f(o_2)) \leq 2r \leq 2div_k(T)$$

and the lemma is proved. Otherwise f is a 1-to-1 mapping. Now if $div(O) \leq 3r \leq 3div_k(T)$ then in this case the lemma is proved as well. Otherwise, we can assume that for any pair of points $o_1, o_2 \in O$, $dist(o_1, o_2) \geq 3r$ and thus $div(O) \geq 3r$. Hence, by triangle inequality

$$\begin{aligned} &dist(f(o_1), f(o_2)) \\ &\geq dist(o_1, o_2) - dist(o_1, f(o_1)) - dist(o_2, f(o_2)) \\ &\geq div(O) - 2r \\ &\geq div(O) - 2div(O)/3 \\ &\geq div(O)/3 \end{aligned}$$

since this holds for any pair o_1, o_2, the set $\{f(o_1), \cdots, f(o_k)\}$ has diversity at least $div(O)/3$ and thus $div_k(T) \geq div(O)/3$ and the lemma is proved. □

3.2 Remote Clique, Remote Star and Remote Bipartition

In this section, we show that the local search algorithm gives a constant-factor approximation for the following diversity notions: Remote Clique, Remote Star and Remote Bipartition.

LEMMA 2. *The local search algorithm computes a constant-factor approximate composable core-set for the remote-clique problem.*

PROOF. We run the Local Search algorithm on each of the sets S_i and let $T_i = LS(S_i)$ be the point set returned by the Local Search and let r_i represent the normalized diversity of the corresponding sets T_i, i.e., $r_i = \frac{1}{\binom{k}{2}} div(T_i)$ and set $r = \max_i r_i$.

Claim 1. There exists a 1-to-1 mapping $f : O \to T$ such that $dist(o, f(o)) \leq 25r$ for any $o \in O$

PROOF. Build an unweighted bipartite graph $G_x = (V_O, U_T, E_x)$ with vertices of one side corresponding to O and vertices of the other side corresponding to T as follows. For any $o \in O$ and $s \in T$, we connect $v_o \in V_O$ to $u_s \in U_T$ iff $dist(o, s) \leq x \times r$. Now, take any $o \in O$ and suppose that $o \in O_i \setminus T_i$, that is, o is in the ith instance but has not been selected by *LocalSearch* algorithm. However, since no more improvement on the set T_i could be made, we have

$$\sum_{s \in T_i} dist(o, s) \leq (k-1)(1 + \frac{\epsilon}{n}) r_i \leq kr$$

Note that since $|T_i| = k$, thus for at least $(1 - 1/x)$ fraction of the values s in the above equation, we have $dist(o, s) \leq xr$ and therefore the corresponding edges in the graph G_x exist. Thus the degree of each vertex v_o corresponding to $o \in O \setminus T$ is at least $k(1 - 1/x)$.

First, take the graph G_3. If G_3 has a matching which saturates the vertices of V_O, then the claim is proved. Otherwise, let M be a maximal matching in G_3 such that for any point $o \in O \cap T$, the corresponding vertices v_o and u_o are matched together. This means that the points corresponding to the set of unmatched vertices in U_T (which we denote by $T \setminus M$) is disjoint from O, and also $O \setminus M$ is disjoint from T. Let $A = O \setminus M$ be the set of points which corresponds to the unmatched vertices. Then for any point $a \in A$, since $a \notin T$, the degree of v_a is at least $2k/3$, and since M is a maximal matching, all the neighbors of v_a should be matched in M. Therefore there are at least $2k/3$ points $o \in O \setminus \{a\}$ such that $dist(o, a) \leq 6r$.

Now take the graph G_{25}. If all vertices in $V_A = V_O \setminus M$ are neighbors to all vertices in $U_T \setminus M$, then clearly G_{25} has a saturating matching for O and thus the claim is proved. Otherwise there exists a point $a \in A$ and $s \in T \setminus M$ such that $dist(a, s) > 25r$.

Let $B \subset O$ be the set of points whose distance is at most $6r$ from a. Then as we proved earlier $|B| > 2k/3$. Hence, if we replace the point a in the set O with the point s to get the set O' (note that since $T \setminus M$ is disjoint from O, we have $s \notin O$), the diversity will increase as follows.

$$\begin{aligned} div(O') - div(O) &= \sum_{o \in O \setminus \{a\}} dist(s, o) - dist(a, o) \\ &= \sum_{o \in B \setminus \{a\}} dist(s, o) - dist(a, o) \\ &+ \sum_{o \in O \setminus B} dist(s, o) - dist(a, o) \\ &\geq \sum_{o \in B \setminus \{a\}} dist(a, s) - 2dist(a, o) \\ &- \sum_{o \in O \setminus B} dist(a, s) \\ &\geq \frac{2k}{3} \times (dist(a, s) - 12r) - \frac{k}{3} \times dist(a, s) \\ &= \frac{k}{3}(dist(a, s) - 24r) \geq kr/3 \end{aligned}$$

which contradicts the fact that O has the optimal diversity. Therefore the claim holds. □

As claim 1 suggests, there is a 1-to-1 mapping between the vertices of O and the vertices of T such that for each $o \in O$ we have $dist(o, f(o)) \leq 25r$. First of all note that if $\binom{k}{2} \times r \geq div(O)/51$ the theorem is proved since for one of the T_i we have $div(T_i) = \binom{k}{2} \times r$ and thus

$$div_k(T) \geq div(T_i) = \binom{k}{2} \times r \geq div(O)/51$$

Otherwise, we have that

$$\begin{aligned} div_k(T) &\geq \sum_{o_1,o_2 \in O} dist(f(o_1), f(o_2)) \\ &\geq \sum_{o_1,o_2 \in O} dist(o_1, o_2) - dist(o_1, f(o_1)) - dist(o_2, f(o_2)) \\ &\geq div(O) - \binom{k}{2} \times 50r \\ &\geq div(O)(1 - 50/51) = div(O)/51 \end{aligned}$$

So the lemma is proved and the algorithm computes a 51-approximate core-set of size k.

COROLLARY 1. *Local Search algorithm computes a constant factor core-set for the minimum star and minimum bipartition problems as well.*

PROOF. First note that for a set of k points Q, a star is the tree achieved by connecting one point to all the others, and its weight is sum of the weights of its edges. Also a bipartition of Q is a bipartite graph which divides the vertices of Q into two parts of cardinality $k/2$ and its weight is the sum of all the edges between the two parts. It can easily be seen that

- by symmetry $wt(\text{minimum star}(Q)) \leq 2wt(\text{ clique}(Q))/k$
- by triangle inequality

$$wt(\text{ clique}(Q)) \leq k \times wt(\text{minimum star}(Q))$$

and that

- $wt(\text{minimum bipartition}(Q)) \leq wt(\text{ clique}(Q))$
- by triangle inequality

$$wt(\text{ clique}(Q)) \leq 5 \times wt(\text{minimum bipartition}(Q))$$

Therefore the same algorithm computes a constant factor core-set for these two problems as well. □

3.3 Remote tree, Remote Cycle, Remote t-trees and Remote t-cycles

LEMMA 3. *The GMM algorithm computes a 6-approximate core-set for the remote-tree problem.*

PROOF. We run the GMM algorithm on each of the sets S_i and let $T_i = GMM(S_i)$ be the point set returned by the GMM and we let r_i denote the radius of T_i. Let $T = \bigcup_{i=1}^{L} T_i$ denote the union of the core-sets, and set $r = \max_i r_i$ to be the maximum radius over the instances. Now define a mapping (this time not a 1-to-1) $f : O_i \rightarrow T_i$ which maps each point $o \in O_i$ to one of its closest points in the set T_i, i.e., $dist(o, f(o)) = dist(o, T_i)$. By anticover property of GMM we have $dist(o, f(o)) \leq r_i \leq r$.

It is easy to see that for any i, $div_k(T) \geq div(T_i) \geq (k-1)r_i$ (since the minimum pairwise distance in T_i is r_i), and thus $div_k(T) \geq (k-1)r$. Now if $div(O) \leq 3(k-1)r \leq 3div_k(T)$, then the lemma is proved. Otherwise let $F = range(f) = \{f(o) | o \in O\}$ (note that F is a subset of T), and let $F^+ \subset T$ be an arbitrary superset of F of size k. Then by triangle inequality and shortcutting

$$\begin{aligned} div(O) = wt(MST(O)) &\leq wt(MST(F)) + kr \\ &\leq wt(MST(F)) + 2(k-1)r \end{aligned}$$

which uses the fact that $k > 1$, otherwise any one point is a solution. Next, note that given the $MST(F^+)$, we can double the edges and traverse them using DFS and remove the vertices not in F by shortcutting. Hence, by triangle inequality, we find a Hamiltonian cycle of length at most $2wt(MST(F^+))$ on the set F, therefore we have $wt(MST(F)) \leq 2wt(MST(F^+))$ and thus

$$\begin{aligned} div_k(T) &\geq wt(MST(F^+)) \\ &\geq wt(MST(F))/2 \\ &\geq \frac{1}{2}[div(O) - 2(k-1)r] \\ &\geq \frac{div(O)}{2} - \frac{div(O)}{3} \\ &\geq \frac{div(O)}{6} \end{aligned}$$

□

LEMMA 4. *The same algorithm computes a 6 core-set for the Remote-t-tree. The proof is very similar to that for the Remote tree and hence moved to Appendix B.*

COROLLARY 2. *Note that since the minimum TSP tour is within a factor 2 of the MST, the above algorithm also computes a constant factor core-set for the remote-cycle problem and remote t-cycle problem.*

3.4 Remote Pseudoforest and Remote Matching

LEMMA 5. *The GMM algorithm computes a $O(\log k)$ core-set for the remote-pseudoforest problem.*

PROOF. We run the GMM algorithm on each of the sets S_i and let $T_i = GMM(S_i)$ be the point set returned by the GMM. Let $T = \bigcup_{i=1}^{L} T_i$ denote the union of the core-sets.

It is shown in page 11 of the paper [13] that when we run the Prefix algorithm on an input set A, the diversity achieved by this algorithm is at least $q \cdot r_q/4$ and that $q \cdot r_q/4 \geq div_k(A)/O(\log k)$. Next, we compare running the PREFIX algorithm on the set S and on the set T. Let $r_1^S, \cdots, r_k^S$ be the radii defined in line 1 of Algorithm 2.3 , and let q^S be the index chosen in line 2, when we run it on the set S. Similarly, let us define $r_1^T, \cdot, r_k^T$ and q^T, when we run the algorithm on the set T.

However by Lemma 1, GMM algorithm computes a core-set for minimum pairwise distances. Together with the fact that running GMM in the Prefix algorithm on the sets S and T preserves the radii upto a constant factor, we get that $r_i^T \geq r_i^S/c$, for any value of $i \leq k$ and some constant c. The diversity achieved by the prefix algorithm is therefore $div_k(T) \geq q^T \cdot r_{q^T}^T/4 \geq q^S \cdot r_{q^S}^T/4 \geq q^S \cdot r_{q^S}^S/(4c) \geq \frac{div_k(S)}{O(\log k)}$ □

For the same reason the GMM algorithm computes a $O(\log k)$ core-set for the remote-matching problem as well with the only difference that the value of the matching achieved by the prefix algorithm when we run in on the input set A is at least $qr_q/8$ instead of $qr_q/4$.

4. NON-EXISTENCE OF CORESET FOR THE MAX K-COVERAGE

An instance of the max k-coverage problem is a collection of sets. The objective is to find k sets in this collection whose union has the maximum size.

THEOREM 1. *For any $\alpha < \frac{\sqrt{k}}{\log k}$ and any constant $\beta > 1$, there is no α-approximate core-set of size k^β for the max k-coverage problem.*

PROOF. Let $\mathcal{U} = \{1, \ldots, N\}$ for a large N and $k = m^2$. We construct a number of instances of the problem as follows: For every subset $S \subset \mathcal{U}$ of size m^2, we have an instance I_S consisting of all m-subsets of S. Assume, for contradiction, that there is an α-approximate core-set, and let C_S denote the core-set on the instance I_S.

Now, fix a m^2-set S, and let R be a random m-subset of S. For each fixed $A \in C_S$, the random variable $|A \cap R|$ is distributed according to the binomial distribution $Bin(m, \frac{1}{m})$. The probability that the value of this variable is at least t is at most $\binom{m}{t}\frac{1}{m^t} < \frac{1}{t!}$. With $t = \log m$, this probability is at most $O(m^{-c})$ for every constant c. Using the union bound and the fact that $|C_S| \leq m^{2\beta}$, we get: $\Pr[\exists A \in C_S : |A \cap R| > \log m] < O(m^{2\beta - c})$ for every constant c. We say that R is an easy subset of S if $\exists A \in C_S : |A \cap R| > \log m$. Therefore for every S, at most a $O(m^{-\gamma})$ fraction of the m-subsets of S are easy, for every γ.

We construct a graph whose vertex set is the set of all m^2 subsets of $\mathcal{U}$. Two m^2-sets S_1 and S_2 in this graph are adjacent if $|S_1 \setminus S_2| = m$. We say that S_1 marks a neighbor S_2 as *bad* if $S_1 \setminus S_2$ is an easy subset of S_1. By the above argument, each vertex S_1 marks at most an $O(m^{-\gamma})$ fraction of its neighbors as bad. Since the total indegree of nodes in a graph is equal to the total outdegree, there must be a vertex S_1 in this graph such that at most an $O(m^{-\gamma})$ fraction of its neighbors have marked S_1 as bad. Therefore, at most an $O(m^{-\gamma})$ fraction of the neighbors of S_1 have either marked S_1 as bad or S_1 has marked them as bad. We call these neighbors the *bad* neighbors of S_1, and the remaining neighbors the *good* ones.

We now pick a collection of m^2-sets $S_1, S_2, \ldots$ as follows: S_1 is the vertex defined above. S_2 is an arbitrary good neighbor of S_1. S_{i+1} is a good neighbor of S_1 such that $S_{i+1} \setminus S_1$ does not intersect any of the sets $S_j \setminus S_1$ for $j \leq i$. We argue that for any $i < m^2$, there is a set S_{i+1} with the above properties that we can pick. This is because for any $x \in \mathcal{U} \setminus S_1$, the fraction of neighbors of S_1 that contain x is precisely $\frac{m}{N-m^2}$. Therefore, by the union bound, the fraction of neighbors of S_1 that contain any of the elements of $S_j \setminus S_1$ for $j \leq i$ is at most $\frac{m^2 i}{N-m^2}$, which is less than 1/2 for $N > 3m^4$. This means that at most a $\frac{1}{2} + O(m^{-\gamma}) < 1$ fraction of neighbors of S_1 either have intersection with some $S_j \setminus S_1$ for $j \leq i$ or are bad. Thus, we can find S_{i+1} with the desired properties, for $i < m^2$.

Now, consider the union of the instances $I_{S_1}, I_{S_2}, \ldots, I_{S_{m^2-m}}$. This instance has a perfect k-coverage solution: pick m non-overlapping m-subsets of S_1 to cover S_1, and for every $i > 1$, pick the m-subset $S_i \setminus S_1$. The total number of subsets picked is $m + m^2 - m = k$, and all of the $O(m^3)$ elements in $S_1 \cup \cdots \cup S_{m^2-m}$ are covered. On the other hand, by our construction, we know that for every $i > 1$, $S_i \setminus S_1$ is not an easy subset of S_i. Therefore, any set in C_{S_i} covers at most $\log m$ elements of $S_i \setminus S_1$, and for $j \neq i$, C_{S_j} does not cover any element of $S_i \setminus S_1$. Thus, a collection of k sets in $\bigcup_i C_{S_i}$ can cover at most $k \log m$ elements in $\bigcup_i (S_i \setminus S_1)$ plus m^2 elements of S_1. This means that the ratio of the best solution on the union of these instances and the solution that is limited to the union of the core-sets is at most $\frac{m^2 \log m + m^2}{m^3} < \frac{\log k}{\sqrt{k}}$. □

5. CONCLUSIONS AND OPEN PROBLEMS

In this paper we presented constructions of composable core-sets for a wide range of diversity measures. As described in the introduction and Appendix A, our core-sets can be directly used to obtain constant-factor approximation algorithms (for the respective diversity measures) in the context of data stream computation, distributed data processing and diverse nearest neighbor search. Some of those implications are essentially known (in particular, the streaming and distributed algorithms for the remote-edge and the remote-star measures [22, 12, 23] and the nearest neighbor search algorithms for the remote-edge measure [2]). Other results and implications are, to the best of our knowledge, new.

Our work raises several interesting open questions. Are there any other applications of composable core-sets, in addition to the ones listed in this paper ? Is there a general characterization of diversity measures for which small composable core-sets exist ? Is it possible to obtain better approximation factors ?

Acknowledgments.
This work was supported in part by grants from MADALGO Center and NSF.

6. REFERENCES

[1] S. Abbar, S. Amer-Yahia, P. Indyk, and S. Mahabadi. Real-time recommendation of diverse related articles. In *WWW*, pages 1–12, 2013.

[2] S. Abbar, S. Amer-Yahia, P. Indyk, S. Mahabadi, and K. R. Varadarajan. Diverse near neighbor problem. In *SoCG*, pages 207–214, 2013.

[3] Z. Abbassi, V. S. Mirrokni, and M. Thakur. Diversity maximization under matroid constraints. In *KDD*, pages 32–40, 2013.

[4] P. K. Agarwal, G. Cormode, Z. Huang, J. Phillips, Z. Wei, and K. Yi. Mergeable summaries. In *Proceedings of the 31st symposium on Principles of Database Systems*, pages 23–34. ACM, 2012.

[5] P. K. Agarwal, S. Har-Peled, and K. R. Varadarajan. Approximating extent measures of points. *Journal of the ACM (JACM)*, 51(4):606–635, 2004.

[6] A. Anagnostopoulos, A. Z. Broder, and D. Carmel. Sampling Search-Engine Results. In *WWW*, 2006.

[7] A. Angel and N. Koudas. Efficient diversity-aware search. In *Proceedings of the 2011 international conference on Management of data*, SIGMOD '11, pages 781–792, New York, NY, USA, 2011. ACM.

[8] M.-F. Balcan, S. Ehrlich, and Y. Liang. Distributed clustering on graphs. In *NIPS*, page to appear, 2013.

[9] S. Bhattacharya, S. Gollapudi, and K. Munagala. Consideration set generation in commerce search. In *WWW*, pages 317–326, 2011.

[10] A. Borodin, H. C. Lee, and Y. Ye. Max-sum diversification, monotone submodular functions and dynamic updates. In *PODS*, pages 155–166, 2012.

[11] J. Carbonell and J. Goldstein. The use of MMR, diversity-based reranking for reordering documents and producing summaries. In *SIGIR*, 1998.

[12] , M. Charikar, C. Chekuri, T. Feder and R. Motwani. Incremental Clustering and Dynamic Information Retrieval. SIAM J. Comput. 33(6), 2004.

[13] B. Chandra and M. M. Halldórsson. Approximation algorithms for dispersion problems. *Journal of algorithms*, 38(2):438–465, 2001.

[14] Z. Chen and T. Li. Addressing Diverse User Preferences in SQL-Query-Result Navigation. In *SIGMOD*, 2007.

[15] F. Chierichetti, R. Kumar, and A. Tomkins. Max-cover in map-reduce. In *WWW*, pages 231–240, 2010.

[16] G. Cormode, H. J. Karloff, and A. Wirth. Set cover algorithms for very large datasets. In *CIKM*, pages 479–488, 2010.

[17] J. Dean and S. Ghemawat. Mapreduce: Simplified data processing on large clusters. In *OSDI*, pages 137–150, 2004.

[18] M. Drosou and E. Pitoura. Search result diversification. *SIGMOD Record*, pages 41–47, 2010.

[19] U. Feige. A threshold of ln for approximating set cover. *J. ACM*, 45(4):634–652, 1998.

[20] S. Gollapudi and A. Sharma. An axiomatic framework for result diversification. In *WWW*, pages 381–390, 2009.

[21] T. F. Gonzalez. Clustering to minimize the maximum intercluster distance. *Theoretical Computer Science*, pages 293–306, 1985.

[22] S. Guha, N. Mishra, R. Motwani, and L. O'Callaghan. Clustering data streams. *STOC*, 2001.

[23] S. Guha, Tight results for clustering and summarizing data streams. *ICDT*, 2009.

[24] R. Hassin, S. Rubinstein, and A. Tamir. Approximation algorithms for maximum dispersion. *Oper. Res. Lett.*, 21(3):133–137, 1997.

[25] R. K. Iyer and J. A. Bilmes. Submodular optimization with submodular cover and submodular knapsack constraints. In *Advances in Neural Information Processing Systems*, pages 2436–2444, 2013.

[26] A. Jain, P. Sarda, and J. R. Haritsa. Providing diversity in k-nearest neighbor query results. In *PAKDD*, pages 404–413, 2004.

[27] M. W. Jones, J. A. Baerentzen, and M. Sramek. 3d distance fields: A survey of techniques and applications. *Visualization and Computer Graphics, IEEE Transactions on*, 12(4):581–599, 2006.

[28] H. J. Karloff, S. Suri, and S. Vassilvitskii. A model of computation for mapreduce. In *SODA*, pages 938–948, 2010.

[29] R. Kumar, B. Moseley, S. Vassilvitskii, and A. Vattani. Fast greedy algorithms in mapreduce and streaming. In *SPAA*, pages 1–10, 2013.

[30] K. Kummamuru, R. Lotlikar, S. Roy, K. Singal, and R. Krishnapuram. A Hierarchical Monothetic Document Clustering Algorithm for Summarization and Browsing Search Results. In *WWW*, 2004.

[31] S. Lattanzi, B. Moseley, S. Suri, and S. Vassilvitskii. Filtering: a method for solving graph problems in mapreduce. In *SPAA*, pages 85–94, 2011.

[32] H. Lin, J. Bilmes, and S. Xie. Graph-based submodular selection for extractive summarization.

[33] G. L. Nemhauser, L. A. Wolsey, and M. L. Fisher. An analysis of approximations for maximizing submodular set functions, 1978.

[34] F. Radlinski and S. T. Dumais. Improving Personalized Web Search using Result Diversification. In *SIGIR*, 2006.

[35] D. Rafiei, K. Bharat, and A. Shukla. Diversifying web search results. In *WWW*, pages 781–790, 2010.

[36] S. S. Ravi, D. J. Rosenkrantz, and G. K. Tayi. Facility dispersion problems: Heuristics and special cases. *Algorithms and Data Structures*, pages 355–366, 1991.

[37] R. Sibson. Slink: an optimally efficient algorithm for the single-link cluster method. *The Computer Journal*, 16(1):30–34, 1973.

[38] M. J. Welch, J. Cho, and C. Olston. Search result diversity for informational queries. In *WWW*, pages 237–246, 2011.

[39] D. Xin, H. Cheng, X. Yan, and J. Han. Extracting Redundancy-Aware Top-k Patterns. In *SIGKDD 2006*, 2006.

[40] C. Yu, L. V. S. Lakshmanan, and S. Amer-Yahia. Recommendation diversification using explanations. In *ICDE*, pages 1299–1302, 2009.

[41] C.-N. Ziegler, S. M. McNee, J. A. Konstan, and G. Lausen. Improving recommendation lists through topic diversification. In *WWW*, 2005.

APPENDIX

A. APPLICATION TO APPROXIMATE NEAREST NEIGHBOR

In this section, we briefly describe how we can apply the aforementioned core-sets to solve k-diverse near neighbor problem. The problem is defined as follows. Given a query point $q \in \Delta$, the goal is to report the maximum diversity set S of k points in the ball of radius r around q. The points in the set S are chosen from a dataset of points $P \subset \Delta$ of size n which is given to the algorithm at the preprocessing time. We would like to answer queries in sublinear time which necessitates solving the approximate problem. The approximate k-diverse Near Neighbor is defined as follows. For some approximation factors $c > 1$ and $\alpha > 1$, we allow the points of the reported set S to be within distance cr of the query point, i.e., $S \subset P \cap B(q, cr)$. Moreover, we require that the diversity of the set S is within an α factor of the k-diversity of the optimal set, i.e., $div(S) \geq \frac{1}{\alpha} div_k(P \cap B(q, r))$.

The definitions and algorithm mentioned here are from [1, 2] and are only included for completeness. Please see the original papers for the detailed theoretical [2] or experimental [1] analysis of its performance. The algorithm uses the techniques of *locality-sensitive hashing*. Its basic idea is to hash the data and query points in a way that the probability of collision is much higher for points that are close to each other, than for those which are far apart. Formally, we require the following.

Definition 3. A family $\mathcal{H} = h : \Delta \to U$ is (r_1, r_2, p_1, p_2)-sensitive for $(\Delta, dist)$, if for any $p, q \in \Delta$, we have

- if $dist(p,q) \leq r_1$, then $Pr_{\mathcal{H}}[h(q) = h(p)] \geq p_1$
- if $dist(p,q) \leq r_2$, then $Pr_{\mathcal{H}}[h(q) = h(p)] \leq p_2$

In order for a locality sensitive family to be useful, it has to satisfy inequalities $p_1 > p_2$ and $r_1 < r_2$.

Given an LSH family, the algorithm creates L hash functions $g_1, g_2, \cdots, g_L$, as well as the corresponding hash arrays $A_1, A_2, \cdots, A_L$. Each hash function is of the form $g_i =< h_{i,1}, \cdots, h_{i,K} >$, where $h_{i,j}$ is chosen uniformly at random from $\mathcal{H}$. Then each point p is stored in bucket $g_i(p)$ of A_i for all $1 \leq i \leq L$. In order to answer a query q, we then search points in $A_1[g_1(q)] \cup \cdots \cup A_L[g_L(q)]$. That is, in each array, we only retrieve points from the single bucket which corresponds to the query point q.

The aforementioned algorithm does not limit the number of points stored in a bucket, and hence its running time is unbounded. To avoid this problem we proceed as follows. During the preprocessing stage, for each of the buckets in all arrays A_i, we replace the bucket content by its core-set, using the algorithms presented in this paper. Then, given a query point q, we collect the core-set points from the corresponding buckets of q, i.e, $T = \bigcup_i c(A_i[g_i(q)])$. Since the core-sets has polynomial size in k, and the total number of hash functions L is sublinear in n, then the total number of points we collect in T is sublinear in n. By properties of core-sets, the k-diversity of the set T is comparable to k-diversity of the set $S = \bigcup_i A_i[g_i(q)]$. Moreover, one can set the parameters of LSH (i.e., L and K) such that with high probability the two following conditions hold:

- $P \cap B(q,r) \subset S$, every point in the r-neighborhood of q is included in the set S.
- $S \subset B(q, cr)$, any retrieved point is in the cr-neighborhood of q, i.e., there are no outliers.

Thus, if β shows the approximation factor of the core-set, then the value of $div_k(T)$ is within β factor of the value $div_k(S)$. Since S is a superset of $(P \cap B(q,r))$, we get that $div_k(T)$ is within β-factor of $div_k(P \cap B(q,r))$. Therefore we can run the "offline" algorithm on the set T to get an approximate k-diverse subset of T whose diversity approximates the diversity of the optimal set.

More specifically, if β' shows the best approximation factor for the "offline" version of diversity approximation, with running time of $T(m)$ on m points, we can get final bounds as follows. We can achieve approximation factor $\alpha = \beta\beta'$, with query time of

$$O(T(k(\log k)^{\frac{c}{c-1}} n^{\frac{1}{c-1}}) + \frac{d}{r}(\log k)^{\frac{c}{c-1}} n^{\frac{1}{c-1}} \log n)$$

and data structure space equal to $O((n \log k)^{1+\frac{1}{c-1}} + nd)$.

B. PROOF OF LEMMA 4

Let $wt(MST_t(A))$ of a set of points A, denote the minimum sum of the weights of spanning trees achieved by dividing A into t sets, i.e., $\min_{A=A_1|\ldots|A_t} \sum_{i=1}^{t} wt(MST(A_i))$, where $A = A_1|\ldots|A_t$ is a partition of A into t sets.

We run the GMM algorithm on each of the sets S_i and let $T_i = GMM(S_i)$ be the point set returned by the GMM and we let r_i denote the radius of T_i. Let $T = \bigcup_{i=1}^{L} T_i$ denote the union of the core-sets, and set $r = \max_i r_i$ to be the maximum radius over the instances. Now define a mapping (not necessarily a 1-to-1) $f : O_i \to T_i$ which maps each point $o \in O_i$ to one of its closest points in the set T_i, i.e., $dist(o, f(o)) = dist(o, T_i)$. By properties of GMM we have $dist(o, f(o)) \leq r_i \leq r$.

First of all, note that it only makes sense if $t \leq k/2$ otherwise in any optimum solution, at least $2t - k$ of the partitions include exactly one of the k points and therefore incur no cost. So instead we could consider the problem of choosing $k' = k - t$ points and having $t' = 2(k-t)$ partitions in which $t' \leq k'/2$.

It is easy to see that for any i, $div_k(T) \geq div(T_i) \geq (k - t)r_i$ (since the minimum pairwise distance in T_i is r_i), and thus $div_k(T) \geq (k-t)r$. Now if $div(O) \leq 3(k-t)r \leq 3div_k(T)$, then the lemma is proved. Otherwise let $F = range(f) = \{f(o) | o \in O\}$ (note that F is a subset of T), and let $F^+ \subset T$ be an arbitrary superset of F of size k. Then by triangle inequality and shortcutting

$$\begin{aligned} div(O) = wt(MST_t(O)) &\leq wt(MST_t(F)) + kr \\ &\leq wt(MST_t(F)) + 2(k-t)r \end{aligned}$$

which uses the fact that $t \leq k/2$. Next, note that given the $MST_t(F^+)$, we can double the edges and traverse them using DFS and remove the vertices not in F by shortcutting. Hence, by triangle inequality, we find a Hamiltonian cycle in each part of the partition with total length at most $2wt(MST_t(F^+))$ on the set F, therefore we have $wt(MST_t(F)) \leq 2wt(MST_t(F^+))$ and thus

$$\begin{aligned} div_k(T) \geq wt(MST_t(F^+)) &\geq wt(MST_t(F))/2 \\ &\geq \frac{1}{2}[div(O) - 2(k-t)r] \\ &\geq div(O)/2 - div(O)/3 \\ &\geq div(O)/6 \end{aligned}$$

Is Min-Wise Hashing Optimal for Summarizing Set Intersection?

Rasmus Pagh *
IT University of Copenhagen
pagh@itu.dk

Morten Stöckel *
IT University of Copenhagen
mstc@itu.dk

David P. Woodruff
IBM Research - Almaden
dpwoodru@us.ibm.com

ABSTRACT

Min-wise hashing is an important method for estimating the size of the intersection of sets, based on a succinct summary (a "min-hash") independently computed for each set. One application is estimation of the number of data points that satisfy the conjunction of $m \geq 2$ simple predicates, where a min-hash is available for the set of points satisfying each predicate. This has applications in query optimization and for approximate computation of COUNT aggregates. In this paper we address the question: *How many bits is it necessary to allocate to each summary in order to get an estimate with $1 \pm \varepsilon$ relative error?* The state-of-the-art technique for minimizing the encoding size, for any desired estimation error, is b-bit min-wise hashing due to Li and König (Communications of the ACM, 2011). We give new lower and upper bounds:

- Using information complexity arguments, we show that b-bit min-wise hashing is *space optimal* for $m = 2$ predicates in the sense that the estimator's variance is within a constant factor of the smallest possible among all summaries with the given space usage. But for conjunctions of $m > 2$ predicates we show that the performance of b-bit min-wise hashing (and more generally any method based on "k-permutation" min-hash) deteriorates as m grows.
- We describe a new summary that nearly matches our lower bound for $m \geq 2$. It asymptotically outperform all k-permutation schemes (by around a factor $\Omega(m/\log m)$), as well as methods based on subsampling (by a factor $\Omega(\log n_{\max})$, where $n_{\max}$ is the maximum set size).

Categories and Subject Descriptors

F.2.0 [**Analysis of Algorithms and Problem Complexity**]: General

*Pagh and Stöckel are supported by the Danish National Research Foundation under the Sapere Aude program.

PODS'14, June 22–27, 2014, Snowbird, UT, USA.

http://dx.doi.org/10.1145/2594538.2594554.

1. INTRODUCTION

Many basic information processing problems can be expressed in terms of intersection sizes within a preprocessed collection of sets. For example, in databases and data analytics, aggregation queries often use a conjunction of several simple conditions such as *"How many sales occurred in June 2013, in Sweden, where the sold object is a car?"* In this paper we consider the problem of quickly *estimating* the size of the intersection of several sets, where a succinct precomputed summary of s bits is available for each set. Specifically, we answer the question:

How many bits is it necessary to allocate to each summary in order to get an estimate with $1 \pm \varepsilon$ relative error?

Note that we require the summaries to be *independently* computed, which for example prevents solutions based on precomputing all answers. This restriction is motivated by yielding scalable and flexible methods for estimating intersection sizes, with no need for a centralized data structure.

Motivation.

Estimates of intersection size can be used directly as part of algorithms with approximation guarantees, but are also useful for exact computation. For example, when evaluating conjunctive database queries the order in which intersections are computed can have a large impact on performance. Good estimates of intersection sizes allow a query optimizer to make a choice that is near-optimal. In other settings, estimates of intersection sizes can be used as a filter to skip parts of an exact computation that would not influence the output (e.g., we might only be interested in a particular sales figure if it exceeds some threshold).

In data warehouses it is common to perform extensive precomputation of answer sets and summaries of simple queries, so that these can be combined to answer more complex queries quickly (see e.g. [26, 29]). At PODS 2011 Wei and Yi [31] showed that a number of different summaries of sets fulfilling a range condition can be efficiently extracted from augmented B-tree indexes. The number of I/Os for creating a summary of all data in a given range is close to the number of I/Os needed for reading a precomputed summary of the same size. That is, the efficiency is determined by the size of each summary, which motivates the question of how small a summary can be. Though Wei and Yi do not consider this explicitly, it is easy to see that (at least when efficient updates of data is not needed) their ideas apply to the kind of summaries, based on min-wise hashing, that we consider in the upper bounds of this paper.

1.1 Brief history

Motivated by document similarity problems encountered in AltaVista, Broder [5] pioneered algorithms for estimating set intersection sizes based on independently pre-computed "summaries" of sets. More specifically he presented a summary technnique called "min-wise hashing" where, given summaries $k_{\min}(A)$ and $k_{\min}(B)$ of sets A and B, it is possible to compute a low-variance, (asymptotically) unbiased estimator of the *Jaccard similarity* $J(A, B) = |A \cap B|/|A \cup B|$. Assuming that $|A|$ and $|B|$ are known, an estimate of $J(A, B)$ with small relative error can be used to compute a good estimate of $|A \cap B|$, and vice versa. In fact, we state many of our results in terms of the ratio between the size of the intersection and the largest set, which is $\Theta(J)$.

Li and König [20] presented "b-bit min-wise hashing", a refinement of Broder's approach that reduces the summary representation size by storing a vector of b-bit hash values of elements from $k_{\min}(X)$. Even though the resulting hash collisions introduce noise in the estimator, this can be compensated for by a small increase in the size of $k_{\min}(X)$, yielding a significantly smaller summary with the same variance. Specifically, with $b = 1$ and using s bits of space, the variance is $2(1-J)/s$.[1] In order to get an estimation error of at most εJ with probability (say) 1/2, by Chebychev's inequality it suffices that $(1 - J)/s < (\varepsilon J)^2$, i.e., $s > (1 - J)/(\varepsilon J)^2$. It is not hard to show that the estimator is well-concentrated, and this bound is tight up to constant factors. Increasing the value of b (while keeping the space usage fixed) does not improve the variance.

1.2 Our contribution

First, we show that the variance of *any* estimator for Jaccard similarity based on summaries of s bits must be $\Omega(1/s)$ for fixed J between 0 and 1. More specifically, there exists a distribution of input sets such that with constant probability any such estimator makes an error of $\Omega(\sqrt{1/s})$ with constant probability. This means that b-bit min-wise hashing cannot be substantially improved when it comes to estimating intersection size (or Jaccard similarity) of two sets, except perhaps when J is asymptotically close to 0 or 1.

Second, we show that it *is* possible to improve existing estimators for the intersection size of $m = \omega(1)$ preprocessed sets. In fact, we show that estimators (such as b-bit min-wise hashing) that are based on many permutations are inherently less precise than their one-permutation counterpart when considering the intersection of many sets. We then show that a suitable approximate encoding of one-permutation min-wise hashing summaries is always competitive with b-bit min-wise hashing, while reducing the space required for accurately estimating the intersection size of many sets.

2. PREVIOUS WORK

Problem definition. Let $S_1, S_2, \ldots$ be sets of size $n_i = |S_i|$ where all $S_i \subseteq [u]$ and the largest set is $n_{\max} = \max n_i$. A query is a subset $I \subseteq \mathbb{N}$ of the set indices and the output to the query is the intersection size $|\bigcap_{i \in I} S_i|$. For ease of notation we assume that the query is $I = \{1, \ldots, m\}$ and intersection size to estimate is then $t = |S_1 \cap \ldots \cap S_m|$.

In this paper we consider estimators for the intersection size t. As previously noted we focus on the setting where the sets $S_1, S_2, \ldots, S_m$ are available for *individual* pre-processing. Storing only a small summary of each set, which requires not even approximate knowledge of t, we provide an estimator for the intersection size t. Note that in this model, we allow ourselves only to pre-process the sets independently of each other, i.e., intersection sizes or other information that rely on more than the set currently being pre-processed cannot be stored. See [13] for work on (exact) set intersection in the model where information about all sets can be used in the pre-processing phase.

For the applications, we seek to obtain bounds that are parameterized on the size of the summary required of each set as a function of largest set $n_{\max}$, the intersection size t, and the relative error ε. Further, let s denote the space in bits stored per set and k the number of permutations or number values taken from one permutation for k-permutation and one-permutation min-wise hashing respectively.

2.1 Lower bounds

Several well-known problems in communication complexity imply lower bounds for special cases of the set intersection problem:

In the Index problem Alice is given a subset of $\{1, \ldots, n\}$, and Bob is given a set of size 1. The task is to determine whether the intersection size is 0 or 1. It is known that even for randomized protocols with error probability 1/3, the one-way communication complexity of this problem is $\Omega(n)$ bits (see [19]). Informally, this shows that the cost of estimating set intersection grows with the ratio between the intersection size t and the size $n_{\max}$ of the largest set.

In the GapAnd problem Alice and Bob are both given subsets of $\{1, \ldots, n\}$, and the task is to determine if the intersection size is below $n/4 - \sqrt{n}$ or above $n/4 + \sqrt{n}$ (if it is in-between, any result is okay). This is a variant of the well-studied GapHamming problem, for which the randomized one-way communication complexity is $\Omega(n)$ bits [16, 32]. In fact, the randomized two-way communication complexity for this problem is also $\Omega(n)$ bits [8], though in our application of first preprocessing the sets in order to then answer queries, we will only need the result for one-way communication. Informally, this lower bound means that the cost of estimating set intersection is inversely proportional with the square of the relative error.

Informally, our lower bound shows that these results generalize and compose, such that the lower bound is the *product* of the cost due to Index and the cost due to GapAnd, each with constant error probability. That is, our lower bound will be $\Omega(n_{\max}\varepsilon^{-2}/t)$, which we can use to bound the variance of any estimator for Jaccard similarity. The intuitive idea behind the lower bound is to compose the two problems such that each "bit" of GapAnd is encoded as the result of an Index problem. Unlike typical arguments in information complexity, see, e.g., the PODS 2010 tutorial by Jayram [17], we instead measure the information a protocol reveals about *intermediate bits* in Claim 13, rather than about the inputs themselves. See the beginning of Section 3 for a more detailed intuition.

We note that using the output bits of multiple instances of one problem as the input bits to another problem was also

[1]The variance bound stated in [20] is more complex, since it deals with min-wise hashing based on permutations, which introduces correlations. By replacing this with full independence one arrives at the stated variance.

Method	Required space (bits)	Time
INCLUSION-EXCLUSION	$s \geq \varepsilon^{-2}(mn/t)^2 + \log n$	2^m
SUBSAMPLING	$s \geq \varepsilon^{-2}(n/t)\log m \log^2 n$	sm
b-BIT MIN-WISE HASHING*	$s \geq \varepsilon^{-2}(mn/t)$	sm
NEW UPPER BOUND	$s \leq \varepsilon^{-2}(n/t)\log(m)\log(n/\varepsilon t)$	sm
GENERAL LOWER BOUND	$s \geq \varepsilon^{-2}(n/t)$	-

Table 1: **Comparison of estimators of intersection size t for relative error ε and constant error probability, with m sets of maximum size n. Bounds on the summary size s ignore constant factors. The subsampling bound assumes that no knowledge of t is available, and thus $\log n$ levels of subsampling are needed. *The bound for b-bit min-wise hashing assumes that the number of hash functions needed in the analysis of min-wise summaries is optimal, see appendix A.**

used in [33], though not for our choice of problems, which are specific to and arguably very useful for one-way communication given the widespread usage of Index and GapAnd problems in proving encoding size or "sketching" lower bounds. We note that our problems may become trivial for 2-way communication, if e.g., one set has size $n_{\max}$ while the other set has size 1, while the lower bounds for the problems considered in [33] are qualitatively different, remaining hard even for 2-way communication.

2.2 Min-wise hashing techniques

Min-wise hashing was first considered by Broder [5] as a technique for estimating the similarity of web pages. For completeness, below we define min-wise independence along with the standard algorithm to compute an unbiased estimator for resemblance.

DEFINITION 1 ([6, EQ. 4]). *Let S_n be the set of all permutations on $[n]$. Then a family $\mathcal{F} \subseteq S_n$ is* min-wise independent *if for any set $X \subseteq [n]$ and any $x \in X$, when permutation $\pi \in \mathcal{F}$ is chosen at random we have*

$$\mathbf{Pr}[\min \pi(X) = x] = 1/|X| \ .$$

In particular, for two sets $X, Y \subseteq [n]$ and a randomly chosen permutation $\pi \in \mathcal{F}$ we have

$$\mathbf{Pr}(\min \pi(X) = \min \pi(Y)) = J = \frac{|X \cap Y|}{|X \cup Y|}.$$

This can be used to compute an estimate of the Jaccard similarity. Specifically, given k independent min-wise permutations $\pi_1, \ldots, \pi_k$ then

$$\hat{J} = \frac{1}{k}\sum_{i=1}^{k}[\min \pi_i(X) = \min \pi_i(Y)]$$

is an unbiased estimator of J (where $[\alpha]$ is Iverson Notation for the event α) with variance $\text{Var}(\hat{J}) = J(1-J)/k$.

In both theory and practice it is often easier to use a hash function with a large range (e.g. size u^3) instead of a random permutation. The idea is that the probability of a collision among the elements of a given set should be negligible, meaning that with high probability the order of the hash values induces a random permutation on the set. We will thus use the (slightly misleading) term "one-permutation" to describe methods using a single hash value on each set element.

Min-wise summaries. For a given set X the *k-permutation* min-wise summary of size k is the vector

$$(\min \pi_1(X), \ldots, \min \pi_k(X)).$$

The *one-permutation* min-wise summary (sometimes called bottom-k sketch) of size k for a permutation π is the set $k_{\min}(X) = \{\pi(x) \mid x \in X, \pi(x) < \tau\}$, where τ is the $k+1$'th largest permutation rank (hash value) of the elements in X. That is, intuitively k-permutation summaries store the single smallest value independently for each of k permutations, while one-permutation summaries store the k smallest values for one permutation. It is not hard to show that $|k_{\min}(X \cup Y) \cap k_{\min}(X) \cap k_{\min}(Y)|/k$ is a good estimator for J, where $k_{\min}(X \cup Y)$ can be computed from $k_{\min}(X)$ and $k_{\min}(Y)$. For k-permutation min-wise summaries, if $\pi_1, \ldots, \pi_k$ are independent min-wise permutations then

$$\frac{1}{k}\sum_{1}^{k} |\min \pi_i(X) \cap \min \pi_i(Y)|$$

is analogously an estimator for J.

2.3 Previous results on set intersection

For m sets $S_1, \ldots S_m$ let the *generalized* Jaccard similarity be $J = |\cap_i S_i|/|\cup_i S_i|$. If we multiply an estimate of the generalized Jaccard similarity of several sets and an estimate of the size of the union of the sets, we obtain an estimate of the intersection size. Using existing summaries for distinct element estimation (also based on hashing, e.g. [18, 15]) we get that previous work on (generalized) Jaccard similarity implies results on intersection estimation [6, 7, 5, 9]. Recently, b-bit variations of min-wise hashing were proposed [22] but so far it is not clear how they can be used to estimate Jaccard similarity of more than three sets [21]. See Section 5.2 for further discussion.

The problem of computing aggregate functions (such as set intersection) over sets when hash functions are used to sample set elements has been widely studied [10, 12, 11]. In the general case of arbitrary aggregate functions, Cohen and Kaplan [11] characterizes for a given aggregate function f if an unbiased estimator for f with finite variance can be achieved using one- or k-permutation summaries. For the specific case of set intersection, *RC* (Rank Conditioning) estimators [10, 12] have been shown to provide an unbiased estimator based on both one- and k-permutation summaries and these can be extended to work with limited precision, analogous to b-bit min-wise hashing. Further, experimental work show that estimators based on one-permutation summaries outperform those based on k-permutation summaries [10] on the data sets used.

In contrast, this paper provides an explicit worst-case analysis of the space requirement needed to achieve ε error with error probability at most δ for set intersection using one-permutation summaries, where signatures (5.2) are used to shave off a logarithmic factor for the upper bound, making the bound close to being tight.

Table 1 shows the performance of different algorithms along with our estimator based on one-permutation min-wise hashing. The methods are compared by time/space used to achieve an (ε, δ)-estimate of the intersection size t of m sets of maximum size n for constant δ.

DEFINITION 2. *Let $z \in \mathbb{R}$ and let $\hat{z}$ be a random variable. We say that $\hat{z}$ is an (ε, δ)-estimate of z if* $\mathbf{Pr}\left[|\hat{z} - z| \geq \varepsilon z\right] \leq \delta$. *We use ε-estimate as shorthand for $(\varepsilon, 1/3)$-estimate.*

The Jaccard estimator computed using k-permutation min-wise hashing, as described in Section 2.2, can trivially be used to estimate intersection when cardinality estimate of the union of the sets is given (by simply multiplying by the union estimate). However, there are instances of sets where J can be as low as $t/(t + m(n - t))$ for a "sunflower", i.e., m sets of n elements that are disjoint except for the t intersection elements. Following from Chernoff bounds, such an instance requires to store $\frac{1}{J\varepsilon^2}$ elements to get an ε-estimation of J with constant probability. See Appendix A for a discussion of the bound for "b-bit min-wise hashing" in Table 1.

In contrast, the one-permutation approach described in this paper stores $s \geq \frac{n}{t} \frac{\log m \log u}{\varepsilon^2}$ bits for m sets of maximum size n, while maintaining estimation time sm. Recent work investigated a *different* way of doing min-wise hashing using just one permutation [23], but this method seems to have the same problem as k-permutation min-wise hashing for the purpose of m-way set intersection. Intersection estimation can also be done by applying inclusion-exclusion to union size estimates of all subset unions of the m sets. To achieve error εt then by Chernoff bounds for sampling without replacement we need sample size $s > \left(\sum_i n_i/(\varepsilon t)\right)^2$. As there are $2^m - 1$ estimates to do for m sets this yields time $2^m s$. Bloom filters [3] also support set intersection operations, and cardinality estimation, but to work well need the assumption that the sets have similar size. Therefore we will not discuss them further.

3. OUR RESULTS

We show a lower bound for the size of a summary for two-way set intersection by a reduction from one-way communication complexity. More specifically, any summary that allows a $(1 + \varepsilon)$-approximation of the intersection size implies a one-way communication protocol for a problem we call GapAndIndex, which we think of as the composition of the Index and GapAnd communication problems. Namely, Alice has $r = \Theta(1/\varepsilon^2)$ d-bit strings $x^1, \ldots, x^r$, while Bob has r indices $i_1, \ldots, i_r \in [d]$, together with bits $b_1, \ldots, b_r$. Bob's goal is to decide if the input falls into one of the following cases, for a constant $C > 0$:

a For at least $\frac{r}{4} + C\varepsilon r$ of the $j \in [r]$, we have $x^j_{i_j} \wedge b_j = 1$.

b For at most $\frac{r}{4} - C\varepsilon r$ of the $j \in [r]$, we have $x^j_{i_j} \wedge b_j = 1$.

If neither case occurs, Bob's output may be arbitrary (i.e., this is a *promise* problem).

A straightforward reduction shows that if you have an algorithm that can $(1 + \varepsilon)$-approximate the set intersection size $|A \cap B|$ for sets A and B, then you can solve GapAndIndex with the parameter d roughly equal to $|A|/t$ and $|B| \leq 4t$. Let the randomized communication complexity $R^{1-way}_{1/3}(\mathsf{f})$ of problem f be the minimal communication cost (maximum message transcript) of any protcol computing f with error probability at most $1/3$.

The crux of our lower bound argument is to show:

THEOREM 3. *For $r = \Theta(1/\varepsilon^2)$, $d = n_{max}/t$,*

$$R^{1-way}_{1/3}(\mathsf{GapAndIndex}) = \Omega(dr).$$

In terms of the parameters of the original set intersection problem, the space lower bound is proportional to the ratio d between the largest set size and the intersection size multiplied by ε^{-2}. Since $d = \Theta(1/J)$ this is $\Omega(\varepsilon^{-2}/J)$, which is a lower bound on the space needed for a $1 \pm \varepsilon$ approximation of J. If we consider the problem of estimating J with *additive* error $\leq \varepsilon_{\text{add}}$ with probability $2/3$, observe that in this case $\varepsilon = \Theta(\varepsilon_{\text{add}}/J)$, so the lower bound becomes $\Omega(J/\varepsilon^2_{\text{add}})$. Conversely, for fixed $J > 0$ and space usage s we get $\varepsilon_{\text{add}} = \Omega(1/\sqrt{s})$ with probability $1/3$ so the variance is $\Omega(1/s)$.

Our second result is a simple estimator for set intersection of an arbitrary number of sets, based on one-permutation min-wise hashing. The intuition behind our result is that when using k-permutation min-wise hashing, the probability of sampling intersection elements relies on the size of the union, while in contrast our one-permutation approach depends on the maximum set size, hence we save almost a factor of the number of input sets in terms of space. We show the following:

THEOREM 4. *Let sets $S_1, \ldots, S_m \subseteq [u]$ be given and let $n_{max} = \max_i |S_i|$, $t = |S_1 \cap \ldots \cap S_m|$ and k be the summary size $|k_{\min}(S_i)|$. For $0 < \varepsilon < 1/4$, $0 < \delta < 1/\sqrt{k}$, consider the estimator*

$$X = \frac{\left|\bigcap_{i \in [m]} k_{\min}(S_i)\right| n_{\max}}{k}.$$

With probability at least $1 - \delta\sqrt{k}$:

$$t \in \begin{cases} [X/(1+\varepsilon); X/(1-\varepsilon)] & \text{if } X > 3n_{\max}\log(2m/\delta)/k\varepsilon^2 \\ [0; 4n_{\max}\log(2m/\delta)/k\varepsilon^2] & \text{otherwise} \end{cases}$$

That is, we either get an (ε, δ)-estimate or an upper bound on t. Whenever $k \geq \frac{4n_{\max}\log(2m/\delta)}{\varepsilon^2 t}$ we are in the first case with high probability. We note that the lower and upper bounds presented are parameterized on the estimand t, i.e., the bounds depend on the size of what we are estimating. This means that the error bound ε will depend of t, so the relative error is smaller for larger t.

Theorem 4 follows from two main arguments: First we show that if the summary of each set is constructed by selecting elements independently using a hash function then we get a good estimate with high probability. As our summaries are of fixed size, there is a dependence between the variables denoting whether an element is picked for a summary or not. The main technical hurdle is then to bound the error introduced by the dependence.

We then extend the use of signatures, which are well-known to reduce space for k-permutation min-wise hashing, to one-permutation min-wise hashing as used in our estimator. This reduces the number of bits s by a logarithmic factor. Section 5.2 discusses this further.

4. LOWER BOUND

4.1 Preliminaries

We summarize terms and definitions from communication complexity that are used in the lower bound proof.

Communication model. We consider two-player one-way communication protocols: Alice is given input x, Bob is given input y and they need to compute function $f(x,y)$. Each player has his/her own private randomness, as well as a shared uniformly distributed public coin $\mathbf{W}$ of some finite length. Since the protocol is 1-way, the *transcript* of protocol Π consists of Alice's single message to Bob, together with Bob's output bits. For a protocol Π, the maximum transcript length in bits over all inputs is called the *communication cost* of Π. The *communication complexity* $R_\delta(f)$ of function f is the minimal communication cost of a protocol that computes f with probability at least $1-\delta$.

Mutual information. For random variables X and Y with support $\mathcal{X}$ and $\mathcal{Y}$ and let $p(x,y), p(x), p(y)$ be the joint and marginal distributions respectively. The *entropy* and *conditional entropy* are defined as:

$$H(X) = -\sum_{x\in\mathcal{X}} p(x)\log p(x)$$

$$H(X \mid Y) = \sum_{x\in\mathcal{X},y\in\mathcal{Y}} p(x,y)\log\frac{p(y)}{p(x,y)}$$

The *mutual information* is given as:

$$I(X;Y) = H(X) - H(X \mid Y) = \sum_{x\in\mathcal{X},y\in\mathcal{Y}} p(x,y)\log\frac{p(x,y)}{p(x)p(y)}$$

We make use of the following rule:

FACT 5. *(Chain Rule) For discrete random variables X, Y, Z it holds that $I(X,Y;Z) = I(X;Z) + I(X;Y \mid Z)$.*

For a protocol Π that uses public random coins $\mathbf{W}$ and has transcript $\Pi(X,Y,Z)$ for random variables $X,Y,Z \sim \mu$, the *conditional information cost* of Π with respect to distribution μ is $I(X,Y,Z;\Pi(X,Y,Z) \mid \mathbf{W})$. For function f we have that the *conditional information complexity* $CIC^\mu_\delta(f)$ is the minimal conditional information cost of any δ-error protocol Π with respect to distribution μ.

Fano's inequality. We make use of Fano's equality which intuitively relates the error probabiliy of a function between random variables to the conditional entropy between them.

DEFINITION 6. *Given domains $\mathcal{X}$ and $\mathcal{Y}$ and random variables X, Y on these domains with distribution μ, we say a function $g : \mathcal{Y} \to \mathcal{X}$ has error δ_g if*

$$\mathbf{Pr}_{X,Y\sim\mu}[g(Y) = X] \geq 1 - \delta_g.$$

FACT 7. *Let X and Y be a random variables chosen from domains $\mathcal{X}$ and $\mathcal{Y}$ respectively according to distribution μ. There is a deterministic function $g : \mathcal{Y} \to \mathcal{X}$ with error δ_g, where $\delta_g \leq 1 - \frac{1}{2^{H(X \mid Y)}}$.*

FACT 8. *(Fano's inequality.) Let X and Y be a random variables chosen from domains $\mathcal{X}$ and $\mathcal{Y}$ respectively according to distribution μ. For any reconstruction function $g : \mathcal{Y} \to \mathcal{X}$ with error δ_g,*

$$H_b(\delta_g) + \delta_g \log(|\mathcal{X}| - 1) \geq H(X \mid Y).$$

4.2 A Communication Problem and its Application to Set Intersection

Let $r = \Theta(1/\varepsilon^2)$, and $d = n_{max}/t$. We consider a two-party one-way communication problem:

DEFINITION 9. *In the* GapAndIndex *problem, Alice has bit vectors $x^1, \ldots, x^r \in \{0,1\}^d$ while Bob has indices $i^1, \ldots, i^r \in [d]$, where $[d] = \{1, 2, \ldots, d\}$, together with bits $b^1, \ldots, b^r \in \{0,1\}$. Let $\mathbf{x} = (x^1, \ldots, x^r)$, $\mathbf{i} = (i^1, \ldots, i^r)$, and $\mathbf{b} = (b^1, \ldots, b^r)$ and $C > 0$ be a fixed constant. The output of* $\mathsf{GapAndIndex}(\mathbf{x}, \mathbf{i}, \mathbf{b})$ *is:*

$$1 \text{ if } \sum_{j=1}^{r}(x^j_{i^j} \wedge b^j) \geq \frac{r}{4} + C\varepsilon r$$

$$0 \text{ if } \sum_{j=1}^{r}(x^j_{i^j} \wedge b^j) \leq \frac{r}{4} - C\varepsilon r.$$

This is a promise problem, and if neither case occurs, the output can be arbitrary.

If the input $(\mathbf{x}, \mathbf{i}, \mathbf{b})$ is in either of the two cases we say the input *satifies the promise.*

We say a one-way randomized protocol Π for GapAndIndex is δ-error if

$$\forall \mathbf{x}, \mathbf{i}, \mathbf{b} \text{ satisfying the promise}:$$
$$\mathbf{Pr}[\Pi(\mathbf{x}, \mathbf{i}, \mathbf{b}) = \mathsf{GapAndIndex}(\mathbf{x}, \mathbf{i}, \mathbf{b})] \geq 1 - \delta,$$

where the probability is over the public and private randomness of Π.

Let κ be the set of randomized one-way δ-error protocols Π. We note that κ is finite for any problem with finite input, as we can always have one player send his/her entire input to the other player.

Then,

$$R^{1-way}_\delta(\mathsf{GapAndIndex}) = \min_{\Pi\in\kappa} \max_{\substack{\mathbf{x},\mathbf{i},\mathbf{b},\\ \text{randomness of } \Pi}} |\Pi(\mathbf{x}, \mathbf{i}, \mathbf{b})|,$$

where $|\Pi(\mathbf{x}, \mathbf{i}, \mathbf{b})|$ denotes the length of the transcript with these inputs. Since the protocol is 1-way, we can write this length as $|M(\mathbf{x})| + 1$, where $M(\mathbf{x})$ is Alice's message function in the protocol Π given her input $\mathbf{x}$, and we add 1 for Bob's output bit. Here, implicitly M also depends on the private randomness of Alice, as well as the public coin $\mathbf{W}$.

Let μ be the uniform distribution on $\mathbf{x} \in (\{0,1\}^d)^r$. We use the capital letter $\mathbf{X}$ to denote random $\mathbf{x}$ distributed according to μ. We introduce a distribution on inputs solely for measuring the following notion of information cost of the protocol; we still require that the protocol is correct on *every* input satisfying the promise with probability $1-\delta$ over its public and private randomness (for a sufficiently small constant $\delta > 0$).

For a uniformly distributed public coin $\mathbf{W}$, let

$$CIC^{\mu,1-way}_\delta(\mathsf{GapAndIndex}) = \min_{\Pi\in\kappa} I(M(\mathbf{X}); \mathbf{X} \mid \mathbf{W}),$$

where for random variables Y, Z and W, $I(Y;Z \mid W) = H(Y \mid W) - H(Y \mid Z, W)$ is the conditional mutual information. Recall that the conditional entropy $H(Y \mid W) = \sum_w H(Y \mid W = w) \cdot \mathbf{Pr}[W = w]$, where w ranges over all values in the support of W. For any protocol Π,

$$\max_{\mathbf{x},\mathbf{i},\mathbf{b}} |\Pi(\mathbf{x},\mathbf{i},\mathbf{b})| = \max_{\mathbf{x}} |M(\mathbf{x})| + 1$$
$$> \max_{\mathbf{x}} |M(\mathbf{x})|$$
$$\geq H(M(\mathbf{X}) \mid \mathbf{W})$$
$$\geq I(M(\mathbf{X}); \mathbf{X} \mid \mathbf{W}),$$

which implies that

$$R_{\delta}^{1-way}(\mathsf{GapAndIndex}) \geq CIC_{\delta}^{\mu,1-way}(\mathsf{GapAndIndex}).$$

We now consider the application to set intersection. Let $r = 10/\varepsilon^2$ and d be the desired ratio between the intersection size t and the largest set. The idea is to give Alice a subset of elements from $[dr]$, where the characteristic vector of her subset is $x^1, \ldots, x^r$. Also, for each $j \in [r]$, Bob is given the element $d \cdot (j-1) + i^j$ if and only if $b^j = 1$. If Alice and Bob's sets are constructed in this way then the intersection is either of size at most $r/4 - C\varepsilon r$, or of size at least $r/4 + C\varepsilon r$. Hence, a 1-way protocol for approximating the intersection size up to a relative $(1 + \Theta(\varepsilon))$-factor can be used to distinguish these two cases and therefore solve the GapAndIndex promise problem.

To get intersection size t without changing the problem, we duplicate each item $4t/r$ times, which means that the problem becomes distinguishing intersection size at most $t(1 - \Theta(\varepsilon))$ and at least $t(1 + \Theta(\varepsilon))$. By rescaling ε by a constant factor, a 1-way protocol for $(1 + \varepsilon)$-approximating the intersection of Alice and Bob's sets with constant probability can be used to solve GapAndIndex with constant probability. Hence, its space complexity is $\geq CIC_{1/3}^{\mu,1-way}(\mathsf{GapAndIndex})$. This holds for any distribution μ for measuring information, though we shall use our choice of μ above.

4.3 The GapAnd Problem

For bit vectors $\mathbf{z}, \mathbf{z}'$ of the same length, let $\mathrm{AND}(\mathbf{z}, \mathbf{z}')$ be the vector $\mathbf{z}''$ in which $z''_i = z_i \wedge z'_i$. For a vector $\mathbf{z}$, let $\mathrm{wt}(\mathbf{z})$ denote its Hamming weight, i.e., the number of its coordinates equal to 1.

DEFINITION 10. *In the* GapAnd *problem, Alice and Bob have* $\mathbf{z}, \mathbf{z}' \in \{0,1\}^r$, *respectively. We define* GapAnd *to be:*

$$1 \text{ if } wt(AND(\mathbf{z}, \mathbf{z}')) \geq \frac{r}{4} + C\varepsilon r$$
$$0 \text{ if } wt(AND(\mathbf{z}, \mathbf{z}')) \leq \frac{r}{4} - C\varepsilon r.$$

This is a promise problem, and if neither case occurs, the output can be arbitrary.

4.4 The Index Problem

Consider the following Index problem.

DEFINITION 11. *In the* Index *problem, Alice has an input* $\mathbf{Y} \in \{0,1\}^d$ *and Bob has an input* $K \in [d]$, *where* $\mathbf{Y}$ *and* K *are independent and uniformly distributed over their respective domains. We define* Index *to be:*

$$1 \text{ if } Y_K = 1$$
$$0 \text{ if } Y_K = 0$$

Suppose $\mathbf{W}$ is the public coin and κ is the set of randomized one-way δ-error protocols Π. Let γ denote this distribution on the inputs. Say a 1-way protocol Π for Index with private randomness R and public randomness $\mathbf{W}$ is δ-error if

$$\mathbf{Pr}_{(\mathbf{Y},K)\sim\gamma,R,\mathbf{W}}[\Pi(\mathbf{Y}, K, R, \mathbf{W}) = \mathbf{Y}_K] \geq 1 - \delta.$$

Let $M(\mathbf{Y})$ be the message function associated with the 1-way protocol Π (which is a randomized function of R and $\mathbf{W}$). Let

$$CIC_{\delta}^{\gamma,1-way}(\mathsf{Index}) = \min_{\Pi \in \kappa} I(M(\mathbf{Y}); \mathbf{Y} \mid \mathbf{W}).$$

FACT 12. *For* $\delta \leq \frac{1}{2} - \Omega(1)$, $CIC_{\delta}^{\gamma,1-way}(\mathsf{Index}) = \Omega(d)$.

PROOF. We note that this fact is folklore, but existing references, e.g., Theorem 5.5 of [1] only explicitly state the bound for deterministic protocols, whereas we want such a bound for protocols with both private randomness and public randomness $\mathbf{W}$. We provide the simple proof here.

Let Π be a δ-error protocol with (randomized) message function M. Let $Y = (Y_1, \ldots, Y_d)$. By the chain rule,

$$I(M(\mathbf{Y}); \mathbf{Y} \mid \mathbf{W}) = \sum_{i=1}^{d} I(M(\mathbf{Y}); Y_i \mid Y_1, \ldots, Y_{i-1}, \mathbf{W}).$$

By independence and the fact that conditioning cannot increase entropy,

$$\sum_{i=1}^{d} I(M(\mathbf{Y}); Y_i \mid Y_1, \ldots, Y_{i-1}, \mathbf{W}) \geq \sum_{i=1}^{d} I(M(\mathbf{Y}); Y_i \mid \mathbf{W}).$$

If Π is δ-error for $\delta = 1/2 - \Omega(1)$, then by Markov's inequality, for an $\Omega(1)$ fraction of i, $\Pi(\mathbf{Y}, i) = Y_i$ with probability $1/2 + \Omega(1)$. Call such an i *good*. Then

$$\sum_{i=1}^{d} I(M(\mathbf{Y}); Y_i, \mid \mathbf{W}) \geq \Omega(d) \cdot \min_{\text{good } i} I(M(\mathbf{Y}); Y_i, \mid \mathbf{W})$$
$$= \Omega(d) \cdot \min_{\text{good } i} (1 - H(Y_i \mid M(\mathbf{Y}), \mathbf{W})).$$

By Fano's inequality (Fact 8) and using that i is good, we have $H(Y_i \mid M(\mathbf{Y}), \mathbf{W}) = 1 - \Omega(1)$. This completes the proof. ■

4.5 Proof of Theorem 3

PROOF. It suffices to prove the theorem for a sufficiently small constant probability of error δ, since

$$R_{1/3}^{1-way}(\mathsf{GapAndIndex}) = \Theta(R_{\delta}^{1-way}(\mathsf{GapAndIndex}).$$

Let Π be a 1-way randomized (both public and private) δ-error protocol for GapAndIndex. For ease of presentation, we let $M = M(\mathbf{X})$ when the input $\mathbf{X}$ is clear from context. Note that M also implicitly depends on Alice's private coins as well as a public coin $\mathbf{W}$. We need to show that $I(M; \mathbf{X} \mid \mathbf{W})$ is $\Omega(rd)$, for $r = \Theta(\varepsilon^{-2})$.

We start with the following claim, which does not directly look at the information Π conveys about its inputs, but rather the information Π conveys about certain bits in its input.

CLAIM 13. $I(M; X_{i^1}^1, \ldots, X_{i^r}^r \mid \mathbf{W}) = \Omega(r)$.

PROOF. We will need the following fact, which follows from work by Braverman et al. [4].

FACT 14. *([4]) Let ρ be the uniform distribution on bits $c^1, \ldots, c^r$ and $d^1, \ldots, d^r$. Let $\mathbf{C} = (C^1, \ldots, C^r)$ and $\mathbf{D} = (D^1, \ldots, D^r)$ for vectors $\mathbf{C}$ and $\mathbf{D}$ drawn from ρ.*

There is a sufficiently small constant δ for which for any private randomness protocol Π which errs with probability at most δ on GapAnd*, over inputs $\mathbf{C}$ and $\mathbf{D}$ drawn from from ρ and the private randomness of Π and the public randomness $\mathbf{W}$, satisfies*

$$I(\Pi(\mathbf{C}, \mathbf{D}); \mathbf{C}, \mathbf{D} \mid \mathbf{W}) = \Omega(r).$$

PROOF. The work of Braverman et al. [4] establishes this for the problem of deciding if $\sum_{i=1}^r (C^i \oplus D^i) \geq r/2 + \sqrt{r}$ or $\sum_{i=1}^r (C^i \oplus D^i) \leq r/2 - \sqrt{r}$, which corresponds to the Hamming distance $\Delta(\mathbf{C}, \mathbf{D})$ of vectors drawn from ρ.

If $\mathrm{wt}(\mathbf{C})$ denotes the Hamming weight of $\mathbf{C}$, then we have

$$wt(\mathbf{C}) + wt(\mathbf{D}) - 2 \cdot \mathsf{And}(\mathbf{C}, \mathbf{D}) = \Delta(\mathbf{C}, \mathbf{D}),$$

where $\mathsf{And}(\mathbf{C}, \mathbf{D})$ is the number of coordinates i for which $C^i = D^i = 1$. Therefore, if Alice and Bob exchange $\mathrm{wt}(\mathbf{C})$ and $\mathrm{wt}(\mathbf{D})$ using $2 \log r$ bits, then together with a protocol Π for GapAnd, they can solve this Hamming distance problem. It follows that

$$I(\Pi(\mathbf{C}, \mathbf{D}), \mathrm{wt}(\mathbf{C}), \mathrm{wt}(\mathbf{D}); \mathbf{C}, \mathbf{D} \mid \mathbf{W}) = \Omega(r),$$

and so by the chain rule for mutual information one has $I(\Pi(\mathbf{C}, \mathbf{D}); \mathbf{C}, \mathbf{D} \mid \mathbf{W}) = \Omega(r) - I(\mathrm{wt}(\mathbf{C}), \mathrm{wt}(\mathbf{D}); \mathbf{C}, \mathbf{D} \mid \mathbf{W}, \Pi(\mathbf{C}, \mathbf{D})) = \Omega(r) - H(\mathrm{wt}(\mathbf{C}), \mathrm{wt}(\mathbf{D})) = \Omega(r) - 2 \log r = \Omega(r)$. ■

First, observe that if $\mathbf{I}$ denotes a uniformly random value of $\mathbf{i}$, then

$$\begin{aligned} & I(M; X^1_{I^1}, \ldots, X^r_{I^r} \mid \mathbf{I}, \mathbf{W}) \\ &= H(M \mid \mathbf{I}, \mathbf{W}) - H(M \mid X^1_{I^1}, \ldots, X^r_{I^r}, \mathbf{I}, \mathbf{W}) \\ &= H(M) - H(M \mid X^1_{I^1}, \ldots, X^r_{I^r}) \\ &= I(M; X^1_{I^1}, \ldots, X^r_{I^r} \mid \mathbf{W}), \end{aligned}$$

where we use that M and $X^1_{I^1}, \ldots, X^r_{I^r}$ are jointly independent of $\mathbf{I}$, conditioned on $\mathbf{W}$.

Hence, using also the independence of $\mathbf{I}$ and $\mathbf{W}$,

$$\begin{aligned} & I(M; X^1_{I^1}, \ldots, X^r_{I^r} \mid \mathbf{W}) \\ &= I(M; X^1_{I^1}, \ldots, X^r_{I^r} \mid \mathbf{I}, \mathbf{W}) \\ &= \sum_{\mathbf{i}} I(M; X^1_{i^1}, \ldots, X^r_{i^r} \mid \mathbf{I} = \mathbf{i}, \mathbf{W}) \cdot \mathbf{Pr}[\mathbf{I} = \mathbf{i}] \\ &\geq \frac{1}{2} \min_{\mathbf{i}} I(M; X^1_{i^1}, \ldots, X^r_{i^r} \mid \mathbf{I} = \mathbf{i}, \mathbf{W}). \end{aligned}$$

We claim that for each $\mathbf{i}$, $I(M; X^1_{i^1}, \ldots, X^r_{i^r} \mid \mathbf{I} = \mathbf{i}, \mathbf{W}) = \Omega(r)$. To see this, define a 1-way protocol $\Pi_{\mathbf{i}}$ for GapAnd as follows. Alice and Bob are given inputs $\mathbf{C}$ and $\mathbf{D}$ to GapAnd, respectively, distributed according to ρ. For each $j \in [r]$, Alice sets $X^j_{i^j} = C^j$, while Bob sets $B^j = D^j$. Alice then chooses an independent uniform random bit for X^j_k for each j and $k \neq i^j$. The players then run the protocol $\Pi(\mathbf{X}, \mathbf{i}, \mathbf{B})$, and outputs whatever Π outputs.

By construction, $\Pi_{\mathbf{i}}(\mathbf{C}, \mathbf{D}) = \mathsf{GapAnd}(\mathbf{X}, \mathbf{i}, \mathbf{B})$, and so the correctness probability of $\Pi_{\mathbf{i}}$ is at least $1 - \delta$.

Moreover, if $M_{\mathbf{i}}$ denotes the message function of Alice in $\Pi_{\mathbf{i}}$, then by construction we have that for a sufficiently small constant δ,

$$\begin{aligned} & I(M; X^1_{i^1}, \ldots, X^r_{i^r} \mid \mathbf{I} = \mathbf{i}, \mathbf{W}) \\ &= I(M_{\mathbf{i}}(X^1_{i^1}, \ldots, X^r_{i^r}); X^1_{i^1}, \ldots, X^r_{i^r} \mid \mathbf{W}) = \Omega(r) \end{aligned}$$

using Fact 14. ■

By Claim 13 and the chain rule, for $\Omega(1)$ fraction of $j \in [r]$ we have $I(M; X^j_{I^j} \mid X^1_{I^1}, \ldots, X^{j-1}_{I^{j-1}}, \mathbf{W}) = \Omega(1)$. Call such an index j *informative.* For each informative j, a value x of the vector $(X^1_{I^1}, \ldots, X^{j-1}_{I^{j-1}})$ is *informative* if $I(M; X^j_{I^j} \mid (X^1_{I^1}, \ldots, X^{j-1}_{I^{j-1}}) = x, \mathbf{W}) = \Omega(1)$. Since

$$I(M; X^j_{I^j} \mid X^1_{I^1}, \ldots, X^{j-1}_{I^{j-1}}, \mathbf{W}) = \Omega(1),$$

it follows that an $\Omega(1)$ fraction of x are informative for an informative j.

We now lower bound $I(M(\mathbf{X}); \mathbf{X} \mid \mathbf{W})$. Let $\mathbf{X}^{<j} = (X^1, \ldots, X^{j-1})$. Applying the chain rule, as well as the definition of informative and the bounds on informative j and x above,

$$\begin{aligned} & I(M(\mathbf{X}); \mathbf{X} \mid \mathbf{W}) \\ &= \sum_{j=1}^r I(M(\mathbf{X}); X^j \mid \mathbf{X}^{<j}, \mathbf{W}) \\ &\geq \sum_{j=1}^r I(M(\mathbf{X}); X^j \mid X^1_{I^1}, \ldots, X^{j-1}_{I^{j-1}}, \mathbf{W}) \\ &= \sum_{j=1}^r \sum_x I(M(\mathbf{X}); X^j \mid (X^1_{I^1}, \ldots, X^{j-1}_{I^{j-1}}) = x, \mathbf{W}) \\ &\quad \cdot \mathbf{Pr}[(X^1_{I^1}, \ldots, X^{j-1}_{I^{j-1}}) = x] \\ &\geq \sum_{\text{inform.} j, x} I(M(\mathbf{X}); X^j \mid (X^1_{I^1}, \ldots, X^{j-1}_{I^{j-1}}) = x, \mathbf{W}) \\ &\quad \cdot \mathbf{Pr}[(X^1_{I^1}, \ldots, X^{j-1}_{I^{j-1}}) = x] \\ &\geq \Omega(r) \cdot \min_{\text{inform.} j, x} I(M(\mathbf{X}); X^j \mid (X^1_{I^1}, \ldots, X^{j-1}_{I^{j-1}}) = x, \mathbf{W}), \end{aligned}$$

where the first inequality follows from the fact that X^j is independent of $\mathbf{X}^{<j}$, together with the fact that conditioning cannot increase entropy.

We now lower bound

$$\min_{\text{informative } j, x} I(M(\mathbf{X}); X^j \mid (X^1_{I^1}, \ldots, X^{j-1}_{I^{j-1}}) = x, \mathbf{W}).$$

To do so, we build a 1-way protocol $\Pi_{j,x}$ with j and x hardwired, for solving the Index problem with a uniform distribution γ on its inputs. Suppose Alice is given the random input $Y \in \{0,1\}^d$, and Bob is given the random input $K \in [d]$, where Y and K are uniformly distributed over $\{0,1\}^d$ and $[d]$, respectively. Alice and Bob create inputs for protocol Π as follows. Namely, Alice sets $X^j = Y$, and uses the hardwiring of x to set $(X^1_{I^1}, \ldots, X^{j-1}_{I^{j-1}}) = x$. Further, Alice uses her private randomness to fill in the remaining coordinates of $X^1, \ldots, X^{j-1}$, as well as to choose $X^{j+1}, \ldots, X^r$ (all coordinates of such vectors are independent of Bob's inputs and uniformly distributed, so Alice can choose such inputs without any communication). Further, Bob sets $I^j = K$, and chooses $I^{j'}$ for $j' \neq j$ uniformly and independently in $[d]$. Bob also chooses his input $\mathbf{B}$ to be independent of all other inputs and uniformly distibuted.

Given this setting of inputs, in $\Pi_{j,x}$ Alice and Bob then run protocol Π on these inputs, resulting in a message function $M'(\mathbf{Y}) = M(\mathbf{X})$. Since j and x are informative, it follows that $I(M(\mathbf{X}); X^j_{Ij} | (X^1_{I1}, \ldots, X^{j-1}_{Ij-1}) = x, \mathbf{W}) = \Omega(1)$, which implies that $I(M'(\mathbf{Y}); Y_K \mid \mathbf{W}) = \Omega(1)$, or equivalently,

$$H(Y_K | M'(\mathbf{Y}), \mathbf{W}) = 1 - \Omega(1).$$

It follows from Fact 7 that Bob, given $M'(\mathbf{Y})$ and $\mathbf{W}$, can predict Y_k with probability $1/2 + \Omega(1)$, and solve Index on the uniform distribution γ. By Fact 12, it follows that $I(M'(\mathbf{Y}); \mathbf{Y} \mid \mathbf{W}) = \Omega(d)$. Notice, though, that by construction of $\Pi_{j,x}$ that $I(M'(\mathbf{Y}); \mathbf{Y} \mid \mathbf{W}) = I(M(\mathbf{X}); X^j \mid (X^1_{I1}, \ldots, X^{j-1}_{Ij-1}) = x, \mathbf{W})$.

We conclude that $I(M(\mathbf{X}); \mathbf{X} \mid \mathbf{W}) = \Omega(dr)$, which completes the proof. ∎

5. UPPER BOUND

Recall that sets $S_1, S_2, \ldots \subseteq [u]$ of sizes $n_1, n_2, \ldots$ where $n_{\max} = \max_i n_i$ are given, and we wish to obtain an (ε, δ)-estimate of $t = |S_1 \cap \ldots \cap S_m|$ using one-permutation k-min summaries as described in Section 2.2. Theorem 4 defines an estimator (see Figure 1 for pseudocode). In our proof of Theorem 4 we will assume that the hash function used to construct the summaries is random and fully independent. In many applications it will be possible to achieve this by simply maintaining a hash table of values during the construction phase. However, Section 6 shows how to replace the full randomness assumption with concrete hash functions in case the number of different hash values is too large to store.

For an intersection query on m sets the main insight is that our estimator relies only on the maximum set size $n_{\max}$ in contrast to the known k-permutation estimator that depends on the size of the union, making it less accurate given the same space (see Table 1). The space needed to store a summary that gives an (ε, δ)-estimate is $O\left(\frac{n_{\max} \log(m/\delta) \log u}{t\varepsilon^2}\right)$ bits. In Section 5.2 we show that this can be reduced almost by a factor $\log u$ by use of signatures.

5.1 Proof of Theorem 4

Recall that $k_{\min}(S_i)$ denotes the size-k one-permutation min-wise summary of S_i and the indicator variable $\hat{X}^{(i)}_j$ denotes the event that item j is chosen for the size-k one-permutation min-wise summary of S_i as defined below: $\hat{X}^{(i)}_j = 1$ if $j \in k_{\min}(S_i)$ and $\hat{X}^{(i)}_j = 0$ otherwise.

High-level proof strategy. Observe that $\mathbf{Pr}[\hat{X}^{(i)}_j = 1] = k/n_i$. Our algorithm uses size k summaries so for each set S_i we have $\sum_{j=1}^{n_i} \hat{X}^{(i)}_j = k$, which causes negative dependence between the indicator variables [14], i.e., when an item is in the summary of a set then the other items have smaller probability of being in the that summary. The main technical hurdle is showing that even with such a dependence one can use the intersection size between the summaries to estimate the intersection size of the sets.

To do this we analyze the case where for each S_i, the variables $X^{(i)}_1, X^{(i)}_2, \ldots, X^{(i)}_{n_i}$ are independent random variables:

$$X^{(i)}_j = \begin{cases} 1 & \text{if } h(j) \le k/n_i \\ 0 & \text{otherwise} \end{cases} \tag{1}$$

where $h : u \mapsto [0,1]$ is a fully random hash function. Let the setting with negative dependence be called *the dependent case* and the case using (1) be *the independent case*. The independent case conditioned on the sum of the variables being k is identically distributed as the dependent case. Therefore the final step is to bound the additional error probability of going from the independent case to the dependent one.

First we bound the probability of sampling k specific items given the number of sampled items is k. Let $i \in [m]$ and $\tilde{S}_i = \{x \in S_i | h(x) \le k/n_i\}$ be a sample of $S_i \subseteq [u]$ picked according to (1). An important consequence of picking elements to be in summaries is that of *consistent* sampling: If the hash value of an element from the intersection is one of the k smallest hash values computed, it will be guaranteed to be sampled in all sets. The following lemma shows that any specific outcome of a sample has equal probability given we restrict a sample to be size k.

LEMMA 15. *If $S_i \subseteq [u]$ and $\{i_1, i_2, \ldots, i_k\}$ is a specific size k outcome then*

$$\mathbf{Pr}\left[\tilde{S}_i = \{i_1, i_2, \ldots, i_k\} \middle| \sum_{j=1}^{n_i} X^{(i)}_j = k\right] = \frac{1}{\binom{n_i}{k}}$$

PROOF. We have:

$$\mathbf{Pr}\left[\tilde{S}_i = \{i_1, i_2, \ldots, i_{n_i}\}\right] = \left(\frac{k}{n_i}\right)^{n_i}\left(1 - \frac{k}{n_i}\right)^{n_i - k}$$

$$\mathbf{Pr}\left[\sum_{j=1}^{n_i} X^{(i)}_j = k\right] = \binom{n_i}{k}\left(\frac{k}{n_i}\right)^{n_i}\left(1 - \frac{k}{n_i}\right)^{n_i - k}$$

The final step of the lemma follows from Bayes theorem:

$$\mathbf{Pr}\left[\tilde{S}_i = \{i_1, i_2, \ldots, i_k\} \middle| \sum_{j=1}^{n_i} X^{(i)}_j = k\right] = \frac{\mathbf{Pr}\left[\tilde{S}_i = \{i_1, i_2, \ldots, i_{n_i}\}\right]}{\mathbf{Pr}\left[\sum_{j=1}^{n_i} X^{(i)}_j = k\right]} = \frac{1}{\binom{n_i}{k}} .$$

∎

We show the lower bound on the probability of the size of any $\tilde{S}_i$ being equal to its expectation k:

LEMMA 16. *For a sample $\tilde{S}_i$ of S_i we have*

$$\mathbf{Pr}\left[|\tilde{S}_i| = k\right] = \Omega\left(\frac{1}{\sqrt{k}}\right) . \tag{2}$$

PROOF. The mean μ of $|\tilde{S}_i|$ is the most likely outcome, i.e, $\mathbf{Pr}\left[|\tilde{S}_i| = k\right] \ge Pr\left[|\tilde{S}_i| = j\right]$ for $1 \le j \le u$ holds due to $E\left[\sum_{j=1}^{n_i} X^{(i)}_j\right] = k$ and the mode of binomial distributions [24]. Next step is showing that $|\tilde{S}_i|$ is more likely to be within $2\sqrt{k}$ of the mean $\mu = k$ than not, that is, $\mathbf{Pr}\left[\left|\sum_{j=1}^{n_i} X^{(i)}_j - k\right| \ge 2\sqrt{k}\right] \le \frac{1}{2}$ This follows from the Chernoff bounds on the sum $\sum_{j=1}^{n_i} X^{(i)}_j$:

$$\mathbf{Pr}\left[\left|\sum_{j=1}^{n_i} X^{(i)}_j - k\right| \ge 2\sqrt{k}\right] \le 2\exp\left(\frac{-k\left(\frac{2\sqrt{k}}{k}\right)^2}{2}\right)$$

$$\le \frac{1}{2} \;\forall k, i > 0 .$$

∎

Input: Sets $S_1, S_2, \ldots \subseteq [u]$
Output: k-min summaries for all S_i

h $\longleftarrow$ fully independent random hash function
foreach S_i **do**
  $k_i \leftarrow$ the kth smallest $h(x)$ for $x \in S_i$
  $k_{\min}(S_i) \leftarrow \{x \mid x \in S_i \wedge h(x) \le k_i\}$

(a) Pre-processing the sets.

Input: k-min summaries and set sizes $k_{\min}(S_1), n_1 = |S_1|, \ldots$ and query set $M \subseteq \mathbf{N}$
Output: X: An (ε, δ)-estimation of $t = \left|\bigcap_{i \in M} S_i\right|$

$n_{\max} \longleftarrow \max_{i \in M} n_i$
$X \longleftarrow \left|\bigcap_{i \in M} k_{\min}(S_i)\right| n_{\max}/k$

(b) Computing the estimator. The output is an (ε, δ)-estimator whenever $X > 3n_{\max} \log(1/\delta)/k\varepsilon^2$ (See Theorem 4).

Figure 1: Pseudocode for performing pre-processing and computing the estimator.

Let S be the elements of the size-t intersection and $\tilde{S}_{\max}$ be the sample of the largest set $S_{\max}$. We show that if the summary size k satisfies

$$k \ge \frac{2n_{\max} \log\left({}^{2m}/_{\delta}\right)}{\varepsilon^2 t} \tag{3}$$

then properties 1 and 2 below are satisfied.

PROPERTY 1. *$\left|\tilde{S}_{\max} \cap S\right|$ is an $(\varepsilon, {}^{\delta}/_{2})$-estimate of $t\frac{k}{n_{\max}}$.*

PROPERTY 2. *$\forall_i \left|\tilde{S}_i \cap S\right| \ge t(1-\varepsilon)\frac{k}{n_{\max}}$ with probability at least $1 - {}^{\delta}/_{2m}$.*

We show that the given properties hold for sufficiently large k, given by (3).

LEMMA 17. *If (3) and $0 \le \varepsilon, \delta \le 1$ then properties 1 and 2 hold.*

PROOF. We show that property 1 holds when (3) holds. This follows from Chernoff bounds on $\sum_{j=1}^{t} X_j^{(max)}$:

$$\begin{aligned}\gamma_1 &= \mathbf{Pr}\left[|\tilde{S}_i \cap S| \notin \left[t\frac{k}{n_{\max}}(1-\varepsilon), t\frac{k}{n_{\max}}(1+\varepsilon)\right]\right] \\ &< 2\exp\left(-\frac{\varepsilon^2 tk}{3n_{\max}}\right) .\end{aligned}$$

Since $k \ge \frac{2n_{\max}\log(2m/\delta)}{\varepsilon^2 t}$ the error probability is $\gamma_1 \le \frac{\delta}{2}$, thus property 1 holds.
Now we are to show that the given k implies property 2 holds, i.e., the size of the intersection between any single $\tilde{S}_i$ sample and intersection S is at least the expected size of the intersection between the sample of the largest set, $\tilde{S}_{\max}$ and S. The intersection of any sample $\tilde{S}_i$ and S has expectation $\mu = E\left[|\tilde{S}_i \cap S|\right] = t\frac{k}{n_i}$. Since $n_{\max} \ge n_i$, it holds that $\forall_i t\frac{k}{n_{\max}} \le t\frac{k}{n_i}$ and thus we bound error γ_2:

$$\begin{aligned}\gamma_2 &= \mathbf{Pr}\left[\sum_{j=1}^{t} X_j^{(max)} < (1-\varepsilon)t\frac{k}{n_{\max}}\right] \\ &\le \mathbf{Pr}\left[\sum_{j=1}^{t} X_j^{(i)} < (1-\varepsilon)t\frac{k}{|S_i|}\right] \le \exp\left(-\frac{\varepsilon^2 tk}{2n_{\max}}\right) .\end{aligned}$$

Since $k \ge \frac{2n_{\max}\log(2m/\delta)}{\varepsilon^2 t}$ the error probability is $\gamma_2 \le \frac{\delta}{2m}$, thus property 2 holds. ∎

We will now show that the independent case provides an estimator with the desired guarantees.

LEMMA 18. *If (3) holds and for $0 \le \varepsilon, \delta \le 1$ then $\frac{\left|\bigcap_{i\in[m]} \tilde{S}_i\right| n_{\max}}{k}$ is an (ε, δ)-estimate of t.*

PROOF. First we need that $\left|\tilde{S}_{\max} \cap S\right| \le (1+\varepsilon)t\frac{k}{n_{\max}}$ with probability $\ge 1-\delta$. By Lemma 17 this holds, as property 1 holds since k satisifies (3). We now argue:

$$\left|\bigcap_{i\in[m]} \tilde{S}_i\right| \ge (1-\varepsilon)\, t\frac{k}{n_{\max}} \text{ with probability } \ge 1-\delta \ . \tag{4}$$

Let $z = (1-\varepsilon)\, t\frac{k}{n_{\max}}$, then by Lemma 17 we have that for each set S_i its sample $\tilde{S}_i$ contains at least z items from S with probability $\ge 1-\delta/2m$ where these z items are sampled from all sets as they are in S and hence (4) holds. To show that

$$\left|\bigcap_{i\in[m]} \tilde{S}_i\right| \le (1+\varepsilon)\, t\frac{k}{n_{\max}} \text{ with probability } \ge 1-\delta \tag{5}$$

holds we need that $\left|\tilde{S}_{\max} \cap S\right| \le (1+\varepsilon)t\frac{k}{n_{\max}}$ with probability $\ge 1-\delta$. This follows directly from property 1 holding since k satisifies (3) as shown in Lemma 17.

We now show that our estimator computes an (ε, δ)-estimate, i.e., it holds that,

$$\frac{\left|\bigcap_{i\in[m]} \tilde{S}_i\right| n_{\max}}{k} \in [(1-\varepsilon)\, t, (1+\varepsilon)\, t]$$

with probability at least

$$1 - \left(\frac{\delta}{2} + m\frac{\delta}{2m}\right) \ge 1 - \delta \ .$$

By (5) and (4) we have the relative error of at most ε as required. To bound the error probability we apply the union bound on the error probabilities given by Lemma 17. As we have error probability $\delta/2$ on property 1 and error probability $\delta/2m$ on property 2, by the union bound we get $\le (\delta/2 + m\delta/2m) = \delta$ where the factor m on the second term comes from the union bound over all m sets. ∎

For each set S_i let B_i denote the set of samples where property 1 or 2 does *not* hold. We have probability $\mathbf{Pr}\left[\tilde{S}_i \in B_i\right]$ of the estimator based on samples $\tilde{S}_i$ being bad. We now relate the independent case where a sample has expected size k to the case where k-min summaries are used and thus we have samples of strictly size k.

LEMMA 19. *If (3) holds and $0 \le \varepsilon, \delta \le 1$ then*

$$\mathbf{Pr}\left[\tilde{S}_i \in B_i \middle| |\tilde{S}_i| = k\right] \le \delta\sqrt{k} \ .$$

For a specific itemset $I = \{i_1, i_2, \ldots, i_k\}$ we have

$$\mathbf{Pr}\left[\tilde{S}_i = I \,\middle|\, \sum_{j=1}^{n_i} X_j^{(i)} = k\right] = \mathbf{Pr}\left[k_{\min}(S_i) = I\right] = \frac{1}{\binom{n_i}{k}} \quad (6)$$

PROOF. An upper bound of the conditional probability can be obtained through Bayes theorem:

$$\mathbf{Pr}\left[\tilde{S}_i \in B | \left|\tilde{S}_i\right| = k\right] \leq \frac{\mathbf{Pr}\left[\tilde{S}_i \in B\right]}{\mathbf{Pr}\left[|\tilde{S}_i| = k\right]} .$$

The probability of the sample being of size k was bounded in (2) and by union bound on the error probabilities found in Lemma 17 we get.

$$\mathbf{Pr}\left[\tilde{S}_i \in B | \left|\tilde{S}_i\right| = k\right] \leq \frac{\mathbf{Pr}\left[\tilde{S}_i \in B\right]}{\mathbf{Pr}\left[|\tilde{S}_i| = k\right]} \leq \delta / \tfrac{1}{\sqrt{k}} = \delta\sqrt{k} .$$

Now we argue that (6) holds, i.e., that the conditional distribution of any sample $|\tilde{S}_i| = k$ is the same as that of $k_{\min}(S_i)$. This follows directly from Lemma 15 and from $\mathbf{Pr}\left[k_{\min}(S_i) = I\right] = \frac{1}{\binom{n_i}{k}}$. ■

PROOF. (Theorem 4.) By Lemma 18 we have that X is an (ε, δ)-estimate of t in the independent case whenever the expected number of elements k in our summaries satisfy (3). Lemma 19 relates the independent case to the dependent case with fixed summary size, showing that X is an $(\varepsilon, \delta\sqrt{k})$-estimate when (3) holds. To show Theorem 4 we consider two cases for t.

1. If $t \geq 2n_{\max} \log(2m/\delta)/k\varepsilon^2$ then (3) is satisfied, so X is an $(\varepsilon, \delta\sqrt{k})$-estimate of t. Since $\varepsilon < 1/4$ we get that $X < 3n_{\max} \log(2m/\delta)/k\varepsilon^2$ implies

   $$X/(1-\varepsilon) < 4n_{\max} \log(2m/\delta)/k\varepsilon^2 .$$

   So as long as $t \in [X/(1+\varepsilon); X/(1-\varepsilon)]$, which happens with probability $1 - \delta\sqrt{k}$, we get a true answer regardless of whether the first or second answer is returned.

2. If $t < 2n_{\max} \log(2m/\delta)/k\varepsilon^2$ then the probability that $X > 3n_{\max} \log(2m/\delta)/k\varepsilon^2)$ is at most $\delta\sqrt{k}$. This is because X is dominated by an estimator X' derived from X by artificially increasing the intersection size to that required by (3). This means that with probability $1 - \delta\sqrt{k}$ the algorithm correctly reports that t is in the interval $[0; 4n_{\max} \log(2m/\delta)/k\varepsilon^2]$.

■

5.2 Use of signatures for the upper bound

An advantage of k-permutation min-wise hashing is that it can easily be combined with signatures to decrease space usage, i.e., elements from u in the min-hash can be replaced with hash values using significantly fewer bit. As shown by Li and König [22], using b-bit signatures, where b is a small integer, allows us to increase k by a factor $\log(u)/b$ without increasing the space usage. With a suitable estimator that takes the signature collisions into account, the net result is an increase in precision for a given space usage. It is a nontrivial matter to extend the estimator to work for the intersection of more than two sets when b is small. The case of three sets was investigated in [21].

It seems to be less well known that one-permutation hashing allows a similar space saving. The idea is to consider signatures of $\log(k) + b$ bits, and store the *set* of signatures for each set $k_{\min}(X)$. By using an appropriate encoding of the signature set the space usage becomes roughly $k(b + \log e)$ bits, see e.g. [25]. There even exist methods that use word-level parallellism to compute the set of signatures that are in common between two such encodings [2, Lemma 3], meaning that there is a speedup in comparing two summaries that is similar to the factor saved in space usage. At least in theory, this means that the difference between the efficiency of k-permutation and one-permutation schemes compressed using signatures is not so large.

We now argue that if we choose a signature hash function $h : [u] \to \{0,1\}^b$ where $b \geq \log(2k^2/\delta)$, a signature collision that affects the estimate will occur with probability at most $\delta/2$, independent of the number of sets considered. Recall that k is the size of a min-hash, and consider a specific set of min-hashes $k_{\min}(S_j)$, $j = 1, \ldots, m$. If we replace $k_{\min}(S_j)$ by the set $h(k_{\min}(S_j))$ of signatures there is a chance that $|\cap_j h(k_{\min}(S_j))|$ is different from $|\cap_j k_{\min}(S_j)|$ because of collision of elements in some set I with at least one element in each min-hash. We define an *i-cover* as a set I where $|I| = i$ and $\forall j : I \cap k_{\min}(S_j) \neq \emptyset$, i.e., an i-cover is a set of i elements that includes an element from every minhash. We now argue that there is a low probability that there exists an i-cover with $i > 1$ for which all elements have the same signature under h. For now we assume that h is fully random, which means that the probability a particular i-cover colliding is at most

$$(2^{-b})^{i-1} = \left(\frac{\delta}{2k^2}\right)^{i-1} .$$

For $i \leq m$ we have at most k^i possible i-covers, so by a union bound the probability of any colliding i-cover occuring is at most

$$\sum_{i=2}^{m} k^i \left(\frac{\delta}{2k^2}\right)^{i-1} \leq \delta/2 .$$

We conclude that with probability at least $1 - \delta/2$ we end up with exactly $|\bigcap_i k_{\min}(S_i)|$ signatures in the intersection, meaning that the result is the same as when storing the elements of $k_{\min}(S_1), \ldots, k_{\min}(S_m)$. Hence one can simply think of the sets $k_{\min}(S_i)$, with the understanding that they can be replaced by a representation of size roughly $k \log(e2k^2/\delta)$ bits using a suitable encoding of signatures.

6. HASH FUNCTIONS OF LIMITED INDEPENDENCE

Until now we have assumed to have access to a fully random hash function on the sets. In this section we show that there are realizable hash functions of limited independence such that our results hold. Thorup [30] recently showed that for Jaccard similarity (and hence intersection size) estimation with one-permutation min-wise summaries it suffices to use a pairwise independent hash function. However, this does not extend to the setting where we seek the intersection size of many sets (see Theorem 20).

We argue that k-wise independence is sufficient for the hash function used to construct the one-permutation min-wise summaries and that m-wise independence is sufficient for the hash functions used to create signatures as described in Section 5.2.

6.1 Hash functions for one-permutation min-wise summaries

We will argue that k-wise independent hash functions are sufficient for the hash function used to create the summaries.

For n variables $X_1, \ldots X_n$, $X = \sum_i^n X_i$, $\mu = E[X]$ and $\delta > 0$ then by [27] we have that if the variables $X_1, \ldots X_n$ are $\lceil \frac{\mu\delta}{1-\mu/n} \rceil$-wise independent, the Chernoff tail bounds hold. Examining the tail bounds used in Section 5.1 we see that if we impose the additional constraint $\delta \leq 1 - k/n$ then $\lceil \frac{\mu\delta}{1-\mu/n} \rceil \leq k$ and hence k-wise independence is sufficient for the construction of our summaries.

6.2 Hash functions for signatures

We will now argue that m-wise independent hash functions are sufficient to obtain error probability $\leq \delta$ when being used to create signatures. This follows directly from the fact that we consider collisions in terms of i-covers for $i \leq m$ and apply a summation of m terms to bound the error probability to be $\leq \delta/2$. For the family of hash functions we will use the construction of Siegel [28]. This construction gives a RAM data structure of space $O\left(u^{\sqrt{\lg k/\lg u+\varepsilon}} \lg v\right)$ bits when hashing from $\{0, \ldots, u-1\}$ to $\{0, \ldots, v-1\}$. A function from the family can be evaluated in constant worst-case time and it is k-wise independent with high probability. In particular, for $m = k = u^{O(1)}$ we have space usage $O(u^{\varepsilon} \lg v)$ for some constant $\varepsilon > 0$.

6.3 Lower bound for c-wise independent hash functions

Motivated by recent work by Thorup [30] showing 2-wise independent hash functions to work well for Jaccard estimation we will now consider an instance where any estimator based on the k smallest hash values of a c-wise independent hash function will not be unbiased. In particular the argument follows from the existence of small families of hash functions.

THEOREM 20. *Let $[u]$ be the universe of elements and $h : [u] \mapsto 0, \ldots, p-1$ be any c-wise independent hash function for $c = O(1)$. There exists an instance on p^2 sets $S_1, \ldots, S_{p^2}$ with intersection size $t = |\cap_i S_i| = n-k$. For any estimator $\tilde{t}$ for t that guarantees a relative error bound and is based on k size min-wise summaries constructed using h it holds that $\hat{t}$ is not unbiased.*

For Theorem 20 we construct an instance on p^c sets where one of the k one-permutation min-wise summaries will hold no elements from S with high probability.

PROOF. Let $h : [u] \mapsto \{0, \ldots, p-1\}$ be a c-independent hash function where $c < \log_p m$. We will consider an instance on $m > p^c$ sets that has large intersection S, but where an unbiased estimator of the intersection size $|S|$ using the smallest k hash values is not possible with high probability.

For any h there exists a set M_z of size k where $h(M_z) = \{0, \ldots, k-1\}$, i.e., the k elements of M_z map to the k smallest possible hash values. Let $S_i = M_i \cup S$ for $0 \leq i < p^c$ be n-sized sets where S is the intersecting elements to be specified later. We have $h(S_z) = M_z \cup h(S) = \{0, \ldots, k-1\} \cup h(S)$ and $z \in \{0, \ldots, p^c\}$, i.e., by the existence of size p^c families of hash function there is a hash function that hashes k elements from a particular set S_z to the k smallest possible hash values. It follows that if $\forall j \in h(S) j \geq k$ then the set of the k smallest hash values will contain no elements from S, even though we have size $|S| = n-k$. For a uniformly random $n-k$-sized set S we have $\mathbf{Pr}[\forall t \in h(S) t \geq k] = \left(1 - \frac{k}{p}\right)^{n-k}$ which is ≈ 1 for $k \ll n$.

Hence if we consider the intersection S of all $m > p^c$ sets S_i it will hold with high probability that this instance will have intersection size $|S| = n-k$ but no elements from S in the set of the k smallest hash values. Consider the case of there being no elements from S in the set of the k smallest hash values and let $\tilde{t}$ be an estimate of $|S|$. Any estimate $\tilde{t}$ of $|S|$ with relative bounded error that is based on p^c min-wise summaries will be unable to distinguish the case of $|S| = 0$ from $|S| = n-k$ when there are no elements from S in the set of the k smallest hash values. Thus when presented with such a set the estimate will always be that $\tilde{t} = 0$. Let ϕ be the probability of there being no elements in from S in the set of the k smallest hash values. Then let the outcome of the random variable X be the estimate $\tilde{t}$. We have $E[X] \leq \phi 0 + (1-\phi)n$ where $\phi = \left(1 - \frac{k}{p}\right)^{n-k}$.

To obtain an unbiased estimator $E[X] = n-k$ for this instance we need $(1-\phi)n \geq n-k$ hence $\phi < k/n$. By the upper bound $\left(1 - \frac{k}{p}\right)^{n-k} < \left(\frac{k}{p}\right)^{n-k}$ we have that there is a constant w s.t. $n > k^{wn}$ implies $\phi > k/n$. Thus when n is exponential in k we have that ϕ is large enough to make any estimator based on the k smallest hash values biased. ■

7. REFERENCES

[1] Z. Bar-Yossef. *The complexity of massive data set computations.* PhD thesis, University of California at Berkeley, 2002.

[2] P. Bille, A. Pagh, and R. Pagh. Fast evaluation of union-intersection expressions. In *Proceedings of the 18th International Symposium on Algorithms And Computation (ISAAC '07)*, pages 739–750.

[3] B. H. Bloom. Space/time trade-offs in hash coding with allowable errors. *Commun. ACM*, 13(7):422–426, 1970.

[4] M. Braverman, A. Garg, D. Pankratov, and O. Weinstein. Information lower bounds via self-reducibility. In *CSR*, pages 183–194, 2013.

[5] A. Z. Broder. On the resemblance and containment of documents. In *In Compression and Complexity of Sequences (SEQUENCES)*, pages 21–29, 1997.

[6] A. Z. Broder, M. Charikar, A. M. Frieze, and M. Mitzenmacher. Min-wise independent permutations. *Journal of Computer and System Sciences*, 60:327–336, 1998.

[7] A. Z. Broder, S. C. Glassman, M. S. Manasse, and G. Zweig. Syntactic clustering of the web. In *Selected papers from the sixth international conference on World Wide Web*, pages 1157–1166, 1997.

[8] A. Chakrabarti and O. Regev. An optimal lower bound on the communication complexity of gap-hamming-distance. *SIAM J. Comput.*, 41(5):1299–1317, 2012.

[9] F. Chierichetti, R. Kumar, S. Lattanzi, M. Mitzenmacher, A. Panconesi, and P. Raghavan. On compressing social networks. In *Proceedings of the 15th ACM SIGKDD*, KDD '09, pages 219–228, 2009.

[10] E. Cohen and H. Kaplan. In J. R. Douceur, A. G. Greenberg, T. Bonald, and J. Nieh, editors, *SIGMETRICS/Performance*, pages 251–262.

[11] E. Cohen and H. Kaplan. What you can do with coordinated samples. In *APPROX-RANDOM*, volume 8096 of *Lecture Notes in Computer Science*, pages 452–467. Springer Berlin Heidelberg, 2013.

[12] E. Cohen, H. Kaplan, and S. Sen. Coordinated weighted sampling for estimating aggregates over multiple weight assignments. *Proc. VLDB Endow.*, 2(1):646–657, Aug. 2009.

[13] H. Cohen and E. Porat. Fast set intersection and two-patterns matching. In *Proceedings of the 9th Latin American Conference on Theoretical Informatics*, LATIN'10, pages 234–242, Berlin, Heidelberg, 2010. Springer-Verlag.

[14] D. Dubhashi and D. Ranjan. Balls and bins: A study in negative dependence. *RANDOM STRUCTURES & ALGORITHMS*, 13:99–124, 1996.

[15] P. Flajolet, E. Fusy, O. Gandouet, and F. Meunier. Hyperloglog: the analysis of a near-optimal cardinality estimation algorithm.

[16] P. Indyk and D. P. Woodruff. Tight lower bounds for the distinct elements problem. In *Proceedings of Foundations of Computer Science (FOCS)*, pages 283–288, 2003.

[17] T. S. Jayram. Information complexity: a tutorial. In *PODS*, pages 159–168, 2010.

[18] D. M. Kane, J. Nelson, and D. P. Woodruff. An optimal algorithm for the distinct elements problem. In *Proceedings of the 29th Symposium on Principles of Database Systems (PODS)*, pages 41–52, 2010.

[19] I. Kremer, N. Nisan, and D. Ron. On randomized one-round communication complexity. *Computational Complexity*, 8(1):21–49, 1999.

[20] P. Li and A. C. König. Theory and applications of b-bit minwise hashing. *Commun. ACM*, 54(8):101–109, Aug. 2011.

[21] P. Li, A. C. König, and W. Gui. *b*-bit minwise hashing for estimating three-way similarities. In *Proceedings of Annual Conference on Neural Information Processing Systems (NIPS)*, pages 1387–1395, 2010.

[22] P. Li and C. König. b-bit minwise hashing. In *Proceedings of the 19th international conference on World wide web*, WWW '10, pages 671–680, 2010.

[23] P. Li, A. Owen, and C.-H. Zhang. One permutation hashing for efficient search and learning. *CoRR*, abs/1208.1259, 2012.

[24] P. Neumann. Über den Median der Binomial- und Poissonverteilung. *Wissenschaftliche Zeitschrift der Humboldt-Universität zu Berlin. Reihe Mathematik/Naturwissenschaften*, 16:62–64, 1967.

[25] R. Pagh. Low redundancy in static dictionaries with constant query time. *SIAM Journal of Computing*, 31(2):353–363, 2001.

[26] F. Rusu and A. Dobra. Sketches for size of join estimation. *ACM Trans. Database Syst.*, 33(3), 2008.

[27] J. P. Schmidt, A. Siegel, and A. Srinivasan. Chernoff-hoeffding bounds for applications with limited independence. *SIAM J. Discret. Math.*, 8(2):223–250, May 1995.

[28] A. Siegel. On universal classes of extremely random constant-time hash functions. *SIAM J. Comput.*, 33(3):505–543, Mar. 2004.

[29] R. R. Sinha and M. Winslett. Multi-resolution bitmap indexes for scientific data. *ACM Trans. Database Syst.*, 32(3):16, 2007.

[30] M. Thorup. Bottom-k and priority sampling, set similarity and subset sums with minimal independence. *STOC*, 2013.

[31] Z. Wei and K. Yi. Beyond simple aggregates: indexing for summary queries. In M. Lenzerini and T. Schwentick, editors, *PODS*, pages 117–128. ACM, 2011.

[32] D. P. Woodruff. Optimal space lower bounds for all frequency moments. In *SODA*, pages 167–175, 2004.

[33] D. P. Woodruff and Q. Zhang. Tight bounds for distributed functional monitoring. In *STOC*, pages 941–960, 2012.

APPENDIX

A. SPACE OF K-PERMUTATION MIN-WISE SUMMARIES ON SUNFLOWER SETS

Sunflower sets. (Section 2.3). This hard instance gives the upper bound for k-permutation min-wise hashing of Table 1. For m sets $S_1 \dots S_m$ each of size n, let $t = |\cap_i S_i|$ be the intersection size of all sets. Then a sunflower instance has the property $\forall_{i \neq j} |S_i \cap S_j| = t$, i.e., the m sets are disjoint except for the t intersection elements. The union size of such an instance is $|\cup_i S_i| = t + mn - mt = t + m(n-t)$ as there are t elements in the intersection and each of the m sets hold additional $n-t$ elements. It follows that the Jaccard similarity for a sunflower instance is $t/(t+m(n-t))$.

LEMMA 21. *Given m sets of size n with intersection size t. To obtain an $(\epsilon, O(1))$-estimate of t using k-permutation min-wise hashing one needs to store $O\left(\frac{mn}{t\epsilon^2}\right)$ elements from each set.*

PROOF. The upper bound for k-permutation min-wise hashing of Table 1 is derived as follows. Let $X_1 \dots X_c$ be independent Bernoulli trials where $\mathbf{Pr}[X_i] = J$ and let $X = \sum_{i=1}^{c} X_i$ and $\mu = E[X] = cJ$. There exists a c for which there is constant probability of the event that the outcome of X is a relative factor ε from $E[X]$. This can be bounded applying a Chernoff-Hoeffding bound on X as follows.

$$\mathbf{Pr}\left[|X - E[X]| \geq (1+\varepsilon)E[X]\right] = \mathbf{Pr}\left[|X - cJ| \geq (1+\varepsilon)cJ\right] = \delta \geq 2e^{(-cJ\varepsilon^2)/3}$$

Then isolating c we have $c \geq \frac{3\log(2/\delta)}{J\varepsilon^2}$, which for $\delta = O(1)$ is $O\left(\frac{1}{J\varepsilon^2}\right) = O\left(\frac{t+m(n-t)}{t\varepsilon^2}\right)$ following from the Jaccard similarity of the sunflower instance above. For $t < n/2$ we have $c = O\left(\frac{mn}{t\varepsilon^2}\right)$, the sample size required for k-permutation min-wise summaries. ■

We conjecture that this bound is tight, by tightness of Chernoff bounds.

Enumerating Answers to First-Order Queries over Databases of Low Degree

Arnaud Durand
CNRS and ENS Cachan
www.logique.jussieu.fr/~durand/

Nicole Schweikardt
Goethe-Universität Frankfurt
www.tks.cs.uni-frankfurt.de/schweika

Luc Segoufin
INRIA and ENS Cachan
http://pages.saclay.inria.fr/luc.segoufin/

ABSTRACT

A class of relational databases has low degree if for all δ, all but finitely many databases in the class have degree at most n^δ, where n is the size of the database. Typical examples are databases of bounded degree or of degree bounded by $\log n$.

It is known that over a class of databases having low degree, first-order boolean queries can be checked in pseudo-linear time, i.e. in time bounded by $n^{1+\varepsilon}$, for all ε. We generalise this result by considering query evaluation.

We show that counting the number of answers to a query can be done in pseudo-linear time and that enumerating the answers to a query can be done with constant delay after a pseudo-linear time preprocessing.

Categories and Subject Descriptors

H.2.4 [**Database Management**]: Systems—*Query processing*; H.2.3 [**Database Management**]: Languages—*Query languages*

General Terms

Theory; Algorithms

Keywords

query evaluation; enumeration; low degree; algorithm

1. INTRODUCTION

Query evaluation is a fundamental task in databases and a vast literature is devoted to the complexity of this problem. However, for more demanding tasks such as producing the whole set of answers or computing aggregates on the query result (such as counting the number of answers), complexity bounds are often simply extrapolated from those for query evaluation; and until recently, few specific methods and tools had been developed to tackle these problems. Given a database $\mathcal{A}$ and a first-order query q, it may be not satisfactory enough to express complexity results in terms of the sizes of $\mathcal{A}$ and q as it is often the case. The fact that the solution set $q(\mathcal{A})$ may be of size exponential in the query is intuitively not sufficient to make the problem hard, and alternative complexity measures had to be found for query answering. In this direction, one way to define tractability is to assume that tuples of the query result can be generated one by one with some regularity, for example by ensuring a fixed delay between two consecutive outputs once a necessary precomputation has been done to construct a suitable index structure. This approach, that considers query answering as an enumeration problem, has deserved some attention over the last few years. In this vein, the best that one can hope for is constant delay, i.e., the delay depends only on the size of q (but not on the size of $\mathcal{A}$). Surprisingly, a number of query evaluation problems have been shown to admit constant delay algorithms, usually preceded by a preprocessing phase that is linear or almost linear. This is the case when queries are evaluated over the class of structures of bounded degree [5, 13] or, more generally, over the class of structures of "bounded expansion" [14]. Similar results have been shown for monadic second-order logic over structures of bounded tree-width [4, 1, 15] or for fragments of first-order logic over arbitrary structures [2, 3]. However, as shown in [2], the fact that evaluation of boolean queries is easy does not guarantee the existence of such efficient enumeration algorithms in general: under some reasonable complexity assumption, there is no constant delay algorithm with linear preprocessing enumerating the answers of acyclic conjunctive queries (although it is well-known that the model checking of boolean acyclic queries can be done in linear time [19]).

In this paper, we investigate the complexity of the enumeration, counting, and testing problems for first-order queries over classes of low degree. A class of relational databases has low degree if for all $\delta > 0$, all sufficiently large databases in the class have degree at most n^δ, where n is the size of the database. Databases of bounded degree or of degree bounded by $(\log n)^c$, for any fixed constant c, are examples of low degree classes. However, it turns out to be incomparable with the class of databases of bounded expansion mentioned above.

It has been proved in [11] that over a class of databases of low degree, first-order boolean queries can be checked in pseudo-linear time, i.e., in time bounded by $O(n^{1+\varepsilon})$, for all $\varepsilon > 0$. In this paper, we prove that counting the number of answers to a query can be done in pseudo-linear time, and that enumerating the answers to a query can be done with constant delay after a pseudo-linear time preprocessing. We also prove that testing membership of a tuple to a query result can be done in constant time after a pseudo-linear time preprocessing. We adopt a uniform approach to prove all these results by using at the heart of the preprocessing phases a quantifier elimination method that reduces our different problems to their analog but for coloured graphs and quantifier-free queries. With such a tool, we can then focus within each specific task on very simple instances.

PODS'14, June 22–27, 2014, Snowbird, UT, USA.

ACM 978-1-4503-2375-8/14/06 ...$15.00.
http://dx.doi.org/10.1145/2594538.2594539.

Over a class of databases of low degree, the difficulty is to handle queries requiring that in all its answers, some of its components are far away from each other. When this is not the case, for instance when in all answers all its components are within short distance from the first component, then the low degree assumption implies that there are only few answers in total and those can be computed in pseudo-linear time. In the difficult case, the number of answers may be exponential in the arity of the query and the naive evaluation algorithm may spend too much time processing tuples with components close to each other. To avoid this situation, we introduce suitable functions that can be precomputed in pseudo-linear time, and that allow us to jump in constant time from a tuple with components close to each other to a correct answer.

Related work. Enumerating the answers to a boolean query q over a database $\mathcal{A}$ amounts to testing whether q holds on $\mathcal{A}$, a problem also known as the model checking problem. An enumeration algorithm with constant delay after a preprocessing phase taking pseudo-linear time, or even polynomial time, induces a model checking algorithm that is *fixed-parameter tractable* (FPT), i.e, works in time $f(q)\cdot\|\mathcal{A}\|^c$ for some constant c and some function f depending only on the class of databases. There is a vast literature studying the model checking problem for first-order logic aiming at finding FPT algorithms for larger and larger classes of databases. Starting from the class of databases of bounded degree, or bounded treewidth, FPT algorithms were derived for databases having bounded expansion [6] (see also [14]). Actually, very recently an FPT algorithm has been obtained for a class of databases known as "nowhere dense", generalising all the previously known results [12]. This last result is in a sense "optimal" as it is known that if a class of databases is closed under substructures and has no FPT model checking algorithm then it is somewhere dense [16], modulo some reasonable complexity hypothesis.

Classes of databases of low degree do not belong to this setting. It is easy to see that they are neither nowhere dense nor closed under substructures (see Section 2.3). Our algorithms build on the known model checking algorithm for low degree databases [11]. They generalise the known enumeration algorithms for databases of bounded degree [5, 13]. However, they differ significantly from those and actually require an extra assumption on our computational model (see Section 2.2).

Organisation. We fix the basic notation and formulate our main results in Section 2. In Section 3 we present the algorithms for counting, testing, and enumerating answers to first-order queries over classes of structures of low degree. These algorithms rely on a particular preprocessing which transforms a first-order query on a database into a quantifier-free query on a coloured graph. The result is stated in Section 3.2, while its proof is presented in Section 4. We conclude in Section 5.

2. PRELIMINARIES AND MAIN RESULTS

We write $\mathbb{N}$ to denote the set of non-negative integers, and we let $\mathbb{N}_{\geqslant 1} := \mathbb{N} \setminus \{0\}$. $\mathbb{Q}$ denotes the set of rationals, and $\mathbb{Q}_{>0}$ is the set of positive rationals.

2.1 Databases and queries

A database is a finite relational structure. A *relational signature* σ is a finite set of relation symbols R, each of them associated with a fixed *arity* $ar(R) \in \mathbb{N}_{\geqslant 1}$. A *relational structure* $\mathcal{A}$ over σ, or a σ-structure (we omit to mention σ when it is clear from the context) consists of a non-empty finite set $dom(\mathcal{A})$ called the *domain* of $\mathcal{A}$, and an $ar(R)$-ary relation $R^{\mathcal{A}} \subseteq dom(\mathcal{A})^{ar(R)}$ for each relation symbol $R \in \sigma$. We define the *size* $\|\mathcal{A}\|$ of $\mathcal{A}$ as $\|\mathcal{A}\| = |\sigma| + |dom(\mathcal{A})| + \sum_{R\in\sigma} |R^{\mathcal{A}}|\cdot ar(R)$. It corresponds to the size of a reasonable encoding of $\mathcal{A}$. The cardinality of $\mathcal{A}$, i.e. the cardinality of its domain, is denoted by $|\mathcal{A}|$.

By *query* we mean a formula of FO(σ), the set of all first-order formulas of signature σ, for some relational signature σ (again we omit σ when it is clear from the context). For $\varphi \in$ FO, we write $\varphi(\bar{x})$ to denote a query whose free variables are $\bar{x}$, and the number of free variables is called the *arity of the query*. A *sentence* is a query of arity 0. Given a structure $\mathcal{A}$ and a query φ, an *answer* to φ in $\mathcal{A}$ is a tuple $\bar{a}$ of elements of $dom(\mathcal{A})$ such that $\mathcal{A} \models \varphi(\bar{a})$. We write $\varphi(\mathcal{A})$ for the set of answers to φ in $\mathcal{A}$, i.e. $\varphi(\mathcal{A}) = \{\bar{a} : \mathcal{A} \models \varphi(\bar{a})\}$. As usual, $|\varphi|$ denotes the size of φ.

Let C be a class of structures. The model checking problem of FO over C is the computational problem of given a **sentence** $\varphi \in$ FO and a database $\mathcal{A} \in C$ to test whether $\mathcal{A} \models \varphi$ or not.

Given a k-ary query φ, we care about "enumerating" $\varphi(\mathcal{A})$ efficiently. Let C be a class of structures. The *enumeration problem of φ over C* is, given a database $\mathcal{A} \in C$, to output the elements of $\varphi(\mathcal{A})$ one by one with no repetition. The time needed to output the first solution is called the *preprocessing time*. The maximal time between any two consecutive outputs of elements of $\varphi(\mathcal{A})$ is called *the delay*. We are interested here in enumeration algorithms with pseudo-linear preprocessing time and constant delay. We now make these notions formal.

2.2 Model of computation and enumeration

We use Random Access Machines (RAMs) with addition and uniform cost measure as a model of computation. For further details on this model and its use in logic see [7, 10].

In the sequel we assume that the input relational structure comes with a linear order on the domain. If not, we use the one induced by the encoding of the structure as an input to the RAM. Whenever we iterate through all nodes of the domain, the iteration is with respect to the initial linear order.

Our algorithms over RAMs will take as input a query φ of size k and a structure $\mathcal{A}$ of size n. We then say that an algorithm runs in *linear time* (respectively, *constant time*) if it outputs the solution within $f(k)\cdot n$ steps (respectively, $f(k)$ steps), for some function f. We also say than an algorithm runs in *pseudo-linear time* if, for all $\varepsilon \in \mathbb{Q}_{>0}$ it outputs the solution within $f(k,\varepsilon)\cdot n^{1+\varepsilon}$ steps, for some function f.

We make the following important hypothesis on our RAM model. This hypothesis was not necessary in [14, 13, 5] for enumerating queries over classes of structures of bounded degree or bounded expansion, but we need it here for the case of structures of low degree (our proofs make crucial use of it; we don't know, though, whether this hypothesis is actually unavoidable).

If n is the size of the input structure, we assume available a total amount of memory of size $O(n^3)$.[1] Because our algorithms will be linear or pseudo-linear time, they will access only a small fraction of this memory, but it is important that this total memory is available. It turns out that we can assume without loss of generality that this memory is initialised to 0. If this were not the case, it could be achieved by using the so called *lazy array initialisation technique* (cf., e.g., the textbook [18]): During the run of the algorithm, a time-stamp is associated to each memory cell indicating the time of its first initialisation. At the same time we maintain an inverted list indicating for each time-stamp which memory cell was initialised. Then, a memory cell is initialised iff the entry for its associated time-stamp in the inverted list is the memory cell itself.

An important consequence of this assumption is that, modulo linear time preprocessing, we can assume available the adjacency

[1]Actually we need a memory of $O(n^{2+\varepsilon})$ for all $\varepsilon \in \mathbb{Q}_{>0}$

matrix of a graph given by the list of its edges. We do this by scanning all its edges and setting to 1 the corresponding entry in the matrix. As all other entries can be assumed to be 0, we can then test in constant time whether there is an edge between a given pair. We will implement this over graphs of size $O(n^{1+\varepsilon})$.

We say that the *enumeration problem* of FO over a class C of structures can be solved with *constant delay after a pseudo-linear preprocessing*, if it can be solved by a RAM algorithm which, on input $q \in$ FO and $\mathcal{A} \in C$, can be decomposed into two phases:

- a preprocessing phase that is performed in pseudo-linear time, and
- an enumeration phase that outputs $q(\mathcal{A})$ with no repetition and a delay depending only on q between any two consecutive outputs. The enumeration phase has full access to the output of the preprocessing phase and can use extra memory whose size depends only on q.

Notice that if we can enumerate q with constant delay after a pseudo-linear preprocessing, then all answers can be output in time $f(|q|, \varepsilon) \cdot (\|\mathcal{A}\|^{1+\varepsilon} + |q(\mathcal{A})|)$, for some function f, and the first solution is computed in pseudo-linear time. In the particular case of boolean queries, the associated model checking problem must be solvable in pseudo-linear time.

EXAMPLE 1. *To illustrate these notions, consider the binary query $q(x, y)$ over coloured graphs computing the pairs of nodes (x, y) such that x is* blue, *y is* red *and there is no edge from x to y. It can be expressed in* FO *by*

$$B(x) \wedge R(y) \wedge \neg E(x, y).$$

A naive algorithm for evaluating q would iterate through all blue nodes, then iterate through all red nodes, check if they are linked by an edge and, if not, output the resulting pair, otherwise try the next pair.

With our RAM model, after a linear preprocessing, we can easily iterate through all blue nodes and through all red nodes with a constant delay between any two of them. Our extra assumption allows us to test in constant time whether there is an edge between any two nodes. The problem with the above algorithm is that many pairs of appropriate colour may be false hits. Hence the delay between two consecutive outputs may be arbitrarily large.

If the degree is assumed to be bounded, then the above algorithm enumerates all answers with constant delay, since the number of false hits for each blue node is bounded by the degree. We will see that for structures of low degree we can modify the algorithm in order to achieve the same result.

2.3 Classes of structures of low degree

The degree of a structure $\mathcal{A}$, denoted *degree*$(\mathcal{A})$, is the degree of the Gaifman graph associated with $\mathcal{A}$ (i.e., the undirected graph with vertex set *dom*$(\mathcal{A})$ where there is an edge between two nodes if they both occur in a tuple that belongs to a relation of $\mathcal{A}$). In the sequel we only consider structures of degree $\geqslant 2$. As structures of degree 1 are quite trivial, this is without loss of generality.

Intuitively a class C of structures has *low degree* if for all $\delta > 0$, all but finitely many structures $\mathcal{A}$ of C have degree at most $|\mathcal{A}|^{\delta}$ (see [11]). More formally, C has low degree if for every $\delta \in \mathbb{Q}_{>0}$ there is an $n_\delta \in \mathbb{N}_{\geqslant 1}$ such that all structures $\mathcal{A} \in C$ of cardinality $|\mathcal{A}| \geqslant n_\delta$ have *degree*$(\mathcal{A}) \leqslant |\mathcal{A}|^{\delta}$.

For example, for every fixed number $c > 0$, the class of all structures of degree at most $(\log n)^c$ is of low degree. Clearly, an arbitrary class C of structures can be transformed into a class C' of low degree by padding each $\mathcal{A} \in C$ with a suitable number of isolated elements (i.e., elements of degree 0). Therefore classes of low degree are usually *not* closed under taking substructures. In particular if we apply the padding trick to the class of cliques, we obtain a class of low degree that is not in any of the class with known low evaluation complexity such as the "nowhere dense" case mentioned in the introduction.

Notice that *degree*$(\mathcal{A}) \leqslant |\mathcal{A}|^{\delta}$ implies that $\|\mathcal{A}\| \leqslant c{\cdot}|\mathcal{A}|^{1+\delta \cdot r}$, where r is the maximal arity of the signature and c is a number only depending on σ. Therefore all our bounds concerning databases in a class of low degree could be expressed using $|\mathcal{A}|$ instead of $\|\mathcal{A}\|$ modulo a small change of the parameters.

It is known that on classes of graphs of low degree, model checking of first-order sentences can be done in pseudo-linear time:

THEOREM 2 (GROHE [11]). *Let C be a class of structures of low degree. There is an algorithm which, on input of a structure $\mathcal{A} \in C$ and a sentence $q \in$ FO, tests in pseudo-linear time whether $\mathcal{A} \models q$.*

REMARK 3. Actually [11] proved a slightly stronger result. Let $k = |q|$. For each $\varepsilon > 0$, the algorithm of [11] runs in time $f(k){\cdot}n^{1+\varepsilon}$ if n is bigger than n_δ, where δ can be computed from k and ε, n_δ is the number given by the fact that C has low degree, and f is a *computable* function that does not depend on ε. If n is smaller than n_δ then the algorithm works in time bounded by $f(k){\cdot}n_\delta^3$. Altogether the algorithm then works in time $g(k, \varepsilon){\cdot}n^{1+\varepsilon}$ for some function g that is computable if the function associating n_δ from δ is computable. In any case it is pseudo-linear according to our definition. For readability we decided to state all our results using the pseudo-linear shorter variant but we actually prove the stronger versions as explained in this remark.

2.4 Our results

We are now ready to state our main results, which essentially lift Theorem 2 to non-boolean queries and to counting, testing, and enumerating their answers.

We start with counting the number of answers to a query.

THEOREM 4. *Let C be a class of structures of low degree. There is an algorithm that, given $\mathcal{A} \in C$ and $\varphi \in$ FO, computes $|\varphi(\mathcal{A})|$ in pseudo-linear time.*

We move to testing whether a given tuple is part of the answers.

THEOREM 5. *Let C be a class of structures of low degree. There is an algorithm that, given $\mathcal{A} \in C$ and $\varphi \in$ FO, computes in pseudo-linear time a data structure such that, on input of any $\bar{a}$, one can then test in constant time whether $\bar{a} \in \varphi(\mathcal{A})$.*

Finally, we consider enumerating the answers to a query.

THEOREM 6. *Let C be a class of structures of low degree. The enumeration problem of* FO *over C can be solved with constant delay after a pseudo-linear preprocessing.*

2.5 Further notation

We close this section by fixing technical notations that will be used throughout this paper.

For a structure $\mathcal{A}$ we write *dist*$^{\mathcal{A}}(a, b)$ for the distance between two nodes a and b of the Gaifman graph of $\mathcal{A}$. For an element $a \in$ *dom*$(\mathcal{A})$ and a number $r \in \mathbb{N}$, the *r-ball* around a is the set $N_r^{\mathcal{A}}(a)$ of all nodes $b \in$ *dom*$(\mathcal{A})$ with *dist*$^{\mathcal{A}}(a, b) \leqslant r$. The *$r$-neighbourhood* around a is the induced substructure $\mathcal{N}_r^{\mathcal{A}}(a)$ of $\mathcal{A}$ on $N_r^{\mathcal{A}}(a)$. Note that if $\mathcal{A}$ is of degree $\leqslant d$ for $d \geqslant 2$, then $|N_r^{\mathcal{A}}(a)| \leqslant \sum_{i=0}^{r} d^i < d^{r+1}$.

3. EVALUATION ALGORITHMS

In this section, we present our algorithms for counting, testing, and enumerating the solutions to a query (see Sections 3.3, 3.4, and 3.5). They all build on the same preprocessing algorithm which runs in pseudo-linear time and which essentially reduces the input to a quantifier-free query over a suitable signature (see Section 3.2). However, before presenting these algorithms, we start with a very simple case.

3.1 Warming up

As a warm-up for working with classes of structures of low degree, we first consider the simple case of queries which we call *connected conjunctive queries*, and which are defined as follows.

A *conjunction* is a query γ which is a conjunction of relational atoms and potentially negated *unary* atoms. Note that the query of Example 1 is not a conjunction as it has a binary negated atom. With each conjunction γ we associate a *query graph* H_γ. This is the undirected graph whose vertices are the variables $x_1, \ldots, x_k$ of γ, and where there is an edge between two vertices x_i and x_j iff γ contains a relational atom in which both x_i and x_j occur. We call the conjunction γ *connected* if its query graph H_γ is connected.

A *connected conjunctive query* is a query $q(\bar{x})$ of the form $\exists \bar{y}\, \gamma(\bar{x}, \bar{y})$, where γ is a *connected conjunction* in which all variables of $\bar{x}, \bar{y}$ occur (here, $|\bar{y}| = 0$ is allowed).

The next simple lemma implies that over a class of structures of low degree, connected conjunctive queries can be evaluated in pseudo-linear time. It will be used in several places throughout this paper: in the proof of Proposition 8, and in the proofs for our counting and enumeration results in Sections 3.3 and 3.5.

LEMMA 7. *There is an algorithm which, at input of a structure $\mathcal{A}$ and a connected conjunctive query $q(\bar{x})$ computes $q(\mathcal{A})$ in time $O(|q| \cdot n \cdot d^{h(|q|)})$, where $n = |dom(\mathcal{A})|$, $d = degree(\mathcal{A})$, and h is a computable function.*

PROOF. Let $q(\bar{x})$ be of the form $\exists \bar{y}\, \gamma(\bar{x}, \bar{y})$, for a connected conjunction γ. Let $k = |\bar{x}|$ be the number of free variables of q, let $\ell = |\bar{y}|$, and let $r = k + \ell$.

Note that since γ is connected, for every tuple $\bar{c} \in \gamma(\mathcal{A})$ the following is true, where a is the first component of $\bar{c}$. All components c' of $\bar{c}$ belong to the r-neighbourhood $\mathcal{N}_r^{\mathcal{A}}(a)$ of a in $dom(\mathcal{A})$. Thus, $q(\mathcal{A})$ is the disjoint union of the sets

$$S_a := \{\, \bar{b} \in q(\mathcal{N}_r^{\mathcal{A}}(a)) \ :\ \text{the first component of } \bar{b} \text{ is } a \,\},$$

for all $a \in dom(\mathcal{A})$. For each $a \in dom(\mathcal{A})$, the set S_a can be computed as follows:

(1) Initialise $S_a := \emptyset$.

(2) Compute $\mathcal{N}_r^{\mathcal{A}}(a)$.

Since $\mathcal{A}$ has degree $\leqslant d$, this neighbourhood's domain contains at most d^{r+1} elements of $dom(\mathcal{A})$. Thus, by using breadth-first search, $\mathcal{N}_r^{\mathcal{A}}(a)$ can be computed in time $O(d^{h(|q|)})$, for a computable function h.

(3) Use a brute-force algorithm that enumerates all k-tuples $\bar{b}$ of elements in $\mathcal{N}_r^{\mathcal{A}}(a)$ whose first component is a.

For each such tuple $\bar{b}$, use a brute-force algorithm that checks whether $\mathcal{N}_r^{\mathcal{A}}(a) \models q(\bar{b})$. If so, insert $\bar{b}$ into S_a

Note that the number of considered tuples $\bar{b}$ is $\leqslant d^{(r+1)(k-1)}$. And checking whether $\mathcal{N}_r^{\mathcal{A}}(a) \models q(\bar{b})$ can be done in time $O(|\gamma| \cdot d^{(r+1)\ell})$: for this, enumerate all ℓ-tuples $\bar{c}$ of elements in $\mathcal{N}_r^{\mathcal{A}}(a)$ and take time $O(|\gamma|)$ to check whether $\gamma(\bar{x}, \bar{y})$ is satisfied by the tuple $(\bar{b}, \bar{c})$.

Thus, we are done after $O(|\gamma| \cdot d^{(r^2)})$ steps.

In summary, we can compute $q(\mathcal{A}) = \bigcup_{a \in A} S_a$ in time $O(n \cdot |q| \cdot d^{h(|q|)})$, for a computable function h. □

As an immediate consequence we obtain the following:

PROPOSITION 8. *Let C be a class of structures of low degree. Given a structure $\mathcal{A} \in C$ and a connected conjunctive query q, one can compute $q(\mathcal{A})$ in pseudo-linear time.*

PROOF. We use the algorithm provided in Lemma 7. To see that the running time is as claimed, we use the assumption that C is of low degree: for every $\delta > 0$ there is an $m_\delta \in \mathbb{N}_{\geqslant 1}$ such that every structure $\mathcal{A} \in C$ of cardinality $|\mathcal{A}| \geqslant m_\delta$ has $degree(\mathcal{A}) \leqslant |\mathcal{A}|^\delta$.

For a given $\varepsilon > 0$ we let $\delta := \frac{\varepsilon}{h(|q|)}$ and define $n_\varepsilon := m_\delta$. Then, every $\mathcal{A} \in C$ with $|\mathcal{A}| \geqslant n_\varepsilon$ has $degree(\mathcal{A}) \leqslant |\mathcal{A}|^{\varepsilon/h(|q|)}$. Thus, on input of $\mathcal{A}$ and q, the algorithm from Lemma 7 has running time $O(|q| \cdot |\mathcal{A}|^{1+\varepsilon})$ if $|\mathcal{A}| \geqslant n_\varepsilon$ and takes time bounded by $O(|q| \cdot n_\varepsilon^{1+h(q)})$ otherwise. □

The method of the proof of Proposition 8 above will be used for several times in the paper.

3.2 Quantifier elimination and normal form

In this section, we make precise the quantifier elimination approach that is at the heart of the preprocessing phase of the query evaluation algorithms of our paper.

A signature is *binary* if all its relation symbols have arity at most 2. A *coloured graph* is a finite relational structure over a binary signature.

PROPOSITION 9. *There is an algorithm which, at input of a structure $\mathcal{A}$ and a first-order query $\varphi(\bar{x})$, produces a binary signature τ (containing, among other symbols, a binary relation symbol E), a coloured graph $\mathcal{G}$ of signature τ, an $\mathrm{FO}(\tau)$-formula $\psi(\bar{x})$, and a mapping f such that the following is true for $k = |\bar{x}|$, $n = |dom(\mathcal{A})|$, $d = degree(\mathcal{A})$ and h some computable function:*

1. *ψ is quantifier-free. Furthermore, ψ is of the form $(\psi_1 \wedge \psi_2)$, where ψ_1 states that no distinct free variables of ψ are connected by an E-edge, and ψ_2 is a positive boolean combination of unary atoms.*

2. *τ and ψ are computed in time and space $h(|\varphi|) \cdot n \cdot d^{h(|\varphi|)}$. Moreover, $|\tau| \leqslant h(|\varphi|)$ and $|\psi| \leqslant h(|\varphi|)$.*

3. *$\mathcal{G}$ is computed in time and space $h(|\varphi|) \cdot n \cdot d^{h(|\varphi|)}$. Moreover, $degree(\mathcal{G}) \leqslant d^{h(|\varphi|)}$.*

4. *f is an injective mapping from $dom(\mathcal{A})^k$ to $dom(\mathcal{G})^k$ such that f is a bijection between $\varphi(\mathcal{A})$ and $\psi(\mathcal{G})$.*

   Furthermore, on input of any tuple $\bar{v} \in \psi(\mathcal{G})$, the tuple $f^{-1}(\bar{v})$ can be computed in time and space $O(k^2)$.

   Using time $O(n \cdot d^{h(|\varphi|)})$ and space $O(n^2)$, we can furthermore construct a data structure such that, on input of any $\bar{a} \in dom(\mathcal{A})^k$, $f(\bar{a})$ can be computed in time $O(k^2)$.

The proof of Proposition 9 is long and technical and of a somewhat different nature than the results we now describe. It is postponed to Section 4. However, this proposition is central in the proofs of the results below.

3.3 Counting

Here we consider the problem of counting the number of solutions to a query on low degree structures.

A *generalised conjunction* is a conjunction of relational atoms and negated relational atoms (hence, also atoms of arity bigger than one may be negated, and the query of Example 1 is a generalised conjunction).

EXAMPLE 10. *Before moving to the formal proof of Theorem 4, consider again the query q from Example 1. Recall that it computes the pairs of blue-red nodes that are not connected by an edge. To count its number of solutions over a class of structures of low degree we can proceed as follows. We first consider the query $q'(x, y)$ returning the set of blue-red nodes that* are *connected. In other words, q' is*

$$B(x) \wedge R(y) \wedge E(x, y).$$

Notice that this query is a connected conjunction. Hence, by Proposition 8 its answers can be computed in pseudo-linear time and therefore we can also count its number of solutions in pseudo-linear time. It is also easy to compute in pseudo-linear time the number of pairs of blue-red nodes. The number of answers to q is then the difference between these two numbers.

The proof sketch for Theorem 4 goes as follows. Using Proposition 9 we can assume modulo a pseudo-linear preprocessing that our formula is quantifier-free and over a binary signature. Each connected component is then treated separately and we return the product of all the results. For each connected component we eliminate the negated symbols one by one using the trick illustrated in Example 10. The resulting formula is then a connected conjunction that is treated in pseudo-linear time using Proposition 8.

LEMMA 11. *There is an algorithm which, at input of a coloured graph $\mathcal{G}$ and a generalised conjunction $\gamma(\bar{x})$, computes $|\gamma(\mathcal{G})|$ in time $O(2^m \cdot |\gamma| \cdot n \cdot d^{h(|\gamma|)})$, where h is a computable function, m is the number of negated binary atoms in γ, $n = |dom(\mathcal{G})|$, and $d = degree(\mathcal{G})$.*

PROOF. By induction on the number m of *negated* binary atoms in γ. The base case for m=0 is obtained as follows. We start by using $O(|\gamma|)$ steps to compute the query graph H_γ and to compute the connected components of H_γ.

In case that H_γ is connected, we can use Lemma 7 to compute the entire set $\gamma(\mathcal{G})$ in time $O(|\gamma| \cdot n \cdot d^{h(|\gamma|)})$, for a computable function h. Thus, counting $|\gamma(\mathcal{G})|$ can be done within the same time bound.

In case that γ is not connected, let $H_1, \ldots, H_\ell$ be the connected components. For each $i \in \{1, \ldots, \ell\}$ let $\bar{x}_i$ be the tuple obtained from $\bar{x}$ by removing all variables that do not belong to H_i. Furthermore, let $\gamma_i(\bar{x}_i)$ be the conjunction of all atoms or negated unary atoms of γ that contain variables in H_i. Note that $\gamma(\bar{x})$ is equivalent to $\bigwedge_{i=1}^{\ell} \gamma_i(\bar{x}_i)$, and

$$|\gamma(\mathcal{G})| \quad = \quad \prod_{i=1}^{\ell} |\gamma_i(\mathcal{G})|.$$

Since each γ_i is connected, we can compute $|\gamma_i(\mathcal{G})|$ in time $O(|\gamma_i| \cdot n \cdot d^{h(|\gamma_i|)})$ by using the algorithm of Lemma 7. We do this for each $i \in \{1, \ldots, \ell\}$ and output the product of the values. In summary, we are done in time $O(|\gamma| \cdot n \cdot d^{h(|\gamma|)})$ for the base case $m = 0$.

For the induction step, let γ be a formula with m+1 negated binary atoms. Let $\neg R(x, y)$ be a negated binary atom of γ, and let γ_1 be such that

$$\gamma \quad = \quad \gamma_1 \wedge \neg R(x, y), \qquad \text{and let}$$
$$\gamma_2 \quad := \quad \gamma_1 \wedge R(x, y).$$

Clearly, $|\gamma(\mathcal{G})| = |\gamma_1(\mathcal{G})| - |\gamma_2(\mathcal{G})|$. Since each of the formulas γ_1 and γ_2 has only m negated binary atoms, we can use the induction hypothesis to compute $|\gamma_1(\mathcal{G})|$ and $|\gamma_2(\mathcal{G})|$ each in time $O(2^m \cdot |\gamma| \cdot n \cdot d^{h(|\gamma|)})$. The total time used for computing $|\gamma(\mathcal{G})|$ is thus $O(2^{m+1} \cdot |\gamma| \cdot n \cdot d^{h(|\gamma|)})$. □

By using Proposition 9, we can lift this to arbitrary structures and first-order queries:

PROPOSITION 12. *There is an algorithm which at input of a structure $\mathcal{A}$ and a first-order query $\varphi(\bar{x})$ computes $|\varphi(\mathcal{A})|$ in time $h(|\varphi|) \cdot n \cdot d^{h(|\varphi|)}$, for a computable function h, where $n = |dom(\mathcal{A})|$ and $d = degree(\mathcal{A})$.*

PROOF. We first use the algorithm of Proposition 9 to compute the according graph $\mathcal{G}$ and the quantifier-free formula $\psi(\bar{x})$. This takes time $h(|\varphi|) \cdot n \cdot d^{h(|\varphi|}$ for a computable function h. And we also know that $|\psi| \leqslant h(|\varphi|)$. By Proposition 9 we know that $|\varphi(\mathcal{A})| = |\psi(\mathcal{G})|$.

Next, we transform $\psi(\bar{x})$ into disjunctive normal form

$$\bigvee_{i \in I} \gamma_i(\bar{x}),$$

such that the conjunctive clauses γ_i exclude each other (i.e., for each $\bar{v} \in \psi(\mathcal{G})$ there is exactly one $i \in I$ such that $\bar{v} \in \gamma_i(\mathcal{G})$). Clearly, this can be done in time $O(2^{|\psi|})$. Each γ_i has length at most $|\psi|$, and $|I| \leqslant 2^{|\psi|}$.

Obviously, $|\psi(\mathcal{G})| = \sum_{i \in I} |\gamma_i(\mathcal{G})|$. We now use, for each $i \in I$, the algorithm from Lemma 11 to compute the number $s_i = |\gamma_i(\mathcal{G})|$ and output the value $s = \sum_{i \in I} s_i$.

By Lemma 11 we know that for each $i \in I$ the computation of s_i can be done in time $O(2^m \cdot |\gamma_i| \cdot \tilde{n} \cdot \tilde{d}^{h_0(|\gamma_i|)})$, where m is the number of binary atoms in γ, $\tilde{n} = |dom(\mathcal{G})|$, $\tilde{d} = degree(\mathcal{G})$, and h_0 is some computable function.

By Proposition 9 we know that $\tilde{n} \leqslant h(|\varphi|) \cdot n \cdot d^{h(|\varphi|)}$ and $\tilde{d} \leqslant d^{h(|\varphi|)}$. Since also $|\gamma_i| \leqslant |\psi| \leqslant h(|\varphi|)$, the computation of s_i, for each $i \in I$, takes time $h_1(|\varphi|) \cdot n \cdot d^{h_1(|\varphi|)}$, for some computable function h_1 (depending on h and h_0).

To conclude, since $|I| \leqslant 2^{|\psi|}$, the total running time for computing $|\varphi(\mathcal{A})| = \sum_{i \in I} s_i$ is $h_2(|\varphi|) \cdot n \cdot d^{h_2(|\varphi|)}$, for a suitably chosen computable function h_2. Hence, we meet the required bound. □

Theorem 4 is an immediate consequence of Proposition 12 (following the arguments of the proof of Proposition 8).

3.4 Testing

Here we consider the problem of testing whether a given tuple is a solution to a query. By Proposition 9 it is enough to consider quantifier-free formulas. Those are treated using the lazy array initialisation technique mentioned in Section 2.

PROPOSITION 13. *There is an algorithm which at input of a structure $\mathcal{A}$ and a first-order query $\varphi(\bar{x})$, has a preprocessing phase of time $h(|\varphi|) \cdot n \cdot d^{h(|\varphi|)}$ in which it computes a data structure such that, on input of any $\bar{a} \in dom(\mathcal{A})^k$ for $k = |\bar{x}|$, it can be tested in time $h(|\varphi|)$ whether $\bar{a} \in \varphi(\mathcal{A})$, where h is a computable function, $n = |dom(\mathcal{A})|$, and $d = degree(\mathcal{A})$.*

PROOF. We first use the algorithm of Proposition 9 to compute the graph $\mathcal{G}$, the quantifier-free formula $\psi(\bar{x})$ and the data structure for function f. For some computable function h, this takes time and space $h(|\varphi|){\cdot}n{\cdot}d^{h(|\varphi|)}$, and furthermore, $|\psi| \leqslant h(|\varphi|)$ and $degree(\mathcal{G}) \leqslant d^{h(|\varphi|)}$. Note that $\|\mathcal{G}\| \leqslant h(|\varphi|){\cdot}n{\cdot}d^{h(|\varphi|)}$. By construction, we furthermore know for all $\bar{a} \in dom(\mathcal{A})^k$ that $\bar{a} \in \varphi(\mathcal{A}) \iff f(\bar{a}) \in \psi(\mathcal{G})$.

Recall from Proposition 9 that $\psi(\bar{x})$ is a quantifier-free formula built from atoms of the form $E(y,z)$ and $C(y)$ for unary relation symbols C. Thus, checking whether a given tuple $\bar{v} \in dom(\mathcal{G})^k$ belongs to $\psi(\mathcal{G})$ can be done easily, provided that one can check whether unary atoms $C(u)$ and binary atoms $E(u,u')$ hold in $\mathcal{G}$ for given nodes u, u' of $\mathcal{G}$.

To enable checking whether $E(u,u')$ holds in $\mathcal{G}$, we construct the following data structure. W.l.o.g. we assume that $dom(\mathcal{G}) = \{1,\dots,\tilde{n}\}$ for

$$\tilde{n} := |dom(\mathcal{G})| \leqslant \|\mathcal{G}\| \leqslant h(|\varphi|){\cdot}n{\cdot}d^{h(|\varphi|)}.$$

We use an $(\tilde{n} \times \tilde{n})$-array A_E that is initialised to 0. By looping through all edges $E(u,u')$ of $\mathcal{G}$, we then update the array entry $A_E[u,u']$ to 1. This way, using time $O(\|\mathcal{G}\|)$, we ensure that for all nodes u, u' of $\mathcal{G}$ we have $A_E[u,u'] = 1$ if $E(u,u')$ holds in $\mathcal{G}$, and $A_E[u,u'] = 0$ otherwise.

In a similar way, within time $O(\|\mathcal{G}\|)$ we can build, for each unary relation symbol C, a 1-dimensional array A_C of length $\tilde{n}$ such that for all nodes u of $\mathcal{G}$ we have $A_C[u] = 1$ if $C(u)$ holds in $\mathcal{G}$, and $A_C[u] = 0$ otherwise.

All these arrays are constructed in time $O(\|\mathcal{G}\|)$, which is $O(h(|\varphi|){\cdot}n{\cdot}d^{h(|\varphi|)})$. This completes the preprocessing phase.

Note that using the arrays A_E and A_C, testing whether a given tuple $\bar{v} \in dom(\mathcal{G})^k$ belongs to $\psi(\mathcal{G})$ can be done in time $O(|\psi|)$, since each atomic statement of ψ can be checked in constant time by a simple look-up of the according array entry.

Finally, the testing algorithm works as follows. Given a tuple $\bar{a} \in dom(\mathcal{A})^k$, we first construct $\bar{v} := f(\bar{a})$ and then check whether $\bar{v} \in \psi(\mathcal{G})$. Building $\bar{v} := f(\bar{a})$ can be done in time $O(k^2)$ (see Proposition 9), and checking whether $\bar{v} \in \psi(\mathcal{G})$ requires time $O(|\psi|)$, which is $O(h(|\varphi|))$. Hence, we meet the required bound for testing. □

Theorem 5 is an immediate consequence of Proposition 13 (following the arguments of the proof of Proposition 8).

3.5 Enumeration

Here we consider the problem of enumerating the solutions to a given query. We first illustrate the proof of Theorem 6 with our running example.

EXAMPLE 14. *Consider again the query q of Example 1. In order to enumerate q with constant delay over a class of low degree we proceed as follows. During the preprocessing phase we precompute those blue nodes that contribute to the answer set, i.e. such that there is a red node not connected to it. This is doable in pseudo-linear time because our class has low degree and each blue node is connected to few red nodes. We call green the resulting nodes. We then order the green nodes and the red nodes in order to be able to iterate through them with constant delay. Finally, we compute the binary function $skip(x,y)$ associating to each green node x and red node y such that $E(x,y)$ the smallest red node y' such that $y < y'$ and $\neg E(x,y')$, where $<$ is the order on red nodes precomputed above. From Proposition 8 it follows that computing skip can be done in pseudo-linear time. It is crucial here that the domain of skip has pseudo-linear size.*

The enumeration phase now goes as follows: We iterate through all green nodes. For each of them we iterate through all red nodes. If there is no edge between them, we output the result and continue with the next red node. If there is an edge, we apply skip to this pair and the process continues with the resulting red node. Note that the new red node immediately yields an answer. Note also that all the red nodes that will not be considered are safely skipped as they are linked to the current green node.

The proof of Theorem 6 can be sketched as follows. By Proposition 9 it is enough to consider quantifier-free formulas looking for tuples of nodes that are disconnected and have certain colours. Hence the query q described in Example 1 corresponds to the binary case. For queries of larger arities we proceed by induction on the arity. By induction we can enumerate the answers of the query projecting out the last variable from the initial query. For each tuple $\bar{u}$ obtained by induction, we iterate through all the red nodes that are a potential completion. We then proceed as in Example 14. If the current red node a is not connected to $\bar{u}$, then $\bar{u}a$ forms an answer and we proceed to the next red node. If a is connected to $\bar{u}$ then we need to jump in constant time to the next red node that yields an answer. This is done by precomputing a suitable function *skip* that depends on the arity of the query and is slightly more complex that the one described in Example 14. The design and computation of this function is the main technical originality of the proof.

We now turn to the technical details that are summarised in the next proposition.

PROPOSITION 15. *There is an algorithm which at input of a structure $\mathcal{A}$ and a first-order query $\varphi(\bar{x})$ enumerates $\varphi(\mathcal{A})$ with delay $h(\varphi)$ after a preprocessing of time $h(\varphi){\cdot}n{\cdot}d^{h(\varphi)}$, where $n = |dom(\mathcal{A})|$, $d = degree(\mathcal{A})$, and h is a computable function.*

PROOF. The proof is by induction on the number $k := |\bar{x}|$ of free variables of φ. In case that $k = 0$, the formula φ is a sentence, and we are done using Theorem 2. In case that $k > 0$ we proceed as follows.

We first use the algorithm of Proposition 9 to compute the according coloured graph $\mathcal{G}$ and the quantifier-free formula $\psi(\bar{x})$. This takes time $g(|\varphi|){\cdot}n{\cdot}d^{g(|\varphi|)}$ for a computable function g. And we know that $|\psi| \leqslant g(|\varphi|)$, that $\mathcal{G}$ has degree $\tilde{d} \leqslant d^{g(|\varphi|)}$, and that $dom(\mathcal{G})$ has $\tilde{n}$ elements, where $\tilde{n} \leqslant g(|\varphi|){\cdot}n{\cdot}d^{g(|\varphi|)}$.

From Item 1 of Proposition 9 we know that the formula $\psi(\bar{x})$ is of the form $(\psi_1 \wedge \psi_2)$, where ψ_1 states that no distinct free variables of ψ are connected by an E-edge and ψ_2 is a positive boolean combination of unary atoms.

We let $\bar{x} = (x_1,\dots,x_k)$. In case that $k = 1$, $\psi(x_1) = \psi_2(x_1)$ is a positive boolean combination of unary atoms. We can use Lemma 7 for each unary atom in order to compute $\psi(\mathcal{G})$ in time $O(|\psi|{\cdot}\tilde{n}{\cdot}\tilde{d}^{g(|\psi|)})$ for a computable function g. This is time $h(\varphi){\cdot}n{\cdot}d^{h(\varphi)}$, for a computable function h, and can thus be done during the preprocessing phase. In the enumeration phase, we then simply loop through the list of all elements in $\bar{v} \in \psi(\mathcal{G})$, compute $\bar{a} := f^{-1}(\bar{v})$, and output $\bar{a}$. Due to Item 4 of Proposition 9, the delay is $O(k^2)$, and we are done.

The case for $k \geqslant 2$ requires much more elaborate constructions. We let $\bar{x}_{k-1} := (x_1,\dots,x_{k-1})$. To enable enumeration of $\psi(\mathcal{G})$ (and hence also $\varphi(\mathcal{A})$, by translating each result $\bar{v} \in \psi(\mathcal{G})$ to $\bar{a} := f^{-1}(\bar{v})$), we first transform ψ into a normal form $\bigvee_{j\in J} \theta_j(\bar{x})$ such that the formulas θ_j exclude each other (i.e., for each $\bar{v} \in \psi(\mathcal{G})$ there is exactly one $j \in J$ such that $\bar{v} \in \theta_j(\mathcal{G})$), and each $\theta_j(\bar{x})$ is of the form

$$\phi_j(\bar{x}_{k-1}) \land P_j(x_k) \land \gamma(\bar{x}), \qquad \text{where}$$

$$\gamma(\bar{x}) := \bigwedge_{i=1}^{k-1} \big(\neg E(x_i, x_k) \land \neg E(x_k, x_i)\big),$$

$P_j(x_k)$ is a boolean combination of unary atoms regarding x_k, and $\phi_j(\bar{x}_{k-1})$ is a formula with only $k{-}1$ free variables. Note that the transformation into this normal form can be done easily, using the particularly simple form of the formula ψ.

Clearly, we can enumerate $\psi(\mathcal{G})$ by enumerating $\theta_j(\mathcal{G})$ for each $j \in J$. In the following, we therefore restrict attention to the enumeration of $\theta_j(\mathcal{G})$ for a fixed $j \in J$. For θ_j we shortly write

$$\theta(\bar{x}) = \phi(\bar{x}_{k-1}) \land P(x_k) \land \gamma(\bar{x}).$$

We let $\theta'(\bar{x}_{k-1}) := \exists x_k\, \theta(\bar{x})$. By the induction hypothesis (since θ' only has $k{-}1$ free variables), we can enumerate $\theta'(\mathcal{G})$ with delay $h(\theta')$ after a preprocessing phase of time $h(\theta')\cdot\tilde{n}\cdot\tilde{d}^{h(\theta')}$.

Since $P(x_k)$ is a boolean combination of unary atoms on x_k, we can use Lemma 7 to compute $P(\mathcal{G})$ in time $O(|P|\cdot\tilde{n}\cdot\tilde{d}^{g(|P|)})$ for a computable function g. Afterwards, we have available a list of all nodes v of $\mathcal{G}$ that belong to $P(\mathcal{G})$. In the following, we will write $\leqslant^P$ to denote the linear ordering of $P(\mathcal{G})$ induced by this list, and we write *first*^{P} for the first element in this list, and *next*^{P} for the successor function, such that for any node $v \in P(\mathcal{G})$, *next*$^P(v)$ is the next node in $P(\mathcal{G})$ in this list (or the value *void*, if v is the last node in the list).

We extend the signature of $\mathcal{G}$ by a unary relation symbol P and a binary relation symbol *next*, and let $\hat{\mathcal{G}}$ be the expansion of $\mathcal{G}$ where P is interpreted by the set $P(\mathcal{G})$ and *next* is interpreted by the successor function *next*^{P} (i.e., *next*(v, v') is true in $\hat{\mathcal{G}}$ iff $v' = \textit{next}^P(v)$). Note that $\hat{\mathcal{G}}$ has degree $\hat{d} = \tilde{d}{+}2$, which is $\leqslant d^{g(|\varphi|)}$ for a computable function g.

We now start the key idea of the proof, i.e., the function that will help us skipping over irrelevant nodes. To this end consider the first-order formulas $E_1, \ldots, E_k$ defined inductively as follows, where $E'(x, y)$ is an abbreviation for $(E(x, y) \lor E(y, x))$. The reason for defining these formulas will become clear only later on, in the proof of Claim 1.

$$E_1(u, y) := P(y) \land E'(u, y), \qquad \text{and}$$

$$E_{i+1}(u, y) := E_i(u, y) \lor \exists z \exists z' \exists v\, \big(E'(z, u) \land \textit{next}(z', z) \land E'(v, z') \land E_i(v, y)\big).$$

A simple induction shows that for $E_i(u, y)$ to hold, y must be at distance $\leqslant 3(i{-}1) + 1 < 3i$ from u.

In our enumeration algorithm we will have to test, given nodes $u, v \in \textit{dom}(\mathcal{G})$, whether $(u, v) \in E_k(\hat{\mathcal{G}})$. Since E_k is a first-order formula, Theorem 5 implies that, after preprocessing time $g'(|E_k|)\cdot\tilde{n}\cdot\hat{d}^{g'(|E_k|)}$ (for some computable function g'), testing membership in $E_k(\hat{\mathcal{G}})$, for any given $(u, v) \in \textit{dom}(\mathcal{G})^2$, is possible within time $g'(|E_k|)$.

By our knowledge on the formula E_k and the size of the parameters $\tilde{n}$ and $\hat{d}$ we know that the preprocessing time is bounded by $g''(|\varphi|)\cdot n\cdot d^{g''(|\varphi|)}$, for a suitable computable function g'', and that each membership test can be done in time $g''(|\varphi|)$.

The last step of the precomputation phase computes the function *skip* that associates to each node $y \in P(\mathcal{G})$ and each set V of at most $k{-}1$ nodes that are related to y via E_k, the smallest (according to the order $\leqslant^P$ of $P(\mathcal{G})$) element $z \geqslant^P y$ in $P(\mathcal{G})$ that is *not* connected by an E-edge to any node in V. More precisely: For any node $y \in P(\mathcal{G})$ and any set V with $0 \leqslant |V| < k$ and $(v, y) \in E_k(\hat{\mathcal{G}})$ for all $v \in V$, we let

$$\textit{skip}(y, V) := \min\{z \in P(\mathcal{G}) : y \leqslant^P z \text{ and } \forall v \in V : (v, z) \notin E(\mathcal{G}) \text{ and } (z, v) \notin E(\mathcal{G})\},$$

respectively, *skip*$(y, V) :=$ *void* if no such z exists.

Notice that the nodes of V are related to y via E_k and hence are at distance $< 3k$ from y. Hence for each y, we only need to consider at most $\hat{d}^{(3k^2)}$ such sets V.

For each set V, *skip*(y, V) can be computed by running consecutively through all nodes $z \geqslant^P y$ in the list $P(\mathcal{G})$ and test whether $\big(E(z, v) \lor E(v, z)\big)$ holds for some $v \in V$. To perform the latter test in constant time, we precompute an $(\tilde{n}\times\tilde{n})$-array A_E such that $A_E[z, v] = 1$ if $(z, v) \in E^{\mathcal{G}}$, and $A_E[z, v] = 0$ otherwise, in the same way as in the proof of Theorem 5.

Since $|V| \leqslant k$ and each $v \in V$ is of degree at most $\tilde{d}$ in $\mathcal{G}$, the value *skip*(y, V) can be found in time $O(k^2\cdot\tilde{d})$. Therefore, the entire *skip*-function can be computed, and stored in an array, in time $O(\tilde{n}\cdot\hat{d}^{(3k^2)}\cdot g''(|\varphi|)\cdot k^2\cdot\tilde{d})$, which is time $g(|\varphi|)\cdot n\cdot d^{g(|\varphi|)}$ for a suitable computable function g. During the enumeration phase we will use this array such that for given y and V, the value *skip*(y, V) can be looked-up within constant time.

We are now done with the preprocessing phase. Altogether it took

1. the time to compute ψ and $\mathcal{G}$, which is $g(|\varphi|)\cdot n\cdot d^{g(|\varphi|)}$, for a computable function g

2. the time to compute $\bigvee_{j\in J}\theta_j$, which is $g(|\varphi|)$, for a computable function g

3. for each $j \in J$ and $\theta := \theta_j$, it took

   (a) the preprocessing time for enumerating $\theta'(\mathcal{G})$, which is $h(\theta')\cdot\tilde{n}\cdot\tilde{d}^{h(\theta')}$, for the computable function h in the Proposition's statement

   (b) the time for computing $P(\mathcal{G})$, which is $g(|\varphi|)\cdot n\cdot d^{g(|\varphi|)}$, for a computable function g

   (c) the preprocessing time for testing membership in $E_k(\hat{\mathcal{G}})$ and for producing the array A_E, which can be done in time $g(|\varphi|)\cdot n\cdot d^{g(|\varphi|)}$, for a computable function g

   (d) and the time for computing the *skip*-function, which is $g(|\varphi|)\cdot n\cdot d^{g(|\varphi|)}$, for a computable function g.

It is straightforward to see that, by suitably choosing the computable function h, all the preprocessing steps can be done within time $h(\varphi)\cdot n\cdot d^{h(\varphi)}$.

We now turn to the enumeration phase. We will describe how to enumerate $\theta(\mathcal{G})$ with delay $h(\varphi)$. Note that this will immediately lead to the desired enumeration algorithm for $\varphi(\mathcal{G})$ by doing the following: Loop through all $j \in J$ to enumerate $\theta_j(\mathcal{G})$; however, instead of outputting a tuple $\bar{v} \in \theta_j(\mathcal{G})$, compute the tuple $\bar{a} := f^{-1}(\bar{v})$ and output $\bar{a}$.

In the rest of this proof, we will therefore restrict attention to enumerating $\theta(\mathcal{G})$. We first describe the enumeration algorithm, then analyse its running time, and finally prove that it outputs, without repetition, all the tuples in $\theta(\mathcal{G})$.

Algorithm for enumerating $\theta(\mathcal{G})$:

1. Let $\bar{u}$ be the first output produced in the enumeration of $\theta'(\mathcal{G})$.
   If $\bar{u} = void$ then STOP with output *void*,
   else let $(u_1, \dots, u_{k-1}) = \bar{u}$ and goto line 2.
2. Let $y := first^P$ be the first element in the list $P(\mathcal{G})$.
3. Let $V := \{v \in \{u_1, \dots, u_{k-1}\} : (v, y) \in E_k(\hat{\mathcal{G}})\}$.
4. Let $z := skip(y, V)$.
5. If $z \neq void$ then OUTPUT $(\bar{u}, z)$ and goto line 9.
6. If $z = void$ then
   7. Let $\bar{u}'$ be the next output produced in the enumeration of $\theta'(\mathcal{G})$.
   8. If $\bar{u}' = void$ then STOP with output *void*,
      else let $\bar{u} := \bar{u}'$ and goto line 2.
9. Let $y := next^P(z)$.
10. If $y = void$ then goto line 7, else goto line 3.

Note that the algorithm never outputs any tuple more than once. Before proving that this algorithm enumerates exactly the tuples in $\theta(\mathcal{G})$, let us first show that it operates with delay at most $h(\varphi)$.

By the induction hypothesis, the execution of line 1 and and each execution of line 7 takes time at most $h(\theta')$. Furthermore, each execution of line 3 takes time $(k-1) \cdot g'(|E_k|)$. Concerning the remaining lines of the algorithm, each execution can be done in time $O(1)$.

Furthermore, before outputting the first tuple, the algorithm executes at most 5 lines (namely, lines 1–5; note that by our choice of the formula θ' we know that when entering line 5 before outputting the first tuple, it is guaranteed that $z \neq void$, hence an output tuple is generated).

Between outputting two consecutive tuples, the algorithm executes at most 12 lines (the worst case is an execution of lines 9, 10, 3, 4, 5, 6, 7, 8, 2, 3, 4, 5; again, by our choice of the formula θ', at the last execution of line 5 it is guaranteed that $z \neq void$, hence an output tuple is generated).

Therefore, by suitably choosing the function h, we obtain that the algorithm enumerates with delay at most $h(\varphi)$.

Concerning the correctness of the output, let us first show that every tuple $(\bar{u}, z)$ that is produced as an output, does belong to $\theta(\mathcal{G})$:

Recall that $\theta(\bar{x}) = \phi(\bar{x}_{k-1}) \wedge P(x_k) \wedge \gamma(\bar{x})$. We know that $\bar{u} \in \theta'(\mathcal{G})$, and thus, in particular, $\phi(\bar{u})$ is satisfied.

Furthermore, if the tuple $(\bar{u}, z)$ is output in line 5 (this is the only OUTPUT instruction present in the algorithm), we know that $V = \{v \in \{u_1, \dots, u_{k-1}\} : (v, y) \in E_k(\hat{\mathcal{G}})\}$ and $z = skip(y, V)$. Hence, z belongs to $P(\mathcal{G})$, and we know that z is not connected by an E-edge to any node in V. By the next claim (Claim 1) we obtain that z is not connected by an E-edge to any node in $\{u_1, \dots, u_{k-1}\}$, and hence $\gamma(\bar{u}, z)$ is satisfied and the tuple $(\bar{u}, z)$ belongs to $\theta(\mathcal{G})$. This is the key of our enumeration algorithm.

CLAIM 1. *Let U be a set of at most $k-1$ nodes of $\mathcal{G}$. Let $y \in P(\mathcal{G})$, let $V := \{v \in U : (v, y) \in E_k(\hat{\mathcal{G}})\}$, and let $z := skip(y, V) \neq void$. Then,*

$$z = \min\{w \in P(\mathcal{G}) \;:\; y \leqslant^P w \text{ and } \forall u \in U : (u, w) \notin E(\mathcal{G}) \text{ and } (w, u) \notin E(\mathcal{G})\}.$$

PROOF OF CLAIM 1. By definition of *skip*(y, V) we have

$$z = \min\{z \in P(\mathcal{G}) \;:\; y \leqslant^P z \text{ and } \forall v \in V : (v, z) \notin E(\mathcal{G}) \text{ and } (z, v) \notin E(\mathcal{G})\}.$$

Since $V \subseteq U$, we thus know that

$$z \leqslant^P \min\{w \in P(\mathcal{G}) \;:\; y \leqslant^P w \text{ and } \forall u \in U : (u, w) \notin E(\mathcal{G}) \text{ and } (w, u) \notin E(\mathcal{G})\}.$$

All that remains to be done is to show that for all $u \in U \setminus V$ we have $(u, z) \notin E(\mathcal{G})$ and $(z, u) \notin E(\mathcal{G})$.

In case that $z = y$, this is true because $U \setminus V$ only contains vertices that are *not* connected to y by an E_k-edge, and hence also not connected to y by an E-edge.

In case that $z \neq y$, we know that $y <^P z$, and thus $y \leqslant^P z' <^P z$ for the immediate predecessor z' of z, i.e., the node $z' \in P(\mathcal{G})$ with $next^P(z') = z$.

For contradiction, assume that for some $u \in U \setminus V$ we have $(u, z) \in E(\mathcal{G})$ or $(z, u) \in E(\mathcal{G})$. Thus, $E'(z, u)$ is satisfied in $\hat{\mathcal{G}}$. Also, $next(z', z)$ is satisfied in $\hat{\mathcal{G}}$. Since $y \leqslant^P z' <^P z$ (i.e., z' is skipped by *skip*(y, V)), we furthermore know that z' is connected by an E-edge to some node $v \in V$, i.e., $E'(v, z')$ is true in $\hat{\mathcal{G}}$.

Assume now that also $E_{k-1}(v, y)$ is true in $\hat{\mathcal{G}}$. Recalling the definition of the formula E_k, note that we thus have found witnesses showing that $E_k(u, y)$ holds in $\hat{\mathcal{G}}$, i.e., $(u, y) \in E_k(\hat{\mathcal{G}})$. This, however, implies that $u \in V$, contradicting the assumption that $u \in U \setminus V$.

To conclude the proof of Claim 1 it remains to show that $E_{k-1}(v, y)$ is indeed true in $\hat{\mathcal{G}}$, i.e., $(v, y) \in E_{k-1}(\hat{\mathcal{G}})$. To this end, for all $j \leqslant k$, let $V_j := \{v' \in V : (v', y) \in E_j(\hat{\mathcal{G}})\}$. Clearly, $V_k = V$. By the choice of the formulas E_j we know that $\emptyset \subseteq V_1 \subseteq \dots \subseteq V_k$. Moreover, it is straightforward to see that the definition of the formulas $E_1, \dots, E_k$ ensures that the following is true: if $V_j = V_{j+1}$, for some $j < k$, then $V_j = \dots = V_k$. Thus, there is a $j \leqslant k$ such that

$$(*): \qquad \emptyset \subseteq V_1 \subsetneq \dots \subsetneq V_j = \dots = V_k = V.$$

Since $V \subseteq U$, $|U| \leqslant k-1$, and $u \in U \setminus V$, we know that $|V| \leqslant k-2$. Hence, $(*)$ implies that $j \leqslant k-1$. Thus, $V_{k-1} = V$. Since $v \in V$, we therefore obtain that v belongs to V_{k-1}, i.e., $E_{k-1}(v, y)$ is true in $\hat{\mathcal{G}}$. This completes the proof of Claim 1. □

To finish the proof of Proposition 15, we need to verify that every tuple in $\theta(\mathcal{G})$ is eventually output by the algorithm. Let $(u_1, \dots, u_k)$ be an arbitrary tuple in $\theta(\mathcal{G})$. Then, in particular, for $\bar{u} := (u_1, \dots, u_{k-1})$, we have that $\bar{u} \in \theta'(\mathcal{G})$, Thus, by the induction hypothesis, the enumeration algorithm for θ' will eventually output the tuple $\bar{u}$. Let $z_1 <^P \dots <^P z_m$ be an ordered list of all elements such that the enumeration algorithm for $\theta(\mathcal{G})$ outputs the tuple $(\bar{u}, z_i)$ for $i \in \{1, \dots, m\}$. Clearly, it suffices to show that u_k is one of the z_i's.

Let $U := \{u_1, \dots, u_{k-1}\}$. Since $(\bar{u}, u_k) \in \theta(\mathcal{G})$ we, in particular, have that $u_k \in P(\mathcal{G})$ and u_k is not connected to any $u \in U$ by an E-edge.

In case that $u_k \leqslant^P z_1$, by construction of the algorithm we know that $z_1 = skip(y, V)$ for $y := first^P$. By Claim 1, we furthermore know that z_1 is the *minimum* element $w \in P(\mathcal{G})$ with $y \leqslant^P w$, which is not connected to any $u \in U$ by an E-edge. Thus, $z_1 \leqslant^P u_k$, and hence $u_k = z_1$.

In case that $z_{i-1} <^P u_k \leqslant^P z_i$, we know for $y := next^P(z_{i-1})$ that $z_i = skip(y, V)$. Since $y \leqslant^P u_k$, we obtain from Claim 1 that $z_i \leqslant^P u_k$, and hence $u_k = z_i$.

The case that $z_m <^P u_k$ cannot occur since, by construction of the algorithm, the following is true: Either z_m is the largest element w.r.t. $\leqslant^P$ or for the element $y := \mathit{next}^P(z_m)$, we have $\mathit{skip}(y, V) = \mathit{void}$, whereas according to the definition of the *skip*-function, $\mathit{skip}(y, V)$ would have to be an element $\leqslant^P u_k$. This concludes the proof of Proposition 15

Theorem 6 follows immediately from Proposition 15 (following again the arguments of the proof of Proposition 8).

4. PROOF OF QUANTIFIER ELIMINATION AND NORMAL FORM

This section is devoted to the proof of Proposition 9. The proof consists of several steps, the first of which relies on a transformation of $\varphi(\bar{x})$ into an equivalent formula in Gaifman normal form, i.e., a boolean combination of basic-local sentences and formulas that are local around $\bar{x}$. A formula $\lambda(\bar{x})$ is *r-local* around $\bar{x}$ (for some $r \geqslant 0$) if every quantifier is relativized to the r-neighbourhood of $\bar{x}$. A *basic-local sentence* is of the form

$$\exists y_1 \cdots \exists y_\ell \bigwedge_{1\leqslant i<j\leqslant \ell} \mathit{dist}(y_i, y_j) > 2r \ \wedge\ \bigwedge_{i=1}^{\ell} \theta(y_i),$$

where $\theta(y)$ is r-local around y. By Gaifman's well-known theorem we obtain an algorithm that transforms an input formula $\varphi(\bar{x})$ into an equivalent formula in Gaifman normal form [9].

The rest of the proof can be sketched as follows. Basic-local sentences can be evaluated on structures of low degree in pseudo-linear time by Theorem 2, so it remains to treat formulas that are local around their free variables. By the Feferman-Vaught Theorem (cf., e.g. [17]), we can further decompose local formulas into formulas that are local around *one* of their free variables. The latter turns out to have a small answer set that can be precomputed in pseudo-linear time. The remaining time is used to compute the structures useful for reconstructing the initial answers from their components. We now give the details.

PROOF OF PROPOSITION 9.
Step 1: transform $\varphi(\bar{x})$ into a local formula $\varphi'(\bar{x})$.

We first transform $\varphi(\bar{x})$ into an equivalent formula $\varphi^G(\bar{x})$ in Gaifman normal form. For each basic-local sentence χ occurring in $\varphi^G(\bar{x})$, check whether $\mathcal{A} \models \chi$ and let $\chi' := \mathit{true}$ if $\mathcal{A} \models \chi$ and $\chi' := \mathit{false}$ if $\mathcal{A} \not\models \chi$. Let $\varphi'(\bar{x})$ be the formula obtained from $\varphi^G(\bar{x})$ by replacing every basic-local sentence χ occurring in $\varphi^G(\bar{x})$ with χ'. By using Gaifman's theorem and Theorem 2, all this can be done in time and space $O(h(|\varphi|){\cdot}n{\cdot}d^{h(|\varphi|)})$, for a computable function h.

Clearly, for every $\bar{a} \in \mathit{dom}(\mathcal{A})^k$ we have $\mathcal{A} \models \varphi'(\bar{a})$ iff $\mathcal{A} \models \varphi(\bar{a})$. Note that there is a number $r \geqslant 0$ such that $\varphi'(\bar{x})$ is r-local around $\bar{x}$, and this number can easily be computed given $\varphi^G(\bar{x})$.

Step 2: transform $\varphi'(\bar{x})$ into a disjunction $\bigvee_{P\in\mathcal{P}} \psi'_P(\bar{x})$.

Let $\bar{x} = (x_1, \ldots, x_k)$. A *partition* of the set $\{1, \ldots, k\}$ is a list $P = (P_1, \ldots, P_\ell)$ with $1 \leqslant \ell \leqslant k$ such that

- $\emptyset \neq P_j \subseteq \{1, \ldots, k\}$, for every $j \in \{1, \ldots, \ell\}$,
- $P_1 \cup \cdots \cup P_\ell = \{1, \ldots, k\}$,
- $P_j \cap P_{j'} = \emptyset$, for all $j, j' \in \{1, \ldots, \ell\}$ with $j \neq j'$,
- $\min P_j < \min P_{j+1}$, for all $j \in \{1, \ldots, \ell{-}1\}$.

Let $\mathcal{P}$ be the set of all partitions of $\{1, \ldots, k\}$. Clearly, $|\mathcal{P}| \leqslant k!$. For each $P = (P_1, \ldots, P_\ell) \in \mathcal{P}$ and each $j \leqslant \ell$ let $\bar{x}_{P_j}$ be the tuple obtained from $\bar{x}$ by deleting all those x_i with $i \notin P_j$.

For every partition $P = (P_1, \ldots, P_\ell) \in \mathcal{P}$ let $\varrho_P(\bar{x})$ be an FO(σ)-formula stating that each of the following is true:

1. The r-neighbourhood around $\bar{x}$ in $\mathcal{A}$ is the disjoint union of the r-neighbourhoods around $\bar{x}_{P_j}$ for $j \leqslant \ell$. I.e., $\delta_P(\bar{x}) :=$

$$\bigwedge_{1\leqslant j<j'\leqslant \ell}\ \bigwedge_{(i,i')\in P_j\times P_{j'}} \mathit{dist}(x_i, x_{i'}) > 2r{+}1.$$

2. For each $j \leqslant \ell$, the r-neighbourhood around $\bar{x}_{P_j}$ in $\mathcal{A}$ is connected, i.e., satisfies the formula $\gamma_{P_j}(\bar{x}_{P_j}) :=$

$$\bigvee_{\substack{E\subseteq P_j\times P_j \text{ such that the}\\ \text{graph } (P_j, E) \text{ is connected}}}\ \bigwedge_{(i,i')\in E} \mathit{dist}(x_i, x_{i'}) \leqslant 2r{+}1.$$

Note that the formula $\varrho_P(\bar{x}) := \delta_P(\bar{x}) \wedge \bigwedge_{j=1}^{\ell} \gamma_{P_j}(\bar{x}_{P_j})$ is r-local around $\bar{x}$. Furthermore, $\varphi'(\bar{x})$ obviously is equivalent to the formula $\bigvee_{P\in\mathcal{P}} \big(\varrho_P(\bar{x}) \wedge \varphi'(\bar{x})\big)$.

Using the Feferman-Vaught Theorem (see e.g. [17]), we can, for each $P = (P_1, \ldots, P_\ell) \in \mathcal{P}$, compute a decomposition of $\varphi'(\bar{x})$ into r-local formulas $\vartheta_{P,j,t}(\bar{x}_{P_j})$, for $j \in \{1, \ldots, \ell\}$ and $t \in T_P$, for a suitable finite set T_P, such that the formula $\big(\varrho_P(\bar{x}) \wedge \varphi'(\bar{x})\big)$ is equivalent to

$$\varrho_P(\bar{x}) \wedge \bigvee_{t\in T_P} \big(\, \vartheta_{P,1,t}(\bar{x}_{P_1}) \wedge \cdots \wedge \vartheta_{P,\ell,t}(\bar{x}_{P_\ell})\,\big)$$

which, in turn, is equivalent to $\psi'_P := (\psi'_{P,1} \wedge \psi'_{P,2})$, where $\psi'_{P,1} := \delta_P(\bar{x})$ and

$$\psi'_{P,2} := \Big(\bigwedge_{j=1}^{\ell} \gamma_{P_j}(\bar{x}_{P_j})\Big) \wedge \bigvee_{t\in T_P} \Big(\bigwedge_{j=1}^{\ell} \vartheta_{P,j,t}(\bar{x}_{P_j})\Big).$$

In summary, $\varphi'(\bar{x})$ is equivalent to $\bigvee_{P\in\mathcal{P}} \psi'_P(\bar{x})$, and for every tuple $\bar{a} \in \mathit{dom}(\mathcal{A})^k$ with $\mathcal{A} \models \varphi'(\bar{a})$, there is exactly one partition $P \in \mathcal{P}$ such that $\mathcal{A} \models \psi'_P(\bar{a})$ (since $\mathcal{A} \models \varrho_P(\bar{a})$ is true for only one such $P \in \mathcal{P}$).

Step 3: defining $\mathcal{G}$, f, and ψ.

We define the domain G of $\mathcal{G}$ to be the disjoint union of the sets A and V, where $A := \mathit{dom}(\mathcal{A})$, and V consists of a "dummy element" $v_\perp$, and an element $v_{(\bar{b},\iota)}$

- for each $\bar{b} \in A^1 \cup \cdots \cup A^k$ such that $\mathcal{A} \models \gamma_{P_j}(\bar{b})$ for $P_j := \{1, \ldots, |\bar{b}|\}$ and
- for each injective mapping $\iota : \{1, \ldots, |\bar{b}|\} \to \{1, \ldots, k\}$.

Note that the first item ensures that the r-neighbourhood around $\bar{b}$ in $\mathcal{A}$ is connected. The second item ensures that we can view ι as a description telling us that the i-th component of $\bar{b}$ shall be viewed as an assignment for the variable $x_{\iota(i)}$ (for each $i \in \{1, \ldots, |\bar{b}|\}$).

We let f be the function from A^k to V^k defined as follows: For each $\bar{a} \in A^k$ let $P = (P_1, \ldots, P_\ell)$ be the unique element in $\mathcal{P}$ such that $\mathcal{A} \models \varrho_P(\bar{a})$. For each $j \leqslant \{1, \ldots, \ell\}$, we write $\bar{a}_{P_j}$ for the tuple obtained from $\bar{a}$ by deleting all those a_i with $i \notin P_j$. Furthermore, we let ι_{P_j} be the mapping from $\{1, \ldots, |P_j|\}$ to $\{1, \ldots, k\}$ such that for any $i \in \{1, \ldots, |P_j|\}$, $\iota(i)$ is the i-th smallest element of P_j. Then,

$$f(\bar{a}) := \big(v_{(\bar{a}_{P_1}, \iota_{P_1})}, \ldots, v_{(\bar{a}_{P_\ell}, \iota_{P_\ell})}, v_\perp, \ldots, v_\perp\big),$$

where the number of $v_\perp$-components is $(k{-}\ell)$. It is straightforward to see that f is injective.

We let τ_1 be the signature consisting of a unary relation symbol $C_\perp$, and a unary relation symbol C_ι for each injective mapping $\iota : \{1,\dots,s\} \to \{1,\dots,k\}$ for $s \in \{1,\dots,k\}$.

In $\mathcal{G}$, the symbol $C_\perp$ is interpreted by the singleton set $\{v_\perp\}$, and each C_ι is interpreted by the set of all nodes $v_{(\bar{b},\hat{\iota})} \in V$ with $\hat{\iota} = \iota$.

We let E be a binary relation symbol which is interpreted in $\mathcal{G}$ by the set of all tuples $(v_{(\bar{b},\iota)}, v_{(\bar{c},\hat{\iota})}) \in V^2$ such that there are elements $b' \in A$ in $\bar{b}$ and $c' \in A$ in $\bar{c}$ such that $dist^{\mathcal{A}}(b',c') \leqslant 2r+1$.

For each $P = (P_1,\dots,P_\ell) \in \mathcal{P}$, each $j \in \{1,\dots,\ell\}$, and each $t \in T_P$ we let $C_{P,j,t}$ be a unary relation symbol which, in $\mathcal{G}$, is interpreted by the set of all nodes $v_{(\bar{b},\iota)} \in V$ such that $\iota = \iota_{P_j}$ and $\mathcal{A} \models \vartheta_{P,j,t}(\bar{b})$.

We let τ_2 be the signature consisting of all the unary relation symbols $C_{P,j,t}$.

We let $\bar{y} = (y_1,\dots,y_k)$ be a tuple of k distinct variables, and we define $\psi_1(\bar{y})$ to be the FO(E)-formula

$$\psi_1(\bar{y}) \ := \bigwedge_{\substack{1 \leqslant j,j' \leqslant k \\ \text{with } j \neq j'}} \neg E(y_j, y_{j'}).$$

For each $P = (P_1,\dots,P_\ell)$ we let $\psi_P(\bar{y})$ be the FO$(\tau_1 \cup \tau_2)$-formula defined as follows:

$$\psi_P(\bar{y}) \ := \ \Big(\bigwedge_{j=1}^{\ell} C_{\iota_{P_j}}(y_j)\Big) \wedge \Big(\bigwedge_{j=\ell+1}^{k} C_\perp(y_j)\Big) \wedge \bigvee_{t \in T_P} \Big(\bigwedge_{j=1}^{\ell} C_{P,j,t}(y_j)\Big).$$

It is straightforward to verify that the following is true:

(1) For every $\bar{a} \in A^k$ with $\mathcal{A} \models \psi'_P(\bar{a})$, we have $\mathcal{G} \models (\psi_1 \wedge \psi_P)(f(\bar{a}))$.

(2) For every $\bar{v} \in G^k$ with $\mathcal{G} \models (\psi_1 \wedge \psi_P)(\bar{v})$, there is a (unique) tuple $\bar{a} \in A^k$ with $\bar{v} = f(\bar{a})$, and for this tuple we have $\mathcal{A} \models \psi'_P(\bar{a})$.

Finally, we let

$$\psi(\bar{y}) \ := \ (\psi_1(\bar{y}) \wedge \psi_2(\bar{y})) \quad \text{with} \quad \psi_2(\bar{y}) \ := \bigvee_{P \in \mathcal{P}} \psi_P(\bar{y}).$$

It is straightforward to see that f is a bijection between $\varphi(\mathcal{A})$ and $\psi(\mathcal{G})$.

In summary, we now know that items 1 and 2, as well as the first statement of item 4 of Proposition 9 are true.

To achieve the second statement of item 4, we use additional binary relation symbols $F_1,\dots,F_k$ which are interpreted in $\mathcal{G}$ as follows: Start by initialising all of them to the empty set. Then, for each $v = v_{(\bar{b},\iota)} \in V$ and each $j \in \{1,\dots,|\bar{b}|\}$, add to $F^{\mathcal{G}}_{\iota(j)}$ the tuple (v,a), where a is j-th component of $\bar{b}$. This completes the definition of $\mathcal{G}$ and τ, letting $\tau := \tau_1 \cup \tau_2 \cup \{E, F_1,\dots,F_k\}$.

Using the relations $F_1,\dots,F_k$ of $\mathcal{G}$, in time and space $O(k)$ we can, upon input of $v = v_{(\bar{b},\iota)} \in V$ compute the tuple $\bar{b}$ and the mapping ι (for this, just check for all $i \in \{1,\dots,k\}$ whether node v has an outgoing F_i-edge). Using this, it is straightforward to see that upon input of $\bar{v} \in \psi(\mathcal{G})$, the tuple $f^{-1}(\bar{v}) \in A^k$ can be computed in time and space $O(k^2)$, thus proving the second statement of item 4.

Step 4: proving item 3.

First of all, note that for each $v_{(\bar{b},\iota)} \in V$, the tuple $\bar{b}$ is of the form $(b_1,\dots,b_s) \in A^s$ for some $s \leqslant k$, such that all components of the tuple belong to the $\hat{r}$-neighbourhood $\mathcal{N}^{\mathcal{A}}_{\hat{r}}(b_1)$ of b_1 in $\mathcal{A}$, for $\hat{r} := k(2r+1)$. Since $\mathcal{A}$ has degree d, $N^{\mathcal{A}}_{\hat{r}}(b_1)$ contains at most $d^{\hat{r}+1}$ elements of A. And by using breadth-first search, $\mathcal{N}^{\mathcal{A}}_{\hat{r}}(b_1)$ can be computed in time $d^{O(\hat{r}+1)}$.

Thus, the set V, along with the relations $C_\perp$, C_ι and $F_1,\dots,F_k$ of $\mathcal{G}$, can be computed as follows: Start by letting $V := \{v_\perp\}$ and initialising all relations to the empty set. Let $C^{\mathcal{G}}_\perp := \{v_\perp\}$. Then, for each $a \in A$, compute the $\hat{r}$-neighbourhood $\mathcal{N}^{\mathcal{A}}_{\hat{r}}(a)$ of a in $\mathcal{A}$, and compute (by a brute-force algorithm), for each $s \in \{1,\dots,k\}$, the set of all s-tuples $\bar{b}$ of elements from this neighbourhood, which satisfy the following: The first component of $\bar{b}$ is a, and $\mathcal{N}^{\mathcal{A}}_{\hat{r}}(a) \models \gamma_{P_j}(\bar{b})$ for $P_j = \{1,\dots,s\}$. For each such tuple $\bar{b}$ do the following: For each injective mapping $\iota : \{1,\dots,s\} \to \{1,\dots,k\}$ add to V a new element $v_{(\bar{b},\iota)}$, add this element to the relation $C^{\mathcal{G}}_\iota$, and for each $j \in \{1,\dots,s\}$, add to $F^{\mathcal{G}}_{\iota(j)}$ the tuple $(v_{(\bar{b},\iota)}, a)$, where a is the j-th component of $\bar{b}$.

This way, the domain $G = A \cup V$ of $\mathcal{G}$, along with the relations C_ι and $F_1,\dots,F_k$ of $\mathcal{G}$, can be computed in time and space $O(h(|\varphi|) \cdot n \cdot d^{h(|\varphi|)})$, for a computable function h.

For computing the unary relations $C_{P,j,t}$ of $\mathcal{G}$, start by initialising all of them to the empty set. For each $v_{(\bar{b},\iota)} \in V$ do the following: Compute (by using the relations $F_1,\dots,F_k$) the tuple $\bar{b}$ and the mapping ι. Let a be the first component of $\bar{b}$. Compute the $\tilde{r}$-neighbourhood $\mathcal{N}^{\mathcal{A}}_{\tilde{r}}(a)$ of a in $\mathcal{A}$, for $\tilde{r} := \hat{r}+r$. For each $P = (P_1,\dots,P_\ell) \in \mathcal{P}$, each $j \in \{1,\dots,\ell\}$ such that $\iota_{P_j} = \iota$, and each $t \in T_P$, check whether $\mathcal{N}^{\mathcal{A}}_{\tilde{r}}(a) \models \theta_{P,t,j}(\bar{b})$. If so, add the element $v_{(\bar{b},\iota)}$ to the relation $C_{P,j,t}$ of $\mathcal{G}$. (This is correct, since the formula $\theta_{P,j,t}$ is r-local around its free variables, and the radius of the neighbourhood is large enough.)

This way, $\mathcal{G}$'s relations $C_{P,j,t}$ can be computed in time and space $O(h(|\varphi|) \cdot n \cdot d^{h(|\varphi|)})$, for a computable function h.

To compute the E-relation of $\mathcal{G}$, note that for all tuples $(v_{(\bar{b},\iota)}, v_{(\bar{c},\hat{\iota})}) \in E^{\mathcal{G}}$, we have $dist^{\mathcal{A}}(a, c_j) \leqslant (2k+1)(2r+1)$, for all components c_j of $\bar{c}$, where a is the first component of $\bar{b}$. Thus, the E-relation of $\mathcal{G}$ can be computed as follows: Start by initialising this relation to the empty set. For each $v_{(\bar{b},\iota)} \in V$ do the following: Compute (by using the relations $F_1,\dots,F_k$) the tuple $\bar{b}$. Let a be the first component of $\bar{b}$. Compute the r'-neighbourhood $\mathcal{N}^{\mathcal{A}}_{r'}(a)$ of a in $\mathcal{A}$, for $r' := r + (2k+1)(2r+1)$. Use a brute-force algorithm to compute all tuples $\bar{c}$ of elements in $\mathcal{N}^{\mathcal{A}}_{r'-r}(a)$, such that $|\bar{c}| \leqslant k$ and $\mathcal{N}^{\mathcal{A}}_{r'}(a) \models \gamma_{P_j}(\bar{c})$ for $P_j = \{1,\dots,|\bar{c}|\}$. Check if there are components b' of $\bar{b}$ and c' of $\bar{c}$ such that $dist^{\mathcal{N}^{\mathcal{A}}_{r'}(a)}(b',c') \leqslant 2r+1$. If so, add to $E^{\mathcal{G}}$ the tuple $(v_{(\bar{b},\iota)}, v_{(\bar{c},\hat{\iota})})$ for each injective mapping $\hat{\iota} : \{1,\dots,|\bar{c}|\} \to \{1,\dots,k\}$.

This way, the E-relation of $\mathcal{G}$ can be computed in time and space $O(h(|\varphi|) \cdot n \cdot d^{h(|\varphi|)})$, for a computable function h.

In summary, we obtain that $\mathcal{G}$ is computable from $\mathcal{A}$ and φ within the desired time and space bound.

To finish the proof of item 3, we need to give an upper bound on the degree of $\mathcal{G}$. As noted above, $(v_{(\bar{b},\iota)}, v_{(\bar{c},\hat{\iota})}) \in E^{\mathcal{G}}$ implies that $dist^{\mathcal{A}}(a, c_j) \leqslant r'$ for $r' := (2k+1)(2r+1)$, for all components c_j of $\bar{c}$, where a is the first component of $\bar{b}$. Thus, for each fixed $v_{(\bar{b},\iota)} \in V$, the number of elements $v_{(\bar{c},\hat{\iota})}$ such that $(v_{(\bar{b},\iota)}, v_{(\bar{c},\hat{\iota})}) \in E^{\mathcal{G}}$ is at most

$$k! \cdot \sum_{s=1}^{k} |\mathcal{N}^{\mathcal{A}}_{r'}(a)|^s \leqslant k! \cdot |\mathcal{N}^{\mathcal{A}}_{r'}(a)|^{k+1} \leqslant k! \cdot d^{(r'+1)(k+1)}.$$

Thus, since $E^{\mathcal{G}}$ is symmetric, its degree is $\leqslant 2k!d^{(r'+1)(k+1)}$.

Similarly, for each tuple $(v_{(\bar{b},\iota)}, a) \in F^{\mathcal{G}}_i$ (with $i \in \{1,\dots,k\}$) we know that a is the $\iota^{-1}(i)$-th component of $\bar{b}$ and each component of $\bar{b}$ belongs to the $\hat{r}$-neighbourhood of a in $\mathcal{A}$, for $\hat{r} = k(2r+1)$. Thus, for each fixed $a \in A$, the number of elements $v_{(\bar{b},\iota)} \in V$ such that $(v_{(\bar{b},\iota)}, a) \in F_i^{\mathcal{G}}$ is at most $k! \cdot \sum_{s=1}^{k} |\mathcal{N}_{\hat{r}}^{\mathcal{A}}(a)|^s \leqslant k! \cdot d^{(\hat{r}+1)(k+1)}$. In summary, we thus obtain that $\mathcal{G}$ is of degree at most $d^{h(|\varphi|)}$ for a computable function h.

Step 5: proving the third statement of item 4.

For $\bar{a} \in A^k$ we know that

$$f(\bar{a}) := \big(v_{(\bar{a}_{P_1}, \iota_{P_1})}, \ldots, v_{(\bar{a}_{P_\ell}, \iota_{P_\ell})}, v_\perp, \ldots, v_\perp\big),$$

for the unique partition $P = (P_1, \ldots, P_\ell) \in \mathcal{P}$ such that $\mathcal{A} \models \varrho_P(\bar{a})$. The number of $v_\perp$-components in $f(\bar{a})$ is $(k-\ell)$. To compute the partition P for a given tuple $\bar{a} = (a_1, \ldots, a_k)$, we can proceed as follows:

Construct an undirected graph H with vertex set $\{1, \ldots, k\}$, where there is an edge between $i \neq j$ iff $dist^{\mathcal{A}}(a_i, a_j) \leqslant 2r+1$. Compute the connected components of H. Let ℓ be the number of connected components of H. For each $j \in \{1, \ldots, \ell\}$ let P_j be vertex set of the j-th connected component, such that $\min P_j < \min P_{j+1}$ for all $j \in \{1, \ldots, \ell-1\}$.

Once the edge set of H is constructed, all further steps of this algorithm can be performed in time $O(k^2)$.

After having constructed the partition $P = (P_1, \ldots, P_\ell)$, further $O(k^2)$ steps suffice to construct the tuples $\bar{a}_{P_1}, \ldots, \bar{a}_{P_\ell}$, the mappings $\iota_{P_1}, \ldots, \iota_{P_\ell}$, and the according tuple $f(\bar{a})$. Hence, we can compute $f(\bar{a})$ in time $O(k^2)$, provided that the edge set of H can be computed in time $O(k^2)$.

To enable the fast computation of the edge set of H, we precompute an $(n \times n)$-array D such that for any two elements $a, b \in A = \{1, \ldots, n\}$ we have $D[a, b] = 1$ if $a \neq b$ and $dist^{\mathcal{A}}(a, b) \leqslant 2r+1$, and $D[a, b] = 0$ otherwise. Once D is available, we can compute the edge set of H in time $O(k^2)$ by checking, for all $i, j \in \{1, \ldots, k\}$ whether $D[a_i, a_j] = 1$. To precompute the array D, we can proceed as follows: In the standard RAM-model, when starting the RAM D is initialised to 0 for free (in a model where this initialisation is not for free, we can avoid initialisation by using the *lazy array technique* described in Section 2). For each $a \in A$, we use time $d^{O(2r+1)}$ to compute the $(2r+1)$-neighbourhood of a in $\mathcal{A}$, and for each element $b \neq a$ in this neighbourhood we let $D[a, b] := 1$. In summary, the computation of the array D thus is done in time $O(n \cdot d^{h(|\varphi|)})$ for a computable function h. This completes the proof of Proposition 9. □

5. CONCLUSION

For classes of databases of low degree, we presented an algorithm which enumerates the answers to first-order queries with constant delay after pseudo-linear preprocessing. An inspection of the proof shows that the constants involved are non-elementary in the query size. In the bounded degree case the constants are triply exponential in the query size [13]. In the (unranked) tree case the constants are provably non-elementary [8] (modulo some complexity assumption). We do not know what is the situation for classes of low degree. It would also be interesting to know whether we can enumerate the answers to a query using the *lexicographical* order (as it is the case over structures of bounded expansion [14]). Finally it would be interesting to know whether the memory assumption that we use for our RAMs can be avoided.

6. REFERENCES

[1] G. Bagan. MSO queries on tree decomposable structures are computable with linear delay. In *Proc. 20th International Workshop/15th Annual Conference of the EACSL (CSL'06)*, pages 167–181, 2006.

[2] G. Bagan, A. Durand, and E. Grandjean. On acyclic conjunctive queries and constant delay enumeration. In *Proc. 21st International Workshop/16th Annual Conference of the EACSL (CSL'07)*, pages 208–222, 2007.

[3] J. Brault-Baron. A negative conjunctive query is easy if and only if it is beta-acyclic. In *Proc. 26th International Workshop/21st Annual Conference of the EACSL (CSL'12)*, pages 137–151, 2012.

[4] B. Courcelle. Linear delay enumeration and monadic second-order logic. *Discrete Applied Mathematics*, 157(12):2675–2700, 2009.

[5] A. Durand and E. Grandjean. First-order queries on structures of bounded degree are computable with constant delay. *ACM Transactions on Computational Logic*, 8(4), 2007.

[6] Z. Dvořák, D. Král, and R. Thomas. Deciding First-Order Properties for Sparse Graphs. In *Proc. 51st Annual IEEE Symposium on Foundations of Computer Science (FOCS'10)*, pages 133–142, 2010.

[7] J. Flum and M. Grohe. *Parameterized Complexity Theory*. Springer-Verlag, 2006.

[8] M. Frick and M. Grohe. The complexity of first-order and monadic second-order logic revisited. *Annals of Pure and Applied Logic*, 130(1-3):3–31, 2004.

[9] H. Gaifman. On local and nonlocal properties. In J. Stern, editor, *Logic Colloquium'81*, pages 105–135. North-Holland, 1982.

[10] E. Grandjean and F. Olive. Graph properties checkable in linear time in the number of vertices. *Journal of Computer and System Sciences*, 68(3):546–597, 2004.

[11] M. Grohe. Generalized model-checking problems for first-order logic. In *Proc. 18th Annual Symposium on Theoretical Aspects of Computer Science (STACS'01)*, pages 12–26, 2001.

[12] M. Grohe, S. Kreutzer, and S. Siebertz. Deciding first-order properties of nowhere dense graphs. In *Proc. 46th Symposium on Theory of Computing (STOC'14)*, 2014. Preliminary version: CoRR abs/1311.3899 (2013).

[13] W. Kazana and L. Segoufin. First-order query evaluation on structures of bounded degree. *Logical Methods in Computer Science*, 7(2), 2011.

[14] W. Kazana and L. Segoufin. Enumeration of first-order queries on classes of structures with bounded expansion. In *Proc. 32nd ACM Symposium on Principles of Database Systems (PODS'13)*, pages 297–308, 2013.

[15] W. Kazana and L. Segoufin. Enumeration of monadic second-order queries on trees. *ACM Transactions on Computational Logic*, 14(4), 2013.

[16] S. Kreutzer and A. Dawar. Parameterized complexity of first-order logic. *Electronic Colloquium on Computational Complexity (ECCC)*, 16:131, 2009.

[17] J. A. Makowsky. Algorithmic uses of the Feferman-Vaught Theorem. *Annals of Pure and Applied Logic*, 126(1-3):159–213, 2004.

[18] B. M. E. Moret and H. D. Shapiro. *Algorithms from P to NP. Volume 1: Design & Efficiency*. Benjamin/Cummings, 1990.

[19] M. Yannakakis. Algorithms for acyclic database schemes. In *Proc. 7th International Conference on Very Large Data Bases (VLDB'81)*, pages 82–94, 1981.

Counting Solutions to Conjunctive Queries: Structural and Hybrid Tractability

Gianluigi Greco
Dept. of Mathematics and Computer Science
University of Calabria - Rende, Italy
ggreco@mat.unical.it

Francesco Scarcello
DIMES
University of Calabria - Rende, Italy
scarcello@dimes.unical.it

ABSTRACT

Counting the number of answers to conjunctive queries is an intractable problem, formally #P-hard, even over classes of *acyclic* queries. However, Durand and Mengel have recently introduced the notion of *quantified star size* that, combined with hypertree decompositions, identifies islands of tractability for the problem. They also wonder whether such a notion precisely characterizes those classes for which the counting problem is tractable. We show that this is the case only for bounded-arity simple queries, where relation symbols cannot be shared by different query atoms.

Indeed, we give a negative answer to the question in the general case, by exhibiting a more powerful structural method based on the novel concept of *#-generalized hypertree decomposition.* On classes of queries with bounded #-generalized hypertree width, counting answers is shown to be feasible in polynomial time, after a fixed-parameter polynomial-time preprocessing that only depends on the query structure. A weaker variant (but still more general than the technique based on the quantified starsize) is also proposed, for which tractability is established without any exponential dependency on the query size.

Based on #-generalized hypertree decompositions, a "hybrid" decomposition method is eventually conceived, where structural properties of the query are exploited in combination with properties of the given database, such as keys or other (weaker) dependencies among attributes that limit the allowed combinations of values. Intuitively, such features may induce different structural properties that are not identified by the "worst-possible database" perspective of purely structural methods.

Categories and Subject Descriptors

H.2.4 [**Database Management**]: Systems—*Query processing; Relational databases*; F.2.2 [**Analysis of Algorithms and Problem Complexity**]: Nonnumerical Algorithms and Problems—*Computations on discrete structures*

PODS'14, June 22–27, 2014, Snowbird, UT, USA.
Copyright 2014 ACM 978-1-4503-2375-8/14/06 ...$15.00.
http://dx.doi.org/10.1145/2594538.2594559.

Keywords

Counting problems; Structural decomposition methods

1. INTRODUCTION

1.1 Structural Decomposition Methods

Conjunctive Queries. Answering conjunctive queries, i.e., Select-Project-Join SQL queries, is a well-known NP-hard problem with respect to both the *combined* and the *query complexity* settings, that is whenever the query is given as input (and its size is not bounded by a fixed constant). This calls for methods and algorithms tailored to design efficient query optimizers. In fact, motivated by the tractability of *acyclic* conjunctive queries [41], i.e., of queries Q whose associated hypergraph $\mathcal{H}_Q$ (whose hyperedges one-to-one correspond with the sets of variables in atoms of Q) is acyclic, *structural decomposition methods* have been proposed in the literature to transform any cyclic query into an equivalent acyclic one, by organizing its atoms or variables into a polynomial number of clusters and by arranging these clusters as a tree, called a *decomposition tree.* The original query is then evaluated via this tree, with a cost that is exponential in the cardinality of the largest cluster, also called *width* of the decomposition, and polynomial if the width is bounded by a constant (see, e.g., [19, 29, 28, 22, 26, 16, 33]).

Several deep and useful results are known for *Boolean* conjunctive queries. In particular, over classes **C** of *bounded-arity* Boolean queries (and under standard complexity theoretic assumptions), the tractability frontier has precisely been charted [28]. It emerged that the notion of *tree decomposition* [36] plays a crucial role, since query answering is tractable on **C** if, and only if, the *cores* of the queries in **C** have *bounded treewidth.* Instead, its natural counterpart over *unbounded-arity* classes, that is, the notion of *generalized hypertree decomposition* [19, 21], fails to capture all classes of tractable instances [29]. However, tight characterizations are known for those classes of instances that can be evaluated in fixed-parameter polynomial time, where the parameter is the size of the query [33].

Enumeration Problems. In real-world applications, conjunctive queries hardly appear in the Boolean form. The "select" part of an SQL query allows users to specify a set of output variables, so that query answering amounts at *enumerating* all solutions rather than just deciding whether there is any. In [3], it has been shown that the enumeration problem where all variables are output variables (i.e., "SELECT *" queries where no variable is projected out) can be solved in polynomial time on a class **C** of queries if, and only if, the number of solutions is always polynomial, and that this is the case, if and only if, the queries in **C** have bounded *fractional edge cover number*. Similar tight worst-case bounds for conjunctive queries with arbitrary sets of output variables have been derived in [20]. Note however that even easy instances may have an exponential number of solutions. Therefore, for enumeration problems it is sensible to propose algorithms computing solutions with *polynomial delay*, or even with *linear delay* [4]. Again, acyclicity has been shown to be a key for tractability in this setting [41, 30, 31, 4], and generalizing these results to decomposition methods is an active area of research (see, e.g., [5, 25]).

Counting Problems. Closely related to the enumeration problem is the problem of *counting* the number of query answers, which occurs in the presence of SQL queries specifying "COUNT" aggregates. Note that these queries are very often at the basis of decision support systems examining large volumes of data in order to get insights on critical business questions. For instance, in the well-known TPC-H decision support benchmark,[1] consisting of business-oriented complex queries over which structural decomposition methods can exhibit their effectiveness [24], 6 out of 22 queries involve counting. Moreover, counting problems are at the basis of OLAP systems and can play a role in data exchange systems, too [38]. And, finally, they occur in the related field of constraint satisfaction problems, constituting an active area of research there (see, e.g, [7, 8, 18, 34]).

In fact, structural decomposition techniques have been applied to counting problems, too. On bounded-arity queries and if no projection is allowed, counting is known to be tractable over a class **C** if, and only if, queries in **C** have bounded treewidth [12, 17]—hence, cores play no role here. Moreover, without projections, most commonly considered structural restrictions generalizing acyclicity yield tractable counting problems, even without fixing any arity bound [35]. However, in almost all practical applications, there are variables that are crucial to join different relations in the query, but that are irrelevant to the user, i.e., they are not required in the output and their instantiations must not be counted. In this paper, we focus precisely on this general setting, whose recent advances in the literature can be summarized as follows:

- Pichler and Skritek [35] observed that classical decomposition methods are not helpful when projections are allowed. Indeed, they showed that counting answers is #P-hard in this case, even for acyclic queries. Moreover, they exhibited an algorithm counting the answers of an acyclic query Q in $O(|Q| \times m^2 \times 4^m)$, with m being the size of the largest database relation. Therefore, the evaluation is tractable w.r.t. the query complexity (where the database is not in input). The result can be easily extended to the *(generalized) hypertree decomposition method* [19].
- Durand and Mengel [14] showed that counting problems are tractable on classes of acyclic queries (or having bounded generalized hypertree width) having also bounded *quantified star size*, a novel structural parameter being introduced to measure how the variables that are not required in the output are spread over the query. Moreover, they proved that this is the best possible notion, whenever *classes of hypergraphs* (representing all possible queries sharing such structures) having bounded edge-size are considered. However, it is left as an open problem whether or not this notion actually characterizes the classes of bounded-arity queries for which the counting problem is tractable.

[1] http://www.tpc.org/tpch/default.asp

1.2 Contributions

In the paper, we look for the identification of novel islands of tractability for the problem of counting query answers. The problem is addressed from two perspectives.

Structural Tractability. We consider the standard setting where decomposition methods are used to identify classes of queries that are tractable over *all* possible databases. The analysis moves from the question left open by Durand and Mengel [14] and leads to the following contributions:

- ► We define a novel decomposition method, based on the concept of *#-covering*. It is based on the core of a suitably *colored* query rather than on the query itself. Moreover, it is defined in the general *tree projections* framework [23, 26], where we are given a set of *views*, i.e., resources that are available to answer the query, and the goal is to arrange some of them in a tree-like structure. Recall that generalized and fractional hypertree decompositions are just special instances of this framework.
- ► We show that if a decomposition computed according to this method (a *#-decomposition*) is given, then counting problems can be solved in polynomial time. Moreover, we show that deciding whether there is a #-decomposition (and compute one, if any) is a fixed-parameter tractable (FPT) problem w.r.t. the size of the given query.
- ► We study #-coverings when generalized hypertree decompositions are considered in place of arbitrary tree projections. On classes of queries having bounded #-generalized hypertree width, counting answers is fixed-parameter tractable w.r.t. the size of the query (actually, it is feasible in polynomial time, after an FPT preprocessing step depending only on the query structure and not involving the database).
- ► We introduce the notion of weak #-generalized hypertree decomposition, and we show that the classes of queries having bounded weak #-generalized hypertree width can be evaluated in polynomial time. These classes of queries include tractable classes that are not recognized according to Durand and Mengel's approach, thereby providing a negative answer to their question.
- ► Finally, we restrict the analysis to *simple* queries, i.e., to queries where there are no multiple occurrences of the same relation symbol. In this case, (weak) #-generalized hypertree decompositions and quantified star size (combined with generalized hypertree decompositions) identify the same classes of tractable instances. Moreover, it turns out that the notions chart the tractability frontier for bounded-arity simple queries (unless FPT = W[1]).

"Hybrid" Tractability. Motivated by the goal of designing algorithms that can be applied over a wide range of real world settings, we explore the identification of islands of tractability for counting problems by looking not only at the structure of the query, but also at the database given at hand. The idea is to adopt a new hybrid approach where decomposition techniques "adaptively" exploit information about the database to keep under control critical query fragments via structural techniques, and use Pichler and Skritek's approach [35] where such techniques do not work. With this respect, our results are as follows:

- We introduce the *boundedness* value of a database DB with respect to a (query plan formalized in terms of a) hypertree decomposition HD.
- We show that the algorithm by Pichler and Skritek scales exponentially with respect to the boundedness value only, which in many cases is significantly smaller than m. This motivates the question of computing a DB-*optimal width-k hypertree decomposition*, i.e., a decomposition leading to the best possible boundedness value. While the problem is shown to be intractable in general, it turns out that it is feasible in polynomial time when restricted over classes of decompositions in *normal form* [39, 27].
- We define the new hybrid notion of $\#_b$-hypertree decomposition, which exploits #-coverings to "attack" in a structural way the portions of the query which would determine a high boundedness value w.r.t. the given database. On the remaining parts (with a low boundedness value), the evaluation approach for DB-optimal decompositions is adopted. Note that the choices of fragments to keep under control change in general the structural properties of the query, so that we have an additional source of complexity here. Nevertheless, we show that dealing with this notion is fixed-parameter tractable, too.

2. PRELIMINARIES

Hypergraphs and Acyclicity. A *hypergraph* $\mathcal{H}$ is a pair (V, H), where V is a finite set of nodes and H is a set of hyperedges such that, for each $h \in H$, $h \subseteq V$. In the following, we denote V and H by $nodes(\mathcal{H})$ and $edges(\mathcal{H})$, respectively.

A hypergraph $\mathcal{H}$ is *acyclic* (more precisely, α-acyclic [15]) if, and only if, it has a join tree [6], i.e., a tree $\mathcal{JT}$ whose vertices are the hyperedges of $\mathcal{H}$ such that, whenever a node $X \in V$ occurs in two hyperedges h_1 and h_2 of $\mathcal{H}$, then h_1 and h_2 are connected in $\mathcal{JT}$, and X occurs in each vertex on the unique path linking h_1 and h_2. In words, the set of vertices where X occurs induces a connected subtree of $\mathcal{JT}$.

Tree Projections. For two hypergraphs $\mathcal{H}_1$ and $\mathcal{H}_2$, we say that $\mathcal{H}_2$ *covers* $\mathcal{H}_1$, denoted by $\mathcal{H}_1 \leq \mathcal{H}_2$, if each hyperedge of $\mathcal{H}_1$ is contained in at least one hyperedge of $\mathcal{H}_2$. Assume that $\mathcal{H}_1 \leq \mathcal{H}_2$. Then, a *tree projection* of $\mathcal{H}_1$ with respect to $\mathcal{H}_2$ is an acyclic hypergraph $\mathcal{H}_a$ such that $\mathcal{H}_1 \leq \mathcal{H}_a \leq \mathcal{H}_2$. Whenever such a hypergraph $\mathcal{H}_a$ exists, we say that the pair of hypergraphs $(\mathcal{H}_1, \mathcal{H}_2)$ has a tree projection.

Relational Structures. Let $\mathcal{U}$ and $\mathcal{X}$ be disjoint infinite sets that we call the *universe of constants* and the *universe of variables*, respectively. A (relational) vocabulary τ is a finite set of relation symbols of specified finite arities. A *relational structure* $\mathcal{A}$ over τ (short: τ-structure) consists of a universe $A \subseteq \mathcal{U} \cup \mathcal{X}$ and, for each relation symbol r in τ, of a relation $r^{\mathcal{A}} \subseteq A^{\rho}$, where ρ is the arity of r.

Let $\mathcal{A}$ and $\mathcal{B}$ be two τ-structures with universes A and B, respectively. A *homomorphism* from $\mathcal{A}$ to $\mathcal{B}$ is a mapping $h : A \mapsto B$ such that $h(c) = c$ for each constant c in $A \cap \mathcal{U}$, and such that, for each relation symbol r in τ and for each tuple $\langle a_1, \ldots, a_\rho \rangle \in r^{\mathcal{A}}$, it holds that $\langle h(a_1), \ldots, h(a_\rho) \rangle \in r^{\mathcal{B}}$. For any mapping h (not necessarily a homomorphism), $h(\langle a_1, \ldots, a_\rho \rangle)$ is used, as usual, as a shorthand for $\langle h(a_1), \ldots, h(a_\rho) \rangle$.

A τ-structure $\mathcal{A}$ is a substructure of a τ-structure $\mathcal{B}$ if $A \subseteq B$ and $r^{\mathcal{A}} \subseteq r^{\mathcal{B}}$, for each relation symbol r in τ.

Relational Databases. Let τ be a given vocabulary. A *database instance* (or, simply, a database) DB over $D \subseteq \mathcal{U}$ is a finite τ-structure DB whose universe is the set D of constants. For each relation symbol r in τ, r^{DB} is a *relation instance* (or, simply, relation) of DB. Sometimes, we adopt the logical representation of a database [40, 1], where a tuple $\langle a_1, ..., a_\rho \rangle$ of values from D belonging to the ρ-ary relation (over symbol) r is identified with the *ground atom* $r(a_1, ..., a_\rho)$. Accordingly, a database DB can be viewed as a set of ground atoms.

Conjunctive Queries. A *conjunctive query* Q is a first order formula $\exists \mathbf{X} \Phi$ where $\Phi = r_1(\mathbf{u_1}) \wedge \ldots \wedge r_m(\mathbf{u_m})$ is a conjunction of atoms, $r_1, ..., r_m$ (with $m > 0$) are relation symbols, $\mathbf{u_1}, ..., \mathbf{u_m}$ are lists of terms (i.e., variables or constants), and $\mathbf{X} = X_1, ..., X_n$ is the list of quantified variables of Φ. We say that the query Q is *simple* if every atom is defined over a distinct relation symbol. The conjunction Φ is denoted by $form(Q)$, while the sets of all atoms in Q is denoted by $atoms(Q)$. For any set A of atoms, $vars(A)$ is the set of all variables in A, and $vars(Q)$ is used for short in place of $vars(atoms(Q))$. Moreover, we define $free(Q) = vars(Q) \setminus \{X_1, ..., X_n\}$ as the set of the free variables in Q.

For a database DB over D, Q^{DB} denotes the set of all substitutions $\theta : vars(Q) \mapsto D$ such that for each $i \in \{1, ..., m\}$, $\theta'(r_{\alpha_i}(\mathbf{u_i})) \in$ DB, where $\theta'(t) = \theta(t)$ if $t \in vars(Q)$ and $\theta'(t) = t$ otherwise (i.e., if the term t is a constant).

Note that the conjunction $form(Q)$ can be viewed as a relational structure $\mathcal{Q}$, whose vocabulary τ_Q and universe U_Q are the set of relation symbols and the set of terms occurring in its atoms, respectively. For each symbol $r_i \in \tau_Q$, the relation $r_i^{\mathcal{Q}}$ contains a tuple of terms $\mathbf{u}$, for any atom of the form $r_i(\mathbf{u}) \in atoms(Q)$ defined over r_i. In the special case of simple queries, every relation $r_i^{\mathcal{Q}}$ of $\mathcal{Q}$ contains just one tuple of terms. According to this view, elements in Q^{DB} are in a one-to-one correspondence with homomorphisms from $\mathcal{Q}$ to DB_Q, where the latter is the (maximal) substructure of DB over the (sub)vocabulary τ_Q. Hereinafter, for the sake of presentation, we freely use interchangeably queries and databases with their relational structures, e.g., we may use Q and DB in place of $\mathcal{Q}$ and DB_Q. Moreover, $||Q||$ and $||\mathrm{DB}||$ denote the sizes of the underlying relation structures, according to their standard encoding (see, e.g., [28]).

A query Q' is a *core* of Q if it is a minimal substructure of Q such that there is a homomorphism from Q to Q'—note that the quantification of the variables in Q' is immaterial here. The set of all cores of Q is denoted by $\mathtt{cores}(Q)$. Elements in $\mathtt{cores}(Q)$ are *isomorphic* to each other.

Relational Algebra. For any set $W \subseteq vars(Q)$ of variables and set S of substitutions, we denote by $\pi_W(S)$ the set of the restrictions of the substitutions in S over the variables in W. If θ is a substitution with domain W, then we denote by $\sigma_\theta(S)$ the set $\{\theta' \in S \mid \pi_W(\{\theta'\}) = \{\theta\}\}$. If S_1 and S_2 are sets of substitutions with domains W_1 and W_2, respectively, then we denote by $S_1 \bowtie S_2$ the set of all substitutions θ over $W_1 \cup W_2$ such that $\pi_{W_1}(\{\theta\}) \subseteq S_1$ and $\pi_{W_2}(\{\theta\}) \subseteq S_2$. We use $S_1 \ltimes S_2$ as a shorthand for $\pi_{W_1}(S_1 \bowtie S_2)$.

Hypergraphs and atoms. There is a very natural way to associate a hypergraph $\mathcal{H}_\mathcal{V} = (N, H)$ with any set $\mathcal{V}$ of atoms: the set N of nodes consists of all variables occurring in $\mathcal{V}$; for each atom in $\mathcal{V}$, the set H of hyperedges contains a hyperedge including all its variables; and no other hyperedge is in H. For a query Q, the hypergraph associated with $atoms(Q)$ is denoted by $\mathcal{H}_Q$.

Counting. According to the above notation, $\pi_{free(Q)}(Q^{\mathrm{DB}})$ is the set of answers of the conjunctive query Q on the database DB (over the *output* variables $free(Q)$). We denote by count(Q, DB) the problem of computing the cardinality of this set, i.e., the number of (distinct) answers of Q on DB.

3. STRUCTURAL ANALYSIS

Let Q be a conjunctive query, and let $\mathcal{V}$ be a set of atoms each one defined over a specific relation symbol not occurring in Q. These atoms play the role of additional resources that can be used to answer (counting problems on) Q.

Following the framework in [26], we say that $\mathcal{V}$ is a *view set* for Q if, for each atom $q \in atoms(Q)$, $\mathcal{V}$ contains an atom w_q with the same list of variables as q (but with a different relation symbol). Each atom in $\mathcal{V}$ is called a *view*; in particular, atoms of the form w_q are called *query views*. The set of all query views will be denoted by $views(Q)$. Let DB be a database whose vocabulary includes all relation symbols in Q and $\mathcal{V}$. We say that DB is a *legal* database (on $\mathcal{V}$ w.r.t. Q) if (i) $w_q^{\mathrm{DB}} \subseteq q^{\mathrm{DB}}$ holds, for each query view $w_q \in views(Q)$; and (ii) $w^{\mathrm{DB}} \supseteq \pi_{vars(w)}(Q^{\mathrm{DB}})$, for each view $w \in \mathcal{V}$. Intuitively, all original "constraints" are there, and views are not more restrictive than the original query.

Note that we are abstracting here all purely *structural decomposition methods* proposed in the literature, which just differ in how they define and build the set of such available resources. Indeed, given a query Q and a database DB, decomposition methods compute a view set $\mathcal{V}$ and enlarge DB by including the relations associated with the views in order to make the resulting database legal. In particular, query views are often initialized with the same tuples as their associated query atoms (i.e., $w_q^{\mathrm{DB}} = q^{\mathrm{DB}}$) while, for any other view $w \in \mathcal{V}$, w^{DB} are initialized by including solutions of some subquery over the variables in w. The goal is then to decide whether (parts of) the views can be arranged as to form a *sandwich query* Q_a, i.e., an acyclic query such that $\mathcal{H}_{Q_a}$ is a tree projection of $\mathcal{H}_Q$ w.r.t. $\mathcal{H}_{\mathcal{V}}$. Indeed, it is well-known that, by projecting the tuples of any legal database DB over the parts of the views used in Q_a, a novel database DB_a can be obtained such that $Q_a^{\mathrm{DB}_a} = Q^{\mathrm{DB}}$. That is, answering Q can be reduced to answering an acyclic query [23].

It is worthwhile noting that views can be useful even without any actual knowledge of a tree projection (and of a sandwich query). For instance, consider the following algorithm for the decision problem of deciding whether Q^{DB} is empty or not: output "empty" if, and only if, no tuple survives after enforcing the *local consistency property* on the legal database DB, i.e., after repeatedly applying semijoin operations over the views to delete tuples that are useless (in that they do not belong to any query answer), till a fixpoint is reached. It is known that this simple polynomial-time algorithm returns the correct answer for the decision problem whenever a tree projection exists (even if it is not given at hand). In fact, such an approach works even for computation problems, and we shall use indeed in the paper a more general and tight characterization of query answering problems that can be solved by just enforcing local consistency [26].

In this section, we will move from answering problems to counting problems, by looking for "structural" restrictions to Q guaranteeing that count(Q, DB) can be solved efficiently via the available views in the set $\mathcal{V}$.

3.1 #-covered Queries

The first ingredient in the analysis is to "color" Q in order to take into account in its structure the role played by the free variables. Formally, the *coloring of* Q is the query $color(Q)$ having the same set of variables as Q (with the same quantifications) and the same atoms as Q, plus an additional atom $r_X(X)$ for each variable $X \in free(Q)$, with r_X being a fresh relation symbol. Thus, in a colored query, the atom $r_X(X)$ associated with a free variable X allows us to distinguish its actual domain with respect to other variables occurring in query atoms over shared relation symbols.

EXAMPLE 3.1. Consider the conjunctive query $Q_0 = \exists D, ..., I\ \Phi$ with $free(Q_0) = \{A, B, C\}$ and where

$$\Phi = \begin{array}{l} r_1(A,B,I) \wedge r_2(B,D) \wedge r_3(B,E) \wedge r_4(D,C) \wedge \\ r_5(D,F) \wedge r_5(D,G) \wedge r_5(G,H) \wedge r_5(F,H) \wedge r_6(D,H). \end{array}$$

Then, $color(Q_0)$ is the query $\exists D, ..., I\ \Phi \wedge \Phi_f$, where

$$\Phi_f \ = \ r_A(A) \wedge r_B(B) \wedge r_C(C).$$

Figure 1(a) reports the hypergraph associated with $\mathcal{H}_{Q_0}$, plus the three dashed hyperedges $\{A\}$, $\{B\}$, and $\{C\}$, additionally occurring in the hypergraph $\mathcal{H}_{color(Q_0)}$. ◁

The concept of coloring is next applied within the tree projection framework. In particular, we focus on tree projections where a special condition holds over the quantified variables, which keeps their interaction with free variables "under control". To state this condition, some further concepts and notations are required.

Let $\mathcal{H}$ be a hypergraph with $nodes(\mathcal{H}) \subseteq vars(Q)$—so, we hereinafter use the term variables also to denote nodes. Let X and Y be two variables in $vars(Q)$, and let $\bar{W} \subseteq vars(Q)$ be a set of variables. We say that X is $[\bar{W}]$-adjacent in $\mathcal{H}$ to Y if there is a hyperedge $h \in edges(\mathcal{H})$ such that $\{X, Y\} \subseteq (h \setminus \bar{W})$. Moreover, X and Y are $[\bar{W}]$-connected (in $\mathcal{H}$) if there is a sequence $X = X_0, \ldots, X_\ell = Y$ such that X_i is $[\bar{W}]$-adjacent to X_{i+1}, for each $i \in \{0, ..., \ell\text{-}1\}$. Any maximal $[\bar{W}]$-connected non-empty set of variables from $nodes(\mathcal{H}) \setminus \bar{W}$ is a $[\bar{W}]$-component. For a set H of hyperedges, let $nodes(H)$ denote the set $\bigcup_{h \in H} h$, and for any $[\bar{W}]$-component C, let $edges(C)$ denote the set $\{h \in edges(\mathcal{H}) \mid h \cap C \neq \emptyset\}$.

For any set $\bar{W}$ of variables and for any variable Y, define the *frontier* $Fr(Y, \bar{W}, \mathcal{H})$ of Y w.r.t. $\bar{W}$ in $\mathcal{H}$ (or, shortly, $Fr(Y, \bar{W})$ if $\mathcal{H}$ is understood) as follows: if $Y \in \bar{W}$, $Fr(Y, \bar{W}) = \emptyset$; otherwise, $Fr(Y, \bar{W}) = \bar{W} \cap nodes(edges(C))$, where C is the $[\bar{W}]$-component of $\mathcal{H}$ where Y occurs. For any query Q' with $vars(Q') \subseteq vars(Q)$, define the *frontier hypergraph* $\mathcal{FH}(Q', \bar{W}) = (vars(Q') \cup \bar{W}, H)$, whose set of hyperedges is $H = \{Fr(Y, \bar{W}, \mathcal{H}_{Q'}) \mid Y \in vars(Q')\}$.

DEFINITION 3.2. A *#-decomposition of* Q *w.r.t.* $\mathcal{V}$ is a tree projection $\mathcal{H}_a$ for $(\mathcal{H}_{Q'}, \mathcal{H}_{\mathcal{V}})$ that covers the frontier hypergraph $\mathcal{FH}(Q', free(Q))$, where Q' is some core of $color(Q)$. Therefore, $\mathcal{H}_a$ is an acyclic hypergraph such that $\mathcal{H}_{Q'} \leq \mathcal{H}_a \leq \mathcal{H}_{\mathcal{V}}$ and $\mathcal{FH}(Q', free(Q)) \leq \mathcal{H}_a$.

Whenever a #-decomposition exists, we say that Q is *#-covered w.r.t.* $\mathcal{V}$. □

Note that, in the above definition, we talk about "some" core of the colored query rather than just about "the" core,

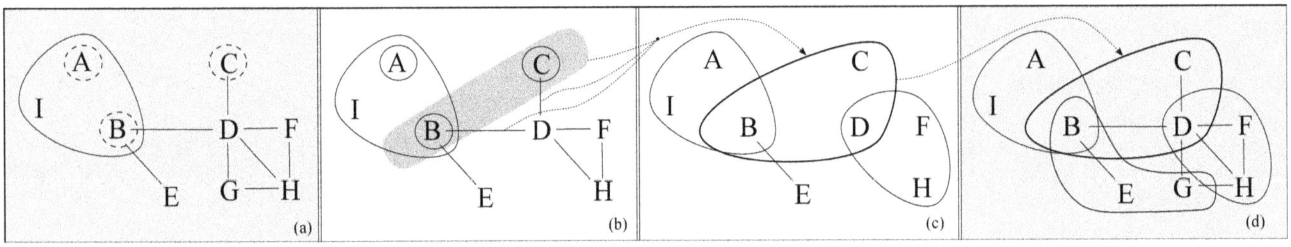

Figure 1: Structures in Example 3.1 and Example 3.3: (a) The hypergraphs $\mathcal{H}_{Q_0}$ and $\mathcal{H}_{color(Q_0)}$; (b) The hypergraph $\mathcal{H}_{Q'_0}$, where the frontier $Fr(D, free(Q'_0)) = Fr(F, free(Q'_0)) = Fr(H, free(Q'_0))$ is in gray; (c) A #-decomposition of Q_0 w.r.t. $\mathcal{V}_0$; (d) The hypergraph $\mathcal{H}_{\mathcal{V}_0}$.

because in this general framework different cores might behave differently w.r.t. the available views [26].

EXAMPLE 3.3. Consider again the query $color(Q_0)$ of Example 3.1, and the query $Q'_0 = \Phi' \wedge \Phi_f$ where

$$\Phi' = r_1(A,B,I) \wedge r_2(B,D) \wedge r_3(B,E) \wedge r_4(D,C) \wedge r_5(D,F) \wedge r_5(F,H) \wedge r_6(D,H).$$

Note that Q'_0 is a core of $color(Q_0)$, and its associated hypergraph is reported in Figure 1(b). In particular, $\mathcal{H}_{Q'_0}$ coincides with $\mathcal{H}_{color(Q_0)}$, but for the hyperedges $\{D, G\}$ and $\{G, H\}$ whose underlying relations disappeared in Q'_0.

Consider the variables in the set $vars(Q'_0) \setminus free(Q_0) = \{D, E, F, H, I\}$. Each of these variables is associated with a non-empty hyperedge in $\mathcal{FH}(Q'_0, free(Q_0))$. In particular, $Fr(E, free(Q'_0)) = \{B\}$, $Fr(D, free(Q'_0)) = \{B, C\}$, $Fr(F, free(Q'_0)) = \{B, C\}$, $Fr(H, free(Q'_0)) = \{B, C\}$, and $Fr(I, free(Q'_0)) = \{A, B\}$ hold. Since each of these frontiers must be covered by some hyperedge of a #-decomposition, B and C should be dealt with together. Moreover, as they are both connected to D in the query hypergraph, the variables in $\{B, C, D\}$ has to be treated by a #-decomposition as they were all included in some query atom.

Consider a set $\mathcal{V}_0$ of views such that $\mathcal{H}_{\mathcal{V}_0}$ is the hypergraph depicted in Figure 1(d), and check that the hypergraph in Figure 1(c) is a tree projection of $\mathcal{H}_{Q'_0}$ w.r.t. $\mathcal{H}_{\mathcal{V}_0}$. Note that the triangle over nodes B, C, and D is covered by the hyperedge $\{B, C, D\}$, which in its turn occurs in $\mathcal{H}_{\mathcal{V}_0}$. Similarly, note that the (true) clique over D, F, and H is absorbed by a hyperedge in $edges(\mathcal{H}_{\mathcal{V}_0})$. The existence of this tree projection witnesses that Q_0 is #-covered w.r.t. $\mathcal{V}_0$.

Finally, observe that the choice of the core does matter. Indeed, the query $Q''_0 = \Phi'' \wedge \Phi_f$ where

$$\Phi'' = r_1(A,B,I) \wedge r_2(B,D) \wedge r_3(B,E) \wedge r_4(D,C) \wedge r_5(D,G) \wedge r_5(G,H) \wedge r_6(D,H),$$

is another core of $color(Q_0)$, but there is no tree projection of $\mathcal{H}_{Q''_0}$ w.r.t. $\mathcal{H}_{\mathcal{V}_0}$, because there is no hyperedge in $edges(\mathcal{H}_{\mathcal{V}_0})$ that can cover the clique over D, G, and H. $\lhd$

Computing a #-decomposition is clearly NP-hard in general, because both dealing with cores and tree projections are hard tasks. However, in database applications it is important to study what happens if queries are not too large, which is often modeled by assuming that they are fixed, as in data-complexity analysis, or at least quite small. With this respect, we next provide a positive result for #-decompositions, by showing that their computation, parameterized by the size of the query, is fixed-parameter tractable.

THEOREM 3.4. *The following problem, parameterized by the query size, is in* FPT*: Given a query Q and a view set $\mathcal{V}$, decide whether there exists a #-decomposition of Q w.r.t. $\mathcal{V}$, and compute one (if any).*

PROOF SKETCH. Let $k = ||Q||$ and let Q' be any core of $color(Q)$. Consider the hypergraph $\mathcal{H}' = (V, H)$ where $V = vars(Q)$ and $H = edges(\mathcal{H}_{Q'}) \cup edges(\mathcal{FH}(Q', free(Q)))$. Observe that any acyclic hypergraph $\mathcal{H}_a$ such that $\mathcal{H}' \leq \mathcal{H}_a \leq \mathcal{H}_\mathcal{V}$ is a #-decomposition of Q w.r.t. $\mathcal{V}$. Therefore the problem is reduced now to computing a standard tree projection of $\mathcal{H}'$ with respect to $\mathcal{H}_\mathcal{V}$, which is known to be in FPT if the number of nodes occurring in the smaller hypergraph (here $vars(Q') \leq k$) is used as a parameter [26]. Finally, the cores of $color(Q)$ can be enumerated in time $f(k)$, for a computable (exponential) function $f(\cdot)$. □

3.2 Tractability of Counting

We can now relate the concept of #-covering with the tractability of the counting problem. The computational costs here and elsewhere in the paper are reported assuming unit cost for arithmetic operations, as usual in this context.

THEOREM 3.5. *Let Q be a query, let $\mathcal{V}$ be a view set for it, and let* DB *be a legal database. If a #-decomposition $\mathcal{H}_a$ of Q w.r.t. $\mathcal{V}$ is also given, then* count(Q, DB) *can be solved in polynomial time (w.r.t. $||Q||$, $||\mathcal{V}||$, $||\mathrm{DB}||$, and $||\mathcal{H}_a||$).*

PROOF IDEA. Let Q_c be any core of $color(Q)$, and let Q' be its uncolored version where the special coloring atoms have been removed. Note that Q' is a subquery of Q containing all its free variables (because of colors) and, as pointed out in [25], $\pi_{free(Q)}(Q'^{\mathrm{DB}}) = \pi_{free(Q)}(Q^{\mathrm{DB}})$. Therefore, the solution of count(Q', DB) is the same as the solution of count(Q, DB). Moreover, note that Q_c and Q' have the same hypergraph $\mathcal{H}_{Q'}$ (but for the singleton edges associated with colors, which are subsets of other edges, and hence are irrelevant as far as the existence of tree projections is concerned). Assume w.l.o.g. that the given acyclic hypergraph $\mathcal{H}_a$ is a tree projection of this hypergraph $\mathcal{H}_{Q'}$ w.r.t. $\mathcal{H}_\mathcal{V}$, and that $\mathcal{H}_a$ covers the frontier hypergraph $\mathcal{FH}(Q', free(Q))$.

We can show the existence of a query Q_f without quantified variables and a database DB″ such that $Q_f^{\mathrm{DB}''} = \pi_{free(Q)}(Q'^{\mathrm{DB}}) = \pi_{free(Q)}(Q^{\mathrm{DB}})$. Roughly, the idea is to use the fact that all frontiers in Q' are covered, and that such coverings somehow contain the relevant information about all subqueries associated with components of quantified variables. Thus, the query Q_f can be obtained by removing from Q' these subqueries, but adding atoms corresponding to those hyperedges of $\mathcal{H}_a$ that cover frontiers of quantified variables occurring in Q'.

Because the only atoms in Q_f that do not belong to Q' come precisely from hyperedges of $\mathcal{H}_a$, it follows that the tree projection $\mathcal{H}_a$ for $\mathcal{H}_{Q'}$ is a tree projection for $\mathcal{H}_{Q_f}$, too. Moreover, since Q_f does not contain any quantified variable, even the acyclic hypergraph $\mathcal{H}'_a$ obtained from $\mathcal{H}_a$ by removing all (nodes associated with) quantified variables is a tree projection for $\mathcal{H}_{Q_f}$.

Finally, we define an acyclic query Q'_a whose associated hypergraph is $\mathcal{H}'_a$ (hence without quantified variables). Then, by using the local-consistency tools described in [26], even if Q_f is actually unknown we are able to compute in polynomial time a database DB'_a such that $\pi_{free(Q)}(Q_a'^{\mathrm{DB}'_a}) = Q_f^{\mathrm{DB}''} = \pi_{free(Q)}(Q^{\mathrm{DB}})$. Eventually, the counting problem is known to be feasible in polynomial time for acyclic queries without quantified variables [35]. □

As a relevant specialization of the concept of #-covering, we now consider the view set $\mathcal{V}_Q^k$ that characterizes the well-known *generalized hypertree decomposition* method. Recall that, for a given query Q, $\mathcal{V}_Q^k$ is the view set built by including, for each subset $C \subseteq atoms(Q)$ with $|C| \leq k$, a fresh atom w_C over the variables $vars(C)$. It is well-known and easy to see that every tree projection of $\mathcal{H}_Q$ w.r.t. the hypergraph associated with $\mathcal{V}_Q^k$ corresponds to a width-k generalized hypertree decomposition of Q, and vice versa (see, e.g., [26]). Accordingly, we use the two notions interchangeably.

Example 3.6. Each hyperedge of the hypergraph $\mathcal{H}_{\mathcal{V}_0}$ in Figure 1(d) is defined over variables occurring in at most two atoms of Q_0. So, $edges(\mathcal{H}_{\mathcal{V}_0})$ is a subset of the edges of the hypergraph associated with $\mathcal{V}_{Q_0}^2$, and the tree projection in Figure 1(c) witnesses that the generalized hypertree width of the cyclic query Q'_0 is 2. ◁

Hereinafter, we say that Q has a width-k *#-generalized hypertree decomposition* if it is #-covered w.r.t. $\mathcal{V}_Q^k$. A class **C** has bounded *#-generalized hypertree width* if there exists some finite natural number k such that every query $Q \in \mathbf{C}$ has a width-k #-generalized hypertree decomposition.

We next show that these classes have nice computational properties, as the counting problem is fixed-parameter tractable over them. In fact, we can say something more, because after a preprocessing step whose cost depends on the query structure only, the actual evaluation over the given database has no exponential dependency on the parameter (query size). This is of course a nice feature for database applications where the query is usually assumed to be very small, while the database size is large.

Theorem 3.7. *Let* **C** *be a class of queries having bounded #-generalized hypertree width. Then, for each* $Q \in \mathbf{C}$ *and for each database* DB, count(Q, DB) *can be solved in time* $f(||Q||) + poly(||Q|| + ||\mathrm{DB}||)$*, for a computable function* $f(\cdot)$ *and some polynomial* $poly(\cdot)$*. The problem parameterized by the query size is thus in* FPT.

3.3 On the Quantified Starsize

Recently, a method to solve counting problems over classes of queries having (standard) generalized hypertree width bounded by some fixed constant has been proposed by [14]. It is founded on the concept of *quantified star size*, which is defined (with our notation) as the cardinality of the maximum independent set over the frontiers $Fr(Y, free(Q), \mathcal{H}_Q)$, for any quantified variable $Y \in vars(Q) \setminus free(Q)$. In particular, recall that $I \subseteq Fr(Y, free(Q), \mathcal{H}_Q)$ is an independent set if there is no hyperedge $h \in edges(\mathcal{H}_Q)$ such that $|h \cap I| > 1$.

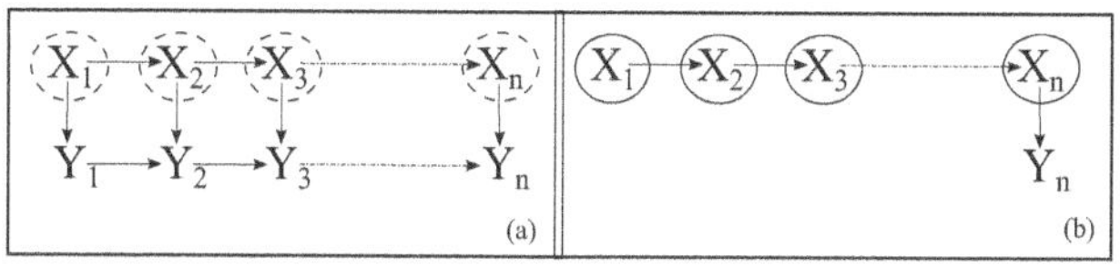

Figure 2: The hypergraphs $\mathcal{H}_{Q_1^n}$ and $\mathcal{H}_{\hat{\Phi}_1^n}$ in Example 3.9. Edge orientation reflects the position of the variables in the relation r.

Proposition 3.8 (cf. [14]). *Let k and ℓ be fixed natural numbers. Given any query Q having quantified star size at most ℓ, together with a generalized hypertree decomposition of Q of width at most k,* count(Q, DB) *can be solved in polynomial time, for every database* DB.

Contrast Theorem 3.5 and Definition 3.2 with the above result, by noticing that this latter does not take into account the concept of core, hence failing to recognize simple classes of tractable instances as evidenced in the following example.

Example 3.9. Consider the class of queries $\{Q_1^n = \exists Y_1, ..., Y_n \Phi_n \mid n > 0\}$, with $free(Q_1^n) = \{X_1, ..., X_n\}$ and $\Phi_n = \bigwedge_{i=1}^n r(X_i, Y_i) \wedge \bigwedge_{i=1}^{n-1} r(X_i, X_{i+1}) \wedge \bigwedge_{i=1}^{n-1} r(Y_i, Y_{i+1})$.

The (hyper)graph associated with Q_1^n is shown in Figure 2(a), where dashed hyperedges correspond to the free variables. Every query in the class has generalized hypertree width 2. However, the quantified star size is $\lceil n/2 \rceil$, because all the free variables $X_1, ..., X_n$ belong to the frontier of, e.g., the quantified variable Y_1. Hence, this class is not recognized as tractable according to Proposition 3.8.

Note now that the acyclic (sub)query $\hat{\Phi}_1^n = r(X_n, Y_n) \wedge \bigwedge_{i=1}^{n-1} r(X_i, X_{i+1}) \wedge \bigwedge_{i=1}^n r_{X_i}(X_i)$ is the core of $color(Q_1^n)$, where each variable Y_i, with $i \in \{1, ..., n-1\}$, is mapped to X_{i+1}. Its associated hypergraph is shown in Figure 2(b). There, check that Y_n is the only quantified variable and that its frontier is the singleton $\{X_n\}$. So, Q_1^n is #-covered w.r.t. $\mathcal{V}_{Q_1^n}^1$ and, by Theorem 3.5, we get its tractability. ◁

We say that a class of queries **C** has *bounded hypertree width and bounded quantified star size* if there are two finite natural numbers k and ℓ such that each query $Q \in \mathbf{C}$ has quantified star size at most ℓ, and there exists a generalized hypertree decomposition of Q of width at most k.

A problem left open by [14] is whether, at least over bounded-arity instances, such classes of bounded hypertree width and bounded quantified star size queries are precisely those classes that are fixed-parameter tractable (parameterized by the query size), and in polynomial-time, too. Example 3.9 provides a first negative answer to the question, by showing a class of FPT instances having unbounded quantified star size. In fact, it turns out that the notion of #-generalized hypertree width allows us to identify larger classes of fixed-parameter tractable queries.

Theorem 3.10. *Any class of queries having bounded hypertree width and bounded quantified star size has bounded #-generalized hypertree width. However, there are classes having bounded #-generalized hypertree width, but unbounded hypertree width and unbounded quantified star size.*

We next pinpoint that such big differences cannot occur on *simple* queries.

3.4 Simple Queries

Let us focus on classes of simple queries, where no relation symbol can be reused in different atoms (so that the concept of core is immaterial). We observe that in this case the #-generalized hypertree decomposition method and the combination of the (standard) generalized hypertree decomposition method with the notion of quantified star size identify the same classes of tractable queries.

THEOREM 3.11. *Let* $\mathbf{C}$ *be any class of simple queries. Then,* $\mathbf{C}$ *has bounded #-generalized hypertree width if, and only if, it has bounded hypertree width and bounded quantified star size.*

Note that deciding whether the core of a query has generalized hypertree width below some fixed threshold k is an NP-hard problem even for simple queries (where cores do not matter) [22]. Nevertheless, by using this notion over simple queries we are able to refine Theorem 3.5 in a form where no decomposition must be known in advance. To establish the result, we use Theorem 3.5 combined with the purely graph-theoretic fact that if $(\mathcal{H}_Q, \mathcal{V}_Q^k)$ has a tree projection, then there is constant factor $(3 \times k + 1)$ approximation [2], formally, a "special" form of tree projection (called *hypertree decomposition*) for $\mathcal{H}_Q$ w.r.t. the hypergraph associated with $\mathcal{V}_Q^{3\times k+1}$, which can be moreover computed in polynomial time—in Section 4, we shall have a closer look at the properties of hypertree decompositions.

THEOREM 3.12. *Let* k *be a fixed natural number. There is a polynomial time algorithm that, for any given simple query* Q*, either solves* count(Q, DB) *or correctly states that* Q *has no width-*k *#-generalized hypertree decompositions.*

We conclude by noting that, if simple queries having bounded arity are considered, the above tractability result is the best possible one (under the assumption that FPT $\neq W[1]$). We recall that a very similar result has been recently proved in [14] for the technique based on quantified star size. This previous result is however given over classes $\mathbf{C}_h$ of pairs $(\mathcal{H}, S)$, where $\mathcal{H}$ is a hypergraph whose edges have bounded size and S is a set of vertices, which means over all possible queries with any possible relational structure, whose free variables are taken from S and whose associated hypergraph is $\mathcal{H}$, for some $(\mathcal{H}, S) \in \mathbf{C}_h$.

The next dichotomy is instead given on classes of simple queries, and it can be viewed as a refinement of the above result (just note that every such a class $\mathbf{C}_h$ of pairs always contains an infinite number of classes of simple queries). More importantly, together with the fixed-parameter tractability result of Theorem 3.7, this dichotomy makes more clear what is still missing to chart the frontier of tractability in general.

THEOREM 3.13. *Assume* FPT $\neq$ W[1]. *Let* $\mathbf{C}$ *be any recursively-enumerable class of bounded-arity simple queries. Then, the following statements are equivalent.*

(1) $\mathbf{C}$ *has bounded #-generalized hypertree width.*

(2) For each $Q \in \mathbf{C}$ *and every database* DB, count(Q, DB) *can be solved in polynomial time.*

Observe that the above polynomial-time tractability results exploit the fact that we focus on simple queries. We next look for islands of tractability for the general case.

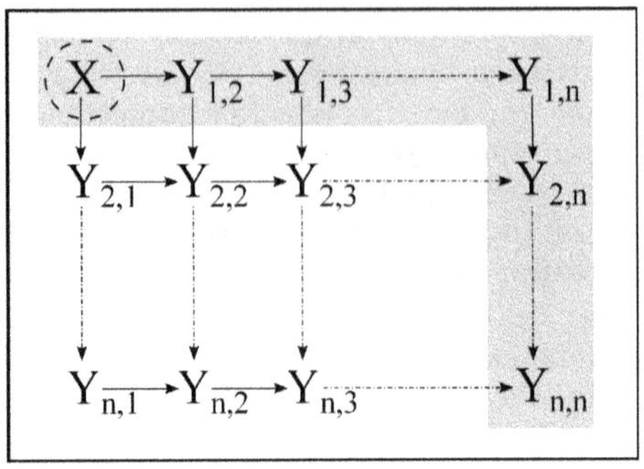

Figure 3: The hypergraph $\mathcal{H}_{Q_1^{n\times n}}$ in Example 3.15.

3.5 Weak Coverings and Tractability

So far, we know from Theorem 3.7 that counting is fixed-parameter tractable (in fact, polynomial-time, after an FPT preprocessing) over classes having bounded #-generalized hypertree width. While this is often enough in database applications, we might still want to end up with a tractability result having no exponential dependency on the query size. To this end, we introduce the following (weaker) variant.

DEFINITION 3.14. A width-k *weak* #-hypertree decomposition of Q is a tree projection $\mathcal{H}_a$ for $(\mathcal{H}_{Q'}, \mathcal{H}_{\mathcal{V}_Q^k})$ covering $\mathcal{FH}(Q, \mathit{free}(Q))$, where Q' is a core of $\mathit{color}(Q)$. □

Note that, in the above definition, the frontier hypergraph is defined w.r.t. the original query Q, rather than w.r.t. the core Q' as in Definition 3.2. Thus, the method exploits only partially the power of the core. For instance, the reader might check that the class of queries in Example 3.9 does not have bounded weak #-generalized hypertree width. Indeed, being the frontier independent of cores in this notion, all the variables in $\{X_1, ..., X_n\}$ must be covered together by some vertex of any hypertree decomposition—see again Figure 2. However, by using weak #-generalized hypertree decompositions, we are able to deal with subproblems over the existential variables having large hypertree width, but whose cores are instead decomposable.

EXAMPLE 3.15. Consider the class $\{Q_1^{n\times n} \mid n > 0\}$ with $\mathit{vars}(Q_1^{n\times n}) = \{X\} \cup \bigcup_{i+j>1}^{n} \{Y_{i,j}\}$ and $\mathit{free}(Q_1^{n\times n}) = \{X\}$.

Atoms in $Q_1^{n\times n}$ are defined over a unique binary relation symbol, and the associated (hyper)graph is the one in Figure 3, where edge orientation reflects the ordering of occurrences of the variables in the atoms. Basically, we have an $n \times n$ grid so that the class does not have bounded generalized hypertree width. However, the (sub)query $\hat{Q}_1^{n\times n} = r(X, Y_{1,2}) \wedge \bigwedge_{j=2}^{n-1} r(Y_{1,j}, Y_{1,j+1}) \wedge \bigwedge_{i=1}^{n-1} r(Y_{i,n}, Y_{i+1,n})$ is a core of $Q_1^{n\times n}$ and it is acyclic, as it is witnessed by the gray area in the figure. Moreover, the set of frontiers consists of the one singleton $\{X\}$. Therefore, $Q_1^{n\times n}$ has a width-1 weak #-generalized hypertree decomposition. ◁

Tractability results for #-decompositions are inherited by their weak variant. Moreover, for this variant we are able to refine Theorem 3.5 in a form where no decomposition must be given, as long as one exists. That is, we have a tractability result for a *promise problem*. Note that this is the best we can hope to do over arbitrary, i.e., not necessarily simple, queries (because of the intractability of the core).

THEOREM 3.16. *Let* $\mathbf{C}$ *be a class of queries having bounded weak #-generalized hypertree width. Then, for each* $Q \in \mathbf{C}$, $\text{count}(Q, \text{DB})$ *can be solved in polynomial time, for every database* DB.

PROOF SKETCH. Let $\mathbf{C}$ be a class of queries for which there exists some finite natural number $\bar{k}$ such that all queries in $\mathbf{C}$ have some weak #-generalized hypertree decomposition of width at most $\bar{k}$. Consider a problem instance $\text{count}(Q, \text{DB})$ with $Q \in \mathbf{C}$, having some weak #-generalized hypertree decomposition of Q of width $k' \leq \bar{k}$.

With reference to the proof of Theorem 3.5, we would like to compute the query Q_f without quantified variables with its database DB_f, and a generalized hypertree decomposition of constant width for Q_f. Indeed, Q_f is solution equivalent to Q, i.e., ${Q_f}^{\text{DB}_f} = \pi_{free(Q)} Q^{\text{DB}}$. So, by using a generalized hypertree decomposition, we can solve the instance in polynomial time by counting the answers of ${Q_f}^{\text{DB}_f}$.

Because $Q \in \mathbf{C}$, we know that there exists a generalized hypertree decomposition of some core of $color(Q)$ having width at most k' that covers all the frontiers (i.e., each set of the form $Fr(Y, free(Q), \mathcal{H}_Q)$ for some $Y \in vars(Q) \setminus free(Q)$). It follows (cf. proof of Theorem 3.5) that this is also a generalized hypertree decomposition of Q_f. Then, starting with $k = 1$ we try to compute a width-k hypertree decomposition of Q_f by using any polynomial-time algorithm for computing such bounded width decompositions (see, e.g. [19]). By the approximation factor shown in [2], we must succeed for some k such that $k' \leq k \leq 3 \times k' + 1$, which is again bounded by a constant independent of the input instance.

Now, we have to compute in polynomial time the database DB_f, in fact just the relations for the fresh atoms that "guard" the frontiers of quantified variables, because the remaining relations are available from the input database DB. This is not an easy task, because such relations are involved in subqueries determined by some core Q' of $color(Q)$, and we know neither Q' nor any decomposition for it. To face these issues, we first compute the view set $\mathcal{V}_Q^k$. Then, we build the legal database DB^k obtained from DB by adding, for each view $w \in \mathcal{V}_Q^k$ defined over a set C_w of atoms ($|C_w| \leq k$), the corresponding relation instance consisting of all substitutions in the answer of the conjunction of the atoms in C_w over DB. Local consistency is enforced on this database by repeatedly taking the semijoin of every pair of views having some variable in common, until a fixpoint is reached. It is well-known that this takes polynomial time, w.r.t. $\mathcal{V}_Q^k$ and DB^k. Let us call DB' the resulting database for $\mathcal{V}_Q^k$, which is known to be still legal with respect to Q.

Now recall that $k' \leq k$. This entails the existence of a weak #-generalized hypertree decomposition of Q having width k. That is, there exists a width-k generalized hypertree decomposition $\mathcal{H}_a$ of some core Q' of $color(Q)$ such that, for every $Y \in (vars(Q) \setminus free(Q))$, $Fr(Y, free(Q), \mathcal{H}_Q) \subseteq vars(h_Y)$ for some edge h_Y of $\mathcal{H}_a$, which is in its turn covered by some view of $w_Y \in \mathcal{V}_Q^k$ such that $h_Y \subseteq vars(w_Y)$. From the results in [26], for each of the above frontier sets, say O, and every view $w \in \mathcal{V}_Q^k$ such that $O \subseteq vars(w)$, $\pi_O(w^{\text{DB}'}) = \pi_O(Q'^{\text{DB}})$. Therefore, we can compute a relation for any atom of the form $atom(\bar{X}_Y)$ by projecting the relation of some available view. More formally, we can define $atom(\bar{X}_Y)^{\text{DB}_f} = \pi_{\bar{X}_Y}(w_Y^{\text{DB}'}) = \pi_{\bar{X}_Y}(Q'^{\text{DB}})$. Thus, in polynomial time, we computed the relations for all atoms "guarding" the frontiers of quantified variables. □

Note that this novel notion is still strictly more powerful than the (standard) hypertree decomposition method combined with the quantified star size (see Example 3.15).

THEOREM 3.17. *Any class of queries having bounded hypertree width and bounded quantified star size has bounded weak #-generalized hypertree width. However, there are classes having bounded weak #-generalized hypertree width, but having unbounded (generalized) hypertree width.*

For completeness, note that all tractability results given in this section can be equivalently stated for the more general notion of fractional hypertree decomposition [29], by using for the construction of the view set the $O(k^3)$ approximation described in [32] (instead of the $3 \times k + 1$ approximation used for generalized hypertree decompositions).

4. HYBRID TRACTABILITY

Since we are dealing with a setting where the query and the database are both given as input (neither is constant), it is meaningful to consider decomposition techniques that are able to exploit structural properties of the query in combination with properties of the given data, such as functional dependencies or any other feature that may simplify the evaluation. Intuitively, such features may induce different structural properties that are not identified by the "worst-possible database" perspective of purely structural methods. The motivating idea is to end up with algorithms that can be applied over a wide range of real world settings where, in particular, the previous methods do not suffice alone.

4.1 An Algorithm for "Bounded" Databases

Pichler and Skritek [35] have recently proposed an algorithm for counting answers to acyclic conjunctive queries, whose scaling is in the worst case exponential w.r.t. the maximum number of tuples over the database relations, denoted by m hereinafter. In fact, they also shown that counting query answers remains #P-hard over this structurally simple class (of course, they considered acyclic queries where existential variables are not "guarded", in the sense described in the previous section). Moreover, they pointed out that their algorithm can be extended to queries that are not necessarily acyclic, but have bounded *hypertree width* [19]. Our first step towards proposing a hybrid decomposition method for counting problems is to analyze such an extension.

A *hypertree decomposition* [19] of Q is a generalized hypertree decomposition enjoying an additional property, often called *descendant condition*. It is now convenient to recall its direct definition (instead of using a view set for Q). Formally, a *hypertree* for a query Q is a triple $\langle T, \chi, \lambda \rangle$, where T is a rooted tree, and χ and λ are labeling functions associating each vertex p of T with two sets $\chi(p) \subseteq vars(Q)$ and $\lambda(p) \subseteq atoms(Q)$. The set of the vertices of T is denoted by $vertices(T)$, whereas its root is denoted by $root(T)$. Moreover, for any $p \in N$, we denote by T_p the subtree of T rooted at p (hence, $T = T_{root(T)}$), and by $\chi(T_p)$ the set of all variables occurring in the χ labeling of T_p.

A *hypertree decomposition* of Q is a hypertree $\text{HD} = \langle T, \chi, \lambda \rangle$ for Q such that: (1) for each $q \in atoms(Q)$, there exists $p \in vertices(T)$ such that $vars(q) \subseteq \chi(p)$; (2) for each $X \in vars(Q)$, the set $\{p \in vertices(T) \mid X \in \chi(p)\}$ induces a (connected) subtree of T; (3) for each $p \in vertices(T)$, $\chi(p) \subseteq vars(\lambda(p))$; and (4) for each $p \in vertices(T)$,

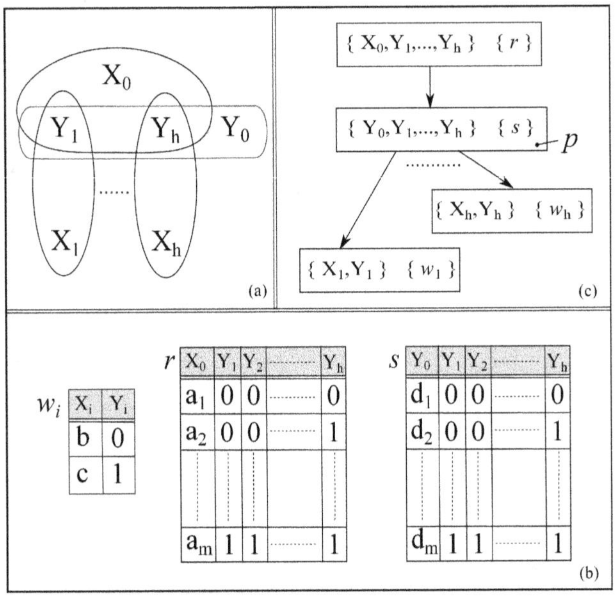

Figure 4: Structures in Example 4.1: (a) The hypergraph $\mathcal{H}_{Q_2^h}$; (b) The database DB_2; (c) A hypertree decomposition HD_2 for the query Q_2^h.

$vars(\lambda(p)) \cap \chi(T_p) \subseteq \chi(p)$ (descendant condition). The decomposition HD is said *complete* if for each atom $q \in atoms(Q)$, there exists $p \in vertices(T)$ such that $q \in \lambda(p)$. The *width* of HD is the cardinality of its largest λ label, i.e., $\max_{p \in vertices(T)} |\lambda(p)|$. The *hypertree width* of Q is the minimum width over all its hypertree decompositions.

This notion is a true generalization of acyclicity, as acyclic queries are precisely those having hypertree width 1. Importantly, for any fixed natural number $k \geq 1$, deciding whether a query has hypertree width at most k is in LOGCFL, and thus it is a tractable and highly parallelizable problem [19].

EXAMPLE 4.1. For any natural number $h \geq 1$, consider the query $Q_2^h = \exists Y_0, ..., Y_h\ r(X_0, Y_1, ..., Y_h) \wedge s(Y_0, Y_1, ..., Y_h) \wedge \bigwedge_{i \in \{1,...,h\}} w_i(X_i, Y_i)$, whose hypergraph is in Figure 4(a).

It is immediate to check that Q_2^h is acyclic, which is also witnessed by the complete width-1 hypertree decomposition HD_2 for Q_2^h, reported in Figure 4(c).

However, the frontier of any existentially quantified variable is the whole set $\{X_0, X_1, ..., X_h\}$ of the free variables. Hence, Q_2^h is not #-covered w.r.t. $\mathcal{V}_Q^k$, for each $k < h+1$. $\lhd$

Because the running time of the algorithm in [35] is in general exponential w.r.t. m (the maximum number of tuples over the database relations), the following notion is then introduced to keep under control such a blow-up.

DEFINITION 4.2. Let $b \geq 0$ be a natural number and let $\mathrm{HD} = \langle T, \chi, \lambda \rangle$ be a hypertree (not necessarily decomposition) of a query Q. We say that a database DB is *b-unbound for Q w.r.t.* HD if there is a vertex v of T and a substitution $\theta \in \pi_{free(Q)}(r_v)$ such that

$$|\sigma_\theta(r_v)| > b, \quad \text{where } r_v = \pi_{\chi(v)}(\bowtie_{q \in \lambda(v)} q^{\mathrm{DB}}).$$

The minimum b for which DB is not b-unbound is the *boundedness* of DB for Q w.r.t. HD, and it is shortly denoted by $bound(\mathrm{DB}, \mathrm{HD})$. $\Box$

Intuitively, the boundedness value $bound(\mathrm{DB}, \mathrm{HD})$ for Q provides an estimate on the size of the information that is required to flow along the given hypertree decomposition HD in order to answer a counting problem over DB.

THEOREM 4.3. *Let $\mathrm{HD} = \langle T, \chi, \lambda \rangle$ be a width-k hypertree decomposition of Q, and let DB be a database such that $bound(\mathrm{DB}, \mathrm{HD}) \leq h$. Then,* count$(Q, \mathrm{DB})$ *can be solved in $O(|vertices(T)| \times m^{2 \times k} \times 4^h)$.*

EXAMPLE 4.4. Consider the query Q_2^h in Example 4.1, the database DB_2 in Figure 4(b), and the hypertree decomposition HD_2 in Figure 4(c). The vertex p in the hypertree does not cover any free variable. Hence, $\pi_{free(Q)}(r_v)$ contains only the trivial substitution ϕ with empty domain so that $|\sigma_\phi(r_p)| = m$, with $m = 2^h$, witnessing that $bound(\mathrm{DB}_2, \mathrm{HD}_2) = m$. In fact, it can be checked that there is no width-1 hypertree decomposition HD such that $bound(\mathrm{DB}_2, \mathrm{HD}) < m$, because of the relation s.

However, even if $bound(\mathrm{DB}_2, \mathrm{HD}_2) = m$, this instance is not that hard. Indeed, consider the hypertree decomposition HD_2' obtained from HD_2, by "merging" the root with its child into a vertex p' such that $\chi(p') = \{X_0, Y_0, Y_1, ..., Y_h\}$ and $\lambda(p') = \{r, s\}$. Then, $\pi_{free(Q)}(r_{p'})$ is the set $\{\theta_1, ..., \theta_m\}$, where each θ_i maps X_0 to the constant a_i. Moreover, $|\sigma_{\theta_i}(r_{p'})| = 1$. Therefore, we have $bound(\mathrm{DB}_2, \mathrm{HD}_2') = 1$, and by Theorem 4.3 we know that the counting problem can be efficiently solved over DB_2 by using HD_2'. $\lhd$

As the above example pointed out, to end up with better boundedness values, it could also be convenient to use higher values of the width. Indeed the two parameters subtly interplay. Hence, we next face the natural problem of computing an optimal decomposition.

DEFINITION 4.5. Let Q be a query, let DB be a database, and let $\mathcal{C}$ be a class of hypertree decompositions. Then, a hypertree decomposition $\mathrm{HD} \in \mathcal{C}$ of Q is DB-*optimal over* $\mathcal{C}$ if there is no hypertree decomposition $\mathrm{HD}' \in \mathcal{C}$ of Q such that $bound(\mathrm{DB}, \mathrm{HD}') < bound(\mathrm{DB}, \mathrm{HD})$. $\Box$

Let $\mathcal{C}_k$ denote the class of all width-k hypertree decompositions. We first show a negative result for the computation of optimal decompositions over $\mathcal{C}_k$, due to a too liberal interplay between the structure and the data in Definition 4.5.

THEOREM 4.6. *Let $k \geq 8$ be any natural number. Computing* DB-*optimal decompositions over $\mathcal{C}_k$ is* NP-*hard.*

Intuitively, the source for the above intractability is that, according to its definition, a hypertree decomposition might mix together in some vertex variables and atoms that might instead be evaluated independently. Usually, this is not a main issue. Indeed, *normal forms* have been defined [39, 27], which typically correspond to more efficient decompositions, and it has been shown that focusing on normal forms is not restrictive, as any given hypertree decomposition can be transformed into a normal form one by preserving its width. Here things are different as, by mixing in some vertex variables and atoms that might be evaluated independently, we can in principle end up with a better boundedness value. Our intuition is confirmed by the result below, evidencing that over normal form decompositions the picture is completely different. Let $\mathcal{C}_k^{nf}$ be the class of all width-k hypertree decompositions in normal form.

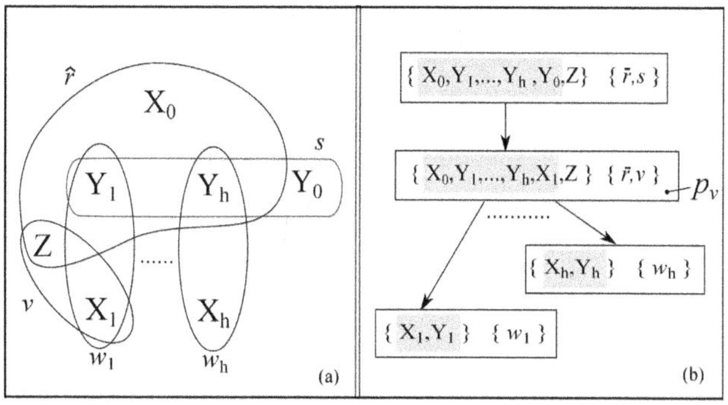

Figure 5: Structures in Example 4.8: (a) The hypergraph $\mathcal{H}_{\hat{Q}_2^h}$; (b) A width-2 $\#_h$-hypertree decomposition decomposition of $\hat{Q}_h^2$.

THEOREM 4.7. *Computing* DB*-optimal decompositions over* $\mathcal{C}_k^{nf}$ *is feasible in polynomial time.*

PROOF SKETCH. Let Q be a query and let DB a database for it. Deciding whether Q has a hypertree decomposition in $\mathcal{C}_k^{nf}$ is feasible in polynomial time [19]. We show how to compute a DB-optimal decomposition in normal form therein.

Let $\mathcal{N}$ be the set of all possible vertices of any width-k hypertree decomposition $\langle T, \chi, \lambda\rangle$ for the query Q.

Consider the function $v_{\rm DB} : \mathcal{N} \mapsto \mathbb{N}$ such that, $\forall p \in \mathcal{N}$,

$$v_{\rm DB}(p) = \max_{\theta \in \pi_{free(Q)}(r_p)} (w+1)^{|\sigma_\theta(r_p)|},$$

where $r_p = \pi_{\chi(p)}(\bigwedge_{q\in\lambda(p)} q)^{\rm DB}$ and $w = |atoms(Q)|$.

Note that $|\sigma_\theta(r_p)| \le m$ holds for each $\theta \in \pi_{free(Q)}(r_p)$, so that $v_{\rm DB}(p)$ is polynomial w.r.t. m. Moreover, consider the aggregate function $F_{Q,\rm DB}$ associating with each hypertree HD $= \langle T, \chi, \lambda\rangle$ of Q in $\mathcal{C}_k^{nf}$ the natural number $F_{Q,\rm DB} = \sum_{p\in vertices(T)} v_{\rm DB}(p)$.

Consider now the hypertree HD$^* \in \mathcal{C}_k^{nf}$ of Q such that $F_{Q,\rm DB}({\rm HD}^*) < F_{Q,\rm DB}({\rm HD}')$, for each hypertree HD$' \in \mathcal{C}_k^{nf}$ of Q. We claim that HD* is DB-optimal over $\mathcal{C}_k^{nf}$. Indeed, let $h = bound({\rm DB}, {\rm HD}^*)$, and observe that $F_{Q,\rm DB}({\rm HD}^*) \ge (w+1)^h$. Assume, for the sake for contradiction, that HD* is not DB-optimal over $\mathcal{C}_k^{nf}$ and let HD$' \in \mathcal{C}_k^{nf}$ be another hypertree decomposition of Q such that $bound({\rm DB}, {\rm HD}') = h' \le h-1$. Since HD$'$ is in normal form, then it has at most w vertices (in fact, the number of its vertices is bounded by the minimum between the number of atoms and the number of variables occurring in Q)[39, 27]. Let $n_{h'}$ be the number of vertices p of HD$'$ such that $v_{\rm DB}(p) = h'$, and observe that:

$$F_{Q,\rm DB}({\rm HD}') \le n_{h'} \times (w+1)^{h'} + (w - n_{h'}) \times (w+1)^{h'-1}.$$

Hence, $F_{Q,\rm DB}({\rm HD}') \le w \times (w+1)^{h'} < (w+1)^{h'+1} \le (w+1)^h \le F_{Q,\rm DB}({\rm HD}^*)$ holds, which is impossible.

To conclude, we point out that the function $F_{Q,\rm DB}$ fits the framework of the weighted hypertree decompositions defined in [39]. There, it is shown that such a hypertree HD* can be computed in polynomial time, for any fixed natural number k, so that our result follows from the above claim. □

4.2 Putting It All Together

We now describe a hybrid decomposition approach, which exploits information on the data to look at the structure under different perspectives. In fact, we have so far analyzed two approaches (in Section 3 and Section 4.1) to identify islands of tractability. The example below illustrates a scenario where they both fail, if considered in isolation.

EXAMPLE 4.8. Consider a slight modification of the setting discussed in Example 4.4. We have a class of instances count$(\hat{Q}_2^h, \hat{\rm DB}_2^m)$, for any pair of natural numbers h and m, where queries have the following form:

$$\hat{Q}_2^h = \exists Y_0, ..., Y_h, Z\ \hat{r}(X_0, Y_1, ..., Y_h, Z) \wedge s(Y_0, Y_1, ..., Y_h) \wedge \bigwedge_{i\in\{1,...,h\}} w_i(X_i, Y_i)\ \wedge v(Z, X_1).$$

That is, we have here an atom $\hat{r}(X_0, Y_1, ..., Y_h, Z)$ instead of $r(X_0, Y_1, ..., Y_h)$, plus the atom $v(Z, X_1)$. Similarly to Q_2^h, the purely structural methods discussed in Section 3 are not very helpful, because there is no bounded guard for the frontiers of existential variables—see Figure 5(a).

The associated relation instances in $\hat{\rm DB}_2^m$ include those in DB$_2$. Moreover, we define $\hat{r}^{\hat{\rm DB}_2^m} = r^{\hat{\rm DB}_2^m} \times \{\theta_1, ..., \theta_m\}$, where θ_i maps Z to a distinguished constant z_i, for each $i \in \{1, ..., m\}$; and we define $v^{\hat{\rm DB}_2^m}$ as $\{\theta_b, \theta_c\} \times \{\theta_1, ..., \theta_m\}$, where θ_b (resp., θ_c) maps X_1 to the constant b (resp., c). Note that the variable Z can be arbitrarily mapped to any value in its domain. So, the boundedness value of $\hat{\rm DB}_2^m$ is m, no matter of the chosen hypertree decomposition, and the techniques in Section 4.1 cannot be applied fruitfully. ◁

In the above example, the presence of the variable Z that can take m distinct values is a crucial factor determining the high boundedness value for $\hat{\rm DB}_2^m$. However, from a structural viewpoint, the interactions of this variable with the free variables are quite limited. In particular, we can look at the variables $Y_0, Y_1, ..., Y_h$ as free ones, because we know that they can be kept "under control" on the specific database instance given at hand (see, again, Example 4.4). Accordingly, we can view the frontier of Z as just consisting of the nodes X_0 and X_1, so that we might define a method that "attacks" the variable Z in a purely structural way, and the rest of the query with the techniques discussed in Section 4.1. In general, whenever we identify existential variables that are not dangerous from the point of view of the boundedness value, we may choose to treat them as if they were free variables. This way, the connectivity properties of the quantified variables do change, and it is possible that their (new) frontiers admit some guards, and a suitable decomposition.

For the sake of presentation, we provide the definition of the new notion in the framework and with the notations used for hypertree decompositions. However, its generalization to arbitrary view sets and tree projections is straightforward (together with the related tractability results).

For any set $\bar{S} \subseteq vars(Q)$, define $Q[\bar{S}]$ as the query over the same atoms and variables as Q, but where $free(Q[\bar{S}]) = \bar{S}$.

DEFINITION 4.9. Let HD $= \langle T, \chi, \lambda\rangle$ be a hypertree of a query Q. Assume that a set $\bar{S} \subseteq vars(Q)$ of variables with $free(Q) \subseteq \bar{S}$ exists such that:

(1) HD is a width-k $\#$-generalized hypertree decomposition of $Q[\bar{S}]$; (more formally, its hypergraph $\mathcal{H}_a$ with $edges(\mathcal{H}_a) = \{\chi(p) \mid p \in vertices(T)\}$);
(2) $bound({\rm DB}, \langle T, \chi_{\bar{S}}, \lambda\rangle) \le b$, where $\chi_{\bar{S}}(p) = \chi(p) \cap \bar{S}$.

Then, $\langle {\rm HD}, \bar{S}\rangle$ is called a width-k $\#_b$-generalized hypertree decomposition of Q w.r.t. DB. □

Note that condition (1) requires the existence of a width-k #-generalized hypertree decomposition for a query where all variables in $\bar{S}$ are treated as if they were free ones (in addition to the true free variables). Thus, variables in $vars(Q)\setminus\bar{S}$ are attacked in a purely structural way, and the frontier of each of them has to be covered in the decomposition. In particular, note that frontiers are calculated w.r.t. the core of $color(Q[\bar{S}])$, that is, the connected components of the quantified variables in the core depend on the choice of variables in $\bar{S}$. Instead, condition (2) is meant to exploit the boundedness condition over the query restricted to the variables in $\bar{S}$. Therefore, the propagation algorithm discussed in the previous section can lead to a controlled exponential blow-up w.r.t. b only over these variables.

Observe that, for $b = 0$, we can set $\bar{S} = free(Q)$ and we are back to the purely structural method, as condition (2) is immaterial. Instead, for any (sufficiently high) value of b, we can set $\bar{S} = vars(Q)$ and condition (1) reduces to the standard (generalized) hypertree decomposition method (tractability in the query complexity setting). Intermediate values of b define cases where the two optimization techniques discussed in the paper are synergically integrated.

EXAMPLE 4.10. Consider again the class of instances $\text{count}(\hat{Q}_2^h, \hat{\text{DB}}_2^m)$, for any pair of natural numbers h and m, described in Example 4.8. We observe that there exists a $\#_1$-generalized hypertree decomposition $\langle\langle T, \chi, \lambda\rangle, \bar{S}\rangle$ of $\hat{Q}_2^h$ w.r.t. $\hat{\text{DB}}_2^m$ having width 2. Such a decomposition is depicted in Figure 5(b), where $\bar{S} = free(Q) \cup \{Y_0, Y_1, ..., Y_h\}$—the elements in the $\chi_{\bar{S}}$-labeling are emphasized. Note that both conditions in Definition 4.9 are satisfied. Indeed, Z is the only quantified variable that is not in $\bar{S}$, and its frontier is covered by a vertex of the decomposition (the vertex p_v, in the decomposition tree shown in the figure).

In particular, to see that condition (2) holds, recall from Example 4.4 that the boundedness value is 1 over DB_2, for any decomposition where s is attacked together with r. Now, consider the root, say p_r, in Figure 5(b) covering the atoms defined over s and $\hat{r}$. Because $Z \notin \chi_{\bar{S}}(p_r) = \chi(p_r) \cap \bar{S}$, it will be projected out when this vertex will be evaluated. Then, without Z, X_0 still acts as a key for the relation computed for evaluating p_r (as it coincides with that considered in Example 4.4). Similarly, in the vertex p_v, where again Z does not occur in the $\chi_{\bar{S}}$-labeling, the variable X_0 keeps under control the quantified variables $Y_1, ..., Y_h$. So, the boundedness value is still 1 over $\hat{\text{DB}}_2^m$ and the given hypertree. ◁

By suitably combining the results in the previous section, we can show that the above hybrid notion is able to guarantee the tractability of the counting problem.

THEOREM 4.11. *Let k and b be fixed natural numbers. If a width-k $\#_b$-generalized hypertree decomposition* HD *of Q w.r.t.* DB *is given, then* count(Q, DB) *can be solved in polynomial time (w.r.t. $||Q||$, $||\text{DB}||$, and $||\text{HD}||$).*

This result can be useful in many practical applications. As suggested by Example 4.10, a noticeable case is when some functional dependencies occur in the database. For instance, if some (often all) existential variables are functionally determined by keys (over which we want to count the solutions), then their boundedness value is always 1, so that the technique may freely use them as if they were free variables, if this is convenient to decompose the given query. More generally, the approach is also effective in the presence of *quasi-keys*, i.e., attributes whose values identify a small subset of all the substitutions in a relation.

Our second result is that computing an optimal hybrid decomposition is fixed-parameter tractable.

THEOREM 4.12. *Let k be a fixed natural number. The following problem, parameterized by the query size, is in* FPT*: Given a query Q and a database* DB*, compute a width-k $\#_b$-generalized hypertree decomposition of Q w.r.t.* DB *(if any), having the minimum boundedness value b.*

Let $\mathbf{C}_h$ be a class of pairs (Q, DB), where Q is a query and DB a database. We say that $\mathbf{C}_h$ has bounded *hybrid generalized hypertree width* if there are two finite numbers k and b such that, for each $(Q, \text{DB}) \in \mathbf{C}_h$, there is a width-$k$ $\#_b$-generalized hypertree decomposition of Q w.r.t. DB. For instance, this is the case of the class in Example 4.10. From the above results, we immediately get that the counting problem is fixed parameter tractable for such classes.

COROLLARY 4.13. *Let $\mathbf{C}_h$ be a class having bounded hybrid generalized hypertree width. Then, for each $(Q, \text{DB}) \in \mathbf{C}_h$, the problem* count$(Q, \text{DB})$*, parameterized by the query size, is in* FPT.

5. CONCLUSION

In the paper, we have studied islands of tractability for the problem of counting answers to conjunctive queries, from the classical purely-structural perspective as well as from a hybrid perspective. Concerning our structural results, the question emerges about whether the notion of #-generalized hypertree decomposition charts the frontier of fixed-parameter tractability over classes of bounded-arity queries. It is worthwhile noting that, unlike the problem of evaluating Boolean conjunctive queries, we have a complexity gap here. Indeed, we provide a polynomial-time tractability result only for the classes of queries having bounded *weak* #-generalized hypertree width, which are properly contained in the classes of queries having bounded #-generalized hypertree width. A possible viable approach to fill the gap is showing that the tractability result holds for the more general notion, too. This requires some clever way to deal (in polynomial time) with frontiers of quantified variables that depend on the cores of the query (colored by the free variables). Concerning the hybrid decomposition methods, a natural avenue of further research is to incorporate them within concrete query optimizers (as in [24]).

We point out that all the results in the paper can be used for the related area of (finite) constraint satisfaction problems (CSPs), which are in fact equivalent to conjunctive queries. With this respect, we recall that "hybrid" approaches (quite different from ours) have also been proposed for evaluating CSPs, where tractable and intractable classes are determined by certain "forbidden patterns" in the constraint data (see, e.g., [10, 11] and the references therein).

6. REFERENCES

[1] S. Abiteboul, R. Hull, and V. Vianu. *Foundations of Databases.* Addison-Wesley, 1995.

[2] I. Adler, G. Gottlob, and M. Grohe. Hypertree-Width and Related Hypergraph Invariants. *European Journal of Combinatorics*, 28, pp. 2167–2181, 2007.

[3] A. Atserias, M. Grohe, and D. Marx. Size bounds and query plans for relational joins. *SIAM Journal on Computing*, 42(4):1737–1767, 2013.

[4] G. Bagan, A. Durand, and E. Grandjean. On acyclic conjunctive queries and constant delay enumeration. In *Proc. of CSL'07*, pp. 208–222, 2007.

[5] A. Bulatov, V. Dalmau, M. Grohe, and D. Marx. Enumerating Homomorphisms. *Journal of Computer and System Sciences*, 78(2): 638–650, 2012.

[6] P.A. Bernstein and N. Goodman. The power of natural semijoins. *SIAM Journal on Computing*, 10(4), pp. 751–771, 1981.

[7] A.A. Bulatov. The complexity of the counting constraint satisfaction problem. *Journal of the ACM*, 60(5), Article 34, 2013.

[8] A.A. Bulatov, M. Dyer, L.A. Goldberg, M. Jerrum, and C. Mcquillan. The expressibility of functions on the boolean domain, with applications to counting CSPs. *Journal of the ACM*, 60(5), Article 32, 2013.

[9] C. Chekuri and A. Rajaraman. Conjunctive query containment revisited. *Theoretical Computer Science*, 239(2), pp. 211–229, 2000.

[10] D.A. Cohen, M.C. Cooper, P. Creed, D. Marx, and A.Z. Salamon. The tractability of CSP classes defined by forbidden patterns. *Journal of Artificial Intelligence Research*, 45:47–78, 2012.

[11] M.C. Cooper, P.G. Jeavons, and A.Z. Salamon. Generalizing constraint satisfaction on trees: Hybrid tractability and variable elimination. *Artificial Intelligence*, 174(9-10):570–584, 2010.

[12] V. Dalmau and P. Jonsson. The complexity of counting homomorphisms seen from the other side. *Theor. Computer Science*, 329(1-3), pp. 315–323, 2004.

[13] R. Downey and M. Fellows. *Parameterized Complexity*. Springer, 1999.

[14] A.Durand and S. Mengel. Structural Tractability of Counting of Solutions to Conjunctive Queries. In *Proc. of ICDT'13*, pp. 81–92, 2013.

[15] R. Fagin. Degrees of acyclicity for hypergraphs and relational database schemes. *Journal of the ACM*, 30(3):514–550, 1983.

[16] J. Flum, M. Frick, and M. Grohe. Query evaluation via tree-decompositions. *Journal of the ACM*, 49(6):716–752, 2002.

[17] J. Flum and M. Grohe. The parameterized complexity of counting problems, *SIAM Journal on Computing*, 33:892–922, 2004.

[18] C.P. Gomes, W.J. Van Hoeve, A. Sabharwal, and B. Selman. Counting CSP solutions using generalized XOR constraints. In *Proc. of AAAI'07*, pp. 204–209.

[19] G. Gottlob, N. Leone, and F. Scarcello. Hypertree decompositions and tractable queries. *Journal of Computer and System Sciences*, 64(3):579–627, 2002.

[20] G. Gottlob, S. Tien Lee, G. Valiant, and P. Valiant. Size and Treewidth Bounds for Conjunctive Queries. *Journal of the ACM*, 59(3), 2012.

[21] G. Gottlob, N. Leone, and F. Scarcello. Robbers, marshals, and guards: game theoretic and logical characterizations of hypertree width. *Journal of Computer and System Sciences*, 66(4):775–808, 2003.

[22] G. Gottlob, Z. Miklós, and T. Schwentick. Generalized hypertree decompositions: NP-hardness and tractable variants. *Journal of the ACM*, 56(6), Article 16, 2009.

[23] N. Goodman and O. Shmueli. The tree projection theorem and relational query processing. *Journal of Computer and System Sciences*, 29(3):767–786, 1984.

[24] L. Ghionna, L.Granata, G. Greco, and F. Scarcello. Hypertree Decompositions for Query Optimization. In *Proc. of ICDE '07*, pp. 36–45, 2007.

[25] G. Greco and F. Scarcello. Structural tractability of enumerating CSP solutions. *Constraints*, 18(1):8–74, 2013.

[26] G. Greco and F. Scarcello. The power of tree projections: local consistency, greedy algorithms, and larger islands of tractability. In *Proc. of PODS'10*, pp. 327–338, 2010. Full version available as CoRR technical report *1205.3321*.

[27] G. Greco and F. Scarcello. Tree Projections: Hypergraph Games and Minimality. In *Proc. of ICALP'08*, pp. 736–747, 2008.

[28] M. Grohe. The complexity of homomorphism and constraint satisfaction problems seen from the other side. *Journal of the ACM*, 54(1), Article 1, 2007.

[29] M. Grohe and D. Marx. Constraint solving via fractional edge covers. In *Proc. of SODA'06*, pp. 289–298, 2006.

[30] C. Koch. Processing queries on tree-structured data efficiently. In *Proc. of PODS'06*, pp. 213–224, 2006.

[31] B. Kimelfeld and Y. Sagiv. Incrementally computing ordered answers of acyclic conjunctive formulas. In *Proc. of NGITS'06*, pp. 33–38, 2006.

[32] D. Marx. Approximating fractional hypertree width. *ACM Tran. on Algorithms*, 6(2), Article 29, 2010.

[33] D. Marx. Tractable Hypergraph Properties for Constraint Satisfaction and Conjunctive Queries. In *Proc. of STOC'10*, pp. 735–744, 2010.

[34] G. Pesant. Counting solutions of CSPs: a structural approach. In *Proc. of IJCAI'05*, pp. 260–265, 2005.

[35] R. Pichler and A. Skritek. Tractable Counting of the Answers to Conjunctive Queries. *Journal of Computer and System Sciences*, 79(6):984–1001, 2013.

[36] N. Robertson and P.D. Seymour. Graph minors III: Planar tree-width. *Journal of Combinatorial Theory, Series B*, 36:49–64, 1984.

[37] N. Robertson and P.D. Seymour. Graph minors V: Excluding a planar graph. *Journal of Combinatorial Theory, Series B*, 41:92–114, 1986.

[38] D. Saccà, E. Serra, and A. Guzzo. Count Constraints and the Inverse OLAP Problem: Definition, Complexity and a Step toward Aggregate Data Exchange. In *Proc. of FOIKS'12*, pp. 352–369, 2012.

[39] F. Scarcello, G. Greco, and N. Leone. Weighted Hypertree Decompositions and Optimal Query Plans. In *Proc. of PODS'04*, pp. 210–221, 2004.

[40] J. D. Ullman. *Principles of Database and Knowledge Base Systems*. Computer Science Press, 1989.

[41] M. Yannakakis. Algorithms for acyclic database schemes. In *Proc. of VLDB'81*, pp. 82–94, 1981.

A Dichotomy for Non-repeating Queries with Negation in Probabilistic Databases

Robert Fink
University of Oxford

Dan Olteanu
University of Oxford & LogicBlox Inc.

ABSTRACT

This paper shows that any non-repeating conjunctive relational query with negation has either polynomial time or #P-hard data complexity on tuple-independent probabilistic databases. This result extends a dichotomy by Dalvi and Suciu for non-repeating conjunctive queries to queries with negation. The tractable queries with negation are precisely the *hierarchical* ones and can be recognised efficiently.

1. INTRODUCTION

Charting the tractability frontier of query evaluation lies at the foundation of probabilistic databases [23]. Existing probabilistic database management systems, such as MystiQ [6] and MayBMS/SPROUT [15], fundamentally rely on query tractability results as they provide exact evaluation techniques for tractable queries and approximate techniques for intractable queries. Thus far, complexity dichotomies are known for non-repeating conjunctive queries (a.k.a. conjunctive queries without self-joins) [6] and union of conjunctive queries [9] on tuple-independent probabilistic databases: The data complexity of any query in each of these languages is either #P-hard or in polynomial time.

This paper shows a similar complexity dichotomy for queries with negation in probabilistic databases. All tractable queries are precisely the *hierarchical* ones and can be recognised in LOGSPACE in the size of the query.

The query language considered in this paper is that of *relational algebra* queries constructed using non-repeating relation symbols, equi-joins, projections, and difference (union not allowed). We denote this language by $1RA^-$. By non-repeating we mean that a relation symbol can occur at most once in the query. We also discuss extensions of $1RA^-$, in particular non-repeating *relational calculus* queries with or without union, and their implications for tractability.

Following earlier work on query tractability in probabilistic databases, this paper considers the *tuple-independent model*, where every tuple in the input database is annotated by a Boolean random variable stating the probability of the existence of that tuple, and any two such variables are independent. For more complex probabilistic models, query tractability is quickly lost: for block-independent disjoint tables, tractability analysis essentially falls back to that for tuple-independent databases by restricting joins to key attributes, while for the general model of probabilistic c-tables, already selection or projection queries can be #P-hard [23].

The following theorem states the main result of this paper:

THEOREM 1. *The data complexity of any $1RA^-$ query Q on tuple-independent databases is polynomial time if Q is hierarchical and #P-hard otherwise.*

We next define the hierarchical property. Let Q be a $1RA^-$ query. We denote by $[A]$ the equivalence class of attribute A in Q, as enforced by join and difference operators; for instance, given relations over schemas $X(A)$ and $Y(B)$, both the join $X \bowtie_{A=B} Y$ and the difference $X -_{A \leftrightarrow B} Y$ under the attribute mapping $A \leftrightarrow B$ enforce that $[A] = [B]$.

DEFINITION 1. *A $1RA^-$ query Q is* hierarchical *if for every pair of attribute classes $[A]$ and $[B]$ that have no attributes in Q's result, there is no triple of relation symbols R, S, and T in Q such that R has attributes in $[A]$ and not in $[B]$, S has attributes in both $[A]$ and $[B]$, and T has attributes in $[B]$ and not in $[A]$.*

The hierarchical property can be decided for $1RA^-$ queries in LOGSPACE [7, 12]. In the special case of queries without the difference operator, the notion of hierarchical queries defaults to the one introduced previously for non-repeating conjunctive queries and also characterises all tractable queries within that class [6]. While the syntactic characterizations are equivalent, the tractability and hardness proofs for $1RA^-$ are non-trivial generalizations of those for conjunctive queries. Careful treatment is needed for the interaction of projection and difference operators, which can encode universal quantification and can lead to hardness already for cases where one single input relation is probabilistic and all other relations are deterministic. A further source of complexity is the lack of commutativity and associativity of the difference operator, which leads to many incomparable minimal hard query patterns made out of difference and join operators. We next exemplify techniques used in the hardness and tractability proofs.

Hardness proof for non-hierarchical queries

We prove that every non-hierarchical query Q has #P-hard data complexity by reduction from the #P-hard model-counting problem for positive bipartite DNF formulas: Given any

PODS'14, June 22–27, 2014, Salt Lake City, UT, USA.

ACM 978-1-4503-2375-8/14/06. $15.00. http://dx.doi.org/10.1145/2594538.2594549.

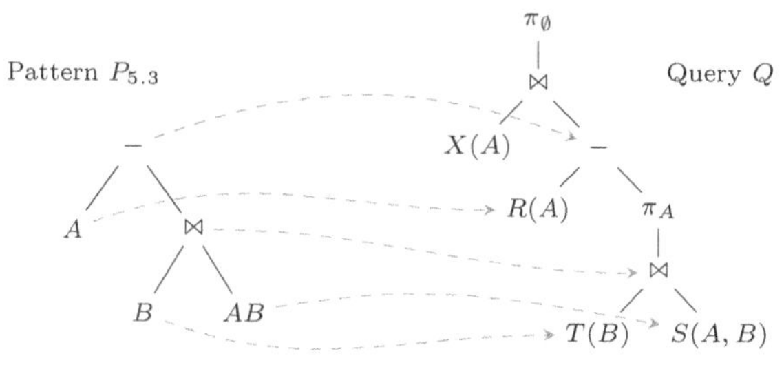

Figure 1: A query (right) matches a pattern (left).

R, X

A	Φ
1	$\top$
2	$\top$

S

A	B	Φ
1	x_1	$\top$
1	y_1	$\top$
1	y_2	$\bot$
2	x_1	$\top$
2	y_1	$\bot$
2	y_2	$\top$

$T \bowtie S$

A	B	Φ
1	x_1	$\neg\mathbf{x}_1$
1	y_1	$\neg\mathbf{y}_1$
1	y_2	$\bot$
2	x_1	$\neg\mathbf{x}_1$
2	y_1	$\bot$
2	y_2	$\neg\mathbf{y}_2$

$\pi_A(T \bowtie S)$

A	Φ
1	$\neg\mathbf{x}_1 \vee \neg\mathbf{y}_1$
2	$\neg\mathbf{x}_1 \vee \neg\mathbf{y}_2$

T

B	Φ
x_1	$\neg\mathbf{x}_1$
y_1	$\neg\mathbf{y}_1$
y_2	$\neg\mathbf{y}_2$

$R - \pi_A(T \bowtie S)$

A	Φ
1	$\mathbf{x}_1\mathbf{y}_1$
2	$\mathbf{x}_1\mathbf{y}_2$

Figure 2: Sketch of a hardness reduction for query Q in Figure 1. To avoid clutter (and in contrast to the naming convention used in Section 4), Q uses the same attribute names across multiple relations.

formula Ψ and the query Q, we construct an input database whose input tuples are annotated with variables in Ψ such that the result of Q becomes annotated with Ψ. To count the models of Ψ, we call an oracle that computes the probability P_Q of the query Q on a tuple-independent database where each variable has probability 1/2. The number of models $\#\Psi$ is then $2^n P_Q$, where n is the number of variables in Ψ.

The starting point of our analysis is an alternative characterisation of the hierarchical property of queries via *matching* one of 48 minimal patterns; for each query, we craft a specific reduction depending on which pattern is matched. A *pattern* is a concise graphical representation of an infinite class of queries that satisfy certain structural properties. For example, the query Q in Figure 1 (right) is non-hierarchical as witnessed by the three relations R, S, T, and it matches the pattern shown in Figure 1 (left). Intuitively, the query matches the pattern, because the arrangement of the three relation symbols $R(A)$, $S(A,B)$, $T(B)$ and the operators connecting them in the query correspond to the structure of the attributes A and B and the operators in the pattern.

Example 1. We exemplify the reduction for query Q in Figure 1 and the formula $\Psi = x_1y_1 \vee x_1y_2$. The input relations and intermediate query results are shown in Figure 2. Each relation has a special column Φ that holds Boolean annotation formulas over variables in Ψ: Relations R and X have only true ($\top$) annotations, S has true and false ($\bot$) annotations, and all other relations have non-trivial annotations. Whereas the input relations are tuple-independent, the intermediate results exhibit correlated annotations. The query result is the projection on the empty set of the bottom-right relation; the annotation associated with the nullary result tuple is Ψ. Our filling of input tables may use variables as constants, e.g., for attribute B in tables S and T.

The reduction strategy is determined solely by the pattern matched by Q. The key challenge is to specify a database for the relation symbols that establish the match (R, S, T, in this example) such that they give rise to formula Ψ when Q is evaluated over this database. The remaining relation symbols (X, in this example) are populated such that they leave the annotations introduced by R, S, T unaltered. □

Example 1 shows the power of negation: Our query Q can compute $\#\Psi$ for any positive 2DNF formula Ψ and is thus #P-hard already when *one* of its relations is uncertain (here, T) and all others are standard certain relations. In contrast, hardness can only be achieved for conjunctive queries when at least two input relations are uncertain.

Efficient algorithm for hierarchical queries

Our evaluation approach for hierarchical $1RA^-$ queries is to compile formulas annotating the query result into ordered binary decision diagrams (OBDDs), whose probabilities can be computed in time linear in their sizes [26]. While for hierarchical non-repeating conjunctive queries the OBDD sizes are independent of the query size and linear in the database size since the resulting formulas admit read-once representations [19], this is not the case for hierarchical $1RA^-$ queries, where the OBDD sizes remain linear in the database size, but may depend exponentially on the query size.

Example 2. The annotation of the result of the hierarchical Boolean query Q' on the database $\mathcal{D}$ in Figure 3 is

$$\Psi = r_1\left[t_1(\neg u_1 \vee \neg v_1) \vee t_2(\neg u_1 \vee \neg v_2)\right] \vee r_2\left[t_1(\neg u_2 \vee \neg v_1) \vee t_2(\neg u_2 \vee \neg v_2)\right].$$

The difference operator entangles the annotations of the participating relations in such a way that the resulting annotation Ψ is not a read-once formula; this entanglement is the pivotal intricacy introduced by the difference operator.

We show in Section 3 that for every tuple-independent database $\mathcal{D}$, the annotation of the result of Q' on $\mathcal{D}$ admits an OBDD of size $\mathcal{O}(|\mathcal{D}| \cdot f(Q))$, where $f(Q)$ is the OBDD *width* and only depends on the query size $|Q|$.

The underlying idea is to translate Q' into an equivalent disjunction of disjunction-free existential relational calculus queries such that each of the disjuncts gives rise to a compact OBDD and all OBDDs have compatible variable orders and can be combined efficiently into a single OBDD. We denote the language of such queries by $RC^{\exists}$. For Q', this translation yields the $RC^{\exists}$ query

$$Q_{RC} = \underbrace{\exists_A\big(R(A) \wedge \neg U(A)\big) \wedge \exists_B T(B)}_{Q_1} \vee \underbrace{\exists_A R(A) \wedge \exists_B\big(T(B) \wedge \neg V(B)\big)}_{Q_2}.$$

The formulas annotating the results of the two queries Q_1 and Q_2 on the database $\mathcal{D}$ from Figure 3 are

$$\Psi_1 = (r_1\neg u_1 \vee r_2\neg u_2) \wedge (t_1 \vee t_2)$$
$$\Psi_2 = (r_1 \vee r_2) \wedge (t_1\neg v_1 \vee t_2\neg v_2).$$

and clearly $\Psi_1 \vee \Psi_2 \equiv \Psi$. The $RC^{\exists}$ expressions Q_1 and Q_2 can be written such that (i) for each quantifier $\exists_X(Q')$ every relation symbol in Q' contains variable X, and (ii) the nesting order of the quantifiers is the same in both Q_1 and Q_2. Property (i) ensures that the formulas Ψ_1 and Ψ_2 admit OBDDs of size $\mathcal{O}(|\mathcal{D}|)$, as exemplified in the diagrams

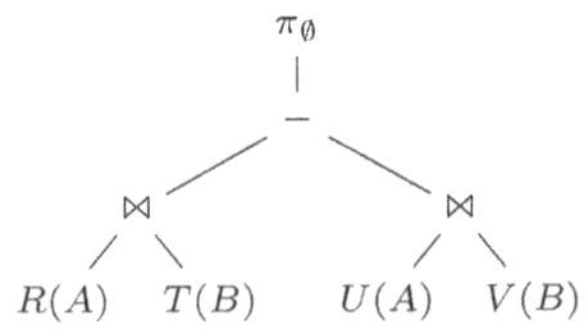

R	
A	Φ
1	r_1
2	r_2

T	
B	Φ
1	t_1
2	t_2

U	
A	Φ
1	u_1
2	u_2

V	
B	Φ
1	v_1
2	v_2

$R \bowtie T$		
A	B	Φ
1	1	r_1t_1
1	2	r_1t_2
2	1	r_2t_1
2	2	r_2t_2

$R \bowtie T - U \bowtie V$		
A	B	Φ
1	1	$r_1t_1\neg(u_1v_1)$
1	2	$r_1t_2\neg(u_1v_2)$
2	1	$r_2t_1\neg(u_2v_1)$
2	2	$r_2t_2\neg(u_2v_2)$

Figure 3: Hierarchical query Q' and a database $\mathcal{D} = (R, T, U, V)$. The tables $R \bowtie T$ and $R \bowtie T - U \bowtie V$ show how the annotations of R, T, U, V are propagated by Q'.

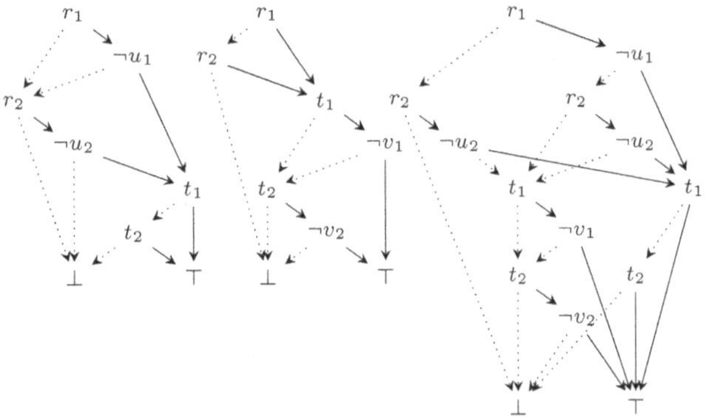

Figure 4: From left to right: OBDDs for Ψ_1, Ψ_2, and $\Psi = \Psi_1 \vee \Psi_2$ in Example 2.

of Figure 4. Property (ii) implies that these OBDDs can be constructed under the same global variable order, and it follows from classic results [26] that we can efficiently combine them via disjunctions and conjunctions. □

2. PRELIMINARIES

Due to lack of space, we defer the introduction of terminology for propositional formulas, their probabilistic interpretation when taken over Boolean random variables, as well as for probabilistic c-tables and annotation semirings to the extended version of this paper [12] and a recent monograph [23]. We next introduce a few necessary notions on the $1RA^-$ and $RC^\exists$ query languages and OBDDs.

The relational algebra query language $1RA^-$. We assume database schemas with unique attribute names. The set of attributes of a relation R is $\mathrm{sch}(R)$. A query Q is *non-repeating* if each relation symbols occurs at most once in Q.

$1RA^-$ is the class of non-repeating, union-free relational algebra queries composed of: *Relation symbols*; *Equi-join*: $Q_1 \bowtie_\rho Q_2$, where ρ is a conjunction of equality conditions $\rho = (A_1{=}B_1) \wedge \cdots \wedge (A_n{=}B_n)$ such that all A_i are attributes of Q_1 and all B_i are attributes of Q_2; *Projection*: $\pi_{A_1,\ldots,A_n}$ for attributes $A_1, \ldots, A_n$, or $\pi_{\bar{A}}$ for a set $\bar{A}$ of attributes; *Difference*: $Q_1 -_\rho Q_2$, where the attributes exported by Q_1 and Q_2 are $\{A_1, \ldots, A_n\}$ and $\{B_1, \ldots, B_n\}$ respectively, and ρ is the following conjunction of attribute mappings $(A_1{\leftrightarrow}B_1) \wedge \cdots \wedge (A_n{\leftrightarrow}B_n)$.

In $Q_1 \bowtie_\rho Q_2$ and $Q_1 -_\rho Q_2$, we write $A \in \rho$ to express that ρ contains an equality condition on A, and $(A{=}A') \in \rho$ or $(A{\leftrightarrow}A') \in \rho$ to express that ρ contains the equality condition $A{=}A'$ or $A{\leftrightarrow}A'$, respectively. When no confusion arises, we choose a schema with suggestive unique attribute names like $R(A_r), S(A_s, B_s), T(B_t)$ and then write the queries $R \bowtie_{A_r=A_s} S$ and $(R \bowtie T) -_{A_r \leftrightarrow A_s \wedge B_t \leftrightarrow B_s} S$ more concisely as $R \bowtie S$ and $(R \bowtie T) - S$.

We interchangeably use algebraic expressions and their ordered parse trees when referring to queries; in the latter case, the leaves are relations and inner nodes are algebra operators. Given a query Q and an operator Op in Q, Op has *even polarity* if the number of "$-$" operators between Op (exclusive) and the root of Q (inclusive), for which Op is a right descendant, is even, and has *odd polarity* otherwise. The pol function captures this notion: $\mathrm{pol}(Q, Op)$ is 1 if Op has odd polarity in Q, and 0 otherwise.

The equivalence class $[A]$ of an attribute A in Q is defined as in the introduction, where we consider the difference operators as joins on all attributes of its operands.

The attributes *exported* by a query Q, denoted $\mathcal{E}(Q)$, are defined recursively on the query structure:

If $Q = Q_1 \bowtie_\rho Q_2$,	then $\mathcal{E}(Q) = \mathcal{E}(Q_1) \cup \mathcal{E}(Q_2)$
If $Q = Q_1 -_\rho Q_2$,	then $\mathcal{E}(Q) = \mathcal{E}(Q_1)$
If $Q = \pi_{\bar{A}}(Q_1)$,	then $\mathcal{E}(Q) = \bar{A}$
If $Q = \sigma_\rho(Q_1)$,	then $\mathcal{E}(Q) = \mathcal{E}(Q_1)$
If $Q = R$,	then $\mathcal{E}(Q) = \mathrm{sch}(R)$

A query Q *exports* $[A]$ if there exists $A' \in [A]$ such that $A' \in \mathcal{E}(Q)$. Conversely, Q *does not export* $[A]$ if for all $A' \in [A]$ it holds that $A' \notin \mathcal{E}(Q)$. By $Q^{[A]}$, $Q^{[\neg B]}$, and $Q^{[A][\neg B]}$ we denote a query Q that exports $[A]$, does not export $[B]$, and respectively exports $[A]$ and not $[B]$.

We use $\pi_{-A_1,\cdots,-A_n}(Q)$ as syntactic sugar for discarding $A_1, \ldots, A_n$, i.e., $\pi_{-A_1,\ldots,-A_n}(Q) = \pi_{\mathcal{E}(Q)-\{A_1,\ldots,A_n\}}(Q)$. Similarly, for an attribute A, the operator $\pi_{[A]}$ is a shortcut for $\pi_{A'}$ for any $A' \in [A]$, and the operator $\pi_{-[A]}$ denotes $\pi_{-A_1,\ldots,-A_n}$ where $[A] = \{A_1, \ldots, A_n\}$.

The relational calculus query language $RC^\exists$ is the class of queries that are expressions $\{\bar{H} \mid F\}$, where the query body F is a formula defined by the following grammar:

$$F ::= R(\bar{X}) \mid \exists_X(F_1) \mid F_1 \wedge F_2 \mid F_1 \vee F_2 \mid \neg(F_1),$$

and the query head $\bar{H}$ is the tuple of variable symbols that occur unquantified in F. In the sequel, we represent a query by its formula F alone. The *size* $|Q|$ of a query Q is the number of its relation symbols. A variable X is *root* in a query $\exists_X(Q)$ if X occurs in every relation symbol in Q [8].

DEFINITION 2. *An $RC^\exists$ query Q is* canonicalised *if every occurrence of a relation symbol $R(\bar{X})$ in Q has the same query variables $\bar{X}$.*

Binary decision diagrams (BDDs) form a representation system for Boolean propositional formulas such as the annotations used in probabilistic databases. A BDD over a set $\mathbf{X}$ of variables is a directed acyclic graph where inner nodes are labeled with variables from $\mathbf{X}$ and terminal nodes are true ($\top$) and false ($\bot$). Each inner node has two outgoing edges, for the case its variable is set to true (solid edge) and false (dotted edge) respectively. Each root-to-leaf path in a BDD is a (possibly partial) assignment of variables.

A BDD is *ordered* (OBDD) if there is a total order Π on its variables such that the variables visited by each path are in Π-order. A *level* in an OBDD corresponds to all nodes labeled with the same variable. The *width*[1] of a BDD is the maximum number of edges crossing the section of the OBDD between the nodes of any two consecutive levels, where edges incident to the same node are counted as one.

In this paper, we make use of the following results:

LEMMA 1 ([26]). *Let Φ_1, Φ_2 be two formulas, Π be a fixed variable order on their variables, and O_1 and O_2 be Π-OBDDs of width w_1 and w_2 for Φ_1 and Φ_2, respectively. Then, Π-OBDDs for $\Phi_1 \wedge \Phi_2$ and for $\Phi_1 \vee \Phi_2$ can be constructed in time $O(|O_1| \cdot |O_2|)$ and have width at most $w_1 \cdot w_2$.*

Given an OBDD for a formula Ψ, the probability P_Ψ can be computed in time linear in the size of the OBDD.

EXAMPLE 3. Figure 4 shows three OBDDs under the same variable order $r_1, u_1, r_2, u_2, t_1, v_1, t_2, v_2$. Solid lines denote the *true*-edges and dotted lines the *false*-edges. The path $r_1 \xrightarrow{\top} \neg u_1 \xrightarrow{\bot} r_2 \xrightarrow{\bot} \bot$ encodes that under any truth assignment ν with $\nu(r_1) = \top$ and $\nu(\neg u_1) = \nu(r_2) = \bot$, the expression $\Psi_1 = (r_1 \neg u_1 \vee r_2 \neg u_2) \wedge (t_1 \vee t_2)$ becomes false. The width of the left two OBDDs is three: There are three edges with different sinks crossing from level of r_2 to $\neg u_2$ and respectively from t_1 to $\neg v_1$. The rightmost OBDD represents the disjunction of the two leftmost OBDDs (using the ITE algorithm [4]) and has width five. □

3. HIERARCHICAL 1RA$^-$ QUERIES

We show in this section the following result:

LEMMA 2. *Any hierarchical 1RA$^-$ query on tuple-independent databases has polynomial-time data complexity.*

PROOF. We prove the lemma via a sequence of steps:

Q_{RA} is a hierarchical 1RA$^-$ query

$\Rightarrow$ Lemma 3

Q_{RA} is equivalent to an RC$^\exists$ query Q_{RC} that is RC-hierarchical and $\exists$-consistent

$\Rightarrow$ Lemma 4

For any database $\mathcal{D}$, we can find an OBDD of size $\mathcal{O}(|\mathcal{D}| \cdot 2^{|Q_{RC}|})$ for the annotation Φ of the result $Q_{RC}(\mathcal{D})$

$\Rightarrow$ Corollary 1

The probability of Φ can be computed in $\mathcal{O}(|\mathcal{D}| \cdot 2^{|Q_{RC}|})$.

The reason for translating 1RA$^-$ queries to RC$^\exists$ queries is that relational calculus is more flexible and allows to unfold negated expressions as per $\neg(Q_1 \wedge Q_2) \equiv \neg Q_1 \vee \neg Q_2$. Since the 1RA$^-$ query Q_{RA} and the RC$^\exists$ query Q_{RC} are equivalent for any input database $\mathcal{D}$, the formulas annotating their results are equivalent too and thus have the same probability. We then show how Q_{RC}'s annotation can be compiled into an OBDD of size $\mathcal{O}(|\mathcal{D}| \cdot 2^{|Q_{RC}|})$.

The RC$^\exists$ query Q_{RC} is a disjunction of disjunction-free RC$^\exists$ expressions. In contrast to Q_{RA}, Q_{RC} may have repeating relation symbols. It is hierarchical in a syntactically more restricted sense:

[1]There is a different notion of BDD width in the literature that refers to the maximum number of nodes in any level.

DEFINITION 3. *An RC$^\exists$ query Q is* RC-hierarchical *if for every sub-query $\exists_X(Q')$ in Q it holds that X is root in Q'.*

Recall from Section 2 that a variable X is *root* in Q' if it appears in every relation symbol in Q', and that an RC$^\exists$ query is *canonicalised* if each relation symbol occurs only with the same variable symbols. In addition, the RC$^\exists$ queries obtained via rewriting can be written such that the nesting order of the existential quantifiers is the same over all of their disjunction-free expressions.

DEFINITION 4. *A canonicalised RC$^\exists$ query is* $\exists$-consistent *if there exists a total order $>_\exists$ of the variable symbols in Q such that $X >_\exists Y$ implies that there is no sub-query of the form $\exists_Y Q'(\exists_X)$ in Q.*

Intuitively, $\exists$-consistency for an RC$^\exists$ query that is a conjunction or disjunction of sub-queries means that these sub-queries have compatible join orders (i.e., non-contradicting $>_\exists$ orders). This means that their annotations, as well as the conjunction, disjunction, and negation of their annotations, can be compiled into OBDDs over the same variable order. In addition, the RC-hierarchical property effectively helps inferring from the order of quantifiers in the query a variable order for the OBDD that keeps its size only linear in the number of variables and thus in the database size but possibly exponential in the query size. We next illustrate these concepts via an example.

EXAMPLE 4. Consider the following three RC$^\exists$ queries:

$$Q_1 = \exists_A \big(M(A) \wedge \neg R(A)\big) \wedge \exists_B N(B)$$
$$Q_2 = \exists_A M(A) \wedge \exists_B \big(N(B) \wedge \neg T(B)\big)$$
$$Q_3 = \exists_A \big(M(A) \wedge U(A)\big) \wedge \exists_B \big(N(B) \wedge V(B)\big)$$

All three queries are RC-hierarchical since for each occurrence of $\exists_A$ and $\exists_B$, A and B, respectively, are root variables. Let us evaluate the queries over the database $\mathcal{D}$, viz:

M		N		R		T		U		V	
A	Φ	B	Φ	A	Φ	B	Φ	A	Φ	B	Φ
1	m_1	1	n_1	1	r_1	1	t_1	1	u_1	1	v_1
2	m_2	2	n_2	2	r_2	2	t_2	2	u_2	2	v_2

The annotations Φ_i of Q_i $(i = 1, 2, 3)$ evaluated on $\mathcal{D}$ are

$$\Phi_1 = (m_1\bar{r}_1 \vee m_2\bar{r}_2) \wedge (n_1 \vee n_2)$$
$$\Phi_2 = (m_1 \vee m_2) \wedge (n_1\bar{t}_1 \vee n_2\bar{t}_2)$$
$$\Phi_3 = (m_1u_1 \vee m_2u_2) \wedge (n_1v_1 \vee n_2v_2)$$

and can be represented by OBDDs of width 2 under the respective variable orders Π_1, Π_2, Π_3:

$$\Pi_1 : m_1, r_1, m_2, r_2, n_1, n_2$$
$$\Pi_2 : m_1, m_2, n_1, t_1, n_2, t_2$$
$$\Pi_3 : m_1, u_1, m_2, u_2, n_1, v_1, n_2, v_2$$

Now consider the query $Q_{123} = Q_1 \vee Q_2 \vee Q_3$; this query is canonicalised, RC-hierarchical, and $\exists$-consistent. The variable orders Π_1, Π_2, and Π_3 are compatible in the sense that they can be extended into an order Π_{123} over all variables:

$$\Pi_{123} : m_1, r_1, u_1, m_2, r_2, u_2, n_1, t_1, v_1, n_2, t_2, v_2$$

In the light of Lemma 1, the OBDDs of Φ_1, Φ_2, and Φ_3 can be combined to yield an OBDD of width at most 2^3 for the annotation $\Phi_1 \vee \Phi_2 \vee \Phi_3$ of query Q_{123}. □

3.1 From 1RA$^-$ to RC$^\exists$

At the core of the evaluation algorithm for hierarchical 1RA$^-$ queries is a rewriting of 1RA$^-$ queries into equivalent safe RC$^\exists$ queries. The rewriting procedure $[\![\cdot]\!]$ is the standard recursive inside-out translation from relational algebra to safe relational calculus (Lemma 5.3.11, [1]), with the addition that after each recursive translation step we "flatten" the resulting RC$^\exists$ query as follows:

- Every $\exists$ operator is pushed as deep as possible in the RC$^\exists$ query without pushing it past a $\neg$ operator: $\exists_X$ distributes over disjunctions and is pushed past conjuncts in which X does not appear. Lemma 3 shows that every $\exists_X$ operator can be pushed until X becomes root, i.e., X occurs in all relation symbols in its scope.
- Every $\neg$ operator is recursively pushed (as per $\neg(A \wedge B) \rightarrow \neg A \vee \neg B$ and its dual) as deep as possible in the RC$^\exists$ query without pushing it past an $\exists$ operator.
- Conjunctions of disjunctions are eagerly expanded into disjunctions of conjunctions as per

$$(A \vee B) \wedge (C \vee D) \rightarrow AB \vee AC \vee BC \vee BD.$$

Our translation has several desirable properties:

LEMMA 3. *For any hierarchical 1RA$^-$ query Q_{RA}, the translated RC$^\exists$ query $Q_{RC} = [\![Q_{RA}]\!]$ satisfies the following:*

(a) Q_{RC} is equivalent to Q_{RA}.

(b) Q_{RC} is canonicalised.

(c) Q_{RC} is a disjunction of disjunction-free RC$^\exists$ queries.

(d) For every variable X in Q_{RC}, Q_{RC} has no sub-query of the form $\exists_X(Q) \wedge Q'(\exists_X)$; here, $Q(\exists_X)$ denotes a query Q in which $\exists_X$ occurs.

(e) Q_{RC} is RC-hierarchical.

(f) The quantifiers in Q_{RC} can be ordered such that Q_{RC} is $\exists$-consistent.

Condition (d) permits sub-queries of the form $\neg\exists_X(Q) \wedge \neg\exists_X(Q')$ or $\exists_X(Q) \vee \exists_X(Q')$, but disallows, e.g., $\exists_X(Q) \wedge \exists_X(Q')$, $\exists_X(Q) \wedge \neg\exists_X(Q')$, $\exists_X(Q) \wedge \neg\exists_Y(Q'' \wedge \neg\exists_X(Q'''))$.

EXAMPLE 5. Consider the following two 1RA$^-$ queries:

$$Q_a = \pi_\emptyset\Big[M(A) \bowtie N(B) - \big[R(A) \bowtie T(B) - U(A) \bowtie V(B)\big]\Big]$$

$$Q_b = \pi_\emptyset\Big[\pi_A\big(M(A) \bowtie N(B)\big) - \pi_A\big[R(A) \bowtie T(B) - U(A) \bowtie V(B)\big]\Big].$$

Query Q_a translates to Q_{123} from Example 4 (subsumed sub-queries removed to avoid clutter). Q_b is similar to Q_a, but with additional projections on A on both sides of the top-most difference operator, and translates to

$$\begin{aligned}[\![Q_b]\!] = {} & \exists_A\big(M(A) \wedge \neg R(A)\big) \wedge \exists_B N(B) \quad \vee \\ & \exists_A M(A) \wedge \exists_B N(B) \wedge \neg\exists_B T(B) \quad \vee \\ & \exists_A\big(M(A) \wedge U(A)\big) \wedge \exists_B N(B) \wedge \neg\exists_B\big(T(B) \neg V(B)\big).\end{aligned}$$

Like Q_{123}, the RC$^\exists$ query $[\![Q_b]\!]$ has three disjuncts, but the nesting orders of $\neg$ and $\exists_B$ operators in the second and third conjuncts differ from the corresponding order in Q_{123}. The translations of Q_a and Q_b satisfy Lemma 3: For example, for every operator $\exists_A$ (or $\exists_B$), A (or B) is a root variable in its scope (Property (e)), and the nesting orders of $\exists_A$ and $\exists_B$ are consistent in all sub-queries (Property (f)). □

The query translation can lead to large RC$^\exists$ queries: A conservative upper bound on their sizes would be a non-elementary function of the size of the input 1RA$^-$ query, explained by the rapid increase in the size and number of disjuncts when pushing down negations, projections, and conjunctions. A singly-exponential upper bound holds for 1RA$^-$ queries where for all projections $\pi_{-X}(Q)$ that are right descendants of a difference operator, attributes in the equivalence class $[X]$ occur in all relation symbols of Q (i.e., X is root in Q). The query Q_a in Example 5 satisfies this condition trivially, since it has no projection that is a right descendant of a difference operator. While this conservative upper bound suffices for the *data*-complexity argument in Lemma 2 since the blowup is in the size of the query only, it is not practical and better translation algorithms, which avoid the generation of subsumed disjuncts, are called for.

3.2 OBDD Construction

The last step in the proof of Lemma 2 is the OBDD compilation of the annotation Φ of the RC$^\exists$ query Q_{RC} obtained from Q_{RA} as per Lemma 3. This OBDD has a total order Π over the Boolean variables annotating the input tuples that can be derived from the structure of Q_{RC}. Let us first exemplify the construction of this order.

EXAMPLE 6. Consider the query

$$Q = \exists_X\big[R(X) \wedge \exists_Y(S(X,Y) \wedge \neg T(X,Y))\big].$$

Since X is a root variable, the OBDDs for different values of X are independent and can be concatenated. For each value a in the active domain of X, we construct the OBDD for the query $R(a) \wedge \exists_Y(S(a,Y) \wedge \neg T(a,Y))$; one good variable order for this OBDD is the sequence of the annotation of $R(a)$ and all annotations of $S(a,b)$ and of $T(a,b)$ for all values b in the active domain of Y. If we write $R(1)$ for the annotation of tuple (1) in R, and similarly for S and T (all values being positive integers), then the overall variable order is

$$R(\mathbf{1}), S(\mathbf{1},1), T(\mathbf{1},1), S(\mathbf{1},2), T(\mathbf{1},2), S(\mathbf{1},3), T(\mathbf{1},3)\ldots,$$
(tuples with $X = \mathbf{1}$)
$$R(\mathbf{2}), S(\mathbf{2},1), T(\mathbf{2},1), S(\mathbf{2},2), T(\mathbf{2},2), S(\mathbf{2},3), T(\mathbf{2},3)\ldots,$$
(tuples with $X = \mathbf{2}$) and so on.

The annotations are ordered in lexicographically ascending order: We first consider all annotations with $X = 1$, then all annotations with $X = 2$, etc. For all annotations with $X = 1$, we first consider those with $Y = 1$, then those with $Y = 2$, etc. This variable order leads to a compact OBDD because the order of random variables annotating bindings of query variables X, Y in the relations R, S, T is compatible with the nesting order of the quantifiers $\exists_X$ and $\exists_Y$. □

LEMMA 4. *For any RC$^\exists$ query Q_{RC} that satisfies the properties of Lemma 3, the annotation Φ of Q_{RC} on a tuple-independent database $\mathcal{D}$ can be represented by an OBDD of size $\mathcal{O}(|\mathcal{D}| \cdot 2^{|Q_{RC}|})$.*

PROOF. We prove the lemma for Boolean queries Q_{RC}; the general case follows trivially. Let the relation symbols in Q_{RC} be $R_1, \ldots, R_n$, the variables be $X_1, \ldots, X_m$, and let $\text{ADom}(X_i)$ be the active domain of variable X_i. The annotation of tuple $\bar{A}$ of relation R_i is denoted by $R_i(\bar{A})$, e.g., the annotation of tuple (a, b) in relation R_1 is $R_1(a, b)$. We assume without loss of generality that the order of the query variables $X_1, \ldots, X_m$ is such that $X_i >_\exists X_j \Leftrightarrow i < j$ with respect to the nesting order $>_\exists$ defined by the $\exists$-consistency of Q_{RC}; that is, $i < j$ allows for the quantifier nesting $\exists_{X_i} Q(\exists_{X_j})$, but not $\exists_{X_j} Q(\exists_{X_i})$. Since Q_{RC} is canonicalised and $\exists$-consistent (Lemma 3), we can assume without loss of generality that in each relation symbol R the query variables occur in $>_\exists$ order (we can always relabel the query and database schema such that the query variables occur in $>_\exists$-order). For example, Q_{RC} may contain $R(X_1, X_5, X_7)$, but not $R(X_7, X_1, X_5)$. Furthermore, we assume a total order over the active domain of the database such that for any $x_i \in \text{ADom}(X_i)$ and $x_j \in \text{ADom}(X_j)$ it holds that $x_i < x_j \Leftrightarrow i < j$; similarly for relation names: $R_1 < R_2 < \cdots < R_n$, where in addition the relation names are not part of the active domains of query variables and occur before the domain constants in this order.

We define a total order Π on the annotations of the tuples in $\mathcal{D}$ as follows. We first associate with every annotation $R(\bar{A})$ the string $\text{string}(R(\bar{A})) = \bar{A}R$, e.g., annotation $R_2(A_7, B_2, C_7)$ is associated with the string $A_7B_2C_7R_2$. The order Π is then defined as

$$R(\bar{A}) <_\Pi R'(\bar{A}') \Leftrightarrow \text{string}(R(\bar{A})) <_{\text{lex}} \text{string}(R(\bar{A}'))$$

where $<_{\text{lex}}$ is the lexicographic order on strings as defined by the total order of the active domain of the database and the relation names. Note that Π is uniquely defined by the order of the relation symbols and the order on the active domain of $\mathcal{D}$. However, different orders on the former and the latter give rise to different orders Π.

We show by structural induction over Φ that it has a Π-OBDD of width $2^{|Q_{RC}|}$ where $|Q_{RC}|$ denotes the number of relation symbols in Q_{RC}:

- The base case is a relation symbol $R(\bar{A})$ which corresponds to a trivial Π-OBDD with one variable $R(\bar{A})$ and width 2.
- If $Q_{RC} = Q_1 \wedge Q_2$ or $Q_{RC} = Q_1 \vee Q_2$, then by induction hypothesis the annotations of Q_1 and Q_2 have Π-OBDDs of width $2^{|Q_1|}$ and $2^{|Q_2|}$, respectively. Then by Lemma 1, the annotation of Q_{RC} has a Π-OBDD of width $2^{|Q_1|} \cdot 2^{|Q_2|} = 2^{|Q_{RC}|}$.
- If $Q_{RC} = \neg Q$, then by induction hypothesis Q has a Π-OBDD of width $2^{|Q|}$. Swapping the $\top$ and $\bot$ nodes in this OBDD yields the required Π-OBDD for Q_{RC}.
- If $Q_{RC} = \exists_{X_i} Q$, then for every $A_l \in \text{ADom}(X_i)$ the annotations Φ_l of queries $Q[A_l/X_i]$ are over disjoint sets of variables because Q_{RC} is RC-hierarchical by Lemma 3 and hence X_i is root in Q. Moreover, each Φ_l has a Π-OBDD of width $2^{|Q|}$ by induction hypothesis. Let $\text{ADom}(X_i) = \{A_1, \ldots, A_h\}$ such that $A_k <_{\text{lex}} A_l$ if and only if $k < l$. The annotation Φ of Q_{RC} is the disjunction $\bigvee_{A_l \in \text{ADom}(X_i)} \Phi_l$. Since the formulas Φ_l are over disjoint sets of variables for distinct values of l, an OBDD for their disjunction is obtained by their concatenation in which the $\bot$ node of the OBDD for Φ_l is replaced by the root node of the OBDD for Φ_{l+1}.

It remains to show that this construction yields an OBDD over order Π. First, note that the OBDD for each Φ_l is over order Π by induction hypothesis; we next show that for any two annotations $R(\bar{A}_k)$ in Φ_k and $R'(\bar{A}_l)$ in Φ_l with $k < l$, it holds that $R'(\bar{A}_k) <_\Pi R'(\bar{A}_l)$; by the definition of $<_\Pi$, this is equivalent to showing $\bar{A}_k R <_{\text{lex}} \bar{A}_l R'$. The strings $\bar{A}_k$ and $\bar{A}_l$ are identical in the first $i-1$ places since, by construction, the variables X_j with $j < i$ are set to the same constants. The lexicographic order of $\bar{A}_k$ and $\bar{A}_l$ — and hence the Π-order of $R(\bar{A}_k)$ in Φ_k and of $R'(\bar{A}_l)$ in Φ_l — is determined by the values of X_i in $\bar{A}_k$ and in $\bar{A}_l$; this value is A_l in $\bar{A}_l$ and A_k in $\bar{A}_k$. Since we concatenate the OBDDs in the order $\Phi_1 \to \cdots \to \Phi_h$ and since $A_1 <_{\text{lex}} \cdots <_{\text{lex}} A_h$ it follows that $\bar{A}_k <_{\text{lex}} \bar{A}_l$ and thus $R(\bar{A}_k) <_\Pi R'(\bar{A}_l)$. The constructed OBDD has width $2^{|Q_{RC}|} = 2^{|Q|}$, because the concatenation leaves the width unchanged. □

The OBDD construction in the above proof shows that conjunction, disjunction, negation, and existential quantification of $\text{RC}^\exists$ queries representing rewritings of 1RA^- queries correspond to analogous operations on OBDDs representing the annotations of such queries. In particular, the width of the resulting OBDD is bounded above by the product of the widths of the input OBDDs. This is a conservative upper bound that allows a uniform and simple treatment of $\text{RC}^\exists$ operations in the proof. A tighter bound can be obtained via a more specific analysis: Any non-repeating RC-hierarchical $\text{RC}^\exists$ query Q admits an OBDD of width at most $|Q|$ and size linear in the input database size and independent of the query size [19]. This tighter bound on the OBDD width can be immediately extended to $\exists$-consistent conjunction and disjunction of such queries $Q_1, \ldots, Q_n$: The resulting OBDD has width $|Q_1| \cdot \ldots \cdot |Q_n|$, which is smaller than $2^{|Q_1|+\cdots+|Q_n|}$ as used in the proof.

We can now use both Lemmata 1 and 4 to obtain the polynomial-time computation of query probability:

COROLLARY 1 (LEMMATA 1, 4). *Let Q_{RC} be a $RC^\exists$ query satisfying the properties of Lemma 3. For any tuple-independent database $\mathcal{D}$, the probability of the query result $Q_{RC}(\mathcal{D})$ can be computed in time $\mathcal{O}(|\mathcal{D}| \cdot 2^{|Q_{RC}|})$.*

4. NON-HIERARCHICAL 1RA^- QUERIES

We show in this section the following result:

LEMMA 5. *The data complexity of any non-hierarchical $1RA^-$ query is #P-hard.*

PROOF. Given a 1RA^- query Q and any 2DNF formula Ψ, we use a reduction from the model-counting problem $\#\Psi$ by means of a construction of a database $\mathcal{D}$ such that Ψ and the query result $Q(\mathcal{D})$ have the same probability. The reduction depends on structural properties of Q. We show that the non-hierarchical property is equivalent to *matching a pattern* from the list of all possible patterns made up of inner nodes that are difference or join operators and leaves that correspond to three relations $R^{[A][\neg B]}$, $S^{[A][B]}$, and $T^{[B][\neg A]}$ for two distinct attribute classes $[A]$ and $[B]$. The notion of a match is then refined to that of an *annotation-preserving*

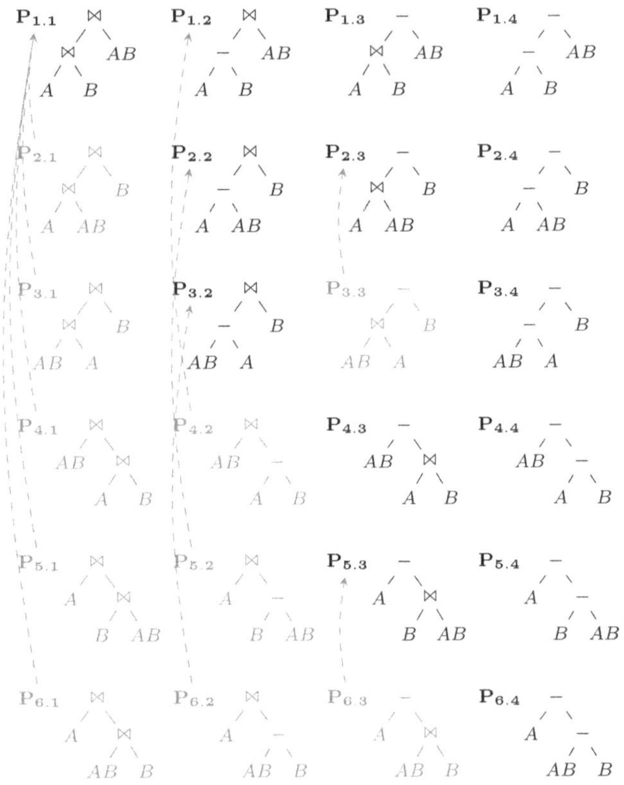

Figure 5: The 24 query patterns $P_{1.1}$, ..., $P_{6.4}$. The 10 grey patterns can by reduced to other patterns as indicated by the arrows, since the labels A and B are symmetric and can be swapped, and the join ($\bowtie$) operator is commutative and its sub-queries can also be swapped. Further 24 patterns can be obtained by swapping A and B in the above patterns.

match, for which a database construction scheme is possible such that the query result becomes annotated by Ψ.

The proof steps are summarised as follows:

Q is non-hierarchical
$\Leftrightarrow$ (Proposition 1)
Q has a match with a pattern in Figure 5
$\Leftrightarrow$ (Lemma 7)
Q has an annotation-preserving match with a pattern
$\Rightarrow$ (Lemma 8)
Q is hard for #P. □

4.1 Database construction scheme

Our database construction scheme prescribes how to populate relations used in a non-hierarchical query such that the query result is annotated with a desired 2DNF formula. It particularly focuses on two distinguished attributes $[A]$ and $[B]$ that witness the non-hierarchical property of the query.

We assume two finite sets of constants, $\mathbf{A}$ and $\mathbf{B}$, and a constant ■ distinct from those in $\mathbf{A}$ and $\mathbf{B}$. In this section, the projection operator π_A^Φ is used to symbolise the projection on attribute A and the annotation column Φ; in contrast, π_A selects only column A, neglecting the annotations of tuples. The notation $(a_1, \ldots, a_n | \Phi(a_1, \ldots, a_n))$ denotes a tuple $(a_1, \ldots, a_n)$ annotated with formula $\Phi(a_1, \ldots, a_n)$.

Preserving the data of one attribute

We commence by analysing queries with one distinguished attribute A. Let Φ be a total function on $\mathbf{A}$. A relation Q is *A-reducible to* $(\mathbf{A}, \Phi)$ if the $[A]$-attributes of Q are filled with all values from $\mathbf{A}$, all non-$[A]$-attributes are filled with ■, and the annotation of a tuple identified by $a \in \mathbf{A}$ is $\Phi(a)$:

$$\pi_{[A]}^{\Phi}(Q) = \{(a|\Phi(a)) \mid a \in \mathbf{A}\}$$
$$\pi_C(Q) = \{(■)\} \quad \text{for any attribute } C \text{ with } C \notin [A].$$

By $\text{red}_A(Q) = \mathbf{A}|\Phi$ we denote that Q is A-reducible to $(\mathbf{A}, \Phi)$. Queries that do not export $[A]$ are called $\emptyset$-reducible to a nullary function Φ (denoted $\text{red}_\emptyset(Q) = ■|\Phi$) if

$$\pi_\emptyset^\Phi(Q) = \{(\Phi)\}$$
$$\pi_C(Q) = \{(■)\} \quad \text{for any attribute } C.$$

We next define three classes of relations $\mathcal{Q}^A$, $\mathcal{Q}_{\text{fill}}$, and $\mathcal{Q}_\emptyset$ that are characterised by their A-reductions; let $\Phi_\top$ be the constant function $\Phi_\top(.) = \top$.

$$Q^{[A]} \in \mathcal{Q}^A \quad \text{if} \quad \text{red}_A(Q) = \mathbf{A}|\Phi \tag{1}$$
$$Q^{[A]} \in \mathcal{Q}_{\text{fill}} \quad \text{if} \quad \text{red}_A(Q) = \mathbf{A}|\Phi_\top \tag{2}$$
$$Q^{[\neg A]} \in \mathcal{Q}_{\text{fill}} \quad \text{if} \quad \text{red}_\emptyset(Q) = ■|\Phi_\top \tag{3}$$
$$Q \in \mathcal{Q}_\emptyset \quad \text{if} \quad Q = \emptyset \tag{4}$$

In Equation (1), Φ can also be $\neg\Phi$. Queries $\mathcal{Q}^A$ are relations in which the values of $[A]$-attributes are populated with values from $\mathbf{A}$, and values for non-$[A]$-attributes are set to ■. There is a functional dependency $[A] \to \Phi$ such that every tuple is represented by its $[A]$-value a and has a corresponding annotation $\Phi(a)$ or $\neg\Phi(a)$. Queries $\mathcal{Q}_{\text{fill}}$ are similar to Q_A-queries, but every tuple is annotated with $\top$. Queries $\mathcal{Q}_\emptyset$ are simply empty relations.

Example 7. Given the domain $\mathbf{A} = \{x_1, x_2, x_3\}$, the following relation X over the distinguished attribute A and two attributes B, C with $B, C \notin [A]$ satisfies the properties of a $\mathcal{Q}^A$-query, and relation Y is a $\mathcal{Q}_{\text{fill}}$-query.

$\mathcal{Q}^A$-relation X

A_x	B_x	C_x	Φ
x_1	■	■	$\mathbf{x_1}$
x_2	■	■	$\mathbf{x_2}$
x_3	■	■	$\mathbf{x_3}$

$\mathcal{Q}_{\text{fill}}$-relation Y

A_y	B_y	C_y	Φ
x_1	■	■	$\top$
x_2	■	■	$\top$
x_3	■	■	$\top$

In relation X we use the same symbols x_i both as data values for A and annotations; the functional dependency $A_x \to \Phi$ is thus trivially satisfied by $\Phi(x_i) = \mathbf{x_i}$. □

Figure 6 shows how $\mathcal{Q}^A$, $\mathcal{Q}_{\text{fill}}$, and $\mathcal{Q}_\emptyset$-queries are propagated through query operators: Given query classes $\mathcal{Q}_1$ and $\mathcal{Q}_2$, the right-most column ($\mathcal{Q}_1$ *Op* $\mathcal{Q}_2$) in the table shows the class to which a query that combines two queries from those respective classes by operator *Op* belongs.

Example 8. Continuing Example 7, the equi-join $X \bowtie Y$ (on the corresponding A, B, C attributes) of $\mathcal{Q}^A$-query X and $\mathcal{Q}_{\text{fill}}$-query Y yields the following relation:

$\mathcal{Q}^A$-query $X \bowtie Y$

A_x	A_y	B_x	B_y	C_x	C_y	Φ
x_1	x_1	■	■	■	■	$\mathbf{x_1}$
x_2	x_2	■	■	■	■	$\mathbf{x_2}$
x_3	x_3	■	■	■	■	$\mathbf{x_3}$

$\mathcal{Q}_1$	Op	$\mathcal{Q}_2$	$\mathcal{Q}_1\ Op\ \mathcal{Q}_2$
$\mathcal{Q}^A$	$\bowtie$	$\mathcal{Q}_{\text{fill}}$	$\mathcal{Q}^A$
	$-$	$\mathcal{Q}_\emptyset$	$\mathcal{Q}^A$
$\mathcal{Q}^{AB}$	$\bowtie$	$\mathcal{Q}_{\text{fill}}$	$\mathcal{Q}^{AB}$
	$-$	$\mathcal{Q}_\emptyset$	$\mathcal{Q}^{AB}$
$\mathcal{Q}_{\text{fill}}$	$\bowtie$	$\mathcal{Q}^A$	$\mathcal{Q}^A$
		$\mathcal{Q}^{AB}$	$\mathcal{Q}^{AB}$
		$\mathcal{Q}_{\text{fill}}$	$\mathcal{Q}_{\text{fill}}$
	$-$	$\mathcal{Q}^A$	$\mathcal{Q}^A$
		$\mathcal{Q}^{AB}$	$\mathcal{Q}^{AB}$
		$\mathcal{Q}_\emptyset$	$\mathcal{Q}_{\text{fill}}$

Figure 6: Class membership of queries connecting classes $\mathcal{Q}^A$, $\mathcal{Q}_{\text{fill}}$, and $\mathcal{Q}_\emptyset$ with operators $\bowtie$, $-$.

This join satisfies the conditions of a $\mathcal{Q}^A$-query as suggested by the rule $\mathcal{Q}^A \bowtie \mathcal{Q}_{\text{fill}} \to \mathcal{Q}^A$ in Figure 6. Similarly, the difference of $Y - X$ is also a $\mathcal{Q}^A$-query:

$\mathcal{Q}^A$-query $Y - X$

A_y	B_y	C_y	Φ
x_1	■	■	$\neg\mathbf{x_1}$
x_2	■	■	$\neg\mathbf{x_2}$
x_3	■	■	$\neg\mathbf{x_3}$

Now let $Q^{[A]}$ be a query that contains a $\mathcal{Q}^A$-relation $X^{[A]}$. We can populate the relations of Q such that Q is a $\mathcal{Q}^A$-query, i.e., that Q satisfies the above properties for $\mathcal{Q}^A$:

LEMMA 6. *Given a query Q, a distinguished attribute A of Q, and a distinguished relation X^A of Q that satisfies Equation* (1), *the remaining relations of Q can be filled such that Q satisfies Equation* (1).

PROOF. We first identify the set $\mathcal{OP}_-$ of difference operators in Q that do not have X as a right descendant and partition the relations of Q into three sets:

$$\text{rels}_X = \{X\}$$
$$\text{rels}_\emptyset = \text{relations right descendants of a } \mathcal{OP}_- \text{ operator}$$
$$\text{rels}_{\text{fill}} = \text{all other relations}$$

We populate every $\text{rels}_{\text{fill}}$ relation as a $\mathcal{Q}_{\text{fill}}$-query, and every $\text{rels}_\emptyset$ relation as a $\mathcal{Q}_\emptyset$-query. For the former, it suffices to populate each $[A]$ attribute of a $\text{rels}_{\text{fill}}$-relation with $\mathbf{A}$, and each non-$[A]$-attribute with ■. The following inductive argument shows that every operator on the path in Q between X and the root of Q is a $\mathcal{Q}^A$-query: First, this trivially holds at X itself. Now let Op be an operator on the path between X and the root of Q. We have the cases:

- $Q_L \bowtie Q_R$, where without loss of generality Q_L contains X. Then, Q_L is a $\mathcal{Q}^A$-query, Q_R contains a relation from $\text{rels}_{\text{fill}}$ and is a $\mathcal{Q}_{\text{fill}}$-query. Hence, $Q_L \bowtie Q_R$ is a $\mathcal{Q}^A$-query.

- $Q_L - Q_R$, where Q_L contains X. Then the difference operator is in $\mathcal{OP}_-$ and Q_R is a $\mathcal{Q}_\emptyset$-query, Q_L is a $\mathcal{Q}^A$-query, and hence $Q_L - Q_R$ is a $\mathcal{Q}^A$-query.

- $Q_L - Q_R$, where Q_R contains X. Then, Q_R is a $\mathcal{Q}^A$-query, Q_L contains a relation from $\text{rels}_{\text{fill}}$ and is a $\mathcal{Q}_{\text{fill}}$-query. Hence, $Q_L - Q_R$ is a $\mathcal{Q}^A$-query. □

If X has even polarity in Q, then the annotation $\Phi_Q(a)$ of a tuple (a) in $\pi_{[A]}(Q)$ is the same as the corresponding annotation $\Phi_X(a)$ of a tuple (a) in $\pi_{[A]}(X)$; if X has odd polarity in Q, then $\Phi_Q(a) = \neg\Phi_X(a)$.

Preserving the data of two attributes

We can extend the above technique to queries that contain relations over two distinguished attributes A and B whose values we would like to preserve; we only sketch this next.

Let Φ^{AB} be a total function on $\mathbf{A}\times\mathbf{B}$, and let Φ^A be a total function on $\mathbf{A}\cup\mathbf{A}\times\mathbf{B}$ such that $\Phi^A(a) \equiv \bigvee_{b\in\mathbf{B}} \Phi^A(a,b)$ for all $a \in \mathbf{A}$. As before, a relation Q is *A-reducible to* $(\mathbf{A}, \Phi^A)$ if

$$\pi^{\Phi}_{[A]}(Q) = \{(a|\Phi^A(a)) \mid a \in \mathbf{A}\}$$
$$\pi_C(Q) = \{(■)\} \qquad \text{for any attribute } C \text{ with } C \notin [A].$$

Similarly, Q is AB-reducible to $(\mathbf{A}\times\mathbf{B}, \Phi^{AB})$ if

$$\pi^{\Phi}_{[A][B]}(Q) = \{(a,b|\Phi^{AB}(a,b)) \mid a \in \mathbf{A}, b \in \mathbf{B}\}$$
$$\pi_C(Q) = \{(■)\} \text{ for any attribute } C \text{ with } C \notin [A] \cup [B].$$

By $\text{red}_{AB}(Q) = \mathbf{A}\times\mathbf{B}|\Phi^{AB}$ we denote that Q is AB-reducible to $(\mathbf{A}\times\mathbf{B}, \Phi^{AB})$. We define additional classes of queries:

$$Q^{[A][\neg B]} \in \mathcal{Q}^A \text{ if } \text{red}_A(Q) = \mathbf{A}|\Phi^A \tag{5}$$
$$Q^{[A][B]} \in \mathcal{Q}^A \text{ if } \text{red}_{AB}(Q) = \mathbf{A}\times\mathbf{B}|\Phi^A \tag{6}$$
$$Q^{[A][B]} \in \mathcal{Q}^{AB} \text{ if } \text{red}_{AB}(Q) = \mathbf{A}\times\mathbf{B}|\Phi^{AB} \tag{7}$$
$$Q^{[A][\neg B]} \in \mathcal{Q}_{\text{fill}} \text{ if } \text{red}_A(Q) = \mathbf{A}|\Phi_\top \tag{8}$$
$$Q^{[A][B]} \in \mathcal{Q}_{\text{fill}} \text{ if } \text{red}_{AB}(Q) = \mathbf{A}\times\mathbf{B}|\Phi_\top \tag{9}$$
$$Q^{[\neg A][\neg B]} \in \mathcal{Q}_{\text{fill}} \text{ if } \text{red}_\emptyset(Q) = ■|\Phi_\top \tag{10}$$
$$Q \in \mathcal{Q}_\emptyset \text{ if } Q = \emptyset \tag{11}$$

In Equations (5)–(7), Φ^A and Φ^{AB} can also be negated. Queries from these classes are propagated by query operators as depicted in Figure 6. Lemma 6 can be extended to the case of two attributes A and B:

- For a distinguished relation $X^{A\neg B}$ of Q that satisfies Equation (5), the remaining relations of Q can be filled such that Q satisfies Equation (5) if Q exports $[A]$ but not $[B]$, or Equation (6) if Q exports $[A]$ and $[B]$.

- For a distinguished relation X^{AB} of Q, the remaining relations in Q can be filled such that Q satisfies Equation (7) if Q exports $[A]$ and $[B]$.

4.2 Patterns and matches

We next define hard minimal query patterns and matches.

DEFINITION 5. *A* (query) pattern P *over attributes A, B and relational operators Op_1, $Op_2 \in \{\bowtie, -\}$ is a binary tree with leaves A, B, AB, root node Op_1, and inner node Op_2.*

There are $2 \cdot 2 \cdot 2 \cdot 6 = 48$ different patterns: There are two distinct unlabeled binary trees with three leaves, the two operators can each be either $\bowtie$ or $-$, and there are 6 possible orders of the labels A, AB, and B. Figure 5 shows 24 of the 48 patterns and omits for each pattern the symmetric pattern obtained by swapping leaves A and B.

DEFINITION 6. *A $1RA^-$ query Q* matches *a pattern P over attributes A and B if there is mapping from the nodes A, B, AB, Op_1, and Op_2 of P to relations $R^{[A][\neg B]}$, $T^{[\neg A][B]}$, $S^{[A][B]}$, and operators Op_1 and respectively Op_2 in the parse tree of Q that preserves ancestor-descendant relationships.*

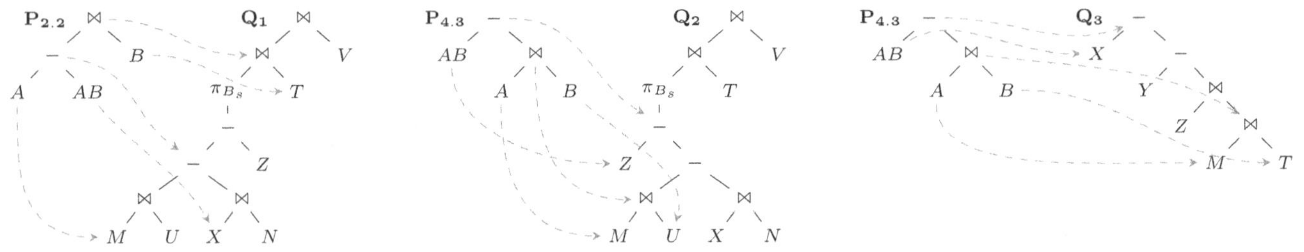

Figure 7: Patterns $P_{2.2}$ and $P_{4.3}$ and parse trees of queries Q_1, Q_2, Q_3 over the schema $M(A_m)$, $N(A_n)$, $T(B_t, C_t)$, $U(B_u)$, $V(B_v, C_v)$, $X(A_x, B_x)$, $Y(A_y, B_y)$, $Z(A_z, B_z)$. Q_1 is an (M, X, T)-match of pattern $P_{2.2}$; it also matches other patterns and is an annotation-preserving (M, X, T)-match of $P_{2.2}$, since Op_2 (the least common ancestor of M and X) is left-deep. Although Q_2 is an (M, X, T)-match of $P_{2.2}$, it is not an annotation-preserving match of $P_{2.2}$, since Op_2 is a right descendant of the top-most difference operator. However, Q_2 is an annotation-preserving (M, Z, U)-match of pattern $P_{4.3}$. Query Q_3 is an annotation-preserving (M, X, T)-match of pattern $P_{4.3}$.

We also say that Q is an (R, S, T)-match of P to emphasise which relations establish the match. Figures 1 and 7 show examples of queries matching patterns. Pattern matching is intimately linked to the non-hierarchical property:

PROPOSITION 1. *A $1RA^-$ query is non-hierarchical if and only if it matches one of the patterns in Figure 5.*

The notion of a match is further specialised to that of an *annotation-preserving match.* Whereas the database construction scheme detailed in Section 4.1 does not work for general matches, it does work for annotation-preserving matches. We first define left-deep operators.

DEFINITION 7. *An operator Op is* left-deep *in a $1RA^-$ query Q if Op is a* left *descendant of every difference operator on the path between the root of Q and Op.*

EXAMPLE 9. In Figure 7, the bottom-most difference operator in Q_1 is left-deep, while the bottom-most difference operator in Q_2 is not left-deep. □

DEFINITION 8. *A $1RA^-$ query Q is an* annotation-preserving match *of a pattern P over attributes A and B if:*

1. *Q is an (R, S, T)-match of P;*
2. *For every difference operator Op_- in Q, if Op_1 is a right descendant of Op_-, then Op_- does not export $[A]$ or $[B]$.*
3. *If Op_2 is a left descendant of Op_1 in Q, then Op_2 is left-deep in the sub-query rooted at Op_1.*

We say that Q is an *annotation-preserving (R, S, T)-match* of P to emphasise the relations establishing the match. Figure 7 shows examples of annotation-preserving matches.

We next look closer at the connection between matches and annotation-preserving matches. Lemma 7 establishes next that any query that matches a pattern necessarily also has an annotation-preserving match with a (possibly different) pattern; furthermore, the relation symbols that establish the annotation-preserving match can be found by exploring the query tree in left-to-right depth-first in-order.

LEMMA 7. *Let Q be a $1RA^-$ query and $o_1, \ldots, o_n$ be the sequence of its parse tree nodes in left-to-right depth-first in-order, and $Q_1, \ldots, Q_n$ be the corresponding sequence of sub-queries rooted at $o_1, \ldots, o_n$. If Q_i is the first sub-query in the above order that matches a pattern in Figure 5, then Q_i is an annotation-preserving match with a pattern.*

EXAMPLE 10. Consider query Q_2 in Figure 7. The sub-query rooted at the top-most difference operator is the first one to match a pattern and also has an annotation-preserving (M, Z, U)-match with $P_{4.3}$. □

4.3 Hardness reductions

The 24 patterns in Figure 5 are the smallest hard patterns for $1RA^-$, and any query that is an annotation-preserving match of one of them is hard for #P.

LEMMA 8. *The data complexity of any $1RA^-$ query that is an annotation-preserving match of one of the patterns in Figure 5 is #P-hard.*

Putting together Proposition 1 and Lemmata 7 and 8, we obtain that the data complexity of all non-hierarchical $1RA^-$ queries is #P-hard.

The proof of Lemma 8 goes over each pattern case and shows hardness via a reduction from the #2DNF problem: Let Q be a query that is an annotation-preserving (R, S, T)-match for a pattern P, and let $\Psi = \bigvee_{(i,j)\in E} x_i y_j$ be a 2DNF formula with $|E|$ clauses over disjoint variable sets $\mathbf{X}$ and $\mathbf{Y}$. We construct in polynomial time a tuple-independent database $\mathcal{D}$ using the database construction scheme in Section 4.1 such that the annotation of the query result $Q(\mathcal{D})$ is either Ψ and hence $P_{Q(\mathcal{D})} = P_\Psi = \#\Psi \cdot 2^{-|\text{vars}(\Psi)|}$, or $\neg\Psi$ and then $P_{Q(\mathcal{D})} = 1 - P_\Psi$.

We next give reductions for patterns $P_{4.3}$ and $P_{5.3}$; all reductions are given in an extended paper [12]. Pattern $P_{1.1}$ is the only one needed to show hardness of non-hierarchical $1RA^-$ queries without difference, i.e., of non-repeating conjunctive queries studied in prior work [6]. The reduction for pattern $P_{5.3}$ establishes that a query matching $P_{5.3}$ can be hard already when constrained to databases in which one relation is probabilistic and all other relations are certain.

Reduction for pattern $P_{4.3}$. We use the illustration of a query matching $P_{4.3}$ in Figure 8(left). By Definition 8, a query Q that is an annotation-preserving match of $P_{4.3}$

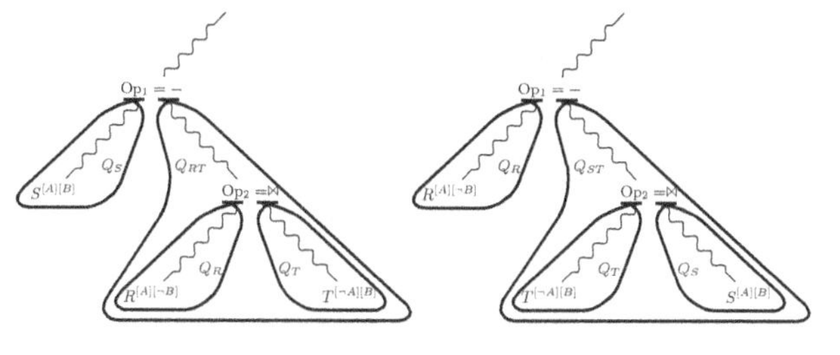

Figure 8: Schematic illustration of a query that is an annotation-preserving match of pattern $P_{4.3}$ (left) or $P_{5.3}$ (right). A curly path indicates that other operators may occur on it.

satisfies the following structural constraint: If Op_1 is a right descendant of a difference operator, then this operator does not export $[A]$ or $[B]$. Furthermore, attributes $[A]$ and $[B]$ are exported by every operator on the paths from S to R and from S to T, respectively. We encode the 2DNF formula Ψ as a database $\mathcal{D}$ such that the annotation of the query result $Q(\mathcal{D})$ is Ψ, if the polarity of Op_2 is odd in Q_{RT}. In case of even polarity, we derive a database $\mathcal{D}$ and another formula Υ from Ψ such that $P_{Q(\mathcal{D})} = P_\Upsilon$ and linearly many calls to an oracle for P_Υ suffice to compute $\#\Psi$.

Case 1: Odd polarity (pol$(Q_{RT}, Op_2) = 1$). We fill the relations R, S, T such that Q_R is a $\mathcal{Q}^A$-query, Q_T is a $\mathcal{Q}^B$-query, and Q_S is a $\mathcal{Q}^{AB}$-query, and for all three relations the annotation functions are the identity. In other words, R consists of a tuple with A-value x_i and annotation x_i for each variable $x_i \in \mathbf{X}$ that occurs in Ψ; T consists of a tuple with B-value y_j and annotation y_j for each variable $y_j \in \mathbf{Y}$ that occurs in Ψ; S consists of a tuple with (A, B)-values (x_i, y_j) and annotation $\top$ for each clause $x_i y_j$ in Ψ. Note that when used outside annotations, the variables are considered constants in relations R, S, T. For the remaining relations, we distinguish two cases: (1) Any relation that appears on the right side of a difference operator different from Op₁ and Op₂, is set to $\emptyset$. (2) Any relation with an $[A]$ attribute and no $[B]$ attribute is filled like R, but with annotations $\top$. Symmetrically, any relation with a $[B]$ attribute and no $[A]$ attribute is filled like T, but with annotations $\top$. Relations with both $[A]$ and $[B]$ attributes are filled with the Cartesian product of $\mathbf{X}$ and $\mathbf{Y}$ and annotations $\top$. In all of the above cases, any attribute that is neither in $[A]$ nor in $[B]$ is filled with constant ■.

Since Op_2 has odd polarity in Q_{RT} and since both $[A]$ and $[B]$ are exported by every operator on the path between Op_1 and Op_2, Q_{RT} and $Q_S - Q_{RT}$ are $\mathcal{Q}^{AB}$-queries with annotations

$$\text{red}_{AB}(Q_{RT}) = \mathbf{X} \times \mathbf{Y} | \neg\Phi_{RT}, \Phi_{RT}(x_i, y_i) = x_i y_i$$
$$\text{red}_{AB}(Q_S - Q_{RT}) = \mathbf{X} \times \mathbf{Y} | \Phi_{RST},$$
$$\Phi_{RST}(x_i, y_j) = \begin{cases} x_i y_j & \text{if } (i,j) \in E \\ \bot & \text{if } (i,j) \notin E. \end{cases}$$

The final projection $\pi_{-[A]-[B]}$ yields one answer tuple, whose annotation is the disjunction of all clauses in Ψ.

Case 2: Even polarity (pol$(Q_{RT}, Op_2) = 0$). Let Θ be the set of assignments of variables $\mathbf{X} \cup \mathbf{Y}$. Then the number of models of Ψ is defined by $\#\Psi = \sum_{\theta \in \Theta : \theta \models \Psi} 1$. If we partition Θ into disjoint sets $\Theta_0 \cup \cdots \cup \Theta_{|E|}$, such that $\theta \in \Theta_i$ if and only if θ satisfies exactly i clauses of Ψ, then this sum can equivalently by written as

$$\#\Psi = \sum_{\theta \in \Theta_1 : \theta \models \Psi} 1 + \cdots + \sum_{\theta \in \Theta_m : \theta \models \Psi} 1 = |\Theta_1| + \cdots + |\Theta_{|E|}|.$$

We next show how to compute $|\Theta_i|$ (and hence $\#\Psi$) using an oracle for P_Υ, with Υ defined below. Let $\mathbf{Z} = \{z_1, \ldots, z_{|E|}\}$ be a set of variables disjoint from $\mathbf{X} \cup \mathbf{Y}$ and define Υ as

$$\Upsilon = \bigvee_{i=1}^{|E|} \neg z_i \wedge \neg\psi_i \quad \text{or, equivalently} \quad \neg\Upsilon = \bigwedge_{i=1}^{|E|} (z_i \vee \psi_i) \quad (12)$$

We fix the probabilities of variables in $\mathbf{X}$ and $\mathbf{Y}$ to $1/2$ and of variables in $\mathbf{Z}$ to $p_z \in [0, 1]$. The probability $1 - P_\Upsilon = P_{\neg\Upsilon}$ can be expressed by conditioning on the number of satisfied clauses of Ψ:

$$P_{\neg\Upsilon} = \sum_{k=0}^{|E|} \underbrace{P\left(\neg\Upsilon \middle| \begin{array}{l}\text{exactly } k \text{ clauses} \\ \text{of } \Psi \text{ are satisfied}\end{array}\right)}_{p_z^{|E|-k}} \cdot \underbrace{P\left(\begin{array}{l}\text{exactly } k \text{ clauses} \\ \text{of } \Psi \text{ are satisfied}\end{array}\right)}_{\frac{1}{2}^{|\mathbf{X}|+|\mathbf{Y}|} \cdot |\Theta_k|}$$

$$= \frac{1}{2}^{|\mathbf{X}|+|\mathbf{Y}|} \sum_{k=0}^{|E|} p_z^{|E|-k} |\Theta_k|$$

Intuitively, the first term simplifies to $p_z^{|E|-k}$, because if exactly k clauses ψ_i are satisfied in $\neg\Upsilon$, then in order to satisfy the remaining $|E| - k$ clauses $(z_i \vee \psi_i)$ at least $|E| - k$ of the z_i must be satisfied, and this occurs with probability $p_z^{|E|-k}$. This is a polynomial in p_z of degree $|E|$, with coefficients $|\Theta_0|, \ldots, |\Theta_{|E|}|$. The $|E| + 1$ coefficients can be derived from $|E| + 1$ pairs (p_z, P_Υ) using Lagrange's polynomial interpolation formula. We conclude that $|E| + 1$ oracle calls to P_Υ suffice to determine $\#\Psi = \sum_{i=0}^{|E|} |\Theta_i|$.

It remains to show how Υ can be encoded as the annotation of a query that is an annotation-preserving match of $P_{4.3}$; given this encoding, any algorithm that evaluates $P_{Q(\mathcal{D})}$ constitutes the above oracle. Formula Υ is encoded using the database construction scheme from Case 1, where the annotation of a tuple with (A, B)-values (x_i, y_j) corresponding to clause $\psi_k = x_i y_j$ in Ψ becomes $\neg z_k$. Then, the annotation of a tuple with (A, B)-values (x_i, y_j) in the result of the sub-query rooted at Op₁, i.e., $Q_S - Q_{RT}$, becomes $\neg z_k \wedge \neg\psi_k$. The final projection $\pi_{-[A]-[B]}$ yields one result tuple, whose annotation is the disjunction of the annotation of $Q_S - Q_{RT}$ which is exactly Υ.

Reduction for pattern $P_{5.3}$. We use the illustration of a query matching $P_{5.3}$ in Figure 8 (right). We only describe here the case when $[B]$ is not exported by Op_1, in which case the sub-query Q_{ST} contains a projection operator $Op_\pi = \pi_{-[B]}$ such that every operator between Op_π and Op_1 exports $[A]$ but not $[B]$, and every operator between Op_π and Op_2 exports $[A]$ and $[B]$. Let Q_π be the sub-query rooted at Op_π.

The first step is to show that one may without loss of generality assume that Op_2 is left-deep in Q_π. Assume to the contrary that there is a difference operator Op_- between Op_π and Op_2 that has Op_2 as a right descendant; clearly, Op_- exports $[A]$ and $[B]$ and hence its left sub-query contains relations $X^{[A][\neg B]}$ and $Y^{[\neg A][B]}$ or it contains a relation $Z^{[A][B]}$. In the former case, Q is an annotation-preserving (R, S, Y)-match of pattern $P_{5.4}$; in the latter case, Q is an

R

A_r	Φ
1	$\top$
2	$\top$

T

B_t	Φ
x_1	$\neg\mathbf{x_1}$
y_1	$\neg\mathbf{y_1}$
y_2	$\neg\mathbf{y_2}$

S

A_s	B_s	Φ
1	x_1	$\top$
1	y_1	$\top$
1	y_2	$\bot$
2	x_1	$\top$
2	y_1	$\bot$
2	y_2	$\top$

$Q_T \bowtie Q_S$

A_s	B_s	Φ
1	x_1	$\neg\mathbf{x_1}$
1	y_1	$\neg\mathbf{y_1}$
1	y_2	$\bot$
2	x_1	$\neg\mathbf{x_1}$
2	y_1	$\bot$
2	y_2	$\neg\mathbf{y_2}$

$Q_\pi = Q_{ST}$

A_s	Φ
1	$\neg\mathbf{x_1} \vee \neg\mathbf{y_1}$
2	$\neg\mathbf{x_1} \vee \neg\mathbf{y_2}$

Q_{RST}

A_r	Φ
1	$\mathbf{x_1 y_1}$
2	$\mathbf{x_1 y_2}$

Figure 9: Relations R, S, T for the hardness reduction of a query with an annotation-preserving match for pattern $P_{5.3}$ where (1) Op_1 does not export $[B]$ and (2) the projection operator $\pi_{-[B]}$ on the path between Op_1 and Op_2 has even polarity in Q_{ST} (the sub-query containing both relations S and T). Only attributes $[A]$ and $[B]$ are depicted, and it is assumed that R, S, T have even polarity in their respective sub-queries Q_R, Q_S, and Q_T. The database is with respect to the formula $\Psi = \psi_1 \vee \psi_2 = x_1y_1 \vee x_1y_2$.

annotation-preserving (R, Z, T)-match of pattern $P_{6.4}$. In both cases, the new Op_2 is Op_- and left-deep in Q_π.

Next, two cases need to be analysed separately depending on the polarity of Op_π in Q_{ST}.

Case 1: Even polarity ($\text{pol}(Q_{ST}, Op_\pi) = 0$). Let $\mathbf{N} = \{1, \ldots, |E|\}$ be the set of integers that numbers consecutively the clauses in Ψ: $\Psi = \psi_1 \vee \cdots \vee \psi_{|E|}$. We set relation R to contain a tuple (n) annotated with $\top$ for every clause number $n \in \mathbf{N}$. Relation S contains all tuples (n, v) where $n \in \mathbf{N}$ is a clause number and $v \in \mathbf{X} \cup \mathbf{Y}$ is a variable from Ψ; (n, v) is annotated with $\top$ if clause n contains variable v, and with $\bot$ otherwise. Relation T has a tuple (v) annotated with $\neg v$ for each variable v in Ψ. Figure 9 exemplifies how R, S, T are filled for a query matching $P_{5.3}$ and for formula $\Psi = x_1y_1 \vee x_1y_2$ and how these annotations are propagated through the query.

Case 2: Odd polarity ($\text{pol}(Q_{ST}, Op_\pi) = 1$). Intuitively, since the number of difference operators between the root of the query and the relations S and T is even, they act equivalently to a sequence of join operators for query annotations: We fill the relations such that Q_T is a $\mathcal{Q}^B$-query, Q_S is a $\mathcal{Q}^{AB}$-query, Q_R is a $\mathcal{Q}^A$-query, and then Q_{ST} is a $\mathcal{Q}^A$-query, where for relations R and T the annotation functions are the identity and for relation S, the anotation function is $\top$ for all tuples (x_i, y_j) corresponding to clauses in Ψ and $\bot$ otherwise.

5. BEYOND 1RA$^-$ QUERIES

In this section we discuss the effect of various extensions of 1RA$^-$ on query tractability.

A dichotomy for full relational algebra seems unattainable since key reasoning tasks for such queries, such as equivalence, emptiness, or subsumption, are undecidable: Given two equivalent queries, one hard and one tractable, we thus cannot decide whether their union is tractable. Restrictions on the use of negation, e.g., guarded negation [3], enable decidability of query equivalence and can pave the way to a complexity dichotomy for (possibly repeating) relational queries with guarded negation in probabilistic databases.

5.1 Non-repeating relational algebra

If we add the union operator to the language 1RA$^-$, we need a different syntactic characterisation of the tractable queries, since the hierarchical property is not defined for queries with union. An immediate attempt would consider all (union-free) sub-queries obtained by choosing one term at each union and checking whether all of them are hierarchical. This approach fails since such sub-queries are not necessarily $\exists$-consistent. For instance, the non-repeating relational algebra query $Q = \pi_\emptyset[S(A, B) - (R(A) \bowtie S_1(A, B) \cup T(B) \bowtie S_2(A, B))]$ has two hierarchical union-free sub-queries under $\pi_\emptyset$: $S(A, B) - (R(A) \bowtie S_1(A, B))$ and $S(A, B) - (T(B) \bowtie S_2(A, B))$. However, these sub-queries cannot be rewritten to $\exists$-consistent RC$^\exists$ queries, since they have roots A and B respectively; it can be further shown that Q is #P-hard.

An alternative characterisation would be to check $\exists$-consistency and the RC$^\exists$-hierarchical property of the RC$^\exists$ expression Q_r representing the rewriting of a non-repeating relational algebra query Q described in Section 3.1. Then Q is tractable when Q_r is $\exists$-consistent and RC-hierarchical. Checking these properties can be done efficiently in the size of the input RC$^\exists$ query, yet Q_r may be much larger than Q (as per discussion at the end of Section 3.1). It is open whether the characterisation of tractable non-repeating relational algebra queries can be done more efficiently than following this procedure via $\exists$-consistency, which incurs the non-trivial time to rewrite the input query.

5.2 Non-repeating RC$^\exists$

There are subtle differences between 1RA$^-$ and non-repeating RC$^\exists$ that revolve around RC$^\exists$'s flexibility to allow disjunction and negation on sub-queries of different schemas. For instance, the non-repeating RC$^\exists$ queries $S(x, y) \wedge \neg R(x)$ and $S(x, y) \wedge (R(x) \vee T(y))$ cannot be expressed in 1RA$^-$. Whereas the former query is tractable, the latter is #P-hard: This means that 1RA$^-$ cannot express both tractable and hard queries that are expressible in non-repeating RC$^\exists$.

For non-repeating RC$^\exists$, the RC-hierarchical property alone does *not* characterise the tractable queries, even when we take away disjunction. Indeed, the RC$^\exists$ query equivalent to the 1RA$^-$ query from Figure 3, i.e., $Q = \exists_A \exists_B R(A) \wedge S(B) \wedge \neg(U(A) \wedge V(B))$, does not satisfy the RC-hierarchical property since neither A nor B are root in the expression and they cannot be pushed further down. However, as for 1RA$^-$ queries, we can rewrite a non-repeating RC$^\exists$ query Q into an RC$^\exists$ query Q_r as outlined in Section 3.1, e.g., $Q_r = \exists_A[R(A) \wedge \neg U(A)] \wedge \exists_B S(B) \vee \exists_A R(A) \wedge \exists_B[S(B) \wedge \neg V(B)]$ for the above query Q, and then again Q is tractable when Q_r is RC-hierarchical and $\exists$-consistent.

6. RELATED WORK

Negation is a substantial source of complexity already for databases with incomplete information and without probabilities [2]. In probabilistic databases, the MystiQ system supports a limited class of NOT EXISTS queries [25]. A framework for the exact and approximate evaluation of full relational algebra queries (thus including negation) in probabilistic databases is part of SPROUT [13, 11]. Further work looks at approximating queries with negation [18].

Our dichotomy is in line with and contributes to a succession of complexity results for queries on probabilistic databases: Starting from a first example of a #P-hard query [14], polynomial-time/#P-hard dichotomies have been established by Dalvi and Suciu for non-repeating conjunctive queries [5] and unions of conjunctive queries (UCQs) [9]; a trichotomy has been proven for positive queries with HAVING aggregates [22]; the precise tractability frontier for so-called quantified queries such as relational division and set equivalence, which can be expressed as repeating queries with nested negation, is also known [13]. Our result strictly generalises the dichotomy for non-repeating conjunctive queries. It corrects an earlier statement by the authors (Theorem 6.4 in [13]). Whereas tractable $1RA^-$ queries can be characterised efficiently by the hierarchical syntactic property, for UCQs no such efficient decision procedure is known. Further complexity results are known for inequality joins [19, 20] and queries with aggregates and group-by clauses [10].

The closest in spirit to the proof techniques in this paper are those for the UCQ dichotomy result [9]. The algorithm for tractable UCQ queries translates them into relational calculus expressions that have root variables and satisfy properties similar to what we call *canonicalised*. These properties are captured by the notion of *separator* variables. Similar to the case of root variables in our algorithm, the existence of a separator variable ensures that the annotations of the query expression are independent for different valuations of the separator variable. Our notion of $\exists$-consistency for queries with negation is inspired by the notion of inversion-freeness for UCQ queries.

The vast majority of hardness reductions in the above works are from the #P-hard model-counting problem for positive (2)DNF formulas [24, 21]. The complexity class #P was originally defined by Valiant [24].

OBDDs have been proposed by Bryant [4]. The first connection between polysize OBDDs and tractable queries has been shown for hierarchical non-repeating conjunctive queries [19]. The class of inversion-free UCQs is equivalent to the class of UCQ queries that admit polysize OBDDs [17]. UCQs with inequalities have also been characterised in terms of their corresponding OBDDs [16].

An overview of various topics in probabilistic databases has been compiled recently [23].

Acknowledgment. The authors would like to thank Dan Suciu for discussions on this work.

7. REFERENCES

[1] S. Abiteboul, R. Hull, and V. Vianu. *Foundations of Databases*. Addison-Wesley, 1995.

[2] S. Abiteboul, P. Kanellakis, and G. Grahne. On the representation and querying of sets of possible worlds. *Theor. Comput. Sci.*, **78**(1), 1991.

[3] V. Bárány, B. ten Cate, and M. Otto. Queries with guarded negation. *PVLDB*, 5(11), 2012.

[4] R. E. Bryant. Graph-based algorithms for boolean function manipulation. *IEEE Trans. Computers*, 35(8), 1986.

[5] N. Dalvi and D. Suciu. Efficient Query Evaluation on Probabilistic Databases. In *VLDB*, 2004.

[6] N. Dalvi and D. Suciu. Efficient query evaluation on probabilistic databases. *VLDB J.*, **16**(4), 2007.

[7] N. Dalvi and D. Suciu. Management of probabilistic data: Foundations and challenges. In *PODS*, 2007.

[8] N. Dalvi and D. Suciu. "The Dichotomy of Conjunctive Queries on Probabilistic Structures". In *PODS*, 2007.

[9] N. N. Dalvi and D. Suciu. The dichotomy of probabilistic inference for unions of conjunctive queries. *J. ACM*, 59(6), 2012.

[10] R. Fink, L. Han, and D. Olteanu. Aggregation in probabilistic databases via knowledge compilation. *PVLDB*, 5(5), 2012.

[11] R. Fink, J. Huang, and D. Olteanu. Anytime approximation in probabilistic databases. *VLDB J.*, 22(6), 2013.

[12] R. Fink and D. Olteanu. A dichotomy for non-repeating queries with negation in probabilistic databases. Technical report, U. Oxford, 2014.

[13] R. Fink, D. Olteanu, and S. Rath. Providing Support for Full Relational Algebra Queries in Probabilistic Databases. In *ICDE*, 2011.

[14] E. Grädel, Y. Gurevich, and C. Hirsch. The complexity of query reliability. In *PODS*, 1998.

[15] J. Huang, L. Antova, C. Koch, and D. Olteanu. MayBMS: A probabilistic database management system. In *SIGMOD*, 2009.

[16] A. K. Jha and D. Suciu. On the tractability of query compilation and bounded treewidth. In *ICDT*, 2012.

[17] A. K. Jha and D. Suciu. Knowledge compilation meets database theory: Compiling queries to decision diagrams. *Theory Comput. Syst.*, 52(3), 2013.

[18] S. Khanna, S. Roy, and V. Tannen. Queries with difference on probabilistic databases. *PVLDB*, 4(11), 2011.

[19] D. Olteanu and J. Huang. Using OBDDs for efficient query evaluation on probabilistic databases. In *SUM*, 2008.

[20] D. Olteanu and J. Huang. Secondary-storage confidence computation for conjunctive queries with inequalities. In *SIGMOD*, 2009.

[21] J. S. Provan and M. O. Ball. The complexity of counting cuts and of computing the probability that a graph is connected. *SIAM J. Comput.*, 12(4), 1983.

[22] C. Ré and D. Suciu. The Trichotomy of HAVING Queries on a Probabilistic Database. *VLDB J*, 18(5), 2009.

[23] D. Suciu, D. Olteanu, C. Ré, and C. Koch. *Probabilistic Databases*. Morgan & Claypool Publishers, 2011.

[24] L. Valiant. The complexity of enumeration and reliability problems. *SIAM J. Comput.*, **8**, 1979.

[25] T.-Y. Wang, C. Ré, and D. Suciu. Implementing NOT EXISTS predicates over a probabilistic database. In *QDB/MUD*, 2008.

[26] I. Wegener. BDDs–design, analysis, complexity, and applications. *Discrete Applied Mathematics*, 138(1-2), 2004.

Database Principles in Information Extraction

Benny Kimelfeld*
LogicBlox, Inc.
Berkeley, CA, USA
bennyk@gmail.com

ABSTRACT

Information Extraction commonly refers to the task of populating a relational schema, having predefined underlying semantics, from textual content. This task is pervasive in contemporary computational challenges associated with Big Data. This tutorial gives an overview of the algorithmic concepts and techniques used for performing Information Extraction tasks, and describes some of the declarative frameworks that provide abstractions and infrastructure for programming extractors. In addition, the tutorial highlights opportunities for research impact through principles of data management, illustrates these opportunities through recent work, and proposes directions for future research.

Categories and Subject Descriptors

H.2.1 [**Database Management**]: Logical Design—*Data models*; H.2.4 [**Database Management**]: Systems—*Textual databases, Relational databases, Rule-based databases*; I.5.4 [**Pattern Recognition**]: Applications—*Text processing*; F.4.3 [**Mathematical Logic and Formal Languages**]: Formal Languages—*Algebraic language theory, Classes defined by grammars or automata, Operations on languages*; F.1.1 [**Computation by Abstract Devices**]: Models of Computation—*Automata, Relations between models*

General Terms

Theory

Keywords

Information extraction, document spanners, regular expressions, finite-state transducers, database inconsistency, database repairs, prioritized repairs

*The work of the author mentioned in this paper was done while at IBM Almaden – Research.

PODS'14, June 22–27, 2014, Snowbird, UT, USA.
Copyright 2014 ACM 978-1-4503-2375-8/14/06 ...$15.00.
http://dx.doi.org/10.1145/2594538.2594563 .

1. INTRODUCTION

Information Extraction (IE) refers to the task of discovering structured information in textual content. More precisely, the goal in IE is to populate a predefined relational schema that has predetermined underlying semantics, by correctly detecting the values of records in a given text document or a collection of text documents. Popular tasks in the space of IE include *named entity recognition* [60] (identify proper names in text, and classify those into a predefined set of categories such as *person* and *organization*), *relation extraction* [67] (extract tuples of entities that satisfy a predefined relationship, such as *person-organization*), *event extraction* [3] (find events of predefined types along with their key players, such as *nomination* and *nominee*), *temporal information extraction* [21,44] (associate mentions of facts with mentions of their validity period, such as *nomination-date*), and *coreference resolution* [53] (match between phrases that refer to the same entity, such as "Obama," "the President," and "him").

As a discipline, IE had its start with the DARPA Message Understanding Conference in 1987 [29]. While early work in the area focused largely on military applications, this task is nowadays pervasive in a plethora of computational challenges, in particular those associated with Big Data, such as social media analysis [7], machine data analysis [26], healthcare analysis [66], customer relationship management [2], and indexing for semantic search [69]. Within a typical text-analytics pipeline (e.g., [65]), the output of IE is fed into a cleaning and/or fusion component, such as an entity-resolution algorithm, that in turn produces input for a global processing phase (e.g., statistical analysis or data mining). Contemporary business models like cloud computing, along with analytics platforms like Hadoop, facilitate such data analyses for a broad range of individuals and organizations.

This tutorial focuses on foundations of data management systems that involve IE over textual content. In Section 2 we give an overview of the methodologies used for carrying out IE tasks; we also highlight some programming paradigms and abstractions for developing IE solutions. Section 3 describes our recent work on a formal framework for IE, where we leverage known principles of database management. We conclude with Section 4, where we propose directions for future research.

2. PARADIGMS AND METHODOLOGIES FOR INFORMATION EXTRACTION

A plethora of methodologies have been proposed, studied and practiced for carrying out IE. We identify four main categories of methodologies: (1) rule invocation, (2) inference over probabilistic graphical models, (3) inference under soft logical constraints, and (4) classification. The approaches in the first category deploy various rule languages as high-level specifications of deterministic IE programs. Within the second category, the IE task is encoded as a probabilistic model that combines the text tokens, annotations, and features as random variables with inter-dependencies, while the actual result is obtained by means of inference (e.g., finding the most likely assignment to the variables). The third category can be viewed as a combination of the former two: rules are specified, yet can be violated, and are in fact means of specifying a probability space over possible results (where the probability is measured by the cases of violation and satisfaction of the rules). Approaches in the fourth category treat the extraction task as a classification problem on candidate tuples. In each of these categories, components of the solution, such as rules and weight parameters, can be either manually encoded or automatically constructed from examples (by means of machine learning). Interestingly, a recent study [15] highlights and quantifies a contrast between the dominance of probabilistic approaches in scientific publications on IE in the research community of Natural Language Processing (NLP), and the dominance of rule-based approaches in industrial solutions.

Our focus here is on the first aforementioned category of methodologies for IE, namely rule invocation. Next, we describe the ideas underlying representative rule-based formalisms and systems. For completeness, we also give an overview of concepts in the other categories. The interested reader is referred to published tutorials and surveys on IE, such as Sarawagi's [57], for in-depth discussions on approaches to IE.

2.1 Rule Invocation

A typical rule-based system for IE supports two kinds of rules. Rules of the first kind declare the manner by which spans (intervals within the document) are annotated when scanning the text. Such a rule is usually a *finite-state transducer* that is represented by means of a pattern in some grammar. We refer to such rules as *direct extractors*. Rules of the second kind operate on top of the annotations produced by the direct extractors, and determine how those should be combined (e.g., by joining annotations into richer tuples, or by resolving conflicts among extracted tuples). In RAPIER [12], for instance, the rules are mostly direct extractors, and a rule is specified through three patterns: a *filler* that matches the extracted span, a *pre-filler* that matches the text right before the filler, and a *post-filler* that matches the text right after the filler. Each of these patterns is phrased as a regular expression (in a restricted grammar) over the words and part-of-speech tags. As another example, in WHISK [60] the transducers are defined as regular expressions with *capture variables*, which are embedded variables that are assigned the substrings that match the corresponding parts of the text; it also deploys rules to filter out conflicting extracted tuples (for example, different tuples should not contain overlapping spans), by imposing a special behavior of the transducers. As a third example, in FASTUS [4] the transducers are applied in two different phases, where the first phase ("Recognizing Phrases") produces annotations that are referenced by the rules of the second phase ("Recognizing Patterns"); following these two phases, the system applies rules that merge tuples produced by the second phase.

The earlier rule-based systems evolved into development platforms for programming IE. One of the most popular such platforms is the General Architecture for Text Engineering (GATE) [19], an open-source project by the University of Sheffield. GATE is an instantiation of the *cascaded finite-state transducers* specified by the *Common Pattern Specification Language* (CPSL) [5]. The core IE engine of GATE, called JAPE, processes a document via a sequence of *phases* (or *cascades*), each annotating spans with types by applying grammar rules over previous annotations and user-defined Java procedures. Another such a system is Xlog [59], which extends (non-recursive) Datalog with *documents* and *spans* as primitive data types, and built-in extractors (e.g., matchers of regular expressions) of spans from documents, and features a query plan optimizer. A system with substantial industrial and academic impact is SystemT [14], which evolved from the Avatar project [36, 54] and supports an SQL-like declarative language named *AQL* (Annotation Query Language). SystemT also includes a query-plan optimizer [54] and development tooling [45]. Conceptually, AQL provides a collection of direct extractors of relations from text (e.g., tokenizer, dictionary lookup, matchers of regular expressions, part-of-speech tagger, and other morphological analyzers), along with an algebra for relational manipulation.

There are also rule systems for IE that are designed for natural language, as their rules can be applied to structured data that expose pre-applied linguistic analyses. Examples include LIEP [33] (which exposes restricted linguistic information obtained through simple patterns) and INSTAREAD [30] (which exposes more thorough text processing such as deep parsing, coreference resolution, and named-entity recognition). Both of these systems use variants of (non-recursive) Datalog over base relations (EDB predicates) that store the linguistic information.

A significant research effort has been made towards the automation (or semi-automation) of rule engineering for IE. Such automation includes *dictionary learning*, *rule refinement*, and *rule induction*. In dictionary learning, a given seed dictionary is automatically expanded from a text corpus [17, 56]. Rule refinement aims to improve existing rules by (at least conceptually) exploring the space of syntactic revisions to the rules and observing the resulting impact on the performance on labeled data [45]. In rule induction, the rules are produced from scratch by learning from training data. The induction techniques include incremental rule specification (i.e., *top-down* induction), where the algorithm begins with high-recall rules and gradually restricts the rules to account for false positives [24, 60]; they also include the analogous rule generalization (i.e., *top-down* induction, where the algorithm generalizes rules that initially overfit the examples) [12, 16], and techniques from inductive logic programming [1, 47].

2.2 Inference and Classification

Designing rules to properly capture the given IE problem may be overly tedious and expensive, depending on the nature of the task and domain. In natural-language text, for example, there is a great variety of ways of expressing the same information, and the extraction should account for typical mistakes due to practices such as grammatical errors, jargon, slang, wishful thinking and sarcasm. An alternative approach, which has been extensively explored, is to capture the problem by means of a probabilistic model, where the actual IE task is done through inference over the probabilistic space. An important advantage of this approach is due to the fact that, very often, a significant portion of the specification of the probabilistic model (e.g., numeric parameters) can be effectively learned automatically by using well studied machine-learning techniques. Hence, machine learning can replace much of the work that would otherwise be done by the developer. IE development then entails labeling of examples (or generation of such examples from available resources) and engineering of *features* (informative components in the specification of the probabilistic model). Labeling of examples may be overly expensive if the learning technique requires too much training, and there have been approaches to reduce the effort of labeling, such as *weak supervision* [31]. Different methodologies within the probabilistic approach differ in the language and structure that specify the probabilistic model, and consequently, in the deployed training and inference algorithms.

An example of a probabilistic model for IE is a *Naive Bayes classifier*, where the label of each token is determined independently by features of a (bounded-length) window that surrounds the token [25]. This model can be viewed as a simple case of *probabilistic graphical model*, which is a model where the text tokens, features, hidden states and annotations are presented as random variables organized in a graph structure, where edges represent probabilistic correlations using the Markov property stating that a node is independent from the rest of the nodes, given its neighbors. Such graph models that have been applied to IE include *Hidden Markov Models* [8,9,27,42] and *Maximum Entropy Markov Models* [39,46], which are Bayesian networks (i.e., directed acyclic graphical models) that can be viewed as generative models of text (in the former) or annotations (in the latter). A highly successful graph model is that of *Conditional Random Fields* [13, 41, 64], which is a non-generative model where the underlying graph is undirected.

Rules (or constraints) with soft interpretation provide means to program extractors by combining the simplicity and expressiveness of rules (allowing the developer to easily express her domain knowledge and insights) with the ability of probabilistic models to capture the uncertain nature of text extraction and to utilize techniques from machine learning. The deployed rules are logical formulas with free variables. An example of such a rule is the following: "If a location name y occurs in a sentence at most 3 tokens after a person name x, and one of these tokens is *born*, then $\mathsf{BornIn}(x, y)$ is true." The rules can be *grounded* by replacing the free variables with actual values (which are obtained by, e.g., deterministic rule invocation). For instance, a possible grounding of our example rule replaces x with "Einstein" and y with "Germany." These rules are usually weighted in order to express a-priory reliability therein. A *possible world* can be viewed as a collection of grounded predicates such as BornIn(Einstein, Germany).

Different notions of soft constraints weight (that is, assign a certainty or probability measure to) a possible world by applying aggregate measures on the grounded rules that are satisfied and those that are violated. SOFIE [63], for example, attempts to satisfy the grounded rules to a maximum extent, using a MAX-SAT solver; hence, under this approach the probability of a possible world is (proportional to) the sum of weights across all the satisfied grounded rules. *Probabilistic Soft Logic* (PSL) [10] and *Markov Logic Networks* [50, 55] (MLNs), which have also been applied to IE [48, 51, 58], apply different such aggregate functions (which we do not define here) over the groundings. Interestingly, recent work has drawn strong connections between MLN inference and database research: Niu et al. [48] showed how a relational query engine can be used to improve the efficiency of inference over MLNs, and Jah and Suciu [37] showed that inference in MLNs can be carried out via a reduction to the problem of query evaluation over *tuple-independent probabilistic databases* [20]. Such probabilistic databases have been used by Dylla et al. [21] directly for IE.

An IE task can also be cast as a classification problem on candidate tuples. In such an approach, one first produces a set of candidate tuples by some simple means of extraction (featuring high recall but possibly low precision), and then applies classification to distinguish the correct tuples from the wrong ones (and therefore increase the precision). In standard classification, every instance (candidate tuple in our case) is mapped into a vector of features, each describing some property of the instance, and the classifier operates over that vector. The features can be either defined manually [35,43] or produced automatically from linguistic information, typically by graph querying (e.g., a feature is a sequence of labels on a path that connects the spans of a tuple in the dependency tree) [62] or *graph kernels* that translate a large (implicitly defined) space of features over graphs (e.g., paths connecting spans) to various measures of *similarity* to the training examples [11, 18].

3. THE FRAMEWORK OF DOCUMENT SPANNERS

In this section, we review a recent work by Fagin et al. [22, 23] who established a formal framework for IE programs, conducted an investigation of expressiveness, and proposed concepts that unify key mechanisms in existing rule systems by making connections to known principles from database research.

As mentioned earlier, a typical rule in an IE program expresses two kinds of functions. Functions of the first kind are *direct extractors* that produce tuples of spans by directly processing the text, usually via specified transducers (e.g., a regular expression with capture variables, or a dictionary lookup). Functions of the second kind apply *relational manipulation* to the relations obtained from the direct extraction. In XLog [59] and INSTAREAD [30] the relational manipulation is expressed through the (non-recursive) Datalog syntax and semantics, and in SystemT [14] the manipulation is by a variation of SQL. In CPSL [5] and JAPE [19], each cascade consists of transducer specifications that can reference the annotations of previous cascades; these specifications combine the two kinds of functions, but they can be viewed, conceptually, as relational joins between direct extractors in different cascades. Later, we will also discuss *cleaning* mechanisms that SystemT and JAPE further provide.

A rule language that features the above two kinds of functions can be abstracted as an ordinary relational query language, except that the base relations are replaced with the direct extractors. The framework of *document spanners* (or just *spanners* for short) is based on this abstraction, and in particular, aims to explore the relationship between the direct extraction (by different mechanisms) and the relational manipulation (through various relational operators); for example, a natural question to ask is to what extent the relational manipulation adds expressive power to the direct extractors. Next, we describe the spanner framework.

3.1 Spanners

We first need some notation. We assume a fixed, finite alphabet Σ. A *document* is a finite string over Σ (i.e., a member of the set Σ^*). A *span* of a document $\mathbf{d} = \sigma_1 \cdots \sigma_n$ represents the range of a substring of $\mathbf{d}$, and if has the form $[i, j\rangle$, where $1 \leqslant i \leqslant j \leqslant n+1$. The substring of $\mathbf{d}$ *spanned by* $[i, j\rangle$ is the string $\sigma_i \cdots \sigma_{j-1}$. For example, if $\mathbf{d}$ is `ACM_PODS_2013`, then the span $[5, 9\rangle$ refers to the part of $\mathbf{d}$ from the fifth to the eighth symbols inclusive, spanning the substring `PODS`. The *variables* we use in this framework are all assigned spans. A *spanner* extracts from a string a relation over its spans, and it is formally defined as follows. Let V be a finite set of *variables*. A $(V, \mathbf{d})$*-tuple* is a mapping that assigns a span of $\mathbf{d}$ to each variable in V. A $(V, \mathbf{d})$*-relation* is a set of $(V, \mathbf{d})$-tuples. Note that in a $(V, \mathbf{d})$-relation, the variables of V are playing the roles of the attribute names, and the spans themselves are used as attribute values. When V and $\mathbf{d}$ are clear from the context, we may write just *tuple* and *relation* instead of $(V, \mathbf{d})$-tuple and $(V, \mathbf{d})$-relation, respectively. A *spanner* is a mapping that is associated with a set V of variables, and that maps every document $\mathbf{d}$ to a $(V, \mathbf{d})$-relation.

As an example, Figure 1 depicts a document $\mathbf{d}$. The alphabet Σ consists of the lowercase and uppercase letters from the English alphabet (i.e., `a`,...,`z` and `A`,...,`Z`), the comma symbol (","), and the underscore symbol ("_") that stands for whitespace. (We use a

`Carter_from_Plains,_Georgia,_Washington_from_Westmoreland,_Virginia`

1 2 3 4 5 6 7 8 9 10 11 12 13 14 15 16 17 18 19 20 21 22 23 24 25 26 27 28 29 30 31 32 33 34 35 36 37 38 39 40 41 42 43 44 45 46 47 48 49 50 51 52 53 54 55 56 57 58 59 60 61 62 63 64 65 66 67

Figure 1: Example of a document

$\rho_{\mathsf{loc}}(\mathbf{d})$

	x_1	x_2	y
μ_1	$[13, 19\rangle$	$[21, 28\rangle$	$[13, 28\rangle$
μ_2	$[21, 28\rangle$	$[30, 40\rangle$	$[21, 40\rangle$
μ_3	$[46, 58\rangle$	$[60, 68\rangle$	$[46, 68\rangle$

Figure 2: The result of applying the spanner ρ_{loc} to the document d of Figure 1

restricted alphabet for simplicity.) The figure also depicts the index of each character in $\mathbf{d}$. Later, we will define a spanner ρ_{loc}. Figure 2 shows the result of ρ_{loc} over $\mathbf{d}$; this result is a $(V, \mathbf{d})$-relation, where $V = \{x_1, x_2, y\}$.

Fagin et al. [22] focus on representations of spanners, and their associated expressive power. The main representation system they consider consists of the following.

- *Direct extractors* are defined by regular expressions with *capture variables* (and with some natural syntactic restrictions), which they call *regex formulas*. These regex formulas take the role of the base relations in the relational model.
- *Relational manipulation* is done by algebraic operators such as natural join, projection, union, difference, and different kinds of selection. Note that projection is based on *span* equality rather than *string* equality.

We do not give the formal definition of a regex formula here, but rather provide examples. For a formal definition of a regex formula, the reader is referred to the paper of Fagin et al. [22]. The following regex formula extracts tokens (which, for simplicity of presentation, are simply complete words) from text.

$$\gamma_{\mathsf{tkn}}[x] := \quad (1)$$
$$\big(\epsilon \vee (\Sigma^* \cdot \_)\big) \cdot x\{[\mathtt{a-zA-Z}]^+\} \cdot \big(((,\vee\_) \cdot \Sigma^*) \vee \epsilon\big)$$

In the syntax of regex formulas, "ϵ" denotes the empty string, "$\vee$" denotes disjunction, "$*$" denotes Kleene star, "$+$" is the same as "$*$" with the exclusion of zero occurrences, and "$\cdot$" denotes concatenation. We often omit concatenation for readability. We are also using the convention that Σ denotes the disjunction over all the symbols, $[\mathtt{a-z}]$ denotes the disjunction $\mathtt{a} \vee \cdots \vee \mathtt{z}$, $[\mathtt{A-Z}]$ denotes the disjunction $\mathtt{A} \vee \cdots \vee \mathtt{Z}$, and $[\mathtt{a-zA-Z}]$ denotes the disjunction $[\mathtt{a-z}] \vee [\mathtt{A-Z}]$. Observe that the formula is applied to the entire document $\mathbf{d}$ (as opposed to every substring of $\mathbf{d}$).

The above regex formula (1) defines a spanner with the variable set $V = \{x\}$. The expression to the left of x matches either the empty string (meaning that x is a prefix of the document) or a string that ends with an underscore. The expression to the right of x matches either the empty string (meaning that x is a suffix of the document), or a string that begins with an underscore or a comma. The expression $[\mathtt{a-zA-Z}]^+$ inside $x\{\cdot\}$ means that x is a nonempty string that consists of only English letters (where each letter is in either lowercase or uppercase). When applied to the document $\mathbf{d}$ of Figure 1, the resulting $(V, \mathbf{d})$-tuples map x to $[1, 7\rangle$, $[8, 12\rangle$, and so on.

The following regex formula extracts spans that begin with a capital letter.

$$\gamma_{\mathsf{1Cap}}[x] := \Sigma^* \cdot x\{[\mathtt{A-Z}] \cdot \Sigma^*\} \cdot \Sigma^*$$

When applied to the document $\mathbf{d}$ of Figure 1, the resulting spans include $[1, 7\rangle$, $[1, 3\rangle$, $[13, 19\rangle$, $[13, 20\rangle$, and so on.

The following regex formula extracts all the triples (x_1, x_2, y) of spans such that the string ",_" separates between x_1 and x_2, y is the span that begins where x_1 begins and ends where x_2 ends, and both x_1 and x_2 are tokens that begin with a capital letter.

$$\rho_{\mathsf{loc}}[x_1, x_2, y] := (\Sigma^* \cdot y\{x_1\{\Sigma^*\},\_x_2\{\Sigma^*\}\} \cdot \Sigma^*) \quad (2)$$
$$\bowtie \gamma_{\mathsf{tkn}}[x_1] \bowtie \gamma_{\mathsf{tkn}}[x_2] \bowtie \gamma_{\mathsf{1Cap}}[x_1] \bowtie \gamma_{\mathsf{1Cap}}[x_2]$$

The result of applying $\rho_{\mathsf{loc}}[x_1, x_2, y]$ to the document $\mathbf{d}$ of Figure 1 is depicted in Figure 2. Note that the natural join is realized by using the same variable (namely x_1 or x_2) in multiple regex formulas.

All of the regex formulas given so far define what we call *hierarchical spanners*; this means that in every extracted $(V, \mathbf{d})$-tuple μ, and for every two variables $x, y \in V$, at least one of the following holds.

- $\mu(x)$ is contained in $\mu(y)$;
- $\mu(y)$ is contained in $\mu(x)$;
- $\mu(x)$ and $\mu(y)$ are disjoint.

An example of a non-hierarchical spanner is given by the following expression, which we will later reference in a different context. This spanner extract all the pairs (y, y') of spans, such that y and y' are different spans with a nonempty intersection (overlap), and either y begins before y' or y' is a prefix of y.

$$\pi_{y,y'}\Big(\big(\Sigma^* \cdot y\{\Sigma^+ \cdot z\{\Sigma^+\} \cdot \Sigma^*\} \cdot \Sigma^*\big) \bowtie \quad (3)$$
$$\big(\Sigma^* \cdot y'\{z\{\Sigma^+\} \cdot \Sigma^*\} \cdot \Sigma^*\big)\Big) \cup$$
$$\big(\Sigma^* \cdot y\{y'\{\Sigma^+\} \cdot \Sigma^+\} \cdot \Sigma^*\big)$$

Note that in the left operand of the union ($\cup$), the variable z represents a nonempty prefix of y', such that z is contained in y but is not a prefix of y. Also note that the spanner defined by this operand does not have the variable z, since z is projected out by the operation $\pi_{y,y'}$.

3.2 Expressiveness

To investigate the expressiveness of spanners defined by regex formulas and relational algebra, Fagin et al. [22] studied representation systems for spanners by means of simple transducers. Intuitively, those transducers are ordinary nondeterministic finite automata that open and close variables along their run, with the restriction that every variable should be opened and later closed precisely once. One such type of a transducer is the *variable-set automaton*, abbreviated *vset-automaton*. Figure 3 depicts an example of a vset-automaton. Observe that some of the transitions open variables (e.g., $x_1 \vdash$) and some close variables (e.g., $\dashv x_1$). A vset-automaton is a nondeterministic machine, and it can have multiple accepting runs over a document $\mathbf{d}$; each accepting run defines a beginning and an end index in $\mathbf{d}$ for each variable. The spanner defined by a vset-automaton produces one $(V, \mathbf{d})$-tuple (where V is the set of variables that occur in the automaton) for each accepting run. As an example, the vset-automaton of Figure 3 defines the same spanner as the one defined by the regex formula ρ_{loc} defined

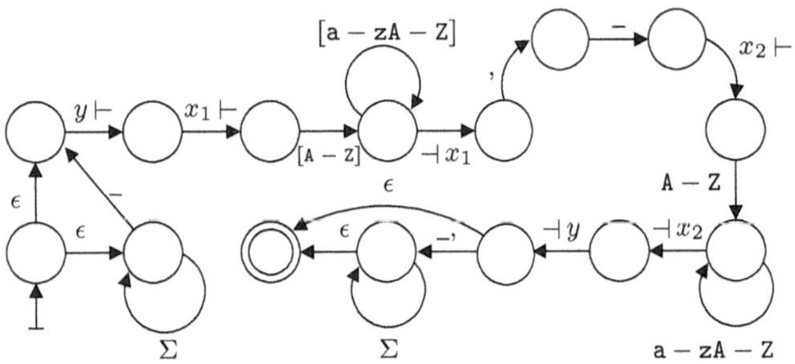

Figure 3: An example of a vset-automaton

in (2). Again, the reader is referred to Fagin et al. [22] for a precise definition of a vset-automaton and its translation into a spanner.

A vset-automaton can represent spanners that are not definable by any regex formula. In particular, regex formulas can define only hierarchical spanners, whereas it is easy to construct a vset-automaton that defines a non-hierarchical spanner. Fagin et al. [22] proved the following theorem, stating the relationship between regex formulas and vset-automata.

THEOREM 3.1. [22] *The following hold.*

1. *The class of spanners that are representable by regex formulas is precisely the class of* hierarchical *spanners that are representable by vset-automata.*
2. *The class of spanners that are representable by vset-automata is precisely the closure of the regex formulas under difference, natural join, projection, and union.*

Spanners representable by vset-automata are called *regular spanners*. Based on the above theorem, Fagin et al. [22] established additional results. For example, they proved that the expressive power of regular spanners is fully captured even without the difference operator in Part 2 of the theorem. They also give various fundamental results on the expressive power gained by adding *string equality* of spans (e.g., x and y span the same string, even though they may be different spans) as a selection operator; as an example, they show that in the presence of string equality, the difference operator strictly increases the expressive power.

3.3 Cleaning Inconsistencies through Database Repairs

Databases often involve inconsistency, due to human errors, integration of heterogeneous resources, imprecision entailed in Extract-Transform-Load (ETL) flows, and so on. The database research community has proposed principled ways to capture and manage data inconsistency [6]. A well-studied notion of inconsistency is the violation of *denial constraints* [6]; such constraints forbid cases such as two persons having the same driver's license number, or a person having multiple residential addresses. In IE tasks, inconsistency occurs even at a lower level. For example, an extractor may annotate multiple person mentions inside *"Martin Luther King Jr"*: *Martin Luther, Luther King, Martin Luther King Jr.*, etc. Moreover, all of these annotated spans may be contained in the larger span *"1805 Martin Luther King Jr Way, Berkeley, CA 94709,"* which by itself is annotated as an address, and which should not overlap with person mentions. As another example, consider again Figure 2, showing the result of applying the spanner (represented by) ρ_{loc} to the document $\mathbf{d}$ of Figure 1. If the goal is to extract locations, then the fact that the tuples μ_1 and μ_2 have overlapping assignments for y can be viewed as inconsistency, since we expect mentions of different locations to be disjoint spans.

To handle inconsistency, IE systems often provide cleaning mechanisms. JAPE [19], for instance, provides a collection of "controls" that represent different cleaning policies. These policies apply to unary annotators (that is, spanners with a single variable), and their specifications explain how the grammar should be translated into procedures (transducers) that avoid conflicts. As an example, in the Appelt control the procedure scans the document left to right; when at a specific location, it applies only the longest annotation, and continues scanning right after that annotation. In the Brill control, scanning is also done left to right, and when at a specific location, all the annotations that begin there are retained; but after that, scanning still continues after the longest annotation. In AQL [14], this cleaning mechanism comes in the form of "consolidation." Specifically, the AQL declaration of a view may include a command to filter out tuples by applying a consolidation policy to one of the columns. There is a built-in collection of such policies, like LeftToRight, which is similar to Appelt, and ContainedWithin that retains only the spans that are not strictly contained in other spans (but other than that, overlaps are permitted). WHISK [60] does not expose cleaning operations, but deploys implicit ones. For example, it deploys a rule which states that the substring captured by the wildcard ("*") should be as short as possible. Another rule states that after producing a tuple, the scan for the next tuple should proceed after (i.e., to the right of) all the spans of the first tuple (to avoid overlaps). In a sense, the well known POSIX semantics for matching regex formulas [34] can be viewed as an extreme cleaning policy that retains at most one tuple from the result.

The above cleaning mechanisms have been collected in an ad-hoc fashion in the course of use cases. Ideally, we would like to allow IE developers to declare their own policies. But the above policies are defined in a procedural way and, hence, it is not clear how to extend the built-in operations without requiring low-level coding of internal or external functions. In a recent work, Fagin et al. [23] used the framework of spanners to establish a formalism for declarative cleaning of inconsistencies in IE. This formalism unifies all of the above cleaning policies by adopting the concept of *prioritized repairs* [61], which extends the traditional notion of database repairs [6] with priorities among conflicting facts. Next, we briefly review this formalism.

In the framework of prioritized repairs, a relational database is augmented with two components. The first component is that of *integrity constraints*. To represent such constraints, Staworko et al. [61] use the conventional formalism of *denial constraints*, which are monotonic constraints (i.e., every subinstance of a consistent database instance is also consistent) that generalize common constraints such as functional dependencies (and key constraints in particular). The second component is a *priority* relation $\succ$, which is a binary relation over the facts; the meaning of $f_1 \succ f_2$ is that the fact f_1 is prioritized over the fact f_2. A *partial repair* of an inconsistent database instance I is a consistent subinstance J (i.e., J satisfies all the integrity constraints). A partial repair J is a *Pareto improvement* of a partial repair J' if J contains a fact f, such that $f \in J \setminus J'$, and $f \succ f'$ for every fact $f' \in J' \setminus J$. A *Pareto-optimal* repair (referred to as just *optimal* here) is a partial repair that does not have any Pareto improvement.[1] Conceptually, an inconsistent database instance is viewed as representing a set of consistent *possible worlds*—those are the optimal repairs.

[1]There are other notions of prioritized repairs, but here we consider only the Pareto semantics for simplicity of presentation. For a discussion on the relationship to other notions, see the work of Fagin et al. [23].

To adopt the concept of prioritized repairs, Fagin et al. [23] investigate extraction programs that are phrased as acyclic Datalog queries, where the *EDB predicates* (i.e., the relational symbols representing the base relations) are replaced with spanners. To phrase integrity constraints and priorities, they propose various formalisms. Constraints are specified by a spanner variant of denial constraints. Priority is specified by the formalism of *priority generating dependencies (pgds)*, which is a spanner variant of the well known tuple-generating dependencies (tgds). The *denial pgds* jointly represent denial constraints and pgds. For simplicity, we will discuss only the latter formalism, namely pgds. An example of what one can express with a denial pgd is the following:

$$\mathsf{overlap}[x, y] \rightarrow \mathit{Address}(x) \rhd \mathit{Person}(y)$$

Here, $\mathsf{overlap}[x, y]$ is the spanner that produces all the pairs of overlapping spans, and *Address* and *Person* are unary relations that store extracted spans. This denial pgd states that whenever two facts $\mathit{Address}(x)$ and $\mathit{Person}(y)$ are such that x and y are overlapping spans, these two facts are in conflict, and moreover, the fact on the left side, namely $\mathit{Address}(x)$, has priority over the fact on the right side, namely $\mathit{Person}(y)$. (This can be due to the fact that the address extractor is deemed more precise than the person extractor.) Note, however, that the fact that $\mathit{Address}(x)$ and $\mathit{Person}(y)$ are in conflict does not necessarily mean that $\mathit{Person}(y)$ is excluded from every optimal repair; it may be the case that $\mathit{Address}(x)$ is excluded due to another declared denial pgd, in which case $\mathit{Person}(y)$ may survive.

As another example, consider again the spanner ρ_{loc} in (2). Suppose that R is a ternary relation that represents the result of the spanner ρ_{loc}; in the case of the document $\mathbf{d}$ of Figure 1, the relation R is given by the table in Figure 2. Let $\rho[y, y']$ denote the spanner defined in (3). Now consider the following denial pgd.

$$\rho[y, y'] \rightarrow \left(R(x_1, x_2, y) \rhd R(x'_1, x'_2, y')\right)$$

Similarly to the previous example, this denial pgd states that in R, whenever two facts $R(x_1, x_2, y)$ and $R(x'_1, x'_2, y')$ are such that the pair (y, y') is extracted by ρ, these two facts are in conflict, and moreover, $R(x_1, x_2, y)$ has priority over $R(x'_1, x'_2, y')$. This denial pgd actually captures the Appelt control of JAPE (as well as the LeftToRight consolidator of AQL). When applying this denial pgd to our example of R (Figure 2), we get a single optimal repair (possible world), namely the relation that consists of the tuples μ_1 and μ_3.

The property of defining a single optimal repair has practical importance, since systems are often not designed to support multiple possible worlds. Fagin et al. [23] explore the problem of whether a given specification with denial pgds (and/or a combination of denial constraints and pgds) is such that a single possible world is assured on every document. Unfortunately, they show undecidability results, such as the following one.

THEOREM 3.2. [23] *The following is undecidable. Given a denial pgd of the form $\rho[x, y] \rightarrow (R(x) \rhd R(y))$, where ρ is a regular spanner, is there an optimal repair for every document $\mathbf{d}$, assuming that R contains all the spans of $\mathbf{d}$?*

Practically, this theorem implies that more restricted safety conditions should be deployed. That work shows some tractable variants of this problem, but the exploration of robust variants that capture real-life examples is left for future research.

Another question they explore is whether the cleaning operations increase the expressive power of the extraction language (in the case of a single optimal repair). They show that in the case of regular spanners, it is possible to define a denial pgd that strictly increases the expressive power. Yet, interestingly, all of the policies mentioned in this section (include POSIX) do not increase the expressive power of regular spanners (but they increase the expressive power if string equality is allowed) [23]. This means that if the program uses only regular spanners with cleaning declarations, then it can be translated into an equivalent program that has no cleaning declarations. For some of the policies (e.g., ContainedWithin), this result is a special case of a more general phenomenon (in particular, this result holds for every transitive denial pgd that is phrased by means of a regular spanner). Also, for some of these cases (e.g., Appelt), this result required a fairly intricate proof.

4. CHALLENGES FOR FUTURE WORK

There are quite a few research challenges to pursue on the foundations and realization of data management systems that effectively incorporate IE. This section focuses on challenges that relate the framework of document spanners.

The theoretical research on spanners is still in its early stage, and some fundamental questions are still open. One class of such questions relates to the computational complexity of spanners: understanding the complexity of spanner evaluation under different representation systems, the complexity of translating spanners between representations (e.g., from algebraic expressions to and from automata with variables), and the complexity of traditional static-analysis questions such as emptiness, containment and equivalence of spanners. Another important direction is the extension of spanner representations with recursion. Specifically, we believe that some algorithms for IE can be naturally represented as recursive Datalog programs with spanner rules (while existing Datalog representations [23, 30, 59] do not support recursion). Another important direction is the incorporation of spanners within a more general database that may include multiple documents and ordinary relational data, as in Xlog [59]. Finally, Fagin et al. [23] leave open some questions on the expressive power of spanners, such as the effect of allowing both string equality and difference in the relational algebra. Obviously, some of these directions involve challenging system aspects towards the application to real-life data and tasks.

To maintain high precision, rule specifications such as spanners need to be highly elaborate, which often comes at the expense of recall and/or software complexity (e.g., many rules need to be deployed). It is then conceivable that in some practical scenarios one would like to enhance the rules with an inference engine that would reason about the precision of the rules and conflicts thereof. In principle, one could naturally extend the framework of spanners with notions of soft constraints, such as the aforementioned MLNs [50, 55]. It has been shown that MLNs properly capture the uncertainty involved in some IE tasks [48, 58]. We believe that an important research direction is to explore the foundations of a probabilistic database systems that combine Datalog, spanners and MLNs. This direction will hopefully allow us to leverage the research on learning soft constraints (e.g., [28, 40, 52]) within the task of rule induction for IE. A related direction is the application of spanners to probabilistic text (rather than deterministic text as discussed here), in a manner similar to the work of Kimelfeld and Ré [38] on the application of transducers to *Markov sequences*. This is especially useful when the text is generated by procedures that involve uncertainty, such as speech recognition [32], image processing [49], and normalization of informal text [68].

Acknowledgments

The author is grateful to Ronald Fagin for providing helpful comments on this paper.

5. REFERENCES

[1] J. S. Aitken. Learning information extraction rules: An inductive logic programming approach. In *ECAI*, pages 355–359. IOS Press, 2002.

[2] J. Ajmera, H.-I. Ahn, M. Nagarajan, A. Verma, D. Contractor, S. Dill, and M. Denesuk. A CRM system for social media: challenges and experiences. In *WWW*, pages 49–58, 2013.

[3] C. Aone and M. Ramos-Santacruz. Rees: A large-scale relation and event extraction system. In *ANLP*, pages 76–83, 2000.

[4] D. E. Appelt, J. R. Hobbs, J. Bear, D. J. Israel, and M. Tyson. FASTUS: A finite-state processor for information extraction from real-world text. In *IJCAI*, pages 1172–1178. Morgan Kaufmann, 1993.

[5] D. E. Appelt and B. Onyshkevych. The common pattern specification language. In *Proceedings of the TIPSTER Text Program: Phase III*, pages 23–30, Baltimore, Maryland, USA, 1998.

[6] M. Arenas, L. E. Bertossi, and J. Chomicki. Consistent query answers in inconsistent databases. In *PODS*, pages 68–79, 1999.

[7] E. Benson, A. Haghighi, and R. Barzilay. Event discovery in social media feeds. In *ACL*, pages 389–398, 2011.

[8] D. M. Bikel, S. Miller, R. M. Schwartz, and R. M. Weischedel. Nymble: a high-performance learning name-finder. In *ANLP*, pages 194–201, 1997.

[9] V. R. Borkar, K. Deshmukh, and S. Sarawagi. Automatic segmentation of text into structured records. In *SIGMOD Conference*, pages 175–186. ACM, 2001.

[10] M. Bröcheler, L. Mihalkova, and L. Getoor. Probabilistic similarity logic. In *UAI*, pages 73–82. AUAI Press, 2010.

[11] R. C. Bunescu and R. J. Mooney. Subsequence kernels for relation extraction. In *NIPS*, 2005.

[12] M. E. Califf and R. J. Mooney. Relational learning of pattern-match rules for information extraction. In *AAAI/IAAI*, pages 328–334. AAAI Press / The MIT Press, 1999.

[13] F. Chen, X. Feng, C. Re, and M. Wang. Optimizing statistical information extraction programs over evolving text. In *ICDE*, pages 870–881. IEEE Computer Society, 2012.

[14] L. Chiticariu, R. Krishnamurthy, Y. Li, S. Raghavan, F. Reiss, and S. Vaithyanathan. SystemT: An algebraic approach to declarative information extraction. In *ACL*, pages 128–137, 2010.

[15] L. Chiticariu, Y. Li, and F. R. Reiss. Rule-based information extraction is dead! Long live rule-based information extraction systems! In *EMNLP*, pages 827–832. ACL, 2013.

[16] F. Ciravegna. Adaptive information extraction from text by rule induction and generalisation. In *IJCAI*, pages 1251–1256. Morgan Kaufmann, 2001.

[17] A. Coden, D. Gruhl, N. Lewis, M. A. Tanenblatt, and J. Terdiman. Spot the drug! An unsupervised pattern matching method to extract drug names from very large clinical corpora. In *HISB*, pages 33–39. IEEE Computer Society, 2012.

[18] A. Culotta and J. S. Sorensen. Dependency tree kernels for relation extraction. In *ACL*, pages 423–429. ACL, 2004.

[19] H. Cunningham. GATE, a general architecture for text engineering. *Computers and the Humanities*, 36(2):223–254, 2002.

[20] N. N. Dalvi and D. Suciu. Efficient query evaluation on probabilistic databases. In *VLDB*, pages 864–875. Morgan Kaufmann, 2004.

[21] M. Dylla, I. Miliaraki, and M. Theobald. A temporal-probabilistic database model for information extraction. *PVLDB*, 6(14):1810–1821, 2013.

[22] R. Fagin, B. Kimelfeld, F. Reiss, and S. Vansummeren. Spanners: a formal framework for information extraction. In *PODS*, pages 37–48. ACM, 2013.

[23] R. Fagin, B. Kimelfeld, F. Reiss, and S. Vansummeren. Cleaning inconsistencies in information extraction via prioritized repairs. In *PODS*. ACM, 2014.

[24] D. Freitag. Toward general-purpose learning for information extraction. In *COLING-ACL*, pages 404–408, 1998.

[25] D. Freitag. Machine learning for information extraction in informal domains. *Machine Learning*, 39(2/3):169–202, 2000.

[26] Q. Fu, J.-G. Lou, Y. Wang, and J. Li. Execution anomaly detection in distributed systems through unstructured log analysis. In *ICDM*, pages 149–158, 2009.

[27] S. Ginsburg and X. S. Wang. Regular sequence operations and their use in database queries. *J. Comput. Syst. Sci.*, 56(1):1–26, 1998.

[28] V. Gogate, W. A. Webb, and P. Domingos. Learning efficient Markov networks. In *NIPS*, pages 748–756. Curran Associates, Inc., 2010.

[29] R. Grishman and B. Sundheim. Message understanding conference 6: A brief history. In *COLING*, pages 466–471, 1996.

[30] R. Hoffmann. *Interactive Learning of Relation Extractors with Weak Supervision*. PhD thesis, University of Washington, 2012.

[31] R. Hoffmann, C. Zhang, X. Ling, L. S. Zettlemoyer, and D. S. Weld. Knowledge-based weak supervision for information extraction of overlapping relations. In *ACL*, pages 541–550. The Association for Computer Linguistics, 2011.

[32] X. D. Huang, Y. Ariki, and M. A. Jack. *Hidden Markov models for speech recognition*, volume 2004. Edinburgh university press Edinburgh, 1990.

[33] S. B. Huffman. Learning information extraction patterns from examples. In S. Wermter, E. Riloff, and G. Scheler, editors, *Learning for Natural Language Processing*, volume 1040 of *Lecture Notes in Computer Science*, pages 246–260. Springer, 1995.

[34] Institute of Electrical and Electronic Engineers and the Open group. The open group base specifications issue 7, 2013. IEEE Std 1003.1, 2013 Edition.

[35] H. Isozaki and H. Kazawa. Efficient support vector classifiers for named entity recognition. In *COLING*, 2002.

[36] T. S. Jayram, R. Krishnamurthy, S. Raghavan, S. Vaithyanathan, and H. Zhu. Avatar information extraction system. *IEEE Data Eng. Bull.*, 29(1):40–48, 2006.

[37] A. K. Jha and D. Suciu. Probabilistic databases with MarkoViews. *PVLDB*, 5(11):1160–1171, 2012.

[38] B. Kimelfeld and C. Ré. Transducing Markov sequences. In *PODS*, pages 15–26. ACM, 2010.

[39] D. Klein and C. D. Manning. Conditional structure versus conditional estimation in NLP models. In *EMNLP*, pages 9–16. Association for Computational Linguistics, 2002.

[40] S. Kok and P. Domingos. Using structural motifs for learning Markov logic networks. In *Statistical Relational Artificial*

Intelligence, volume WS-10-06 of *AAAI Workshops*. AAAI, 2010.

[41] J. D. Lafferty, A. McCallum, and F. C. N. Pereira. Conditional random fields: Probabilistic models for segmenting and labeling sequence data. In *ICML*, pages 282–289, 2001.

[42] T. R. Leek. Information extraction using hidden Markov models. Master's thesis, UC San Diego, 1997.

[43] Y. Li, K. Bontcheva, and H. Cunningham. SVM based learning system for information extraction. In *Deterministic and Statistical Methods in Machine Learning*, volume 3635 of *Lecture Notes in Computer Science*, pages 319–339. Springer, 2004.

[44] X. Ling and D. S. Weld. Temporal information extraction. In *AAAI*. AAAI Press, 2010.

[45] B. Liu, L. Chiticariu, V. Chu, H. V. Jagadish, and F. Reiss. Automatic rule refinement for information extraction. *PVLDB*, 3(1):588–597, 2010.

[46] A. McCallum, D. Freitag, and F. C. N. Pereira. Maximum entropy Markov models for information extraction and segmentation. In *ICML*, pages 591–598, 2000.

[47] A. Nagesh, G. Ramakrishnan, L. Chiticariu, R. Krishnamurthy, A. Dharkar, and P. Bhattacharyya. Towards efficient named-entity rule induction for customizability. In *EMNLP-CoNLL*, pages 128–138. ACL, 2012.

[48] F. Niu, C. Ré, A. Doan, and J. W. Shavlik. Tuffy: Scaling up statistical inference in Markov logic networks using an RDBMS. *PVLDB*, 4(6):373–384, 2011.

[49] R. Plamondon and S. N. Srihari. On-line and off-line handwriting recognition: A comprehensive survey. *IEEE Trans. Pattern Anal. Mach. Intell.*, 22(1):63–84, 2000.

[50] H. Poon and P. Domingos. Joint inference in information extraction. In *AAAI'07: Proceedings of the 22nd national conference on Artificial intelligence*, pages 913–918. AAAI Press, 2007.

[51] J. Pujara, H. Miao, L. Getoor, and W. Cohen. Knowledge graph identification. In *International Semantic Web Conference (1)*, volume 8218 of *Lecture Notes in Computer Science*, pages 542–557. Springer, 2013.

[52] L. D. Raedt and K. Kersting. Statistical relational learning. In C. Sammut and G. I. Webb, editors, *Encyclopedia of Machine Learning*, pages 916–924. Springer, 2010.

[53] K. Raghunathan, H. Lee, S. Rangarajan, N. Chambers, M. Surdeanu, D. Jurafsky, and C. D. Manning. A multi-pass sieve for coreference resolution. In *EMNLP*, pages 492–501. ACL, 2010.

[54] F. Reiss, S. Raghavan, R. Krishnamurthy, H. Zhu, and S. Vaithyanathan. An algebraic approach to rule-based information extraction. In *ICDE*, pages 933–942, 2008.

[55] M. Richardson and P. Domingos. Markov logic networks. *Machine Learning*, 62(1-2):107–136, 2006.

[56] E. Riloff and R. Jones. Learning dictionaries for information extraction by multi-level bootstrapping. In *AAAI/IAAI*, pages 474–479. AAAI Press / The MIT Press, 1999.

[57] S. Sarawagi. Information extraction. *Foundations and Trends in Databases*, 1(3):261–377, 2008.

[58] S. Satpal, S. Bhadra, S. Sellamanickam, R. Rastogi, and P. Sen. Web information extraction using Markov logic networks. In *KDD*, pages 1406–1414. ACM, 2011.

[59] W. Shen, A. Doan, J. F. Naughton, and R. Ramakrishnan. Declarative information extraction using datalog with embedded extraction predicates. In *VLDB*, pages 1033–1044, 2007.

[60] S. Soderland. Learning information extraction rules for semi-structured and free text. *Machine Learning*, 34(1-3):233–272, 1999.

[61] S. Staworko, J. Chomicki, and J. Marcinkowski. Prioritized repairing and consistent query answering in relational databases. *Ann. Math. Artif. Intell.*, 64(2-3):209–246, 2012.

[62] F. M. Suchanek, G. Ifrim, and G. Weikum. Combining linguistic and statistical analysis to extract relations from web documents. In *KDD*, pages 712–717. ACM, 2006.

[63] F. M. Suchanek, M. Sozio, and G. Weikum. SOFIE: a self-organizing framework for information extraction. In *WWW*, pages 631–640. ACM, 2009.

[64] D. Z. Wang, M. J. Franklin, M. N. Garofalakis, J. M. Hellerstein, and M. L. Wick. Hybrid in-database inference for declarative information extraction. In *SIGMOD Conference*, pages 517–528. ACM, 2011.

[65] R. Wisnesky, M. A. Hernández, and L. Popa. Mapping polymorphism. In *ICDT*, ACM International Conference Proceeding Series, pages 196–208. ACM, 2010.

[66] H. Xu, S. P. Stenner, S. Doan, K. B. Johnson, L. R. Waitman, and J. C. Denny. Application of information technology: Medex: a medication information extraction system for clinical narratives. *JAMIA*, 17(1):19–24, 2010.

[67] D. Zelenko, C. Aone, and A. Richardella. Kernel methods for relation extraction. *Journal of Machine Learning Research*, 3:1083–1106, 2003.

[68] C. Zhang, T. Baldwin, H. Ho, B. Kimelfeld, and Y. Li. Adaptive parser-centric text normalization. In *ACL (1)*, pages 1159–1168. The Association for Computer Linguistics, 2013.

[69] H. Zhu, S. Raghavan, S. Vaithyanathan, and A. Löser. Navigating the intranet with high precision. In *WWW*, pages 491–500, 2007.

Cleaning Inconsistencies in Information Extraction via Prioritized Repairs

Ronald Fagin
IBM Research – Almaden
San Jose, CA, USA
fagin@us.ibm.com

Benny Kimelfeld*
LogicBlox, Inc.
Berkeley, CA, USA
bennyk@gmail.com

Frederick Reiss
IBM Research – Almaden
San Jose, CA, USA
frreiss@us.ibm.com

Stijn Vansummeren
Université Libre de Bruxelles (ULB)
Bruxelles, Belgium
stijn.vansummeren@ulb.ac.be

ABSTRACT

The population of a predefined relational schema from textual content, commonly known as Information Extraction (IE), is a pervasive task in contemporary computational challenges associated with Big Data. Since the textual content varies widely in nature and structure (from machine logs to informal natural language), it is notoriously difficult to write IE programs that extract the sought information without any inconsistencies (e.g., a substring should not be annotated as both an address and a person name). Dealing with inconsistencies is hence of crucial importance in IE systems. Industrial-strength IE systems like GATE and IBM SystemT therefore provide a built-in collection of *cleaning* operations to remove inconsistencies from extracted relations. These operations, however, are collected in an ad-hoc fashion through use cases. Ideally, we would like to allow IE developers to declare their own policies. But existing cleaning operations are defined in an algorithmic way and, hence, it is not clear how to extend the built-in operations without requiring low-level coding of internal or external functions.

We embark on the establishment of a framework for declarative cleaning of inconsistencies in IE, though principles of database theory. Specifically, building upon the formalism of *document spanners* for IE, we adopt the concept of *prioritized repairs*, which has been recently proposed as an extension of the traditional database repairs to incorporate priorities among conflicting facts. We show that our framework captures the popular cleaning policies, as well as the POSIX semantics for extraction through regular expressions. We explore the problem of determining whether a cleaning declaration is unambiguous (i.e., always results in a single repair), and whether it increases the expressive power of the extraction language. We give both positive and negative results, some of which are general, and some of which apply to policies used in practice.

Categories and Subject Descriptors

H.2.1 [**Database Management**]: Logical Design—*Data models*; H.2.4 [**Database Management**]: Systems—*Textual databases, Relational databases, Rule-based databases*; I.5.4 [**Pattern Recognition**]: Applications—*Text processing*; F.4.3 [**Mathematical Logic and Formal Languages**]: Formal Languages—*Algebraic language theory, Classes defined by grammars or automata, Operations on languages*; F.1.1 [**Computation by Abstract Devices**]: Models of Computation—*Automata, Relations between models*

General Terms

Theory

Keywords

Information extraction, document spanners, regular expressions, extraction inconsistency, database repairs, prioritized repairs

*Work done while at IBM Almaden – Research.

PODS'14, June 22–27, 2014, Snowbird, UT, USA.

ACM 978-1-4503-2375-8/14/06 ...$15.00.
http://dx.doi.org/10.1145/2594538.2594540.

1. INTRODUCTION

Information Extraction (IE) conventionally refers to the task of automatically extracting structured information from text. While early work in the area focused largely on military applications [22], this task is nowadays pervasive in a plethora of computational challenges (especially those associated with Big Data), including social media analysis [4], machine data analysis [21], healthcare analysis [40], customer relationship management [1], and indexing for semantic search [41]. Moreover, analytics platforms like Hadoop make the analysis of data more accessible to a broad range of users. The techniques used for implementing IE tasks include rule engineering [20,35,37], rule learning [11,28], probabilistic graph models [25,27,30], and other statistical models such as Markov Logic Networks [31,33] and probabilistic databases [12]. There are also general frameworks for the development and scalable execution of IE programs, such as UIMA [18], the General Architecture for Text Engineering (GATE) [9], Xlog [36] and SystemT [7].

GATE and SystemT are highly relevant to this paper. GATE, an open-source project by the University of Sheffield, is an instantiation of the *cascaded finite-state transducers* [2]. The core IE engine of GATE, called JAPE, processes a document via a sequence of *phases* (*cascades*), each annotating spans (intervals within the document) with types by processing previous annotations by applying grammar rules and user-defined Java procedures. SystemT exposes an SQL-like declarative language named *AQL* (Annotation Query Language), along with a query plan optimizer [34] and development tooling [28]. Conceptually, AQL supports a collection of "direct" extractors of relations from text (e.g., tokenizer, dictionary lookup, regex matcher, part-of-speech tagger, and other morphological analyzers), along with an algebra for relational manipulation.

Databases often contain inconsistent data, due to human errors, integration of heterogeneous resources, imprecision in ETL flows, and so on. The database research community has proposed principled ways to capture, manage and resolve data inconsistency [3,5,6, 15–17,29,38]. Here, the identification and capturing of inconsistencies is usually done through the use of specialized constraints and dependencies [3,15,16,29,38]. A prominent formalism for specifying inconsistencies in this respect are the *denial constraints* [3,38] that can specify, for example that no two persons can have the same driver's license number, or that no single person can have multiple residential addresses. To manage and resolve data inconsistencies, the database research community has proposed a wide variety of methods, ranging from consistent query answering [3], to formalisms for the declarative specification of conflict resolution by means of prioritized repairs [38], to data cleaning and data fusion tools that introduce domain-specific operators for removing data inconsistencies [5, 6, 17].

In IE tasks, inconsistencies occur at a low level. For example, an extractor may annotate multiple person mentions inside *"Martin Luther King Jr"*, namely: *Martin Luther, Luther King, Martin Luther King Jr.*, etc. Moreover, all of these annotated spans may be contained in the larger span *"1805 Martin Luther King Jr Way, Berkeley, CA 94709,"* which is annotated as an address, and which should not overlap with person mentions.

To handle inconsistency, nearly all rule-based IE systems integrate a cleaning mechanism as a core element of the rule language. For example, the CPSL standard, which underpins many commonly-used systems, stipulates that "at each [token position]... one of the matching rules is selected as a 'best match' and is applied" [2]. JAPE, which implements CPSL, generalizes this "best match" to a collection of "controls" that represent different cleaning policies. Every JAPE rule must include a specification of which control applies to matches of the rule. As an example, in the Appelt control of JAPE the annotation procedure (transducer) scans the document left to right; when at a specific location, it applies only the longest annotation, and continues scanning right after that annotation. In the Brill control, scanning is also left to right, and when at a specific location, all the annotations that begin there are retained; but after that, scanning still continues after the longest annotation. In AQL, this cleaning mechanism comes in the form of "consolidation." Specifically, the AQL declaration of a view can include a command to filter out tuples by applying a consolidation policy to one of the columns. There is a built-in collection of such policies, like LeftToRight, which is similar to Appelt, and ContainedWithin that retains only the spans that are not strictly contained in other spans. The Appelt control of JAPE, as well as the ContainedWithin consolidator of AQL, can involve explicitly specified priorities that we ignore here for simplicity; we discuss those in Section 5.2.

The goal of this work is to establish principles for declarative cleaning of inconsistencies in IE programs. We build upon our recent work [14], where we proposed the framework of *document spanners* (or just *spanners* for short) that captures the relational philosophy of AQL. Intuitively, a spanner extracts from a document $\mathbf{d}$ (which is a string over a finite alphabet) a relation over the spans of $\mathbf{d}$. An example of a spanner representation is a *regex formula*: a regular expression with embedded capture variables that are viewed as relational attributes. A *regular* spanner is one that can be expressed in the closure of the regex formulas under relational algebra. We extend the spanners into *extraction programs*, which are non-recursive Datalog programs that can use spanners in the premises of the rules. We then include denial constraints (again phrased using spanners) to specify integrity constraints within the program. In the presence of denial constraints, a *repair* of a schema instance is a subset of facts that satisfies all the constraints, and is not strictly contained in any other such subset [3].

Denial constraints do not provide means to discriminate among repairs, and are therefore insufficient to capture common cleaning policies in IE like the ones aforementioned (Appelt and Brill, etc.); those cleaning policies imply not only which sets of facts are in conflict, but also which facts should remain and which facts should be dropped. To accommodate preferences, we adopt the *prioritized repairs* of Staworko et al. [38], which extend the concept of repairs with priorities among facts that, eventually, translate into priorities among repairs. More precisely, Staworko et al. assume that in addition to denial constraints, the inconsistent database is associated with a binary relation $\succ$, called *priority*, over the facts (where $f_1 \succ f_2$ means that f_1 has priority over f_2). We say that a repair J *can be improved* if we can add to J a new database fact f and retain consistency of J by removing only facts that are inferior to f (according to the priority). The idea is to restrict the set of repairs to those that are *Pareto-optimal* (or just *optimal* hereafter), where an optimal repair is one that cannot be improved.[1]

Staworko et al. [38] made the assumption that the priority relation $\succ$ is given in an explicit manner, and did not provide any syntax for declaring priority at the schema level. Here, we need such a syntax, and we propose what we call a *priority generating dependency*, or just *pgd* for short. A pgd has the logical form $\psi(\mathbf{x}) \rightarrow (\varphi_1(\mathbf{x}) \succ \varphi_2(\mathbf{x}))$, where $\mathbf{x}$ is a sequence of variables, all universally quantified (and all assigned spans in our framework), $\psi(\mathbf{x})$ represents a spanner with variables in $\mathbf{x}$, and the $\varphi_i(\mathbf{x})$ are atomic formulas over the relational schema. A *cleaning update* in an extraction program is specified by a collection of denial constraints and pgds, and it instructs the program to branch into the optimal repairs (which are viewed as possible worlds). In Section 5 we show that common strategies for cleaning inconsistencies in IE, like all those used in JAPE and AQL, can be phrased in our framework, where all involved spanners are regular. We further show that the POSIX semantics for regex formulas is expressible in our framework. The POSIX semantics can be viewed as an extreme cleaning policy for a regex formula, dictating that the evaluation on a string always results in a single match [24].

One difference between the ordinary repairs and the prioritized repairs is that the latter give rise to interesting cases where a *single* optimal repair exists. This is a significant difference, since data management systems are usually not designed to support multiple possible worlds. Here, we refer to this property as *unambiguity*. An extraction program is *unambiguous* if, for all input documents, the result consists of exactly one possible world. This property holds in all of the IE cleaning policies mentioned thus far. The next problem we study is that of deciding whether a given extraction program is unambiguous. We prove that, for the class of programs that use regular spanners, this property is undecidable. To prove that, we give an intermediate result of independent interest: it is undecidable to determine whether a two-way two-head deterministic finite automaton [23] has any immortal finite configuration.

Staworko et al. [38] show that under two conditions, unambiguity is guaranteed. The first condition (which they assume throughout their paper) is that the priority relation induces an acyclic graph. The second condition is *totality*: every two facts that are jointly involved in a conflict are also comparable in the priority relation. In Section 4 we improve that result by relaxing totality into what we call the *minimum property*: every conflict has a least prioritized member. In our setting, an important example where the minimum property (and, in fact, totality) is guaranteed is the special case of

[1] Staworko et al. [38] also study *global optimality* as an alternative to Pareto optimality. As we discuss in Section 3, it turns out that all the results in this paper hold true even if we adopt global optimality instead of the Pareto one.

a cleaning update consisting of binary conflicts, such that the pgds are specified *precisely* for those pairs in conflict. In fact, we define a special syntax to capture this case: a *denial pgd* is an expression of the form $\psi(\mathbf{x}) \rightarrow (\varphi_1(\mathbf{x}) \rhd \varphi_2(\mathbf{x}))$, which has the same semantics as a pgd, but it also specifies that $\varphi_1(\mathbf{x})$ and $\varphi_2(\mathbf{x})$ are in conflict (and the former is of higher priority). We then look again at extraction programs that use regular spanners. We prove that it is decidable to determine whether the minimum property is guaranteed by a given cleaning update. However, it turns out that it is undecidable to determine whether a pgd guarantees acyclicity of the priority relation. The conclusion is that other (stronger) conditions need to be imposed if we want to automatically verify unambiguity of an extraction program (an example might be by using a potential function, e.g., as in [13]). Such conditions are beyond the scope of this paper, and are left as important directions for future work.

An extreme example of an unambiguous extraction program is a program that does not use cleaning updates (hence, never branches). Given that one is interested in the content of a single relation of the program (which we assume as part of our definition of an extraction program), an unambiguous program can be viewed simply as a representation of a spanner. The next question we explore is whether cleaning updates increase the expressive power (when used in unambiguous programs). We define the property of *disposability* of a cleaning update that, intuitively, means that we can replace the cleaning update with a collection of non-cleaning (ordinary) rules. As usual, this definition is parameterized by the representation system we use for the involved spanners. In the case of unambiguous programs using regular spanners, if all the cleaning updates are disposable, then the spanner defined by the program is also regular. However, we show that there exists an unambiguous program that uses regular spanners and a single cleaning update, such that the resulting spanner is not regular. Moreover, in the case of *core spanners* (which extend the regular spanners with the string-equality selection [14]), each of JAPE's cleaners, as well as the POSIX one, strictly increase the expressive power.

In Section 5 we explore special cases of cleaning updates in extraction programs with regular spanners. The first case is that of acyclic and transitive denial pgds. An example of such a denial pgd is the ContainedWithin consolidation policy mentioned earlier in this section. The second case is the denial pgds that declare the different controls of JAPE. The third case is the POSIX policy for regex formulas, where we show how it is simulated by a sequence of denial pgds. It follows from our results that an extraction program that uses only cleaning updates among the three cases is unambiguous. We prove that all of these cleaning updates are disposable. We find these results interesting, since we can now draw the following conclusions. First, the extraction programs that use regular spanners, as well as cleaning updates among the three cases, have the same expressive power as the regular spanners. Second, for every regex formula γ there exists a regex formula γ', such that when evaluated over a document, γ' (without any cleaning applied) gives the same result as γ under the POSIX semantics. We are not aware of any result in the literature showing that the POSIX semantics can be "compiled away" in this sense.

2. DOCUMENT SPANNERS

In this section, we give some preliminary definitions and notation, and recall the formalism of *document spanners* [14].

2.1 Strings and Spans

We fix a finite alphabet Σ of *symbols*. We denote by Σ^* the set of all finite strings over Σ, and by Σ^+ the set of all finite strings of length at least one over Σ. For clarity of context, we will often refer to a string in Σ^* as a *document*. A *language over* Σ is a subset of Σ^*. Let $\mathbf{d} = \sigma_1 \cdots \sigma_n \in \Sigma^*$ be a document. The length n of $\mathbf{d}$ is denoted by $|\mathbf{d}|$. A *span* identifies a substring of $\mathbf{d}$ by specifying its bounding indices. Formally, a span of $\mathbf{d}$ has the form $[i, j\rangle$, where $1 \leqslant i \leqslant j \leqslant n + 1$. If $[i, j\rangle$ is a span of $\mathbf{d}$, then $\mathbf{d}_{[i,j\rangle}$ denotes the substring $\sigma_i \cdots \sigma_{j-1}$. Note that $\mathbf{d}_{[i,i\rangle}$ is the empty string, and that $\mathbf{d}_{[1,n+1\rangle}$ is $\mathbf{d}$. The more standard notation would be $[i, j)$, but we use $[i, j\rangle$ to distinguish spans from intervals. For example, $[1, 1)$ and $[2, 2)$ are both the empty interval, hence equal, but in the case of spans we have $[i, j\rangle = [i', j'\rangle$ if and only if $i = i'$ and $j = j'$ (and in particular, $[1, 1\rangle \neq [2, 2\rangle$). We denote by $\mathsf{Spans}(\mathbf{d})$ the set of all the spans of $\mathbf{d}$. Two spans $[i, j\rangle$ and $[i', j'\rangle$ of $\mathbf{d}$ *overlap* if $i \leqslant i' < j$ or $i' \leqslant i < j'$, and are *disjoint* otherwise. Finally, $[i, j\rangle$ *contains* $[i', j'\rangle$ if $i \leqslant i' \leqslant j' \leqslant j$.

EXAMPLE 2.1. In all of the examples throughout the paper, we consider the example alphabet Σ which consists of the lowercase and capital letters from the English alphabet (i.e., a,...,z and A,...,Z), the comma symbol (" , "), and the underscore symbol ("_") that stands for whitespace. (We use a restricted alphabet for simplicity.) Figure 1 depicts an example document $\mathbf{d}$ in Σ^*. For ease of later reference, it also depicts the index of each character in $\mathbf{d}$. Figure 2 shows two tables containing spans of $\mathbf{d}$. Observe that the spans in the left table are those that correspond to words in $\mathbf{d}$ that are names of US states (Georgia, Washington and Virginia). For example, the span $[21, 28\rangle$ corresponds to Georgia. We will further discuss the meaning of these tables later. □

2.2 Document Spanners

We fix an infinite set SVars of *span variables*; spans may be assigned to these span variables. The sets Σ^* and SVars are disjoint. For a finite set $V \subseteq \mathsf{SVars}$ of variables and a document $\mathbf{d} \in \Sigma^*$, a $(V, \mathbf{d})$*-tuple* is a mapping $\mu\colon V \rightarrow \mathsf{Spans}(\mathbf{d})$ that assigns a span of $\mathbf{d}$ to each variable in V. A $(V, \mathbf{d})$*-relation* is a set of $(V, \mathbf{d})$-tuples. A *document spanner* (or just *spanner* for short) is a function P that is associated with a finite set V of variables, denoted $\mathsf{SVars}(P)$, and that maps every document $\mathbf{d}$ to a $(V, \mathbf{d})$-relation.

EXAMPLE 2.2. Throughout our running example (which started in Example 2.1) we will define several spanners. Two of those are denoted as $[\![\rho_{\mathsf{stt}}]\!]$ and $[\![\rho_{\mathsf{loc}}]\!]$, where $\mathsf{SVars}([\![\rho_{\mathsf{stt}}]\!]) = \{x\}$ and $\mathsf{SVars}([\![\rho_{\mathsf{loc}}]\!]) = \{x_1, x_2, y\}$. Later we will explain the meaning of the brackets, and specify what exactly each spanner extracts from a given document. For now, the span relations (tables) in Figure 2 show the results of applying the two spanners to the document $\mathbf{d}$ of Figure 1. □

Let P be a spanner with $\mathsf{SVars}(P) = V$. Let $\mathbf{d} \in \Sigma^*$ be a document, and let $\mu \in P(\mathbf{d})$ be a $(V, \mathbf{d})$-tuple. We say that μ is *hierarchical* if for all variables $x, y \in \mathsf{SVars}(P)$ one of the following holds: *(1)* the span $\mu(x)$ contains $\mu(y)$, *(2)* the span $\mu(y)$ contains $\mu(x)$, *or (3)* the spans $\mu(x)$ and $\mu(y)$ are disjoint. As an example, the reader can verify that all the tuples in Figure 2 are hierarchical. We say that P is *hierarchical* if μ is hierarchical for all $\mathbf{d} \in \Sigma^*$ and $\mu \in P(\mathbf{d})$. Observe that for two variables x and y of a hierarchical spanner, it may be the case that, over the same document, one tuple maps x to a subspan of y, another tuple maps y to a subspan of x, and a third tuple maps x and y to disjoint spans.

2.3 Spanner Representation Systems

By a *spanner representation system* we refer collectively to any manner of specifying spanners through finite objects. In previous work [14] we defined several representation systems (by means of

```
Carter_from_Plains,_Georgia,_Washington_from_Westmoreland,_Virginia
1 2 3 4 5 6 7 8 9 10 11 12 13 14 15 16 17 18 19 20 21 22 23 24 25 26 27 28 29 30 31 32 33 34 35 36 37 38 39 40 41 42 43 44 45 46 47 48 49 50 51 52 53 54 55 56 57 58 59 60 61 62 63 64 65 66 67
```

Figure 1: Document d in the running example

regular expressions, special types of automata, and relational algebra). Here, we recall the definition of the *regex formula* system, as well as its closure under relational algebra.

A *regular expression with capture variables*, or just *variable regex* for short, is an expression in the following syntax that extends that of regular expressions:

$$\gamma := \emptyset \mid \epsilon \mid \sigma \mid \gamma \vee \gamma \mid \gamma \cdot \gamma \mid \gamma^* \mid x\{\gamma\} \qquad (1)$$

The added alternative is $x\{\gamma\}$, where $x \in \mathsf{SVars}$. We denote by $\mathsf{SVars}(\gamma)$ the set of variables that occur in γ. We use γ^+ as abbreviations of $\gamma \cdot \gamma^*$.

A variable regex can be matched against a document in multiple ways, or more formally, there can be multiple parse trees showing that a document matches a variable regex. Each such a parse tree naturally associates variables with spans. It is possible, however, that in a parse tree a variable is not associated with any span, or is associated with multiple spans. If every variable is associated with precisely one span, then the parse tree is said to be *functional*. A variable regex is called a *regex formula* if it has only functional parse trees on every input document. An example of a variable regex that is *not* a regex formula is $(x\{\mathtt{a}\})^*$, because a match against aa assigns x to two spans. We refer to Fagin et al. [14] for the full formal definition of regex formulas. By RGX we denote the class of regex formulas. A regex formula γ is naturally viewed as representing a spanner, and by $[\![\gamma]\!]$ we denote the spanner that is represented by γ. Following are examples of spanners represented as regex formulas.

EXAMPLE 2.3. In the regex formulas of our running examples we will use the following conventions.

- [a-z] denotes the disjunction a $\vee \cdots \vee$ z;
- [A-Z] denotes the disjunction A $\vee \cdots \vee$ Z;
- and [a-zA-Z] denotes the disjunction [a-z] $\vee$ [A-Z].

We now define several variable regexes that we will use throughout the paper.

The following regex formula extracts tokens (which for our purposes now are simply complete words) from text. (Note that this is a simplistic extraction for the sake of presentation.)

$$\gamma_{\mathsf{tkn}} := \big(\epsilon \vee (\Sigma^* \cdot \_)\big) \cdot x\{\texttt{[a-zA-Z]}^+\} \cdot \Big(\big((, \vee \_) \cdot \Sigma^*\big) \vee \epsilon\Big)$$

When applied to the document $\mathbf{d}$ of Figure 1, the resulting spans include $[1,7\rangle$, $[8,12\rangle$, $[13,19\rangle$ and so on.

The following variable regex extracts spans that begin with a capital letter.

$$\gamma_{\mathsf{1Cap}} := \Sigma^* \cdot x\{\texttt{[A-Z]} \cdot \Sigma^*\} \cdot \Sigma^*$$

$[\![\rho_{\mathsf{stt}}]\!](\mathbf{d})$			$[\![\rho_{\mathsf{loc}}]\!](\mathbf{d})$		
	x		x_1	x_2	y
μ_1	$[21,28\rangle$	μ_5	$[13,19\rangle$	$[21,28\rangle$	$[13,28\rangle$
μ_2	$[30,40\rangle$	μ_4	$[21,28\rangle$	$[30,40\rangle$	$[21,40\rangle$
μ_3	$[60,68\rangle$	μ_6	$[46,58\rangle$	$[60,68\rangle$	$[46,68\rangle$

Figure 2: Results of spanners in the running example

When applied to the document $\mathbf{d}$ of Figure 1, the resulting spans include $[1,7\rangle$, $[1,3\rangle$, $[13,19\rangle$, $[13,20\rangle$, and so on.

The following regex formula extracts all the spans that span names of US states. For simplicity, we include just the three in Figure 1. For readability, we omit the concatenation symbol $\cdot$ between two alphabet symbols.

$$\gamma_{\mathsf{stt}} := \Sigma^* \cdot x\{\texttt{Georgia} \vee \texttt{Virginia} \vee \texttt{Washington}\} \cdot \Sigma^*$$

When applied to the document $\mathbf{d}$ of Figure 1, the resulting spans are $[21,28\rangle$, $[30,40\rangle$, and $[60,68\rangle$.

The following regex formula extracts all the triples (x_1, x_2, y) of spans such that the string ",_" separates between x_1 and x_2, and y is the span that starts where x_1 starts and ends where x_2 ends.

$$\gamma_{,\_} := \Sigma^* \cdot y\{x_1\{\Sigma^*\} \cdot , \_ \cdot x_2\{\Sigma^*\}\} \cdot \Sigma^*$$

Let $\mathbf{d}$ be the document of Figure 1, and let V be the set $\{x_1, x_2, y\}$ of variables. The $(V, \mathbf{d})$-tuples that are obtained by applying $\gamma_{,\_}$ to $\mathbf{d}$ map (x_1, x_2, y) to triples like $([13,19\rangle, [21,28\rangle, [13,28\rangle)$, and in addition, triples that do not necessarily consist of full tokens, such as the triple $([9,19\rangle, [21,23\rangle, [9,23\rangle)$. □

We denote by REG the class of expressions in the closure of RGX under union ($\cup$), projection ($\pi_{\mathbf{x}}$ where $\mathbf{x}$ is a sequence of variables) and natural join ($\bowtie$). Note that natural join is based on span equality, not on string equality, since our relations contain spans. A spanner is *regular* if it is definable in REG. Fagin et al. [14] proved that the class of regular spanners is closed under the difference operator. As usual, by $[\![\rho]\!]$ we denote the spanner that is represented by the REG expression ρ.

Let ρ be an expression in REG and let $\mathbf{x} = x_1, \ldots, x_n$ be a sequence of n distinct variables containing all the variables in $\mathsf{SVars}(\rho)$ (and possibly additional variables). Let $\mathbf{y} = y_1, \ldots, y_n$ be a sequence of distinct variables of the same length as $\mathbf{x}$. We denote by $\rho[\mathbf{y}/\mathbf{x}]$ the expression ρ' that is obtained from ρ by replacing every occurrence of x_i with y_i. If $\mathbf{x}$ is clear from the context, then we may write just $\rho[\mathbf{y}]$.

EXAMPLE 2.4. Using γ_{tkn}, γ_{stt} and $\gamma_{,\_}$ from Example 2.3, we define several regular spanners.

- The spanner ρ_{stt} extracts all the tokens that are names of US states: $\rho_{\mathsf{stt}} := \gamma_{\mathsf{tkn}} \bowtie \gamma_{\mathsf{stt}}$.
- The spanner ρ_{1Cap} extracts all the tokens beginning with a capital letter: $\rho_{\mathsf{1Cap}} := \gamma_{\mathsf{tkn}} \bowtie \gamma_{\mathsf{1Cap}}$.
- The spanner ρ_{loc} extracts spans of strings like "*city, state*": $\rho_{\mathsf{loc}} := \rho_{\mathsf{1Cap}}[x_1/x] \bowtie \rho_{\mathsf{stt}}[x_2/x] \bowtie \gamma_{,\_}$.

The results of applying the spanners $[\![\rho_{\mathsf{stt}}]\!]$ and $[\![\rho_{\mathsf{loc}}]\!]$ to the document $\mathbf{d}$ of Figure 1 are in Figure 2. □

Fagin et al. [14] proved the following.

THEOREM 2.5. [14] *A spanner is definable in* RGX *if and only if it is regular and hierarchical.*

Both RGX and REG are spanner representation systems that we shall study. In addition, in our proofs we shall later discuss other spanner representation systems, including ones based on automata and ones that extend the system of regular spanners.

3. EXTRACTION PROGRAMS

In the previous section we introduced spanners, along with the representation systems RGX and REG. Here we will use spanners as building blocks for specifying what we call *extraction programs* that involve direct extraction of relations, specification of inconsistencies, and resolution of inconsistencies. We begin with an adaptation of the standard notions of *signature* and *instances* to text extraction.

3.1 Signatures and Instances

A *signature* is a finite sequence $\mathbf{S} = \langle R_1, \dots, R_m \rangle$ of distinct *relation symbols*, where each R_i has an arity $a_i > 0$. In this work, the *data* is a document $\mathbf{d}$, and entries in the instances of a signature are spans of $\mathbf{d}$. Formally, for a signature $\mathbf{S} = \langle R_1, \dots, R_m \rangle$ and a document $\mathbf{d} \in \Sigma^*$, a $\mathbf{d}$*-instance* (*over* $\mathbf{S}$) is a sequence $\langle r_1, \dots, r_m \rangle$, where each r_i is a relation of arity a_i over $\mathsf{Spans}(\mathbf{d})$; that is, r_i is a subset of $\mathsf{Spans}(\mathbf{d})^{a_i}$. A $\mathbf{d}$*-fact* (*over* $\mathbf{S}$) is an expression of the form $R(s_1, \dots, s_a)$, where R is a relation symbol of $\mathbf{S}$ with arity a, and each s_i is a span of $\mathbf{d}$. If f is a $\mathbf{d}$-fact $R(s_1, \dots, s_a)$ and I is a $\mathbf{d}$-instance, both over the signature $\mathbf{S}$, then we say that f is *a fact of* I if $(s_1, \dots, s_a)$ is a tuple in the relation of I that corresponds to R. For convenience of notation, we identify a $\mathbf{d}$-instance with the set of its facts.

EXAMPLE 3.1. The signature $\mathbf{S}$ we will use for our running example consists of three relation symbols:

- The unary relation symbol Loc that stands for *location*;
- The unary relation symbol Per that stands for *person*;
- The binary relation symbol PerLoc that associates persons with locations.

We continue with our running example. Figure 3 shows a $\mathbf{d}$-instance over $\mathbf{S}$, where $\mathbf{d}$ is the document of Figure 1. This instance has 12 facts, and for later reference we denote them by $f_1, \dots, f_{12}$. Note that there are quite a few mistakes in the table (e.g., the annotation of `Virginia` as a person by fact f_9); in the next section we will show how these are dealt with in the framework of this paper. □

3.2 Conflicts and Priorities

The database research community has established the concept of *repairs* as a mechanism for handling inconsistencies in a declarative fashion [3]. Conventionally, *denial constraints* are specified to declare sets of facts that cannot co-exist in a consistent instance. A *minimal repair* of an inconsistent instance is a consistent subinstance that is not properly contained in any other consistent subinstance. Each minimal repair is then viewed as a *possible world* (and the notion of *consistent query answers* can then be applied). Here, we will adapt the concept of denial constraints to our setting. In Section 5 we will illustrate the generality of these constraints w.r.t. conflict resolutions that take place in real life. However, in the world of IE the minimal repairs are not necessarily all equal. In fact, in every example we are aware of, the developer has a clear preference as to which facts to exclude when a denial constraint fires. Therefore, instead of the traditional repairs, we will use the notion of *prioritized repairs* of Staworko et al. [38] that extends repairing by incorporating priorities.

Let $\mathbf{S}$ be a signature, let $\mathbf{d}$ be a document, and let I be a $\mathbf{d}$-instance over $\mathbf{S}$. A *conflict hypergraph* for I is a hypergraph H over the facts of I; that is, $H = (V, E)$ where V is the set of I's facts and E is a collection of hyperedges (subsets of V). Intuitively, the hyperedges represent sets of facts that together are in conflict. A *priority relation* for I is a binary relation $>$ over the facts of I.

Loc

f_1	$[13, 28\rangle$
f_2	$[21, 40\rangle$
f_3	$[46, 68\rangle$

Per

f_4	$[1, 7\rangle$
f_5	$[13, 19\rangle$
f_6	$[21, 28\rangle$
f_7	$[30, 40\rangle$
f_8	$[46, 58\rangle$
f_9	$[60, 68\rangle$

PerLoc

f_{10}	$[1, 7\rangle$	$[13, 28\rangle$
f_{11}	$[1, 7\rangle$	$[46, 68\rangle$
f_{12}	$[30, 40\rangle$	$[46, 68\rangle$

Figure 3: A d-instance I over the signature of the running example

If f and f' are facts of I, then $f > f'$ means intuitively that f is preferred to f'. A *repair* of I is a subinstance of I that does not contain any hyperedge of H. To accommodate priorities in cleaning, we use the notion of *Pareto optimality* [38]: a repair J is an *improvement* of a repair J' if there is a fact $f \in J \setminus J'$ such that $f > f'$ for all $f' \in J' \setminus J$; an *optimal repair* is a repair that has no improvement.

COMMENT 3.2. Another notion of optimality in [38] is *global optimality*, where a repair J is an *improvement* of a repair J' if for every fact $f' \in J' \setminus J$ there is a fact $f \in J \setminus J'$ such that $f > f'$. As before, an *optimal repair* is a repair that has no improvement. When *(1)* all conflicts are binary and *(2)* the priority relation includes all the pairs in conflict, then it follows from results in [38] that if we also make the natural assumption of acyclicity of the priority relation, we have that global optimality and Pareto optimality coincide. Assumptions *(1)* and *(2)* hold in all our results that involve optimal repairs, except for Theorem 4.3 where the same proof works for both notions of optimality. □

EXAMPLE 3.3. Recall the instance I of our running example (Figure 3). Figure 4 shows both a conflict hypergraph (which is a graph in this case) and a priority relation over I. Specifically, the figure has two types of edges. Dotted edges (with small arrows) define priorities, where $f_i \rightarrow f_j$ denotes that $f_i > f_j$. Later, we shall explain the preferences (such as $f_1 > f_4$). Solid edges (with bigger arrows) define both conflicts and priorities: $f_i \rightarrow f_j$ denotes that $\{f_i, f_j\}$ is an edge of the conflict hypergraph, and that $f_i > f_j$.

Consider the following sets of facts.

- $J_1 = \{f_2, f_3, f_4, f_5, f_{11}\}$;

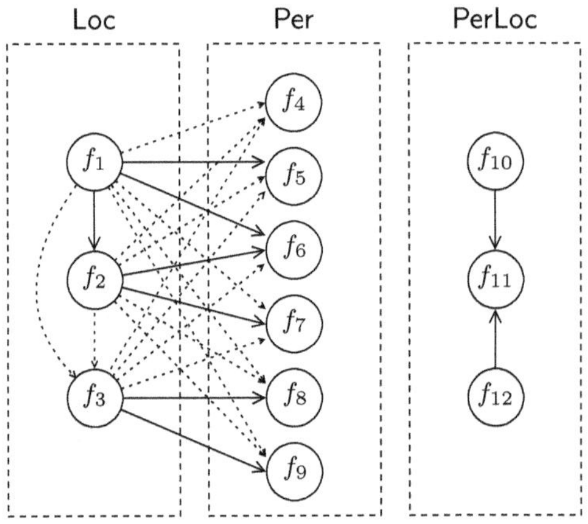

Figure 4: A conflict graph with priorities in the running example

Loc		Per		PerLoc		
f_1	$[13,28\rangle$	f_4	$[1,7\rangle$	f_{10}	$[1,7\rangle$	$[13,28\rangle$
f_3	$[46,68\rangle$	f_7	$[30,40\rangle$	f_{12}	$[30,40\rangle$	$[46,68\rangle$

Figure 5: A d-instance J_3 over the signature of the running example

- $J_2 = \{f_1, f_3, f_4, f_7, f_{11}\} = (J_1 \cup \{f_1, f_7\}) \setminus \{f_2, f_5\}$;
- $J_3 = \{f_1, f_3, f_4, f_7, f_{10}, f_{12}\} = (J_2 \cup \{f_{10}, f_{12}\}) \setminus \{f_{11}\}$.

Observe that each J_i is a repair of I. The repair J_2 is an improvement of J_1, since both $f_1 \succ f_2$ and $f_1 \succ f_5$ hold. The repair J_3 is an improvement of J_2, since $f_{10} \succ f_{11}$ (and $f_{12} \succ f_{11}$). Note that J_3 is not an improvement of J_1, since no fact in J_3 is preferred to both f_2 and f_{11}. Thus, "is an improvement of" is not transitive. The reader can verify that J_3 is an optimal repair. In fact, it can easily be verified (and it also follows from Theorem 4.3 below) that J_3 is the *unique* optimal solution. The instance J_3 is depicted in Figure 5. □

3.3 Denial Constraints and Priority Generating Dependencies

We now discuss the syntactic declaration of conflicts and priorities.

To specify a conflict hypergraph at the signature level (i.e., to say how to define the conflict hypergraph for every instance), we use the formalism of denial constraints. Let $\mathbf{S}$ be a signature, and let $\mathcal{R}$ be a spanner representation system. A *denial constraint* in $\mathcal{R}$ *(over* $\mathbf{S}$), or just $\mathcal{R}$*-dc* (or simply *dc*) for short, has the form $\forall \mathbf{x}[P \rightarrow \neg\Psi(\mathbf{x})]$, where $\mathbf{x}$ is a sequence of variables in SVars, P is a spanner specified in $\mathcal{R}$ with all variables in $\mathbf{x}$, and Ψ is a conjunction of atomic formulas $\varphi(\mathbf{x})$ over $\mathbf{S}$. (Note that an *atomic formula* φ is an expression of the form $R(x_1, \dots, x_a)$, where R is an a-ary relation symbol in $\mathbf{S}$.) We usually omit the universal quantifier, and specify a dc simply by $P \rightarrow \neg\Psi(\mathbf{x})$.[2]

EXAMPLE 3.4. We now define dcs in our running example. We denote by precede the regex formula $\Sigma^* \cdot x\{\Sigma^*\} \cdot \Sigma^* \cdot y\{\Sigma^*\} \cdot \Sigma^*$. Hence, precede states that x terminates before y begins. We denote by disjoint the regex formula precede$[x,y] \vee$ precede$[y,x]$. We denote by overlap an expression in REG that represents the complement of disjoint. Note that overlap is indeed expressible by a regular spanner, since regular spanners are closed under complement [14]. Finally, we denote by overlap$_{\neq}$ an expression in REG that restricts the pairs in overlap to those (x,y) satisfying $x \neq y$ (i.e., x and y are not the same span). It is easy to verify that overlap$_{\neq}$ indeed is expressible by a regular spanner.

The following dc, denoted d_{loc}, states that the spans of locations are disjoint.

$$d_{\mathsf{loc}} := \mathsf{overlap}_{\neq}[x,y] \rightarrow \neg\big(\mathsf{Loc}(x) \wedge \mathsf{Loc}(y)\big)$$

Similarly, the following dc, denoted d_{lp}, states that spans of locations are disjoint from spans of persons.

$$d_{\mathsf{lp}} := \mathsf{overlap}[x,y] \rightarrow \neg\big(\mathsf{Loc}(x) \wedge \mathsf{Per}(y)\big) \quad \Box$$

[2]We note that instead of being written as $P \rightarrow \neg\Psi(\mathbf{x})$, denial constraints are typically written (as in [38]) in the equivalent form $\neg(P \wedge \Psi(\mathbf{x}))$. In the literature, the premise P is typically taken to be a conjunction of atomic formulas, whereas for us P represents a spanner.

To specify a priority relation $\succ$, we propose what we call here a *priority generating dependency*, or just *pgd* for short. Let $\mathbf{S}$ be a signature, and let $\mathcal{R}$ be a spanner representation system. A pgd in $\mathcal{R}$ (for $\mathbf{S}$) has the form $\forall \mathbf{x}[P \rightarrow (\varphi(\mathbf{x}) \succ \varphi'(\mathbf{x}))]$, where $\mathbf{x}$ is a sequence of variables in SVars, P is a spanner specified in $\mathcal{R}$ with all variables in $\mathbf{x}$, and φ and φ' are atomic formulas over $\mathbf{S}$. Again, we usually omit the universal quantifier and write just $P \rightarrow (\varphi(\mathbf{x}) \succ \varphi'(\mathbf{x}))$.

EXAMPLE 3.5. The following pgd, denoted p_{loc}, states that for spans in the unary relation Loc, spans that start earlier are preferred, and moreover, when two spans begin together, the longer one is preferred.

$$p_{\mathsf{loc}} := \rho[x,y] \rightarrow \big(\mathsf{Loc}(x) \succ \mathsf{Loc}(y)\big)$$

Here, $\rho[x,y]$ is the following expression in REG.

$$\pi_{x,y}\Big(\big(\Sigma^* \cdot x\{z\{\epsilon\} \cdot \Sigma^*\} \cdot \Sigma^*\big) \bowtie \big(\Sigma^* \cdot z\{\epsilon\} \cdot \Sigma^+ \cdot y\{\Sigma^*\} \cdot \Sigma^*\}\big)\Big) \vee \big(\Sigma^* \cdot x\{y\{\Sigma^*\}\Sigma^+\} \cdot \Sigma^*\big)$$

Intuitively, the first disjunct says that x begins before y, because x begins with the empty span z, and y begins strictly after z begins. The second disjunct says that x and y begin together, but x ends strictly after y ends.

The following pgd, denoted p_{lp}, states that all the facts of Loc are preferred to all the facts of Per (e.g., because the extraction made for Loc is deemed more precise). We use the Boolean spanner true that is true on every document.

$$p_{\mathsf{lp}} := \mathsf{true} \rightarrow \big(\mathsf{Loc}(x) \succ \mathsf{Per}(y)\big) \quad \Box$$

As we will discuss in Section 5, common resolution strategies translate into a dc and a pgd, such that the dc is binary, and the pgd defines priorities precisely on the facts that are in conflict. To refer to such a case conveniently, we write $P \rightarrow (\varphi(\mathbf{x}) \rhd \varphi'(\mathbf{x}))$ to jointly represent the dc $P \rightarrow \neg(\varphi(\mathbf{x}) \wedge \varphi'(\mathbf{x}))$ and the pgd $P \rightarrow (\varphi(\mathbf{x}) \succ \varphi'(\mathbf{x}))$. We call such a constraint a *denial pgd*.

EXAMPLE 3.6. We denote by contains$_{\neq}[x,y]$ a regex formula that produces all pairs (x,y) of spans where x strictly contains y. Let encloses$[z,x,y]$ denote a specification in REG that produces all the triples (z,x,y), such that z begins where x begins and ends where y ends. For presentation's sake, we avoid the precise specification of these formulas.

The following denial pgd, denoted dp_{enc}, states that in the relation PerLoc, two facts are in conflict if the span that covers the two elements of the one strictly contains that span of the other; in that case, the smaller span is prioritized (since a smaller span indicates closer relationship between the person and the location).

$$\mathsf{encloses}[z,x,y] \bowtie \mathsf{encloses}[z',x',y'] \bowtie \mathsf{contains}_{\neq}[z',z] \rightarrow \mathsf{PerLoc}[x,y] \rhd \mathsf{PerLoc}[x',y'] \quad \Box$$

EXAMPLE 3.7. Consider again the $\mathbf{d}$-instance I of Figure 3. The reader can verify that dcs d_{loc} and d_{lp} from Example 3.4, the pgds p_{loc} and p_{lp} in Example 3.5 and the denial pgd dp_{enc} of Example 3.6, together define the conflicts and priorities discussed in Example 3.3 (Figure 4). □

3.4 Extraction Programs

Let $\mathcal{R}$ be a spanner representation system. An *extraction program in* $\mathcal{R}$, or just $\mathcal{R}$*-program*, for short, is a triple $\langle \mathbf{S}, U, \varphi \rangle$, where

$\mathbf{S}$ is a signature, U is a finite sequence $u_1, \dots, u_m$ of *updates*, and φ is an atomic formula over $\mathbf{S}$ (representing the result of the program). There are two types of updates u_i:

1. **CQ updates**. These updates are conjunctive queries of the form $R(y_1, \dots, y_a)$:– $\alpha_1 \wedge \cdots \wedge \alpha_k$, where R is a relation symbol of $\mathbf{S}$ of arity a, and each α_i is either an atomic formula over $\mathbf{S}$ or a spanner in $\mathcal{R}$. The α_i are called *atoms*. We make the requirement that each y_i occurs in at least one atom.

2. **Cleaning updates**. A cleaning update is an update of the form $\text{CLEAN}(\delta_1, \dots, \delta_d)$, where each δ_i is a dc or a pgd (for convenience, we will also allow denial pgds).

In the program of the following example, we specify an extraction program $\langle \mathbf{S}, U, \varphi \rangle$ using only U along with a special RETURN statement that specifies φ. We then assume that $\mathbf{S}$ consists of precisely the relation symbols that occur in the program.

EXAMPLE 3.8. We now define the REG-program $\mathcal{E}$ of our running example. Intuitively, the goal of the program is to extract pairs (x, y), where x is a person and y is a location associated with x.[3] The signature is, as usual, that of Example 3.1. The sequence U of updates is the following. Note that we are using the notation we established in the previous examples.

1. $\mathsf{Loc}(x)$:– $\rho_{\mathsf{loc}}[x]$ (see example 2.4)

2. $\mathsf{Per}(y)$:– $\rho_{\mathsf{1Cap}}[y]$ (see example 2.4)

3. $\text{CLEAN}(d_{\mathsf{loc}}, d_{\mathsf{lp}}, p_{\mathsf{loc}}, p_{\mathsf{lp}})$ (see Examples 3.4 and 3.5)

4. $\mathsf{PerLoc}(x, y)$:– $\mathsf{Per}(x) \wedge \mathsf{Loc}(y) \wedge \mathsf{precede}[x, y]$ (see Example 3.4)

5. $\text{CLEAN}(dp_{\mathsf{enc}})$ (see Example 3.6)

6. RETURN $\mathsf{PerLoc}(x, y)$

Note that lines 1, 2 and 4 are CQ updates, whereas lines 3 and 5 are cleaning updates. □

We now define the semantics of evaluating an extraction program over a document. Let $\mathcal{E} = \langle \mathbf{S}, U, \varphi \rangle$ be an $\mathcal{R}$-program with $U = \langle u_1, \dots, u_m \rangle$, and let $\mathbf{d} \in \Sigma^*$ be a document. Let $\mathbf{I}_0$ be the singleton $\{I_\varnothing\}$, where $I_\varnothing$ is the empty instance over $\mathbf{S}$. For $i = 1, \dots, m$, we denote by $\mathbf{I}_i$ the result of executing the updates $u_1, \dots, u_i$ as we describe below. Since the cleaning operation can result in multiple instances (optimal repairs), each $\mathbf{I}_i$ is a *set* of $\mathbf{d}$-instances, rather than a single one. For $i > 0$ we define the following.

1. If u_i is the CQ update $R(x_1, \dots, x_a)$:– $\alpha_1 \wedge \cdots \wedge \alpha_k$, then $\mathbf{I}_i$ is obtained from $\mathbf{I}_{i-1}$ by adding to each $I \in \mathbf{I}_{i-1}$ all the facts (over R) that are obtained by evaluating the CQ over I.

2. If u_i is the cleaning $\text{CLEAN}(\delta_1, \dots, \delta_d)$, then $\mathbf{I}_i$ is obtained from $\mathbf{I}_{i-1}$ by replacing each $I \in \mathbf{I}_{i-1}$ with all the optimal repairs of I, as defined by the conflict hypergraph and priorities implied by all the δ_j.

Recall that a spanner is a function that maps a document into a $(V, \mathbf{d})$-relation (see Section 2). An extraction program acts similarly, except that a document is mapped into a set of $(V, \mathbf{d})$-relations (since it branches into multiple repairs). Later, we are going to investigate cases where the extraction program produces precisely one $(V, \mathbf{d})$-relation, and then we will view the extraction program simply as a spanner. Next, we define the output of an extraction program $\mathcal{E} = \langle \mathbf{S}, U, \varphi \rangle$, where $U = \langle u_1, \dots, u_m \rangle$ and $\varphi = R(x_1, \dots, x_a)$. Let $V = \{x_1, \dots, x_a\}$ be the set of variables in φ. From a $\mathbf{d}$-instance I over $\mathbf{S}$ (that does not involve any variables) we naturally obtain a $(V, \mathbf{d})$-relation (that involves the variables in V): the $(V, \mathbf{d})$-relation consisting of all the assignments $\mu : V \to \mathsf{Spans}(\mathbf{d})$ such that $R(\mu(x_1), \dots, \mu(x_a))$ is a fact in I. We denote this relation by $I[\varphi]$. The *result* $\mathcal{E}(\mathbf{d})$ of evaluating the program $\mathcal{E}$ over the document $\mathbf{d}$ is the set of all the $(V, \mathbf{d})$-relations $I[\varphi]$ with $I \in \mathbf{I}_m$, where $\mathbf{I}_m$ is the result (as defined earlier) of the last update u_m.

EXAMPLE 3.9. Consider again the REG-program $\mathcal{E}$ of Example 3.8. We will now follow the steps of evaluating the program $\mathcal{E}$ on the document $\mathbf{d}$ of our running example (Figure 1). It turns out that, in this example, each $\mathbf{I}_i$ is a singleton, since every cleaning operation results in a unique optimal repair. Hence, we will treat the $\mathbf{I}_i$ as instances.

1. In $\mathbf{I}_1$, the relation Loc is as shown in Figure 3, and the other two relations are empty.

2. In $\mathbf{I}_2$, the relations Loc and Per are as shown in Figure 3, and PerLoc is empty.

3. In $\mathbf{I}_3$, the relations Loc and Per are as shown in Figure 5, and PerLoc is empty. The cleaning process is described throughout Sections 3.2 and 3.3.

4. In $\mathbf{I}_4$, the relations Loc and Per are as in $\mathbf{I}_3$, and PerLoc is as shown in Figure 3.

5. $\mathbf{I}_5$ is the instance shown in Figure 5.

The result $\mathcal{E}(\mathbf{d})$ is the (singleton containing the) $(\{x, y\}, \mathbf{d})$-relation that has two mappings: the first maps (x, y) to $([1, 7\rangle, [13, 28\rangle)$, and the second to $([30, 40\rangle, [46, 48\rangle)$. □

4. PROPERTIES OF REGULAR PROGRAMS

In this section, we discuss some fundamental properties of extraction programs, and focus on the class of REG-programs, which we refer to as *regular programs*.

4.1 Unambiguity

Recall that a spanner maps a document $\mathbf{d}$ into a $(V, \mathbf{d})$-relation, for a set V of variables, while an extraction program maps $\mathbf{d}$ into a *set* of $(V, \mathbf{d})$-relations. The first property we discuss for extraction programs is that of *unambiguity*, which is the property of having a single possible world when the program is evaluated over any given document. Formally, we say that extraction program $\mathcal{E}$ is *unambiguous* if $\mathcal{E}(\mathbf{d})$ is a singleton $(V, \mathbf{d})$-relation for every document $\mathbf{d}$. We may view an unambiguous extraction program $\mathcal{E}$ simply as a specification of spanner.

Let $\mathcal{R}$ be a spanner representation system. An $\mathcal{R}$-program is said to be *non-cleaning* if it does not contain cleaning updates (hence, it consists of only CQ updates). Clearly, if an extraction program is non-cleaning, then it is unambiguous. The following proposition states that in the case where $\mathcal{R}$ is REG or RGX, the non-cleaning $\mathcal{R}$-programs do not have any expressive power beyond the regular spanners. The proof is straightforward from the definitions.

[3] In real life, such a program would of course be much more involved; here it is extremely simplistic, for the sake of presentation.

PROPOSITION 4.1. *Let P be a spanner. The following are equivalent: (1) P is representable by a non-cleaning* REG*-program, (2) P is representable by a non-cleaning* RGX*-program, and (3) P is regular.*

The following theorem states that, unfortunately, in the presence of cleaning updates unambiguity cannot be verified for regular extraction programs.

THEOREM 4.2. *Whether a* REG*-program is unambiguous is co-recursively enumerable but not recursively enumerable. In particular, it is undecidable.*

The proof of Theorem 4.2 is an adaptation of the proof of Theorem 4.6 that we later present and discuss in detail.

Let I be a $\mathbf{d}$-instance over a signature $\mathbf{S}$. Let H and $\succ$ be a conflict hypergraph and a priority relation over I, respectively. Staworko et al. [38] give the following sufficient condition for the existence of a single optimal solution (under the assumption that there are no empty hyperedges). Suppose that (1) $\succ$ is acyclic, and that (2) $\succ$ is total on every hyperedge of H. Then there is exactly one optimal repair. We have obtained an improvement of this result. We say that $(\succ, H)$ satisfies the *minimum property* if every hyperedge h of H contains a minimum element, that is, an element a such that $b \succ a$ for every member of h other than a. Intuitively, for every conflict, the minimum element is a natural candidate to remove to break the conflict. It is clear that, in the presence of acyclicity (and the absence of empty hyperedges), totality on every hyperedge is strictly more restrictive than our minimum property. We have the following.

THEOREM 4.3. *Let I be a $\mathbf{d}$-instance over a schema $\mathbf{S}$. Let H and $\succ$ be a conflict hypergraph and a priority relation over I, respectively. Suppose that (1) $\succ$ is acyclic, and that (2) the pair $(\succ, H)$ satisfies the minimum property. Then there is exactly one optimal repair.*

The proof of Theorem 4.3 goes by way of contradiction; specifically, it shows how, in the presence of (1) and (2), when given two distinct optimal repairs we can construct an improvement of one of the two (contradicting its optimality). The theorem suggests the following condition for when a cleaning update does not introduce ambiguity. Let u be a cleaning update. We say that u is *acyclic* if, for every document $\mathbf{d}$ and $\mathbf{d}$-instance I over $\mathbf{S}$, the priority relation implied by the pgds of u is acyclic. We say that u is *minimum generating* if, for every document $\mathbf{d}$ and $\mathbf{d}$-instance I over $\mathbf{S}$, for the priority relation $\succ$ implied by the pgds of u and the conflict hypergraph H implied by u, we have that $(\succ, H)$ satisfies the minimum property. As an example, if u consists of only denial pgds, then u is minimum generating (since the hyperedges are all of size 2). From Theorem 4.3 we conclude the following.

COROLLARY 4.4. *Let $\mathcal{E}$ be an $\mathcal{R}$-program for some spanner representation system $\mathcal{R}$. If every cleaning update of $\mathcal{E}$ is acyclic and minimum generating, then $\mathcal{E}$ is unambiguous.*

The good news is that testing whether a regular cleaning update is minimum generating is a decidable problem.

THEOREM 4.5. *Whether a cleaning update in* REG *is minimum generating is decidable.*

Establishing finer complexity classes for this and later decidability results is the subject of future work. In the proof of Theorem 4.5, we show how to construct, from a regular cleaning update u, a regular spanner P, represented as a *variable-set automaton* [14], such that u is minimum generating if and only if P is empty. We then use results of Fagin et al. [14] that imply a procedure to test whether a given variable-set automaton is empty.

Unfortunately, acyclicity is an undecidable property of regular cleaning updates. Moreover, undecidability remains even if the update consists of a single denial pgd.

THEOREM 4.6. *Whether a denial pgd in* REG *is acyclic is co-recursively enumerable but not recursively enumerable. In particular, it is undecidable.*

In Section 4.1.1 we discuss our proof of Theorem 4.6.

What about the decidability of the two conditions (1) and (2) of Theorem 4.3 together? Those two together are also undecidable, since as we observed, denial pgds are automatically minimum generating, and so Theorem 4.6 implies that deciding whether a denial pgd in REG satisfies conditions (1) and (2) of Theorem 4.3 together is undecidable.

4.1.1 Proof of Undecidability

The proof of Theorem 4.2 is a variation of the proof of Theorem 4.6. To prove the latter, we use results on the emptiness of multi-head automata [23], and prove an intermediate result of independent interest. To present this intermediate result, we need some definitions.

Let k be a natural number. A *nondeterministic two-way k-head finite automaton* (or just *2NFA(k)* for short) is a tuple of the form $\langle \Theta, Q, \delta, q_0, F \rangle$ where Θ is a finite alphabet, Q is a finite set of states, δ is a transition function that maps each element in $Q \times (\Theta \cup \{\vdash, \dashv\})^k$ to a subset of $Q \times \{\mathsf{l}, \mathsf{r}, \mathsf{h}\}^k$, $q_0 \in Q$ is the initial state, and $F \subseteq Q$ is a set of accepting states. The symbols $\vdash$ and $\dashv$ are the left and right endmarkers of input strings, respectively, and are not in Θ. If the image of δ consists of only singletons and the empty set, then A is *deterministic* and we may replace "NFA" with "DFA."

The semantics of a 2NFA(k) $A = \langle \Theta, Q, \delta, q_0, F \rangle$ is as follows. Let $\mathbf{s} \in \Theta^*$ be a string, and denote it as $s_1, \dots, s_n$. The machine A does not read $\mathbf{s}$ directly, but rather the augmentation $\vdash\mathbf{s}\dashv$ (i.e., endpoints are marked), which we denote by $s_0, s_1, \dots, s_n, s_{n+1}$. The machine has a single current state and k heads, each on some symbol in $\vdash\mathbf{s}\dashv$. In the initial configuration, the state is q_0 and all the heads are on s_0. The transition $(q', t_1, \dots, t_k) \in \delta(q, a_1, \dots, a_k)$, where $t_i \in \{\mathsf{l}, \mathsf{r}, \mathsf{h}\}$ and $a_i \in \Theta \cup \{\vdash, \dashv\}$, means that if the current state is q and the ith head is on the symbol a_i, then in a possible next configuration the state is q' and each head i acts according to t_i: moves one left (l), moves one right (r), or holds in place (h). If t_i moves the head outside the input, it is treated as h. A *halting* configuration is one without possible next configurations (because $\delta(q, a_1, \dots, a_k) = \emptyset$). A halting configuration is *accepting* if its state q is in F; otherwise, the halting configuration is *rejecting*. We say that A *accepts* a sting $\mathbf{s}$ if there is a run (legal sequence of configurations) on $\vdash\mathbf{s}\dashv$ that starts with the initial configuration and ends with an accepting configuration.

Let $\mathbf{C}$ be a class of multi-head automata (e.g., 2DFA(2)). The *finite mortality problem* for $\mathbf{C}$ is the following. Given an automaton $A \in \mathbf{C}$, determine whether A terminates on every input string from every possible configuration; in that case, we say that *A has no immortal configurations*. We can prove the following lemma.[4]

[4]In private communication with the authors, Martin Kutrib independently proved this result.

LEMMA 4.7. *For 2DFA(2), the finite mortality problem is co-recursively enumerable but not recursively enumerable. In particular, it is undecidable.*

The proof of Lemma 4.7 uses a result by Holzer et al. [23], stating that the emptiness problem (i.e., whether no string is accepted) is undecidable for 1DFA(2). Specifically, the proof reduces the emptiness problem for 1DFA(2) to the finite mortality problem for 2DFA(2), where the main idea is to "restart" the run of the given 1DFA(2) whenever it enters an accepting configuration.

Lemma 4.7 is used in the proof of Theorem 4.6 as follows. From an input 2DFA(2) A, we construct a binary regular spanner $\rho[x, y]$. Given a document $\mathbf{d}$, we view the spans in $[\![\rho]\!](\mathbf{d})$ as representing configurations of A over some input string, and $(a, b) \in [\![\rho]\!](\mathbf{d})$ implies that b is the next configuration following a. We then define the denial pgd $\rho[x, y] \to (R(y) \rhd R(x))$, where R is a unary relation symbol. It then follows that A has no immortal configurations if and only if this pgd is acyclic.

4.2 Disposability

Next, we address the question of whether cleaning updates increase the expressive power of extraction programs.

Let $\mathcal{R}$ be a spanner representation system. A cleaning update u defined in $\mathcal{R}$ is said to be *$\mathcal{R}$-disposable* if the following holds: for every $\mathcal{R}$-program $\mathcal{E}$ that has u as its single cleaning update, there exists a non-cleaning $\mathcal{R}$-program that is equivalent to $\mathcal{E}$. Of course, we have the following.

PROPOSITION 4.8. *Let $\mathcal{R}$ be a spanner representation system and let $\mathcal{E}$ be an $\mathcal{R}$-program. If every cleaning update of $\mathcal{E}$ is $\mathcal{R}$-disposable, then $\mathcal{E}$ is equivalent to a non-cleaning $\mathcal{R}$-program.*

We say that a denial pgd p is *$\mathcal{R}$-disposable* if the cleaning update that consists of only p is $\mathcal{R}$-disposable. The following theorem implies that cleaning updates, and in fact a single acyclic denial pgd, increase the expressive power of regular extraction programs. Recall that a program that uses an acyclic denial pgd as its single cleaning update is unambiguous (Theorem 4.3).

THEOREM 4.9. *There exists an acyclic denial pgd in* REG *that is not* REG*-disposable.*

In the proof of Theorem 4.9, we build a REG-program $\mathcal{E}$ with a single cleaning update u. We then assume, by contradiction, that $\mathcal{E}'$ is a non-cleaning REG-program that is equivalent to $\mathcal{E}$, and then we show how to construct from $\mathcal{E}'$ an NFA that accepts the language $\mathcal{L}$ of all the strings $\mathbf{s}\#\mathbf{t}$ where $\mathbf{s}$ and $\mathbf{t}$ are in $\{0, 1\}^*$, and their lengths are equal and even. But it follows immediately from the literature on regular languages that $\mathcal{L}$ is not regular (hence, no NFA accepts it), and we therefore have a contradiction.

In Section 5, we are going to discuss specific regular cleaning updates that are, in fact, REG-disposable. We will also discuss some general conditions that suffice for REG-disposability.

5. SPECIAL CLEANING STRATEGIES

In this section, we discuss several classes of cleaning strategies that are used in practice. We will show that the strategies in each class are expressible through the use of a regular spanner in the premise. Moreover, we will prove that all of these cleaning updates are REG-disposable.

5.1 Transitive Denial Pgds

A denial pgd is *transitive* if the relationship "fact f is in conflict with and has priority over fact g" is transitive. More formally, let p be a denial pgd $P \to (\varphi(\mathbf{x}) \rhd \varphi'(\mathbf{x}))$ over a schema $\mathbf{S}$. Let I be a $\mathbf{d}$-instance over $\mathbf{S}$, and let f and f' be two facts in I. By $p \models f \rhd f'$ we denote the fact that there is a span assignment for $\mathbf{x}$ that is true on P, and that maps $\varphi(\mathbf{x})$ and $\varphi'(\mathbf{x})$ to f and f', respectively. We say that p is *transitive* if for every $\mathbf{d}$-instance I over $\mathbf{S}$ and for every three facts f_1, f_2 and f_3 in I, if $p \models f_1 \rhd f_2$ and $p \models f_2 \rhd f_3$ then $p \models f_1 \rhd f_3$.

An example of a transitive denial pgd is the *maximal container* denial pgd, which has the form $\mathsf{contains}_{\neq}[x, y] \to (R(\mathbf{x}) \rhd R(\mathbf{y}))$, where R is a relation symbol, and $\mathbf{x}$ and $\mathbf{y}$ are disjoint sequences of variables that contain x and y, respectively. This denial pgd is among the standard collection of "consolidation" strategies provided by SystemT [7], along with the analogous *minimal contained* (that favors shorter strings, and is expressed by the denial pgd dp_{enc} in Example 3.6), which is also transitive. Another example of a transitive denial pgd that captures a popular strategy is that of *rule priority*, and it has the form $P \to (R(\mathbf{x}) \rhd S(\mathbf{y}))$, where P is a spanner, and R and S are *distinct* relation symbols. Hence, the rule states that if the condition P holds (e.g., some attributes overlap), the fact that is from R is preferred to the fact that is from S (perhaps because the source of R is more trusted). Here, transitivity holds in a vacuous manner. Later in this section we will encounter additional transitive denial pgds.

Next, we give results about transitive denial pgds in REG. The first result states that transitivity is a decidable property.

THEOREM 5.1. *The following are decidable for a given denial pgd p in* REG. (1) *Determine whether p is transitive;* (2) *Determine whether p is both transitive and acyclic.*

Like in the proof of Theorem 4.5, the proof here shows how to reduce each of the two conditions to the emptiness of variable-set automata.

Recall that every cleaning update that consists of a single acyclic denial pgd is unambiguous. Interestingly, if that denial pgd is a transitive denial pgd in REG, then the cleaning update is also REG-disposable.

THEOREM 5.2. *If p is a transitive denial pgd in* REG, *then p is* REG*-disposable.*

To prove Theorem 5.2 we use the observation that, under the condition of the theorem, the single optimal repair is the one that consists of only the maximal elements under $\rhd$. Then we show how to construct a spanner that selects those maximal elements from the relevant relations.

5.2 JAPE Controls

JAPE [10] is an instantiation of the Common Pattern Specification Language (CPSL) [2], a rule based framework for IE. A JAPE program (or "phase") can be viewed as an extraction program where all the relation symbols are unary. This system has several built-in cleaning strategies called "controls." Here, we will define these strategies in our own terminology—denial pgds.

JAPE provides four controls (in addition to the All control stating that no cleaning is to be applied). These translate to the following denial pgds. Here, R is assumed to be a unary relation in an extraction program.

- Under the Appelt control, $R(x) \rhd R(y)$ holds if *(1)* x and y overlap and x starts earlier than y, *or (2)* x and y start at the same position but x is longer than y. The same strategy is used is also provided by SystemT [7] (as a "consolidator"). This control also involves *rule priority*, which we ignore for now and discuss later.

- The Brill control is similar to Appelt, with the exclusion of option (2); that is, $R(x) \rhd R(y)$ holds if x and y overlap and x starts earlier than y.
- The First control is similar to Appelt with "longer" replaced with "shorter."
- The Once control states that a single fact should remain in R (unless R is empty), which is the one that starts earliest, where a tie is broken by taking the one that ends earliest. Hence, $R(x) \rhd R(y)$ if and only if x is that remaining fact and $x \neq y$.

EXAMPLE 5.3. Suppose that $\Sigma = \{0, 1\}$, and that R is defined by the following regex formula:

$$\Sigma^* \cdot x\{1^+0^+1^+\} \cdot \Sigma^*$$

Now, consider the following two documents:

$$\mathbf{d}^1 = 100110100101 \quad \mathbf{d}^2 = 000110100101$$

Note that the two documents differ only in their first symbol. The spans in R for $\mathbf{d}^1$ are $[1,5\rangle$, $[1,6\rangle$, $[4,8\rangle$, $[5,8\rangle$, $[7,11\rangle$, and $[10,13\rangle$. The spans in R for $\mathbf{d}^2$ are $[4,8\rangle$, $[5,8\rangle$, $[7,11\rangle$, and $[10,13\rangle$.

- By applying the Appelt control, the spans that remain in R for $\mathbf{d}^1$ are $[1,6\rangle$ and $[7,11\rangle$, and the spans that remains in R for $\mathbf{d}^2$ are $[4,8\rangle$ and $[10,13\rangle$.
- By applying the Brill control, the spans that remain in R for $\mathbf{d}^1$ are $[1,5\rangle$, $[1,6\rangle$ and $[7,11\rangle$, and the spans that remains in R for $\mathbf{d}^2$ are $[4,8\rangle$ and $[10,13\rangle$.
- By applying the First control, the spans that remain in R for $\mathbf{d}^1$ are $[1,5\rangle$, $[5,8\rangle$ and $[10,13\rangle$, and the spans that remains in R for $\mathbf{d}^2$ are $[4,8\rangle$ and $[10,13\rangle$.
- By applying the Once control, the span that remains in R for $\mathbf{d}^1$ is $[1,5\rangle$, and the span that remains in R for $\mathbf{d}^2$ is $[4,8\rangle$.

As can be seen in the example, the change in the first symbol of the document affects the extracted spans all over the document. □

It is easy to show that each of the above denial pgds is acyclic, and can be expressed in REG. For example, the Applet control is presented in Example 3.5 with R being the relation symbol Loc. We can also show the following.

THEOREM 5.4. *Each of the denial pgds that correspond to the four JAPE controls is* REG*-disposable.*

In the case of Once, the proof of Theorem 5.4 is by using Theorem 5.2 (since the corresponding denial pgd is transitive in a vacuous sense). The challenging part of the theorem is for Appelt, Brill and First. To handle the three cases, we prove Lemma 5.5 below that is of independent interest. We first need a definition.

Let P be a unary spanner. Define the *Kleene star* of P, denoted P^*, to be the spanner Q with $\mathsf{SVars}(P) = \mathsf{SVars}(Q)$, where for each document $\mathbf{d}$, we have that $Q(\mathbf{d})$ consists of those spans $[a, a'\rangle$ such that the following holds: there are indices $a_1 \leqslant \cdots \leqslant a_n$ where $n \geqslant 1$, $a_1 = a$, $a_n = a'$, and $[a_i, a_{i+1}\rangle$ is in $P(\mathbf{d})$ for all $i = 1, \ldots, n-1$. Observe that for all documents $\mathbf{d}$, every empty span $[a, a\rangle$ is in P^*; this is obtained by letting $a' = a$ and $n = 1$.

LEMMA 5.5. *Let P be a unary spanner. If P is regular, then P^* is regular.*

The proof of Lemma 5.5 is by constructing a variable-set automaton that simulates an unbounded number runs of the variable-set automaton that specifies P.

We now sketch a proof that the denial pgd for the Appelt control is REG-disposable. The proofs for the Brill and First denial pgds are similar. Given the unary spanner P, let Q be a regular spanner that gives the strict prefixes of spans from P. By closure of regular spanners under complement [14], the complement Q' of Q is a regular spanner. Now define M to be a regular spanner that gives spans in $P \cap Q'$. So M gives the right-maximal spans from P (which means the spans that are maximal when we ignore possible extensions to the left). Next, let T be the regular spanner that gives spans that contain a starting point for spans of P. Let us denote the complement of T by N. By closure under complement, N is also a regular spanner. Intuitively, N gives the spans that do not contain any starting point for spans of P. Next, define K to be the spanner $(M \cup N)^*$. Intuitively, K gives us a sequence of right-maximal spans, possibly preceded by or followed by spans that do that do not contain any starting point for a span of P. By closure of regular spanners under union and the Kleene star (Lemma 5.5), we know that K is a regular spanner. Finally, define S to be the spanner that gives those spans from M that are preceded by a span from K. Then S is a regular spanner that gives those spans in the result of Appelt cleaning.

5.2.1 Rule Priority

In its general form, Appelt involves rule priority. In JAPE, the priority of a rule is determined by an explicit numerical priority (e.g., `Priority:20`) and, in the case of ties, the position of the rule in the program definition. In our terminology, we have n unary view definitions $R_1, \ldots, R_n$ (ordered by decreasing priority), and we apply the cleaning of Appelt simultaneously to all of these (that is, as if applying it to the union of these), and in the end remove from each R_i all the spans that occur in $R_1 \cup \cdots \cup R_{i-1}$.

We can extend Theorem 5.4 to include priorities, as follows. We first define R as the union of the R_i (which we can do in an extraction program). Next, we apply Appelt, as previously defined, to R, and then join each R_i with R using $R_i(x) :- R_i(x) \wedge R(x)$. Finally, we apply the (transitive) cleaners $\text{CLEAN}(\mathsf{true} \rightarrow R_i(x) \rhd R_j(x))$ for $1 \leqslant i < j \leqslant n$, one by one, in order of increasing i.

5.3 POSIX Disambiguation

Recall from Section 2.3 that a regex formula γ defines a spanner by considering all possible ways that the input document $\mathbf{d}$ can be matched by γ; that is, it considers all possible parse trees of γ on $\mathbf{d}$. Each such parse tree generates a new $(V, \mathbf{d})$-tuple, where $V = \mathsf{SVars}(\gamma)$, in the resulting span relation. In contrast, regular-expression pattern-matching facilities of common UNIX tools, such as `sed` and `awk`, or programming languages such as Perl, Python, and Java, do not construct all possible parse trees. Instead, they employ a *disambiguation policy* to construct only a single parse tree among the possible ones. As a result, a regex formula in these tools always yields a single $(V, \mathbf{d})$-tuple per matched input document $\mathbf{d}$ instead of multiple such tuples.[5]

In this section, we take a look at the POSIX disambiguation policy [19, 24], which is followed by all POSIX compliant tools such as `sed` and `awk`. Formalizations of this policy have been proposed by Vansummeren [39] and Okui and Suzuki [32], and multiple efficient algorithms for implementing the policy are known [8, 26, 32]. We show in particular that the POSIX disambiguation policy can

[5]While our syntax $x\{\gamma\}$ for variable binding is not directly supported in these tools, it can be mimicked through the use of so-called *parenthesized expressions* and *submatch addressing*.

be expressed in our framework as a REG-program that uses only cleaning updates with transitive denial pgds. Other disambiguation policies, such as the first and greedy match policy followed by Perl, Python, and Java (see, e.g. [39] for a description of this policy) are left for future work.

POSIX essentially disambiguates as follows when matching a document $\mathbf{d}$ against regex formula γ.[6] A formal definition may be found in [32, 39]. If γ is one of $\emptyset$, ϵ, or $\sigma \in \Sigma$ then at most one parse tree exists; disambiguation is hence not necessary. If γ is a disjunction $\gamma_1 \vee \gamma_2$, then POSIX first tries to match $\mathbf{d}$ against γ_1 (recursively, using the POSIX disambiguation policy to construct a unique parse tree for this match). Only if this fails it tries to match against γ_2 (again, recursively). If, on the other hand, γ is a concatenation $\gamma_1 \cdot \gamma_2$ then POSIX first determines the longest prefix $\mathbf{d_1}$ of $\mathbf{d}$ that can be matched by γ_1 such that the corresponding suffix $\mathbf{d_2}$ of $\mathbf{d}$ can be matched by γ_2. Then, $\mathbf{d_1}$ (respectively, $\mathbf{d_2}$) is recursively matched under the POSIX disambiguation policy by γ_1 (respectively, γ_2) to construct a unique parse tree for γ. If γ is a Kleene closure δ^* and $\mathbf{d}$ is nonempty, then POSIX views γ as equivalent to its expansion $\delta \cdot \delta^*$. In line with the rule for concatenation, it hence first determines the longest prefix $\mathbf{d_1}$ of $\mathbf{d}$ that can be matched by δ such that the corresponding suffix $\mathbf{d_2}$ of $\mathbf{d}$ can be matched by δ^*. Then, a unique parse tree for $\mathbf{d}$ against γ is constructed by matching $\mathbf{d_1}$ recursively against δ and $\mathbf{d_2}$ against δ^*. If, on the other hand, $\mathbf{d}$ is empty, then a special parse tree is constructed for this case. The following example illustrates the policy.

EXAMPLE 5.6. Consider $\gamma = x\{(0 \vee 01)\} \cdot y\{(1 \vee \epsilon)\}$ and $\mathbf{d} = 01$. Under the POSIX disambiguation policy, subexpression $x\{(0 \vee 01)\}$ will match as much of $\mathbf{d}$ as possible while still allowing the rest of the expression, namely $y\{(1 \vee \epsilon)\}$, to match the remainder of $\mathbf{d}$. As such, $x\{(0 \vee 01)\}$ will match $\mathbf{d}$ entirely, and $y\{(1 \vee \epsilon)\}$ will match the empty string. We hence bind x to the span $[1, 3\rangle$ and y to $[3, 3\rangle$.

In contrast, when $\gamma = (x\{0\} \cdot y\{(1 \vee \epsilon)\}) \vee (x\{01\} \cdot y\{(1 \vee \epsilon\})$ and $\mathbf{d} = 01$, under the POSIX disambiguation policy we bind x to the span $[1, 2\rangle$ and y to the span $[2, 3\rangle$. □

By $\mathsf{posix}[\gamma]$ we denote the spanner represented by the regex formula γ under the POSIX disambiguation policy; this is the spanner such that $\mathsf{posix}[\gamma](\mathbf{d})$ is empty if $\mathbf{d}$ cannot be matched by γ, and consists of the unique $(V, \mathbf{d})$-tuple resulting from matching $\mathbf{d}$ against γ under the POSIX disambiguation policy otherwise. We can prove the following.

LEMMA 5.7. *For every regex formula γ there exists a* REG-*program $\mathcal{E}$ such that $\mathcal{E}(\mathbf{d}) = \{\mathsf{posix}[\gamma](\mathbf{d})\}$, for every document $\mathbf{d}$. Furthermore, all cleaning updates in $\mathcal{E}$ are of the form* CLEAN(p) *where p is a transitive denial pgd.*

The proof proceeds by induction on γ, showing how to encode the POSIX policy by means of transitive denial pgds.

Since every transitive denial pgd is REG-disposable by Theorem 5.2, we immediately obtain from Lemma 5.7 that the spanner $\mathsf{posix}[\gamma]$ is regular, for every regex formula γ. Moreover, since it is easily verified that $\mathsf{posix}[\gamma]$ is hierarchical, it follows by Theorem 2.5 that $\mathsf{posix}[\gamma]$ is itself definable in RGX by a regex formula δ. While $[\![\gamma]\!]$ may produce many tuples for a given input document, $[\![\delta]\!]$ is always guaranteed to produce only one—corresponding to the tuple defined by the γ-parse constructed by the POSIX disambiguation policy.

[6]For simplicity, we restrict ourselves here to the setting where the entire input is required to match γ. Our results naturally extend to the setting where partial matches of $\mathbf{d}$ against γ are sought.

THEOREM 5.8. *For every regex formula γ, the spanner $\mathsf{posix}[\gamma]$ is definable in* RGX.

5.4 Core Spanners

Recall that REG is the closure of RGX under union, projection, and natural join. The class Core of *core spanners* [14] is obtained by adding to this list of operators the *string-equality selection*, denoted $\varsigma^=$. Formally, given an expression ρ in REG and two variables $x, y \in \mathsf{SVars}(\rho)$, the spanner defined by $\varsigma^=_{x,y}(\rho)$ selects all those tuples from ρ in which x and y span equal strings (though x and y can be different spans). The following theorem implies that the results given earlier in this section to not extend to the core spanners.

THEOREM 5.9. *If p is the maximal-container denial pgd or one of the JAPE denial pgds, then p is* not *Core-disposable.*

To prove Theorem 5.9, we use the following definition. Let p be a denial pgd of the form $\rho[x, y] \rightarrow R(x) \rhd S(y)$, where R and S are not-necessarily distinct unary relation symbols. We say that *p favors strict containers* if for all spans a and b, if b is contained in a, and b is neither a prefix or a suffix of a, then $R(a) \rhd S(b)$ is implied by p. Note that all the denial pgds in Theorem 5.9 favor strict containers. It also applies to POSIX, which we did not define formally as a denial pgd. Our proof is by showing that if p favors strict containers, then p is *not* Core-disposable. In particular, if a denial pgd that favors strict containers is Core-disposable, then there is a Boolean core spanner that recognizes the language of all the strings $\mathbf{s}\#\mathbf{t}$ where $\mathbf{s}, \mathbf{t} \in \{0, 1\}^+$ and $\mathbf{s}$ is *not* a substring of $\mathbf{t}$. Then, we use the result of Fagin et al. [14] stating that no such core spanner exists. Note that Theorem 5.9 does not mention any *rule priority* denial pgd (Section 5.1), since this rule is underspecified. Nevertheless, we can show that the cleaning update consisting of the denial pgd $\mathsf{true} \rightarrow (R(x) \rhd S(x))$, where R and S are distinct unary relation symbols, is not Core-disposable.

6. CONCLUSIONS

By incorporating the concept of prioritized repairs, we have generalized the framework of spanners into extraction programs that involve cleaning updates. We showed that existing cleaning policies can be represented, in a unified formalism, as denial pgds in REG. We discussed the problem of unambiguity, and showed that it is undecidable for REG-programs, as is the related problem of deciding if a given pgd in is acyclic. We also investigated disposability (i.e., whether a cleaning update can be simulated by CQ updates alone). We showed that cleaning updates in REG (and denial pgds as special cases) are not always REG-disposable, even if the program is unambiguous. Hence, cleaning updates increase the expressive power of unambiguous REG-programs as a representation system for spanners. Finally, we looked at special cases of cleaning updates in REG, namely transitive denial pgds, JAPE controls and POSIX, and showed that they all are REG-disposable. Of course, this does not mean that the programs that simulate these cleaners are of manageable sizes; the complexity of simulating disposable cleaners is a direction left here for future investigation. Another direction derived directly from this work is the challenge of devising a sufficient condition for unambiguity of cleaners, featuring low complexity, and robustness to realistic needs. Finally, we believe that it is of importance to explore the impact of *recursion* on our extraction programs (and in particular, associating an ordinary, order-independent Datalog semantics to our programs), either with or without cleaning updates.

Acknowledgments

We are extremely grateful to Phokion G. Kolaitis for suggestions that had significant impact on the paper. We also thank Martin Kutrib and Frank Neven for insightful discussions on multi-head automata.

7. REFERENCES

[1] J. Ajmera, H.-I. Ahn, M. Nagarajan, A. Verma, D. Contractor, S. Dill, and M. Denesuk. A CRM system for social media: challenges and experiences. In *WWW*, pages 49–58, 2013.

[2] D. E. Appelt and B. Onyshkevych. The common pattern specification language. In *Proceedings of the TIPSTER Text Program: Phase III*, pages 23–30, Baltimore, Maryland, USA, 1998.

[3] M. Arenas, L. E. Bertossi, and J. Chomicki. Consistent query answers in inconsistent databases. In *PODS*, pages 68–79, 1999.

[4] E. Benson, A. Haghighi, and R. Barzilay. Event discovery in social media feeds. In *ACL*, pages 389–398, 2011.

[5] L. E. Bertossi, S. Kolahi, and L. V. S. Lakshmanan. Data cleaning and query answering with matching dependencies and matching functions. *Theory Comput. Syst.*, 52(3):441–482, 2013.

[6] J. Bleiholder and F. Naumann. Data fusion. *ACM Comput. Surv.*, 41(1), 2008.

[7] L. Chiticariu, R. Krishnamurthy, Y. Li, S. Raghavan, F. Reiss, and S. Vaithyanathan. SystemT: An algebraic approach to declarative information extraction. In *ACL*, pages 128–137, 2010.

[8] R. Cox. Regular expression matching: the virtual machine approach. digression: Posix submatching, December 2009. http://swtch.com/ rsc/regexp/regexp2.html.

[9] H. Cunningham. Gate, a general architecture for text engineering. *Computers and the Humanities*, 36(2):223–254, 2002.

[10] H. Cunningham, D. Maynard, and V. Tablan. JAPE: a Java Annotation Patterns Engine (Second Edition). Research Memorandum CS–00–10, Department of Computer Science, University of Sheffield, November 2000.

[11] G. DeJong. An overview of the frump system. In W. G. Lehnert and M. H. Ringle, editors, *Strategies for natural language processing*, pages 149–176. Lawrence Erlbaum Associates, 1982.

[12] M. Dylla, I. Miliaraki, and M. Theobald. A temporal-probabilistic database model for information extraction. *PVLDB*, 6(14):1810–1821, 2013.

[13] R. Fagin, B. Kimelfeld, Y. Li, S. Raghavan, and S. Vaithyanathan. Rewrite rules for search database systems. In *PODS*, pages 271–282, 2011.

[14] R. Fagin, B. Kimelfeld, F. Reiss, and S. Vansummeren. Spanners: a formal framework for information extraction. In *PODS*, pages 37–48, 2013.

[15] W. Fan. Dependencies revisited for improving data quality. In *PODS*, pages 159–170, 2008.

[16] W. Fan, H. Gao, X. Jia, J. Li, and S. Ma. Dynamic constraints for record matching. *VLDB J.*, 20(4):495–520, 2011.

[17] W. Fan, J. Li, S. Ma, N. Tang, and W. Yu. Interaction between record matching and data repairing. In *SIGMOD Conference*, pages 469–480, 2011.

[18] D. A. Ferrucci and A. Lally. UIMA: an architectural approach to unstructured information processing in the corporate research environment. *Natural Language Engineering*, 10(3-4):327–348, 2004.

[19] G. Fowler. An interpreation of the posix regex standard (2003), 2003. http://gsf.cococlyde.org/download/re-interpretation.tgz.

[20] D. Freitag. Toward general-purpose learning for information extraction. In *COLING-ACL*, pages 404–408, 1998.

[21] Q. Fu, J.-G. Lou, Y. Wang, and J. Li. Execution anomaly detection in distributed systems through unstructured log analysis. In *ICDM*, pages 149–158, 2009.

[22] R. Grishman and B. Sundheim. Message understanding conference-6: A brief history. In *COLING*, pages 466–471, 1996.

[23] M. Holzer, M. Kutrib, and A. Malcher. Multi-head finite automata: Characterizations, concepts and open problems. In *CSP*, volume 1 of *EPTCS*, pages 93–107, 2008.

[24] Institute of Electrical and Electronic Engineers and the Open group. The open group base specifications issue 7, 2013. IEEE Std 1003.1, 2013 Edition.

[25] J. D. Lafferty, A. McCallum, and F. C. N. Pereira. Conditional random fields: Probabilistic models for segmenting and labeling sequence data. In *ICML*, pages 282–289, 2001.

[26] V. Laurikari. Efficient submatch addressing for regular expressions. Master's thesis, Helsinki University of Technology, 2001.

[27] T. R. Leek. Information extraction using hidden markov models. Master's thesis, UC San Diego, 1997.

[28] B. Liu, L. Chiticariu, V. Chu, H. V. Jagadish, and F. Reiss. Automatic rule refinement for information extraction. *PVLDB*, 3(1):588–597, 2010.

[29] S. Ma, W. Fan, and L. Bravo. Extending inclusion dependencies with conditions. *Theor. Comput. Sci.*, 515:64–95, 2014.

[30] A. McCallum, D. Freitag, and F. C. N. Pereira. Maximum entropy markov models for information extraction and segmentation. In *ICML*, pages 591–598, 2000.

[31] F. Niu, C. Ré, A. Doan, and J. W. Shavlik. Tuffy: Scaling up statistical inference in Markov Logic Networks using an RDBMS. *PVLDB*, 4(6):373–384, 2011.

[32] S. Okui and T. Suzuki. Disambiguation in regular expression matching via position automata with augmented transitions. In M. Domaratzki and K. Salomaa, editors, *CIAA*, volume 6482 of *Lecture Notes in Computer Science*, pages 231–240, 2010.

[33] H. Poon and P. Domingos. Joint inference in information extraction. In *AAAI*, pages 913–918. AAAI Press, 2007.

[34] F. Reiss, S. Raghavan, R. Krishnamurthy, H. Zhu, and S. Vaithyanathan. An algebraic approach to rule-based information extraction. In *ICDE*, pages 933–942, 2008.

[35] E. Riloff. Automatically constructing a dictionary for information extraction tasks. In *AAAI*, pages 811–816, 1993.

[36] W. Shen, A. Doan, J. F. Naughton, and R. Ramakrishnan. Declarative information extraction using datalog with embedded extraction predicates. In *VLDB*, pages 1033–1044, 2007.

[37] S. Soderland, D. Fisher, J. Aseltine, and W. G. Lehnert. CRYSTAL: Inducing a conceptual dictionary. In *IJCAI*, pages 1314–1321, 1995.

[38] S. Staworko, J. Chomicki, and J. Marcinkowski. Prioritized repairing and consistent query answering in relational databases. *Ann. Math. Artif. Intell.*, 64(2-3):209–246, 2012.

[39] S. Vansummeren. Type inference for unique pattern matching. *ACM Trans. Program. Lang. Syst.*, 28(3):389–428, 2006.

[40] H. Xu, S. P. Stenner, S. Doan, K. B. Johnson, L. R. Waitman, and J. C. Denny. Application of information technology: Medex: a medication information extraction system for clinical narratives. *JAMIA*, 17(1):19–24, 2010.

[41] H. Zhu, S. Raghavan, S. Vaithyanathan, and A. Löser. Navigating the intranet with high precision. In *WWW*, pages 491–500, 2007.

Nested Dependencies: Structure and Reasoning

Phokion G. Kolaitis
UC Santa Cruz & IBM
kolaitis@cs.ucsc.edu

Reinhard Pichler
TU Vienna
pichler@dbai.tuwien.ac.at

Emanuel Sallinger
TU Vienna
sallinger@dbai.tuwien.ac.at

Vadim Savenkov
TU Vienna
savenkov@dbai.tuwien.ac.at

ABSTRACT

During the past decade, schema mappings have been extensively used in formalizing and studying such critical data interoperability tasks as data exchange and data integration. Much of the work has focused on GLAV mappings, i.e., schema mappings specified by source-to-target tuple-generating dependencies (s-t tgds), and on schema mappings specified by second-order tgds (SO tgds), which constitute the closure of GLAV mappings under composition. In addition, nested GLAV mappings have also been considered, i.e., schema mappings specified by nested tgds, which have expressive power intermediate between s-t tgds and SO tgds.

Even though nested GLAV mappings have been used in data exchange systems, such as IBM's Clio, no systematic investigation of this class of schema mappings has been carried out so far. In this paper, we embark on such an investigation by focusing on the basic reasoning tasks, algorithmic problems, and structural properties of nested GLAV mappings. One of our main results is the decidability of the implication problem for nested tgds. We also analyze the structure of the core of universal solutions with respect to nested GLAV mappings and develop useful tools for telling apart SO tgds from nested tgds. By discovering deeper structural properties of nested GLAV mappings, we show that also the following problem is decidable: given a nested GLAV mapping, is it logically equivalent to a GLAV mapping?

Categories and Subject Descriptors

H.2.4 [**Database Management**]: Systems—*Relational databases*; H.2.5 [**Database Management**]: Heterogeneous Databases—*Data translation*

General Terms

Theory, Languages, Algorithms

PODS'14, June 22–27, 2014, Snowbird, UT, USA.

http://dx.doi.org/10.1145/2594538.2594544 .

Keywords

Schema mappings, data integration, data exchange, nested dependencies, second-order dependencies

1. Introduction

Schema mappings are high-level specifications, typically expressed in some logical formalism, that describe the relationship between two database schemas, called the source schema and the target schema. During the past decade, schema mappings have been extensively used in formalizing and studying such critical data interoperability tasks as data exchange and data integration. Much of the work has focused on two classes of schema mappings: GLAV mappings and mappings specified by SO tgds. A GLAV mapping is specified by a finite set of source-to-target tuple-generating dependencies (s-t tgds), which are first-order formulas of the form $\forall \vec{x}(\varphi(\vec{x}) \rightarrow \exists \vec{y}\psi(\vec{x},\vec{y}))$ with $\varphi(\vec{x})$ a conjunction of atoms over the source schema and $\psi(\vec{x},\vec{y})$ a conjunction of atoms over the target schema. As the name suggests, a second-order tuple-generating dependency (SO tgd) is a second-order formula; it starts with a string of existential function quantifiers that is followed by a conjunction of first-order formulas that resemble s-t tgds, but allow function terms in atomic formulas and also equalities between such terms. As shown in [8], SO tgds are the *right* language for expressing the composition of GLAV schema mappings. The study of GLAV mappings and mappings specified by SO tgds has spanned a wide range of problems, from expressive power and algorithms to optimization and structural properties; for recent overviews of the literature, see [1, 13].

In addition to GLAV mappings and mappings specified by SO tgds, two other classes of schema mappings of intermediate expressive power have also been considered. The first is the class of nested GLAV mappings that are specified by finitely many nested tgds, that is, first-order formulas that, informally, are obtained by a finite "nesting" of s-t tgds inside other s-t tgds. For example, the expression

$$\forall x_1 x_2(S(x_1,x_2) \rightarrow \exists y\, (S(y,x_2) \wedge \forall x_3(S(x_1,x_3) \rightarrow R(y,x_3))))$$

is a nested tgd. The second is the class of plain SO tgds, which consists of those SO tgds that contain no nested terms (i.e., no functional terms that have other functional terms as arguments) and no equalities between terms. For example, the expression

$$\exists f\, \forall x \forall y\, (S(x,y) \rightarrow R(f(x), f(y)))$$

is a plain SO tgd. We now describe the different reasons and motivation that led to the introduction of these two classes of schema mappings.

Nested GLAV mappings were introduced in [10] and demonstrated in [12] as an enhancement of the specification language of the Clio system, which, at that time, was being developed at the IBM Almaden Research Center, and is now part of IBM's InfoSphere BigInsights suite. Clio is a system that supports both the automatic or semi-automatic derivation of schema mappings from a visual specification and the subsequent generation of executable transformations for exchanging data between source and target. The main argument in favor of nested GLAV mappings over GLAV mappings given in [10, 12] is that they produce specifications that are more compact and also reflect more accurately the correlations between data; moreover, since they are specified in first-order logic, nested GLAV mappings give rise to transformations that, like those arising from GLAV mappings, can be implemented using SQL queries.

Plain SO tgds were introduced and studied in depth quite recently in [2] with a very different motivation in mind. Specifically, the goal was to find a "good" language for handling both composition and inversion of GLAV mappings. The results in [2] make a strong case that plain SO tgds form the *right* language for handling CQ-composition and inversion of GLAV mappings, where CQ-composition is a variant of the composition operator in which two schema mappings are considered to be equivalent if they give rise to the same certain answers for conjunctive queries (the notion of CQ-composition was introduced in [16]).

In terms of expressive power, nested GLAV mappings are strictly more expressive than GLAV mappings and strictly less expressive than mappings specified by plain SO tgds. As a matter of fact, it is known that the nested tgd given earlier is not logically equivalent to any finite set of s-t tgds, while the plain SO tgd given earlier is not logically equivalent to any finite set of nested tgds. Nested GLAV mappings and plain SO tgds share several desirable structural properties, such as admitting universal solutions and being closed under target homomorphisms [17, 2]. These similarities notwithstanding, it should be kept in mind that nested tgds and SO tgds belong to intrinsically different logical formalisms (first-order logic vs. second-order logic), a fact that may translate to different algorithmic behavior. For instance, the data complexity of the model checking problem of nested tgds is in LOGSPACE, while the data complexity of plain SO tgds is NP-complete.

Even though nested GLAV mappings were introduced several years ago and were incorporated into data exchange systems, no systematic investigation of nested tgds in their own right has been carried out to date. Our goal in this paper is to embark on such an investigation by focusing on the basic reasoning tasks, algorithmic problems, and deeper structural properties of nested GLAV mappings. Our first main result is that the implication problem (and, hence, the equivalence problem) for nested tgds is decidable. This should be contrasted with the state of affairs for SO tgds, for which the logical equivalence problem (hence also the implication problem) is undecidable. In fact, there is no algorithm even for deciding whether a given SO tgd is logically equivalent to a given finite set of s-t tgds, see [3, 9]. As for plain SO tgds, it is not known whether the implication problem and the logical equivalence problem are decidable.

Our decision procedure for the implication problem for nested tgds is rather elaborate and entails a delicate analysis of the properties of the chase procedure for nested tgds.

After this, we address the problem of telling apart nested tgds from s-t tgds. To that end, we show that the following problem is decidable: given a nested GLAV mapping, is it logically equivalent to some GLAV mapping? The situation is less clear regarding the problem of telling apart plain SO tgds from nested tgds. Indeed, at present, it is not known whether or not the following problem is decidable: given a plain SO tgd, is it logically equivalent to some nested GLAV mapping? Even though we do not settle the decidability of this problem here, we succeed in providing useful and easy-to-use sufficient conditions for telling that a given plain SO tgd is not logically equivalent to a nested GLAV mapping.

The aforementioned algorithm for telling apart nested tgds from s-t tgds, as well as the aforementioned sufficient conditions for telling apart a plain SO tgd from nested tgds, are derived by analyzing the structure of the cores of universal solutions with respect to nested GLAV mappings. In carrying out this analysis, we discover several deeper properties of nested tgds that enable their comparison with both s-t tgds and plain SO tgds. We believe that these properties are of interest in their own right and may play a role in structural characterizations of schema-mapping languages.

Finally, we study settings where key dependencies or, more generally, equality generating dependencies (egds) over the source schema are present. By revisiting the fundamental decision problems of logical equivalence and of telling apart schema mappings in different formalisms, we unveil further significant differences between nested tgds and plain SO tgds. In [9], the logical equivalence problem for plain SO tgds was shown undecidable if the source schema contains key dependencies. In contrast, here we show that the implication problem (and, hence, the logical equivalence problem) for nested tgds remains decidable even in the presence of arbitrary source egds. Likewise, we show that the problem of deciding if a given nested GLAV mapping is logically equivalent to some GLAV mapping remains decidable if arbitrary source egds are allowed. Again, this is in sharp contrast to plain SO tgds, for which we prove undecidability of the following problems in the presence of source key dependencies: given a plain SO tgd, is it logically equivalent to a GLAV mapping (or to a nested GLAV mapping, respectively)?

The remainder of the paper is organized as follows. Section 2 contains the definitions of the basic concepts and background material. Section 3 is devoted to the implication problem for nested tgds. Section 4 contains the analysis of the core of the universal solutions with respect to nested GLAV mappings, and the applications of this analysis to differentiating nested tgds from s-t tgds, and also to differentiating plain SO tgds from nested tgds. Section 5 revisits the problems studied in earlier sections when source key constraints are also present in the specification of the schema mappings at hand. Finally, the paper concludes with a discussion of open problems and directions for future research.

2. Preliminaries

Schemas, Instances, and Homomorphisms. A *schema* $\mathbf{R}$ is a finite sequence $\langle R_1, \ldots, R_k \rangle$ of relation symbols, where each R_i has a fixed arity. An *instance* I over $\mathbf{R}$, or an $\mathbf{R}$-*instance*, is a sequence $(R_1^I, \ldots, R_k^I)$, where each R_i^I is a finite relation of the same arity as R_i. We will often use R_i to denote both the relation symbol and the relation R_i^I that instantiates it. A *fact* of an instance I (over $\mathbf{R}$) is an expression $R_i^I(v_1, \ldots, v_m)$ (or simply $R_i(v_1, \ldots, v_m)$), where R_i is a relation symbol of $\mathbf{R}$ and $(v_1, \ldots, v_m) \in R_i^I$.

Let $\mathbf{S}$ and $\mathbf{T}$ be two schemas with no relation symbols in common. We refer to $\mathbf{S}$ as the *source schema*, and $\mathbf{T}$ as the *target schema*. Similarly, we refer to $\mathbf{S}$-instances as *source instances*, and $\mathbf{T}$-instances as *target instances*. We assume the presence of two kinds of values, namely *constants* and *(labeled) nulls*. We also assume that the active domains of source instances consists of constants; the active domains of target instances may consist of constants and nulls.

Let J be a target instance. The *Gaifman graph of facts* of J is the graph whose nodes are the facts of J and there is an edge between two facts if they have a null in common. We say that a target instance J is *connected* if the Gaifman graph of facts of J is connected. A *fact block (f-block)* of J is a connected component of the Gaifman graph of facts of J. The *fact block size (f-block size)* of J is the maximum cardinality of the f-blocks of J.

Let J_1 and J_2 be two target instances. A function h is a *homomorphism* from J_1 to J_2 if the following hold: (i) for every constant c, we have that $h(c) = c$; and (ii) for every relation symbol R in $\mathbf{R}$ and every tuple $(a_1, \ldots, a_n) \in R^{J_1}$, we have that $(h(a_1), \ldots, h(a_n)) \in R^{J_2}$. We use the notation $J_1 \rightarrow J_2$ to denote that there is a homomorphism from J_1 to J_2. We say that J_1 is *homomorphically equivalent* to J_2, written $J_1 \leftrightarrow J_2$, if $J_1 \rightarrow J_2$ and $J_2 \rightarrow J_1$. The *core* of an instance J, denoted *core*(J), is the smallest subinstance of J that is homomorphically equivalent to J. If there are multiple cores of J, then they are all isomorphic [11].

Schema mappings. A *schema mapping* is a triple $\mathcal{M} = (\mathbf{S}, \mathbf{T}, \Sigma)$, where $\mathbf{S}$ is the source schema, $\mathbf{T}$ is the target schema, and Σ is a set of constraints (typically, formulas in some logic) that describe the relationship between $\mathbf{S}$ and $\mathbf{T}$. We say that $\mathcal{M}$ is *specified by* Σ; often, we will use the set Σ of constraints to denote the mapping $\mathcal{M}$ specified by Σ.

If I is a source instance and J is a target instance such that the pair (I, J) satisfies Σ (written $(I, J) \models \Sigma$), then we say that J is a *solution* of I w.r.t. $\mathcal{M}$. We say that J is a *universal solution for I w.r.t. $\mathcal{M}$* if J is a solution for I and for every solution J' for I, we have $J \rightarrow J'$. If $\mathcal{C}$ is a class of schema mappings, we say that $\mathcal{C}$ *admits universal solutions* if for every schema mapping $\mathcal{M}$ in $\mathcal{C}$ and every source instance I, a universal solution for I w.r.t. $\mathcal{M}$ exists.

s-t tgds. A *source-to-target tuple-generating dependency* (in short, *s-t tgd*) is a first-order sentence of the form $\forall \vec{x}(\varphi(\vec{x}) \rightarrow \exists \vec{y} \psi(\vec{x}, \vec{y}))$, where $\varphi(\vec{x})$ is a conjunction of atoms over $\mathbf{S}$, each variable in $\vec{x}$ occurs in at least one atom in $\varphi(\vec{x})$, and $\psi(\vec{x}, \vec{y})$ is a conjunction of atoms over $\mathbf{T}$ with variables in $\vec{x}$ and $\vec{y}$. For simplicity, we will often suppress writing the universal quantifiers $\forall \vec{x}$ in the above formula. Another name for s-t tgds is *global-and-local-as-view* (GLAV) constraints (see [14]). We refer to a schema mapping specified entirely by a finite set of GLAV constraints as a *GLAV mapping*. As shown in [5], the class of GLAV mappings admits universal solutions. Moreover, if $\mathcal{M}$ is a GLAV mapping, then given a source instance I, a canonical universal solution *chase*$(I, \mathcal{M})$ can be produced via the *oblivious chase procedure*. That is, whenever the antecedent of an s-t tgd in $\mathcal{M}$ becomes true, fresh null values are introduced and facts involving these nulls are added to *chase*$(I, \mathcal{M})$ so that the conclusion of the s-t tgd becomes true.

SO tgds and Plain SO tgds. *Second-Order tgds*, or *SO tgds*, were introduced in [8], where it was shown that SO tgds are exactly the dependencies needed to specify the composition of an arbitrary number of GLAV mappings. Before we formally define SO tgds, we need to define *terms*. Given collections $\vec{x}$ of variables and $\vec{f}$ of function symbols, a *term (based on $\vec{x}$ and $\vec{f}$)* is defined recursively as follows: (1) Every variable in $\vec{x}$ is a term; (2) If f is a k-ary function symbol in $\vec{f}$ and $t_1, \ldots, t_k$ are terms, then $f(t_1, \ldots, t_k)$ is a term.

Let $\mathbf{S}$ be a source schema and $\mathbf{T}$ a target schema. A *second-order tuple-generating dependency (SO tgd)* is a formula of the form:

$$\exists \vec{f}((\forall \vec{x}_1(\varphi_1 \rightarrow \psi_1)) \wedge ... \wedge (\forall \vec{x}_n(\varphi_n \rightarrow \psi_n))), \text{where}$$

(1) Each member of $\vec{f}$ is a function symbol. (2) Each φ_i is a conjunction of (i) atoms $S(y_1, ..., y_k)$, where S is a k-ary relation symbol of schema $\mathbf{S}$ and $y_1, \ldots, y_k$ are variables in $\vec{x}_i$, not necessarily distinct, and (ii) equalities of the form $t = t'$ where t and t' are terms based on $\vec{x}_i$ and $\vec{f}$. (3) Each ψ_i is a conjunction of atoms $T(t_1, ..., t_l)$, where T is an l-ary relation symbol of schema $\mathbf{T}$ and $t_1, \ldots, t_l$ are terms based on $\vec{x}_i$ and $\vec{f}$. (4) Each variable in $\vec{x}_i$ appears in some atom formula of φ_i. As an example, the formula

$$\exists f(\forall e(Emp(e) \rightarrow Mgr(e, f(e))) \wedge \\ \forall e(Emp(e) \wedge (e = f(e)) \rightarrow SelfMgr(e)))$$

expresses the property that every employee has a manager, and if an employee is the manager of himself/herself, then this employee is a self-manager.

Note that SO tgds allow for nested terms and for equalities between terms. A nested term is a functional term which contains a functional term as an argument. A *plain SO tgd* is an SO tgd that contains no nested terms and no equalities. For example, the preceding SO tgd is not plain, while the following SO tgd is plain

$$\exists f \forall x \forall y(S(x, y) \rightarrow R(f(x), f(y)))$$

The properties of plain SO tgds were recently investigated in [2]. It is easy to see that every GLAV schema mapping is logically equivalent to a plain SO tgd. Moreover, as shown in [8], the class of SO tgds admits universal solutions, hence the same holds true for the class of plain SO tgds. In fact, the chase procedure can be extended to SO tgds, so that if σ is an SO tgd and I is a source instance, then *chase*(I, σ) is a canonical universal solution for I w.r.t. σ.

In what follows, we will often suppress writing the existential second-order quantifiers and the universal first-order quantifiers in front of SO tgds.

Nested tgds. Fix a partition of the set of first-order variables into two disjoint infinite sets, X and Y. A *nested tgd* is a first-order sentence that can be generated by the following recursive definition:

$$\chi ::= \alpha \mid \forall \vec{x}\,(\beta_1 \wedge \ldots \wedge \beta_k \rightarrow \exists \vec{y}\,(\chi_1 \wedge \ldots \wedge \chi_\ell))$$

where each $x_i \in X$, each $y_i \in Y$, α is an atomic formula over the target schema, and each β_j is an atomic formula over the source schema containing only variables from X, such that each x_i occurs in some β_j. As an example, the formula

$$\forall x_1 x_2 (S(x_1,x_2) \rightarrow \exists y\,(R(y,x_2) \wedge \forall x_3 (S(x_1,x_3) \rightarrow R(y,x_3))))$$

is a nested tgd. It is known that this nested tgd is not logically equivalent to any finite set of s-t tgds (see [8, 17]).

A nested tgd σ contains a number of *parts* σ_i. Informally, σ_i is an implicational formula that corresponds to the recursive option of the production rule for χ, where each χ_i is the conjunction of atoms given by the non-recursive option. Thus, σ_i is syntactically similar to an s-t tgd, but may have free variables; moreover, the conclusion may be an empty conjunction, in which case it evaluates to $\top$ (true). As an example, the parts of the preceding nested tgd are

- $\forall x_1 x_2 (S(x_1,x_2) \rightarrow \exists y\, R(y,x_2))$ and
- $\forall x_3 (S(x_1,x_3) \rightarrow R(y,x_3))$

In our examples, we refer to parts of nested tgds using labels. The way of inline labeling of parts which we use throughout this paper is illustrated below by a nested tgd σ with four parts $\sigma_1,\ldots,\sigma_4$:

$$\begin{array}{ll} \sigma_1: & \forall x_1 \big(S_1(x_1) \rightarrow \exists y_1 \qquad (*) \\ \sigma_2: & \quad \big(\forall x_2 (S_2(x_2) \rightarrow R_2(y_1,x_2)) \wedge \\ \sigma_3: & \quad\quad \forall x_3 (S_3(x_1,x_3) \rightarrow (R_3(y_1,x_3) \wedge \\ \sigma_4: & \quad\quad\quad \forall x_4 (S_4(x_3,x_4) \rightarrow \exists y_2 R_4(y_2,x_4))))\big)\end{array}$$

For $i > 1$, by $parent(\sigma_i)$ we denote the part where σ_i is nested: for instance, for the above dependency σ, we have $parent(\sigma_2) = parent(\sigma_3) = \sigma_1$, and $parent(\sigma_4) = \sigma_3$. The ancestors $anc(\sigma_i)$ of σ_i are defined via the transitive closure of *parent*. For example $anc(\sigma_4) = \{\sigma_1, \sigma_3\}$. Symmetrically, we define $child(\sigma_i)$ to be the set of parts nested directly under (σ_i). For example, we have $child(\sigma_1) = \{\sigma_2, \sigma_3\}$ for the dependency σ above. Again, we define the descendants $desc(\sigma_i)$ to be the transitive closure of *child*, e.g., $desc(\sigma_1) = \{\sigma_2, \sigma_3, \sigma_4\}$.

It is sometimes convenient to consider *Skolemized nested tgds*, in which every existential variable y is replaced by the Skolem term $f(\vec{x})$ where f is a fresh function symbol and $\vec{x}$ is the vector of universally quantified variables in the part σ_i in which $\exists y$ occurs, and in the ancestors of σ_i. Note that we assume existential variables in different parts to be renamed apart. The Skolemized version of σ has the following form:

$$\begin{array}{ll} \sigma_1: & \forall x_1 \big(S_1(x_1) \rightarrow \\ \sigma_2: & \quad \big(\forall x_2 (S_2(x_2) \rightarrow R_2(f(x_1),x_2)) \wedge \\ \sigma_3: & \quad\quad \forall x_3 (S_3(x_1,x_3) \rightarrow (R_3(f(x_1),x_3) \wedge \\ \sigma_4: & \quad\quad\quad \forall x_4 (S_4(x_3,x_4) \rightarrow R_4(g(x_1,x_3,x_4),x_4))))\big)\end{array}$$

We write $\forall \vec{x}(\varphi(\vec{x},\vec{x}_0) \rightarrow \psi(\vec{x},\vec{x}_0))$ to express a part σ_i of a Skolemized nested tgd, where $\vec{x}_0$ is the vector of universally quantified variables stemming from $anc(\sigma_i)$. For instance, the part σ_4 can be expressed as $\forall \vec{x}(\varphi_4(\vec{x},\vec{x}_0) \rightarrow \psi_4(\vec{x},\vec{x}_0))$ where $\vec{x} = \langle x_4 \rangle$ and $\vec{x}_0 = \langle x_1, x_3 \rangle$.

It is easy to see that every Skolemized nested tgd is a plain SO tgd. Thus, the class of nested tgds contains the class of s-t tgds and is contained in the class of plain SO tgds. A *nested GLAV mapping* is a schema mapping $\mathcal{M} = (\mathbf{S}, \mathbf{T}, \Sigma)$, where Σ is a finite set of nested tgds.

3. The Implication Problem

Let Σ and Σ' be two finite sets of source-to-target constraints expressed in some logical formalism (e.g., SO tgds, nested tgds, s-t tgds). We say that Σ implies Σ', denoted by $\Sigma \models \Sigma'$, if for every source instance I and every target instance J such that $(I,J) \models \Sigma$, we have that $(I,J) \models \Sigma'$. The *implication problem* asks: given two finite sets Σ and Σ' of source-to-target constraints, does $\Sigma \models \Sigma'$ hold? Analogously, the *(logical) equivalence problem* asks if $\Sigma \equiv \Sigma'$ holds, i.e., if Σ and Σ' are satisfied by exactly the same pairs (I,J) of source and target instances.

Note that, since all instances considered are finite, this is the implication (and equivalence) problem *in the finite*. The main result of this section is as follows.

Theorem 3.1 *The implication problem for nested tgds is decidable.*

The decision procedure behind Theorem 3.1 requires the introduction of several key concepts and the development of new technical tools that are presented in what follows.

Chase Forest. We begin by introducing the *chase forest* of a nested tgd, which represents the process of chasing a source instance with a nested tgd.

Let σ be a nested tgd and I a source instance. The oblivious chase *chase*(I,σ) of I with σ can be described as a sequence of recursive *triggerings*: Each triggering t is associated with a part $\sigma_i : \forall \vec{x} \varphi(\vec{x},\vec{x}_0) \rightarrow \psi(\vec{x},\vec{x}_0)$ and with the variable assignment $\vec{a}$ to the variables in $\vec{x}$.

If the part σ_i is the top-level part of σ, then the vector $\vec{x}_0$ is empty and t is called a *root triggering*. Otherwise, the triggering t of σ_i has a unique *parent triggering* t', associated with the part $parent(\sigma_i)$ and the partial assignment to the variables in $\vec{x}_0$. The transitive closure over parent triggerings gives the set of *ancestor triggerings* of t. All variables in $\vec{x}_0$ are bound in ancestor triggerings. The corresponding assignment $\vec{a}_0$ for $\vec{x}_0$ is called the *input assignment* of t.

Let $\forall \vec{x}(\varphi(\vec{x},\vec{x}_0) \rightarrow \psi(\vec{x},\vec{x}_0))$ be a part σ_i of σ, and suppose that there exists a chain of triggerings of parts in $anc(\sigma_i)$ that has bound all variables in $\vec{x}_0$ yielding an assignment $\vec{a}_0$. A necessary and sufficient condition to activate the triggering t of σ_i is $I \models \varphi(\vec{a},\vec{a}_0)$, for some assignment $\vec{a}$ for $\vec{x}$. The result of t is the instantiation $\psi(\vec{a},\vec{a}_0)$ of the conclusion atoms of σ_i, which are then added to the instance *chase*(I,σ). In this instantiation, Skolem terms are considered as null labels. The parts in $child(\sigma_i)$ are then triggered recursively. The set of all triggerings recursively called from t is denoted by $rec(t)$.

The collection of the triggerings in the chase of I with a finite set Σ of nested tgds constitutes the *chase forest of I with* σ: root triggerings t_r are associated with the top-level parts of nested tgds in Σ, and each set of triggerings called recursively from t_r constitutes the *chase tree* rooted at t_r.

An immediate consequence of the definition of the chase is that triggerings in distinct chase trees produce facts which share no nulls. This is one of the key underpinnings of our decidability result: namely, reasoning about nested tgds may be restricted to source instances that give rise to a single chase tree. The second underpinning is that only chase trees of bounded fanout need to be considered, as we explain next.

Patterns. The algorithm behind Theorem 3.1 is described in the displayed decision procedure IMPLIES. We now introduce the notions used in this procedure.

Definition 3.2 (Pattern) Let σ be a nested tgd and $\mathcal{T}$ a chase tree of some source instance I with σ.

A *pattern* of σ is a tree whose nodes are labeled by identifiers of tgd parts in such a way that the parent-child re-

Procedure IMPLIES(Σ,σ)

Data: Set Σ of nested tgds, nested tgd σ
Result: *true* if $\Sigma \models \sigma$, *false* otherwise

```
Skolemize σ and Σ in a standard way;
Let v_σ be the number of distinct Skolem functions in σ;
Let w_Σ be the maximum number of universally
  quantified variables in a nested tgd in Σ;
Let k = v_σ · w_Σ + 1;
Let P_k(σ) be the set of k-patterns of σ;
for each k-pattern p_k ∈ P_k(σ) do
  | Produce I_{p_k} and J_{p_k}, the canonical source and,
  | respectively, the canonical target instances of p_k;
  | if no homomorphism J_{p_k} → chase(I_{p_k}, Σ) exists
  | then
  |   | return false;
  | end
end
return true;
```

lationship between nodes coincides with the nesting of the tgd parts at the labels of respective nodes.

The *pattern of chase tree* $\mathcal{T}$ is the tree obtained from $\mathcal{T}$ by ignoring the assignments to the universal variables and using solely the identifiers of tgd parts as node markers. $\triangleleft$

We also use the notion of subtree in a pattern and the "cloning" operation on subtrees, defined in an intuitive way.

Definition 3.3 (Subtree, Cloning, k-pattern) Let σ be a nested tgd and let p be a pattern of σ. By a *subtree* of a pattern p, we always mean a subtree closed under child relation. That is, there is a single subtree rooted at each node n, namely the one containing all descendant nodes of n.

A subtree t' is called a *clone* of a subtree t if the roots of t' and t are siblings in p and the two subtrees are isomorphic. Appending a clone of a subtree t to the parent of its root node is called *cloning* t.

Let $\mathcal{C}_t$ denote the set of all clones of t in p. If for each subtree t, $|\mathcal{C}_t| \leq k$, we call p a *k-pattern*. The set of all k-patterns of σ is denoted $\mathcal{P}_k(\sigma)$. $\triangleleft$

Example 3.4 We point out that not every pattern of a nested tgd can be realized in a chase forest. Consider the nested tgd $\forall x_1\, S_1(x_1) \to ((S_2(x_1) \to T_2(x_1))$ with a single nested part. This tgd can only generate chase trees with patterns having two nodes. This is because the assignment of the only variable x_1 is determined by the root triggering and thus only a single triggering of the nested part is possible, using the same assignment. $\triangleleft$

Ignoring realizability of patterns simplifies the presentation of the decision procedure and can be shown not to affect its correctness.

We now show how to enumerate k-patterns. We identify trees with the pairs $\langle \sigma_j, \mathcal{T}^\mu \rangle$ where σ_j is a part of σ associated with the root of the tree and $\mathcal{T}^\mu$ is a *multiset* of subtrees nested under σ_j, given by the set $\mathcal{T}$ of distinct subtrees and the multiplicity function $\mu : \mathcal{T} \to 1 \ldots k$. We now define the set $\mathcal{P}^*_k(\sigma_j)$ associated with a part σ_j of σ as follows:

- If $child(\sigma_j)$ is empty, define $\mathcal{P}^*_k(\sigma_j) = \{\langle \sigma_j, \emptyset \rangle\}$.
- Otherwise, assume $child(\sigma_j) = \{\sigma_{i_1}, \ldots \sigma_{i_\ell}\}$; define

$$\mathcal{P}^*_k(\sigma_j) = \{\langle \sigma_j, \textstyle\bigcup_{\alpha=1}^{\ell} P_\alpha^{\mu_\alpha} \rangle \mid P_\alpha \subseteq \mathcal{P}^*_k(\sigma_{i_\alpha}) \text{ and } \mu_\alpha \text{ is a function } P_\alpha \to 1 \ldots k\}.$$

The inductive step of the above definition constructs the set of all possible trees rooted at a node labeled with σ_j and having as subtrees at most k clones of some trees in $\mathcal{P}^*(\sigma_{i_\alpha})$, for every part σ_{i_α} nested at σ_j.

Proposition 3.5 *Let k be an integer, σ be a nested tgd and let σ_1 be the top-level part of σ. Then, the set $\mathcal{P}_k(\sigma)$ of k-patterns of σ coincides with $\mathcal{P}^*_k(\sigma_1)$.*

Example 3.6 Recall the nested tgd σ with four parts from Section 2 marked with (*). The set $\mathcal{P}_1(\sigma) = \{p_1, \ldots, p_8\}$ containing 1-patterns of σ is shown in Figure 1. $\triangleleft$

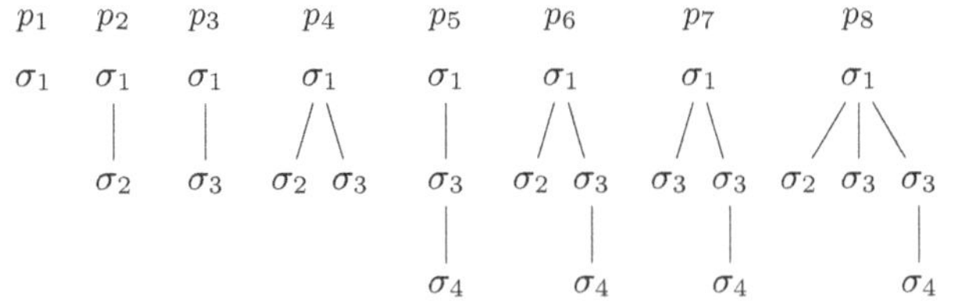

Figure 1: 1-patterns of the tgd σ from Section 2.

It follows from the definition of the set $\mathcal{P}^*_k(\sigma_j)$ used in Proposition 3.5 that for each fixed k, the maximum size of k-patterns in $\mathcal{P}_k(\sigma)$ is bounded, albeit non-elementary in the nesting depth of σ, and so is the size of $\mathcal{P}_k(\sigma)$ itself.

The only missing component for the decision procedure IMPLIES is now the notion of the canonical instance of a pattern. It is defined next.

Definition 3.7 (Canonical instances of a pattern) Let p be a pattern representing a sequence of recursive triggerings of a nested tgd σ. The *canonical source instance* I_p *of* p and the *canonical target instance* J_p *of* p are obtained by adding, for each node associated with the part $\sigma_i : \forall \vec{x}(\varphi(\vec{x}, \vec{x}_0) \to \psi(\vec{x}, \vec{x}_0))$, the atoms of $\varphi(\vec{a}, \vec{a}_0)$ to I_p and the atoms of $\psi(\vec{a}, \vec{a}_0)$ to J_p, where $\vec{a}$ assigns distinct fresh constants to the variables of $\vec{x}$, and $\vec{a}_0$ is the assignment used to instantiate the parts in $anc(\sigma_i)$. $\triangleleft$

Note that we speak of *the* canonical source and target instances, even though the constants used to create them can be arbitrary. The justification is that such instances are unique up to renaming of constants and thus are indistinguishable for nested tgds, which have no constants, according to the definition in Section 2.

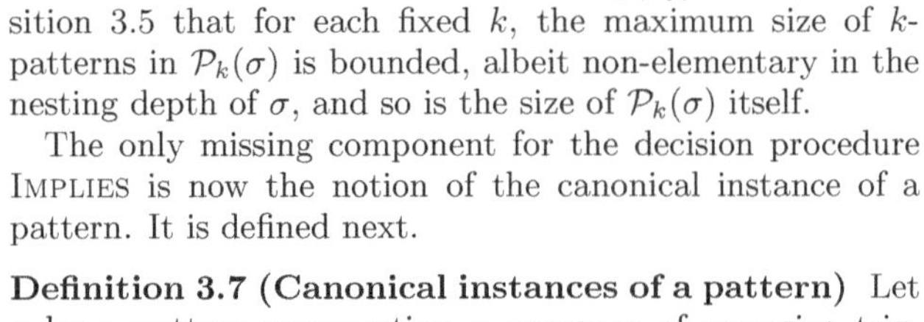

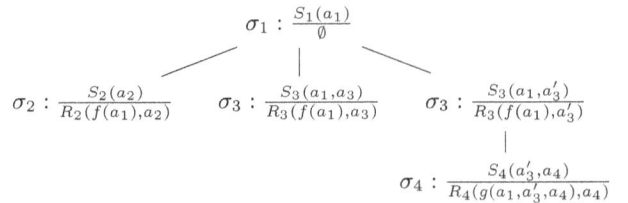

Figure 2: Facts of the canonical source instance I_{p_8} (above the bars) and the canonical target instance J_{p_8} (below the bars) of the pattern p_8.

Example 3.8 The canonical source instance and the canonical target instance of the 1-pattern p_8 from Example 3.6 are respectively I_{p_8} and J_{p_8} arranged in a tree in Figure 2. ◁

The next example shows the canonical source instance of a pattern containing clones of subtrees.

Example 3.9 One possible 3-pattern based on the 1-pattern p_8 from Example 3.8, in which one clone of the node σ_2 and two clones of the node σ_4 are added, is shown in Figure 3, along with the facts of its canonical source instance. ◁

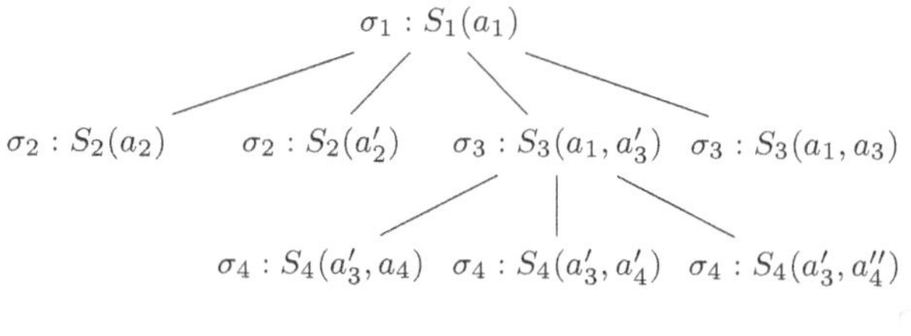

Figure 3: A 3-pattern and the facts constituting its canonical source instance.

Finally, we have the stage set to put the procedure IMPLIES into action.

Example 3.10 Consider the nested tgd τ and the s-t tgds τ' and τ'':

$$\tau : \forall x_1\,(S_1(x_1) \to \exists y(\forall x_2 S_2(x_2) \to R(x_2, y)))$$
$$\tau' : \forall x_2\,(S_2(x_2) \to \exists z R(x_2, z))$$
$$\tau'' : \forall x_1 \forall x_2\,(S_1(x_1) \wedge S_2(x_2) \to R(x_2, x_1))$$

It is easy to see that $\tau' \not\models \tau$ and $\tau'' \models \tau$. We now verify that procedure IMPLIES yields the same answers. The Skolemization of the nested tgd τ has the form:

$$\begin{array}{ll} \tau_1: & \forall x_1 (S_1(x_1) \to \\ \tau_2: & \qquad \forall x_2 (S_2(x_2) \to R_2(x_2, f(x_1)))) \end{array}$$

According to line 4 of the procedure, the bound k on the number of clones should be 2 for testing $\tau' \models \tau$ and 3 for testing $\tau'' \models \tau$, since we have $v_\sigma = 1$, $w_{\{\tau'\}} = 1$, and $w_{\{\tau''\}} = 2$. The set $\mathcal{P}_3(\tau)$ has two 1-patterns $\{p', p''\}$, of which only p'' has a non-empty canonical target instance. Based on p'', the 2-pattern p''_2 and the 3-pattern p''_3 can be obtained. One can then check that the set $\{p', p'', p''_2, p''_3\}$ is actually the complete set of 3-patterns of τ.

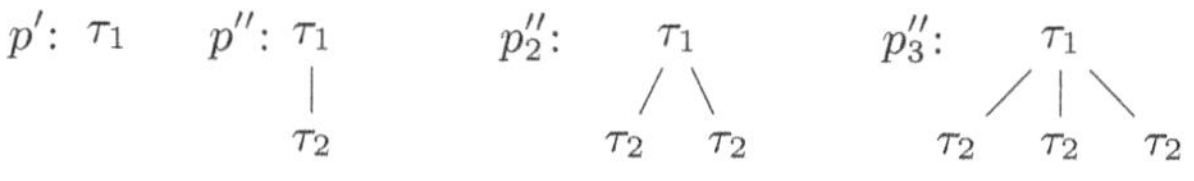

Figure 4: Patterns used to test $\tau' \models \tau$ and $\tau'' \models \tau$.

Let I_p and J_p denote the canonical source resp. canonical target instance of a pattern p of τ with $p \in \{p', p'', p''_2, p''_3\}$. Let Σ be one of $\{\tau'\}$ or $\{\tau''\}$. To test if $\Sigma \models \tau$, the procedure IMPLIES checks the existence of a homomorphism $J_p \to chase(I_p, \Sigma)$ for the patterns p', p'', p''_2 and p''_3 (for the case $\Sigma = \{\tau''\}$). For p', this check is trivial since p' has an empty canonical target instance. We illustrate the check for the pattern p''_2. The canonical source and target instances for this pattern are as follows:

$$I_{p''_2} = \{S_1(a_1), S_2(a_2), S_2(a'_2)\}$$
$$J_{p''_2} = \{R_2(a_2, f(a_1)), R_2(a'_2, f(a_1))\}$$

Let us check $\tau' \not\models \tau$. The Skolemization of τ' is

$$\tau' : \forall x_2\,(S_2(x_2) \to R(x_2, g(x_2)))$$

The chase of $I_{p''_2}$ with τ' results in $J_{\tau'} = \{R(a_2, g(a_2)), R(a'_2, g(a'_2))\}$. Due to the absence of a homomorphism from $J_{p''_2}$ to $J_{\tau'}$, IMPLIES($\{\tau'\}$,τ) outputs *false*, as it should.

We now check that $\tau'' \models \tau$ holds. The chase of $I_{p''_2}$ with τ'' results in $J_{\tau''} = \{R(a_2, a_1), R(a'_2, a_1)\}$. The mapping $[f(a_1) \mapsto a_1]$ is a homomorphism $J_{p''_2} \to J_{\tau''}$, and thus the check in the IMPLIES procedure for the pattern p''_2 passes successfully. One can verify that so does the check for the patterns p'' and p''_3. Therefore, IMPLIES($\{\tau''\}$,τ) outputs *true*, as it should. ◁

Proof of Theorem 3.1 (Idea). Two ideas underlie the correctness of the decision procedure IMPLIES, and thus of Theorem 3.1. The first is a well-known property of schema mappings which are closed under target homomorphisms and for which a chase procedure producing universal solutions exists. Namely, $\Sigma \models \sigma$ if and only if for every source instance I, we have that $chase(I, \sigma) \to chase(I, \Sigma)$ holds, which is the case when every f-block of $chase(I, \sigma)$ can be homomorphically embedded in $chase(I, \Sigma)$ [7]. The second idea is specific to nested tgds. It uses the fact that $chase(I, \sigma) \to chase(I, \Sigma)$ holds for arbitrary I if for every k-pattern $p_k \in \mathcal{P}_k(\sigma)$, the homomorphism $J_{p_k} \to chase(I_{p_k}, \Sigma)$ exists, where k is a constant depending on σ and Σ, as defined at line 4 of the decision procedure IMPLIES, and I_{p_k} and J_{p_k} are the canonical source instance and, respectively, the canonical target instance of p_k.

The rationale for choosing k is based on the following claim. Let t_1 and t_2 be two triggerings in a chase tree of σ such that neither triggering is an ancestor of the other one. Then, the facts generated by t_1 and t_2 can only share nulls that instantiate Skolem terms based on variables bound in the common ancestor triggerings of t_1 and t_2. Based on that, one can show that any large f-block B generated by a nested tgd via chase must be "stitched together" from small fragments having a small number of common nulls. Namely, there are at most v_σ such nulls, where v_σ is the number of distinct Skolem terms in σ. A homomorphism $h : B \to chase(I, \Sigma)$ maps every such null either to a constant or to a null created by Σ. In the latter case, this null corresponds to some Skolem term in Σ. A Skolem term can be based on at most w_Σ variables, where w_Σ is the maximum number of variables in any tgd in Σ. Now, let B contain $k = v_\sigma \cdot w_\Sigma + 1$ fragments corresponding to clones of some pattern subtree. Using the pigeonhole principle one can show that if facts corresponding to yet further clones of the same subtree are added to B, the homomorphism h can be extended to such an increased f-block. Thus, the property $chase(I, \sigma) \to chase(I, \Sigma)$ for arbitrary I can be ensured by inspecting f-blocks of canonical instances corresponding to chase trees with at most k clones of any subtree. Such chase tree patterns are among the k-patterns of σ. □

We conclude this section by discussing an immediate consequence of Theorem 3.1.

Corollary 3.11 *The logical equivalence problem for nested tgds is decidable.*

In contrast, it is known that the logical equivalence problem for SO tgds is undecidable, according to Theorem 1 in [9], which builds on [3]. As a matter of fact, an examination of the proof of Theorem 1 in [9] reveals that the following problem is undecidable: given an SO tgd σ and a finite set Σ' of s-t tgds, is $\sigma \equiv \Sigma'$? Hence, the following problem is undecidable as well: given an SO tgd σ and a finite set Σ' of nested tgds, is $\sigma \equiv \Sigma'$? Therefore, Corollary 3.11 contributes significantly to the delineation of the boundary between decidability and undecidability for the logical equivalence problem.

4. The Structure of the Core and Applications

As mentioned in Section 2, the class of nested tgds contains the class of s-t tgds and is, in turn, contained in the class of plain SO tgds. Moreover, it is known that both containments are proper. In this section, we produce powerful tools that allow us to tell apart nested tgds from s-t tgds, and also plain SO tgds from nested tgds. The main result of this section is an algorithm for telling whether or not a given finite set of nested tgds is logically equivalent to a finite set of s-t tgds. In addition, we give useful and easy-to-apply sufficient conditions for a plain SO tgd to be not logically equivalent to any finite set of nested tgds.

The results in this section are obtained by analyzing the structure of the core of the universal solutions of nested GLAV mappings. We embark on this analysis next, which we believe is of interest in its own right.

4.1 Nested GLAV Mappings vs. GLAV Mappings

Recall that every schema mapping $\mathcal{M}$ specified by an SO-tgd admits universal solutions. Moreover, for every source instance I, a canonical universal solution $chase(I, \mathcal{M})$ for I w.r.t. $\mathcal{M}$ can be obtained via the chase procedure. Since all universal solutions for a given source instance I are homomorphically equivalent, it follows that their cores are unique up to isomorphism, hence we can take $core(chase(I, \mathcal{M}))$ as *the* core of the universal solutions for I w.r.t. $\mathcal{M}$ [7]. Note that, in general, $core(chase(I, \mathcal{M}))$ need not be a universal solution for I w.r.t. $\mathcal{M}$ [6]. However, if $\mathcal{M}$ is specified by a plain SO tgd, then $core(chase(I, \mathcal{M}))$ is a universal solution for I w.r.t. $\mathcal{M}$. The reason for this is that, as shown in [2], every schema mapping $\mathcal{M}$ specified by a plain SO tgd is *closed under target homomorphisms*, which means that if J is a solution for I w.r.t. $\mathcal{M}$ and if there is a homomorphism from J to J' that is the identity on constants, then J' is also a solution for I w.r.t. $\mathcal{M}$. Moreover, $core(chase(I, \mathcal{M}))$ is the smallest universal solution for I w.r.t. $\mathcal{M}$. In particular, the above facts hold true for nested GLAV mappings (hence also for GLAV mappings).

We will make extensive use of the following notion, which was introduced in [6]. A schema mapping $\mathcal{M}$ specified by an SO tgd has *bounded f-block size* if there is a positive integer b such that for every source instance I, the f-block size of $core(chase(I, \mathcal{M}))$ is at most b; otherwise, we say that $\mathcal{M}$ has *unbounded f-block size*. The following result follows immediately from Proposition 3.14 and Theorem 4.10 in [6].

Theorem 4.1 ([6]) *A schema mapping $\mathcal{M}$ specified by a plain SO tgd is logically equivalent to a GLAV schema mapping if and only if $\mathcal{M}$ has bounded f-block size. In particular, this holds true for every nested GLAV schema mapping.*

The preceding Theorem 4.1 will be used to prove the main result in this section, which we now state formally.

Theorem 4.2 *The following problem is decidable: given a nested GLAV mapping $\mathcal{M}$, is there a GLAV mapping $\mathcal{M}'$ such that $\mathcal{M}$ is logically equivalent to $\mathcal{M}'$?*

In view of Theorem 4.1, it suffices to give an algorithm that, given a nested GLAV schema mapping $\mathcal{M}$, determines whether or not $\mathcal{M}$ has bounded f-block size. To this end, we introduce a crucial property of mappings and show that nested GLAV mappings have this property.

Definition 4.3 Let $\mathcal{C}$ be a class of schema mappings. We say that $\mathcal{C}$ has *effective threshold for f-block size* if there exists a recursive function $f : \mathcal{C} \to \mathbb{N}$, where $\mathbb{N}$ is the set of natural numbers, s.t. every mapping $\mathcal{M} \in \mathcal{C}$ either has f-block size at most $f(\mathcal{M})$ or has unbounded f-block size. ◁

Theorem 4.4 *The class of nested GLAV mappings has effective threshold for f-block size.*

Proof (Idea). We show that if the size of an f-block in the core is above a certain threshold that depends on the maximum size of a 1-pattern, then two siblings in the chase tree of that f-block have isomorphic subtrees (up to variable bindings). After that, we "clone" a third subtree, and show that this strictly increases the f-block size. Finally, we show that the claimed f-block with increased size indeed persists in the core of an extended source instance. It is then clear that, by successively increasing the size of this f-block, the size can increase beyond any bound. □

The following statement was claimed in [4].

Claim 4.5 *There is an algorithm for the following problem: Given an SO tgd σ and a positive integer b, is the f-block size of σ bounded by b?*

Our desired Theorem 4.2 would follow immediately by combining Theorem 4.1 and Theorem 4.4 with Claim 4.5. Alas, while the algorithm for Claim 4.5 presented in [4, Theorem 5.2] appears to be correct, the proof of correctness of the algorithm given there has a flaw, which will be pointed out in the sequel. It should be noted that the above claim would also follow from Theorem 3 in [16] together with Theorem 4.10 in [6]; however, Theorem 3 in [16] is stated without proof. In view of this state of affairs, we prove that Claim 4.5 indeed holds for nested GLAV mappings. For this purpose, we introduce the following concept.

Definition 4.6 A schema mapping $\mathcal{M}$ is said to have a *bounded anchor* if there exists an integer a such that for every source instance I and for every connected target instance J with $J \subseteq core(chase(I, \mathcal{M}))$, there are a source instance I' and a connected target instance J' such that

- $|I'| \leq a|J|$;
- $|J'| \geq |J|$ and $J' \subseteq core(chase(I', \mathcal{M}))$.

We say that *the bounded anchor of $\mathcal{M}$ is witnessed by a.* ◁

We extend this notion to classes of schema mappings.

Definition 4.7 Let $\mathcal{C}$ be a class of schema mappings. We say that $\mathcal{C}$ has *effective bounded anchor*, if there exists a recursive function $a : \mathcal{C} \to \mathbb{N}$ such that every schema mapping $\mathcal{M}$ in $\mathcal{C}$ has bounded anchor witnessed by $a(\mathcal{M})$. ◁

For understanding the intuition behind the concept of bounded anchor, let us consider an example that was brought to our attention by R. Fagin.

Example 4.8 Let σ be the following plain SO tgd:

$$\exists f\, \forall x \forall y\, (S(x,y) \rightarrow R(f(x), f(y)) \wedge R(f(y), f(x)))$$

Suppose we want to determine whether σ has a bounded anchor. Let $I_n = \{S(1,2), S(2,3), \ldots, S(n,1)\}$ be the source instance consisting of a directed cycle of length n. Then $chase(I_n, \sigma)$ is the undirected cycle of length n. Let n be an odd number. It follows that $core(chase(I_n, \sigma))$ is also the undirected cycle of length n, which we depict on the left side of Figure 5 for $n > 5$ (each arc, whether it is solid or dashed, denotes an R-atom).

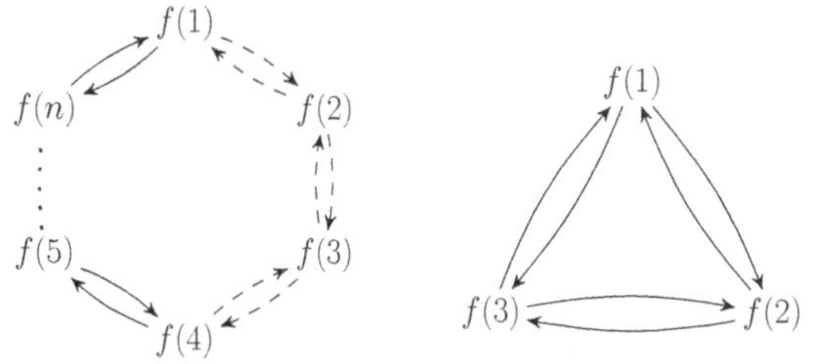

Figure 5: The undirected cycle of length n on the left side, and of length 3 on the right side.

We now take J to be the subinstance of $core(chase(I_n, \sigma))$ consisting of the dashed edges on the left side of Figure 5 (i.e., 6 R-atoms denoted by the 6 dashed arcs). Intuitively, the definition of bounded anchor requires us to find a "small" source instance I' that gives rise to a connected J' of size at least $|J| = 6$ such that J' is contained in $core(chase(I', \sigma))$. Here, "small" means that the size of I' may depend on the size of J but not on n. Now observe that no such small source instance can be constructed using the atoms of I_n: if I' is *any* proper subinstance of I_n, then $core(chase(I', \sigma))$ is just an undirected R-edge. However, we can meet the requirements in the definition of bounded anchor by taking $I' = I_3$ (note that for each $n > 3$, $I_3 \not\subseteq I_n$ holds). Indeed, $core(chase(I_3, \sigma))$ is the undirected cycle of size 3, as depicted on the right side of Figure 5. $\triangleleft$

Note that Example 4.8 yields a counter-example to a step in the proof of correctness of the algorithm in Theorem 5.2 in [4], where the search for I' and J' was confined to subsets of the given instances I and J.

Example 4.8 also illustrates that it is not always easy to find a bounded anchor. However, we show next that the class of nested tgds indeed has effective bounded anchor.

Theorem 4.9 *The class of nested GLAV mappings has effective bounded anchor.*

Proof (Idea). Given I and J, we first construct an overestimation I_b and J_b, where J_b fulfills the lower bound of the bounded anchor definition, but I_b is too large. Intuitively, this J_b is of the size of the f-block B in which the connected subinstance J is contained. From this overestimation, we compute an underestimation I_0 and J_0, where I_0 fulfills the upper bound of the bounded anchor definition, but J_0 is too small. I_0 and J_0 are, respectively, the canonical source and target instances of a k-pattern from which the pattern of J_b can be obtained by cloning of subtrees. Here, k is defined as in the procedure IMPLIES in Section 3. From this underestimation, we compute our final I' and J' according to the definition of bounded anchor by a suitable cloning of subtrees. Based on the ideas underpinning the proof of Theorem 3.1, J' can be shown to satisfy the required properties of an anchor. $\square$

The computation of the function for the effective bounded anchor in the preceding Theorem 4.9, as well as the function witnessing effective threshold in Theorem 4.4, utilize the concept of a k-pattern introduced in Section 3. Hence, by the considerations in Section 3, we have that both are non-elementary in the depth of the nested tgd.

Having shown that the class of nested GLAV mappings has effective bounded anchor, we can now prove that Claim 4.5 indeed holds for the class of nested GLAV mappings.

Theorem 4.10 *Let $\mathcal{C}$ be a class of schema mappings that has effective bounded anchor. Then the following problem is decidable: given a schema mapping $\mathcal{M}$ in $\mathcal{C}$ and a positive integer b, is the f-block size of $\mathcal{M}$ at most b?*

Proof (Sketch). Let a be a witness of the bounded anchor of $\mathcal{M}$. We test for all source instances I with $|I| \leq a(b+1)$ whether the f-block size of $core(chase(I, \Sigma))$ is at most b. There are finitely many such instances (up to isomorphism) and each test itself is decidable by computing and inspecting the core. If at least one of these tests returns an f-block size greater than b, we return that the f-block size is greater than b. Otherwise, we return that the f-block size is at most b. $\square$

Now, by exploiting the fact that nested GLAV mappings have both effective threshold and effective bounded anchor, there is an algorithm for deciding whether the f-block size of a nested GLAV mapping is bounded.

Theorem 4.11 *Let $\mathcal{C}$ be a class of schema mappings having both effective threshold for f-block size and effective bounded anchor. Then the following problem is decidable: given a schema mapping $\mathcal{M}$ in $\mathcal{C}$, does $\mathcal{M}$ have bounded f-block size?*

Proof Let f be the recursive function providing the effective threshold for f-block size for schema mappings in $\mathcal{C}$. Consider the following algorithm: given a mapping $\mathcal{M}$ in $\mathcal{C}$, compute the bound $b = f(\mathcal{M})$ for the effective threshold for f-block size. Since $\mathcal{C}$ has effective bounded anchor, we can use the algorithm in Theorem 4.10 to test whether $\mathcal{M}$ has f-block size bounded by b. If it does, we return that $\mathcal{M}$ has bounded f-block size; otherwise, we return that $\mathcal{M}$ has unbounded f-block size. $\square$

By assembling all the preceding machinery, we can now prove the main result of this section.

Proof of Theorem 4.2 By Theorem 4.4 and Theorem 4.9, the class of nested GLAV mappings has both effective threshold for f-block size and effective bounded anchor. Therefore, by Theorem 4.11, the following problem is decidable: given a nested GLAV mapping, does it have bounded f-block size? Thus, together with Theorem 4.1, we get the decidability result stated in Theorem 4.2. $\square$

4.2 Plain SO tgds vs. Nested GLAV Mappings

We have just seen that there is an algorithm to differentiate between nested GLAV mappings and GLAV mappings. It is not known, however, whether there is an algorithm to differentiate between plain SO tgds and nested GLAV mappings. In other words, it is not known whether or not the

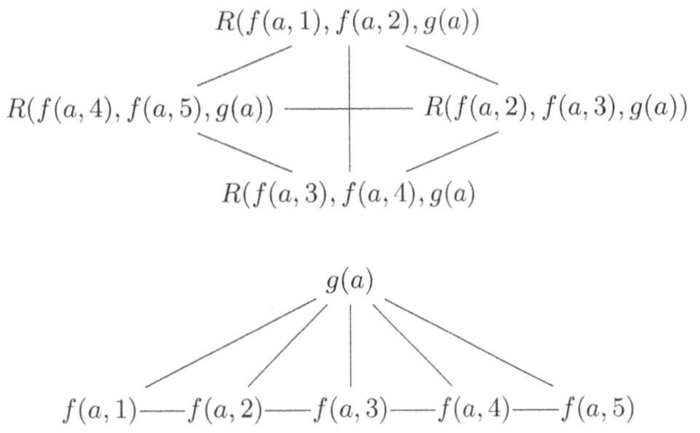

Figure 6: Gaifman graph of facts (top) and Gaifman graph of nulls (bottom) of Example 4.14 for a successor relation of length 5.

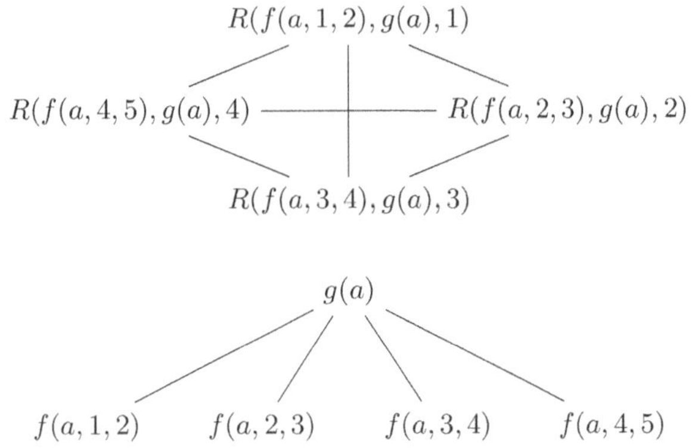

Figure 7: Gaifman graph of facts (top) and Gaifman graph of nulls (bottom) of Example 4.15 for a successor relation of length 5.

following problem is decidable: given a plain SO tgd σ, is there a nested GLAV mapping $\mathcal{M}$ such that σ is logically equivalent to $\mathcal{M}$?

What tools are there for showing that a particular plain SO tgd σ is not logically equivalent to any nested GLAV mapping? Since plain SO tgds are expressible in second-order logic while nested GLAV mappings are expressible in first-order logic, it suffices to show that σ is not first-order expressible. The standard method for doing this are Ehrenfeucht-Fraïssé games or locality methods (see [15]). In fact, essentially this method is behind the proof in [2] that the plain SO tgd

$$\exists f\, \forall x \forall y\, (S(x,y) \to R(f(x), f(y)))$$

is not logically equivalent to any nested GLAV mapping. In what follows, we take a totally different approach and give two different sufficient conditions for showing that a given SO tgd is not logically equivalent to any nested GLAV mapping. The idea behind these conditions is as follows. Suppose we suspect that a given plain SO tgd σ is not logically equivalent to any nested GLAV mapping. In this case, σ is not equivalent to any GLAV mapping either and, hence, σ has unbounded f-block size by Theorem 4.1. Now, a schema mapping may have unbounded f-block size for a number of different reasons. However, we will show that a nested GLAV mapping can have unbounded f-block size only for certain specific reasons that are not shared by all plain SO tgds. Therefore, if the given SO tgd σ falls in one of these categories, then we can conclude that indeed σ is not logically equivalent to any nested GLAV mapping.

Before stating the first result of this section, we need to relativize the notion of bounded f-block size to a class of source instances.

Assume that $\mathcal{M}$ is a schema mapping specified by an SO tgd and $\mathcal{C}$ is a class of source instances. We say that $\mathcal{M}$ has *bounded f-block size on* $\mathcal{C}$ if there is a positive integer b such that for every source instance I in $\mathcal{C}$, the f-block size of *core*(*chase*($I, \mathcal{M}$)) is at most b; otherwise, we say that $\mathcal{M}$ has *unbounded f-block size on* $\mathcal{C}$. Clearly, $\mathcal{M}$ has bounded f-block size if it has bounded f-block size on the class of all source instances.

If G is an undirected graph and v is a node of G, then the *degree of* v is the number of edges incident to v. The *degree of* G is the maximum degree of its nodes. We say that a schema mapping has *bounded f-degree on* $\mathcal{C}$ if there is a positive integer d such that for every source instance I in $\mathcal{C}$, the degree of every f-block of *core*(*chase*($I, \mathcal{M}$)) is at most d; otherwise, we say that $\mathcal{M}$ has *unbounded f-degree on* $\mathcal{C}$.

Theorem 4.12 *Let $\mathcal{M}$ be a nested GLAV mapping and $\mathcal{C}$ a class of source instances. Then $\mathcal{M}$ has bounded f-block size on $\mathcal{C}$ if and only if $\mathcal{M}$ has bounded f-degree on $\mathcal{C}$.*

Informally, the preceding theorem asserts that nested tgds can achieve unbounded f-block size on a class of source instances only because some null value appears unboundedly often in the core of the universal solutions of such instances. In contrast, plain SO tgds can achieve unbounded f-block size in more complex ways, as evidenced by the next result.

Proposition 4.13 *There is a plain SO tgd τ and a class $\mathcal{C}$ of source instances such that τ has unbounded f-block size on $\mathcal{C}$, but bounded f-degree on $\mathcal{C}$.*

Proof Let τ be the plain SO tgd

$$\exists f\, \forall x \forall y\, (S(x,y) \to R(f(x), f(y)))$$

and let $\mathcal{C}$ be the class of all source instances I such that S is a successor relation. If $I \in \mathcal{C}$, then *core*(*chase*(I, τ)) consists of a single f-block of the same size as S in which no null occurs more than twice. Thus, the f-block size of τ on $\mathcal{C}$ is unbounded, but the f-degree of τ on $\mathcal{C}$ is 2. □

It follows that the plain SO tgd τ in Proposition 4.13 is not logically equivalent to any nested GLAV mapping. Altogether, f-degree is an easy-to-use tool for showing that a schema mapping is not logically equivalent to a nested GLAV mapping. However, it is not always sufficient for dealing with for more complex schema mappings, as the next example shows.

Example 4.14 Consider the following plain SO tgd σ:

$$\exists f\, \forall x \forall y \forall z\, (S(x,y) \wedge Q(z) \to R(f(z,x), f(z,y), g(z)))$$

It will turn out that σ is not logically equivalent to any nested GLAV mapping. However, it is easy to see that each f-block is a clique, which implies that for every class $\mathcal{C}$ of source instances, σ has unbounded f-block size on $\mathcal{C}$ if and only if it has unbounded f-degree on $\mathcal{C}$. For example, if $\mathcal{C}$

is the class of source instances in which S is a successor relation and Q is a singleton, then each f-block is a clique of the form depicted in the upper part of of Figure 6. Thus, Theorem 4.12 cannot be used to show that σ is not logically equivalent to any finite set of nested tgds. $\triangleleft$

The preceding example shows that, in addition to Theorem 4.12, a different structural tool is needed to differentiate between plain SO tgds and nested GLAV mappings. To appreciate how delicate this differentiation can be, we note that a plain SO tgd and a nested tgd may have the same f-blocks on some classes of instances, yet the plain SO tgd is not logically equivalent to any finite set of nested tgds.

Example 4.15 Consider the following plain SO tgd σ':

$$\exists f \exists g \, \forall x \forall y \forall z \, (S(x,y) \wedge Q(z) \rightarrow R(f(z,x,y), g(z), x))$$

This dependency is logically equivalent to the following nested tgd:

$$\forall z \, (Q(z) \rightarrow \exists u \, (\forall x \forall y \, (S(x,y) \rightarrow \exists v \, R(v,u,x))))$$

For the source instances in which S is a successor relation, the f-blocks are the same as those for the plain SO tgd σ in Example 4.14, i.e., they are complete graphs (see Figure 6 and 7). Yet, as we are about to discover, σ is not logically equivalent to any finite set of nested tgds. $\triangleleft$

To cope with this situation, we need to look beyond the Gaifman graph of facts. Recall that the Gaifman graph of facts (in short, fact graph) is the graph whose nodes are the facts and there is an edge between two facts if they share a null. Let J be a target instance. The Gaifman graph of nulls of J (in short, null graph), is the graph whose nodes are the nulls of J, and there is an edge between two nulls if they occur in the same fact in J.

It turns out that properties of the null graph can be used to show inexpressibility in situations where the structure of the fact graph is of no help. More formally, the *path length* of an undirected graph G is the length of the longest simple path in G, where a simple path is a path that visits each node in G at most once. We say that a schema mapping $\mathcal{M}$ specified by an SO tgd has *bounded path length* if there is a positive integer l such that for every source instance I, the path length of the null graph of $core(chase(I, \mathcal{M}))$ is at most l; otherwise, we say that $\mathcal{M}$ has *unbounded path length.*

Theorem 4.16 *Every nested GLAV mapping has bounded path length.*

Equipped with Theorem 4.16, we now have a tool to show that the plain SO tgd σ of Example 4.14 is not logically equivalent to any nested GLAV mapping. This is so because σ has unbounded path length, which can be checked using successor relations in S as source instances (see the bottom part of Figure 6, where the null graph contains a simple path of length 4).

5. Adding Source Constraints

In the previous section, we showed that it is decidable whether a schema mapping based on nested tgds is equivalent to a GLAV mapping. The decidability of whether an SO tgd is equivalent to a GLAV mapping is still open. In this section, we give evidence that the problem may indeed be harder for SO tgds: It is undecidable whether a plain SO tgd is equivalent to a GLAV mapping in the presence of a single source key dependency. In contrast, for nested tgds and in the presence of arbitrary source egds, equivalence to GLAV is still decidable. Completing the picture, we also show that the implication problem of nested tgds discussed in Section 3 remains decidable in the presence of source egds.

Recall that Theorem 4.1 reduces the problem of whether a plain SO tgd is equivalent to a GLAV mapping to the problem of deciding whether it has bounded f-block size. This theorem, which is derived from Proposition 3.14 and Theorem 4.10 in [6], thus played an important role in Section 4. A close inspection of the proofs of Proposition 3.14 and Theorem 4.10 in [6] shows that these results (and therefore Theorem 4.1) still hold in the presence of source egds. We make use of this fact below.

Theorem 5.1 *It is undecidable whether a given plain SO tgd is equivalent to a GLAV mapping in the presence of a single source key dependency.*

Proof (Idea). By the above comments it suffices to show the undecidability of the problem if, given a plain SO tgd and a source key dependency, the mapping has bounded f-block size. Our proof is by reduction from the halting problem.

Thus for a given Turing machine, we construct an SO tgd that "simulates" the computation of the Turing machine. The basic structure for our construction is to represent a run of a Turing machine (state and tape configurations) together with a successor relation in the source instance. We construct a key dependency to ensure that in the supposed successor relation, each element has a unique predecessor. The SO tgd then guarantees that the f-block size is bounded if and only if the Turing machine halts.

The particular challenge of this reduction is how to handle incorrect and missing information in the source instance. For incorrect information, we define "guards" that lead to a collapse of f-block size. The more problematic part is missing information, for which we define a specific one-dimensional enumeration of the two-dimensional (time and tape space) structure of the Turing machine's run in the target. When we reach a certain point of this enumeration, we know that no essential information is missing up to that point.

The final challenge is how to handle the effects of unintended structure of the successor relation given in the source instance. While the single key dependency gives us some control over the structure, we define "traps" that address the effects of deviating from the successor relation in the target in ways not handled by that single key dependency. □

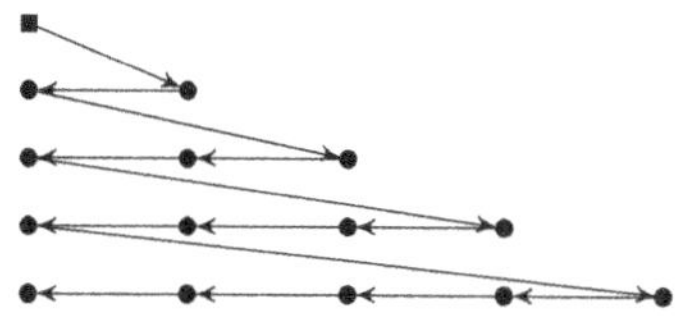

Figure 8: Intended enumeration represented in the target instance. Arrows denote N atoms.

Missing Information. To give a bit of the flavor of the construction in the proof of Theorem 5.1, we highlight one of the main challenges, namely how to handle missing information. The enumeration of the configurations we materialize in the target instance is illustrated in Figure 8. The vertical axis represents time and the horizontal axis the tape. Note that it is only necessary to represent this triangular part of the configuration matrix, as a Turing machine can in, e.g., 4 steps in time at most reach the 4th tape cell.

The first key fact about this enumeration is that it uses the successor relation, both in space and in time, only in one direction (the "backwards" direction). This is necessary because with a single key dependency we can only guarantee that one direction allows correct navigation (in our case, we guarantee unique predecessors). The only other navigation step we can ensure to be correct is "jumping to the diagonal" (the time and space index coincide) as illustrated by the diagonal arrows in Figure 8.

What we have to show is that we can indeed, using the successor relation only in correct ways, generate this enumeration using SO tgds. Assume that S represents a successor relation and Z represents the initial element ("'zero") of that successor relation. During the construction, we define an abbreviation $check_{\pi_{good}}[x, y]$ that checks whether the Turing machine at time instant x and at tape position y represents a certain locally correct (π_{good}) configuration. It is a complex definition that does not give major insights, so we do not give it here. The crucial parts are the following two plain SO tgds:

$check_{\pi_{good}}[x, y] \wedge S(y, y') \rightarrow N(f(x, y'), f(x, y))$
$check_{\pi_{good}}[x', x'] \wedge S(x, x') \wedge Z(y) \rightarrow N(f(x, y), f(x', x'))$

The first SO tgd realizes the $\leftarrow$ step in Figure 8, while the second SO tgd realizes the $\searrow$ step (which can be seen by the term $f(x', x')$, the "diagonal"). Note that they are mutually exclusive as one checks for a predecessor via S, and the other one for the initial element using Z.

To sum up, while each step in the enumeration guarantees that locally the configuration is correct, the full unbroken enumeration thus guarantees that globally, the computation of the Turing machine is correct. In particular, if we have missing information, the enumeration will break. Finally, recall that we are interested in the f-block size. What our construction ensures through appropriate graph gadgets is that a part of the enumeration that is not connected to the origin (the square node in Figure 8) will collapse in the core, thus not contribute to the f-block size.

The Turing machine construction of Theorem 5.1 can be used to give an alternative proof of the undecidability of the equivalence of plain SO-tgds in the presence of source key dependencies, which was originally shown in [9] by a reduction from the domino problem.

Also, we note that the SO tgd simulating a Turing machine computation can produce a core with f-blocks of arbitrary size but with bounded f-degree if the Turing machine does not halt. In this case, by Theorem 4.12, the SO tgd cannot be equivalent to a nested GLAV mapping. This immediately gives us the following undecidability result:

Theorem 5.2 *It is undecidable whether a given plain SO tgd is equivalent to a nested GLAV mapping in the presence of a single source key dependency.*

Nested tgds. We now show that in contrast, the problem of deciding whether a set of nested tgds is equivalent to a GLAV mapping is decidable even in the presence of source egds.

The proof strategy of Theorem 4.2 is still valid, namely showing that the class of schema mappings has (1) effective threshold, (2) effective bounded anchor as well as that (3) a mapping is logically equivalent to a GLAV mapping iff f-block size is bounded. We already mentioned that (3) still holds in the presence of source egds. It thus remains to show that also (1) and (2) hold if source egds are allowed.

We now show that nested tgds have effective threshold for f-block size also in the presence of source egds. However, a straightforward extension of Theorem 4.4 is not possible, as the following example illustrates.

Example 5.3 Consider the following nested tgd σ:

$$\forall z\, (Q(z) \rightarrow \exists y\, \forall x_1 \forall x_2 \\ (P_1(z, x_1) \wedge P_2(z, x_2) \rightarrow R(y, x_1, x_2)))$$

and the set Σ_s of source dependencies given by

$$P_1(z, x_1) \wedge P_1(z, x_1') \rightarrow x_1 = x_1'$$

Now consider the source instance I given as

$$\{Q(a), P_1(a, b), P_2(a, b), P_2(a, c)\}$$

The proof of Theorem 4.4 depends on "cloning" parts of the source instance. Intuitively, in our example this means constructing a source instance $I' = I \cup I[b \mapsto d]$, where $[b \mapsto d]$ denotes replacing all occurrences of b by d. That is, we have $I' = I \cup \{Q(a), P_1(a, d), P_2(a, d), P_2(a, c)\}$. But while both I and $I[b \mapsto d]$ satisfy Σ_s, the combined instance I' does not. Indeed, $\{P_1(a, b), P_1(a, d)\}$ violates Σ_s. ◁

Still, it is possible to show effective threshold also in this case. The key tool for this result and further results in this section is an adapted notion of canonical instances that takes source dependencies into account.

Definition 5.4 Consider a nested tgd σ defined for the source schema **S** and a target schema **T**, such that a set of integrity constraints Σ_s consisting of egds is associated with **S**. Given a pattern p of a chase tree with σ, we define the *legal canonical source resp. target instances* I_p^s, J_p^s as the instances obtained from the canonical source resp. target instances I_p and J_p of σ and p as follows: I_p^s results from chasing I_p with Σ_s, and J_p^s results from J_p by enforcing all equalities between constants of I_p implemented in I_p^s. ◁

Similarly to the case without source dependencies, we speak of *the* legal canonical source resp. target instances, since irrespectively of the choice of constants used to produce such instances, they are unique up to constant renaming. We are now able to show our desired result.

Theorem 5.5 *The class of nested tgds with source egds has effective threshold for f-block size.*

Proof (Idea). This is shown by adapting the proof of Theorem 4.4 through using legal canonical instances. Additional claims are needed to show that the equalities present in a legal canonical target instance do not interfere with the "cloning" process needed to increase the f-block size. □

Furthermore, the argumentation in the proof of Theorem 4.9 that nested tgds have effective bounded anchor still holds in the presence of source egds, by using legal canonical instances. We can thus extend Theorem 4.2:

Theorem 5.6 *It is decidable whether a given nested GLAV mapping is equivalent to a GLAV mapping in the presence of source egds.*

Finally, we show that also the implication problem remains decidable in the presence of source egds.

Theorem 5.7 *The implication problem for nested tgds is decidable in the presence of source egds.*

Proof (Idea). It turns out that in the presence of source egds, all results of Section 3 required to show the correctness of the procedure IMPLIES remain valid, with the provision that legal canonical instances are used instead of canonical instances. The adaptations necessary to ensure correctness complicate the proof considerably, but the intuition behind the machinery introduced in Section 3 persists. □

This result clearly separates the complexity of reasoning tasks for nested and plain SO tgds, since as shown in [9], equivalence — and thus also implication — of plain SO tgds is undecidable even in the presence of a single source key dependency.

6. Concluding Remarks

In this paper, we initiated the study of fundamental reasoning tasks and structural properties of nested tgds. On the positive side, we showed that the following problems are decidable: the implication problem (and hence the equivalence problem) of nested tgds, and the problem of deciding whether a given nested GLAV mapping is equivalent to some GLAV mapping. We also showed that these problems remain decidable even if source egds are allowed. In contrast, we established that the problem whether a given plain SO tgd is equivalent to some GLAV mapping becomes undecidable as soon as a single key dependency is allowed in the source schema.

For future work, the decidability of the equivalence problem for plain SO tgds and of the problem of determining whether a given plain SO tgd is equivalent to some GLAV mapping (resp. to some nested GLAV mapping) remains open. Moreover, the aforementioned decidability results for nested tgds call for further study: all of our decidability results depend on the notion of k-patterns introduced in Section 3. As pointed out in that section, the number of k-patterns and the maximum size of k-patterns for a given nested tgd are non-elementary in the depth of the nested tgd, and so are all algorithms utilizing patterns. It is worth investigating whether this high complexity is inherent in these problems or more efficient algorithms can be designed.

Another important direction for future research is concerned with structural characterizations of schema mappings along the lines of [17]. In this paper, we discovered necessary conditions (via the notions of unbounded f-degree and bounded path length) of schema mappings that are logically equivalent to some nested GLAV mapping. These properties sometimes provide an easy argument for telling apart plain SO tgds from nested GLAV mappings. It remains open whether these properties can be extended to a sufficient condition for the expressibility by a finite set of nested tgds. For instance, are all plain SO tgds with unbounded f-degree and/or bounded path length equivalent to a nested GLAV mapping? A structural characterization of plain SO tgds (raised in [2]) also remains an interesting open problem.

Acknowledgements. Kolaitis' research on this paper was partially supported by NSF Grant IIS-1217869. The research of Pichler, Sallinger, and Savenkov was supported by the Austrian Science Fund (FWF):P25207-N23.

7. References

[1] M. Arenas, P. Barceló, L. Libkin, and F. Murlak. *Relational and XML Data Exchange*. 2010.

[2] M. Arenas, J. Pérez, J. Reutter, and C. Riveros. The language of plain SO-tgds: Composition, inversion and structural properties. *JCSS*, 79(6):763 – 784, 2013.

[3] M. Arenas, J. Pérez, and C. Riveros. The recovery of a schema mapping: Bringing exchanged data back. *ACM TODS*, 34(4), 2009.

[4] R. Fagin and P. G. Kolaitis. Local transformations and conjunctive-query equivalence. In *PODS*, pages 179–190, 2012.

[5] R. Fagin, P. G. Kolaitis, R. J. Miller, and L. Popa. Data Exchange: Semantics and Query Answering. *TCS*, 336(1):89–124, 2005.

[6] R. Fagin, P. G. Kolaitis, A. Nash, and L. Popa. Towards a theory of schema-mapping optimization. In *PODS*, pages 33–42, 2008.

[7] R. Fagin, P. G. Kolaitis, and L. Popa. Data Exchange: Getting to the Core. *ACM TODS*, 30(1):174–210, 2005.

[8] R. Fagin, P. G. Kolaitis, L. Popa, and W. C. Tan. Composing schema mappings: Second-order dependencies to the rescue. *ACM TODS*, 30(4):994–1055, 2005.

[9] I. Feinerer, R. Pichler, E. Sallinger, and V. Savenkov. On the undecidability of the equivalence of second-order tuple generating dependencies. In *AMW*, 2011.

[10] A. Fuxman, M. A. Hernández, C. T. H. Ho, R. J. Miller, P. Papotti, and L. Popa. Nested mappings: Schema mapping reloaded. In *VLDB*, pages 67–78, 2006.

[11] P. Hell and J. Nešetřil. The Core of a Graph. *Discrete Mathematics*, 109:117–126, 1992.

[12] M. A. Hernández, H. Ho, L. Popa, A. Fuxman, R. J. Miller, T. Fukuda, and P. Papotti. Creating nested mappings with Clio. In *ICDE*, pages 1487–1488, 2007.

[13] P. G. Kolaitis, M. Lenzerini, and N. Schweikardt, editors. *Data Exchange, Integration, and Streams*, volume 5 of *Dagstuhl Follow-Ups*. Schloss Dagstuhl - Leibniz-Zentrum für Informatik, 2013.

[14] M. Lenzerini. Data Integration: A Theoretical Perspective. In *PODS*, pages 233–246, 2002.

[15] L. Libkin. *Elements of Finite Model Theory*. Springer, 2004.

[16] J. Madhavan and A. Y. Halevy. Composing mappings among data sources. In *VLDB*, pages 572–583, 2003.

[17] B. ten Cate and P. G. Kolaitis. Structural characterizations of schema-mapping languages. In *ICDT*, pages 63–72, 2009.

Does Query Evaluation Tractability Help Query Containment?

Pablo Barceló
Department of Computer Science, Universidad de Chile
pbarcelo@dcc.uchile.cl

Miguel Romero
Department of Computer Science, Universidad de Chile
mromero@dcc.uchile.cl

Moshe Y. Vardi
Department of Computer Science, Rice University
vardi@cs.rice.edu

ABSTRACT

While checking containment of Datalog programs is undecidable, checking whether a Datalog program is contained in a union of conjunctive queries (UCQ), in the context of relational databases, or a union of conjunctive 2-way regular path queries (UC2RPQ), in the context of graph databases, is decidable. The complexity of these problems is, however, prohibitive: 2EXPTIME-complete. We investigate to which extent restrictions on UCQs and UC2RPQs, which have been known to reduce the complexity of query containment for these classes, yield a more "manageable" single-exponential time bound, which is the norm for several static analysis and verification tasks.

Checking containment of a UCQ Θ' in a UCQ Θ is NP-hard, in general, but better bounds can be obtained if Θ is restricted to belong to a *tractable* class of UCQs, e.g., a class of bounded treewidth or hypertreewidth. Also, each Datalog program Π is equivalent to an infinite union of CQs. This motivated us to study the question of whether restricting Θ to belong to a tractable class also helps alleviate the complexity of checking whether Π is contained in Θ.

We study such question in detail and show that the situation is much more delicate than expected: First, tractability of UCQs does not help in general, but further restricting Θ to be acyclic and have a bounded number of shared variables between atoms yields better complexity bounds. As corollaries, we obtain that checking containment of Π in Θ is in EXPTIME if Θ is of treewidth one, or it is acyclic and the arity of the schema is fixed. In the case of UC2RPQs we show an EXPTIME bound when queries are acyclic and have a bounded number of edges connecting pairs of variables. As a corollary, we obtain that checking whether Π is contained in UC2RPQ Γ is in EXPTIME if Γ is a strongly acyclic UC2RPQ. Our positive results for UCQs and UC2RPQs are optimal, in a sense, since slightly extending the conditions turns the problem 2EXPTIME-complete.

Categories and Subject Descriptors

H.2.3 [**Database Management**]: Languages—*Query Languages*

SIGMOD/PODS'14, June 22–27, 2014, Salt Lake City, UT, USA.
Copyright ACM 978-1-4503-2375-8/14/06?$15.00.
http://dx.doi.org/10.1145/2594538.2594553.

Keywords

Containment; conjunctive queries; datalog; conjunctive regular path queries; tree automata.

1. INTRODUCTION

Query containment is a basic static analysis task that amounts to check whether the evaluation of a query q is necessarily contained in the evaluation of another query q' (often written as $q \subseteq q'$). Several database tasks crucially depend on the ability to check query containment; these include, e.g., query optimization, view-based query answering, querying incomplete databases, integrity checking, and implication of dependencies: cf. [6, 11, 20, 22, 23, 27].

Checking containment between queries is difficult computationally. For instance, the containment problem is undecidable for queries expressible in first-order logic (FO), and, thus, for any relational language that contains FO (such as SQL). Decidability results can be obtained for syntactically restricted classes of FO formulas. In the context of databases, the most important such restriction is defined by the class of conjunctive queries (CQs), or, equivalently, the expressions defined by the select-project-join operators of relational algebra. It follows from the seminal work of Chandra and Merlin [10] that CQ containment and CQ evaluation are polynomially equivalent problems and both are NP-complete. The NP upper bound is not affected if we extend the language to also consider unions of CQs (UCQs).

Extending the class of UCQs with recursion yields the important language of Datalog, which has gained renewed attention in the last years due to its applications in areas such as distributed computing, ontological reasoning, cluster computing, graph databases, and data exchange (cf. [19, 2] for a broad description of current applications of Datalog in academia and industry). This extension, however, has a crucial drawback: the containment problem for Datalog is undecidable [33]. This has motivated the search for relevant restrictions of the problem that can be effectively decided, ideally at a reasonable computational cost.

Since containment for UCQs is decidable, a natural restriction of the Datalog containment problem is when one of the two queries is a UCQ. This actually yields positive results in any of the two possible cases: Checking whether a UCQ Θ is contained in a Datalog program Π is EXPTIME-complete [16], while the opposite, deciding whether the Datalog program Π is contained in the UCQ Θ, is 2EXPTIME-complete [12]. From this we obtain that the important problem of checking whether the recursive program Π is equivalent to the nonrecursive (and, thus, typically easier to evaluate and optimize) query Θ can be solved in 2EXPTIME.

While the decidability of containment of Datalog in UCQs is of theoretical importance, it is impractical due to the unavoidable double exponential cost. In addition, the 2EXPTIME lower bound holds even for UCQs of fixed arity, and, therefore, it implies "real" intractability. This raised the interest in identifying which parameters of the input affect its complexity. In particular, Chaudhuri and Vardi [13] and Benedikt et al. [5] performed a fine analysis of the complexity of the problem for restricted classes of Datalog programs (e.g. monadic, linear, single-rule and non-persistent programs), identifying cases that lead to better bounds.

In this paper we study the opposite question: To what extent is it possible to obtain more practical bounds for the problem by restricting the syntactic shape of UCQs, while retaining the full expressive power of Datalog programs? Our goal is identifying relevant restrictions on UCQs for which the double-exponential time procedure from [12] can be replaced by a more "acceptable" single-exponential time one, which is the norm in many static analysis and verification questions [28, 30].

Consider first the problem of checking whether $\theta \subseteq \theta'$ for CQs θ and θ'. This problem is NP-complete, but it follows from [10] that it can be solved efficiently if θ' belongs to a *tractable* class of CQs; that is, a class of CQs whose evaluation problem can be solved in polynomial time. Due to a flurry of activity in the last two decades, we have by now a fairly complete picture of what these classes are:

1. Chekuri and Rajaraman [14] (see also [18]) proved that each level of the hierarchy

$$\mathsf{TW}(1) \subset \mathsf{TW}(2) \subset \cdots \subset \mathsf{TW}(k) \subset \cdots,$$

where $\mathsf{TW}(k)$ is the set of CQs of *treewidth* at most k, is tractable. Treewidth is a well-studied notion that provides a measure for the *tree-likeness* of a CQ.

2. The treewidth of a CQ is defined in terms of its *underlying graph*, but this is too restrictive when the schema is not fixed. In such case, it is more convenient to measure the tree-likeness of a CQ in terms of its underlying *hypergraph*. Gottlob et al. [24] identified an appropriate correlate of treewidth in this context – called *hypertreewidth* – and proved that each level of the hierarchy

$$\mathsf{HW}(1) \subset \mathsf{HW}(2) \subset \cdots \subset \mathsf{HW}(k) \subset \cdots,$$

where $\mathsf{HW}(k)$ corresponds to the class of CQs of *hypertreewidth* at most k, is tractable. Interestingly, the first level of this hierarchy, $\mathsf{HW}(1)$, corresponds to the well-known class AC of *acyclic* CQs [36]. (See [25] for some extensions of this line of work.)

We can easily extend these two notions to UCQs: A UCQ Θ is in $\mathsf{TW}(k)$ (resp. $\mathsf{HW}(k)$) iff each one of the CQs in Θ is in $\mathsf{TW}(k)$ (resp. $\mathsf{HW}(k)$). Tractability results for query evaluation and containment extend to these classes [31].

Returning to the problem of checking containment of a Datalog program Π in a UCQ Θ, it is well-known that each Datalog program Π is equivalent to an *infinite* union $\bigcup_{i\geq 1} \theta_i$ of (uniformly generated) CQs, and, therefore, checking if $\Pi \subseteq \Theta$ amounts to checking if $\bigcup_{i\geq 1} \theta_i \subseteq \Theta$. Restricting Θ to belong to one of the tractable classes $\mathsf{TW}(k)$ and $\mathsf{HW}(k)$ reduces the complexity of containment when the left-hand side of the containment problem is a *finite* union of CQs. So far, however, the question of whether such restriction also helps alleviate the cost of checking containment of the infinite union $\bigcup_{i\geq 1} \theta_i$ (and, thus, of Π) in Θ has not been addressed. We study this question in depth in this paper.

Somewhat surprisingly, we prove that the situation is more delicate than expected:

1. First, we show that none of the tractable restrictions of UCQs that have been studied to date – save for $\mathsf{TW}(1)$ – helps to reduce the complexity of the Datalog containment problem. That is, checking whether $\Pi \subseteq \Theta$, for Π a Datalog program and Θ a UCQ, continues to be 2EXPTIME-complete even if (a) Θ is of $\mathsf{TW}(2)$, or (b) Θ is in $\mathsf{HW}(1)$, and, thus, acyclic. (This does not follow from known hardness results.)

2. Second, in order to obtain better complexity bounds we have to unveil a finer hierarchy of queries inside the class of acyclic UCQs. This hierarchy is

$$\mathsf{AC}_1 \subset \mathsf{AC}_2 \subset \cdots \subset \mathsf{AC}_k \subset \cdots,$$

where AC_k denotes the class of UCQs Θ in AC such that no two atoms in Θ share more than k variables. We prove that checking $\Pi \subseteq \Theta$, for Θ in AC_k, can be solved in EXPTIME (being complete for this class).

As corollaries, we obtain that checking $\Pi \subseteq \Theta$ can be solved in EXPTIME when Θ is an acyclic UCQ of *fixed* arity and when it is of treewidth 1. These results are optimal, since we prove that checking $\Pi \subseteq \Theta$ is 2EXPTIME-complete, even if Θ is a UCQ in $\mathsf{HW}(2)$ or $\mathsf{TW}(2)$ of *fixed* arity.

In the second part of the paper we switch to study the containment problem over graph databases [1, 35]. The analogue of UCQs in this context are the unions of *conjunctive two-way regular path queries*, UC2RPQs [7], that extend UCQs with the ability to check whether two nodes in a graph database are linked by a path that satisfies a regular condition. Calvanese et al. [8] proved that containment of Datalog in UC2RPQ is still decidable in 2EXPTIME.

Evaluation of UC2RPQs is also NP-complete, but tractability can be obtained by considering the class ACR of *acyclic* UC2RPQs [3]. These are the UC2RPQs whose underlying CQs are acyclic (or, equivalently, of treewidth one, since $\mathsf{AC} = \mathsf{TW}(1)$ over graph databases). Since containment of Datalog in UCQs in $\mathsf{TW}(1)$ can be solved in EXPTIME, it is natural to study whether the restriction to acyclic UC2RPQs also helps alleviate the complexity of the containment problem in this context. We show that, again, the situation is more delicate than expected:

1. First, acyclicity in this case does not help to reduce the complexity. That is, containment of a Datalog program Π in a UC2RPQ Γ is 2EXPTIME-complete, even if Γ is a UC2RPQ in ACR.

2. Again, in order to obtain better complexity bounds we need to unveil the finer structure of the class of acyclic UC2RPQs. In order to do that, we first identify a hierarchy

$$\mathsf{ACR}^1 \subset \mathsf{ACR}^2 \subset \cdots \subset \mathsf{ACR}^k \subset \cdots,$$

where ACR^k is the class of UC2RPQs $\Gamma \in \mathsf{ACR}$ in which each pair of variables is connected by at most k atoms, and then prove that $\Pi \subseteq \Gamma$ can be solved in EXPTIME if Γ belongs to ACR^k, for $k \geq 1$. Queries in ACR^1 have been previously studied in the literature under the name of *strongly* acyclic UC2RPQs [1].

This result is, in a sense, optimal, since containment of Datalog in UC2RPQs Γ of (hyper-)treewidth two is 2EXPTIME-complete, even if each pair of variables in Γ is connected by at most one atom.

Organization. We present preliminaries in Section 2 and tractable classes of UCQs in Section 3. Results on containment of Datalog in tractable UCQs are in Section 4, while Section 5 is devoted to the study of containment of Datalog in acyclic UC2RPQs. We finish in Section 6 with our concluding remarks.

2. PRELIMINARIES

Conjunctive queries. We assume familiarity with relational schemas σ and databases $\mathcal{D}$. Recall that a conjunctive query (CQ) over σ is a logical formula in the $\exists, \wedge$-fragment of FO, i.e., a formula θ of the form

$$\exists \bar{y}(R_1(\bar{x}_1) \wedge \cdots \wedge R_m(\bar{x}_m)),$$

where each $R_i(\bar{x}_i)$ is an atom over σ ($1 \leq i \leq m$). We write $\theta(\bar{x})$ to denote that $\bar{x}$ are the *free* variables of θ, i.e., those that are not mentioned in the tuple $\bar{y}$.

As usual, the semantics of CQs is defined in terms of *homomorphisms*. Formally, a homomorphism h from a CQ θ of the form $\exists \bar{y}(R_1(\bar{x}_1) \wedge \cdots \wedge R_m(\bar{x}_m))$ to a database $\mathcal{D}$ over σ is a mapping from the set of variables that appear in the $\bar{x}_i$'s (for $1 \leq i \leq m$) to the elements of $\mathcal{D}$, such that $R_i(h(\bar{x}_i)) \in \mathcal{D}$ for each $1 \leq i \leq m$. The evaluation of θ over $\mathcal{D}$, denoted $\theta(\mathcal{D})$, consists of the set of all tuples $h(\bar{x})$, for h a homomorphism from θ to $\mathcal{D}$.

A union of CQs (UCQ) Θ over σ is a set $\{\theta_1(\bar{x}), \ldots, \theta_k(\bar{x})\}$ of CQs over σ with the same free variables. We define $\Theta(\mathcal{D})$ to be $\bigcup_{1 \leq j \leq k} \theta_j(\mathcal{D})$, for each database $\mathcal{D}$.

Datalog. Extending UCQs with recursion yields the Datalog language. Formally, a Datalog *program* Π consists of a finite set of rules of the form

$$S(\bar{x}) \leftarrow R_1(\bar{x}_1), \ldots, R_m(\bar{x}_m),$$

where $S(\bar{x})$ and $R_i(\bar{x}_i)$ are atoms, for each $1 \leq i \leq m$, and each variable in $\bar{x}$ appears in some of the $\bar{x}_i$'s ($1 \leq i \leq m$). The atom $S(\bar{x})$ is the *head* of this rule, while its *body* is $R_1(\bar{x}_1), \ldots, R_m(\bar{x}_m)$. We denote by Rels($\Pi$) the set of relation symbols that appear in Π and by IRels(Π) the set of *intensional* relation symbols of Π, i.e., the set of symbols $S \in$ Rels(Π) such that there is an atom of the form $S(\bar{x})$ in the head of some rule in Π.

The semantics of a Datalog program Π is defined as follows. Let $\mathcal{D}$ be a database over Rels(Π). Then $\mathcal{F}(\mathcal{D})$ is a database over Rels(Π) that consists of all facts $S(\bar{t})$ such that Π contains a rule of the form $S(\bar{x}) \leftarrow R_1(\bar{x}_1), \ldots, R_m(\bar{x}_m)$ that satisfies that $\bar{t}$ belongs to the evaluation of the CQ $\theta(\bar{x}) := \exists \bar{y}(R_1(\bar{x}_1) \wedge \cdots \wedge R_m(\bar{x}_m))$ over $\mathcal{D}$. We define the *result of applying* Π *to* $\mathcal{D}$ to be $\mathcal{F}^\infty(\mathcal{D}) := \bigcup_{i \geq 0} \mathcal{F}^i(\mathcal{D})$, where

$$\mathcal{F}^0(\mathcal{D}) := \mathcal{D} \text{ and } \mathcal{F}^{i+1}(\mathcal{D}) := \mathcal{F}(\mathcal{F}^i(\mathcal{D})) \cup \mathcal{F}^i(\mathcal{D}),$$

for $i \geq 0$. Clearly, for every database $\mathcal{D}$ we have $\bigcup_{i \geq 0} \mathcal{F}^i(\mathcal{D}) = \bigcup_{0 \leq i \leq j} \mathcal{F}^i(\mathcal{D})$, for some $j \geq 0$, and, thus, $\mathcal{F}^\infty(\mathcal{D})$ is finite.

A Datalog program Π is *over the schema* σ, if $\sigma =$ Rels(Π) $\setminus$ IRels(Π) and there is a distinguished symbol Q in IRels(Π). If $\mathcal{D}$ is a database over σ, we define the evaluation $\Pi(\mathcal{D})$ of Π over $\mathcal{D}$ to be the set of tuples $\bar{t}$ such that $Q(\bar{t}) \in \mathcal{F}^\infty(\mathcal{D})$ (assuming that the interpretation in $\mathcal{D}$ of each $R \in$ IRels(Π) is empty).

EXAMPLE 1. This example is taken from [29]. Imagine a scenario in which we have compulsive consumers that buy everything they like, plus anything that is trendy in case they have bought something before. The shopping carts of these consumers can be defined by the Datalog program Π_c that consists of rules

$$buys(x, y) \leftarrow likes(x, y)$$
$$buys(x, y) \leftarrow trendy(x), buys(z, y).$$

The program Π_c is over the schema that consists of symbols $trendy$ and $likes$. The distinguished symbol is $buys$. □

Containment of queries. Let q_1 and q_2 be queries over the same schema σ in one of the query languages we introduced before. Then q_1 is *contained* in q_2, denoted $q_1 \subseteq q_2$, if and only if $q_1(\mathcal{D}) \subseteq q_2(\mathcal{D})$ for every database $\mathcal{D}$ over σ. Notice that q_1 is equivalent to q_2 iff $q_1 \subseteq q_2$ and $q_2 \subseteq q_1$.

Let $\mathcal{C}_1$ and $\mathcal{C}_2$ be two classes of queries, e.g. CQs, UCQs, Datalog, or some of the classes we introduce in the paper. We define the containment problem of $\mathcal{C}_1$ in $\mathcal{C}_2$ as follows:

PROBLEM :	CONT($\mathcal{C}_1$,$\mathcal{C}_2$).
INPUT :	Queries $q_1 \in \mathcal{C}_1$ and $q_2 \in \mathcal{C}_2$ over same schema σ.
QUESTION :	Is $q_1 \subseteq q_2$?

We also study the complexity of this problem for schemas of fixed arity. Formally, let c be a positive integer. We then write CONT$_c$($\mathcal{C}_1$,$\mathcal{C}_2$) to denote the restriction of the problem CONT($\mathcal{C}_1$,$\mathcal{C}_2$) to inputs in which the arity of σ is at most c.

Containment of UCQs. It has long been known that containment and evaluation of CQs are polynomially equivalent problems. In fact, let $\theta(\bar{x})$ and $\theta'(\bar{x})$ be CQs over σ and assume that θ is of the form $\exists \bar{y}(R_1(\bar{x}_1), \ldots, R_m(\bar{x}_m))$. Let $\mathcal{D}_\theta$ be the *canonical database* of θ, i.e.,

$$\mathcal{D}_\theta := \{R_i(\bar{x}_i) \mid 1 \leq i \leq m\}.$$

It follows from the seminal work of Chandra and Merlin [10] that $\theta \subseteq \theta'$ iff $\bar{x} \in \theta'(\mathcal{D}_\theta)$. Furthermore, Sagiv and Yannakakis proved that if Θ and Θ' are UCQs, then $\Theta \subseteq \Theta'$ iff for every CQ $\theta \in \Theta$ there exists a CQ $\theta' \in \Theta'$ such that $\theta \subseteq \theta'$ [31]. Since CQ evaluation is NP-complete [10], we obtain the following:

THEOREM 1. [10, 31] CONT(UCQ,UCQ) *is* NP-*complete.*

Containment of Datalog in UCQ. As opposed to the case of UCQs, checking containment for Datalog programs is undecidable [33]. This has motivated the search for relevant restrictions of the problem that can be effectively decided (ideally at a reasonable computational cost). We study in this paper one of the most important of such decidable restrictions: containment of Datalog in UCQs [12], CONT(Datalog,UCQ). In full generality, this is a computationally expensive problem, even for schemas of fixed arity.

THEOREM 2. [12] CONT(Datalog,UCQ) *is in* 2EXPTIME. *There is* $c \geq 1$ *such that the problem* CONT$_c$(Datalog,UCQ) *is* 2EXPTIME-*complete.*

EXAMPLE 2. Consider the compulsive consumers program Π_c from Example 1. It can be shown to be contained (and, in fact, it is equivalent to) the following UCQ:

$$\{likes(x, y),\ \exists z(trendy(x) \wedge likes(z, y))\}. \quad \Box$$

3. TRACTABLE CONTAINMENT FOR UCQ

While in general UCQ containment is an NP-complete problem, we obtain tractability by imposing that UCQs Θ' in the right-hand side of the containment problem belong to a *tractable* class; that is, to a class $\mathcal{C}$ of UCQs for which there is a polynomial time algorithm that given a UCQ $\Theta(\bar{x})$ in $\mathcal{C}$, a database $\mathcal{D}$, and a tuple $\bar{t}$ of the same arity than $\bar{x}$, checks whether $\bar{t} \in \Theta(\mathcal{D})$. Formally:

PROPOSITION 1. [10, 31] *Let* $\mathcal{C}$ *be a tractable class of UCQs. Then* CONT(UCQ,$\mathcal{C}$) *is in* PTIME.

Due to a myriad of papers in the last two decades, we have by now a very good understanding of which classes of UCQs are tractable. These include classes of bounded *treewidth* [14], *hypertreewidth* [24], *generalized* hypertreewidth [24], *fractional* hypertreewidth [25], etc. We concentrate on the first two, which are defined next.

UCQs of bounded treewidth. An important tractable class of UCQs can be obtained by restricting the *treewidth* of the *Gaifman graph* of queries [14]. Formally, the Gaifman graph of a CQ θ of the form $\exists\bar{y}(R_1(\bar{x}_1),\ldots,R_m(\bar{x}_m))$ is the undirected graph G_θ whose nodes are the variables of θ, and there is an edge in G_θ from variable x to x' iff there is $1 \leq i \leq m$ such that both x and x' appear in the tuple $\bar{x}_i$.

A *tree decomposition* of an undirected graph $G = (V, E)$ is a pair (T, λ), where T is a tree and $\lambda : T \to 2^V$, that satisfies the following:

1. For each $v \in V$ the set $\{t \in T \mid v \in \lambda(t)\}$ is a connected subset of T.

2. Each edge of E is contained in one of the sets $\lambda(t)$, for $t \in T$.

The *width* of (T, λ) is $\max(\{|\lambda(t)| \mid t \in T\})-1$. The *treewidth* of G is the minimum width of its tree decompositions. Intuitively, the treewidth of G measures its *tree-likeness*. Notice that G is acyclic iff it is of treewidth one.

The treewidth of the UCQ Θ is the maximum treewidth of G_θ, for $\theta \in \Theta$. We denote by $\mathsf{TW}(k)$ the class of UCQs of treewidth at most k, for $k \geq 1$.

EXAMPLE 3. The CQ $E(x_1,x_2) \wedge \cdots \wedge E(x_{n-1},x_n)$ is in $\mathsf{TW}(1)$, for each $n \geq 3$. In fact, its Gaifman graph is a path, and, thus, acyclic. Adding $E(x_1,x_n)$ increases the treewidth to two. Adding all atoms of the form $E(x_i,x_j)$, for $1 \leq i < j \leq n$, yields a CQ whose Gaifman graph is a clique of size n. The treewidth of this CQ is $n-1$. □

It follows from [14] (see also [18]) that each layer of the hierarchy $\mathsf{TW}(1) \subset \mathsf{TW}(2) \subset \cdots \subset \mathsf{TW}(k) \subset \cdots$ is tractable. From Proposition 1 we thus have:

THEOREM 3. *Let* $k \geq 1$. *Then* CONT(UCQ,TW(k)) *can be solved in* PTIME.

UCQs of bounded hypertreewidth. The notion of treewidth is defined in terms of the Gaifman graph of a CQ, but this is too restrictive when the arity of the schemas is not fixed in advance. In order to overcome this limitation, Gottlob et al. [24] proposed studying syntactic restrictions of the class of CQs based on properties of the *underlying hypergraph* of queries. The analogue of treewidth in this context is the notion of hypertreewidth, which, like the former, leads to tractability of query evaluation. In particular, each layer of the hierarchy $\mathsf{HW}(1) \subset \mathsf{HW}(2) \subset \cdots \subset \mathsf{HW}(k) \subset \cdots$, where $\mathsf{HW}(k)$ is the class of UCQs of hypertreewidth at most k, is tractable [24]. We skip the definition of the $\mathsf{HW}(k)$'s since it is rather technical and not crucial for our purposes (the interested reader can find the definition in [24]).

Since the $\mathsf{HW}(k)$'s are tractable, we obtain from Proposition 1 the tractability of CONT(UCQ,HW(k)):

THEOREM 4. *Let* $k \geq 1$. *Then* CONT(UCQ,HW(k)) *can be solved in* PTIME.

It is important for us to notice that the lowest level $\mathsf{HW}(1)$ of the hierarchy coincides with the well-known class AC of *acyclic* UCQs [36], which admits a simple definition. A UCQ Θ is in AC iff each CQ $\theta \in \Theta$ can be represented as a *join tree* [4]. The latter means that there is a tree T whose nodes are the atoms of θ, such that for each variable x in θ it is the case that the set of nodes in which x is mentioned is a connected subset of T.

The notions of bounded treewidth and acyclicity are incomparable. For instance, consider the class $\mathcal{C} = \{\theta_n \mid n \geq 2\}$, where $\theta_n := \bigwedge_{1\leq i<j\leq n} E(x_i,x_j) \wedge T_n(x_1,\ldots,x_n)$. Each CQ $\theta_n \in \mathcal{C}$ is acyclic; this is witnessed by the join tree T whose root r corresponds to the atom $T_n(x_1,\ldots,x_n)$ and there is a child of r for each atom of the form $E(x_i,x_j)$, for $1 \leq i < j \leq n$. On the other hand, the treewidth of the CQs in $\mathcal{C}$ is not bounded by a constant. Consider now the class $\mathcal{C}$ of queries $\{E(x_1,x_2)\wedge\cdots\wedge E(x_{n-1},x_n)\wedge R(x_1,x_n) \mid n \geq 3\}$. Each CQ in $\mathcal{C}$ is in $\mathsf{TW}(2)$, but no such CQ is acyclic.

4. CONTAINMENT OF DATALOG IN TRACTABLE CLASSES OF UCQS

It is well-known that each Datalog program Π can be expressed as an infinite union $\bigcup_{i\geq 1}\theta_i^\Pi$ of CQs. The θ_i^Π's are called the *expansions* of Π (see, e.g., [29]). Therefore, checking containment of Π in a UCQ Θ reduces to checking containment of the infinite UCQ $\bigcup_{i\geq 1}\theta_i^\Pi$ in Θ. Restricting Θ to belong to one of the tractable classes $\mathsf{TW}(k)$ and $\mathsf{HW}(k)$ reduces the complexity of containment when the left-hand side of the containment problem is a *finite* union of CQs (Theorems 3 and 4). On the other hand, it is not known whether such restriction also helps alleviate the cost of checking containment of the infinite union $\bigcup_{i\geq 1}\theta_i^\Pi$ (and, thus, of Π) in Θ. We show in this section that the situation is much more delicate than expected. But before doing so, it is important to explain how expansions can be represented using *expansion trees*, and how containment of Datalog programs in UCQs can be checked using those expansion trees.

Expansion trees. We quickly recall the notion of (unfolding) expansion tree from [12]. Let Π be a Datalog program over σ with distinguished symbol Q. Then:

1. The nodes of an expansion tree of Π are labeled with instances of rules in Π.

2. The root of an expansion tree of Π is labeled with a rule whose head is of the form $Q(\bar{x})$.

3. For every node u of an expansion tree such that u is labeled ρ and $R_1(\bar{x}_1),\ldots,R_\ell(\bar{x}_\ell)$ are the atoms of the body of ρ over the schema IRels(Π), it is the case that u has exactly ℓ children $u_1,\ldots,u_\ell$ in the expansion tree and each u_j is labeled with an instance ρ_j of a rule in Π whose head is $R_j(\bar{x}_j)$, for $1 \leq j \leq \ell$.

   Therefore, leaves of expansion trees have to be labeled with instances of rules of Π with no intensional atoms.

4. For every node u of an expansion tree labeled ρ, it is the case that every variable y mentioned in the body of ρ either appears in the head of ρ or it does not appear in any node above u in the expansion tree.

   This is a technical condition that ensures that when creating children of nodes in expansion trees in order to unify intensional atoms, only "fresh" instances of rules in Π can be used.

Clearly, the number of different expansion trees of a program Π might be infinite (in particular, when Π is *recursive*).

Each expansion tree τ represents a CQ θ_τ over σ: this is obtained by taking the conjunction of all atoms over σ that label the nodes of τ. Assume that the root of τ is labeled with a rule whose head is $Q(\bar{x})$. Then $\bar{x}$ is the tuple of free variables of θ_τ. The CQs of the form θ_τ, for τ an expansion tree of Π, are precisely the expansions of Π, i.e. the CQs θ_i^Π such that Π is equivalent to $\bigcup_{i\geq 1}\theta_i^\Pi$ [12]. It follows that Π is contained in a UCQ Θ iff for each expansion tree τ of Π with associated CQ $\theta_\tau(\bar{x})$ there is a a CQ $\theta' \in \Theta$ such that $\theta_\tau \subseteq \theta'$, or equivalently, $\bar{x} \in \theta'(\mathcal{D}_{\theta_\tau})$.

This last condition is usually rephrased in terms of the existence of a *containment mapping* from θ' to τ [12], i.e. a mapping μ from the variables of θ' to the variables that label the atoms of τ, such that (i) μ is the identity over $\bar{x}$, and (ii) for each atom $R(\bar{y})$ in θ' it is the case that $R(\mu(\bar{y}))$ appears in the label of a node of τ. Clearly, $\bar{x} \in \theta'(\mathcal{D}_{\theta_\tau})$ iff there is a containment mapping from θ' to τ. Summing up:

PROPOSITION 2. *Let Π be a Datalog program and Θ a UCQ. Then $\Pi \subseteq \Theta$ iff for every expansion tree τ of Π there is a CQ $\theta \in \Theta$ and a containment mapping from θ to τ.*

Several of our proofs rely on this characterization.

4.1 Tractable UCQs are not enough

We show that tractable restrictions on UCQs do not help, in general, to reduce the complexity of CONT(Datalog,UCQ). In particular, we prove that 2EXPTIME-hardness for checking containment of a Datalog program Π in a UCQ Θ holds even if Θ is in $\mathsf{HW}(1) = \mathsf{AC}$, or it is in $\mathsf{TW}(2)$. These negative results are quite resilient: They hold even for UCQs in $\mathsf{TW}(2)$ or $\mathsf{HW}(2)$ over schemas of fixed arity. Formally:

THEOREM 5. *The following problems are* 2EXPTIME*-hard:*

1. CONT(Datalog,AC).
2. CONT$_2$(Datalog,HW(2)).
3. CONT$_2$(Datalog,TW(2)).

None of these results follows from existing hardness results for CONT(Datalog,UCQ) in the literature [5, 12]. Instead, we have to carefully refine the techniques in [12] to obtain these stronger lower bounds. Next, we sketch the proof of 2EXPTIME-hardness for CONT(Datalog,AC).

Proof (Sketch): We reduce from the following 2EXPTIME-complete problem: Given an alternating Turing machine M and a positive integer n, decide whether M accepts the empty tape using 2^n space. Recall that alternating Turing machines M have existential and universal states. We assume w.l.o.g. that (1) the initial state of M is existential, (2) M always alternates between existential and universal states, and (3) every configuration of M has two possible successors, a *left* successor and a *right* successor, defined by two deterministic transitions functions δ^ℓ and δ^r. An accepting computation of M is a tree of configurations, where each configuration is a successor of its parent, a universal configuration has both of its successors as children, and all leaves are accepting.

A configuration of M can be described as a string of length 2^n. The symbols of the string are either symbols of the alphabet or *composite* symbols. A composite symbol is a pair (q, e), where q is a state of M and e is in the alphabet of M. Intuitively, a symbol (q, e) indicates that M is in state q and is scanning the symbol e. It is well known that the successor relation between configurations depends only on local constraints: we can associate with δ^ℓ two ternary relations I^ℓ, F^ℓ and a 4-ary relation B^ℓ on symbols that characterize the left successor relation. If $\bar{a} = a_1 \cdots a_m$ and $\bar{b} = b_1, \cdots, b_m$ are two configurations, then $\bar{b}$ is a left successor of $\bar{a}$ iff $(a_1, a_2, b_1) \in I^\ell$, $(a_{m-1}, a_m, b_m) \in F^\ell$ and $(a_{i-1}, a_i, a_{i+1}, b_i) \in B^\ell$, for each $1 < i < m$. Analogously, we associate with δ^r the relations I^r, F^r and B^r.

We construct a Datalog program Π and a UCQ Θ in AC that encode accepting computations of M. The expansions of Π will correspond to configuration trees, and each disjunct in Θ will detect a particular *error* that prevents an expansion from being an accepting computation. Thus, if an expansion τ does not correspond to an accepting computation, we will have that $\tau \subseteq \Theta$. Therefore, $\Pi \subseteq \Theta$ if and only if the machine M does not accept the empty tape using 2^n space. In our construction, we need to compare corresponding positions in successive configurations in order to detect transition errors. This is achieved by identifying each position in a configuration with an n-bit address.

Schema. The schema of Π and Θ consists of a symbol A of arity $n+8$, a unary symbol $Start$ and a unary symbol Q_s, for each possible symbol s. The intuition behind the predicate A is as follows: (1) The first two arguments of A act as the constants 0 and 1, (2) the third and fourth arguments of A link successive addresses, (3) the next n arguments of A encode the address, (4) the next three arguments of A link successive configurations, and (5) the last argument indicates whether the current configuration is existential or universal.

Program Π. The program Π contains an intensional relation symbol B of arity $n+7$ and a 0-ary distinguished symbol C. Expansion trees of Π correspond to computation trees of M. In an expansion tree, the predicate B propagates the information while it generates atoms of the form $A(x, y, z, z', a_1, \ldots, a_n, u, v, w, t), Q_s(z)$. Intuitively, this represents that, in the current configuration, the position at address $a_1 \cdots a_n$ contains the symbol s.

For $1 \leq i \leq n$, the program Π contains the following rules:

$$B(x,y,z,a_1,\ldots,a_n,u,v,w,t) \leftarrow B(x,y,z,a_1,\ldots a_{i-1},x,a_{i+1}\ldots,a_n,u,v,w,t).$$
$$B(x,y,z,a_1,\ldots,a_n,u,v,w,t) \leftarrow B(x,y,z,a_1,\ldots a_{i-1},y,a_{i+1}\ldots,a_n,u,v,w,t).$$

Intuitively, each unfolding of these rules modifies the i-th address bit: x encodes the bit 0, and y the bit 1.

For each symbol s, Π contains the rule:

$$B(x,y,z,a_1,\ldots,a_n,u,v,w,t) \leftarrow A(x,y,z,z',a_1,\ldots,a_n,u,v,w,t), Q_s(z), B(x,y,z',a_1,\ldots,a_n,u,v,w,t).$$

These rules determine the symbols in the configurations.

To encode transitions from configuration to configuration, we have to check whether the source configuration is existential or universal. For existential configurations we have rules of the form:

$$B(x,y,z,a_1,\ldots,a_n,u,v,w,x) \leftarrow A(x,y,z,z',a_1,\ldots,a_n,u,v,w,x), Q_s(z), B(x,y,z',a_1,\ldots,a_n,u',u,w',y).$$
$$B(x,y,z,a_1,\ldots,a_n,u,v,w,x) \leftarrow A(x,y,z,z',a_1,\ldots,a_n,u,v,w,x), Q_s(z), B(x,y,z',a_1,\ldots,a_n,u',v',u,y).$$

Note that u moves either one or two positions to the right in the B predicate. A one-position movement corresponds to a transition to a left successor, while a two-position movement corresponds to a transition to the right successor.

Equivalently, for universal configurations we have rules :

$$\begin{aligned}B(x,y,z,a_1,\ldots,a_n,u,v,w,y) \\ \leftarrow A(x,y,z,z',a_1,\ldots,a_n,u,v,w,y), Q_s(z) \\ B(x,y,z',a_1,\ldots,a_n,u',u,w',x), \\ B(x,y,z',a_1,\ldots,a_n,u',v',u,x).\end{aligned}$$

To encode the start of the computation we use the rule:

$$C \leftarrow Start(z), B(x,y,z,x,\ldots,x,u,v,w,x).$$

To encode the end of the computation, we use rules:

$$\begin{aligned}B(x,y,z,a_1,\ldots,a_n,u,v,w,t) \\ \leftarrow Q_s(z), A(x,y,z,z',a_1,\ldots,a_n,u,v,w,t),\end{aligned}$$

for symbols $s = (q, e)$ such that q is an accepting state.

The UCQ Θ. Now we show how to detect errors in the expansion trees of Π using a Boolean acyclic UCQ Θ. Each disjunct of Θ detects a particular type of error. There are first some simple errors that prevent the expansion tree from being a configuration tree: (a) the first address is not $0, \ldots, 0$, (b) there are two consecutive addresses $\bar{a}$ and $\bar{b}$ such that $\bar{b} \neq \bar{a} + 1 \pmod{2^n}$, (c) a configuration does not change when the address is $1, \ldots, 1$, and (d) a configuration changes when the address is not $1, \ldots, 1$. For each one of them we can easily adapt techniques from [12] and build an acyclic CQ that detects it.

We have so far ensured that the expansion tree is a configuration tree. Now we have to ensure that the tree is a valid computation of the machine M. In order to force the first configuration to be the initial configuration, we can again apply techniques from [12]. On the other hand, to detect errors in the transitions δ^ℓ and δ^r we cannot directly apply those techniques. This is because the CQs constructed in [12] to detect those errors are not acyclic. We use, instead, the following idea.

For each $(a,b,c,d) \notin B^\ell$ we add the CQ that is defined by the conjunction of every atom in the set:

$$\begin{aligned}\Phi(a,b,c,d) := \{&A(x,y,z_1,z_2,\bar{a}_1,u,v,w,u_1), Q_a(z_1), \\ &A(x,y,z_2,z_3,\bar{a}_2,u,v,w,u_2), Q_b(z_2), \\ &A(x,y,z_3,z_4,\bar{a}_3,u,v,w,u_3), Q_c(z_3), \\ &A(x,y,z,z',\bar{a}_2,u',u,w',u_4), Q_d(z)\}.\end{aligned}$$

The pattern of the z_i's variables and the u, v, w variables ensures that the first three atoms are mapped in three successive positions in the same configuration E. The pattern "u', u, w'" ensures that the last atom is mapped to the left successor of E. The reuse of $\bar{a}_2$ ensures that the second and the last atom are mapped to the same address. Note that each one of these queries is actually acyclic, as witnessed by the join tree in which the first three A-atoms form a path and the last A-atom is a child of the second one. We define similar CQs in AC for each $(a,b,c) \notin I^\ell$, for each $(a,b,c) \notin F^\ell$, and for detecting errors in δ^r.

It is not hard to prove now that $\Pi \subseteq \Theta$ iff M does not accept the empty tape in space 2^n. Since the construction of Π and Θ can be carried out in polynomial time, it follows that CONT(Datalog,AC) is 2EXPTIME-hard. □

4.2 Better bounds for queries in AC_k

Since restricting to a tractable class of UCQs the right-hand side of the problem CONT(Datalog,UCQ) does not help, in general, to reduce its computational cost, we look for further restrictions on UCQs that yield better bounds.

A big source of complexity for CONT(Datalog,AC) is the existence of pairs of atoms in CQs that share an unbounded number of variables (in the proof of Theorem 5 this is witnessed, for instance, in the CQs of the form $\Phi(a,b,c,d)$, for $(a,b,c,d) \notin B^\ell$). By restricting this parameter we unveil a new hierarchy inside the class of acyclic UCQs, that consists of the acyclic UCQs with a *bounded number of common variables between atoms*. We prove that containment of Datalog in any of the levels of this hierarchy can be solved in EXPTIME (and it is actually complete for this class).

Formally, let us define AC_k, for $k \geq 1$, to be the class of queries Θ in AC such that no two distinct atoms in a CQ in Θ share more than k variables. Clearly:

$$\mathsf{AC}_1 \subset \mathsf{AC}_2 \subset \cdots \subset \mathsf{AC}_k \subset \cdots \subset \mathsf{AC}.$$

EXAMPLE 4. The CQ $\bigwedge_{1 \leq i < n} E(x_i, x_{i+1})$, for $n \geq 2$, is in AC_1. The CQ $\bigwedge_{1 \leq i < j \leq n} E(x_i, x_j) \wedge T_n(x_1, \ldots, x_n)$, for $n \geq 2$, is in AC_2. □

We prove next that CONT(Datalog,AC_k) can be solved in single-exponential time, for each $k \geq 1$.

THEOREM 6. *Let $k \geq 1$. Then* CONT(Datalog,AC_k) *is* EXPTIME-*complete.*

Proof (Sketch): We only sketch the upper bound. We assume familiarity with standard (one-way) *nondeterministic tree automata* [32], 1NTA, and *two-way alternating tree automata* [34], 2ATA, which extend 1NTA with both upward moves and alternation.

Overall idea. It is known that each expansion tree of a Datalog program Π can be represented as a ranked tree over a finite alphabet Σ_Π. Such representations are called the *proof trees* of Π. The language of all proof trees of Π can be defined by a 1NTA $\mathcal{A}_\Pi$ over Σ_Π, such that $\mathcal{A}_\Pi$ can be constructed in single exponential time from Π [12]. Consider first the case when Θ is an arbitrary UCQ (i.e., not necessarily in AC_k). Then it is possible to construct in single exponential time from Π and a UCQ Θ, a 1NTA $\mathcal{A}_\Pi^\Theta$ that accepts precisely the proof trees ν of Π such that there is a CQ $\theta \in \Theta$ and a containment mapping from θ to the expansion tree τ represented by ν [12]. (Both $\mathcal{A}_\Pi$ and $\mathcal{A}_\Pi^\Theta$ can be of exponential size). Thus, in order to check if $\Pi \subseteq \Theta$, it is sufficient to check whether the language defined by the 1NTA $\mathcal{A}_\Pi$ is contained in the one defined by $\mathcal{A}_\Pi^\Theta$. The latter can be done in double exponential time in the size of Π and Θ [32].

In our case, that is, when Θ belongs to AC_k, we can follow a slightly different approach and check containment of Π in Θ in single exponential time. We start again by constructing in EXPTIME the 1NTA $\mathcal{A}_\Pi$ over Σ_Π that defines the set of proof trees of Π. The difference is that we now construct in exponential time from Π and Θ a 2ATA $\mathcal{B}_\Pi^\Theta$ of *polynomial size*[1], that accepts all trees T over Σ_Π such that there exists a CQ $\theta \in \Theta$ and a *strong* containment mapping from θ to T. Notice that, in opposition to $\mathcal{A}_\Pi^\Theta$, the 2ATA $\mathcal{B}_\Pi^\Theta$ may accept trees over Σ_Π that are not proof trees of Π.

Checking whether $\Pi \subseteq \Theta$ reduces to check if the language defined by $\mathcal{A}_\Pi$ is contained in the one defined by $\mathcal{B}_\Pi^\Theta$. In order to

[1]This means that even if $|\Sigma_\Pi|$ is exponential, both the set of states $\mathcal{S}$ of $\mathcal{B}_\Pi^\Theta$ and the sets of the form $\delta(s,a)$, where δ is the transition function of $\mathcal{B}_\Pi^\Theta$, $s \in \mathcal{S}$ and $a \in \Sigma_\Pi$, are of polynomial size.

do the latter, we first compute from $\mathcal{B}_\Pi^\Theta$ a 1NTA that defines the complement of $\mathcal{B}_\Pi^\Theta$, and then check for nonemptiness the intersection of this 1NTA with $\mathcal{A}_\Pi$. This tells us whether $\Pi \not\subseteq \Theta$. The result now follows from EXPTIME being closed under complement and the following facts: (1) A 1NTA that defines the complement of $\mathcal{B}_\Pi^\Theta$ can be constructed in single exponential time from Π and Θ [17], and (2) checking if the language defined by the intersection of this 1NTA with $\mathcal{A}_\Pi$ is nonempty can be solved in time exponential in the size of Π and Θ.

Technical details of the construction. Proof trees of Π describe expansion trees of Π using a finite number of labels. Formally, let r be a rule of Π and $nv(r)$ be the number of variables in r. We define $nv(\Pi)$ to be twice the maximum of $nv(r)$, for all rules r in Π. Let $vars(\Pi)$ be a set of variables of cardinality $nv(\Pi)$. A proof tree ν of Π is simply an expansion tree that does not satisfy the last condition of the definition (that is, variables in ν can be reused), and all the variables used in ν come from $vars(\Pi)$.

In an expansion tree, when we "unfold" a node we take a "fresh" copy of a rule r in Π. In a proof tree, we take instead an instance of r over $vars(\Pi)$. Since the number of variables in $vars(\Pi)$ is twice the number of variables in any rule of Π, we can instantiate the variables in the body of r that do not appear in its head by variables different from those in the head. Notably, the set of proof trees of Π can be described by a tree automaton $\mathcal{A}_\Pi$. Formally, let Σ_Π be the alphabet that consists of all instances of rules of Π that can be formed with variables from $vars(\Pi)$. Then:

LEMMA 1. [12] *There exists an* EXPTIME *algorithm that, given a Datalog program Π, constructs a 1NTA $\mathcal{A}_\Pi$ over Σ_Π such that the language defined by $\mathcal{A}_\Pi$ is precisely the set of proof trees of Π.*

Before following with the construction, it is necessary to understand when two occurences of the same variable in a proof tree ν denote the same element in the expansion tree represented by ν. Let T be a tree over Σ_Π (e.g., T might be a proof tree of Π). Assume n_1 and n_2 are nodes of T with lowest common ancestor n, and x_1 and x_2 are occurences of the same variable x from $vars(\Pi)$ in n_1 and n_2, respectively. Then x_1 and x_2 are *connected* in T, if there is an occurrence of x in the head of the label of every node, except perhaps for n, in the simple path from n_1 to n_2 in T. An occurrence x_1 of x in T is *distinguished*, if it is connected to an occurrence of x in the head of the label of the root of T.

Containment of Π in Θ can be rephrased in terms of the existence of *strong* containment mappings from the CQs in Θ to trees T over Σ_Π [12]. Let $\theta(\bar{x})$ be a CQ in Θ and T a tree over Σ_Π such that the head of the rule that labels the root of T is $Q(\bar{x}')$, for $|\bar{x}| = |\bar{x}'|$. A strong containment mapping μ from $\theta(\bar{x})$ to T maps occurrences of variables in θ to occurrences of variables in $vars(\Pi)$, in such a way that the following holds: (i) if y_1 and y_2 are two occurences of the same variable in θ, then $\mu(y_1)$ and $\mu(y_2)$ are connected occurrences of the same variable in T, (ii) for each occurence x of the i-th variable x_i of $\bar{x}$ in θ, it is the case that $\mu(x)$ is a distinguished occurence in T of the i-th variable x'_i of $\bar{x}'$, and (iii) for each atom in θ of the form $R(\bar{y})$, we have that $R(\mu(\bar{y}))$ appears in the label of some node of T.

Intuitively, a strong containment mapping from θ to a proof tree ν enforces that different occurences of the same variable y in θ are mapped to the same element in the expansion tree τ represented by ν. With this idea in mind, it is not hard to prove that there is a strong containment mapping from θ to ν iff there is a containment mapping from θ to τ. We obtain the following from Proposition 2:

LEMMA 2. [12] *Let Π be a Datalog program and Θ a UCQ. Then $\Pi \subseteq \Theta$ iff for every proof tree ν of Π there is a CQ $\theta \in \Theta$ and a strong containment mapping from θ to ν.*

In order to complete the proof of the theorem, it will be sufficient to prove Lemma 3 below. This lemma states that, if $\Theta \in \mathsf{AC}_k$, for $k \geq 1$, it is possible to construct in single exponential time a 2ATA $\mathcal{B}_\Pi^\Theta$ of polynomial size, that accepts precisely the trees T over Σ_Π for which there is a CQ $\theta \in \Theta$ and a strong containment mapping from θ to T. It will follow then from Lemmas 1, 2 and 3, that checking $\Pi \subseteq \Theta$ reduces to checking $\mathcal{A}_\Pi \subseteq \mathcal{B}_\Pi^\Theta$. As mentioned before, this can be done in EXPTIME using known techniques.

LEMMA 3. *Let $k \geq 1$. There is an* EXPTIME *algorithm that, given a Datalog program Π and a UCQ $\Theta \in \mathsf{AC}_k$, constructs a 2ATA $\mathcal{B}_\Pi^\Theta$, whose size is polynomial in the size of Π and Θ, such that the language defined by $\mathcal{B}_\Pi^\Theta$ is the set of trees T over Σ_Π for which there is a CQ $\theta \in \Theta$ and a strong containment mapping from θ to T.*

The 2ATA $\mathcal{B}_\Pi^\Theta$ looks for a strong containment mapping from some CQ in Θ to the tree T. In order to do this, it first guesses a CQ $\theta \in \Theta$, and then operates in a top-down fashion over the join tree of θ (which exists since θ is acyclic). At each point, $\mathcal{B}_\Pi^\Theta$ is in a state that summarizes the following information: the atom A of the join tree of θ that is being scanned (which is the one that $\mathcal{B}_\Pi^\Theta$ is currently trying to match in T), and an assignment M from the variables of θ that have already been mapped to the variables of T (which restricts the possible matchings for A in T, since some of the variables of A may belong to the domain of M). A transition results in either the mapping of the current atom or a movement to an adjacent node in T.

The 2ATA $\mathcal{B}_\Pi^\Theta$ is defined as $\bigcup_{\theta \in \Theta} \mathcal{B}_\Pi^\theta$. We define 2ATAs of the form $\mathcal{B}_\Pi^\theta$ below. Let J be a join tree of θ. We write J also to refer to the set of atoms of θ. Assume that $x_1, \dots, x_m$ are the distinguished variables of θ. For an atom A of θ, we define $dvar(A)$ to be the set of indices in $\{1, \dots, m\}$ such that x_i appears in A.

The state set $\mathcal{S}$ of $\mathcal{B}_\Pi^\theta$ consists of two types of states: (1) *atom* states in $J \times \mathcal{M}_k$, where $\mathcal{M}_k$ consists of all partial mappings from the variables of θ to $vars(\Pi)$ whose domain has at most k elements, and (2) *variable* states in the set $\{1, \dots, m\} \times vars(\Pi)$ (recall that m is the number of distinguished variables in θ). There is also an accepting state $accept$. The initial state of $\mathcal{B}_\Pi^\theta$ is the atom state $(A_r, \emptyset)$, where A_r is the root of J and $\emptyset$ denotes the empty mapping.

Since $\mathcal{B}_\Pi^\theta$ is a 2ATA, the transition function of $\mathcal{B}_\Pi^\theta$ maps each pair (s, r), where $s \in \mathcal{S}$ and $r \in \Sigma_\Pi$, to a positive formula ϕ in DNF over the set $\{-1, 0, 1, \dots, \ell\} \times \mathcal{S}$, where ℓ is the maximum number of intensional atoms in a rule of Π. Intuitively, when $\mathcal{B}_\Pi^\theta$ is in state s reading symbol r, it first chooses a conjunction in ϕ, and then for each literal in this conjunction of the form $\langle c, s' \rangle$, for $c \in \{-1, 0, 1, \dots, \ell\}$ and $s' \in \mathcal{S}$, it launches a new copy of itself in the direction suggested by c starting in state s'.

The transition function δ of $\mathcal{B}_\Pi^\theta$ is (in broad terms) defined as follows. Consider first a pair $((A, M), R(\bar{t}) \leftarrow \rho) \in \mathcal{S} \times \Sigma_\Pi$, where (A, M) is an atom state, i.e., $A \in J$ and $M \in \mathcal{M}_k$, and $R(\bar{t}) \leftarrow \rho$ is an instance of a rule in Π over $vars(\Pi)$. Then:

1. It is the case that $\delta((A, M), R(\bar{t}) \leftarrow \rho)$ contains an *atom mapping* transition of the form:

$$\langle 0, (A_1, M_1) \rangle \wedge \dots \wedge \langle 0, (A_n, M_n) \rangle \wedge \\ \langle 0, (j_1, x'_{j_1}) \rangle \wedge \dots \wedge \langle 0, (j_p, x'_{j_p}) \rangle,$$

   if $A_1, \dots, A_n$ are the children of A in J and the following conditions hold:

   (a) There is a mapping M' consistent with M that maps the atom A to an atom in ρ.

(b) For each $1 \leq i \leq n$, the mapping M_i is precisely the restriction of M' to the common variables between A and A_i.

(c) $dvar(A) = \{j_1, \ldots, j_p\}$ and $x'_{j_i} = M'(x_{j_i})$, for each $1 \leq i \leq p$.

Intuitively, this transition maps A to the current node of T, and then launches new copies of $\mathcal{B}^{\theta}_{\Pi}$ that check that each one of the children A_i of A in J is matched in T ($1 \leq i \leq n$). Since J is a join tree, the mapping M_i is the only information the automaton needs to store in order to continue consistently mapping in T the subtree J_i of J rooted in A_i. This is represented by the atom $\langle 0, (A_i, M_i)\rangle$ in the transition. In addition, if A mentions a distinguished variable x_{j_i}, we have to ensure that it is mapped to a distinguished occurrence of x'_{j_i}. This is enforced with the atom $\langle 0, (j_1, x'_{j_1})\rangle$ in the atom mapping transition, as we will see below.

2. It is the case that $\delta((A, M), R(\bar{t}) \leftarrow \rho)$ contains a *moving* transition $\langle j, (A, M)\rangle$, for $j \in \{-1, 1, \ldots, \ell\}$, if one of the following condition holds:

(a) $j \in \{1, \ldots, \ell\}$ and, if $R_{i_j}(\bar{t}_{i_j})$ is the j-th intensional atom of ρ, then for each variable appearing both in A and the domain of M it is the case that its image under M is in $\bar{t}_{i_j}$.

(b) $j = -1$ and for each variable appearing both in A and the domain of M it is the case that its image under M appears in $\bar{t}$.

This transition moves the automaton to an adjacent node in T. It is applied when the current atom A cannot be mapped to the current node of T. The value of M must be propagated through the head of the rule to which the automaton moves. This allows to ensure that M satisfies the connectedness condition in the definition of strong containment mapping.

Consider now a pair $((j, x), R(\bar{t}) \leftarrow \rho)$, where (j, x) is a variable atom, i.e. $j \in \{1, \ldots, m\}$ and $x \in vars(\Pi)$, and $R(\bar{t}) \leftarrow \rho$ is an instance of a rule of Π over $vars(\Pi)$. Then $\delta((j, x), R(\bar{t}) \leftarrow \rho)$ contains a "variable checking" transition $\langle -1, (j, x)\rangle$ if the variable x is in $\bar{t}$. In addition, it contains a *variable checking* transition $\langle 0, accept\rangle$ if the j-th variable of $\bar{t}$ is x. The goal of the *variable checking* transitions is to ensure that each distinguished occurence of a variable x in θ is mapped to a distinguished occurrence of the corresponding distinguished variable of T.

It can be proved that this construction is correct, that is, that $\mathcal{B}^{\theta}_{\Pi}$ defines the set of trees T over Σ_{Π} for which there is a strong containment mapping from θ to T. Notice that the number of states of $\mathcal{B}^{\theta}_{\Pi}$ is $O(||\theta||^{k+1}||\Pi||^{k})$, i.e., it is polynomial in the size of Π and θ. Also, for each state s of $\mathcal{B}^{\theta}_{\Pi}$ and symbol $a \in \Sigma_{\Pi}$, the size of $\delta(s, a)$ is polynomial. This finishes our sketch. □

4.2.1 *Results for* AC *and* TW(1)

Theorem 5 states that both problems CONT(Datalog,AC) and CONT(Datalog,TW(2)) are complete for 2EXPTIME, and that for TW(2) and HW(2) this holds even for schemas of fixed arity. This leaves the following two cases open: (1) CONT(Datalog,TW(1)), and (2) CONT$_c$(Datalog,AC), for $c \geq 1$. We obtain that both can be solved in EXPTIME as corollaries of Theorem 6.

COROLLARY 1. *The following problems are complete for* EXPTIME*:*

1. CONT$_c$(Datalog,AC)*, for each* $c \geq 1$.

2. CONT(Datalog,TW(1)).

Proof (Sketch): We concentrate on upper bounds. Consider first CONT$_c$(Datalog,AC), for $c \geq 1$. Each input consists of a Datalog program Π and a UCQ Θ over σ, where the arity of σ is bounded by c. It follows that $\Theta \in \mathsf{AC}_c$, and therefore that $\Pi \subseteq \Theta$ can be checked in EXPTIME (from Theorem 6).

Consider now CONT(Datalog,TW(1)). We use the following fact, which has a simple proof: $\mathsf{TW}(1) \subseteq \mathsf{AC}_2$. The result now follows from Theorem 6. □

4.2.2 *Results about equivalence*

Checking containment of UCQ in Datalog is decidable in EXPTIME [16]. Together with Theorem 6 this implies that checking if a Datalog program is equivalent to a UCQ in AC_k is decidable in EXPTIME, for each $k \geq 1$.

COROLLARY 2. *Let* $k \geq 1$. *The following problem is complete for* EXPTIME*: Given a Datalog program* Π *and a UCQ* Θ *in* AC_k*, decide if* Π *is equivalent to* Θ.

4.2.3 *Queries in* AC_k *modulo equivalence*

Tractability results for $\mathsf{TW}(k)$ and $\mathsf{HW}(k)$ are invariant modulo equivalence, i.e., they continue to hold for the classes $\mathcal{H}(\mathsf{TW}(k))$ and $\mathcal{H}(\mathsf{HW}(k))$ of UCQs that are equivalent to one in $\mathsf{TW}(k)$ and $\mathsf{HW}(k)$, respectively [18, 15]. Interestingly, our single-exponential time bound for the problem CONT(Datalog,AC_k) is also invariant modulo equivalence for queries in AC_k. Let $\mathcal{H}(\mathsf{AC}_k)$ be the set of all UCQs that are equivalent to one in AC_k, for $k \geq 1$. Then:

PROPOSITION 3. *Let* $k \geq 1$. *Then* CONT(Datalog,$\mathcal{H}(\mathsf{AC}_k)$) *can be solved in* EXPTIME.

Proof: First, we introduce the notion of *strong induced subqueries*. A CQ θ' is a strong induced subquery of a CQ θ if:

1. The set $V_{\theta'}$ of variables mentioned in θ' is contained in the set V_{θ} of variables mentioned in θ.

2. The atoms of θ' are exactly the atoms of θ induced by the variables in $V_{\theta'}$.

3. The free variables of θ' are exactly the free variables of θ.

4. If A is an atom in θ but not in θ' and V_A are the variables in A that belong to $V_{\theta'}$, then there exists an atom A' in θ' that contains all the variables in V_A.

As it turns out, the class AC_k is closed under taking strong induced subqueries. Indeed, let θ be a CQ in AC_k and θ' a strong induced subquery of θ. Since each atom of θ' is an atom of θ, it follows that no two distinct atoms in θ' share more than k variables. It thus suffices to prove that θ' has a join tree.

Let T be a join tree of θ. It is convenient in this case to switch back and forth between two different ways of viewing at T: the traditional one in which each node of T is an atom A of θ, and another one – based on the fact that T can also be interpreted as a tree decomposition of θ – in which each such node is associated with the set of variables in V_{θ} that are mentioned in A. Consider now a node of T that is associated with some atom A that is not in θ'. Assume that the set of variables mentioned in A is S (notice that $S \not\subseteq V_{\theta'}$, since θ' is a strong induced subquery of θ). Let

$S_{\theta'}$ be the restriction of S to $V_{\theta'}$, and assume for the time being that node A is replaced in T by $S_{\theta'}$. By condition (4), there is a node of T that is associated with some set S' of variables such that $S_{\theta'} \subseteq S' \subseteq V_{\theta'}$. Thus, $S_{\theta'}$ is subsumed by node S', which in turn only contains variables in θ'. Since $S_{\theta'}$ is contained in S', we can apply standard tree decomposition techniques (see, e.g., [21]), and transform T into a new tree T' by "contracting" the node $S_{\theta'}$ into the node S' (that is, $S_{\theta'}$ but not S' is removed from T), in such a way that the connectivity properties of the variables in $V_{\theta'}$ are preserved in T'. It is easy to see that by iteratively applying this transformation to each node of T associated with an atom A in θ but not in θ', we will end up with a join tree for θ'.

We show next that if $\theta \in \mathsf{AC}_k$, then its *core* [26, 10] θ' is a strong induced query. It follows from well-known core properties [26] that conditions (1), (2) and (3) hold. We prove next that condition (4) also holds. Again by well-known properties of cores [26], we have that there is a homomorphism μ from θ to $\mathcal{D}_{\theta'}$ such that $\mu(x) = x$, for each $x \in V_{\theta'}$. Let $A(x_1, \ldots, x_m)$ be an atom in θ but not in θ'. Then it is the case that $A(\mu(x_1), \ldots, \mu(x_m))$ is an atom of θ'. Since μ is the identity in V_A, we conclude that condition (4) holds.

Now, it is easy to prove the following observation: A CQ θ is in $\mathcal{H}(\mathsf{AC}_k)$ iff its core θ' is in AC_k. In fact, assume first that $\theta' \in \mathsf{AC}_k$. Since θ is equivalent to θ', we have that $\theta \in \mathcal{H}(\mathsf{AC}_k)$. Assume, on the other hand, that θ is equivalent to a CQ θ^* in AC_k. It is well-known that cores of equivalent CQs are isomorphic [26]. But the core of θ^* is in AC_k (since θ^* is in AC_k), and, therefore, the core of θ' is in AC_k.

The latter can be used to prove the following: Let $k \geq 1$. There is an EXPTIME algorithm that, given a UCQ $\Theta \in \mathcal{H}(\mathsf{AC}_k)$, constructs a UCQ $\Theta^* \in \mathsf{AC}_k$ such that (i) Θ^* is equivalent to Θ, and (ii) the size of Θ^* is at most the size of Θ. In fact, let $\Theta \in \mathcal{H}(\mathsf{AC}_k)$. Then there exists an equivalent $\Theta' \in \mathsf{AC}_k$. Let Θ_{min} be a subset of the CQs in Θ such that (1) Θ_{min} is equivalent to Θ, and (2) no proper subset of Θ_{min} is equivalent to Θ. Analogously, we define Θ'_{min} to be "minimally" equivalent to Θ'. By minimality, there are no distinct CQs θ_1 and θ_2 in Θ_{min} such that $\theta_2 \subseteq \theta_1$. Moreover, since Θ_{min} and Θ'_{min} are equivalent, it follows that, for each $\theta \in \Theta_{min}$, there is an equivalent CQ θ' in Θ'_{min}. Thus, each $\theta \in \Theta_{min}$ belongs to $\mathcal{H}(\mathsf{AC}_k)$. Let Θ^* be the UCQ Θ_{min}, where each CQ is replaced by its core. By our previous observations, it follows that $\Theta^* \in \mathsf{AC}_k$. Moreover, Θ^* is equivalent to Θ and its size is at most the size of Θ. The algorithm then proceeds as follows: It first computes Θ_{min} from Θ, and then it constructs Θ^* from Θ_{min}. It is not hard to prove that each step of the algorithm can be carried out in single exponential time.

This implies that in order to check if the Datalog program Π is contained in the UCQ $\Theta \in \mathcal{H}(\mathsf{AC}_k)$, we can first construct Θ^* from Θ in EXPTIME, and then check whether $\Pi \subseteq \Theta^*$. The latter can be done in EXPTIME from Theorem 6. □

Is it decidable to check membership in $\mathcal{H}(\mathsf{AC}_k)$? It follows from the techniques developed in the proof of the previous proposition that this is indeed the case. In addition, those techniques allow us to pinpoint the precise complexity of the problem.

PROPOSITION 4. *Let $k \geq 1$. Then checking if an UCQ Θ is in $\mathcal{H}(\mathsf{AC}_k)$ is* NP*-complete.*

5. CONTAINMENT OF DATALOG IN TRACTABLE CLASSES OF UC2RPQS

We now switch to study the containment problem in the context of graph databases. We start by introducing the basic notions used in this section.

5.1 Preliminaries

Graph databases. Let Σ be a finite alphabet. A *graph database* $\mathcal{G}$ over Σ is a pair (V, E), where V is a finite set of nodes and $E \subseteq V \times \Sigma \times V$. Thus, each edge in $\mathcal{G}$ is a triple $(v, a, v') \in V \times \Sigma \times V$, whose interpretation is an a-labeled edge from v to v' in $\mathcal{G}$. A *path* in a graph database $\mathcal{G} = (V, E)$ is a sequence

$$\eta = v_0 a_0 v_1 a_1 v_2 \cdots v_{k-1} a_{k-1} v_k,$$

for $k \geq 0$, such that (v_{i-1}, a_{i-1}, v_i) is in E, for each i with $1 \leq i \leq k$. The *label* of η, denoted $\lambda(\eta)$, is the string $a_0 a_1 \cdots a_{k-1} \in \Sigma^*$. Notice that v is a path, for each $v \in V$. The label of such path is the empty string ϵ.

C2RPQs and Datalog. Queries over graph databases are typically navigational, in the sense that they allow to recursively traverse the edges of the graph while checking for the existence of paths satisfying a regular condition (see, e.g., [1, 35]).

The basic mechanism for querying graph databases is the class of *two-way regular path queries*, or 2RPQs [9]. A 2RPQ L over Σ is a regular expression over the alphabet $\Sigma^{\pm}$ that extends Σ with the *inverse* a^- of each symbol $a \in \Sigma$. To define the semantics of 2RPQs we use the notion of the *completion* of a graph database $\mathcal{G}$, denoted $\mathcal{G}^{\pm}$. This is the graph database over $\Sigma^{\pm}$ that is obtained from $\mathcal{G} = (V, E)$ by adding the edge (u, a^-, v), for each $(v, a, u) \in E$. We define the evaluation $L(\mathcal{G})$ of 2RPQ L over $\mathcal{G}$ to be the set of pairs (v, v') of nodes in V such that there is a path η in $\mathcal{G}^{\pm}$ from v to v' whose label $\lambda(\eta)$ satisfies L.

The analogue of CQs in the context of graph databases is the class of *conjunctive* 2RPQs, or C2RPQs [7], that closes 2RPQs under joins and projection. Formally, a C2RPQ γ over Σ is an expression of the form

$$\exists \bar{z}(L_1(x_1, y_1) \wedge \cdots \wedge L_m(x_m, y_m)),$$

where each L_i is a 2RPQ over Σ, for $1 \leq i \leq m$, the x_i's and y_i's are variables, and $\bar{z}$ is a tuple of variables among the x_i's and y_i's. Again, $\gamma(\bar{x})$ denotes that $\bar{x}$ is the tuple of free variables of γ.

A homomorphism from a C2RPQ $\gamma = \exists \bar{z}(L_1(x_1, y_1) \wedge \cdots \wedge L_m(x_m, y_m))$ to a graph database $\mathcal{G} = (V, E)$ is a mapping h from the set of variables used in γ to V, such that $(h(x_i), h(y_i)) \in L_i(\mathcal{G})$, for each $1 \leq i \leq m$. The evaluation $\gamma(\mathcal{G})$ of $\gamma(\bar{x})$ over $\mathcal{G}$ is the set of tuples $h(\bar{x})$, for h a homomorphism from γ to $\mathcal{G}$.

A UC2RPQ Γ is a finite set $\{\gamma_1(\bar{x}), \ldots, \gamma_k(\bar{x})\}$ of C2RPQs over Σ with the same free variables. In addition, we define $\Gamma(\mathcal{G})$ to be $\bigcup_{1 \leq i \leq k} \gamma_i(\mathcal{G})$, for each graph database $\mathcal{G}$.

It is clear that each graph database $\mathcal{G} = (V, E)$ over Σ can be represented as a relational database $\mathcal{D}(\mathcal{G})$ over the schema $\sigma(\Sigma)$ that consists of one binary relation symbol E_a, for each symbol $a \in \Sigma$: The database $\mathcal{D}(\mathcal{G})$ consists of all facts of the form $E_a(v, v')$ such that $(v, a, v') \in E$ (where $v, v' \in V$ and $a \in \Sigma$). We identify Datalog programs Π over Σ with Datalog programs over $\sigma(\Sigma)$, and define $\Pi(\mathcal{G})$ to be $\Pi(\mathcal{D}(\mathcal{G}))$, for each graph database $\mathcal{G}$. Notice that while each symbol in $\sigma(\Sigma)$ is binary, the intensional symbols used in Π can be of arbitrary arity. It is a well-known fact that Datalog subsume UC2RPQs over graph databases.

Containment of Datalog in UC2RPQs. In this section we study the containment problem of Datalog in classes $\mathcal{C}$ of UC2RPQs, which (by slightly abusing notation) we denote by CONT(Datalog,$\mathcal{C}$). Formally, CONT(Datalog,$\mathcal{C}$) is defined as follows: Given a Datalog program Π and a UC2RPQ $\Gamma \in \mathcal{C}$ over the same finite alphabet Σ, is it the case that $\Pi \subseteq \Gamma$ (that is, $\Pi(\mathcal{G}) \subseteq \Gamma(\mathcal{G})$ for every graph database $\mathcal{G}$)?

Calvanese et al. proved that CONT(Datalog,UC2RPQ) is in general not only decidable, but also not more expensive than the problem CONT(Datalog,UCQ).

THEOREM 7. [8] *The problem* CONT(Datalog,UC2RPQ) *is complete for* 2EXPTIME.

5.2 Containment of Datalog in Acyclic UC2RPQs

In general, evaluation of C2RPQs is NP-complete [1], but a tractable class can be obtained by restricting the syntactic shape of queries to be *acyclic* [3]. This notion is typically defined in terms of the acyclicity of its *underlying conjunctive query*. Let $\gamma = \exists \bar{y} \bigwedge_{1 \le i \le m} L_i(x_i, y_i)$ be a C2RPQ. Its underlying CQ is the query over the schema of binary relation symbols $T_1, \ldots, T_m$ defined as: $\exists \bar{y} \bigwedge_{1 \le i \le m} T_i(x_i, y_i)$. Intuitively, this underlying conjunctive query represents the structure of γ when the regular languages that label the atoms of γ are turned into relation symbols. A C2RPQ is *acyclic* if its underlying CQ is acyclic (or, equivalently, if it belongs to TW(1), since AC = TW(1) for binary schemas). A UC2RPQ is acyclic if each one of its C2RPQs is acyclic. We denote by ACR the class of acyclic UC2RPQs.

EXAMPLE 5. Let L_1, L_2 and L_3 be regular expressions over Σ. The C2RPQ $L_1(x, x) \wedge L_2(x, y) \wedge L_3(y, x)$ is acyclic. The C2RPQ $L_1(x, y) \wedge L_2(y, z) \wedge L_3(z, x)$ is not acyclic. □

We proved in Theorem 6 that containment of Datalog in UCQs in TW(1) is in EXPTIME. Since acyclic UC2RPQs are those that contain only C2RPQs whose underlying CQ is of treewidth one, it is natural to study whether the restriction to queries in ACR also helps alleviate the complexity of CONT(Datalog,UC2RPQs). We prove that this is not the case, by showing that the 2EXPTIME-hardness proof for CONT(Datalog,UC2RPQ) in [8] can be carried out even with UC2RPQs in ACR.

THEOREM 8. *The problem* CONT(Datalog,ACR) *is complete for* 2EXPTIME.

5.3 Better bounds for queries in ACR^k

In the case of CONT(Datalog,AC), a big source of complexity was the presence of pairs of atoms in queries in AC that share an unbounded number of variables. In the case of CONT(Datalog,ACR) we identify a different source of complexity, which is the existence of queries in ACR with an unbounded number of atoms connecting the same variables. By restricting this parameter we again obtain a hierarchy inside the class of acyclic queries, which in this case is defined by queries in ACR with a *bounded number of atoms connecting pairs of distinct variables*. We prove that containment of Datalog in any of the levels of this hierarchy is in EXPTIME (and it is actually complete for this class).

Formally, let us define ACR^k, for $k \ge 1$, to be the class of queries Γ in ACR such that for each C2RPQ $\gamma \in \Gamma$ and pair (x, x') of distinct variables in γ, there are at most k atoms of the form $L(x, x')$ or $L(x', x)$ in γ. Clearly:

$$\mathsf{ACR}^1 \subset \mathsf{ACR}^2 \subset \cdots \subset \mathsf{ACR}^k \subset \cdots \subset \mathsf{ACR}.$$

Interestingly, queries in ACR^1 have been previously studied under the name of *strongly acyclic* UC2RPQs [1].

EXAMPLE 6. The C2RPQ $L_1(x, x) \wedge L_2(x, y) \wedge L_3(y, x)$ is in ACR^2. □

We prove next that CONT(Datalog,ACR^k) can be solved in single-exponential time, for each $k \ge 1$.

THEOREM 9. *Let* $k \ge 1$. *Then* CONT(Datalog,ACR^k) *is complete for* EXPTIME.

Proof (Sketch): Containment of a Datalog program Π in a UC2RPQ Γ can be stated in terms of the existence of strong containment mappings from the *expansions* of the C2RPQs in Γ to the proof trees of Π. An expansion of a C2RPQ $\gamma = \exists \bar{z} \bigwedge_{1 \le i \le m} L_i(x_i, y_i)$ over Σ is a CQ over $\sigma(\Sigma^{\pm})$ of the form $\phi = \exists \bar{z} \bigwedge_{1 \le i \le m} \theta_i(x_i, y_i)$, where for each i with $1 \le i \le m$ it is the case that $\theta_i(x_i, y_i)$ is of the form:

$$\exists u_1 \cdots u_{n-1}(E_{a_1}(x_i, u_1) \wedge E_{a_2}(u_1, u_2) \wedge \cdots \wedge E_{a_n}(u_{n-1}, y_i)),$$

for $a_1 a_2 \cdots a_n$ a word over $\Sigma^{\pm}$ that satisfies L_i. We assume no two distinct θ_i's share an existentially quantified variable. Strong containment mappings μ from the expansion ϕ to the proof tree ν of Π are defined as in the proof of Theorem 6, save for condition (iii) that is restated as follows: for each atom A in θ we have that if A is of the form $E_a(x, y)$, for $a \in \Sigma$, then $E_a(\mu(x), \mu(y))$ appears in ν, and if A is of the form $E_{a^-}(x, y)$, for $a \in \Sigma$, then $E_a(\mu(y), \mu(x))$ appears in ν. Then:

LEMMA 4. [8] *It is the case that* $\Pi \subseteq \Gamma$ *iff for every proof tree* ν *of* Π *there is a C2RPQ* $\gamma \in \Gamma$, *an expansion* ϕ *of* γ, *and a strong containment mapping from* ϕ *to* ν.

Consider the 1NTA $\mathcal{A}_\Pi$ over Σ_Π constructed in the proof of Theorem 6. Assume that $\Gamma \in \mathsf{ACR}^k$, for $k \ge 1$. We construct in EXPTIME a 2ATA $\mathcal{B}_\Pi^\Gamma := \bigcup_{\gamma \in \Gamma} \mathcal{B}_\Pi^\gamma$, whose size is polynomial in the size of Π and Γ, such that $\mathcal{B}_\Pi^\gamma$ satisfies the following: Given a proof tree ν over Σ_Π, the 2ATA $\mathcal{B}_\Pi^\gamma$ accepts ν iff there is an expansion ϕ of γ and a strong containment mapping from ϕ to ν. It follows from Lemmas 1 and 4 that $\Pi \subseteq \Gamma$ iff $\mathcal{A}_\Pi \subseteq \mathcal{B}_\Pi^\Gamma$. It is known that the latter can be checked in EXPTIME from Π and Γ [34].

We explain now how to construct $\mathcal{B}_\Pi^\gamma$. For each pair (x, x') of variables in γ, we denote by $\gamma(x, x')$ the set of atoms of the form $L(x, x')$ or $L(x', x)$ in γ. Consider the undirected graph G_γ whose vertices are the variables of γ, and there is an undirected edge between x and x' in G_γ iff $\gamma(x, x')$ is nonempty. Since γ is acyclic, the graph G_γ is a tree. We assume for the sake of this sketch that G_γ is connected and contains no loops, but both cases can be handled at the cost of a more cumbersome construction.

The 2ATA $\mathcal{B}_\Pi^\gamma$ reads G_γ in a top-down fashion, looking for the existence of an expansion ϕ of γ and a strong containment mapping μ from ϕ to ν. After scanning node x in G_γ, the automaton stores the value of $\mu(x)$, and then makes a universal transition to check that for each child y of x in G_γ the mapping μ can be extended to a strong containment mapping from some expansion of the atoms in $\gamma(x, y)$ to ν.

Suppose first that γ belongs to ACR^1. Then there is exactly one atom in $\gamma(x, y)$, for each child y of x in G_γ. Assume without loss of generality that $\gamma(x, y) = \{L(x, y)\}$. Thus, in order to check that μ can be extended to a strong containment mapping μ_L from an expansion of $L(x, y)$ to ν, the automaton $\mathcal{B}_\Pi^\gamma$ proceeds as follows: (1) It first guesses an expansion $E_{a_1}(u_0, u_1) \wedge \cdots \wedge E_{a_n}(u_{n-1}, u_n)$ of the C2RPQ $L(x, y)$, where $u_0 = x$ and $u_n = y$, and then (2) checks, iteratively from $i = 1$ to $i = n$, that $E_{a_i}(u_{i-1}, u_i)$ can be mapped to ν. If $1 \le i \le n$, the invariant in each iteration is that $\mu_L(u_{i-1})$ is already known and the automaton looks for a value $\mu_L(u_i)$ that satisfies $E_{a_i}(u_{i-1}, u_i)$. If such a value does not exist in the rule r, where r labels the node in ν currently being scanned by the automaton, then it moves to an adjacent node while checking that $\mu_L(u_{i-1})$ can be propagated through the head of the rule to which the automaton moves. This ensures that the two occurrences of u_{i-1} in $E_{a_{i-1}}(u_{i-2}, u_{i-1})$ and $E_{a_i}(u_{i-1}, u_i)$ are actually connected.

Suppose now that γ belongs to ACR^k, for $k \geq 2$, and, in particular, that $\gamma(x, y)$ contains more than just a single atom. Assume for the sake of the argument that $\gamma(x, y)$ consists only of two different atoms, $L_1(x, y)$ and $L_2(x, y)$. This case is more difficult than the previous one, since we now have to check that $\mu_{L_1}(y)$ and $\mu_{L_2}(y)$ are *connected* occurrences of the same variable in ν. We explain next how to do this without incurring in an exponential blowup in the construction of $\mathcal{B}_\Pi^\gamma$ (recall that $\mathcal{B}_\Pi^\gamma$ must be of polynomial size).

The 2ATA $\mathcal{B}_\Pi^\gamma$ processes the atoms $L_1(x, y)$ and $L_2(x, y)$ simultaneously; this allows to check that $\mu_{L_1}(y)$ and $\mu_{L_2}(y)$ correspond to connected occurrences of the same variable in ν. This idea is implemented in $\mathcal{B}_\Pi^\gamma$ using *multiedge* states and transitions, which interact with *atom* states. We only provide an idea of how these states and transitions are used, since the actual construction of $\mathcal{B}_\Pi^\gamma$ is intricate (and left to the full version of the paper).

We assume that L_1 and L_2 are given as nondeterministic finite automata (NFA). For states s and s' in L_1, we denote by $(L_1)_s$ the NFA that is obtained from L_1 by setting s to be the initial state, and by $(L_1)_{s,s'}$ the NFA obtained from L_1 by setting s and s' to be the initial and final state, respectively. Similarly for L_2. For $i \in [1, 2]$, the atom states associated with L_i in $\mathcal{B}_\Pi^\gamma$ are of the form $(L_i)_{s,s'}(u, v)$ or $(L_i)_s(u, v)$, where s and s' are states in L_i, and u and v are variables mentioned in ν (i.e., $u, v \in vars(\Pi)$). When the automaton is in state $(L_i)_{s,s'}(u, v)$ (the case $(L_i)_s(u, v)$ is analogous), then u and v are variables in the rule r that labels the node currently being scanned by $\mathcal{B}_\Pi^\gamma$. The 2ATA $\mathcal{B}_\Pi^\gamma$ then looks for an expansion $\theta = \exists u_1 \ldots \exists u_{n-1}(E_{a_1}(x', u_1) \wedge \cdots \wedge E_{a_n}(u_{n-1}, y'))$ of the C2RPQ $(L_i)_{s,s'}(x', y')$, where x' and y' are fresh variables, and a strong containment mapping μ_θ from θ to ν such that $\mu_\theta(x')$ corresponds to an occurence of u in ν that is connected to the occurrence of u in r, and similarly for $\mu_\theta(y')$ and v. Although the implementation of atom states requires some work, we can adapt techniques from [8] in order to construct the modules of $\mathcal{B}_\Pi^\gamma$ that implement them.

Now we explain how to process the atoms $L_1(x, y)$ and $L_2(x, y)$ in $\gamma(x, y)$ simultaneously. The multiedge states associated with $\gamma(x, y)$ in $\mathcal{B}_\Pi^\gamma$ are of the form $\gamma_{x,y}(s_1, s_2; u_1, u_2)$, where s_1 and s_2 are states of L_1 and L_2, respectively, and u_1 and u_2 are variables mentioned in ν. When processing $\gamma(x, y)$, the automaton looks for expansions θ_1 and θ_2 of $L_1(x, y)$ and $L_2(x, y)$, respectively, and a strong containment mapping μ_{L_1,L_2} from these expansions to ν. The mapping μ_{L_1,L_2} must be consistent: the two occurrences of y in θ_1 and θ_2 must be mapped to connected occurrences of the same variable in ν. Intuitively, a multiedge state indicates the "suffixes" of the expansions θ_1 and θ_2 that remain to be mapped to ν. When processing $\gamma(x, y)$, the automaton starts in state $\gamma_{x,y}(i_1, i_2; u_x, u_x)$, where i_1 and i_2 are the initial states of L_1 and L_2, respectively, and u_x is a variable in the rule r that is currently being scanned by $\mathcal{B}_\Pi^\gamma$, such that the strong containment mapping constructed so far from the expansion ϕ of G_γ to ν maps x to u_x (formally, each image via this mapping of an occurrence of x in γ is connected to the occurrence of u_x in r).

When $\mathcal{B}_\Pi^\gamma$ is in state $\gamma_{x,y}(s_1, s_2; u_1, u_2)$, for u_1 and u_2 variables that appear in the rule r currently being scanned, the automaton looks for expansions θ_1' of $(L_1)_{s_1}(z_1, y)$ and θ_2' of $(L_2)_{s_2}(z_2, y)$, where z_1, z_2 are fresh variables, and strong containment mappings μ_{L_1}' and μ_{L_2}' from θ_1' and θ_2' to ν, respectively, such that (1) $\mu_{L_1}'(z_1)$ is an occurence of u_1 that is connected to the occurence of u_1 in r, and similarly for $\mu_{L_2}'(z_2)$ and v_2, and (2) $\mu_{L_1}'(y)$ and $\mu_{L_2}'(y)$ are connected occurrences of the same variable w in ν. We explain next how this is done.

We consider two cases:

1. The rule r currently being scanned contains an occurence of w that is connected to $\mu_{L_1}'(y)$ and $\mu_{L_2}'(y)$. This case is simple since we can continue processing θ_1' and θ_2' independently from the current node. This is done by performing a universal transition $\langle 0, (L_1)_{s_1}(u_1, w)\rangle \wedge \langle 0, (L_2)_{s_2}(u_2, w)\rangle$.

2. Otherwise, it is easy to prove that there is $j \in \{-1, 1, \ldots \ell\}$, where ℓ is the number of intensional predicates in the rule r, such that both $\mu_{L_1}'(y)$ and $\mu_{L_2}'(y)$ belong to the subtree ν_j of ν rooted at the j-th child of the node currently being scanned, if $j \geq 1$, and to the subtree ν_{-1} of ν induced by all descendants of the proper ancestors of the current node, if $j = -1$.

   One might be tempted to apply a "moving" transition (see the proof of Theorem 6) in direction j, and check that u_1 and u_2 are propagated through the head of the rule in such direction. Nevertheless, it could be the case that ν_j does not contain any occurrence of a variable connected to u_1 or u_2. Indeed, some "prefixes" of the expansions θ_1' and θ_2' could be mapped outside ν_j. Therefore, before moving in direction j, we have to update the state $\gamma_{x,y}(s_1, s_2; u_1, u_2)$. Intuitively, the automaton $\mathcal{B}_\Pi^\gamma$ guesses "prefixes" of the expansions θ_1' and θ_2' that are mapped outside ν_j via μ_{L_1}' and μ_{L_2}', and continues processing the corresponding "suffixes".

   More formally, let A be the first atom in the expansion θ_1' that is mapped via μ_{L_1}' inside ν_j. If A is the first atom in the expansion θ_1', then we let u_1' to be u_1. Otherwise, let A' be the atom that precedes A in θ_1' (notice that A' must be mapped via μ_{L_1}' outside ν_j). In this case, we let u_1' to be the one variable A' and A have in common. Analogously, we define u_2' with respect to θ_2' and μ_{L_2}'. Notice that rule r must contain occurrences of u_1' and u_2'. Moreover, the subtree ν_j must contain occurrences of u_1' and u_2' that are connected to the occurrences of u_1' and u_2' in r, respectively. Now the automaton $\mathcal{B}_\Pi^\gamma$ is ready to move in direction j. This is done by performing the following universal transitions:

   - $\langle 0, (L_1)_{s_1,s_1'}(u_1, u_1')\rangle$ and $\langle 0, (L_2)_{s_2,s_2'}(u_2, u_2')\rangle$, for s_1' and s_2' suitable states in L_1 and L_2, respectively.
   - $\langle j, \gamma_{x,y}(s_1', s_2'; u_1', u_2')\rangle$. This corresponds to guessing the "suffixes" of the expansions that will be processed in future transitions.

Note that case (1) can only apply a finite number of times. After this, case (2) applies, and the expansions θ_1 and θ_2 of $L_1(x, y)$ and $L_2(x, y)$ have been correctly mapped to ν.

In general, the number of multiedges states is $O(||\gamma||^{k+1}||\Pi||^k)$, and the number of atoms states is $O(||\gamma||^2||\Pi||^2)$. Therefore, the number of states in $\mathcal{B}_\Pi^\gamma$ is polynomial in the size of Π and γ. In addition, there is a polynomial that bounds the size of $\delta(t, a)$, for each state t of $\mathcal{B}_\Pi^\gamma$ and symbol $a \in \Sigma_\Pi$. This finishes the sketch of the proof . □

Notice that containment in the opposite direction, that is, checking if a query in ACR is contained in a Datalog program, is undecidable [8] (same for equivalence).

5.3.1 Queries of larger treewidth

We prove here that it is not possible to extend this positive result to classes of UC2RPQs of larger treewidth. Formally, let $\mathsf{TWR}(2)$ be the class of UC2RPQs Γ such that for each C2RPQ $\gamma \in \Gamma$ we have that (1) the underlying CQ of γ is of treewidth at most two, and (2) there is at most one atom of the form $L(x,x')$ or $L(x',x)$ in γ for each pair (x,x') of distinct variables. Then:

PROPOSITION 5. *The problem* CONT(Datalog,TWR(2)) *is complete for* 2EXPTIME.

6. CONCLUSIONS

Our results convey two messages: (1) Traditional restrictions on UCQs and UC2RPQs that have been used for reducing the complexity of the UCQ and UC2RPQ evaluation problem are not adequate for reducing the complexity of CONT(Datalog,UCQ) and CONT(Datalog,UC2RPQ). (2) Adequate restrictions can be identified by unveiling new hierarchies of acyclic UCQs and UC2RPQs.

We are currently investigating what is the impact of applying the traditional notion of bounded (hyper-)treewidth in restricted versions of our problem. For instance, it has recently been proved that checking containment of the Datalog program Π in the UCQ Θ is 2EXPTIME-complete even if Π is *monadic*, i.e., it contains only monadic intensional symbols [5]. It is by no means clear whether better complexity bounds for this problem can be obtained by restricting Θ to be in $\mathsf{TW}(k)$ or $\mathsf{HW}(k)$, for $k \geq 1$.

Acknowledgments Barceló is funded by Fondecyt grant 1130104. Romero is funded by CONICYT Ph.D. Scholarship.

7. REFERENCES

[1] P. Barceló. Querying graph databases. In *PODS* 2013, pages 175-188.
[2] P. Barceló, R. Pichler (Eds.). *Datalog in Academia and Industry.* LNCS 7494, Springer 2012.
[3] P. Barceló, M. Romero, M. Y. Vardi. Semantic acyclicity on graph databases. In *PODS* 2013, pages 237-248.
[4] C. Beeri, R. Fagin, D. Maier, A. O. Mendelzon, J. D. Ullman, M. Yannakakis. Properties of acyclic database schemes. In *STOC* 1981, pages 355-362.
[5] M. Benedikt, P. Bourhis, P. Senellart. Monadic datalog containment. In *ICALP* 2012, pages 79-91.
[6] P. Buneman, S. B. Davidson, G. G. Hillebrand, D. Suciu. A query language and optimization techniques for unstructured data. In *SIGMOD* 1996, pages 505-516.
[7] D. Calvanese, G. de Giacomo, M. Lenzerini, M. Y. Vardi. Containment of conjunctive regular path queries with inverse. In *KR'00*, pages 176–185.
[8] D. Calvanese, G. de Giacomo, M. Y. Vardi. Decidable containment of recursive queries. *Theor. Comput. Sci.* 336(1), pages 33-56, 2005.
[9] D. Calvanese, G. de Giacomo, M. Lenzerini, M. Y. Vardi. Rewriting of regular expressions and regular path queries. *JCSS*, 64(3):443–465, 2002.
[10] A. Chandra, Ph. Merlin. Optimal implementation of conjunctive queries in relational data bases. In *STOC* 1977, pp. 77-90.
[11] S. Chaudhuri, R. Krishnamurthy, S. Potamianos, K. Shim. Optimizing queries with materialized views. In *ICDE* 1995, pages 190-200.
[12] S. Chaudhuri, M. Y. Vardi. On the equivalence of recursive and nonrecursive Datalog programs. *J. Comput. Syst. Sci.* 54(1), pages 61-78, 1997.
[13] S. Chaudhuri, M. Y. Vardi. On the complexity of equivalence between recursive and nonrecursive Datalog programs. In *PODS* 1994, pages 107-116.
[14] C. Chekuri, A. Rajaraman. Conjunctive query containment revisited. *Theor. Comput. Sci.* 239(2), pages 211-229, 2000.
[15] H. Chen, V. Dalmau. Beyond hypertree width: Decomposition methods without decompositions. In *CP* 2005, pages 167-181.
[16] S. S. Cosmadakis, P. C. Kanellakis. Parallel Evaluation of Recursive Rule Queries. In *PODS* 1986, pages 280-293.
[17] S. S. Cosmadakis, H. Gaifman, P. C. Kanellakis, M. Y. Vardi. Decidable optimization problems for database logic programs (Preliminary report). In *STOC* 1988, pages 477-490.
[18] V. Dalmau, P. Kolaitis, M. Vardi. Constraint satisfaction, bounded treewidth, and finite-variable logics. In *CP* 2002, pp. 310-326.
[19] O. de Moor, G. Gottlob, T. Furche, A. J. Sellers (Eds.). *Datalog Reloaded.* LNCS 6702, Springer 2011.
[20] M. F. Fernández, D. Florescu, A. Y. Levy, D. Suciu. Verifying integrity constraints on web sites. In *IJCAI* 1999, pages 614-619.
[21] J. Flum and M. Grohe. *Parameterized Complexity Theory.* Springer, 2006.
[22] M. Friedman, A. Y. Levy, T. D. Millstein. Navigational plans For data integration. In *AAAI/IAAI* 1999, pages 67-73.
[23] R. Fagin, M. Y. Vardi. The theory of data dependencies - An overview. In *ICALP* 1984, pages 1-22.
[24] G. Gottlob, N. Leone, F. Scarcello. Hypertree decompositions and tractable queries. *J. Comput. Syst. Sci.* 64(3), pages 579–627, 2002.
[25] M. Grohe, D. Marx. Constraint solving via fractional edge covers. In *SODA* 2006, pages 289-298.
[26] P. Hell, J. Nešetřil. The core of a graph. *Discr. Math.* 109, 1995.
[27] T. Imielinski, W. Lipski Jr. Incomplete information in relational databases. *J. of the ACM* 31(4), pages 761-791, 1984.
[28] S. Malik and L. Zhang. Boolean satisfiability: from theoretical hardness to practical success. *CACM* 52(8), 76–82, 2009.
[29] J. Naughton. Data independent recursion in deductive databases. *JCSS* 38, pages 259-289, 1989.
[30] A. Robinson, A. Voronkov, eds. *Handbook of Automated Reasoning.* The MIT Press, 2001.
[31] Y. Sagiv and M. Yannakakis. Equivalences among relational expressions with the union and difference operator. *J. of the ACM* 27(4), 1980, pages 633–655.
[32] H. Seidl. Deciding equivalence of finite tree automata. *SIAM J. Comput.* 19(3), pages 424-437, 1990.
[33] O. Shmueli. Equivalence of DATALOG queries is undecidable. em J. Log. Program. 15(3), pages 231-241, 1993.
[34] G. Slutzki. Alternating tree automata. *TCS* 41, pp. 305-318, 1985.
[35] P. T. Wood. Query languages for graph databases. *SIGMOD Record* 41(1), pages 50-60, 2012.
[36] M. Yannakakis. Algorithms for acyclic database schemes. In *VLDB* 1981, pages 82-94.

Generating Low-cost Plans From Proofs *

Michael Benedikt
Oxford University

Balder ten Cate
LogicBlox Inc. & UC Santa Cruz

Efthymia Tsamoura
Oxford University

ABSTRACT

We look at generating plans that answer queries over restricted interfaces, making use of information about source integrity constraints, access restrictions, and access costs. Our method can exploit the integrity constraints to find low-cost access plans even when there is no direct access to relations appearing in the query. The key idea of our method is to move from a search for a plan to a search for a proof that a query is answerable, and then *generate a plan from a proof*. Discovery of one proof allows us to find a single plan that answers the query; exploration of several alternative proofs allows us to find low-cost plans. We start by mapping out a correspondence between proofs and restricted-interface plans in the context of arbitrary first-order constraints, based on interpolation. The correspondence clarifies the connection between preservation and interpolation theorems in predicate logic and reformulation problems, and generalizes it in several dimensions. We then provide algorithms for schemas based on tuple-generating dependencies. These algorithms perform interpolation, but generate plans directly. Finally, we show how the direct plan-generation approach can be adapted to take into account the cost of plans.

1. INTRODUCTION

This work concerns answering queries in the presence of integrity constraints, where the datasources may vary in terms of their access restrictions and access costs. Examples of restricted interfaces include web forms, web services, and legacy databases. Examples of access cost include the monetary cost of accessing certain services, and the cost in time of accessing data through web service calls, by iteratively filling out web forms, or using particular indices. Our goal is getting plans which (a) give *complete answers to queries* while (b) *minimizing the access cost*. The first condition means that, for a query asking for the office number of all Professors with last name "Smith", we want a plan that returns all tuples in the answer, even if access to the Professor relation is limited. The second condition means that our goal is not merely to get a complete answer, but also to take into account the cost of making accesses to the sources, which we assume will dominate the cost of local query processing. An obvious question arises: if access to a source is restricted, how can one hope to get complete answers, or any answers at all? *Relationships between sources* can help us find plans that can answer a query.

*Benedikt and Tsamoura are supported by EPSRC grant EP/H017690/1. Ten Cate is supported by NSF grant IIS-1217869.

PODS'14, June 22–27, 2014, Snowbird, UT, USA.
Copyright 2014 ACM 978-1-4503-2375-8/14/06 ...$15.00.
http://dx.doi.org/10.1145/2594538.2594550.

EXAMPLE 1. *Consider a* Profinfo *table containing information about faculty, including their last names, office number, and employeeid, but with a restricted interface that requires giving an employeeid as an input. The query Q asking for ids of faculty named smith cannot be completely answered over this schema.*

If another source has a Udirect *table containing the employeeid and last name of every university employee, with unrestricted access, then Q* is *completely answerable: one plan pulls all tuples from the* Udirect *table and check them with the* Profinfo *table.*

The above example shows that complete answers may or may not be obtainable, and that information on source overlap, which we can formalize using *referential integrity constraints*, can play an important role in determining whether and how queries can be completely answered. The simple example above involves two kinds of inferences to see that the query is answerable: reasoning about the logical relations between relations (referential constraints, mappings, view definitions), and also reasoning concerning what kinds of access we have to the data. The latter must account for the fact that some relations, such as materialized views, are freely accessible, while others (base relations hidden behind views, virtual relations within a data integration schema) may not be directly accessible at all. Or as above, it may capture finer notions of access – e.g. that a relation can be accessed only via certain indexes. In Example 1, the reasoning was straightforward, but in the presence of more complex schemas we may have to chain several inferences:

EXAMPLE 2. *We consider two telephone directory datasources with overlapping information. One source exposes information from* Direct1(uname, addr, uid) *via an access requiring a* uname *and* uid. *There is also a table* Ids(uid) *with no access restriction, that makes available the set of* uids *(hence a referential constraint from* Direct1 *into* Ids *on* uid*). The other source exposes* Direct2(uname, addr, phone)*, requiring a* uname *and* addr, *and also a table* Names(uname) *with no access restriction that reveals all* unames *in* Direct2 *(that is, a referential constraint from* Direct2 *to* Names*). There is also a referential constraint from* Direct1 *to* Direct2 *on* uname *and* addr. *Consider a query asking for all phone numbers in the second directory:*

$Q = \{\mathsf{phone} \mid \exists\ \mathsf{uname}\ \mathsf{addr}\ \mathsf{Direct2}(\mathsf{uname}, \mathsf{addr}, \mathsf{phone})\}$.

There is a plan that answers this query: it gets all the uids *from* Ids *and* unames *from* Names *first, puts them into the access on* Direct1, *then uses the* uname *and* addr *of the resulting tuples to get the phone numbers in* Direct2.

We will begin with the case of arbitrary first-order logic constraints. We show that existence of a plan for a query is equivalent to an entailment between formulas, with the entailment holding relative to a set of rules that encode both integrity constraints and access/availability restrictions. We show that by "tweaking" the axioms, we can characterize the existence of a plan that uses only positive relational algebra operators, and a plan that uses positive relational algebra operators and the difference operator restricted to atomic relations. Our equivalence theorems are closely-related to interpolation and preservation theorems in first-order logic. On the one hand, we generalize results of Nash, Segoufin, and Vianu [18] to show that several of the main preservation theorems in first-order model theory correspond to results that characterize which queries can be reformulated over restricted interfaces. Futhermore, we show that these results have effective content, allowing us to compute a reformulation from a proof of a certain entailment. Finally, our results on first-order constraints show that the connection between interpolation and reformulation applies not only to the setting of view definitions, but to the more refined notion of restricted interface given by access patterns, and in the presence of arbitrary first-order integrity constraints. The latter extension is obtained via a new interpolation theorem, which is of independent interest as it generalizes existing interpolation theorems in the literature and provides the first constructive proof of a prior theorem.

We go on to show that for a wide class of constraints used in databases, tuple-generating dependencies, plan-generation from a proof can be done via a particularly simple algorithm, which produces plans that are efficient in terms of number of accesses made. We provide algorithms for relational algebra plans, along with an algorithm geared towards plans that use conjunctive queries. This latter algorithm generalizes the decidability of conjunctive reformulation over views (a seminal result of Levy et al. [14]) and is the basis for the work on low-cost plans in the remainder of the paper.

Our initial plan-generation algorithm would generate the "obvious plans" for either of the examples above, thus satisfying requirement (a) in the first paragraph above. But what about (b)? In the setting of overlapping datasources, there can be many plans with very distinct costs. Consider a variant of Example 1 in which there are two tables $\mathsf{Udirect}_1$ and $\mathsf{Udirect}_2$ that contain the necessary information. In this case we would have at least three plans: one that first accesses Udirect1 as above and then checks the results in Profinfo, another that first accesses $\mathsf{Udirect}_2$, and a third that accesses both $\mathsf{Udirect}_1$ and $\mathsf{Udirect}_2$ and intersects the results in middleware before doing the check in Profinfo. Which of these is best will depend on how costly access is to each of the directory tables, and what percentage of the tuples in the two directory tables match a result in Profinfo. Notice that these plans are not variants of one another, and one cannot be obtained from the other by applying algebraic transformations.

A salient fact about our algorithms is that they can directly produce physical plans whose structure mirrors the structure of proofs. We can thus search for a good physical plan while searching through the space of proofs, rather than having separate reformulation and optimization phases. We discuss how to use this approach to find the lowest-cost plan, thus addressing requirement (b), in the setting where we may have complex constraints, and a "generic" cost function on access plans. The main idea is to *explore the full space of proofs, but guiding the search by cost as well as proof structure.* The notion of searching simultaneously in "proof space" and "plan space" is a key contribution – we believe that it is applicable in a wide variety of query reformulation settings, unifying cases with very distinct integrity constraints and optimisation requirements.

Related Work. The goal here of plans that get *complete answers* to queries contrasts with much work in data integration and knowledge representation, which deals with the more general problem of getting the maximal number of answers possible (the *certain answers*) or the best plan in a certain language (the *maximal contained rewriting*). For example, in the setting of the semantic web it is generally assumed that sources are inherently incomplete, and thus one cannot hope to get the complete answers. Although we believe our techniques can apply to this broader problem, by restricting to the "completely answerable" setting we circumvent many complications: for example, the resulting plans will never require recursion [3]. This restriction will allow us to focus on the basic ideas in our approach to query reformulation via proof exploration.

We are interested not just in getting the complete answers, but in getting them with the lowest possible cost. The impact of access restrictions on cost-based optimization has been considered before. Florescu et al. [12] look at integrating access restrictions into a cost-based optimizer, following up on earlier cost-agnostic work on querying with access patterns by Li and Chang [16]. In the absence of integrity constraints, querying with access patterns amounts to a limitation on the search space, restricting the ordering of atoms within a query plan. In contrast, we allow schemas that can simultaneously restrict the search space (via access restrictions) and extend it (via integrity constraints, which allow relations outside of the query to become relevant) in comparison to the search space of traditional query optimizers.

Our approach starts by connecting plan generation with interpolation and preservation properties, building on the work of Nash, Segoufin, and Vianu [18]. [18] introduces the idea of going from a preservation property (in their case, determinacy of a query by views) to a plan (in their case, a rewriting of the query over the set of views). We give theorems for plan-generation over arbitrary first-order constraints, which work via new preservation and interpolation theorems. The results connecting preservation properties and existence of a plan can be seen as generalizations of [18] to the setting with access patterns and constraints, as explained later on. We also show how this connection can be "pushed down" to smaller classes of constraints, generating plans directly, rather than going via queries, and how this approach can be combined with cost considerations.

Several works provide algorithms for querying in the presence of both access patterns and integrity constraints, usually in the context of computing maximal answers rather than complete answers. Duschka et al. [11] include access patterns in their Datalog-based approach to data integration. They observe, following [15], that the accessible data can be "axiomatized" using recursive rules. We will make use of this axiomatization (see the "accessibility axioms" defined later on) but establish a tighter relationship between proofs that use these axioms and query plans.

Much closer to our work is the chase and backchase (C&B) method elaborated in work of Popa [21], Tannen, and Deutsch (e.g., [10, 9]) for reformulating queries on a physical schema while exploiting constraints. The main idea is to produce a "universal plan" (the chase) and then simplify it (back-chasing). Our work connects the approach via preservation of Nash, Segoufin and Vianu with the C&B method, while pointing out new applications. The proof-to-plan approach here applies to logics beyond dependencies (where the chase is not applicable), and to dependencies where the chase does not converge. We demonstrate this flexibility by discussing a cost-aware plan-generation algorithm for *guarded dependencies.* This class of constraints is orthogonal to those in [21, 10], which use an OO model that includes both TGDs and EGDs (e.g. keys), but relying on chase termination. In the special case of TGDs where the chase terminates, our algorithm can be seen as a way of combining the cost-based C&B described in Chapter 6 of Popa's thesis [21] with the access-method extension of C&B given in the work of Deutsch, Ludäscher, and Nash [8]. We note that unlike [21, 9] the cost-based algorithm outlined in this paper is not targeted towards generating physical plans on a single source (and thus we do not assume, as in these works, a fine model of how physical and logical schemas interact) – instead we are interested in optimizing the performance of expensive queries on top of sources, using a DBMS in the middleware.

Chapter 5 of the book of Toman and Weddell [22] (see also [5]) outlines an approach to reformulating queries with respect to a physical schema that is based on proofs. They discuss proofs using the chase algorithm, as well as an extended proof system connected to Craig Interpolation, remarking as we do that the latter can synthesize plans that are not conjunctive. Our results give a finer look at how plan-generation is impacted by the expressiveness of integrity constraints, axioms for capturing access restrictions, and the chosen proof system.

The recent work [3] studies the complexity of "complete answerability" for constraints in guarded logics. We will use several tools from [3], but our focus is exploring the relationship of proofs to plans: in the general first-order setting as well as for restricted constraint classes; finding optimal plans in addition to finding some plan; checking if a plan exists and finding plans efficiently.

Summary of Contributions. In summary, this work outlines a new perspective on implementing queries over restricted interfaces, by generating plans from proofs.

- We prove theorems characterizing the existence of a plan for a query. These results can be read as semantics-to-syntax results

– if a query has a certain preservation property then it can be rewritten in a certain form. They have an alternative effective reading, providing a recipe for deriving a plan from a proof.
- We show that these results generalize a number of theorems concerning views, and give a parallel between reformulation results for queries in databases and preservation and definability theorems in classical logic.
- We provide a new constructive interpolation theorem for predicate logic that generalizes many prior results, and provides a powerful new tool in the study of query reformulations.
- For TGDs, we give algorithms that produce plans directly from chase proofs. Informally, these algorithms perform interpolation directly over a plan language. We show that the proof-generated plans are as efficient as arbitrary plans based on conjunctive queries.
- We show how the direct proof-to-plan approach outlined for TGDs can be extended to find the lowest cost plan, even in the case of TGDs where the chase does not converge.

2. DEFINITIONS

Our starting point will be a *schema* which describes a querying scenario, consisting of:

- A collection of relations, each of a given arity. A *position* of a relation R is a number $\leq arity(R)$.
- A finite collection C of *schema constants* ("smith", 3, ...). Informally, these represent a fixed set of values that a querier might use as test values in accesses. For example, if the user is performing a query involving the string "smith", we would assume that "smith" was a schema constant – but not arbitrary unrelated strings.
- For each relation R, a collection (possibly empty) of *access methods*. Each method mt is associated with a collection of positions of R – the *input positions* of mt.
- A collection of *integrity constraints*, which we will always assume are given by sentences of first-order logic (interpreted under the active domain semantics [1]), using only relations and constants from the schema.

  We will give particular attention to constraints given by *tuple-generating dependencies* (TGDs), given syntactically as

$$\forall \mathbf{x} \varphi(\mathbf{x}) \rightarrow \exists \mathbf{y} \rho(\mathbf{x}, \mathbf{y})$$

  where φ and ρ are conjunctions of relational atoms, possibly including constants.

  A special subclass consists of *Guarded TGDs*, in which φ is of the form $R(\mathbf{x}) \wedge \varphi'$ where $R(\mathbf{x})$ contains all variables of φ'. These subsume *inclusion dependencies* (IDs): where φ is of the form $R(\mathbf{x})$ in which no variables are repeated and there are no constants, while ρ is also a single atom with no repeated variables or constants. IDs are also called "referential constraints".

Informally, the access methods give restrictions on how relations can be accessed. A standard example of relations with access methods comes from Web forms, where the input positions represent mandatory fields of the form.

We will use standard terminology for describing queries in first-order logic, including the notion of free variable, quantifiers, connectives, etc. [1]. A database instance (or just database) I for schema S assigns to every relation R in S a collection of tuples $I(R)$ of the right arity, in such a way that any integrity constraints of S are satisfied. An association of a database relation R with a tuple $\mathbf{c}$ of the proper arity will be referred to as a *fact*. A database instance can equivalently be seen as a collection of facts.

We consider *conjunctive queries* (CQs) $Q(\mathbf{x}) = \exists \mathbf{y}(A_1 \wedge \cdots \wedge A_n)$, where A_i is an atom using a relation of the schema and variables from $\mathbf{x}$ and $\mathbf{y}$ and/or constants from the schema as arguments. These are equivalent to *ESPJ* queries in relational algebra (defined below), and we will freely move back-and-forth between logic-based notation and relational algebra notation, and also between positional and attribute-based notation for components of a tuple. Given a conjunctive query Q and instance I, $Q(I)$ is the result of evaluating Q on I.

Access plans and costs. We look at plans for answering a query respecting the access methods.

An *access command* over a schema S with access methods consists of an access method mt from S on some relation R, a relational algebra expression E over some set of relations not in S ("temporary relations" henceforward), a bijective mapping b_{in} taking output attributes of E to the input positions of mt, an output temporary relation T and a binary relation b_{out} relating positions of R to positions of T, such that every position of T is in the range of b_{out}.

We will generally omit the mappings in the notation (and it will be clear from context in the examples), and we write an access command as $T \Leftarrow \mathsf{mt} \Leftarrow E$, denoting that mt is invoked with inputs produced by relational algebra expression E with the result going into T. For example, a plan for the query in Example 2 might begin with a command $T_1 \Leftarrow \mathsf{mt}_{\mathsf{Ids}} \Leftarrow \emptyset$, where $\mathsf{mt}_{\mathsf{Ids}}$ is the input-free access to table Ids, T_1 is a temporary table with a single column, and $\emptyset$ (by convention) represents no input.

A *middleware query command* is of the form $T := E$, where T is a temporary relation and E is a relational algebra expression. The input relations of E are temporary relations filled by other access commands, while the relation T may be used as input in further commands.

An *RA-plan* consists of a sequence of access and middleware query commands, along with a distinguished final output relation T_{fin}. We can similarly talk about *SPJ-plans*, where the expressions in access and middleware query commands are built up from relational algebra operators SELECT, PROJECT, and JOIN, *USPJ-plans* that allow UNION in addition to SPJ operators, and $USPJ^{\neg}$*-plans* that allow the difference operator $E - E'$ to be applied only in taking the output tuples of E and subtracting out tuples that are in some relation R, where R has at least one method. Hence $USPJ^{\neg}$-plans implement queries that use the difference operator only when the second argument is a relation. Similarly we can talk about plans for other relational algebra fragments. We allow for the use of inequalities in selections and join conditions, and we denote by *ESPJ* the fragment of SPJ where only equality conditions are allowed. *EUSPJ* and $EUSPJ^{\neg}$ are defined analogously.

The semantics of plans is straightforward. Given a database instance I that interprets a relation R with access method mt having input positions $j_1 \dots j_m$, and also interpreting the relations mentioned in expression E, an access command $T \Leftarrow \mathsf{mt} \Leftarrow E$ is executed by performing the query E on I and "accessing mt on every result tuple". That is, each output tuple of E is mapped to a tuple $t_{j_1} \dots t_{j_m}$ using the input mapping. For each tuple $\mathbf{t} = t_1 \dots t_n \in R$ that "matches" (i.e. that extends) $t_{j_1} \dots t_{j_m}$, $\mathbf{t}$ is transformed to a tuple $\mathbf{t}'$ added to T using the output mapping b_{out}. If b_{out} maps one position of R to multiple positions in T, the values t_i are duplicated in $\mathbf{t}'$. If b_{out} maps positions p, p' of R to the same position in T, then a tuple $\mathbf{t}'$ is only added to T if $t_p = t_{p'}$. A middleware query command $T := E$ executes query E on the current contents of the temporary tables mentioned in E, and then places the result in temporary table T. A plan is evaluated on an instance of S by evaluating each command in sequence, starting with all temporary relations initially empty. The *output* of the plan on an input database is the content of the table T_{fin}.

Given a schema S with access methods and constraints, a plan *answers* a query Q *(over all instances)* if for every instance I satisfying the constraints of S, the output of the plan on I is the same as the output of Q. We say that the plan *answers* Q *over finite instances* if this holds for every finite instance I satisfying the constraints.

For general constraints, answering over all instances is not always the same as answering over finite instances, and in this work *we will always deal, by default, with the unrestricted notion of answering.* We will discuss the modification for the finite case later in the paper, and in particular we will show that for the main class of constraints we work with in our implementation (Guarded TGDs) the two notions of answerability coincide.

The requirement that the plan generate *all* outputs of Q on *every* instance formalizes our notion of "complete answerability" mentioned in the introduction.

Cost. We will be interested in finding plans that minimize a *plan cost function*, which associates every plan with a real-valued cost. Our framework can work with a "black box" cost function on plans that is monotone as additional access commands are concatenated to the plan.

If no information about the underlying sources is available, a default cost metric would associate each access method mt with a positive rational cost c_{mt}, and then the total cost of a plan whose access commands are calls to $\mathsf{mt}_1 \dots \mathsf{mt}_n$ (with possibly the same method repeated with different arguments) would be defined as $\Sigma_{i \leq n} c_{\mathsf{mt}_i}$. We refer to these as *simple cost functions* in the remainder, and we will provide refinements of the algorithms for this case.

3. FROM FO PROOFS TO PLANS

We describe how to generate plans that correspond to proofs that a query can be answered, in the setting of arbitrary first-order integrity constraints. Two kinds of reasoning are needed to know whether a query can be answered. One concerns the semantic relationships between tables, captured by integrity constraints. Another concerns what sort of access we have to relations. We formalize this second type of reasoning by revisiting and extending a prior technique for *axiomatizing properties of accesses in rules* (see [11, 8]).

Given schema S_0, the *Accessible Schema for* S_0, denoted $\mathsf{AcSch}(S_0)$, is the schema without any access restrictions, such that:

- The constants are those of S_0.
- The relations are those of S_0, a copy of each relation R denoted $\mathsf{Accessed}R$ (the "accessible version of R"), a unary relation $\mathsf{accessible}(x)$ ("x is an accessible value") plus another copy of each relation R of S_0 called $\mathsf{InferredAcc}R$ – the "inferred accessible version of R". We refer to the relations of the form $\mathsf{Accessed}R$ and the relation $\mathsf{accessible}$ as the "accessible copy of S_0" .
- The constraints are those of S_0 (referred to as "original constraints" below) along with the following constraints (dropping universal quantifiers on the outside for brevity)
  - A "defining axiom" for the relation accessible:

$$\mathsf{Accessed}R(\mathbf{x}) \rightarrow \mathsf{accessible}(x_i)$$

  for every R and x_i in $\mathbf{x}$. Informally, this says that accessible is the active domain of all accessible facts.
  - *accessibility axioms*: for each access method mt on relation R of arity n with input positions $j_1 \dots j_m$ we have a rule:

$$\mathsf{accessible}(x_{j_1}) \wedge \dots \wedge \mathsf{accessible}(x_{j_m}) \wedge R(x_1 \dots x_n) \rightarrow \mathsf{Accessed}R(x_1 \dots x_n)$$

  In addition, we have $\mathsf{accessible}(c)$ for each constant c of S_0.
  - *inferred accessible fact rules*, which are of two forms. First we have rules:

$$\mathsf{Accessed}R(\mathbf{x}) \rightarrow \mathsf{InferredAcc}R(\mathbf{x})$$

  Secondly, we have a copy of each of the original integrity constraints, with each relation R replaced by $\mathsf{InferredAcc}R$.

Informally, the accessible versions of relations represent the facts that can be explicitly retrieved from the access methods, while $\mathsf{accessible}(c)$ indicates that the value c can be returned by some access. The inferred accessible relations represent facts that can be derived from the accessible facts using reasoning. Thus the accessible schema represents the rules that allow one to move from a "hidden fact" (e.g. $R(c_1 \dots c_n)$) to an accessible fact ($\mathsf{Accessed}R(c_1 \dots c_n)$), and from there – using the constraints – to an inferred fact (e.g. $\exists y\ \mathsf{InferredAcc}S(c_1 \dots c_n, y)$). From the structure of the rules it is easy to see that "inferred accessible rules" can fire based upon facts generated by other kinds of rules, but not vice versa.

Given a query Q, its *inferred accessible version* $\mathsf{InferredAcc}Q$ is obtained by replacing each relation R by $\mathsf{InferredAcc}R$ and adding the atom $\mathsf{accessible}(x)$ for every free variable. $\mathsf{InferredAcc}Q$ represents the fact that the existence of a witness to Q can be obtained through making accesses and reasoning.

We say that Q *entails* Q' with respect to a set of integrity constraints if in any instance that satisfies the constraints $\forall \mathbf{x} (Q(\mathbf{x}) \rightarrow Q'(\mathbf{x}))$ holds. As with other notions, by default, we deal here with arbitrary instances, not necessarily finite.

In particular, if Q entails $\mathsf{InferredAcc}Q$, this means that we can infer from Q holding in a hidden database that Q's truth can be learned by a user via accesses and reasoning with constraints.

EXAMPLE 3. *The query Q from Example 1 can be expressed as* $\exists \mathsf{onum}\ \mathsf{Profinfo}(\mathsf{eid}, \mathsf{onum}, \textit{"smith"})$. *Therefore* $\mathsf{InferredAcc}Q$ *is* $\mathsf{accessible}(\mathsf{eid}) \wedge \exists \mathsf{onum}\ \mathsf{InferredAccProfinfo}(\mathsf{eid}, \mathsf{onum}, \textit{"smith"})$. *The accessible schema includes rules:*

- $\mathsf{Profinfo}(\mathsf{eid}, \mathsf{onum}, \mathsf{lname}) \rightarrow \mathsf{Udirect}(\mathsf{eid}, \mathsf{lname})$
- $\mathsf{Udirect}(\mathsf{eid}, \mathsf{lname}) \rightarrow \mathsf{AccessedUdirect}(\mathsf{eid}, \mathsf{lname})$
- $\mathsf{AccessedUdirect}(\mathsf{eid}, \mathsf{lname}) \rightarrow \mathsf{accessible}(\mathsf{eid}) \wedge \mathsf{accessible}(\mathsf{lname})$
- $\mathsf{Profinfo}(\mathsf{eid}, \mathsf{onum}, \mathsf{lname}) \wedge \mathsf{accessible}(\mathsf{eid}) \rightarrow \mathsf{AccessedProfinfo}(\mathsf{eid}, \mathsf{onum}, \mathsf{lname})$
- $\mathsf{AccessedProfinfo}(\mathsf{eid}, \mathsf{onum}, \mathsf{lname}) \rightarrow \mathsf{InferredAccProfinfo}(\mathsf{eid}, \mathsf{onum}, \mathsf{lname})$

One can see that Q entails $\mathsf{InferredAcc}Q$ *with respect to these rules.*

The relationship between entailment using the accessible schema and plans is encoded in the following theorem:

THEOREM 1. *For any conjunctive query Q and schema S_0 containing constraints specified in first-order logic and access restrictions, there is a complete USPJ-plan for Q (over databases in S_0) if and only if Q entails* $\mathsf{InferredAcc}Q$ *with respect to* $\mathsf{AcSch}(S_0)$.

Furthermore, if the constraints of S_0 are specified by equality-free first-order formulas (e.g., TGDs), then we can replace USPJ-plan with $EUSPJ$-plan in the above statement.

Theorem 1 gives a correspondence between Q entailing $\mathsf{InferredAcc}Q$ and the existence of complete plans based on unions of conjunctive queries. Its proof, discussed further down, yields an algorithm for generating plans, given a proof witnessing that Q entails $\mathsf{InferredAcc}Q$. But for first-order constraints such proofs cannot be found effectively. We will look at plan-generation algorithms for more restricted constraints in the next section.

Extending to larger classes of plans. The proof/plan correspondence is not limited to USPJ plans. Let $\mathsf{AcSch}^{\leftrightarrow}(S_0)$ extend the axioms of $\mathsf{AcSch}(S_0)$ with the axioms $\forall \mathbf{x}\ \mathsf{Accessed}R(\mathbf{x}) \rightarrow R(\mathbf{x})$ and the following axioms (universal quantifiers omitted):

$$\bigwedge_{i \leq m} \mathsf{accessible}(x_{j_i}) \wedge \mathsf{InferredAcc}R(x_1 \dots x_n) \rightarrow \mathsf{Accessed}R(x_1 \dots x_n)$$

Above, R is a relation of S_0 having an access method with input positions $j_1 \dots j_m$. Notice that these rules are obtained from those of $\mathsf{AcSch}(S_0)$ by switching the roles of $\mathsf{InferredAcc}R$ and R, resulting in a rule set where the original schema and the $\mathsf{InferredAcc}$ copy are treated symmetrically. The following result shows that provability with these "bi-directional axioms" corresponds to existence of a relational algebra plan:

THEOREM 2. *For any relational query Q and schema S_0 containing access restrictions and constraints specified in first-order logic, there is an RA-plan answering Q (over databases in S_0) if and only if Q entails* $\mathsf{InferredAcc}Q$ *with respect to the rules in* $\mathsf{AcSch}^{\leftrightarrow}(S_0)$.

In between the RA and USPJ versions, we have a version for queries that allow atomic negation: allowing the difference operator $E - R$, but where R must be a relation. Let $\mathsf{AcSch}^{\neg}(S_0)$ extend $\mathsf{AcSch}(S_0)$ with the following "negative accessibility axioms", for all relations R that have some access method:

$$\bigwedge_{i \leq n} \mathsf{accessible}(x_i) \wedge \neg R(x_1 \dots x_n) \rightarrow \neg \mathsf{InferredAcc}R(x_1 \dots x_n)$$

Intuitively, the rule says that if the hidden database does *not* include a hidden fact, and all the values in the fact are known to a user, then the user can infer that the fact does not hold using accesses. The result below shows that this axiom system characterizes $USPJ^{\neg}$ plans:

THEOREM 3. *For any relational algebra query Q and schema S_0 containing access restrictions and constraints specified in first order logic, there is a complete $USPJ^{\neg}$-plan for Q (over databases in S_0) if and only if Q entails* InferredAcc$Q$ *with respect to* $\mathsf{AcSch}^{\neg}(S_0)$.

Furthermore, if the constraints of S_0 are equality-free then we can replace $USPJ^{\neg}$-plan with $EUSPJ^{\neg}$-plan.

Proofs of the main first-order theorems. We now begin the proofs of these three theorems, beginning with two main tools, executable queries and an interpolation theorem that can produce executable queries.

Executable queries and plans. In creating our plans that witness the proof-to-plan direction of the theorems, we will sometimes find it convenient to produce not a plan, but an *executable FO rewriting*. For us, an *executable FO query* (relative to a schema with access methods) is a first-order formula built up from equalities and the formula True using arbitrary boolean operations and the quantifiers:

$$\forall \mathbf{y}\ [(R(\mathbf{x},\mathbf{y}) \rightarrow \varphi(\mathbf{x},\mathbf{y},\mathbf{z})] \quad \text{and} \quad \exists \mathbf{y}\ R(\mathbf{x},\mathbf{y}) \wedge \varphi(\mathbf{x},\mathbf{y},\mathbf{z})$$

where R has an access method mt such that, in $R(\mathbf{x},\mathbf{y})$ above, all of the input positions of mt are occupied by some x_i. An executable FO rewriting of Q (relative to a schema S_0 with access methods and constraints) is an executable FO query for S_0 that is equivalent to Q over instances that satisfy the constraints of S_0. To improve readability, we will drop the schema S_0 from the terminology, and just talk about executable FO queries and rewritings henceforward.

The intuition is that these queries are such that given an input tuple matching the free variables, we can use the access methods to verify whether it satisfies the query. In particular, executable boolean RA queries can be easily converted directly to RA-plans via induction.

PROPOSITION 1. *There is a linear time procedure converting an executable boolean FO query into an RA-plan. Furthermore, if the FO query is existential (resp. existential without inequalities) the result is a $USPJ^{\neg}$ (resp. $EUSPJ^{\neg}$)-plan, while if the query is positive existential, the result is a USPJ (resp. EUSPJ)-plan*

Interpolation. The next key element of our proofs will be *interpolation theorems*. The Craig interpolation theorem states that if φ_1 and φ_2 are first-order formulas such that φ_1 entails φ_2, then there exists a first-order formula φ such that φ_1 entails φ and φ entails φ_2, and φ uses only relation symbols occurring in both φ_1 and φ_2.

Variants of the Craig interpolation theorem exist that allow one to make further conclusions about the interpolant. For example, the Lyndon interpolation theorem [17] restricts the relations that occur positively (resp. negatively) in the interpolant to those occurring positively and negatively on both the left and right. More recently Otto [20] has proven a more powerful *relativized interpolation theorem* that not only controls the polarity of relations, but the pattern of quantification that occurs within them. Inspired by Otto's result, we prove a version of Craig interpolation that allows us to relate the "binding patterns" used in the interpolant φ with those used in φ_1 or φ_2. When we apply this theorem to the entailment of InferredAcc$Q$ by Q, we will be able to conclude that the interpolant is an executable query.

We associate to first-order formulas the set of binding patterns used in quantification, where a binding pattern is a relation and a subset of the positions. This is done by induction on the formula:

$$\begin{array}{lll}
\mathsf{BindPatt}(\top) = \mathsf{BindPatt}(x=y) & = & \emptyset \\
\mathsf{BindPatt}(R(t_1,\ldots,t_n)) & = & \{(R,\{1,\ldots,n\})\} \\
\mathsf{BindPatt}(\neg\varphi) & = & \mathsf{BindPatt}(\varphi) \\
\mathsf{BindPatt}(\varphi \wedge \psi) & = & \mathsf{BindPatt}(\varphi) \cup \mathsf{BindPatt}(\psi) \\
\mathsf{BindPatt}(\varphi \vee \psi) & = & \mathsf{BindPatt}(\varphi) \cup \mathsf{BindPatt}(\psi) \\
\mathsf{BindPatt}(\exists \mathbf{x}(R(t_1,\ldots,t_n) \wedge \varphi)) & = & \mathsf{BindPatt}(\varphi) \cup \{(R,\{i \mid t_i \notin \mathbf{x}\})\} \\
\mathsf{BindPatt}(\forall \mathbf{x}(R(t_1,\ldots,t_n) \rightarrow \varphi)) & = & \mathsf{BindPatt}(\varphi) \cup \{(R,\{i \mid t_i \notin \mathbf{x}\})\}
\end{array}$$

Intuitively, BindPatt(φ) describes the kind of access that is used if φ is evaluated in an instance using a straightforward inductive evaluation procedure. For example,

$$\mathsf{BindPatt}(\exists xy(Rxy \wedge \forall z(Sxyz \rightarrow Uxyz))) = \{(R,\emptyset),(S,\{1,2\}),(U,\{1,2,3\})\}$$

In particular, if each pattern in BindPatt(φ) is represented by a method in a schema S_0, then φ is an executable FO query for S_0.

Note that, for formulas φ containing unrestricted quantifiers, such as $\exists x\ \neg P(x)$, BindPatt(φ) is undefined. However, every conjunctive query can be viewed (modulo minor syntactic transformations) as having no unrestricted quantifiers, and, furthermore, under the active domain semantics, every formula is equivalent to one without unrestricted quantifiers.

We say that a relation symbol R *occurs positively* (*negatively*) in a formula φ if some occurrence of R in φ is in the scope of an even (odd) number of negations. For the purpose of this definition, we view the implication symbol as a shorthand: $\psi \rightarrow \chi$ stands for $\neg\psi \vee \chi$. Thus, for example, in the formula $\forall x(P(x) \rightarrow \exists y R(x,y))$, the relation symbol P occurs negatively and R occurs positively.

THEOREM 4 (ACCESS INTERPOLATION). *Let φ_1 and φ_2 be first-order sentences such that φ_1 entails φ_2. Then there exists a first-order sentence φ such that*
1. *φ_1 entails φ and φ entails φ_2,*
2. *A relation symbol occurs positively (negatively) in φ only if it occurs positively (negatively) in both φ_1 and φ_2.*
3. *A constant symbol occurs in φ only if it occurs both in φ_1 and φ_2*
4. *If* BindPatt(φ_1) *and* BindPatt(φ_2) *are both defined, then* BindPatt(φ) $\subseteq$ BindPatt(φ_1) $\cup$ BindPatt(φ_2).
5. *If φ_1 and φ_2 are both equality-free, then φ is equality-free.*

Furthermore, ψ can be computed in polynomial time from a proof (in a suitable proof system) of the entailment $\varphi_1 \rightarrow \varphi_2$.

The proof of the Access interpolation theorem, deferred to the full paper, is constructive (in fact, polynomial time), producing an interpolant inductively from a proof that φ_1 entails φ_2 in a particular proof system. Both the proof system used (tableaux) and the technique used to extract the interpolant follow along the lines of a standard technique for interpolation, annotating the proof elements with a "bias" and extracting an interpolant bottom-up on the proof tree (e.g. [2, 4]). The new component is an analysis of the relationship between binding patterns in the output formula and those in the input formula.

$\mathsf{AcSch}^{\leftrightarrow}$ and RA-plans. We now begin with the proofs, starting with Theorem 2, because it is the simplest of the results, and will establish a template used in the proofs of the other two results.

Recall that given a schema S_0 with constraints and access restrictions, the set of constraints $\mathsf{AcSch}^{\leftrightarrow}(S_0)$ includes all constraints of $\mathsf{AcSch}(S_0)$, as well as the additional rules:

$$\forall x_1 \ldots x_n\ \mathsf{Accessed}R(x_1 \ldots x_n) \rightarrow R(x_1 \ldots x_n)$$

and also the rules:

$$\forall x_1 \ldots x_n\ \mathsf{InferredAcc}R(x_1 \ldots x_n) \wedge \mathsf{accessible}(x_{j_1}) \ldots \mathsf{accessible}(x_{j_m}) \rightarrow \mathsf{Accessed}R(x_1 \ldots x_n)$$

for every relation R with an access method mt on positions $j_1 \ldots j_m$.

For simplicity, in this proof, as well as others in the section, we deal with the case where Q is boolean and there are no constants in the schema.

We recall several notions from [3]. Given an instance I for schema S_0 the *accessible part of I*, denote AccPart(I) consists of all the facts over I that can be obtained by starting with empty relations and iteratively entering values into the access methods. Formally, it is a database containing a set of facts Accessed$R(v_1 \ldots v_n)$, where R is a relation and $v_1 \ldots v_n$ are values in the domain of I such that $R(v_1 \ldots v_n)$ holds in I, obtained by starting with relations AccessedR_0 and $\mathsf{accessible}_0$ empty [1], and then iterating the following process until a fixpoint is reached:

- $\mathsf{accessible}_{i+1} = \mathsf{accessible}_i \cup \bigcup_{R \text{ a relation},\ j<arity(R)} \pi_j(\mathsf{Accessed}_i(R))$

[1]In the presence of schema constants, we would start with $\mathsf{accessible}_0$ consisting of the schema constants

- $\mathsf{Accessed}_{i+1}(R) = \mathsf{Accessed}_i(R) \cup \bigcup_{\substack{(R,\{j_1,\ldots,j_m\}) \\ \text{a method of } S_0}} \{(v_1 \ldots v_n) \in I(R) \mid v_{j_i} \in \mathsf{accessible}_i \text{ for all } i \leq m\}$

where $\pi_j(\mathsf{Accessed}_i(R))$ is the j-th projection of $\mathsf{Accessed}_i(R)$.

Above we consider $\mathsf{AccPart}(I)$ as a database instance for the schema with relations accessible and Accessed$R$. Below we will sometimes refer to the values in the relation accessible as the *accessible values of I*. An immediate observation is that if we expand the database I with the interpretations of accessible and the Accessed$R$ from $\mathsf{AccPart}(I)$, the result will satisfy all the axioms of $\mathsf{AcSch}^{\leftrightarrow}(S_0)$ that relate the original relations R to accessible and the relations Accessed$R$.

The following proposition states that an instance and its accessible part agree on executable FO queries.

PROPOSITION 2. *For any instance I of S_0, let I' be the accessible part of I, seen as a structure for the relations of S_0: that is, the relations R is interpreted in I' by* Accessed$R$ *in the accessible part of I. Then for executable FO formula ρ and any binding $\mathbf{b}$ of the variables in ρ to elements in* $\mathsf{AccPart}(I)$, *ρ is true on $I, \mathbf{b}$ iff ρ is true on $I', \mathbf{b}$. In particular, I and I' agree on all executable boolean FO queries.*

The proposition can be proven straightforwardly via induction on ρ, or via the appropriate back-and-forth game.

Q is said to be *access-determined* over S_0 if for all instances I and I' satisfying the constraints of S_0 with $\mathsf{AccPart}(I) = \mathsf{AccPart}(I')$ we have $Q(I) = Q(I')$. If a query is *not* access-determined, it is obvious that it cannot be answered through any plan, since it is easy to see that any plan can only read accessible tuples. The following claim restates our entailment hypothesis in terms of this preservation property.

CLAIM 1. *The following are equivalent (for any schema consisting of first-order constraints and access restrictions):*
1. *Q entails* InferredAcc$Q$ *with respect to the rules in* $\mathsf{AcSch}^{\leftrightarrow}(S_0)$
2. *Q is access-determined over S_0*

PROOF. We prove that the first item implies the second. Fix I and I' satisfying the schema with the same accessible part, and assume I satisfies Q. Consider the instance I'' for the accessible schema formed by interpreting the relations R as in I, each relation Accessed$R$ by the accessible tuples that R has in I (that is, the relation Accessed$R$ of the accessible part of I, defined via the fixpoint process described above), the relation accessible by the accessible values of I, and each InferredAcc$R$ by the interpretation of R in I'. Then one can easily verify that I'' satisfies the constraints of $\mathsf{AcSch}^{\leftrightarrow}(S_0)$. Since I (and hence I'') satisfies Q, and we are assuming that Q entails InferredAcc$Q$ with respect to $\mathsf{AcSch}^{\leftrightarrow}(S_0)$ we can conclude that I'' must satisfy InferredAcc$Q$. Thus Q holds in I' as required.

We now argue from the second item to the first, which will complete the proof of the claim. Suppose Q does not imply InferredAcc$Q$ with respect to the rules in $\mathsf{AcSch}^{\leftrightarrow}(S_0)$. Hence there is an instance $I^{\mathsf{AcSch}^{\leftrightarrow}}$ satisfying the rules of $\mathsf{AcSch}^{\leftrightarrow}(S_0)$ and also satisfying $Q \wedge \neg$InferredAcc$Q$. Let I_1 consist of the restriction of $I^{\mathsf{AcSch}^{\leftrightarrow}}$ to the original schema relations. Let I_2 consist of the inferred accessible relations from $I^{\mathsf{AcSch}^{\leftrightarrow}}$, renamed to the original schema. We first claim that a fact $F = R(e_1 \ldots e_n)$ of the accessible part of I_1 is in the accessible part of I_2. We prove this by induction on the iteration of the fixpoint where F appears. F must be generated by an access using elements $e_{j_1} \ldots e_{j_m}$ which in turn satisfy accessible facts generated earlier in the fixpoint iteration. Thus by induction these earlier facts are in the accessible part of I_2, and in particular $e_{j_1} \ldots e_{j_m}$ are accessible values of I_2. Using the axioms we have that InferredAcc$R(e_1 \ldots e_n)$ holds, and thus $R(e_1 \ldots e_n)$ holds in I_2. Using the definition of accessible part, we conclude that F is in the accessible part of I_2 as required. Arguing symmetrically, we have that I_1 and I_2 have the same accessible part, and hence they contradict access-determinacy. □

From this claim, we easily see the "plan-to-proof" direction of Theorem 2. Suppose Q does not imply InferredAcc$Q$ with respect to the rules in $\mathsf{AcSch}^{\leftrightarrow}(S_0)$. By Claim 1, Q is not access-determined, and thus no plan can answer Q.

Note that Claim 1 allows us to restate Theorem 2 as: *A query Q has an RA-plan iff Q is access-determined.* Thus, we can think of the theorem as a kind of preservation theorem (see the comparison with earlier results below).

We now prove the "proof-to-plan" direction of Theorem 2: assuming Q entails InferredAcc$Q$, we construct an RA-plan that answers Q.

We can remove the relation accessible from the schema, modifying the rules of $\mathsf{AcSch}^{\leftrightarrow}(S_0)$ by breaking up the relation accessible as a disjunction of relations Accessed$S$. That is, we could replace every accessibility axiom

$$\bigwedge_{i \leq m} \mathsf{accessible}(x_{j_i}) \wedge R(\mathbf{x}) \rightarrow \mathsf{Accessed}R(\mathbf{x})$$

by all axioms of the form

$$\alpha_1(x_{j_1}) \wedge \cdots \wedge \alpha_n(x_{j_n}) \wedge R(\mathbf{x}) \rightarrow \mathsf{Accessed}R(\mathbf{x}))$$

where $\alpha_i(x_{j_i})$ is of the form Accessed$S(\mathbf{y}, x_{j_i}, \mathbf{z})$ for some S and fresh $\mathbf{y}, \mathbf{z}$.

Thus from now on we will assume that accessible does not appear.

We can rephrase the assumption as:

$$Q \wedge \Sigma_1 \text{ entails } (\Sigma_2 \rightarrow \mathsf{InferredAcc}Q)$$

where Σ_1 is the set of constraints in $\mathsf{AcSch}^{\leftrightarrow}(S_0)$ mentioning only the original relations and the relations Accessed$R$, while Σ_2 contains all constraints mentioning relations of the form InferredAcc$R$. As observed above, we can assume that Σ (and hence Σ_1, Σ_2) do not use unrestricted quantification.

By the Access interpolation theorem there is a first-order sentence φ using only relations of the form Accessed$R$ such that:
1. $Q \wedge \Sigma_1$ entails φ
2. φ entails $\Sigma_2 \rightarrow$ InferredAcc$Q$
3. φ only uses binding patterns occurring in $Q \wedge \Sigma_1$ or in $\Sigma_2 \rightarrow$ InferredAcc$Q$

For a formula ρ using only the relations Accessed$R$, let deacc(ρ) be obtained be replacing each relation Accessed$R$ of ρ with R. Note that since the binding patterns of the accessibility axioms are all compatible with some method of the schema (inputs of the pattern are contained in the input positions of the method) deacc(φ) is an executable FO query. Further, Proposition 2 implies that deacc(φ) holds on I iff φ holds on $\mathsf{AccPart}(I)$.

We claim that deacc(φ) is an executable FO rewriting of Q (and hence can be converted to an RA-plan using Proposition 1). We prove this by looking at the case where Q holds on an instance I of S_0 and the case where Q does not hold on I. If Q is true on I, then letting I' be the extension of I with relations Accessed$R$ interpreted as in $\mathsf{AccPart}(I)$, we have that $I + \mathsf{AccPart}(I)$ satisfies $Q \wedge \Sigma_1$. So by the first condition above we will have φ is true on $\mathsf{AccPart}(I)$, and thus deacc(φ) is true on I. On the other hand, if deacc(φ) is true on I then φ is true on $\mathsf{AccPart}(I)$. Consider the database instance I'' interpreting each Accessed$R$ as in $\mathsf{AccPart}(I)$ and each InferredAcc$R$ by R in I. I'' satisfies Σ_2. Thus applying the second condition on φ to I'', we get that InferredAcc$Q$ holds in I'', and hence Q holds in I.

This completes the proof of Theorem 2.

AcSch and USPJ-plans. We now turn to the proof of Theorem 1. As before, we will assume for simplicity that Q is a boolean query and there are no schema constants present.

We will again translate entailment in our axiom schema into a preservation property of models.

We say Q is *subinstance-access-determined* over S_0 if for all instances I and I' satisfying the constraints of S_0 with every fact of $\mathsf{AccPart}(I)$ contained in $\mathsf{AccPart}(I')$ (that is, $\mathsf{AccPart}(I)$ is a subinstance of $\mathsf{AccPart}(I')$), if I satisfies Q, then I' satisfies Q.

That is, we have weakened the hypothesis of access-determinacy to require only containment of facts, not equality.

The following claim now relates these notions to our axioms, analogously to Claim 1. Its proof follows along the lines of Claim 1, and is given in the full paper.

CLAIM 2. *The following are equivalent (for any schema consisting of first-order constraints and access restrictions):*
1. Q entails InferredAcc$Q$ *with respect to the rules in* AcSch(S_0)
2. Q is subinstance-access-determined w.r.t. S_0

Assuming this claim, Theorem 1 can be restated as saying that a query is subinstance-access-determined iff it has a USPJ-plan. The proof of Theorem 1 follows along the lines of the proof of Theorem 2, with the direction from plan to proof using Claim 2, and the proof to plan applying the Access interpolation theorem to the entailment.

The schema AcSch$^{\neg}$ and $USPJ^{\neg}$-plans. Finally, we discuss the proof of Theorem 3. We need a characterization corresponding to Claim 1 for AcSch$^{\neg}$.

Recall that given an instance I, an *accessible value* is an element in the domain of I that occurs in some fact Accessed$R(\mathbf{c})$ of AccPart(I). Equivalently, it is an element that satisfies the relation accessible in AccPart(I).

Given instances I and I', we say AccPart(I) is an *induced subinstance* of AccPart(I') if *(i)* every fact Accessed$R(\mathbf{c})$ of AccPart(I) is in AccPart(I') and *(ii)* for every $\mathbf{c}$ with each c_i an accessible value of I, if $R(\mathbf{c})$ is a fact of AccPart(I') then Accessed$R(\mathbf{c})$ is in AccPart(I).

We say that Q is *induced-subinstance-access-determined* with respect to S_0 if *whenever we have two instances I, I' satisfying the constraints of the schema S_0, I satisfies Q, and* AccPart(I) *is an induced subinstance of* AccPart(I')*, then I' satisfies Q.*

The following claim, whose proof follows along the lines of the earlier ones, relates this new preservation property to provability in the axiom schema AcSch$^{\neg}$.

CLAIM 3. *The following are equivalent (for any schema consisting of first-order constraints and access restrictions):*
1. Q entails InferredAcc$Q$ *with respect to the rules in* AcSch$^{\neg}(S_0)$
2. Q is induced-subinstance-access-determined w.r.t. S_0

The proof of Theorem 3 uses the claim above in one direction and Access interpolation in the other.

Consequences in the case of views, and comparison with preservation theorems.. We will now look at what the prior theorems say in the simpler case of *view-based access restrictions*. By this we mean that there is a subcollection of relations in the schema that are designated as fully accessible, and the integrity constraints just state that these relations are equivalent to first-order queries defining them. We will see that our results in this case are closely-related to preservation theorems in classical model theory.

Let us start with looking at Theorem 2, concerning RA-plans, in the setting of view-based access restrictions. In this simpler setting the notion of access-determinacy degenerates to the notion of *query-view determinacy* of Nash, Segoufin, and Vianu [18]. Theorem 2 then says that if a query is determined (over all instances) it is first-order rewritable over the views – a basic observation of [18], and one which is almost a restatement of the Projective Beth Definability Theorem of first-order logic. The proof of our Theorem 2 follows the proof of the Projective Beth Theorem via interpolation due to Craig [7]. Note that, unlike [18], the significance of this result for us is not as a "completeness theorem" (first-order logic suffices to express all rewritings), but as a way to obtain rewritings: we can begin to explore proofs, and from the proofs we can efficiently read off the rewritings.

The generalization for access patterns and arbitrary first-order constraints given in Theorem 2 has not been stated before, but it is very similar to results already proven in [3]: Theorem 4.5 of [3] starts with a preservation property of a query and concludes that the query has an "FO-k-rewriting", which is syntactically different from having an RA-plan.

Let us now look at Theorem 1, which concerns USPJ-plans, in the special case of view-based access restrictions. In this case the notion of subinstance-access-determinacy is again one considered by [18], the notion of *monotonicity*. Given a boolean relational algebra query Q and a set of relational algebra queries $Q_1 \ldots Q_n$, we say that Q is *monotone in* $Q_1 \ldots Q_n$, with respect to a set of constraints, if for any two instances I, I' satisfying the constraints, if I satisfies Q and for each $i \leq n$, the tuples returned by Q_i on I are a subset of those returned by Q_i on I', then Q is true on I. In the setting of finite instances, where there are no constraints, the proof of Theorem 5.6 of [18] shows that CQ Q is monotone in CQs $Q_1 \ldots Q_n$ iff there is a rewriting of Q as a CQ in terms of the $Q_1 \ldots Q_n$.

A corollary of the proof of Theorem 1 is the following variant for arbitrary RA queries in the presence of first-order constraints (where monotonicity is required over all instances):

COROLLARY 1. *Q is monotone in $Q_1 \ldots Q_n$ iff there is a USPJ-rewriting of Q in terms of $Q_1 \ldots Q_n$.*

That is, queries monotone in a set of views are USPJ-rewritable. For RA queries and arbitrary FO constraints, this requirement of monotonicity over all instances is needed. But when Q and the Q_i are CQs and the constraints come only from view definitions, we will see later that it can be weakened. Again, we want to emphasize the effective aspect of this: from a proof witnessing monotonicity, we can derive a rewriting.

As with the results on views, our theorem and also the special case above for views are closely related to a theorem in classical model theory, the Lyndon Preservation Theorem, which states that formulas preserved under surjective homomorphism are equivalent to positive formulas. Roughly speaking, the special case above is a version of Lyndon's Theorem that deals with the active domain semantics (which is what allows us to move from "positive" to "positive existential") and which is "projective" – allowing Q to be preserved under mappings preserving only a subset of the relations, and concluding that it has a nice rewriting using only the subset.

We now turn to Theorem 3. To our knowledge, the notion of preservation/determinacy considered in this theorem does not have any analog in in the earlier literature on views. But as with Theorem 1, the proof of Theorem 3 can be applied to characterize queries that are $USPJ^{\neg}$-rewritable in terms of a distinguished set of view relations in the presence of constraints. We modify the definition of monotonicity to require that, for each $i \leq n$, $Q_i(I')$ is obtained from $Q_i(I)$ by adding facts, but never adding facts all of whose elements lie in some $Q_j(I)$ for $j \leq n$. If we call such queries *induced-subinstance-monotone* we can then conclude:

COROLLARY 2. *A conjunctive query is induced-subinstance-monotone over a set of queries $\{Q_1 \ldots Q_n\}$ exactly when it is $USPJ^{\neg}$ rewritable over relations V_i for each Q_i.*

Again, there is an analogous result to Theorem 3 in classical model theory, namely the Łoś-Tarski Theorem, which characterizes existential formulas as those that are preserved under the notion of "model extension" used in classical model theory. Compared to this classical theorem, the corollary of Theorem 3 for views given just above differs in being "projective", and being used in the context of active-domain semantics.

Alternative proofs of the main first-order theorems. We mention here that all of these theorems can be proven directly from Otto's relativized interpolation theorem [20] and the compactness theorem of first-order logic. Applying Otto's theorem to the entailment of InferredAcc$Q$ by Q, what we obtain is that Q can be answered by a first-order sentence φ of the appropriate form (e.g. existential for Theorem 3) that is to be evaluated over the accessible part of the instance. Computing the accessible part requires a recursive query, but the compactness theorem can be applied to show that only k "levels" of the accessible part are necessary (see the notion of "k-accessible part" in [3]). There is an $EUSPJ$-plan P_k that will produce this truncation of the accessible part: P simply performs k rounds of making every possible access with values produced by the previous round. Since RA-plans are allowed to run arbitrary RA queries in the middleware, the composition of a first-order query φ with P_k is also given by an RA-plan. Similar reasoning shows that an existential query composed with P_k is implementable by a USPJ plan, and so forth.

In fact, if we apply this alternative approach to the most basic result, Theorem 2, we see that for this theorem we do not need Otto's theorem but only the determinacy-implies-rewriting theorem of Nash, Segoufin, and Vianu (Theorem 3.1 of [18]), whose proof in turn makes use of Otto's theorem.

One drawback of this alternative approach is that it is non-constructive, since the proof of Otto's result in [20] is non-constructive, and also because it appeals to the compactness theorem. But even with a constructive proof of Otto's result and a bound on k, it has limitations: even when one can find short proofs effectively, the plans resulting from this technique will begin by doing every possible access up to k iterations, which is certainly not feasible. We thus find the approach via Access interpolation more promising for implementation, and also closer to the direct algorithms used for TGDs. In addition, we believe that the Access interpolation theorem is of independent interest.

Finite instances and restricted constraints. The results above related existence of a plan for a query Q that works over all instances that satisfy the constraints of schema S_0 with entailment of $\mathsf{InferredAcc}Q$ from Q relative to a schema derived from S_0. But suppose we want a method that will check existence of a plan that answers Q only over all *finite* instances? One can construct example schemas, even using TGD constraints, where there is an RA-plan that works over finite instances, but no plan that works over all instances.

Using standard counterexamples in finite model theory, we can show that if we restrict to finite instances Theorem 1, Theorem 2, and Theorem 3 all fail. Indeed, there can not even be any effective *semi-decision* procedure that will check given a schema with first-order constraints and a CQ Q, whether Q has a plan (RA, USPJ, etc.) over finite instances. Thus the problem here is intrinsic to the hardness of reformulating queries in the presence of first-order logic constraints over finite structures, not specific to our approach via proofs. This follows easily from the fact that the valid first-order sentences can not be computably enumerated.

If we restrict our constraints to "finitely controllable" fragments (e.g. Guarded TGDs, Guarded Fragment), then we can regain completeness in the finite. For example, if the constraints of a schema are inclusion dependencies and our CQs are boolean, then Theorem 1–3 all hold when only finite instances are considered, and the method of plans-from-proofs will always generate a plan for any query that has a plan over finite instances. The key observation here is that when the constraints of S_0 are in these finitely-controllable fragments, then $\mathsf{AcSch}(S_0)$ is as well.

Decidability and complexity. The correspondences in Theorem 1, Theorem 2, and Theorem 3 deal with arbitrary first-order constraints, where both existence of a proof and the existence of a plan are undecidable. But since access interpolation can be done effectively, it follows that for any subclass S of first-order logic, we can decide if a plan exists whenever containment of CQs is decidable in the corresponding class of accessible schemas. Using this we can get decidability for "tame" integrity constraint classes studied in the literature. For example, for Guarded TGDs, which we will deal with later on in the paper, the derived schema $\mathsf{AcSch}^{\leftrightarrow}$ also consists only of Guarded TGDs, and a 2EXPTIME upper bound follows from bounds on querying with respect to Guarded TGDs. On the other hand, a reduction from query answering can be used to show that when constraints are Guarded TGDs deciding if a plan exists is 2EXPTIME-hard.

4. PLANS FROM TGD PROOFS

The previous results give a correspondence between entailment of $\mathsf{InferredAcc}Q$ from Q and the existence of a query that abides by the access restrictions. We will now focus on making this transformation from proofs more concrete, and also making the corresponding proof search more practical, restricting our attention now to constraints in the form of TGDs. For TGDs we can make use of a "forward-chaining" proof system known in the database literature as *the chase*. A proof can be rephrased as a sequence of database instances, beginning with the *canonical database* of query Q: the database whose elements are the constants of Q plus copies c_1 of each variable x_1 in Q and which has a fact $R(c_1 \ldots c_n)$ for each atom $R(x_1 \ldots x_n)$ of Q. These databases evolve by *firing rules*. Given a set of facts I and a TGD $\delta = \forall x_1 \ldots x_j \varphi(\mathbf{x}) \to \exists y_1 \ldots y_k \rho(\mathbf{x}, \mathbf{y})$ a *candidate match for* δ is a $\mathbf{e}$ such that $\varphi(\mathbf{e})$ holds but there is no $\mathbf{f}$ such that $\rho(\mathbf{e}, \mathbf{f})$ holds in I. A *rule firing* for this candidate match adds facts to I that make $\rho(\mathbf{e}, \mathbf{f})$ true, where $f_1 \ldots f_k$ are new constants ("chase constants").

A *chase sequence* following a set of dependencies Σ consists of a sequence of instances $F_i : 1 \leq i \leq n$, where F_{i+1} is obtained from F_i by some rule firing of a dependency in Σ. Thus each $1 \leq i \leq n$ is associated to a set of facts F_i (which we sometimes refer to as a *chase configuration*), to a rule firing, and to a set of *newly-generated facts* – the ones produced by the last rule firing. A homomorphism of a query Q' into the configuration of a chase sequence is called a *match* for Q' in the configuration.

We now have the following well-known result: for any conjunctive queries Q and Q' (with the same free variables), and any TGD constraints Σ, Q entails Q' w.r.t. Σ iff there is a chase sequence following Σ beginning with the canonical database of Q, leading to a configuration that has a match for Q', mapping the free variables of Q' to the same constants corresponding to the free variables of Q. In particular Q entails $\mathsf{InferredAcc}Q$ exactly when there is a chase sequence beginning with the canonical database of Q leading to an element that has a match for $\mathsf{InferredAcc}Q$.

We know from the previous section that for schemas S_0 with arbitrary first-order constraints, applying interpolation to a proof of $\mathsf{InferredAcc}Q$ from Q using $\mathsf{AcSch}(S_0)$ gives a query that can be converted to a USPJ-plan for Q. We will show that when S_0 has only TGDs, and we use forward-chaining proofs as our proof system, we can generate SPJ-plans directly from a proof using $\mathsf{AcSch}(S_0)$.

Given a chase sequence, let C_∞ be the set of chase constants generated by firings of original constraints of S_0 within this sequence. Our plans will make use of temporary tables T_j whose attributes correspond to a subset C_j of C_∞; informally, rows of these tables will store possible homomorphisms that map the chase constants into the instance being queried. The C_j will be monotonic in j under inclusion as j increases.

We will construct the commands in the plan by induction on the number of rule firings of an accessibility axiom in the chase sequence.

We will maintain as an invariant that the set of attributes C_j are exactly the set of constants $c \in C_\infty$ such that $\mathsf{accessible}(c)$ holds in the configuration of the last element of the sequence. We will also restrict to *eager proofs*: those which do not have a firing at some step i of an accessibility axiom, and then at a later step a rule firing involving the initial integrity constraints or their copies on the relations $\mathsf{InferredAcc}R$ that was already applicable at step i. Informally, in eager proofs, we always perform "cost-free rules" before we perform a rule firing that corresponds to an access. It is clear that any proof can be turned into an eager proof by re-arranging the proof steps.

In the induction step, we consider an eager chase sequence ending with the firing of a rule:

$$\mathsf{accessible}(c_{j_1}) \wedge \ldots \mathsf{accessible}(c_{j_m}) \wedge R(c_1 \ldots c_n) \\ \to \mathsf{Accessed}R(c_1 \ldots c_n)$$

associated with method mt on relation R having input positions $j_1 \ldots j_m$. Let v_{j-1} be the chase configuration prior to the firing of this rule. Note that by the inductive invariant, each c_{j_i} must be an attribute of table T_{j-1} associated to the sequence prior to the firing. We define the *commands that correspond to this rule firing*, denoted $\mathsf{Comms}(v_{j-1}, R(c_1 \ldots c_n), \mathsf{mt})$. We will focus on the case where no c_{j_i} are schema constants, no constant is repeated in $R(c_1 \ldots c_n)$, and $R(c_1 \ldots c_n)$ is the unique R-fact of v_{j-1} that has c_{j_i} at position j_i for each $i \leq m$; we defer the additional cases to the full paper. We first generate an access command whose input expression is the projection of T_{j-1} onto $c_{j_1} \ldots c_{j_m}$, with the input mapping b_{in} taking column c_{j_i} of T_{j-1} to input position j_i of mt. The command's output relation will be a table T_j with attributes $C_j = C_{j-1} \cup \{c_1 \ldots c_n\}$. We follow the access command by a middleware query command that sets T_j to the join of itself with T_{j-1}, again using the mapping associating the ith position in an output tuple with the attribute c_i in T_j.

Let C_{ret} be the set of chase constants c corresponding to the free variables of Q. If the configuration of the element v has a match for InferredAcc$Q$ in its configuration, we will add a query that will set a final table T_{fin} to the projection of T_j on C_{ret}. In the special case that Q is boolean, the final query amounts to checking that the table T_j is non-empty.

EXAMPLE 4. *Consider the same schema as in Example 1. Let* $Q = \exists \text{eid onum lname Profinfo(eid,onum,lname)}$. *Using the chase, we get the following* **proof***:*

1. *Create the canonical database, which in this case contains the single fact* $\text{Profinfo}(\text{eid}_0, \text{onum}_0, \text{lname}_0)$
2. *One of the initial integrity constraints matches* $\text{Profinfo}(\text{eid}_0, \text{onum}_0, \text{lname}_0)$*, and by firing the rule, we derive* $\text{Udirect}(\text{eid}_0, \text{lname}_0)$.
3. $\text{Udirect}(\text{eid}_0, \text{lname}_0)$ *matches an accessibility axiom, and the rule firing generates* $\text{AccessedUdirect}(\text{eid}_0, \text{lname}_0)$*, which in turn generates* $\text{InferredAccUdirect}(\text{eid}_0, \text{lname}_0)$ *and* $\text{accessible}(eid_0)$.
4. *An accessibility axiom matches* $\text{Profinfo}(\text{eid}_0, \text{onum}_0, \text{lname}_0) \wedge \text{accessible}(\text{eid}_0)$*, creating the fact* $\text{AccessedProfinfo}(\text{eid}_0, \text{onum}_0, \text{lname}_0)$*, which in turn generates* $\text{InferredAccProfinfo}(\text{eid}_0, \text{onum}_0, \text{lname}_0)$.
5. *We now have a match for* InferredAcc$Q$*, so we have a successful sequence.*

Here is the generated **plan***:*

1. *The firing of the accessibility axiom on the third line above generates access command* $T_1 \Leftarrow \text{mt}_{\text{Udirect}} \Leftarrow \emptyset$*, where* T_1 *is a table with attributes for* eid_0 *and* lname_0.
2. *The accessibility axiom on the fourth line generates commands* $T_2 \Leftarrow \text{mt}_{\text{Profinfo}} \Leftarrow T_1$ *and* $T_2 := T_2 \bowtie T_1$.
3. *The match at the end generates the command output* $\pi_\emptyset(T_2)$*, which returns non-empty if* T_2 *is non-empty.*

That is, we do an input-free access on Udirect *and put all the results into* Profinfo.

The following theorem shows the soundness of this approach to generating plans from proofs:

THEOREM 5. *For every chase sequence proving* InferredAcc$Q$ *from conjunctive query* Q *using the rules above, the corresponding SPJ-plan produced by the translation above answers* Q.

Thus every query that is completely answerable can be answered by a proof-based plan. We want to emphasize that this approach does not depend on any acyclicity condition on the constraints – thus the set of possible chase sequences can be infinite.

The proof, deferred to the full paper, proceeds by showing an invariant on the intermediate chase configurations F_j and associated partial plans PL_j produced by the algorithm, each of which outputs a temporary table T_j. Focusing on the case where Q is boolean, let $\text{Accessed}(F_j)$ be the conjunctive query formed by taking the conjunction of all facts of the form InferredAcc$R(\mathbf{c})$ in F_j and turning them into an existentially quantified conjunction of facts $R(\mathbf{w})$, changing the chase constants c that satisfy $\text{accessible}(c)$ to free variables and the other chase constants to existentially quantified variables. Note that if F_j has a match for InferredAcc$Q$, then AccessedF_j entails Q. The attributes C_j of T_j will be all chase constants such that the relation accessible holds in F_j – hence these match the free variables of $\text{Accessed}(F_j)$. Let $T_j(I)$ be the instance of table T_j produced by PL_j when run on an instance I of schema S_0. The key invariant is that the following holds for any instance I of the schema:

1. If Q returns a non-empty result on I, then $T_j(I)$ is non-empty.
2. $T_j(I)$ is a subset of the tuples in $\text{Accessed}(F_j)(I)$.

This implies the theorem, since on the final configuration, $\text{Accessed}(F_j)$ entails Q, as noted above. The two assertions above can be thought of as saying that PL_j interpolates between Q and $\text{Accessed}(F_j)$, in the sense of the Craig Interpolation Theorem.

Decidability, the case of views, and finite instances. For general TGDs, one cannot decide the existence of a proof or a plan, just as for general FO constraints: thus there is no advantage in "worst-case effectiveness" by restricting to TGDs. But whenever the class of accessible schemas is tame enough, we get decidability. For many restricted classes the chase on the accessible schema *terminates* (see, [19] for a survey) – there is a point after which no rules can add new facts. One important case is where the access restrictions in schema S_0 are given by a set of view relations which are fully accessible, with the constraints merely relating each view relation V_i to a conjunctive query Q_i that defines it. In this case the TGDs in the generated schema $\text{AcSch}(S_0)$ will terminate after polynomially many steps.

Thus we can search for a chase-based proof to decide if Q can be conjunctively reformulated over the views. One can also show that whenever the chase terminates in the schema $\text{AcSch}(S_0)$, our technique for determining a plan is complete for *finite instances*. Thus in particular, we have the following corollary, which implies the seminal result of Levy et. al. [14] on finding conjunctive reformulations over a set of views:

THEOREM 6. *Let schema* S_0 *have TGD constraints stating that each view relations* V_i *is equivalent to the result of a conjunctive query* Q_i *over some base signature* B*, for* $i \leq k$*. Then for any conjunctive query* Q *over* B*, we can determine whether or not* Q *can be rewritten as a conjunctive query over* $V_i : i \leq n$ *(over finite instances, equivalently over all instances) by performing the chase on* Q *using* $\text{AcSch}(S_0)$ *until it terminates, and then checking* $\text{InferredAcc}(Q)$ *on the result.*

RA-plans for schemas with TGDs. The proof-to-plan algorithm above focused on generating SPJ-plans. It is known [18] that there are conjunctive queries that have rewritings over a set of views defined by conjunctive queries, but the rewritings require the relational difference operator. From this it follows that there are schemas S_0 consisting of access restrictions and TGDs and conjunctive queries Q that have RA-plans but no SPJ-plans. From Theorem 2, we know that Q has an RA-plan with respect to S_0 iff Q entails InferredAcc$Q$ with respect to $\text{AcSch}^{\leftrightarrow}(S_0)$. We now give a slight extension of the prior algorithm to read off a RA-plan from a chase proof using the rules of $\text{AcSch}^{\leftrightarrow}(S_0)$. For convenience we assume that our queries are boolean, our constraints contain no schema constants, and that our queries and constraints contain no repeated variables in atoms – thus the chase proofs will not produce any configurations that contain such facts.

Algorithm Description. The algorithm proceeds by backward induction on the size of the proof. We group proofs into

- the firing of integrity constraints from the schema or their copies on the InferredAcc$R$ relations are fired.
- the firing of rules $R(\mathbf{x}) \wedge \bigwedge_i \text{accessible}(x_{j_i}) \rightarrow \text{Accessed}R(\mathbf{x})$, where there is at least one method mt with input $j_1 \dots j_m$ on relation R. We assume these are immediately followed by the corresponding firing of the rule $\text{Accessed}R(\mathbf{x}) \rightarrow \text{InferredAcc}R(\mathbf{x})$, and consider this to be a single step. If such a rule is applied to $R(\mathbf{c})$ we refer to this as "a positive accessibility axiom firing exposing fact $R(\mathbf{c})$".
- the firing of rules $\text{InferredAcc}R(\mathbf{x}) \wedge \bigwedge_i \text{accessible}(x_{j_i}) \rightarrow \text{Accessed}R(\mathbf{x})$, which we assume are immediately followed by the corresponding firing of the rule $\text{Accessed}R(\mathbf{x}) \rightarrow R(\mathbf{x})$. If such a rule is applied to $R(\mathbf{c})$ we refer to this as "a negative accessibility axiom firing and exposing fact $\text{InferredAcc}R(\mathbf{c})$".

The algorithm takes as input a proof beginning with some configuration C_i and produces an executable FO query $P_i(\mathbf{x})$, where $\mathbf{x}$ are variables indexed by the accessible constants in C_i. If the proof is trivial (only one configuration), the algorithm returns a plan that always returns true. Otherwise the algorithm analyzes the first rule firing in the proof.

- No commands are generated by rules of the first type above, so the algorithm just proceeds to the remaining rules.
- We consider a proof $C_i \dots$ where the transition from C_i to C_{i+1} is formed via a positive accessibility axiom firing exposing fact $R(\mathbf{c})$. We generate the executable query that does an access to R using the projection of $\mathbf{x}$ to the chase constants $c_{j_1} \dots c_{j_m}$, then returns true only if for some tuple $\mathbf{w}$ in the result, $\mathbf{w}$ joins with $\mathbf{x}$ to give $\mathbf{u}$ and $P_{i+1}(\mathbf{u})$ returns true.

- We now consider a proof $C_i \dots$ where the transition from C_i to C_{i+1} is formed via a negative accessibility axiom firing exposing fact $\mathsf{InferredAcc}R(\mathbf{c})$. We generate an executable rewriting that does an access to R with the projection of $\mathbf{x}$ to the chase constants $c_{j_1} \dots c_{j_m}$, and returns true only if, for *every* tuple $\mathbf{w}$ in the result of the access that joins with $\mathbf{x}$ giving joined tuple $\mathbf{u}$, $P_{i+1}(\mathbf{u})$ returns true.

The reader should note that this algorithm is extremely close to the one given in the view case by Nash, Segoufin, and Vianu (page 21:29 of [18]). But the proof of correctness introduces several new subtleties: one needs a much more complex invariant than that used in the proof of Theorem 5.

In the case of views given by conjunctive queries, the chase using the constraints in $\mathsf{AcSch}^{\leftrightarrow}(S_0)$ does not necessarily converge, since facts propagate in both directions. Indeed, the question of deciding whether a query can be reformulated using a relational algebra query over a set of views is open.

Also note that the algorithm will produce a $USPJ^{\neg}$ plan in the case where the proof used only accessibility axioms in the restricted schema $\mathsf{AcSch}^{\neg}(S_0)$. Hence we have:

THEOREM 7. *For any schema S_0 using TGDs and CQ Q, for every chase proof using $\mathsf{AcSch}^{\leftrightarrow}(S_0)$, the algorithm above produces an RA-plan that completely answers Q. If the proof uses only rules in $\mathsf{AcSch}^{\neg}(S_0)$, the result is a $USPJ^{\neg}$-plan.*

5. LOW-COST PLANS VIA PROOFS

We now look at finding efficient plans, focusing for the remainder of the paper on generating SPJ-plans with respect to schemas consisting of TGDs, and letting the function Plan be the one described using AcSch in the beginning of the previous section. We first note that the proof-based plans that were generated by the SPJ algorithm are as access-efficient as arbitrary plans, and thus we can focus on these.

A plan PL *makes fewer accesses* than plan PL′ if for every pair consisting of a method mt and method input **t** that is executed in running PL on instance I of the schema, the same pair is also accessed in running PL′ on I. Thus "fewer" means "no more than". The following result captures the claim proof-based plans are no more costly than general plans; it is proven by first finding a proof-based plan PL′ that mimics the given plan PL on the chase, then using universality properties of the chase to argue that PL′ behaves as well as PL on all instances.

THEOREM 8. *For conjunctive query Q and schema with TGD constraints Σ and access restrictions, for every SPJ-plan* Plan *that answers Q, there is a chase sequence v proving* InferredAcc$Q$ *from Q, such that* Plan(v) *makes fewer access than* Plan.

Note that this theorem does not imply anything about the cost of proof-based plans versus arbitrary plans according to particular cost functions, since cost functions look at plans statically, and are thus not necessarily monotone in the set of (method, input) pairs produced at runtime. For example, what we call simple cost functions are based on the set of access commands (that is, bulk accesses) that are performed.

The proof works by taking a plan PL and constructing a chase proof that mimics its behavior, in terms of accesses that are made and facts exposed, when applied to the canonical database for the input query Q. This plan is constructed inductively, firing one accessibility axiom at a time until all the facts exposed by PL are present in the chase proof. We then argue, using the universality of the chase, that the plan generated from this proof will make fewer access than PL on arbitrary inputs.

Adding cost to plan search. Theorem 8 implies that the plans produced from proof-to-plan algorithms are optimal in a certain sense. Moreover the SPJ algorithm of Section 4 generates physical plans directly, rather than going via queries, with the structure of the plans directly reflecting the structure of the firing of accessibility axioms. We can thus apply a plan cost function to partial plans while searching for a proof, thus merging the proof search with the search for a low cost plan. This is the last main idea of the paper: *we can find low-cost plans by exploring the space of proofs.*

Our search will maintain a *partial proof tree* – a tree consisting of chase sequences, ordered by extension. We refer to the configuration (set of facts) of the final element in the chase sequence associated with a node v as config(v). The plan associated with v is the one generated by the proof-to-plan algorithm given previously, while by the cost of v we mean the cost of the associated plan. We now give an algorithm for extending the tree to find new proofs.

For node v if there is a fact $R(c_1 \dots c_m)$ in config(v) with Accessed$R(c_1 \dots c_m)$ not yet in config(v) and there is an access method mt on R with input positions $j_1 \dots j_m$ such that accessible$(c_{j_1}) \dots$ accessible(c_{j_m}) all hold in config(v), then we call $R(c_1 \dots c_m)$ a *candidate for exposure* at v, and mt an *exposing method for* $R(c_1 \dots c_m)$. Note that if a fact is a candidate for exposure, then firing an accessibility axiom will add that fact to the associated chase sequence.

When we explore the impact of making an access, we want to include all relevant consequences that do not involve further accesses, thus producing an eager proof (as defined in Section 4). This corresponds to the following requirements on the configurations in a partial proof tree:

- (Original Schema Reasoning First) The configuration of the root node (henceforward "initial configuration") corresponds to the canonical instance of Q plus the result of firing integrity constraints of the original schema S_0 until a termination condition is reached – the termination condition will be explained further below.
- (Fire Inferred Accessible Rules Immediately) For a non-root node v, there is a candidate fact for exposure $R(c_1 \dots c_m)$ in its parent with exposing method mt such that config(v) is obtained from the parent by
  - adding the *facts induced by firing* mt *with* $c_{j_1} \dots c_{j_m}$ – that is, all facts Accessed$R(d_1 \dots d_m)$ such that $R(d_1 \dots d_m)$ is in the parent configuration and **d** agrees with **c** on the input positions of mt. Note that there may be several such facts, but they will include $R(c_1 \dots c_m)$.
  - firing inferred accessible axioms on the result until some termination condition is reached.

Thus the successive configurations are connected by firing a rule associated with an accessibility axiom, firing additional accessibility rules corresponding to the other facts exposed by the same access and exploring the cost-free consequences. Thus we can also characterize a node v by the sequence of rule firings of accessibility axioms leading to it.

We also label a node as *successful* if InferredAcc$Q$ holds in the corresponding configuration (preserving free variables in the non-boolean case).

The idea is that we have labelled each node with a configuration of the proof, and whenever we choose an access to fire, after firing we immediately fire all the relevant rules that do not generate accesses.

We explore downward from a node v of a partial proof tree by choosing a *candidate fact for exposure* at config(v) along with the methods that expose the fact. A node is *terminal* if it is either successful or has no candidate facts. Note that non-terminal nodes do not have to be leaves of the tree.

The basic search structure is outlined in Algorithm 1. At each iteration of the while loop at line 5 we have a partial proof/plan tree satisfying the properties above. We look for a node v corresponding to a partial proof that is not yet successful, has not yet exhausted the maximum number of accesses we allow, and for which the firings of accessibility axioms can add new facts. We non-deterministically choose such a path and such a rule (lines 6-7), and calculate both the new configuration that comes from firing the rule, the commands that will be added to the corresponding plan, and the cost via a call to the "blackbox" cost function, denoted AtomicCost (lines 8-9). We update the candidate list (line 11) and determine whether the new path is successful, recording whether this gives the new lowest cost plan (lines 12-15).

Search order and termination conditions. The non-deterministic algorithm above leaves open a number of issues. The first is how the non-terminal node is chosen. Our policy is to do this *depth-first*: always pick the leaf of the leftmost branch (where left is defined using some ordering on facts) as long as it does not go past a

Algorithm 1: generic search

Input: query Q, schema S, depth d
Output: plan BestPlan

ProofTree := an initial node v_0 labelled with the configuration obtained by firing original integrity constraint rules up to termination condition.
Set Candidates(v_0) = all pairs $(R(c_1 \ldots c_n), \mathsf{mt})$, $R(c_1 \ldots c_n)$ a fact in the original configuration, mt a method on R.
BestPlan := $\bot$
BestCost := ∞
while *there is a non-terminal node v at depth at most d in* ProofTree **do**
    Choose such a node v.
    Choose a candidate fact and method $(R(c_1 \ldots c_n), \mathsf{mt}) \in$ Candidates(v) with accessible(c_{j_1})...accessible(c_{j_m}) $\in$ config(v) and mt having inputs $j_1 \ldots j_m$.
    Add a new node v' as a child of v with configuration formed by adding all the accessible facts induced by exposing $R(c_1 \ldots c_n)$ with mt and then closing under sufficiently many firings of the "inferred accessible rules".
    Set Cost(Plan(v')) using call to AtomicCost.
    Remove $(R(d_1 \ldots d_n), \mathsf{mt})$ with $\mathbf{d}$ extending $c_{j_1} \ldots c_{j_m}$ from Candidates(v), marking v as terminal if it has no more candidates.
    Determine if v' is successful by checking if InferredAcc$Q$ holds, and if so also mark it as terminal.
    if *v' is successful and* Cost(Plan(v')) < BestCost **then**
        BestPlan := Plan(v')
        BestCost := Cost(Plan(v'))
return BestPlan;

threshold d on access commands that is assumed to be provided as an input. In this way we explore the paths with the most accesses, which maximizes our chances of finding a match. The second question is which candidate fact to choose when there is more than one at a node. One policy chooses a candidate node of minimal derivation depth, where the derivation depth of a fact represents the number of rule firings needed to generate in it within this sequence– that is, its depth in the dependency graph associated with the chase sequence. Finally, we must determine the order with which we choose the exposure method mt for relations where there is more than one method. Here we assume some fixed priority for the methods – e.g. based on some notion of expected cost.

Algorithm 1 describes firing "all" rules that involve only reasoning with constraints – but such rules can fire a large number of times, even infinitely often for cyclic collections of referential constraints. For Guarded TGDs, we do not require any chase termination condition on our constraints, but instead rely on a "local blocking condition" for safely terminating such rules, a variant on the technique used within theorem-proving for guarded sublogics of first-order logic (see, e.g. [13, 6]). We organize every configuration into a tree of "guarded bags" – sets of facts B such that there is an atom $R(\mathbf{c})$ containing every chase constant appearing in B. We consider only rule firings that match within a single bag B. Any fact generated from this firing that contains a fresh constant will be added into a new child B$'$ of B, while facts $F(\mathbf{c})$ containing only constants of B will be both added to B$'$ and propagated back up the tree, added recursively to any other elements that contain all elements of $\mathbf{c}$. We abort the rule firing if the generated bag B$'$ is "blocked" by a previously existing B$''$ – that is, there is a homomorphism h of B$'$ into B$''$ such that for every query Q' based on quantifying a subset of the conjuncts of InferredAcc$Q$, if Q' is satisfied in the configuration by constants $\mathbf{c}$ of B$'$, then it is satisfied by $h(\mathbf{c})$ in the configuration. We refresh the set of rule firings that need to be considered whenever the state (facts and subqueries of InferredAcc$Q$) of the parent bag B changes.

The blocking condition guarantees that any rule firing that occurs in B$'$ would have also occurred in B$''$, and that these firings will lead to a match for some $\mathbf{c}$ in B$'$ iff they lead to a match for $h(\mathbf{c})$ in B$''$. The approach is very naive compared to the optimized blocking strategies available in the description logic community (which study logics incomparable in expressiveness with Guarded TGDs). But even this simple version suffices to guarantee termination, since a bound on the number of guarded bags implies a bound on the depth of a path with no blocked nodes.

The algorithm given before can be applied to any cost function. But we will need assumptions on the cost to prove that it obtains the optimal plan. In this work, we state an optimality result only for simple cost functions:

THEOREM 9. *For all schemas S consisting of access restrictions and Guarded TGDs, for all simple cost functions, for all conjunctive queries Q, and for all numbers d, Algorithm 1 will always return a plan with the lowest cost, among all those SPJ plans that completely answer Q w.r.t. S and which make at most d access commands.*

Note that one important class of constraints, those generated from view definitions, are generally not expressible as Guarded TGDs. But for the constraints generated via view definitions over CQs, the chase on AcSch(S_0) will terminate quickly (see comments before Theorem 6). Thus we can avoid using blocking in this case.

Optimizations. The prior algorithm performs exhaustive search of proofs up to some level. We defer a discussion of a more realistic implementation to a later paper, but make a few observations about pruning the search space.

Notions of reducing the search space must consider at *proof structure* and *cost analysis*, both individually and in combination. Looking at proof structure in isolation, we should prune paths that cannot lead to a valid proof while preferring ones that are more likely to lead to a proof. As an example of an optimization related only to cost, we always assume monotonicity of cost functions, and exploit it by aborting exploration of a node if the corresponding partial plan has cost that is already worse than the cost of a known successful plan.

As an example of the interaction of proof structure and cost analysis, we will wish to abort the search below a node if it is "worse than" another node in the search tree. Consider the case where we are at a node v in the search space, and have a candidate fact c at v and method mt for exposing c, such that when we generate a new node v' from c we find that there is a node v'' already in ProofTree such that config(v'') has "at least as many useful facts" as config(v') and we know that Plan(v'') is "at least as efficient" than Plan(v'). Then there is no need to generate v', since if a sequence of further accesses added on to the actions of v' generates a complete plan, the same sequence will generate a complete plan with no higher cost when added on to the actions of v''. The notion "at least as many useful facts" can be formalized via the existence of a mapping from chase constants of v' to those of v'' that preserves facts over relations of the original schema and those of the form InferredAcc$R$. For simple cost functions, the notion of efficiency is captured by the notion of having lower cost. For general cost functions the notion of "worse plan" must be more complex, since v' might produce some temporary relations that are smaller than those of v'', and the size of these relations may diminish the cost of later accesses. In our follow-up work, we investigate heuristic notions of comparison for more general cost-functions, and their relationship with notions used in traditional query optimization.

EXAMPLE 5. *Let us return to the setting of Example 1, assuming we have 3 directory sources* Udirect$_1$, Udirect$_2$, Udirect$_3$. *The integrity constraints contain:*

$$\mathsf{Profinfo}(\mathsf{eid}, \mathsf{onum}, \mathsf{lname}) \rightarrow \mathsf{Udirect}_i(\mathsf{eid}, \mathsf{lname})$$

for $i = 1, 2, 3$, with Profinfo *having an access that requires all arguments to be given and each* Udirect$_i$ *having unrestricted access. Consider the query* $Q = \exists \mathsf{eid}\ \mathsf{onum}\ \mathsf{lname}\ \mathsf{Profinfo}(\mathsf{eid}, \mathsf{onum}, \mathsf{lname})$.

Figure 1 illustrates the exploration. The canonical database of Q consists of the fact Profinfo(eid_0, onum_0, lname_0). *The proof configuration of the initial node n_0 will then add* Udirect$_i$(eid_0, lname_0) *for*

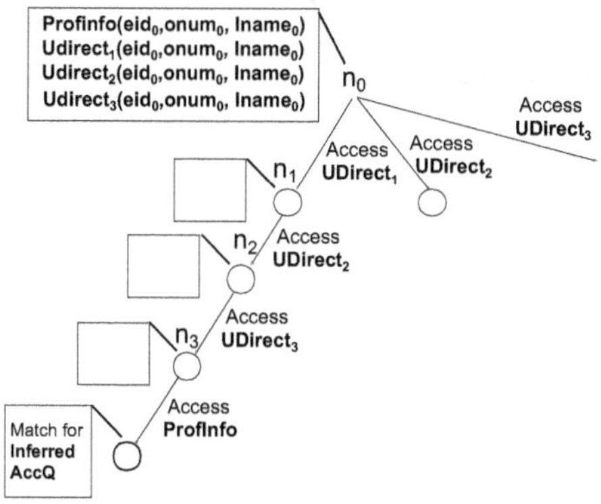

Figure 1: Exploration in the running example

$i = 1,2,3$. There are thus three candidates facts to expose, corresponding to firing accessibility axioms that expose $\mathsf{Udirect}_i(\mathsf{eid}_0, \mathsf{lname}_0)$: *$i = 1,2,3$ in the initial node.*

Assuming that we have a heuristic that tells us to prefer to explore access to $\mathsf{Udirect}_i$ *before access to* $\mathsf{Udirect}_j$ *for $i < j$, we will choose fact* $\mathsf{Udirect}_1(\mathsf{eid}_0, \mathsf{lname}_0)$ *to expose first. This creates a child proof configuration n_1. The transition from parent to child is associated with a plan command performing input-free access to* $\mathsf{Udirect}_1$*, putting the output into a table T_1 with attributes* $\{\mathsf{eid}_0, \mathsf{lname}_0\}$*. The associated proof configuration for n_1 (shown as a box to the upper left) adds the exposed fact* $\mathsf{AccessedUdirect}_1(\mathsf{eid}_0, \mathsf{lname}_0)$*, and then immediately the fact* $\mathsf{InferredAccUdirect}_1(\mathsf{eid}_0, \mathsf{lname}_0)$.

In n_1 there are three candidate facts to expose via accessibility axioms: $\mathsf{Udirect}_2(\mathsf{eid}_0, \mathsf{lname}_0), \mathsf{Udirect}_3(\mathsf{eid}_0, \mathsf{lname}_0)$ *and now also* $\mathsf{Profinfo}(\mathsf{eid}_0, \mathsf{onum}_0, \mathsf{lname}_0)$*, since there is an accessibility axiom that would expose this last fact now. The highest priority one is* $\mathsf{Udirect}_2(\mathsf{eid}_0, \mathsf{lname}_0)$*. Thus a child n_2 will be generated (again including the exposed fact* $\mathsf{AccessedUdirect}_2(c_0)$ *and one inferred fact). The transition to n_2 will be associated with an input-free access command on* $\mathsf{Udirect}_2$ *and a command joining the results with the previous table.*

The node n_2 will have the facts $\mathsf{Udirect}_3(\mathsf{eid}_0, \mathsf{lname}_0)$ *and* $\mathsf{Profinfo}(\mathsf{eid}_0, \mathsf{onum}_0, \mathsf{lname}_0)$ *as candidates for exposure, of which* $\mathsf{Udirect}_3(\mathsf{eid}_0, \mathsf{lname}_0)$ *has highest priority. We will thus generate a child n_3, whose configuration adds the exposed fact and the corresponding inferred accessible fact.*

The node n_3 will have only one candidate fact, corresponding to $\mathsf{Profinfo}(\mathsf{eid}_0, \mathsf{onum}_0, \mathsf{lname}_0)$*, so a child n_4 will be generated. The access associated with the edge from n_3 to n_4 will be of the form* $T_4 \Leftarrow \mathsf{mt}_{\mathsf{Profinfo}} \Leftarrow T_3$*, where T_3 will be a table with attributes* $\mathsf{eid}_0, \mathsf{lname}_0$ *containing the intersection of the outputs of the 3 prior accesses. The query* $\mathsf{InferredAcc}Q$ *matches the configuration of n_4, so it is designated a success node, and hence is terminal.*

Now the search can go back up the tree to a node with more candidates to explore – e.g. following the "depth-first on nodes" approach, it will move to n_3, and pick the highest priority child of n_3 to explore. Note that at some point in the process, the tree extension process will consider creating a node n''' corresponding to firing the first two axioms in the reverse order than in the path above – exposing first fact $\mathsf{Udirect}_2(\mathsf{eid}_0, \mathsf{lname}_0)$ *then* $\mathsf{Udirect}_1(\mathsf{eid}_0, \mathsf{lname}_0)$*. This chase node would have the same configuration as the node n_2 above; assuming it has no larger cost, n''' will be determined to be "no better than" n_2, and hence would not be generated.*

6. CONCLUSIONS AND FUTURE WORK

The main goal of this work is to introduce a means for generating query plans from "proofs of answerability of a query". By exploring many proofs, one can guide the search for good query plans by the structure of proofs. The technique is particularly useful in the presence of rich integrity constraints, which cannot be exploited by traditional query planners. The further presence of access restrictions can make the use of constraints essential for finding any plan, and crucial for finding a good plan.

We have stressed the continuity between the general technique based on interpolation and the direct algorithms for TGDs based on the chase. We have implemented a proof-to-plan generator in the setting of forward-chaining proofs. While we gave a flavor of the system here, an overview of the prototype and a full description of the system are in preparation. But note that proof systems exist that are very different from forward-chaining ones, such as those used in proving the Access interpolation theorem – e.g. tableaux,backward-chaining systems, saturation-based procedures that compute all provable sequences of a given form. We wish to investigate how the correspondence between proofs and plans works for each of these proof schemes.

7. REFERENCES

[1] S. Abiteboul, R. Hull, and V. Vianu. *Foundations of Databases.* Addison-Wesley, 1995.

[2] C. Areces, P. Blackburn, and M. Marx. Hybrid logic: Characterization, interpolation and complexity. *J.Symb. Log.*, 66(3):977–1010, 2001.

[3] V. Bárány, M. Benedikt, and P. Bourhis. Access restrictions and integrity constraints revisited. In *ICDT*, 2013.

[4] P. Blackburn and M. Marx. Constructive interpolation in hybrid logic. *J. Symb. Log.*, 68(2):463–480, 2003.

[5] A. Borgida, J. de Bruijn, E.Franconi, I. Seylan, U. Straccia, D. Toman, and G. E. Weddell. On finding query rewritings under expressive constraints. In *SEBD*, 2010.

[6] A. Calì, T. Lukasiewicz, and G. Gottlob. A general datalog-based framework for tractable query answering over ontologies. *J. Web Sem.*, 14(0), 2012.

[7] W. Craig. Three uses of the Herbrand-Gentzen theorem in relating model theory and proof theory. *J. Symb. Log.*, 22(3):269–285, 1957.

[8] A. Deutsch, B. Ludäscher, and A. Nash. Rewriting queries using views with access patterns under integrity constraints. *TCS*, 371(3):200–226, 2007.

[9] A. Deutsch, L. Popa, and V. Tannen. Physical data independence, constraints, and optimization with universal plans. In *VLDB*, 1999.

[10] A. Deutsch, L. Popa, and V. Tannen. Query reformulation with constraints. *SIGMOD Record*, 35(1):65–73, 2006.

[11] O. Duschka, M. Genesereth, and A. Levy. Recursive query plans for data integration. *JLP*, 43(1):49 – 73, 2000.

[12] D. Florescu, A. Y. Levy, I. Manolescu, and D. Suciu. Query optimization in the presence of limited access patterns. In *SIGMOD*, 1999.

[13] C. Hirsch and S. Tobies. A tableau algorithm for the clique guarded fragment. In *Adv. Modal Logic*, 2000.

[14] A. Y. Levy, A.O. Mendelzon, Y. Sagiv, and D. Srivastava. Answering queries using views. In *PODS*, 1995.

[15] C. Li. Computing complete answers to queries in the presence of limited access patterns. *VLDB Journal*, 12(3):211–227, 2003.

[16] C. Li and E. Chang. Answering queries with useful bindings. *TODS*, 26(3):313–343, 2001.

[17] Roger C. Lyndon. An interpolation theorem in the predicate calculus. *Pacific J. Math.*, 9:129–142, 1959.

[18] A. Nash, L. Segoufin, and V. Vianu. Views and queries: Determinacy and rewriting. *TODS*, 35(3), 2010.

[19] A. Onet. The chase procedure and its applications in data exchange. In *DEIS*, 2013.

[20] M. Otto. An interpolation theorem. *B. Symb. Log.*, 6(4):447–462, 2000.

[21] L. Popa. *Object/Relational Query Optimization with Chase and Backchase.* PhD thesis, U. Penn., 2000.

[22] D. Toman and G. Weddell. *Fundamentals of Physical Design and Query Compilation.* Morgan Claypool, 2011.

Skew in Parallel Query Processing

Paul Beame, Paraschos Koutris and Dan Suciu
University of Washington, Seattle, WA
{beame,pkoutris,suciu}@cs.washington.edu

ABSTRACT

We study the problem of computing a conjunctive query q in parallel, using p of servers, on a large database. We consider algorithms with one round of communication, and study the complexity of the communication. We are especially interested in the case where the data is skewed, which is a major challenge for scalable parallel query processing. We establish a tight connection between the *fractional edge packing* of the query and the *amount of communication* in two cases. First, in the case when the only statistics on the database are the cardinalities of the input relations, and the data is skew-free, we provide matching upper and lower bounds (up to a polylogarithmic factor of p) expressed in terms of fractional edge packings of the query q. Second, in the case when the relations are skewed and the heavy hitters and their frequencies are known, we provide upper and lower bounds expressed in terms of packings of *residual queries* obtained by specializing the query to a heavy hitter. All our lower bounds are expressed in the strongest form, as number of bits needed to be communicated between processors with unlimited computational power. Our results generalize prior results on uniform databases (where each relation is a matching) [4], and lower bounds for the MapReduce model [1].

Categories and Subject Descriptors

H.2.4 [**Systems**]: Parallel Databases

Keywords

Parallel Computation; Skew; Lower Bounds

1. INTRODUCTION

While in traditional query processing the main complexity is dominated by the disk access time, in modern massively distributed systems the dominant cost is that of the communication. A data analyst will use a cluster with sufficiently many servers to ensure that the entire data fits in main memory. Unlike MapReduce [6], which stores data on disk between the Map and the Reduce phase for recovery purposes, newer systems like Spark [17] and its SQL-extension Shark [14] perform the entire computation in main memory, and use replay to recover. In these systems the new complexity parameter is the communication cost, which depends on both the amount of data sent and the number of rounds.

A key requirement in such systems is that the data be uniformly partitioned on all servers, and this requirement is challenging to enforce when the input data is *skewed*. A value in the database is skewed, and is called a *heavy hitter*, when it occurs with much higher frequency than some predefined threshold. Since data reshuffling is typically done using hash-partitioning, all records containing a heavy hitter will be sent to the same server, causing it to be overloaded. Skew for parallel joins has been studied intensively since the early days of parallel databases, see [13]. The standard parallel join algorithm that handles skew is the *skew join* [11], which consists of first detecting the heavy hitters (e.g. using sampling), then treating them differently from the others values, e.g. by partitioning tuples with heavy hitters on the other attributes; a detailed description is in [15]. None of these algorithms has been proven to be optimal in any formal sense, and to the best of our knowledge there are no lower bounds for the communication required to compute a join in the presence of skew.

Complex queries often involve multiple joins, and the traditional approach that computes one join at a time leads to a number of communication rounds at least as large as the depth of the query plan. It is possible, however, to compute a multiway join in a single communication round, using a technique that can be traced back to Ganguli, Silberschatz, and Tsur [8, Sec.7], and was described by Afrati and Ullman [2] in the context of MapReduce algorithms. We will refer to this technique as the HYPERCUBE *algorithm*, following [4]. The p servers are organized into a hypercube with k dimensions, where k is the number of variables in the query. During a single reshuffling step, every tuple is sent to all servers in a certain subcube of the hypercube (with as many dimensions as the number of query variables missing from the tuple). One challenge in this approach is to determine the size of the hypercube in each of the k dimensions. In [2] this is treated as a non-linear optimization problem and solved using Lagrange multipliers. In [4] it is shown that, in the case where all relations have the same cardinality, the optimal dimensions can be expressed in terms of the optimal fractional vertex cover of the query. All hypercube-based techniques described in [2, 4], and elsewhere (e.g. in [12] for computing triangles) assume that the

PODS'14, June 22–27, 2014, Snowbird, UT, USA.

ACM 978-1-4503-2375-8/14/06 ...$15.00.
http://dx.doi.org/10.1145/2594538.2594558 .

data has no skew. The behavior of the algorithm on skewed data has not been studied before and no techniques for addressing skew have been proposed.

Our Contribution. In this paper we study the problem of computing a full conjunctive query (multi-way join query) when the input data may have arbitrary skew. We are given p servers that have to compute a query on a database with m tuples; we assume that $m \gg p$. We prove upper and lower bounds for the amount of communication needed to compute the query in one round. We assume the following statistics on the input database to be known: the cardinality of each input relation, the identity of the heavy hitters, and their (approximate) frequency in the data. We note that this is a reasonable assumption in today's distributed query engines. In our settings there are at most $O(p)$ heavy hitters because we choose a threshold for the frequency of heavy hitters that is $\geq m/p$, and therefore the number of heavy hitters is tiny compared to the size of the database. We assume that at the beginning of the computation all servers know the identity of all heavy hitters, and the (approximate) frequency of each heavy hitter. Given these statistics, we present upper and lower bounds for the amount of communication needed to compute the query on the class of databases satisfying those statistics. There is a small gap remaining between the upper and lower bound; for the join query, however, we prove that the bounds match. Our results are significant extensions of our previous results [4], which hold only in the absence of skew and for relations of the same cardinality.

Grohe and Marx [9] and Atserias et al. [3] give upper bounds on the query size in terms of a fractional *edge cover*; this is also a lower bound on the running time of any sequential algorithm that computes the query. Recently, Ngo at al. [10] described a sequential algorithm that matches that bound. Thus, the sequential complexity of a query is captured by the edge cover; our results show that the communication complexity for parallel evaluation is instead captured by the *edge packing*.

Overview of the results. Our analysis of skew starts with an analysis of skew-free databases, but with unequal cardinalities. Consider a simple cartesian product, $q(x, y) = S_1(x), S_2(y)$, of two relations with cardinalities m_1, m_2. Assume $1/p \leq m_1/m_2 \leq p^1$. Let $p_1 = \sqrt{m_1 p/m_2}$, $p_2 = \sqrt{m_2 p/m_1}$ and assume that they are integer values. Organize the p servers into a $p_1 \times p_2$ rectangle, and assign to each server two coordinates $(i, j) \in [p_1] \times [p_2]$. During the communication phase, the algorithm uses two random hash functions h_1, h_2 and sends every tuple $S_1(x)$ to all servers with coordinates $(h_1(x), j)$, $j \in [p_2]$ (thus, every server receives with high probability $O(m_1/p_1) = O(\sqrt{m_1 m_2/p})$ tuples from S_1), and sends every tuple $S_2(y)$ to all servers with coordinates $(i, h_2(y))$, $i \in [p_1]$. The load per server is $L = O(\sqrt{m_1 m_2/p})$, and it is not hard to see that this is optimal[2]. This observation generalises to any u-way cartesian product: the minimum load per server needed to compute $S_1 \times \ldots \times S_u$ is $\Omega((m_1 m_2 \cdots m_u/p)^{1/u})$

Consider now some arbitrary full conjunctive query q over relations $S_1, \ldots, S_\ell$, and assume that the cardinality of S_j is m_j. Choose some subset $S_{j_1}, S_{j_2}, \ldots, S_{j_u}$; the subset is called an *edge packing*, or an *edge matching*, if no two relations share a common variable. Any one-round algorithm that computes the query correctly must also compute the cartesian product of the relations $S_{j_1}, S_{j_2}, \ldots, S_{j_u}$. Indeed, since no two relations share variables, any tuple in their cartesian product could potentially be part of the query answer; without knowing the content of the other relations, the input servers that store (fragments of) $S_{j_1}, S_{j_2}, \ldots$ must ensure that any combination reaches some output server. Therefore, the load per server of any one-round algorithm is at least $\Omega((m_{j_1} \cdots m_{j_u}/p)^{1/u})$. Thus, every edge packing gives a lower bound for computing q. For example the load per server needed to compute the query $q(x, y, z, w) = S_1(x, y), S_2(y, z), S_3(z, w)$ is at least $L \geq \sqrt{m_1 m_3/p}$, because of the packing $\{S_1, S_3\}$; it must also be $L \geq m_2/p$, because of the packing $\{S_2\}$. We prove in this paper that this property extends to any *fractional edge packing*. Let M_j denote the number of bits needed to represent the relation S_j. We show:

THEOREM 1.1. *Let $\mathbf{u} = (u_1, \ldots, u_\ell)$ be any fractional edge packing for the query q, and $u = \sum_j u_j$. Let $K(\mathbf{u}, \mathbf{M}) = \prod_j M_j^{u_j}$ and $L(\mathbf{u}, \mathbf{M}, p) = (K(\mathbf{u}, \mathbf{M})/p)^{1/u}$. If an algorithm computes q in one step, then at least one server has a load $\Omega(L(\mathbf{u}, \mathbf{M}, p))$. Conversely, let $L_{lower} = \max_{\mathbf{u}} L(\mathbf{u}, \mathbf{M}, p)$ be the maximum over all fractional edge packings. Then, there exists a randomized algorithm for q (*HyperCube *or HC algorithm) whose maximum load per server is $O(L_{lower} \ln^k p)$ with high probability on all databases without skew.*

In the case when all relations have the same size M, then the lower bound is $L_{lower} = \max_{\mathbf{u}}(M/p^{1/u}) = M/p^{1/\tau^*}$, where τ^* is the value of the maximal fractional edge packing, and is equal to the *fractional vertex covering* number for q; thus, we recover our prior result in [4], which was stated for the special case when all relations are *matchings* and have equal cardinalities.

Theorem 1.1 completes the analysis of the HC algorithm on skew-free databases with arbitrary cardinalities. In addition, we prove a rather surprising result: the HC algorithm is resilient to skew, in the sense that, even on skewed databases, it can still offer a non-trivial upper bound for the maximum load per server: namely $L = O(M/p^{1/k})$, where M is the size of the largest relation, and k the total number of variables in the query. For example, using HC one can compute the join of two relations and guarantee a maximum load of $O(M/p^{1/3})$, *even without any knowledge about skew or heavy hitters*. In contrast, a standard hash-join algorithm may incur a load of $\Omega(M)$ when the join attributes have a single value.

Next, we consider the case when information about heavy hitters is known. In addition to knowing the cardinalities of the input relations, we assume that the identities of the heavy hitters are known, and that the frequency in the data of every heavy hitter is also known. For example, if the relation S_j contains an attribute x, then we assume to know the set of heavy hitters H, together with the frequencies $m_j(h) = |\sigma_{x=h}(S_j)|$, which, by definition, are $\geq m_j/p$.

[1]if $m_1 < m_2/p$ then we can broadcast S_1 to all servers and compute the query with a load increase of at most m_2/p per server thus at most double that of any algorithm, because m_2/p is the load required to store S_2.

[2]Let a_i, b_i be the number of S_1-tuples and S_2-tuples received by server $i \in [p]$. On one hand $\sum_i a_i b_i = \langle \bar{a}, \bar{b} \rangle \geq m_1 m_2$ because the servers must report all $m_1 m_2$ tuples; on the other hand $\langle \bar{a}, \bar{b} \rangle \leq \|\bar{a} + \bar{b}\|_2^2/4 \leq p\|\bar{a} + \bar{b}\|_\infty^2/4 = pL^2/4$.

For this setting, we generalize the results for skew-free databases by proving both lower bound and upper bounds. Our lower bound is an elegant generalization of that in Theorem 1.1, and is expressed in terms of fractional edge packings of *residual queries*: for each set of variables $\mathbf{x}$, the residual query $q_{\mathbf{x}}$ is obtained from q by simply removing the variables $\mathbf{x}$. The upper bound is based on the idea of running the main query on the subset of the database that consists of light hitters, then handling each heavy hitter separately, by computing a residual query. The algorithm is difficult, because of two challenges. First, one needs to consider sets of attributes of each relation S_j that may be heavy hitters jointly, even if none of them is a heavy hitter by itself. Second, an attribute value may become a heavy hitter in the residual query even though it was light in the main query. Our algorithm addresses these challenges by creating, for each subset of attributes of each relation, $O(\log p)$ bins of heavy hitters, where all heavy hitters in a bin have frequencies that differ by at most a factor of two (because of this it suffices for our algorithm to have access only to approximate frequencies of heavy hitters). By considering separately all combinations of bins, we can run residual queries on databases where the frequencies are guaranteed to be uniform, thus avoiding the difficulties that arise from recursion. Denote $M_j(h)$ the number of bits needed to represent the subset $\sigma_{x=h}(S_j)$ of S_j. Our second main result is:

THEOREM 1.2. *Consider all database instances defined by a set of statistics consisting of the cardinalities of the relations, the set of heavy hitters, and the frequency of each heavy hitter. For a set of variables* $\mathbf{x}$ *and any packing* $\mathbf{u}$ *of the residual query* $q_{\mathbf{x}}$ *that saturates the variables in* $\mathbf{x}$*, let* $L_{\mathbf{x}}(\mathbf{u}, \mathbf{M}, p) = \left(\sum_{\mathbf{h}} K(\mathbf{u}, \mathbf{M}(\mathbf{h}))/p\right)^{1/u}$*: then any deterministic algorithm that computes q on these databases must have a load* $\geq L_{\mathbf{x}}(\mathbf{u}, \mathbf{M}, p)$.

Moreover, there exists a randomized algorithm for computing q with maximum load $O(L_{\text{upper}} \log^{O(1)} p)$ *with high probability, where* $L_{\text{upper}} = \max_{\mathbf{x},\mathbf{u}} L_{\mathbf{x}}(\mathbf{u}, \mathbf{M}, p)$ *and* $\mathbf{u}$ *now ranges over all packings of the residual query* $q_{\mathbf{x}}$.

The gap between the upper and lower bound comes from the fact that in the upper bound the possible edge packings for $q_{\mathbf{x}}$ are not restricted to only those which saturate the variables in $\mathbf{x}$.

As a final contribution of our paper, we discuss the connection between our results in the MPC model and the results of [1] on models for computation in MapReduce. We show that our results provide new upper and lower bounds for computing conjunctive queries in [1], and in a stronger computational model.

The paper is organized as follows. We describe the computational model and review the basic definitions from [4] in section 2, then present in section 3 our results for the case when the statistics known about the database are restricted to cardinalities. The case of databases with known heavy hitters is discussed in section 4. We present the connection with [1] in section 5 and finally conclude in section 6. Several proofs are relegated to the full version of the paper [5].

2. PRELIMINARIES

2.1 Massively Parallel Communication

We define here the MPC model. The computation is performed by p servers connected by a complete network of private[3] channels. The input data is initially distributed evenly among the p servers. The computation proceeds in rounds, where each round consists of *local computation* at the servers interleaved with *global communication*. The servers have unlimited computational power, but may be limited in the amount of bits they receive. In this paper, we discuss query evaluation in this model, and consider a single round of communication. The *load* of a server is the number of bits received by the server during the communication; we write L for the maximum load among all servers.

If the size of the input is M bits, an ideal algorithm would split the data equally among the servers, and so we would like to have $L = M/p$; in this case, the total amount of data communicated is M and thus there is no *replication*. Depending on the query, L is higher than the ideal M/p by some factor called *replication factor*. In [4] we considered the case when the input data is perfectly uniform and all relations have the same size, and showed that the replication factor for any conjunctive query is $O(p^{\varepsilon})$, where $0 < \varepsilon \leq 1$ is a constant that depends only on the query. In this work we consider arbitrary input data, and the replication factor becomes a more complex formula that depends on the database statistics.

Randomization. The MPC model allows randomization during the computation. The random bits are available to all servers at the beginning of computation, and are independent of the input data.

Random Instances and Yao's Lemma. Our lower bounds are stated by showing that, if the database instance is chosen at random from some known probability space, then any algorithm with a load less than a certain bound can report only $o(1)$ fraction of the expected number of answers to the query. Using Yao's lemma [16] this implies that for any randomized algorithm there exists an instance on which the algorithm will fail with high probability; see [4] for details.

Input Servers. In our upper bounds we assume that the input relations S_j are initially partitioned uniformly on the servers: all our algorithms treat tuples in S_j independently of other tuples. For our lower bounds, we assume a more powerful model, where at the beginning of the algorithm each relation S_j is stored on a separate server, called an *input server*, which can examine the entire relation in order to determine what message to send. These assumptions are the same as in [4].

Database Statistics. In this paper we assume that all input servers know certain database statistics. *Simple database statistics* consists of the cardinalities m_j of all input relations S_j; we discuss this case in section 3. *Complex database statistics* add information about heavy hitters; we discuss these in the rest of the paper. The size of these statistics is $O(1)$ in the first case, and $O(p)$ in the second. Both upper and lower bounds assume that these statistics are available to all input servers.

2.2 Conjunctive Queries

We study the problem of computing answers to conjunctive queries over an input database in the MPC model. We fix an input vocabulary $S_1, \ldots, S_\ell$, where each relation S_j has arity a_j; let $a = \sum_{j=1}^{\ell} a_j$. The input data consists of one relation instance for each symbol. We consider full con-

[3]"Private" means that when server i sends a message to server j no other server sees its content.

junctive queries without self-joins[4]:

$$q(x_1,\dots,x_k) = S_1(\bar{x}_1),\dots,S_\ell(\bar{x}_\ell) \quad (1)$$

The query is *full*, meaning that every variable in the body appears in the head (for example $q(x) = S(x,y)$ is not full), and *without self-joins*, meaning that each relation name S_j appears only once (for example $q(x,y,z) = S(x,y), S(y,z)$ has a self-join). The *hypergraph* of a query q is defined by introducing one node for each variable in the body and one hyperedge for each set of variables that occur in a single atom. With some notational abuse we write $i \in S_j$ to mean that the variable x_i occurs in the the variables $vars(S_j)$ of the atom S_j.

Fractional Edge Packing. A *fractional edge packing* (also known as a *fractional matching*) of a query q is any feasible solution $\mathbf{u} = (u_1,\dots,u_\ell)$ of the following linear constraints:

$$\forall i \in [k] : \sum_{j:i\in S_j} u_j \le 1 \quad (2)$$

$$\forall j \in [\ell] : u_j \ge 0$$

The edge packing associates a non-negative weight u_j to each atom S_j such that for every variable x_i, the sum of the weights for the atoms that contain x_i do not exceed 1. If all inequalities are satisfied as equalities by a solution to the LP, we say that the solution is *tight*.

For a simple example, an edge packing of the query $L_3 = S_1(x_1,x_2), S_2(x_2,x_3), S_3(x_3,x_4)$ is any solution to $u_1 \le 1$, $u_1 + u_2 \le 1$, $u_2 + u_3 \le 1$ and $u_3 \le 1$. In particular, the solution $(1,0,1)$ is a tight and feasible edge packing. A *fractional edge cover* is a feasible solution $\mathbf{u} = (u_1,\dots,u_\ell)$ to the system above where $\le$ is replaced by $\ge$ in Eq.2. Every tight fractional edge packing is a tight fractional edge cover, and vice versa.

2.3 Friedgut's Inequality

Friedgut [7] introduces the following class of inequalities. Each inequality is described by a hypergraph, which in our paper corresponds to a query, so we will describe the inequality using query terminology. Fix a query q as in (1), and let $n > 0$. For every atom $S_j(\bar{x}_j)$ of arity a_j, we introduce a set of n^{a_j} variables $w_j(\mathbf{a}_j) \ge 0$, where $\mathbf{a}_j \in [n]^{a_j}$. If $\mathbf{a} \in [n]^k$, we denote by $\mathbf{a}_j$ the vector of size a_j that results from projecting on the variables of the relation S_j. Let $\mathbf{u} = (u_1,\dots,u_\ell)$ be a fractional *edge cover* for q. Then:

$$\sum_{\mathbf{a}\in[n]^k} \prod_{j=1}^{\ell} w_j(\mathbf{a}_j) \le \prod_{j=1}^{\ell} \left(\sum_{\mathbf{a}_j\in[n]^{a_j}} w_j(\mathbf{a}_j)^{1/u_j} \right)^{u_j} \quad (3)$$

We illustrate Friedgut's inequality on C_3:

$$C_3(x,y,z) = S_1(x,y), S_2(y,z), S_3(z,x) \quad (4)$$

C_3 has cover $(1/2,1/2,1/2)$. Thus, we obtain the following, where a,b,c stand for w_1,w_2,w_3 respectively:

$$\sum_{x,y,z\in[n]} a_{xy}\cdot b_{yz}\cdot c_{zx} \le \sqrt{\sum_{x,y\in[n]} a_{xy}^2 \sum_{y,z\in[n]} b_{yz}^2 \sum_{z,x\in[n]} c_{zx}^2}$$

Friedgut's inequalities immediately imply a well known result developed in a series of papers [9, 3, 10] that give an upper bound on the size of a query answer as a function on the cardinality of the relations. For example in the case of C_3, consider an instance S_1, S_2, S_3, and set $a_{xy} = 1$ if $(x,y) \in S_1$, otherwise $a_{xy} = 0$ (and similarly for b_{yz}, c_{zx}). We obtain then $|C_3| \le \sqrt{|S_1|\cdot|S_2|\cdot|S_3|}$.

3. SIMPLE DATABASE STATISTICS

In this section we consider the case when the statistics on database consist of the cardinalities $m_1,\dots,m_\ell$ of the relations $S_1,\dots,S_\ell$. All input servers know these statistics. We denote $\mathbf{m} = (m_1,\dots,m_\ell)$ the vector of cardinalities, and $\mathbf{M} = (M_1,\dots,M_\ell)$ the vector of the sizes expressed in bits, where $M_j = a_j m_j \log n$, and n is the size of the domain of each attribute.

3.1 The HyperCube Algorithm

We present here the HyperCube (HC) algorithm and its analysis.

The HC algorithm, first described in [2], expresses the number of servers p as $p = p_1 \cdot p_2 \cdots p_k$, where each p_i is called the *share* for the variable x_i. The algorithm uses k independently chosen random hash functions $h_i : [n] \to [p_i]$, one for each variable x_i. During the communication step, the algorithm sends every tuple $S_j(\mathbf{a}_j) = S_j(a_{i_1},\dots,a_{i_{r_j}})$ to all servers $\mathbf{y} \in [p_1]\times\cdots\times[p_k]$ such that $h_{i_m}(a_{i_m}) = \mathbf{y}_{i_m}$ for any $1 \le m \le r_j$. In other words, for every tuple in S_j, after applying the hash functions the algorithm knows the coordinates for the dimensions $i_1,\dots,i_{r_j}$ in the hypercube, but does not know the other coordinates, and it simply replicates the tuple along those other dimensions. The algorithm finds all answers, because each potential output tuple $(a_1,\dots,a_k)$ is known by the server $\mathbf{y} = (h_1(a_1),\dots,h_k(a_k))$.

Since the HC algorithm is parametrized by the choice of shares, we next address two issues. First, we choose the shares p_i so as to minimize the expected load per server. Second, we prove that, with high probability on the choices of the random hash functions, the expected load is not exceeded by more than a factor for any server. We start with the latter, which was not addressed in [2], and was addressed only in a limited setting in [4]: our analysis reveals a previously unknown property of the HC algorithm.

Analysis of the Load Per Server. Our analysis is based on the following lemma about hashing.

Lemma 3.1. *Let $R(A_1,\dots,A_r)$ be a relation of arity r with m tuples. Let $p_1,\dots,p_r$ be integers and denote $p = \prod_i p_i$ where $m \ge p^2$. Suppose that we hash each tuple $(a_1,\dots,a_r)$ to the bucket $(h_1(a_1),\dots,h_r(a_r))$, where $h_1,\dots,h_r$ are independent and perfectly random hash functions. Then:*

1. *The expected load in every bucket is m/p.*
2. *If for every $i \in [r]$ every value of the attribute A_i occurs at most once, then the maximum load per bucket is $O(m/p)$ with high probability*[5].
3. *If for every $S \subseteq [r]$, every tuple of values of attributes $(A_i)_{i\in S}$ occurs at most $am/\prod_{i\in S} p_i$ times, for $a \ge e^3/\ln(p)$ then the maximum load is $O((\frac{12a\ln p}{\ln\ln p+\ln(3a)})^r m/p)$ with high probability.*
4. *The maximum load per bucket is $O(m/\min_i(p_i))$ with high probability, independent of the instance.*

[4]For queries with self-joins, the upper bounds hold unchanged, while the lower bounds hold up to constant factor.

[5]high probability means polynomially small in p

We prove this lemma in the full paper [5]. The proof of the lemma is based on the balls-into-bins framework. The bounds provided for the case where $r \geq 2$ require novel arguments, to the best of our knowledge.

We apply the lemma to analyze the behavior of the HC algorithm under two conditions: over skew-free databases, and over arbitrary databases. For a vector of shares $(p_1, \ldots, p_k)$, we say that a relation S_j is *skew-free* w.r.t. the shares if for every subset of variables $\mathbf{x} \subseteq vars(S_j)$, every value has frequency at most $m_j / \prod_{x_i \in \mathbf{x}} p_i$. Our prior analysis in [4] was only for the special case when the frequency of each value at each attribute is at most 1.

COROLLARY 3.2. *Let $\mathbf{p} = (p_1, \ldots, p_k)$ be the shares of the HC algorithm.*
(i) If S_j is skew-free w.r.t. $\mathbf{p}$, then with high probability the maximum load per server is

$$O\left(\max_j \frac{M_j}{\prod_{i:i \in S_j} p_i} \ln^k(p)\right)$$

(ii) For any given database, with high probability the maximum load per server is

$$O\left(\max_j \frac{M_j}{\min_{i:i \in S_j}(p_i)}\right)$$

In [2], it is assumed that the database is skew-free and that the load per server is the expected load; item (i) of our result confirms that the load does not exceed the expected load by more than a poly-log factor with high probability, and defines precisely the skew threshold that gives the optimal behavior. Item (ii) is novel, because it describes how the HC algorithm behaves on skewed data: it shows that the algorithm is resilient to skew, and gives an upper bound even on skewed databases. We illustrate with an example.

EXAMPLE 3.3. *Let $q(x, y, z) = S_1(x, z), S_2(y, z)$ be a simple join, where both relations have cardinality m. We show two instances of the HC algorithm, the first optimized for skewed databases, and the second optimized for skew-free databases. The first share allocation is $p_1 = p_2 = p_3 = p^{1/3}$, thus every processor is identified by $(w_1, w_2, w_3) \in [p_1] \times [p_2] \times [p_3]$. The algorithm sends every tuple $S_1(a, c)$ to all processors $(h_1(a), w_2, h_3(c))$ for $w_2 \in [p_3]$ and every tuple $S_2(b, c)$ to all processors $(w_1, h_2(b), h_3(c))$ for $w_1 \in [p_1]$. By Corollary 3.2, on skew-free databases the load per server is $O(m/p^{2/3})$ (times some polylog factor). But even on skewed database the load per server is $O(m/p^{1/3})$. The second algorithm allocates shares $p_1 = p_2 = 1, p_3 = p$. This corresponds to a standard hash-join on the variable z. On a skew-free database (equivalently, when every value of z has frequency at most m/p in both relations) the load per server is $O(m/p)$ with high probability. However, if it is skewed, then the load can be as bad as $O(m)$: this occurs when all tuples have the same value z.*

Generalizing the example, for every conjunctive query with k variables, we can execute the HC algorithm with equal shares $p_1 = \ldots = p_k = p^{1/k}$. Then, the algorithm achieves a maximum load per server of at most $O(\max_j M_j / p^{1/k})$.

However, in practice, in applications where skew is expected, it is better to design specialized algorithms, as we further discuss in section 4. Therefore, we focus our analysis on skew-free databases, and optimize the expected load.

Choosing the Shares. Here we discuss how to compute the shares p_i to optimize the expected load per server. Afrati and Ullman compute the shares by optimizing the total load $\sum_j m_j / \prod_{i:i \in S_j} p_i$ subject to the constraint $\prod_i p_i = 1$, which is a non-linear system that can be solved using Lagrange multipliers. Here we take a different approach. First, we write the shares as $p_i = p^{e_i}$ where $e_i \in [0, 1]$ is called the *share exponent* for x_i, and denote L the maximum load per server, thus $M_j / \prod_{i:i \in S_j} p_i \leq L$ for every j. Denote $\lambda = \log_p L$ and $\mu_j = \log_p M_j$ (we will assume w.l.o.g. that $m_j \geq p$, hence $\mu_j \geq 1$ for all j). Then, we optimize the LP:

$$\begin{aligned} \text{minimize} \quad & \lambda \\ \text{subject to} \quad & \sum_{i \in [k]} -e_i \geq -1 \\ & \forall j \in [\ell] : \sum_{i \in S_j} e_i + \lambda \geq \mu_j \\ & \forall i \in [k] : e_i \geq 0, \quad \lambda \geq 0 \end{aligned} \tag{5}$$

Denote $L_{\text{upper}} = p^{e^*}$ where e^* is the objective value of the optimal solution to the above LP. We have:

THEOREM 3.4. *For a query q and p servers, with statistics $\mathbf{M}$, let $\mathbf{e} = e_1, \ldots, e_k$ be share exponents that are optimal for the above LP. Then, the expected load per server is L_{upper}. Moreover, if every S_j is skew-free w.r.t. to $\mathbf{e}$, then the maximum load per server is $O(L_{\text{upper}} \cdot \ln^k(p))$ with high probability.*

In subsection 3.3 we will give a closed form expression for L_{upper} and also provide an example. But first, we prove a matching lower bound.

3.2 The Lower Bound

We prove a lower bound for the maximum load per server over databases with statistics $\mathbf{M}$. Fix some constant $0 < \delta < \min_j\{a_j\}$, and assume that for every relation S_j its cardinality satisfies $m_j \leq n^{\delta}$, where n is the domain size of each attribute.

Consider the probability space where each relation S_j is chosen independently and uniformly at random from all subsets of $[n]^{a_j}$ with exactly m_j tuples. Denote $\mathbf{E}[|q(I)|]$ the expected number of answers to q: we can show that $\mathbf{E}[|q(I)|] = n^{k-a} \prod_{j=1}^{\ell} m_j$.

Fix a query q and a fractional edge packing $\mathbf{u}$ of q. Denote $u = \sum_{j=1}^{\ell} u_j$ the value of the packing, and:

$$K(\mathbf{u}, \mathbf{M}) = \prod_{j=1}^{\ell} M_j^{u_j} \tag{6}$$

$$L(\mathbf{u}, \mathbf{M}, p) = \left(\frac{K(\mathbf{u}, \mathbf{M})}{p}\right)^{1/u} \tag{7}$$

Further denote $L_{\text{lower}} = \max_{\mathbf{u}} L(\mathbf{u}, \mathbf{M}, p)$, where $\mathbf{u}$ ranges over all fractional edge packings for q. Let c be a constant, $c = \frac{a_j - \delta}{3a_j}$, where a_j is the maximum arity of all relations. We prove in the full paper:

THEOREM 3.5. *Fix statistics $\mathbf{M}$, and consider any deterministic MPC algorithm that runs in one communication round on p servers. Let $\mathbf{u}$ be any edge packing of q. Any* *server i with load L_i reports at most*

$$\frac{L_i^u}{c^u K(\mathbf{u}, \mathbf{M})} \cdot \mathbf{E}[|q(I)|]$$

answers in expectation, where I is a randomly chosen database with statistics $\mathbf{M}$. Therefore, the p servers of the algorithm report at most

$$\left(\frac{L}{c \cdot L(\mathbf{u}, \mathbf{M}, p)}\right)^u \cdot \mathbf{E}[|q(I)|]$$

answers in expectation, where L is the maximum load.

As a consequence, any algorithm that computes q correctly over any database with statistics $\mathbf{M}$ must have load $L \geq cL_{lower}$ bits[6].

In our previous work [4], we presented a matching lower and upper bound for computing q on some restricted database instances, where the relations S_j are *matchings* and have the same cardinalities; the proof of Theorem 3.5 is an extension of the lower bound proof in [4]. We explain here the relationship. When all cardinalities are equal, $M_1 = \ldots = M_\ell = M$, then $L_{\text{lower}} = M/p^{1/u}$, and this quantity is maximized when $\mathbf{u}$ is a maximum fractional edge packing, whose value is denoted τ^*: by duality, this is equal to the fractional vertex covering number for q. The bound in [4] is $c'M/p^{1/\tau^*}$ (the constant c' in [4] is tighter). Theorem 3.5 generalizes the lower bound to arbitrary cardinalities, in which case $L(\mathbf{u}, \mathbf{M}, p)$ is not necessarily maximized at τ^*. In the rest of this section we prove that $L_{\text{lower}} = L_{\text{upper}}$.

3.3 Proof of Equivalence

The feasible solutions of the edge packing constraints in (2) define a feasible and bounded convex polytope. An *extreme point* of a polytope is one that cannot be written as a convex combination of two other distinct points of the polytope. Each extreme point can be obtained by choosing k constraints, transform them into equalities and solve the corresponding linear system. The set of extreme points for (2), denoted $pk(q)$, is thus finite and can be bounded by $|pk(q)| \leq \binom{k+\ell}{k}$, *i.e.* it depends only on the query.

We prove here:

THEOREM 3.6. *For any vector of statistics $\mathbf{M}$ and number of processors p , we have:*

$$L_{lower} = L_{upper} = \max_{\mathbf{u} \in pk(q)} L(\mathbf{u}, \mathbf{M}, p)$$

Before we prove the theorem we discuss its implications. We start with an example.

EXAMPLE 3.7. *Consider the triangle query*

$$C_3 = S_1(x_1, x_2), S_2(x_2, x_3), S_3(x_3, x_1)$$

and assume the three cardinalities are m_1, m_2, m_3. Then, $pk(C_3)$ has four vertices, and each gives a different value for $L(\mathbf{u}, \mathbf{M}, p)$:

$\mathbf{u}$	$L(\mathbf{u}, \mathbf{M}, p)$
$(1/2, 1/2, 1/2)$	$(M_1 M_2 M_3)^{1/3}/p^{2/3}$
$(1, 0, 0)$	M_1/p
$(0, 1, 0)$	M_2/p
$(0, 0, 1)$	M_3/p

The first vertex is the solution to $u_1 + u_2 = u_1 + u_3 = u_2 + u_3 = 1$; the second the solution to $u_1 + u_2 = 1, u_2 = u_3 = 0$, etc. Thus, the load of the algorithm is the largest of these four quantities, and this is also the lower bound of any algorithm. In other words, the optimal solution to the LP (5) can be given in closed form, as the maximum over four expressions.

Next, we use the theorem to compute the *space exponent*. In [4] we showed that, for every query q, the optimal load over databases restricted to matchings of equal size M is $O(M/p^{1-\varepsilon})$, where $0 \leq \varepsilon < 1$ is called the space exponent for q. Consider now a database with arbitrary statistics, and denote $M = \max_j M_j$. Thus, we may assume w.l.o.g. that for every j, $M_j = M/p^{\nu_j}$ for some $\nu_j \geq 0$. Then, $L(\mathbf{u}, \mathbf{M}, p) = M/p^{(\sum_j \nu_j u_j + 1)/u}$. To obtain the optimal load, one needs to find $\mathbf{u} \in pk(q)$ that minimizes $v = (\sum_j \nu_j u_j + 1)/(\sum_j u_j)$. Denoting v^* the minimal value, the load is M/p^{v^*}. Thus, the space exponent for given statistics is $1 - v^*$.

PROOF OF THEOREM 3.6. Recall that L_{upper} is p^{e^*}, where e^* is the objective value of the optimal solution to the *primal* LP problem (5). Consider its *dual* LP:

$$\begin{aligned} \text{maximize} \quad & \sum_{j \in [\ell]} \mu_j f_j - f \\ \text{subject to} \quad & \sum_{j \in [\ell]} f_j \leq 1 \\ \forall i \in [k] : & \sum_{j : i \in S_j} f_j - f \leq 0 \\ \forall j \in [\ell] : & f_j \geq 0, \quad f \geq 0 \end{aligned} \tag{8}$$

By the primal-dual theorem, the objective is also maximized at e^*. Writing $u_j = f_j/f$ and $u = 1/f$, we transform it into the following non-linear optimization problem:

$$\begin{aligned} \text{maximize} \quad & \frac{1}{u} \cdot \left(\sum_{j \in [\ell]} \mu_j u_j - 1\right) \\ \text{subject to} \quad & \sum_{j \in [\ell]} u_j \leq u \\ \forall i \in [k] : & \sum_{j : i \in S_j} u_j \leq 1 \\ \forall j \in [\ell] : & u_j \geq, 0 \quad u \geq 0 \end{aligned} \tag{9}$$

The optimal solution of the above non-linear problem, with value u^*, must satisfy $u = \sum_j u_j$, otherwise we simply replace u with $\sum_j u_j$ and obtain a feasible solution with at least as good objective function (indeed, $\mu_j \geq 1$ for any j, and hence $\sum_j \mu_j u_j \geq \sum_j u_j \geq 1$, since any optimal $\mathbf{u}$ will have sum at least 1). Therefore, the optimal is given by a fractional edge packing $\mathbf{u}$. Furthermore, for any packing $\mathbf{u}$, the objective function $\sum_j \frac{1}{u} \cdot (\mu_j u_j - 1)$ is $\log_p L(\mathbf{u}, \mathbf{M}, p)$. To conclude the proof of the theorem, we show that (a) $e^* = u^*$ and (b) the optimum is obtained when $\mathbf{u} \in pk(q)$. This follows from:

LEMMA 3.8. *Let $F : \mathbf{R}^{k+1} \to \mathbf{R}^{k+1}$: $F(x_0, x_1, \ldots, x_k) = (1/x_0, x_1/x_0, \ldots, x_k/x_0)$. Then:*

- *F is its own inverse, $F = F^{-1}$.*

[6]This follows by observing that, when $L(\mathbf{u}, \mathbf{M}, p)$ is maximized, then $u = \sum_j u_j \geq 1$.

- *F maps any feasible solution to (8) to a feasible solution to (9), and conversely.*
- *F maps a convex set to a convex set.*

PROOF. If $y_0 = 1/x_0$ and $y_j = x_j/x_0$, then obviously $x_0 = 1/y_0$ and $x_j = y_j/y_0$. The second item can be checked directly. For the third item, it suffices to prove that F maps a convex combination $\lambda\mathbf{x} + \lambda'\mathbf{x}'$ where $\lambda + \lambda' = 1$ into a convex combination $\mu F(\mathbf{x}) + \mu' F(\mathbf{x}')$, where $\mu + \mu' = 1$. Assuming $\mathbf{x} = (x_0, x_1, \ldots, x_k)$ and $\mathbf{x}' = (x_0', x_1', \ldots, x_k')$, this follows by setting $\mu = x_0/(\lambda x_0 + \lambda x_0')$ and $\mu' = x_0'/(\lambda x_0 + \lambda x_0')$. $\square$

This completes the proof of Theorem 3.6.

4. COMPLEX DATABASE STATISTICS

In this section, we discuss algorithms and lower bounds for the case where the input servers are provided by additional information regarding skew.

4.1 A Simple Case: Join

We start with a simple example, the join of two tables, $q(x, y, z) = S_1(x, z), S_2(y, z)$, to illustrate the main algorithmic and proof ideas. Let m_1, m_2 be the cardinalities of S_1, S_2. For any value $h \in [n]$ that variable z may assume, let $m_j(h)$ denote the frequency of h in S_j, $j = 1, 2$; h is called a *heavy hitter* in S_j if $m_j(h) \geq m_j/p$. For general queries, the threshold for a heavy hitter will differ. We assume that heavy hitters and their frequencies are known initially by the algorithm.

The algorithm uses the same principle popular in virtually all parallel join implementations to date: identify the heavy hitters and treat them differently. However, the analysis and optimality proof is new, to the best of our knowledge.

The Algorithm. Let H denote the set of heavy hitters either in S_1 or in S_2. Note that $|H| \leq 2p$. The algorithm will deal with the tuples that have no heavy hitter values (*light tuples*) by running the vanilla HC algorithm. However, it will adapt its function for heavy hitters.

To compute q, the algorithm must compute for each $h \in H$ the subquery $q[h/z] = S_1(x, h), S_2(y, h)$, which is equivalent to computing the cartesian product $q_z = S_1'(x), S_2'(z)$, where $S_1'(x) = S_1(x, h)$ and $S_2'(y) = S_2(y, h)$, and the relations have cardinality $m_1(h)$ and $m_2(h)$ respectively (and size in bits $M_1(h), M_2(h)$). We call q_z the *residual query*. The algorithm will allocate p_h servers to compute $q[h/z]$ for each $h \in H$, such that $\sum_{h \in H} p_h = \Theta(p)$. Since the unary relations have no skew, Theorem 3.6 says that the maximum load L_h for each h is given by

$$L_h = \tilde{O}\left(\max_{\mathbf{u} \in pk(q_z)} L(\mathbf{u}, \mathbf{M}(h), p_h)\right)$$

where $\tilde{O}$ hides the polylog dependence on p. One can compute that $pk(q_z) = \{(1, 1), (1, 0), (0, 1)\}$. At this point, since p_h is not specified, it is not clear which edge packing maximizes the above quantity for each h. To overcome this problem, we further refine the assignment of servers to heavy hitters: we allocate $p_{h,\mathbf{u}}$ servers to each h and each $\mathbf{u} \in pk(q_z)$, such that $p_h = \sum_{\mathbf{u}} p_{h,\mathbf{u}}$.

Now, for a given $\mathbf{u} \in pk(q)$, we can evenly distribute the load among the heavy hitters by choosing $p_{h,\mathbf{u}}$ such that for any $h, h' \in H$, we have $L(\mathbf{u}, \mathbf{M}(h), p_{h,\mathbf{u}}) = L(\mathbf{u}, \mathbf{M}(h'), p_{h',\mathbf{u}})$. In particular, we will choose the server allocation proportionally to the "heaviness" of executing the residual query:

$$p_{h,\mathbf{u}} = \left\lceil p \cdot \frac{K(\mathbf{u}, \mathbf{M}(h))}{\sum_{h' \in H} K(\mathbf{u}, \mathbf{M}(h'))} \right\rceil$$

It is easy to check that the total number of servers will be $\Theta(p)$, and that the load L_h will be

$$L_h = \tilde{O}\left(\max_{\mathbf{u} \in pk(q_z)} \left(\frac{\sum_{h \in H} M_1(h)^{u_1} M_2(h)^{u_2}}{p}\right)^{1/(u_1+u_2)}\right)$$

By plugging in the possible values of $pk(q_z)$, as well as the load for the vanilla HC algorithm that runs on the light tuples, we obtain that the maximum load will be

$$\tilde{O}\left(\max\left\{\frac{M_1}{p}, \frac{M_2}{p}, \left(\frac{\sum_{h \in H} M_1(h) M_2(h)}{p}\right)^{1/2}\right\}\right) \tag{10}$$

The first two terms are exactly what we would get from the analysis of the HC algorithm, and do not depend on the occurrence of heavy hitters, while the third term depends on the frequencies of the heavy hitters and can be much larger than the first two. In the extreme, a single heavy hitter h with $m_j(h) = m_j$ for $j = 1, 2$ will demand maximum load equal to $\tilde{O}(\sqrt{M_1 M_2/p})$.

The Lower Bound. We show here that the above algorithm is optimal within a polylog factor of p. Recall that in section 3 we have shown that any algorithm that computes correctly a query q must have maximum load at least $\Omega(\max_{\mathbf{u} \in pk(q)} \{L(\mathbf{u}, \mathbf{M}, p)\})$. Since $pk(q) = \{(1, 0), (0, 1)\}$ in the case of the join, we already have a lower bound of $\Omega(\max\{M_1/p, M_2/p\})$ for the load.

Hence, to show optimality it suffices to show that the load L is further lower bounded by the third term of (10). We sketch here the main idea of the proof. Recall that in section 3 we constructed a uniformly random instance to show the lower bound. For skewed data, we have to construct a random instance I that agrees with the frequency information $m_j(h)$ for each $h \in [n]$. To do this, we create I by choosing a uniformly random subinstance for each residual query $q[h/z]$. Notice that, by our construction, the size of the join will be $\sum_{h \in [n]} m_1(h) m_2(h)$.

Now, let $L_j^s(h)$ denote the expected number of tuples from the subinstance $S_j(h)$ that are known by some server s ($s = 1, \ldots, p$) after communication. We show in subsection 4.3 that, in order for the servers to report correctly all join tuples, we must have that for each $h \in [n]$:

$$\sum_{s=1}^{p} L_1^s(h) L_2^s(h) \geq m_1(h) m_2(h)$$

We can now sum up the above inequalities for all $h \in [n]$:

$$\sum_{h \in [n]} m_1(h) m_2(h) \leq \sum_{h \in [n]} \sum_{s=1}^{p} L_1^s(h) L_2^s(h)$$

$$= \sum_{s=1}^{p} \sum_{h \in [n]} L_1^s(h) L_2^s(h) \leq \sum_{s=1}^{p} \left(\sum_{h \in [n]} L_1^s(h)\right) \left(\sum_{h \in [n]} L_2^s(h)\right)$$

Observe that $\sum_h L_j^s(h)$ denotes the expected number of tuples from S_j known by a server s. Since s will receive at most L bits, it can be shown (details in subsection 4.3) that

$\sum_h L_j^s(h) \leq L/(2c\log(n))$ for some constant c. We now obtain:

$$\sum_{h\in[n]} M_1(h)M_2(h) \leq pL^2$$

which proves our lower bound.

4.2 An Algorithm for the General Case

We now generalize some of the ideas for the simple join to an arbitrary conjunctive query q. Extending the notion for simple joins, for each relation S_j with $|S_j| = m_j$ we say that a partial assignment $\mathbf{h}_j$ to a subset $\mathbf{x}_j \subset vars(S_j)$ is a *heavy hitter* if and only if the number of tuples, $m_j(\mathbf{h}_j)$, from S_j that contain $\mathbf{h}_j$ satisfies $m_j(\mathbf{h}_j) > m_j/p$. As before, there are $O(p)$ such heavy hitters. We will assume that each input server knows the entire set of heavy hitters for all relations.

Bin Combinations. For simplicity we assume that p is a power of 2. We will not produce quite as smooth a bound as we did for the simple join, since we will initially group the frequencies to *bins*, which will add a $\log^{O(1)} p$ factor to the bound. In particular, for each relation S_j and subset of variables $\mathbf{x}_j$, we define $\log_2 p$ bins for the frequencies, or degrees of each of the heavy hitters. The b-th bin, for $b = 1, \ldots, \log_2 p$ will contain all heavy hitters $\mathbf{h}_j$ with $m_j/2^{b-1} \geq m_j(\mathbf{h}_j) > m_j/2^b$. The last bin, a bin of light hitters with $b = \log_2 p + 1$, will contain all assignments $\mathbf{h}_j$ to $\mathbf{x}_j$ that are not heavy hitters. Notice that, when $\mathbf{x}_j = \emptyset$, the only non-empty bin is the first bin, the only heavy hitter is the empty tuple $\mathbf{h}_j = ()$, and $m_j(\mathbf{h}_j) = m_j$.

For a bin b on $\mathbf{x}_j$ define $\beta_b = \log_p(2^{b-1})$; observe that for each heavy hitter bin, there are at most $2p^{\beta_b}$ heavy hitters in this bin, and for the last bin we have $\beta_b = 1$. Instead of identifying each bin using its index b, we identify each bin by β_b, called its *bin exponent*, along with the index of the relation S_j for which it is defined, and the set $\mathbf{x}_j \subset vars(S_j)$. Note that $0 = \beta_1 < \beta_2 < \cdots < \beta_{\log_2 p+1} = 1$.

DEFINITION 4.1 (BIN COMBINATION). *Consider a set of variables $\mathbf{x} \subset V = vars(q)$, and define $\mathbf{x}_j = \mathbf{x} \cap vars(S_j)$. A pair $\mathcal{B} = (\mathbf{x}, (\beta_j)_j)$ is called a* bin combination *if (1) $\beta_j = 0$ for every j where $\mathbf{x}_j = \emptyset$, and (2) there is some consistent assignment $\mathbf{h}$ to $\mathbf{x}$ such that for each j with $\mathbf{x}_j \neq \emptyset$ the induced assignment $\mathbf{h}_j$ to $\mathbf{x}_j$ has bin exponent β_j in relation S_j. We write $C(\mathcal{B})$ for the set of all such assignments $\mathbf{h}$.*

Algorithm BinHC. The algorithm BinHC allocates p virtual processors to each bin combination and handles associated inputs separately. There are $O(\log p)$ bin choices for each relation and therefore the algorithm requires at most $\log^{O(1)} p$ virtual processors in total. Let N_{bc} be the number of possible bin combinations. As in the join algorithm (subsection 4.1), within each bin combination we partition the p servers among the heavy hitters, using $p_{\mathbf{h}} = p/|C(\mathcal{B})|$ servers for heavy hitter $\mathbf{h}$ (note that $p_{\mathbf{h}}$ is independent of $\mathbf{h}$, since we have ensured complete uniformity within a bin combination). Unfortunately, we can only process $\leq p$ heavy hitters in every bin combination, while in genera, we may have $C(\mathcal{B}) > p$: *e.g.* if $\mathbf{x}$ contains variables x_1 in S_1 and x_2 in S_2, there may be up to $p \times p$ heavy hitters in this bin combination.

To solve this issue, for each $\mathcal{B}$ we will define a set $C'(\mathcal{B}) \subseteq C(\mathcal{B})$ with $|C'(\mathcal{B})| \leq p$ and sets $S_j^{(\mathcal{B})} \subseteq S_j$ of tuples for $j \in [\ell]$ that extend $\mathbf{h}_j$ for some $\mathbf{h} \in C'(\mathcal{B})$.

The BinHC algorithm for $\mathcal{B}$, in short BinHC($\mathcal{B}$), will compute all query answers for the subinstance $I_{\mathcal{B}} = (S_j^{(\mathcal{B})})_j$. If $\alpha(\mathcal{B}) = \log_p |C'(\mathcal{B})|$, the algorithm will run the HC algorithm on $p^{1-\alpha(\mathcal{B})}$ virtual processors for each of the heavy hitters $\mathbf{h} \in C'(\mathcal{B})$ so as to compute $q(I_{\mathcal{B}})$.

The share exponents for the HC algorithm will be provided by a modification of the vertex covering primal LP (5), which describes an algorithm that suffices for all light hitters. Recall that in this LP, $\mu_j = \log_p M_j$ and λ is $\log_p L$ for the load L. That LP corresponds to the bin combination $\mathcal{B}_\emptyset$ which has $\mathbf{x} = \emptyset$ and all $\beta_j = 0$. More generally, the LP associated with our algorithm for bin combination $\mathcal{B}$ is:

$$\begin{aligned} &\text{mininimize} \quad \lambda && (11)\\ &\text{subject to} \\ &\forall j \in [\ell]: \ \lambda + \sum_{x_i \in vars(S_j)-\mathbf{x}_j} e_i \geq \mu_j - \beta_j \\ &\sum_{i\in V-\mathbf{x}} e_i \leq 1 - \alpha(\mathcal{B}) \\ &\forall i \in V - \mathbf{x}: \ e_i \geq 0, \quad \lambda \geq 0 \end{aligned}$$

Let $(e_i^{(\mathcal{B})})_{i\in V-\mathbf{x}'})$ be the optimal solution for the above LP and $(\lambda^{(\mathcal{B})}$ the minimum value of the objective function.

To complete the description of BinHC, we need to define $C'(\mathcal{B})$ and $(S_j^{(\mathcal{B})})_j$. We define $C'(\mathcal{B})$ inductively. For the bin combination $\mathcal{B}_\emptyset$, $C'(\mathcal{B}_\emptyset) = C(\mathcal{B}_\emptyset)$ and it has 1 element, the empty partial assignment. For $\mathcal{B} \neq \mathcal{B}_\emptyset$, $C'(\mathcal{B})$ is defined based on optimal solutions to the above LP applied to bin combinations $\mathcal{B}'$ with $\mathbf{x}' \subset \mathbf{x}$ (such solutions may not be unique but we fix one arbitrarily for each bin combination).

For $\mathbf{h}' \in C'(\mathcal{B}')$, we say that a heavy hitter $\mathbf{h}_j$ of S_j that is an extension of $\mathbf{h}'_j$ to $\mathbf{x}_j$ is *overweight* for $\mathcal{B}'$ if there are more than $N_{\text{bc}} \cdot m_j/p^{\beta_j+\sum_{i\in\mathbf{x}_j-\mathbf{x}'_j} e_i^{(\mathcal{B}')}}$ elements of S_j consistent with $\mathbf{h}_j$. $C'(\mathcal{B})$ consists of all assignments $\mathbf{h} \in C(\mathcal{B})$ such that there is some $j \in [\ell]$, some bin combination $\mathcal{B}'$ on set $\mathbf{x}' \subset \mathbf{x}$ such that $\mathbf{x} - \mathbf{x}' \subseteq vars(S_j)$, and some $\mathbf{h}' \in C'(\mathcal{B}')$ such that $\mathbf{h}$ is an extension of $\mathbf{h}'$ and $\mathbf{h}_j$ is an overweight heavy hitter of S_j for $\mathcal{B}'$. The following lemma, which is proved in the full paper, shows that $\alpha(\mathcal{B}) \leq 1$.

LEMMA 4.2. *For all bin combinations $\mathcal{B}$, $|C'(\mathcal{B})| \leq p$.*

Let $A_{\mathcal{B}} \subseteq [\ell]$ be the set of all j such that $\mathbf{x}_j \neq \emptyset$. For each $j \in [\ell] - A_{\mathcal{B}}$, let $S_j^{(\mathcal{B})}$ consist of all tuples in S_j that do not contain any heavy hitter $\mathbf{h}''_j$ of S_j that is overweight for $\mathcal{B}$. For each $j \in A_{\mathcal{B}}$, and $\mathbf{h} \in C'(\mathcal{B})$ let $S_j^{(\mathcal{B})}(\mathbf{h})$ consist of all tuples in S_j that contain $\mathbf{h}_j$ on $\mathbf{x}_j$ (with bin exponent β_j) but do not contain any heavy hitter $\mathbf{h}''_j$ of S_j that is overweight for $\mathcal{B}$ and a proper extension of $\mathbf{h}_j$. $S_j^{(\mathcal{B})}$ will be the union of all $S_j^{(\mathcal{B})}(\mathbf{h})$ for all $\mathbf{h} \in C'(\mathcal{B})$.

Analysis. We analyze here the BinHC algorithm. We show first that it correctly computes all answers to the query q on the relations S_j.

LEMMA 4.3 (CORRECTNESS). *Every tuple in the join of $(S_j)_{j\in[\ell]}$ is contained in a join of subrelations $(S_j^{(\mathcal{B})})_{j\in[\ell]}$ for some bin combination $\mathcal{B}$.*

PROOF. Observe first that every join tuple is vacuously consistent with the empty bin combination $\mathcal{B}_\emptyset$. Therefore the join of $(S_j^{(\mathcal{B}_\emptyset)})_{j\in[\ell]}$ contains all join tuples that do not contain an overweight heavy hitter $\mathbf{h}_j$ for any relation S_j with respect to $\mathcal{B}_\emptyset$ (and therefore contains all join tuples that are not consistent with any heavy hitter). Now fix a join tuple $\mathbf{t}$ that is overweight for $\mathcal{B}_\emptyset$. By definition, there is an associated relation S_{j_1} and $\mathbf{x}^1 \subset vars(S_{j_1})$ such that $\mathbf{h}^1 = (\mathbf{t}_{\mathbf{x}^1})$ is an overweight heavy hitter of S_{j_1} for $\mathcal{B}_\emptyset$. Let $\mathcal{B}_1$ be the bin combination associated with $\mathbf{h}^1$. By definition $\mathbf{h}^1 \in C'(\mathcal{B}_1)$. Now either $\mathbf{t}$ is contained in the join of $(S_j^{(\mathcal{B}_1)})_{j\in[\ell]}$ and we are done or there is some relation S_{j_2} and $\mathbf{x}^2$ such that $\mathbf{x}^2 - \mathbf{x}^1 \subset vars(S_{j_2})$ such that $\mathbf{h}^2 = (\mathbf{t}_{\mathbf{x}^2})$ has the property that $\mathbf{h}^2_{j_2}$ is an overweight heavy hitter of S_{j_2} for $\mathcal{B}_1$. Again, in the latter case, if $\mathcal{B}_2$ is the bin combination associated with $\mathbf{h}^2$ then $\mathbf{h}^2 \in C'(\mathcal{B}_2)$ by definition and we can repeat the previous argument for $\mathcal{B}_2$ instead of $\mathcal{B}_1$. Since the number of variables grows at each iteration, we can repeat this at most k times before finding a first $\mathcal{B}_r$ such that $\mathbf{t}$ is not associated with any overweight heavy hitter for $\mathcal{B}_r$. In this case $\mathbf{t}$ will be computed in the join of $(S_j^{(\mathcal{B}_r)})_{j\in[\ell]}$. □

We next analyze the load for BinHC($\mathcal{B}$), and show that it is within a $\log^{O(1)} p$ factor of $p^{\lambda^{(\mathcal{B})}}$, where $\lambda^{(\mathcal{B})}$ is the optimal value given by the LP for $\mathcal{B}$.

LEMMA 4.4. *Let $\mathbf{h}$ be an assignment to $\mathbf{x}$ that is consistent with bin combination $\mathcal{B}$. If we hash each residual relation $S_j^{(\mathcal{B})}(\mathbf{h})$ on $vars(S_j) - \mathbf{x}_j$ using $p^{e_i^{(\mathcal{B})}}$ values for each $x_i \in vars(S_j) - \mathbf{x}_j$, each processor has load (in bits)*

$$O\left((N_{\mathrm{bc}} \cdot \ln p)^{r'} \cdot M_j / p^{\min(\beta_j + \sum_{i \in vars(S_j)-\mathbf{x}_j} e_i^{(\mathcal{B})}, 1)}\right)$$

with high probability, where $r' = \max_j (r_j - |\mathbf{x}_j|)$.

PROOF. For $j \in [\ell] - A_{\mathcal{B}}$, $S_j^{(\mathcal{B})}$ only contains tuples of S_j that are not overweight for $\mathcal{B}$, which means that for every $\mathbf{x}_j'' \subseteq vars(S_j)$ and every heavy hitter assignment $\mathbf{h}''$ to the variables of $\mathbf{x}_j''$, there are at most

$$N_{\mathrm{bc}} \cdot m_j / p^{\beta_j + \sum_{i \in \mathbf{x}_j''} e_i^{(\mathcal{B})}} = N_{\mathrm{bc}} \cdot m_j / p^{\beta_j + \sum_{i \in \mathbf{x}_j'' - \mathbf{x}_j} e_i^{(\mathcal{B})}}$$

elements of S_j consistent with $\mathbf{h}''$. Every other assignment $\mathbf{h}''$ to the variables of $\mathbf{x}_j''$ is a light hitter and therefore is contained in at most m_j/p consistent tuples of S_j. For $j \in A_{\mathcal{B}}$, we obtain the same bound, where the only difference is that we need to restrict things to extensions of $\mathbf{h}_j$. This bound gives the smoothness condition on $S_j^{(\mathcal{B})}(\mathbf{h})$ necessary to apply Lemma 3.1 to each relation $S_j^{(\mathcal{B})}(\mathbf{h})$ and yields the claimed result. □

As a corollary, we obtain:

COROLLARY 4.5. *Let $L_{min} = \max_j (M_j/p)$. The maximum load of BinHC($\mathcal{B}$) is $O((N_{\mathrm{bc}} \cdot \ln p)^{r_{\max}} \cdot \max(L_{min}, p^{\lambda}))$ with high probability, where $\lambda = \lambda^{(\mathcal{B})}$ is the optimum of the LP for $\mathcal{B}$ and $r_{\max}$ is the maximum arity of any S_j.*

PROOF. There are $p^{1-\alpha(\mathcal{B})}$ processors allocated to each $\mathbf{h}$ and $p^{\alpha(\mathcal{B})}$ such assignments $\mathbf{h}$ so that the maximum load per $\mathbf{h}$ is also the maximum overall load. Given the presence of the L_{min} term, it suffices to show that the maximum load per $\mathbf{h}$ due to relation $S_j^{(\mathcal{B})}(\mathbf{h})$ is at most $(\ln p)^{k-|\mathbf{x}|} \cdot \max(M_j/p, p^{\lambda})$ for each $j \in [\ell]$. Observe that by construction, p^{λ} is the smallest value s.t. $p^{\lambda} \cdot p^{\beta_j + \sum_{x_i \in vars(S_j)-\mathbf{x}_j} e_i^{(\mathcal{B})}} \geq M_j$ for all j and $\sum_{i \in \mathbf{x}} e_i^{(\mathcal{B})} \leq 1 - \alpha(\mathcal{B})$. Lemma 4.4 then implies that the load due to relation $S_j^{(\mathcal{B})}(\mathbf{h})$ is at most a polylogarithmic factor times

$$\max(M_j/p, M_j/p^{\beta_j + \sum_{x_i \in vars(S_j)-H_j} e_i^{(\mathcal{B})}})$$

which is at most $\max(M_j/p, p^{\lambda})$. □

We can now upper bound the maximum load of the BinHC algorithm. Denote $\mathbf{M}(\mathcal{B}) = (M_1/p^{\beta_1}, \ldots, M_\ell/p^{\beta_\ell})$. Then:

THEOREM 4.6 (MAXIMUM LOAD). *The BinHC algorithm has with high probability maximum load*

$$L = O\left(\log^{O(1)} p \cdot \max_{\mathcal{B}, \mathbf{u} \in pk(q_{\mathbf{x}})} L(\mathbf{u}, \mathbf{M}(\mathcal{B}), p^{1-\alpha(\mathcal{B})})\right)$$

PROOF. There are only $\log^{O(1)} p$ choices of $\mathcal{B}$ and for each choice of $\mathcal{B}$, by Corollary 4.5, the load with p virtual processors is $O(\log^{O(1)} p \cdot \max(L_{min}, p^{\lambda^{(\mathcal{B})}}))$. We first show that we can remove the L_{min} term. Indeed, observe that in the original LP which corresponds to an empty bin combination $\mathcal{B}$, we have $\lambda + \sum_{i \in S_j} e_i \geq \mu_j$ for each $j \in [\ell]$ and $\sum_i e_i \leq 1$. This implies that $\lambda \geq \mu_j - 1$ and hence $p^{\lambda} \geq M_j/p$ for each j, so $p^{\lambda} \geq L_{min}$. Finally, by applying a duality argument to (11), we have:

$$\lambda^{(\mathcal{B})} = \max_{\mathbf{u} \in pk(q_{\mathbf{x}})} \{L(\mathbf{u}, \mathbf{M}(\mathcal{B}), p^{1-\alpha(\mathcal{B})})\}$$

This completes the proof. □

4.3 Lower Bound

In this section we give a lower bound for the load of any deterministic algorithm that computes a query q, and generalize the lower bound in Theorem 3.5, which was over databases with cardinality statistics $\mathbf{M}$. Our new lower bound generalizes this to databases with a fixed degree sequence: if the degree sequence is skewed, then the new bounds can be stronger, proving that skew in the input data makes query evaluation harder.

For a relation S_j, let $\mathbf{x}_j \subseteq vars(S_j)$ and $d_j = |\mathbf{x}_j|$. A *statistics of type* $\mathbf{x}_j$, or $\mathbf{x}_j$*-statistics*, is a function $m_j : [n]^{d_j} \to \mathbb{N}$. An instance of S_j satisfies the statistics m_j if for any tuple $\mathbf{h}_j \in [n]^{d_j}$, its frequency is precisely $m_j(\mathbf{h}_j)$, in other words $|\sigma_{\mathbf{x}_j = \mathbf{h}_j}(S_j)| = m_j(\mathbf{h}_j)$. As an example, if $S(x, y)$ is a binary relation, then an x-statistics is a degree sequence $m(1), m(2), \ldots, m(n)$; also, if $\mathbf{x}_j = \emptyset$ then an $\mathbf{x}_j$-statistics consists of a single number, which denotes the cardinality of S_j. In general, the $\mathbf{x}_j$-statistics define uniquely the cardinality of S_j, as $|S_j| = \sum_{\mathbf{h}_j \in [n]^{d_j}} m_j(\mathbf{h}_j)$.

Fix a set of variables $\mathbf{x}$ from q, let $d = |\mathbf{x}|$, and denote $\mathbf{x}_j = \mathbf{x} \cap vars(S_j)$ for every j. A *statistics of type* $\mathbf{x}$ *for the database* is a vector $\mathbf{m} = (m_1, \ldots, m_\ell)$, where each m_j is an $\mathbf{x}_j$-statistics for S_j. We associate with m the function $m : [n]^k \to (\mathbb{N})^\ell$, $m(\mathbf{h}) = (m_1(\mathbf{h}_1), \ldots, m_\ell(\mathbf{h}_\ell))$; here and in the rest of the section, $\mathbf{h}_j$ denotes $\pi_{\mathbf{x}_j}(\mathbf{h})$, *i.e.* the restriction of the tuple $\mathbf{h}$ to the variables in $\mathbf{x}_j$. When $\mathbf{x} = \emptyset$, then m simply consists of ℓ numbers, each representing the cardinality of a relation; thus, a $\mathbf{x}$-statistics generalizes the cardinality statistics from section 3. Recall that we use upper case $\mathbf{M} = (M_1, \ldots, M_\ell)$ to denote the same statistics expressed in bits, i.e. $M_j(\mathbf{h}_j) = a_j m_j(\mathbf{h}_j) \log n$. As before, we fix some constant $0 < \delta < 1$, and assume every relation S_j, has cardinality $\leq n^\delta$.

In this section, we fix $\mathbf{x}$-statistics $\mathbf{M}$ and consider the probability space where the instance is chosen uniformly at random over all instances that satisfy $\mathbf{M}$.

To prove the lower bound we need some notations. Let $q_\mathbf{x}$ be the *residual query*, obtained by removing all variables $\mathbf{x}$, and decreasing the arities of S_j as necessary: the new arity of S_j is $a_j - d_j$. Clearly, every fractional edge packing of q is also a fractional edge packing of $q_\mathbf{x}$, but the converse does not hold in general. Let $\mathbf{u}$ be a fractional edge packing of $q_\mathbf{x}$. We say that $\mathbf{u}$ *saturates* a variable $x_i \in \mathbf{x}$, if $\sum_{j:i\in S_j} u_j \geq 1$; we say that $\mathbf{u}$ saturates $\mathbf{x}$ if it saturates all variables in $\mathbf{x}$. For every fractional edge packing $\mathbf{u}$ of $q_\mathbf{x}$ that saturates $\mathbf{x}$, denote as before $u = \sum_{j=1}^{\ell} u_j$ and, using K defined in (6):

$$L_\mathbf{x}(\mathbf{u}, \mathbf{M}, p) = \left(\frac{\sum_{\mathbf{h}\in[n]^d} K(\mathbf{u}, \mathbf{M}(\mathbf{h}))}{p}\right)^{1/u} \quad (12)$$

Further denote $L_{\texttt{lower}} = \max_\mathbf{u} L_\mathbf{x}(\mathbf{u}, \mathbf{M}, p)$, and let c be the constant $c = \min_j \frac{a_j - d_j - \delta}{3a_j}$.

THEOREM 4.7. *Given a query q, fix statistics $\mathbf{M}$ of type $\mathbf{x}$, where $\mathbf{x}$ is a strict subset of the variables, and consider any deterministic MPC algorithm that runs in one communication round on p servers and has maximum load L. Then, for any edge packing $\mathbf{u}$ of q that saturates $\mathbf{x}$, any algorithm that computes q correctly must have maximum load $L \geq cL_\mathbf{x}(\mathbf{u}, \mathbf{M}, p)$ bits.*

Note that, when $\mathbf{x} = \emptyset$ then $L_\mathbf{x}(\mathbf{u}, \mathbf{M}, p) = L(\mathbf{u}, \mathbf{M}, p)$, defined in (7); therefore, our theorem is a generalization of the simpler lower bound Theorem 3.5. Before we prove the theorem, we show an example.

EXAMPLE 4.8. *We first revisit the lower bound we described in subsection 4.1 for $q(x, y, z) = S_1(x, z), S_2(y, z)$. If $\mathbf{x} = \emptyset$ then the lower bound is $\max_\mathbf{u} L(\mathbf{u}, (M_1, M_2), p)$, which is $\max(M_1/p, M_2/p)$, because there are two packings in $pk(q)$: $(1, 0)$ and $(0, 1)$. For $\mathbf{x} = \{z\}$, the residual query is $q_\mathbf{x} = S_1(x), S_2(y)$ and its sole packing is $(1, 1)$, which saturates the variable z. The packing produces an additional new lower bound: $\sqrt{\sum_{h\in[n]} M_1(h)M_2(h)/p}$. The lower bound is the maximum of these quantities.*

Next, consider C_3. In addition to the lower bounds in Example 3.7, we obtain new bounds by setting $\mathbf{x} = \{x_1\}$. The residual query is $S_1(x_2), S_2(x_2, x_3), S_3(x_3)$ and $(1, 0, 1)$ is a packing that saturates x_1 (while for example $(0, 1, 0)$ does not). This gives us a new lower bound, of the form $\sqrt{\sum_{h\in[n]} m_1(h)m_3(h)/p}$.

In the rest of the section we prove Theorem 4.7. Fix a concrete instance S_j, and let $\mathbf{a}_j \in S_j$. We write $\mathbf{a}_j|\mathbf{h}$ to denote that the tuple $\mathbf{a}_j$ from S_j matches with $\mathbf{h}$ at their common variables, and denote $(S_j)_\mathbf{h}$ the subset of tuples $\mathbf{a}_j$ that match $\mathbf{h}$: $S_j(\mathbf{h}) = \{\mathbf{a}_j \mid \mathbf{a}_j \in S_j, \mathbf{a}_j|\mathbf{h}\}$. Let $I_\mathbf{h}$ denote the restriction of I to $\mathbf{h}$, in other words $I_\mathbf{h} = (S_1(\mathbf{h}), \ldots, S_\ell(\mathbf{h}))$.

When I is chosen at random over the probability space defined by the $\mathbf{x}$-statistics $\mathbf{M}$, then, for a fixed tuple $\mathbf{h} \in [n]^d$, the restriction $I_\mathbf{h}$ is a uniformly chosen instance over all instances with cardinalities $\mathbf{M}(\mathbf{h})$, which is precisely the probability space that we used in the proof of Theorem 3.6. In particular, for every $\mathbf{a}_j \in [n]^{d_j}$ such that $\mathbf{a}_j|\mathbf{h}$, the probability that S_j contains $\mathbf{a}_j$ is $P(\mathbf{a}_j \in S_j) = m_j(\mathbf{h}_j)/n^{a_j - d_j}$; thus, our proof below is an extension of that of Theorem 3.6. We first compute the expected number of answers for q on the subinstance $I_\mathbf{h}$:

LEMMA 4.9. $\mathbf{E}[|q(I_\mathbf{h})|] = n^{k-d} \prod_{j=1}^{\ell} \frac{m_j(\mathbf{h}_j)}{n^{a_j - d_j}}$

PROOF. We can write:

$$\mathbf{E}[|q(I_\mathbf{h})|] = \sum_{\mathbf{a}|\mathbf{h}} P(\bigwedge_{j=1}^{\ell} (\mathbf{a}_j \in S_j)) = \sum_{\mathbf{a}|\mathbf{h}} \prod_{j=1}^{\ell} P(\mathbf{a}_j \in S_j)$$

$$= \sum_{\mathbf{a}|\mathbf{h}} \prod_{j=1}^{\ell} m_j(\mathbf{h}_j) n^{d_j - a_j} = n^{k-d} \prod_{j=1}^{\ell} m_j(\mathbf{h}_j) n^{d_j - a_j}$$

where the last equality follows from the fact that the number of tuples $\mathbf{a}|\mathbf{h}$ is exactly n^{k-d}. □

Single Server.

Let us fix some server and let $m(I)$ be the message the server receives on input I. For any fixed value m of $m(I)$, let $K_m(S_j)$ be the set of tuples from relation S_j *known* by the server. Let $w_j(\mathbf{a}_j)$ to denote the probability that the server knows the tuple $\mathbf{a}_j \in S_j$. In other words $w_j(\mathbf{a}_j) = P(\mathbf{a}_j \in K_{m_j(S_j)}(S_j))$, where the probability is over the random choices of S_j. This is upper bounded by $P(\mathbf{a}_j \in S_j)$:

$$w_j(\mathbf{a}_j|\mathbf{h}) \leq m_j(\mathbf{h}_j)/n^{a_j - d_j} \quad (13)$$

We derive a second upper bound by exploiting the fact that the server receives a limited number of bits.

LEMMA 4.10. *Let L be the number of bits a server receives. If $a_j > d_j$, then $\sum_{\mathbf{a}_j\in[n]^{a_j}} w_j(\mathbf{a}_j) \leq \frac{L}{ca_j \log(n)}$ for some constant $c > 0$.*

PROOF. Since $\sum_{\mathbf{a}_j\in[n]^{a_j}} w_j(\mathbf{a}_j) = \mathbf{E}[|K_{m(S_j)}(S_j)|]$, we will bound the right hand side. Now, notice that:

$$H(S_j) = H(m(S_j)) + \sum_m P(m(S_j) = m) \cdot H(S_j|m(S_j) = m)$$

$$\leq L + \sum_m P(m(S_j) = m) \cdot H(S_j|m(S_j) = m) \quad (14)$$

For every $\mathbf{h}$, let $K_m(S_j(\mathbf{h}))$ denote the known tuples from the restriction of S_j to $\mathbf{h}$. We can now show that:

$$H(S_j|m(S_j) = m) \leq \sum_\mathbf{h} \left(1 - \frac{|K_m(S_j(\mathbf{h}))|}{cm_j(\mathbf{h}_j)}\right) \log \binom{n^{a_j - d_j}}{m_j(\mathbf{h}_j)}$$

$$= H(S_j) - \sum_\mathbf{h} \frac{|K_m(S_j(\mathbf{h}))|}{cm_j(\mathbf{h}_j)} \log \binom{n^{a_j - d_j}}{m_j(\mathbf{h}_j)}$$

$$\leq H(S_j) - \sum_\mathbf{h} \frac{|K_m(S_j(\mathbf{h}))|}{cm_j(\mathbf{h}_j)} m_j(\mathbf{h}_j)(a_j - d_j - \delta) \log(n)$$

$$= H(S_j) - (1/c) \cdot |K_m(S_j)|(a_j - d_j - \delta) \log(n)$$

where the proof for the first inequality is in the full paper. Plugging this in Equation 14, we have:

$$H(S_j) \leq L + H(S_j) - (1/c) \cdot \mathbf{E}[|K_m(S_j)|](a_j - d_j - \delta) \log(n)$$

or equivalently, since $c \leq 3$:

$$\mathbf{E}[|K_m(S_j)|] \leq \frac{3L}{(a_j - d_j - \delta) \log(n)}$$

This concludes our proof. □

In the case where $a_j = d_j$, the instance $I_{\mathbf{h}}$ specifies exactly the relation S_j, and so $w_j(\mathbf{a}_j) \in \{0,1\}$ for every $\mathbf{a}_j$. Denote by $J(\mathbf{x})$ the set of relations S_j for which $a_j > d_j$.

Recall that $\mathbf{u}$ is a fractional edge packing for the residual query $q_{\mathbf{x}}$ that saturates $\mathbf{x}$. Define the *extended query* $q_{\mathbf{x}}{}'$ to consists of $q_{\mathbf{x}}$, where we add a new atom $S_i'(x_i)$ for every variable $x_i \in vars(q_{\mathbf{x}})$. Define $u_i' = 1 - \sum_{j:i \in S_j} u_j$. In other words, u_i' is defined to be the slack at the variable x_i of the packing $\mathbf{u}$. The new edge packing $(\mathbf{u}, \mathbf{u}')$ for the extended query $q_{\mathbf{x}}'$ has no more slack, hence it is both a tight fractional edge packing and a tight fractional edge cover for $q_{\mathbf{x}}$. By adding all equalities of the tight packing we obtain:

$$\sum_{j=1}^{\ell}(a_j - d_j)u_j + \sum_{i=1}^{k-d} u_i' = k - d$$

We next compute how many output tuples from $q(I_{\mathbf{h}})$ will be known in expectation by the server. Note that $q(I_{\mathbf{h}}) = q_{\mathbf{x}}(I_{\mathbf{h}})$, and thus:

$$\begin{aligned}\mathbf{E}[|K_m(q(I_{\mathbf{h}}))|] = \mathbf{E}[|K_m(q_{\mathbf{x}}(I_{\mathbf{h}}))|] &= \sum_{\mathbf{a}\in[n]^{k-d}} \prod_{j=1}^{\ell} w_j(\mathbf{a}_j|\mathbf{h}) \\ &= \sum_{\mathbf{a}\in[n]^{k-d}} \prod_{j=1}^{\ell} w_j(\mathbf{a}_j|\mathbf{h}) \prod_{i=1}^{k-d} w_i'(\mathbf{a}_i) \\ &\leq \prod_{i=1}^{k-d} n^{u_i'} \cdot \prod_{j=1}^{\ell} \left(\sum_{\mathbf{a}\in[n]^{a_j-d_j}} w_j(\mathbf{a}|\mathbf{h})^{1/u_j} \right)^{u_j}\end{aligned}$$

By writing $w_j(\mathbf{a}|\mathbf{h})^{1/u_j} = w_j(\mathbf{a}|\mathbf{h})^{1/u_j-1} w_j(\mathbf{a}|\mathbf{h})$, we can bound the quantity as follows:

$$\begin{aligned}\sum_{\mathbf{a}\in[n]^{a_j-d_j}} w_j(\mathbf{a}|\mathbf{h})^{1/u_j} &\leq \left(\frac{m_j(\mathbf{h}_j)}{n^{a_j-d_j}}\right)^{1/u_j-1} \sum_{\mathbf{a}\in[n]^{a_j-d_j}} w_j(\mathbf{a}|\mathbf{h}) \\ &= (m_j(\mathbf{h}_j) n^{d_j-a_j})^{1/u_j-1} L_j(\mathbf{h})\end{aligned}$$

where $L_j(\mathbf{h}) = \sum_{\mathbf{a}\in[n]^{a_j-d_j}} w_j(\mathbf{a}|\mathbf{h})$. Notice that for every relation S_j, $\sum_{\mathbf{h}_j\in[n]^{d_j}} L_j(\mathbf{h}_j) = \sum_{\mathbf{a}_j\in[n]^{a_j}} w_j(\mathbf{a}_j)$.

$$\begin{aligned}&\mathbf{E}[|K_m(q(I_{\mathbf{h}}))|] \\ &\leq n^{\sum_{i=1}^{k-d} u_i'} \prod_{j=1}^{\ell} \left(L_j(\mathbf{h}) m_j(\mathbf{h}_j)^{1/u_j-1} n^{(d_j-a_j)(1/u_j-1)} \right)^{u_j} \\ &= \prod_{j=1}^{\ell} L_j(\mathbf{h})^{u_j} \cdot \prod_{j=1}^{\ell} m_j(\mathbf{h}_j)^{-u_j} \cdot \mathbf{E}[|q(I_{\mathbf{h}})|]\end{aligned}$$

All Servers.

Let us first index the quantities K_m, L_j with the server $s = 1, \ldots, p$ they correspond to: K_m^s, L_j^s. Let $\mathcal{H}$ be the set of $\mathbf{h} \in [n]^d$ such that for every $j \notin J(\mathbf{x})$, $m_j(\mathbf{h}) = 1$. Observe that if $\mathbf{h} \notin \mathcal{H}$, then for some $j \notin J(\mathbf{x})$ we have $m_j(\mathbf{h}) = 0$, which implies that $q(I_{\mathbf{h}}) = \emptyset$ independent of the random subinstance. For some $\mathbf{h} \in [n]^d$, the expected number of answers that all servers will produce for the subinstance $I_{\mathbf{h}}$ is $\mathbf{E}[|K_m(q(I_{\mathbf{h}}))|] = \sum_s \mathbf{E}[|K_m^s(q(I_{\mathbf{h}}))|]$. If some $\mathbf{h} \in \mathcal{H}$ this number is not at least $\mathbf{E}[|q(I_{\mathbf{h}})|]$, the algorithm will fail to compute $q(I)$ (since any $\mathbf{h} \notin \mathcal{H}$ never produces answers, we do not need to consider it). Consequently, for every $\mathbf{h} \in \mathcal{H}$ we must have that

$$\sum_s \prod_{j\in J(\mathbf{x})} L_j^s(\mathbf{h}_j)^{u_j} \geq \prod_{j\in J(\mathbf{x})} m_j(\mathbf{h}_j)^{u_j} \tag{15}$$

Summing the inequalities for every $\mathbf{h} \in \mathcal{H}$:

$$\begin{aligned}\sum_{\mathbf{h}\in\mathcal{H}} \prod_{j\in J(\mathbf{x})} m_j(\mathbf{h}_j)^{u_j} &\leq \sum_{\mathbf{h}\in\mathcal{H}} \sum_s \prod_{j\in J(\mathbf{x})} L_j(\mathbf{h}_j)^{u_j} \\ &= \sum_s \left(\sum_{\mathbf{h}\in\mathcal{H}} \prod_{j\in J(\mathbf{x})} L_j(\mathbf{h}_j)^{u_j} \right) \\ &\leq \sum_s \prod_{j\in J(\mathbf{x})} \left(\sum_{\mathbf{h}_j} L_j^s(\mathbf{h}_j) \right)^{u_j}\end{aligned}$$

where the last inequality comes from the following application of Friedgut's inequality.

LEMMA 4.11. *If* $\mathbf{u}$ *saturates* $\mathbf{x}$ *in query* q,

$$\sum_{\mathbf{h}} \prod_j L_j(\mathbf{h}_j)^{u_j} \leq \prod_j \left(\sum_{\mathbf{h}_j} L_j(\mathbf{h}_j) \right)^{u_j}$$

Since we have $M_j = a_j m_j \log(n)$, and for any relation where $j \in J(\mathbf{x})$ also $\sum_{\mathbf{h}_j} L_j^s(\mathbf{h}_j) \leq L/(c a_j \log(n))$ (from Lemma 4.10) for every server s, we obtain that :

$$\begin{aligned}\sum_{\mathbf{h}} \prod_{j=1}^{\ell} M_j(\mathbf{h}_j)^{u_j} = \sum_{\mathbf{h}\in\mathcal{H}} \prod_{j\in J(\mathbf{x})} M_j(\mathbf{h}_j)^{u_j} &\leq \sum_s \prod_{j\in J(\mathbf{x})} (L/c)^{u_j} \\ &= p \left(\frac{L}{c}\right)^{\sum_{j\in J(\mathbf{x})} u_j} \leq p \left(\frac{L}{c}\right)^{\sum_j u_j}\end{aligned}$$

which completes the proof of Theorem 4.7.

Upper and Lower Bound Comparison. To compare the lower bound with the upper bound we obtained from the BinHC algorithm in Theorem 4.6, we apply the lower bound for a particular bin combination $\mathcal{B}$ with set $\mathbf{x}$. In this case, the definition of bin exponents implies that $m_j(\mathbf{h}_j) \geq m_j/(2p^{\beta_j})$ for the heavy hitters. Then:

$$\begin{aligned}L &\geq \max_{\mathbf{u}'} \left(\frac{\sum_{\mathbf{h}\in[n]^d} \prod_j M_j(\mathbf{h}_j)^{u_j'}}{p} \right)^{1/u'} \\ &\geq \max_{\mathbf{u}'} \left(\frac{p^{\alpha} \prod_j (M_j/2p^{\beta_j})^{u_j'}}{p} \right)^{1/u'} \\ &= \frac{1}{2} \max_{\mathbf{u}'} \left(\frac{\prod_j (M_j/p^{\beta_j})^{u_j'}}{p^{1-\alpha}} \right)^{1/u'} \\ &= \frac{1}{2} \max_{\mathbf{u}'} \{L(\mathbf{u}', \mathbf{M}(\mathcal{B}), p^{1-\alpha})\}\end{aligned}$$

where, in contrast to Theorem 4.6, the edge packing $\mathbf{u}'$ ranges only over edge packings of the residual query $q_{\mathbf{x}}$ that *saturate* all variables in $\mathbf{x}$.

5. MAP-REDUCE MODELS

In this section, we discuss the connection between the MPC model and the Map-Reduce model presented by Afrati et. al [1]. In contrast to the MPC model, where the number of servers p is the main parameter, in the model of [1] the main parameter is an upper bound q on the number of input tuples a reducer can receive, which is called *reducer size*. Given an input I, a Map-Reduce algorithm is restricted to deterministically send each input tuple independently to some reducer, which will then produce all the outputs that can be extracted from the received tuples. If $q_i \leq q$ is the number of inputs assigned to the i-th reducer, where $i = 1, \ldots, p$, we define the *replication rate* r of the algorithm $r = \sum_{i=1}^{p} q_i/|I|$.

In [1], the authors provide lower and upper bounds on r with respect to q and the size of the input. However, their results are restricted to binary relations where all sizes are equal, and they provide matching upper and lower bounds only for a subclass of such queries. We show next how to apply the results of this paper to remove these restrictions, and further consider an even stronger computation model for our lower bounds.

First, we express the bound on the data received by the reducers in *bits*: let L be the maximum number of bits each reducer can receive. The input size $|I|$ is also expressed in bits. We will also allow any algorithm to use randomization. Finally, we relax the assumption on how the inputs are communicated to the reducers: instead of restricting each input tuple to be sent independently, we assume that the input data is initially partitioned into a number of *input servers* p_0 (where p_0 must be bigger than the query size), and allow the algorithm to communicate bits to reducers by accessing all the data in one such input server. Notice that this setting allows for stronger algorithms that use input statistics to improve communication.

If each reducer receives L_i bits, the replication rate r is defined as $r = \sum_{i=1}^{p} L_i/|I|$. Notice that any algorithm with replication rate r must use $p \geq (r|I|)/L$ reducers. Now, let q be a conjunctive query, where S_j has $M_j = a_j m_j \log n$ bits (n is the size of the domain).

THEOREM 5.1. *Let q be a conjunctive query where S_j has size (in bits) M_j. Any algorithm that computes q with reducer size L, where $L \leq M_j$ for every S_j*[7] *must have replication rate*

$$r \geq \frac{c^u L}{\sum_j M_j} \max_{\mathbf{u}} \prod_{j=1}^{\ell} \left(\frac{M_j}{L}\right)^{u_j}$$

where $\mathbf{u}$ ranges over all fractional edge packings of q.

PROOF. Let f_i be the fraction of answers returned by server i, in expectation, where I is a randomly chosen database with statistics $\mathbf{M}$. By Theorem 3.5, $f_i \leq \frac{L_i^u}{c^u K(\mathbf{u},\mathbf{M})}$. Since we assume all answers are returned,

$$1 \leq \sum_{i=1}^{p} f_i = \sum_{i=1}^{p} \frac{L_i^u}{c^u K(\mathbf{u},\mathbf{M})} = \frac{\sum_{i=1}^{p} L_i L_i^{u-1}}{c^u K(\mathbf{u},\mathbf{M})}$$

$$\leq \frac{L^{u-1}\sum_{i=1}^{p} L_i}{c^u K(\mathbf{u},\mathbf{M})} = \frac{L^{u-1} r|I|}{c^u K(\mathbf{u},\mathbf{M})}$$

where we used the fact that $u \geq 1$ for the optimal $\mathbf{u}$. The claim follows by using the definition of K (6) and noting that $|I| = \sum_j M_j$. $\square$

We should note here that, following from our analysis in section 3, the bound provided by Theorem 5.1 is matched by the HYPERCUBE algorithm with appropriate shares. We illustrate Theorem 5.1 with an example.

EXAMPLE 5.2 (TRIANGLES). *Consider the triangle query C_3 and assume that all sizes are equal to M. In this case, the edge packing that maximizes the lower bound is the one that maximizes $\sum_j u_j$, $(1/2, 1/2, 1/2)$. Thus, we obtain a bound $\Omega(\sqrt{M/L})$ for the replication rate. This is exactly the formula proved in [1], but notice that we can derive bounds even if the sizes are not equal. Further, observe that any algorithm must use at least $\Omega((M/L)^{3/2})$ reducers.*

[7]if $L > M_j$, we can send the whole relation to any reducer without cost

6. CONCLUSIONS

In this paper we have studied the parallel query evaluation problem on databases in two settings: the first with known cardinalities, and the second with additionally known heavy hitters and their frequency. In the first case we have given matching lower and upper bounds (within a polylog factor of p) that are described in terms of *fractional edge packings* of the query. In the second case we have shown both lower and upper bounds described in terms of fractional packings of the residual queries, one residual query for each type of heavy hitter.

Acknowledgements. This work was partially supported by NSF grants IIS-1247469 and CCF-1217099.

7. REFERENCES

[1] F. N. Afrati, A. D. Sarma, S. Salihoglu, and J. D. Ullman. Upper and lower bounds on the cost of a map-reduce computation. *PVLDB*, 6(4):277–288, 2013.

[2] F. N. Afrati and J. D. Ullman. Optimizing joins in a map-reduce environment. In *EDBT*, pages 99–110, 2010.

[3] A. Atserias, M. Grohe, and D. Marx. Size bounds and query plans for relational joins. In *FOCS*, pages 739–748, 2008.

[4] P. Beame, P. Koutris, and D. Suciu. Communication steps for parallel query processing. In *PODS*, pages 273–284, 2013.

[5] P. Beame, P. Koutris, and D. Suciu. Skew in parallel query processing. *CoRR*, abs/1401.1872, 2014.

[6] J. Dean and S. Ghemawat. Mapreduce: Simplified data processing on large clusters. In *OSDI*, pages 137–150, 2004.

[7] E. Friedgut. Hypergraphs, entropy, and inequalities. *American Mathematical Monthly*, pages 749–760, 2004.

[8] S. Ganguly, A. Silberschatz, and S. Tsur. Parallel bottom-up processing of datalog queries. *J. Log. Program.*, 14(1&2):101–126, 1992.

[9] M. Grohe and D. Marx. Constraint solving via fractional edge covers. In *SODA*, pages 289–298, 2006.

[10] H. Q. Ngo, E. Porat, C. Ré, and A. Rudra. Worst-case optimal join algorithms: [extended abstract]. In *PODS*, pages 37–48, 2012.

[11] C. Olston, B. Reed, U. Srivastava, R. Kumar, and A. Tomkins. Pig latin: a not-so-foreign language for data processing. In *SIGMOD Conference*, pages 1099–1110, 2008.

[12] S. Suri and S. Vassilvitskii. Counting triangles and the curse of the last reducer. In *WWW*, pages 607–614, 2011.

[13] C. B. Walton, A. G. Dale, and R. M. Jenevein. A taxonomy and performance model of data skew effects in parallel joins. In *VLDB*, pages 537–548, 1991.

[14] R. S. Xin, J. Rosen, M. Zaharia, M. J. Franklin, S. Shenker, and I. Stoica. Shark: Sql and rich analytics at scale. In *SIGMOD Conference*, pages 13–24, 2013.

[15] Y. Xu, P. Kostamaa, X. Zhou, and L. Chen. Handling data skew in parallel joins in shared-nothing systems. In *SIGMOD Conference*, pages 1043–1052, 2008.

[16] A. C. Yao. Lower bounds by probabilistic arguments. In *FOCS*, pages 420–428, Tucson, AZ, 1983.

[17] M. Zaharia, M. Chowdhury, T. Das, A. Dave, J. Ma, M. McCauley, M. J. Franklin, S. Shenker, and I. Stoica. Resilient distributed datasets: a fault-tolerant abstraction for in-memory cluster computing. In *NSDI*, 2012.

The Input/Output Complexity of Triangle Enumeration

Rasmus Pagh
IT University of Copenhagen
Copenhagen, Denmark
pagh@itu.dk

Francesco Silvestri*
Dept. Information Engineering
University of Padova
Padova, Italy
silvest1@dei.unipd.it

ABSTRACT

We consider the well-known problem of enumerating all triangles of an undirected graph. Our focus is on determining the input/output (I/O) complexity of this problem. Let E be the number of edges, $M < E$ the size of internal memory, and B the block size. The best results obtained previously are $\text{sort}(E^{3/2})$ I/Os (Dementiev, PhD thesis 2006) and $\mathcal{O}\left(E^2/(MB)\right)$ I/Os (Hu et al., SIGMOD 2013), where $\text{sort}(n)$ denotes the number of I/Os for sorting n items. We improve the I/O complexity to $\mathcal{O}\left(E^{3/2}/(\sqrt{M}B)\right)$ expected I/Os, which improves the previous bounds by a factor $\min(\sqrt{E/M}, \sqrt{M})$. Our algorithm is cache-oblivious and also I/O optimal: We show that any algorithm enumerating t distinct triangles must *always* use $\Omega\left(t/(\sqrt{M}B)\right)$ I/Os, and there are graphs for which $t = \Omega\left(E^{3/2}\right)$. Finally, we give a deterministic cache-aware algorithm using $\mathcal{O}\left(E^{3/2}/(\sqrt{M}B)\right)$ I/Os assuming $M \geq E^{\varepsilon}$ for a constant $\varepsilon > 0$. Our results are based on a new color coding technique, which may be of independent interest.

Categories and Subject Descriptors

F.2.2 [**Analysis of Algorithms and Problem Complexity**]: Nonnumerical Algorithms and Problems—*Computations on discrete structures*; H.2.8 [**Database Management**]: Database Applications—*Data Mining*

General Terms

Algorithms; Theory

Keywords

Triangle listing; external memory; cache-oblivious; cache-aware; lower bound

*This work was done while Silvestri was visiting the IT University of Copenhagen.

PODS'14, June 22–27, 2014, Snowbird, UT, USA.

http://dx.doi.org/10.1145/2594538.2594552.

1. INTRODUCTION

Many kinds of information can be naturally represented as graphs, and algorithms for processing information in this format often need to consider small subgraphs such as triangles. Examples of applications in which we need to enumerate all triangles in a graph are found in [24] for studying social processes in networks, [6] for community detection, [12] for solving systems of geometric constraints. See [14, 5] for further discussion and examples.

A classical example from database theory is the following. A database is created to store information on salespeople and the products they sell. Each product is characterized by a brand and a product type, e.g. "ACME vacuum cleaner", where each product type may be available in many brands. An obvious representation in a relational database is a single table `Sells(salesperson,brand,productType)`. However, suppose that a salesperson is characterized by a set B of brands and a set T of product types, and she sells all available products in $B \times T$. Then `Sells` is not in 5th normal form[1], so to avoid anomalies it should be decomposed into three tables, one for each pair of attributes, whose natural join is equal to `Sells`. Viewing each table as a bipartite graph with vertices corresponding to attribute values, computing `Sells` is exactly the task of enumerating all triangles in the union of these three graphs. In other words, to be able to compute the join of three tables that are in 5th normal form we must solve the triangle enumeration problem. Surprisingly, it seems that the challenge of doing this in an I/O-efficient way was not addressed in the database community until the SIGMOD 2013 paper of Hu, Tao and Chung [14], though we note that a pipelined nested loop join does a good job when the edge set almost fits in memory.

In the context of I/O-efficient algorithms it is natural to not require the *listing* of all triangles to external memory. Rather, we simply require that the algorithm *enumerates* all triangles. More precisely, it suffices that for each triangle $\{v_1, v_2, v_3\}$ the algorithm makes exactly one call to a procedure $\texttt{emit}(\cdot,\cdot,\cdot)$ with parameters (v_1, v_2, v_3) at a point of time during the computation where all edges $\{v_1, v_2\}$, $\{v_2, v_3\}$, and $\{v_1, v_3\}$ are present in internal memory. Focusing on enumeration rather than listing is in line with the way the I/O complexity of algorithms in database systems is usually accounted for, where pipelining of operations may mean that it is not necessary to materialize an intermedi-

[1]The 5th normal form reduces redundancy in relational databases recording multi-valued facts. Intuitively, a table is in 5th normal form if it cannot be reconstructed from smaller tables using equijoins [16].

ate result. The same is true for other applications in which enumerating all triangles is a preprocessing step. Since each triangle is emitted at exactly one point in time there is no need for a separate duplicate elimination step.

The algorithm for triangle listing in [14] can be easily adapted to solve the enumeration problem. We recently learned that Hu et al. also make this observation in the journal version [13] of their SIGMOD 2013 paper. However, the algorithm requires $\mathcal{O}(E^2/(MB))$ I/Os for enumerating all triangles. We note that the I/O complexity corresponds to E/M scans of the edge set. The main message of this paper is that it is possible to improve this I/O complexity by a factor $\sqrt{E/M}$, which is significant whenever the data size is much larger than internal memory. Our contributions are the following:

- We present a randomized triangle enumeration algorithm that is cache-oblivious [11], and improves the I/O complexity of previous algorithms by an expected factor $\min\left(\sqrt{E/M}, \sqrt{M}\right)$. This is significant for large graphs in which $E \gg M \gg 1$.
- We present a deterministic and cache-aware triangle enumeration algorithm with the same asymptotic I/O complexity under the mild assumption $M \geq \sqrt{E}$.
- We show that the number of I/Os of our algorithms is within a constant factor of the best possible under the assumption that each triangle output must be "witnessed" by edges stored in internal memory. A similar result has been independently achieved in [13].

Formal statements can be found in Section 1.2.

1.1 State of the art

Algorithms for memory hierarchies, in particular in the external memory model [2], have been widely investigated in the last years and we refer to the excellent survey by Vitter [23] for a complete overview of the state of the art. Cache-oblivious algorithms have been introduced by Frigo et al. [10, 11] and are algorithms that do not use in their specifications the parameters describing the memory hierarchy, but still exhibit an optimal or quasi-optimal I/O complexity.

The triangle listing and enumeration problems are equivalent in flat memory (e.g., the RAM model) since the cost of writing in memory all the enumerated triangles is asymptotically no larger than the cost of triangle generation. However, this is not the case when external storage is used: the cost of writing triangles can significantly increase the I/O complexity in graphs with a large number of triangles.

Several previous papers have considered the problem of listing triangles in the external memory model. Before considering these papers, we observe that since triangle enumeration can be expressed as a natural join of three relations, it is possible to use two block-nested loop joins (in a pipelined fashion) to solve the problem incurring $\mathcal{O}((E/M)^2E/B) = \mathcal{O}(E^3/(M^2B))$ I/Os.

The first two works dealing explicitly with triangle listing in external memory are due to Menegola [18] and Dementiev [9], which give algorithms using $\mathcal{O}\left(E + E^{1.5}/B\right)$ and $\mathcal{O}\left((E^{1.5}/B)\log_{M/B}(E/B)\right)$ I/Os, respectively. Both algorithms incur a large number of I/Os and have weak temporal locality of reference since their bounds have at most a logarithmic dependency on the memory size M. Using graph partitioning ideas, Chu and Cheng [8] improved the bound to $\mathcal{O}\left(E^2/(MB) + t/B\right)$ for a class of graphs, where t is the number of returned triangles. This bound improves the previous ones as soon as $M = \Omega\left(\sqrt{E}\right)$ and is the first to be output sensitive. The class of graphs handled are those for which each subgraph generated by the partitioning fits in memory. Hu, Tao and Chung [14] provided an algorithm reaching the same bound, using very different techniques, working for *arbitrary* graphs. This improves the algorithm based on block-nested loop joins by a factor E/M. It is argued in [14] (and elaborated in the full version [13]) that their algorithm is near-optimal in the sense that it cannot be significantly improved for *all* combinations of E and M. However, the argument leaves open the question of whether a significant improvement can be obtained when $E \gg M$. In contrast, we show matching upper and lower bounds for all combinations of E and M.

As mentioned above, a lower bound on the I/O complexity of triangle enumeration has independently been shown in the unpublished journal article [13]. Although the main interest of the paper is in the listing problem, it provides a $\Omega\left(E^{3/2}/(\sqrt{M}B) + E/B\right)$ lower bound on the I/O complexity that applies also to the enumeration problem. However, in this paper we extend this result to be a best-case lower bound and to be output sensitive, using a shorter and arguably simpler argument. That is, we show that the I/O complexity of any algorithm for enumerating t triangles is $\Omega\left(t/(\sqrt{M}B) + t^{2/3}/B\right)$. Both bounds apply to algorithms that, intuitively, manage edges and vertices as atomic information.

We recall that triangle listing has been widely studied in other models (there is no distinction between enumeration and listing in these works). The relations between listing and other problems have been widely investigated, see for instance Williams and Williams [25] for a reduction to matrix multiplication, and Jafargholi and Viola [15] for 3SUM/3XOR. Parallel algorithms for triangle listing have been addressed in the MapReduce framework by Afrati et al. [1], and by Suri and Vassilvitskii [22]. Triangle listing in certain classes of random graphs has been addressed recently by Berry et al. [5] to explain the empirically good behavior of simple triangle listing algorithms. For the related problem of counting the number of triangles in a graph, we refer to [17] and references therein.

1.2 Our results

Our first main result is a cache-oblivious algorithm for triangle enumeration. In a cache-oblivious algorithm no variables dependent on hardware parameters, such as internal memory size and block length, need to be tuned to achieve optimality (or quasi optimality). The cache-oblivious algorithm is inspired by a recursive approach proposed by Jafargholi and Viola [15], in the context of output sensitive triangle listing in the RAM model. We prove the following claim.

THEOREM 1. *Assume $E \geq M$. Then there exists a cache-oblivious randomized algorithm for triangle enumeration using $\mathcal{O}\left(\frac{E^{3/2}}{\sqrt{M}B}\right)$ I/Os in expectation and $\mathcal{O}(E)$ words on disk.*

By a property of cache-oblivious algorithms [11], we have that the claimed I/O complexity applies to each level of a multilevel cache with an LRU replacement policy.

Our second result is a deterministic cache-aware algorithm with the same I/O complexity as the cache-oblivious algorithm, under the assumption that internal memory has size at least $\sqrt{E}$. This is a reasonable assumption in practice if we are concerned with a graph stored on hard disk or on solid-state drive and M is the capacity of the RAM. The algorithm is based on the derandomization of a simple cache-aware algorithm, described in Section 2. The derandomization uses an idea introduced in [15], though we present a more refined greedy approach that preserves the exponent 3/2 of the algorithm. We conjecture that with some technical adjustments the derandomization can be also applied to the cache-oblivious algorithm.

THEOREM 2. *Assume $E \geq M \geq E^{\epsilon}$, for an arbitrary constant $\epsilon > 0$. Then there exists a deterministic, cache-aware algorithm for triangle enumeration that uses $\mathcal{O}\left(\frac{E^{3/2}}{\sqrt{M}B}\right)$ I/Os and $\mathcal{O}(E)$ words on disk in the worst case.*

Finally, we prove that the I/O complexity of our algorithms is optimal in the external memory model. We assume that information on an edge requires at least one memory word: this assumption is similar to the indivisibility assumption [4] which is usually required for deriving lower bounds on the I/O complexity, or to the witnessing class of the aforementioned lower bound in [13]. With respect to this bound, we remark that our lower bound applies also in the best-case and it is output sensitive.

THEOREM 3. *For any input graph, an algorithm that enumerates t distinct triangles requires, even in the best case, $\Omega\left(\frac{t}{\sqrt{M}B} + \frac{t^{2/3}}{B}\right)$ I/Os .*

The above lower bound on the I/O complexity applies also in the case of a weak definition of the triangle enumeration problem, which requires an algorithm to make *at least* one call to the procedure `emit(·,·,·)` for each triangle. Algorithms for the weak triangle enumeration problem may not be able to compute the exact number of triangles in a graph, while this is not the case of our algorithms.

Although the work of an algorithm is not the main complexity measure in the external memory model, we remark that all our algorithms are also work optimal: indeed, it can be easily proved that each algorithm performs $\mathcal{O}\left(E^{3/2}\right)$ operations in the worst case, matching the naive $\Omega(t)$ lower bound for enumerating t triangles when $t = \Omega\left(E^{3/2}\right)$.

The paper is organized as follows. Section 2 gives a simple cache-aware randomized algorithm. Section 3 describes the claimed cache-oblivious randomized algorithm. The deterministic algorithm is then proposed in Section 4 by derandomizing the previous cache-aware randomized algorithm. Section 5 gives the lower bound on the I/O complexity. We conclude the paper with some final comments in Section 6.

1.3 Preliminaries

We study our algorithms in the *external memory model* [2], which consists of an internal memory of M words and of an external memory of unbounded size. The processor can only use data stored in internal memory and move data from the two memories in chunk of consecutive B words. The *I/O complexity* of an algorithm is defined as the number of input/output blocks performed by the algorithm. We denote the I/O complexity of sorting n entries with $\text{sort}(n) = \mathcal{O}\left(\frac{n\log(n/B)}{B\log M} + \frac{n}{B}\right)$ [23].

A *cache-oblivious* algorithm is an algorithm that does not use in its specification the parameters describing the memory hierarchy (i.e., M and B in our model), but still exhibits an optimal or quasi-optimal I/O complexity. An algorithm that does use at least one of these parameters is said *cache-aware*. In the context of cache-oblivious algorithms, we assume that block transfers between internal and external memories are automatically managed by an optimal replacement policy. However, it can be shown [11, Lemma 6.4] that optimality with an optimal replacement policy implies an optimal number of I/Os on each level of a multilevel cache with LRU replacement, under a regularity condition. This condition says that the I/O complexity $Q(n, M, B)$ satisfies $Q(n, M, B) = \mathcal{O}(Q(n, 2M, B))$. Since our cache-oblivious algorithm for triangle enumeration is optimal and satisfies the regularity condition, we have that this result applies to our algorithm as well. In the paper, we make the standard tall cache assumption $M = \Omega\left(B^2\right)$, which has been shown to be necessary for getting optimal cache-oblivious algorithms, in particular for the problems of sorting [7] and permuting [20].

We consider a simple, undirected graph (no self loops, no parallel edges) with vertex set V and edge set E. Each vertex and edge requires one memory word. For notational convenience and consistency with earlier papers, whenever the context is clear we use E as a shorthand for the *size* of a set E (and similarly for other sets). We denote with $\deg(v)$ the degree of a vertex $v \in V$. We assume that the elements of V are ordered according to degree, breaking ties among vertices of the same degree in an arbitrary but consistent way. We assume that an edge $\{v_1, v_2\}$ is represented by the tuple (v_1, v_2) such that $v_1 < v_2$, and that these tuples are sorted lexicographically (so for each vertex v we have the list of neighbors that come after v in the ordering). If the graph comes in some other representation, it can be converted to this form in sort(E) I/Os. Following [14], for a triangle $\{v_1, v_2, v_3\}$, with $v_1 < v_2 < v_3$, we call the edge $\{v_2, v_3\}$ its *pivot edge*, and the vertex v_1 its *cone vertex*.

The following lemma describes a subroutine that is widely used in the paper for enumerating all triangles containing a given vertex v.

LEMMA 1. *Enumerating all triangles in an edge set E that contain a given vertex v can be done in $\mathcal{O}(sort(E))$ I/Os.*

PROOF. By scanning E, we find the set Γ_v of vertices that are adjacent to v, and we sort it by degree. Then we sort edges in E by the smallest vertex and find the set $E_v \subseteq E$ of edges with the smallest vertex in Γ_v, just by scanning E and Γ_v. Finally, we sort edges in E_v by the largest vertex and compute the set of edges $E'_v \subseteq E_v$ with both vertices in Γ_v with another scan of E_v and Γ_v. By construction we have that, for each $e = \{u, w\} \in E'_v$, there exists a triangle with vertices v, u and w. □

Another subroutine used in the paper is the algorithm given in [14] that efficiently finds all triangles with a pivot edge in a set $E' \subseteq E$. Though this subroutine was presented in [14] as a listing algorithm, it is easy to see that it works for enumeration as well. We sketch the result below for the sake of completeness.

LEMMA 2. *(Hu et al. [14, Algorithm 1, step 2]) The set of triangles in an edge set E with a pivot edge in $E' \subseteq E$ can be enumerated in $\mathcal{O}(E/B + E'E/(MB))$ I/Os.*

PROOF. The algorithm runs in iterations. In each iteration αM new edges from E', for a suitable constant $\alpha \in (0;1)$, are loaded into internal memory. Let Γ_{mem} be the set of vertices that appear in an edge of E' currently stored in internal memory. Then, for each vertex v in the graph, the algorithm computes the set

$$\Gamma_v = \{u \mid (v,u) \in E, u > v, u \in \Gamma_{\text{mem}}\},$$

that is, the set containing all vertices larger than v that are adjacent to v, and appear in an edge of E' stored in internal memory in the current iteration. Then, it enumerates all triangles $\{v,u,w\}$ where $\{u,w\} \in E'$ and $u,w \in \Gamma_v$. It is easy to see that it is possible to compute Γ_v for every vertex v using a single scan of all edges in E, since all edges $\{v,u\} \in E$ with $u > v$ are stored consecutively in external memory. Then, we get the I/O complexity $\mathcal{O}\left(\lceil E'/M\rceil \sum_{v\in V} \deg(v)/B\right)$ which is upper bounded by $\mathcal{O}(E/B + E'E/(MB))$. □

2. CACHE-AWARE ENUMERATION

Our first algorithm is cache-aware, that is, it is given information on the internal memory size M and on the block length B. The algorithm also explicitly manages block transfers. Without loss of generality we assume that $E > M$ and that $\sqrt{E/M}$ is an integer.

2.1 Algorithm overview

Let $V_h = \{v \mid \deg(v) > \sqrt{EM}\}$ be the set of *high-degree* vertices, and $V_l = V \backslash V_h$ be the remaining *low-degree* vertices. There cannot be too many vertices in the set V_h: indeed we have $V_h < \sqrt{E/M}$. We denote with E_h the set of edges incident to at least one vertex in V_h, and with $E_l = E \backslash E_h$ the remaining edges.

The first step of our algorithm enumerates the triangles that involve at least one edge from E_h using the algorithm described in Lemma 1 for each high-degree vertex in V_h. Subsequent steps can then focus on triangles within E_l. Our algorithm will work with a coloring $\xi : V \to \{1,\ldots,c\}$ of the vertex set where the number of colors will be $c = \sqrt{E/M}$. The coloring will partition the edges of E_l into $c^2 = E/M$ sets according to the colors of their vertices. More specifically, for $\tau_1, \tau_2 \in \{1,\ldots,c\}$ let

$$E_{\tau_1,\tau_2} = \{\{v_1,v_2\} \in E_l \mid v_1 < v_2, \xi(v_1) = \tau_1, \xi(v_2) = \tau_2\} .$$

Since the number of partitions is E/M, the average number of edges in a partition is M. If all partitions did indeed have size M, we could easily obtain an algorithm with the desired I/O complexity by considering all c^3 possible coloring of the vertices of a triangle in $\mathcal{O}(M/B)$ I/Os. However, some partitions may be much larger than M, so there is no guarantee that we can fit a large part of a partition in memory.

We are now ready to describe the high-level algorithm:

1. Enumerate all triangles with at least one vertex in V_h using the algorithm of Lemma 1.
2. Choose ξ uniformly at random from a 4-wise independent family of functions, and construct the sets E_{τ_1,τ_2} using a sorting algorithm.
3. For every triple $(\tau_1,\tau_2,\tau_3) \in \{1,\ldots,c\}^3$, enumerate all triangles with a cone vertex of color τ_1 and a pivot edge in E_{τ_2,τ_3}. We use the algorithm in Lemma 2 by setting the pivot edge to E_{τ_2,τ_3}, the edge set to $E_{\tau_1,\tau_2} \cup E_{\tau_1,\tau_3} \cup E_{\tau_2,\tau_3}$, and ignoring triangles where the cone vertex does not have color τ_1.

2.2 Analysis

2.2.1 Correctness

We first argue for correctness of the algorithm. Every triangle that includes at least one vertex in V_h is enumerated in step 1 by Lemma 1. On the other hand, a triangle with vertices $v_1 < v_2 < v_2$, none of which belongs to V_h, is enumerated in step 3, specifically in the iteration where $(\tau_1,\tau_2,\tau_3) = (\xi(v_1), \xi(v_2), \xi(v_3))$.

2.2.2 I/O complexity

We define the random variable X_ξ as follows:

$$X_\xi = \sum_{\tau_1,\tau_2} \binom{E_{\tau_1,\tau_2}}{2} . \qquad (1)$$

This variable denotes the number of pairs of edges in each partition and will be used for bounding the I/Os in step 3. We have the following bound.

LEMMA 3. *Let $\xi : V \to \{1,\ldots,c\}$ be chosen uniformly at random from a 4-wise independent family of functions, where $c = \sqrt{E/M}$. Then*

$$\mathbb{E}[X_\xi] \le \binom{E}{2}/c^2 + \sum_{v\in V_l} \binom{\deg(v)}{2}/c \le EM.$$

PROOF. Define the indicator variable Y_{e_1,e_2} to be 1 if e_1 and e_2 are colored in the same way (i.e., belong to the same set E_{τ_1,τ_2}), and zero otherwise. By linearity of expectation we have:

$$\mathbb{E}[X_\xi] = \sum_{e_1\neq e_2} \mathbb{E}[Y_{e_1,e_2}] = \sum_{e_1\neq e_2} \Pr(Y_{e_1,e_2} = 1) .$$

There are at most $\sum_{v\in V_l} \binom{\deg(v)}{2}$ pairs of edges $\{e_1, e_2\} \subseteq E_l$ that share a vertex, and for those $\mathbb{E}[Y_{e_1,e_2}] \le 1/c$ since the ξ function is chosen uniformly at random from a 4-wise independent family of functions. For the remaining at most $\binom{E}{2}$ pairs the colorings are independent, and hence the probability of having the same coloring is $1/c^2$. Summing up, and using the fact that $\deg(v) \le \sqrt{EM}$ for all $v \in V_l$ gives $X_\xi < E^2/(2c^2) + E\sqrt{EM}/(2c)$. Finally, inserting $c = \sqrt{E/M}$ yields the stated bound. □

THEOREM 4. *Assume $E \ge M \ge E^\epsilon$, for an arbitrary constant $\epsilon > 0$. Then the above cache-aware randomized algorithm for triangle enumeration requires $\mathcal{O}\left(\frac{E^{3/2}}{\sqrt{M}B}\right)$ I/Os in expectation and $\mathcal{O}(E)$ words on disk.*

PROOF. When $M \ge E^\epsilon$, for an arbitrary constant $\epsilon > 0$, the first and second steps together require $\mathcal{O}(V_h \text{sort}(E)) =$

$\mathcal{O}\left(\frac{E^{3/2}}{\sqrt{MB}}\right)$ I/Os, which is upper bounded by the claimed complexity. By setting $E_{\tau_1,\tau_2,\tau_3} = E_{\tau_1,\tau_2} + E_{\tau_1,\tau_3} + E_{\tau_2,\tau_3}$, we get that the I/O complexity $Q(E, M, B)$ of step 3 is by Lemma 2

$$Q(E, M, B) = \mathcal{O}\left(\sum_{(\tau_1,\tau_2,\tau_3)} \frac{E_{\tau_1,\tau_2,\tau_3}}{B} + \frac{E^2_{\tau_1,\tau_2,\tau_3}}{MB}\right).$$

Since $\sum_{(\tau_1,\tau_2)} E_{\tau_1,\tau_2} = E$, the above bound becomes

$$Q(E, M, B) = \mathcal{O}\left(\frac{cE}{B} + \sum_{(\tau_1,\tau_2,\tau_3)} \frac{E^2_{\tau_1,\tau_2} + E^2_{\tau_1,\tau_3} + E^2_{\tau_2,\tau_3}}{MB}\right),$$

and hence

$$Q(E, M, B) = \mathcal{O}\left(\frac{cE}{B} + \frac{c}{MB}\sum_{(\tau_1,\tau_2)} E^2_{\tau_1,\tau_2}\right).$$

Since $E^2_{\tau_1,\tau_2} \leq 4\binom{E_{\tau_1,\tau_2}}{2}$ and by the definition of X_ξ in (1), we get

$$Q(E, M, B) = \mathcal{O}\left(\frac{E^{3/2}}{\sqrt{MB}} + \frac{\sqrt{E}}{M^{3/2}} X_\xi\right).$$

That is, the expected time complexity is governed by the expectation of the random variable X_ξ. By Lemma 3, we have that $\mathbb{E}[X_\xi] \leq EM$ and then the expected I/O complexity of step 3 is $\mathcal{O}\left(E^{3/2}/(\sqrt{MB})\right)$. The algorithm clearly requires $\mathcal{O}(E)$ space on disk. □

3. CACHE-OBLIVIOUS ENUMERATION

In this section we describe a cache-oblivious, randomized algorithm for the enumeration of all triangles in a graph in $\mathcal{O}\left(E^{3/2}/(\sqrt{MB})\right)$ expected I/Os, proving Theorem 1. Optimality of this bound is shown in Section 5. As already noticed, an optimal cache-oblivious algorithm implies an optimal number of I/Os on each level of a multilevel cache with LRU replacement if a regularity condition is verified (i.e., the I/O complexity of the algorithm $Q(n, M, B)$ satisfies $Q(n, M, B) = \mathcal{O}(Q(n, 2M, B))$). Since our cache-oblivious algorithm is optimal and satisfies the regularity condition, we have that this result applies to our algorithm as well.

3.1 Algorithm overview

The cache-oblivious algorithm in this section is inspired by a recursive approach proposed by Jafargholi and Viola [15], in the context of output sensitive triangle listing in a RAM model. To describe the algorithm we define the more general (c_0, c_1, c_2)-enumeration problem. Let $\xi : V \to \mathbb{Z}$ be a coloring of the vertex set, assigning an integer to each vertex. The (c_0, c_1, c_2)-*enumeration problem* with coloring ξ consists of enumerating all triangles colored according to the vector (c_0, c_1, c_2), i.e., triangles with vertices $\{u, v, w\} \subseteq V$ where $u < v < w$, $\xi(u) = c_0$, $\xi(v) = c_1$, and $\xi(w) = c_2$. The enumeration of all triangles simply reduces to the $(1, 1, 1)$-enumeration problem with the constant coloring $\xi(v) = 1$.

A triangle is *proper* if it satisfies the (c_0, c_1, c_2) coloring, and an edge $\{u, v\}$, with $u < v$, is *incompatible* with coloring (c_0, c_1, c_2) if $(\xi(u), \xi(v)) \notin \{(c_0, c_1), (c_1, c_2), (c_0, c_2)\}$. Without loss of generality, we assume that there are no incompatible edges in G and that the color of each vertex is stored within the vertex (these assumptions can be guaranteed by suitably sorting edges without increasing the I/O complexity).

Our algorithm solves the (c_0, c_1, c_2)-enumeration problem with coloring ξ in three steps:

1. The algorithm enumerates all triangles satisfying the (c_0, c_1, c_2) coloring with at least one local high degree vertex. A *local high degree vertex* is a vertex with degree at least $E/8$; there are at most 16 local high degree nodes. For each local high degree vertex v, the algorithm enumerates all triangles containing v with the subroutine in Lemma 1 (using any efficient cache-oblivious sorting algorithm, e.g., the one from [11]). Local high degree vertices and their edges are then removed.

2. A new coloring $\xi' : V \to \mathbb{Z}$ is defined by adding a random bit to the value returned by ξ in the least significant position of the binary representation. Specifically, let $\xi'(v) = 2\xi(v) - b(v)$, where $b : V \to \{0, 1\}$ is chosen uniformly at random from a 4-wise independent family of functions.

3. The remaining triangles that satisfy (c_0, c_1, c_2) under coloring ξ are enumerated by recursively solving 8 subproblems. For each color vector $\zeta \in \{2c_0 - 1, 2c_0\} \times \{2c_1 - 1, 2c_1\} \times \{2c_2 - 1, 2c_2\}$, we recursively solve the ζ-enumeration problem with coloring ξ' on the graph obtained by removing edges incompatible with the color vector.

The recursion ends when E is empty, or at depth $\log_4 E$: in the first base case there are no triangles; in the second base case, triangles are enumerated with the deterministic algorithm by Dementiev [9], which relies on sort and scan operations, and can be trivially made oblivious using any oblivious sorting algorithm. We note that step 1 has an effect also in the recursive calls, since E refers to the number of edges compatible with the given subproblem. In fact, this is the main conceptual difference between our algorithm and the algorithm in [15].

We observe that at the recursive level $i = \log c$, with $c = \sqrt{E/M}$, the behavior of the algorithm is similar to the one of the cache-aware algorithm presented in Section 2: There are c colors and, as we will see below, when $i = \log c$ each vertex with degree at least $\sqrt{EM}$ is expected to be removed, and there are $(E/M)^{3/2}$ subproblems, each of expected size M.

3.2 Analysis

3.2.1 Correctness

We argue that all proper triangles with coloring (c_0, c_1, c_2) are correctly enumerated. Indeed, proper triangles with a local high degree vertex v are found in step 1, and cannot appear again since edges adjacent to v are subsequently removed. The remaining triangles are enumerated in the subproblems. Indeed, each proper triangle is given a coloring in $\{2c_0 - 1, 2c_0\} \times \{2c_1 - 1, 2c_1\} \times \{2c_2 - 1, 2c_2\}$ under ξ', and there is exactly one recursive call reporting each triangle.

3.2.2 I/O Complexity

Suppose the 8^i subproblems at level i, with $0 \leq i \leq \log_4 E$, are arbitrarily numbered. We denote by $E_{i,j}$, $\xi_{i,j}$, $(c^0_{i,j}, c^1_{i,j}, c^2_{i,j})$ the input edge set, the coloring, and the triplet defining proper triangles, respectively, of the jth subproblem at level i, for any $0 \leq i \leq \log_4 E$ and $0 \leq j < 8^i$. We then define $E_{i,j}^{k,l}$, for any $0 \leq k < l \leq 2$, as the set containing each edge $\{u, v\} \in E_{i,j}$, with $u < v$, such that $\xi_{i,j}(u) = c_{i,j}^k$ and $\xi_{i,j}(v) = c_{i,j}^l$. With a slight abuse of notation, we let $E_{i,j}$ and $E_{i,j}^{k,l}$ also denote the size of the respective sets. Since there are no incompatible edges, we have $E_{i,j} \leq E_{i,j}^{0,1} + E_{i,j}^{1,2} + E_{i,j}^{0,2}$.

In order to upper bound the expected I/O complexity of our algorithm we introduce two lemmas. Lemma 4 gives an upper bound on the expected value and variance of each subproblem at a given recursive level. Then, Lemma 5 uses these bounds to limit the probability that a subproblem is larger than the expected size.

LEMMA 4. *For any $0 \leq i \leq \log_4 E$ and $0 \leq j < 8^i$, we have*

$$\mathbb{E}\left[E_{i,j}^{0,1}\right] \leq \frac{E}{4^i}, \qquad Var\left(E_{i,j}^{0,1}\right) \leq \frac{3E^2}{16^i}.$$

The same bounds apply to $E_{i,j}^{1,2}$ and $E_{i,j}^{0,2}$.

PROOF. For the sake of the analysis we do not remove local high degree vertices in step 1, but replace them with vertices of degree one. Specifically, for any removed vertex v with (local) degree $\deg(v)$, we replace it with $\deg(v)$ new vertices v_i of degree 1, and replace each edge $\{v, u\}$ with $\{v_i, u\}$ for a suitable i. This assumption simplifies the analysis since no edges are removed in a recursive level. However, correctness is not affected since the new vertices will not be involved in any proper triangle enumerated in recursive calls as they have degree one. By symmetry we may focus on $E_{i,j}^{0,1}$, the proofs for $E_{i,j}^{1,2}$ and $E_{i,j}^{0,2}$ being analogous.

We now prove by induction that, at any recursive level $0 \leq i \leq \log_4 E$, we have $\mathbb{E}\left[E_{i,j}^{0,1}\right] = X/4^i$ and $\mathrm{Var}\left(E_{i,j}^{0,1}\right) \leq X^2/16^i + 2X/4^i$, where $X = E_{0,0}^{0,1} = E$. The lemma then follows since $X = E$ and $X^2/16^i + 2X/4^i \leq 3X^2/16^i$ as soon as $i \leq \log_4 X$. The claim is trivially verified when $i = 0$ since we get $\mathbb{E}\left[E_{0,0}^{0,1}\right] = E_{0,0}^{0,1} = X$, and $\mathrm{Var}\left(E_{0,0}^{0,1}\right) = 0$.

Now consider a subproblem j at level $i > 0$ and its parent problem j' at level $i - 1$. By the inductive hypothesis, we have for the parent problem that $\mathbb{E}\left[E_{i-1,j'}^{0,1}\right] = X/4^{i-1}$ and $\mathrm{Var}\left(E_{i-1,j'}^{0,1}\right) \leq X^2/16^{i-1} + 2X/4^{i-1}$. Assign to each edge $e \in E_{i-1,j'}^{0,1}$ a random variable Y_e equal to one if $e \in E_{i,j}^{0,1}$ and 0 otherwise. By conditioning on the number of edges in the parent problem, we get

$$\mathbb{E}\left[E_{i,j}^{0,1}\right] = \mathbb{E}\left[\mathbb{E}\left[\sum_{e \in E_{i-1,j'}^{0,1}} Y_e | E_{i-1,j'}^{0,1}\right]\right] = \frac{\mathbb{E}\left[E_{i-1,j'}^{0,1}\right]}{4} = \frac{X}{4^i}$$

since each edge in $E_{i-1,j'}^{0,1}$ is in $E_{i,j}^{0,1}$ with probability $1/4$. The first claim follows.

Now consider the variance. We have

$$\begin{aligned}\mathrm{Var}\left(E_{i,j}^{0,1}\right) &= \mathbb{E}\left[(E_{i,j}^{0,1})^2\right] - \mathbb{E}\left[E_{i,j}^{0,1}\right]^2 \\ &= \mathbb{E}\left[\mathbb{E}\left[(E_{i,j}^{0,1})^2 | E_{i-1,j'}^{0,1}\right]\right] - \mathbb{E}\left[E_{i,j}^{0,1}\right]^2. \qquad (2)\end{aligned}$$

The conditional expectation $\mathbb{E}\left[(E_{i,j}^{0,1})^2 | E_{i-1,j'}^{0,1}\right]$ can be computed as follows. Since $E_{i,j}^{0,1} = \sum_{e \in E_{i-1,j'}^{0,1}} Y_e$ we have:

$$\left(E_{i,j}^{0,1}\right)^2 = \sum_{e \in E_{i-1,j'}^{0,1}} Y_e^2 + \sum_{\substack{e,e' \in E_{i-1,j'}^{0,1} \\ e \neq e', |e \cap e'|=1}} Y_e Y_{e'} + \sum_{\substack{e,e' \in E_{i-1,j'}^{0,1} \\ e \neq e', e \cap e' = \emptyset}} Y_e Y_{e'}.$$

Let $W_{i,j}^{0,1} = \sum_{e,e' \in E_{i-1,j'}^{0,1}, e \neq e', e \cap e' = \emptyset} Y_e Y_{e'}$; note that $W_{i,j}^{0,1}$ denotes the number of edge pairs that do not share any vertex in the j-th subproblem at level i. Two edges sharing a vertex (i.e., $|e \cap e'| = 1$) are in $E_{i,j}^{0,1}$ with probability $1/8$. Also, there are at most $2(E_{i-1,j'}^{0,1})^2/8$ pairs of edges that share exactly one vertex, since the maximum degree after step 2 is $E_{i-1,j'}^{0,1}/8$. Then the conditional expectation becomes

$$\begin{aligned}&\mathbb{E}\left[(E_{i,j}^{0,1})^2 | E_{i-1,j'}^{0,1}\right] = \\ &= \frac{E_{i-1,j'}^{0,1}}{4} + \frac{(E_{i-1,j'}^{0,1})^2}{32} + \mathbb{E}\left[W_{i,j}^{0,1} | E_{i-1,j'}^{0,1}\right], \qquad (3)\end{aligned}$$

We then take the expectation of (3):

$$\begin{aligned}&\mathbb{E}\left[\mathbb{E}\left[(E_{i,j}^{0,1})^2 | E_{i-1,j'}^{0,1}\right]\right] = \\ &= \frac{\mathbb{E}\left[E_{i-1,j'}^{0,1}\right]}{4} + \frac{\mathbb{E}\left[(E_{i-1,j'}^{0,1})^2\right]}{32} + \mathbb{E}\left[W_{i,j}^{0,1}\right] \\ &= \frac{\mathbb{E}\left[E_{i-1,j'}^{0,1}\right]}{4} + \frac{\mathrm{Var}\left(E_{i-1,j'}^{0,1}\right) + \mathbb{E}\left[(E_{i-1,j'}^{0,1})\right]^2}{32} + \mathbb{E}\left[W_{i,j}^{0,1}\right].\end{aligned}$$

By the inductive hypotheses on expectation and variance at level $i - 1$ it follows that

$$\mathbb{E}\left[\mathbb{E}\left[(E_{i,j}^{0,1})^2 | E_{i-1,j'}^{0,1}\right]\right] \leq \frac{X^2}{16^i} + \frac{5X}{4^{i+1}} + \mathbb{E}\left[W_{i,j}^{0,1}\right].$$

The term $\mathbb{E}\left[W_{i,j}^{0,1}\right]$ can be upper bounded assuming that no two input edges share a vertex in $E_{0,0}^{0,1}$. This gives an upper bound since a vertex shared by two edges cannot increase $W_{i,j}^{0,1}$. By induction it follows that $\mathbb{E}\left[W_{i,j}^{0,1}\right] \leq X^2/16^i$: indeed, an edge pair in $E_{i-1,j'}^{0,1}$ is also in $E_{i,j}^{0,1}$ with probability $1/16$. Then we get

$$\mathbb{E}\left[\mathbb{E}\left[(E_{i,j}^{0,1})^2 | E_{i-1,j'}^{0,1}\right]\right] \leq \frac{2X^2}{16^i} + \frac{5X}{4^{i+1}}.$$

Finally, by (2), we get that the variance at level i is:

$$\mathrm{Var}\left(E_{i,j}^{0,1}\right) \leq \frac{2X^2}{16^i} + \frac{5X}{4^{i+1}} - \frac{X^2}{16^i} \leq \frac{X^2}{16^i} + \frac{2X}{4^i}$$

and the claim follows. □

LEMMA 5. *For any $0 \leq i \leq \log_4 E$, $0 \leq j < 8^i$ and $0 \leq k < \log_4 E - i$, we have that*

$$Pr\left(E_{i,j} \geq 9\frac{E}{4^{i-k}}\right) \leq 1/16^k.$$

PROOF. Since $E_{i,j} \leq E_{i,j}^{0,1} + E_{i,j}^{1,2} + E_{i,j}^{0,2}$, we clearly have $\Pr\left(E_{i,j} \geq \beta\frac{E}{4^{i-k}}\right) \leq 3\Pr\left(E_{i,j}^{0,1} \geq \frac{\beta}{3}\frac{E}{4^{i-k}}\right)$. Lemma 4 gives $\mathbb{E}\left[E_{i,j}^{0,1}\right] \leq E/4^i$ and $\mathrm{Var}\left(E_{i,j}^{0,1}\right) \leq 3E^2/(16)^i$. Then, by

Chebyshev's inequality, we get

$$\Pr\left(E_{i,j}^{0,1} \geq \frac{\beta}{3}\frac{E}{4^{i-k}}\right) \leq \Pr\left(\left|E_{i,j}^{0,1} - \mathbb{E}\left[E_{i,j}^{0,1}\right]\right| \geq \frac{(\beta/3-1)E}{4^{i-k}}\right)$$
$$\leq 9\frac{\mathrm{Var}\left(E_{i,j}^{0,1}\right)16^{i-k}}{(\beta-3)^2E^2} \leq \frac{27}{(\beta-3)^2 16^k}.$$

By setting $\beta = 9$ the lemma follows. □

We are now ready to prove the first result of the paper, repeated here for convenience.

THEOREM 1. *Assume $E \geq M$. Then there exists a cache-oblivious randomized algorithm for triangle enumeration using $\mathcal{O}\left(\frac{E^{3/2}}{\sqrt{MB}}\right)$ I/Os in expectation and $\mathcal{O}(E)$ words on disk.*

PROOF. We first argue that the I/O complexity of subproblems with input size not larger than M is asymptotically negligible. Consider a subproblem x whose input size is smaller than M, but its parent y has input size larger than M. Since the data used by x fits in memory, the I/O complexity for solving x (including subproblems generated in x) is $\mathcal{O}(M/B+1)$. On the other hand, in our analysis we assume that the I/O complexity of y is $\Omega(M/B+1)$, and thus the cost for solving x is asymptotically negligible. Since a problem with input larger than M can have at most 8 child subproblems, we can ignore subproblems of size smaller than M without affecting asymptotically the I/O complexity of our algorithm.

We now upper bound the I/O complexity without taking into account the cost of subproblems at level $\log_4 E$ which have a slightly different I/O complexity than a subproblem at level $i < \log_4 E$ — we will later see how to bound this quantity.

Let $Y_{i,s}$ denote the number of subproblems at level i with input size $(E/4^{s+1}, E/4^s]$, for any $0 \leq i \leq \log_4 E$ and $0 \leq s < \log_4(E/M)$. The cost of a subproblem of size $Y_{i,s}$ is dominated by the sorting in step 1, and then we get:

$$Q(E,M,B) = \mathcal{O}\left(\sum_{i=0}^{\log_4 E-1}\sum_{s=0}^{\log_4(E/M)} Y_{i,s}\mathrm{sort}(E/4^s)\right)$$
$$= \mathcal{O}\left(\sum_{s=0}^{\log_4(E/M)}\sum_{i=0}^{\log_4 E-1} Y_{i,s}\mathrm{sort}(E/4^s)\right)$$

Since there are at most $2\cdot 8^s$ subproblems of size no larger than $E/4^s$ at levels $0,\ldots,s$, we get

$$Q(E,M,B) = \mathcal{O}\left(\sum_{s=0}^{\log_4(E/M)}\left(8^s + \sum_{i=s+1}^{\log_4 E-1} Y_{i,s}\right)\mathrm{sort}(E/4^s)\right).$$

By Lemma 5, the probability that a subproblem at level $i > s$ has size at least $E/4^{s+1}$ is

$$\Pr\left(E_{i,j} \geq E/4^{s+1}\right) \leq \Pr\left(E_{i,j} \geq 9E/4^{s+3}\right) \leq 1/16^{i-s-3}.$$

The expected number of subproblems of size larger than $E/4^{s+1}$ at level $i > s$ is $8^i\frac{1}{16^{i-s-3}} = \mathcal{O}\left(16^s/2^i\right)$, which means that

$$\mathbb{E}\left[Y_{i,s}\right] = \mathcal{O}\left(16^s/2^i\right) \text{ and } \mathbb{E}\left[\sum_{i=s+1}^{\log_4 E} Y_{i,j}\right] = \mathcal{O}\left(8^s\right).$$

It follows that the expected value of $Q(E,M,B)$ is

$$\mathbb{E}\left[Q(E,M,B)\right] = \mathcal{O}\left(\sum_{s=0}^{\log_4(E/M)} 2^s\frac{E\log(E/4^s)}{B\log M}\right)$$
$$= \mathcal{O}\left(\frac{E}{B\log M}\int_0^{\log_4(E/M)+1} 2^x\log(E/4^x)dx\right)$$
$$= \mathcal{O}\left(\frac{E}{B\log M}\left.\frac{2^x\left(\ln(E/4^x)+2\right)}{\ln^2 2}\right|_0^{\log_4(E/M)+1}\right)$$
$$= \mathcal{O}\left(\frac{E^{3/2}}{\sqrt{MB}}\right).$$

We now bound the expected number of I/Os required for subproblems at level $i = \log_4 E$. Since we are using the algorithm by Dementiev [9] for solving base cases, the cost of a subproblem with input size in the range $(E/4^{s+1}, E/4^s]$ is $\mathcal{O}\left(\mathrm{sort}\left((E/4^s)^{3/2}\right)\right)$ I/Os. This means that the number $Q'(E,M,B)$ of I/Os required by level $\log_4 E$ is:

$$Q'(E,M,B) = \mathcal{O}\left(\sum_{s=0}^{\log_4(E/M)} Y_{\log_4 E,s}\mathrm{sort}\left((E/4^s)^{3/2}\right)\right).$$

By applying Lemma 5 as before, we get that

$$\mathbb{E}\left[Y_{\log_4 E,s}\right] = \mathcal{O}\left(16^s/2^{\log_4 E}\right).$$

Hence the expected value of $Q'(E,M,B)$ is

$$\mathbb{E}\left[Q'(E,M,B)\right] = \mathcal{O}\left(\sum_{s=0}^{\log_4(E/M)} 2^s\frac{E\log(E/4^s)}{B\log M}\right)$$

which is $\mathcal{O}\left(\frac{E^{3/2}}{\sqrt{MB}}\right)$ as shown before. The I/O complexity of the cache-oblivious algorithm follows by summing the expected values of $Q(E,M,B)$ and $Q'(E,M,B)$.

If the input of a subproblem is stored in a new location, the used space on disk is $\mathcal{O}(E)$ in expectation since the expected size decreases geometrically. However, $\mathcal{O}(E\log E)$ space is required in the worst case (i.e., when there exists only one partition containing all edges). The claimed $\mathcal{O}(E)$ bound follows by noticing that no new space is required for storing subproblem input: before each recursive call, edges are sorted so that the subproblem input is stored in consecutive locations in the input of the parent problem. In this case, just pointers to the initial and final positions are required for denoting the input. □

4. DERANDOMIZATION

We now pursue a derandomization of the cache-aware algorithm in Section 2 via small-bias probability spaces. More specifically, we need to find a balanced coloring ξ such that $X_\xi = \mathcal{O}(EM)$. The idea of using this method to derandomize a triangle enumeration algorithm was previously used in [15], though we present a more refined greedy approach that preserves the exponent 3/2 of the algorithm.

For convenience we round up the number of colors c to the nearest power of 2, which can only decrease $\mathbb{E}[X_\xi]$ for random ξ. We split X_ξ into two terms, $X_\xi = X_\xi^{\mathrm{adj}} + X_\xi^{\mathrm{nonadj}}$, where the two terms are the contributions in the sum defined in (1) from adjacent and non-adjacent edge pairs, respectively.

Our algorithm fixes one bit of the coloring at a time, aiming to approach the coloring guarantee of Lemma 3. Formally we start with the constant coloring ξ_0 that assigns color 1 to every vertex. For $i = 1, \ldots, \log c$ we find a two-coloring $b_{i-1} : V \to \{0,1\}$ such that the coloring $\xi_i(v) = 2\xi_{i-1}(v) - b_{i-1}(v)$ satisfies

$$\frac{4^i X_{\xi_i}^{\text{nonadj}}}{c^2} + \frac{2^i X_{\xi_i}^{\text{adj}}}{c} \leq (1+\alpha)^i EM \ . \qquad (4)$$

Setting $\alpha = 1/\log c$ we have $(1+\alpha)^{\log c} < e$ so for the final coloring $\xi = \xi_{\log c}$, since $c \geq \sqrt{E/M}$ we get $X_{\xi_i} = X_{\xi_i}^{\text{nonadj}} + X_{\xi_i}^{\text{adj}} < eEM$.

It remains to be shown how we select ξ_i to ensure (4) for $i = 0, \ldots, \log c$. For $i = 0$ we have $X_{\xi_0}^{\text{nonadj}} < E^2/2$ and $X_{\xi_0}^{\text{adj}} < E\sqrt{EM}/2$, and inserting $c \geq \sqrt{E/M}$ the claim follows. The function b_{i-1} used for constructing ξ_i for $i > 0$ will be taken from an almost 4-wise independent sample space. We use the following known result:

LEMMA 6. *([3, Theorem 2].) For any $\alpha > 0$ there is a set of $t = \mathcal{O}\left((\log(V)/\alpha)^2\right)$ functions $\beta_1, \ldots, \beta_t : V \to \{0,1\}$ such that: For every four vertices v_1, v_2, v_3, v_4 and each vector $x \in \{0,1\}^4$ the set $\{\beta_j \mid (\beta_j(v_1), \beta_j(v_2), \beta_j(v_3), \beta_j(v_4)) = x\}$ has size at most $(1+\alpha)2^{-4}t$. The space required for computing a value of b_i is $\mathcal{O}(\log(V/\alpha))$ bits.*

We now argue that if (4) holds for ξ_{i-1} there exists a function b_{i-1} from the sample space of Lemma 6 such that (4) holds for ξ_i. To see this, consider the function

$$\xi_i(v) = 2\xi_{i-1}(v) - b_{i-1}(v)$$

where b_{i-1} is chosen at random from the family of Lemma 6. Then $\mathbb{E}\left[X_{\xi_i}^{\text{nonadj}}\right] \leq X_{\xi_{i-1}}^{\text{nonadj}}(1+\alpha)/4$ because each pair contributing to $X_{\xi_{i-1}}^{\text{nonadj}}$ has probability at most $(1+\alpha)/4$ of colliding under ξ_i. Similarly, $\mathbb{E}\left[X_{\xi_i}^{\text{adj}}\right] \leq X_{\xi_{i-1}}^{\text{adj}}(1+\alpha)/2$. This means that

$$\mathbb{E}\left[\frac{4^i X_{\xi_i}^{\text{nonadj}}}{c^2} + \frac{2^i X_{\xi_i}^{\text{adj}}}{c}\right] = \frac{4^i \mathbb{E}\left[X_{\xi_i}^{\text{nonadj}}\right]}{c^2} + \frac{2^i \mathbb{E}\left[X_{\xi_i}^{\text{adj}}\right]}{c} \leq$$

$$\leq (1+\alpha)\left(\frac{4^{i-1} X_{\xi_{i-1}}^{\text{nonadj}}}{c^2} + \frac{2^{i-1} X_{\xi_{i-1}}^{\text{adj}}}{c}\right) \leq (1+\alpha)^i EM.$$

So we conclude that there must exist a choice of b_{i-1} for which (4) holds.

Finally, we need to argue that the right function b_{i-1} can be chosen efficiently. To do this we maintain the list of edges sorted according to color class, such that all edges in

$$E_{\tau_1,\tau_2}^{i-1} = \{\{v_1, v_2\} \in E_l | v_1 < v_2, \ \xi_{i-1}(v_1) = \tau_1, \ \xi_{i-1}(v_2) = \tau_2\}$$

are stored consecutively. Since $X_{\xi_i} = \sum_{\tau_1,\tau_2} \binom{E_{\tau_1,\tau_2}^i}{2}$, in a single scan of the edge list we can compute the value of (4) for every choice of b_{i-1}, using the assumption that M is large enough to hold a constant number of variables for each function in internal memory. In particular, what is needed is keeping track of the number of edges of each color class E_{τ_1,τ_2}^{i-1} that go into each of the four possible new color classes for those edges. We then select the function b_{i-1} that minimizes (4), and split the edge set into new color classes in one additional scan. This concludes the description of our deterministic cache-aware algorithm for triangle enumeration:

THEOREM 2. *Assume $E \geq M \geq E^{\epsilon}$, for an arbitrary constant $\epsilon > 0$. Then there exists a deterministic, cache-aware algorithm for triangle enumeration that uses $\mathcal{O}\left(\frac{E^{3/2}}{\sqrt{MB}}\right)$ I/Os and $\mathcal{O}(E)$ words on disk in the worst case.*

PROOF. If $M > k \log^2 V \log^2(E/M)$ for a sufficiently large constant k, we spend $\mathcal{O}(E/B)$ I/Os for finding the best b_i, and then $\mathcal{O}(\text{sort}(E))$ I/Os to organized edges after fixing the coloring ξ_i, for each $i = 1, \ldots \log c$. Thus the final balance coloring is computed in $\mathcal{O}(E \log(E/M)/B)$ I/Os as soon as $M \geq E^{\epsilon}$. By mimicking the argument of Theorem 4, we get the claim since $X_\xi \leq eEM$. □

5. LOWER BOUND

In this section, we lower bound the I/O complexity of any algorithm for triangle enumeration. We restrict our attention to algorithms where each edge requires at least one memory word. That is, at any point in time there can be at most M edges in memory, and an I/O can move at most B edges to or from memory. This assumption is similar to the indivisibility assumption [4] which is usually required for deriving lower bounds on the I/O complexity. The optimality of our algorithms follows from the following theorem since a clique of $\sqrt{E}$ vertices has $t = \Omega\left(E^{3/2}\right)$ triangles.

THEOREM 3. *For any input graph, an algorithm that enumerates t distinct triangles requires, even in the best case, $\Omega\left(\frac{t}{\sqrt{MB}} + \frac{t^{2/3}}{B}\right)$ I/Os .*

PROOF. In order to emit a triangle, information on the three nodes (or edges) must reside in internal memory at some point in time. Since there are at most M edges in internal memory, it follows from e.g. [1, Section 4.1] that no more than $\mathcal{O}\left(M^{3/2}\right)$ distinct triangles can be emitted without doing any I/O.

Let $\mathcal{A}$ be any (possibly non-deterministic) algorithm for triangle enumeration. For the sake of the lower bound, consider the best execution $\mathcal{A}'$ of algorithm $\mathcal{A}$ for a given input graph on a internal memory of size M and block B. In other words, we consider the execution getting the smallest I/O complexity $Q_{\mathcal{A}'}(E, M, B)$ for a given input: for instance, for a randomized algorithm we take the execution with the most favorable choice of the random values. Since, $\mathcal{A}'$ is an execution, all decisions that can be made by algorithm $\mathcal{A}$ have already been taken.

We simulate the execution $\mathcal{A}'$ on an internal memory of size $2M$ in such a way that the computation advances in epochs, and blocks are read (resp., written) on disk only at the beginning (resp., end) of an epoch. The simulation works as follows. We consider the internal memory to be divided into two non-overlapping parts $\mathcal{M}_0$ and $\mathcal{M}_1$ of size M, where $\mathcal{M}_0$ will be used to simulate the memory of size M used by execution $\mathcal{A}'$, and $\mathcal{M}_1$ will be used for anticipating/delaying block reads/writes. Specifically, each epoch simulates M/B consecutive I/Os of $\mathcal{A}'$: the input blocks are prefetched and stored in $\mathcal{M}_1$ at the beginning of the epoch; the output blocks are temporary stored in $\mathcal{M}_1$ and then written on the external memory at the end of the epoch; the I/Os performed by $\mathcal{A}'$ are then simulated by moving data between $\mathcal{M}_0$ and $\mathcal{M}_1$. By construction, we have that the I/O complexity of the simulation is $Q_{\mathcal{A}'}(E, M, B)$ and the I/O complexity of each epoch is M/B (except the last epoch, which may use fewer I/Os). In an epoch the processor touches at most $2M$ internal memory words and thus $\mathcal{O}\left(M^{3/2}\right)$ distinct triangles can be emitted. Then we have

$$Q_{\mathcal{A}'}(E,M,B) \geq \left\lfloor \frac{t}{\mathcal{O}(M^{3/2})} \right\rfloor \frac{M}{B}.$$

Since $\Omega\left(t^{2/3}\right)$ edges are required for enumerating t distinct triangles, we also have $Q_{\mathcal{A}'}(E,M,B) = \Omega\left(t^{2/3}/B\right)$ and the theorem follows. □

6. CONCLUSION

In this paper we have investigated the I/O complexity of triangle enumeration in external memory. In particular, we have described an optimal cache-oblivious algorithm requiring $\mathcal{O}\left(E^{3/2}/(\sqrt{M}B)\right)$ expected I/Os, which improves previous bounds by a factor $\min(\sqrt{E/M}, \sqrt{M})$.

Recently, it has been shown [21] that the cache-aware randomized algorithm described in Section 2 can be extended to the enumeration of a given subgraph with k vertices in the Alon class [1] (which includes k-cliques) with $\mathcal{O}\left(E^{k/2}/(M^{k/2-1}B)\right)$ expected I/Os if $k \geq 3$ is a constant. The algorithm decomposes the problem into $\mathcal{O}\left((E/M)^{k/2}\right)$ subproblems of expected size $\mathcal{O}(M)$ using the random coloring technique in Section 2; each subproblem is then solved using an extension of the algorithm in [14] that enumerates all cliques of k vertices in $\mathcal{O}\left(E^{k-1}/(M^{k-2}B)\right)$ I/Os.

An interesting open problem is to derive a triangle enumeration algorithm whose I/O complexity is sensitive to the number of triangles in the input graph. Another direction is to extend to more general types of database queries, and consider for example cases of cyclic joins where the sizes of relations differ. Recently Pagh and Stöckel [19] made progress on I/O-efficient join algorithms that make duplicate-eliminating projections. Extending their approach to other types of database queries is also an interesting direction.

Acknowledgments

The authors would like to thank Konstantin Kutzkov and Thomas Dueholm Hansen for discussions in the early stages of this work, Yufei Tao for providing us with a copy of the extended version of [14], and the anonymous reviewers for useful comments. This work was supported by the Danish National Research Foundation under the Sapere Aude program, by MIUR of Italy under project AMANDA, and by the University of Padova under project CPDA121378.

7. REFERENCES

[1] Foto N. Afrati, Anish Das Sarma, Semih Salihoglu, and Jeffrey D. Ullman. Upper and lower bounds on the cost of a Map-Reduce computation. *Proc. VLDB Endow.*, 6(4):277–288, 2013.

[2] Alok Aggarwal and Jeffrey Scott Vitter. The input/output complexity of sorting and related problems. *Commun. ACM*, 31(9), 1988.

[3] Noga Alon, Oded Goldreich, Johan Håstad, and René Peralta. Simple construction of almost k-wise independent random variables. *Random Struct. Algorithms*, 3(3):289–304, 1992.

[4] Lars Arge and Peter Bro Miltersen. On showing lower bounds for external-memory computational geometry problems. In James M. Abello and Jeffrey S. Vitter, editors, *External Memory Algorithms*, pages 139–159. AMS, 1999.

[5] Jonathan Berry, Luke Fostvedt, Daniel Nordman, Cynthia Phillips, C. Seshadhri, and Alyson Wilson. Why do simple algorithms for triangle enumeration work in the real world? In *Proc. 5th Innovations in Theoretical Computer Science*, 2014.

[6] Jonathan W. Berry, Bruce Hendrickson, Randall A. LaViolette, and Cynthia A. Phillips. Tolerating the community detection resolution limit with edge weighting. *Phys. Rev. E*, 83:056119, May 2011.

[7] Gerth S. Brodal and Rolf Fagerberg. On the limits of cache-obliviousness. In *Proc. 35th ACM Symposium on Theory of Computing*, pages 307–315, 2003.

[8] Shumo Chu and James Cheng. Triangle listing in massive networks. *ACM Trans. Knowl. Discov. Data*, 6(4):17:1–17:32, 2012.

[9] Roman Dementiev. *Algorithm engineering for large data sets: hardware, software, algorithms.* PhD thesis, Saarland University, 2007.

[10] Matteo Frigo, Charles E. Leiserson, Harald Prokop, and Sridhar Ramachandran. Cache-oblivious algorithms. In *Proc. 40th Symposium on Foundations of Computer Science*, pages 285–298, 1999.

[11] Matteo Frigo, Charles E. Leiserson, Harald Prokop, and Sridhar Ramachandran. Cache-oblivious algorithms. *ACM Transactions on Algorithms*, 8(1):4, 2012.

[12] Ioannis Fudos and Christoph M. Hoffmann. A graph-constructive approach to solving systems of geometric constraints. *ACM Trans. Graph.*, 16(2):179–216, 1997.

[13] Xiaocheng Hu, Yufei Tao, and Chin-Wan Chung. I/O-efficient algorithms on triangle listing and counting. Full version under submission (Yufei Tao, personal communication), 2013.

[14] Xiaocheng Hu, Yufei Tao, and Chin-Wan Chung. Massive graph triangulation. In *Proc. ACM SIGMOD International Conference on Management of Data*, pages 325–336. ACM, 2013.

[15] Zahra Jafargholi and Emanuele Viola. 3SUM, 3XOR, Triangles. *ArXiv e-prints*, May 2013. 1305.3827.

[16] William Kent. A simple guide to five normal forms in relational database theory. *Commun. ACM*, 26(2):120–125, 1983.

[17] Mihail N. Kolountzakis, Gary L. Miller, Richard Peng, and Charalampos E. Tsourakakis. Efficient triangle counting in large graphs via degree-based vertex partitioning. *Internet Mathematics*, 8(1-2):161–185, 2012.

[18] Bruno Menegola. An external memory algorithm for listing triangles. Technical report, Federal University of Rio Grande Sul, 2010.

[19] Rasmus Pagh and Morten Stöckel. The Input/Output Complexity of Sparse Matrix Multiplication. *ArXiv e-prints*, March 2014. 1403.3551.

[20] Francesco Silvestri. On the limits of cache-oblivious rational permutations. *Theor. Comput. Sci.*, 402(2-3):221–233, 2008.

[21] Francesco Silvestri. Subgraph Enumeration in Massive Graphs. *ArXiv e-prints*, February 2014. 1402.3444.

[22] Siddharth Suri and Sergei Vassilvitskii. Counting triangles and the curse of the last reducer. In *Proc. 20th ACM International Conference on World Wide Web*, pages 607–614, 2011.

[23] Jeffrey S. Vitter. *Algorithms and Data Structures for External Memory.* Now Publishers Inc., Hanover, MA, USA, 2008.

[24] Brooke Foucault Welles, Anne Van Devender, and Noshir S. Contractor. Is a friend a friend?: investigating the structure of friendship networks in virtual worlds. In *Proc.28th International Conference on Human Factors in Computing Systems*, pages 4027–4032, 2010.

[25] V. Vassilevska Williams and Ryan Williams. Subcubic equivalences between path, matrix and triangle problems. In *Proc. 51st Symposium on Foundations of Computer Science*, pages 645–654, 2010.

Beyond Worst-case Analysis for Joins with Minesweeper*

Hung Q. Ngo
SUNY at Buffalo
hungngo@buffalo.edu

Dung T. Nguyen
SUNY at Buffalo
dtn3@buffalo.edu

Christopher Ré
Stanford University
chrismre@stanford.edu

Atri Rudra
SUNY at Buffalo
atri@buffalo.edu

ABSTRACT

We describe a new algorithm, Minesweeper, that is able to satisfy stronger runtime guarantees than previous join algorithms (colloquially, 'beyond worst-case guarantees') for data in indexed search trees. Our first contribution is developing a framework to measure this stronger notion of complexity, which we call *certificate complexity*, that extends notions of Barbay et al. and Demaine et al.; a certificate is a set of propositional formulae that certifies that the output is correct. This notion captures a natural class of join algorithms. In addition, the certificate allows us to define a strictly stronger notion of runtime complexity than traditional worst-case guarantees. Our second contribution is to develop a dichotomy theorem for the certificate-based notion of complexity. Roughly, we show that Minesweeper evaluates β-acyclic queries in time linear in the certificate plus the output size, while for any β-cyclic query there is some instance that takes superlinear time in the certificate (and for which the output is no larger than the certificate size). We also extend our certificate-complexity analysis to queries with bounded treewidth and the triangle query. We present empirical results that certificates can be much smaller than the input size, which suggests that ideas in minesweeper might lead to faster algorithms in practice.

Categories and Subject Descriptors

H.2.4 [**Database Management**]: Systems—*Relational databases*

*We thank LogicBlox, Mahmoud Abo Khamis, Semih Salihoglu and Dan Suciu for many helpful conversations. We thank Jérémy Barbay for bringing helpful references on set intersection to our attention. HQN's work is partly supported by NSF grant CCF-1319402 and a gift from Logicblox. DTN's work is partly supported by NSF grant CCF-0844796 and a gift from Logicblox. CR's work on this project is generously supported by NSF CAREER Award under No. IIS-1353606, NSF award under No. CCF-1356918, the ONR under awards No. N000141210041 and No. N000141310129, Sloan Research Fellowship, Oracle, and Google. AR's work is partly supported by NSF CAREER Award CCF-0844796, NSF grant CCF-1319402 and a gift from Logicblox.

PODS'14, June 22–27, 2014, Snowbird, UT, USA.

http://dx.doi.org/10.1145/2594538.2594547.

General Terms

Algorithms, Theory

Keywords

Join Algorithms; Adaptive Algorithm; Instance Optimality; Certificate; Beta-acyclic queries; Bounded Treewidth; Triangle query

1. INTRODUCTION

Efficiently evaluating relational joins is one of the most well-studied problems in relational database theory and practice. Joins are a key component of problems in constraint satisfaction, artificial intelligence, motif finding, geometry, and others. This paper presents a new join algorithm, called Minesweeper, for joining relations that are stored in order data structures, such as B-trees. Under some mild technical assumptions, Minesweeper is able to achieve stronger runtime guarantees than previous join algorithms.

The Minesweeper algorithm is based on a simple idea. When data are stored in an index, successive tuples indicate *gaps*, i.e., regions in the output space of the join where no possible output tuples exist. Minesweeper maintains gaps that it discovers during execution and infers where to look next. In turn, these gaps may indicate that a large number of tuples in the base relations cannot contribute to the output of the join, so Minesweeper can efficiently skip over such tuples without reading them. By using an appropriate data structure to store the gaps, Minesweeper guarantees that we can find at least one point in the output space that needs to be explored, given the gaps so far. The key technical challenges are the design of this data structure, called the *constraint data structure*, and the analysis of the join algorithm under a more stringent runtime complexity measure.

To measure our stronger notion of runtime, we introduce the notion of a *certificate* for an instance of a join problem: essentially, a certificate is a set of comparisons between elements of the input relations that certify that the join output is exactly as claimed. We use the certificate as a measure of the difficulty of a particular instance of a join problem. That is, our goal is to find algorithms whose running times can be bounded by some function of the *smallest certificate size* for a particular input instance. Our notion has two key properties:

- *Certificate complexity captures the computation performed by widely implemented join algorithms.* We observe that the set of comparisons made by any join algorithm that interacts with the data by comparing elements of the input relations (implicitly) constructs a certificate. Examples of such join algorithms are index-nested-loop join, sort-merge join, hash join, grace join, and block-nested loop join. Hence, our results provide a lower bound for this class of algorithms, as any such algorithm must take at least as many steps as the number of comparisons in a smallest certificate for the instance.

- *Certificate complexity is a strictly finer notion of complexity than traditional worst-case data complexity.* In particular, we show that there is always a certificate that is no larger than the input size. In some cases, the certificate may be much smaller (even constant-sized for arbitrarily large inputs).

These two properties allow us to model a common situation in which indexes allow one to answer a query *without* reading all of the data—a notion that traditional worst-case analysis is too coarse to capture. We believe ours is the first *beyond worst-case analysis* of join queries.

Throughout, we assume that all input relations are indexed consistently with a particular ordering of all attributes called the *global attribute order* (GAO). In effect, this assumption means that we restrict ourselves to algorithms that compare elements in GAO order. This model, for example, excludes the possibility that a relation will be accessed using indexes with multiple search keys during query evaluation.

With this restriction, our main technical results are as follows. Given a β-acyclic query we show that there is some GAO such that Minesweeper runs in time that is essentially optimal in the certificate-sense, i.e., in time $\tilde{O}(|C|+Z)$, where C is a smallest certificate for the problem instance, Z is the output size, and $\tilde{O}$ hides factors that depend (perhaps exponentially) on the query size and at most logarithmically on the input size.[1] Assuming the 3SUM conjecture, this boundary is tight, in the sense that any β-cyclic query (and any GAO) there are some family of instances that require a run-time of $\Omega(|C|^{4/3-\epsilon}+Z)$ for any $\epsilon > 0$ where $Z = O(|C|)$. For α-acyclic join queries, which are the more traditional notion of acyclicity in database theory and a strictly larger class than β-acyclic queries, Yannakakis's seminal join algorithm has a worst-case running time that is linear in the input size plus output size (in data complexity). However, we show that in the certificate world, this boundary has changed: assuming the exponential time hypothesis, the runtime of any algorithm for α-acyclic queries cannot be bounded by any polynomial in $|C|$. In the full version of this paper [37], we show that both worst-case optimal algorithms [38, 50] and Yannakakis's algorithm run in time $\omega(|C|)$ for β-acyclic queries on some family of instances.

We also describe how to extend our results to notions of treewidth. Recall that any ordering of attributes can be used to construct a tree decomposition. Given a GAO that induces a tree decomposition with an (induced) *treewidth* w, Minesweeper runs in time $\tilde{O}(|C|^{w+1}+Z)$. In particular, for a query with *treewidth* w, there is always a GAO that achieves $\tilde{O}(|C|^{w+1}+Z)$. Moreover, we show that no algorithm (comparison-based or not) can improve this exponent by more than a constant factor in w. However, our algorithm does not have an optimal exponent: for the special case of the popular triangle query, we introduce a more sophisticated data structure that allows us to run in time $\tilde{O}(|C|^{3/2}+Z)$, while Minesweeper runs in time $\tilde{O}(|C|^2+Z)$.

Outline of the Remaining Sections. In Section 2, we describe the notion of a certificate and formally state our main technical problem and results. In Section 3, we give an overview of the main technical ideas of Minesweeper, including a complete description of our algorithm and its associated data structures. In Section 4, we describe the analysis of Minesweeper for β-acyclic queries. In Section 5, we then describe how to extend the analysis to queries with low-treewidth and the triangle query. We also present some empirical results to indicate that the certificate size may be much smaller than the input size for some graph queries. In Section 6, we discuss related work. Most of the technical details are provided in the appendix.

[1]The exponential dependence on the query is similar to traditional data complexity; the logarithmic dependence on the data is an unavoidable technical necessity (see Appendix B).

2. PROBLEM AND MAIN RESULT

Roughly, the main problem we study is:

> Given a natural join query Q and a database instance I, compute Q in time $f(|C|,Z)$, where C is the smallest "certificate" that certifies that the output $Q(I)$ is as claimed by the algorithm and $Z = |Q(I)|$.

We will assume that all relations in the input are already indexed. Ideally, we aim for $f(|C|,Z) = O(|C|+Z)$. We make this problem precise in this section.

2.1 The inputs to Minesweeper

We assume a set of attributes $A_1,\ldots,A_n$ and denote the domain of attribute A_i as $\mathbf{D}(A_i)$. Throughout this paper, without loss of generality, we assume that all attributes are on domain $\mathbb{N}$. We define three items: (1) the global attribute order; (2) our notation for order; and (3) our model for how the data are indexed.

The Global Attribute Order. Minesweeper evaluates a given natural join query Q consisting of a set atoms(Q) of relations indexed in a way that is consistent with an ordering $A_1,\ldots,A_n$ of all attributes occurring in Q that we call the *global attribute order* (GAO). To avoid burdening the notation, we assume that the GAO is simply the order $A_1,\ldots,A_n$. We assume that all relations are stored in ordered search trees (e.g., B-trees) where the search key for this tree is consistent with this global order. For example, (A_1,A_3) is consistent, while (A_3,A_2) is not.

Tuple-Order Notation. We will extensively reason about the relative order of tuples and describe notation to facilitate the arguments. For a relation $R(A_{s(1)},\ldots,A_{s(k)})$ where $s:[k]\to[n]$ is such that $s(i) < s(j)$ if $i < j$, we define an *index tuple* $\mathbf{x} = (x_1,\cdots,x_j)$ to be a tuple of positive integers, where $j \leqslant k$. Such tuples index tuples in the relation R. We define their meaning inductively. If $\mathbf{x} = (x_1)$, then $R[\mathbf{x}]$ denotes the x_1'th smallest value in the set $\pi_{A_{s(1)}}(R)$. Inductively, define $R[\mathbf{x}]$ to be the x_j'th smallest value in the set

$$R[x_1,\ldots,x_{j-1},*] := \pi_{A_j}\big(\sigma_{A_{s(1)}=R[x_1],\cdots,A_{s(j-1)}=R[x_1,\ldots,x_{j-1}]}(R)\big).$$

For example, if $R(A_1,A_2) = \{(1,1),(1,8),(2,3),(2,4)\}$ then $R[*] = \{1,2\}$, $R[1,*] = \{1,8\}$, $R[2] = 2$, and $R[2,1] = 3$.

We use the following convention to simplify the algorithm's description: for any index tuple $(x_1,\ldots,x_{j-1})$,

$$R[x_1,\ldots,x_{j-1},0] = -\infty \quad (1)$$

$$R[x_1,\ldots,x_{j-1},|R[x_1,\ldots,x_{j-1},*]|+1] = +\infty. \quad (2)$$

Model of Indexes. The relation R is indexed such that the values of various attributes of tuples from R can be accessed using index tuples. We assume appropriate size information is stored so that we know what the correct ranges of the x_j's are; for example, following the notation described above, the correct range is $1 \leqslant x_j \leqslant |R[x_1,\ldots,x_{j-1},*]|$ for every $j \leqslant \text{arity}(R)$. With the convention specified in (1) and (2), $x_j = 0$ and $x_j = |R[x_1,\ldots,x_{j-1},*]|+1$ are *out-of-range* coordinates. These coordinates are used for the sake of brevity only; an index tuple, by definition, cannot contain out-of-range coordinates.

The index structure for R supports the query $R.\text{FINDGAP}(\mathbf{x},a)$, which takes as input an index tuple $\mathbf{x} = (x_1,\ldots,x_j)$ of length $0 \leqslant j < k$ and a value $a \in \mathbb{Z}$, and returns a pair of coordinates (x_-,x_+) such that

- $0 \leqslant x_- \leqslant x_+ \leqslant |R[(\mathbf{x},*)]| + 1$
- $R[(\mathbf{x},x_-)] \leqslant a \leqslant R[(\mathbf{x},x_+)]$, and
- x_- (resp. x_+) is the maximum (resp. minimum) index satisfying this condition.

Note that it is possible for $x_- = x_+$, which holds when $a \in R[(\mathbf{x},*)]$. We assume throughout that FINDGAP runs in time $O(k \log |R|)$. This model captures widely used indexes including a B-tree [43, Ch.10] or a Trie [50].

2.2 Certificates

We define a *certificate*, which is a set of comparisons that certifies the output is exactly as claimed. We do not want the comparisons to depend on the specific values in the instance, only their order. To facilitate that, we think of $R[\mathbf{x}]$ as a variable that can be mapped to specific domain value by a database instance. We use variables as a perhaps more intuitive, succinct way to describe the underlying morphisms. These variables are only defined for valid index tuples as imposed by the input instance described in the previous section.

A *database instance* I instantiates all variables $R[\mathbf{x}]$, where $\mathbf{x} = (x_1,\ldots,x_j)$, $1 \leqslant j \leqslant \text{arity}(R)$, is an index tuple in relation R. (In particular, the input database instance described in the previous section is such a database instance.) We use $R^I[\mathbf{x}]$ to denote the instantiation of the variable $R[\mathbf{x}]$. Note that each such variable is on the domain of some attribute A_k; for short, we call such variable an A_k-*variable*. A database instance I fills in specific values to the nodes of the search tree structures of the input relations.

Example 2.1. Consider the query $Q = R(A) \bowtie T(A,B)$ on the input instance $I(N)$ defined by $R^{I(N)} = [N]$ and $T^{I(N)} = \{(1,2i) \mid i \in [N]\} \cup \{(2,3i) \mid i \in [N]\}$. This instance can be viewed as defining the following variables: $R[i]$, $i \in [N]$, $T[1]$, $T[2]$, $T[1,i]$, and $T[2,i]$, $i \in [N]$. Another database instance J can define the same index variables but using different constants, in particular, set $R^J[i] = \{2i \mid i \in [N]\}$, $T^J[1] = 2$, $T^J[2] = 4$, $T^J[1,i] = i$, and $T^J[2,i] = 10i$, $i \in [N]$.

We next formalize the notion of certificates. Consider an input instance to Minesweeper, consisting of the query Q, the GAO $A_1,\ldots,A_n$, and a set of relations $R \in \text{atoms}(Q)$ already indexed consistently with the GAO.

Definition 2.2 (Argument). An *argument* for the input instance is a set of symbolic comparisons of the form

$$R[\mathbf{x}]\ \theta\ S[\mathbf{y}], \quad \text{where } R,S \in \text{atoms}(Q) \qquad (3)$$

and $\mathbf{x}$ and $\mathbf{y}$ are two index tuples such that $R[\mathbf{x}]$ and $S[\mathbf{y}]$ are both A_k-variables for some $k \in [n]$, and $\theta \in \{<,=,>\}$. Note that we allow $R = S$. In fact, we need to allow equality constraints between index tuples from the same relation to guarantee that certificates are no larger than the input, which is property (ii) below. A database instance I *satisfies an argument* $\mathcal{A}$ if $R^I[\mathbf{x}]\ \theta\ S^I[\mathbf{y}]$ is true for every comparison $R[\mathbf{x}]\ \theta\ S[\mathbf{y}]$ in the argument $\mathcal{A}$.

An index tuple $\mathbf{x} = (x_1,\ldots,x_r)$ for a relation S is called a *full index tuple* if $r = \text{arity}(S)$. Let I be a database instance for the problem. Then, the full index tuple $\mathbf{x}$ is said to *contribute* to an output tuple $\mathbf{t} \in Q(I) = \bowtie_{R \in \text{atoms}(Q)} R^I$ if $(S[x_1], S[x_1,x_2],\ldots,S[\mathbf{x}])$ is exactly the projection of $\mathbf{t}$ onto attributes in S. A collection X of full index tuples is said to be a *witness* for $Q(I)$ if X has exactly one full index tuple from each relation $R \in \text{atoms}(Q)$, and all index tuples in X contribute to the same $\mathbf{t} \in Q(I)$.

Definition 2.3 (Certificate). An argument $\mathcal{A}$ for the input instance is called a *certificate* iff the following condition is satisfied: if I and J are two database instances of the problem both of which satisfy $\mathcal{A}$, then *every* witness for $Q(I)$ is a witness for $Q(J)$ and vice versa. The *size* of a certificate is the number of comparisons in it.

Example 2.4. Continuing with Example 2.1. Fix an N, the argument $\{R[1] = T[1],\ R[2] = T[2]\}$ is a certificate for $I(N)$. For every database, such as $I = I(N)$ and J in the example, that satisfies the two equalities, the set of witnesses are the same, i.e., the sets $\{1,(1,i)\}$ and $\{2,(2,i)\}$ for $i \in [N]$. Notice we do not need to spell out all of the outputs in the certificate.

Consider the instance K in which $R^K = [N]$, $T^K = \{(1,2i) \mid i \in [N]\} \cup \{(3,3i) \mid i \in [N]\}$. While K is very similar to I, K does *not* satisfy the certificate since $R^K[2] \neq T^K[2]$. The certificate also does not apply to $I(N+1)$ from Example 2.1, since $I(N+1)$ defines a different set of variables from $I(N)$, e.g., $T[1,N+1]$ is defined in $I(N+1)$, but not in $I(N)$.

Properties of optimal certificates. We list three important facts about C, a minimum-sized certificate:

(i) The set of comparisons issued by a very natural class of (non-deterministic) comparison-based join algorithms *is* a certificate; this result not only justifies the definition of certificates, but also shows that $|C|$ is a lowerbound for the runtime of any comparison-based join algorithm.

(ii) $|C|$ can be shown to be at most linear in the input size *no matter what the data and the GAO are*, and in many cases $|C|$ can even be of constant size. Hence, running time measured in $|C|$ is a strictly finer notion of runtime complexity than input-based runtimes; and

(iii) $|C|$ depends on the data and the GAO.

We explain the above facts more formally in the following two propositions. The proofs of the propositions can be found in Appendix A.

Proposition 2.5 (Certificate size as run-time lowerbound of comparison-based algorithms). *Let Q be a join query whose input relations are already indexed consistent with a GAO as described in Section 2.1. Consider any comparison-based join algorithm that only does comparisons of the form shown in* (3). *Then, the set of comparisons performed during execution of the algorithm is a certificate. In particular, if C is an optimal certificate for the problem, then the algorithm must run in time at least $\Omega(|C|)$.*

Proposition 2.6 (Upper bound on optimal certificate size). *Let Q be a general join query on m relations and n attributes. Let N be the total number of tuples from all input relations. Then, no matter what the input data and the GAO are, we have $|C| \leqslant r \cdot N$, where $r = \max\{arity(R) \mid R \in \text{atoms}(Q)\} \leqslant n$.*

In Appendix A, we present examples to demonstrate that $|C|$ can vary any where from $O(1)$ to $\Theta(|\text{input-size}|)$, that the input data or the GAO can change the certificate size, and that same-relation comparisons are needed.

2.3 Main Results

Given a set of input relations already indexed consistent with a fixed GAO, we wish to compute the natural join of these relations as quickly as possible. As illustrated in the previous section, a runtime approaching $|C|$ is optimal among comparison-based algorithms. Furthermore, runtimes as a function of $|C|$ can be sublinear in the input size. Ideally, one would like a join algorithm running in $\tilde{O}(|C|)$-time. However, such a runtime is impossible because for many instances the output size Z is *super*linear in the input size, while $|C|$ is at most linear in the input size. Hence, we will aim for runtimes of the form $\tilde{O}(g(|C|)+Z)$, where Z is the output size and g is some function; a runtime of $\tilde{O}(|C|+Z)$ is essentially optimal.

Our algorithm, called Minesweeper, is a general-purpose join algorithm. Our main results analyze its runtime behavior on various classes of queries in the certificate complexity model. Recall that α-acyclic (often just acyclic) is the standard notion of (hypergraph) acyclicity in database theory [1, p. 128]. A query is β-acyclic, a stronger notion, if every subquery of Q obtained by removing atoms from Q remains α-acyclic.

Let N be the input size, n the number of attributes, m the number of relations, Z the output size, r the maximum arity of input relations, and C any optimal certificate for the instance. Our key results are as follows.

Theorem 2.7. *Suppose the input query is β-acyclic. Then there is some GAO such that Minesweeper computes its output in time* $O\big(2^n m^2 n(4^r|C|+Z)\log N\big)$.

As is standard in database theory, we ignore the dependency on the query size, and the above theorem states that Minesweeper runs in time $\tilde{O}(|C|+Z)$. For β-acyclic queries with a fixed GAO, our results are loose; our best upper bound the complexity uses the treewidth from Section 5.

What about *β-cyclic* queries? The short answer is *no*: we cannot achieve this guarantee. It is obvious that any join algorithm will take time $\Omega(Z)$. Using *3SUM-hardness*, a well-known complexity-theoretic assumption [42], we are able to show the following.

Proposition 2.8. *Unless the 3SUM problem can be solved in sub-quadratic time, for any β-*cyclic *query Q in any GAO, there does not exist an algorithm that runs in time $O(|C|^{4/3-\epsilon}+Z)$ for any $\epsilon > 0$ on all instances.*

We extend our analysis of Minesweeper to queries that have bounded treewidth and to triangle queries in Section 5. These results are technically involved and we only highlight the main technical challenges.

3. THE Minesweeper ALGORITHM

We begin with an overview of the main ideas and technical challenges of the Minesweeper algorithm. Intuitively, Minesweeper probes into the space of all possible output tuples, and explores the gaps in this space where there is no output tuples. These gaps are encoded by a technical notion called constraints, which we describe next.

3.1 Notation for Minesweeper

We need some notation to describe our algorithm. Define the *output space* O of the query Q to be the space $O = \mathbf{D}(A_1)\times\mathbf{D}(A_2)\times\cdots\times\mathbf{D}(A_n)$, where $\mathbf{D}(A_i)$ is the domain of attribute A_i. Recall, we assume $\mathbf{D}(A_i)=\mathbb{N}$ for simplicity. By definition, a tuple $\mathbf{t}$ is an *output tuple* if and only if $\mathbf{t}=(t_1,\ldots,t_n)\in O$, and $\pi_{\bar{A}(R)}(\mathbf{t})\in R$, for all $R\in \text{atoms}(Q)$, where $\bar{A}(R)$ is the set of attributes in R.

Constraints. A *constraint* $\mathbf{c}$ is an n-dimensional vector of the following form: $\mathbf{c}=\langle c_1,\cdots,c_{i-1},(\ell,r),\{*\}^{n-i}\rangle$, where $c_j\in\mathbb{N}\cup\{*\}$ for every $j\in[i-1]$. In other words, each constraint $\mathbf{c}$ is a vector consisting of three types of components:

(1) *open-interval* component (ℓ,r) on the attribute A_i (for some $i\in[n]$) and $\ell,r\in\mathbb{N}\cup\{-\infty,+\infty\}$,

(2) *wildcard* or $*$ component, and

(3) *equality* component of the type $p\in\mathbb{N}$.

In any constraint, there is exactly one interval component. All components after the interval component are wildcards. Hence, we will often not write down the wildcard components that come after the interval component. The prefix that comes before the interval component is called a *pattern*, which consists of any number of wildcards and equality components. The equality components encode the coordinates of the axis parallel affine planes containing the gap. For example, in three dimensions the constraint $\langle *,(1,10),*\rangle$ can be viewed as the region between the affine hyperplanes $A_2=1$ and $A_2=10$; and the constraint $\langle 1,*,(2,5)\rangle$ can be viewed as the strip inside the plane $A_1=1$ between the line $A_3=2$ and $A_3=5$. We encode these gaps syntactically to facilitate efficient insertion, deletion, and merging.

Let $\mathbf{t}=(t_1,\ldots,t_n)\in O$ be an arbitrary tuple from the output space, and $\mathbf{c}=\langle c_1,\ldots,c_n\rangle$ be a constraint. Then, $\mathbf{t}$ is said to *satisfy* constraint $\mathbf{c}$ if for every $i\in[n]$ one of the following holds: (1) $c_i=*$, (2) $c_i\in\mathbb{N}$ and $t_i=c_i$, or (3) $c_i=(\ell,r)$ and $t_i\in(\ell,r)$. We say a tuple $\mathbf{t}$ is *active* with respect to a set of constraints if $\mathbf{t}$ does not satisfy any constraint in the set (Geometrically, no constraint covers the point $\mathbf{t}$).

3.2 A High-level Overview of Minesweeper

We break Minesweeper in two components: (1) a special data structure called the *constraint data structure* (CDS), and (2) an algorithm that uses this data structure. Algorithm 1 gives a high-level overview of how Minesweeper works, which we will make precise in the next section.

The CDS stores the constraints already discovered during execution. For example, consider the query $R(A,B),S(B)$. If Minesweeper determines that $S[4]=20$ and $S[5]=28$, then we can deduce that there is no tuple in the output that has a B value in the open interval $(20,28)$. This observation is encoded as a constraint $\langle *,(20,28)\rangle$. A key challenge with the CDS is to efficiently find an active tuple $\mathbf{t}$, given a set of constraints already stored in the CDS.

The outer algorithm queries the CDS to find active tuples and then probes the input relations. If there is no active $\mathbf{t}$, the algorithm terminates. Given an active $\mathbf{t}$, Minesweeper makes queries into the index structures of the input relations. These queries either report that $\mathbf{t}$ is an output tuple, in which case $\mathbf{t}$ is output, or they discover constraints that are then inserted into the CDS. Intuitively, the queries into the index structures are crafted so that at least one of the constraints that is returned is responsible for ruling out $\mathbf{t}$ in any optimal certificate.

We first describe the interface of the CDS and then the outer algorithm which uses the CDS.

3.3 The CDS

The CDS is a data structure that implements two functions as efficiently as possible: (1) InsConstraint($\mathbf{c}$) takes a new constraint $\mathbf{c}$ and inserts it into the data structure, and (2) getProbePoint() returns an active tuple $\mathbf{t}$ with respect to all constraints that have been inserted into the CDS, or null if no such $\mathbf{t}$ exists.

Algorithm 1 High-level view: Minesweeper algorithm

CDS ← ∅ ▷ No gap discovered yet
While CDS can find **t** not in any stored gap **do**
  If $\pi_{\bar{A}(R)}(\mathbf{t}) \in R$ for every $R \in$ atoms(Q) **then**
    Report **t** and tell CDS that **t** is ruled out
  else
    Query all $R \in$ atoms(Q) for gaps around **t**
    Insert those gaps into CDS

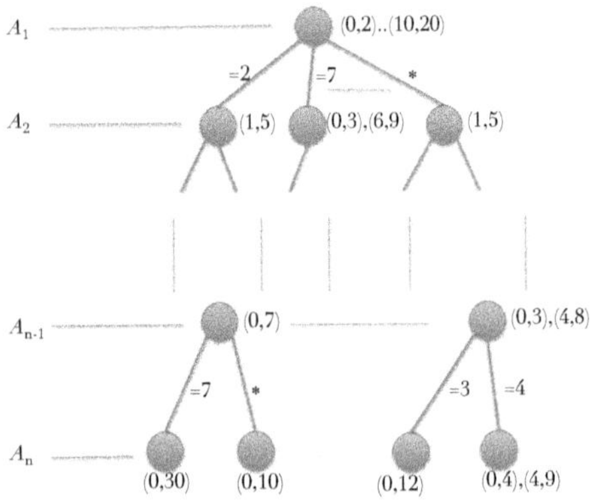

Figure 1: Example of ConstraintTree data structure

Implementation. To support these operations, we implement the CDS using a tree structure called ConstraintTree, which is a tree with at most n levels, one for each of the attributes following the GAO. Figure 1 illustrates such a tree. Each node v in the CDS corresponds to a prefix (i.e. pattern) of constraints; each node has two data structures:

(1) v.equalities is a sorted list with one entry per child of v in the underlying tree. Each entry in the sorted list is labeled with an element of $\mathbb{N}$ and has a pointer to the subtree rooted at the corresponding child. There are two exceptions: (1) if v is a leaf then v.equalities $= \emptyset$, and (2) each v has at most one additional child node labeled with $*$.

(2) v.intervals is a sorted list of disjoint open intervals under that corresponding attribute. A key property is that *given a value u we can, in logarithmic time, output the smallest value $u' \geqslant u$ that is not covered by any interval in v.intervals (via the* Next *function).* We will maintain the invariant that, for every node v in a ConstraintTree, none of the labels in v.equalities is contained in an interval in v.intervals.

The following lemma is straightforward hence we omit the proof. Note that when we insert a new interval that overlaps existing intervals and/or contains values in equalities, we will have to merge them and/or remove the entries in equalities; and hence the cost is amortized.

Proposition 3.1. *The operation* InsConstraint(**c**) *can be implemented in amortized time $O(n \log W)$, where W is total number of constraint vectors already inserted.*

The key challenge is to design an efficient implementation of getProbePoint(). In Sections 4 and 5, we analyze getProbePoint() using properties of the query Q.

3.4 The outer algorithm

Algorithm 2 contains all the details that were missing from the high-level view of Algorithm 1. The full version contains a complete run of Minesweeper on a specific query along with complete end-to-end descriptions of two specific queries, which may help clarify the general algorithm. We prove the following result.

Theorem 3.2. *Let N denote the input size, Z the number of output tuples, $m = |\text{atoms}(Q)|$, and $r = \max_{R \in \text{atoms}(Q)} arity(R)$. Let C be any optimal certificate for the input instance. Then, the total runtime of Algorithm 2 is*

$$O((4^r|C| + rZ)m\log(N)) + T(CDS),$$

where $T(CDS)$ is the total time taken by the constraint data structure. The algorithm inserts $O(m4^r|C| + Z)$ constraints to CDS and issues $O(2^r|C| + Z)$ calls to getProbePoint().

Our proof strategy bounds the number of iterations of the algorithm using an amortized analysis. We pay for each probe point **t** returned by the CDS by either charging a comparison in the certificate C *or* by charging an output tuple. If **t** is an output tuple, we charge the output tuple. If **t** is not an output tuple, then we observe that at least one of the constraints we discovered must rule out **t**. Recall that each constraint is essentially a pair of elements from some base relation. If one element from each such pair is not involved in any comparison in C, then we can perturb the instance slightly by moving the comparison-free element to align with **t**. This means C does not have enough information to rule out **t** as an output tuple, reaching a contradiction. Hence when **t** is not an output tuple, essentially some gap must map to a pair of comparisons. Finally, using the geometry of the gaps, we show that each comparison is charged at most 2^r times and each output tuple is charged $O(1)$ times. Thus, in total the number of iterations is $O(2^r|C| + Z)$.

When C is an optimal-size certificate, the runtime above is about linear in $|C| + Z$ *plus* the total time the CDS takes. Note, however, that $|C|$ can be very small, even constant. Hence, we basically shift all of the burden of join evaluation to the CDS. Thus, one should not hope that there is an efficient CDS for general queries:

Theorem 3.3 (Limitation of any CDS). *Unless the exponential time hypothesis is wrong, no constraint data structure can process the constraints and the probe point accesses in time polynomial (independent of the query) in the number of constraints inserted and probe points accessed.*

In the next sections, we analyze the CDS, specifically the function getProbePoint(). Our analysis exploits properties of the query and the GAO for β-acyclic and bounded treewidth queries.

4. β-ACYCLIC QUERIES

We describe how to implement getProbePoint for β-acyclic queries. In particular, we show that there is some GAO that helps implement getProbePoint in amortized logarithmic time. Hence, by Theorem 3.2 our running time is $\tilde{O}(|C|+Z)$, which we argued previously is essentially optimal.

4.1 Overview

Recall that given a set of intervals, getProbePoint returns an active tuple $\mathbf{t} = (t_1, \dots, t_n) \in \mathcal{O}$, i.e., a tuple **t** that does not satisfy any of the constraints stored in the CDS. Essentially, during execution there may be a large number of constraints, and getProbePoint needs to answer an alternating sequence of constraint satisfaction problems and insertions. The question is: how do we split this work between insertion time and querying time?

In Minesweeper, we take a lazy approach: we insert all the constraints without doing any cleanup on the CDS. Then, when the Minesweeper calls getProbePoint, Minesweeper might have to do hard work to return a new active tuple, applying memoization along

Algorithm 2 Minesweeper for evaluating the query $Q = \bowtie_{R \in \text{atoms}(Q)} R(\bar{A}(R))$

Input: We use the conventions defined in (1) and (2)

Initialize the constraint data structure CDS $= \emptyset$
While $((\mathbf{t} \leftarrow \text{CDS.GETPROBEPOINT}()) \neq \text{NULL})$ **do**
  Denote $\mathbf{t} = (t_1, \ldots, t_n)$
  For each $R \in \text{atoms}(Q)$ **do**
    $k \leftarrow \text{arity}(R)$;
    Let $\bar{A}(R) = (A_{s(1)}, \ldots, A_{s(k)})$ be R's attributes, where $s : [k] \to [n]$ is such that $s(i) < s(j)$ for $i < j$.
    For $p = 0$ **to** $k-1$ **do** ▷ Explore around $\mathbf{t}$ in R
      For each vector $\mathbf{v} \in \{\ell, h\}^p$ **do** ▷ ℓ, h are just symbols, and $\{\ell, h\}^0$ has only the empty vector
        Let $\mathbf{v} = (v_1, \ldots, v_p)$ ▷ $v_j \in \{\ell, h\}, \forall j \in [p]$
        $(i_R^{(\mathbf{v},\ell)}, i_R^{(\mathbf{v},h)}) \leftarrow R.\text{FINDGAP}\Big(\big(i_R^{(v_1)}, i_R^{(v_1,v_2)}, \ldots, i_R^{(v_1,\ldots,v_p)}\big), t_{s(p+1)}\Big)$ ▷ Gap around $(R[\mathbf{i}_R^{(\mathbf{v})}], t_{s(p+1)})$ in R.
  If $R\Big[i_R^{(h)}, i_R^{(h,h)}, \ldots, i_R^{\{h\}^p}\Big] = t_{s(p)}$ for all $p \in [\text{arity}(R)]$ and for all $R \in \text{atoms}(Q)$ **then**
    Output the tuple $\mathbf{t}$
    $\text{CDS.INSCONSTRAINT}\big(\langle t_1, t_2, \ldots, t_{n-1}, (t_n - 1, t_n + 1)\rangle\big)$
  else
    For each $R \in \text{atoms}(Q)$ **do**
      $k \leftarrow \text{arity}(R)$
      For $p = 0$ **to** $k-1$ **do**
        For each vector $\mathbf{v} \in \{\ell, h\}^p$ **do**
          If (all the indices $i_R^{(v_1)}, \ldots, i_R^{(v_1,\ldots,v_p)}$ are **not** out of range) **then**
            $\text{CDS.INSCONSTRAINT}\Big(\Big\langle R\Big[i_R^{(v_1)}\Big], \ldots, R\Big[i_R^{(v_1)}, \cdots, i_R^{(v_1,\ldots,v_p)}\Big], \Big(R[i_R^{(\mathbf{v},\ell)}], R[i_R^{(\mathbf{v},h)}]\Big)\Big\rangle\Big)$
            ▷ Note that the constraint is empty if $R[i_R^{(\mathbf{v},\ell)}] = R[i_R^{(\mathbf{v},h)}]$

the way so the heavy labor does not have to be repeated in the future. When the GAO has a special structure, this strategy helps keep every CDS operation at amortized logarithmic time. We first give an example to build intuition about how our lazy approach works.

Example 4.1. Consider a query with three attributes (A, B, C), and suppose the constraints that are inserted into the CDS are

(i) $\langle a, b, (-\infty, 1)\rangle$ for all $a, b \in [N]$,

(ii) $\langle *, b, (2i-2, 2i)\rangle$ for all $b, i \in [N]$,

(iii) $\langle *, *, (2i-1, 2i+1)\rangle$ for $i \in [N]$,

(iv) and $\langle *, *, (2N, +\infty)\rangle$.

There are $O(N^2)$ constraints, and there is no active tuple of the form (a, b, c) for $a, b \in [N]$. Without memoization, the brute-force strategy will take time $\Omega(N^3)$, because for every pair $(a, b) \in [N]^2$, the algorithm will have to verify in $\Omega(N)$ time that the constraints (ii) forbid all $c = 2i - 1, i \in [N]$, the constraints (iii) forbid all $c = 2i, i \in [N]$, and the constraint (iv) forbid $c > 2N$.

But we can do better by remembering inferences that we have made. Fix a value $a = 1, b = 1$. Minesweeper recognizes in $O(N)$-time that there is no c for which (a, b, c) is active. Minesweeper is slightly smarter: it looks at constraints of the type $(ii), (iii), (iv)$ (for $b = 1$) and concludes in $O(N)$-time that every tuple satisfying those constraints also satisfies the constraint $\langle *, 1, (0, +\infty)\rangle$. Minesweeper remembers this inference by inserting the inferred constraint into the CDS. Then, for $a \geqslant 2$, it takes only $O(1)$-time to conclude that no tuple of the form $(a, 1, c)$ can be active. It does this inference by inserting constraint $\langle a, 1, (0, +\infty)\rangle$, which is merged with (i) to become $\langle a, 1, (-\infty, +\infty)\rangle$. Overall, we need only $O(N^2)$-time to reach the same conclusion as the $\Omega(N^3)$ brute-force strategy.

4.2 Patterns

Recall that GETPROBEPOINT returns a tuple $\mathbf{t} = (t_1, \ldots, t_n) \in O$ such that $\mathbf{t}$ does not satisfy any of the constraints stored in the CDS. We find $\mathbf{t}$ by computing $t_1, t_2, \ldots, t_n$, one value at a time, backtracking if necessary. We need some notation to describe the algorithm and the properties that we exploit.

Let $0 \leqslant k \leqslant n$ be an integer. A vector $\mathbf{p} = \langle p_1, \ldots, p_k\rangle$ for which $p_i \in \mathbb{N} \cup \{*\}$ is called a *pattern*. The number k is the *length* of the pattern. If $p_i \in \mathbb{N}$ then it is an *equality component* of the pattern, while $*$ is a *wildcard component* of the pattern.

A node u at depth k in the tree CONSTRAINTTREE can be identified by a pattern of length k corresponding naturally to the labels on the path from the root of CONSTRAINTTREE down to node u. The pattern for node u is denoted by $P(u)$. In particular, $P(\text{root}) = \epsilon$, the empty pattern.

Let $\mathbf{p} = \langle p_1, \ldots, p_k\rangle$ be a pattern. Then, a *specialization* of $\mathbf{p}$ is another pattern $\mathbf{p}' = \langle p_1', \ldots, p_k'\rangle$ *of the same length* for which $p_i' = p_i$ whenever $p_i \in \mathbb{N}$. In other words, we can get a specialization of $\mathbf{p}$ by changing some of the $*$ components into equality components. If $\mathbf{p}'$ is a specialization of $\mathbf{p}$, then $\mathbf{p}$ is a *generalization* of $\mathbf{p}'$. For two nodes u and v of the CDS, if $P(u)$ is a specialization of $P(v)$, then we also say that node u is a specialization of node v.

The specialization relation defines a partially ordered set. When $\mathbf{p}'$ is a specialization of $\mathbf{p}$, we write $\mathbf{p}' \preceq \mathbf{p}$. If in addition we know $\mathbf{p}' \neq \mathbf{p}$, then we write $\mathbf{p}' \prec \mathbf{p}$.

Let $G(t_1, \ldots, t_i)$ be the *principal filter* generated by $(t_1, \ldots, t_i)$ in this partial order, i.e., it is the set of all nodes u of the CDS such that $P(u)$ is a generalization of $\langle t_1, \ldots, t_i\rangle$ and that $u.\text{INTERVALS} \neq \emptyset$. The key property of constraints that we exploit is summarized by the following proposition.

Proposition 4.2. *Using the notation above, for a β-acyclic query, there exists a GAO such that for each $t_1, \ldots, t_i$ the principal filter $G(t_1, \ldots, t_i)$ is a chain.*

Recall that a chain is a totally ordered set. In particular, $G = G(t_1,\dots,t_i)$ has a smallest pattern $\bar{\mathbf{p}}$ (or bottom pattern). Note that these patterns in G might come from constraints inserted from relations, constraints inserted by the outputs of the join, or even constraints inserted due to backtracking. Thinking of the constraints geometrically, this condition means that the constraints form a collection of axis-aligned affine subspaces of $\mathcal{O}$ where one is contained inside another.

We prove Proposition 4.2 using a result of Brouwer and Kolen [15]. The class of GAOs in the proposition is called a *nested elimination order*. We show that there exists a GAO that is a nested elimination order if and only if the query is β-acyclic. We also show that β-acyclicity and this GAO can be found in polynomial time.

4.3 The GETPROBEPOINT Algorithm

Algorithm 3 describes GETPROBEPOINT algorithm specialized to β-acyclic queries. In turn, this algorithm uses Algorithm 4, which is responsible for efficiently inferring constraints imposed by patterns above this level. We walk through the steps of the algorithm below.

Initially, let v be the root node of the CDS. We set t_1 to the smallest value that does not belong to any interval stored in v.INTERVALS, i.e., $t_1 = v$.INTERVALS.NEXT(-1). We work under the implicit assumption that any interval inserted into CONSTRAINTTREE that contains -1 must be of the form $(-\infty, r)$, for some $r \geqslant 0$. This is because the domain values are in $\mathbb{N}$. In particular, if $t_1 = +\infty$ then the constraints cover the entire output space $\mathcal{O}$ and NULL can be returned.

Inductively, let $(t_1,\dots,t_i)$, $i \geqslant 1$, be the *prefix* of $\mathbf{t}$ we have built thus far. Our goal is to compute t_{i+1}. What we need to find is a value t_{i+1} such that t_{i+1} does not belong to the intervals stored in u.INTERVALS *for every* node $u \in G(t_1,\dots,t_i)$. For this, we call algorithm 4 that uses Prop. 4.2 to efficiently find t_{i+1} or return that there is no such t_{i+1}. We defer its explanation for the moment. We only note that if such a t_{i+1} cannot be found (i.e. if $t_{i+1} = +\infty$ is returned after the search), then we have to *backtrack* because what that means is that every tuple $\mathbf{t}$ that begins with the prefix $(t_1,\dots,t_i)$ satisfies some constraint stored in CONSTRAINTTREE. Line 15 of Algorithm 3 shows how we backtrack. In particular, we save this information (by inserting a new constraint into the CDS) in Line 15 to avoid ever exploring this path again.

Next Chain Value.. The key to Algorithm 4 is that such a t_{i+1} can be found efficiently since one only needs to look through a chain of constraint sets. We write $\mathbf{p} \lessdot \mathbf{p}'$ if $\mathbf{p} \prec \mathbf{p}'$ and there is no pattern $\mathbf{p}''$ such that $\mathbf{p} \prec \mathbf{p}'' \prec \mathbf{p}'$. Every interval from a node $u \in G$ higher up in the chain infers an interval at a node lower in the chain. For instance, in Example 4.1, the chain G consists of three nodes $\langle a,b\rangle$, $\langle *,b\rangle$, and $\langle *,*\rangle$. Further, every constraint of the form $\langle *,*,(2i-1,2i+1)\rangle$ infers a more specialized constraint of the form $\langle *,b,(2i-1,2i+1)\rangle$, which in turns infers a constraint of the form $\langle a,b,(2i-1,2i+1)\rangle$. Hence, if we infer every single constraint downward from the top pattern to the bottom pattern, we will be spending a lot of time. The idea of Algorithm 4 is to infer as large of an interval as possible from a node higher in the chain before specializing it down. Our algorithm will ensure that whenever we infer a new constraint (line 13 of Algorithm 4), this constraint subsumes an old constraint which will never be charged again in a future inference.

4.4 Runtime Analysis

Lemma 4.3. *Suppose the input query Q is β-acyclic. Then, there exists a GAO such that each of the operations* GETPROBEPOINT *and* INSCONSTRAINT *of* CONSTRAINTTREE *takes amortized time $O(n2^n \log W)$, where W is the total number of constraints ever inserted.*

Algorithm 3 CDS.GETPROBEPOINT() for β-acyclic queries

Input: A CONSTRAINTTREE CDS

1: $i \leftarrow 0$
2: **While** $i < n$ **do**
3: $G \leftarrow \{u \in \text{CDS} \mid (t_1,\dots,t_i) \preceq P(u)$ and u.INTERVALS $\neq \emptyset\}$
4: **If** $(G = \emptyset)$ **then**
5: $t_{i+1} \leftarrow -1$
6: $i \leftarrow i+1$
7: **else**
8: Let $\bar{\mathbf{p}} = \langle \bar{p}_1,\dots,\bar{p}_i\rangle$ be the *bottom* of G
9: Let $\bar{u} \in$ CDS be the node for which $P(\bar{u}) = \bar{\mathbf{p}}$
10: $t_{i+1} \leftarrow$ CDS.NEXTCHAINVAL$(-1,\bar{u},G)$
11: $i_0 \leftarrow \max\{k \mid k \leqslant i, \bar{p}_k \neq *\}$
12: **If** $(t_{i+1} = +\infty)$ and $i_0 = 0$ **then**
13: **Return** NULL ▷ No tuple $\mathbf{t}$ found
14: **else If** $(t_{i+1} = +\infty)$ **then**
15: CDS.INSCONSTRAINT$(\langle \bar{p}_1,\dots,\bar{p}_{i_0-1},(\bar{p}_{i_0}-1,\bar{p}_{i_0}+1)\rangle)$
16: $i \leftarrow i_0 - 1$ ▷ Back-track
17: **else**
18: $i \leftarrow i+1$ ▷ Advance i
19: **Return** $\mathbf{t} = (t_1,\dots,t_n)$

The above lemma and Theorem 3.2 leads directly to one of our main results.

Corollary 4.4 (Restatement of Theorem 2.7)**.** *Suppose the input query is β-acyclic then there exists a GAO such that Minesweeper computes its output in time*

$$O\big(2^n m^2 n (4^r|\mathcal{C}| + Z)\log N\big).$$

In particular, its data-complexity runtime is essentially optimal in the certificate complexity world: $\tilde{O}(|\mathcal{C}| + Z)$.

Beyond β-acyclic queries, we show that we cannot do better modulo a well-known complexity theoretic assumption.

Proposition 4.5 (Re-statement of Proposition 2.8)**.** *Unless the* 3SUM *problem can be solved in sub-quadratic time, for any β-cyclic query Q in any GAO, there does not exist an algorithm that runs in time $O(|\mathcal{C}|^{4/3-\epsilon} + Z)$ for any $\epsilon > 0$ on all instances.*

Comparison with Worst-Case Optimal Algorithms. It is natural to wonder if Yannakakis' worst-case optimal algorithm for α-acyclic queries or the worst-case optimal algorithms of [38] (henceforth, NPRR) or [50] (henceforth LFTJ) can achieve runtimes of $\tilde{O}(|\mathcal{C}| + Z)$ for β-acyclic queries. We outline the intuition about why this cannot be the case.

Yannakakis' algorithm performs pairwise semijoin reducers. If we pick an instance where $|\mathcal{C}| = o(N)$ such that there is a relation pair involved each with size $\Omega(N)$, then Yannakakis's algorithm will exceed the bound. For NPRR and LFTJ, consider the family of instances in which one computes all paths of length ℓ (some constant) in a directed graph $G = (V,E)$ (this can be realized by a "path" query of length ℓ where the relations are the edge set of G). Now consider the case where the longest path in G has size at most $\ell - 1$. In this case the output is empty and since each relation is E, we have $|\mathcal{C}| \leqslant O(|E|)$ and by Corollary 4.4, we will run in time $\tilde{O}(|E|)$. Hence, when G has many paths (at least $\omega(|E|)$) of

Algorithm 4 CDS.NEXTCHAINVAL(x, u, G), where G is a chain

Input: A CONSTRAINTTREE CDS, a node $u \in G$
Input: A chain G of nodes, and a starting value x
Output: the smallest value $y \geqslant x$ not covered by *any* v.INTERVALS, for all $v \in G$ such that $P(u) \preceq P(v)$

```
If there is no v ∈ G for which P(u) ≺ P(v) then   ▷ At the top of the chain G
    Return u.INTERVALS.NEXT(x)
else
    y ← x
    repeat
        Let v ∈ G such that P(u) ≺ P(v)
                                        ▷ Next node up the chain
        z ← CDS.NEXTCHAINVAL(y, v, G)
                    ▷ first "free value" ≥ y at all nodes up the chain
        y ← u.INTERVALS.NEXT(z)
                                        ▷ first "free value" ≥ z at u
    until y = z
    CDS.INSCONSTRAINT(⟨P(u), (x − 1, y)⟩)
    Return y
```

length at most ℓ, then both NPRR and LFTJ will have to explore all $\omega(|E|)$ paths leading to an $\omega(|C|)$ runtime.

In the full version of this paper, we exhibit a family of β-acyclic queries and a family of instances that combines both of the ideas above to show that all the three worst-case optimal algorithms can have arbitrarily worse runtime than Minesweeper. In particular, even running those worst-case algorithms in parallel is not able to achieve the certificate-based guarantees.

5. EXTENSIONS

We extend in two ways: queries with bounded tree width and we describe faster algorithms for the triangle query.

5.1 Queries with bounded tree-width

While Proposition 2.8 shows that $O(|C|^{4/3-\epsilon} + Z)$-time is not achievable for β-cyclic queries, we are able to show the following analog of the treewidth-based runtime under the traditional worst-case complexity notion [6, 18].

Theorem 5.1 (Minesweeper for bounded treewidth queries). *Suppose that the GAO has an* elimination width *bounded by w. Then, Minesweeper runs in time*

$$O\left(m^3 n^3 4^n \left(nm^{w+1} 8^{n(w+1)} |C|^{w+1} + Z\right) \log N\right).$$

In particular, if we ignore the dependence on the query size, the runtime is $\tilde{O}\left(|C|^{w+1} + Z\right)$. *Furthermore, if the treewidth of the input query Q is bounded by w, then there exists a GAO for which Minesweeper runs in the above time.*

The overall structure of the algorithm remains identical to the β-acyclic case, the only change is in GETPROBEPOINT. For general queries, the GETPROBEPOINT algorithm remains similar in structure to that of the β-acyclic case (Algorithm 3), and if the input query is β-acyclic (with a nested elimination order as the GAO), then the general GETPROBEPOINT algorithm is *exactly* Algorithm 3. The new issue we have to deal with is the fact that the poset G at each depth is not necessarily a chain. Our solution is simple: we mimic the behavior of Algorithm 3 on a shadow of G that *is* a chain and make use of both the algorithm and the analysis for the β-acyclic case.

Query	com-Orkut		soc-Epinions1		soc-LiveJournal1	
	N	$\lvert C\rvert$	N	$\lvert C\rvert$	N	$\lvert C\rvert$
Star	352M	214K	1.5M	1.1K	207M	172K
3-path	352M	119K	1.5M	0.8K	207M	138K
Tree	469M	2.8M	2M	3.4K	276M	2.7M

Table 1: Input size (N) versus Certificate size ($|C|$). Units are Million(M) and Thousand(K). The three graph datasets are from Orkut, Epinions, and LiveJournal network `http://snap.stanford.edu/data/`.

It is natural to wonder if Theorem 5.1 is tight. In addition to the obvious $\Omega(Z)$ dependency, the next result indicates that the dependence on w also cannot be avoided, *even if* we just look at the class of α-acyclic queries.

Proposition 5.2. *Unless the* exponential time hypothesis *is false, for every large enough constant $k > 0$, there is an α-acyclic query Q_k for which there is no algorithm with runtime $|C|^{o(k)}$. Further, Q_k has treewidth $k-1$.*

Our analysis of Minesweeper is off by at most 1 in the exponent.

Proposition 5.3. *For every $w \geqslant 2$, there exists an (α-acyclic) query Q_w with treewidth w with the following property. For every possible global ordering of attributes, there exists an (infinite family of) instance on which the Minesweeper algorithm takes $\Omega(|C|^w)$ time.*

5.2 An implementation of Minesweeper

With the help of LogicBlox, we implemented Minesweeper inside the LogicBlox engine. Our results are preliminary: it is implemented for main memory data and all experiments are run in a multi-threaded mode. We run three queries: a star query, a small path query, and a tree query, which are described below, on three data sets Orkut online social network, Who-trusts-whom network of Epinions.com, and LiveJournal online social network.

- Star query: $Q = R_1(A) \bowtie S(A,B) \bowtie S(A,C) \bowtie S(A,D) \bowtie R_2(B) \bowtie R_3(C) \bowtie R_4(D)$.
- 3-path query: $Q = S(A,B) \bowtie S(B,C) \bowtie S(C,D) \bowtie R_5(A) \bowtie R_6(B) \bowtie R_7(C) \bowtie R_8(D)$.
- Tree query: $Q = S(A,B) \bowtie S(B,C) \bowtie S(B,D) \bowtie S(D,E) \bowtie R_9(A) \bowtie R_{10}(C) \bowtie R_{11}(D) \bowtie R_{12}(E)$.

For each query and each dataset, relation S is a graph dataset, while every R_i relation contains a subset of vertices from that graph dataset, where every vertex is chosen with a probability 0.001. Table 1 shows the input size versus certificate size on different queries and different graph datasets. The upper bound of the certificate size is measured by counting the number of FINDGAP operations during computing join queries. These numbers show that certificate size is very small compared to input size and so it indicates that a practical implementation might be obtained.

5.3 The Triangle Query

We consider the triangle query $Q_\triangle = R(A,B) \bowtie S(B,C) \bowtie T(A,C)$ that can be viewed as enumerating triangles in a given graph. Using the CDS described so far, Minesweeper computes this query in time $\tilde{O}(|C|^2 + Z)$, and this analysis is tight. (A straightforward application of our more general analysis given in Theorem 5.1, which gives $\tilde{O}(|C|^3 + Z)$.) The central inefficiency is that the CDS wastes time determining that many tuples with the same prefix (a,b) have been ruled out by existing constraints. In particular, the CDS considers all possible pairs (a,b) (of which there can be $\Omega(|C|^2)$ of them). By designing a smarter CDS, our improved CDS explores $O(|C|)$ such pairs. We can prove the following result.

Theorem 5.4. *We can solve the triangle query, Q_Δ in time $O\left(\left(|C|^{3/2}+Z\right)\log^{7/2} N\right)$.*

6. RELATED WORK

Our work touches on a few different areas, and we structure the related work around each of these areas: join processing, certificates for set intersection, and complexity measures that are finer than worst-case complexity.

6.1 Join Processing

Many positive and negative results regarding conjunctive query evaluation also apply to natural join evaluation. On the negative side, both problems are NP-hard in terms of expression complexity [16], but are easier in terms of data complexity [47] (when the query is assumed to be of fixed size). They are W[1]-complete and thus unlikely to be fix-parameter tractable [31,41].

On the positive side, a large class of conjunctive queries (and thus natural join queries) are tractable. In particular, the classes of acyclic queries and bounded treewidth queries can be evaluated efficiently [17,26,29,51,52]. For example, if $|q|$ is the query size, N is the input size, and Z is the output size, then Yannakakis' algorithm can evaluate acyclic natural join queries in time $\tilde{O}(\text{poly}(|q|)(N\log N+Z))$. Acyclic conjunctive queries can also be evaluated efficiently in the I/O model [40], and in the RAM model even when there are inequalities [51]. For queries with treewidth w, it was recognized early on that a runtime of about $\tilde{O}(N^{w+1}+Z)$ is attainable [18,27]. our result strictly generalizes these results. We able to show that Yannakakis' algorithm does not meet our notion of certificate optimality.

The notion of treewidth is loose for some queries. For instance, if we replicate each attribute x times for every attribute, then the treewidth is inflated by a factor of x; but by considering all duplicate attributes as one big compound attribute the runtime should only be multiplied by a polynomial in x and there should not be a factor of x in the exponent of the runtime. Furthermore, there is an inherent incompatibility between treewidth and acyclicity: an acyclic query can have very large treewidth, yet is still tractable. A series of papers [2,17,26,29,30] refined the treewidth notion leading to generalized hyper treewidth [29] and ultimately *fractional hypertree width* [36], which allows for a unified view of tractable queries. (An acyclic query, for example, has fractional hypertree width at most 1.)

The fractional hypertree width notion comes out of a recent tight worst-case output size bound in terms of the input relation sizes [7]. An algorithm was presented that runs in time matching the bound, and thus it is worst-case optimal in [38]. Given a tree decomposition of the input query with the minimum fractional edge cover over all bags, we can run this algorithm on each bag, and then Yannakakis algorithm [52] on the resulting bag relations, obtaining a total runtime of $\tilde{O}(N^{w^*}+Z)$, where w^* is the fractional hyper treewidth. The *leap-frog triejoin* algorithm [50] is also worst-case optimal and runs fast in practice; it is based on the idea that we can efficiently skip unmatched intervals. The indices are also built or selected to be consistent with a chosen GAO. We are able to show that neither Leapfrog nor the algorithm from [38] can achieve the certificate guarantees of Minesweeper for β-acyclic queries.

Notions of acyclicity. There are at least five notions of acyclic hypergraphs, four of which were introduced early on in database theory (see e.g, [23]), and at least one new one introduced recently [21]. The five notions are *not* equivalent, but they form a strict hierarchy in the following way:

$$\text{Berge-acyclicity} \subsetneq \gamma\text{-acyclicity} \subsetneq \text{jtdb} \subsetneq \beta\text{-acyclicity} \subsetneq \alpha\text{-acyclicity}$$

Acyclicity or α-acyclicity [11,12,25,28,35] was recognized early on to be a very desirable property of data base schemes; in particular, it allows for a data-complexity optimal algorithm in the worst case [52]. However, an α-acyclic hypergraph may have a sub-hypergraph that is not α-acyclic. For example, if we take *any* hypergraph and add a hyperedge containing all vertices, we obtain an α-acyclic hypergraph. This observation leads to the notion of β-acyclicity: a hypergraph is β-acyclic if and only if every one of its sub-hypergraph is (α-) acyclic [23]. It was shown (relatively) recently [39] that SAT is in P for β-acyclic CNF formulas and is NP-complete for α-acyclic CNF formulas. Extending the result, it was shown that negative conjunctive queries are poly-time solvable if and only if it is β-acyclic [14]. The separation between γ-acyclicity and β-acyclicity showed up in logic [20], while Berge-acyclicity is restrictive and, thus far, is of only historical interest [13].

Graph triangle enumeration. In social network analysis, computing and listing the number of triangles in a graph is at the heart of the clustering coefficients and transitivity ratio. There are four decades of research on computing, estimating, bounding, and lower-bounding the number of triangles and the runtime for such algorithms [5,33,34,46,48,49]. This problem can easily be reduced to a join query of the form $Q = R(A,B) \bowtie S(B,C) \bowtie T(A,C)$.

6.2 Certificates for Intersection

The problem of finding the union and intersection of two sorted arrays using the fewest number of comparisons is well-studied, dated back to at least Hwang and Lin [32] since 1972. In fact, the idea of skipping elements using a binary-search jumping (or leap-frogging) strategy was already present in [32]. Demaine et al. [19] used the leap-frogging strategy for computing the intersection of k sorted sets. They introduced the notion of proofs to capture the intrinsic complexity of such a problem. Then, the idea of gaps and certificate encoding were introduced to show that their algorithm is average case optimal.

DLM's notion of proof inspired another adaptive complexity notion for the set intersection problem called partition certificate by Barbay and Kenyon in [8, 9], where instead of a system of inequalities essentially a set of gaps is used to encode and verify the output. Barbay and Kenyon's idea of a partition certificate is very close to the set of intervals that Minesweeper outputs. In the analysis of Minesweeper for the set intersection problem, we (implicitly) show a correspondence between these partition certificates and DLM's style proofs. In addition to the fact that join queries are more general than set intersection, our notion of certificate is value-oblivious; our certificates do not depend on specific values in the domain, while Barbay-Kenyon's partition certificate does.

It should be noted that these lines of inquiries are not only of theoretical interest. They have yielded good experimental results in text-datamining and text-compression [10].

6.3 Beyond Worst-case Complexity

There is a fairly large body of work on analyzing algorithms with more refined measures than worst-case complexity. (See, e.g., the excellent lectures by Roughgarden on this topic [44].) This section recalls the related works that are most closely related to ours.

A fair amount of work has been done in designing *adaptive* algorithms for sorting [22], where the goal is to design a sorting algorithm whose runtime (or the number of comparisons) matches a notion of difficulty of the instance (e.g. the number of inversions, the length of longest monotone subsequence and so on – the survey [22] lists at least eleven such measures of *disorder*). This line of work is similar to ours in the sense that the goal is to run in time proportional to the difficulty of the input. The major difference is that in these lines of work the main goal is to avoid the logarithmic factor over the linear runtime whereas in our work, our potential gains are of much higher order and we ignore log-factors.

Another related line of work is on self-improving algorithms of Ailon et al. [4], where the goal is to have an algorithm that runs on inputs that are drawn i.i.d. from an *unknown* distribution and in expectation converge to a runtime that is related to the entropy of the distribution. In some sense this setup is similar to online learning while our work requires worst-case per-instance guarantees.

The notion of instance optimal join algorithms was (to the best of our knowledge) first explicitly studied in the work of Fagin et al. [24]. The paper studies the problem of computing the top-k objects, where the ranking is some aggregate of total ordering of objects according to different attributes. (It is assumed that the algorithm can only iterate through the list in sorted order of individual attribute scores.) The results in this paper are stronger than ours since Fagin et al. give $O(1)$-optimality ratio (as opposed to our $O(\log N)$-optimality ratio). On the other hand the results in the Fagin et al. paper are for a problem that is arguably narrower than the class we consider of join algorithms.

The only other paper with provable instance-optimal guarantees that we are aware of is the Afshani et al. results on some geometric problems [3]. Their quantitative results are somewhat incomparable to ours. On the one hand their results get a constant optimality ratio: on the other hand, the optimality ratio is only true for *order oblivious* comparison algorithms (while our results with $O(\log N)$ optimality ratio hold against all comparison-based algorithms).

7. CONCLUSION AND FUTURE WORK

We described the Minesweeper algorithm for processing join queries on data that is stored ordered in data structures modeling traditional relational databases. We showed that Minesweeper can achieve stronger runtime guarantees than previous algorithms; in particular, we believe Minesweeper is the first algorithm to offer beyond worst-case guarantees for joins. Our analysis is based on a notion of certificates, which provide a uniform measure of the difficulty of the problem that is independent of any algorithm. In particular, certificates are able to capture what we argue is a natural class of comparison-based join algorithms.

Our main technical result is that, for β-acyclic queries there is some GAO such that Minesweeper runs in time that is linear in the certificate size. Thus, Minesweeper is optimal (up to an $O(\log N)$ factor) among comparison-based algorithms. Moreover, the class of β-acyclic queries is the boundary of complexity in that we show no algorithm for *β-cyclic* queries runs in time linear in the certificate size. And so, we are able to completely characterize those queries that run in linear time for the certificate and hence are optimal in a strong sense. Conceptually, certificates change the complexity landscape for join processing as the analogous boundary for traditional worst-case complexity are α-acyclic queries, for which we show that there is no polynomial bound in the certificate size (assuming the strong form of the exponential time hypothesis). We then considered how to extend our results using treewidth. We showed that our same Minesweeper algorithm obtains $\tilde{O}(|C|^{w+1}+Z)$ runtime for queries with treewidth w. For the triangle query (with treewidth 2), we presented a modified algorithm that runs in time $\tilde{O}(|C|^{3/2}+Z)$.

Future Work. We are excited by the notion of certificate-based complexity for join algorithms; we see it as contributing to an emerging push beyond worst-case analysis in theoretical computer science. We hope there is future work in several directions for joins and certificate-based complexity.

Indexing and Certificates. The interplay between indexing and certificates may provide fertile ground for further research. For example, the certificate size depends on the order of attributes. In particular, a certificate in one order may be smaller than in another order. We do not yet have a handle on how the certificate-size changes for the same data in different orders. Ideally, one would know the smallest certificate size for any query and process in that order. Moreover, we do not know how to use of multiple access paths (eg. Btrees with different search keys) in either the analysis or the algorithm. These indexes may result in dramatically faster algorithms and new types of query optimization.

Fractional Covers. A second direction is that join processing has seen a slew of powerful techniques based on increasingly sophisticated notions of covers and decompositions for queries. We expect that such covers (hypergraph, fractional hypergraph, etc.) could be used to tighten and improve our bounds. For the triangle query, we have the fractional cover bound, i.e., $\tilde{O}(|C|^{3/2})$. But is this possible for all queries?

8. REFERENCES

[1] S. Abiteboul, R. Hull, and V. Vianu, *Foundations of Databases*, Addison-Wesley, 1995.

[2] I. Adler, G. Gottlob, and M. Grohe, *Hypertree width and related hypergraph invariants*, European J. Combin., 28 (2007).

[3] P. Afshani, J. Barbay, and T. M. Chan, *Instance-optimal geometric algorithms*, in FOCS, 2009, pp. 129–138.

[4] N. Ailon, B. Chazelle, K. L. Clarkson, D. Liu, W. Mulzer, and C. Seshadhri, *Self-improving algorithms*, SIAM J. Comput., 40 (2011), pp. 350–375.

[5] N. Alon, *On the number of subgraphs of prescribed type of graphs with a given number of edges*, Israel J. Math., 38 (1981).

[6] S. Arnborg and A. Proskurowski, *Linear time algorithms for NP-hard problems restricted to partial k-trees*, Discrete Appl. Math., 23 (1989), pp. 11–24.

[7] A. Atserias, M. Grohe, and D. Marx, *Size bounds and query plans for relational joins*, 2008, pp. 739–748.

[8] J. Barbay and C. Kenyon, *Adaptive intersection and t-threshold problems*, in SODA, 2002, pp. 390–399.

[9] ———, *Alternation and redundancy analysis of the intersection problem*, ACM Transactions on Algorithms, 4 (2008).

[10] J. Barbay and A. López-Ortiz, *Efficient algorithms for context query evaluation over a tagged corpus*, in SCCC, M. Arenas and B. Bustos, eds., IEEE Computer Society, 2009, pp. 11–17.

[11] C. Beeri, R. Fagin, D. Maier, A. Mendelzon, J. Ullman, and M. Yannakakis, *Properties of acyclic database schemes*, in STOC, New York, NY, USA, 1981, ACM, pp. 355–362.

[12] C. Beeri, R. Fagin, D. Maier, and M. Yannakakis, *On the desirability of acyclic database schemes*, J. ACM, 30 (1983), pp. 479–513.

[13] C. Berge, *Graphs and Hypergraphs*, Elsevier Science Ltd, 1985.

[14] J. Brault-Baron, *A Negative Conjunctive Query is Easy if and only if it is Beta-Acyclic*, in CSL 12, vol. 16, 2012, pp. 137–151.

[15] A. Brouwer and A. Kolen, *A super-balanced hypergraph has a nest point*, (1980). Tech. Report.

[16] A. K. Chandra and P. M. Merlin, *Optimal implementation of conjunctive queries in relational data bases*, in STOC, 1977.

[17] C. Chekuri and A. Rajaraman, *Conjunctive query containment revisited*, Theor. Comput. Sci., 239 (2000), pp. 211–229.

[18] R. Dechter and J. Pearl, *Tree clustering for constraint networks.*, Artificial Intelligence, 38 (1989), pp. 353–366.

[19] E. D. Demaine, A. López-Ortiz, and J. I. Munro, *Adaptive set intersections, unions, and differences*, in SODA, 2000, pp. 743–752.

[20] D. Duris, *Hypergraph acyclicity and extension preservation theorems*, in LICS, 2008, pp. 418–427.
[21] ———, *Some characterizations of γ and β-acyclicity of hypergraphs.*, Information Processing Letters, 112 (2012).
[22] V. Estivill-Castro and D. Wood, *A survey of adaptive sorting algorithms*, ACM Comput. Surv., 24 (1992), pp. 441–476.
[23] R. Fagin, *Degrees of acyclicity for hypergraphs and relational database schemes*, J. ACM, 30 (1983), pp. 514–550.
[24] R. Fagin, A. Lotem, and M. Naor, *Optimal aggregation algorithms for middleware*, J. Comput. Syst. Sci., 66 (2003), pp. 614–656.
[25] R. Fagin, A. O. Mendelzon, and J. D. Ullman, *A simplied universal relation assumption and its properties*, TODS, 7 (1982).
[26] J. Flum, M. Frick, and M. Grohe, *Query evaluation via tree-decompositions*, J. ACM, 49 (2002), pp. 716–752.
[27] E. C. Freuder, *Complexity of k-tree structured constraint satisfaction problems*, in AAAI, AAAI'90, AAAI Press, 1990, pp. 4–9.
[28] N. Goodman and O. Shmueli, *Tree queries: a simple class of relational queries*, ACM Trans. Database Syst., 7 (1982).
[29] G. Gottlob, N. Leone, and F. Scarcello, *Hypertree decompositions and tractable queries*, J. Comput. Syst. Sci., 64 (2002), pp. 579–627.
[30] G. Gottlob, Z. Miklós, and T. Schwentick, *Generalized hypertree decompositions: Np-hardness and tractable variants*, J. ACM, 56 (2009), pp. 30:1–30:32.
[31] M. Grohe, *The parameterized complexity of database queries*, in PODS, 2001, pp. 82–92.
[32] F. K. Hwang and S. Lin, *A simple algorithm for merging two disjoint linearly ordered sets*, SIAM J. Comput., 1 (1972), pp. 31–39.
[33] A. Itai and M. Rodeh, *Finding a minimum circuit in a graph*, SIAM J. Comput., 7 (1978), pp. 413–423.
[34] M. N. Kolountzakis, G. L. Miller, R. Peng, and C. E. Tsourakakis, *Efficient triangle counting in large graphs via degree-based vertex partitioning*, Internet Mathematics, 8 (2012), pp. 161–185.
[35] D. Maier and J. D. Ullman, *Connections in acyclic hypergraphs: extended abstract*, in PODS, ACM, 1982, pp. 34–39.
[36] D. Marx, *Approximating fractional hypertree width*, ACM Transactions on Algorithms, 6 (2010).
[37] H. Q. Ngo, D. T. Nguyen, C. Ré, and A. Rudra, *Beyond worst-case analysis for joins with minesweeper*, CoRR, abs/1302.0914 (2014).
[38] H. Q. Ngo, E. Porat, C. Ré, and A. Rudra, *Worst-case optimal join algorithms: [extended abstract]*, in PODS, 2012, pp. 37–48.
[39] S. Ordyniak, D. Paulusma, and S. Szeider, *Satisfiability of Acyclic and Almost Acyclic CNF Formulas*, in FSTTCS 2010, vol. 8, 2010.
[40] A. Pagh and R. Pagh, *Scalable computation of acyclic joins*, in PODS, 2006, pp. 225–232.
[41] C. H. Papadimitriou and M. Yannakakis, *On the complexity of database queries*, in PODS, 1997, pp. 12–19.
[42] M. Pătraşcu, *Towards polynomial lower bounds for dynamic problems*, in STOC, 2010, pp. 603–610.
[43] R. Ramakrishnan and J. Gehrke, *Database Management Systems*, McGraw-Hill, Inc., New York, NY, USA, 3 ed., 2003.
[44] T. Roughgarden, *Lecture notes for CS369N "beyond worst-case analysis"*. http://theory.stanford.edu/ tim/f09/f09.html, 2009.
[45] ———, *Problem set #1 (CS369N: Beyond worst-case analysis)*. http://theory.stanford.edu/ tim/f11/hw1.pdf, 2011.
[46] S. Suri and S. Vassilvitskii, *Counting triangles and the curse of the last reducer*, in WWW, 2011, pp. 607–614.
[47] M. Y. Vardi, *The complexity of relational query languages (extended abstract)*, in STOC, 1982, pp. 137–146.
[48] V. Vassilevska and R. Williams, *Finding a maximum weight triangle in $n^{3-\delta}$ time, with applications*, in STOC, 2006, pp. 225–231.
[49] V. Vassilevska and R. Williams, *Finding, minimizing, and counting weighted subgraphs*, in STOC, ACM, 2009, pp. 455–464.
[50] T. L. Veldhuizen, *Leapfrog triejoin: a worst-case optimal join algorithm*, ICDT, (2014). To Appear.
[51] D. E. Willard, *An algorithm for handling many relational calculus queries efficiently*, J. Comput. Syst. Sci., 65 (2002), pp. 295–331.
[52] M. Yannakakis, *Algorithms for acyclic database schemes*, in VLDB, 1981, pp. 82–94.

APPENDIX

A. CERTIFICATES

The full version of this paper contains a handful of examples to illustrate the subtlties of certificates. For completeness, we include the following proofs.

A.1 Proof of Proposition 2.5

Proof. To prove this proposition, it is sufficient to show that the set of comparisons issued by an execution of a comparison-based algorithm is a certificate. To be concrete, we model a comparison-based join algorithm by a decision tree. Every branch in the tree corresponds to a comparison of the form (3). An execution of the join algorithm is a path through this decision tree, reaching a leaf node. At the leaf node, the result $Q(I)$ is labeled. The label at a leaf is the set of tuples the algorithm deems the output of the query applied to database instance I. The collection of comparisons down the path is an argument $\mathcal{A}$ which we want to prove a certificate.

First, note that for every tuple $\mathbf{t} = (t_1, \dots, t_n) \in Q(I)$, the values t_i have to be one of the values $R^I[\mathbf{x}]$ for some $R \in \text{atoms}(Q)$. If this is not the case, then we can perturb the instance I as follows: for every attribute A_i let M_i be the maximum value occurring in any A_i-value overall tuples in the input relations. Now, add $M_i + 1$ to every A_i-value. Then, all A_i-values are shifted the same positive amount. In this new database instance J, all of the comparisons in the argument have the same Boolean value, and hence the output has to be the same. Hence, if there was a value t_i in some output tuple not equal to $R[\mathbf{x}]$, the output would be wrong.

Second, we show that every output tuple can be uniquely identified with a witness, independent of the input instance I. Recall that a collection X of (full) index tuples is said to be a *witness* for $Q(I)$ if X has exactly one full index tuple from each relation $R \in \text{atoms}(Q)$, and all index tuples in X contribute to the same $\mathbf{t} \in Q(I)$.

Fix an input instance I and an output tuple $\mathbf{t} = (t_1, \dots, t_n)$. Note as indicated above that the t_i can now be thought of as a variable $R[\mathbf{x}]$ for some index tuple $\mathbf{x}$ (not necessarily full) and some relation $R \in \text{atoms}(Q)$. By definition of the natural join operator, there has to be a witness X for this output tuple $\mathbf{t}$.

Consider, for example, a full index tuple $\mathbf{y} = (y_1, \dots, y_k)$ from some relation S which is a member of the witness X. Suppose the relation S is on attributes $(A_{s(1)}, A_{s(2)}, \dots, A_{s(k)})$. We show that, for every $j \in [k]$, the argument $\mathcal{A}$ must imply via the transitivity of the equalities in the argument that $S[y_1, \dots, y_j] = t_{s(j)}$.

Suppose to the contrary that this is not the case. Let V be the set of all variables transitively connected to the variable $S[y_1, \dots, y_j]$ by the equality comparisons in $\mathcal{A}$.

Now, construct an instance J from instance I by doing the following

- set $R^J[\mathbf{x}] = 2R^I[\mathbf{x}] + 1$ for all variables $R[\mathbf{x}]$ appearing in the argument $\mathcal{A}$ but $R[\mathbf{x}]$ is not in V.
- set $R^J[\mathbf{x}] = 2R^I[\mathbf{x}] + 2$ for all variables $R[\mathbf{x}]$ appearing in V.

Then, any comparison between a pair of variables both not in V or both in V have the same outcome in both databases I and J. For a pair of variables $R[\mathbf{x}] \in V$ and $T[\mathbf{y}] \notin V$ the comparison cannot be an equality from the definition of V, and hence the $<$ or $>$ relationship still holds true. This is because if a and b are natural numbers, then $a < b$ implies $2a + 2 < 2b + 1$ and $2a + 1 < 2b + 2$. Consequently, the instance J also satisfies all comparisons in the argument $\mathcal{A}$. However, at this point $S[\mathbf{y}]$ can no longer be contributing to $\mathbf{t}$. More importantly, **no** full index tuple from S can contribute to $\mathbf{t}$ in $Q(J)$. Because,

$$\begin{aligned} S^J[y_1,\ldots,y_{j-1},y_j-1] &\leqslant 2S^I[y_1,\ldots,y_{j-1},y_j-1]+1 \\ &\leqslant 2(S^I[y_1,\ldots,y_{j-1},y_j]-1)+1 \\ &= 2S^I[y_1,\ldots,y_{j-1},y_j]-1 \\ &= 2t^I_{s(j)}-1 \\ &< t^J_{s(j)}. \end{aligned}$$

(The first inequality is an equality except when $y_j = 1$.) Similarly,

$$\begin{aligned} S^J[y_1,\ldots,y_{j-1},y_j+1] &\geqslant 2S^I[y_1,\ldots,y_{j-1},y_j+1]+1 \\ &\geqslant 2(S^I[y_1,\ldots,y_{j-1},y_j]+1)+1 \\ &= 2S^I[y_1,\ldots,y_{j-1},y_j]+3 \\ &= 2t^I_{s(j)}+3 \\ &> t^J_{s(j)}. \end{aligned}$$

(Except when $y_j = |S[y_1,\ldots,y_{j-1},*]|$, the first inequality is an equality.) □

A.2 Proof of Proposition 2.6

Proof. We construct a certificate C as follows. For each attribute A_i, let $v_1 < v_2 < \cdots < v_p$ denote the set of *all* possible A_i-values present in any relations from atoms(Q) which has A_i as an attribute. More concretely,

$$\{v_1,v_2,\ldots,v_p\} := \bigcup_{R\in\text{atoms}(Q),A_i\in\bar{A}(R)} \pi_{A_i}(R).$$

For each $k \in [p]$, let T_k denote the set of all tuples from relations containing A_i such that the tuple's A_i-value is v_k. Note that the tuples in T_k can come from the same or different relations in atoms(Q). Next, add to C at most $|T_k| - 1$ equalities connecting all tuples in T_k asserting that their A_i-values are equal. (The reason we may not need exactly $|T_k| - 1$ equalities is because there might be many tuples from the same relation R that share the A_i-value, and A_i comes earlier than other attributes of R in the total attribute order.)

Then, for each $k \in [p]$, pick an arbitrary tuple $\mathbf{t}_k \in T_k$ and add $p-1$ inequalities stating that $\mathbf{t}_1.A_i < \mathbf{t}_2.A_i < \cdots < \mathbf{t}_p.A_i$. (Depending on which relation $\mathbf{t}_k$ comes from, the actual syntax for $\mathbf{t}_k.A_i$ is used correspondingly. For example, if $\mathbf{t}_k$ is from the relation $R[A_j,A_i,A_\ell]$, then $\mathbf{t}_k.A_i$ is actually $R[x_j,x_i]$.)

Overall, for each A_i the total number of comparisons we added is at most the number of tuples that has A_i as an attribute. Hence, there are at most rN comparisons added to the certificate C, and they represent all the possible relationships we know about the data. The set of comparisons is thus a certificate for this instance. □

B. RUNNING TIME ANALYSIS

In this paper, we use the following notion to benchmark the runtime of join algorithms.

Definition B.1. We say a join algorithm $\mathcal{A}$ for a join query Q to be instance optimal for Q with optimality ratio α if the following holds. For every instance for Q, the runtime of the algorithm is bounded by $O_{|Q|}(\alpha \cdot |C|)$, where $O_{|Q|}(\cdot)$ ignores the dependence on the query size and C be the certificate of the smallest size for the given input instance. We allow α to depend on the input size N. Finally, we refer to an instance optimal algorithm for Q with optimality ratio $O(\log N)$ simply as near instance optimal for Q.

Technically we should be call such algorithms *near instance optimal* for certificate-based complexity but for the sake of brevity we drop the qualification. Further, we use the term near instance optimal to mirror the usage of the term near linear to denote runtimes of $O(N \log N)$.

Next, we briefly justify our definition above. First note that we are using the size of the optimal certificate as a benchmark to quantify the performance of join algorithms. We have already justified this as a natural benchmark to measure the performance of join algorithms in Section 2.2. In particular, recall that Proposition 2.5 says that $|C|$ is a valid lower bound on the number of comparisons made by any comparison-based algorithm that "computes" the join Q. Even though this choice makes us compare performance of algorithms in two different models (the RAM model for the runtime and the comparison model for certificates), this is a natural choice that has been made many times in the algorithms literature: most notably, the claim that algorithms to sort n numbers that run in $O(n \log n)$ time are optimal in the comparison model. (This has also been done recently in other works [3,4].)

Second, the choice to ignore the dependence on the query size is standard in database literature. In particular, in this work we focus on the data complexity of our join algorithms.

Perhaps the more non-standard choice is to call an algorithm with optimality ratio $O(\log N)$ to be (near) instance optimal. We made this choice because this is *unavoidable* for comparison-based algorithm. In particular, there exists a query Q so that every (deterministic) comparison-based join algorithm for Q needs to make $\Omega(\log N \cdot |C|)$ many comparisons on *some* input instance. This follows from the easy-to-verify fact for the selection problem (given N numbers $a_1,\ldots,a_N$ in sorted order, check whether a given value v is one of them), every comparison-based algorithm needs to make $\Omega(\log N)$ many comparisons while every instance can be "certified" with constant many comparisons [45, Problem 1(a)]. For the sake of completeness we sketch the argument below.

Consider the query $Q = R(A) \bowtie S(A)$. Now consider the instance where $R(A) = \{a_1,\ldots,a_N\}$ and $S(A) = \{v\}$. Note that for this instance, we have $|C| \leqslant O(1)$ (and that the output of Q is empty if and only if v does not belong to $\{a_1,\ldots,a_N\}$). However, given any sequence of $\lfloor \log N \rfloor - 1$ comparisons between (the only) element of S and some element of R, there always exists two instantiation of $a_1,\ldots,a_N$ and v such that in one case the output of Q is empty and is non-empty in the other case. (Basically, the adversary will always answer the comparison query in a manner that forces v to be in the larger half of the "unexplored" numbers.)

Finally, we remark that even though this $\Omega(\log N)$ lower bound on the optimality ratio is stated for the specific join query Q above, it can be easily extended to any join query Q' where at least two relations share an attribute (by "embedding" the above simple set intersection query Q into Q').

Independent Range Sampling

Xiaocheng Hu Miao Qiao Yufei Tao

Department of Computer Science and Engineering
Chinese University of Hong Kong
New Territories, Hong Kong
{xchu, mqiao, taoyf}@cse.cuhk.edu.hk

ABSTRACT

This paper studies the *independent range sampling* problem. The input is a set P of n points in $\mathbb{R}$. Given an interval $q = [x, y]$ and an integer $t \geq 1$, a query returns t elements uniformly sampled (with/without replacement) from $P \cap q$. The sampling result must be *independent* from those returned by the previous queries. The objective is to store P in a structure for answering all queries efficiently.

If P fits in memory, the problem is interesting when P is dynamic (i.e., allowing insertions and deletions). The state of the art is a structure of $O(n)$ space that answers a query in $O(t \log n)$ time, and supports an update in $O(\log n)$ time. We describe a new structure of $O(n)$ space that answers a query in $O(\log n + t)$ expected time, and supports an update in $O(\log n)$ time.

If P does not fit in memory, the problem is challenging even when P is static. The best known structure incurs $O(\log_B n + t)$ I/Os per query, where B is the block size. We develop a new structure of $O(n/B)$ space that answers a query in $O(\log^\star(n/B) + \log_B n + (t/B) \log_{M/B}(n/B))$ amortized expected I/Os, where M is the memory size, and $\log^\star(n/B)$ is the number of iterative $\log_2(.)$ operations we need to perform on n/B before going below a constant. We also give a lower bound argument showing that this is nearly optimal—in particular, the multiplicative term $\log_{M/B}(n/B)$ is necessary.

Categories and Subject Descriptors

F.2.2 [**Analysis of algorithms and problem complexity**]: Nonnumerical Algorithms and Problems—*computations on discrete structures*; H.3.1 [**Information storage and retrieval**]: Content analysis and indexing—*indexing methods*

Keywords

Independent range sampling, range reporting, lower bound

PODS'14, June 22–27, 2014, Snowbird, UT, USA.

http://dx.doi.org/10.1145/2594538.2594545.

1. INTRODUCTION

A *reporting* query, in general, retrieves from a dataset all the elements satisfying a condition. In the current big data era, such a query easily turns into a "big query", namely, one whose result contains a huge number of elements. In this case, even the simple task of enumerating all these elements can prove to be problematic. For example, assuming that a hard disk can write 4k bytes in one millisecond, it takes an hour to write a query result of 4 billion integers. Note that a query result of 4 billion elements is actually rather small on a tera-byte scale dataset, while a tera bytes of data could hardly be counted as "big" by today's standard.

This phenomenon naturally brings back the notion of *query sampling*, a classic concept that was introduced to the database community several decades ago. The goal of query sampling is to return, instead of an entire query result, only a random sample set of the elements therein. The usefulness of such a sample set has long been recognized even in the non-big-data days (see an excellent survey in [12]). The unprecedented gigantic data volume we are facing nowadays has only strengthened the importance of query sampling. Particularly, this is an effective technique in dealing with the big-query issue mentioned earlier in many scenarios where acquiring a query result in its entirety is not compulsory.

This work aims to endow query sampling with *independence*; namely, the samples returned by each query should be independent from the samples returned by the previous queries. In particular, we investigate how to achieve this purpose on *range reporting*, as it is a very fundamental query in the database and data structure fields. Formally, the problem we study can be stated as follows:

PROBLEM 1 (**Independent Range Sampling (IRS)**). *Let P be a set of n points in $\mathbb{R}$. Given an interval $q = [x, y]$ in $\mathbb{R}$ and an integer $t \geq 1$, we define two types of queries:*

- *A* **with replacement (WR) query** *returns a sequence of t points, each of which is taken uniformly at random from $P(q) = P \cap q$.*
- *Requiring $t \leq |P(q)|$, a* **without replacement (WoR) query** *returns a subset R of $P(q)$ with $|R| = t$, which is taken uniformly at random from all the size-t subsets of $P(q)$. The query may output the elements of R in an arbitrary order.*

In both cases, the output of the query must be independent from the outputs of all previous queries.

Guaranteeing independence among the sampling results of all queries ensures a strong sense of fairness: the elements satisfying a query predicate always have the same chance of being reported (regardless of the samples returned previously), as is a desirable feature in battling the "big-query issue". Furthermore, the independence requirement also offers convenience in statistical analysis and algorithm design. In particular, it allows one to issue the *same* query multiple times to fetch different samples. This is especially useful when one attempts to test a property by sampling, but is willing to accept only a small failure probability of drawing a wrong conclusion. The independence guarantees that the failure probability decreases exponentially with the number of times the query is repeated.

Computation Models. We study IRS in both the scenarios where the input set P fits or does not fit in memory, respectively. In the former scenario, we discuss algorithms on a *random access machine* (RAM), where it takes constant time to perform a comparison, a + operation, and to access a memory location. For randomized algorithms, we make the standard assumption that it takes constant time to generate a random integer in $[0, 2^w - 1]$, where w is the length of a word.

In the latter scenario (where P does not fit in memory), we adhere to the standard *external memory* (EM) model [2], where a machine has M words of memory and a disk that has been formatted into blocks of size B words. It always holds that $M \geq 2B$. An I/O either reads a block of data into memory, or writes B words in memory to a disk block. The cost of an algorithm is the number of I/Os performed (CPU time is free), while the space of a structure is the number of disk blocks occupied.

Finally, we define $\log^{(0)} x = x$, and $\log^{(i+1)} x = \log_2(\log^{(i)} x)$ for any integer $i \geq 0$. Define $\log^* x$ to be the smallest i such that $\log^{(i)} x \leq 2$.

Existing Results. Next we review the literature on IRS, assuming first the WR semantics. In internal memory, the problem is trivial when P is static. Specifically, we can simply store the points of P in ascending order using an array A. Given a query with parameters $q = [x, y]$ and t, we can first perform binary search to identify the subsequence in A that consists of the elements covered by q. Then, we can simply sample from the subsequence by generating t random ranks and accessing t elements. The total query cost is $O(\log n + t)$.

The problem becomes much more interesting when P is dynamic, namely, it admits insertions and deletions of elements. This problem was first studied more than two decades ago. The best solution to this date uses $O(n)$ space, answers a query in $O(t \log n)$ time, and supports an update in $O(\log n)$ time (see [12] and the references therein). This can be achieved by creating a "rank structure" on P that allows us to fetch the i-th (for any $i \in [1, n]$) largest element of P in $O(\log n)$ time. After this, we can then simulate the static algorithm described earlier by spending $O(\log n)$ time, instead of $O(1)$, fetching each sample.

In external memory, the IRS problem is challenging even when P is static. Note that accessing t random positions from a disk-resident array is expensive: it takes $O(t)$ I/Os when the array size is large. As a result, the RAM algorithm we discussed earlier incurs $O(\log_B n + t)$ I/Os in external memory, assuming a B-tree on the array A. This is nearly a factor of B higher than the $\Theta(t/B)$ cost needed to write t samples. Going back to the baseline solution, one can always retrieve the entire $P(q) = P \cap q$, and then sample t elements from $P(q)$ using a standard algorithm [7, 15]. Assuming $t \leq k$, the query cost is $O(\log_B n + (k/B) \log_{M/B}(k/B))$, where $k = |P(q)|$. This cost is not necessarily better than $O(\log_B n + t)$ because t can be arbitrarily smaller than k.

We are not aware of work that tackles specifically WoR queries. However, we will see later that a WoR query with parameters q, t can be answered by a constant number (in expectation) of WR queries having parameters $q, 2t$. Hence, the aforementioned performance guarantees also hold on WoR queries in expectation.

The above represent the current state of the art on the IRS problem. It is worth mentioning that if one does not require independence of the sampling results of different queries, query sampling can be supported as follows. For each $i = 0, 1, ..., \lceil \log n \rceil$, maintain a set P_i by independently including each element of P with probability $1/2^i$. Given a query with interval $q = [x, y]$, $P_i \cap q$ serves as a sample set where each element in $P(q)$ is taken with probability $1/2^i$. However, by issuing the same query again, one always gets back the same samples, thus losing the benefits of IRS mentioned before.

Also somewhat relevant is the recent work of Wei and Yi [16], in which they studied how to return various statistical summaries (e.g., quantiles) on the result of range reporting. They did not address the problem of query sampling, let alone how to enforce the independence requirement. At a high level, IRS may be loosely classified as a form of *online aggregation* [8], because most research on this topic has been devoted to the maintenance of a random sample set of a long-running query (typically, aggregation from a series of joins); see [10] and the references therein. As far as IRS is concerned, we are not aware of any work along this line that guarantees better performance than the solutions surveyed previously.

It is worth mentioning that sampling algorithms have been studied extensively in various contexts (for entry points into the literature, see [1, 4, 5, 6, 7, 11, 14, 15]). These algorithms aim at efficiently producing sample sets for different purposes over a static or evolving dataset. Our focus, on the other hand, is to design data structures for sampling the results of arbitrary range queries.

Our Results. We present several new results on the IRS problem. In Section 2, we give a dynamic RAM structure of $O(n)$ space that answers a WR or WoR query in $O(\log n + t)$ expected time, and supports an update in $O(\log n)$ time. All the expectations in this paper depend only on the random choices made by our algorithms.

In EM, we first establish in Section 3 a lower bound showing that one cannot hope to achieve a query cost such as $O(\log_B n + t/B)$ using a structure of reasonable space even when P is static. Specifically, we prove that, whenever $\log_{M/B}(n/B) \leq B$, any structure occupying $n^{O(1)}$ blocks must perform $\Omega((t/B) \log_{M/B}(n/B))$ expected I/Os answering a WR query with parameters $q = (-\infty, \infty)$ and $t \in [B, n]$. In fact, this is true even if query cost is *amortized*. That is, there is a sequence of queries such that every structure of $n^{O(1)}$ space must incur $\Omega(m \cdot (t/B) \log_{M/B}(n/B))$ I/Os in expectation processing the entire sequence, where m is the number of queries in the sequence. A similar lower bound also holds on WoR queries, except for $t \in [B, n^{1-\epsilon}]$, where $\epsilon > 0$ is an arbitrarily small constant.

As a second step, in Section 4 we develop a structure that uses $O(n/B)$ space, and answers a WR or WoR query in $O(\log^\star(n/B) + \log_B n + (t/B)\log_{M/B}(n/B))$ amortized I/Os in expectation. Our lower bound shows that the query cost is optimal within only an additive factor of $O(\log^\star(n/B) + \log_B n)$.

Interestingly, our RAM and EM structures are based on different technical ideas. In RAM, our structure essentially stores the elements of the input set P in a number of arrays of various sizes. This idea, however, does not work in EM due to the expensive I/O overhead of sampling directly from an array. Instead, we develop an approach that precomputes independent samples even before a query comes. Those samples are stored inside our data structure, which is modified every time a query is answered so that we can ensure there are always enough samples for the next query. We show how to balance the work of sample computation among the queries so that the amortized query cost remains low.

The concept of *independent query sampling* can be integrated with any reporting queries (e.g., multidimensional range reporting, stabbing queries on intervals, half-plane reporting, etc.), and defines a new variant for every individual problem. All these variants are expected to play increasingly crucial roles in countering the big-query issue. The techniques developed in this paper pave the foundation for further studies in this line of research.

2. RAM STRUCTURES

Our discussion will assume WR queries by default because as we will see there is an efficient reduction from WoR to WR. Recall that a query specifies two parameters: a range $q = [x, y]$ and the number t of samples. We say that the query is *one-sided* if $x = -\infty$ or $y = \infty$; otherwise, the query is *two-sided*. Next, we will first describe a structure for one-sided queries, before attending to two-sided ones.

2.1 A One-Sided Structure

Structure. We build a *weight-balanced B-tree* (WBB-tree) [3] on the input set P with leaf capacity $b = 4$ and branching parameter $f = 8$. In general, a WBB-tree parameterized by b and f is a B-tree where

- data elements are stored in the leaves. We label the leaf level as level 0; if a node is at level i, then its parent is at level $i + 1$.
- a non-root node u at the i-th level has between $bf^i/4$ and bf^i elements stored in its subtree. We denote by $P(u)$ the set of those elements. This property implies that an internal node has between $f/4$ and $4f$ child nodes.

Each node u is naturally associated with an interval $I(u)$ defined as follows. If u is a leaf, then $I(u) = (e', e]$ where e (or e', resp.) is the largest element stored in u (or the leaf preceding u, resp.); specially, if no leaf precedes u, then $e' = -\infty$. If u is an internal node, then $I(u)$ unions the intervals of all the child nodes of u.

Let z_ℓ be the leftmost leaf (i.e., the leaf containing the smallest element of P). Denote by Π_ℓ the path from the root to z_ℓ. For every node u on Π_ℓ, store all the elements of $P(u)$ in an array $A(u)$. Note that the element ordering in $A(u)$ is arbitrary. The total space of all arrays is $O(n)$, noticing that the arrays' sizes shrink geometrically as we descend Π_ℓ.

Query. A one-sided query with parameters $q = (-\infty, y]$ and t is answered as follows. We first identify the lowest node u on Π_ℓ such that $I(u)$ fully covers q. If u is a leaf, we obtain the entire $P(q) = P \cap q$ from u in constant time, after which the samples can be obtained trivially in $O(t)$ time. If u is an internal node, we obtain a sequence $\mathcal{R}$ by repeating the next step until the length of $\mathcal{R}$ is t: select uniformly at random an element e from $A(u)$, and append e to $\mathcal{R}$ if e is covered by q. We return $\mathcal{R}$ as the query's output. Note that the $\mathcal{R}$ computed this way is independent from all the past queries.

We argue that the above algorithm runs in $O(\log\log n + t)$ expected time, focusing on the case where u is not a leaf. Let $k = |P(q)|$. Node u can be found in $O(\log\log n)$ time by creating a binary search tree on the intervals of the nodes on Π_ℓ. It is easy to see that the size of $A(u)$ is at least k but at most ck for some constant $c \geq 1$. Hence, a random sample e from $A(u)$ has at least $1/c$ probability of falling in q. This implies that we expect to sample no more than $ct = O(t)$ times before filling up $\mathcal{R}$.

Update. Recall the well-known fact that an array can be maintained in $O(1)$ time per insertion and deletion[1]—this is true even if the array's size needs to grow or shrink—provided that the element ordering in the array does not matter. The key to updating our structure lies in modifying the secondary arrays along Π_ℓ. Whenever we insert/delete an element e in the subtree of a node u on Π_ℓ, e must be inserted/deleted in $A(u)$ as well. Insertion is easy: simply append e to $A(u)$. To delete e, we first locate e in $A(u)$, swap it with the last element of $A(u)$, and then shrink the size of $A(u)$ by 1. The problem, however, is how to find the location of e; although hashing does this trivially, the update time becomes $O(\log n)$ expected.

The update time can be made worst case by slightly augmenting our structure. For each element $e \in P$, we maintain a linked list of all its positions in the secondary arrays. This linked list is updated in constant time whenever a position changes (this requires some proper bookkeeping, e.g., pointers between a position in an array and its record in a linked list). In this way, when e is deleted, we can find all its array positions in $O(\log n)$ time. Taking care of other standard details of node balancing (see [3]), we have arrived at:

THEOREM 1. *For the IRS problem, there is a RAM structure of $O(n)$ space that can answer a one-sided WR query in $O(\log\log n + t)$ expected time, and can be updated in $O(\log n)$ worst-case time per insertion and deletion.*

2.2 A 2-Sided Structure of $O(n \log n)$ Space

By applying standard range-tree ideas to the one-sided structure in Theorem 1, we obtain a structure for two-sided queries with space $O(n \log n)$ and query time $O(\log n + t)$ expected. However, it takes $O(\log^2 n)$ time to update the structure. Next, we give an alternative structure with improved update cost.

[1]A deletion needs to specify where the target element is in the array.

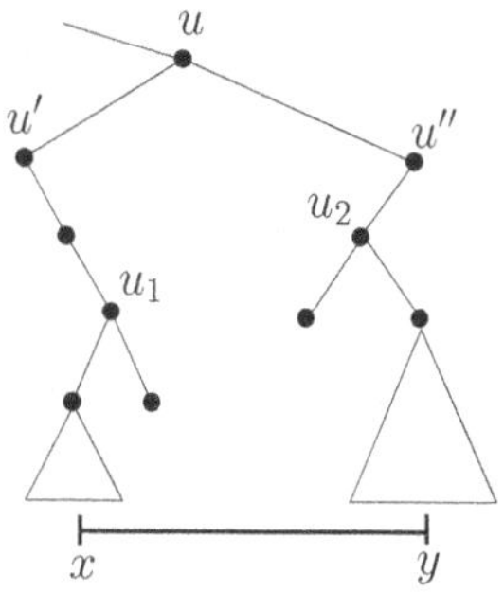

Figure 1: Answering a query at two nodes

Structure. Again, we build a WBB-tree T on the input set P with leaf capacity $b = 4$ and branching parameter $f = 8$. At each node u in the tree, we keep a count equal to $|P(u)|$, i.e., the number of elements in its subtree. We also associate u with an array $A(u)$ that stores all the elements of $P(u)$; the ordering in $A(u)$ does not matter. The overall space consumption is clearly $O(n \log n)$.

Query. We will see how to use the structure to answer a query with parameters $q = [x, y]$ and t. Let $k = |P(q)|$. Since we aim at query time of $\Omega(\log n)$, it suffices to consider only $k > 0$ (one can check whether $k > 0$ easily with a separate "range count" structure). The crucial step is to find at most two nodes u_1, u_2 satisfying two conditions:

c1 $I(u_1)$ and $I(u_2)$ are disjoint, and their union covers q;

c2 $|P(u_1)| + |P(u_2)| = O(k)$.

These nodes can be found as follows. First, identify the lowest node u in T such that $I(u)$ covers q. If u is a leaf node, setting $u_1 = u$ and $u_2 = nil$ satisfies both conditions.

Now, suppose that u is an internal node. If q spans the interval $I(u')$ of at least one child u' of u, then once again setting $u_1 = u$ and $u_2 = nil$ satisfies both conditions. Now, consider that q does not span the interval of any child of u. In this case, x and y must fall in the intervals of two consecutive child nodes u', u'' of u, respectively. Define $q_1 = q \cap I(u')$ and $q_2 = q \cap I(u'')$. We decide u_1 (u_2, resp.) as the lowest node in the subtree of u' (u'', resp.) whose interval covers q_1 (q_2, resp.); see Figure 1 for an illustration. The lemma below shows that our choice is correct.

LEMMA 1. *The u_1 and u_2 we decided satisfy conditions* **c1** *and* **c2**.

PROOF. We will focus on the scenario where u is an internal node. Let k_1 (k_2, resp.) be the number of elements in the subtree of u' (u'', resp.) covered by q. Clearly, $k = k_1 + k_2$. It suffices to show that $|P(u_1)| = O(k_1)$ and $|P(u_2)| = O(k_2)$. We will prove only the former due to symmetry. In fact, if u_1 is a leaf, then both k_1 and $|P(u_1)|$ are $O(1)$. Otherwise, q definitely spans the interval of a child node, say $\hat{u}$, of u_1. Hence, $|P(u_1)| = O(|P(\hat{u})|) = O(k_1)$. □

Let us continue the description of the query algorithm, given that u_1 and u_2 are already found. We conceptually append $A(u_1)$ to $A(u_2)$ to obtain a concatenated array A. Then, we repetitively perform the following step until an initially empty sequence $\mathcal{R}$ has length t: sample uniformly at random an element e from A, and append e to $\mathcal{R}$ if it lies in q. Note that since we know both $|A(u_1)|$ and $|A(u_2)|$, each sample can be obtained in constant time. Since A has size $O(k)$ and at least k elements covered by q, we expect to sample $O(t)$ elements before filling up $\mathcal{R}$. The total query cost is therefore $O(\log n + t)$ expected.

Update. The key to updating our structure is to modify the secondary arrays, as can be done using the ideas explained in Section 2.1 for updating our one-sided structure. The overall update time is $O(\log n)$.

LEMMA 2. *For the IRS problem, there is a RAM structure of $O(n \log n)$ space that can answer a two-sided WR query in $O(\log n + t)$ expected time, and can be updated in $O(\log n)$ worst-case time per insertion and deletion.*

2.3 A 2-Sided Structure of $O(n)$ Space

In this subsection, we improve the space of our two-sided structure to linear using a two-level sampling idea.

Structure. Let s be an integer between $\log_2 n - 1$ and $\log_2 n + 1$. We divide the domain $\mathbb{R}$ into a set $\mathcal{I}$ of $g = \Theta(n/\log n)$ disjoint intervals $\mathcal{I}_1, ..., \mathcal{I}_g$ such that each $\mathcal{I}_i$ ($1 \leq i \leq g$) covers between $s/2$ and s points of P. Define $\mathcal{C}_i = \mathcal{I}_i \cap P$, and call it a *chunk*. Store the points of each $\mathcal{C}_i$ in an array (i.e., one array per chunk).

We build a structure T of Lemma 2 on $\{\mathcal{I}_1, ..., \mathcal{I}_g\}$. T allows us to sample at the chunk level, when given a query range $q^* = [x^*, y^*]$ aligned with the intervals' endpoints (in other words, q^* equals the union of several consecutive intervals in $\mathcal{I}$). More specifically, given a query with such a range q^* and parameter t, we can use T to obtain a sequence S of t chunk ids, each of which is taken uniformly at random from the ids of the chunks whose intervals are covered by q^*. We slightly augment T such that whenever a chunk id i is returned in S, the chunk size $|\mathcal{C}_i|$ is always returned along with it. The space of T is $O(g \log g) = O(n)$.

We will also need a rank structure on P, which (as explained in Section 1) allows us to obtain t samples from any query range in $O(t \log n)$ time.

Query. We answer a query with parameters $q = [x, y]$ and t as follows. First, in $O(\log n)$ time, we can identify the intervals $\mathcal{I}_i$ and $\mathcal{I}_{i'}$ that contain x and y, respectively. If $i = i'$, we answer the query bruteforce by reading all the $O(\log n)$ points in $\mathcal{C}_i$.

If $i \neq i'$, we break q into three disjoint intervals $q_1 = [x, x^*]$, $q_2 = [x^*, y^*]$, and $q_3 = [y^*, y]$, where x^* (y^*, resp.) is the right (left, resp.) endpoint of $\mathcal{I}_i$ ($\mathcal{I}_{i'}$, resp.). In $O(\log n)$ time (using the rank structure on P), we can obtain the number of data points in the three intervals: $k_1 = |q_1 \cap P|$, $k_2 = |q_2 \cap P|$, and $k_3 = |q_3 \cap P|$. Let $k = k_1 + k_2 + k_3$.

We now determine the numbers t_1, t_2, t_3 of samples to take from q_1, q_2, and q_3, respectively. To do so, generate t random integers in $[1, k]$; t_1 equals how many of those integers fall in $[1, k_1]$, t_2 equals how many in $[k_1 + 1, k_1 + k_2]$, and t_3 how many in $[k_1 + k_2 + 1, k]$. We now proceed to take the desired number of samples from each interval (we will clarify how to do so shortly). Finally, we randomly permute the t samples in $O(t)$ time, and return the resulting permutation.

Sampling t_1 and t_3 elements from q_1 and q_3 respectively can be easily done in $O(\log n)$ time. Next, we concentrate on taking t_2 samples from q_2. If $t_2 \leq 6 \ln 2$, we simply obtain t_2 samples from the rank structure in $O(t_2 \log n) = O(\log n)$

time. For $t_2 > 6 \ln 2$, we first utilize T to obtain a sequence S of $4t_2$ chunk ids for the range $q_2 = [x^*, y^*]$. We then generate a sequence $\mathcal{R}$ of samples as follows. Take the next id j from S. Toss a coin with head probability $|C_j|/s$.[2] If the coin tails, do nothing; otherwise, append to $\mathcal{R}$ a point selected uniformly at random from C_j. The algorithm finishes as soon as $\mathcal{R}$ has collected t_2 samples. It is possible, however, that the length of $\mathcal{R}$ is still less than t_2 even after having processed all the $4t_2$ ids in S. In this case, we restart the *whole* query algorithm from scratch.

We argue that the expected cost of the algorithm is $O(\log n + t)$. As $|C_j|/s \geq 1/2$ for any j, the coin we toss in processing S heads at least $4t_2/2 = 2t_2$ times in expectation. A simple application of Chernoff bounds shows that the probability it heads less than t_2 times is at most $1/2$ when $t_2 > 6 \ln 2$. This means that the algorithm terminates with probability at least $1/2$. Each time the algorithm is repeated, its cost is bounded by $O(\log n + t)$ (regardless of whether another round is needed). Therefore, overall, the expected running time is $O(\log n + t)$.

Update. T is updated whenever a chunk (either its interval or the number of points therein) changes. This can be done in $O(\log n)$ time per insertion/deletion of a point in P. A chunk overflow (i.e., size over s) or underflow (below $s/2$) can be treated in $O(s)$ time by a chunk split or merge, respectively. Standard analysis shows that each update bears only $O(1)$ time amortized. Finally, to make sure s is between $\log_2 n - 1$ and $\log_2 n + 1$, we rebuild the whole structure whenever n has doubled or halved, and set $s = \log_2 n$. Overall, the amortized update cost is $O(\log n)$. The amortization can be removed by standard techniques [13]. We have now established:

THEOREM 2. *For the IRS problem, there is a RAM structure of $O(n)$ space that can answer a two-sided WR query in $O(\log n + t)$ expected time, and can be updated in $O(\log n)$ worst-case time per insertion and deletion.*

2.4 Reduction from WoR to WR

We will need the fact below (see appendix for a proof):

LEMMA 3. *Let S be a set of k elements. Consider taking $2s$ samples uniformly at random from S with replacement, where $s \leq k/(3e)$. The probability that we get at least s distinct samples is at least $1/2$.*

A two-sided WoR query with parameters q, t on dataset P can be answered using a structure of Theorem 2 as follows. First, check whether $t \geq k/(3e)$ where $k = |P(q)|$ can be obtained in $O(\log n)$ time. If so, we run a sampling WoR algorithm (e.g., [15]) to take t samples from $P(q)$ directly, which requires $O(\log n + k) = O(\log n + t)$ time. Otherwise, we run a WR query with parameters $q, 2t$ to obtain a sequence $\mathcal{R}$ of samples in $O(\log n + t)$ expected time. If $\mathcal{R}$ has at least t distinct samples (which can be checked in $O(t)$ expected time using hashing), we collect all these samples into a set S, and sample WoR t elements from S; the total running time in this case is $O(\log n + t)$. On the other hand, if $\mathcal{R}$ has less than t distinct elements, we repeat the above by issuing another WR query with parameters $q, 2t$.

[2]This can be done without division: generate a random integer in $[1, s]$ and check if it is smaller than or equal to $|C_j|$.

By Lemma 3, a repeat is necessary with probability at most $1/2$. Therefore, overall the expected query time remains $O(\log n + t)$.

Similarly, a one-sided WoR query can be answered using a structure of Theorem 1 in $O(\log \log n + t)$ expected time.

3. A TIGHT I/O LOWER BOUND

Having gained some experience about IRS, we now turn our attention to external memory, where the problem is much more challenging. The first question we will answer is: would it be possible to achieve a query cost such as $O(\log_B n + t/B)$ with a small-space structure, especially given the RAM result in Theorem 2?

For this purpose, it suffices to look at a special instance of the IRS problem where all queries' search intervals are fixed to $q = (-\infty, \infty)$. Formally, our objective is to preprocess a set S of n elements such that all queries of the following form can be answered efficiently: given an integer $t \geq 1$, randomly sample t elements WR or WoR from S. We refer to this special instance as the *set sampling problem.*

We will prove a query cost lower bound under the *indivisibility assumption* that every element in S must always be stored as an atom. This assumption was first introduced to prove a sorting lower bound in EM [2] (which still remains the best today), and is a key assumption in the *indexability model* [9] which encapsulates almost all the existing lower bounds on EM data structures. Specifically, our result is:

THEOREM 3. *Let c be an arbitrary constant. For the set sampling problem, when $n \geq B^2$, every structure occupying at most n^c blocks must incur*

$$\Omega\left(\min\left\{t, \frac{t}{B}\log_{M/B}\frac{n}{B}\right\}\right)$$

amortized I/Os in expectation answering:

- *a WR query with parameter $t \in [B, n]$.*
- *a WoR query with parameter $t \in [B, n^{1-\epsilon}]$, where $\epsilon > 0$ is an arbitrarily small constant.*

Notice that the lower bound is on amortized query cost (and hence, stronger than a worst-case lower bound). In other words, a structure is allowed to balance the work among queries in an attempt to keep the cost low on average, but the lower bound says that the average cost must still be high. Furthermore, note that the bound holds rules out any structure of $O(n^c)$ space on the IRS problem with query cost $O(\log_B n + t/B)$—such a structure can be used to answer a set sampling query with $t \geq B \log_B n$ in $O(t/B)$ I/Os.

Also notice that the ranges of t are different for WR and WoR queries in Theorem 3. In fact, the two types of queries are indeed separated in terms of hardness for t close to n. This is most intuitive when $t = n$, in which case a (set sampling) WoR query can simply return the entire dataset S in $O(n/B)$ I/Os, whereas a WR query must (essentially) produce a random permutation of S, and incur $\Omega((n/B)\log_{M/B}(n/B))$ I/Os as shown in the theorem.

As a second step, we will match the lower bound with a set sampling structure:

THEOREM 4. *For the set sampling problem, there is a structure of $O(n/B)$ space that answers a WR or WoR query in $O(1 + (t/B)\log_{M/B}(n/B))$ amortized I/Os.*

It is worth mentioning that one can always answer a WR query in $O(t)$ I/Os by sampling directly from an array (i.e., just apply a RAM algorithm by ignoring blocking), and answer a WoR query in $O(t)$ expected I/Os by resorting to the reduction in Section 2.4. Thus, both cases of the query cost in Theorem 3 are tight. The rest of the section gives our proofs for the two theorems.

3.1 Proof of Theorem 3

WoR Lower Bound for $t \in [B, n^{1-\epsilon}]$. We will first prove the WoR branch of Theorem 3. At a high level, our proof works as follows. We issue m queries of the same parameter t for some large m to be chosen later, and ask them to write their retrieved sample sets sequentially in the disk. At the end, we get a *final sequence* of m sample sets[3]. Because of queries' independence, the number of possible final sequences is huge. On the other hand, if the amortized query cost has to be low, then the query algorithm can perform only a small number of I/Os in total, such that it will not be able to produce that many possible final sequences. This puts a constraint on how low the query cost can possibly be. The complication, however, is that the data structure is randomized (no deterministic structure can solve the problem). To make the above idea work, we need to argue that the structure must nonetheless still produce numerous final sequences from at least one "initial state".

We will regard each block as a set of elements (i.e., ignoring the ordering of the elements therein). Denote by Σ the set of all possible final sequences. It is easy to see that $|\Sigma| = \binom{n}{t}^m$. We define an *initial state* of a randomized data structure as the sequence of non-empty blocks in memory followed by those in the disk at the time the structure answers the first query. Let Π be the set of all possible initial states. Since an initial state has at most $M/B + n^c < n^{c+1}$ blocks, we know that $|\Pi| < \binom{n}{B}^{n^{c+1}}$.

Given a final sequence $\sigma \in \Sigma$ and an initial state $\pi \in \Pi$, define $cost(\sigma, \pi)$ as the minimum I/O cost of all possible algorithms (of an indivisible structure) to produce σ, when the memory and disk currently have the contents π. For each σ, define its best initial state—denoted as π_σ—as the π with the smallest $cost(\sigma, \pi)$.

Let H be the expected cost of the structure in processing all the m queries we issued. It suffices to consider $H \le nm$.[4] We observe:

LEMMA 4. $\sum_{\sigma\in\Sigma} cost(\sigma, \pi_\sigma) \le H \cdot |\Sigma|$.

PROOF. Let X be a random variable that equals the final sequence produced by the structure. Since queries are independent and each query returns a size-t WoR sample set of S, we know that $\mathbf{Pr}[X = \sigma] = 1/|\Sigma|$ for each $\sigma \in \Sigma$. Let Y be another random variable that equals the actual number of I/Os the structure performs. We know that

$$H = \mathbf{E}[Y] = \sum_{\sigma\in\Sigma} \mathbf{E}[Y \mid X = \sigma] \cdot \mathbf{Pr}[X = \sigma].$$

By definition, $cost(\sigma, \pi_\sigma) \le \mathbf{E}[Y \mid X = \sigma]$. The lemma then follows. □

Let Σ^* be the set of all such $\sigma \in \Sigma$ that $cost(\sigma, \pi_\sigma) \le 2H$. Lemma 4 implies that $|\Sigma^*| \ge |\Sigma|/2$. Given an initial state $\pi \in \Pi$, let its *power*—denoted as $power(\pi)$—be the number of final sequences $\sigma \in \Sigma^*$ that finds π as their best initial state, namely, $\pi = \pi_\sigma$. Let π^* be the initial state with the greatest power. Obviously:

$$power(\pi^*) \ \ge\ |\Sigma^*|/|\Pi|.$$

Let us define the *final state* of a structure as the combination of (i) the set of elements in memory, and (ii) the sequence of occupied blocks in the disk, both at the moment when it has answered all m queries. Starting from π^*, how many different final states can we leave the structure in after $2H$ I/Os? By a standard permutation argument [2], the answer is at most $(2(n^c + 2H)\binom{M}{B})^{2H} \le (2(n^c + 2nm)\binom{M}{B})^{2H}$. As this number must be at least $power(\pi^*)$, we have:

$$\begin{aligned}\left(2(n^c + 2nm)\binom{M}{B}\right)^{2H} &\ge |\Sigma^*|/|\Pi| \\ &\ge \frac{(1/2)\binom{n}{t}^m}{\binom{n}{B}^{n^{c+1}}} \\ (\text{by } t \in [B, n^{1-\epsilon}]) &\ge \frac{1}{2}\binom{n}{t}^{m-n^{c+1}}.\end{aligned}$$

Now we fix $m = 2n^{c+1}$ so that the above gives

$$\begin{aligned}\left(n^{c+3}\binom{M}{B}\right)^{2H} &\ge \frac{1}{2}\binom{n}{t}^{m/2} \\ \Rightarrow \frac{H}{m} &\ge \frac{(t/8)\ln(n/t)}{(c+3)\ln n + B(1 + \ln(M/B))}.\end{aligned}$$

Note that $\ln(n/t) = \Omega(\log n)$, and that when $n \ge B^2$, $\ln(n/B) = \Theta(\log n)$. Hence, the above inequality implies that $H/m = \Omega(\min\{t, (t/B)\log_{M/B}(n/B)\})$ as claimed.

WR Lower Bound for $t \in [B, n]$. We now prove the WR branch of Theorem 3. Let us start with $t = B$. In fact, this follows immediately from the reduction in Section 2.4; namely, when $n \ge B^2$, if there is an algorithm answering a WR query with $t = B$ in H amortized expected I/Os, we can apply the algorithm to answer a WoR query with $t = B$ in $O(H)$ amortized expected I/Os. Hence, a WR query with $t = B$ must incur $\Omega(\min\{B, \log_{M/B}(n/B)\})$ amortized cost in expectation.

Now consider any $t \in [B, n]$. Observe that if an algorithm can answer a WR query with parameter $t = \tau > B$ in H amortized expected I/Os, we can use it to answer a WR query with $t = B$ in $O(HB/\tau)$ amortized expected I/Os. This is because by running a $t = \tau$ query once we get enough samples for the next $\lfloor \tau/B \rfloor$ queries of $t = B$. With this, we have completed the whole proof of Theorem 3.

3.2 Proof of Theorem 4

We prove the theorem by developing such a structure. We store all the elements of S in an arbitrary order using an array. In addition, we also take n samples WR from S, and store these samples in a separate array A, which is called the

[3]Note that this is a sequence of *sets*; the ordering of the elements in the same sample set does not matter.

[4]Otherwise, $H/m > n > t$, in which case our claim $\Omega(\min\{t, (t/B)\log_{M/B}(n/B)\})$ already holds.

sample pool. With sorting, all these samples can be obtained in $O((n/B)\log_{M/B}(n/B))$ I/Os.

When the structure is newly built, all samples are marked as *clean.* To answer a query with parameter t, we simply return the next t clean samples from the pool, and mark them *dirty.* When the pool runs out of clean samples, we rebuild it in $O((n/B)\log_{M/B}(n/B))$ I/Os. The cost can be amortized on the n samples already returned, so that each of them is charged only $O((1/B)\log_{M/B}(n/B))$ I/Os. The amortized query cost is therefore $O(1+(t/B)\log_{M/B}(n/B))$.

4. I/O-EFFICIENT IRS STRUCTURES

In this section, we present I/O-efficient structures for solving the IRS problem, focusing on the scenario where the input set P is static. We will discuss only WR queries because the extension to WoR queries is straightforward by the reduction in Section 2.4.

4.1 A One-Sided Structure

The one-sided RAM structure in Section 2.1 can be adapted to work in EM, by still using a constant fanout for the base tree, and replacing each secondary array with a set sampling structure of Theorem 4. It answers an IRS query in $O(\log_B \log_2 n + (t/B)\log_{M/B}(n/B))$ amortized expected I/Os[5]. Next, we improve the query cost to $O(\log_B \log_B n + (t/B)\log_{M/B}(n/B))$. The improvement owes to a new idea we call *sample replenishing.* This idea also lies at the core of our other EM structures.

Structure. We build a B-tree T on P with leaf capacity and branching parameter both set to B. Let Π_ℓ be the path from the root to the leftmost leaf. For each node u that either is the root or has its parent on Π_ℓ, we build a set sampling structure $\mathcal{T}(u)$ of Theorem 4 on $P(u)$ (the set of elements in the subtree of u). All the set sampling structures occupy $O(n/B)$ space in total.

Given an internal node u, we use $u[i]$ to denote the i-th child node of u, counting from the left. Consider now u as an internal node on Π_ℓ with f child nodes. For each $i \in [1, f]$, we record in u the value of $|P(u[i])|$. We also store $\log_2 f$ bags (i.e., multi-sets) of samples at u but of different sizes such that in total all the samples occupy $O(f)$ blocks. Specifically, for each $l = 1, 2, ..., \log_2 f$, we store a bag $\mathcal{S}_u(l)$ of $2^l B$ samples, each of which is an element randomly taken WR from $\bigcup_{i=1}^{2^l} P(u[i])$. All samples are marked as clean at this point. It is easy to see that the overall space of our structure still remains $O(n/B)$.

Query. As before, given a node u in T, we use $I(u)$ to represent the interval associated with u. To answer a one-sided IRS query with parameters $q = (-\infty, x]$ and t, we first identify in $O(\log_B \log_B n)$ I/Os the lowest node u on Π_ℓ such that $I(u)$ covers q. Let l be the smallest integer such that q is contained in the union of the intervals of the leftmost 2^l child nodes of u. We repeat the following step to generate a bag $\mathcal{R}$ of t samples: take the next clean sample e from $\mathcal{S}_u(l)$, and add it to $\mathcal{R}$ if e falls in q. We mark e dirty regardless of whether it has been added to $\mathcal{R}$. Due to the choice of l, we expect to repeat the step at most $2t$ times. The total query cost is therefore $O(\log_B \log_B n + t/B)$ expected so far.

When $\mathcal{S}_u(l)$ runs out of clean samples, we launch a *replenishing process* to re-compute a new bag $\mathcal{S}_u(l)$ of $2^l B$ samples. For this purpose, we first determine how many samples to get from each child node of u, by generating $2^l B$ random ranks from 1 to $\sum_{i=1}^{2^l} |P(u[i])|$. Then, for every $u[i]$ with $i \in [1, 2^l]$, we take the desired number of samples from $P(u[i])$ using the set sampling structure $\mathcal{T}(u[i])$. By Theorem 4, doing so to all the 2^l child nodes requires $O(2^l + (2^l B/B)\log_{M/B}(n/B)) = O(2^l \log_{M/B}(n/B))$ amortized I/Os in total. Finally, we generate a random permutation of the $2^l B$ samples in $O(2^l \log_{M/B}(n/B))$ I/Os [7], and store the permutation as the newly computed $\mathcal{S}_u(l)$. All these samples are marked as clean.

Overall, replenishing $\mathcal{S}_u(l)$ takes $O(2^l \log_{M/B}(n/B))$ amortized I/Os. However, $2^l B$ samples must have been reported from $\mathcal{S}_u(l)$ since its last replenishment. We can thus amortize the cost over those samples, so that each of them bears only $O((1/B)\log_{M/B}(n/B))$ I/Os. Therefore, the amortized query cost is bounded by $O(\log_B \log_B n + (t/B)\log_{M/B}(n/B))$ expected.

THEOREM 5. *For the IRS problem, there is a structure of $O(n/B)$ space that answers a one-sided WR or WoR query in $O(\log_B \log_B n + (t/B)\log_{M/B}(n/B))$ amortized I/Os in expectation.*

4.2 A 2-Sided Structure of Near-Linear Space

In this subsection, we will give a structure of $O((n/B)\log^\star(n/B))$ space that answers a 2-sided IRS query in $O(\log_B n + (t/B)\log_{M/B}(n/B))$ amortized expected I/Os. We achieve this by utilizing our set sampling and 1-sided structures, and the sample replenishing technique.

Structure. We will build a tree T on P of $h = 1 + \log^\star(n/B)$ levels where the fanout decreases very rapidly as we descend the tree. First, create a root node, and associate it with all the points in P. In general, a node u at level $h - i$ ($0 \le i \le h$) is associated with a set $P(u)$ of at most $2B\log^{(i)}(n/B)$ points in an interval $I(u)$ satisfying:

- $P(u) = I(u) \cap P$
- the intervals of all nodes at the same level are disjoint, and their union is $\mathbb{R}$.

If u is the root, $i = 0$, $P(u) = P$, and $I(u) = \mathbb{R}$. For $i < h$, we obtain the child nodes of u as follows. Divide $I(u)$ into a set of intervals, such that each interval covers exactly $\lfloor B\log^{(i+1)}(n/B) \rfloor$ points in $P(u)$, except possibly the last one which is allowed to have between $\lfloor B\log^{(i+1)}(n/B) \rfloor$ and $2\lfloor B\log^{(i+1)}(n/B) \rfloor$ points. Create a child node of u for each interval, and associate it with the points covered.

Now, consider an internal node u in T. Let $u[1], ..., u[f]$ be the child nodes of u (the value of f depends on the level of u). We store $|P(u)|$ at u, and associate u with some secondary structures:

- A set sampling structure of Theorem 4 on $P(u)$.
- A one-sided structure of Theorem 5 on $P(u)$.
- A binary search tree $\mathcal{T}(u)$ on the intervals $I(u[1]), ..., I(u[f])$. Let v be a node in $\mathcal{T}(u)$, and suppose that $I(u[j]), ..., I(u[j'])$ are the intervals covered in the subtree of v. Define $I(v)$ as the union

[5]We adopt the convention that $O(\log_b x)$ should be understood as $O(\max\{1, \log_b x\})$.

of these intervals, and $P(v) = P(u[j]) \cup ... \cup P(u[j'])$ (clearly, $P(v) = I(v) \cap P$). We store at v the value of $|P(v)|$, and a bag $\mathcal{S}(v)$ of $(j' - j + 1)B$ samples, each of which is taken randomly WR from $P(v)$.

To analyze the space, let u be an internal node at level $h - i$. The number f of its child nodes is at most $\frac{2B \log^{(i)}(n/B)}{\lfloor B \log^{(i+1)}(n/B) \rfloor} = O(\frac{\log^{(i)}(n/B)}{\log^{(i+1)}(n/B)})$. $\mathcal{T}(u)$ as well as all the sample bags in its nodes occupy $O(f \log f)$ blocks. As there are at most $n/\lfloor B \log^{(i)}(n/B) \rfloor$ nodes at level $h - i$, all their secondary structures occupy

$$\begin{aligned} & \frac{n}{\lfloor B \log^{(i)}(n/B) \rfloor} \cdot O(f \log f) \\ = & \ O\left(\frac{n}{B \log^{(i)}(n/B)} \cdot \frac{\log^{(i)}(n/B)}{\log^{(i+1)}(n/B)} \log \log^{(i)}(n/B)\right) \\ = & \ O(n/B). \end{aligned}$$

Therefore, the overall space is $O((n/B) \log^\star(n/B))$.

Query. To answer a 2-sided query with parameters $q = [x, y]$ and t, we first identify the lowest node u in T such that $I(u)$ covers q. This can be done in $O(\log_B n)$ I/Os, because the fanout is exponentially lower every level down. If u is a leaf, we answer the query by reading all the $O(B)$ points in $P(u)$.

If u is an internal node, then based on the intervals of the child nodes of u, we can break the query into two 1-sided queries (which will be answered at two child nodes of u), and a 2-sided query with a range q^* that is aligned with the intervals' endpoints. We can process each query separately, after determining appropriately how many samples to take from them, respectively, and then perform a random permutation on all the collected t samples in $O((t/B) \log_{M/B}(t/B))$ I/Os. The samples are then output in the permuted order. Given Theorem 5, it suffices to explain how to handle the query with q^*.

Suppose that we want to take t^* samples from q^*. Let $k^* = |P \cap q^*|$. Using the approach explained in Section 2.2, we can identify two nodes v_1, v_2 in $\mathcal{T}(u)$ such that (i) $I(v_1)$ and $I(v_2)$ are disjoint, and their union covers q, and (ii) $|P(v_1)| + |P(v_2)| = O(k^*)$. This can be done in $O(\log_B n)$ I/Os by applying the standard idea of packing the routing information of multiple nodes of $\mathcal{T}(u)$ in a block. We then generate a bag $\mathcal{R}$ of t^* samples by repeating the following two-step procedure. First, take t^* samples WR from $P(v_1) \cup P(v_2)$ (we will discuss how to do so shortly). Second, add to $\mathcal{R}$ all the samples falling in q^*. We can fill up $\mathcal{R}$ by running the procedure only $O(1)$ times in expectation.

Next, we clarify how to obtain t^* samples from $P(v_1) \cup P(v_2)$. From $|P(v_1)|$, $|P(v_2)|$, and t^*, we can decide how many samples to take from $P(v_1)$ and $P(v_2)$, respectively, by generating random ranks in memory. Then, we simply pull the desired number of samples from $\mathcal{S}(v_1)$ and $\mathcal{S}(v_2)$, respectively. If $\mathcal{S}(v_1)$ has been exhausted (the case with $\mathcal{S}(v_2)$ is similar), we perform sample replenishing as follows. Let $u[j]$, ..., $u[j']$ be the child nodes of u whose intervals are covered by $I(v_1)$. Recall that $\mathcal{S}(v_1)$ had $(j'-j+1)B$ samples after it was newly computed. We obtain a new $\mathcal{S}(v_1)$ of this size from $P(u[j]) \cup ... \cup P(u[j'])$ in two steps:

1. Decide how many samples to take from each of $P(u[j]), ..., P(u[j'])$. For this purpose, generate $(j' - j + 1)B$ random ranks from 1 to $|P(v_1)|$, sort them, and see how many ranks fall in each of those subtrees according to the values of $|P(u[j])|, ..., |P(u[j'])|$. This can be done in $O((j' - j + 1) \log_{M/B}(n/B))$ I/Os.
2. Query the set sampling structures of $u[j]$, ... $u[j']$ to get the desired numbers of samples, and then carry out a random permutation over all the samples. This demands $O((j' - j + 1) \log_{M/B}(n/B))$ amortized I/Os.

Each sample already output is thus amortized only $O((1/B) \log_{M/B}(n/B))$ I/Os. This completes the description of our query algorithm.

LEMMA 5. *For the IRS problem, there is a structure of $O((n/B) \log^\star(n/B))$ space that answers a two-sided WR or WoR query in $O(\log_B n + (t/B) \log_{M/B}(n/B))$ amortized I/Os in expectation.*

4.3 Two-Level IRS

This subsection tackles a separate problem which we call *two-level IRS*, whose solution is the key to obtaining an $O(n/B)$-space structure for 2-sided IRS queries.

In the two-level IRS problem, we have a set $\mathcal{I}$ of g disjoint intervals $\mathcal{I}_1, ..., \mathcal{I}_g$ whose union is $\mathbb{R}$. Each interval $\mathcal{I}_i$ ($1 \le i \le g$) covers a set $\mathcal{C}_i$ of points (whose concrete locations within $\mathcal{I}_i$ are irrelevant). We refer to $\mathcal{C}_i$ as a *chunk*. Define $P = \bigcup_{i=1}^{g} \mathcal{C}_i$, and $n = |P|$. A query specifies an integer $t \ge 1$ and a range $q = [x, y]$ that is always aligned with the intervals' endpoints (namely, q always equals the union of several consecutive intervals in $\mathcal{I}$). The query returns t samples each taken randomly WR from $P(q) = P \cap q$.

One can apply Lemma 5 to solve this problem, but we aim to meet a different space budget:

LEMMA 6. *For the two-level IRS problem, there is a structure of $O(n/B + g \log^\star g)$ space that answers a query in $O(\log_B n + (t/B) \log_{M/B}(n/B))$ amortized I/Os in expectation.*

The rest of the subsection proves the lemma by describing such a structure.

Structure. We create a set sampling structure of Theorem 4 on each $\mathcal{C}_i$ ($i \in [1, g]$). They occupy $O(g + n/B)$ blocks in total. We also need a separate structure at the chunk level, which is similar to the one in Section 4.2, but differs in the secondary structures, as explained next.

We build a tree T on $\mathcal{I}$ of $h = 1 + \log^\star g$ levels such that a node u at level $h - i$ ($0 \le i \le h$) is associated with an interval $I(u)$ with all the properties below:

- $I(u)$ is the union of between $\lfloor \log^{(i)} g \rfloor$ and $2 \log^{(i)} g$ consecutive intervals in $\mathcal{I}$.
- The nodes at the same level have disjoint intervals, whose union is $\mathbb{R}$.
- The interval of an internal node is always the union of its child nodes' intervals.

Define $P(u) = I(u) \cap P$.

Now consider an internal node u. Let $\mathcal{I}_j, \mathcal{I}_{j+1}, ..., \mathcal{I}_{j'}$ be the intervals covered by $I(u)$ in ascending order, and $\lambda = j' - j + 1$. We associate u with several secondary structures:

- The first one allows us to do set sampling on $P(u)$, that is, to extract t random samples WR from $P(u)$ in $O(1 + (t/B) \log_{M/B}(n/B))$ amortized I/Os. Our aim, however, is to use only $O(\lambda)$ blocks; thus, we cannot simply create a set sampling structure of Theorem 4 on $P(u)$. Instead, we store a pool of λB samples from $P(u)$. Upon a set sampling request, we simply return the next t samples from the pool. When the pool is exhausted, a new pool of λB samples is generated by querying the set sampling structures of chunks $\mathcal{C}_j, \mathcal{C}_{j+1} ..., \mathcal{C}_{j'}$, and then performing a random permutation in $O(\lambda \log_{M/B}(n/B))$ amortized I/Os.

- The second one allows us to answer a one-sided query on $P(u)$. The space budget is still $O(\lambda)$, and thus disallows a direct application of Theorem 5. Instead, we apply once again an idea developed in Section 4.1: prepare $\log_2 \lambda$ bags of samples of size B, $2B$, $4B$, ..., λB, respectively, where the l-th bag ($1 \le l \le \lceil \log_2 \lambda \rceil$) of samples is taken from $\mathcal{C}_j \cup ... \cup \mathcal{C}_{j+2^l-1}$. A one-sided query can be answered in $O(\log_B \log_2 \lambda + (t/B) \log_{M/B}(n/B))$ amortized expected I/Os from an appropriate bag. When a bag is exhausted, replenish it by querying the set sampling structures of the relevant chunks and a random permutation.

- Let $u[1], ..., u[f]$ be the child nodes of u. The third secondary structure allows us to answer a two-sided query whose query interval is the union of several continuous intervals in $\{I(u[1]), ..., I(u[f])\}$. For this purpose, we directly use the same structure $\mathcal{T}(u)$ as described in Section 4.2.

T has $O(g/\log^{(i)} g)$ nodes at level $h - i$ ($0 \le i \le h$), each with at most $f = O(\frac{\log^{(i)} g}{\log^{(i+1)} g})$ child nodes, and thus requiring $O(f \log f)$ blocks for its secondary structures. Hence, all these nodes occupy $O(g)$ blocks in total. Overall, T requires $O(g \log^\star g)$ space.

Query. The query algorithm is completely the same as the one in Section 4.2 (remember that each node u in T has been given secondary structures with the same functionality as those in the previous subsection). We thus conclude the proof of Lemma 6.

4.4 A 2-Sided Structure of Linear Space

We are now ready to describe our $O(n/B)$-space structure for answering two-sided IRS queries. Set $s = B \log^\star(n/B)$. We divide $\mathbb{R}$ into a set $\mathcal{I}$ of $g = \Theta(n/s)$ intervals $\mathcal{I}_1, ..., \mathcal{I}_g$. Each interval covers exactly s points of the input set P, except possibly the last one which can contain between s and $2s$ points of P. In any case, define $\mathcal{C}_i = \mathcal{I}_i \cap P$ for each $i \in [1, g]$. Build a structure of Lemma 6 on the two-level IRS problem defined by $\mathcal{I}$ and $\mathcal{C}_1, ..., \mathcal{C}_g$. This structure occupies $O(n/B + g \log^\star g) = O(n/B)$ blocks.

Now we explain how to process a query with parameter $q = [x, y]$ and t. If q is covered by some interval $\mathcal{I}_i$, we answer it within chunk $\mathcal{C}_i$. First, scan $\mathcal{C}_i$ to obtain $S = \mathcal{C}_i \cap q$, and store S in an array; this requires $O(s/B)$ I/Os. Second, generate t random ranks in the range $[1, |S|]$, and sort them in ascending order. Third, obtain t samples by merging the rank list and S in $O(s/B)$ I/Os. Finally, compute a random permutation of the t samples. Therefore, the total query cost is $O(\log^\star(n/B) + \log_B n + (t/B) \log_{M/B}(t/B))$, where the second term is for finding $\mathcal{I}_i$.

If q intersects at least two intervals in $\mathcal{I}$, we break the query into two one-sided queries (each of which will be answered within a chunk) and one two-sided query with a range q^* that equals the union of several intervals in $\mathcal{I}$. We process the two one-sided queries by the "within-chunk" algorithm we have just described, and the query with range q^* by the two-level IRS structure, after deciding the sample sizes for these queries appropriately. Finally, we perform a random permutation of all the samples fetched. The query cost is $O(\log^\star(n/B) + \log_B n + (t/B) \log_{M/B}(n/B))$ amortized expected. We have thus established the last main result of this paper:

THEOREM 6. *For the IRS problem, there is a structure of $O(n/B)$ space that answers a two-sided WR or WoR query in $O(\log^\star(n/B) + \log_B n + (t/B) \log_{M/B}(n/B))$ amortized I/Os in expectation.*

ACKNOWLEDGEMENTS

This work was supported in part by projects GRF 4165/11, 4164/12, and 4168/13 from HKRGC.

5. REFERENCES

[1] S. Acharya, P. B. Gibbons, and V. Poosala. Congressional samples for approximate answering of group-by queries. In *Proceedings of ACM Management of Data (SIGMOD)*, pages 487–498, 2000.

[2] A. Aggarwal and J. S. Vitter. The input/output complexity of sorting and related problems. *Communications of the ACM (CACM)*, 31(9):1116–1127, 1988.

[3] L. Arge and J. S. Vitter. Optimal external memory interval management. *SIAM Journal of Computing*, 32(6):1488–1508, 2003.

[4] V. Braverman, R. Ostrovsky, and C. Zaniolo. Optimal sampling from sliding windows. *Journal of Computer and System Sciences (JCSS)*, 78(1):260–272, 2012.

[5] P. Efraimidis and P. G. Spirakis. Weighted random sampling with a reservoir. *Information Processing Letters (IPL)*, 97(5):181–185, 2006.

[6] R. Gemulla, W. Lehner, and P. J. Haas. Maintaining bernoulli samples over evolving multisets. In *Proceedings of ACM Symposium on Principles of Database Systems (PODS)*, pages 93–102, 2007.

[7] J. Gustedt. Efficient sampling of random permutations. *Journal of Discrete Algorithms*, 6(1):125–139, 2008.

[8] J. M. Hellerstein, P. J. Haas, and H. J. Wang. Online aggregation. In *Proceedings of ACM Management of Data (SIGMOD)*, pages 171–182, 1997.

[9] J. M. Hellerstein, E. Koutsoupias, D. P. Miranker, C. H. Papadimitriou, and V. Samoladas. On a model of indexability and its bounds for range queries. *Journal of the ACM (JACM)*, 49(1):35–55, 2002.

[10] C. Jermaine, S. Arumugam, A. Pol, and A. Dobra. Scalable approximate query processing with the dbo engine. *ACM Transactions on Database Systems (TODS)*, 33(4), 2008.

[11] S. Nath and P. B. Gibbons. Online maintenance of very large random samples on flash storage. *The VLDB Journal*, 19(1):67–90, 2010.
[12] F. Olken. *Random Sampling from Databases.* PhD thesis, University of California at Berkeley, 1993.
[13] M. H. Overmars. *The Design of Dynamic Data Structures.* Springer-Verlag, 1983.
[14] A. Pol, C. M. Jermaine, and S. Arumugam. Maintaining very large random samples using the geometric file. *The VLDB Journal*, 17(5):997–1018, 2008.
[15] J. S. Vitter. Random sampling with a reservoir. *ACM Trans. Math. Softw.*, 11(1):37–57, 1985.
[16] Z. Wei and K. Yi. Beyond simple aggregates: indexing for summary queries. In *Proceedings of ACM Symposium on Principles of Database Systems (PODS)*, pages 117–128, 2011.

Appendix: Proof of Lemma 3

Denote by R the set of samples we obtain after eliminating duplicates. Consider any $t < s$, and an arbitrary subset S' of S with $|S'| = t$. Thus, $\mathbf{Pr}[R \subseteq S'] = (t/k)^{2s}$. Hence, the probability that $R = S'$ is at most $(t/k)^{2s}$. Therefore:

$$\begin{aligned}
\mathbf{Pr}[|R| < s] &= \sum_{t=1}^{s-1} \mathbf{Pr}[|R| = t] \\
&\le \sum_{t=1}^{s-1} \binom{k}{t} (t/k)^{2s} \\
&\le \sum_{t=1}^{s-1} (ek/t)^t \cdot (t/k)^{2s} \\
\text{(by } e^t < e^s < e^{2s-t}\text{)} &< \sum_{t=1}^{s-1} (et/k)^{2s-t} \\
&< \sum_{t=1}^{s-1} (es/k))^{2s-t} \\
&\le \frac{es/k}{1 - es/k} \le \frac{1/3}{2/3} = 1/2.
\end{aligned}$$

The lemma thus follows.

A Dynamic I/O-Efficient Structure for One-Dimensional Top-k Range Reporting

Yufei Tao
CUHK
Hong Kong
taoyf@cse.cuhk.edu.hk

ABSTRACT

We present a structure in external memory for *top-k range reporting*, which uses linear space, answers a query in $O(\lg_B n + k/B)$ I/Os, and supports an update in $O(\lg_B n)$ amortized I/Os, where n is the input size, and B is the block size. This improves the state of the art which incurs $O(\lg_B^2 n)$ amortized I/Os per update.

Categories and Subject Descriptors

F.2.2 [**Analysis of algorithms and problem complexity**]: Nonnumerical Algorithms and Problems—*computations on discrete structures*; H.3.1 [**Information storage and retrieval**]: Content analysis and indexing—*indexing methods*

Keywords

Top-k, range reporting, dynamic data structure

1. INTRODUCTION

In the *top-k range reporting problem*, the input is a set S of n points in $\mathbb{R}$, where each point $e \in S$ carries a distinct[1] real-valued *score*, denoted as *score*(e). Given an interval $q = [x_1, x_2]$ and an integer k, a query returns the k points in $S(q) = S \cap q$ with the highest scores. If $|S(q)| < k$, the entire $S(q)$ should be returned. The goal is to store S in a structure so that queries can be answered efficiently.

Motivation. Top-k search in general is widely acknowledged as an important operation in a large variety of information systems (see an excellent survey [9]). It plays a central role in applications where an end user wants only a small number of elements with the best competitive quality, as opposed to all the elements satisfying a query predicate. Top-k range reporting—being an extension of classic range reporting—is one of the most fundamental forms of top-k search. A representative query on a hotel database is "*find the 10 best-rated hotels whose prices are between 100 and 200 dollars per night*". Here, each point $e \in S$ represents the price of a hotel, with *score*(e) corresponding to the hotel's user rating. In fact, queries like the above are so popular that database systems nowadays strive to make them first-class citizens with direct algorithm support. This calls for a space-economic structure that can guarantee attractive query and update efficiency.

Computation Model. We study the problem in the *external memory* (EM) model [2]. A machine is equipped with M words of memory, and a disk of unbounded size that has been formatted into *blocks* of size B words. An I/O either reads a block of data from the disk to memory, or conversely, writes B words in memory to a disk block. The *space* of a structure is the number of blocks it occupies, whereas the *time* of an algorithm is the number of I/Os it performs. CPU calculation is for free. A word has $\Omega(\lg n)$ bits, where $n \geq B$ is the input size of the problem at hand. The values of M and B satisfy the condition $M = \Omega(B)$.[2]

Throughout this paper, a space/time complexity holds in the worst case by default. A logarithm $\lg_b x$ is defined as $\max\{1, \log_b x\}$, and $b = 2$ if omitted. *Linear* cost should be understood as $O(n/B)$ whereas *logarithmic* cost as $O(\lg_B n)$.

1.1 Previous Work

Top-k range reporting was first studied by Afshani, Brodal and Zeh [1], who gave a static structure of $O(n/B)$ space that answers a query in $O(\lg_B n + k/B)$ I/Os. The query cost is optimal, as can be shown via a reduction from predecessor search [12]. They also analyzed the space-query tradeoff for an *ordered* variant of the problem, where the top-k elements need to be sorted by score. Their result suggests that when the space usage is linear, one can achieve nearly the best query efficiency by simply solving the unordered version in $O(\lg_B n + k/B)$ I/Os, and then sorting the retrieved elements (see [14] for more details). For the unordered version, Sheng and Tao [14] proposed a dynamic structure that has the

[1] This is a standard assumption [1, 14] to guarantee the uniqueness of a top-k result. See [14] for two semantic extensions to remove the assumption, and how to reduce those extensions to the standard top-k problem with distinct weights.

[2] M can be as small as $2B$ in the model defined in [2]. However, any algorithm that works on $M = cB$ with constant $c > 2$ can be adapted to work on $M = 2B$ with only a constant blowup in space and time. Therefore, one might as well consider that $M = \Omega(B)$.

PODS'14, June 22–27, 2014, Snowbird, UT, USA.

Http://dx.doi.org/10.1145/2594538.2594543.

same space and query cost as [1], but supports an update in $O(\lg_B^2 n)$ amortized I/Os.

In internal memory, by combining a priority search tree [10] and Frederickson's selection algorithm [7] on heaps, one can obtain a pointer-machine structure that uses $O(n)$ words, answers a query in $O(\lg n + k)$ time, and supports an update in $O(\lg n)$ time. In RAM, Brodal, Fagerberg, Greve and Lopez-Ortiz [5] considered a special instance of the problem where the input points of S are from the domain $[1, n]$. They gave a linear-size structure with $O(1 + k)$ query time (which holds also for the ordered version).

It is worth mentioning that top-k search has received considerable attention in many other contexts. We refer the interested readers to recent works [11, 13] for entry points into the literature.

1.2 Our Results

We improve the state of the art [14] by presenting a new structure with logarithmic update cost:

THEOREM 1. *For top-k range reporting, there is a structure of $O(n/B)$ space that answers a query in $O(\lg_B n + k/B)$ I/Os, and supports an insertion and a deletion in $O(\lg_B n)$ I/Os amortized.*

We achieve logarithmic updates by combining three methods. The first one adapts the aforementioned pointer machine structure—which combines a priority search tree with Frederickson's heap selection algorithm—to external memory. This gives a linear-size structure that can be updated in $O(\lg_B n)$ amortized I/Os, but answers a query in $O(\lg n + k/B)$ I/Os (note that the log base is 2). We use the structure to handle $k \geq B \lg n$ in which case its query cost is $O(\lg n + k/B) = O(k/B)$.

The second method applies directly the structure of [14]. Looking at their analysis carefully, one sees that their amortized update cost is in fact $O(\lg_B n + \frac{\lg n}{B^{1/6}} \lg_B n)$. In other words, when $\lg n \leq B^{1/6}$, the structure already achieves logarithmic update cost.

The most difficult case arises when $\lg n > B^{1/6}$, or equivalently, $B < \lg^6 n$. We observe that, since $k \geq B \lg n$ has already been taken care of, it remains to target $k < B \lg n < \lg^7 n$. Motivated by this, we develop a linear-size structure that can be updated in $O(\lg_B n)$ I/Os, and answers a query with $k = O(\text{polylg}\, n)$ in $O(\lg_B n + k/B)$ I/Os. The most crucial idea behind this structure is to use a suite of "RAM-reminiscent" techniques to unleash the power of manipulating individual bits.

Theorem 1 can now be established by putting together the above three structures using standard global rebuilding techniques.

2. A STRUCTURE FOR $k = \Omega(B \lg n)$

In this section, we will prove:

LEMMA 1. *For top-k range reporting, there is a structure of $O(n/B)$ space that answers a query in $O(\lg n + k/B)$ I/Os, and supports an insertion and a deletion in $O(\lg_B n)$ I/Os amortized.*

Top-k range reporting has a geometric interpretation. We can convert S to a set P of points, by mapping each element

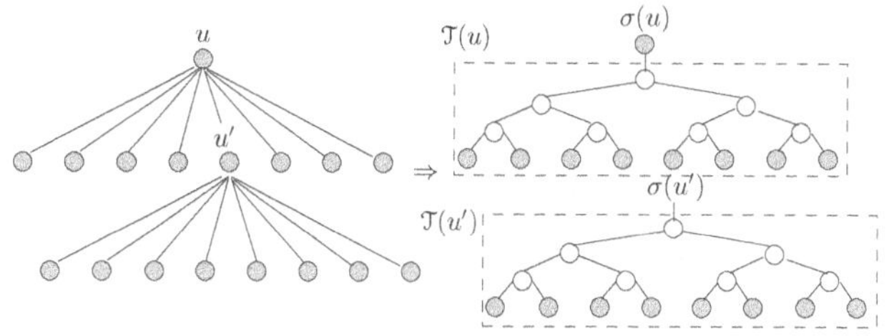

Figure 1: Concatenating secondary binary trees

$e \in S$ to a 2d point $(e, score(e))$. Then, a top-k query with $q = [x_1, x_2]$ equivalently reports the k highest points of P in the vertical slab $q \times (-\infty, \infty)$. This is the perspective we will take to prove Lemma 1.

Our structure is essentially an *external priority search tree* [3] on P with a constant fanout. However, we make two contributions. First, we develop an algorithm using this structure to answer top-k range queries. Second, we explain how to update the structure in $O(\lg_B n)$ I/Os. Note that an update by the standard algorithm of [3] requires $O(\lg n)$ I/Os.

Structure. Let T be a *weight balanced B-tree* (WBB-tree) [4] on the x-coordinates of the points in P. The leaf capacity and branching parameter of T are both set to B. We number the levels of T bottom up, with the leaves at level 0. For each node u in T, we use $P(u)$ to denote the set of points whose x-coordinates are stored in the subtree of u. As a property of the WBB-tree, if u is at level i, then $|P(u)|$ falls between $B^{i+1}/4$ and B^{i+1}; if $|P(u)|$ is outside this range, u becomes *unbalanced* and needs to be remedied.

Each node u naturally corresponds to a vertical *slab* $\sigma(u)$ with $P(u) = \sigma(u) \cap P$.[3] Let u, u' be child nodes of the same parent. We say that u' is a *right sibling* of u if $\sigma(u')$ is to the right of $\sigma(u)$. Otherwise, u' is a *left sibling* of u. Note that a node can have multiple left/right siblings, or none (if it is already the left/right most child).

Consider now u as an internal node with child nodes $u_1, ..., u_f$ where $f = O(B)$ (we always follow the left-to-right order in listing out child nodes). We associate u with a binary search tree $\mathcal{T}(u)$ of f leaves, which correspond to $\sigma(u_1), ..., \sigma(u_f)$, respectively. Let v be an internal node in $\mathcal{T}(u)$. We define $\sigma(v) = \cup_{j=j_1}^{j_2} \sigma(u_j)$, where $\sigma(u_{j_1}), \sigma(u_{j_1+1}), ..., \sigma(u_{j_2})$ are the leaves of $\mathcal{T}(u)$ below v, and accordingly, define $P(v) = \sigma(v) \cap P$.

Notice that we can view T insteads as one big tree $\boldsymbol{T}$ that concatenates the secondary binary trees of all the nodes in T. Specifically, if u' is a child of u in T, the concatenation makes the root of $\mathcal{T}(u')$ the only child of the leaf $\sigma(u')$ of $\mathcal{T}(u)$. See Figure 1. $\boldsymbol{T}$ is almost a binary tree except that some internal nodes have only one child which is an internal node itself. However, this is only a minor oddity because any path in $\boldsymbol{T}$ of 3 nodes must contain at least one node with two children. The height of $\boldsymbol{T}$ is $O(\lg n)$.

[3]Precisely, the slab of a leaf node u is $[x, x') \times (-\infty, \infty)$ where x is the smallest x-coordinate stored at u, and x' is the smallest x-coordinate in the leaf node u' succeeding u. If u' does not exist, $x' = \infty$. The slab of an internal node unions those of all its child nodes.

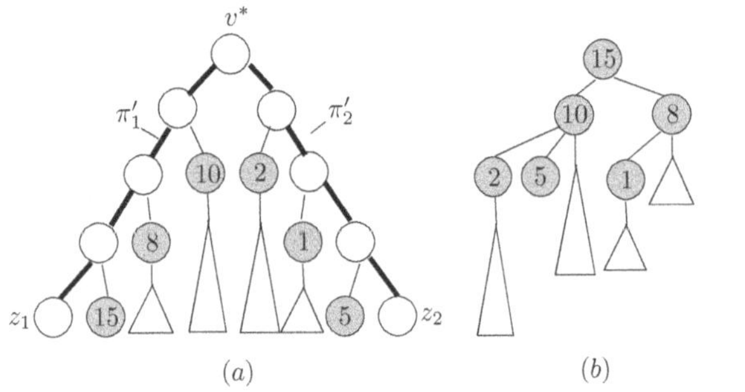

Figure 2: The gray nodes in Figure (a) constitute set Π. Each number is a node's sorting key in the heap rooted at that node. Figure (b) shows H after heap concatenation.

Each node v in $\boldsymbol{T}$ is associated with a set—denoted as *pilot*(v)—of *pilot points* satisfying two conditions:

- The points of *pilot*(v) are the highest among all points $p \in P(v)$ that are not stored in any *pilot*$(\hat{v})$, where $\hat{v}$ is a proper ancestor of v in $\boldsymbol{T}$.
- If less than $B/2$ points satisfy the above condition, *pilot*(v) includes all of them. Otherwise, $B/2 \leq |pilot(v)| \leq 2B$. In any case, *pilot*$(v)$ is stored in $O(1)$ blocks.

The lowest point in *pilot*(v) is called the *representative* of *pilot*(v).

Finally, for each internal node u in T, we collect the representatives of the pilot sets of all the nodes in $\mathcal{T}(u)$, and store these $O(B)$ representatives in $O(1)$ blocks—referred to as the *representative blocks* of u.

Query. Given a top-k query with range $q = [x_1, x_2]$, we descend two root-to-leaf paths π_1 and π_2 in $\boldsymbol{T}$ to reach the leaf nodes z_1 and z_2 whose slabs' x-ranges cover x_1 and x_2, respectively. In $O(\lg n)$ I/Os, we retrieve all the $O(B \lg n)$ pilot points of the nodes on $\pi_1 \cup \pi_2$, and eliminate those outside $q \times (-\infty, \infty)$. Let Q_1 be the set of remaining points.

Let v^* be the least common ancestor of z_1 and z_2. Define π'_1 (π'_2) as the path from v^* to z_1 (z_2). Let Π be the set of nodes v satisfying two conditions:

(i) $v \notin \pi'_1 \cup \pi'_2$, but the parent of v is in $\pi'_1 \cup \pi'_2$;

(ii) The x-range of $\sigma(v)$ is covered by q.

For every such v, we can regard its subtree as a max-heap $H(v)$ as follows. First, $H(v)$ includes all the nodes v' in the subtree of v (in $\boldsymbol{T}$) with non-empty pilot sets. Second, the sorting key of v' is the y-coordinate of the representative of *pilot*(v'). In this way, we have identified at most $|\Pi|$ non-empty max-heaps, each rooted at a distinct node in Π. Concatenate these heaps into one, by organizing their roots into a binary max-heap based on the sorting keys of those roots. This can be done in $O(\lg n)$ I/Os[4]. Denote by H the resulting max-heap after concatenation. See Figure 2.

Set ϕ to a sufficiently large constant. We now invoke Frederickson's algorithm to extract the set R of $\phi \cdot (\lg n + k/B)$ representatives in H with the largest y-coordinates; this entails $O(\lg n + k/B)$ I/Os. Let S_R be the set of nodes whose representatives are collected in R. Gather all the pilot points of the nodes of S_R into a set Q_2.

Define a set S^*_R of nodes as follows. For each node $v \in S_R$, we first add to S^*_R all such siblings v' of v (in $\boldsymbol{T}$) that (i) $v' \notin S_R$, and (ii) the x-range of $\sigma(v')$ is contained in q. Second, if v is an internal node, add all its child nodes in $\boldsymbol{T}$ to S^*_R. Note that $|S^*_R| = O(|S_R|) = O(\lg n + k/B)$. We now collect the pilot points of all the nodes of S^*_R into a set Q_3.

At this moment, we have collected three sets Q_1, Q_2, Q_3 with a total size of $O(B \log n + k)$. We can now report the k highest points in $Q_1 \cup Q_2 \cup Q_3$ in $O(\lg n + k/B)$ I/Os. The query algorithm performs $O(\lg n + k/B)$ I/Os in total. Its correctness is ensured by the fact below:

LEMMA 2. *Setting $\phi = 16$ ensures that $Q_1 \cup Q_2 \cup Q_3$ includes the k highest points in $q \times (-\infty, \infty)$.*

PROOF. We will focus on the scenario that the heap H has at least $\phi \cdot (\lg n + k/B)$ representatives. Otherwise, P has $O(B \lg n + k)$ points in $q \times (-\infty, \infty)$, and all of them are in $Q_1 \cup Q_2$ (Q_3 is empty).

We will first show that $|Q_1 \cup Q_2| \geq k$. This is very intuitive because $Q_1 \cup Q_2$ collects the contents of $\Omega(\lg n + k/B)$ pilot sets. However, a formal proof requires some effort because the pilot set of a node v can have arbitrarily few points (in this case all the nodes in the proper subtree of v must have empty pilot sets). We need a careful argument to address this issue.

We say that a representative in R is *poor* if its pilot set has less than $B/8$ points; otherwise, it is *rich*. Consider a poor representative r in R; and suppose that it is a pilot point of node v, and its x-coordinate is stored in leaf node z. Note that z stores the x-coordinates of at least $B/4$ points, all of which fall in q. By the fact that r represents less than $B/8$ points, we know that at least $B/8$ points (with x-coordinates) in z are pilot points of some proper ancestors of v in $\boldsymbol{T}$, and therefore, appear in either Q_1 or Q_2. We associate those $B/8$ points with r. On the other hand, we associate each rich representative with the at least $B/8$ points in its pilot set.

Thus, the $\phi \cdot (\lg n + k/B)$ representatives in R are associated with at least $(\phi/8)(B \lg n + k)$ points in $Q_1 \cup Q_2$. Each point $p \in Q_1 \cup Q_2$, on the other hand, can be associated with at most 2 representatives: the representative of the node where p is a pilot point, and a poor representative whose x-coordinate is stored in the same leaf as p.[5] This implies $|Q_1 \cup Q_2| \geq (\phi/16)(B \lg n + k)$. Hence, $\phi = 16$ ensures $|Q_1 \cup Q_2| \geq k$.

Finally, the inclusion of Q_3 ensures that no pilot point in $q \times (-\infty, \infty)$ but outside $Q_1 \cup Q_2 \cup Q_3$ can be higher than the lowest point in $Q_1 \cup Q_2$. The lemma then follows. ☐

Insertion. To insert a point p, first update the B-tree T by inserting the x-coordinate of p. Let us assume for the time being that no rebalancing in T is required. Then, we identify the node v in $\boldsymbol{T}$ whose pilot set should incorporate p. This can be achieved in $O(\lg_B n)$ I/Os by descending a

[4]Using a linear-time "make-heap" algorithm; see [6].

[5]No two poor representatives can have their x-coordinates stored in the same leaf.

single root-to-leaf path in T (note: not $\boldsymbol{T}$), and inspect the representative blocks of the nodes on the path. We add p to $pilot(v)$.

We say that a pilot set *overflows* if it has more than $2B$ points. If $pilot(v)$ overflows, we carry out a *push-down* operation at v, which moves the $|pilot(v)| - B$ lowest points of $pilot(v)$ to the pilot sets of its at most 2 child nodes in $\boldsymbol{T}$. The resulting $pilot(v)$ has size B. If the pilot set of a child v' now overflows, we treat it in the same manner by performing a push-down at v'. We will analyze the cost of push-downs later.

Deletion. To delete a point p, we identify the node v in $\boldsymbol{T}$ whose pilot set contains p. This can be done in $O(\lg_B n)$ I/Os by inspecting the representative blocks. We then remove p from $pilot(v)$.

We say that a pilot set *underflows* if it has less than $B/2$ points, and yet, one of its child nodes has a non-empty pilot set. To remedy this, we define a *pull-up* operation at node v' in $\boldsymbol{T}$ as one that moves the $\min\{B/2, B-|pilot(v')|\}$ highest points from

$$\bigcup_{\text{child } v'' \text{ of } v' \text{ in } \boldsymbol{T}} pilot(v'') \quad (1)$$

to $pilot(v')$. If (1) has less than the requested number of points, the pull-up moves all the points of (1) into $pilot(v)$, after which all proper descendants of v' have empty subsets; we call such a pull-up a *draining* one.

In general, if the pilot set of a node v' underflows, we carry out at most two pull-ups at v' until either $|pilot(v')| = B$, or a draining pull-up has been performed. After the first pull-up, if the pilot set at a child node of v' underflows, we should remedy that first (in the same manner recursively) before continuing with the second pull-up at v'. We will analyze the cost of pull-ups later.

It is worth mentioning that we do not remove the x-coordinate of p from the base tree T. This does not create a problem because we will rebuild the whole T periodically, as clarified later.

Rebalancing. It remains to clarify how to rebalance T. Let $u^\star$ be the highest node in T that becomes unbalanced after inserting p. Let $\hat{u}$ be the parent of $u^\star$. We rebuild the whole subtree of $\hat{u}$ in T, and the corresponding portion in $\boldsymbol{T}$. Let l be the level of $\hat{u}$ in T. Our goal is to complete the reconstruction in $O(B^l)$ I/Os. A standard argument with the WBB-tree shows that every insertion accounts for $O(\lg_B n)$ I/Os of all the reconstructions.

Let $\hat{v}$ be the root of $\mathcal{T}(\hat{u})$. Essentially, we need to rebuild the subtree of $\hat{v}$ in $\boldsymbol{T}$, which has $O(B^l)$ nodes. The first step of our algorithm is to distribute all the pilot points stored in the subtree of $\hat{v}$ down to the leaves where their x-coordinates are stored, respectively. For this purpose, we simply push down all the pilot points of $\hat{v}$ to its child nodes in $\boldsymbol{T}$, and do so recursively at each child. We call this a *pilot grounding* process.

We now reconstruct the subtrees of $\hat{u}$ and $\hat{v}$. First, it is standard to create all the nodes of T in the subtree of $\hat{u}$, and all the nodes of $\boldsymbol{T}$ in the subtree of $\hat{v}$ in $O(B^l)$ I/Os. What remains to do is to fill in the pilot sets. We do so in a bottom up manner. Suppose that we are to fill in the pilot set of v, knowing that the pilot sets of all the proper descendants of v (in $\boldsymbol{T}$) have been computed properly. We populate $pilot(v)$ using the same algorithm as treating a pilot set underflow at v.

Next, we prove that the whole reconstruction takes $O(B^l)$ I/Os. Let us first analyze the pilot grounding process. We say that a *demotion event* occurs when a point moves from the pilot set of a parent node to that of a child. If N_d represents the number of such events, we can bound the total cost of pilot grounding as $O(B^l + N_d/B)$.

To bound N_d, first consider a level-1 node u in T. A node at level $j \geq 1$ of $\mathcal{T}(u)$ triggers $O(jB)$ demotion events. Hence, the number of demotion events triggered by all the nodes of $\mathcal{T}(u)$ is $\sum_{j=1}^{O(\lg B)} O(B/2^j) \cdot O(jB) = O(B^2)$. As the subtree of $\hat{u}$ has $O(B^{l-1})$ level-1 nodes, they trigger $O(B^2 \cdot B^{l-1}) = O(B^{l+1})$ demotion events in total.

Now consider u as a level-i node of T with $i \geq 2$. Each of the B nodes in $\mathcal{T}(u)$ can trigger $O(iB \lg B)$ demotion events, resulting in a total event count of $O(iB^2 \lg B)$ for u. Since there are $O(B^{l-i})$ nodes at level i, the number of demotion events due to the nodes from level 2 to level l is at most

$$\sum_{i=2}^{l} O(B^{l-i}) \cdot O(iB^2 \lg B) = O(B^l \lg B).$$

Therefore, $N_d = O(B^{l+1} + B^l \lg B) = O(B^{l+1})$. It follows that the pilot grounding process requires $O(B^l + N_d/B) = O(B^l)$ I/Os.

The cost of filling pilot sets can be analyzed in the same fashion, by looking at *promotion events*—namely, a point moves from the pilot set of a child to that of the parent. If N_p represents the number of such events, we can bound the cost of pilot set filling as $O(B^l + N_p/B)$. By an argument analogous to the one on N_d, one can derive that $N_p = O(B^{l+1})$.

Push-Downs and Pull-Ups. Next, we will prove that each update accounts for only $O(\frac{1}{B} \lg n)$ I/Os incurred by push-downs and pull-ups. At first glance, this is quite intuitive: inserting a point into a pilot set may "edge out" an existing point there to the next level of $\boldsymbol{T}$, which may then create a cascading effect every level down. Viewed this way, an insertion creates $O(\lg n)$ demotion events, and reversely, a deletion creates $O(\lg n)$ promotion events. As $\Omega(B)$ such events are handled by a push-down or pull-up using $O(1)$ I/Os, the cost amortized on an update should be $O(\frac{1}{B} \lg n)$. What complicates things, however, is the fact that pilot points may bounce up and down across different levels. Below we give an argument to account for this complication.

We imagine some conceptual *tokens* that can be passed by a node to a child in $\boldsymbol{T}$, but never the opposite direction. Specifically, the *rules* for creating, passing, and deleting tokens are:

1. When a point p is being inserted into $\boldsymbol{T}$, we give v an *insertion token* if p is placed in $pilot(v)$.

2. When a point p is deleted from $\boldsymbol{T}$, we give v a *deletion token* if p is removed from $pilot(v)$.

3. In a push-down, when a point p is moved from $pilot(v)$ to $pilot(v')$ (where v' is a child of v), we take away an

insertion token from v, and give it to v'. We will prove shortly that v always has enough tokens to make this possible.

4. In a pull-up, when a point p is moved from $pilot(v')$ to $pilot(v)$ (where v' is a child of v), we take away a deletion token from v, and give it to v'. Again, we will prove shortly that this is always do-able.

5. When an insertion/deletion token reaches a leaf node, it disappears.

6. After a draining pull-up is performed at v, all the tokens in the subtree of v disappear.

7. When the subtree of a node v is reconstructed, all the tokens in the subtree disappear.

LEMMA 3. *Our update algorithms enforce two invariants at all times:*

- *Invariant 1: every internal node v in $\boldsymbol{T}$ has at least $|pilot(v)| - B$ insertion tokens.*
- *Invariant 2: every internal node v in $\boldsymbol{T}$ has at least $B - |pilot(v)|$ deletion tokens, unless all proper descendants of v in $\boldsymbol{T}$ have empty pilot sets.*

Notice that, by Invariant 1, a node v with $|pilot(v)| \leq B$ is not required to hold any insertion tokens; likewise, by Invariant 2, a node v with $|pilot(v)| \geq B$ is not required to hold any deletion tokens. Furthermore, the two invariants ensure that the token passing described in Rules 3 and 4 is always do-able.

PROOF OF LEMMA 3. Both invariants hold on v right after the subtree of v has been reconstructed because at this moment either (i) $|pilot(v)| = B$, or (ii) $|pilot(v)| < B$ and meanwhile all proper descendants of v in $\boldsymbol{T}$ have empty pilot sets.

Inductively, assuming that the invariants are valid currently, next we will prove that they remain valid after applying our update algorithms.

- Putting a newly inserted point p into $pilot(v)$ gives v a new insertion token, which accounts for the increment of $|pilot(v)| - B$. Hence, Invariant 1 still holds. Invariant 2 also holds because $B - |pilot(v)|$ has decreased.
- Physically deleting a point $p \in pilot(v)$ from $\boldsymbol{T}$ gives v a new deletion token, which accounts for the increment of $B - |pilot(v)|$. Hence, Invariant 2 still holds. Invariant 1 also holds because $|pilot(v)| - B$ has decreased.
- Consider a push-down at node v. After the push-down, $|pilot(v)| = B$; thus, Invariants 1 and 2 trivially hold on v. Let v' be a child of v. Invariant 1 still holds on v' because v' gains as many insertion tokens as the increase of $|pilot(v')| - B$. Invariant 2 also continues to hold on v' because the value of $B - |pilot(v')|$ has decreased.
- Consider a pull-up at node v. After the pull-up, $|pilot(v)| \leq B$; hence, Invariant 1 trivially holds on v. Invariant 2 also holds on v because v loses as many deletion tokens as the decrease of $B - |pilot(v)|$. Let v' be a child of v. Invariant 1 continues to hold on v' because the value of $|pilot(v')| - B$ has decreased. Invariant 2 also holds on v' because v' gains as many deletion tokens as the increase of $B - |pilot(v')|$.

□

Recall that a push-down is necessitated at a node v only if $pilot(v) > 2B$. Therefore, by Invariant 1, after the operation $|pilot(v)| - B = \Omega(|pilot(v)|)$ insertion tokens must have descended to the next level of $\boldsymbol{T}$. The operation itself takes $O(|pilot(v)|/B)$ I/Os; after amortization, each of those insertion tokens bears only $O(1/B)$ I/Os of that cost.

Now consider the moment when a pilot set underflow happens at v. By Invariant 2, v must be holding at least $B/2$ deletion tokens at this time. Our algorithm performs one or two pull-ups at v using $O(1)$ I/Os. We account for such cost as follows. If neither of the two pull-ups is a draining one, at least $B/2$ deletion tokens must have descended to the next level; we charge the cost on those tokens, each of which bears $O(1/B)$ I/Os. On the other hand, if a draining pull-up occurred, at least $B/2$ deletion tokens must have disappeared; each of them is asked to bear $O(1/B)$ I/Os.

In summary, each token before its disappearance is charged $O(\frac{1}{B}\lg n)$ I/Os in total. Since an update creates only one token, the amortized update cost only needs to increase by $O(\frac{1}{B}\lg n)$ to cover the cost of push-downs and pull-ups.

Remark. The above analysis has assumed that the height of T remains $\Theta(\lg n)$. This assumption can be removed by the standard technique of global rebuilding. With this, we have completed the proof of Lemma 1.

3. A STRUCTURE FOR $k = O(\text{polylg}\, n)$

In this section, we will prove:

LEMMA 4. *For top-k range reporting with $k = O(\text{polylg}\, n)$, there is a structure of $O(n/B)$ space that answers a query in $O(\lg_B n + k/B)$ I/Os, and supports an insertion and a deletion in $O(\lg_B n)$ I/Os amortized.*

As explained in Section 1.2, Theorem 1 follows from the combination of Lemmas 1 and 4, and a structure of [14]. To prove Lemma 4, we will first introduce two relevant problems in Sections 3.1 and 3.2. Our final structure—presented in Section 3.3—is built upon solutions to those problems.

3.1 Approximate Union-Rank Selection

Let L be a set of real values. Given a real value e, we define its *rank* in L as $|\{e' \in L \mid e' \geq e\}|$. Note that the largest element of L has rank 1.

In *approximate union-rank selection* (AURS), we are given m disjoint sets $L_1, ..., L_m$ of real values, such that each L_i ($1 \leq i \leq m$) can be accessed only by the following operators:

- MAX: Returns the largest element of L_i in $cost_{max}$ I/Os.
- RANK: Given a real-valued parameter $\rho \in [1, \frac{1}{c_1}|L_i|]$ where $c_1 \geq 2$ is a constant, this operator returns in $cost_{rank}$ I/Os an element $e \in L_i$ whose rank in L_i falls in $[\rho, c_1\rho)$.

Given an integer k satisfying

$$1 \leq k \leq (1/c_1) \cdot \min\{|L_1|, ..., |L_m|\}, \quad (2)$$

a query returns an element $e \in \bigcup_{i=1}^{m} L_i$ whose rank in $\bigcup_{i=1}^{m} L_i$ falls in $[k, c'k]$, where $c' > 1$ is a constant dependent only on c_1.

AURS is reminiscent of a rank selection problem defined by Frederickson and Johnson [8]. However, their algorithm assumes a more powerful RANK operator that returns an element in L_i with a *precise* rank. In the appendix, we show how to adapt their algorithm to obtain the result below:

LEMMA 5. *Each query in the AURS problem can be answered in $O(m(cost_{max} + cost_{rank}))$ I/Os.*

3.2 Approximate (f, l)-Group k-Selection

Given integers f and l, we define an *(f, l)-group $\boldsymbol{G}$* as a sequence of f disjoint sets $G_1, ..., G_f$, where each G_i $(1 \leq i \leq f)$ is a set of at most l real values. Let $N \geq fl$ be an integer such that a word has $\Omega(\lg N)$ bits.

In the *approximate (f, l)-group k-selection problem*—henceforth, the *(f, l)-problem* for short—the input is an (f, l)-group $\boldsymbol{G}$, where the values of f, l, N, and B (block size) satisfy all of the following:

- $l = O(\text{polylg}\, N)$
- $f \leq \sqrt{B} \lg^{\epsilon} N$ where ϵ is a constant satisfying $0 < \epsilon < 1$.

A query is given:

- an interval $q = [\alpha_1, \alpha_2]$ with $1 \leq \alpha_1 \leq \alpha_2 \leq f$,
- and a real value $k \in [1, |\bigcup_{i \in q} G_i|]$;

it returns a real value x whose rank in $\bigcup_{i \in q} G_i$ falls in $[k, c_2 k)$, where $c_2 \geq 2$ is a constant. It is required that x should be either $-\infty$ or an element in $\bigcup_{i \in q} G_i$.

The following lemma is a crucial result that stands at the core of our final structure. Its proof is non-trivial and delegated to Section 4.

LEMMA 6. *For the (f, l)-problem, we can store $\boldsymbol{G}$ in a structure of $O(fl/B)$ space that answers a query in $O(\lg_B(fl))$ I/Os, and supports an insertion and deletion in $O(\lg_B(fl))$ I/Os amortized.*

3.3 Proof of Lemma 4

We are now ready to elaborate on the structure claimed in Lemma 4. It suffices to focus on the *approximate range k-selection problem*:

> The input is the same set S of points as in top-k range reporting. Given an interval $q = [x_1, x_2]$ and an integer k satisfying $1 \leq k \leq |S \cap q|$, a query returns a point $e \in S \cap q$ such that between k and $O(k)$ points in $S \cap q$ have scores at least *score*(e).

Suppose that there is a structure solving the above problem with query time t_q and amortized update time t_u. Then, we immediately obtain a structure of asymptotically the same space for top-k range reporting with query time $O(t_q + \lg_B n + k/B)$ and amortized update time $O(t_u + \lg_B n)$ (see [14]). A structure with $t_q = \lg_B n$ and $t_u = \lg_B^2 n$ was given in [14].

Fix an integer $l = O(\text{polylg}\, n)$. Next, assuming $k \leq l$, we describe a linear-size structure with $t_q = t_u = O(\lg_B n)$, which therefore yields a structure of Lemma 4.

Structure. We build a WBB-tree T on S with branching parameter $f = \sqrt{B \lg n}$, and leaf capacity $b = flB$. Each node u naturally corresponds to an x-range in $\mathbb{R}$. If u is an internal node with child nodes $u_1, ..., u_f$, define a *multi-slab* to be the union of the x-ranges of $u_i, u_{i+1}, ..., u_j$ for some meaningful i, j.

Given an (internal/leaf) node u, let S_u be the set of elements stored in the subtree of u. Define G_u as the set of $c_2 l$ highest scores of the elements in S_u, where c_2 is the constant mentioned in the definition of the (f, l)-problem in Section 3.2.

For each leaf node u, maintain a structure of [14] to support approximate range k-selection on S_u. Consider now u as an internal node with child nodes $u_1, ..., u_f$. We

- maintain an *$(f, c_2 l)$-structure* of Lemma 6 on the $(f, c_2 l)$-group $\boldsymbol{G}_u = (G_{u_1}, ..., G_{u_f})$, with N fixed to some integer in $[n, 4n]$ (this will be guaranteed by our update algorithms).
- store $G_{u_1} \cup ... \cup G_{u_f}$ in a (slightly augmented) B-tree so that, for any $1 \leq \alpha_1 \leq \alpha_2 \leq f$, the maximum score in $\bigcup_{i \in [\alpha_1, \alpha_2]} G_{u_i}$ can be found in $O(\lg_B(fl))$ I/Os.

There are $O(n/(fb))$ internal nodes, each of which occupies $O(fl/B)$ blocks. Hence, all the internal nodes use altogether $O(\frac{n}{fb} \cdot \frac{fl}{B}) = o(n/B)$ space. The overall space cost is therefore $O(n/B)$.

Query. Given a query with parameters $q = [x_1, x_2]$ and k, search T in a standard way to identify a minimum set C of $O(\lg_f n)$ disjoint *canonical ranges* whose union covers q, such that each canonical range is either the x-range of a leaf node or a multi-slab.

Define $S_m = m \cap S$ for each multi-slab $m \in C$. Perform AURS with parameter k on $\{S_m \mid m \in C\}$. At each internal node u on which a multi-slab $m \in C$ is defined, the $(f, c_2 l)$-structure of u and the B-tree on $\boldsymbol{G}_u$ allow us to implement the RANK and MAX operators on S_m in $O(\lg_B(fl))$ I/Os, respectively. Therefore, by Lemma 5[6], the AURS finishes in $O(\lg_f n \cdot \lg_B(fl)) = O(\lg_B n)$ I/Os. Denote by e the element returned[7].

For each leaf node z whose x-range is in C, perform approximate range k-selection on S_z using q in $O(\lg_B b) = O(\lg_B n)$ I/Os. There are at most two such leaf nodes; let e_1, e_2 be the results of approximate range k-selection on them, respectively. We return $\max\{e, e_1, e_2\}$ as the final answer.

[6]The constant c_1 in the RANK operator's definition (see Section 3.1) equals c_2 here, as is guaranteed by the $(f, c_2 l)$-structures. Given that we focus on $k \leq l$ while each G_u has size $c_2 l$, we know that the condition stated in (2) always holds.

[7]The AURS returns only the score of e, but it is easy to fetch e by the score in $O(\lg_B n)$ I/Os.

Update. The update algorithm (which is relatively standard) can be found in the appendix.

4. SOLVING THE (f, l)-PROBLEM

We devote this section to proving Lemma 6. Henceforth, by "query", we refer to a query in the (f, l)-problem. When no ambiguity can arise, we use $\boldsymbol{G}$ to denote also the union of G_1, ... G_f.

4.1 A Static Structure

We will need a tool called the *logarithmic sketch*—henceforth, *sketch*—developed in [14]. Let L be a set of l real values. Its sketch Σ is an array of size $\lfloor \lg l \rfloor + 1$, where the j-th ($1 \le j \le \lfloor \lg l \rfloor + 1$) entry $\Sigma[j]$—called a *pivot*—is an element in L whose rank in L falls in $[2^{j-1}, 2^j)$; any such element can be used as $\Sigma[j]$.

LEMMA 7 ([14]). *Let $L_1, ..., L_m$ be m disjoint sets of real values. Given their sketches and a real value k satisfying $1 \le k \le |\bigcup_{i=1}^m L_i|$, we can find in $O(m)$ I/Os a real value x whose rank in $\bigcup_{i=1}^m L_i$ is between k and $c_3 k$ (where $c_3 \ge 2$ is a constant). Furthermore, x is either $-\infty$ or an element in $\bigcup_{i=1}^m L_i$.*

Create a sketch Σ_i for each G_i ($1 \le i \le f$). Call the set $\{\Sigma_1, ..., \Sigma_f\}$ a *sketch set.* We store a compressed form of the sketch set as follows. Describe each pivot $e \in \Sigma_i$ by its *global rank* in $\boldsymbol{G}$ using $\lg(fl)$ bits, and by its *local rank* in G_i using $\lg l$ bits. Hence, each Σ_i requires $\lg l \cdot 2\lg(fl)$ bits. A compressed sketch set occupies $f \lg l \cdot 2\lg(fl) = \sqrt{B} \cdot \lg^\epsilon N \cdot O((\lg\lg N)^2)$ bits, and thus fits in a block (which has $B \cdot \Omega(\lg N)$ bits).

Given a query, we first spend an I/O reading the compressed sketched set, and then run the algorithm of Lemma 7 on it in memory. Suppose that this algorithm outputs x. If $x = -\infty$, we simply return $-\infty$ as our final answer. Otherwise, x is equal to the global rank of an element in $\boldsymbol{G}$. To convert the global rank to an actual element, we index all the elements of $\boldsymbol{G}$ with a B-tree, which supports such a conversion in $O(\lg_B(fl))$ I/Os. The overall space is $O(fl/B)$ (due to the B-tree); and the query cost is $O(\lg_B(fl))$. Notice that the constant c_2 in Section 3.2 equals the constant c_3 stated in Lemma 7.

4.2 Supporting Insertions

To facilitate updates, we store the elements of each G_i ($1 \le i \le f$) in a B-tree that allows us to obtain the element of any specific local rank in $O(\lg_B l)$ I/Os. In addition, we also maintain a structure of the following lemma, whose proof is deferred to Section 4.4:

LEMMA 8. *We can store an (f, l)-group $\boldsymbol{G} = (G_1, ..., G_f)$ in a structure of $O(fl/B)$ space such that, in one I/O, we can read into memory a single block, from which we can obtain for free the global rank of the element with local rank r in G_i, for every $r \in [1, \sqrt{B}\lg_B(fl)]$ and every $i \in [1, f]$. The structure supports an insertion and a deletion in $O(\lg_B(fl))$ I/Os.*

Suppose that an element e_{new} is to be inserted in G_i for some $i \in [1, f]$. Let r_{new} be the rank of e_{new} in $\boldsymbol{G}$. We observe that, except perhaps a single pivot, the new compressed sketch set (after the update) can be deduced from: the current compressed sketch set, r_{new} and i. To understand this, consider first a compressed sketch $\Sigma_{i'}$ where $i' \ne i$. Each pivot whose global rank is at least r_{new} now has its global rank increased by 1 (its local rank is unaffected). Regarding the compressed Σ_i, the same is true, but additionally every such pivot should also have its local rank increased by 1. Furthermore, a new pivot is needed in Σ_i if $|G_i|$ reaches a power of 2 after the insertion—in such a case we say that Σ_i *expands*; the new pivot is the only one in the compressed sketch set that cannot be deduced (because its global rank is unknown).

Motivated by this observation, to insert e_{new} in G_i, we first obtain r_{new} from the B-tree of $\boldsymbol{G}$ in $O(\lg_B(fl))$ I/Os, and then update the new compressed sketch set as described earlier in 1 I/O. Next, e_{new} is inserted in the B-trees of $\boldsymbol{G}$ and G_i using $O(\lg_B(fl))$ I/Os. If now $|G_i|$ is a power of 2, we retrieve the global rank of the smallest element in G_i in $O(\lg_B(fl))$ I/Os, and add the element to Σ_i in memory.

Recall that, the j-th ($1 \le j \le \lfloor \lg l \rfloor + 1$) pivot of Σ_i should have its local rank confined to $[2^{j-1}, 2^j)$. If this is not true, we say that it is *invalidated.* The insertion may have invalidated one or more pivots, (all of which can be found with no I/O because Σ_i in memory). Upon the invalidation of $\Sigma_i[j]$, we replace it as the element $e \in G_i$ with local rank $\lfloor \frac{3}{2} \cdot 2^{j-1} \rfloor$ so that $\Omega(2^j)$ updates in G_i are needed to invalidate $\Sigma_i[j]$ again. For the replacement to proceed, it remains to obtain the global rank of e. We do so by distinguishing two cases:

- *Case* $2^j \ge \sqrt{B}\lg_B(fl)$. We simply fetch e from the B-tree on G_i, and obtain its global rank from the B-tree on $\boldsymbol{G}$. We can now update $\Sigma_i[j]$ in memory.

  In total, the invalidated pivot is fixed with $O(\lg_B(fl)) = O(2^j/\sqrt{B})$ I/Os. Since $\Omega(2^j)$ updates must have occurred in G_i to trigger the invalidity of $\Sigma_i[j]$, each of those updates accounts for $O(1/\sqrt{B})$ I/Os of the pivot recomputation. As an update can be charged at most $O(\lg l)$ times this way (i.e., once for every $j \ge \sqrt{B}\lg_B(fl)$), its amortized cost is increased by only $O(\frac{1}{\sqrt{B}} \lg l) = O(\lg_B l)$.

- *Case* $2^j < \sqrt{B}\lg_B(fl)$. There are $O(\lg(\sqrt{B}\lg_B(fl))$ such invalidated pivots in Σ_i. We can recompute *all* of them together in $O(1)$ I/Os using Lemma 8.

Overall, an insertion requires $O(\lg_B(fl))$ I/Os amortized.

4.3 Supporting Deletions

Suppose that an element e_{old} is to be deleted from G_i for some $i \in [1, f]$. Let r_{old} be the rank of e_{old} in $\boldsymbol{G}$. Except possibly for only one pivot, the new compressed sketch set can be deduced based only on the current compressed sketch set, r, and i. To see this, consider first $\Sigma_{i'}$ where $i' \ne i$. Each pivot whose global rank is larger than r_{old} now needs to have its global rank decreased by 1. Regarding Σ_i, the same is true, and every such pivot should also have its local rank decreased by 1. Furthermore, the last pivot of Σ_i should be discarded if $|G_i|$ was a power of 2 before the deletion: in such a case, we say that Σ_i *shrinks*. Finally, if e_{old} happens to be a pivot of Σ_i, a new pivot needs to be computed to replace it—this is the only pivot that cannot be deduced; we call it a *dangling* pivot.

The concrete steps of deleting e_{old} are as follows. After fetching its global rank r_{old} in $O(\lg_B(fl))$ I/Os, we update the compressed sketch set in memory according to the above discussion. If Σ_i shrinks, we delete the last pivot Σ_i in memory. If e_{old} was a pivot (say, the j-th one for some j), we retrieve the element e with local rank $\lfloor \frac{3}{2} \cdot 2^{j-1} \rfloor$ in G_i, and obtain its global rank using $O(\lg_B(fl))$ I/Os. We then replace the dangling pivot $\Sigma_i[j]$ with e in memory.

Finally, recompute the invalidated pivots (if any) in the same way as in an insertion. As analyzed in Section 4.2, such recomputation increases the amortized update cost by only $O(\lg_B l)$.

4.4 Proof of Lemma 8

Let us define the list of the $\sqrt{B}\lg_B(fl)$ largest elements of G_i ($1 \le i \le f$) as the *prefix* of G_i, and denote it as P_i. Let $\boldsymbol{P}$ be the union of $P_1, .., P_f$; we refer to $\boldsymbol{P}$ as a *prefix set.* $\boldsymbol{P}$ contains at most $f\sqrt{B}\lg_B(fl)$ points.

We compress $\boldsymbol{P}$ by describing each element e (say, $e \in P_i$ for some i) in $\boldsymbol{P}$ using its global rank in $\boldsymbol{G}$ and its local rank in G_i, for which purpose $O(\lg(fl))$ bits suffice. Hence, $\boldsymbol{P}$ can be described by $f \cdot \sqrt{B}\lg_B(fl) \cdot O(\lg(fl)) = \sqrt{B}\lg^{\epsilon} N \cdot \sqrt{B} \cdot O((\lg\lg N)^2) = B \cdot \lg^{\epsilon} N \cdot O((\lg\lg N)^2)$ bits, which fit in a block. After loading this block into memory, we can obtain the global rank of the r-th largest element of G_i for free, regardless of $r \in [1, \sqrt{B}\lg_B(fl)]$ and i.

Besides the aforementioned block, we also maintain a B-tree on each G_i ($1 \le i \le f$) and a B-tree on $\boldsymbol{G}$. The space consumed is $O(fl/B)$.

Insertion. Suppose that we need to insert an element e_{new} into G_i. First, we update the B-trees of G_i and $\boldsymbol{G}$ in $O(\lg_B(fl))$ I/Os. With the same cost, we can also decide whether e_{new} should enter P_i. If not, the insertion is complete.

Otherwise, we find the global rank r_{new} of e_{new} and its local rank r'_{new} in G_i with $O(\lg_B(fl))$ I/Os. Load the compressed prefix set $\boldsymbol{P}$ into memory with 1 I/O. Then, the new compressed prefix set can be determined for free based on $\boldsymbol{P}$, i, r_{new}, and r'_{new}. To see this, first consider a compressed prefix $P_{i'}$ with $i' \ne i$: if an element has global rank at least r_{new}, it should have its global rank increased by 1. Regarding the compressed prefix P_i, the same is true; furthermore, all such elements in P_i should also have their local ranks increased by 1. Finally, we add e_{new} into P_i; if P_i has a size over $\sqrt{B}\lg_B(fl)$, we discard its smallest element.

Deletion. Suppose that we need to delete an element e_{old} from G_i. Using the B-tree on $\boldsymbol{G}$, we find its global rank r_{old} in $O(\lg_B(fl))$ I/Os. Then, e_{old} is removed from the B-trees of G_i and $\boldsymbol{G}$ in $O(\lg_B(fl))$ I/Os.

If $e_{old} \notin P_i$, the deletion is done. Otherwise, we load the compressed prefix set in 1 I/O, and then update it, except for a single element, in memory. Specifically, in a compressed prefix $P_{i'}$ with $i' \ne i$, if an element has global rank at least r_{old}, it should have its global rank decreased by 1. Regarding the compressed prefix P_i, the same is true; furthermore, all such elements in P_i should also have their local ranks decreased by 1.

The last element of P_i is the only one that cannot be inferred directly at this point. But it can be filled in simply by retrieving the element with local rank $\sqrt{B}\lg_B(fl)$ in G_i, and then its global rank in $\boldsymbol{G}$, all in $O(\lg_B(fl))$ I/Os.

5. ACKNOWLEDGEMENTS

This work was supported in part by projects GRF 4165/11, 4164/12, and 4168/13 from HKRGC. The author would like to thank Xiaocheng Hu for proofreading the paper and his comments on how the presentation can be simplified.

6. REFERENCES

[1] P. Afshani, G. S. Brodal, and N. Zeh. Ordered and unordered top-k range reporting in large data sets. In *Proceedings of the Annual ACM-SIAM Symposium on Discrete Algorithms (SODA)*, pages 390–400, 2011.

[2] A. Aggarwal and J. S. Vitter. The input/output complexity of sorting and related problems. *Communications of the ACM (CACM)*, 31(9):1116–1127, 1988.

[3] L. Arge, V. Samoladas, and J. S. Vitter. On two-dimensional indexability and optimal range search indexing. In *Proceedings of ACM Symposium on Principles of Database Systems (PODS)*, pages 346–357, 1999.

[4] L. Arge and J. S. Vitter. Optimal external memory interval management. *SIAM Journal of Computing*, 32(6):1488–1508, 2003.

[5] G. S. Brodal, R. Fagerberg, M. Greve, and A. Lopez-Ortiz. Online sorted range reporting. In *International Symposium on Algorithms and Computation (ISAAC)*, pages 173–182, 2009.

[6] T. H. Cormen, C. E. Leiserson, R. L. Rivest, and C. Stein. *Introduction to Algorithms, Second Edition.* The MIT Press, 2001.

[7] G. N. Frederickson. An optimal algorithm for selection in a min-heap. *Information and Computation*, 104(2):197–214, 1993.

[8] G. N. Frederickson and D. B. Johnson. The complexity of selection and ranking in x+y and matrices with sorted columns. *Journal of Computer and System Sciences (JCSS)*, 24(2):197–208, 1982.

[9] I. F. Ilyas, G. Beskales, and M. A. Soliman. A survey of top-k query processing techniques in relational database systems. *ACM Computing Surveys*, 40(4), 2008.

[10] E. M. McCreight. Priority search trees. *SIAM Journal of Computing*, 14(2):257–276, 1985.

[11] G. Navarro and Y. Nekrich. Top-k document retrieval in optimal time and linear space. In *Proceedings of the Annual ACM-SIAM Symposium on Discrete Algorithms (SODA)*, pages 1066–1077, 2012.

[12] M. Patrascu and M. Thorup. Time-space trade-offs for predecessor search. In *Proceedings of ACM Symposium on Theory of Computing (STOC)*, pages 232–240, 2006.

[13] R. Shah, C. Sheng, S. V. Thankachan, and J. S. Vitter. Top-k document retrieval in external memory. In *Proceedings of European Symposium on Algorithms (ESA)*, pages 803–814, 2013.

[14] C. Sheng and Y. Tao. Dynamic top-k range reporting in external memory. In *Proceedings of ACM Symposium on Principles of Database Systems (PODS)*, 2012.

Appendix

Proof of Lemma 5

In this proof, set $c = c_1$ and $L = \cup_{i=1}^{m} L_i$. Given an element $e \in L_i$ ($1 \le i \le m$), we refer to its rank in L_i as its *local rank*, and its rank in L as its *global rank*.

Case $k \ge m$. Our algorithm executes in $\lceil \lg_c m \rceil$ rounds. In the j-th round ($1 \le j \le \lceil \lg_c m \rceil$), $\lceil m/c^{j-1} \rceil$ sets among $L_1, ..., L_m$ are *active*, while the others are *inactive*. At the beginning, $L_1, ..., L_m$ are all active.

In round $j \in [1, \lceil \lg_c m \rceil]$, we execute RANK on each active set L_i with parameter $\rho = c^j k/m$. Remember that the operator can return any element whose local rank falls in $[c^j k/m, c^{j+1} k/m)$.[8] Let P' be the set of elements fetched. We call each element in P' a *marker*, and assign it a *weight* equal to

- $\lceil ck/m \rceil$ if $j = 1$;
- $\lceil c^j k/m \rceil - \lceil c^{j-1} k/m \rceil$ if $j > 1$.

The $\lceil m/c^j \rceil$ largest markers in P' are taken as *pivots*, among which the smallest is the *cutoff pivot* of this round. An active set remains active in the next round if its marker is a pivot, whereas the other active sets become inactive.

Denote by P_j the set of pivots taken in the j-th round ($1 \le j \le \lceil \lg_c m \rceil$), and by P the union of $P_1, P_2, ..., P_{\lceil \lg_c m \rceil}$. It is clear that $|P| = \sum_{j=1}^{\lceil \lg_c m \rceil} \lceil m/c^j \rceil = O(m)$.

Consider a pivot $p \in P_j$, and suppose that it comes from L_i for some $i \in [1, m]$. Define the *local prefix weight* of p as the sum of the weights of the first j pivots fetched from L_i. By how we define weights, it is easy to verify that the local prefix weight of p is $\lceil c^j k/m \rceil$. For each pivot $p \in P$, define its *prefix weight* as the total weight of all the pivots that are larger than or equal to p.

OBSERVATION 1. *Every cutoff pivot has a prefix weight at least k.*

PROOF. Consider the cutoff pivot p^* of round $j \in [1, \lceil \lg_c m \rceil]$. Let P'_j be the set of $\lceil m/c^j \rceil$ pivots of P_j greater than or equal to p^*. The prefix weight of p^* is at least the sum of the local prefix weights of all the pivots in P'_j, which is at least $\lceil m/c^j \rceil \lceil c^j k/m \rceil \ge k$. □

We perform a *weighted selection* to find the largest pivot $v \in P$ whose prefix weight is at least k (v definitely exists by the previous observation). The algorithm terminates by returning v.

The algorithm performs in $O(m \cdot cost_{rank})$ I/Os because the j-th round takes $O((m/c^{j-1}) \cdot cost_{rank})$ I/Os (i.e., geometrically decreasing with j), while the weighted selection needs only $O(m/B)$ I/Os. Next, we prove that the algorithm is correct, namely, the global rank of v is in $[k, c'k]$ for some constant c' dependent only on c.

OBSERVATION 2. *The prefix weight of v is at most $(1 + 2c)k$.*

PROOF. We define v' as the smallest pivot in P that is larger than v. By definition, we know that the prefix weight of v' is smaller than k. Define p'_i as the smallest pivot in L_i that is larger than or equal to v'; $p'_i = nil$ if no such pivot exists. Defining the local prefix weight of a *nil* point to be 0, we have:

$$\begin{aligned} \text{prefix weight of } v' &= \sum_{i=1}^{m} \text{local prefix weight of } p'_i \\ &< k. \end{aligned} \tag{3}$$

Clearly, it also holds that

$$\begin{aligned} \text{prefix weight of } v &= \text{prefix weight of } v' + \text{weight of } v \\ &< k + \text{weight of } v \end{aligned} \tag{4}$$

Let i^* be such that $v \in L_{i^*}$. We distinguish two cases:

Case 1: $p'_{i^*} = nil$. This means that v was taken in the first round of our algorithm; hence, its weight is $\lceil ck/m \rceil < 2ck$ (recall that $c \ge 2$). Therefore, by (4) the prefix weight of v is less than $k + 2ck$.

Case 2: $p'_{i^*} \ne nil$. Then, the weight of v is less than $2c$ times the local prefix weight of p'_{i^*}. Together with (3), this implies that the weight of v is less than $2ck$. Therefore, once again, (4) tells us that the prefix weight of v is less than $k + 2ck$. □

By Observation 1 and the definition of v, all cutoff pivots are smaller than or equal to v. Hence, every L_i has at least one marker smaller than or equal to v. We will refer to the largest such marker as the *succeeding marker* of L_i, and denote it as e_i. Note that e_i is not necessarily a pivot.

Let p_i be the smallest pivot of L_i that is larger than or equal to v. If p_i exists, we say that L_i is *pivotal*; otherwise, L_i is *non-pivotal*. For a pivotal L_i, define:

- r_i = the local prefix weight of p_i.
- S_i = the set of elements in L_i that are larger than or equal to v.
- S'_i = the set of elements in L_i that are larger than or equal to p_i.

OBSERVATION 3. $r_i \le |S'_i| \le |S_i| < c^2 \cdot r_i$.

PROOF. Let j be such that p_i was taken in the j-th round of our algorithm. $|S'_i|$ is exactly the local rank of p_i, which must fall in $[c^j k/m, c^{j+1} k/m)$. Hence, it follows that $|S'_i| \ge \lceil c^j k/m \rceil = r_i$.

As e_i was taken in the $(j+1)$-st round, its local rank is less than $c^{j+2} k/m$. Since the local rank e_i is an upper bound of $|S_i|$, it follows that $|S_i| < c^{j+2} k/m \le c^2 r_i$. □

In the pivotal sets, the total number of elements larger than or equal to v equals:

$$\begin{aligned} \sum_{i \text{ s.t. } L_i \text{ is pivotal}} |S_i| &\le c^2 \sum_{i \text{ s.t. } L_i \text{ is pivotal}} r_i \\ &= c^2 \cdot (\text{prefix weight of } v) \\ \text{(by Observation 2)} &< c^2(1 + 2c)k. \end{aligned}$$

Each non-pivotal set L_i has less than $c^2 k/m$ elements larger than or equal to v. It thus follows that the global rank of v is less than $(c^2 k/m)m + c^2(1 + 2c)k = c^2(2 + 2c)k$.

On the lower side, the global rank of v is at least

$$\begin{aligned} \sum_{i \text{ s.t. } L_i \text{ is pivotal}} |S_i| &\ge \sum_{i \text{ s.t. } L_i \text{ is pivotal}} r_i \\ &= \text{prefix weight of } v \\ &\ge k. \end{aligned}$$

[8] Such an element definitely exists because $c^j k/m \le ck \le |L_i|$.

Case $k < m$. From each L_i, we use MAX to request the largest element in L_i. Let P' be the set of elements fetched (i.e., one from each L_i). Obtain the k-th largest element v' in P'. Make set L_i inactive if its largest element is smaller than v'; otherwise, L_i is active. Run the above algorithm on the k active sets. Suppose that the algorithm outputs v. We then return $\max\{v, v'\}$ as the final answer. It is easy to prove that the algorithm is correct, and runs in $O(m(cost_{rank} + cost_{max}))$ I/Os.

The Update Algorithm in Section 3.3

To support updates, for each internal node u, build a B-tree on the scores in $\boldsymbol{G}_u$. For each leaf node z, build a B-tree on the scores of the elements in S_z. Refer to these B-trees as *score B-trees*. Denote by $parent(u)$ the parent of u.

To insert a point e in S, first descend a root-to-leaf path π to the leaf node z whose x-range covers e. At z, update all its secondary structures in $O(\lg_B^2 b) = O((\lg_B \lg n)^2) = O(\lg_B n)$ amortized I/Os. Next, we fix the secondary structures of the nodes along π in a bottom up manner. If $score(e)$ enters G_z, at $parent(z)$, delete the lowest score in G_z, and then insert $score(e)$ in G_z. The secondary structures of $parent(z)$ are then updated accordingly. In general, after updating an internal node u, we check using the score B-tree of u whether $score(e)$ should enter G_u. If so, at $parent(u)$, delete the lowest score in G_u, insert $score(e)$ in G_u, and update the secondary structures of $parent(u)$. By Lemma 6, we spend $O(\lg_B(fl))$ amortized I/Os at each node, and hence, $O(\lg_B n)$ amortized I/Os in total along the whole π.

We now explain how to handle node splits. Suppose that a leaf node z splits into z_1, z_2. First, build the secondary structures of z_1 and z_2 in $O(b \lg_B^2 b)$ I/Os. At $v = parent(z)$, destroy G_z, and include G_{z_1} and G_{z_2} into $\boldsymbol{G}_v$. Rebuild all the secondary structures at v in $O(fl \cdot \lg_B(fl)) = O(b \lg_B b)$ I/Os (Lemma 6). This cost can be amortized over the $\Omega(b)$ updates that must have taken place in z, such that each update is charged only $O(\lg_B^2 b) = O(\lg_B n)$ I/Os.

A split at an internal level can be handled in a similar way. Suppose that an internal node u splits into u_1, u_2. Divide $\boldsymbol{G}_u$ into $\boldsymbol{G}_{u_1}$ and $\boldsymbol{G}_{u_2}$ in $O(fl/B)$ I/Os, and then rebuild the secondary structures of u_1, u_2 in $O(fl \cdot \lg_B(fl))$ I/Os. After discarding G_u but including G_{u_1}, G_{u_2}, we rebuild the secondary structures of $parent(u)$ in $O(fl \cdot \lg_B(fl))$ I/Os. On the other hand, $\Omega(fl)$ updates must have taken place in the subtree of u (recall that the base tree is a WBB-tree). Hence, each of those updates bears $O(\lg_B(fl))$ I/Os for the split cost. As an update bears such cost for at most one node per level, the amortized update cost increases by only $O(\lg_B n)$.

An analogous algorithm can be used to handle a deletion in $O(\lg_B n)$ amortized I/Os. After n has doubled or halved, we destroy the entire structure, reset N to $2n$, and rebuild everything in $O(n \lg_B n)$ I/Os. The amortized update cost is therefore $O(\lg_B n)$.

Categorical Range Maxima Queries*

Manish Patil
Louisiana State University, USA
mpatil@csc.lsu.edu

Sharma V. Thankachan
University of Waterloo, Canada
thanks@uwaterloo.ca

Rahul Shah
Louisiana State University, USA
rahul@csc.lsu.edu

Yakov Nekrich
University of Waterloo, Canada
yakov.nekrich@gmail.com

Jeffrey Scott Vitter
The University of Kansas, USA
jsv@ku.edu

ABSTRACT

Given an array $A[1...n]$ of n distinct elements from the set $\{1, 2, ..., n\}$ a range maximum query $\text{RMQ}(a, b)$ returns the highest element in $A[a...b]$ along with its position. In this paper, we study a generalization of this classical problem called *Categorical Range Maxima Query* (CRMQ) problem, in which each element $A[i]$ in the array has an associated category (color) given by $C[i] \in [\sigma]$. A query then asks to report each distinct color c appearing in $C[a...b]$ along with the highest element (and its position) in $A[a...b]$ with color c. Let p_c denote the *position* of the highest element in $A[a...b]$ with color c. We investigate two variants of this problem: a threshold version and a top-k version. In threshold version, we only need to output the colors with $A[p_c]$ more than the input threshold τ, whereas top-k variant asks for k colors with the highest $A[p_c]$ values.

In the word RAM model, we achieve linear space structure along with $O(k)$ query time, that can report colors in sorted order of $A[\cdot]$. In external memory, we present a data structure that answers queries in optimal $O(1+\frac{k}{B})$ I/O's using almost-linear $O(n \log^* n)$ space, as well as a linear space data structure with $O(\log^* n + \frac{k}{B})$ query I/Os. Here k represents the output size, $\log^* n$ is the iterated logarithm of n and B is the block size. CRMQ has applications to document retrieval and categorical range reporting – giving a one-shot framework to obtain improved results in both these problems. Our results for CRMQ not only improve the existing best known results for three-sided categorical range reporting but also overcome the hurdle of maintaining color uniqueness in the output set.

Categories and Subject Descriptors

E.1 [**Data Structures**]: Trees; Tables; F.2 [**ANALYSIS OF ALGORITHMS AND PROBLEM COMPLEXITY**]: Tradeoffs among Complexity Measures

Keywords

I/O Efficiency, Categorical Queries

1. INTRODUCTION

Given an array A of n elements from a totally ordered set, a natural question is to ask for the position of a maximum element between two specified indices a and b. Queries of this form are known as range maximum queries (RMQ). Consider a sample query: "Give me the highest paid employee within age group 18 to 22 years". By arranging all employees in a age-sorted array with his/her salary as the key, this query translates into an RMQ problem. Being an important tool in designing data structures for numerous problems in string processing and computation geometry, RMQ has been extensively studied in the literature [5, 4, 10]. There are several variants of the problem, the most prominent being the one where the array is static and known in advance. The current best known result for such a scenario is by Fischer and Heun [10], where they present a $2n + o(n)$-bit structure capable of answering queries in constant time.

However, in many applications, the standard RMQ problem does not suffice. Consider the generalization of the above query as a motivating example: "Give me the list of highest paid employees for different job positions (one per job position) with age between 18 to 22 years". This problem can obviously be solved by maintaining age-sorted array of employees as before for each designation in the organizational hierarchy and then issuing a RMQ for all of them. However, this solution may be very inefficient as the job positions held by employees within the specified age group can be only a fraction of all listed positions for the organization. We call the above problem to be an instance of *Categorical Range Maxima Query* (CRMQ). For CRMQ, we assume that each element in the input array A is assigned a color. The goal is to preprocess the array and maintain a data structure, such that given a query range $[a, b]$, one can efficiently report each distinct color c in the query range along with the highest element in $A[a...b]$ with color c. Further continuing the example under consideration, lets say we only need to output the job positions where the highest paid employee with that designation earns more than \$80,000 per year. This natural extension of CRMQ called "threshold-CRMQ" problem is formally defined below.

*This work is supported in part by National Science Foundation (NSF) Grants CCF–1017623 (R. Shah and J. S. Vitter) and CCF–1218904 (R. Shah).

PODS'14, June 22–27, 2014, Snowbird, UT, USA.

PROBLEM 1. *[Threshold-CRMQ] Let $A[1...n]$ be an array of n distinct integers in $[1,n]$ with each element $A[i]$ associated with a color $C[i] \in [\sigma]$. Then, goal is to build a data structure such that, given a query (a,b,τ), we can report the triplet $(c, p_c, A[p_c])$ for those colors $c \in [\sigma]$ with $A[p_c] \geq \tau$. Here $A[p_c]$ represents the highest element in $A[a...b]$ with color c. If there does not exist an element in $A[a...b]$ with color c, then $A[p_c] = -\infty$.*

Top-k queries are widely popular in database and information retrieval systems as they allow end-users to focus on the most important (top-k) outputs amongst those which satisfy the query. We study top-k version of CRMQ problem (top-CRMQ) as well, where the query input consists of a range $[a,b]$ and an integer $k \leq \sigma$, and we are required to output only k colors with the highest $A[p_c]$ values.

PROBLEM 2. *[Top-CRMQ] Let $A[1...n]$ be an array of n distinct integers in $[1,n]$ with each element $A[i]$ associated with a color $C[i] \in [\sigma]$. Then, goal is to build a data structure such that, given a query (a,b,k), we can report k triplets $(c, p_c, A[p_c])$ for colors $c \in [\sigma]$ with the highest $A[p_c]$ values, where $A[p_c]$ represents the highest element in $A[a...b]$ with color c. If there does not exist an element in $A[a...b]$ with color c, then $A[p_c] = -\infty$.*

In this article, we focus on top-CRMQ as our central problem. We distinguish between the sorted and unsorted version of this problem. In the sorted version, a triplet $(c, p_c, A[p_c])$ is reported before $(c', p_{c'}, A[p_{c'}])$, if $A[p_c] > A[p_{c'}]$, whereas unsorted version do not place any such restrictions. We focus on sorted version in Word-RAM model and unsorted version in external memory. Our main results are summarized in following theorems.

THEOREM 1. *There exists a linear space (in words) and optimal $O(k)$ time solution for the (sorted) top-CRMQ problem in Word-RAM model.*

THEOREM 2. *There exists an external memory structure of $O(n \log^* n)$ space and optimal $O(1+\frac{k}{B})$ query I/Os for the top-CRMQ problem, where $\log^* n$ is the iterated logarithm of n and B is the block size.*

THEOREM 3. *There exists an external memory structure of linear-space and near-optimal $O(\log^* n + \frac{k}{B})$ query I/Os for the top-CRMQ problem, where $\log^* n$ is the iterated logarithm of n and B is the block size.*

We improve the query I/O bound of the linear space solution in the above theorem by trading off space to achieve space-time bounds with Inverse Ackermann function. We summarize the result in following theorem with its proof deferred to Appendix D.

THEOREM 4. *The top-CRMQ problem can answered in near-optimal $O(\alpha^3 + \frac{k}{B})$ I/Os using an $O(n\alpha)$-word space structure, α being the Inverse Ackermann function of n.*

Answering Threshold-CRMQ: Data structures for answering top-CRMQ as summarized in theorems above, can be used for answering the threshold-CRMQ as well. Given a threshold-CRMQ (a,b,τ), we issue multiple top-CRMQ's as follows. Assume, we are using the I/O-optimal structure in Theorem 2, then we choose $K_j = 2^j B$ and issue top-CRMQ (a,b,K_j) for $j = 0,1,2,3,...$ until we find the smallest K_j (say K') where at least one of the triplet $(x, p_x, A[p_x])$ in the output set violates the condition $A[x] \geq \tau$. Then all those triplets corresponding to the output of top-CRMQ (a,b,K') satisfying the condition $A[\cdot] \geq \tau$ can be reported as the final answers. The number of I/O's required is $O(1+2+4+...+K'/B) = O(1+K'/B) = O(1+k/B)$, where k is the output size. If we are using the linear-space structure, we use the same procedure, with $K_j = 2^j B \log^* n$ and the query I/Os can be bounded by $O(\log^* n + (1+2+4+...+k/B)) = O(\log^* n + k/B)$. In conclusion, results in Theorem 2 and Theorem 3 are applicable for threshold-CRMQ as well.

Outline: Section 2 introduces a few existing data structures for several orthogonal range searching problems and give a brief summary of the external-memory model [2]. While CRMQ is an interesting problem in its own right, it is also closely related to other important problems. In Section 3 we describe the applications of our results to categorical range reporting and document retrieval. Section 4- 7 are dedicated for deriving external memory data structures for the top-CRMQ problem. We begin by reducing the problem under consideration to a geometric problem in Section 4. Using the equivalent geometric formulation, we present a simple external memory solution for top-CRMQ in Section 5. We build upon this solution incrementally in Section 6 and 7 to obtain I/O optimal and linear space structures. Internal memory result for top-CRMQ is discussed in Section 8. Finally we conclude in Section 9.

2. PRELIMINARIES

2.1 External Memory Model

The external memory (EM) model [2, 27] is a popular model for analyzing the performance of algorithms when input data set is too large to be accommodated in internal memory and hence resides on the disk. In EM, the CPU is connected directly to an internal memory, which is then connected to a much slower disk. The disk is of an unbounded size and is formatted into disjoint blocks, each of which contains B consecutive words. An I/O operation reads a block of data from the disk into memory, or conversely, writes a block of memory information into the disk. Main memory can accommodate M words and is assumed to have at least two blocks, i.e., $M \geq 2B$. The cost of answering a query is measured in the number of I/Os performed by the algorithm.

2.2 Three-dimensional Dominance Reporting

Given a set S of n points in three dimensions and query point $q = (q_1, q_2, q_3)$, the three-dimensional dominance reporting asks for all the points $s = (x_1, x_2, x_3) \in S$ such that $x_i < q_i$, $1 \leq i \leq 3$. The best known result for the problem is by Afshani [1] which achieves linear space along with optimal $O(\log_B n + k/B)$ query I/Os.

2.3 Three-sided Orthogonal Range Reporting

Given a set S of n points in two dimensions, three-sided orthogonal range reporting asks for all points inside a query rectangle of the form $[x_1, x_2] \times (-\infty, y]$. The best I/O model solution to this range reporting problem is due to Arge et al. [3] which takes linear space and report all the points the query rectangle in $O(\log_B n + k/B)$ I/Os. When the two-dimensional points are on the $[n] \times [n]$ grid, Larsen et. al [17] achieve improved query bound of $O(1 + k/B)$ I/Os.

3. APPLICATIONS OF CRMQ

3.1 Categorical Range Reporting Without Duplicates

In the categorical (or colored) range reporting problem the set of input points is partitioned into categories and stored in a data structure; a query asks for categories of points that belong to the query range. The problem has been extensively studied in computational geometry and database communities [14, 12, 6, 20, 16, 23, 17, 18].

In three-sided color reporting, the query asks to report the set of colors of the points in an input region $[a, b] \times [\tau, +\infty)$. Without loss of generality, we assume that the points are in rank-space ‖. The first external memory result for this problem was given by Nekrich [23]. His results on this problem were further improved by Larsen and Walderveen [18], where they presented an $O(nh)$-word data structure with $O(\log^{(h)} n + \frac{k}{B})$ query cost, k being the output size, $1 \leq h \leq \log^* n, \log^{(h)} n = \log\log^{(h-1)} n$ and $\log^{(1)} n = \log n$. Thus by choosing $h = \log^* n$, an I/O-optimal structure can be obtained. On the other-hand, a linear space structure can be obtained by choosing $h = O(1)$.

The data structures described in [23, 18] have a limitation that can compromise their usefulness in some situations: the list of colors in the output set may contain several (yet constant) occurrences of the same color. Eliminating such duplicates (in the current settings) needs extra I/Os (sorting is inevitable in these solutions, which makes these results less-optimal in terms of query I/Os). In [23], another data structure that uses linear space and reports every color exactly once is described. Unfortunately, this data structure needs $O((\frac{n}{B})^{\varepsilon} + \frac{k}{B})$ I/Os to answer a query, where ε is an arbitrarily small positive constant. This makes the design of an efficient external data structure that reports every color exactly once an important open problem, and we provide the following solution for it.

THEOREM 5. *A three-sided color reporting query on a set of n points in rank-space can be answered in $O(1 + \frac{k}{B})$ I/Os using an $O(n \log^* n)$-word structure, or in $O(\log^* n + \frac{k}{B})$ I/Os using an $O(n)$-word structure, such that the output set contains* exactly one copy of each answer, *where k is the output size, $\log^* n$ is the iterated logarithm of n and B is the block size.*

PROOF. Let $P = \{(i, y_i) | i = 1, 2, 3, ..., n\}$ be the set of points, then construct the array A, where $A[i] = y_i$ and its color is same as that of (i, y_i). Then the output of any three-sided color reporting query on P with $[a, b] \times [\tau, +\infty)$ as an input is the same as that of a threshold-CRMQ (a, b, τ) on A. Thus, we obtain the results summarized in above theorem using Theorem 2 and Theorem 3. □

Consequently, we achieve a smaller (non-optimal) term of $\log^* n$ in the I/O bound of the linear-space structure compared to the $(\frac{n}{B})^{\varepsilon}$ or $\log^{(O(1))} n$ terms in the existing solutions. Further, using standard techniques [23, 18] in conjunction with results in Theorem 2, Theorem 3, we obtain following results for (two dimensional) four-sided color reporting problem. Although this improves the known results of the problem [18], the output set may contain multiple (at most two) copies of the same color.

THEOREM 6. *A four-sided color reporting query on a set of n points in an $[n] \times [n]$ grid can be answered in $O(1 + \frac{k}{B})$ I/Os using an $O(n \log n \log^* n)$-word structure, or in $O(\log^* n + \frac{k}{B})$ I/Os using an $O(n \log n)$-word structure. Here k is the output size, $\log^* n$ is the iterated logarithm of n and B is the block size.*

Hardness of color counting: In a color counting problem, our task is to simply report the cardinality of the output set of the corresponding reporting problem. Color counting problems are considered to be much harder than the reporting counterparts. For example, the best known space-time trade-off for two-dimensional four-sided color counting is $O(n^2 \log^2 n)$ words and $O(\log^2 n)$ time [12, 15]. In [18], Larsen and Walderveen show that two-dimensional range counting problem is equivalent to one-dimensional color counting problem. Using a simple extension of their techniques, we can obtain a similar result for three-sided color counting problem as summarized below.

THEOREM 7. *Three-sided color counting problem (in two dimension) is at least as hard as three-dimensional orthogonal range counting problem.*

3.2 Ranked Document Retrieval

Suppose that we want to store a collection $\mathcal{D} = \{d_1, d_2, ..., d_D\}$ of D documents (strings) of total n characters, so that for a given query string P all documents containing P can be reported. This problem can be reduced to one-dimensional color reporting problem and can be solved optimally [20]. A more general and arguably the most important query, known as the *top-k document retrieval query* asks to find those k documents in $\mathcal{D}$ which are most relevant to P, where k is also an input parameter. The relevance of a document d w.r.t a pattern P is captured using a predefined ranking function $w(P, d)$, which is dependent on the set of occurrences of P in d. A popular example is the *term frequency*, where $w(P, d)$ is the number of occurrences of P in d. This problem has been studied extensively in string searching community (See [21] for an excellent survey) and linear-space and optimal query time internal memory results are known [13, 22]. Whereas in external memory, the best known linear space index is given by Shah et al. [25], however the query I/O bound is $O(\frac{|P|}{B} + \log_B n + \log^{(h)} n + \frac{k}{B})$ I/Os for any constant $h \geq 1$. We show that our solution for top-CRMQ can be used to obtain the following new result. Please refer to Appendix B for more details.

THEOREM 8. *If the ranking function is such that, the relevance of a document w.r.t. a pattern is not more that its relevance w.r.t. to any prefix of the same pattern, then we can construct a linear-space structure for answering top-k document retrieval queries in $O(\frac{|P|}{B} + \log_B n + \log^* B + \frac{k}{B})$ I/Os, where P is the input pattern.*

Although, our results require relevance to be a monotonic function (less general than the one considered by Shah et al. [13]), the most popular relevance measures such as term-frequency, term-proximity, Page-Rank etc. are monotonic.

‖By rank-space we assume that the points are in $[n] \times [n]$ grid, and the projections of any two points to any axis is different. If the points are in a $[U] \times [U]$ grid, we can reduce them to $[n] \times [n]$ grid using standard techniques. However the space will increase by an $O(n)$ words and the query cost by $O(\log\log_B U)$ I/Os (or $O(\log\log U)$ time). If the coordinate values are unbounded, the extra term in space is again $O(n)$, but in the query cost is $O(\log_B n)$ I/Os (or $O(\log n)$ time).

3.3 Sorted Reporting

In this problem we want to report all elements of an array A in sorted order. Suppose that we want to store an array A in a data structure such that for any query range $[a, b]$ all elements $A[i]$, $a \leq i \leq b$, can be reported in sorted order. Brodal et al. [7] described a linear space data structure that answers such queries in $O(b-a+1)$ time: moreover their data structure can be also used to report k highest points in the range in sorted order. Karpinski and Nekrich [16] considered the same problem in the color scenario: elements of the array are also assigned colors. We assume that colors are from an ordered set; now the query answer must report the k highest colors that occur in the query range and colors must be reported in the reverse order. We observe that the optimal data structure described in Theorem 1 generalizes the result of [16, 7]. This result is obtained using a new data structure for sorted three-dimensional dominance queries, which may be of independent interest. The result is summarized below (Proof is deferred to Appendix C).

THEOREM 9. *A given set of n three-dimensional points can be stored as an $O(n)$-word data structure that can answer a three-dimensional dominance reporting query in $O(\log n +$ output$)$ time in Word-RAM model, with outputs reported in the sorted order of z coordinate.*

4. THE FRAMEWORK

For color listing problem i.e., to simply enumerate all distinct colors in $C[a...b]$, Muthukrishnan [20] proposed the *chaining* idea, where each occurrence of a particular color points to (or chains to) its predecessor of the same color ¶. Therefore, among all occurrences of a particular color $c \in [\sigma]$ occurring in $C[a...b]$, only the first ones chain will be pointing outside the range $[a, b]$. Based on this observation, he reduced the problem to a (two-dimensional) three-sided range reporting query, which can be solved optimally using known structures. We introduce a generalization of this approach for solving our top-CRMQ problem. Formally, for each position $i \in [1, n]$ in the array A, we define *previous* and *next* pointers as follows:

$$prev(i) = max\{\{j \in [1, i) | A[j] > A[i], C[j] = C[i]\} \cup \{-\infty\}\}$$
$$next(i) = min\{\{j \in (i, n] | A[j] > A[i], C[j] = C[i]\} \cup \{+\infty\}\}$$

Using these pointers, for each position $i \in [1, n]$ in A we obtain a (weighted) interval-pair with $(prev(i), i)$ as a backward interval, $(i, next(i))$ as a forward interval, and $A[i]$, $C[i]$ being the weight and color associated with the interval-pair respectively. We represent such an interval-pair by a pentuple $(i, A[i], C[i], prev(i), next(i))$. The following is a key observation for the *two-sided chaining* just introduced.

LEMMA 1. *For a given range $[a, b]$ and a color c, let $S_{a,b,c} = \{i_1, i_2, ..., i_r\}$ be the (possibly empty) set of all positions within $[a, b]$ such that $C[i_1] = C[i_2] = ... = C[i_r] = c$. If $S_{a,b,c}$ is not an empty set, then exactly one element $p_c \in S_{a,b,c}$ satisfies the following: $prev(p_c) < a, b < next(p_c)$, where $A[p_c] = max\{A[i_1], A[i_2], ..., A[i_r]\}$.*

In order to utilize the above lemma for answering top-CRMQ, we use an $O(n)$-word structure that can compute a threshold $\tau^k_{a,b}$ for a given top-CRMQ (a, b, k) in $O(1)$ time such that size of $Out_\tau = \{(c, p_c, A[p_c]) \mid c \in \sigma, A[p_c] \geq \tau^k_{a,b}\}$ is bounded by $\hat{k} = k + O(k)$, where $A[p_c]$ represents the highest element in $A[a...b]$ with color c (see Appendix A for details). Then, Lemma 1 suggests that if a triplet $(c, p_c, A[p_c])$ is an answer for a top-CRMQ, then the pentuple $(p_c, A[p_c]$, $C[p_c]$, $prev(p_c), next(p_c))$ satisfies the following conditions, and vice versa: $p_c \in [a, b]$, $prev(p_c) < a$, $next(p_c) > b$ and $A[p_c] \geq \tau^k_{a,b}$. Therefore, top-CRMQ can be reduced to a new problem as defined below.

PROBLEM 3. *Store a set $\mathcal{I}$ of n interval-pairs of the form $(i, A[i], C[i], prev(i), next(i))$ in a data structure, such that given a query $(a, b, k, \tau^k_{a,b})$, we can efficiently report all those interval-pairs with weight $\geq \tau^k_{a,b}$ and its backward, forward intervals stabbed by a, b respectively. i.e., output the interval-pairs satisfying the following five constraints:*
(1) $prev(i) < a$ (2) $a \leq i$
(3) $i \leq b$ (4) $b < next(i)$ (5) $A[i] \geq \tau$

Notice that the output set Out_τ for the above problem, is a super set of the output set Out_k of our top-CRMQ, because $\hat{k} \geq k$. Therefore, in order to answer a top-CRMQ, we first find the triplet $(c^*, p_{c^*}, A[p_{c^*}]) \in Out_\tau$ using a selection algorithm such that the number of triplets $(c, p_c, A[p_c]) \in Out_\tau$ with $A[p_{c^*}] \leq A[p_c]$ is k. This takes only $O(\hat{k}/B) = O(k/B)$ I/Os [26]. Then, all those triplets in Out_τ with $A[p_{c^*}] \leq A[p_c]$ can be reported as the final outputs. Both the problems being equivalent, we use the term "top-CRMQ" to refer to either of these problems. In particular, by top-CRMQ (a, b, k) we refer to Problem 2 whereas by top-CRMQ $(a, b, k, \tau^k_{a,b})$ we refer to the Problem 3. Moreover, for notational simplicity, input to the Problem 3 is defined as a quadruple (a, b, k, τ).

5. INTERVAL TREE BASED SOLUTION

In this section, we present a simple interval-tree based external memory data structure and achieve the result summarized in following lemma.

LEMMA 2. *A given set $\mathcal{I}$ of interval-pairs can be maintained as an $O(|\mathcal{I}|)$-space structure such that given a top-CRMQ (a, b, k, τ), we can report all interval-pairs $(i, A[i], C[i]$, $prev(i), next(i)) \in \mathcal{I}$ with $i \in [a, b]$, $prev(i) < a$, $next(i) > b$ and $A[i] \geq \tau$ using $O(\log^3(|\mathcal{I}|/B) + \frac{k}{B})$ I/Os.*

We begin by describing a linear space external memory interval tree (which is not optimal, but is sufficient for our purpose) and then use it to answer top-CRMQ.

5.1 Linear Space Interval Tree

Given a set $\mathcal{I}$ of n intervals of the form (s_i, e_i), where s_i and e_i represent the start and end points, the output of an interval stabbing query is the set of intervals stabbed by a input point q; i.e., we need to output all those intervals (s_j, e_j) such that $q \in [s_j, e_j]$. For simplicity we assume all start and end points to be distinct; otherwise ties can be broken arbitrarily.

The proposed interval tree construction begins with building a balanced binary search tree (BST) of n nodes over all end points e_i of set $\mathcal{I}$. Thus each node u in BST is associated with a unique end point which we denote as $stab(u)$**.

¶If there is no such predecessor, then points to $-\infty$.

**For any given nodes u_1 and u_2, $stab(u_1) \leq stab(u_2)$ if u_1 comes before u_2 during the in-order traversal of BST.

Further each node u is associated with a set of intervals $\mathcal{I}(u) = \{(s_i, e_i) | stab(u) \in [s_i, e_i], stab(v) \notin [s_i, e_i]$, where v is any ancestor of $u\}$. Let $size(u)$ represent the number of leaves in the subtree of u. We finish the construction by making each node u with $size(u) \leq B$, $size(parent(u)) > B$, a leaf node by first setting $\mathcal{I}(u) = \cup_{v \in subtree(u)} \mathcal{I}(v)$ and then pruning its subtree. We emphasize that, in this interval tree, for each leaf u, $\mathcal{I}(u)$ is bounded by $O(B)$[††]. The size of interval tree can now be bounded as $O(n)$ words since $\sum_u |\mathcal{I}(u)| = |\mathcal{I}| = n$. To answer a stabbing query, we first identify the node u_q such that value $stab(u_q)$ is the predecessor of q. Then any interval stabbed by a query point q will be associated with one of the $O(\log(\frac{n}{B}))$ nodes on the path from the root to node u_q. We summarize this property in the following lemma.

LEMMA 3. *Given a query point q, we can obtain a set of $O(\log(\frac{n}{B}))$ nodes in the proposed linear space interval tree in $O(\log(\frac{n}{B}))$ I/Os such that any interval stabbed by q is associated with one of these nodes.*

For query point q and each interval (s_j, e_j) associated with any of the $O(\log(\frac{n}{B}))$ nodes obtained by the above lemma, either $s_j \leq q$ or $q \leq e_j$ is true. The interval stabbing query can now be answered by issuing $O(\log(\frac{n}{B}))$ single-constraint queries (i.e., check if $q \leq e_j$ in the case one already knows $s_j \leq q$, and vice versa) on these nodes. Therefore, Lemma 3 can be rewritten as follows.

LEMMA 4. *A set $\mathcal{I}$ of n intervals can be categorized into subsets using an interval tree structure, such that an interval stabbing query (with two constraints) can be decomposed into $O(\log(\frac{n}{B}))$ queries with a single constraint.*

5.2 Interval Tree within an Interval Tree

Taking a clue from Lemma 4, we aim to decompose top-CRMQ problem into a set of simpler queries. Intuitively, we can maintain an interval tree structure with respect to the backward intervals of all interval-pairs and reduce the original problem (which is a five-constraints query) to $O(\log(\frac{n}{B}))$ four-constraints queries. Each of these four-constraints query can be further reduced to $O(\log(\frac{n}{B}))$ three-constraints queries by employing another interval tree structure with respect to the forward intervals on a smaller set of interval-pairs. We elaborate on such an interval-tree-within-an-interval-tree approach below to achieve the result summarized in Lemma 2.

Data Structure: The proposed data structure consists of three components described as follows:

- Backward interval tree: This is an interval tree based on backward intervals of all the interval-pairs in $\mathcal{I}$ as described earlier in the beginning of this section.
- Forward interval trees: The backward interval tree partitions the set $\mathcal{I}$ of interval-pairs into disjoint sets such that each of the set is associated with some node in the interval tree. Let $\mathcal{I}(u_b)$ be such a set associated with node u_b in backward interval tree. We maintain an interval tree at each node u_b based on the forward intervals of all interval-pairs in $\mathcal{I}(u_b)$.
- Dominance structures: Let $\mathcal{I}(u_b, v_f)$ be the set of the interval-pairs associated with node v_f in forward interval tree that is in turn associated with node u_b in backward interval tree. For each possible set $\mathcal{I}(u_b, v_f)$ we maintain data structures for answering the three-dimensional dominance queries [1] listed below.

Q_1 : (1) $prev(i) < a$, (4) $b < next(i)$ and (5) $A[i] \geq \tau$
Q_2 : (2) $a \leq i$, (3) $i \leq b$ and (5) $A[i] \geq \tau$
Q_3 : (2) $a \leq i$, (4) $b < next(i)$ and (5) $A[i] \geq \tau$
Q_4 : (1) $prev(i) < a$, (3) $i \leq b$ and (5) $A[i] \geq \tau$

With each of the above three components occupying linear space total space required for the proposed data structure can be bounded by $O(|\mathcal{I}|)$ words. Space requirement of the backward interval tree is $O(|\mathcal{I}|)$ words (Lemma 3). By the same argument space requirement of a forward interval tree associated with node u_b of backward interval tree is bounded by $O(|\mathcal{I}(u_b)|)$. Thus the total space required for all forward interval trees is $O(|\mathcal{I}|)$ words. Moreover since each interval-pair belongs to exactly one of the $\mathcal{I}(u_b, v_f)$ set, all dominance structures collectively occupy linear space as well.

Query Algorithm: We begin by employing the standard interval tree algorithm (Lemma 3) to identify $O(\log(|\mathcal{I}|/B))$ nodes in the backward interval tree such that any interval-pair that has its backward interval stabbed by a is associated with one of these $O(\log(|\mathcal{I}|/B))$ nodes. We then apply the same algorithm to each of the forward interval tree associated with these $O(\log(|\mathcal{I}|/B))$ nodes to obtain $O(\log(|\mathcal{I}|/B))$ nodes in a single forward interval tree and $O(\log^2(|\mathcal{I}|/B))$ nodes overall such that any interval-pair that has its backward interval stabbed by a and forward interval stabbed by b is associated with one of these $O(\log^2(|\mathcal{I}|/B))$ nodes. We call these nodes candidate nodes and the set of interval-pairs associated with these nodes candidate sets. We now need to further explore only the retrieved candidate sets to get the desired outputs.

For each candidate node v_f belonging to a forward interval tree that in turn is associated with the node u_b in the backward interval tree, let $stab(v_f)$ and $stab(u_b)$ be the end points maintained at nodes v_f and u_b respectively. Then, each interval-pair in $\mathcal{I}(u_b, v_f)$ is stabbed by $stab(u_b)$ and $stab(v_f)$ on its backward and forward interval respectively. By careful examination of the relative values of $a, b, stab(u_b)$ and $stab(v_f)$, we can eliminate two constraints out of five for top-CRMQ and is one of the crucial observations of our paper. We classify node v_f into one the following categories based on which two constraints are satisfied by the interval-pairs in set $\mathcal{I}(u_b, v_f)$:

T_1 : $a \leq stab(u_b) \leq stab(v_f) \leq b$
T_2 : $stab(u_b) \leq a \leq b \leq stab(v_f)$
T_3 : $stab(u_b) \leq a \leq stab(v_f) \leq b$
T_4 : $a \leq stab(u_b) \leq b \leq stab(v_f)$

It can be easily verified that each of these categories lead to the query types Q_1, Q_2, Q_3, and Q_4 respectively on set $\mathcal{I}(u_b, v_f)$ to obtain the interval-pairs satisfying all five constraints required for top-CRMQ problem.

Thus, by first obtaining the candidate nodes and then applying appropriate three-dimensional dominance query on each of them all desired outputs can be retrieved. Using Lemma 3, number of I/Os spent on querying backward interval tree as well as each of the forward interval trees are bounded by $O(\log(|\mathcal{I}|/B))$ I/Os. Therefore all candidate

[††]For any node u, the total number of intervals assigned to nodes in its subtree is $O(size(u))$. This fact follows because (1) all our start and end points are distinct, and (2) for any interval assigned to node u, both its start and end points should be some value associated with one of its descendants.

nodes can be obtained by spending $O(\log^2(|\mathcal{I}|/B))$ I/Os. Moreover, data structure from [1] used for dominance query also requires additional $O(\log_B |\mathcal{I}|)$ I/Os. Therefore total number of I/Os required is $O(\log^2(|\mathcal{I}|/B)\log_B|\mathcal{I}|+\frac{k}{B}) = O(\log^3(|\mathcal{I}|/B)+\frac{k}{B})$. This completes the proof of Lemma 2.

6. BOOTSTRAPPING

The I/O bound in Lemma 2 is optimal for the case $k \geq B\log^3(n/B)$. In the present section, we bootstrap this result to optimally answer "special" top-CRMQ. We start by introducing a blocking scheme that forms the basis of all subsequent external memory results.

Blocking Scheme: Let blocking factor $\delta_j = B(\log^{(j)}(\frac{n}{B}))^5$ and $k_j = B(\log^{(j)}(\frac{n}{B}))^3$ for $j = 1, 2, 3, ..., \log^*(\frac{n}{B})$. Without loss of generality, we further assume that both δ_j and k_j are always rounded to the next highest power of 2 [§]. We partition the array $A[1...n]$ into $\frac{n}{\delta_j}$ disjoint blocks each of size δ_j such that block $A_{j,t} = A[(t-1)\delta_j+1...t\delta_j]$. Define $f_{j,t}$ to denote the left boundary of the block $A_{j,t}$. We say that a block of size δ_j is δ_j-block and a blocking boundary of partitioning based on δ_j (i.e., $f_{j,t}$) is δ_j-boundary. For consistency, fix $\delta_0 = n$ and $A_{0,1} = A[1...n]$. Given a range $[a, b]$, let $A[a^j...b^j]$ be the longest span of δ_j blocks that is completely within $A[a...b]$. Suppose query range $[a, b]$ intersects blocks $A_{j,l}, A_{j,l+1}, ..., A_{j,t}$ then $a^j = f_{j,l+1}$ and $b^j = f_{j,t} - 1$. We prove the following results in the remainder of this section.

LEMMA 5. *A top-CRMQ (a, b, k, τ) can be answered in $O(\frac{k_{\mu+1}}{B} + \frac{k}{B})$ I/Os using an $O(n\log^* n)$-space structure if the span $A[a...b]$ is completely within a δ_μ-block for $\mu \in [0, \log^*(\frac{n}{B})]$.*

LEMMA 6. *A top-CRMQ (a, b, k, τ) can be answered in $O(\frac{k_{\mu+1}}{B} + \frac{k}{B} + \log^* n)$ I/Os using an $O(n)$-space structure if the span $A[a...b]$ is completely within a δ_μ-block for $\mu \in [0, \log^*(\frac{n}{B})]$.*

6.1 Proof of Lemma 5

For each block $A_{j,t}$, we maintain a data structure $IT_{j,t}$ (of size $|IT_{j,t}|$ words) summarized in Lemma 2 [‡]. The total space occupancy is $O(\sum_j \sum_t |IT_{j,t}|) = O(n\log^* n)$ space. Then the δ_μ-block containing span $A[a...b]$ i.e., $A_{\mu,t}$ with $t = \lceil \frac{a}{\delta_\mu} \rceil$ can be queried using structure $IT_{\mu,t}$ to obtain the desired answers in $O(\log^3(\frac{\delta_\mu}{B}) + \frac{k}{B}) = O(\frac{k_{\mu+1}}{B} + \frac{k}{B})$ I/Os.

6.2 Proof of Lemma 6

The space blowup in Lemma 5 comes from the fact that, each interval-pair in $\mathcal{I}$ is repeated $\log^*(\frac{n}{B})$ times as a part of $\log^*(\frac{n}{B})$ number of $IT_{\{\cdot,\cdot\}}$'s. We introduce a categorization technique based on the blocking scheme described earlier that avoids this space blowup, though at the cost of (acceptable) slow-down in query performance. We categorize the input interval-pairs in set $\mathcal{I}$ into $\log^*(\frac{n}{B})+1$ types based on the following rule:

> *An interval-pair $(i, \cdot, \cdot, \cdot)$ is categorized as type-j if its both intervals (i.e., backward and forward) are stabbed by a δ_j-boundary, but at least one of them is not stabbed by a δ_{j-1}-boundary.*

Taking into account the boundary conditions, an interval-pair is termed as type-1 if its both intervals are stabbed by a δ_1-boundary, whereas for an interval-pair of type-$(\log^*(\frac{n}{B})+1)$, none of its intervals is stabbed by any boundary i.e., i and $prev(i)/next(i)$ are within the same $\delta_{\log^*(\frac{n}{B})}$-block (which is of size $\Theta(B)$). Let n_j represent the number of type-j interval-pairs, then $n_1 + n_2 + ... + n_{\log^*(\frac{n}{B})+1} = n$.

We now describe the data structure and query algorithm to achieve the result in Lemma 6. Intuitively, our idea is to make separate linear space data structures for interval-pairs in each type thereby restricting the total space to $O(n)$ words. However, this requires multiple structures to be queried incurring an additive $\log^*(\frac{n}{B})$ term in query I/Os.

Data Structure: We maintain the following substructures.

- For each block $A_{j,t}$ maintain a structure $IT_{j,t}$ summarized in Lemma 2 by considering only type-$(j+1)$ and type-$(j+2)$ interval-pairs. This occupies a total of $O(\sum_j(n_{j+1} + n_{j+2})) = O(n)$ space.
- We create a collection of two-dimensional points by mapping each type-j interval-pair $(i, A[i], prev(i), next(i))$ to a point $(i, A[i])$. Then we apply rank space reduction to these two-dimensional points and maintain a three-sided range reporting structure TS_j by Larsen et al. [17] on this collection. All those type-j interval pairs within $i \in [a, b]$ and $A[i] \geq \tau$ for any given a, b, and τ can be answered in optimal I/Os using TS_j. Further, we associate each two-dimensional point with its corresponding interval-pair, so that the interval-pairs corresponding to the points reported by structure from [17] can be obtained without spending any additional I/Os. Moreover, to be able to query data structure in [17] we need to map the boundary points (a and b) and the threshold τ to rank space. This can be achieved in constant time by maintaining two bit vectors (along with rank-select structure [24]) of length n. Total space required for this component is bounded by $O(n_j)$ words + $O(n)$ bits $= O(n_j + \frac{n}{\log n})$ words. Thus over all space corresponding to $j = 0, 1, 2, ..., \log^*(\frac{n}{B}) + 1$ is $O(n)$ words.
- We also maintain a list A' of all interval pairs $(i, \cdot, \cdot, \cdot)$ in the ascending order of i. Space occupancy is $O(n)$ words.

As each of the components described above occupies $O(n)$ words the overall space requirement is linear.

Query Algorithm: As before, let $A_{\mu,t}$ with $t = \lceil \frac{a}{\delta_\mu} \rceil$ be the δ_μ-block containing $A[a...b]$. Then we query $IT_{\mu,t}$ by spending $O(\frac{k_{\mu+1}}{B} + \frac{k}{B})$ I/Os. However, this will give only the outputs of type $(\mu+1)$ and $(\mu+2)$. It remains to show how to retrieve the outputs of type-h, for $h \leq \mu$ or $h \geq \mu+3$.

We first demonstrate how type-h outputs with $h \leq \mu$ are retrieved when span $A[a...b]$ is known to be completely within a δ_μ block i.e., $A_{\mu,t}$. We note that any type-h link $(i, \cdot, \cdot, \cdot)$ with $h \leq \mu$ and i falling within the block $A_{\mu,t}$ (i.e., $i \in [f_{\mu,t}, f_{\mu,t+1} - 1]$), both its forward as well as backward intervals are stabbed by δ_μ-boundaries ($f_{\mu,t}$ and $f_{\mu,t+1}$ respectively). Therefore, such an interval-pair implicitly satisfies constraints $prev(i) < a$, $b < next(i)$. Hence, for $h \leq \mu$ we only need to take into account the position and weight constraint of the interval-pair (i.e., $i \in [a, b]$ and $A[i] \geq \tau$) and all such type-h outputs can be obtained in optimal I/Os by querying structure TS_h. Therefore, overall I/Os required for retrieving all type-h outputs for $h \leq \mu$ are bounded by $O(\mu + \frac{k}{B}) = O(\log^*(\frac{n}{B}) + \frac{k}{B})$.

[§]In order to ensure δ_{j-1} is always divisible by δ_j

[‡]$IT_{j,t}$ is the structure in Lemma 2 over the following set of interval-pairs $\mathcal{I}_{j,t} = \{(i, \cdot, \cdot, \cdot) \in \mathcal{I} | i \in [(t-1)\delta_j + 1, t\delta_j]\}$.

Finally all type-h outputs for $h \geq \mu + 3$ can be efficiently retrieved using the following key observation. Any type-h interval-pair $(i, \cdot, \cdot, \cdot, \cdot)$, with $h \geq \mu + 3$ is an output, only if i falls within a $\delta_{\mu+1}$-block that contains either a or b. Otherwise at-least one of two conditions $prev(i) < a$, $b < next(i)$ will be violated. Therefore, the number of candidate interval-pairs in this case is only $2\delta_{\mu+2}$, and the output interval-pairs can be obtained by scanning the two $\delta_{\mu+2}$-blocks in A' to evaluate the five conditions listed in Observation 1 for each of the candidate. The I/Os required in this step are bounded by $O(\frac{\delta_{\mu+2}}{B}) = o(\frac{k_{\mu+1}}{B})$.

Putting together all pieces, the number of I/Os required to answer a top-CRMQ (a, b, k, τ) with $A[a...b]$ completely within a δ_μ-block, can be bounded by $O(\frac{k_{\mu+1}}{B} + \frac{k}{B} + \log^* n)$.

7. THE FINAL DATA STRUCTURES

This section is dedicated to proving Theorem 2 and Theorem 3. Given a top-CRMQ (a, b, k), the structure presented in Lemma 2 can be maintained in $O(n)$-space to optimally handle queries with $k = \Omega(B \log^3(n/B))$. Otherwise, we find the parameter $\pi \in [1, \log^*(n/B)]$, where $k_{\pi+1} < k \leq k_\pi$ (for consistency, assume $k_{\log^*(n/B)+1} = 0$). Then we decompose the original query into following subqueries:

1. top-CRMQ $(a, a^\pi - 1, k, \tau)$
2. top-CRMQ (a^π, b^π, k)
3. top-CRMQ $(b^\pi + 1, b, k, \tau)$

Here $A[a^\pi ... b^\pi]$ represents the longest span of δ_π blocks that is completely within $A[a...b]$. Let Out_i represent the set of answers corresponding to the above queries for $i = 1, 2, 3$ (a procedure to obtain them will be described later). Notice that these are disjoint sets and cardinality of each of them is $O(k)$. Moreover, $\cup_{i=1}^{3} Out_i$ is a superset of final answers for the original query (a, b, τ). Therefore, those interval-pairs $(i, A[i], C[i], prev(i), next(i)) \in \cup_{i=1}^{3} Out_i$ with $prev(i) < a$, $next(i) > b$ and $A[i] \geq \tau$ can be *uniquely* reported as the final answers (the condition $i \in [a, b]$ is satisfied implicitly).

It remains to show, how to retrieve the output set for each of the subqueries efficiently. Both Out_1 and Out_3 can be obtained in $O(k_{\pi+1}/B + k/B) = O(1 + k/B)$ I/Os by maintaining an $O(n \log^* n)$-space structure (refer to Lemma 5). By querying on the structure described in the following lemma, Out_2 also can be obtained in optimal I/Os. This completes the proof of Theorem 2.

LEMMA 7. *There exists an $O(n \log^* n)$-space structure that supports a top-CRMQ (α, β, K) in optimal $O(1 + K/B)$ I/Os if $A[\alpha...\beta]$ is a span of several δ_π-blocks and $K \leq k_\pi$ for $\pi \in [0, \log^*(\frac{n}{B})]$.*

Similarly, using the linear space structure in Lemma 6, both Out_1 and Out_3 can be obtained in $O(k_{\pi+1}/B + k/B + \log^* n) = O(\log^* n + k/B)$ I/Os. Combining this with the following lemma for retrieving Out_2, we achieve the result summarized in Theorem 3.

LEMMA 8. *There exists an $O(n)$-space structure that supports a top-CRMQ (α, β, K) in $O(\log^* n + K/B)$ I/Os if $A[\alpha...\beta]$ is a span of several δ_π-blocks and $K \leq k_\pi$ for $\pi \in [0, \log^*(\frac{n}{B})]$.*

The remaining part of this section is dedicated to prove these two lemmas i.e., Lemma 7 and 8.

7.1 Proofs of Lemma 7 and Lemma 8

We identify the parameter θ as the smallest i such that, there exists a δ_i-boundary in $[\alpha, \beta]$. Using θ we decompose top-CRMQ (α, β, K) further into the following subqueries, and obtain the desired answers by merging the outputs of individual subqueries.

- Q_{left}: top-CRMQ $(\alpha, \alpha^\theta - 1, K)$
- O_{middle}: top-CRMQ $(\alpha^\theta, \beta^\theta, K)$
- Q_{right}: top-CRMQ $(\beta^\theta + 1, \beta, K)$

Here $A[\alpha^\theta ... \beta^\theta]$ represents the longest span of δ_θ blocks that is completely within $A[\alpha...\beta]$. We now describe the necessary structure for handling each of these queries, followed by the query algorithm.

7.1.1 *Answering Q_{middle}*

Data Structure: Starting from left boundary of each block $A_{j,t}$ i.e., $f_{j,t}$, consider the spans covering $1, 2, 4, 8, ...$ blocks of size δ_j such that it does not cross the first δ_{j-1}-boundary that follows $f_{j,t}$. We maintain the top-k_j answers (i.e., the corresponding pentuples) for each of these spans explicitly (in descending order of weight) i.e., we maintain the list $ML(j, t, i)$ that contains the answers for top-CRMQ with k_j as an input on the span $A[f_{j,t} ... f_{j,t+2^i} - 1]$ for any $1 \leq j \leq \log^*(\frac{n}{B})$, $1 \leq t \leq \frac{n}{\delta_j}$ and $i = 0, 1, 2, ..., \log(\frac{\delta_{j-1}}{\delta_j})$. Overall space requirement for such a storage is $O(\sum_j (\frac{n}{\delta_j}) k_j \log(\frac{\delta_{j-1}}{\delta_j}))$ $= O(\sum_j \frac{n}{\log^{(j)}(\frac{n}{B})}) = O(n)$ words.

Query Algorithm: We represent $A[\alpha^\theta ... \beta^\theta]$ as union of two overlapping spans each of which covers 2^i δ_θ-blocks for some integer i. Let $[f_{\theta,l'}, f_{\theta,l'+2^i} - 1]$ and $[f_{\theta,t'-2^i}, f_{\theta,t'} - 1]$ be the ranges for these overlapping spans such that $f_{\theta,l'} = \alpha^\theta$ and $f_{\theta,t'} - 1 = \beta^\theta$. It is evident that any top-K answer for $A[\alpha^\theta ... \beta^\theta]$ should also be in top-K answers of either of the overlapping spans i.e., it should be present in either $ML(j, l', i)$ or $ML(j, t' - 2^i, i)$. Top-K answers (in sorted order) for these two overlapping spans can be directly retrieved from the maintained precomputed answers in $O(\frac{k}{B})$ I/Os. Further, the two lists can be merged to obtain the outputs for Q_{middle} by a simple scan. However, before merging we discard any answer belonging to the region of overlap between two ranges (i.e., span $A[f_{\theta,t'-2^i} ... f_{\theta,l'+2^i} - 1]$) from either of the answer lists to ensure uniqueness of reported answers. In conclusion, Q_{middle} can be answered optimally using an $O(n)$-space structure.

7.1.2 *Answering Q_{left} and Q_{right}*

I/O-Optimal Structure: For each $A_{j,t}$ and $h < j$ we maintain top-k_j answers (in descending order of weight) for the span bounded by $f_{j,t}$ and the first δ_h-boundary that follows $f_{j,t}$. Similarly, top-k_j answers for the span bounded by $f_{j,t+1} - 1$ and the first δ_h-boundary that precedes it are maintained. These answers are maintained in two lists SL_r and SL_l. The list $SL_r(j, t, h)$ and $SL_l(j, t, h)$ contains the answer to top-CRMQ with k_j as an input on the span $[f_{j,t}, f_{h,t'+1} - 1]$ and $[f_{h,t'}, f_{j,t+1} - 1]$ respectively for any $1 \leq j \leq \log^*(\frac{n}{B})$, $1 \leq t \leq \frac{n}{\delta_j}$ and $h < j$ with $t' = \lceil \frac{t}{(\delta_h/\delta_j)} \rceil$. Here t' is the δ_h-block that contains the δ_j-block t. Overall space usage for maintaining these inter-level answers can be bounded by $O(\sum_j \frac{n}{\delta_j} k_j (j - 1)) = O(\sum_j \frac{nj}{(\log^{(j)}(\frac{n}{B}))^2}) =$ $O(n \log^* n)$ words.

Desired answers for the top-CRMQ query on desired spans $A[\alpha...\alpha^\theta - 1]$ and $A[\beta^\theta + 1...\beta]$ are simply the first K entries in the appropriate lists $SL_r(\pi, \cdot, \theta)$, $SL_l(\pi, \cdot, \theta)$ respectively and the I/Os needed for retrieving are $O(\frac{K}{B})$. Combing this result along with $O(n)$-space structure capable of answering Q_{middle}, we prove Lemma 7.

Linear Space Structure: To achieve linear space, we do the following modification to the data structure just described: maintain $SL_r(j, \cdot, \cdot)$ and $SL_l(j, \cdot, \cdot)$ only for those $j \le \phi \le \log^*(\frac{n}{B})$, where $\log^{(\phi)}(\frac{n}{B}) \ge \log^*(\frac{n}{B}) > \log^{(\phi+1)}(\frac{n}{B})$. Then space can be bounded by $O(\frac{n}{(\log^{(2)}(\frac{n}{B}))^2} + \frac{2n}{(\log^{(3)}(\frac{n}{B}))^2} + \frac{3n}{(\log^{(4)}(\frac{n}{B}))^2} + ... + \frac{(\phi-1)n}{(\log^{(\phi)}(\frac{n}{B}))^2}) = O(\frac{n}{\log^*(\frac{n}{B})})$ words. In addition, we maintain all $SL_r(\phi + 1, \cdot, \phi)$ and $SL_l(\phi + 1, \cdot, \phi)$ as well occupying $O(\frac{n}{(\log^{(\phi+1)}(\frac{n}{B}))^2}) = o(n)$ words. Further, we also assume the availability of the linear space data structure described in Lemma 6. Thus overall space is bounded by $O(n)$-words. In order to answer a query, we consider the following cases:

1. *If* $\pi \le \phi$: Obtain answers from the appropriate $SL_r(\pi, \cdot, \theta)$ and $SL_l(\pi, \cdot, \theta)$ in $O(\frac{K}{B})$ I/Os.
2. *If* $\pi = \phi + 1$: Obtain answers from appropriately chosen lists $SL_r(\phi+1, \cdot, \phi)$, $SL_r(\phi, \cdot, \theta)$ and then merge them by spending $O(\frac{K}{B})$ I/Os. Similarly appropriate lists $SL_l(\phi+1, \cdot, \phi)$, $SL_l(\phi, \cdot, \theta)$ can be accessed to obtain the desired results.
3. *If* $\pi > \phi + 1$: We first obtain answers for the span $A[\alpha^{\phi+1}...\alpha^\theta - 1]$ and $A[\beta^\theta + 1...\beta^{\phi+1}]$ from appropriate SL_r and SL_l structures in $O(\frac{K}{B})$ I/Os. Whereas answers for $A[\alpha...\alpha^{\phi+1} - 1]$ (resp., $A[\beta^{\phi+1} + 1...\beta]$) can be obtained in $O(\log^3(\frac{\delta_{\phi+1}}{B}) + \frac{K}{B} + \log^*(\frac{n}{B})) = O(\log^*(\frac{n}{B}) + \frac{K}{B})$ I/Os as it is completely within a block of size $\delta_{\phi+1}$ (from Lemma 6).

Therefore, total number of I/Os required to answer Q_{left} and Q_{right} is bounded by $O(\log^*(\frac{n}{B}) + \frac{K}{B})$, when linear space data structure is used. Result summarized in Lemma 8 can now be obtained by using this structure in addition to $O(n)$-space structure for answering Q_{middle}.

8. CRMQ IN INTERNAL MEMORY

In this section, we show how to modify our external memory data structures to achieve the result in Theorem 1. We again begin with an interval tree based solution and obtain internal memory version of Lemma 2 by simply substituting B by 2. i.e., $O(n)$-word space and $O(\log^3 n + k)$ query time. However, outputs are not sorted. Recall that this result is obtained by querying $O(\log^2 n)$ three-dimensional dominance structures. By using our new three-dimensional dominance structure (Theorem 9) instead of the one by Afshani [1], the outputs from each of those three-dimensional dominance queries can be obtained in sorted order. Further, these outputs can be merged to get a complete list of all answers in sorted order using a heap structure. For our purpose, we use an atomic heap [11] that can perform all heap operations in $O(1)$ in Word-RAM model provided the heap size is $\log^{O(1)} n$. By putting everything together, we obtain an $O(n)$-word space and $O(\log^3 n + k)$ query time data structure for the sorted version of Problem 2.

We now apply blocking scheme with a single blocking factor $\delta_1 = \log^4 n$, and maintain the above described interval-tree based structure over each block $A_{1,t} = A[(t-1)\delta_1 + 1...t\delta_1]$ as $IT_{1,t}$, taking overall $O(n)$ space. Recall that $\delta_0 = n$ and we also maintain $IT_{0,1}$. Further we maintain, the structures $ML(\cdot, \cdot, \cdot)$ as described in Section 7.1.1 occupying $O(n)$ word space i.e., from each δ_1-boundary $f_{1,t}$ consider the spans covering $1, 2, 4, 8, ...$ δ_1-blocks and maintain top-k_1 answers ($k_1 = \log^3 n$) for each of these spans explicitly. Whenever query input $k \ge \log^3 n$, it can be answered optimally using $IT_{0,1}$. For $k < \log^3 n$ and the input range $[a, b]$ completely within a δ_1-block, query can be answered in $O(\log^3 \log n + k)$ time only using appropriate $IT_{1,t}$ structure. Otherwise, we can retrieve top-k answers from fringe spans $A[a...a^1 - 1]$, $A[b^1...b]$ and a middle span $A[a^1...b^1 - 1]$ (refer Section 7.1.1, 7.1.2) and merge them to report final top-k answers with identical query time of $O(\log^3 \log n + k)$. The non-optimal $O(\log^3 \log n)$-additive factor is due to the time for querying the interval tree based structure maintained over each δ_1 block. Therefore, for improving the case where $k < \log^3 \log n$ and the query span $A[a...b]$ is completely within a δ_1 blocks, we maintain the following additional structure. Given a δ_1-block $A_{1,t}$, for every span $A[f_{1,t} + i, f_{1,t} + i + 2^j - 1]$ for $i \in 0, 1, 2, 3, ..., (\delta_1 - 1)$ and $j = 0, 1, 2, ..., \log \delta_1$, maintain top-($\log^3 \log n$) answers (in sorted order). Instead of explicitly maintaining, an output element $A[r]$ (or its location r) for a particular span, we simply encode it as an offset from the left boundary of the span i.e., $r - f_{1,t} + i$ in $O(\log \delta_1) = O(\log \log n)$ bits. Thus overall space requirement can be bounded by $o(n \log n)$ bits. Now any span $A[a...b]$ with both a as well as b in the same δ_1-block can be partitioned into two overlapping spans $A[a...y]$ and $A[x...b]$ where $a < x \le y < b$, such that the top-k answers of these overlapping spans are precomputed and can be retrieved in optimal time. Finally, by merging these answers, we obtain the final output.

9. CONCLUSIONS

In this paper we introduced the problem of colored (categorical) range maxima that generalizes the fundamental problem of computing maxima in a query range to the colored scenario. We show that this problem is related to or generalizes other important problems, such as reporting most relevant documents containing a given string and three-sided categorical range reporting. We provide an optimal solution of the colored range maxima problem in internal memory. Our external memory data structure uses $O(n)$ space and answers queries in $O(\log^* n + k/B)$ I/Os. Design of a linear space data structure with constant query cost or proving a lower bound for this problem remains an interesting open question.

10. REFERENCES

[1] P. Afshani. On dominance reporting in 3d. In *ESA*, pages 41–51, 2008.

[2] A. Aggarwal and J. S. Vitter. The input/output complexity of sorting and related problems. *Communications of the ACM*, 31(9):1116–1127, 1998.

[3] L. Arge, V. Samoladas, and J. S. Vitter. On two-dimensional indexability and optimal range search indexing. In *PODS*, pages 346–357, 1999.

[4] M. A. Bender, M. Farach-Colton, G. Pemmasani, S. Skiena, and P. Sumazin. Lowest common ancestors in trees and directed acyclic graphs. *J. Algorithms*, 57(2):75–94, 2005.

[5] O. Berkman and U. Vishkin. Recursive star-tree parallel data structure. *SICOMP*, 22(2):221–242, 1993.

[6] P. Bozanis, N. Kitsios, C. Makris, and A. K. Tsakalidis. New upper bounds for generalized intersection searching problems. In *ICALP*, pages 464–474, 1995.

[7] G. S. Brodal, R. Fagerberg, M. Greve, and A. López-Ortiz. Online sorted range reporting. In *ISAAC*, pages 173–182, 2009.

[8] B. Chazelle and H. Edelsbrunner. Linear space data structures for two types of range search. *DCG*, 2:113–126, 1987.

[9] P. Ferragina and R. Grossi. The String B-tree: A new data structure for string searching in external memory and its application. *JACM*, 46(2):236–280, 1999.

[10] J. Fischer and V. Heun. A new succinct representation of RMQ-information and improvements in the enhanced suffix array. In *ESCAPE*, pages 459–470, 2007.

[11] M. L. Fredman and D. E. Willard. Trans-dichotomous algorithms for minimum spanning trees and shortest paths. *J. Comput. Syst. Sci.*, 48(3):533–551, 1994.

[12] P. Gupta, R. Janardan, and M. H. M. Smid. Further results on generalized intersection searching problems: counting, reporting, and dynamization. *J. Algorithms*, 19(2):282–317, 1995.

[13] W.-K. Hon, R. Shah, and J. S. Vitter. Space-efficient framework for top-k string retrieval problems. In *FOCS*, pages 713–722, 2009.

[14] R. Janardan and M. A. Lopez. Generalized intersection searching problems. *IJCGA*, 3(1):39–69, 1993.

[15] H. Kaplan, N. Rubin, M. Sharir, and E. Verbin. Efficient colored orthogonal range counting. *SICOMP*, 38(3):982–1011, 2008.

[16] M. Karpinski and Y. Nekrich. Top-k color queries for document retrieval. In *SODA*, pages 401–411, 2011.

[17] K. G. Larsen and R. Pagh. I/O-efficient data structures for colored range and prefix reporting. In *SODA*, pages 583–592, 2012.

[18] K. G. Larsen and F. van Walderveen. Near-optimal range reporting structures for categorical data. In *SODA*, pages 256–276, 2013.

[19] C. Makris and A. K. Tsakalidis. Algorithms for three-dimensional dominance searching in linear space. *IPL*, 66(6):277–283, 1998.

[20] S. Muthukrishnan. Efficient algorithms for document retrieval problems. In *SODA*, pages 657–666, 2002.

[21] G. Navarro. Spaces, trees and colors: The algorithmic landscape of document retrieval on sequences. In *CoRR abs/304.6023*, 2013.

[22] G. Navarro and Y. Nekrich. Top-k document retrieval in optimal time and linear space. In *SODA*, 2012.

[23] Y. Nekrich. Space-efficient range reporting for categorical data. In *PODS*, pages 113–120, 2012.

[24] R. Raman, V. Raman, and S. S. Rao. Succinct indexable dictionaries with applications to encoding k-ary trees, prefix sums and multisets. *TALG*, 2007.

[25] R. Shah, C. Sheng, S. V. Thankachan, and J. S. Vitter. Top-k document retrieval in external memory. In *ESA*, 2013.

[26] J. F. Sibeyn. External selection. In *STACS*, pages 291–301, 1999.

[27] J. S. Vitter. Algorithms and data structures for external memory. *Foundations and Trends in Theoretical Computer Science*, 2(4):305–474, 2008.

[28] P. Weiner. Linear pattern matching algorithms. In *SWAT*, pages 1–11, 1973.

APPENDIX

A. TOP TO THRESHOLD MAPPING

Data Structure: We partition the array $A[1...n]$ into $\lceil \frac{n}{\log^2 n} \rceil$ disjoint blocks each of size $\log^2 n$ (possibly except for the rightmost block). Starting from each blocking boundary, we consider spans (of length at most n) covering $1, 2, 4, 8, ...$ blocks, and for each such span $S = A[x, y]$, we maintain $\tau^k_{x,y}$ for $k = 1, 2, 4, 8, ..., n$. Here $\tau^k_{x,y} \in \{A[j] | j \in [x, y]\}$ with k as the output size of the threshold-CRMQ $(x, y, \tau^k_{a,b})$. This takes $O(n)$ space. Further, we divide each block into sub-blocks of size $\log^2 \log n$, and starting from each sub-block boundary, we consider spans (of length at most $\log^2 n$) covering $1, 2, 4, 8, ...$ sub-blocks. Again, for each such span $S' = [x', y']$, we maintain $\tau^k_{x',y'}$ for $k = 1, 2, 4, 8, ..., \Theta(\frac{\log^2 n}{\log^2 \log n})$. Notice that the explicit storage of $\tau^k_{x',y'}$'s (in $\log n$ bits per element) is costly. Therefore, we simply encode its relative position within that span in lesser number of $O(\log(\log^2 n)) = O(\log \log n)$ bits. i.e., total $O(n)$-space. Finally answers for the query (a, b, k) where both a, b are completely within a sub-block can be maintained in $o(n)$ bits using tables.

Query Answering: In order to compute the threshold $\tau^k_{a,b}$ corresponding to the input (a, b, k), we get k' by approximating k to the next highest power of 2 i.e., $k' = 2^{\lceil \log k \rceil}$. Then the input range $[a, b]$ can be partitioned into (at most) 6 spans $[a, a' - 1], [a', a'' - 1], [a'', b''], [b'' + 1, b'], [b' + 1, b]$ such that (1) both $[a, a' - 1]$, $[b' + 1, b]$ are within a sub-block, (2) $[a', a'' - 1]$, $[b'' + 1, b']$ are covered by spans of sub-blocks and (3) $[a'', b'']$ is covered by two possibly overlapping spans of blocks. The $\tau^{k'}_{\{\cdot,\cdot\}}$ for each of these spans can be retrieved in constant time and we choose the maximum among them as our threshold $\tau^k_{a,b}$. It can be easily verified that $\hat{k} \le 6k' < 12k$ and $\hat{k} \ge min(k, dcol)$, where $dcol$ denotes the number of distinct colors in $C[a...b]$.

B. TOP-*k* DOCUMENT RETRIEVAL

In this problem, we are given a set of D string documents $\{d_1, d_2, ..., d_D\}$ of total length n. We need to index these documents so as to answer the query (P, k) that requires us to output k documents with the highest $w(P, d_j)$. The relevance $w(P, d_j)$ depends only on the set of occurrences of P in d_j i.e., $Occ(P, d_j)$ and the document itself. Whenever a relevance measure satisfies the monotonicity property (either $w(P, d_j)$ is always $\le w(P', d_j)$ or it is always $\ge w(P', d_j)$, where P' is a prefix of P), top-k string retrieval problem can be reduced to top-CRMQ

First, construct a generalized suffix tree [28] of the document collection. Then we mark nodes with document-ids as follows: a leaf node ℓ is marked with document d_j if the suffix represented by ℓ belongs to d_j. An internal node u is marked with d_j if it is the lowest common ancestor of two leaves marked with d_j. Notice that a node can be marked with multiple documents. For each node u (with pre-order rank $rank(u)$) and each of its marked documents d_j, we define a triplet $(rank(u), w(path(u), d_j), d_j)$, where $path(u)$ represents the concatenation of edge labels on the path from root to u. Let (x_i, y_i, d_{c_i}) represents the i-th triplet, where $x_i \leq x_{i+1}$, then we construct A and C as follows: $A[i] = y_i$ and $C[i] = c_i \in [1, D]$. The top-k documents corresponding to the query (P, k) are same as the output colors for top-CRMQ (a, b, k), where $[a, b]$ represents the maximal range such that for all triplets $(x_i, \cdot, \cdot)$ with $i \in [a, b]$, the node with pre-order rank x_i is in the subtree of u_P. Here u_P represents the locus of P, the node closest to root with P as a prefix of $path(u_P)$. Using a String B-tree [9] and some auxiliary structures occupying $O(n)$-word space over all, we can compute u_P in $O(\log_B n + \frac{|P|}{B})$ I/Os.

C. PROOF OF THEOREM 9

Our data structure is based on the same approach as in [8, 19]. But we will also need additional ideas to output points in sorted order.

We associate sets of points $P(v)$ with nodes v of a binary tree T. Let $\max_{xy}(S)$ denote those points of a set S whose projections on the xy-plane are maximal. We set $S(w_r) = S$ for the root w_r of T. In every node v starting with the root, we store set $P(v) = \max_{xy} S(v)$. Then, we divide all points from $S(v) \setminus P(v)$ into two equal parts according to their z-coordinates and associate them with children v_l, v_r of v. In other words, points from $S(v) \setminus P(v)$ are distributed among $S(v_l)$ and $S(v_r)$ so that (1) $p_l.z < p_r.z$ for any $p_l \in S(v_l)$ and $p_r \in S(v_r)$, (2) $|S(v_r)| \leq |S(v_l)| \leq |S(v_r)| + 1$. Finally, we recursively apply the same procedure to $S(v_l)$ and $S(v_r)$.

For every node v, we keep all points of $P(v)$ sorted by their x-coordinates in an array $A(v)$. We also maintain a data structure from [7] that supports sorted reporting queries on $A(v)$: for any query interval $[a, b]$, $D(v)$ reports all points $p \in A[i]$, such that $a \leq i \leq b$ and $p.z \geq c$, sorted in decreasing order of their z-coordinates. As described in [7], $D(v)$ uses $O(|P(v)|)$ space and answers queries in $O(k+1)$ time, where k is the number of reported points. We also store structures $D_x(v)$ and $D_y(v)$ that enable us to answer predecessor and successor queries on x- and y-coordinates of points in $P(v)$.

Using $D(v)$, $D_x(v)$, and $D_y(v)$, we can answer a sorted dominance query $Q = [a, +\infty] \times [b, +\infty] \times [c, +\infty]$ on $P(v)$. Since $P(v)$ contains maximal points with respect to their x- and y-coordinates, all $p_1, p_2 \in P(v)$ have the following property: if $p_1.x > p_2.x$, then $p_1.y < p_2.y$. That is, y-coordinates of points in $P(v)$ decrease monotonously with increasing x-coordinates. Let p_l be the point in $P(v)$ with the smallest x-coordinate, such that $p_l.x \geq a$; let p_r be the point in $P((v)$ with the smallest y-coordinate, such that $p_r.y \geq b$. Let i_l and i_r denote the x-ranks[‡‡] of p_l and p_r respectively. All points p stored in $A[i_l...i_r]$ and only those points satisfy $p.x \geq a$ and $p.y \geq b$. Hence, we can answer a query Q on $P(v)$ by reporting all points in $A[i_l...i_r]$ in decreasing order of their z-coordinates until all points p, $p.z \geq c$, are output.

The same sorted dominance query on S is answered as follows. Let Π_q denote the search path for c in T. We report all points $p \in P(v)$ for all nodes $v \in \Pi_q$. For every node u that is a right sibling of $v \in \Pi_q$, we must report relevant points stored in u and its descendants. First, we answer the dominance queries on $P(u)$; if at least one point was reported, we visit both children of u and recursively process both children of u. Let $L(u)$ denote the list of points in $P(u) \cap Q$ sorted by their z-coordinates. The union of $L(u)$ for all visited nodes u contains all points in $S \cap Q$: all points p, $p.z \geq c$, are stored in nodes $v \in \Pi_q$ or in right siblings of nodes $v \in \Pi_q$ and their descendants. Our procedure visits all nodes $v \in \Pi_q$ and their right siblings; our procedure also visits all descendants of the right siblings that contain at least one point $p \in Q$, as can be concluded from the following observation.

OBSERVATION 1. *Suppose that u is the right sibling of some node $v \in \Pi_q$ or a descendant of the right sibling of some $v \in \Pi_q$. If $P(u) \cap Q = \emptyset$, then $P(w) \cap Q = \emptyset$ for all descendants w of u.*

Every list $L(u)$ is generated in $O(|L(u)| + 1)$ time: using fractional cascading, we can find indices i_l and i_r in any visited node u in constant time. When i_l and i_r are known, data structure $D(u)$ reports all points $p \in A(u)$, $p.z \geq c$ in $O(|L(u)| + 1)$ time. The total number of nodes u for which lists $L(u)$ were generated is bounded by $O(\log n + k)$. Hence, the total time needed to generate all lists $L(u)$ is $O(\log n + k)$. It remains to show how to merge all $L(u)$ so that the output is sorted by z-coordinates. We will say that a node u is situated to the right of a node v if u and v are stored in respectively the right and the left subtrees of their lowest common ancestor.

OBSERVATION 2. *If $p_u.z > p_w.z$ for some $p_u \in P(u)$ and $p_w \in P(w)$, then u is an ancestor of w or u is situated to the right of w in T.*

Let V denote the set of all visited nodes. Since the height of T is $O(\log n)$, we can use sweepline approach for sorting points in the query range: we maintain the *current path* Π_c, and report points stored in $P(u)$, $u \in \Pi_c$, in sorted order. Suppose that we work with the current path Π_c at some time. Then this means that all nodes $u \in V$ to the right of Π_c were already processed and points from lists $L(u)$ are already in sorted order. To initialize the path Π_c, we start at the root and move down the tree until a leaf is reached or the currently visited node u has no child $u_i \in V$. In every visited node u, we move to its right child u_r if $u_r \in V$; otherwise, we move to its left child u_l. Thus Π_c is initialized to the rightmost path that consists of nodes $u \in V$.

We extract the first point (i.e., the point with the highest z-coordinate) from every $L(u)$, $u \in \Pi_c$, and insert them into a priority queue Q. The following steps are repeated until all points in all $L(u)$, $u \in V$, are sorted. We extract the highest point p from Q and add it to the sorted list of points. If the list $L(u)$, such that $p \in L(u)$, is not empty, we extract the next point p' from $L(u)$ and add it to Q. When some list $L(w)$, $w \in \Pi_c$, becomes empty, we might need to update the path Π_c. If $L(w)$ is empty and w is the lowest node in Π_c, we remove w from Π_c. If w is the right child of its parent and its left sibling v is in V, we also append new nodes to Π_c. This is done by traversing a downward path that starts in v. In every visited node u, starting with v, we add u to Π_c and move down the tree if at least one child of u is in V; if both children of u are in V, we always select the right child. For every new node u in Π_c, we extract the highest point $p \in L(u)$ and add it to Q. Otherwise, if w has

[‡‡]The x-rank of a point p in a set P is the number of points $p' \in P$ such that $p'.x \leq p.x$.

no left sibling or the left sibling of w is not in Π_c, then we move up in the tree and consecutively examine all ancestors w' of w starting with the parent. If $L(w')$ for an ancestor w' of w is empty, we remove w' from Π_c. If w' has a left sibling $w'' \in V$, we append the rightmost path starting at w'' to Π_c as described above. Otherwise, we examine the ancestors of w' until a node u, $L(u) \neq \emptyset$, is reached. When Π_c and Q are empty, we have generated the sorted list of all points in $S \cap Q$. Correctness of our procedure follows from Observation 2. Suppose that a point $p_1 \in L(u_1)$ was reported before $p_2 \in L(u_2)$, then either (1) u_1 is to the right of u_2, or (2) u_1 is an ancestor of u_2, or (3) u_2 is ancestor of u_1. In the case (1) $p_1.z \leq p_2.z$ by Observation 2. In the case (2) u_1 is an ancestor of u_2. If p_1 was reported before u_2 was inserted into Π_c, then $p_1.z \geq p_3.z$ for some $p_3 \in L(u_3)$, where u_3 is to the right of u_2. Hence, $p_1.z \geq p_3.z \geq p_2.z$. If p_1 was reported after u_2 had been included into Π_c, then it follows from the description that $p_1.z \geq p_2.z$. Case (3) is identical with the second part of case (2).

We implement Q using the atomic heap data structure [11]; Since Q contains $O(\log n)$ elements, all operations on Q can be supported in $O(1)$ time. By keeping the depths of all non-empty nodes $u \in \Pi_c$ in another atomic heap, we can determine whether there are non-empty nodes $u' \in \Pi_c$ below a given node u in $O(1)$ time. Thus we can sort all points $p \in L(v)$, $v \in V$, by their z-coordinates in $O(|V| + \sum_{v \in V} |L(v)|)$ time. This completes the proof of Theorem 9.

D. PROOF OF THEOREM 4

To achieve the result in Theorem 4 we once again rely on the blocking scheme and interval-pair categorization introduced in the Section 6. We begin by partitioning the input range $[a, b]$ into disjoint spans as described in Section 7 and investigate each of them independently: $A[a^\theta...b^\theta]$ as middle span, $A[a^\pi...a^\theta - 1]$ and $A[b^\theta + 1...b^\pi]$ as side spans and $A[a...a^\pi - 1]$, $A[b^\pi + 1...b]$ as fringe spans. Recall that $k_{\pi+1} < k \leq k_\pi$, both a and b are within a single $\delta_{\theta-1}$-block but belong to two distinct δ_θ-blocks and $\theta \leq \pi$. With structure described in Section 7.1.1 capable of querying the middle span within the desired space-time complexity, we focus on fringe and side spans below. We the following notation in this section: $\log^{*^0}(\cdot) = \log(\cdot)$, $\log^{*^h}(\cdot)$ is the number of times function $\log^{*^{h-1}}(\cdot)$ must be iteratively applied before the result is less than or equal to 2 for $h \geq 1$ and $\alpha(\cdot)$ is the minimum h, where $\log^{*^h}(\cdot) \leq 2$. We use α to denote $\alpha(n)$ for simplicity i.e., α is the Inverse Ackermann function of n.

D.1 Handling Fringe Spans

A close look at the Lemma 6 reveals that the additive $\log^*(\frac{n}{B})$ factor in query I/Os is due to the necessity to access as many three-sided range reporting structures. Recall that each such structure TS_j was built by only considering the type-j interval-pairs. Intuitively, additional three-sided range reporting structures $TS_{i,j}$ can be maintained over a collection of type-m interval-pairs for $m = i, i+1, ..., j$ trading off space for better query performance.

To formalize this intuition we begin by proving following lemma that summarizes the way to group the interval-pairs of different types so as to build a collective three-sided range reporting structure over them. We extend the notation used for blocking factor δ_j as below for the purpose of this subsection: $\delta_j(n) = B(\log^{(j)}(\frac{n}{B}))^5$ and we use δ_j for $\delta_j(n)$ simplicity. By choosing $h = \alpha$ in the lemma, we can obtain a set $U(n, \alpha)$ such that each element of $S(n, \alpha) = \{\delta_1, \delta_2, ..., \delta_{\log^*(\frac{n}{B})}\}$ belongs to at most α sets in $U(n, \alpha)$. We now simply maintain a collective three-sided structure for each element U_e in $U(n, \alpha)$ considering all type-j interval-pairs such that $\delta_j \in U_e$. The overall space requirement of such storage can be bounded by $O(n\alpha)$. Moreover the total number of three-sided structures we need to access in query algorithm of Lemma 6 is now bounded by $2\alpha^2 \log(\frac{\delta_\pi}{B}) = \Theta(\alpha^2(\frac{k_{\pi+1}}{B})^{1/3}) = O(\alpha^2(\frac{k}{B})^{1/3})$. Thus the query I/Os can be bounded by $O(\alpha^2(\frac{k}{B})^{1/3} + \frac{k}{B})$.

LEMMA 9. *Given a set $S(n, h) = \{\delta_1, \delta_2, ..., \delta_x\}$ such that $\log^{(x)}(\frac{n}{B}) \geq \log^{*^h}(\frac{n}{B}) > \log^{(x+1)}(\frac{n}{B})$, we can obtain a set $U(n, h)$ with each of its element being a subset of $S(n, h)$ satisfying following conditions:*

- *any element of $S(n, h)$ belongs to at the most $h+1$ sets in $U(n, h)$*
- *set $Q_x = \{\delta_1, \delta_2, ..., \delta_x\}$ can be expressed as a union of h sets in $U(n, h)$*
- *any set $Q_\mu = \{\delta_1, \delta_2, ..., \delta_\mu\}$ with $\mu < x$ can be expressed as a union of $P(n, h, \mu) \leq 2h^2 \log(\frac{\delta_\mu(n)}{B})$ sets in $U(n, h)$*

PROOF. For the base case with $h = 1$ we have $\delta_x \geq B(\log^* \frac{n}{B}) > \delta_{x+1}$. Then construct $U(n, 1) = \{\{\delta_1\}, \{\delta_2\}, ..., \{\delta_{x-1}\}, \{\delta_1, \delta_2, ..., \delta_x\}\}$. Clearly the first and second statements in the Lemma are true. For any $\mu \leq x - 1$, the set Q_x can be expressed as a union of μ sets in $U(n, h)$, where μ can be upper bounded by $\log(\frac{\delta_\mu(n)}{B}) \leq P(1)$ in this case. This is because $\mu \leq \log^*(\frac{n}{B}) < \frac{\delta_x}{B} \leq \log(\frac{\delta_\mu(n)}{B})$ for any $\mu \leq x - 1$. We now assume that the desired $U(n, h)$ can be obtained for $h = 1, 2, ..., m$ and show how $U(n, m+1)$ can be obtained for $S(n, m+1)$.

We use an important property expressed by equality $\delta_{j+1} = \delta_1(\delta_j)$ to obtain $U(n, m+1)$. Let $\log^{(\phi_1)}(\frac{n}{B}) \geq \log^{*^m}(\frac{n}{B}) > \log^{(\phi_1+1)}(\frac{n}{B})$ then $S(n, m) = \{\delta_1, \delta_2, ..., \delta_{\phi_1}\}$. Further we define $\phi_2, \phi_3, ..., \phi_r$ with $\log^{(\phi_j)}(\frac{n}{B}) \geq \log^{*^m} \log^{*^m} ...j\ times ...(\frac{n}{B}) > \log^{(\phi_j+1)}(\frac{n}{B})$ for $j = 1, 2, 3, ..., r$, and $\log^{(\phi_r)}(\frac{n}{B}) \geq \log^{(x')}(\frac{n}{B}) \geq \log^{*^{m+1}}(\frac{n}{B}) > \log^{(x'+1)}(\frac{n}{B}) > \log^{(\phi_r+1)}(\frac{n}{B})$. Then $S(n, m+1)$ can be written as follows:

$$\begin{aligned}
S(n, m+1) &= \{\delta_1, \delta_2, ..., \delta_{x'}\} \\
&= \{\delta_1, ..., \delta_{\phi_1}\} \cup \{\delta_{\phi_1+1}, ..., \delta_{\phi_2}\} \cup \{\delta_{\phi_2+1}, ..., \delta_{\phi_3}\} \\
&\cup ... \cup \{\delta_{\phi_r+1}, ..., \delta_{x'}\} \\
&= \{\delta_1(n), \delta_2(n), ...\} \cup \{\delta_1(\delta_{\phi_1}), \delta_2(\delta_{\phi_1}), ...\} \\
&\cup \{\delta_1(\delta_{\phi_2}), \delta_2(\delta_{\phi_2}), ...\} \cup ... \cup \{\delta_1(\delta_{\phi_r}), \delta_2(\delta_{\phi_r}), ...\} \\
&= S(n, m) \cup S(\delta_{\phi_1}, m) \cup S(\delta_{\phi_2}, m) \cup ... \cup S'(\delta_{\phi_r}, m)
\end{aligned}$$

Note that the last set $S'(\delta_{\phi_r}, m) = \{\delta \geq B \log^{*^{m+1}}(n/B) | \delta \in S(\delta_{\phi_r}, m)\}$. After constructing $U(\cdot, m)$ for each of the $S(\cdot, m)$ in the above equation (using our recursive method for $h = m$ case), we obtain $U(n, m+1) = U(n, m) \cup U(\delta_{\phi_1}, m) \cup U(\delta_{\phi_2}, m) \cup ... \cup U'(\delta_{\phi_r}, m) \cup \{\delta_{\phi_1}, ..., \delta_{x'}\}$.

It can be easily verified that each element in $S(n, m+1)$ belongs to at the most $m+2$ sets in $U(n, m+1)$ thus proving the first statement in Lemma. The second statement also verifiable since $Q_{x'}$ can be expressed as a union of $S(n, m)$ and $\{\delta_{\phi_1}, ..., \delta_{x'}\} \in U(n, m+1)$, where $S(n, m)$ can in-turn be expressed as a union of $m+1$ sets in $U(n, m) \in U(n, m+1)$. Finally the remaining case, where $\mu < x'$ can be proved as follows: let $\phi_j + 1 \leq \mu \leq \phi_{j+1}$, the set Q_μ

can be expressed as $S(n,m) \cup S(\delta_{\phi_1},m) \cup S(\delta_{\phi_2},m) \cup ... \cup S(\delta_{\phi_j},m) \cup \{\delta_{\phi_j+1},...,\delta_\mu\}$. As each $S(.,m)$ can be expressed as the union of m sets in $U(n,m+1)$, $S(n,m) \cup S(\delta_{\phi_1},m) \cup S(\delta_{\phi_2},m) \cup ... \cup S(\delta_{\phi_j},m)$ can be expressed as a union of $(j+1)m$ sets in $U(n,m+1)$. Moreover $j \le \log^{*^{m+1}}(\frac{n}{B}) \le \log(\frac{\delta_\mu(n)}{B})$ for all $\mu < x'$, therefore $(j+1)m \le (\log(\frac{\delta_\mu(n)}{B})+1)m$. The remaining elements in Q_μ, i.e., $\{\delta_{\phi_j+1},...,\delta_\mu\}$ can be represented as the union of $P(\delta_{\phi_j},m,\mu-\phi_j) \le P(n,m,\mu)$ sets in $U(\delta_{\phi_j},m)$. By putting every thing together, $P(n,m+1,\mu) \le P(n,m,\mu) + m\log(\frac{\delta_\mu(n)}{B}) + m \le 2(m+1)^2\log(\frac{\delta_\mu}{B})$. This completes the proof. □

D.2 Handling Side Spans

We demonstrate the proposed data structures for the span $A[a^\pi...a^\theta-1]$ below and note that the span $A[b^\theta+1...b^\pi]$ can handled in a symmetric way. We take a different approach for handling the side spans and instead of obtaining the top-k answers for the query $(a^\pi, a^\theta-1, k)$ as before, we instead choose to retrieve only those outputs from set $Output(a,b,k)$ of size k which belong to the span $A[a^\pi...a^\theta-1]$. This can be achieved by using the index summarized in following lemma. By choosing $h=\alpha$, we obtain linear space index with $O(\alpha\log_B k + \frac{k}{B})$ query I/Os.

LEMMA 10. *There exists an $S(n,h) = O(n/\log^{*^h}(n/B))$ space data structure for answering the following query in $T(n,h)+O(\frac{k'}{B})$ I/Os where $T(n,h) = T(n,h-1)+O(\log_B k)$: Given a top-$k$ categorical maxima query (a,b,k) retrieve the $k' \le k$ outputs in the set $Output(a,b,k)$ which belong to the span $A[a^{dn}...a^{up}-1]$ such that $a \le a^{dn} \le a^{up}-1 \le b$, $\log^{*^h}(\frac{n}{B}) \le \log^{(dn)}(\frac{n}{B}) < \log^{(up)}(\frac{n}{B})$ and $k \le k_{dn} < k_{up}$.*

PROOF. Before moving to the proof recall that, if query range $[a,b]$ intersects blocks $A_{j,l}, A_{j,l+1},...,A_{j,t}$ then $a^j = f_{j,l+1}$. We now prove the above result using induction. The base case for $h=1$ can be proved as follows: for each $A_{j,t}$ with $j \le \phi \le \log^*(\frac{n}{B})$, $\log^{(\phi)}(\frac{n}{B}) \ge \log^*(\frac{n}{B}) > \log^{(\phi+1)}(\frac{n}{B})$ and $i<j$ we maintain top-k_j answers for the span bounded by $f_{j,t}$ and the first δ_i-boundary that follows $f_{j,t}$. Instead of maintaining these k_j answers as a single list $SL(j,t,i)$ as before, we view it as a collection of multiple lists $SL(j,t,i,\overline{k_j})$ storing top-$\overline{k_j}$ answers for $\overline{k_j} = 1,2,4,...k_j$ and maintain a three-dimensional dominance structure for each of these lists over the $prev(.)$, $next(.)$ and $weight(.)$ fields. Thus $S(n,1)$ can be bounded by $O(\frac{n}{(\log^{(2)}(\frac{n}{B}))^2} + \frac{2n}{(\log^{(3)}(\frac{n}{B}))^2} + \frac{3n}{(\log^{(4)}(\frac{n}{B}))^2} + ... + \frac{(\phi-1)n}{(\log^{(\phi)}(\frac{n}{B}))^2}) = O(\frac{n}{\log^*(\frac{n}{B})})$ words. In order to answer a query, we use the dominance structure corresponding to the list $SL(dn,t,up,\overline{k})$ with $t = \lceil\frac{a^{dn}}{\delta_{dn}}\rceil$ and $k \le \overline{k} < 2k$. Note that an answer from any list $SL(dn,t,up,.)$ belongs to the span $A[a^{dn}...a^{up}-1]$. Then such an answer only needs to satisfy the conditions $prev(.) < a$, $b < next(.)$ and $A[.] \ge \tau^k_{a,b}$ to be reported as an output for the query (a,b,k). Total query I/Os needed can bounded by $O(\log_B \overline{k} + \frac{k'}{B})$ and $T(n,1) = O(\log_B k)$.

Next we prove the result for $h=m+1$ assuming the claim to be true for all previous cases (i.e., $h=1,2,...,m$). Let r be such that $\log^{*^m}\log^{*^m}$ ... r *times* ...$(\frac{n}{B}) \ge \log^{*^{m+1}}(\frac{n}{B}) > \log^{*^m}\log^{*^m}$ ... $(r+1)$ *times* ...$(\frac{n}{B})$. Then for $j=1,2,3,...,r-1$, define ϕ_j as follows: $\log^{(\phi_j)}(\frac{n}{B}) \ge \log^{*^m}\log^{*^m}$ ... j *times* ...$(\frac{n}{B}) > \log^{(\phi_j+1)}(\frac{n}{B})$. Where as ϕ_r is defined as the largest integer (say g) with $\log^{*^m}(\log^{(\phi_r)}(\frac{n}{B})) \ge \log^{*^{m+1}}(\frac{n}{B})$. Note that for $j=1,2,3,...,r-2$, $\log^{*^m}(\log^{(\phi_j)}(\frac{n}{B})) = \log^{(\phi_{j+1})}(\frac{n}{B})$. We consider the following two cases:

Case 1. $\delta_{\phi_x+1} < \delta_{dn} < \delta_{up} \le \delta_{\phi_x}$: To answer a query in this scenario, we simply maintain the structure $S(.,m)$ for each $A_{\phi_j,t}$ occupying overall space of $O(\frac{n}{\log^{(\phi_1)}(\frac{n}{B})} + \frac{n}{\log^{(\phi_2)}(\frac{n}{B})} + ... + \frac{n}{\log^{*^m}\log^{(\phi_r)}(\frac{n}{B})}) = O(\frac{n}{\log^{*^{m+1}}(\frac{n}{B})})$ words. Since both a^{dn} and a^{up} belong to the same δ_x-block in this case, query can be answered using the structure maintained over the points in that δ_{ϕ_x}-block in $T(\delta_x,m) \le T(n,m)$ time.

Case 2. $\delta_{\phi_x+1} < \delta_{dn} \le \delta_{\phi_x} \le \delta_{y+1} < \delta_{up} \le \delta_y$: We maintain two components described below.

- For each $A_{\phi_j,t}$ and $i<j$ for $j=1,2,3,..,r$, we maintain top-k_{ϕ_j} answers for the span bounded by $f_{\phi_j,t}$ and the first δ_{ϕ_i}-boundary that follows it. Again these k_{ϕ_j} answers are maintained as a collection of three-dimensional dominance structures over the multiple lists $SL(\phi_j,t,\phi_i,\overline{k_{\phi_j}})$ for $\overline{k_{\phi_j}} = 1,2,4,...,k_{\phi_j}$. The overall space (in words) of this component can be bounded as follows: $O(\frac{n}{\log^{(\phi_2)}(\frac{n}{B})} + \frac{2n}{\log^{(\phi_3)}(\frac{n}{B})} + ... + \frac{(r-1)n}{\log^{(\phi_r)}(\frac{n}{B})}) = O(\frac{n}{\log^{*^{m+1}}(\frac{n}{B})})$. Here note that $r \le \log^{*^{m+1}}(\frac{n}{B})$ and $\log^{(\phi_r)}(\frac{n}{B}) = \Omega((\log^{*^{m+1}}(\frac{n}{B}))^2)$.
- Consider a blocking factor δ_z in our blocking scheme such that $\delta_{\phi_j+1} < \delta_z < \delta_{\phi_j}$. Then for each δ_z-boundary i.e., $f_{z,t}$ we maintain top-k_z answers for the span bounded by $f_{z,t}$ and the first δ_{ϕ_j}-boundary that follows it. Once again it is in the form of three-dimensional dominance structures over the lists $sl(z,t,\phi_j,\overline{k_z})$ for $\overline{k_z} = 1,2,4,...,k_z$ occupying $O(\frac{n}{(\log^{(z)}(\frac{n}{B}))^2})$ space. Such pre-computed answers are stored for each δ_z, where $\log^{(z)}(\frac{n}{B}) \ge \log^{*^{m+1}}(\frac{n}{B})$. Therefore total space can be bounded by $o(\frac{n}{\log^{*^{m+1}}(\frac{n}{B})})$.

In order to answer the query, we partition that span $A[a^{dn}...a^{up}-1]$ into three disjoint spans and answer each of them separately as discussed below.

- The first span is bounded by a^{dn} and the first δ_{ϕ_x}-boundary that follows it. By slight abuse of notation let such a δ_{ϕ_x}-boundary be denoted by a^{ϕ_x}. Recall that $\delta_{\phi_x+1} < \delta_{dn} \le \delta_{\phi_x}$. Hence the desired answers can be obtained by querying dominance structure on the list $sl(dn,t,\phi_x,\overline{k})$ with $t = \lceil\frac{a^{dn}}{\delta_{dn}}\rceil$ and $k \le \overline{k} < 2k$ by spending $O(\log_B k + \frac{k''}{B})$.
- To get the outputs for the query (a,b,k) in the span $A[a^{\phi_x}...a^{\phi_y+1}-1]$ we need to query appropriate SL list (three-dimensional dominance structure associated with it). Here a^{ϕ_y+1} represents the first δ_{ϕ_y+1}-boundary that follows a^{ϕ_x} and number of I/Os required for querying SL are bounded by $O(\log_B k + \frac{k'''}{B})$.
- The remaining span for the range a^{ϕ_y+1}, a^{up} falls into the case 1 studied earlier as the range will be completely contained in a δ_{ϕ_y}-block. Therefore I/Os needed in this case are given by $T(n,m) + \frac{k''''}{B}$.

We note that $k' = k''+k'''+k''''$ and total query I/Os are bounded by $T(n,m)+O(\log_B k + \frac{k'}{B})$. Putting all the pieces together, $S(n,m+1) = O(\frac{n}{\log^{*^{m+1}}(\frac{n}{B})})$ and $T(n,m+1) = T(n,m)+O(\log_B k) = O(m\log_B k)$. □

By putting every thing together, we obtain an $O(n\alpha)$-word data structure with $O(\alpha^2(\frac{k}{B})^{1/3}+\alpha\log_B\alpha+\frac{k}{B}) = O(\alpha^3+\frac{k}{B})$ query I/Os. This completes the proof of Theorem 4.

Cost-Oblivious Storage Reallocation

Michael A. Bender
Computer Science,
Stony Brook University
and Tokutek, Inc.
USA
bender@cs.stonybrook.edu

Martin Farach-Colton
Computer Science,
Rutgers University
and Tokutek, Inc.
USA
farach@cs.rutgers.edu

Sándor P. Fekete
Computer Science
TU Braunschweig
Germany
s.fekete@tu-bs.de

Jeremy T. Fineman
Computer Science
Georgetown University
USA
jfineman@cs.georgetown.edu

Seth Gilbert
Computer Science
National University of Singapore
Singapore
seth.gilbert@comp.nus.edu.sg

ABSTRACT

Databases allocate and free blocks of storage on disk. Freed blocks introduce holes where no data is stored. Allocation systems attempt to reuse such deallocated regions in order to minimize the footprint on disk. When previously allocated blocks cannot be moved, this problem is called the ***memory allocation*** problem. It is known to have a logarithmic overhead in the footprint size.

This paper defines the ***storage reallocation*** problem, where previously allocated blocks can be moved, or ***reallocated***, but at some cost. This cost is determined by the allocation/reallocation ***cost function***. The algorithms presented here are ***cost oblivious***, in that they work for a broad and reasonable class of cost functions, even when they do not know what the cost function actually is.

The objective is to minimize the storage footprint, that is, the largest memory address containing an allocated object, while simultaneously minimizing the reallocation costs. This paper gives asymptotically optimal algorithms for storage reallocation, in which the storage footprint is at most $(1+\varepsilon)$ times optimal, and the reallocation cost is at most $O((1/\varepsilon)\log(1/\varepsilon))$ times the original allocation cost, which is asymptotically optimal for constant ε. The algorithms are ***cost oblivious***, which means they achieve these bounds with no knowledge of the allocation/reallocation cost function, as long as the cost function is subadditive.

This research was supported in part by NSF grants IIS 1247726, CCF 1217708, CCF 1114809, CCF 0937822, IIS 1247750, CCF 1114930, CCF 1218188, by DFG grant FE407/17-1, and by Singapore NUS FRC R-252-000-443-133.

PODS'14, June 22–27, 2014, Snowbird, UT, USA.

ACM 978-1-4503-2375-8/14/06 ...$15.00.
http://dx.doi.org/10.1145/2594538.2594548.

Categories and Subject Descriptors

F.2.2 [**Analysis of Algorithms and Problem Complexity**]: Nonnumerical Algorithms and Problems—*Sequencing and scheduling*

Keywords

Reallocation, storage allocation, scheduling, physical layout, cost oblivious

1. INTRODUCTION

Databases, and more generally storage systems, need to allocate and free blocks of storage on disk. Freed data introduces holes where no data is stored. Allocation systems attempt to reuse such deallocated regions in order to minimize the footprint on disk.

The problem of allocating and freeing storage is well studied as the ***memory allocation*** problem. In this formulation, allocated objects cannot be moved. The ***competitive ratio*** is defined as the maximum possible ratio of the allocated memory (largest allocated memory address) to the sum of the sizes of allocated segments [34–36]. The lower bound on the competitive ratio is roughly logarithmic in the number of requests and in the ratio of the largest to smallest request [35].

The logarithmic lower bound renders traditional memory allocation too blunt a theoretical tool for understanding storage in many settings. Furthermore, as we show, this lower bound is a consequence of the requirement that allocated storage cannot be moved. But many actual systems have no such restriction. Storage systems typically define a mapping from a logical address space to a physical address space, and this layer of indirection allows storage to be reallocated, at a cost.

Storage reallocation. This paper generalizes memory allocation by allowing the allocator to move previously allocated objects. We call this generalization ***storage reallocation***. Storage reallocation can take place on any physical medium for allocating objects, e.g., main memory, rotating disks, or flash memory.

Thus, garbage collection [31] is a type of in-core storage reallocation. Our own interest in memory reallocation stems for our experience in building the TokuDB [45] and TokuMX [46] databases, in which memory segments are accessed via a so-called "block translation layer," which translates between the block name, which is immutable, and the block address in storage, which may change.

Cost-oblivious storage reallocation. An algorithm for storage reallocation must contend with the tradeoff between storage footprint size and the amount (and cost) of reallocation. It should come as no surprise that a storage reallocator that is designed for main memory is unlikely to work well if the objects are allocated on a rotating device instead—and vice versa. This is because the cost model depends on where the objects are stored.

The question is therefore how to model the cost of reallocating memory objects. Faithful cost models are hard to come by because the memory hierarchy has a hard-to-quantify impact on run time. In RAM, moving an object is roughly proportional to w, the object size. On disk, moving a small object may be dominated by the seek time, while moving a large object may be dominated by the disk bandwidth. In both cases, there are cache effects, both in memory and in storage and in their interaction. The performance characteristics for each aspect of memory vary by brand and model.

Rather than model these complex interactions, this paper specifies a class of cost functions that subsumes them. We give universal reallocators, independent of the particulars of the reallocation cost. We say that a universal reallocator is ***cost oblivious*** with respect to a class of cost functions if it is optimal or near optimal for all cost functions in that class. Our reallocation algorithms are cost oblivious with respect to the class of cost functions that are ***subadditive***, monotonically increasing functions of the object size.[1]

To summarize, in storage reallocation, there is an online sequence of insert (malloc) and delete (free) requests. Objects are allocated to locations in an arbitrarily large array (address space). The cost of allocating or moving (reallocating) a size-w object is some unknown (monotonically increasing) subadditive function $f(w)$.

Storage reallocation is thus a bicriteria optimization problem. The first objective is to store objects in an array so that the largest allocated memory address—which we call the ***footprint***—is approximately minimized. The second objective is to minimize the amortized reallocation cost per new request. In this paper, we consider the problem of minimizing the amortized reallocation cost, while using a memory footprint that is at most a constant factor larger than optimal.

Storage reallocation in a database. Databases have many moving parts, and any system that changes the way that storage is allocated needs to interact gracefully with the other requirements of the storage system.

[1]A (monotonically increasing) function $f(x)$ is ***subadditive***, if $f(x+y) \leq f(x) + f(y)$ for any positive x and y. (All monotonically increasing concave functions are subadditive.) The restriction to subadditivity is not severe. While there exist corner cases where a storage system is temporarily superadditive, most mechanisms employed by operating systems, such as prefetching for latency hiding, rely on the subadditivity of costs.

A common constraint in storage (re)allocation is that updates be ***nonoverlapping***, i.e., when an object is moved, its new location must be disjoint from its old location. In databases, object writes are not atomic, so nonoverlapping reallocation is necessary for durability[2].

The nonoverlapping constraint is only part of the mechanism for durability. Another consideration is that when an object is moved, the translation table between logical and physical addresses is updated. It is then written to disk during a ***checkpoint***. Only then are blocks that have been freed since the last checkpoint available for reuse. Therefore, the allocator may not write to a location that has been freed since the last checkpoint.

Finally, new memory requests arrive at unpredictable times. It is undesirable for an allocation request to block on a long sequence of reallocations, even if the average throughput is high. A good reallocation algorithm provides some guarantee on the worst-case cost of individual operations, while still maintaining (near) optimal throughput.

Formalization. An ***online execution*** is a sequence of requests of the form $\langle$INSERTOBJECT, *name*, *length*$\rangle$ and $\langle$DELETEOBJECT, *name*$\rangle$. After each request, the reallocator outputs an allocation for the objects in the system. We say that an object is ***active*** at time t if it has been inserted by one of the first t requests, but not deleted by the end of request t. (Note that an object being deleted remains active until the reallocator completes the delete request.)

If $\mathcal{S}$ and $\mathcal{S}'$ are the allocations immediately before and after request p, then the ***reallocation cost of p*** is the sum of the reallocation costs of all objects moved between $\mathcal{S}$ and $\mathcal{S}'$.

A reallocator A is ***(f,a,b)-competitive*** for cost function $f()$, if (1) the footprint size is always optimized within an a-factor of optimal, and (2) the reallocation cost is at most b times the sum of the allocation costs of every object inserted thus far (including those that have subsequently been deleted). Since every object must be allocated at least once, the cost of such a reallocator is clearly within a factor of b of optimal.

Let $\mathcal{C}$ be a set of cost functions. A reallocation algorithm A is ***cost oblivious*** if it does not depend on $f()$.[3] A cost-oblivious reallocator A is ***$(\mathcal{C},a,b)$-competitive*** if it is (f,a,b)-competitive for every $f \in \mathcal{C}$; we abbreviate to ***(a,b)-competitive*** if the set $\mathcal{C}$ is unambiguous. We say that A is ***optimally cost-oblivious*** if it is ***(a,b)-competitive*** for some $a, b \in O(1)$. Let $\mathcal{F}_{sa}$ be the class of subadditive functions.

Results. Our reallocation algorithms are tunable to achieve an arbitrarily good competitive ratio $1+\varepsilon$, $(0 < \varepsilon \leq 1/2)$ with respect to the footprint size. All objects have integral length, and Δ denotes the length of the longest object. We establish the following:

- We give a cost-oblivious algorithm for storage reallocation that is $(\mathcal{F}_{sa}, 1+\varepsilon, O((1/\varepsilon)\log(1/\varepsilon))$-competitive.

[2]This is also relevant in other contexts: In SSDs, the nonoverlapping constraint is enforced by the hardware, because memory locations must be erased between writes. In FPGAs, satisfying this constraint allows interruption-free reallocations of modules [23].

[3]This means not only that $f()$ is not a parameter to algorithm A, but also A learns nothing about $f()$ as A executes.

This allocator is amortized in the sense that it might reallocate every existing object between servicing two requests.

- As a corollary, we give a defragmenter that is cost oblivious with respect to $\mathcal{F}_{sa}$. The defragmenter takes as input a comparison function, a set of objects having total length V and consuming space $(1+\varepsilon)V$. The defragmenter sorts the objects using $(1+\varepsilon)V+\Delta$ working space, moving each object $O((1/\varepsilon)\log(1/\varepsilon))$ times.
- We extend the storage reallocator to support checkpointing. With an additional $O(\Delta)$ space, we guarantee that each operation completes within $O(1/\varepsilon)$ checkpoints. (An immediate consequence is that all reallocations are non-overlapping.)
- We also partially deamortize the storage reallocator so that the worst-case reallocation cost (and therefore the worst-case time blocking for a new size-w allocation) is reduced to $O((1/\varepsilon)wf(1)+f(\Delta))$.

Related work. We now briefly review the related work.
Dynamic memory allocation. There is an extensive literature on memory allocation [34–36, 38–40, 52] where object reallocation is disallowed. There are upper and lower bounds on the competitive ratio of the memory footprint that are roughly logarithmic in the number of requests and in the ratio of the largest to smallest request. These papers generally analyze traditional strategies such as Best Fit, First Fit, and the Buddy System [33], but also propose alternatives. Traditional memory-allocation strategies often have analogs in bin-packing [17–20, 25], but an enumeration of such results lies beyond the scope of this paper.

Memory allocation where reallocation *is allowed* appears often in the literature on garbage collection [31]. There is a long and important line of literature studying dynamic memory allocation with differing compaction mechanisms, exploring the time/space trade-off between the amount of compaction performed and the total memory used. Ting [44] develops a mathematical model for examining this trade-off for different compaction algorithms; Błażewicz et al. [14] develop a "partial" compaction algorithm for segments of two different sizes that reallocates only a limited number of segments per compactions. More recently Bendersky and Petrank [13] and Cohen and Petrank [21] have more fully explored the trade-offs inherent in partial compaction.

These papers on dynamic memory allocation with compaction are instances of storage reallocation, as addressed in this paper, where the reallocation cost is (typically) linear: the cost of compaction is directly proportional to the amount of memory that is moved. (These papers often address other problems that arise in garbage collection, such as how to update pointers to memory that has moved.) For example, Bendersky and Petrank [13] show that when the cost function is linear, one can achieve constant amortized reallocation cost with memory size that is within a constant-factor of optimal.

In this paper, by contrast, we focus on cost-oblivious algorithms that tolerate the range of cost functions found in external storage systems. Cost obliviousness bears a passing resemblance to similar notions in the memory hierarchy, particularly the cache-oblivious/ideal-cache [24, 37], hierarchical memory [1], and cache-adaptive [8] models. With the exception of the underlying paging [43], work in these models is about writing algorithms that are memory-hierarchy universal rather than analyzing resource allocation.
Other related work. We note that storage reallocation has other applications besides databases. For example, Fekete et al. [23] address the storage reallocation problem in the context of FPGAs, and Bender et al. [10] give (not cost-oblivious) algorithms for constant reallocation cost.

Sparse table data structures [6,7,11,12,16,28,29,32,49–51] also solve the storage reallocation problem and are easily adapted to deal with different-sized objects and linear reallocation cost. But they do so while maintaining the constraint that the object order does not change, which makes the problem harder and the reallocation cost correspondingly larger.
Scheduling/planning interpretation. The storage reallocation problem can be viewed as a reallocation problem in scheduling/planning. In this interpretation, we have an online sequence of requests to insert a new job j into the schedule or to delete an exiting job j. Each job has a length w_j and the rescheduling cost is $f(w_j)$. The goal is to maintain a uniprocessor schedule that (approximately) minimizes the makespan (latest completion time of any job), while simultaneously guaranteeing the overall reallocation cost is approximated minimized. We can abbreviate this scheduling problem as $1|f(w)$ *realloc* $|C_{\max}$, generalizing standard scheduling notation [26]. The goal is actually not to *run* the schedule, but rather to plan a schedule subject to an online sequence of requests.

We thus (briefly) review related work in scheduling and combinatorial optimization. Several papers explore related notions of scheduling reallocation (although to the best of our knowledge, not cost-universal scheduling reallocation). Bender et al. [9] study reallocation scheduling with unit-length jobs having release times and deadlines. Their reallocator maintains a feasible multiprocessor schedule while servicing inserts and deletes.

In the area of robust optimization, the goal is to develop solutions for combinatorial optimization problems that are (near) optimal, and that can be readily updated if the instance changes. In this context, many papers have looked at the problem of minimizing reallocation costs for specific optimization problems (e.g., [23,27,47]). For example, Davis et al. [22] study a reallocation problem, where an allocator divides resources among a set of users, updating the allocation as the users' constraints change. The goal is to minimize the number of changes to the allocation. As another example, Sanders et al. [41] look at the problem of assigning jobs to processors, minimizing the reallocation as new jobs arrive. Jansen et al. [30] look at robust algorithms for online bin packing that minimize migration costs. See Verschae [48] for more details on robust optimization.

Shachnai et al. [42] explore a slightly different notion of reallocation for combinatorial problems. Given an input, an optimal solution for that input, and a modified version of the input, they develop algorithms that find the minimum-cost modification of the optimal solution to the modified input. A difference between their setting and ours is that we measure the ratio of reallocation cost to allocation cost, whereas they measure the ratio of the actual transition cost to the optimal transition cost resulting in a good solution. Also, we focus on a sequence of changes, which means we amortize the expensive changes against a sequence of updates.

There also exist reoptimization problems, which address the goal of minimizing the computational cost for incrementally updating the schedule [2–5, 15]. By contrast, in reallocation, we focus on the cost of reallocating resources rather than the computational cost of generating the allocation.

2. FOOTPRINT MINIMIZATION

In this section we give a cost-oblivious algorithm for footprint minimization in storage reallocation. The footprint always has size at most $(1+\varepsilon)V_t$, where V_t denotes the ***volume***, or total size, of all allocated objects at time t, i.e., of the active objects after the tth operation completes. A size-w object has an amortized reallocation cost of $O(f(w)\cdot(1/\varepsilon)\log(1/\varepsilon))$, where $f(w)$ is the (unknown) cost for allocating an object of size w.

THEOREM 1. *For any constant ε with $0<\varepsilon\leq 1/2$, there exists a cost-oblivious storage-reallocation algorithm that is $(1+\varepsilon, O((1/\varepsilon)\log(1/\varepsilon)))$-competitive with respect to $\mathcal{F}_{sa}$, the class of subadditive cost functions.*

Thus, the storage reallocation algorithm is asymptotically optimal for any constant $\varepsilon<1/2$.

Intuition and cost-function-specific algorithms. We begin by considering some simple cases where the cost function is known in advance. First suppose that the reallocation cost is linear in the object size, i.e., $f(w)=w$. A simple logging-and-compressing strategy attains a $(2,2)$-competitive algorithm for linear cost functions. Specifically, allocate objects from left to right. Upon a deletion, leave a hole where the object used to be. Whenever a deallocation causes the footprint to reach $2V_t$, remove all holes by compacting. The cost to reallocate the entire volume V_t is paid for by the V_t's worth of elements that were deallocated since the last compaction.

Logging and compressing does not work well for constant reallocation cost, i.e., $f(w)=1$. To see why, suppose the deleted objects have size Δ, and the reallocated elements have size 1. We may need to spend amortized $\Theta(\Delta)$ reallocation cost per deletion.

There do exist good reallocators for constant reallocation cost [10]. Conceptually, round the sizes of object up to the next power of 2, to form ***size classes***, where objects have size 2^i for $i=1,\ldots,\log\Delta$. Now group the objects by increasing size. Between the ith and $(i+1)$st size class, is either a gap of size 2^i or no gap. To insert an object of size 2^i, put the object into the gap after the ith size class, if one exists, or displace a larger object to make space. Then recursively reinsert the larger object. The amortized reallocation cost is $O(1)$, because the costs per unit volume to displace the recursively larger objects form a geometric series.

It can be shown, however, that with linear reallocation cost this strategy is only $(2, O(\log\Delta))$-competitive.

This section gives a single algorithm that works for $f(w)=w$, $f(w)=1$, and all other subadditive cost functions. The algorithm keeps the objects partially sorted by size. Since the cost function is subadditive, small objects are the most expensive to move per unit size. We therefore want to guarantee that when an object is inserted or deleted, it can only trigger the movement of larger (less expensive per unit size) objects. Specifically, small objects with total volume W will be able to cause the movements of big objects with total volume $O(W)$, but not the other way around. At the same time, we need to avoid cascading reinserts, which can happen with the algorithm for unit cost described above.

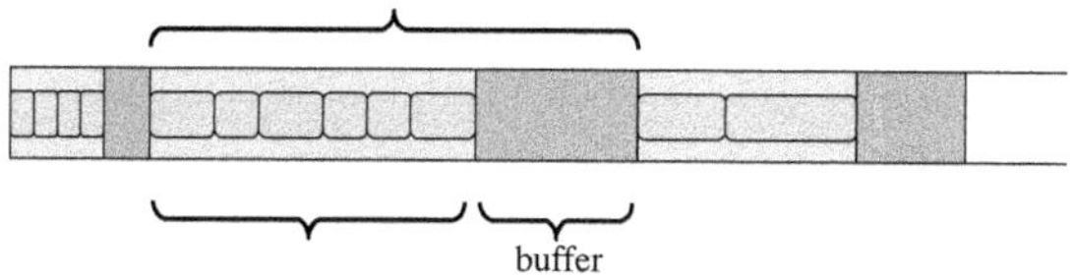

Figure 1: The layout of the data structure when the buffer segments are empty, with $\varepsilon'=1/2$. The light-gray are the payload segments, and the dark-gray areas are the buffer segments. The orange rectangles are objects currently in the data structure.

Overview and invariants. Objects are categorized into $\lfloor\lg\Delta\rfloor+1$ ***size classes***, where objects have size at least 1 and at most Δ. The value of Δ need not be set in advance. The ith size class contains objects of size w where $2^{i-1}\leq w<2^i$. For size class i, $V_t(i)$ denotes the ***volume*** (total size) of all objects active at time t in size class i. If t is understood, we use $V(i)$.

The array (address space) is divided into $\lfloor\lg\Delta\rfloor+1$ regions, as illustrated in Figure 1. The ith region is dedicated to the ith size class and comprises two subregions, a ***payload segment*** followed by a ***buffer segment***. The ith payload segment contains only objects belonging to the ith size class, whereas the ith buffer segment may contain objects that are in the ith size class or earlier (smaller) size classes.

Whenever (potentially large) reallocations are taking place, we utilize one last region at the end of the array, the ***overflow segment***. The overflow segment is used for temporarily rearranging the objects, as described later.

INVARIANT 2. *The following properties are maintained throughout the execution of the algorithm:*

1. *The ith region ($i=1,\ldots,\lfloor\lg\Delta\rfloor+1$) comprises the ith payload and ith buffer segment.*
2. *The ($\lfloor\lg\Delta\rfloor+2$)nd region, the overflow segment, stores elements temporarily during reallocation.*
3. *The ith payload segment only stores elements from the ith size class.*
4. *The ith buffer segment only stores elements from size classes $\ell\leq i$.*

Allocating and deallocating. When a new size-w object that belongs to an existing size class i is allocated, it is stored at the end of the earliest buffer $j\geq i$ that has sufficient unoccupied space. (Recall that this object cannot be inserted into any buffer in a segment $<i$.)

When there is not enough available space in any of these buffers, a ***buffer flush*** operation is triggered, after which the object is inserted.[4] During a buffer flush, all objects in

[4]As described in this section, $V_t(i)$ immediately increases to count the new object, but the object is not yet placed in the array. Next, the flush occurs, and finally the new object is placed in the array. Our extension in Section 3 places the

some suffix of buffers get moved to their proper payload segments and the segment and region boundaries get redefined.

If the new size-w object belongs to a larger size class than any other active object, then we instead create a new payload segment and buffer segment for the new size class located immediately after the last size class's segment, increasing the total space used by at most an additive $w + \varepsilon' w$, for some constant ε'. (The overflow segment is empty, as it is only used during a buffer flush, and hence is implicitly moved to after the new size class.)

When an active size-w object is deleted, it leaves a hole until the next buffer flush occurs. A dummy deletion request is added to the buffer and forced to consume w space. This buffered dummy request is not freed until the next buffer flush. Since both inserting and deleting a job of size w reduces the space in the buffer by w, we can analyze insertions and deletions as a single case.

INVARIANT 3. *The overflow segment is empty except during buffer flush operations.*

INVARIANT 4. *When a flush of the ith buffer segment occurs at time t, the object and segment boundaries move in such a way as to guarantee that:*

1. *the space occupied by the ith payload segment after the buffer flush completes is exactly $V_t(i)$, and*
2. *the space occupied by the ith buffer segment after the buffer flush completes is $\lfloor \varepsilon' V_t(i) \rfloor$, for $\varepsilon' = \Theta(\varepsilon)$.*

Immediately following this flush, the size-$\lfloor \varepsilon' V_t(i) \rfloor$ buffer contains no objects. (This space is reserved to accommodate future insertions and deletions.)

Buffer flush. A buffer flush updates the segment boundaries in a suffix of regions, moving all objects to their proper payload segments, and leaving all buffer segments empty to accommodate future insertions.

To execute a buffer flush, first determine the ***boundary size class*** b and then flush all buffers for size classes $i \geq b$. The value b is defined as the maximum value such that all objects in buffers $i \geq b$ and the object being inserted/deleted belong to size classes $\geq b$. To determine b, iterate from the largest to the smallest region, examining every object in the region's buffer. If any object belongs to a size class $s < b$, then update b with the size class s. This continues until reaching size class b, where no object from a smaller size class has been encountered.

To flush the size classes $i \geq b$ at time t, first calculate $V_t(i)$ for all $i \geq b$. The goal is to redistribute these size classes to take space at most $S = (1 + \varepsilon') \sum_{i \geq b} V_t(i)$, i.e., space $V_t(i)$ for the ith payload segment and $\lfloor \varepsilon' V_t(i) \rfloor$ for the ith buffer, while moving all objects from buffers into payload segments.

A flush can be implemented to include at most two moves per object in the flushed size classes.

1. First identify the new array suffix of size S to accommodate payload and buffer segments. Temporarily move all objects from buffer segments to empty space immediately after this suffix (or after the current suffix, if the current suffix is longer due to deletes), removing any dummy delete records from buffers. These objects make up the overflow segment. This first step increases space usage by at most $\sum_{i \geq b} \varepsilon' V_t(i)$.

object before performing the flush; this extension requires an additive Δ working space during the flush procedure.

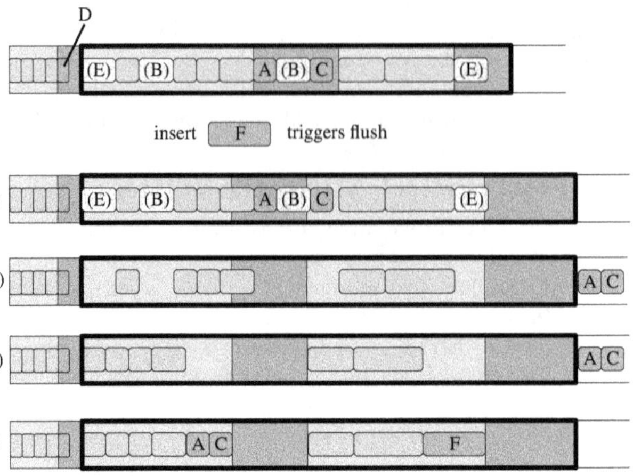

Figure 2: Example of a flush, starting from Figure 1. The lavender rectangles are updates to the data structure, with parentheses and light shading denoting a delete or delete record. (i) The state after insert A, delete B, insert C, insert D, and delete E in that order. (ii)–(v) show a flush that occurs when inserting F. The heavy outline shows the region affected by the flush, i.e., size classes 2 and 3. (ii) The new boundaries for the 2nd and 3rd size class. (iii) The state after moving buffered objects out of the way and dropping deleted objects. (iv) The state after rearranging the payload segments. (v) The state after putting all buffered objects to their proper locations. Observe that for the flushed classes, the buffers are now empty.

2. Next, iterate over payload segments from smallest to largest, moving objects as early as possible, thus removing any gaps left by deleted objects or emptied buffers. At the end of this step, all the objects are packed as far left as possible with no gaps, beginning at the start of region b.
3. Then, iterate over payload segments from largest to smallest, moving each object to its final destination in the redistributed array (which is no earlier than its current location). The final destination can be determined by looking at the values $\{V_t(i)\}$; this step reintroduces gaps to accommodate any not-yet-placed objects in the overflow segment and the empty size-$\lfloor \varepsilon' V_t(i) \rfloor$ buffers.
4. Finally, iterate over all objects in the overflow segment, placing them in their final destination at the end of the appropriate payload segments.

Analysis. The proof of Theorem 1 follows from Lemmas 5 and 6 given below, by fixing $\varepsilon' = \Theta(\varepsilon)$ appropriately. Lemma 5 states that the space used is $1 + O(\varepsilon')$ times the optimal space usage. Lemma 6 states that the reallocation cost is no worse than $O((1/\varepsilon') \lg(1/\varepsilon'))$ times the optimal reallocation cost.

LEMMA 5. *After processing allocation/deallocation requests $1, 2, \ldots, t$, the space used by the storage-reallocation algorithm is $(1 + O(\varepsilon'))V$, where $V = \sum_i V_t(i)$.*

PROOF. Let $f_i \leq t$ be the previous time the ith buffer was flushed. The space used by the buffers and payload segments is at most $(1+\varepsilon') \sum_i V_{f_i}(i)$ by construction, and it may grow to $(1 + O(\varepsilon')) \sum_i V_{f_i}(i)$ during the present buffer flush.

To prove the lemma, we need only to show that $\sum_i V_{f_i}(i)$ is not much different from $\sum_i V_t(i)$. The difference is reflected precisely by those objects in buffers (including delete records), which correspond to at most an $\varepsilon' \sum_i V_{f_i}(i)$ total volume of objects. Thus, we have $\left|\sum_i V_t(i) - \sum_i V_{f_i}(i)\right| \leq \varepsilon' \sum_i V_{f_i}(i)$.

The worst case ratio overhead occurs when all buffered objects are deletions, in which case we have $\sum_i V_t(i) \geq (1 - \varepsilon') \sum_i V_{f_i}(i)$.

We thus have at most $(1 + O(\varepsilon')) \sum_i V_{f_i}(i)$ space storing at least $(1 - \varepsilon') \sum_i V_{f_i}(i)$ active objects. Observing that $(1 + O(\varepsilon'))/(1 - \varepsilon') = 1 + O(\varepsilon')$ for $\varepsilon' \leq 1/2$ completes the proof. □

LEMMA 6. *For subadditive cost functions f, the amortized cost of inserting or deleting an object of size w is $O(f(w) \cdot (1/\varepsilon) \lg(1/\varepsilon))$.*

PROOF. Consider a buffer-flush operation, and let b be the boundary size class (i.e., all size classes $i \geq b$ have their buffers flushed). There are two cases:

Case 1: The ith buffer contains $\Omega(\varepsilon' V(i))$ volume of objects, for concreteness, say at least $\varepsilon' V(i)/2$ volume.

Case 2: The ith buffer is ***underfull***, i.e., contains less than $\varepsilon' V(i)/2$ volume. Case 2 occurs because of various kinds of roundoff. Specifically, $\varepsilon' V(i)$ may not be large enough to accommodate even one object in size-class i.

We first deal with Case 1. We need to show that the initial allocation cost of objects in the buffer is sufficient to pay for the reallocation cost of objects in the payload segment. Since the objects in the buffer belong to the ith or earlier size classes, they can each have size at most 2^i. For monotonic subadditive functions, $f(x)/x$ (the cost per unit) is nonincreasing, so the cost of allocating the objects in the buffer is at least $\Omega((f(2^i)/2^i)(\varepsilon' V(i)))$. Since f is subadditive, we have $f(2^i) = O(f(2^{i-1}))$, which implies that this buffer cost is at least $\Omega((f(2^{i-1})/2^{i-1})(\varepsilon' V(i)))$. If we charge each buffered object for $\Theta(1/\varepsilon')$ reallocations, it follows that we can afford the total cost of at most $(f(2^{i-1})/2^{i-1})V(i)$ to reallocate all objects in the payload segment. Observing that each object is only flushed once (after an object moves to the payload segment, it stays there until deallocated) completes this case.

We next deal with Case 2, where buffer i is underfull. Buffer i participates in the buffer-flush operation because some object belonging to size class $i' \leq i$ is placed in some buffer for size class $j > i$. We charge that object for flushing any underfull buffers between size class i' and size class j. (There may be many such objects, which only decreases the cost per object—we pessimistically charge only a single object.)

The main question, then, is: what is the maximum reallocation cost due to underfull buffers that can be charged against an object in size-class i'? Size-class i may only be charged against the object if $2^{i'} > \varepsilon' V(i)/2$. This implies that $V(i) = O(2^{i'}/\varepsilon')$, and hence the cost of moving every object in size-class i is at most $O(1/\varepsilon')$ times the cost of allocating a single object in size-class i'. Because each successive size class doubles in size, and a size class only has a payload segment (and buffer segment) if there is at least one object in the size class, only the $O(\lg(1/\varepsilon'))$ nearest size classes may satisfy $2^{i'} > \varepsilon' V(i)/2$—in particular, $\varepsilon' 2^{i'+\lceil \lg(1/\varepsilon') \rceil + 1}/2 \geq 2^{i'}$, and hence if any larger size-class is underfull, it will not be "skipped over" by an object in size-class i'.

To conclude, buffered objects in size-class i' may be charged for $O(1/\varepsilon')$ reallocations in $O(\lg(1/\varepsilon'))$ different size classes, for a total cost of $O((1/\varepsilon') \lg(1/\varepsilon'))$ allocations. □

Corollary: Defragmenting/Sorting

A corollary of cost-oblivious storage reallocation is a cost-oblivious defragmentation algorithm, i.e., a cost-oblivious algorithm for sorting the objects while simultaneously respecting constraints on the space usage.

We first compare with naïve defragmentation. If $2V$ working space is allowed, then defragmentation is trivial with two movements per object. First crunch the objects into the rightmost V space, using one move per object. Then place each object directly in its final destination within the leftmost V region of space.

The following theorem shows that defragmentation is possible even using $(1+\varepsilon)V + \Delta$ space by applying cost-oblivious storage reallocation as a black box.

THEOREM 7. *For any $0 < \varepsilon \leq 1/2$ there exists a cost-oblivious defragmentation algorithm that takes as input (1) an arbitrary comparison function, (2) a set of objects with volume V, and (3) a current allocation of the objects using space at most $(1+\varepsilon)V$. The algorithm sorts the objects according to the comparison function, subject to:*

- *the total space usage at any time never exceeds $(1 + \varepsilon)V + \Delta$ space, and*
- *the total cost is at most $O((1/\varepsilon) \log(1/\varepsilon))$ times the cost to allocate all of the objects.*

PROOF. First crunch the objects into the rightmost V space, leaving a size-$\lfloor \varepsilon V \rfloor$ prefix of the array empty. We reserve this prefix to run the cost-universal storage-reallocation algorithm. Starting with the leftmost object in the suffix, remove it from the suffix, store it temporarily in the Δ additional space, and then insert it into the prefix as per cost-universal storage reallocation. Since the storage reallocation guarantees at most $(1 + \varepsilon)W$ space usage, for W total volume of objects in the prefix, at no point does the size-$\leq (1 + \varepsilon)W$ prefix overlap the size-$(V - W)$ suffix. When this process completes, the suffix is empty and all objects are in the cost-universal-storage data structure.

Next, move elements back to the suffix in reverse sorted order. Specifically, delete each object from the prefix (using the cost-universal storage-reallocation algorithm), which implicitly compacts the space used, and place the object just before its successor in the suffix. Again, at any time if W is the remaining volume of objects in the prefix, the prefix uses at most $(1 + \varepsilon)W$ space, and the suffix uses exactly $V - W$ space, so the prefix does not overlap the suffix. □

3. FOOTPRINT MINIMIZATION IN A DATABASE CONTEXT

This section extends the storage-reallocation algorithm to the database setting by addressing two key issues: durability and blocking. To provide durability, we extend the algorithm to work with a checkpointing mechanism. Specifically, we show how to complete a buffer flush in $O(1/\varepsilon)$

checkpoints. During a flush, the memory footprint increases by an additive Δ term, up to $(1+\varepsilon)V+\Delta$, where V is the total length of all active objects, and Δ is the length of the longest object. The additive Δ is unavoidable due to the fact that when a large object is moved, its new location cannot overlap its old location.

To prevent updates from blocking for too long, we present a (partially) deamortized version. The deamortized data structure has the same amortized reallocation cost and memory footprint as the original, but it also has a worst-case reallocation cost of $O((1/\varepsilon)wf(1)+f(\Delta))$ for inserting/deleting a size-w object. That is, on each update, the total length of jobs reallocated is roughly proportional to the size of the object being inserted/deleted. Viewed differently, the deamortized bound says the desired footprint bound can be maintained with nonblocking updates, as long as the rate of updates is sufficiently lower than the speed of the machine.

3.1 Overview of the Checkpointing Model

Recall that moving an object updates the map that is maintained between logical and physical addresses. From time to time, and specifically during a checkpoint, this map is written to disk, so that a database that is recovering from a crash has access to the updated map. Suppose an object is reallocated. Then the map must be updated. But if a crash occurs before the next checkpoint, the updated map will not be available to the database on recovery. Therefore, we must maintain two copies of the data—at the old and new locations—until the next checkpoint has completed. Only then is it safe to assume that the database knows, in a durable fashion, the new location of the data.

The consequence for designing a reallocator is that from time to time, the database will perform a checkpoint and all the space that was freed since the last checkpoint will become available. If our algorithm would like to write to a freed but not checkpointed location it will block. Therefore, a reallocation algorithm is better if it requires fewer checkpoints to compete. For example, if we were to write the data to completely new locations, the algorithm would not block on any checkpoints, because we would not be reusing any space. However, the competitive ratio of the footprint would be at least two. We show below that we can achieve our bound of $(1+\varepsilon)$ competitive ratio while blocking on at most $O(1/\varepsilon)$ checkpoints.

The frequency of checkpointing is dependent on many considerations beyond the needs for reallocation, so we assume that checkpoints are initiated by the system, rather than our algorithm. There are other models of checkpointing, such as log-trimming through incremental checkpointing. A complete treatment of checkpointing is beyond the scope of this paper, though it would be interesting to see how different types of checkpointing interact with reallocation.

3.2 Flushing with Checkpoints

The goal of the flush here is identical to in Section 2, but the implementation details differ to accommodate the checkpointing model. Namely, the space used increases by an additive Δ, and the flush itself proceeds in several rounds with checkpoints in between. Another improvement here is that an inserted element gets inserted *before* the flush completes, whereas in Section 2 we assumed for simplicity that the insert blocked until the flush completed. The memory footprint at the end of the flush is identical to that of the previous algorithm.

Note that the additional Δ working space is unavoidable when reallocating large objects. To see this fact, consider a single size-Δ object. This object cannot be moved unless the target location is not overlapping with the original location. That is, if we have less than 2Δ space to work with, the object can never be moved as every target location overlaps its current location.

Inserting (allocating) and deleting (deallocating). Since objects only move during a buffer flush, the insert and delete procedure is almost identical to Section 2. The only difference here is that we insert the object *before* triggering a flush.

To insert an object, place it in the appropriate buffer segment as before. If there is insufficient space to place the object in any following buffer segment, place it at the end of the last buffer segment (filling and exceeding the buffer capacity) and trigger a flush. When deleting an object, a dummy delete request is inserted as in Section 2. If this delete request would overflow the last buffer, then trigger the flush without using space for the dummy delete request.

Buffer flush. A flush proceeds as follows. First identify the boundary size class b as before. Recall that the flush proceeds on size classes $i \geq b$. Let L denote the endpoint of the last object *before* the insert/delete that triggers the flush, i.e., if the total space is S including a newly inserted size-w object, then $L = S - w$.[5] Let L' be the desired memory footprint after the flush, but subtracting off the size of any flush-triggering insert.[6] That is, if the final data structure should take S' space after the flush, then $L' = S' - w$, where w is the size of the last insert if the flush was triggered by an insert. Let B be the total space occupied by the buffers involved in the flush. Move all objects from buffer segments $i \geq b$ to the end of the array, starting from location $(\max\{L, L'\} + B + \Delta)$. The important observation here is that $L+\Delta$ exceeds the location of the newly inserted object, so none of the target locations overlap any of the current objects. And hence all of these movements can be performed within a single checkpoint. The order in which the buffered objects are moved does not matter. This step of the flush is similar to Section 2, except the starting location is up to $B+\Delta$ slots later in the array.

Next, iterate over payload segments from largest to smallest, moving objects as late as possible in the array ending at location $(\max\{L, L'\} + B + \Delta)$. After this step, flushed payload segments are packed as late as possible before location $(\max\{L, L'\} + B + \Delta)$, and flushed buffer segments (including the newly inserted object) are packed as early as possible after $(\max\{L, L'\} + B + \Delta)$.

This payload-packing step, however, moves objects to locations in the array that may have previously been occupied, which would violate the checkpointing model. Instead, break these movements into phases with checkpoints between each phase. Move at least $B+1$ and at most $B+\Delta$ volume of objects in each phase. (That is, move as many objects as

[5]This detail of subtracting off the newly inserted object is important to obtain a space usage of $(1+\varepsilon)V+\Delta$ throughout the flush rather than $(1+\varepsilon)V+O(\Delta)$.

[6]Similar to the procedure for "S" discussed in Section 2, L' can be calculated by first computing $\sum_{i \geq b}(V_t(i) + \lfloor \varepsilon' V_t(i) \rfloor)$.

possible before exceeding $B + \Delta$ volume. Since the largest object has size Δ, the minimum amount moved is $B + 1$.) As we shall prove, the movements within a phase do not overlap, and the total number of phases is $O(1/\varepsilon')$. Aside from checkpointing, this step differs from the version in Section 2 in that objects are packed later in the array rather than earlier, and hence the movements iterate from largest-to-smallest size class rather than smallest-to-largest. The reason for this change is to take advantage of the $B + \Delta$ working space available at the end of the region.

Next, iterate over payload segments from smallest to largest, moving the objects exactly where they should go in the array. This step, again, may move objects to space that was previously occupied, so we again break it into phases consisting of the next $B + 1$ to $B + \Delta$ target locations with a checkpoint following each phase.

Finally, move the buffered elements to their target locations. Since all buffered elements are currently located after $(\max\{L, L'\} + B + \Delta)$, and all target locations are before $L' + \Delta$, none of these movements overlap, and they can be performed within a single checkpoint.

Analysis. Note that the number of reallocations is similar to that in Section 2, with the only difference being one reallocation for the flush-triggering item. Hence the reallocation cost of Lemma 6 holds for this version of the algorithm. The space used after a flush completes is also identical to Section 2. It remains to prove three facts: 1) the space used during a flush is $(1+O(\varepsilon'))V+\Delta$ where V is the total volume of active jobs, 2) the object movements between checkpoints only move objects to nonoverlapping locations, and 3) the number of checkpoints is $O(1/\varepsilon')$ per flush.

LEMMA 8. *While processing any allocation/deallocation request, the total footprint used by the algorithm is at most $(1 + O(\varepsilon'))V + \Delta$, where V denotes the total volume of all currently active objects.*

PROOF. Let V_{before} and V_{after} denote the total volume of objects before and after the operation, respectively. Let S_{before} and S_{after} denote the total space of the data structure before and after the operation, respectively. According to Lemma 5, we have $S_{before} \leq (1 + O(\varepsilon'))V_{before}$, and $S_{after} \leq (1 + O(\varepsilon'))V_{after}$. The question is what happens during the operation, notably during a flush operation.

Suppose the flush is triggered by a size-w insertion. The volume during the flush is thus $V = V_{before} + w = V_{after}$. The space used to store all buffered objects, including the newly inserted object, is at most $w+B$, where B is the total amount of space devoted to buffers before the flush. Note that since the buffers are sized to less than an ε' fraction of the total space, we have $B \leq \varepsilon' S_{before}$.

Case 1: $S_{before} \geq S_{after}$. Then these objects are written at an offset of $(S_{before} + B + \Delta)$, meaning that the total space during the flush is at most

$$\begin{aligned}
& (S_{before} + B + \Delta) + (w + B) \\
\leq\ & (1 + 2\varepsilon')S_{before} + w + \Delta && \text{// upper bound on } B \\
\leq\ & (1 + 2\varepsilon')\left[(1 + O(\varepsilon'))V_{before}\right] + w + \Delta && \text{// Lemma 5} \\
\leq\ & (1 + O(\varepsilon'))V_{before} + w + \Delta && \text{// larger const in big-O} \\
\leq\ & (1 + O(\varepsilon'))(V_{before} + w) + \Delta \\
=\ & (1 + O(\varepsilon'))V + \Delta\,.
\end{aligned}$$

Case 2: $S_{before} < S_{after}$. Then these objects are written at an offset of $(S_{after} - w) + B + \Delta$. And the total space during the flush is at most $S_{after} + 2B + \Delta \leq (1+O(\varepsilon'))V_{after} + \Delta = (1+O(\varepsilon'))V + \Delta$, where the steps follow from analogous steps in Case 1.

In the case of a deletion, the argument is similar, except w becomes 0 in all the expressions, and $V = V_{before}$ throughout the flush. That is, the deleted object is considered active until the flush completes. □

LEMMA 9. *During a single phase of object movements between two checkpoints, all object starting locations are disjoint from all object ending locations.*

PROOF. First, consider the payload-packing step, where payload segments are packed to the right. At the start of the jth phase, let ℓ_j denote the last cell occupied by the payload segments that have yet to be packed, and let r_j denote the first occupied cell later than ℓ_j. We claim that at the start of each phase $r_j \geq \ell_j + B + \Delta$, which we shall prove by induction. If true, the claim implies disjointness: if the space between r_j and ℓ_j is at least $B+\Delta$, then we can pack up to $B + \Delta$ volume of jobs in front of ℓ_j during the jth phase before overlapping the ending position of jobs at ℓ_j.

We prove the claim by induction. The claim holds initially because $\ell_0 \leq L$, and $r_0 \geq L+B+\Delta$. For the inductive step, observe that if X volume of objects are moved in phase j, then $\ell_{j+1} \leq \ell_j - X$, and $r_{j+1} = r_j - X$. Combined with the inductive assumption that $r_j \geq \ell_j + B + \Delta$, we get $r_{j+1} \geq (\ell_j+B+\Delta)-X \geq ((\ell_{j+1}+X)+B+\Delta)-X = \ell_{j+1}+B+\Delta$.

We next consider the unpacking step, where the payload segments are moved to their final positions. Let ℓ_j denote the last cell occupied by unpacked payload segments at the start of the jth phase of movements, and let r_j denote the first cell occupied by the yet-to-be unpacked payload objects. We claim that $\ell_j + B + \Delta \leq r_j$ (but this time we shall prove it by contradiction). If the claim holds, then we can afford to increase ℓ_j by $B + \Delta$ in each phase without violating the disjointness.

To prove the claim, suppose for the sake of contradiction that $\ell_j > r_j - B - \Delta$, and let X be the total volume remaining in the packed region. Then the final position of the last payload segment can end no earlier than $\ell_j + X > r_j + X - B - \Delta$ after the unpacking, and hence the space desired by these payload segments is at least $L' > (r_j + X) - B - \Delta$. We also have $r_j + X = \max\{L', L\} + B + \Delta$ is the offset at which the buffered objects were moved, which we simplify to $r_j + X \geq L' + B + \Delta$. Combining these two facts, we get $L' > (r_j + X) - B - \Delta \geq (L' + B + \Delta) - B - \Delta = L'$, i.e., $L' > L'$, which is a contradiction. □

LEMMA 10. *The number of checkpoints occurring during a flush is $O(1/\varepsilon')$.*

PROOF. The checkpoints are dominated by the packing and unpacking steps. Let $P(i)$ denote the total space of the ith payload segment at the time of the flush, i.e., the volume of jobs that were in this size class the last time a flush occurred. Then the total size of flushed buffers is $B = \sum_{i \geq b} \lfloor \varepsilon' P(i) \rfloor$, and the total space of the region being flushed is $S = \sum_{i \geq b}(P(i) + \lfloor \varepsilon' P(i) \rfloor)$. Since each movement phase does more than B work, showing that $B = \Omega(\varepsilon' S)$ would be sufficient. The only difficulty is the floor in the expression, so we shall consider the case of large $P(i)$ and small $P(i)$ separately.

Case 1: sufficiently large P. More precisely, suppose $B = \sum_{i \geq b} \lfloor \varepsilon' P(i) \rfloor \geq \sum_{i \geq b} \varepsilon' P(i)/2$. Then $B = \Omega(\varepsilon' S)$, since $\sum_{i \geq b} P(i) \geq S/2$ for $\varepsilon < 1$.

Case 2: small P. Suppose $B < \sum_{i \geq b} \varepsilon' P(i)/2$. Note that $B = \sum_{i \geq b} \lfloor \varepsilon' P(i) \rfloor \geq \sum_{i \geq b} \varepsilon' P(i) - \Theta(\lg \Delta)$, since there are only $\Theta(\lg \Delta)$ size classes. It follows that $B < \sum_{i \geq b} \varepsilon' P(i)/2$ implies $\sum_{i \geq b} \varepsilon' P(i) = O(\lg \Delta)$, and hence $S = O((1/\varepsilon') \lg \Delta)$. The algorithm tries to move as many objects as it can until exceeding $B + \Delta$ volume, and hence every consecutive pair of phases moves at least $\Delta/2 = \Omega(\lg \Delta) = \Omega(\varepsilon' S)$ volume. □

3.3 Deamortizing the Data Structure

As described so far, the data structure is amortized—the average reallocation cost per update is low, but on some updates *every* active object may need to be reallocated (i.e., when all size classes are involved in a flush). This section improves the worst-case reallocation cost of a size-w update to $O((1/\varepsilon) w f(1) + f(\Delta))$, without hurting the amortized update cost or the maximum footprint.

Note that the deamortization described here builds on the checkpointing modification, yielding a worst-case $O(1/\varepsilon)$ checkpoints per operation.

Modifications to the algorithm. The main idea of our deamortization is that if a buffer flush performs a total of X reallocations by volume, then this work is spread across the subsequent $\varepsilon' X$ updates by volume. The question, however, is where to place new objects that are inserted during a flush. If, for example, an insert could trigger a smaller flush while a larger flush is still ongoing, that would present even more challenges. We tackle these problems by adding two more buffers to the data structure and modifying the flush, which serve to avoid the issue of nested flushes.

Augment the data structure to include one size-$\lfloor \varepsilon' V_f \rfloor$ buffer, called the ***tail buffer***, following all the size-class segments, where V_f is the total volume of all jobs active at the start of the previous buffer flush. The tail buffer is like any other buffer: objects are only placed in the tail buffer if all earlier buffers are too full, and a buffer flush is only triggered once the tail buffer becomes full. The point of the large tail buffer is to enable the flush to complete before triggering another flush.

When a flush is triggered, calculate the desired space and the temporary working space as before.[7] We treat all space immediately following the temporary working space as another buffer called the ***log***.

The flush process resembles the previous flush process (with or without checkpointing), except that:

1. Objects may be inserted/deleted during a flush. These updates are placed at the end of the log.
2. The work of the flush is spread across these subsequent updates. Specifically, on an insertion/deletion of a size-w object, perform (just over) the next $(4/\varepsilon')w$ steps of the flush by volume. Since a fractional object cannot be moved, the amount of volume processed may be as high $(4/\varepsilon')w + \Delta$.
3. There is an extra phase at the end. During this phase, all objects in the log are moved to their appropriate buffers, i.e., they are re-inserted/re-deleted. This phase proceeds in order from the beginning of the log. Updates may continue to be recorded at the end of the log during this phase. Since the volume moved is significantly larger than the size of the update, the re-insertion/re-deletion will eventually "catch up" to the end of the log, at which point the flush terminates and the log disappears.

[7]But the space is slightly larger now due to the $\lfloor \varepsilon' V \rfloor$ space necessary for the tail buffer.

Analysis. To show correctness of the new flush protocol, we argue that the log is drained completely before another flush gets triggered, i.e., before the tail buffer fills. Note that if the last update during a flush involves a large object, that update may finish the previous flush and trigger the next one. The point is only that the tail buffer cannot overflow before that time.

LEMMA 11. *Let V_f be the total volume of active objects at the time a flush is triggered. For any $\varepsilon' < 1$, the flush completes by the time the subsequent volume of updates first exceeds $\varepsilon' V_f$.*

PROOF. In the worst case, a flush may move every object twice. Specifically, the buffered elements are moved out of the buffers temporarily, then to their final location. Similarly, the payload segments are packed once and then unpacked to their final location. The total volume of reallocations of preexisting elements is thus at most $2V_f$. (Any delete records do not have to be reallocated; these are just destroyed.)

It follows that by the time $(\varepsilon'/2)V_f$ volume of updates are logged, all preexisting elements have been moved to their final locations. But this analysis does not take into account the elements logged during the flush. The next $(\varepsilon'/2)V_f$ volume of updates more than suffice to move all objects from the log to a buffer. □

The following lemmas bound the space and reallocation costs of the updated algorithm.

LEMMA 12. *After each allocation/deallocation request is processed, the total space used by the data structure is at most $(1 + O(\varepsilon'))V + \Delta$, where V denotes the total volume of all currently active objects. If a flush is not in progress, this space improves to $(1 + O(\varepsilon'))V$.*

PROOF. The only significant difference in space between this algorithm and the amortized one is the tail buffer and the log. The tail buffer has size at most $\varepsilon' V_f$, where V_f was the volume at the last flush. According to Lemma 11, the log also has size at most $\varepsilon' V_f$. Combined, the total increase to space is an additive $O(\varepsilon')V_f$. To complete the argument, we need only argue that $V_f = \Theta(V)$, where V is the current volume of active jobs, which is done in the proof of Lemma 5. □

LEMMA 13. *For subadditive cost function f, the amortized cost of inserting or deleting a size-w object is $O(f(w) \cdot (1/\varepsilon') \lg(1/\varepsilon'))$. Moreover, the worst-case cost of an insert or delete is $O((1/\varepsilon') w f(1) + f(\Delta))$.*

PROOF. The worst-case upper bound follows by construction. The algorithm only reallocates $(4/\varepsilon')w$ volume of objects per update, plus up to one last object to exceed this volume. In the worst case, these objects are size-1 objects except the last which is size-Δ, for a total cost of $O((1/\varepsilon)wf(1) + f(\Delta))$.

As for the amortized bound, adding a larger buffer to the data structure only improves the amortized cost. Specifically, proof of Lemma 6 relied on *lower bounding* the volume of buffered objects, so the same analysis applies once an object is placed in a buffer. The deamortized data structure has an additional reallocation for each object that is placed in the log, moving it from the log to a buffer, but this only occurs once per object. □

Lower bound on worst-case cost. Note that $\Omega(f(\Delta))$ is a lower bound on the worst-case reallocation cost when maintaining a $(1+\varepsilon)V$ footprint size, as exhibited by the following lemma. It is not obvious whether $\Omega(wf(1))$ is also a lower bound on the worst-case reallocation cost of any algorithm. If so, then our deamortized structure's worst-case cost would be asymptotically optimal for constant ε. Although not a general lower bound, an $\Omega(wf(1))$ worst-case cost appears to be unavoidable for any algorithm that stores "enough" small objects after large objects. (And storing objects out of order in this way seems crucial for obtaining a *cost-oblivious* algorithm.) Informally, deleting a size-w object leaves a large hole in the array. To maintain the desired footprint, this hole must be filled by later objects. If all later objects are small (size-1), then a size-w delete may cause $\Omega(w)$ size-1 objects to move.

LEMMA 14. *For any reallocation algorithm that maintains a footprint of $(1 + 1/2)V$ and subadditive cost function f, there exists an update sequence such that at least one update has a reallocation cost of $\Omega(f(\Delta))$. This lower bound applies even if the reallocation algorithm knows f and the full update sequence.*

PROOF. Here is the sequence. First insert one size-Δ object. Then insert Δ size-1 objects. Then delete the size-Δ object. There are two cases to show the lower bound.
Case 1: some small-object insertion causes the large object to be reallocated. Then that insert has a reallocation cost of at least $f(\Delta)$.
Case 2: the large object does not get reallocated. Then the large object must end before position $(3/2)\Delta$ to achieve the footprint bound, and hence there must be at least $\Delta/2$ small objects appearing after the large one. When deleting the large object, those small objects must move in order to restore the $(3/2)\Delta$ footprint bound. Hence the cost of deleting the large objects is $\Omega(\Delta \cdot f(1)) = \Omega(f(\Delta))$ for subadditive f. □

4. REFERENCES

[1] A. Aggarwal, B. Alpern, A. K. Chandra, and M. Snir. A model for hierarchical memory. In *Proc. 19th Annual ACM Symposium on Theory of Computing (STOC)*, pages 305–314, 1987.

[2] C. Archetti, L. Bertazzi, and M. G. Speranza. Reoptimizing the Traveling Salesman Problem. *Networks*, 42(3):154–159, 2003.

[3] C. Archetti, L. Bertazzi, and M. G. Speranza. Reoptimizing the 0-1 knapsack problem. *Disc. Appl. Math.*, 158(17):1879–1887, 2010.

[4] G. Ausiello, V. Bonifaci, and B. Escoffier. Complexity and approximation in reoptimization. In *Proc. CiE*, 2007.

[5] G. Ausiello, B. Escoffier, J. Monnot, and V. T. Paschos. Reoptimization of minimum and maximum traveling salesman's tours. *J. Disc. Alg.*, 7(4):453–463, 2009.

[6] M. A. Bender, R. Cole, E. D. Demaine, and M. Farach-Colton. Scanning and traversing: Maintaining data for traversals in a memory hierarchy. In *Proc. 10th European Symposium on Algorithms (ESA)*, pages 139–151, 2002.

[7] M. A. Bender, E. D. Demaine, and M. Farach-Colton. Cache-oblivious B-trees. *SIAM J. Comp.*, 35(2):341–358, 2005.

[8] M. A. Bender, R. Ebrahimi, J. T. Fineman, G. Ghasemiesfeh, R. Johnson, and S. McCauley. Cache-adaptive algorithms. In *Proc. 25th ACM-SIAM Symposium on Discrete Algorithms (SODA)*, pages 958–971, 2014.

[9] M. A. Bender, M. Farach-Colton, S. P. Fekete, J. T. Fineman, and S. Gilbert. Reallocation problems in scheduling. In *Proc. 25th ACM Symposium on Parallelism in Algorithms and Architectures (SPAA)*, pages 271–279, 2013.

[10] M. A. Bender, S. P. Fekete, T. Kamphans, and N. Schweer. Maintaining arrays of contiguous objects. In *Proc. 17th International Symposium on Fundamentals of Computation Theory (FCT)*, pages 14–25, 2009.

[11] M. A. Bender and H. Hu. An adaptive packed-memory array. In *Proc. 25th ACM SIGMOD-SIGACT-SIGART Symposium on Principles of Database Systems (PODS)*, pages 20–29, 2006.

[12] M. A. Bender and H. Hu. An adaptive packed-memory array. *Trans. Datab. Syst.*, 32(4), 2007.

[13] A. Bendersky and E. Petrank. Space overhead bounds for dynamic memory management with partial compaction. *ACM Trans. Program. Lang. Syst.*, 34(3):13, 2012.

[14] J. Błażewicz and J. Nawrocki. Dynamic storage allocation with limited compaction - complexity and some practical implications. *Discrete Applied Mathematics*, 10(3):241 – 253, 1985.

[15] H.-J. Böckenhauer, L. Forlizzi, J. Hromkovic, J. Kneis, J. Kupke, G. Proietti, and P. Widmayer. Reusing optimal TSP solutions for locally modified input instances. In *Proc. Fourth IFIP International Conference on Theoretical Computer Science (TCS)*, pages 251–270, 2006.

[16] J. Bulánek, M. Koucký, and M. Saks. Tight lower bounds for the online labeling problem. In *Proc. 44th Symposium on Theory of Computing (STOC)*, pages 1185–1198, 2012.

[17] E. G. Coffman, Jr., M. R. Garey, and D. S. Johnson. Dynamic bin packing. *SIAM J. Comput.*, 12(2):227–258, 1983.

[18] E. G. Coffman, Jr., M. R. Garey, and D. S. Johnson. Approximation algorithms for np-hard problems. chapter Approximation Algorithms for Bin Packing: A Survey, pages 46–93. PWS Publishing Co., 1997.

[19] E. G. Coffman, Jr., D. S. Johnson, P. W. Shor, and R. R. Weber. Markov chains, computer proofs, and average-case analysis of best fit bin packing. In *Proc. Twenty-Fifth Annual ACM Symposium on Theory of Computing (STOC)*, pages 412–421, 1993.

[20] E. G. Coffman, Jr., D. S. Johnson, P. W. Shor, and R. R. Weber. Bin packing with discrete item sizes, part ii: Tight bounds on first fit. *Random Struct. Algorithms*, 10(1-2):69–101, 1997.

[21] N. Cohen and E. Petrank. Limitations of partial compaction: towards practical bounds. In *Proc. ACM SIGPLAN Conference on Programming Language Design and Implementation (PLDI)*, pages 309–320, 2013.

[22] S. Davis, J. Edmonds, and R. Impagliazzo. Online algorithms to minimize resource reallocations and network communication. In *Proc. APPROX-RANDOM*, pages 104–115, 2006.

[23] S. P. Fekete, T. Kamphans, N. Schweer, C. Tessars, J. C. van der Veen, J. Angermeier, D. Koch, and J. Teich. Dynamic defragmentation of reconfigurable devices. *ACM Trans. Reconf. Technol. Syst.*, 5(2):8:1–8:20, June 2012.

[24] M. Frigo, C. E. Leiserson, H. Prokop, and S. Ramachandran. Cache-oblivious algorithms. In *Proc. 40th Annual Symposium on Foundations of Computer Science (FOCS)*, pages 285–297, 1999.

[25] G. Galambos and G. J. Woeginger. On-line bin packing - a restricted survey. *Math. Meth. of OR*, 42(1):25–45, 1995.

[26] R. Graham, E. Lawler, J. Lenstra, and A. Kan. Optimization and approximation in deterministic sequencing and scheduling: a survey. *Ann. Disc. Math.*, 5:287 – 326, 1979.

[27] N. G. Hall and C. N. Potts. Rescheduling for new orders. *Op. Res.*, 52(3), 2004.

[28] A. Itai and I. Katriel. Canonical density control. *Inf. Process. Lett.*, 104(6):200–204, 2007.

[29] A. Itai, A. G. Konheim, and M. Rodeh. A sparse table implementation of priority queues. In *Proc. International Colloquium on Automata, Languages, and Programming (ICALP)*, pages 417–431, 1981.

[30] K. Jansen and K.-M. Klein. A robust afptas for online bin packing with polynomial migration,. In *Proc. 40th International Colloquium on Automata, Languages, and Programming (ICALP)*, pages 589–600, 2013.

[31] R. Jones, A. Hosking, and E. Moss. *The Garbage Collection Handbook: The Art of Automatic Memory Management.* CRC Applied Algorithms and Data Structures Series. Chapman and Hall/CRC, 2011.

[32] I. Katriel. Implicit data structures based on local reorganizations. Master's thesis, Technion – Isreal Inst. of Tech., Haifa, May 2002.

[33] K. C. Knowlton. A fast storage allocator. *Commun. ACM*, 8(10):623–624, Oct. 1965.

[34] D. E. Knuth. *The Art of Computer Programming: Fundamental Algorithms*, volume 1. Addison-Wesley, third edition, 1997.

[35] M. G. Luby, J. Naor, and A. Orda. Tight bounds for dynamic storage allocation. *SIAM J. Disc. Math.*, 9:155–166, 1996.

[36] J. Naor, A. Orda, and Y. Petruschka. Dynamic storage allocation with known durations. *Disc. Appl. Math.*, 3:203–213, 2000.

[37] H. Prokop. Cache-oblivious algorithms. Master's thesis, Department of Electrical Engineering and Computer Science, Massachusetts Institute of Technology, June 1999.

[38] J. M. Robson. An estimate of the store size necessary for dynamic storage allocation. *J. ACM*, 18(3):416–423, July 1971.

[39] J. M. Robson. Bounds for some functions concerning dynamic storage allocation. *J. ACM*, 21(3):491–499, July 1974.

[40] J. M. Robson. Worst case fragmentation of first fit and best fit storage allocation strategies. *Comput. J.*, 20(3):242–244, 1977.

[41] P. Sanders, N. Sivadasan, and M. Skutella. Online scheduling with bounded migration. *Math. Oper. Res.*, 34(2):481–498, 2009.

[42] H. Shachnai, G. Tamir, and T. Tamir. A theory and algorithms for combinatorial reoptimization. In *Proc. 10th Latin American Theoretical INformatics Symposium (LATIN)*, pages 618–630, 2012.

[43] D. D. Sleator and R. E. Tarjan. Amortized efficiency of list update and paging rules. *Communications of the ACM*, 28(2):202–208, February 1985.

[44] D. W. Ting. Allocation and compaction - a mathematical model for memory management. In *Proc. ACM SIGMETRICS Conference on Computer Performance Modeling Measurement and Evaluation (SIGMETRICS)*, pages 311–317, 1976.

[45] Tokutek, Inc. TokuDB: MySQL Performance, MariaDB Performance. `http://www.tokutek.com/products/tokudb-for-mysql/`.

[46] Tokutek, Inc. TokuMX—MongoDB Performance Engine. `http://www.tokutek.com/products/tokumx-for-mongodb/`.

[47] A. T. Unal, R. Uzsoy, and A. S. Kiran. Rescheduling on a single machine with part-type dependent setup times and deadlines. *Ann. Op. Res.*, 70, 1997.

[48] J. C. Verschae. *The Power of Recourse in Online Optimization Robust Solutions for Scheduling, Matroid and MST Problems The Power of Recourse in Online Optimization: Robust Solutions for Scheduling, Matroid and MST Problems.* PhD thesis, Technischen Universität Berlin, June 2012.

[49] D. Willard. Maintaining dense sequential files in a dynamic environment (extended abstract). In *Proc. 14th ACM Symposium on Theory of Computing (STOC)*, pages 114–121, 1982.

[50] D. E. Willard. Good worst-case algorithms for inserting and deleting records in dense sequential files. In *Proc. SIGMOD*, pages 251–260, 1986.

[51] D. E. Willard. A density control algorithm for doing insertions and deletions in a sequentially ordered file in good worst-case time. *Inf. and Comput.*, 97(2):150–204, 1992.

[52] D. Woodall. The bay restaurant–a linear storage problem. *The American Mathematical Monthly*, 81(3):240–246, 1974.

Author Index

www.ingramcontent.com/pod-product-compliance
Lightning Source LLC
Chambersburg PA
CBHW061343210326
41598CB00035B/5871
* 9 7 8 1 4 5 0 3 3 1 0 9 8 *